# Principles
# of
# Risk
# Management
# and
# Insurance

**SIXTH EDITION**

**GEORGE E. REJDA**

**ADDISON-WESLEY**

An imprint of Addison Wesley Longman, Inc.

Reading, Massachusetts • Menlo Park, California • New York • Harlow, England
Don Mills, Ontario • Sydney • Mexico City • Madrid • Amsterdam

Senior Editor:   Denise Clinton
Associate Editor:  Julie Zasloff
Development Editor:  Beverly Peavler
Editorial Assistant:  Emily Meehan
Senior Production Supervisor:  Nancy H. Fenton
Marketing Manager:  Jodi Fazio
Manufacturing Supervisor:  Hugh Crawford
Cover Designer:  Eileen Hoff
Project Coordination: Interactive Composition Corporation

Photo Credits: Part One, © Andrew Lichtenstein/Impact Visuals; Parts Two and Three, © Scott Takushi/St. Paul Pioneer Press/SYGMA; Part Four, © Jim Mahoney/The Image Works; Part Five, © Charles Gupton/Stock Boston; Part Six, © Michael Dwyer/Stock Boston.

Copyright © 1998 by Addison-Wesley Educational Publishers Inc.

All rights reserved. No part of this publication may be reproduced, stored in a retrieval system, or transmitted, in any form or by any means, electronic, mechanical, photocopying, recording, or otherwise, without the prior written permission of the publisher. Printed in the United States of America.

**Library of Congress Cataloging-in-Publication Data**

Rejda, George E., 1931-
    Principles of risk management and insurance / George E. Rejda.—
6th ed.
        p.   cm.
    Includes bibliographical references and index.
    ISBN 0-321-01451-0 (hc)
    1. Insurance.   2. Insurance—United States.   3. Risk (Insurance)
4. Risk management.   I. Title.
HG8051.R44   1997
368—dc21                                                   97-28269
                                                              CIP

1 2 3 4 5 6 7 8 9 10—RNT—01 00 99 98 97

# Contents

*skip for test purposes and studying*

# Preface

In 1995, the federal building in Oklahoma City was bombed—allegedly by anti-government terrorists—causing the deaths of 168 persons and $125 million in insured damages. In 1996, TWA Flight 800 mysteriously exploded shortly after takeoff in New York City, killing all aboard. In 1997, 39 members of the Heavens Gate Cult committed suicide in San Diego. During the same year, raging flood waters in Grand Forks, North Dakota devasted thousands of homes and business firms, causing millions of dollars of property damage and enormous personal hardship. To say that a lot has happened since publication of the fifth edition of *Principles of Risk Management and Insurance* might be an understatement.

The federal government went on to prosecute and convict Timothy McVeigh, who received the death penalty for the Oklahoma City bombing. Federal officials are still investigating the crash of TWA Flight 800; psychologists and psychiatrists continue to debate why cult members commit suicide; and rivers and streams continue to overflow and flood.

The sixth edition of the text deals with similar tragic events that can cause great financial insecurity and enormous emotional grief and suffering for surviving family members. Like earlier editions, the text is designed for a beginning undergraduate course in risk management and insurance with no prerequisites. Thoroughly revised and updated, the sixth edition provides complete and current coverage of major areas in risk management and insurance, including basic concepts of risk and insurance, risk management, legal principles, property and liability insurance, life and health insurance, employee benefits, social insurance, functional and financial operations of insurers, insurance regulation, and current public policy issues, especially those affecting consumers.

As with previous editions, the sixth edition leans toward the insurance consumer and blends basic insurance principles with consumer considerations. Further, it addresses personal risk management and financial planning issues so that students of insurance can apply basic insurance concepts immediately to their own lives.

## MAJOR CHANGES IN THE SIXTH EDITION

1. **Internet resources.** The Internet is becoming increasingly important as a marketing tool for insurers and a convenient source of information for insurance consumers. Many insurance industry associations have established World Wide Web sites. The sixth edition contains numerous web site addresses of insurance organizations for interested students seeking current information or doing research on insurance topics.

2. **Shorter text.** Instructors have requested a shorter, more streamlined text. Through keen editing and judicious rewriting, I have carefully pruned content detail to reduce the text's overall length without sacrificing its usefulness as an insurance resource for years to come.

3. **Clarity in writing.** Insurance as a subject can intimidate some students if set forth in a disjointed or abstract way. Since readability continues to be crucial, I persist in presenting concepts clearly and directly, for the most user-friendly of texts.

4. **New "Insight" boxes.** Instructors and students have enthusiastically endorsed the "Insight" boxes in each chapter of previous editions. Because "Insights" are such powerful learning tools with their real-world applications of the principles at hand, most "Insights" have been replaced with exciting new ones. Readers should look for these grabbers, and then some, throughout the text:

- Using Phone at Wheel Labeled as Dangerous as Drunk Driving
- Cut Your Car Insurance Premiums by as Much as 20%
- Buying Term Insurance is No Simple Task
- The Rip-Off: Vanishing Premium Life, Typical Tab: $2000
- Life Insurers Sidestep Sales-Fraud Taint
- Variable Annuities: Here's to the Winners, and Losers
- Insurance You Can Do Without

- Doctors Can Leave You on Hook as Insurers Cut Back
- Protect Yourself from Bad HMO Practices Even if Your State Doesn't
- Retirement Honing: How Much Should You Have Saved for a Comfortable Life?
- Delaying Social Security Benefits May Not Be as Smart as You Think
- Proposals for Reforming Social Security
- Borrowing from 401(k) Can Be Good Move
- Punitive-Damage Awards Found to Be Generally Modest and Rare
- Computer Crime Called Extraordinarily Widespread
- Webpages Can Be Revolutionary Tools for Insurers
- Auto Insurers Are Trying Out Managed Care
- Dear Mom and Dad: Here's Something That's Easier to Read Than to Discuss

5. **Current issues and up-to-date coverage.** Readers will find in-depth analyses of current issues throughout the text: new developments in managed care plans, analysis of Health Insurance Portability and Accountability Act of 1996, new SIMPLE retirement plan, proposed privatization of Social Security, investing Social Security trust funds in common stocks, the Medicare crisis, increased mergers and consolidation of insurers, deceptive sales practices by life insurers, banks entering insurance, and numerous additional issues. All statistics are updated. Many citations feature recent copyright dates.

6. **Technical accuracy.** As in past editions, numerous insurance specialists and technical experts have reviewed the text for technical accuracy, especially in areas where changes have occurred rapidly or dramatically. Once again, instructors can rely on the sixth edition for the most technically accurate and up-to-date information available.

## CONTENT CHANGES

1. **Law of Large Numbers.** Material dealing with a technical discussion of the Law of Large Numbers has been rewritten and simplified. The new material should be easily grasped by students and appears in the appendix to Chapter 2.

2. **New edition of the commercial general liability policy (CGL).** Chapter 13 discusses the latest 1996 edition of the CGL policy drafted by the Insurance Services Office.

3. **Life insurance.** The number of life insurance policies discussed in Chapter 16 has been reduced. Discussion of older life insurance products that are not widely sold or are obsolete has been deleted, including adjustable life insurance, and the family policy. As a result, students can focus attention of the newer products that have appeared in recent years.

4. **New NAIC Policy Illustration Model Regulation.** Chapter 16 discusses the new policy illustration model regulation drafted by the National Association of Insurance Commissioners (NAIC). The model legislation restricts insurers in the presentation of policy data and is designed to reduce deceptive sales practices.

5. **Continuance provisions.** Chapter 20 discusses the latest continuance provisions that are found in individual medical expense policies. Material on individual disability income contracts has been rewritten and updated. Discussion of the rules for shopping for an individual health insurance policy has been substantially rewritten.

6. **Managed care plans.** Chapter 21 has been substantially rewritten with greater emphasis on managed care plans in group health insurance. Chapter 21 also discusses the newer types of managed care plans. The controversial issues associated with managed care plans are examined in some detail.

7. **Health Insurance Portability and Accountability Act.** Chapter 21 discusses the new Health Insurance Portability and Accountability Act of 1996. The new legislation deals with important health-care issues, including limitations on preexisting conditions, credit for previous group health insurance coverage, and group health insurance for small employers.

8. **Medical savings accounts.** Chapter 21 discusses medical savings accounts that allow in-

sureds to pay premiums with before-tax dollars for a high-deductible major medical policy.

9. **Coordination-of-benefit rules.**    Chapter 21 discusses the latest version of the coordination-of-benefit rules developed by the National Association of Insurance Commissioners (NAIC).    The rules are designed to prevent overinsurance and duplication of benefits if an insured is covered by more than one plan.

10. **Section 401 (k) plans and other retirement plans.** Because of its importance in retirement planning, discussion of Section 401 (k) plans has been moved up and is discussed earlier in Chapter 22. Chapter 22 also discusses the new **SIMPLE retirement plan** for smaller employers as a result of federal legislation enacted in 1996.

11. **Proposed changes in Social Security.** Chapter 23 discusses proposed changes in the Social Security program.    These proposals include privatization of Social Security, investing part of the OASDI trust funds in common stocks, and approaches for reducing the anticipated long-range actuarial deficit. The chapter also discusses the current Medicare financial crisis. The real rate of return beneficiaries can expect to receive under the OASDI program is also treated.

12. **Increased mergers and consolidation of insurers.** Chapter 24 discusses the trend toward mergers and increased consolidation of insurers. The chapter also discussion legislation enacted by some states that allow mutual insurers to reorganize as stock holding companies and have stockholders. Discussion of perpetual mutuals has been deleted.

13. **Deceptive sales practices by life insurers.** Chapter 27 discusses the problem of deceptive sales practices by life insurers, which resulted in class action suits by policyowners, substantial fines by state insurance departments against major life insurers,  and new efforts to control the market conduct of unethical agents.

## SUPPLEMENTS

**Instructor's Manual with Transparency Masters** Prepared by George E. Rejda, the University of Nebraska-Lincoln. Designed to reduce new course start-up costs and to give seasoned instructors some fresh ideas, this comprehensive manual contains teaching notes, lecture outlines, answers to all text questions for discussion and review and case applications, and a set of transparency masters that illustrate  important points in the text.

**Computerized Testing System**    Prepared by Burton T. Beam, Jr., The American College, this computerized version of the test bank enables instructors to construct tests quickly and easily. Instructors can choose existing test items randomly by chapter, question type, and quantity, or manually by specific item number. The program allows instructors to edit test items or add their own questions; print tests in several formats; and incorporate graphs, charts, and tables. The test bank is designed for Macintosh, IBM-PC and compatible computers and is available at no additional cost to text adopters.

**Printed Test Bank**  All test questions from the computerized test bank are available in this bound supplement.

**PowerPoint Presentation**  All figures from the text are available in PowerPoint format.  Use the slides to enhance your classroom presentation of the course material.   For users with the complete PowerPoint software program, customization and the addition of lecture notes is possible.

**Study     Guide** Prepared   by   Michael   J. McNamara, The University of Memphis. This study tool is an improvement over the traditional study guide and contains exercises that  enable students to apply the various concepts to their own insurance programs. The introductory section summarizes the benefits of the guide, and how to use the guide effectively as a learning tool.  Each chapter contains practice items such as objective test questions similar to test bank questions; learning goals organized by objectives listed at the beginning of every text chapter; key-term exercises; worksheets where appropriate for solving end-of-chapter mini-cases; and step-by-step demonstration problems with rationales for each step. Solutions to all questions are found at the end of every chapter for quick reference and self-testing.

## ACKNOWLEDGMENTS

As I have stated in previous editions, a market-leading textbook is never written alone. I owe an enormous intellectual debt to numerous insurance experts and academicians for their kind and gracious assistance. Numerous insurance educators have taken time out of their busy professional schedules to review part or all of the sixth edition, to contribute supplementary materials, or to offer valuable suggestions and comments. They include the following:

Burton T. Beam, Jr., The American College

Joseph M. Belth, Indiana University

Stewart Bonem, Cincinnati State Technical and Community College

James M. Carson, Illinois State University

Patricia A. Chesier, California State University-Sacramento

Deborah S. Gaunt, Georgia State University

Edward E. Graves, The American College

John J. McFadden, The American College

Michael J. McNamara, The University of Memphis

Robert J. Myers, former chief actuary, Social Security Administration

Donald R. Oakes, American Institute for Chartered Property Casualty Underwriters

Robert Schini, attorney-at-law

Eric Wiening, American Institute for Chartered Property Casualty Underwriters.

I also wish to acknowledge the technical assistance of Beaverly Peavler who served as the developmental editor for the sixth edition. I also appreciate the feedback and observations of the people who have helped me, including the supplements team of Burton Beam, Jr., Michael McNamara, and Evelyn Rice.

Finally, the fundamental objective underlying the sixth edition remains the same as earlier editions—I have attempted to write an intellectually stimulating textbook from which students can learn and professors can teach.

*George E. Rejda, Ph.D., CLU*
*V.J. Skutt Distinguished Professor of Insurance*
*University of Nebraska, Lincoln*

# PRINCIPLES OF RISK MANAGEMENT AND INSURANCE

*Part One*

# BASIC CONCEPTS IN RISK MANAGEMENT AND INSURANCE

On-Line Resources

ARIA Web is the World Wide Web site of the **American Risk and Insurance Association,** a professional association and the publisher of *The Journal of Risk and Insurance* and *Risk Management and Insurance Review.* ARIA Web's address is:

    http://www.aria.org/

RIMS on the Web is the site of the **Risk and Insurance Management Society:**

    http://www.rims.org/

**RISK Web** is an electronic mail-based forum in which academics and professionals discuss issues related to risk and insurance:

    http://www.riskweb.com/

For general insurance coverage explanations and definitions of insurance terms, see the **"Complete Glossary of Insurance Coverage Explanations"** at:

    http://www.lcgroup.com/explanations/index.html

**Insurance and Risk Management Central** bills itself as providing "fast, friendly access to all that's insurance on the Internet." Visit the site at:

    http://www.irmcentral.com/

The **Federal Emergency Management Agency (FEMA)** has as its mission "to reduce loss of life and property and protect our nation's infrastructure through a comprehensive, risk-based, emergency management program of mitigation, preparedness, response and recovery." Visit FEMA's web site at:       http://www.fema.gov/

# Chapter 1

# RISK IN OUR SOCIETY

> *"When we take a risk, we are betting on an outcome that will result from a decision we have made, though we do not know for certain what the outcome will be."*
>
> Peter L. Bernstein<br>Against the Gods, The Remarkable Story of Risk

## Student Learning Objectives

After studying this chapter, you should be able to:

- Explain the meaning of risk.
- Define the terms "chance of loss," "peril," and "hazard."
- Distinguish between pure risk and speculative risk.
- Describe the major pure risks that are associated with great financial insecurity.
- Understand how risk is a burden to society.
- Explain the major methods of handling risk.

Most individuals and families have a strong desire for financial security and protection against those events that threaten their financial security. Financial security can be threatened or lost from numerous causes. Some families will be deprived of financial support because the family head is tragically killed in an auto accident. Others will experience destruction of their homes and personal property because of fires, floods, hurricanes, earthquakes, or other disasters. Still others will become disabled because of heart disease, cancer, AIDS, or other disease. Finally, others will be financially ruined because they are sued and cannot pay a liability judgment against them.

It is apparent that certain risks can threaten the financial security of individuals and their families. This chapter discusses the nature and treatment of risk in our society. Specific topics discussed include the meaning of risk, the major types of risk that threaten the financial security of individuals and families, and the basic methods of handling risk.

## MEANING OF RISK

There is no single definition of risk. Economists, behavioral scientists, risk theorists, statisticians, and actuaries each have their own concept of risk. However, risk traditionally has been defined in terms of uncertainty. Based on this concept, **risk** *is defined as uncertainty concerning the occurrence of a loss.*[1] For example, the risk of being killed in an auto accident is present because uncertainty is present. The risk of lung cancer for smokers is present because uncertainty is present. And the risk of flunking a college course is present because there is uncertainty concerning the grade you will earn.

Although risk is defined as uncertainty in this text, employees in the insurance industry often use the term risk to identify the property or life being insured. Thus, in the insurance industry, it is common to hear statements such as "that driver is a poor risk," or "that building is an unacceptable risk."

Finally, when risk is defined as uncertainty, some authors make a careful distinction between objective risk and subjective risk.

## Objective Risk

**Objective risk** *is defined as the relative variation of actual loss from expected loss.* For example, assume that a property insurer has 10,000 houses insured over a long period and, on average, 1 percent, or 100 houses, burn each year. However, it would be rare for exactly 100 houses to burn each year. In some years, as few as 90 houses may burn, while in other years, as many as 110 houses may burn. Thus, there is a variation of 10 houses from the expected number of 100, or a variation of 10 percent. This relative variation of actual loss from expected loss is known as objective risk.

Objective risk declines as the number of exposures increases. More specifically, *objective risk varies inversely with the square root of the number of cases under observation.* In our previous example, 10,000 houses were insured, and objective risk was 10/100, or 10 percent. Now assume that 1 million houses are insured. The expected number of houses that will burn is now 10,000, but the variation of actual loss from expected loss is only 100. Objective risk is now 100/10,000, or 1 percent. Thus, as the square root of the number of houses increased from 100 in the first example to 1000 in the second example (ten times), objective risk declined to one-tenth of its former level.

Objective risk can be statistically measured by some measure of dispersion, such as the standard deviation or coefficient of variation. Because objective risk can be measured, it is an extremely useful concept for an insurer or a corporate risk manager. As the number of exposures increases, an insurer can predict its future loss experience more accurately because it can rely on the law of large numbers. The **law of large numbers** states that as the number of exposure units increases, the more closely will the actual loss experience approach the probable loss experience. For example, as the number of homes under observation increases, the greater is the degree of accuracy in predicting the proportion of homes that will burn. The law of large numbers is discussed in greater detail in Chapter 2.

## Subjective Risk

**Subjective risk** *is defined as uncertainty based on a person's mental condition or state of mind.* For example, a customer who was drinking heavily in a bar may attempt to drive home. The driver may be uncertain whether he or she will arrive home safely without being arrested by the police for drunken driving. This mental uncertainty is called subjective risk.

The impact of subjective risk varies depending on the individual. Two persons in the same situation may have a different perception of risk, and their behavior may be altered accordingly. If an individual experiences great mental uncertainty concerning the occurrence of a loss, that person's behavior may be affected. High subjective risk often results in conservative and prudent behavior, while low subjective risk may result in less conservative behavior. A driver may have been previously arrested for drunk driving and is aware that he or she has consumed too much alcohol. The driver may then compensate for the mental uncertainty by getting someone else to drive him or her home or by taking a cab. Another driver in the same situation may perceive the risk of being arrested as slight. This second driver may drive in a more careless and reckless manner; a low subjective risk results in less conservative driving behavior.

## CHANCE OF LOSS

Chance of loss is closely related to the concept of risk. **Chance of loss** *is defined as the probability that an event will occur.* Like risk, "probability" has both objective and subjective aspects.

## Objective Probability

**Objective probability** *refers to the long-run relative frequency of an event based on the assumptions of an infinite number of observations and of no change in the underlying conditions.* Objective probabilities can be determined in two ways. First, they can be determined by deductive reasoning. These probabilities are called *a priori probabilities.* For example, the probability of getting a head from the toss of a perfectly balanced coin is 1/2 because there are two sides, and only one is a head. Likewise, the probability of rolling a 6 with a single die is 1/6, since there are six sides and only one side has six dots on it.

Second, objective probabilities can be determined by inductive reasoning, rather than by deduction. For example, the probability that a person age 21 will die before age 26 cannot be logically deduced. However, by a careful analysis of past mortality experience, life insurers can estimate the probability of death and sell a five-year term insurance policy issued at age 21.

## Subjective Probability

**Subjective probability** *is the individual's personal estimate of the chance of loss.* Subjective probability need not coincide with objective probability. For example, people who buy a lottery ticket on their birthday may believe it is their lucky day and overestimate the small chance of winning. A wide variety of factors can influence subjective probability, including a person's age, sex, intelligence, education, and the use of alcohol.

In addition, a person's estimate of a loss may differ from objective probability because there may be ambiguity in the way in which the probability is perceived. For example, assume that a slot machine in a gambling casino requires three lemons to win. The person playing the machine may perceive the probability of winning to be quite high. But if there are ten symbols on each reel and only one is a lemon, the objective probability of hitting the jackpot with three lemons is quite small. Assuming that each reel spins independently of the others, the probability that all three will simultaneously show a lemon is the product of their individual probabilities $(1/10 \times 1/10 \times 1/10 = 1/1000)$. This knowledge is advantageous to casino owners, who know that most gamblers are not trained statisticians and are therefore likely to overestimate the objective probabilities of winning.

## Chance of Loss Distinguished from Risk

Chance of loss should be distinguished from objective risk. Chance of loss is the probability that an event will occur. Objective risk is the relative variation of actual loss from expected loss. *The chance of loss may be identical for two different groups, but objective risk may be quite different.* For example, assume that a property insurer has 10,000 homes insured in Los Angeles and 10,000 homes insured in Philadelphia and that the chance of loss in each city is 1 percent. Thus, on average, 100 homes should burn annually in each city. However, if the annual variation in losses ranges from 75 to 125 in Philadelphia, but only from 90 to 110 in Los Angeles, objective risk is greater in Philadelphia even though the chance of loss in both cities is the same.

## PERIL AND HAZARD

The terms *peril* and *hazard* should not be confused with the concept of risk discussed earlier.

### Peril

**Peril** *is defined as the cause of loss.* If your house burns because of a fire, the peril, or cause of loss, is the fire. If your car is damaged in a collision with another car, collision is the peril, or cause of loss. Some common perils that cause property damage or loss include fire, lightning, windstorm, hail, tornadoes, earthquakes, theft, and burglary.

### Hazard

A **hazard** *is a condition that creates or increases the chance of loss.* There are three major types of hazards:

* Physical hazard
* Moral hazard
* Morale hazard

**Physical Hazard** A **physical hazard** *is a physical condition that increases the chance of loss.* Examples of physical hazards are icy roads that increase the chance of an auto accident, defective wiring in a building that increases the chance of fire, and a defective lock on a door that increases the chance of theft.

**Moral Hazard** **Moral hazard** *is dishonesty or character defects in an individual that increase the frequency or severity of loss.* Examples of moral hazard are faking an accident to collect the insurance, submitting a fraudulent claim, inflating the amount of a claim, and intentionally burning unsold merchandise that is insured.

Moral hazard is present in all forms of insurance, and it is difficult to control. Dishonest individuals often rationalize their actions on the grounds that "the insurer has plenty of money." This view is incorrect because the insurer can pay claims only by collecting premiums from other insureds. Because of moral hazard, premiums are higher for everyone.

Insurers attempt to control moral hazard by careful underwriting of applicants for insurance and by various policy provisions, such as deductibles, waiting periods, exclusions, and riders. These provisions are examined in Chapter 5.

**Morale Hazard** Some insurance authors make a distinction between moral hazard and morale hazard. There is a subtle difference between them. Moral hazard refers to dishonesty by an insured that increases the frequency or severity of loss. **Morale hazard** *is carelessness or indifference to a loss because of the existence of insurance.* Some insureds are careless or indifferent to a loss because they have insurance. Examples of morale hazard include leaving car keys in the ignition of an unlocked car and thus increasing the chance of theft, leaving a door unlocked that allows a burglar to enter, and changing lanes suddenly on a congested interstate highway without signaling. Careless acts like these increase the chance of loss.

## BASIC CATEGORIES OF RISK

Risk can be classified into several distinct categories. The major categories of risk are:

- Pure and speculative risks
- Fundamental and particular risks

### Pure and Speculative Risks

**Pure risk** *is defined as a situation in which there are only the possibilities of loss or no loss.* The only possible outcomes are adverse (loss) and neutral (no loss). Examples of pure risks include premature death, job-related accidents, catastrophic medical expenses, and damage to property from fire, lightning, flood, or earthquake.

**Speculative risk** *is defined as a situation in which either profit or loss is possible.* If you purchase 100 shares of common stock, you would profit if the price of the stock increases but would lose if the price declines. Other examples of speculative risks are betting on a horse race, investing in real estate, and going into business for yourself. In these situations, both profit and loss are possible.

It is important to distinguish between pure and speculative risks for three reasons. First, private insurers generally insure only pure risks. With certain exceptions, speculative risks are not considered insurable, and other techniques for coping with risk must be used. (One exception is that some insurers will insure institutional portfolio investments and municipal bonds against loss.)

Second, the law of large numbers can be applied more easily to pure risks than to speculative risks. The law of large numbers is important because it enables insurers to predict loss in advance. In contrast, it is generally more difficult to apply the law of large numbers to speculative risks in order to predict future loss experience. An exception is the speculative risk of gambling, where casino operators can apply the law of large numbers in a most efficient manner.

Finally, society may benefit from a speculative risk even though a loss occurs, but it is harmed if a pure risk is present and a loss occurs. For example, a firm may develop new technology for producing computers more cheaply. As a result, some competitors may be forced into bankruptcy. Despite the bankruptcy, society benefits since the computers are produced at a lower cost. However, society normally does not benefit when a loss from a pure risk occurs, such as a flood or earthquake that devastates an area.

### Fundamental and Particular Risks

A **fundamental risk** *is a risk that affects the entire economy or large numbers of persons or groups within the economy.* Examples include high inflation, cyclical

EXHIBIT 1.1

**The 10 Most Costly Insured Catastrophes**

| Month/Year | Catastrophe | Estimated insured loss |
|---|---|---|
| Aug. 1992 | Hurricane Andrew: wind, flooding, tornadoes | $15,500,000,000 |
| Jan. 1994 | Northridge, Calif., earthquake | 12,500,000,000 |
| Sept. 1989 | Hurricane Hugo: wind, flooding, tornadoes | 4,195,000,000 |
| March 1993 | 20-state winter storm | 1,750,000,000 |
| Oct. 1991 | Oakland, Calif., fire | 1,700,000,000 |
| Sept. 1992 | Hurricane Iniki | 1,600,000,000 |
| Oct. 1989 | Loma Prieta, Calif., earthquake | 960,000,000 |
| Oct./Nov. 1993 | California brush fires | 950,000,000 |
| May 1995 | Texas and New Mexico: wind, hail, flooding | 910,000,000 |
| Dec. 1983 | Wind, snow, freezing, 41 states | 880,000,000 |

SOURCE: *The Fact Book 1996, Property/Casualty Insurance Facts* (New York: Insurance Information Institute), p. 83.

unemployment, and war because large numbers of individuals are affected.

The risk of a natural disaster is another important fundamental risk. Hurricanes, tornadoes, earthquakes, floods, and forest and grass fires can result in billions of dollars in property damage as well as the loss of numerous lives. Exhibit 1.1 shows the 10 most costly insured catastrophes in the United States.

In 1996, Hurricane Fran caused almost $1 billion in property damage in North Carolina, South Carolina, Virginia, and Maryland. More than 1000 tornadoes occur annually in the United States, and cause substantial property damage and the loss of lives.

In addition, earthquakes cause enormous property damage, especially in California. In 1994, an earthquake in Northridge, California resulted in billions of dollars of property damage and the loss of numerous lives. Floods can also devastate an area and cause catastrophic losses. In 1993, severe floods in the Midwest caused millions of dollars in property damage and considerable financial hardship. Most flood losses were uninsured.

In contrast to a fundamental risk, a **particular risk** *is a risk that affects only individuals and not the entire community.* Examples are car thefts, bank robberies, and dwelling fires. Only individuals experiencing such losses are affected, not the entire economy.

The distinction between a fundamental and a particular risk is important since government assistance may be necessary to insure a fundamental risk. Social insurance and government insurance programs, as well as government guarantees and subsidies, may be necessary to insure certain fundamental risks in the United States. For example, the risk of unemployment generally is not insurable by private insurers but can be insured publicly by state unemployment compensation programs. In addition, flood insurance subsidized by the federal government is available to business firms and individuals in flood areas.

## TYPES OF PURE RISK

The major types of pure risk that can create great financial insecurity include personal risks, property risks, and liability risks.

### Personal Risks

**Personal risks** *are risks that directly affect an individual;* they involve the possibility of the complete loss or reduction of earned income, extra expenses, and the depletion of financial assets. There are four major personal risks:[2]

- Risk of premature death
- Risk of insufficient income during retirement
- Risk of poor health
- Risk of unemployment

**Risk of Premature Death  Premature Death** *is defined as the death of a household head with unfulfilled financial obligations.* These obligations can include dependents to support, a mortgage to be paid off, or children to educate. If the surviving family members receive an insufficient amount of replacement income from other sources, or have insufficient financial assets to replace the lost income, they may be financially insecure.

Premature death can cause financial problems only if the deceased has dependents to support or dies with unsatisfied financial obligations. Thus, the death of a child age 10 is not "premature" in the economic sense.

There are at least four costs that result from the premature death of a household head. First, the human life value of the family head is lost forever. The **human life value** *is defined as the present value of the family's share of the deceased breadwinner's future earnings.* This loss can be substantial; the actual or potential human life value of most college graduates can easily exceed $500,000. Second, additional expenses may be incurred because of funeral expenses, uninsured medical bills, probate and estate settlement costs, and estate and inheritance taxes for larger estates. Third, because of insufficient income, some families will experience a reduction in their standard of living. Finally, certain noneconomic costs are also incurred, including emotional grief, loss of a role model, and counseling and guidance for the children.

**Risk of Insufficient Income During Retirement**  The major risk associated with old age is insufficient income during retirement. The vast majority of workers in the United States retire before age 65. When they retire, they lose their earned income. Unless they have sufficient financial assets on which to draw, or have access to other sources of retirement income, such as Social Security or a private pension, they will be exposed to financial insecurity during retirement.

How are the aged 65 and older doing financially? In answering this question, it is a mistake to assume that all aged are wealthy; it is equally wrong to assume that all aged are poor. *The aged are an economically diverse group, and the incomes received are far from uniform.* In 1994, about 31 percent of the aged units 65 and older had incomes under $10,000.

At the other extreme, about 9 percent of the aged units had incomes of $50,000 or more. The median income for all aged units in 1994 was only $15,094.[3] This amount is relatively low and may be insufficient for retired workers with substantial additional expenses, such as high uninsured medical bills, the cost of long-term care in a nursing facility, or high property taxes.

In addition, many middle-aged households and individuals approaching retirement have accumulated an insufficient amount of financial assets. Financial assets are important because the investment income can supplement the retirement income received, and the assets provide a cushion for emergencies. The Rand Corporation has analyzed the financial assets owned by middle-age households with at least one person in their fifties and by individuals ages 51–61. The study showed that in 1993, median financial assets owned by middle-age white households and individuals ages 51–61 were only $17,300 (excluding home equity). Median financial assets owned by middle-age black households in the same age category were only $400, and for Hispanic households, only $150.[4] These amounts are relatively low and will provide only limited amounts of supplemental income during retirement. Financial assets included individual retirement accounts (IRAs), Keogh plans, stocks, mutual funds, savings accounts, certificates of deposit, treasury bills, and other liquid assets.

**Risk of Poor Health**  Poor health is another important personal risk. The risk of poor health includes both the payment of catastrophic medical bills and the loss of earned income. The costs of major surgery have increased substantially in recent years. For example, an open heart operation can cost more than $75,000, a kidney or heart transplant can cost more than $200,000, and the costs of a crippling automobile accident requiring several major operations, plastic surgery, and rehabilitation can exceed $250,000. In addition, long-term care in a nursing home can cost $40,000 or more each year. Unless these persons have adequate health insurance, private savings and financial assets, or other sources of income to meet these expenditures, they will be financially insecure. In particular, the inability of some persons to pay catastrophic medical bills is an important cause of personal bankruptcy.

The loss of earned income is another major cause of financial insecurity if the disability is severe. In cases of long-term disability, there is a substantial loss of earned income, medical bills are incurred, employee benefits may be lost or reduced, savings are often depleted, and someone must take care of the disabled person.

Most workers seldom think about the financial consequences of long-term disability. The probability of becoming disabled before age 65 is much higher than is commonly believed, especially at the younger ages. *For individuals age 25, the 1985 Commissioners Disability Table shows that the probability of being totally disabled for 90 or more days prior to age 65 is 54 percent.*[5] The loss of earned income during an extended disability can be financially very painful. Even if the disabled person carries disability income insurance, the financial consequences can be severe if the insurer refuses to pay the claim.

**Risk of Unemployment**   The risk of unemployment is another major threat to financial security. Unemployment can result from business cycle downswings, technological and structural changes in the economy, seasonal factors, and imperfections in the labor market.

Unemployment at times can be a serious problem in the United States because of several important trends. To hold down labor costs, large corporations have downsized, and their work force has been permanently reduced; employers are increasingly hiring temporary or part-time workers to reduce labor costs; and millions of jobs have been lost to foreign nations because of global competition.

Regardless of the reason, unemployment can cause financial insecurity in at least three ways. First, the worker loses his or her earned income. Unless there is adequate replacement income or past savings on which to draw, the unemployed worker will be financially insecure. Second, because of economic conditions, the worker may be able to work only part-time. The reduced income may be insufficient in terms of the worker's needs. Finally, if the duration of unemployment is extended over a long period, past savings may be exhausted.

## Property Risks

Persons owning property are exposed to the risk of having their property damaged or lost from numerous causes. Real estate and personal property can be damaged or destroyed because of fire, lightning, tornadoes, windstorms, and numerous other causes. There are two major types of loss associated with the destruction or theft of property: direct loss and indirect or consequential loss.

**Direct Loss**   A **direct loss** *is defined as a financial loss that results from the physical damage, destruction, or theft of the property.* For example, if you own a restaurant that is damaged by a fire, the physical damage to the restaurant is known as a direct loss.

**Indirect or Consequential Loss**   An **indirect loss** *is a financial loss that results indirectly from the occurrence of a direct physical damage or theft loss.* Thus, in addition to the physical damage loss, the restaurant would lose profits for several months while it is being rebuilt. The loss of profits would be a consequential loss. Other examples of a consequential loss would be the loss of rents, the loss of the use of the building, and the loss of a local market.

*Extra expenses* are another type of indirect, or consequential, loss. For example, suppose you own a newspaper, bank, or dairy. If a loss occurs, you must continue to operate regardless of cost; otherwise, you will lose customers to your competitors. It may be necessary to set up a temporary operation at some alternative location, and substantial extra expenses would then be incurred.

## Liability Risks

**Liability risks** are another important type of pure risk that most persons face. Under our legal system, you can be held legally liable if you do something that results in bodily injury or property damage to someone else. A court of law may order you to pay substantial damages to the person you have injured.

The United States is a litigious society at the present time. There is a widely held notion that the way to resolve any dispute is to sue. As a result, lawsuits of all types have increased substantially in recent years. Motorists are being held legally liable for the negligent operation of their vehicles; operators of boats and lake owners are being sued because of bodily injury to boat occupants, swimmers, and water skiers. The damages awarded can be substantial (see Insight 1.1). Business firms are also being sued because of defective products that harm or injure

## INSIGHT 1.1

### Water Skier Injured in Accident Wins $1.7 Million Settlement

Boating procedures and skiing regulations were issues in a lawsuit in which an Omaha teen-ager won a $1.7 million settlement.

Jerod Krejci, 18, won the award in Merrick County District Court. Krejci was paralyzed in a water-skiing accident at Sundance Lake, a recreational area south of Clarks, Neb.

Krejci contended that he was injured because of the negligence of a boat driver and lake operators. Defendants maintained that Krejci could have avoided the accident and that lake rules were proper.

Krejci settled with defendants as the trial of the lawsuit was in its ninth day. Krejci's attorney was presenting evidence to the jury.

Krejci sued boat driver Tobin Anderson of York, Sundance Lake Association and Overland Sand and Gravel Co. of Stromsburg.

Anderson is to pay $1 million, the lake association is to pay $500,000, and Overland is to pay $200,000. Insurance companies agreed to the settlements.

The accident happened July 3, 1993. Krejci broke his neck as he struck a sandbar and was paralyzed from the chest down.

Attorney Steve Leininger of Grand Island, who represented Krejci, contended that the boat driver got too close to the shore and failed to keep a proper lookout for the skier.

The lake is a narrow sandpit with an irregular shoreline, Leininger said. Krejci was to the right of the boat when the boat apparently turned suddenly, leaving a sandbar between the boat and skier, Leininger said.

Krejci released the tow rope and glided in shallow water until he struck the sandbar, Leininger said. Krejci broke the top of an arm bone and his neck, Leininger said.

He also contended that the design of the lake was dangerous and that lake operators failed to warn boaters and skiers.

SOURCE: Adapted from Gloria Sunderman, "Water Skier Injured In Accident Wins $1.7 Million Settlement," *Omaha World Herald,* May 2, 1996, pp. 17, 23.

---

customers; physicians, attorneys, accountants, engineers, and other professionals are being sued because of alleged professional malpractice. And new types of lawsuits are constantly emerging. For example, some ministers have been sued by church members who accuse them of giving improper advice.

Liability risks are of great importance for several reasons. *First, there is no maximum upper limit with respect to the amount of the loss.* You can be sued for any amount. In contrast, if you own property, there is a maximum limit on the loss. For example, if your automobile has an actual cash value of $10,000, the maximum physical damage loss is $10,000. But if you are negligent and cause an accident that results in serious bodily injury to the other driver, you can be sued for any amount—$50,000, $500,000, or $1 million or more—by the person you have injured.

*Second, a lien can be placed on your income and financial assets to satisfy a legal judgment.* For example, assume that you injure someone, and a court of law orders you to pay substantial damages to the injured

party. If you cannot pay the judgment, a lien may be placed on your income and financial assets to satisfy the judgment. If you declare bankruptcy to avoid payment of the judgment, your credit rating will be impaired.

*Finally, legal defense costs can be enormous.* If you have no liability insurance, the cost of hiring an attorney to defend you can be staggering. If the suit goes to trial, attorney fees and other legal expenses can be substantial.

## BURDEN OF RISK ON SOCIETY

The presence of risk results in certain undesirable social and economic effects. Risk entails three major burdens on society:

- The size of an emergency fund must be increased.
- Society is deprived of certain goods and services.
- Worry and fear are present.

## Larger Emergency Fund

It is prudent to set aside funds for an emergency. However, in the absence of insurance, individuals and business firms would have to increase the size of their emergency fund in order to pay for unexpected losses. For example, assume you have purchased a $100,000 home and want to accumulate a fund for repairs if the home is damaged by fire, hail, windstorm, or some other peril. Without insurance, you would have to save at least $20,000 annually to build up an adequate fund within a relatively short period of time. Even then, an early loss could occur, and your emergency fund may be insufficient to pay the loss. If you are a middle-income wage earner, you would find such saving difficult. In any event, the higher the amount that must be saved, the more current consumption spending must be reduced, which results in a lower standard of living.

## Loss of Certain Goods and Services

A second burden of risk is that society is deprived of certain goods and services. For example, because of the risk of a liability lawsuit, many corporations have discontinued manufacturing certain products. Numerous examples can be given. Some 250 companies in the world used to manufacture childhood vaccines; today, only a small number of firms manufacture vaccines, due in part to the threat of liability suits. Other firms have discontinued the manufacture of certain products, including asbestos products, football helmets, silicone-gel breast implants, and certain birth-control devices.

## Worry and Fear

A final burden of risk is that worry and fear are present. Numerous examples can illustrate the mental unrest and fear caused by risk. Parents may be fearful if a teenage son or daughter departs on a skiing trip during a blinding snowstorm since the risk of being killed on an icy road is present. Some passengers in a commercial jet may become extremely nervous and fearful if the jet encounters severe turbulence during the flight. A college student who needs a grade of C in a course in order to graduate may enter the final examination room with a feeling of apprehension and fear.

## METHODS OF HANDLING RISK

As we stressed earlier, risk is a burden not only to the individual but to society as well. Thus, it is important to examine some techniques for meeting the problem of risk. There are five major methods of handling risk:

- Avoidance
- Loss control
- Retention
- Noninsurance transfers
- Insurance

## Avoidance

**Avoidance** is one method of handling risk. For example, you can avoid the risk of being mugged in a high-crime rate area by staying out of the area; you can avoid the risk of divorce by not marrying; and a business firm can avoid the risk of being sued for a defective product by not producing the product.

But not all risks should be avoided. For example, you can avoid the risk of death or disability in a plane crash by refusing to fly. But is this practical or desirable? The alternatives, driving or taking a bus or train, are often not appealing. Although the risk of a plane crash is present, the safety record of commercial airlines is excellent, and flying is a reasonable risk to assume.

## Loss Control

**Loss control** is another important method for handling risk. Loss control consists of certain activities that reduce both the frequency and severity of losses. Thus, loss control has two major objectives: loss prevention and loss reduction.

**Loss Prevention**    Loss prevention aims at reducing the probability of loss so that the frequency of losses is reduced. Several examples of personal loss prevention can be given. Automobile accidents can be reduced if motorists take a safe-driving course and drive defensively. The number of heart attacks can be reduced if individuals control their weight, give up smoking, and eat healthy diets.

Loss prevention is also important for business firms. For example, a boiler explosion can be prevented by periodic inspections by a safety engineer;

occupational accidents can be reduced by the elimination of unsafe working conditions and by strong enforcement of safety rules; and fires can be prevented by forbidding workers to smoke in a building where highly flammable materials are being used. In short, the goal of loss prevention is to prevent the loss from occurring.

**Loss Reduction**   Strict loss-prevention efforts can reduce the frequency of losses, yet some losses will inevitably occur. Thus, the second objective of loss control is to reduce the severity of a loss after it occurs. For example, a department store can install a sprinkler system so that a fire is promptly extinguished, thereby reducing the loss; a plant can be constructed with fire-resistant materials to minimize fire damage; fire doors and fire walls can be used to prevent a fire from spreading; and a community warning system can reduce the number of injuries and deaths from an approaching tornado.

From the viewpoint of society, loss control is highly desirable for two reasons. *First, the indirect costs of losses may be large, and in some instances can easily exceed the direct costs.* For example, a worker may be injured on the job. In addition to being responsible for the worker's medical expenses and a certain percentage of earnings (direct costs), the firm may also incur sizable indirect costs: a machine may be damaged and must be repaired; the assembly line may have to be shut down; costs are incurred in training a new worker to replace the injured worker; and a contract may be canceled because goods are not shipped on time. By preventing the loss from occurring, both indirect costs and direct costs are reduced.

*Second, the social costs of losses are reduced.* For example, assume that the worker in the preceding example dies from the accident. Society is deprived forever of the goods and services the deceased worker could have produced. The worker's family loses its share of the worker's earnings and may experience considerable grief and financial insecurity. And the worker may personally experience great pain and suffering before dying. In short, these social costs can be reduced through an effective loss-control program.

## Retention

**Retention** is a third method of handling risk. An individual or a business firm may retain all or part of a given risk. Risk retention can be either active or passive.

**Active Retention**   Active risk retention means that an individual is consciously aware of the risk and deliberately plans to retain all or part of it. For example, a motorist may wish to retain the risk of a small collision loss by purchasing an auto insurance policy with a $250 or higher deductible. A homeowner may retain a small part of the risk of damage to the home by purchasing a homeowners policy with a substantial deductible. A business firm may deliberately retain the risk of petty thefts by employees, shoplifting, or the spoilage of perishable goods. In these cases, a conscious decision is made to retain part or all of a given risk.

Active risk retention is used for two major reasons. First, risk retention can save money. Insurance may not be purchased at all, or it may be purchased with a deductible; either way, there is often a substantial saving in the cost of insurance. Second, the risk may be deliberately retained because commercial insurance is either unavailable or can be obtained only by the payment of prohibitive premiums.

**Passive Retention**   Risk can also be retained passively. Certain risks may be unknowingly retained because of ignorance, indifference, or laziness. Passive retention is very dangerous if the risk retained has the potential for destroying you financially. For example, many workers with earned incomes are not insured against the risk of long-term total and permanent disability under either an individual or group disability income plan. However, the adverse financial consequences of total and permanent disability generally are more severe than premature death. Therefore, people who are not insured against this risk are using the technique of risk retention in a most dangerous and inappropriate manner.

In summary, risk retention is an important technique for handling risk, especially in a modern corporate risk management program, which will be discussed in Chapter 3. Risk retention, however, is appropriate primarily for high-frequency, low-severity risks where potential losses are relatively small. Except under unusual circumstances, risk retention should not be used to retain low-frequency, high-severity risks, such as the risk of catastrophic medical expenses, long-term disability, or a liability lawsuit.

## Noninsurance Transfers

**Noninsurance transfers** are another technique for handling risk. The risk is transferred to a party other than an insurance company. A risk can be transferred by several methods, among which are the following:

- Transfer of risk by contracts
- Hedging price risks
- Incorporation of a business firm

**Transfer of Risk by Contracts**    Unwanted risks can be transferred by contracts. For example, the risk of a defective television or stereo set can be transferred to the retailer by purchasing a service contract, which makes the retailer responsible for all repairs after the warranty expires. The risk of a rent increase can be transferred to the landlord by a long-term lease. The risk of a price increase in construction costs can be transferred to the builder by having a fixed price in the contract.

Finally, a risk can be transferred by a **hold-harmless clause.** For example, if a manufacturer of scaffolds inserts a hold-harmless clause in a contract with a retailer, the retailer agrees to hold the manufacturer harmless in case a scaffold collapses and someone is injured.

**Hedging Price Risks**    Hedging price risks is another example of risk transfer. **Hedging** is a technique for transferring the risk of unfavorable price fluctuations to a speculator by purchasing and selling futures contracts on an organized exchange, such as the Chicago Board of Trade or New York Stock Exchange.

For example, the portfolio manager of a pension fund may hold a substantial position in long-term U.S. Treasury bonds. If interest rates rise, the value of the Treasury bonds will decline. To hedge that risk, the portfolio manager can sell U.S. Treasury bond futures. Assume that interest rates rise as expected, and bond prices decline. The value of the futures contract will decline, which will enable the portfolio manager to make an offsetting purchase at a lower price. The profit obtained from closing out the futures position will partly or completely offset the decline in the market value of the Treasury bonds. Of course, markets do not always move as expected, and the hedge may not be perfect. Transaction costs also are incurred. However, by hedging, the portfolio manager has reduced the potential loss in bond prices if interest rates rise.

**Incorporation of a Business Firm**    **Incorporation** is another example of risk transfer. If a firm is a sole proprietorship, the owner's personal assets can be attached by creditors for satisfaction of debts. If a firm incorporates, personal assets cannot be attached by creditors for payment of the firm's debts. In essence, by incorporation, the liability of the stockholders is limited, and the risk of the firm having insufficient assets to pay business debts is shifted to the creditors.

## Insurance

For most people, insurance is the most practical method for handling a major risk. Although private insurance has several characteristics, three major characteristics should be emphasized. First, *risk transfer* is used since a pure risk is transferred to the insurer. Second, the *pooling technique* is used to spread the losses of the few over the entire group so that average loss is substituted for actual loss. Finally, the risk may be reduced by application of the *law of large numbers* by which an insurer can predict future loss experience with some accuracy. Each of these characteristics is treated in greater detail in Chapter 2.

### SUMMARY

- There is no single definition of risk. Risk traditionally has been defined as uncertainty concerning the occurrence of a loss.

- Objective risk is the relative variation of actual loss from expected loss. Subjective risk is uncertainty based on an individual's mental condition or state of mind. Chance of loss is defined as the probability that an event will occur; it is not the same thing as risk.

- Peril is defined as the cause of loss. Hazard is any condition that creates or increases the chance of loss. There are three types of hazards. Physical hazard is a physical condition present that increases the chance of loss. Moral hazard is dishonesty or character defects in an individual that increase the chance of loss. Morale hazard is carelessness or indifference to a loss because of the existence of insurance.

- The basic categories of risk include the following:

    Pure and speculative risks

    Fundamental and particular risks

    > A pure risk is a risk where there are only the possibilities of loss or no loss. A speculative risk is a risk where either profit or loss is possible.

    > A fundamental risk is a risk that affects the entire economy or large numbers of persons or groups within the economy, such as inflation, war, or recession. A particular risk is a risk that affects only the individual and not the entire community or country.

- The following types of pure risk can threaten an individual's financial security:

    Personal risks

    Property risks

    Liability risks

- Personal risks are those risks that directly affect an individual. Major personal risks include the following:

    Risk of premature death

    Risk of insufficient income during retirement

    Risk of poor health

    Risk of unemployment

- Property risks affect persons who own property. If property is damaged or lost, two principal types of losses may result:

    Direct loss to property

    Indirect, or consequential, loss

    > A direct loss is a financial loss that results from the physical damage, destruction, or theft of the property. An indirect, or consequential, loss is a financial loss that results indirectly from the occurrence of a direct physical damage or theft loss. Examples of indirect losses are the loss of use of the property, loss of profits, loss of rents, and extra expenses.

- Liability risks are extremely important because there is no maximum upper limit on the amount of the loss, and if a person must pay damages, future income and assets can be attached to pay an unsatisfied judgment; substantial legal defense costs and attorney fees may also be incurred.

- Risk entails three major burdens on society:

    The size of an emergency fund must be increased.

    Society is deprived of needed goods and services.

    Worry and fear are present.

- There are five major methods of handling risk:

    Avoidance

    Loss control

    Retention

    Noninsurance transfers

    Insurance

## KEY CONCEPTS AND TERMS

| | |
|---|---|
| Avoidance | Noninsurance transfers |
| Chance of loss | Objective probability |
| Direct loss | Objective risk |
| Fundamental risk | Particular risk |
| Hazard | Peril |
| Hedging | Personal risks |
| Hold-harmless clause | Physical hazard |
| Human life value | Property risks |
| Incorporation | Pure risk |
| Indirect, or consequential, loss | Retention |
| | Risk |
| Liability risks | Speculative risk |
| Loss control | Subjective probability |
| Moral hazard | Subjective risk |
| Morale hazard | |

## QUESTIONS FOR REVIEW

1. Explain briefly the meaning of risk.

2. How does objective risk differ from subjective risk?

3. Define chance of loss.

4. Distinguish between an objective probability and a subjective probability.

5. Define peril, hazard, physical hazard, moral hazard, and morale hazard.

6. Explain the difference between pure and speculative risk and between fundamental and particular risk.

7. Identify the major types of pure risk that are associated with great financial insecurity.

8. Why is pure risk harmful to society?

9. What is the difference between a direct loss and an indirect, or consequential, loss?

10. Describe briefly the five major methods of handling risk. Give an example of each method.

## QUESTIONS FOR DISCUSSION

1. The Apex Insurance Company received an application to provide property insurance on a frame

## CASE APPLICATION

Tyrone is a college senior who is majoring in journalism. He owns a high mileage 1985 Ford that has a current market value of $900. The current replacement value of his clothes, television set, stereo set, and other personal property in a rented apartment total $5,000. He wears disposable contact lenses, which cost $200 for a six-month supply. He also has a waterbed in his rented apartment that has leaked water in the past. Tyrone is an avid runner who runs five miles daily in a nearby public park that has the reputation of being extremely dangerous because of drug dealers, numerous assaults and muggings, and drive-by shootings. Tyrone's parents both work to help him pay his tuition.

For each of the following risks or loss exposures, identify an appropriate risk management technique that could be used to deal with the exposure. Explain your answer.

a. Physical damage to the 1985 Ford because of a collision with another motorist.
b. Liability lawsuit against Tyrone arising out of the negligent operation of his car.
c. Total loss of clothes, television, stereo, and personal property because of a grease fire in the kitchen of his rented apartment.
d. Disappearance of one contact lens.
e. Waterbed leak that causes property damage to the apartment.
f. Physical assault on Tyrone by gang members who are dealing drugs in the park where he runs.
g. Loss of tuition from Tyrone's father who is killed by a drunk driver in an auto accident.

dwelling located near an oil refinery in an industrial section of the city. In considering this property for insurance, the property insurer is concerned with risk, hazard, and chance of loss.

a. (1) Describe several risks to which the frame dwelling is exposed.
   (2) Compare and contrast moral hazard and morale hazard with respect to property insurance on the frame dwelling. Give an example of each.
b. Assume that chance of loss is 3 percent for two different fleets of trucks. Explain how it is possible that objective risk for both fleets can be different even though the chance of loss is identical.

2. Identify the types of financial losses likely to be incurred by each of the following parties.
a. A person who negligently injures another motorist in an automobile accident
b. A restaurant that is shut down for six months because of a tornado
c. A family whose family head dies prematurely
d. An attorney who fails to file a legal brief on time for a client
e. A tenant whose apartment burns in a fire

3. Several methods are available for handling risk. However, certain techniques are more appropriate than others in a given situation.
a. (1) Should retention be used in those situations where both loss frequency and loss severity are high? Explain your answer.
   (2) Explain why loss control is a highly desirable method for handling risk.
b. Explain why chance of loss and risk are not the same thing.

4. Megan operates a pawn shop in a large city. Her shop is in a high-crime area, and the high cost of burglary insurance is threatening the existence of her business. A trade association points out that several methods other than insurance can be used to handle the burglary exposure. Identify and illustrate three different noninsurance methods that might be used to deal with this exposure.

### SELECTED REFERENCES

Berstein, Peter L. *Against the Gods, The Remarkable Story of Risk.* New York: John Wiley & Son, Inc., 1996.
Crowe, Robert M., and Ronald C. Horn. "The Meaning of Risk," *Journal of Risk and Insurance,* 34 (September 1967): 459–74.

Head, George L. "An Alternative to Defining Risk as Uncertainty," *Journal of Risk and Insurance,* 34 (June 1967): 205–14.

Pritchett, S. Travis, et al. *Risk Management and Insurance,* 7th ed. St. Paul, MN.: West Publishing Company, 1996, Chapter 1.

Rejda, George E. *Social Insurance and Economic Security,* 5th ed. Englewood Cliffs, N.J.: Prentice Hall, 1994, Chapter 1.

Rejda, George E., special ed. "Risk and Its Treatment: Changing Societal Consequences," *Annals of the American Academy of Political and Social Science,* 443 (May 1979): 1–144.

## NOTES

1. Risk has also been defined as (1) variability in future outcomes, (2) chance of loss, (3) possibility of an adverse deviation from a desired outcome that is expected or hoped for, (4) the variation in possible outcomes that exist in a given situation, and (5) possibility that a sentient entity can incur a loss. For a critical discussion of the uncertainty theory of risk, the interested student should read George L. Head, "An Alternative to Defining Risk as Uncertainty," *Journal of Risk and Insurance,* 34 (June 1967): 205–14; and Robert M. Crowe and Ronald C. Horn, "The Meaning of Risk," *Journal of Risk and Insurance,* 34 (September 1967): 459–74.

2. This section is based on George E. Rejda, *Social Insurance and Economic Security,* 5th ed. (Englewood Cliffs, N.J.: Prentice Hall, 1994), pp. 6–8.

3. Susan Grad, *Income of the Population Age 55 and Over, 1994* (Washington, D.C.: Social Security Administration, Office of Research and Statistics, January 1996), Table III.1, p. 35.

4. James P. Smith, *Documented Briefing, Unequal Wealth and Incentives to Save* (Santa Monica, CA: RAND, 1995), p. 10.

5. Data based on the 1985 Commissioners Disability Table as cited in Edward E. Graves, ed., *McGill's Life Insurance* (Bryn Mawr, PA.: The American College, 1994), Table 7–2, p. 141.

# Chapter 2

# INSURANCE AND RISK

> *Insurance: An ingenious modern game of chance in which the player is permitted to enjoy the comfortable conviction that he is beating the man who keeps the table.*
>
> Ambrose Bierce

## Student Learning Objectives

After studying this chapter, you should be able to:

■ Define insurance and explain the basic characteristics of insurance.

■ Explain the law of large numbers.

■ Describe the requirements of an insurable risk from the viewpoint of a private insurer.

■ Identify the major insurable and uninsurable risks in our society.

■ Show how insurance differs from gambling and speculation.

■ Describe the major types of insurance.

■ Explain the social benefits and social costs of insurance.

In the previous chapter, major risks that can create great financial insecurity were identified. For most people, insurance is the most important technique for handling risk. Consequently, you should understand how insurance works. This chapter discusses insurance as a major technique for handling risk. Topics discussed include the basic characteristics of insurance, the requirements of an insurable risk, the major types of insurance, and the social benefits and costs of insurance.

## DEFINITION OF INSURANCE

There is no single definition of insurance. Insurance can be defined from the viewpoint of several disciplines, including law, economics, history, actuarial science, risk theory, and sociology. But each possible definition will not be examined at this point. Instead, attention will be focused on those common elements that are typically present in any insurance plan. However, before proceeding, a working definition of insurance—one that captures the essential characteristics of a true insurance plan—must be established.

After careful study, the Commission on Insurance Terminology of the American Risk and Insurance Association has defined insurance as follows.[1] **Insurance** *is the pooling of fortuitous losses by transfer of such risks to insurers, who agree to indemnify insureds for such losses, to provide other pecuniary benefits on their occurrence, or to render services connected with the risk.*

Although this definition may not be acceptable to all insurance scholars, it is useful for analyzing the common elements of a true insurance plan.

## BASIC CHARACTERISTICS OF INSURANCE

Based on the preceding definition, an insurance plan or arrangement typically has certain characteristics. They include the following:

- Pooling of losses
- Payment of fortuitous losses
- Risk transfer
- Indemnification

### Pooling of Losses

Pooling or the sharing of losses is the heart of insurance. **Pooling** *is the spreading of losses incurred by the few over the entire group, so that in the process, average loss is substituted for actual loss.* In addition, pooling involves the grouping of a large number of exposure units so that the law of large numbers can operate to provide a substantially accurate prediction of future losses. Ideally, there should be a large number of similar, but not necessarily identical, exposure units that are subject to the same perils. Thus, pooling implies (1) the sharing of losses by the entire group, and (2) prediction of future losses with some accuracy based on the law of large numbers.

With respect to the first concept—loss sharing—consider this simple example. Assume that 1000 farmers in southeastern Nebraska agree that if any farmer's home is damaged or destroyed by a fire, the other members of the group will indemnify, or cover, the actual costs of the unlucky farmer who has a loss. Assume also that each home is valued at $100,000, and, on average, one home burns each year. In the absence of insurance, the maximum loss to each farmer is $100,000 if the home should burn. However, by pooling the loss, it can be spread over the entire group, and if one farmer has a total loss, the maximum amount that each farmer would have to pay is only $100 ($100,000/1000). In effect, the pooling technique results in the substitution of an average loss of $100 for the actual loss of $100,000.

In addition, by pooling or combining the loss experience of a large number of exposure units, an insurer may be able to predict future losses with some accuracy. From the viewpoint of the insurer, if future losses can be predicted, objective risk is reduced. Thus, another characteristic often found in many lines of insurance is risk reduction based on the law of large numbers.

The **law of large numbers** *states that the greater the number of exposures, the more closely will the actual results approach the probable results that are expected from an infinite number of exposures.*[2] For example, if you flip a balanced coin into the air, the *a priori* probability of getting a head is 0.5. If you flip the coin only ten times, you may get a head eight times. Although the observed probability of getting a head is 0.8, the true probability is still 0.5. If the coin were flipped one million times, however, the actual number of heads would be approximately 500,000. Thus, as the number of random tosses increases, the actual results approach the expected results.

A practical illustration of the law of large numbers is the National Safety Council's prediction of the number of automobile deaths during a typical holiday weekend. Because millions of automobiles are on the road, the National Safety Council has been able to predict with great accuracy the number of motorists who will die during a typical July 4 holiday weekend. For example, 500 to 700 motorists may be expected to die during a typical July 4 weekend. Although individual motorists cannot be identified, the actual number of deaths for the group of motorists as a whole can be predicted with some accuracy.

However, for most insurance lines, the actuary seldom knows the true probability and severity of loss. Therefore, estimates of both the average frequency and the average severity of loss must be based on previous loss experience. If there are a large number of exposure units, the actual loss experience of the past may be a good approximation of future losses. As noted in Chapter 1, objective risk varies inversely with the square root of the number of cases under observation: as the number of exposures increases, the relative variation of actual loss from expected loss will decline. Thus, the insurer can predict future losses with a greater degree of accuracy as the number of exposures increases. This concept is important since an insurer must charge a premium that will be adequate for paying all losses and expenses during the policy period. The lower the degree of objective risk, the more confidence an insurer has that the actual premium charged will be sufficient to pay all claims and expenses and provide a margin for profit.

A more rigorous statement of the law of large numbers can be found in the Appendix at the end of this chapter.

## Payment of Fortuitous Losses

A second characteristic of private insurance is the payment of fortuitous losses. A **fortuitous loss** *is one that is unforeseen and unexpected and occurs as a result of chance*. In other words, the loss must be accidental. The law of large numbers is based on the assumption that losses are accidental and occur randomly. For example, a person may slip on an icy sidewalk and break a leg. The loss would be fortuitous.

## Risk Transfer

Risk transfer is another essential element of insurance. With the exception of self-insurance,[3] a true insurance plan always involves risk transfer. **Risk transfer** *means that a pure risk is transferred from the insured to the insurer, who typically is in a stronger financial position to pay the loss than the insured*. From the viewpoint of the individual, pure risks that are typically transferred to insurers include the risk of premature death, poor health, disability, destruction and theft of property, and liability lawsuits.

## Indemnification

A final characteristic of insurance is indemnification for losses. **Indemnification** *means that the insured is restored to his or her approximate financial position prior to the occurrence of the loss*. Thus, if your home burns in a fire, the homeowners policy will indemnify you or restore you to your previous position. If you are sued because of the negligent operation of an automobile, your automobile liability insurance policy will pay those sums that you are legally obligated to pay. Similarly, if you are seriously disabled, a disability-income policy will restore at least part of the lost wages.

## REQUIREMENTS OF AN INSURABLE RISK

Insurers normally insure only pure risks. However, not all pure risks are insurable. Certain requirements usually must be fulfilled before a pure risk can be privately insured. From the viewpoint of the insurer, there are ideally six requirements of an insurable risk.

- There must be a large number of exposure units.
- The loss must be accidental and unintentional.
- The loss must be determinable and measurable.
- The loss should not be catastrophic.
- The chance of loss must be calculable.
- The premium must be economically feasible.

## Large Number of Exposure Units

*The first requirement of an insurable risk is a large number of exposure units*. Ideally, there should be a large group of roughly similar, but not necessarily identical, exposure units that are subject to the same peril or group of perils. For example, a large number of frame dwellings in a city can be grouped together for purposes of providing property insurance on the dwellings.

The purpose of this first requirement is to enable the insurer to predict loss based on the law of large numbers. Loss data can be compiled over time, and losses for the group as a whole can be predicted with some accuracy. The loss costs can then be spread over all insureds in the underwriting class.

## Accidental and Unintentional Loss

*A second requirement is that the loss should be accidental and unintentional;* ideally, it should be fortuitous and outside the insured's control. This means that if an individual deliberately causes a loss, he or she should not be indemnified for the loss.

The requirement of an accidental and unintentional loss is necessary for two reasons. First, if intentional losses were paid, moral hazard would be substantially increased, and premiums would rise as a result. The substantial increase in premiums could result in relatively fewer persons purchasing the insurance, and the insurer might not have a sufficient number of exposure units to predict future losses.

Second, the loss should be accidental because the law of large numbers is based on the random occurrence of events. A deliberately caused loss is not a random event since the insured knows when the loss will occur. Thus, prediction of future experience may be highly inaccurate if a large number of intentional or nonrandom losses occur.

## Determinable and Measurable Loss

*A third requirement is that the loss should be both determinable and measurable*. This means the loss should be definite as to cause, time, place, and amount. Life insurance in most cases meets this requirement easily. The cause and time of death can be readily determined in most cases, and if the person is insured, the face amount of the life insurance policy is the amount paid.

Some losses, however, are difficult to determine and measure. For example, under a disability-income policy, the insurer promises to pay a monthly benefit to the disabled person if the definition of disability stated in the policy is satisfied. Some dishonest claimants may deliberately fake sickness or injury in order to collect from the insurer. Even if the claim is legitimate, the insurer must still determine whether the insured satisfies the definition of disability stated in the policy. Sickness and disability are highly subjective, and the same event can affect two persons quite differently. For example, two accountants who are insured under separate disability-income contracts may be injured in an automobile accident, and both may be classified as totally disabled. One accountant, however, may be stronger willed and more determined to return to work. If that accountant undergoes rehabilitation and returns to work, the disability-income benefits will terminate. Meanwhile, the other accountant would still continue to receive disability-income benefits according to the terms of the policy. In short, it is difficult to determine when a person is actually disabled. However, all losses ideally should be both determinable and measurable.

The basic purpose of this requirement is to enable an insurer to determine if the loss is covered under the policy, and if it is covered, how much should be paid. For example, Shannon has an expensive fur coat that is insured under a homeowners policy. It makes a great deal of difference to the insurer if a thief breaks into her home and steals the coat, or the coat is missing because her husband stored it in a dry-cleaning establishment but forgot to tell her. The loss is covered in the first example but not in the second.

## No Catastrophic Loss

*The fourth requirement is that ideally the loss should not be catastrophic.* This means that a large proportion of exposure units should not incur losses at the same time. As we stated earlier, pooling is the essence of insurance. If most or all of the exposure units in a certain class simultaneously incur a loss, then the pooling technique breaks down and becomes unworkable. Premiums must be increased to prohibitive levels, and the insurance technique is no longer a viable arrangement by which losses of the few are spread over the entire group.

Insurers ideally wish to avoid all catastrophic losses, but in the real world, this is impossible, since catastrophic losses periodically result from floods, hurricanes, tornadoes, earthquakes, forest fires, and other natural disasters. Fortunately, two approaches are available for meeting the problem of a catastrophic loss. First, reinsurance can be used by which insurance companies are indemnified by reinsurers for catastrophic losses. **Reinsurance** *is the shifting of part or all of the insurance originally written by one insurer to another insurer.* The reinsurer is then responsible for the payment of its share of the loss. Reinsurance is discussed in greater detail in Chapter 25.

Second, insurers can avoid the concentration of risk by *dispersing their coverage over a large geographical area.* The concentration of loss exposures in a geographical area exposed to frequent floods, tornadoes, hurricanes, or other natural disasters can result in periodic catastrophic losses. If the loss exposures are geographically dispersed, the possibility of a catastrophic loss is reduced.

## Calculable Chance of Loss

*Another important requirement is that the chance of loss should be calculable.* The insurer must be able to calculate both the average frequency and the average severity of future losses with some accuracy. This requirement is necessary so that a proper premium can be charged that is sufficient to pay all claims and expenses and yield a profit during the policy period.

Certain losses, however, are difficult to insure because the chance of loss cannot be accurately estimated, and the potential for a catastrophic loss is present. For example, floods, wars, and cyclical unemployment occur on an irregular basis, and prediction of the average frequency and the severity of losses is difficult. Thus, without government assistance, these losses are difficult for private carriers to insure.

## Economically Feasible Premium

*A final requirement is that the premium should be economically feasible.* The insured must be able to afford to pay the premium. In addition, for the insurance to be an attractive purchase, the premiums paid must be substantially less than the face value, or amount, of the policy.

In order to have an economically feasible premium, the chance of loss must be relatively low. One view is that if the chance of loss exceeds 40 percent, the cost of the policy will exceed the amount that the insurer must pay under the contract. For example, an insurer could issue a $1000 life insurance policy on a man age 99, but the pure premium would be about $980, and an additional amount for expenses would have to be added. The total premium would exceed the face amount of the insurance.[4]

Based on these requirements, personal risks, property risks, and liability risks can be privately insured, since the requirements of an insurable risk generally can be met. By contrast, *most market risks, financial risks, production risks, and political risks are normally uninsurable by private insurers.*[5] These risks are uninsurable for several reasons. First, these risks are speculative and so are difficult to insure privately. Second, the potential of each to produce a catastrophic loss is great; this is particularly true for political risks, such as the risk of war. Finally, calculation of the proper premium for such risks may be difficult because the chance of loss cannot be accurately estimated. For example, insurance that protects a retailer against loss because of a change in consumer tastes, such as a style change, generally is not available. Accurate loss data are not available, and there is no accurate way to calculate a premium.

The premium charged may or may not be adequate to pay all losses and expenses. Since private insurers are in business to make a profit, certain risks are uninsurable because of the possibility of substantial losses.

## TWO APPLICATIONS: THE RISKS OF FIRE AND UNEMPLOYMENT

You will understand more clearly the requirements of an insurable risk if you can apply these requirements to a specific risk. For example, consider the risk of fire to a private dwelling. This risk can be privately insured since the requirements of an insurable risk are generally fulfilled (see Exhibit 2.1).

Consider next the risk of unemployment, which generally is not privately insurable at the present time. How well does the risk of unemployment meet the requirement of an insurable risk? As is evident in Exhibit 2.2, the risk of unemployment does not completely meet the requirements.

First, predicting unemployment is difficult because of the different types of unemployment and labor. There are professional, highly skilled, semiskilled, unskilled, blue-collar, and white-collar workers. Moreover, unemployment rates vary significantly by occupation, age, sex, education, marital status, city, state, and by a host of other factors, including government programs and economic policies that frequently change. Also, the duration of

---

EXHIBIT 2.1

### The Risk of Fire as an Insurable Risk

| *Requirements* | *Does the risk of fire qualify as insurable?* |
| --- | --- |
| 1. Large number of exposure units | Yes. Numerous exposure units are present. |
| 2. Accidental and unintentional loss | Yes. With the exception of arson, most fire losses are accidental and unintentional. |
| 3. Determinable and measurable loss | Yes. If there is disagreement over the amount paid, a property insurance policy has provisions for resolving disputes. |
| 4. No catastrophic loss | Yes. Although catastrophic fires have occurred, all exposure units normally do not burn at the same time. |
| 5. Calculable chance of loss | Yes. Chance of fire can be calculated, and the average severity of a fire loss can be estimated in advance. |
| 6. Economically feasible premium | Yes. Premium rate per $100 of fire insurance is relatively low. |

---

### Exhibit 2.2

**The Risk of Unemployment as an Insurable Risk**

| Requirements | Does the risk of unemployment qualify as insurable? |
| --- | --- |
| 1. Large number of exposure units | Not completely. Although there are a large number of employees, predicting unemployment is difficult because of the different types of unemployment and labor. |
| 2. Accidental and unintentional loss | No. A large proportion of unemployment is due to individuals who voluntarily quit their jobs. |
| 3. Determinable and measurable loss | Not completely. The level of unemployment can be determined, but the measurement of loss is difficult. Some unemployment is involuntary; however, some unemployment is voluntary. |
| 4. No catastrophic loss | No. A severe national recession or depressed local business conditions could result in a catastrophic loss. |
| 5. Calculable chance of loss | No. The different types of unemployment generally are too irregular to estimate the chance of loss accurately. |
| 6. Economically feasible premium | No. Adverse selection, moral hazard, and the potential for a catastrophic loss could make the premium unattractive. |

---

unemployment varies widely among the different groups. In addition, since a large number of workers can become unemployed at the same time, a potential catastrophic loss is present. And since the different types of unemployment occur irregularly, it is difficult to calculate the chance of loss accurately. For these reasons, the risk of unemployment generally is not privately insurable, but it can be insured by social insurance programs. Social insurance programs are discussed later in the chapter.

## ADVERSE SELECTION AND INSURANCE

When insurance is sold, insurers must deal with the problem of adverse selection. **Adverse selection** *is the tendency of persons with a higher-than-average chance of loss to seek insurance at standard (average) rates, which if not controlled by underwriting, results in higher-than-expected loss levels.* For example, adverse selection can result from high-risk drivers who seek auto insurance at standard rates, from persons with serious health problems who seek life or health insurance at standard rates, and from business firms that have been repeatedly robbed or burglarized who seek crime insurance at standard rates. If the applicants for insurance with a higher-than-average chance of loss succeed in obtaining the coverage at standard rates, we say that the insurer is "adversely selected against."

If not controlled by underwriting, adverse selection can result in higher-than-expected loss levels.

Although adverse selection can never be completely eliminated, it can be controlled by careful underwriting. **Underwriting** *refers to the process of selecting and classifying applicants for insurance.* Applicants who meet the underwriting standards are insured at standard rates. If the underwriting standards are not met, the insurance is denied, or an extra premium must be paid. Insurers frequently sell insurance to applicants who have a higher-than-average chance of loss, but such applicants must pay higher premiums. The problem of adverse selection arises when applicants with a higher-than-average chance of loss succeed in obtaining the coverage at standard or average rates.

Policy provisions are also used to control adverse selection. Examples are the suicide clause in life insurance, and the preexisting conditions clause in health insurance. These policy provisions are discussed in greater detail later in the text when specific insurance contracts are analyzed.

## INSURANCE AND GAMBLING COMPARED

Insurance is often erroneously confused with gambling. There are two important differences between them. *First, gambling creates a new speculative risk, while insurance is a technique for handling an already existing pure risk.* Thus, if you bet $300 on a horse race, a new speculative risk is created, but if you pay $300 to an insurer for fire insurance, the risk of fire is already present and is transferred to the insurer by a contract. No new risk is created by the transaction.

*The second difference between insurance and gambling is that gambling is socially unproductive, since the winner's gain comes at the expense of the loser.* In contrast, insurance is always socially productive, since neither the insurer nor the insured is placed in a position where the gain of the winner comes at the expense of the loser. The insurer and the insured both have a common interest in the prevention of a loss. Both parties win if the loss does not occur. Moreover, gambling transactions never restore the losers to their former financial position. In contrast, insurance contracts restore the insureds financially in whole or in part if a loss occurs.

## INSURANCE AND SPECULATION COMPARED

In Chapter 1, we discussed the concept of hedging by which risk can be transferred to a speculator by purchase of a futures contract. An insurance contract, however, is not the same thing as speculation. Although both techniques are similar in that risk is transferred by a contract, and no new risk is created, there are some important differences between them. *First, an insurance transaction involves the transfer of insurable risks, since the requirements of an insurable risk generally can be met.* However, speculation is a technique for handling risks that are typically uninsurable, such as protection against a decline in the price of agricultural products and raw materials.

*A second difference between insurance and speculation is that insurance can reduce the objective risk of an insurer by application of the law of large numbers.* As the number of exposure units increases, the insurer's prediction of future losses improves, since the relative variation of actual loss from expected loss will decline. Thus, many insurance transactions reduce objective risk. In contrast, speculation typically involves only risk transfer, not risk reduction. The risk of adverse price fluctuations is transferred to speculators who believe they can make a profit because of superior knowledge of market conditions. The risk is transferred, not reduced, and the

speculator's prediction of loss generally is not based on the law of large numbers.

## TYPES OF INSURANCE

Insurance can be divided into private and government insurance. Private insurance, in turn, can be classified into life and health insurance and property and liability insurance. Government insurance can be classified into social insurance programs and all other government insurance plans. Thus, the major types of insurance, both private and public, can be classified as follows.

- Private insurance
  - Life and health insurance
  - Property and liability insurance
- Government insurance
  - Social insurance
  - Other government insurance

### Private Insurance

**Life and Health Insurance**  At the end of 1995, the number of United States life insurers totaled an estimated 1715.[6] These insurers are extremely important in providing financial security to individuals and families.

Life insurers pay death benefits to designated beneficiaries when the insured dies. The death benefits are designed to pay for funeral expenses, uninsured medical bills, estate taxes, and other expenses as a result of death. The death proceeds can also be arranged to provide periodic income payments to the deceased's dependents. Life insurers also sell both group and individual retirement plans that pay retirement benefits. In addition, life and health insurers sell individual and group health insurance plans that cover medical expenses from sickness or injury. Finally, both types of insurers sell disability-income coverages that pay income benefits during a period of disability.

**Property and Liability Insurance**  At the end of 1993, 3346 property and liability insurers were operating in the United States.[7] Property and liability insurers can be classified by the types of insurance sold. The major types of insurance sold today are listed in Exhibit 2.3.

EXHIBIT 2.3
## Property and Liability Insurance

1. Fire insurance and allied lines
2. Marine insurance
   - Ocean marine
   - Inland marine
3. Casualty insurance
   - Automobile insurance
   - General liability insurance
   - Burglary and theft insurance
   - Workers compensation
   - Glass insurance
   - Boiler and machinery insurance
   - Nuclear insurance
   - Crop-hail insurance
   - Health insurance
   - Other miscellaneous lines
4. Multiple-line insurance
5. Fidelity and surety bonds

---

1. *Fire insurance and allied lines.* Fire insurance covers the loss or damage to real estate and personal property because of fire, lightning, or removal from the premises. Other perils can be added, such as windstorm, hail, tornadoes, and vandalism. Indirect losses can also be covered, including the loss of profits and rents and the extra expenses incurred as a result of a loss from the interruption of business.

2. *Marine insurance.* Marine insurance is often called transportation insurance because it covers goods in transit against most pure risks connected with transportation.

   Marine insurance is divided into ocean marine and inland marine insurance. **Ocean marine insurance** provides protection for all types of ocean-going vessels and their cargoes. Ocean marine insurance is also used to insure vessels and cargo that sail on the Great Lakes and navigable water-ways in the United States. Contracts can also be written to cover the legal liability of the owners and shippers.

   **Inland marine insurance** provides coverage for goods being shipped on land. This includes imports, exports, domestic shipments, and the means of transportation (for example,

bridges, tunnels, and pipelines). In addition, inland marine insurance covers personal property such as fine art, jewelry, and furs.

3. *Casualty insurance.* **Casualty insurance** is a broad field of insurance and covers whatever is not covered by fire, marine, and life insurers.

   **Automobile insurance** covers legal liability arising out of the ownership or operation of an automobile and also provides physical damage insurance on the automobile, medical payments insurance, and protection against uninsured motorists.

   **General liability insurance** covers legal liability arising out of property damage or bodily injury to others. Legal liability may arise out of the ownership of business property, sales or distribution of products, manufacturing or contracting operations, and professional services.

   **Burglary and theft insurance** covers the loss of property, money, and securities because of burglary, robbery, larceny and other crime perils.

   **Workers compensation insurance** covers workers for a job-related accident or disease. The insurance pays for medical bills, disability income benefits, and death benefits to dependents of an employee whose death is job related.

   **Glass insurance** provides broad coverage for glass breakage in covered buildings. **Boiler and machinery insurance** is a highly specialized commercial line that covers boilers, turbines, generators, and other power-producing equipment. **Nuclear insurance** provides protection against losses resulting from nuclear accidents. **Crop-hail insurance** covers the loss of crops because of hail storms and other perils. **Health insurance** similar to the coverages provided by life and health insurers is also sold by casualty insurers. Other miscellaneous lines include **title insurance,** which covers a financial loss because of a legal defect in the title to real estate, and **credit insurance,** which covers manufacturers and wholesalers against loss because an account receivable is not collected.

4. *Multiple-line insurance.* **Multiple-line insurance** combines both property and casualty coverages into one contract. All states have passed multiple-line legislation that permits insurers to write fire and casualty lines in one

contract. For example, a homeowners policy combines fire insurance and other perils with liability insurance in one contract.

5. *Fidelity and surety bonds.* **Fidelity bonds** provide protection against loss caused by the dishonest or fraudulent acts of employees, such as embezzlement and theft of money. **Surety bonds** provide for monetary compensation in case of failure by bonded persons to perform certain acts, such as the failure of a contractor to construct a building on time.

## Government Insurance

Numerous government insurance programs are in operation at the present time. Government insurance can be divided into social insurance programs and other government insurance programs.

**Social Insurance** **Social insurance** programs are government insurance programs with certain characteristics that distinguish them from other government insurance plans. Social insurance programs are financed entirely or in large part by mandatory contributions from employers, employees, or both, and not primarily by the general revenues of government. The contributions are usually earmarked for special funds that are kept separate from ordinary government accounts; the benefits, in turn, are paid from these funds. In addition, the right to receive benefits is ordinarily derived from or linked to the recipient's past contributions or coverage under the program; the benefits and contributions generally vary among the beneficiaries according to their prior earnings, but the benefits are heavily weighted in favor of low-income groups. Moreover, most social insurance programs are compulsory; certain covered workers and employers are required by law to pay contributions and participate in the programs. Finally, qualifying conditions and benefit rights are usually prescribed exactly by statute, leaving little room for administrative discretion in the award of benefits.[8]

Major social insurance programs in the United States include the following:

- Old-Age, Survivors, Disability, and Health Insurance (Social Security)
- Unemployment insurance
- Workers compensation
- Compulsory temporary disability insurance
- Railroad Retirement Act
- Railroad Unemployment Insurance Act

*Old-Age, Survivors, Disability, and Health Insurance (OASDHI)* is a massive income-maintenance program that provides an important layer of income protection to most individuals and families. The OASDHI program provides retirement benefits, survivor benefits, disability income benefits, and Medicare benefits to eligible beneficiaries and family members.

*Unemployment insurance* programs provide weekly cash benefits to eligible workers who experience short-term involuntary unemployment. Regular state unemployment benefits are typically paid up to 26 weeks after certain eligiblity requirements are met. Extended benefits also may be available to unemployed workers who exhaust their regular benefits.

As noted earlier, *workers compensation insurance* covers workers against a job-related accident or disease. Although workers compensation is a casualty line sold by private insurers, it is also an important form of social insurance. The social insurance aspects of workers compensation are discussed in Chapter 23.

In addition, *compulsory temporary disability insurance,* which exists in five states, Puerto Rico, and the railroad industry, provides for the partial replacement of wages that may be lost because of a temporary nonoccupational disability.[9] The *Railroad Retirement Act* provides retirement benefits, survivor benefits, and disability income benefits to railroad workers who meet certain eligibility requirements. Finally, the *Railroad Unemployment Insurance Act* provides unemployment and sickness benefits to railroad employees.

**Other Government Insurance Programs** Other government insurance programs exist at both the federal and state level. However, these programs do not have the distinguishing characteristics of social insurance programs. Important federal insurance programs include the Federal Employees Retirement System, the Civil Service Retirement System, various life insurance programs for veterans, pension termination insurance, insurance on checking and savings accounts in commercial banks and saving and loan associations (Federal Deposit Insurance Corporation), federal flood insurance, federal crop insurance, and numerous other programs.

Government insurance programs also exist at the state level. These programs include the Wisconsin State Life Fund, title insurance programs in a few states, and the Maryland Automobile Insurance Fund. In addition, competitive and monopoly workers compensation funds are in operation in several states. Finally, the majority of states have special health insurance pools that make health insurance available to persons who are uninsurable or substandard in health.

## BENEFITS OF INSURANCE TO SOCIETY

The existence of insurance results in great benefits to society. The major social and economic benefits of insurance include the following:

- Indemnification for loss
- Less worry and fear
- Source of investment funds
- Loss prevention
- Enhancement of credit

### Indemnification for Loss

**Indemnification** permits individuals and families to be restored to their former financial position after a loss occurs. As a result, they can maintain their financial security. Since they are restored either in part or in whole after a loss occurs, they are less likely to apply for public assistance or welfare, or to seek financial assistance from relatives and friends.

Indemnification to business firms also permits firms to remain in business and employees to keep their jobs. Suppliers continue to receive orders, and customers can still receive the goods and services they desire. The community also benefits because its tax base is not eroded. In short, the indemnification function contributes greatly to family and business stability and therefore is one of the most important social and economic benefits of insurance.

### Less Worry and Fear

A second benefit of insurance is that worry and fear are reduced. This is true both before and after a loss. For example, if family heads have adequate amounts of life insurance, they are less likely to worry about the financial security of their dependents in the event of premature death; persons insured for long-term disability do not have to worry about the loss of earnings if a serious illness or accident occurs; and property owners who are insured enjoy greater peace of mind since they know they are covered if a loss occurs. Worry and fear are also reduced after a loss occurs, since the insureds know that they have insurance that will pay for the loss.

### Source of Investment Funds

The insurance industry is an important source of funds for capital investment and accumulation. Premiums are collected in advance of the loss, and funds not needed to pay immediate losses and expenses can be loaned to business firms. These funds typically are invested in shopping centers, hospitals, factories, housing developments, and new machinery and equipment. The investments increase society's stock of capital goods, and promote economic growth and full employment. Insurers also invest in social investments, such as housing, nursing homes, and economic development projects (see Insight 2.1). In addition, because the total supply of loanable funds is increased by the advance payment of insurance premiums, the cost of capital to business firms that borrow is lower than it would be in the absence of insurance.

### Loss Prevention

Insurance companies are actively involved in numerous loss prevention programs and also employ a wide variety of loss prevention personnel, including safety engineers and specialists in fire prevention, occupational safety and health, and products liability. Some important loss prevention activities that property and liability insurers strongly support include the following:

- Highway safety and reduction of automobile deaths.
- Fire prevention
- Reduction of work-related disabilities
- Prevention of automobile thefts
- Prevention and detection of arson losses
- Prevention of defective products that could injure the user
- Prevention of boiler explosions
- Educational programs on loss prevention

## INSIGHT 2.1

# Social Investments of Life and Health Insurers

Life and health insurers invest in numerous social investments. Social investments are those that would not otherwise be made under the insurer's customary lending standards, or those in which social considerations played a substantial part in the investment decision.

Socially responsive investments by life and health insurers totaled $1.8 billion in 1994. The two largest areas of investments were for affordable housing and health facilities. Deposits in minority financial institutions exceeded $1 billion.

### Investments for Socially Desirable Purposes

In Millions—All Reporting Companies—1994

|  | Total $ |
|---|---|
| Housing (1–4 Family) | 359 |
| Housing (Multifamily) | 75 |
| Hospitals | ★ |
| Nursing Homes | 238 |
| Clinics | 1 |
| Commercial | 28 |
| Economic Development | 31 |
| Arts/Cultural | 1 |
| Social Service | 3 |
| Environment | 1 |
| Education (Student Loans) | 7 |
| Education (Facilities) | ★ |
| Other | 68 |
| **Total Investments** | $813 |
| **Minority Financial Institution Deposits** | $1,027 |
| **Overall Total** | $1,840 |

Number of Companies Reporting (194).

*Less than $500,000.

SOURCE: The Life and Health Insurance Industry Annual Report on Community Involvement 1995—Helping Families, Strengthening Communities (Washington, D.C.: Center for Corporate Public Involvement, 1995), pp.12–13.

The loss prevention activities reduce both the direct and indirect, or consequential, losses. Society benefits, since both types of losses are reduced.

## Enhancement of Credit

A final benefit is that insurance enhances a person's credit. Insurance makes a borrower a better credit risk because it guarantees the value of the borrower's collateral, or gives greater assurance that the loan will be repaid. For example, when a house is purchased, the lending institution normally requires property insurance on the house before the mortgage loan is granted. The property insurance protects the lender's financial interest if the property is damaged or destroyed. Similarly, a business firm seeking a temporary loan for Christmas or seasonal business may be required to insure its inventories before the loan is made. And if a new automobile is purchased and financed by a bank or other lending institution, physical damage insurance on the automobile may be required before the loan is made. Thus, insurance can enhance a person's credit.

## COSTS OF INSURANCE TO SOCIETY

Although the insurance industry provides enormous social and economic benefits to society, the social costs of insurance must also be recognized. The major social costs of insurance include the following:

- Cost of doing business
- Fraudulent claims
- Inflated claims

## Cost of Doing Business

One important cost is the cost of doing business. Insurers consume scarce economic resources—land, labor, capital, and business enterprise—in providing insurance to society. In financial terms, an expense loading must be added to the pure premium to cover the expenses incurred by companies in their daily operations. An **expense loading** *is the amount needed to pay all expenses, including commissions, general administrative expenses, state premium taxes, acquisition expenses, and an allowance for contingencies*

*and profit.* Sales and administrative expenses by property and liability insurers account for 23 percent of each premium dollar; operating expenses of life insurers account for 11 percent of each premium dollar. As a result, the total costs to society are increased. For example, assume that a small country with no insurance has an average of $100 million of fire losses each year. If fire insurers now provide fire insurance, assume that the expense loading is 35 percent of the losses. Thus, the total costs to this country are increased to $135 million.

However, these additional costs can be justified for several reasons. First, from the insured's viewpoint, uncertainty concerning the payment of a covered loss is reduced because of insurance. Second, the costs of doing business are not necessarily wasteful, since insurers engage in a wide variety of loss prevention activities. Finally, the insurance industry provides more than 2.2 million jobs to workers in the United States.[10] However, since economic resources are used up in providing insurance to society, a real economic cost is incurred.

## Fraudulent Claims

A second cost of insurance is the submission of fraudulent claims. Examples of fraudulent claims include the following:

- Auto accidents may be faked or staged to collect benefits.
- Dishonest claimants may fake slip and fall accidents.
- Phony burglaries, thefts, or acts of vandalism may be reported to insurers.
- Bodily injuries in auto accidents may be faked.
- False claims may be submitted to collect health insurance benefits.

Numerous additional fraudulent acts are common (see Exhibit 2.4). The payment of fraudulent claims results in higher premiums to all insureds. The presence of insurance also encourages intentional losses to collect benefits. These social costs fall directly on society.

To control the increase in fraudulent claims, insurers are cracking down on fraud rings by hiring additional investigators, by using sophisticated computer systems to track claims, and by using new legal tactics to prosecute fraudulent claimants (see Insight 2.2).

EXHIBIT 2.4

## Types of Insurance Fraud

*Examples of insurance fraud*

■ *Creating a fraudulent claim.*

Staged or caused auto accident.

Staged slip and fall accident.

False claim of foreign object in food or drink.

Faking a death to collect benefits.

Murder for profit.

Phony burglary, theft or vandalism.

Arson or intentional water damage.

Staged theft of auto.

Staged homeowner accident or burglary.

■ *Overstating amount of loss.*

Inflating bodily injuries in auto accident.

Inflating value of items taken in burglary or theft.

Inflating damage claim from minor fender bender.

Medical providers inflating billing or coding of medical procedures.

■ *Misrepresenting facts to receive payment.*

Claiming pre-existing damage occurred in current accident.

Claiming damages to auto when none occurred.

Claiming minor injury creates partial or total disability.

Receiving disability payments and working elsewhere.

■ *Misrepresentation to receive payments.*

Claiming false disability.

Providing unnecessary medical treatment.

Charging for medical tests not carried out.

"Upcoding" for medicine by issuing generic pills and charging for name brands.

Personal injury mills of doctors, lawyers and claimants.

■ *Misrepresentation to obtain a policy or lower premiums.*

Misrepresenting health information on life insurance and then submitting a false claim.

Misrepresenting name, date of birth or Social Security number and then submitting a false claim.

■ *Insider and internal fraud.*

Agent or insurer pocketing premiums, then issuing no policy or a bogus policy.

Agent or insurer issuing fake policies, certificates, ID cards or binders.

Agent or insurer making false entry on document or statement.

SOURCE: Insurance Fraud Prevention Division, Nebraska Insurance Department.

SOURCE: Excerpted from Steve Jordan, "State's New Insurance Fraud Prevention Unit Off to Fast Start," *Sunday World Herald*, February 25, 1996, p. 3-M.

# INSIGHT 2.2

## Insurance Firms Cracking Down on Fraud Rings

On a sunny day in Chicago, Mike Borders and his wife Nancy were just picking up speed on Lake Shore Drive in their Mercedes when a 14-year-old Buick lurched to a halt in front of them.

"I slammed on my brakes," Borders said, "and almost got stopped." But not quite.

The jolt stunned them, but neither was hurt. The three men in the other car seemed OK, too, and so Borders felt grateful that things had not turned out worse. It did not dawn on him then, he said, that he might have been set up, the victim of a staged accident. But after the three men filed medical claims, his insurer, State Farm, linked them to a clinic that the company has accused of being part of a $3 million auto-insurance fraud ring.

These rings have spread across the country in recent years, hiring people to stage crashes and lining up lawyers and doctors to help them file large claims for fictitious injuries.

To trace the tangled paper trails left by these rings, insurers are hiring armies of investigators and adapting computer tracking systems designed for the military and intelligence agencies. And they are deploying new legal tactics to bring to court cases that both insurers and prosecutors long viewed as too time-consuming and expensive to pursue.

The change in strategy is evident in the insurers' detective forces: Allstate Insurance has 600 investigators today, up from about 100 four years ago. State Farm has nearly doubled its anti-fraud force to 1,000 agents.

The old passivity, industry experts say, helped faking accidents grow from a cottage industry into big business.

"By being an easy touch, we gave these people an incentive," said Robert Grove, a claims specialist for the consulting firm of Tillinghast-Towers Perrin. "There are probably hundreds of these rings across the country now."

There were reasons for not pursuing every case. Companies often found that prosecutors, overwhelmed with murders and other violent crimes, were unwilling to divert resources. When cases did go to trial, penalties were often slight. Jail time was rare. More typical was a small fine and probation.

To overcome these obstacles, the industry's National Insurance Crime Bureau is employing 200 investigators and computers to develop fraud cases in detail and then present them to prosecutors.

The computers are used to match telephone numbers, addresses and names from claims filed with many different insurers, to detect such patterns as several people in one city who each file several claims in a short period, using the same lawyers and doctors.

"We present them (prosecutors) with a wonderful package, and they can go into court and get the credit," said Jon Hoch, the bureau's spokesman.

In Florida, Nationwide Insurance Co. is experimenting with a computer program designed for federal intelligence agencies. Not only does it match sets of numbers, but it searches for patterns in types of claims, such as accidents that result in minor damages to cars but generate large medical bills. In another effort to exact meaningful punishment, State Farm filed a civil suit in U.S. District Court in Chicago, using a weapon designed to fight the Mafia—the Racketeer Influenced and Corrupt Organizations Act.

The company's targets were four organizers whom State Farm claimed had hired drivers and passengers to stage accidents, and three lawyers, 11 doctors and chiropractors and 10 clinics that the insurer said had helped build fictitious medical bills and file fraudulent claims. The conspiracy, State Farm says, cost it $3 million in false claims.

The suit is likely to take three or four years and cost State Farm more than $1 million. But a victory would have high impact. The racketeering statute provides for a judgment of up to three times the losses, which in State Farm's case would be $9 million.

"What really hurts these people," said Frank Hall, chief of State Farm's special investigative unit, "is getting at their money, their yachts and their houses."

SOURCE: Adapted from Joseph B. Treaster, "Insurance Firms Cracking Down On Fraud Rings," *Omaha World Herald*, November 23, 1996, pp. 29, 33.

## Inflated Claims

Many claims are inflated because of insurance. The loss may not be intentionally caused by the insured, but the claim may be inflated; in other words, it may exceed the actual financial loss experienced by the insured. Examples of inflated claims include the following:

- Attorneys for plaintiffs may seek high liability judgments that often exceed the true economic loss of the victim.
- Physicians may charge higher fees for surgical procedures covered by major medical health insurance.
- Disabled persons may malinger to collect disability-income benefits for a longer duration.
- Insureds may inflate the amount of an automobile collision loss to cover the deductible in an auto insurance policy.

These inflated claims must be recognized as an important social cost of insurance. Premiums must be increased to cover the losses, and disposable income and the consumption of other goods or services is thereby reduced.

In summary, the social and economic benefits of insurance generally outweigh the social costs. Insurance reduces worry and fear; the indemnification function contributes greatly to social and economic stability; financial security of individuals and firms is preserved; and from the viewpoint of insurers, objective risk in the economy is reduced. The social costs of insurance can be viewed as the sacrifice that society must make to obtain these benefits.

## SUMMARY

- There is no single definition of insurance. However, a typical insurance plan contains four elements:

    Pooling of losses
    Payment of fortuitous losses
    Risk transfer
    Indemnification

    Pooling means that the losses of the few are spread over the group, and average loss is substituted for actual loss. Fortuitous losses are unforeseen and unexpected and occur as a result of chance. Risk transfer involves the transfer of a pure risk to an insurer. Indemnification means that the victim of a loss is restored in whole or in part by payment, repair, or replacement by the insurer.

- The law of large numbers states that as the number of exposures increases, the more likely it is that the actual results will approach the expected results. The law of large numbers permits an insurer to estimate future losses with some accuracy.

- There are several ideal requirements of an insurable risk.

    There must be a large number of exposure units.
    The loss must be accidental and unintentional.
    The loss must be determinable and measurable.
    The loss should not be catastrophic.
    The chance of loss must be calculable.
    The premium must be economically feasible.

- Personal risks, property risks, and liability risks can be privately insured, since the requirements of an insurable risk generally can be met. However, market risks, financial risks, production risks, and political risks generally are uninsurable, since these requirements are difficult to meet.

- Adverse selection is the tendency of persons with a higher-than-average chance of loss to seek insurance at average rates, which if not controlled by underwriting, results in higher-than-expected loss levels.

- Insurance is not the same as gambling. Gambling creates a new speculative risk, while insurance deals with an existing pure risk. Also, gambling is socially unproductive, since the winner's gain comes at the expense of the loser. Insurance is always socially productive since both the insured and insurer win if the loss does not occur.

- Insurance is not the same as speculation. Insurance involves the transfer of a pure risk, whereas speculation involves the transfer of a speculative risk. Also, insurance may reduce objective risk because of the law of large numbers. Speculation typically involves only risk transfer and not risk reduction.

- Insurance can be divided into private and government insurance. Private insurance consists of life and health insurance and property and liability insurance. Government insurance consists of social insurance and other government insurance programs.

- The major benefits of insurance to society are as follows:

    Indemnification for loss
    Less worry and fear

Source of investment funds

Loss prevention

Enhancement of credit

* Insurance entails certain social costs to society, which include the following:

Cost of doing business

Fraudulent claims

Inflated claims

## KEY CONCEPTS AND TERMS

| | |
|---|---|
| Adverse selection | Ocean marine insurance |
| Casualty insurance | Pooling |
| Expense loading | Property and liability |
| Fidelity and surety bonds | insurance |
| Fortuitous loss | Reinsurance |
| Indemnification | Requirements of an |
| Inland marine insurance | insurable risk |
| Insurance | Risk transfer |
| Law of large numbers | Social insurance |
| Life and health insurance | Underwriting |
| Multiple-line insurance | |

## QUESTIONS FOR REVIEW

1. Explain the major characteristics of a typical insurance plan.

2. Why is the pooling technique essential to insurance?

3. Explain the law of large numbers and show how the law of large numbers can be used by an insurer to estimate future losses.

4. Explain the major requirements of an insurable risk.

5. Why are most market risks, financial risks, production risks, and political risks considered to be uninsurable by private insurers?

6. How does insurance differ from gambling?

7. How does insurance differ from speculation?

8. Identify the major fields of private and government insurance.

9. How is insurance beneficial to society?

10. Explain the social costs of insurance to society.

## QUESTIONS FOR DISCUSSION

1. Although no risk completely meets all of the ideal requirements of an insurable risk, some risks come much closer to meeting them than others.

a. Identify the ideal requirements of an insurable risk.

b. Compare and contrast automobile collisions and war in terms of how well they meet the requirements of an insurable risk.

2. One author states that "the law of large numbers forms the basis of insurance." Do you agree or disagree with this statement? Explain your answer.

3. a. Private insurers provide numerous benefits to society. Explain how private insurance produces each of the following benefits:

(1) Indemnification

(2) Enhancement of credit

(3) Capital accumulation and investment

b. One critic of private insurance states that "private insurance cannot be justified economically because the industry uses scarce economic resources that could be used to provide additional goods and services to society." Do you agree or disagree with this statement? Explain your answer.

4. The potential for adverse selection is present in all forms of insurance. Underwriting is one technique that is used to control adverse selection.

a. Explain the meaning of "adverse selection."

b. Why are insurers concerned about adverse selection?

c. Explain how underwriting can be used to control adverse selection.

5. Explain how insurance is socially productive while gambling is socially unproductive.

## SELECTED REFERENCES

Gibbons, Robert J., George E. Rejda, and Michael W. Elliott. *Insurance Perspectives.* Malvern, Pa.: American Institute for Chartered Property Casualty Underwriters, 1992, chapters 1 and 2.

Rejda, George E., Constance M., Cheryl L. Ferguson, and Donald R. Oakes. *Personal Insurance,* 3rd ed. Malvern, Pa.: Insurance Institute of America, 1997, chapter 1.

Smith, Barry D. *How Insurance Works: An Introduction to Property and Liability Insurance.* Malvern, Pa.: Insurance Institute of America, 1994.

## NOTES

1. *Bulletin of the Commission on Insurance Terminology of the American Risk and Insurance Association,* 1 (October 1965), p. 1.

2. Robert I. Mehr and Sandra G. Gustavson, *Life Insurance: Theory and Practice,* 4th ed. (Plano, Texas: Business Publications, 1987), p. 31.

3. Self-insurance is discussed in Chapter 3.

4. Robert I. Mehr, Emerson Cammack, and Terry Rose, *Principles of Insurance,* 8th ed. (Homewood, Ill.: Richard D. Irwin, 1985), pp. 36–37.

5. Market risks include the risks of adverse price changes in raw materials, general price level changes (inflation), changes in consumer tastes, new technology, and increased competition from competitors. Financial risks include the risks of adverse price changes in the price of securities, adverse changes in interest rates, and the inability to borrow on favorable terms. Production risks include shortages of raw materials, depletion of natural resources, and technical problems in production. Finally, political risks include the risks of war, overthrow of government, adverse government regulations, and the nationalization of foreign plants by a hostile government.

6. *1996 Life Insurance Fact Book* (Washington, D.C.: American Council of Life Insurance, 1996), p. 108.

7. *The Fact Book 1996, Property/Casualty Insurance Facts* (New York: Insurance Information Institute), p. 7.

8. George E. Rejda, *Social Insurance and Economic Security,* 5th ed. (Englewood Cliffs, N.J.: Prentice Hall, 1994), pp. 12–13.

9. The five states are California, Hawaii, New Jersey, New York, and Rhode Island.

10. *The Fact Book 1996, Property/Casualty Insurance Facts,* p. 5.

## CASE APPLICATION

There are numerous definitions of insurance. Based on the definition of insurance stated in the text, indicate whether each of the following guarantees is considered insurance.

a. A television set is guaranteed by the manufacturer against defects for 90 days.

b. A new set of radial tires is guaranteed by the manufacturer against road defects for 50,000 miles.

c. A builder of new homes gives a ten-year guarantee against structural defects in the home.

d. A cosigner of a note agrees to pay the loan balance if the original debtor defaults on the payments.

e. A large group of homeowners agree to pay for losses to homes that burn during the year because of a fire.

# *Appendix* \*

# BASIC STATISTICS AND THE LAW OF LARGE NUMBERS

In no industry is the application of probability and statistics more important than in the insurance industry. Insurance actuaries constantly face a tradeoff when determining the premium to charge for coverage: the premium must be high enough to cover expected losses and expenses, but low enough to remain competitive with premiums charged by other insurers. Actuaries apply statistical analysis to determine expected loss levels and expected deviations from these loss levels. Through the application of the Law of Large Numbers, insurers reduce their risk of adverse outcomes.

In this appendix we review some statistical concepts that are important to insurers, including probability, central tendency, and dispersion. Next we examine the Law of Large Numbers—its derivation and how insurance companies apply the law of large numbers to reduce risk.

## PROBABILITY AND STATISTICS

In order to determine expected losses, insurance actuaries apply probability and statistical analysis to given loss situations. The probability of an event is simply the long-run relative frequency of the event, given an infinite number of trials with no changes in the underlying conditions. The probability of some events can be determined without experimentation. For example, if a "fair" coin is flipped in the air, the probability the coin will come up "heads" is 50 percent, and the probability it will come up "tails" is

*Prepared by Michael J. McNamara, The University of Memphis.

also 50 percent. Other probabilities, such as the probability of dying during a specified year or the probability of being involved in an auto accident, can be estimated from past loss data.

A convenient way of summarizing events and probabilities is through a probability distribution. A probability distribution lists events that could occur and the corresponding probability of each occurrence. Probability distributions may be discrete, meaning that only distinct outcomes are possible, or continuous, meaning that any outcome over a range of outcomes could occur.[1]

Probability distributions are characterized by two important measures: central tendency and dispersion. Although there are several measures of central tendency, the measure most often employed is the mean ($\mu$) or expected value ($EV$) of the distribution.[2] The mean or expected value is found by multiplying each outcome by the probability of occurrence, and then summing the resulting products:

$$\mu \text{ or } EV = \Sigma\, X_i P_i$$

For example, assume that an actuary estimates the following probabilities of various losses for a certain risk:

| Amount of Loss ($X_i$) | | Probability of Loss ($P_i$) | | $X_i P_i$ |
|---|---|---|---|---|
| $ 0 | × | .30 | = | $0 |
| $360 | × | .50 | = | $180 |
| $600 | × | .20 | = | $120 |
| | | $\Sigma X_i P_i$ | = | $300 |

Thus, we could say that the mean or expected loss given the probability distribution is $300.

Although the mean value indicates central tendency, it does not tell us anything about the riskiness or dispersion of the distribution. Consider a second probability-of-loss distribution:

| Amount of Loss ($X_i$) | | Probability of Loss ($P_i$) | | $X_iP_i$ |
|---|---|---|---|---|
| $225 | $\times$ | .40 | = | $90 |
| $350 | $\times$ | .60 | = | $210 |
| | | $\Sigma\, X_iP_i$ | = | $300 |

This distribution also has a mean loss value of $300. However, the first distribution is riskier because the range of possible outcomes is from $0 to $600. With the second distribution, the range of possible outcomes is only $125 ($350 − $225), so we are more certain about the outcome with the second distribution.

Two standard measures of dispersion are employed to characterize the variability or dispersion about the mean value. These measures are the variance ($\sigma^2$) and the standard deviation ($\sigma$). The variance of a probability distribution is the sum of the squared differences between the possible outcomes and the expected value, weighted by the probability of the outcomes:

$$\sigma^2 = \Sigma\, P_i\,(X_i - EV)^2$$

So the variance is the average squared deviation between the possible outcomes and the mean. Because the variance is in "squared units," it is necessary to take the square root of the variance so that the central tendency and dispersion measures are in the same units. The square root of the variance is the standard deviation. The variance and standard deviation of the first distribution are:

$$\sigma^2 = .30(0 - 300)^2 + .50(360 - 300)^2 + .20(600 - 300)^2$$
$$= 27,000 + 1,800 + 18,000$$
$$= 46,800$$
$$\sigma = \sqrt{46,800} = 216.33$$

For the second distribution, the variance and standard deviation are:

$$\sigma^2 = .40(225 - 300)^2 + .60(350 - 300)^2$$
$$= 2,250 + 1,500$$
$$= 3,750$$
$$\sigma = \sqrt{3,750} = 61.24$$

Thus, while the means of the two distributions are the same, the standard deviations are significantly different. *Higher standard deviations, relative to the mean, are associated with greater uncertainty of loss; therefore, the risk is higher. Lower standard deviations, relative to the mean, are associated with less uncertainty of loss; therefore, the risk is lower.*

The two probability distributions used in the discussion of central tendency and dispersion are "odd" in that only 3 and 2 possible outcomes, respectively, could occur. In addition, specific loss levels corresponding to the probabilities are assigned. In practice, estimating the frequency and severity of loss is difficult. Insurers can employ both actual loss data and theoretical loss distributions in estimating losses.[3]

## THE LAW OF LARGE NUMBERS

Even if the characteristics of the population were known with certainty, most insurers do not insure populations. Rather, they select a sample from the population and insure the sample. Obviously the relationship between population parameters and the characteristics of the sample (mean and standard deviation) is important for insurers, since actual experience may vary significantly from the population parameters. The characteristics of the sampling distribution help to illustrate the Law of Large Numbers, the mathematical foundation of insurance.

It can be shown that the average losses for a random sample of $n$ exposure units will follow a normal distribution because of the Central Limit Theorem. The Central Limit Theorem states:

> If you draw random samples of $n$ observations from any population with mean $\mu_x$ and standard deviation $\sigma_x$, and $n$ is sufficiently large, the distribution of sample means will be approximately normal, with the mean of the distribution equal to the mean of the population ($\mu_{\bar{x}} = \mu_x$), and the standard error of the sample mean ($\sigma_{\bar{x}}$) equal to the standard deviation of the population ($\sigma_x$) divided by the square root of $n$ ($\sigma_{\bar{x}} = \sigma_x/\sqrt{n}$). This approximation becomes increasingly accurate as the sample size, $n$, increases.

The Central Limit Theorem has two important implications for insurers. First, it is clear that the sample distributions of means does not depend on

**Sampling Distribution vs. Sample Size**

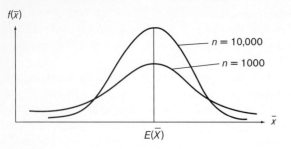

**Standard Error of the Sampling Distribution vs. Sample Size**

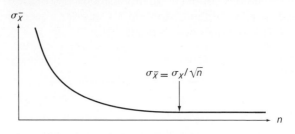

| $n$ | $\sigma_{\bar{x}}$ |
|---|---|
| 10 | 110.67 |
| 100 | 35.00 |
| 1,000 | 11.07 |
| 10,000 | 3.50 |

the population distribution, provided $n$ is sufficiently large. *In other words, regardless of the population distribution (bimodal, unimodal, symmetric, skewed right, skewed left, etc.), the distribution of sample means will approach the normal distribution as the sample size increases.* This result is shown in Exhibit A.1.

The normal distribution is a symmetric, bell-shaped curve. It is defined by the mean and standard deviation of the distribution. About 68 percent of the distribution lies within one standard deviation of the mean, and about 95 percent of the distribution lies within two standard deviations of the mean. The normal curve has many statistical applications (hypothesis testing, confidence intervals, etc.), and is easy to use.

The second important implication of the Central Limit Theorem for insurers is that the standard error of the sample mean distribution declines as the sample size increases. Recall that the standard error is defined as:

$$\sigma_{\bar{x}} = \sigma_x / \sqrt{n}$$

In other words, the standard error of the sample mean loss distribution is equal to the standard deviation of the population divided by the square root of the sample size. Because the population standard deviation is independent of the sample size, *the standard error of the sampling distribution, $\sigma_{\bar{x}}$, can be reduced by simply increasing the sample size.* For example, an insurer selecting a sample to insure from a population that has a mean loss of $500 and a standard deviation of $350 can reduce the standard error of the sampling distribution simply by insuring more units:

This result is shown graphically in Exhibit A.2.

A brief example demonstrates the application of the Law of Large Numbers. Assume, based on previous losses for a certain rating category, that an insurer expects 40 drivers out of a sample of 100 drivers in a rating category will report a physical damage claim during the year. Further assume that the standard deviation of the estimate is 20 drivers.

A second insurer writes coverage on 10,000 drivers in this category. Obviously the underwriting risk for the second insurer is greater as there are 10,000 units that could report a loss. If the rate of loss does not change, the second insurer should expect 4,000 losses (.40 × 10,000) to occur. However, the standard deviation does not increase proportionately. Rather, it increases only by a factor of 10, to 200.[4] While the second insurer increased its exposure to loss by insuring a larger sample, the predictability of the outcome also increased.

The coefficient of variation $(CV)$ is a composite statistic expressing the standard deviation as a percentage of the expected value. For the first insurer, the $CV$ is .50 (20/40). For the second insurer, the $CV$ is only .05 (200/4,000). In the first case, 95 percent of the distribution of expected losses (two standard deviations) lies between 0 and 80 losses with a mean of 40. For the second insurer, 95 percent of the distribution lies between

3,600 and 4,400; with a mean of 4,000. Obviously the per-unit risk in the second case is reduced by insuring a larger sample.

Insurance companies are in the loss business—they expect some losses to occur. It is the deviaiton between actual losses and expected losses that is the major concern. By insuring large samples, insurers reduce their objective risk. There truly is "safety in numbers" for insurers.

## NOTES

1. The number of runs scored in a baseball game is a discrete measure as partial runs cannot be scored. Speed and temperature are continuous measures as all values over the range of values can occur.
2. Other measures of central tendency are the median, which is the middle observation in a probability distribution; and the mode, which is the observation that occurs most often.
3. Introductory statistics texts discuss several popular theoretical distributions, such as the binomial and Poisson distributions, that can be used to estimate losses. Another popular distribution, the normal distribution, is discussed in the next section.
4. The underwriting risk for the insurer is equal to the number of units insured, $n$, multiplied by the standard error of the average loss distribution, $\sigma_{\bar{x}}$. Recalling that $\sigma_{\bar{x}}$ is equal to $\sigma_x / \sqrt{n}$, we can rewrite the expression for underwriting risk as:

$$n \times \sigma_{\bar{x}} = n \times \sigma_x / \sqrt{n} = \sqrt{n} \times \sigma_x$$

Thus while underwriting risk increases with an increase in a sample size, it does not increase proportionately. Rather it increases by the square root of the increase in the sample size.

# Chapter 3

# RISK MANAGEMENT

*"Risk management deals with the systematic identification of a company's exposure to the risk of loss."*

*Insurance Company of North America*
Risk Management: Some Professional Considerations

## Student Learning Objectives

After studying this chapter, you should be able to:

■ Define risk management.

■ Explain the basic objectives of risk management.

■ Describe the four steps in the risk management process.

■ Explain the various methods for treating loss exposures, including

    avoidance
    loss control
    retention
    noninsurance transfers
    insurance.

■ Give an example of each of the above methods and show how it is used in
a risk management program.

Corporations, small employers, farmers, state and local governments, and even students are exposed to risk in one form or another. Although insurance can be effectively used to manage risk, other techniques are also available. Risk management is a method for handling pure risks to which an organization or individual is exposed. Risk management attempts to identify the pure risks or pure loss exposures faced by a firm or organization and uses a number of methods, including insurance, for treating these exposures.

In this chapter, the fundamentals of corporate risk management are explored in some detail. This involves a discussion of the meaning of risk management, the objectives of risk management, steps in the risk management process, and the various techniques that can be used to treat loss exposures.

## RISK MANAGEMENT

**Risk management** *is defined as a systematic process for the identification and evaluation of pure loss exposures faced by an organization or individual, and for the selection and implementation of the most appropriate techniques for treating such exposures.* It is a discipline that systematically identifies and analyzes the various loss exposures faced by a firm or organization, and the best methods of treating the loss exposures consistent with the organization's goals and objectives. As a general rule, the risk manager is concerned only with the management of pure risks, not speculative risks. All pure risks are considered, including those that are uninsurable.

## Risk Management and Insurance Management

Risk management should not be confused with insurance management. Risk management is a broader concept and differs from insurance management in several respects. First, risk management places greater emphasis on the identification and analysis of pure loss exposures and techniques for dealing with these exposures. Second, in addition to insurance, risk management uses other techniques to treat loss exposures, which include avoidance, loss control, retention, and noninsurance transfers. Finally, risk management has a greater impact on the firm than insurance management. A successful risk management program requires the cooperation of numerous individuals and departments throughout the firm. Insurance management involves a smaller number of persons.

## Objectives of Risk Management

Risk management has several important objectives that can be classified into two categories: preloss objectives and postloss objectives.[1]

**Preloss Objectives**    A firm or organization has several risk management objectives prior to the occurrence of a loss. The most important include economy, the reduction of anxiety, and meeting externally imposed obligations.

The first goal means that the firm should prepare for potential losses in the most *economical way* possible. This involves an analysis of safety program expenses, insurance premiums, and the costs associated with the different techniques for handling losses.

The second objective, the *reduction of anxiety,* is more complicated. Certain loss exposures can cause greater worry and fear for the risk manager, key executives, and stockholders than other exposures. For example, the threat of a catastrophic lawsuit from a defective product can cause greater anxiety and concern than a possible small loss from a minor fire. However, the risk manager wants to minimize the anxiety and fear associated with all loss exposures.

The third objective is to meet any *externally imposed obligations.* This means the firm must meet certain obligations imposed on it by outsiders. For example, government regulations may require a firm to install safety devices to protect workers from harm. Similarly, a firm's creditors may require that property pledged as collateral for a loan must be insured. The risk manager must see that these externally imposed obligations are met.

**Postloss Objectives**    The first and most important postloss objective is *survival of the firm.* Survival means that after a loss occurs, the firm can at least resume partial operation within some reasonable time period if it chooses to do so.

The second postloss objective is to *continue operating.* For some firms, the ability to operate after a severe loss is an extremely important objective. This is particularly true of certain firms, such as a public utility firm, which must continue to provide service. The ability to operate is also important for firms that may lose customers to competitors if they cannot operate after a loss occurs. This would include banks, bakeries, dairies, and other competitive firms.

*Stability of earnings* is the third postloss objective. The firm wants to maintain its earnings per share after a loss occurs. This objective is closely related to the objective of continued operations. Earnings per share can be maintained if the firm continues to operate. However, there may be substantial costs involved in achieving this goal (such as operating at another location), and perfect stability of earnings may not be attained.

The fourth postloss objective is *continued growth* of the firm. A firm may grow by developing new products and markets or by acquisitions and mergers. The risk manager must consider the impact that a loss will have on the firm's ability to grow.

Finally, the goal of *social responsibility* is to minimize the impact that a loss has on other persons and on society. A severe loss can adversely affect employees, customers, suppliers, creditors, taxpayers, and the community in general. For example, a severe loss that requires shutting down a plant in a small community for an extended period can lead to

EXHIBIT 3.1

**Steps in the Risk Management Process**

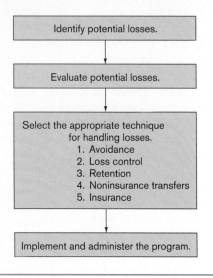

- Liability losses
- Death or disability of key people
- Job-related injuries or disease
- Fraud, criminal acts, and employee dishonesty
- Employee benefits loss exposures
- International loss exposures (plants, property, and personnel in foreign countries)

Most large corporations operate globally, and the risk manager may also be involved in the identification of major loss exposures in foreign countries. As corporations expand their overseas operations, the role of risk managers in international risk management is increasing.

A risk manager has several sources of information that can be used to identify major and minor loss exposures. *Physical inspection* of company plants and operations can identify major loss exposures. Extensive *risk analysis questionnaires* can be used to discover hidden loss exposures that are common to many firms. *Flow charts* that depict production and delivery processes can reveal production bottlenecks where a loss can have severe financial consequences to the firm. *Financial statements* can be used to identify the major assets that must be protected. Finally, *departmental and historical claims data* can be invaluable in identifying major loss exposures.

Risk managers must also be aware of new loss exposures that may be emerging. More recently, misuse of the internet and e-mail transmissions by employees have exposed employers to potential legal liability because of transmission of pornographic material, theft of confidential information, and copyright infringement (see Insight 3.1).

depressed business conditions and substantial unemployment in the community.

## THE RISK MANAGEMENT PROCESS

In order to have an effective risk management program, the risk manager must take certain steps. There are four steps in the risk management process: (1) identify potential losses, (2) evaluate potential losses, (3) select the appropriate technique, or combination of techniques, for treating loss exposures, and (4) implement and administer the program (see Exhibit 3.1). Each of these steps is discussed in some detail in the following section.

## IDENTIFYING POTENTIAL LOSSES

The first step in the risk management process is to identify all pure loss exposures. This involves a painstaking identification of all potential losses. The risk manager must identify several types of potential losses, including the following:

- Property losses
- Business income losses

## EVALUATING POTENTIAL LOSSES

The second step in the risk management process is to evaluate and measure the impact of losses on the firm. This involves an estimation of the potential frequency and severity of loss. **Loss frequency** *refers to the probable number of losses that may occur during some given time period.* **Loss severity** *refers to the probable size of the losses that may occur.*

Once the risk manager estimates the frequency and severity of loss for each type of loss exposure, the various loss exposures can be ranked according to their relative importance. For example, a loss

# INSIGHT 3.1

## Internet Misuse Can Leave Companies Exposed

Imagine a workplace in which employees send pornographic pictures via electronic mail throughout the office, creating an atmosphere of sexual harassment.

Next imagine the lawsuits that could be filed by angry female employees.

Finally, imagine attorneys recovering the e-mail transmissions and using them as evidence against an employer.

Welcome to the brave new world of Internet and Intranet liability.

According to two panelists at the Vermont Captive Insurance Association's annual meeting in Burlington, such situations are a reality.

Human nature being what it is makes managing Internet liabilities a daunting task for risk managers and companies, said Frederick Lane, III, a Vermont attorney and principal with ProSeComputing, Inc. in Burlington.

Situations like the one above can occur, said Mr. Lane, and can open naive companies to significant legal liability. Indeed, he cited the legal doctrine of *respondeat superior,* which holds an employer responsible for all the intentional torts of its employees.

To show attendees how easy it is for employees to access pornographic material on the Internet, Mr. Lane demonstrated a search on the Internet that revealed thousands of sites from which such information can be downloaded.

Other potential liabilities include theft of confidential information, copyright infringement and computer viruses, he noted.

Mr. Lane said the key to reducing the risks associated with the Internet is setting up a formal policy and education program that shows employees its proper, as well as its inappropriate uses.

He said companies also can use special software developed to help track employee access to different sites on the Internet. Software filters also can be used to prevent employees from getting access to certain sites deemed inappropriate.

Mr. Lane also explained to the audience that attorneys are beginning to understand how useful e-mail can be as a litigation tool against defendant companies. Because e-mail is extremely difficult to destroy, he said searches of it can be used to provide evidence of improper activity in lawsuits against companies.

Solutions include educating employees about the proper uses of e-mail and noting to employees that their e-mail transmissions are owned by the company and subject to review.

E-mail transmissions also expose companies to electronic espionage by competitors. He said devices also are available to block outside access to e-mail transmissions.

Technology is available to allow companies to encrypt certain Internet transmissions, though its use is currently banned by the federal government, according to John Foehl, chief financial officer and treasurer of Housing Authority Insurance, Inc., a Cheshire, Conn.-based risk management service provider to housing authorities.

In the meantime, Mr. Foehl said he expects the Internet to become a full-fledged electronic marketplace for insurance products. Indeed, he said at least one company—Pioneer Ins. Co.—already offers online quotes.

He said such electronic insurance commerce—which will enable companies to sell policies to anyone, anywhere—raises serious questions about how it should be regulated.

More importantly, he said state insurance regulators are ill-equipped to deal with such problems.

Although he noted that the National Association of Insurance Commissioners recently established a new working group to look into Internet insurance sales, he said that technology is changing so rapidly, state regulators will always be playing catch-up.

SOURCE: Adapted from Dan Lonkevich, "Internet Misuse Can Leave Companies Exposed," *National Underwriter,* Property & Casualty/Risk and Benefits Management Edition, August 26, 1996, p. 17.

exposure with the potential for bankrupting the firm is much more important in a risk management program than an exposure with a small loss potential.

In addition, the relative frequency and severity of each loss exposure must be estimated so that the risk manager can select the most appropriate technique, or combination of techniques, for handling loss exposures. For example, if certain losses occur regularly and are fairly predictable, they can be budgeted out of a firm's income and treated as a normal operating expense. However, if the annual loss experience of a certain type of exposure fluctuates widely, an entirely different approach may be required.

Although the risk manager must consider both loss frequency and loss severity, severity is more important, since a single catastrophic loss could wipe out the firm. Therefore, the risk manager must also consider all losses that can result from a single event. Both the maximum possible loss and maximum probable loss must be estimated. The **maximum possible loss** *is the worst loss that could possibly happen to the firm during its lifetime.* The **maximum probable loss** *is the worst loss that is likely to happen.*[2] For example, if a plant is totally destroyed in a flood, the risk manager may estimate that replacement cost, debris removal, demolition costs, and other costs will total $10 million. Thus, the maximum possible loss is $10 million. The risk manager also estimates that a flood causing more than $8 million of damage to the plant is so unlikely that such a flood would not occur more than once in 50 years. The risk manager may choose to ignore events that occur so infrequently. Thus, for this risk manager, the maximum probable loss is $8 million.

Catastrophic losses are difficult to predict because they occur infrequently. However, their potential impact on the firm must be given high priority. In contrast, certain losses, such as physical damage losses to automobiles and trucks, occur with greater frequency, are usually relatively small, and can be predicted with greater accuracy.

## SELECTING THE APPROPRIATE TECHNIQUE FOR TREATING LOSS EXPOSURES

The third step in the risk management process is to select the most appropriate technique, or combination of techniques, for treating each loss exposure.

The major techniques for treating loss exposures are the following:[3]

- Avoidance
- Loss control
- Retention
- Noninsurance transfers
- Insurance

Avoidance and loss control are called **risk control** techniques because they attempt to reduce the frequency and severity of accidental losses to the firm. Retention, noninsurance transfers, and insurance are called **risk financing** techniques because they provide for the funding of accidental losses after they occur.

### Avoidance

**Avoidance** *means that a certain loss exposure is never acquired, or an existing loss exposure is abandoned.* For example, a firm can avoid a flood loss by not building a plant in a flood plain. An existing loss exposure may also be abandoned. For example, a pharmaceutical firm that produces a drug with dangerous side effects may stop manufacturing that drug.

The major advantage of avoidance is that the chance of loss is reduced to zero if the loss exposure is not acquired. In addition, if an existing loss exposure is abandoned, the possibility of loss is either eliminated or reduced because the activity or product that could produce a loss has been abandoned.

Avoidance, however, has two disadvantages. First, it may not be possible to avoid all losses. For example, a company cannot avoid the premature death of a key executive. Second, it may not be practical or feasible to avoid the exposure. For example, a paint factory can avoid losses arising from the production of paint. However, without any paint production, the firm will not be in business.

### Loss Control

**Loss control** is another method for handling loss in a risk management program. *Loss-control activities are designed to reduce both the frequency and severity of losses.* Unlike the avoidance technique, loss control deals with an exposure that the firm does not wish to abandon. *The purpose of loss-control activities is to change the characteristics of the exposure so that it is more acceptable to the firm;* the firm wishes to keep the exposure but wants to reduce the frequency and severity of losses.

Several examples can illustrate how loss-control measures can reduce the frequency and severity of losses. Measures that reduce loss frequency are quality-control checks, driver examinations, strict enforcement of safety rules, and improvements in product design. Measures that reduce loss severity are the installation of an automatic sprinkler or burglar alarm system, early treatment of injuries, limiting the amount of cash on the premises that can be stolen, and rehabilitation of injured workers.

## Retention

Retention is another important technique for handling losses. **Retention** *means that the firm retains part or all of the losses that result from a given loss exposure.*

Retention can be effectively used in a risk management program when three conditions exist.[4] *First, no other method of treatment is available.* Insurers may be unwilling to write a certain type of coverage, or the coverage may be too expensive. Noninsurance transfers may not be available. In addition, although loss control can reduce the frequency of loss, all losses cannot be eliminated. In these cases, retention is a residual method. If the exposure cannot be insured or transferred, then it must be retained.

*Second, the worst possible loss is not serious.* For example, physical damage losses to automobiles in a large firm's fleet will not bankrupt the firm if the automobiles are separated by wide distances and are not likely to be simultaneously damaged.

*Finally, losses are highly predictable.* Retention can be effectively used for workers' compensation claims, physical damage losses to automobiles, and shoplifting losses. Based on past experience, the risk manager can estimate a probable range of frequency and severity of actual losses. If most losses fall within that range, they can be budgeted out of the firm's income.

**Determining Retention Levels**    If retention is used, the risk manager must determine the firm's retention level, *which is the dollar amount of losses that the firm will retain.* A financially strong firm can have a higher retention level than one whose financial position is weak.

A number of methods can be used to determine the retention level, but only two methods are summarized here.[5] First, a corporation can determine the maximum uninsured loss it can absorb without adversely affecting the company's earnings and dividend policy. One rough rule is that the maximum retention can be set at 5 percent of the company's annual earnings before taxes from current operations.

A second approach is to determine the maximum retention as a percentage of the firm's net working capital, such as between 1 and 5 percent. Although this method does not reflect the firm's overall financial position for absorbing a loss, it does measure the firm's ability to fund a loss.

**Paying Losses**    If retention is used, the risk manager must have some method for paying losses.[6] The firm can pay losses out of its *current net income,* with the losses treated as expenses for that year. However, a large number of losses could exceed current net income, and other assets may then have to be liquidated to pay losses.

Another method for paying losses is an *unfunded or funded reserve.* An unfunded reserve is a bookkeeping account that is charged with the actual or expected losses from a given exposure. A funded reserve is the setting aside of liquid funds to pay losses. Funded reserves are not widely used by private employers in their risk management programs, since the funds may yield a much higher rate of return by being used in the business.[7]

A third method is to *borrow* the necessary funds from a bank. A line of credit is established and used to pay losses as they occur. However, interest must be paid on the loan, and loan repayments can aggravate cash flow problems the firm may have.

A captive insurer can also be used to pay losses. A **captive insurer** *is an insurer established and owned by a parent firm for the purpose of insuring the parent firm's loss exposures.* If the captive is owned by only one parent, such as a corporation, it is known as a *pure captive.* If the captive is owned by a sponsoring organization, such as a trade association, it is called an *association or group captive.* Many captive insurers are located in the Carribbean because of favorable regulatory climate, low capitalization requirements, and low taxes. Captive insurers are also domiciled in certain states in the United States.

Captive insurers are formed for several reasons, including the following:

- *Difficulty in obtaining insurance.* The parent firm may have difficulty in obtaining certain types of insurance from commercial insurers, so it forms its own captive insurer to write the coverage. This is especially true for global firms that may be unable to purchase certain coverages from commercial insurers, including liability insurance and political risk insurance (see Insight 3.2). Establishing a captive may also reduce insurance costs because of lower operating expenses, avoidance of an agent's or broker's commission, and interest earned on invested premiums and reserves that otherwise would be received by commercial insurers.
- *Greater stability of earnings.* A captive insurer can provide for greater stability of earnings, since the adverse impact of chance fluctuations on the firm's income is reduced.
- *Easier access to a reinsurer.* A captive insurer has easier access to reinsurance, since many reinsurers will deal only with insurance companies and not with insureds.
- *Profit center.* A captive insurer can be a source of profit by insuring other parties as well as providing insurance to the parent firm and subsidiaries.
- *Possible tax advantages.* As a general rule, the Internal Revenue Service has take the position that premiums paid to a captive insurer are not income-tax deductible. The IRS argues that there is no substantial transfer of risk to an insurer, and that the premiums paid are similar to contributions to a self-insurance reserve, which is not tax deductible. However, there are certain exceptions. In 1992, a federal appeals court ruled that a corporation can deduct premiums paid to an in-house or captive insurer if the captive obtains at least 30 percent of its business from outsiders.[8] Also, in 1992, the Internal Revenue Service ruled that a corporation could deduct premiums paid to a captive insurer for group life insurance and accident and health insurance provided to company employees.[9]

**Self-Insurance**  Our discussion of retention would not be complete without a brief discussion of self-insurance. The term self-insurance is commonly used by risk managers in their risk management programs. However, self-insurance is a misnomer since it is technically not insurance, and a pure risk is not transferred to an insurer. **Self-insurance** *is a special form of planned retention by which part or all of a given loss exposure is retained by the firm.* A better name for self-insurance is self-funding, which expresses more clearly the idea that losses are funded and paid by the firm.

Self-insurance is widely used in workers compensation insurance (see Exhibit 3.2). Self-insurance is also used by employers to provide group health, dental, vision, and prescription drug benefits to employees. Firms often self-insure their group health-insurance benefits because they can save money and control health-care costs.

Finally, self-insured plans are typically protected by some type of stop-loss insurance that limits the employer's out-of-pocket costs once losses exceed certain limits.

**Risk Retention Groups**  Federal legislation enacted in 1981 and 1986 allows employers, trade groups, governmental units, and other parties to form risk retention groups to self-insure products liability and other commercial liability insurance (except workers compensation). A **risk retention group** *is a group captive that writes commercial liability insurance and products liability insurance for employers who have had difficulty in obtaining such insurance.* For example, a group of taxicab drivers may find commercial liability insurance too expensive to purchase. They can self-insure their general liability loss exposures by forming a risk retention group.

Risk retention groups are exempt from many state insurance laws that apply to other insurers. However, the risk retention group must be licensed as a liability insurer in at least one state.

**Advantages and Disadvantages of Retention**  The retention technique has both advantages and disadvantages in a risk management program.[10] The major advantages are as follows:

- *Save money.* The firm can save money in the long run if its actual losses are less than the loss allowance in the insurer's premium.

## INSIGHT 3.2

## Globalization May Spur Formation of New Captives

A recent survey by Liberty Mutual Group of Boston of approximately 220 risk managers for multinational companies revealed that adequate international insurers are difficult to find.

Among other coverages, property and political risk insurance are particularly hard to get for global operations. Not surprisingly, the "International Issues and Risk Management" survey also disclosed that the risk managers find liability claims the most difficult to manage on a worldwide basis because of local laws and settlement practices.

The prudent risk manager who cannot assemble a borderless risk management program in the traditional market probably owes it to himself or herself and the company to investigate a captive option.

A few courageous risk managers are actually creating tailormade captives today to fit their companies' specialized needs.

For example, a Canadian-based multinational petroleum company formed a captive when it could not find viable commercial insurance covering political risk exposures in Libya.

Not every company, however, is necessarily suited to this type of solution. Multinational firms considering the captive route will generally have a decentralized risk management practice, but a centralized risk department. Companies need the centralized function to add value to the captive solution. But the decentralized practice fosters a risk-sensitive culture in each locale, which is desirable for maximizing the benefits of a captive program.

Besides resolving an immediate insurance availability problem, a "global" captive offers other advantages for those companies with the right set of conditions. Not only can a captive focus on tailoring coverage for a worldwide exposure, but it can also develop an excellent specialized risk management program. One of the key areas where a captive can excel is loss control.

Self-insurance also motivates greater loss control activity than does traditional insurance. However, by going with a captive, the risk manager is better able to pre-plan loss control data collection and claims administration.

Under a captive, the risk manager has the flexibility to select the risk management information system to go along with the other things that assist in loss prevention and cost allocations.

Captives can also offer cost advantages. Usually, an agent's or broker's commission is avoided. Operating expenses are decreased if a captive manager is hired instead of hiring staff and creating a huge bureaucracy. Buying reinsurance directly from the reinsurer can also lower costs.

Captives involved in liability exposures provide more cost benefits than captives linked to property insurance. The long-tail element allows the captive to establish technical reserves, replicating the tax advantages that insurers enjoy. The earnings on reserve investments can be retained within the captive and used to offset losses.

SOURCE: Adapted from Ed Pouzar, "Globalization May Spur New Captives," *National Underwriter*, Property & Casualty/Risk & Benefits Management Edition, August 19, 1996, p. 9.

- *Lower expenses.* The services provided by the insurer may be provided by the firm at a lower cost. Some expenses may be reduced, including loss-adjustment expenses, general administrative expenses, commissions and brokerage fees, loss control expenses, taxes and fees, and the insurer's profit.
- *Encourage loss prevention.* Since the exposure is retained, there may be a greater incentive for loss prevention.

- *Increase cash flow.* Cash flow may be increased, since the firm can use the funds that normally would be held by the insurer.

The retention technique, however, has several disadvantages:

- *Possible higher losses.* The losses retained by the firm may be greater than the loss allowance in the insurance premium that is saved by not purchasing the insurance. Also, in the short run,

## Exhibit 3.2

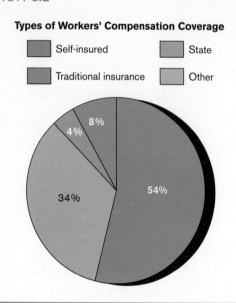

**Types of Workers' Compensation Coverage**

- Self-insured
- Traditional insurance
- State
- Other

8%
4%
34%
54%

SOURCE: Excerpted from Andy McIlvaine, "State of Workers' Comp," *Risk and Insurance,* November 1996, p. 20. Data are based on 303 respondents to the 4th Annual Workers' Compensation Survey conducted jointly by *Risk and Insurance* and *Human Resource Executive* magazines.

there may be great volatility in the firm's loss experience.

- *Possible higher expenses.* Expenses may actually be higher. Outside experts such as safety engineers may have to be hired. Insurers may be able to provide loss control services less expensively.
- *Possible higher taxes.* Income taxes may also be higher. The premiums paid to an insurer are income-tax deductible. However, if retention is used, only the amounts actually paid out for losses are deductible. Contributions to a funded reserve are not income-tax deductible.

## Noninsurance Transfers

Noninsurance transfers can also be used to handle losses. **Noninsurance transfers** *are methods other than insurance by which a pure risk and its potential financial consequences are transferred to another party.* Examples of noninsurance transfers include contracts, leases, and hold-harmless agreements. For example, a company's contract with a construction firm to build a new plant can specify that the construction firm is responsible for any damage to the

plant while it is being built. A firm's computer lease can specify that maintenance, repairs, and any physical damage loss to the computer are the responsibility of the computer firm. Or a firm may insert a hold-harmless clause in a contract, by which one party assumes legal liability on behalf of another party. Thus, a publishing firm may insert a hold-harmless clause in a contract, by which the author, and not the publisher, is held legally liable if the publisher is sued for plagiarism.

In a risk management program, noninsurance transfers have several advantages:[11]

- The risk manager can transfer some potential losses that are not commercially insurable.
- Noninsurance transfers often cost less than insurance.
- The potential loss may be shifted to someone who is in a better position to exercise loss control.

However, noninsurance transfers have several disadvantages. They are summarized as follows:

- The transfer of potential loss may fail because the contract language is ambiguous. Also, there may be no court precedents for the interpretation of a contract that is tailor-made to fit the situation.
- If the party to whom the potential loss is transferred is unable to pay the loss, the firm is still responsible for the claim.
- Noninsurance transfers may not always reduce insurance costs, since an insurer may not give credit for the transfers.

## Insurance

Commercial insurance is also used in a risk management program. Insurance is appropriate for loss exposures that have a low probability of loss but the severity of loss is high.

**Risk Management and Insurance**    If the risk manager uses insurance to treat certain loss exposures, five key areas must be emphasized. They are as follows:[12]

- Selection of insurance coverages
- Selection of an insurer
- Negotiation of terms

- Dissemination of information concerning insurance coverages
- Periodic review of the insurance program

*First, the risk manager must select the insurance coverages needed.* Since there may not be enough money in the risk management budget to insure all possible losses, the need for insurance can be divided into several categories depending on importance. One useful approach is to classify the need for insurance into three categories: (1) essential, (2) desirable, and (3) available. **Essential insurance** *includes those coverages required by law or by contract, such as workers compensation insurance.* Essential insurance also includes those coverages that will protect the firm against a catastrophic loss or a loss that threatens the firm's survival; commercial general liability insurance would fall into that category. **Desirable insurance** *is protection against losses that may cause the firm financial difficulty, but not bankruptcy.* **Available insurance** *is coverage for slight losses that would merely inconvenience the firm.*

The risk manager must also determine if a deductible is needed and the size of the deductible. A **deductible** is a provision by which a specified amount is subtracted from the loss payment otherwise payable. *A deductible is used to eliminate small claims and the administrative expense of adjusting these claims.* As a result, substantial premium savings are possible. In essence, a deductible is a form of risk retention.

Most risk management programs combine the retention technique discussed earlier with commercial insurance. In determining the size of the deductible, the firm may decide to retain only a relatively small part of the maximum possible loss. The insurer normally adjusts any claims, and only losses in excess of the deductible are paid.

Another approach is to purchase **excess insurance.** A firm may be financially strong and may wish to retain a relatively larger proportion of the maximum possible loss. *Under an excess insurance plan, the insurer does not participate in the loss until the actual loss exceeds the amount a firm has decided to retain.* The retention limit may be set at the maximum probable loss (not maximum possible loss). For example, a retention limit of $1 million may be established for a single fire loss to a plant valued at $25 million. The $1 million would be viewed as the maximum probable loss. In the unlikely event of a total loss, the firm would absorb the first $1 million of loss, and the commercial insurer would pay the remaining $24 million.

*Second, the risk manager must select an insurer or several insurers.* Several important factors come into play here. These include the financial strength of the insurer, risk management services provided by the insurer, and the cost and terms of protection. The insurer's financial strength is determined by the size of policyowners' surplus, underwriting and investment results, adequacy of reserves for outstanding liabilities, types of insurance written, and the quality of management. Several trade publications are available to the risk manager for determining the financial strength of a particular insurer. One of the most important are the ratings published by the A. M. Best Company, which rates insurers based on their relative financial strength.

The risk manager must also consider the availability of risk management services in selecting a particular insurer. An insurance agent or broker can provide the desired information concerning the risk management services available from different insurers. These services include loss control services, assistance in identifying loss exposures, and claim adjustment services.

The cost and terms of insurance protection must also be considered. All other factors being equal, the risk manager would prefer to purchase insurance at the lowest possible price. Many risk managers will solicit competitive premium bids from several insurers to get the necessary protection and services at the lowest price.

*Third, after the insurer or insurers are selected, the terms of the insurance contract must be negotiated.* If printed policies, endorsements, and forms are used, the risk manager and insurer must agree on the documents that will form the basis of the contract. If a specially tailored **manuscript policy**[13] is written for the firm, the language and meaning of the contractual provisions must be clear to both parties. In any case, the various risk management services the insurer will provide must be clearly stated in the contract. Finally, if the firm is large, the premiums may be negotiable between the firm and insurer. In many cases, an agent or broker will be involved in the negotiations.

*In addition, information concerning insurance coverages must be disseminated to others in the firm.* The firm's employees and managers must be informed about the insurance coverages, the various records that must be kept, the risk management services that the insurer will provide, and the changes in hazards that could result in a suspension of insurance. Those persons responsible for reporting a loss must also be informed. The firm must comply with policy provisions concerning how notice of a claim is to be given and how the necessary proofs of loss are to be presented.

*Finally, the insurance program must be periodically reviewed.* The entire process of obtaining insurance must be evaluated periodically. This involves an analysis of agent and broker relationships, coverages needed, cost of insurance, quality of loss-control services provided, whether claims are paid promptly, and numerous other factors. Even the basic decision—whether to purchase insurance—must be reviewed periodically.

**Advantages of Insurance**   The use of commercial insurance in a risk management program has certain advantages:[14]

- The firm will be indemnified after a loss occurs. The firm can continue to operate, and there may be little or no fluctuation in earnings.
- Uncertainty is reduced, which permits the firm to lengthen its planning horizon. Worry and fear are reduced for managers and employees, which should improve their performance and productivity.
- Insurers can provide valuable risk management services, such as loss-control services, exposure analysis to identify loss exposures, and claims adjusting.
- Insurance premiums are income-tax deductible as a business expense.

**Disadvantages of Insurance**   The use of insurance also entails certain disadvantages and costs:

- The payment of premiums is a major cost, since the premium consists of a component to pay losses, an amount for expenses, and an allowance for profit and contingencies. There is also an opportunity cost. Under the retention technique discussed earlier, the premium could be invested or used in the business until needed

to pay claims. If insurance is used, premiums must be paid in advance.
- Considerable time and effort must be spent in negotiating the insurance coverages. An insurer or insurers must be selected, policy terms and premiums must be negotiated, the firm must cooperate with the loss-control activities of the insurer, and proof of loss must be filed with the insurer following a loss.
- The risk manager may have less incentive to follow a loss-control program, since the insurer will pay the claim if a loss occurs. Such a lax attitude toward loss control could increase the number of noninsured losses as well.

## Which Method Should Be Used?

In determining the appropriate method or methods for handling losses, a matrix can be used that classifies the various loss exposures according to frequency and severity. The matrix can be useful in determining which risk management method should be used (see Exhibit 3.3).

The first loss exposure is characterized by both low frequency and low severity of loss. One example of this type of exposure would be the potential theft of a secretary's dictionary. This type of exposure can be best handled by retention, since the loss occurs infrequently and, when it does occur, it seldom causes financial harm.

The second type of exposure is more serious. Losses occur frequently, but severity is relatively low. Examples of this type of exposure include physical damage losses to automobiles, workers compensation claims, shoplifting, and food spoilage. Loss

EXHIBIT **3.3**

**Risk Management Matrix**

| Type of loss | Loss frequency | Loss severity | Appropriate risk management technique |
|---|---|---|---|
| 1 | Low | Low | Retention |
| 2 | High | Low | Loss control and retention |
| 3 | Low | High | Insurance |
| 4 | High | High | Avoidance |

control should be used here to reduce the frequency of losses. In addition, since losses occur regularly and are predictable, the retention technique can also be used. However, because small losses in the aggregate can reach sizable levels over a one-year period, excess insurance could also be purchased.

The third type of exposure can be met by insurance. Insurance is best suited for low-frequency, high-severity losses. High severity means that a catastrophic potential is present, while a low probability of loss indicates that the purchase of insurance is economically feasible. Examples of this type of exposure include fires, explosions, natural disasters, and liability lawsuits. The risk manager could also use a combination of retention and commercial insurance to deal with these exposures.

The fourth and most serious type of exposure is one characterized by both high frequency and high severity. This type of exposure is best handled by avoidance. For example, if you have been drinking heavily in a bar and attempt to drive home, the chances are high that you will be in an accident or kill or seriously injure someone. This loss exposure can be avoided by not driving when you drink or by having a designated driver take you home.

## IMPLEMENTING AND ADMINISTRATING THE RISK MANAGEMENT PROGRAM

At this point, three of the four steps in the risk management process have been discussed. The fourth step is implementation and administration of the risk management program.

Typical activities of a risk manager include identifying and evaluating loss exposures, establishing procedures for handling insurance claims, designing and installing employee benefit plans, participating in loss-control and safety programs, and administrating group insurance and self-insurance programs. Thus, risk managers are an important part of the management team, and the salaries paid are relatively high (see Insight 3.3).

### Risk Management Policy Statement

A **risk management policy statement** is necessary in order to have an effective risk management program. *This statement outlines the risk management objectives of the firm, as well as company policy with respect to treatment of loss exposures.* It also educates top-level executives in regard to the risk management process, gives the risk manager greater authority in the firm, and provides standards for judging the risk manager's performance.

In addition, a **risk management manual** may be developed and used in the program. The manual describes in some detail the risk management program of the firm and can be a very useful tool for training new employees who will be participating in the program. Writing the manual also forces the risk manager to state precisely his or her responsibilities, objectives, and available techniques.

### Cooperation with Other Departments

The risk manager does not work alone. Other functional departments within the firm are extremely important in identifying pure loss exposures and methods for treating these exposures. These departments can cooperate in the risk management process in the following ways:

- *Accounting.* Internal accounting controls can reduce employee fraud and theft of cash.
- *Finance.* Information can be provided showing how losses can disrupt profits and cash flow, and the impact that losses will have on the firm's balance sheet and profit and loss statement.
- *Marketing.* Accurate packaging can prevent liability lawsuits. Safe distribution procedures can prevent accidents.
- *Production.* Quality control can prevent the production of defective goods and liability lawsuits. Effective safety programs in the plant can reduce injuries and accidents.
- *Personnel.* This department may be responsible for employee benefit programs, pension programs, and safety programs.

This list indicates how the risk management process involves the entire firm. Indeed, without the active cooperation of the other departments, the risk management program will be a failure.

### Periodic Review and Evaluation

To be effective, the risk management program must be periodically reviewed and evaluated to determine

## INSIGHT 3.3

## How Much Do Risk Managers Earn?

Risk managers in the U.S. average $65,000 per year in total cash compensation, 94 percent of which they receive in base salary. They also average six years as risk managers and 13 years in the risk and insurance profession.

These and other findings are among the first survey of compensation and benefits practices of member organizations released by the Risk and Insurance Management Society Inc. (RIMS) of New York. Nearly 1,000 organizations were surveyed on demographics, administration, compensation, and employee benefits.

In addition to salary, the survey noted that 18 percent of risk managers have an MBA, 30 percent a B.S. and 36 percent a B.A. In addition, the average risk manager supervises three employees and works 45 hours per week.

As for directors of risk management, the total cash compensation average was $85,000—90 percent of it in base salary. Directors have been in the profession for an average of 16 years, supervise six employees and work 47 hours a week. Twenty-four percent hold MBA degrees.

The average annual salaries of six other positions were also noted, including vice president of risk management, at $116,000; employee benefits manager, at $52,000; claims manager, at $51,000; safety manager, at $54,000; risk management analyst, at $38,500; and administrative assistant, at $27,600. RIMS plans to update the survey biennially.

Source: Matt Damsker, "Risk Managers' Salaries Surveyed," *Risk and Insurance*, Vol. 7, No. 5 (May 1996), p. 7.

---

if the objectives are being attained. In particular, risk management costs, safety programs, and loss prevention programs must be carefully monitored. Loss records must also be examined to detect any changes in frequency and severity. In addition, new developments that affect the original decision on handling a loss exposure must be examined. Finally, the risk manager must determine if the firm's overall risk management policies are being carried out, and if the risk manager is receiving the total cooperation of the other departments in carrying out the risk management functions.

### SUMMARY

- Risk management is defined as a systematic process for identifying and evaluating pure loss exposures faced by an organization or individual, and for selecting and administering the most appropriate techniques for treating such exposures. All pure risks are considered, including those that are uninsurable.

- There are several important differences between risk management and insurance management. First, risk management places greater emphasis on the identification and analysis of pure loss exposures. Second, insurance is only one of several methods for handling losses; the risk manager uses numerous methods to handle losses. Third, risk management provides for the periodic evaluation of all methods for meeting losses, not just insurance. Finally, risk management requires the cooperation of other individuals and departments throughout the firm.

- Risk management has several important objectives. Preloss objectives include the goals of economy, reduction of anxiety, and meeting externally imposed obligations. Postloss objectives include survival of the firm, continued operation, stability of earnings, continued growth, and social responsibility.

- There are four steps in the risk management process.

    Potential losses must be identified.

    The potential losses must then be evaluated in terms of loss frequency and loss severity.

    An appropriate method or combination of methods for treating loss exposures must be selected.

    The risk management program must be implemented and properly administered.

- The major methods for treating loss exposures in a risk management program are avoidance, loss control, retention, noninsurance transfers, and insurance.

- The major advantage of avoidance is that the chance of loss is reduced to zero. The major disadvantages are that it may not be possible to avoid all losses, and that it is neither practical nor feasible to avoid all loss exposures.

- Loss control is extremely important in a risk management program. Loss-control activities are designed to reduce both loss frequency and loss severity.

- Retention can be used if no other method of treatment is available, the worst possible loss is not serious, and losses are highly predictable. If retention is used, some method for paying losses must be selected. Losses can be paid out of the firm's current net income; an unfunded or funded reserve can be established to pay losses; the necessary funds can be borrowed; or a captive insurer can be formed.

- A captive insurer may be formed because the firm wants to reduce its premium costs; a captive insurer provides for greater stability of earnings; access to a reinsurer is easier; a captive insurer can be a profit center by selling insurance to other parties; and there may be possible tax advantages.

- The advantages of retention are that the firm may be able to save money on insurance premiums; there may be a reduction in expenses; loss prevention is encouraged; and cash flow may be increased. The major disadvantages are possible greater volatility in losses in the short run, higher expenses if loss control personnel must be hired, and possible higher taxes.

- Self-insurance is a special form of planned retention by which part or all of a given loss exposure is retained by the firm. Another name for self-insurance is self-funding.

- There are several advantages of noninsurance transfers. The risk manager may be able to transfer some uninsurable exposures; noninsurance transfers may cost less than insurance; and the potential loss may be shifted to someone who is in a better position to exercise loss control. However, there are several disadvantages. The transfer of a potential loss may fail because the contract language is ambiguous; the firm is still responsible for the loss if the party to whom the potential loss is transferred is unable to pay the loss; and an insurer may not give sufficient premium credit for the transfers.

- Commercial insurance can also be used in a risk management program. Use of insurance involves a selection of insurance coverages, selection of an insurer, negotiation of contract terms with the insurer, dissemination of information concerning the insurance coverages, and periodic review of the insurance program.

- The major advantages of insurance include indemnification after a loss occurs, reduction in uncertainty, availability of valuable risk management services, and the income-tax deductibility of the premiums. The major disadvantages of insurance include the cost of insurance, time and effort that must be spent in negotiating for insurance, and a possible lax attitude toward loss control because of the presence of insurance.

- A risk management program must be properly implemented and administered. This involves preparation of a risk management policy statement, close cooperation with other individuals and departments, and periodic review of the entire risk management program.

## KEY CONCEPTS AND TERMS

Association or group
  captive
Available insurance
Avoidance
Captive insurer
Deductible
Desirable insurance
Essential insurance
Excess insurance
Loss control
Loss frequency
Loss severity
Manuscript policy
Maximum possible loss

Maximum probable loss
Noninsurance transfers
Pure captive
Retention
Retention level
Risk control
Risk financing
Risk management
Risk management manual
Risk management policy
  statement
Risk retention group
Self-insurance

## QUESTIONS FOR REVIEW

1. Define risk management. How does risk management differ from insurance management?

2. Explain the objectives of a risk management program both before and after a loss.

3. Explain the four steps in the risk management process.

4. How can a risk manager identify potential losses? How does a risk manager evaluate and analyze each potential loss?

5. Explain the various methods for treating loss exposures in a risk management program.

6. What conditions must be fulfilled before retention is used in a risk management program?

7. Define captive insurer and explain why captive insurers are formed.

8. Is self-insurance the same as insurance? Explain.

9. List some examples of loss control and noninsurance transfers.

10. Explain the basic factors that a risk manager must consider if commercial insurance is used in a risk management program.

## QUESTIONS FOR DISCUSSION

1. The Smith Corporation manufactures and sells ladders and scaffolds that are used by construction firms. These products are sold to more than 1000 independent retailers in the United States. The management of Smith Corporation is concerned that the company may be sued if one of its products is defective and someone is injured. Since the cost of products liability insurance has increased sharply in recent years, the Smith Corporation is looking for ways to control its loss exposures.

   a. Describe each of the steps in the risk management process.

   b. For each of the following risk management techniques, describe a specific action using that technique that may be helpful in dealing with the products liability exposure of the Smith Corporation.
      (1) Avoidance
      (2) Loss prevention
      (3) Loss reduction
      (4) Noninsurance transfers

2. a. Captive insurers are a popular approach that many large corporations use to finance retained loss exposures. Explain the advantages of using a captive insurer in a risk management program.

   b. Compare the risk management techniques of avoidance and loss control with respect to the following:
      (1) The effect on the loss exposure itself
      (2) The financing of losses if they should occur

3. The Gem Corporation has 10,000 salespersons and employees in the United States who drive company cars. Lisa Kim, risk manager of the Gem Corporation, has recommended to the firm's management that they should implement a partial retention program for collision losses to the company's cars.

   a. Describe the factors that the Gem Corporation should consider in deciding whether or not it should partially retain the collision loss exposure to company cars.

   b. If the partial retention program is implemented, explain the various methods that the Gem Corporation can use to pay for any collision losses to the company's cars.

   c. Explain the advantages and disadvantages of a partial retention program to the Gem Corporation.

   d. Give an example of a noninsurance transfer that the company could use in its risk management program.

4. Gerald Hanner has just been appointed head of the risk management department of Gates Manufacturing. His first action as a risk manager is to prepare a formal risk management policy statement.

   a. What benefits can the firm expect to receive from a well-prepared risk management policy statement?

   b. Describe the different techniques that Gerald might use to identify the firm's pure loss exposures.

   c. Explain the advantages and disadvantages of using commercial insurance in the company's risk management program.

## CASE APPLICATION

City Bus Corporation provides school bus transportation to private and public schools in Lancaster County. City Bus owns 50 buses that are garaged in three different cities within the county. City Bus is faced with competition from two larger bus companies that operate in the same area. Public school boards and private schools generally award contracts to the lowest bidder; however, the level of service and overall performance are also considered.

a. Briefly describe the steps in the risk management process that should be followed by the risk manager of City Bus.

b. Identify the major loss exposures faced by the City Bus Corporation.

c. For each of the loss exposures identified in (b) above, identify a risk management technique or combination of techniques that could be used to handle the exposure.

d. Describe several sources of funds for paying losses if retention is used in the risk management program.

e. Identify other departments in the City Bus Corporation that would also be involved in the risk management program.

5. The principles of risk management can also be applied to individual or family loss exposures.

   a. Briefly describe three major loss exposures that a typical individual or family faces.

   b. For each of the loss exposures described above, explain an appropriate technique or combination of techniques that can be used to treat the exposure.

## SELECTED REFERENCES

Doherty, Neil A. *Corporate Risk Management: A Financial Exposition,* New York: McGraw-Hill, 1985.

Head, George L., ed. *Essentials of Risk Control,* 3rd ed., vols. 1 and 2. Malvern, Pa.: Insurance Institute of America, 1995.

Head, George L., Michael J. Elliott, and James D. Blinn. *Essentials of Risk Financing,* 3rd ed. Malvern, Pa.: Insurance Institute of America, 1996.

Head, George L., and Stephen Horn II. *Essentials of Risk Management,* 3rd ed., vols. 1 and 2. Malvern, Pa.: Insurance Institute of America, 1997.

*The Risk Funding and Self-Insurance Bulletins (RF&S).* Cincinnati, Ohio: National Underwriter. The bulletins are published quarterly and provide valuable information on self-insurance issues.

Williams, C. Arthur, Jr., Michael L. Smith, and Peter C. Young. *Risk Management and Insurance,* 7th ed. New York: McGraw-Hill, 1995.

Vaughan, Emmett J. *Risk Management.* New York: John Wiley & Sons, Inc., 1996.

## NOTES

1. Robert I. Mehr and Bob A. Hedges, *Risk Management: Concepts and Applications* (Homewood, Ill.: Richard D. Irwin, 1974), chapters 1 and 2. See also C. Arthur Williams, Jr., George L. Head, Ronald C. Horn, and G. William Glendenning, *Principles of Risk Management and Insurance,* 2nd ed., vol. 1 (Malvern, Pa.: American Institute for Property and Liability Underwriters, 1981), pp. 15–18.

2. Williams et al., pp. 158–59.

3. These techniques are analyzed in some detail in Williams et al., chapters 2–5. The author drew heavily on this source in preparing this section.

4. Williams et al., pp. 125–26.

5. *Insurance Decisions Determining Risk Retention Levels* (Philadelphia: Insurance Company of North America, n.d.), pp. 3–12.

6. Williams et al., pp. 135–42.

7. George L. Head and Stephen Horn II, *Essentials of the Risk Management Process,* 2nd ed., vol. 2 (Malvern, Pa.: Insurance Institute of America, 1991), pp. 31–32.

8. *Investors Business Daily,* December 2, 1992, p. 4.

9. L. H. Otis, "IRS Frees Captives for Benefit Risk," *National Underwriter,* Property & Casualty/Risk & Benefits Management ed., March 22, 1993, pp. 9, 42.

10. The advantages and disadvantages of retention are discussed in some detail in Williams et al., pp. 126–33.

11. Williams et al., pp. 103–4.

12. For an extensive discussion of insurance in a risk management program, see Williams et al., pp. 107–23, 146–51.

13. A manuscript policy is one that is specifically designed for a business firm to meet its specific needs and requirements.

14. Williams et al., pp. 108–16.

# Part Two

# LEGAL PRINCIPLES IN RISK AND INSURANCE

**On-Line Resources**

One source of detailed information on contract law, among other areas of law, is the **Legal Information Institute** of the Cornell Law School. The LII's web site can be found at:

`http://www.law.cornell.edu/`

**LawLinks,** the Internet Legal Resource Center, calls itself "the Internet's most comprehensive legal resource site for both attorneys and consumers." Visit the site at:

`http://lawlinks.com`

**Nolo Press** is a publisher of self-help legal information for consumers:

`http://www.nolo.com/`

# Chapter 4

# FUNDAMENTAL LEGAL PRINCIPLES

66 *The education of those engaged in the important functions of the insurance business calls for an understanding of the essentials of insurance law.* 99

*Edwin W. Patterson,*
Essentials of Insurance Law, *2nd ed.*

## Student Learning Objectives

After studying this chapter, you should be able to:

■ Explain the fundamental legal principles that are reflected in insurance contracts, including the

principle of indemnity
principle of insurable interest
principle of subrogation
principle of utmost good faith.

■ Explain how the legal concepts of representations, concealment, and warranty support the principle of utmost good faith.

■ Describe the basic requirements for the formation of a valid insurance contract.

■ Show how insurance contracts differ from other contracts.

■ Explain the law of agency and how it affects the actions of insurance agents.

You probably own at least one insurance policy. Have you ever read the policy? The chances are you have never read an insurance policy, and even if you did, you probably did not understand the coverages provided. Insurance contracts are complex legal documents that reflect both general rules of law and insurance law. When you buy insurance, you expect to be paid for a covered loss. Whether you can collect and the amount paid are governed by insurance law. Thus, you should have some understanding of the legal principles and concepts reflected in insurance contracts. You will understand more clearly the individual insurance contracts that are discussed later in the text if you understand the legal principles discussed in this chapter.

In this chapter, several important areas are emphasized. This includes a discussion of the fundamental legal principles that are reflected in insurance contracts, the legal requirements that must be met to have a valid insurance contract, and the distinct legal characteristics of insurance contracts that distinguish them from other contracts. The chapter concludes with a discussion of the law of agency and how it applies to insurance agents.

## PRINCIPLE OF INDEMNITY

The principle of indemnity is one of the most important legal principles in the field of insurance. The **principle of indemnity** *states that the insured should not profit from a covered loss but should be restored to approximately the same financial position that existed prior to the loss.* Most property insurance contracts are contracts of indemnity. If a covered loss occurs, the insured should not collect more than the actual amount of the loss.

The principle of indemnity has two fundamental purposes. *The first purpose is to prevent the insured from profiting from insurance.* The insured should not profit if a loss occurs, but should be restored to approximately the same financial position that existed before the loss. For example, if Kristin's home is insured for $100,000, and a $20,000 loss occurs, the principle of indemnity would be violated if $100,000 were paid to her. She would be profiting from insurance.

*The second purpose is to reduce moral hazard.* If dishonest insureds can profit from a loss, they may deliberately cause a loss with the intention of collecting the insurance. Thus, if the loss payment does not exceed the actual amount of the loss, the temptation to be dishonest is reduced.

### Actual Cash Value

The concept of **actual cash value** underlies the principle of indemnity. In property insurance, the standard method for indemnifying the insured is based on the actual cash value of the damaged property at the time of loss. The courts have used three major methods to determine actual cash value:

- Replacement cost less depreciation
- Fair market value
- Broad evidence rule

**Replacement Cost Less Depreciation**  Under this rule, **actual cash value** *is defined as replacement cost less depreciation.* This rule has been traditionally used to determine the actual cash value of property in property insurance. It takes into consideration both inflation and depreciation of property values over time. Replacement cost is the current cost of restoring the damaged property with new materials of like kind and quality. Depreciation is a deduction for physical wear and tear, age, and economic obsolescence.

For example, Shannon has a favorite couch that burns in a fire. Assume that she bought the couch five years ago, that the couch is 50 percent depreciated, and that a similar couch today would cost $1000. Under the actual cash value rule, Shannon will collect $500 for the loss of her couch because replacement cost is $1000, but depreciation is $500, or 50 percent. If she were paid the full replacement value of $1000, the principle of indemnity would be violated, because she would be receiving the value of a brand new couch instead of one five years old. In short, the $500 payment represents indemnification for the loss of a five-year-old couch. This can be summarized as follows:

Replacement cost = $1000

Depreciation = $500 (couch is 50 percent depreciated)

Actual cash value = Replacement cost − Depreciation

$500 = $1000 − $500

**Fair Market Value**  Some courts have ruled that fair market value should be used to determine actual cash value of a loss. **Fair market value** *is the price a willing buyer would pay a willing seller in a free market.*

The fair market value of a building may be below its actual cash value based on replacement cost less depreciation. This may be due to several reasons, including a poor location, deteriorating neighborhood, or economic obsolescence of the building. For example, in major cities, large homes in older residential areas often have a market value well below replacement cost less depreciation. If a loss occurs, the fair market value may be used to determine the value of the loss. In one case, a building valued at $170,000 based on the actual cash value rule had a market value of only $65,000 when a loss occurred. The court ruled that the actual cash value of the property should be based on the fair market value of $65,000 rather than on $170,000.[1]

### Broad Evidence Rule

Many states now use the broad evidence rule to determine the actual cash value of a loss. The **broad evidence rule** *means that the determination of actual cash value should include all relevant factors an expert would use to determine the value of the property.* Relevant factors include replacement cost less depreciaton, fair market value, present value of expected income from the property, comparison sales of similar property, opinions of appraisers, and numerous other factors.

Although actual cash value is used in property insurance, different procedures are followed for other types of insurance. In liability insurance, the amount paid for a loss is the actual damage the insured is legally obligated to pay because of bodily injury or property damage to another. In business income insurance, the amount paid is usually based on the loss of profits plus continuing expenses incurred when the firm is shut down because of a loss from a covered peril. In life insurance, the amount paid upon the insured's death is the face amount of the policy.

## Exceptions to the Principle of Indemnity

There are several important exceptions to the principle of indemnity. They include the following:

- Valued policy
- Valued policy laws
- Replacement cost insurance
- Life insurance

### Valued Policy

A **valued policy** *is one that pays the face amount of insurance regardless of actual cash value if a total loss occurs.* Valued policies typically are used to insure antiques, fine arts, rare paintings, and family heirlooms. Because of difficulty in determining the actual value of the property at the time of loss, the insured and insurer both agree on the value of the property when the policy is first issued. For example, you may have a valuable antique clock that was owned by your great-grandmother. Assume that the clock is worth $10,000 today and is insured for that amount. If the clock is totally destroyed in a fire, you would be paid $10,000 and

not the actual cash value. Because the amount paid may exceed the actual cash value, the principle of indemnity is violated.

### Valued Policy Laws

**Valued policy laws** are another exception to the principle of indemnity.[2] The specified perils to which a valued policy law applies vary among the states. Some states cover only fire; others cover fire, lightning, windstorm, and tornado; and a small number of states cover all insured perils. In addition, the laws generally apply only to real property, and the loss must be total. For example, a building insured for $200,000 may have an actual cash value of $175,000. If a total loss from a fire occurs, the face amount of $200,000 would be paid. Because the insured would be paid more than the actual cash value, the principle of indemnity would be violated.

The original purpose of a valued policy law was to protect the insured from an argument with the insurer if an agent had deliberately overinsured property in order to receive a higher commission. After a total loss, the insurer might offer less than the face amount for which the policyowner had paid premiums on the grounds that the building was overinsured. However, the importance of a valued policy law has declined over time because inflation in property values has made overinsurance less of a problem. Underinsurance is now the greater problem, since it results in both inadequate premiums for the insurer and inadequate protection for the insured.

Despite their reduced importance, valued policy laws can lead to overinsurance and an increase in moral hazard. Most buildings are not physically inspected before they are insured. If an insurer fails to inspect a building for valuation purposes, overinsurance and possible moral hazard may result. The insured may not be concerned about loss prevention, or may even deliberately cause a loss to collect the insurance proceeds. Although valued policy laws provide a defense for the insurer when fraud is suspected, the burden of proof is on the insurer to prove fraudulent intent. This is often difficult. For example, in an older case, a house advertised for sale at $1800 was insured for $10,000 under a fire insurance policy. About six months later, the house was totally destroyed by a fire. The insurer denied liability on the grounds of misrepresentation and fraud. However, an appeals court ordered the face amount of insurance to be paid. The court held that nothing prevented the company from inspecting the property to determine its value, and the insured's statement concerning the value of the house was an expression of opinion, not a representation of fact.[3]

*Replacement Cost Insurance*    Replacement cost insurance is a third exception to the principle of indemnity. **Replacement cost insurance** *means no deduction is taken for depreciation in determining the amount paid for a loss.* For example, assume the roof on your home is five years old and has a useful life of 20 years. The roof is damaged by a tornado, and the current cost of replacement is $10,000. Under the actual cash value rule, you would receive only $7500 ($10,000 − $2500 = $7500). Under a replacement cost policy, you would receive the full $10,000 (less any applicable deductible). Since you receive the value of a brand new roof instead of one that is five years old, the principle of indemnity is technically violated.

However, replacement cost insurance is based on the recognition that payment of the actual cash value can still result in a substantial loss to the insured, since few persons budget for depreciation. The deduction for depreciation means that you must come up with the necessary cash to restore the property to its original condition after a loss occurs. In our example, you would have had to pay $2500 to restore the damaged roof, since it was one-fourth depreciated. To deal with this problem, replacement cost insurance can be purchased to insure homes, buildings, and business and personal property.

*Life Insurance*    Life insurance is another exception to the principle of indemnity. A life insurance contract is not a contract of indemnity but is a valued policy that pays a stated sum to the beneficiary upon the insured's death. The indemnity principle is difficult to apply to life insurance for the obvious reason that the historical actual cash value rule (replacement cost less depreciation) is meaningless in determining the value of a human life. Moreover, in order to plan for personal and business purposes, such as the need to provide a specific amount of monthly income to the deceased's dependents, a certain amount of life insurance must be purchased before death occurs. For these reasons, a life insurance policy is another exception to the principle of indemnity.

## PRINCIPLE OF INSURABLE INTEREST

The principle of insurable interest is another important legal principle. The **principle of insurable interest** *states that the insured must lose financially if a loss occurs, or must incur some other kind of harm if the loss takes place.* For example, you have an insurable interest in your automobile since you may lose financially if the car is damaged or stolen. You have an insurable interest in your personal property, such as a television set or VCR, since you may lose financially if the property is damaged or destroyed.

### Purposes of an Insurable Interest

To be legally enforceable, all insurance contracts must be supported by an insurable interest. Insurance contracts must be supported by an insurable interest for the following reasons.[4]

- To prevent gambling
- To reduce moral hazard
- To measure the loss

*First, an insurable interest is necessary to prevent gambling.* If an insurable interest were not required, the contract would be a gambling contract and would be against the public interest. For example, you could insure the property of another and hope for an early loss. You could similarly insure the life of another person and hope for an early death. These contracts clearly would be gambling contracts and would be against the public interest.

*Second, an insurable interest reduces moral hazard.* If an insurable interest is not required, a dishonest person could purchase a property insurance contract on someone else's property and then deliberately cause a loss to receive the proceeds. But if the insured stands to lose financially, nothing is gained by causing the loss. Thus, moral hazard is reduced. In life insurance, an insurable interest requirement reduces the incentive to murder the insured for the purpose of collecting the proceeds.

*Finally, an insurable interest measures the amount of the insured's loss.* In property insurance, most contracts are contracts of indemnity, and one measure of recovery is the insurable interest of the insured. If the loss payment cannot exceed the amount of one's insurable interest, the principle of indemnity is supported.

## Examples of an Insurable Interest

Several situations that satisfy the insurable interest requirement are discussed in this section. However, it is helpful at this point to distinguish between an insurable interest in property and liability insurance and in life insurance.

**Property and Liability Insurance**   *Ownership of property* can support an insurable interest, since owners of property will lose financially if their property is damaged or destroyed.

*Potential legal liability* can also support an insurable interest. For example, a dry-cleaning firm has an insurable interest in the property of the customers, since the firm may be legally liable for damage to the customer's goods because of the firm's negligence.

*Secured creditors* have an insurable interest as well. A commercial bank or savings and loan institution that grants mortgages has an insurable interest in the property pledged. The property serves as collateral for the mortgage, so if the building is damaged, the collateral behind the loan is impaired. A bank that makes an inventory loan to a business firm has an insurable interest in the stock of goods, since it serves as collateral for the loan. However, the courts have ruled that unsecured, or general, creditors normally do not have an insurable interest in the debtor's property.[5]

Finally, a *contractual right* can support an insurable interest. Thus, a business firm that contracts to purchase goods from abroad on the condition that they arrive safely in the United States has an insurable interest in the goods because of the loss of profits if the merchandise does not arrive.

**Life Insurance**   The question of an insurable interest does not arise when you purchase life insurance on your own life. The law considers the insurable interest requirement to be met whenever a person voluntarily purchases life insurance on his or her life. This means that you can purchase as much life insurance as you can afford, subject of course to the insurer's underwriting rules concerning the maximum amount of insurance that can be written on any single life. Also, when you apply for life insurance on your own life, you can name anyone as beneficiary. The beneficiary is not required to have an insurable interest in your life.[6]

If you wish to purchase a life insurance policy on the life of another person, however, you must have an insurable interest in that person's life. Close ties of blood or marriage will satisfy the insurable interest requirement in life insurance. For example, a husband can purchase a life insurance policy on his wife's life and be named as beneficiary. Likewise, a wife can insure her husband and be named as beneficiary. A grandparent can purchase a life insurance policy on the life of a grandchild. However, remote family relationships will not support an insurable interest. For example, cousins cannot insure each other unless a pecuniary relationship is involved.

If a **pecuniary interest** is involved, the insurable interest requirement in life insurance can be met. Even when there is no relationship by blood or marriage, one person may be financially harmed by the death of another. For example, a corporation can insure the life of an outstanding salesperson, since the firm's profit may decline if the salesperson should die. One business partner can insure the life of the other partner in order to purchase the deceased partner's interest if he or she should die.

## When Must an Insurable Interest Exist?

*In property insurance, the insurable interest must exist at the time of the loss.* There are two reasons for this requirement. First, most property insurance contracts are contracts of indemnity. If an insurable interest did not exist at the time of loss, financial loss would not occur. Hence, the principle of indemnity would be violated if payment were made. For example, if José sells his home to Susan, and a fire occurs before the insurance on the home is canceled, José cannot collect since he no longer has an insurable interest in the property. Susan cannot collect either since she is not named as an insured under the policy.

Second, you may not have an insurable interest in the property when the contract is first written, but may expect to have an insurable interest in the future, at the time of possible loss. For example, in ocean marine insurance, it is common to insure a return cargo by a contract entered into prior to the ship's departure. However, the policy may not cover the goods until they are on board the ship as the insured's property. Although an insurable interest does not exist when the contract is first written, you can still collect if you have an insurable interest in the goods at the time of loss.

---

## INSIGHT 4.1

### No Insurable Interest at the Time of Death: Can the Policyowner Collect the Life Insurance Proceeds?

**Legal Facts**

Jack worked for Pioneer Foundry for nine years. The company had an insurable interest in his life and purchased a $50,000 life insurance policy on his life. The company was named as beneficiary. Jack later left the company, but the company continued to pay the premiums until his death. At the time of Jack's death, the company had no insurable interest in his life. Jack's widow sued and claimed the company was not entitled to the proceeds because the insurable interest terminated when Jack left the company. Is the company entitled to the policy proceeds?

**Court Decision**

The court ruled that the company is entitled to the policy proceeds. If the insurable interest requirement is met at the inception of the policy, the death benefit must be paid even though there is no insurable interest at the time of death.[1]

[1]*Secor v. Pioneer Foundry Co., Inc.*, 173 N.W. 2d 780 (Mich. 1970).
SOURCE: Adapted from Joseph L. Frascona, *Business Law, The Legal Environment, Text and Cases*, 3rd ed. (Dubuque, Iowa: Wm. C. Brown Publishers, 1987), p. 1005.

---

*In contrast, in life insurance, the insurable interest requirement must be met only at the inception of the policy, not at the time of death.*[7] Life insurance is not a contract of indemnity but is a valued policy that pays a stated sum upon the insured's death. Since the beneficiary has only a legal claim to receive the policy proceeds, the beneficiary does not have to show that a loss has been incurred by the insured's death. For example, if Michelle takes out a policy on her husband's life and later gets a divorce, she is entitled to the policy proceeds upon the death of her former husband if she has kept the insurance in force. The insurable interest requirement must be met only at the inception of the contract (see Insight 4.1).

## PRINCIPLE OF SUBROGATION

The principle of subrogation strongly supports the principle of indemnity. **Subrogation** *means substitution of the insurer in place of the insured for the purpose of claiming indemnity from a third person for a loss covered by insurance.*[8] This means that the insurer is entitled to recover from a negligent third party any loss payments made to the insured. For example, assume that a negligent motorist fails to stop at a red light and smashes into Jennifer's car, causing damages in the amount of $5000. If she has collision insurance on her car, her company will pay the physical damage loss to the car (less any deductible) and then attempt to collect from the negligent motorist who caused the accident. Alternatively, Jennifer could attempt to collect directly from the negligent motorist for the damage to her automobile. Subrogation does not apply if a loss payment is not made. However, to the extent that a loss payment is made, the insured gives to the insurer legal rights to collect damages from the negligent third party.

### Purposes of Subrogation

Subrogation has three basic purposes. *First, subrogation prevents the insured from collecting twice for the same loss.* In the absence of subrogation, the insured could collect from the insurer and from the person who caused the loss. The principle of indemnity would be violated because the insured would be profiting from a loss.

*Second, subrogation is used to hold the guilty person responsible for the loss.* By exercising its subrogation rights, the insurer can collect from the negligent person who caused the loss.

*Finally, subrogation tends to hold down insurance rates.* Subrogation recoveries can be reflected in the rate-making process, which tends to hold rates below where they would be in the absence of subrogation.

## Importance of Subrogation

You should keep in mind five important corollaries of the principle of subrogation.

1. *The general rule is that by exercising its subrogation rights, the insurer is entitled only to the amount it has paid under the policy.*[9] Some insureds may not be fully indemnified after a loss because of insufficient insurance, satisfaction of a deductible, or legal expenses in trying to recover from a negligent third party. Many policies currently have a provision stating how a a subrogation recovery is to be shared between the insured and insurer. However, in the absence of any policy provision, the courts have used different rules in determining how a subrogation recovery is to be shared. *One commonly held view is that the insured must be reimbursed in full for the loss; the insurer is then entitled to any remaining balance up to the insurer's interest, with any remainder going to the insured.*[10] For example, Andrew has a $100,000 home insured for only $80,000 under a homeowners policy. Assume that the house is totally destroyed in a fire because of faulty wiring by an electrician. The insurer would pay $80,000 to Andrew and then attempt to collect from the negligent electrician. After exercising its subrogation rights against the negligent electrician, the insurer has a net recovery of $50,000 (after deduction of legal expenses). Andrew would receive $20,000, and the insurer can retain the balance of $30,000.

   There are some exceptions to the general rule of full recovery by the insured when the insurer exercises its subrogation rights. In automobile collision insurance, insurers typically will indemnify the insured for the deductible if full recovery is received from the negligent third party. However, if the insurer incurs legal expenses in exercising its subrogation rights, the deductible may be prorated with the insured. Finally, some insurance contracts specify that a subrogation recovery will be shared pro rata between the insured and insurer based on the proportion that the loss incurred by each party bears to the total loss.

2. *The insured cannot impair the insurer's subrogation rights.* The insured cannot do anything after a loss that prejudices the insurer's right to proceed against a negligent third party. For example, if the insured waives the right to sue the negligent party, the right to collect from the insurer for the loss is also waived. This could happen if the insured admits fault in an automobile accident or attempts to settle a collision loss with the negligent driver without the insurer's consent. If the insurer's right to subrogate against the negligent motorist is adversely affected, the insured's right to collect from the insurer is forfeited.[11]

3. *The insurer can waive its subrogation rights in the contract.* To meet the special needs of some insureds, the insurance company may waive its subrogation rights by a contractual provision for losses that have not yet occurred. For example, in order to rent an apartment house, a landlord may agree to release the tenants from potential liability if the building is damaged. If the landlord's insurer waives its subrogation rights, and if a tenant negligently starts a fire, the insurer would have to reimburse the landlord for the loss, but could not recover from the tenant since the subrogation rights were waived.

   The insurer may decide not to exercise its subrogation rights after a loss occurs. The legal expenses may exceed the possible recovery; a counterclaim against the insured or insurer may be filed by the alleged wrongdoer; the insurer may wish to avoid embarrassment of the insured; or the insurer company may wish to maintain good public relations.[12]

4. *Subrogation does not apply to life insurance and to most individual health insurance contracts.* Life insurance is not a contract of indemnity, and subrogation has relevance only for contracts of indemnity. Individual health insurance contracts usually do not contain subrogation clauses.[13] Thus, if Janet is injured in an automobile accident by a negligent driver, she can collect for her medical expenses under an individual health insurance policy and can also sue the negligent motorist for her bodily injuries.

5. *The insurer cannot subrogate against its own insureds.* If the insurer could recover a loss payment for a covered loss, the basic purpose of purchasing the insurance would be defeated.

## PRINCIPLE OF UTMOST GOOD FAITH

An insurance contract is based on the principle of **utmost good faith.** *This means that a higher degree of honesty is imposed on both parties to an insurance contract than is imposed on parties to other contracts.* This principle has its historical roots in ocean marine insurance. The marine underwriter had to place great faith in statements made by the applicant for insurance concerning the cargo to be shipped. The property to be insured may not have been visually inspected, and the contract may have been formed in a location far removed from the covered cargo and ship. Thus, the principle of utmost good faith imposed a high degree of honesty on the applicant for insurance.

The principle of utmost good faith is supported by three important legal doctrines: representations, concealment, and warranty.

### Representations

**Representations** *are statements made by the applicant for insurance.* For example, if you apply for life insurance, you may be asked questions concerning your age, weight, height, occupation, state of health, family history, and other relevant questions. Your answers to these questions are called representations.

The legal significance of a representation is that the insurance contract is voidable at the insurer's option if the representation is (1) material, (2) false, and (3) relied on by the insurer.[14] **Material** *means that if the insurer knew the true facts, the policy would not have been issued, or would have been issued on different terms.* False means that the statement is not true or is misleading. Reliance means that the insurer relies on the misrepresentation in issuing the policy at a specified premium. For example, Scott may apply for life insurance and state in the application that he has not visited a doctor within the last five years. However, he may have undergone surgery for lung cancer six months earlier. In this case, he has made a statement that is both false and material, and the policy is voidable at the insurer's option. If Scott dies shortly after the policy is issued, the company could contest the death claim on the basis of a material misrepresentation. Insight 4.2 provides an additional application of this legal principle.

But if an applicant for insurance states an opinion or belief that later turns out to be wrong, the insurer must prove that the applicant spoke fraudulently and intended to deceive the company before it can deny payment of a claim. For example, assume that you are asked if you have high blood pressure when you apply for health insurance, and you answer no to the question. If the insurer later discovers you have high blood pressure, in order to deny payment of a claim, it must prove that you intended to deceive the company. Thus, a statement of opinion or belief must also be fraudulent before the insurer can refuse to pay a claim.

Finally, an **innocent** (unintentional) **misrepresentation** of a material fact, if relied on by the insurer, also makes the contract voidable.[15] A majority of court opinions have ruled that an innocent misrepresentation of a material fact makes the contract voidable.

### Concealment

The doctrine of concealment also supports the principle of utmost good faith. A **concealment** *is intentional failure of the applicant for insurance to reveal a material fact to the insurer.* Concealment is the same thing as nondisclosure; that is, the applicant for insurance deliberately withholds material information from the insurer. The legal effect of a material concealment is the same as a misrepresentation—the contract is voidable at the insurer's option.

To deny a claim based on concealment, a nonmarine insurer must prove two things: (1) the concealed fact was known by the insured to be material, and (2) the insured intended to defraud the insurer.[16] For example, Joseph DeBellis applied for a life insurance policy on his life. Five months after the policy was issued, he was murdered. The death certificate named the deceased as Joseph DeLuca, his true name. The insurer denied payment on the grounds that Joseph had concealed a material fact by not revealing his true identity, and that he had an extensive criminal record. In finding for the insurer, the court held that intentional concealment of his true identity was material and breached the obligation of good faith.[17]

The doctrine of concealment is applied in a harsher manner in ocean marine insurance. An

---

## INSIGHT 4.2

### Misrepresentation of Material Facts
### Allows Insurer to Deny Liability

**Legal Facts**

Orr applied for an auto insurance policy. He stated in the application he did not use alcohol, had no offenses other than traffic violations, and had never been fined or convicted for a moving vehicle violation. In fact, Orr had a number of convictions for drunkenness, forgery, and traffic violations. The policy was issued. Orr's car later was involved in an auto accident. Orr was not driving the car at the time of the accident. Based on the preceding facts, can Orr's insurer deny liability because of Orr's false statements?

**Court Decision**

The court ruled that the insurer was not liable since Orr made several material misrepresentations. Therefore, the policy was void.[1]

[1]*Countryside Casualty Co. v. Orr*, 523 F. 2d 870 (1975).

SOURCE: Adapted from Joseph L. Frascona, *Business Law, The Legal Environment, Text and Cases,* 3rd ed. (Dubuque, Iowa: Wm. C. Brown Publishers, 1987), p. 1006.

---

ocean marine insurer is not required to prove that the concealment is intentional. Applicants are required to reveal all material facts that pertain to the property to be insured. The applicant's lack of awareness of the materiality of the fact is of no consequence. Thus, an ocean marine insurer can successfully deny payment of a claim if it can show that the concealed fact is material.

### Warranty

The doctrine of warranty also reflects the principle of utmost good faith. A **warranty** *is a statement of fact or a promise made by the insured, which is part of the insurance contract and which must be true if the insurer is to be liable under the contract.*[18] For example, in exchange for a reduced premium, the owner of a liquor store may warrant that an approved burglary and robbery alarm system will be operational at all times. The clause describing the warranty becomes part of the contract.

In its strictest form based on the common law, a warranty is a harsh legal doctrine. Any breach of the warranty, even if minor or not material, allows the insurer to deny payment of a claim. However, the courts and legislation have softened and modified the harsh common law doctrine of warranty. With

the exception of ocean marine insurance, most American courts do not follow the strict common law. Some modifications of the doctrine of warranty are summarized as follows.

- Statements made by the applicant for insurance are considered to be representations and not warranties. Thus, the insurer cannot deny liability for a loss if a misrepresentation is not material.
- Most courts will interpret a breach of warranty liberally in those cases where a minor breach affects the risk only temporarily or insignificantly.
- "Increase in hazard" statutes have been passed that state that the company cannot deny a claim unless the breach of warranty increases the hazard.
- Statutes have been passed that allow the insured to recover unless the breach of warranty actually contributed to the loss.

### REQUIREMENTS OF AN INSURANCE CONTRACT

An insurance policy is based on the law of contracts. To be legally enforceable, an insurance contract must meet four basic requirements: offer and acceptance, consideration, competent parties, and legal purpose.

## Offer and Acceptance

The first requirement of a binding insurance contract is that there must be **an offer and an acceptance** of its terms. In most cases, the applicant for insurance makes the offer, and the company accepts or rejects the offer. An agent merely solicits or invites the prospective insured to make an offer. The requirement of offer and acceptance can be examined in greater detail by making a careful distinction between property and liability insurance, and life insurance.

In property and liability insurance, the offer and acceptance can be oral or written. In the absence of specific legislation to the contrary, oral insurance contracts are valid. However, as a practical matter, most property and liability insurance contracts are in written form. The applicant for insurance fills out the application and pays the first premium (or promises to pay the first premium). This constitutes the offer. The agent then accepts the offer on behalf of the insurance company. In property and liability insurance, agents typically have the power to bind their companies through use of a binder. A **binder** *is a temporary contract for insurance and can be either written or oral.* The binder is used to bind the company immediately prior to receipt of the application and issuance of the policy. Thus, the insurance contract can be effective immediately, since the agent accepts the offer on behalf of the company. This is the usual procedure followed in personal lines of property and liability insurance, including homeowners policies and automobile insurance. However, in some cases, the agent is not authorized to bind the company, and the application must be sent to the company for approval. The company may accept the offer and issue the policy.

In life insurance, the procedures followed are different. A life insurance agent does not have the power to bind the insurer. Therefore, the application for life insurance is always in writing, and the applicant must be approved by the insurer before the life insurance is in force. The usual procedure is for the applicant to fill out the application and pay the first premium. A **conditional premium receipt** is then given to the applicant. The most common conditional receipt is the "insurability premium receipt." If the applicant is found insurable according to the insurer's normal underwriting standards, the life insurance becomes effective as of the date of the application or the date of the medical examination, whichever is later. For example, assume that Aaron applies for a $100,000 life insurance policy on Monday. He fills out the application, pays the first premium, and receives a conditional premium receipt from the agent. On Tuesday morning, he takes a physical examination, and on Tuesday afternoon, he is accidentally killed in a boating accident. The application and premium will still be forwarded to the insurer, as if he were still alive. If he is found insurable according to the insurer's underwriting rules, the life insurance is in force, and $100,000 will be paid to his beneficiary.

However, if the applicant for life insurance does not pay the first premium when the application is filled out, a different set of rules applies. Before the life insurance is in force, the policy must be issued and delivered to the applicant, the first premium must be paid, and the applicant must be in good health when the policy is delivered. Some insurers also require that there must be no interim medical treatment between submission of the application and delivery of the policy. These requirements are considered to be "conditions precedent"—in other words, they must be fulfilled before the life insurance is in force.[19]

## Consideration

The second requirement of a valid insurance contract is **consideration.** Consideration refers to the value that each party gives to the other. The insured's consideration is payment of the first premium (or a promise to pay the first premium) plus an agreement to abide by the conditions specified in the policy. The insurer's consideration is the promise to do certain things as specified in the contract. This can include paying for a loss from an insured peril, providing certain services, such as loss prevention and safety services, or defending the insured in a liability lawsuit.

## Competent Parties

The third requirement of a valid insurance contract is that each party must be **legally competent.** This means the parties must have legal capacity to enter into a binding contract. Most adults are legally competent to enter into insurance contracts, but there are some exceptions. Insane persons, intoxicated persons, and corporations that act outside the scope of their authority cannot enter into enforceable insurance contracts. Minors normally are not legally competent to enter into binding insurance contracts; but most states have enacted laws that permit minors, such as a teenager age 15, to enter into a valid life or health insurance contract.

## Legal Purpose

A final requirement is that the contract must be for a **legal purpose.** An insurance contract that encourages or promotes something illegal or immoral is contrary to the public interest and cannot be enforced. For example, a street pusher of heroin and other hard drugs cannot purchase a property insurance policy that would cover seizure of the drugs by the police. This type of contract obviously is not enforceable since it would promote illegal activities that are contrary to the public interest.

## DISTINCT LEGAL CHARACTERISTICS OF INSURANCE CONTRACTS

Insurance contracts have distinct legal characteristics that make them different from other legal contracts. Several distinctive legal characteristics have already been discussed. As we noted earlier, most property and liability insurance contracts are contracts of indemnity; all insurance contracts must be supported by an insurable interest; and insurance contracts are based on utmost good faith. Other distinct legal characteristics are as follows:

- Aleatory contract
- Unilateral contract
- Conditional contract
- Personal contract
- Contract of adhesion

## Aleatory Contract

An insurance contract is aleatory rather than commutative. An **aleatory contract** *is one in which the values exchanged may not be equal but depend on an uncertain event.* Depending on chance, one party may receive a value out of proportion to the value that is given. For example, assume that Lorri pays a premium of $500 for $100,000 of homeowners insurance on her home. If the home were totally destroyed by fire shortly thereafter, she would collect an amount that greatly exceeds the premium paid. On the other hand, a homeowner may faithfully pay premiums for many years and never have a loss.

In contrast, other commercial contracts are commutative. A **commutative contract** *is one in which the values exchanged by both parties are theoretically even.* For example, the purchaser of real estate normally pays a price that is viewed to be equal to the value of the property.

Although the essence of an aleatory contract is chance, or the occurrence of some fortuitous event, an insurance contract is not a gambling contract. Gambling creates a new speculative risk that did not exist before the transaction. Insurance, however, is a technique for handling an already existing pure risk. Thus, although both gambling and insurance are aleatory in nature, an insurance contract is not a gambling contract because no new risk is created.

## Unilateral Contract

An insurance contract is a unilateral contract. A **unilateral contract** *means that only one party makes a legally enforceable promise.* In this case, only the insurer makes a legally enforceable promise to pay a claim or provide other services to the insured. After the first premium is paid, and the insurance is in force, the insured cannot be legally forced to pay the premiums or to comply with the policy provisions. Although the insured must continue to pay the premiums to receive payment for a loss, he or she cannot be legally forced to do so. However, if the premiums are paid, the insurer must accept them and must continue to provide the protection promised under the contract.

In contrast, most commercial contracts are *bilateral* in nature. Each party makes a legally enforceable promise to the other party. If one party fails to perform, the other party can insist on performance or can sue for damages because of the breach of contract.

## Conditional Contract

An insurance contract is a **conditional contract.** This means the insurer's obligation to pay a claim depends on whether or not the insured or the beneficiary has complied with all policy conditions. *Conditions are provisions inserted in the policy that qualify or place limitations on the insurer's promise to perform.* The conditions section imposes certain duties on the insured if he or she wishes to collect for a loss. Although the insured is not compelled to abide by the policy conditions, he or she must do so in order to collect for a loss. The insurer is not obligated to pay a claim if the policy conditions are not met. For example, under a homeowners policy, the insured must give immediate notice of a loss. If the insured delays for an unreasonable period in reporting the loss, the company can refuse to pay the claim on the grounds that a policy condition has been violated.

## Personal Contract

In property insurance, insurance is a **personal contract,** *which means the contract is between the insured and the insurer.* Strictly speaking, a property insurance contract does not insure property, but insures the owner of property against loss. The owner of the insured property is indemnified if the property is damaged or destroyed. Since the contract is personal, the applicant for insurance must be acceptable to the insurer and must meet certain underwriting standards regarding character, morals, and credit. Since a property insurance contract is a personal contract, it normally cannot be assigned to another party without the insurer's consent. If property is sold to another person, the new owner may not be acceptable to the insurer. *Thus, the insurer's consent is normally required before a property insurance policy can be validly assigned to another party.* In contrast, a life insurance policy can be freely assigned to anyone without the insurer's consent because the assignment does not usually alter the risk and increase the probability of death.

The loss payment can, however, be freely assigned to another party without the property insurer's consent. Although the insurer's consent is not required, the contract may require that the insurer be notified of the assignment of the proceeds to another party.

## Contract of Adhesion

A **contract of adhesion** *means the insured must accept the entire contract, with all of its terms and conditions.* The insurer drafts and prints the policy, and the insured generally must accept the entire document and cannot insist that certain provisions be added or deleted or the contract rewritten to suit the insured. Although the contract can be altered by the addition of endorsements or forms, the endorsements and forms are drafted by the insurer. To redress the imbalance that exists in such a situation, *the courts have ruled that any ambiguities or uncertainties in the contract are construed against the insurer.* If the policy is ambiguous, the insured gets the benefit of the doubt.

The general rule that ambiguities in insurance contracts are construed against the insurer is reinforced by the principle of reasonable expectations. The **principle of reasonable expectations** *states that an insured is entitled to coverage under a policy that he or she reasonably expects it to provide, and that to be effective, exclusions or qualifications must be conspicuous, plain, and clear.*[20] Some courts have ruled that insureds are entitled to the protection that they reasonably expect to have, and that technical restrictions in the contract should not be a hidden pitfall. For example, in one case, a liability insurer refused to defend the insured on the grounds that an intentional act was excluded under the policy. However, the court ruled that the insurer was responsible for the defense costs, because the insured had a reasonable expectation that these costs were covered under the policy since the policy covered other types of intentional acts.[21]

## LAW AND THE INSURANCE AGENT

An insurance contract normally is sold by an agent who represents the principal. An agent is someone who has the authority to act on behalf of someone else. The principal (insurer) is the party for whom action is to be taken. Thus, if Sean has the authority to solicit, create, or terminate an insurance contract on behalf of Apex Fire Insurance, he would be the agent and Apex Fire Insurance would be the principal.

## General Rules of Agency

There are three important rules of law that govern the actions of agents and their relationship to insureds:[22]

- There is no presumption of an agency relationship.
- An agent must have authority to represent the principal.
- A principal is responsible for the acts of agents acting within the scope of employment.

**No Presumption of an Agency Relationship**
There is no presumption that one person legally can act as an agent for another. Some visible evidence of any agency relationship must exist. For example, a person who claims to be an agent for an automobile insurer may collect premiums and then abscond with the funds. The automobile insurer is not legally responsible for the person's actions if it has done nothing to create the impression that an agency relationship is in existence. However, if the person has a calling card, rate book, and application blanks, then it can be presumed that a legitimate agent is acting on behalf of that company.

**Authority to Represent the Principal**  An agent must be authorized to represent the principal. An agent's authority is derived from three sources: (1) express powers, (2) implied powers, and (3) apparent authority.

**Express powers** are powers specifically conferred on the agent. These powers are normally stated in the *agency agreement* between the agent and the principal. The agency agreement may also withhold certain powers. For example, a life insurance agent may be given the power to solicit applicants and arrange for physical examinations. Certain powers, such as the right to extend the time for payment of premiums, or the right to alter contractual provisions in the policy, may be denied.

Agents also have **implied powers.** Implied powers refer to the authority of the agent to perform all incidental acts necessary to fulfill the purposes of the agency agreement. For example, an agent may have the express authority to deliver a life insurance policy to the client. It follows that the agent also has the implied power to collect the first premium.

Finally, an agent may bind the principal by **apparent authority.** If an agent acts with apparent authority to do certain things, and a third party is led to believe that the agent is acting within the scope of reasonable and appropriate authority, the principal can be bound by the agent's actions. Third parties only have to show that they have exercised due diligence in determining the agent's authority based on the agent's actual authority or conduct of the principal. For example, an agent for an auto insurer may frequently grant his or her clients an extension of time to pay overdue premiums. If the insurer has not expressly granted this right to the agent and has not taken any action to deal with the violation of company policy, it could not later deny liability for a loss on the grounds that the agent lacked authority to grant the time extension. The insurer first would have to notify all policyowners of the limitations on the agent's powers.

**Principal Responsible for Acts of Agents**
A final rule of agency law is that the principal is responsible for all acts of agents when they are acting within the scope of their authority. This responsibility also includes fraudulent acts, omissions, and misrepresentations.

*In addition, knowledge of the agent is presumed to be knowledge of the principal with respect to matters within the scope of the agency relationship.* For example, if a life insurance agent knows that an applicant for life insurance is addicted to alcohol, this knowledge is imputed to the insurer even though the agent deliberately omits this information from the application. Thus, if the insurer issues the policy, it cannot later attack the validity of the policy on the grounds of alcohol addiction and the concealment of a material fact.

## Waiver and Estoppel

The doctrines of waiver and estoppel have direct relevance to the law of agency and to the powers of insurance agents. The practical significance of these concepts is that an insurer legally may be required to pay a claim that it ordinarily would not have to pay.

**Waiver** *is defined as the voluntary relinquishment of a known legal right.* If the insurer voluntarily waives a legal right under the contract, it cannot later deny payment of a claim by the insured on the grounds that such a legal right was violated. For example, assume that an insurer receives an application for insurance at its home office, and that the application contains an incomplete or missing answer. The insurer does not contact the applicant for additional information, and the policy is issued. The insurer later could not deny payment of a claim on the basis of an incomplete application. In effect, the insurer has waived its requirement that the application be complete.

The legal term estoppel was derived centuries ago from the English common law. **Estoppel** *occurs when a representation of fact made by one person to another person is reasonably relied on by that person to such an extent that it would be inequitable to allow the first person to deny the truth of the representation.*[23] Stated simply, if one person makes a statement to another person who then relies on the statement to his or her detriment, the first person cannot later deny the statement was made. The law of estoppel is designed to prevent persons from changing their minds to the detriment of another party. For example, assume that Richard's auto insurance premium is due. He calls his agent and asks for an extension of time. The agent states, "Don't worry. The company has a ten-day grace period for overdue premiums." If Richard has an accident during the so-called grace period, the insurer cannot deny liability for the loss on the grounds that the premium was not paid on time. In effect, the insurer would be estopped, or prevented, from denying payment of the claim. Richard has relied on the statement by his agent, and the insurer cannot later change its mind to Richard's detriment.

## SUMMARY

- The principle of indemnity means that the insured should not profit from a covered loss but should be restored to approximately the same financial position that existed prior to the occurrence of the loss.

- There are several exceptions to the principle of indemnity. These exceptions include a valued policy, valued policy laws, replacement cost insurance, and life insurance.

- The principle of insurable interest means that the insured must stand to lose financially if a loss occurs, or must incur some other kind of harm if the loss takes place. All insurance contracts must be supported by an insurable interest to be legally enforceable. There are three purposes of the insurable interest requirement:

  To prevent gambling

  To reduce moral hazard

  To measure the amount of loss

- In property insurance, the ownership of property, potential legal liability, secured creditors, and contractual rights can support the insurable interest requirement. In life insurance, the question of an insurable interest does not arise when a person purchases life insurance on his or her own life. However, if life insurance is purchased on the life of another person, there must be an insurable interest in that person's life. Close ties of love, affection, blood, and marriage, or a pecuniary interest will satisfy the insurable interest requirement in life insurance.

- In property insurance, the insurable interest requirement must be met at the time of loss. In life insurance, the insurable interest requirement must be met only at the inception of the policy.

- The principle of subrogation means that the insurer is entitled to recover from a negligent third party any loss payments made to the insured. The purposes of subrogation are to prevent the insured from collecting twice for the same loss, to hold the negligent person responsible for the loss, and to hold down insurance rates. If the insurer exercises its subrogation rights, the insured generally must be fully restored before the insurer can retain any sums collected from the negligent third party. Also, the insured cannot do anything that might impair the insurer's subrogation rights. However, the insurer can waive its subrogation rights in the contract either before or after the loss. Finally, subrogation does not apply to life insurance contracts and to most individual health insurance contracts.

- The principle of utmost good faith means that a higher degree of honesty is imposed on both parties to an insurance contract than is imposed on parties to other contracts.

- The legal doctrines of representations, concealment, and warranty support the principle of utmost good faith. Representations are statements made by the applicant for insurance. The insurer can deny payment for a claim if the representation is material, false, and is relied on by the insurer in issuing the policy at a specified premium. In the case of statements of belief or opinion, the misrepresentation must also be fraudulent before the insurer can deny a claim. Concealment of a material fact has the same legal effect as a misrepresentation: the contract is voidable at the insurer's option.

- A warranty is a clause in the insurance contract that prescribes, as a condition of the insurer's liability, the existence of a fact stated by the insured that affects the risk. Based on common law, any breach of the warranty, even if not material, allows the insurer to deny payment of a claim. The harsh, common law doctrine of a warranty, however, has been modified and softened by court decisions and statutes.

- In order to have a valid insurance contract, four requirements must be met:

  There must be an offer and acceptance.
  Consideration must be exchanged.
  The parties to the contract must be legally competent.
  The contract must be for a legal purpose.

- Insurance contracts have distinct legal characteristics. An insurance contract is an *aleatory contract* in which the values exchanged may not be equal and depend on the occurrence of an uncertain event. An insurance contract is *unilateral* because only the insurer makes a legally enforceable promise. An insurance contract is *conditional* because the insurer's obligation to pay a claim depends on whether or not the insured or beneficiary has complied with all policy provisions. A property insurance contract is considered to be a *personal contract* between the insured and insurer and cannot be validly assigned to another party without the insurer's consent. A life insurance policy is freely assignable without the insurer's consent. Finally, insurance is a *contract of adhesion,* which means the insured must accept the entire contract, with all of its terms and conditions; however, if there is an ambiguity in the contract, it will be construed against the insurer.

- There are three general rules of agency that govern the actions of agents and their relationship to insureds:

  There is no presumption of an agency relationship.
  An agent must have the authority to represent the principal.
  A principal is responsible for the actions of agents acting within the scope of employment.

- An agent can bind the principal based on express powers, implied powers, and apparent authority.

- Based on the legal doctrines of waiver and estoppel, an insurer legally may be required to pay a claim that it ordinarily would not have to pay.

## KEY CONCEPTS AND TERMS

Actual cash value
Aleatory contract
Apparent authority
Binder
Commutative
 contract
Competent parties
Concealment
Conditional contract
Conditional premium
 receipt
Consideration
Contract of adhesion
Estoppel
Express powers
Implied powers
Innocent
 misrepresentation
Insurable interest

Legal purpose
Material fact
Offer and acceptance
Personal contract
Principle of indemnity
Principle of reasonable
 expectations
Replacement cost
 insurance
Representations
Secured creditors
Subrogation
Unilateral contract
Utmost good faith
Valued policy
Valued policy laws
Waiver
Warranty

## QUESTIONS FOR REVIEW

1. Explain the principle of indemnity. How does the concept of actual cash value support the principle of indemnity?

2. Explain how a valued policy, valued policy laws, replacement cost insurance, and life insurance are exceptions to the principle of indemnity.

3. What is an insurable interest? Why is an insurable interest required in every insurance contract?

4. Explain the principle of subrogation. Why is subrogation used?

5. Explain the principle of utmost good faith. How do the legal doctrines of representations, concealment, and warranty support the principle of utmost good faith?

6. Explain the four requirements that must be met in order to have a valid insurance contract.

7. Insurance contracts have distinct legal characteristics that distinguish them from other contracts. Explain these characteristics.

8. Explain the three general rules of agency that govern the actions of agents and their relationship to insureds.

9. What are the various sources of authority that enable an agent to bind the principal?

10. Explain the meaning of waiver and estoppel.

## QUESTIONS FOR DISCUSSION

1. a. One important purpose of the principle of indemnity is to reduce moral hazard. Explain how the principle of indemnity tends to reduce moral hazard.

   b. What arguments can you present to show that replacement cost insurance does not violate the principle of indemnity?

   c. Why is a valued policy considered to be an exception to the principle of indemnity?

2. Jan borrowed $500,000 from the Gateway Bank to purchase a fishing boat. He keeps the boat at a dock owned by the Marina Company. He uses the boat to earn income by fishing. Jan also has a contract with the Blue Fin Fishing Company to transport shrimp from one port to another.

   a. Do any of the following parties have an insurable interest in Jan or his property? If an insurable interest exists, explain the extent of the interest.

      (1) Gateway Bank

      (2) Marina Company

      (3) Blue Fin Fishing Company

   b. If Jan did not own the boat but operated it on behalf of the Blue Fin Fishing Company, would he have an insurable interest in the boat? Explain.

3. A drunk driver ran a red light and smashed into Cleo's car. Damages were $5000. She has collision insurance on her car with a $250 deductible.

   a. Can Cleo collect from both the negligent driver's insurer and her own insurer? Explain your answer.

   b. Show how Cleo may be reimbursed for the $250 deductible if the loss is paid by her own insurer.

   c. Explain how subrogation supports the principle of indemnity.

4. a. Representations and warranties exist in many contracts, but they are particularly important in insurance contracts. Explain the difference between representations and warranties that are found in insurance contracts, and give an example of each.

   b. Insurance is a *conditional contract.* Explain the meaning of the term.

   c. Explain some additional characteristics of insurance contracts that distinguish them from other contracts.

5. One requirement for the formation of a valid insurance contract is that the contract must be for a legal purpose.

   a. Identify three factors, other than the legal purpose requirement, that are essential to the formation of a binding insurance contract.

   b. Show how each of the three requirements in part (a) is fulfilled when the applicant applies for an automobile liability insurance policy.

   c. In each of the following cases, indicate whether a person is legally competent to enter into a valid insurance contract.

      (1) A young man, age 15, who applies for insurance on his life

      (2) A married woman, age 21, who applies for an automobile policy and is the named insured

      (3) A young woman, age 21, who signs an application for life insurance when she is intoxicated

      (4) A young man, age 21, who has been convicted of drunk driving and has been canceled by an insurer

6. Nicole is applying for a health insurance policy. She has a chronic liver ailment and other health problems. She honestly disclosed the true facts concerning her medical history to the insurance agent. However, the agent did not include all the facts in the application. Instead, the agent stated that he was going to cover the material facts in a separate letter to the insurance company's underwriting department, but the agent did not furnish the material facts to the insurer, and the contract was issued as standard. A claim occurred shortly thereafter. After investigating the claim, the insurer denied payment. Nicole contends that the company should pay the claim since she honestly answered all questions that the agent asked.

   a. On what basis can the insurance company deny payment of the claim?

   b. What legal doctrines can Nicole use to support her argument that the claim should be paid?

## SELECTED REFERENCES

Anderson, Buist M. *Anderson on Life Insurance.* Boston: Little, Brown, 1991. See also *Anderson on Life Insurance, 1996 Supplement.*

Crawford, Muriel L., and William T. Beadles. *Law and the Life Insurance Contract.* 6th ed. Homewood, Ill.: Richard D. Irwin, 1989.

Dobbyn, John F. *Insurance Law in a Nutshell,* 2nd ed. St. Paul, Minn.: West Publishing Company, 1989.

*Fire Casualty & Surety Bulletins.* Fire and Marine Volume. Cincinnati: National Underwriter Company. These bulletins contain interesting cases concerning the meaning of actual cash value, insurable interest, and other legal concepts.

Keeton, Robert E., and Alan I. Widiss. *Insurance Law: A Guide to Fundamental Principles, Legal Doctrines, and Commercial Practices.* Student edition. St. Paul, Minn.: West Publishing Company, 1988.

Lorimer, James J. et al. *The Legal Environment of Insurance.* 4th ed., vols. 1 and 2. Malvern, Pa.: American Institute for Property and Liability Underwriters, 1993.

Patterson, Edwin W. *Essentials of Insurance Law.* 2nd ed. New York: McGraw-Hill, 1957.

Wiening, Eric A., and Donald S. Malecki. *Insurance Contract Analysis.* Malvern, Pa.: American Institute for Chartered Property Casualty Underwriters, 1992, Chapters 1 and 4.

## NOTES

1. *Jefferson Insurance Company of New York v. Superior Court of Alameda County,* 475 P. 2d 880 (1970).
2. Valued policy laws are in force in Arkansas, California (optional), Florida, Georgia, Kansas, Minnesota, Mississippi, Missouri, Montana, Nebraska, New Hampshire, North Dakota, Ohio, South Carolina, South Dakota, Tennessee, Texas, West Virginia, and Wisconsin.
3. *Gamel v. Continental Ins. Co.,* 463 S.W. 2nd 590 (1971). For additional information concerning valued policy laws, the interested student should consult the *Fire Casualty & Surety Bulletins,* Fire and Marine Volume (Cincinnati: National Underwriter Company). The bulletin service is regularly updated and can be found in many libraries.
4. Edwin W. Patterson, *Essentials of Insurance Law,* 2nd ed. (New York: McGraw-Hill, 1957), pp. 109–11, 154–59.
5. Patterson, p. 114.
6. Buist M. Anderson, *Anderson on Life Insurance* (Boston: Little, Brown, 1991), p. 361.
7. Texas is an exception. An individual who takes out a life insurance policy on the life of another person must have an insurable interest in the insured at the maturity of the contract.
8. Patterson, pp. 147–48.
9. James J. Lorimer et al., *The Legal Environment of Insurance,* 3rd ed., vol. 1 (Malvern, Pa.: American Institute for Property and Liability Underwriters, 1987), p. 376.
10. Lorimer et al., p. 377.
11. Patterson, p. 149.
12. C. Arthur Williams, Jr., George L. Head, Ronald C. Horn, and G. William Glendenning, *Principles of Risk Management and Insurance,* 2nd ed., vol. 2 (Malvern, Pa.: American Institute for Property and Liability Underwriters, 1981), p. 228.
13. Group health insurance contracts may contain subrogation clauses.

## CASE APPLICATION

Carmine purchased an automobile service station from Ben. The purchase price included the building, equipment, and other assets. The business was financed by a loan from National Bank, which held a mortgage on the building. Carmine also converted a one-car repair bay into a short-order restaurant. When Carmine applied for property insurance on the business, he did not tell the insurance company about the restaurant because his premiums would have been substantially increased. Six months after the business opened, a car caught fire and damaged the roof over a bay in the service station area.

a. Do any of the following parties have an insurable interest in the business at the time of the fire?
   1. Ben
   2. Carmine
   3. National Bank
b. Ben told Carmine he could save money by taking over Ben's insurance instead of buying a new policy. Would it be appropriate for Carmine to take over Ben's insurance without notifying Ben's insurer? Explain.
c. Investigation of the fire revealed that the car owner knew the gas tank had a leak, but this information was not disclosed to Carmine when the car was brought in for service. Explain how subrogation might apply in this case.
d. Did Carmine show utmost good faith when he applied for property insurance on the business? Explain.
e. Could Carmine's insurer deny coverage for the fire on the basis of a material concealment? Explain.

14. John F. Dobbyn, *Insurance Law,* 2nd ed. (St. Paul, Minn: West Publishing Company, 1989), p. 157.

15. Lorimer et al., p.166.

16. Lorimer et al., pp. 154–55.

17. Lorimer et al., p. 157.

18. Joseph L. Frascona, *Business Law, The Legal Environment, Text and Cases,* 3rd ed. (Dubuque, Iowa: William C. Brown, 1987), p. 1006.

19. Edward E. Graves, ed., *McGill's Life Insurance* (Bryn Mawr, Pa.: The American College, 1994), p. 789.

20. Lorimer et al., pp. 402–3.

21. Lorimer et al., p. 403.

22. Graves, pp. 805–8.

23. Patterson, pp. 495–96.

# Chapter 5

# ANALYSIS OF INSURANCE CONTRACTS

> *"The insurance contract is one of the most important inventions of the human mind in modern times."*
>
> *Edwin W. Patterson,*
> Essentials of Insurance Law, *2nd ed.*

## Student Learning Objectives

After studying this chapter, you should be able to:

■ Explain the basic parts of any insurance contract.

■ Define the insured and show how more than one person can be insured under the same policy.

■ Understand the meaning of endorsements or riders and show how they modify the basic policy.

■ Describe the various types of deductibles and why they are used.

■ Explain the meaning of coinsurance in property insurance and show how coinsurance achieves the fundamental purpose of equity in rating.

■ Explain the meaning of coinsurance (percentage participation clause) in a major medical policy.

■ Show how losses are paid when more than one insurance contract covers the same loss.

The previous chapter discussed important legal principles that are reflected in insurance contracts. In this chapter, we continue our discussion of insurance contracts by examining some important contractual provisions. Although insurance contracts are not identical, they contain some common contractual provisions. Topics discussed in this chapter include the basic parts of an insurance contract, definition of an insured, deductibles, coinsurance, and other-insurance provisions. Understanding these topics will provide a foundation for understanding specific insurance contracts discussed later in the text.

## BASIC PARTS OF AN INSURANCE CONTRACT

Insurance contracts are complex legal documents. Despite their complexities, insurance contracts generally can be divided into six parts.

- Declarations
- Definitions
- Insuring agreement
- Exclusions
- Conditions
- Miscellaneous provisions

Although all insurance contracts do not necessarily contain all six parts in the order given, such a classification provides a simple and convenient framework for analyzing most insurance contracts.

### Declarations

The declarations section is the first part of an insurance contract. **Declarations** *are statements that provide information about the property or activity to be insured.* Information contained in the declarations section is used for underwriting and rating purposes and for identification of the property or activity to be insured. The declarations section usually can be found on the first page of the policy or on a policy insert.

In property insurance, the declarations page contains information concerning the identification of the insurer, name of the insured, location of the property, period of protection, amount of insurance, amount of the premium, size of the deductible (if any), and other relevant information. In life insurance, although the first page of the policy technically is not a declarations page, it contains the insured's name, age, premium amount, issue date, and policy number.

### Definitions

Insurance contracts typically contain a page or section of definitions. Key words or phrases have quotation marks ("...") around them or are in **boldface** type. For example, the insurer is frequently referred to as "we," "our," or "us." The insured is referred to as "you" and "your." The purpose of the various definitions is to define clearly the meaning of key words

or phrases so that coverage under the policy can be determined more easily.

### Insuring Agreement

The insuring agreement is the heart of an insurance contract. The **insuring agreement** *summarizes the major promises of the insurer.* The insurer, in other words, agrees to do certain things, such as paying losses from insured perils, providing certain services (such as loss-prevention services), or agreeing to defend the insured in a liability lawsuit. The promises of the insurer and the conditions under which losses are to be paid are described in the insuring agreement.

There are two basic forms of an insuring agreement in property and liability insurance: (1) named-perils coverage and (2) "all-risks" coverage. *Under a* **named-perils policy,** *only those perils specifically named in the policy are covered.* If the peril is not named, it is not covered. For example, in the homeowners policy, personal property is covered for fire, lightning, windstorm, and certain other named perils. Only losses caused by these perils are covered. Flood damage is not covered, since flood is not a listed peril.

Under an **"all-risks" policy** *(also called an open perils policy), all losses are covered except those losses specifically excluded.* If the loss is not excluded, then it is covered. For example, the physical damage section of the personal auto policy covers physical damage losses to a covered auto. Thus, if a smoker burns a hole in the upholstery, or a bear in a national park tears up the convertible roof of a covered auto, the losses would be covered because they are not excluded.

"All-risks" coverage is generally preferable to a named-perils contract, since the protection is broader with fewer gaps in coverage. If the loss is not excluded, then it is covered. In addition, a greater burden of proof is placed on the insurer to deny a claim. To deny payment, the insurer must prove that the loss is excluded. In contrast, under a named-perils contract, the burden of proof is on the insured to show that the loss is caused by a named peril.

Many insurers and rating organizations have deleted the word *all* in their "all-risks" policy forms or are using special terminology. In the homeowners policy drafted by the Insurance Services Office, the phrase *risk of direct loss to property* is now used instead of the term *"all-risks."* However, this term is interpreted to mean that all losses are covered except those losses specifically excluded. Likewise, the Insurance Services Office has drafted a *special-causes-of-loss form* that is used in commercial property insurance. Once again, this terminology is interpreted to mean that all losses are covered except those losses excluded. The deletion of any reference to an "all-risks" policy is intended to avoid creating unreasonable expectations among policyowners that the policy covers all losses, even those losses that are specifically excluded.

Life insurance is another example of an "all-risks" policy. Most life insurance contracts cover all causes of death whether by accident or by disease. The major exclusions are suicide during the first two years of the contract; certain aviation hazard exclusions, such as military flying, crop dusting, or sports piloting; and in some contracts, death caused by war.

## Exclusions

Exclusions are the fourth basic part of any insurance contract. There are three major types of exclusions: excluded perils; excluded losses; and excluded property.

**Excluded Perils**    The contract may exclude certain perils, or causes of loss. Under a homeowners policy, the perils of flood, earth movement, and nuclear radiation or radioactive contamination are specifically excluded. In the physical damage section of the personal auto policy, collision is specifically excluded if the car is used as a public taxicab. In disability income policies, the peril of war may be excluded.

**Excluded Losses**    Certain types of losses may be excluded. For example, in a homeowners policy, earthquake losses are not covered without a special endorsement. In the personal liability section of a homeowners policy, a liability lawsuit arising out of the negligent operation of an automobile is excluded. Professional liability losses are also excluded; a specific professional liability policy is needed to cover this exposure.

**Excluded Property**    The contract may exclude or place limitations on the coverage of certain property. For example, in a homeowners policy, cer-tain types of personal property are excluded, such as cars, planes, animals, birds, and fish. In a liability insurance policy, property of others in the care, control, and custody of the insured is usually excluded.

**Reasons for Exclusions**    Exclusions are necessary for the following reasons:[1]

- Uninsurable perils
- Presence of extraordinary hazards
- Coverage provided by other contracts
- Moral hazard
- Coverage not needed by typical insureds

*Exclusions are necessary because the peril may be considered uninsurable by commercial insurers.* A given peril may depart substantially from the requirements of an insurable risk, as discussed in Chapter 2. There may be an incalculable catastrophic loss; a loss may be within the direct control of the insured; or a loss may be due to a predictable decline in value; thus these losses are not insurable. Most property and liability insurance contracts exclude losses for potential catastrophic events such as war or exposure to nuclear radiation. A health insurance contract may exclude losses within the direct control of the insured, such as an intentional, self-inflicted injury. Finally, predictable declines in the value of property, such as depreciation, wear and tear, and inherent vice, are not insurable. Inherent vice refers to the destruction or damage of property without any tangible external force, such as the tendency of fruit to rot and the tendency of diamonds to crack.

*Exclusions are also used because extraordinary hazards are present.* A hazard is a condition that increases the chance of loss. Because of an extraordinary increase in hazard, a loss may be excluded. Insurance is based on the pooling of losses. Exposure units with roughly the same loss-producing characteristics are grouped, and losses are pooled or spread over the entire group. In the process, aggregate losses are more easily predictable. The pooling technique is based on the assumption that each exposure unit is charged a premium that accurately reflects the long-run chance of loss. Thus, if an exposure unit faces an extraordinary hazard that is peculiar to it and is not shared by the other exposure units, the premium charged to the exposure unit is too low. This results in an inadequate premium for the insurer and an inequity for the other exposure units, since they are subsidizing the exposure unit faced with the extraordinary increase in hazard.

For example, the premium for liability insurance under a personal auto policy is based on the assumption that the car is normally used for personal and recreational use and not as a taxicab. The chance of an accident, and a resulting liability lawsuit, is much higher if the car is used as a taxicab. Therefore, to provide coverage for a taxicab at the same premium rate for a family car could result in inadequate premiums for the insurer and unfair rate discrimination against other insureds who are not using their vehicles as taxicabs. To avoid this problem, taxicabs are in a separate rating category, and losses due to the operation of the vehicle as a taxicab are specifically excluded under the personal auto policy.

*Exclusions are also necessary because coverage is provided by other contracts.* Exclusions are used to avoid duplication of coverage and to confine the coverage to the policy best designed to provide it. For example, a car is excluded under a homeowners policy because it is covered under the personal auto policy and other auto insurance contracts. If both policies covered the loss, there would be unnecessary duplication.

In addition, certain property is excluded because of moral hazard or difficulty in determining and measuring the amount of loss. For example, homeowner contracts typically limit the coverage of money to $200. If unlimited amounts of money were covered, fraudulent claims could increase. Also, loss-adjustment problems in determining the exact amount of the loss could increase. Thus, because of moral hazard, exclusions are used.

*Finally, exclusions are used because the coverage is not needed by the typical insured.* Since a particular peril may not be common to a large group of persons, the insureds should not be required to pay for coverage they will not use or need. For example, most homeowners do not own private planes. To cover aircraft as personal property under the homeowners policy would be grossly unfair to the majority of insureds who do not own planes because premiums would be substantially higher.

## Conditions

The conditions section is another important part of an insurance contract. **Conditions** *are provisions in*

*the policy that qualify or place limitations on the insurer's promise to perform.* In effect, the conditions section imposes certain duties on the insured if he or she wishes to collect for a loss. If the policy conditions are not met, the insurer can refuse to pay the claim. Common policy conditions include notifying the insurer if a loss occurs, protecting the property after a loss, filing a proof of loss with the insurer, and cooperating with the insurer in the event of a liability suit. Therefore, if your house is on fire, you cannot simply call your agent and tell him or her to fix the house and then call you in Bermuda when the house is repaired. You must actively cooperate with the insurer in determining the amount of loss.

## Miscellaneous Provisions

Insurance contracts also contain certain miscellaneous provisions that are common to all insurance contracts. These provisions deal with the relationship between the insured and insurer, and the relationship and responsibility of the insurer toward third parties. These common provisions also establish working procedures for carrying out the terms of the contract. In property and liability insurance, some common provisions refer to cancellation, subrogation, requirements if a loss occurs, assignment of the policy, and other-insurance provisions. In life and health insurance, some common provisions refer to the grace period, the reinstatement of a lapsed policy, and the misstatement of age. Details of these common provisions are discussed later in the text when specific insurance contracts are analyzed.

## DEFINITION OF THE INSURED

Insurance contracts typically contain a definition of the insured under the policy. The contract must indicate the person or persons for whom the protection is provided. Several possibilities exist concerning the persons who are insured under the policy. First, the policy may insure only *one person.* For example, in many life and health insurance contracts, only one person is specifically named as insured under the policy.

Second, the policy may contain a formal definition of the named insured. The **named insured** *is the person or persons named in the declarations section of the policy, as opposed to someone who may have an* *interest in the policy but is not named as an insured.* For example, the named insured under the personal auto policy includes the person named in the declarations page and his or her spouse if a resident of the same household. Thus, Jennifer may be the named insured under the personal auto policy. Her husband is also included in the definition of the named insured as long as he resides in the same household.

The policy may also cover additional insureds even though they are not specifically named in the policy. For example, in addition to the named insured, a homeowners policy covers resident relatives of the named insured or spouse and any person under age 21 who is in the care of an insured, such as a child in a foster home. The homeowners policy also covers resident relatives who are attending college and are away from home. The personal auto policy covers the named insured and spouse, resident relatives, and any other person using the automobile with the permission of the named insured (see Insight 5.1). In short, a contract may provide broad coverage with respect to the number of persons who are insured under the policy.

## ENDORSEMENTS AND RIDERS

Insurance contracts frequently contain **endorsements** and **riders.** The terms endorsements and riders are often used interchangeably and mean the same thing. *In property and liability insurance, an endorsement is a written provision that adds to, deletes from, or modifies the provisions in the original contract. In life and health insurance, a rider is a document that amends or changes the original policy.*

There are numerous endorsements in property and liability insurance that modify, extend, or delete provisions found in the original policy. For example, a homeowners policy excludes coverage for earthquakes. However, an earthquake endorsement can be added that covers damage from an earthquake or from earth movement.

In life and health insurance, numerous riders can be added that increase or decrease benefits, waive a condition of coverage present in the original policy, or amend the basic policy. For example, a waiver-of-premium provision can be added to a life insurance policy. If the insured should become disabled, all fu-ture premiums are waived after an elimination period of six months, for as long as the insured remains disabled according to the terms of the rider.

An endorsement attached to a contract normally has precedence over any conflicting terms in the contract, unless a law or regulation requires that a standard policy be used or that a policy contain certain provisions. An endorsement cannot be used to circumvent the purpose of legislation by modifying the terms of a standard policy or by changing the wording of a required provision. If an endorsement is contrary to a law or regulation, the policy is read and applied as if that endorsement did not exist.[2]

## DEDUCTIBLES

A deductible is another common policy provision. A **deductible** *is a provision by which a specified amount is subtracted from the total loss payment that otherwise would be payable.* Deductibles typically are found in property, health, and auto insurance contracts. A deductible is not used in life insurance because the insured's death is always a total loss, and a deductible would only reduce the face amount of insurance. Also, a deductible generally is not used in personal liability insurance because the insurer must provide a legal defense, even for a small claim. The insurer wants to be involved from the first dollar of loss in order to minimize its ultimate liability for a claim. Also, the premium reduction that would result from a small deductible in personal types of third-party liability coverages would be relatively small.[3]

### Purposes of Deductibles

Deductibles have several important purposes. They include the following:

- To eliminate small claims
- To reduce premiums
- To reduce moral and morale hazard

*A deductible eliminates small claims that are expensive to handle and process.* For example, an insurer can easily incur expenses of $100 or more in processing a $50 claim. Since a deductible eliminates small claims, the insurer's loss-adjustment expenses are reduced.

## INSIGHT 5.1

### Are You Insured When You Drive Another Person's Car?

College students frequently drive cars owned by friends or roommates. Are you insured when you drive another person's car? To answer that question, we must examine the definition of an insured that appears in the personal auto policy, which reads as follows:

"Insured" as used in this Part means:

1. You or any "family member" for the ownership, maintenance or use of any auto or "trailer."

2. Any person using "your covered auto."

3. For "your covered auto," any person or organization but only with respect to legal responsibility for acts or omissions of a person for whom coverage is afforded under this Part.

4. For any auto or "trailer," other than "your covered auto," any other person or organization but only with respect to legal responsibility for acts or omissions of you or any "family member" for whom coverage is afforded under this Part. This provision applies only if the person or organization does not own or hire the auto or "trailer."

Mike is the named insured under the personal auto policy that contains the above provision. His daughter, Patti, lives in a dormitory during the school year while she attends college away from home. Although she does not presently live at home, she generally would qualify as a family member since her college stay is temporary, and she regards her parents' home as her permanent residence address.

Patti drives a Ford titled in Mike's name. Since she is a family member, she is an insured while driving the Ford because of the policy definition of an "insured." What happens if Patti allows her boyfriend to drive the Ford? Although the boyfriend is not a family member, he nevertheless qualifies as "any person using your covered auto." The boyfriend is an insured.

What if Patti occasionally drives her roommate's car? Assuming she is a family member under her father's policy, Patti is insured while driving any car, including her roommate's.

Suppose Patti is involved in an auto accident while using her car on a field trip sponsored by the college as part of her college studies. The injured party sues both Patti and the college. Patti clearly is an insured and is covered. Is the college also an "insured" under Patti's policy? Yes. The definition of an insured extends coverage to any person or organization who is legally responsible for any acts or omissions by an insured. Thus, the college is considered an insured. Patti's insurer is obligated to defend the college in the suit.

SOURCE: Adapted from Eric A. Wiening and Donald S. Malecki, *Insurance Contract Analysis* (Malvern, Pa.: American Institute for Chartered Property Casualty Underwriters, 1992), pp. 175–76.

*Deductibles are also used to reduce premiums.* Since small losses are eliminated, more of the premium dollar can be used for the larger claims that can cause serious financial insecurity if a loss should occur. Insurance is not an appropriate technique for paying small losses that can be better budgeted out of personal or business income. Insurance should be used to cover large catastrophic events, such as medical expenses of $250,000 from a terminal illness. Insurance that protects against a catastrophic loss can be purchased more economically if deductibles are used. This concept of using insurance premiums to pay for large losses rather than for small losses is often called the **large-loss principle.** The objective is to cover large losses that can financially ruin an individual and exclude small losses that can be budgeted out of the person's income.

Other factors being equal, a large deductible is preferable to a small one. For example, many motorists with auto insurance have policies that contain a $200 deductible for collision losses instead of a $500 or larger deductible. They may not be aware of how expensive the extra insurance really costs. For example, let us assume that you can purchase auto insurance on your car with a $200 collision deductible at an annual premium of $600, while a policy with a $500 deductible can be purchased for an annual premium of $525. If you select the $200 deductible over the $500 deductible, you will obtain an additional $300 of collision insurance, but you must also pay an additional $75 in annual premiums. Using a simple benefit-cost analysis, you are paying an additional $75 for an additional $300 of insurance, which is a relatively expensive increment of insurance. When analyzed in this manner, larger deductibles are preferable to smaller ones.

*Finally, deductibles are used to reduce both moral and morale hazard.* Some dishonest insureds may deliberately cause a loss in order to profit from insurance. Deductibles reduce moral hazard since the insured may not profit if a loss occurs.

Deductibles are also used to reduce morale hazard. Morale hazard is carelessness because insurance is in force, which increases the chance of loss. Deductibles encourage persons to be more careful with respect to the protection of their property and prevention of a loss. Loss prevention is thereby encouraged since the insured must pay part of any loss.

## Deductibles in Property Insurance

The following deductibles are commonly found in property insurance contracts:

- Straight deductible
- Aggregate deductible
- Franchise deductible

**Straight Deductible**  With a **straight deductible,** *the insured must pay a certain number of dollars of loss before the insurer is required to make a payment.* Such a deductible typically applies to each loss. An example can be found in automobile collision insurance. For instance, assume that Tanya has collision insurance on her 1997 Toyota, with a $500 deductible. If a collision loss is $7000, she would receive only $6500.

**Aggregate Deductible**  An **aggregate deductible** *is often used in commercial property insurance, by which all covered losses during the year are added together until they reach a certain level.* If total covered losses are below the aggregate deductible, the insurer pays nothing. Once the deductible is satisfied, all losses thereafter are paid in full. For example, assume that a property insurance contract contains a $1000 aggregate deductible for the calendar year. If a loss of $500 occurs in January, the insurer pays nothing. If a $2000 loss occurs in February, the insurer would pay only $1500. At this point, the aggregate deductible of $1000 has now been satisfied for the year. If a $5000 loss occurs in March, it is paid

in full. Any other covered losses occurring during the year would also be paid in full.

**Franchise Deductible**  A franchise deductible is used in ocean marine insurance and can be expressed either as a percentage or dollar amount. With a **franchise deductible,** *the insurer has no liability if the loss is under a certain amount, but once this amount is exceeded, the entire loss is paid in full.* For example, assume that an exporter is shipping goods valued at $100,000 to England, and a 3 percent franchise deductible is present in the contract. Any loss under $3000 is paid by the insured. However, if the actual loss is $3000 or higher, the entire amount is paid in full by the insurer. In effect, this type of deductible acts as a disappearing deductible, since small losses are not paid, but a large loss exceeding the deductible amount is paid in full. A franchise deductible is used in ocean marine insurance because shippers expect minor losses from bad weather, rolling ships, and the frequent handling of cargo.

## Deductibles in Health Insurance

In health insurance, the deductible can be stated in terms of dollars or time. Some commonly used deductibles in health insurance are the following:

- Calendar-year deductible
- Corridor deductible
- Elimination (waiting) period

**Calendar-year Deductible**  A **calendar-year deductible** is a type of aggregate deductible that is commonly found in basic medical expense and major medical insurance contracts. Eligible medical expenses are accumulated during the calendar year, and once they exceed the deductible amount, the insurer must then pay the benefits promised under the contract. Once the deductible is satisfied during the calendar year, no additional deductibles are imposed on the insured.

**Corridor Deductible**  Employers with basic medical expense plans often wish to supplement the basic benefits with major medical benefits. A **corridor deductible** is a deductible that can be used to integrate a basic medical expense plan with a supplemental major medical expense plan. The corridor deductible must be satisfied before the major medical plan pays any benefits.

*The corridor deductible applies only to eligible medical expenses that are not covered by the basic medical expense plan.* For example, assume that Janet has $10,000 of covered medical expenses, of which $8000 are paid by the basic medical expense plan. If the supplemental major medical plan has a $200 corridor deductible, the supplemental plan will cover the remaining $1800 of expenses, subject to any limitations or coinsurance provisions that may apply.

**Elimination (Waiting) Period**    A deductible can also be expressed as an elimination period. An **elimination period** *is a stated period of time at the beginning of a loss during which no insurance benefits are paid.* An elimination period is appropriate for a single loss that occurs over some time period, such as the loss of work earnings. Elimination periods are commonly used in disability-income contracts. For example, disability-income contracts that replace part of a disabled worker's earnings typically have elimination periods of 30, 60, or 90 days, or even longer.

## COINSURANCE

Coinsurance is a contractual provision that is commonly found in property insurance contracts. This is especially true of commercial property insurance contracts.

### Nature of Coinsurance

A **coinsurance clause** *in a property insurance contract requires the insured to insure the property for a stated percentage of its insurable value. If the coinsurance requirement is not met at the time of loss, the insured must share in the loss as a coinsurer.* The insurable value of the property is the actual cash value, replacement cost, or some other value described in the valuation clause of the policy.[4] If the insured wants to collect in full for a partial loss, the coinsurance requirement must be satisfied. Otherwise, the insured will be penalized if a partial loss occurs.

A coinsurance formula is used to determine the amount paid for a covered loss. The coinsurance formula is as follows:

$$\frac{\text{Amount of insurance carried}}{\text{Amount of insurance required}} \times \text{Loss} = \text{Amount of recovery}$$

For example, assume that a commercial building has an actual cash value of $500,000, and that the owner has insured it for only $300,000. If an 80 percent coinsurance clause is present in the policy, the required amount of insurance based on actual cash value is $400,000. (If a replacement cost policy is used, the required amount of insurance would be based on replacement cost.) Thus, if a $10,000 loss occurs, only $7500 will be paid. This can be illustrated as follows:

$$\frac{\$300,000}{\$400,000} \times \$10,000 = \$7500$$

Since the insured has only three-fourths of the required amount of insurance at the time of loss, only three-fourths of the loss, or $7500, will be paid. Since the coinsurance requirement is not met, the insured must absorb the remaining amount of the loss.

Finally, in applying the coinsurance formula, two additional points should be kept in mind. First, the amount paid can never exceed the amount of the actual loss even though the coinsurance formula produces such a result. This could happen if the amount of insurance carried is greater than the required amount of insurance. Second, the maximum amount paid for any loss is limited to the face amount of insurance.

### Purpose of Coinsurance

*The fundamental purpose of coinsurance is to achieve* **equity in rating.** Most property insurance losses are partial and not total losses. But if everyone insures only for the partial loss rather than for the total loss, the premium rate for each $100 of insurance would be higher. This would be inequitable to insureds who wish to insure their property to full value. For example, if everyone insures to full value, the pure premium rate for fire insurance is 6 cents for each $100 of insurance, ignoring expenses and the profit allowance of the insurer (see Exhibit 5.1).

However, if each property owner insures only for a partial loss, the pure premium rate will increase from 6 cents per $100 of fire insurance to 10 cents per $100 (see Exhibit 5.2). This would be inequitable to property owners who want to insure their buildings to full value. If full coverage is desired, the insured would have to pay a higher rate of 10 cents, which we calculated earlier to be worth only 6 cents. This would be inequitable. *So, if the coinsurance requirement*

---

## EXHIBIT 5.1
### Insurance to Full Value

Assume that 10,000 buildings are valued at $75,000 each and are insured to full value for a total of $750 million of fire insurance. The following fire losses occur:

| | |
|---|---|
| 2 total losses | $150,000 |
| 30 partial losses at $10,000 each | 300,000 |
| Total fire losses paid by insurer | = $450,000 |

$$\text{Pure premium rate} = \frac{\$450,000}{\$750,000,000}$$

$$= 6 \text{ cents per } \$100 \text{ of insurance}$$

---

## EXHIBIT 5.2
### Insurance to Half Value

Assume that 10,000 buildings are valued at $75,000 each and are insured to half value for a total of $375 million of fire insurance. The following fire losses occur:

| | | |
|---|---|---|
| 2 total losses ($150,000) | Insurer pays only | $75,000 |
| 30 partial losses at $10,000 each | | 300,000 |
| Total fire losses paid by insurer | = | $375,000 |

$$\text{Pure premium rate} = \frac{\$375,000}{\$375,000,000}$$

$$= 10 \text{ cents per } \$100 \text{ of insurance}$$

---

*is met, the insured receives a rate discount, and the policy-owner who is underinsured is penalized through application of the coinsurance formula.*

As an alternative to coinsurance, *graded rates* could be used, by which rate discounts would be given as the amount of insurance to value is increased. However, this would require an accurate appraisal of each property to determine the required amount of insurance, which would be extremely expensive for the insurer. In addition, the appraisal method is unsatisfactory if property values fluctuate widely during the policy period. For these reasons, the coinsurance formula, rather than a table of graded rates, is used to achieve equity in rating.

### Coinsurance Problems

Some practical problems arise when a coinsurance clause is present in a contract. First, inflation can result in a serious coinsurance penalty if the amount of insurance is not periodically increased for inflation. The insured may be in compliance with the coinsurance clause when the policy first goes into effect; however, rapid price inflation can cause the replacement cost of the property to increase sharply. The result is that the insured may not be carrying the required amount of insurance at the time of loss, and he or she will then be penalized if a loss occurs. Thus, if a coinsurance clause is present, the amount of insurance carried should be periodically evaluated to determine if the coinsurance requirement is being met.

Second, the insured may incur a coinsurance penalty if property values fluctuate widely during the policy period. For example, there may be a substantial increase in inventory values because of an unexpected arrival of a shipment of goods. If a loss occurs, the insured may not be carrying sufficient insurance to avoid a coinsurance penalty. One solution to this problem is an *agreed amount endorsement,* by which the insurer agrees in advance that the amount of insurance carried meets the coinsurance requirement. Another solution is a *reporting form,* by which property values are periodically reported to the insurer.

Third, if a small loss occurs, the insured may incur a financial hardship if he or she is required to take a physical inventory of the undamaged and damaged goods for purposes of determining if the coinsurance requirement has been met. Under a *waiver of inventory clause,* the insured is relieved of the obligation of taking a physical inventory of the undamaged goods if the loss is less than 2 percent of the amount of insurance.

## COINSURANCE IN HEALTH INSURANCE

Health insurance contracts frequently contain a coinsurance clause, which is technically called a **percentage participation clause.** In particular, major medical policies typically have a coinsurance provision that requires the insured to pay a certain percentage of covered medical expenses in excess of the deductible. A typical plan requires the insured to pay 20 or 25 percent of covered expenses in excess of the deductible. For example, assume that Megan has covered medical expenses in the amount of $50,500, and that she has a major medical policy with a $500 deductible and an 80–20 coinsurance clause. The insurer pays 80 percent of the bill in excess of the deductible, or $40,000, and Megan pays 20 percent, or $10,000 (plus the deductible).

The purposes of coinsurance in health insurance are (1) to reduce premiums and (2) to prevent overutilization of policy benefits. Because the insured pays part of the cost, premiums are reduced. In addition, it is argued that physicians and other health-care providers will be more restrained in setting their fees if the patient pays part of the cost, and the patient will not demand the most expensive medical services if he or she pays part of the cost.

## OTHER-INSURANCE PROVISIONS

**Other-insurance provisions** typically are present in property and liability insurance and health insurance contracts. These provisions apply when more than one contract covers the same loss. *The purpose of these provisions is to prevent profiting from insurance and violation of the principle of indemnity.* If the insured could collect the full amount of the loss from each insurer, there would be profiting from insurance and a substantial increase in moral hazard. Some dishonest insureds would deliberately cause a loss in order to collect multiple benefits.

Some important other-insurance provisions in property and liability insurance include (1) the pro rata liability clause, (2) contribution by equal shares, and (3) primary and excess insurance.

### Pro Rata Liability Clause

The **pro rata liability clause** is a generic term for a provision that applies when two or more policies of the same type cover the same insurable interest in the property. *Each insurer's share of the loss is based on the proportion that its insurance bears to the total amount of insurance on the property.* For example, assume that Luis owns a building and wishes to insure it for $200,000. For underwriting reasons, insurers may limit the amount of insurance they will write on a given property. Assume that an agent places $100,000 of insurance with Company A, $50,000 with Company B, and $50,000 with Company C, for a total of $200,000. If a $10,000 loss occurs, each company will pay only its pro rata share of the loss (see Exhibit 5.3). Thus, Luis would collect $10,000 for the loss and not $30,000.

*The basic purpose of the pro rata liability clause is to preserve the principle of indemnity and to prevent*

---

**EXHIBIT 5.3**
**Pro Rata Liability Clause**

| | | | |
|---|---|---|---|
| **Company A** | $\dfrac{\$100,000}{\$200,000}$ | or  $1/2 \times \$10,000$ | = \$ 5,000 |
| **Company B** | $\dfrac{\$50,000}{\$200,000}$ | or  $1/4 \times \$10,000$ | = \$ 2,500 |
| **Company C** | $\dfrac{\$50,000}{\$200,000}$ | or  $1/4 \times \$10,000$ | = \$ 2,500 |

---

*profiting from insurance.* In the preceding example, if the pro rata liability clause were not present, the insured would collect $10,000 from each insurer, or a total of $30,000 for a $10,000 loss.

### Contribution by Equal Shares

**Contribution by equal shares** is another type of other-insurance provision that is frequently found in liability insurance contracts. Each insurer shares equally in the loss until the share paid by each insurer equals the lowest limit of liability under any policy, or until the full amount of the loss is paid. For example, assume that the amount of insurance provided by Companies A, B, and C is $100,000, $200,000, and $300,000 respectively. If the loss is $150,000 each insurer pays an equal share, or $50,000 (see Exhibit 5.4).

However, if the loss were $500,000, how much would each insurer pay? In this case, each insurer would pay equal amounts until its policy limits are exhausted. The remaining insurers then continue to share equally in the remaining amount of the loss until each insurer has paid its policy limit in full, or until the full amount of the loss is paid. Thus, Company A would pay $100,000, Company B would pay $200,000, and Company C would pay $200,000 (see Exhibit 5.5). If the loss were $600,000, Company C would pay the remaining $100,000.

### Primary and Excess Insurance

**Primary and excess insurance** is another type of other-insurance provision. *The primary insurer pays first, and the excess insurer pays only after the policy limits under the primary policy are exhausted.*

An automobile liability insurance policy is an excellent example of primary and excess coverage. For example, assume that Bob goes on vacation and

EXHIBIT 5.4

**Contribution by Equal Shares**

*Amount of loss = $150,000*

|  | *Amount of insurance* | *Contribution by equal shares* | *Total paid* |
|---|---|---|---|
| **Company A** | $100,000 | $50,000 | $50,000 |
| **Company B** | $200,000 | $50,000 | $50,000 |
| **Company C** | $300,000 | $50,000 | $50,000 |

EXHIBIT 5.5

**Contribution by Equal Shares**

*Amount of loss = $500,000*

|  | *Amount of insurance* | *Contribution by equal shares* | *Total paid* |
|---|---|---|---|
| **Company A** | $100,000 | $100,000 | $100,000 |
| **Company B** | $200,000 | $100,000 + $100,000 | $200,000 |
| **Company C** | $300,000 | $100,000 + $100,000 | $200,000 |

rents a car. He has liability insurance in the amount of $100,000 per person for bodily injury liability under his automobile policy. Also assume that the rental firm carries liability insurance on the rented car, and that the bodily injury liability limits are only $25,000 per person. If Bob negligently injures another person while driving the rental car, both policies will cover the loss. The normal rule is that liability insurance on the borrowed (rental) car is primary, and any other insurance is excess. Thus, if a court of law awards a $100,000 judgment against Bob, the rental firm's insurer will pay the first $25,000 of loss. Bob's policy is excess, so his insurer will pay the remaining $75,000 of loss.

The **coordination-of-benefits provision** in group health insurance is another example of primary and excess coverage. This provision is designed to prevent overinsurance and the duplication of benefits if one person is covered under more than one group health insurance plan.

The majority of states have adopted part or all of the coordination-of-benefits provisions developed by the National Association of Insurance Commissioners (NAIC). The rules are complex, and only two of them are discussed here. *First, coverage as an employee is usually primary to coverage as a dependent.* For example, assume that Jack and Kelly McVay both work, and that each is insured as a dependent under the other's group health insurance plan. If Jack incurs covered medical expenses, his policy pays first as primary coverage. He then submits his unreimbursed expenses (such as the deductible and coinsurance payments) to Kelly's insurer. Kelly's coverage then applies as excess insurance. No more than 100 percent of the eligible medical expenses are paid under both plans.

Second, the birthday rule applies to dependents in families where the parents are married or are not separated. Under this rule, *the plan of the parent whose birthday occurs first during the year is primary.* For example, assume that Kelly's birthday is in January, and Jack's birthday is in July. If their daughter is hospitalized, Kelly's plan is primary. Jack's plan would be excess. The purpose of the birthday rule is to eliminate sex discrimination with respect to coverage of dependents.

## SUMMARY

• There are six basic parts in an insurance contract:
   Declarations
   Definitions
   Insuring agreement

Exclusions

Conditions

Miscellaneous provisions

- Declarations are statements concerning the property or activity to be insured.

- The definitions page or section defines the key words or phrases so that coverage under the policy can be determined more easily.

- The insuring agreement summarizes the promises of the insurer. There are two basic types of insuring agreements:

    Named-perils coverage

    "All-risks" coverage

- All policies contain one or more exclusions. There are three major types of exclusions:

    Excluded perils

    Excluded losses

    Excluded property

Exclusions are necessary for several reasons. The peril may be uninsurable by private insurers; extraordinary hazards may be present; coverage is provided by other contracts; moral hazard is present to a high degree; and coverage is not needed by the typical insureds.

- Conditions are provisions that qualify or place limitations on the insurer's promise to perform. The conditions section imposes certain duties on the insured if he or she wishes to collect for a loss.

- Miscellaneous provisions in property and liability insurance include cancellation, subrogation, requirements if a loss occurs, assignment of the policy, and other insurance provisions.

- The contract also contains a definition of the insured. The contract may cover only one person, or it may cover other persons as well even though they are not specifically named in the policy.

- An endorsement, or rider, is a written provision that adds to, deletes from, or modifies the provisions in the original contract. An endorsement normally has precedence over any conflicting terms in the contract to which the endorsement is attached.

- A deductible is a provision by which a specified amount is subtracted from the total loss payment that otherwise would be payable. Deductibles are used to eliminate small claims, to reduce premiums, and to reduce moral and morale hazard. Examples of deductibles include the straight deductible, aggregate deductible, franchise deductible, calendar-year deductible, corridor deductible, and elimination (waiting) period.

- A coinsurance clause in property insurance requires the insured to insure the property for a stated percentage of its actual cash value at the time of loss. If the coinsurance requirement is not met at the time of loss, the insured must share in the loss as a coinsurer. The fundamental purpose of coinsurance is to achieve equity in rating.

- A coinsurance clause (percentage participation clause) is typically found in major medical policies. A typical provision requires the insurer to pay 80 percent of covered expenses in excess of the deductible, and the insured pays 20 percent.

- Other-insurance provisions are present in many insurance contracts. These provisions apply when more than one policy covers the same loss. The purpose of these provisions is to prevent profiting from insurance and violation of the principle of indemnity. Some important other-insurance provisions include the pro rata liability clause, contribution by equal shares, and primary and excess insurance.

## KEY CONCEPTS AND TERMS

| | |
|---|---|
| Aggregate deductible | Franchise deductible |
| "All-risks" policy | Insuring agreement |
| Calendar-year deductible | Large-loss principle |
| Coinsurance clause | Named insured |
| Conditions | Named-perils policy |
| Contribution by equal shares | Other-insurance provisions |
| Coordination-of-benefits provision | Percentage participation clause (coinsurance) |
| Corridor deductible | Primary and excess insurance |
| Declarations | |
| Deductible | Pro rata liability clause |
| Elimination (waiting) period | Risk of direct loss to property |
| Endorsements and riders | Special-causes-of-loss form |
| Equity in rating | |
| Exclusions | Straight deductible |

## QUESTIONS FOR REVIEW

1. Describe the six basic parts of an insurance contract.

2. Identify the major types of exclusions typically found in insurance contracts. Why are exclusions used by insurers?

3. Define the term *conditions*. What is the significance of the conditions section to the insured?

4. How can an insurance contract cover other persons even though they are not specifically named in the policy?

5. What is an endorsement or rider? If an endorsement conflicts with a policy provision, how is the problem resolved?

6. Why do deductibles appear in insurance contracts? Identify some common deductibles that are found in insurance contracts.

7. Explain how a coinsurance clause in property insurance works. Why is coinsurance used?

8. Describe a typical coinsurance clause (percentage participation clause) in a major medical policy.

9. What is the purpose of other-insurance provisions? Give an example of the pro rata liability clause and contributions by equal shares.

10. Show how a statement in a policy concerning primary and excess insurance can prevent the duplication of policy benefits.

## QUESTIONS FOR DISCUSSION

1. Jason owns a light plane that he flies on weekends. He is upset when you inform him that aircraft are excluded as personal property under the homeowners policy. As an insured, he feels that his plane should be covered just like any other personal property he owns.
   a. Explain to Jason the rationale for excluding certain types of property such as aircraft under the homeowners policy.
   b. Explain some additional reasons why exclusions are present in insurance contracts.

2. a. A manufacturing firm incurred the following insured losses, in the order given, during the current policy year.

   | Loss | Amount of loss |
   |------|----------------|
   | A    | $ 2500         |
   | B    | 3500           |
   | C    | 10,000         |

   How much would the company's insurer pay for each loss if the policy contained the following type of deductible?
   (1) $1000 straight deductible
   (2) $3000 franchise deductible
   (3) $15,000 annual aggregate deductible
   b. Explain the coordination-of-benefits provision that is typically found in group medical expense plans.

3. Malcolm owns a small warehouse that is insured for $200,000 under a commercial property insurance policy. The policy contains an 80 percent coinsurance clause. The warehouse is damaged by fire to the ex-

tent of $50,000. The actual cash value of the warehouse at the time of loss is $500,000.
   a. What is the insurer's liability, if any, for the above loss? Show your calculations.
   b. Assume that Malcolm carried $500,000 of fire insurance on the warehouse at the time of loss. If the amount of loss is $10,000, how much will he collect?
   c. Explain the theory or rationale of coinsurance in a property insurance contract.

4. Gianna owns a commercial office building that is insured under three property insurance contracts. She has $100,000 of insurance in Company A, $200,000 in Company B, and $200,000 in Company C.
   a. If a $100,000 loss occurs, how much will Gianna collect from each insurer? Explain your answer.
   b. What is the purpose of the other-insurance provisions that are frequently found in insurance contracts?

5. a. Assume that a $60,000 liability claim is covered under two liability insurance contracts. Policy A has a $100,000 limit of liability for the claim, while Policy B has a $25,000 limit of liability. Both contracts provide for *contribution by equal shares*.
   (1) How much will each insurer contribute toward the above claim? Explain your answer.
   (2) If the claim were only $10,000, how much would each insurer pay?
   b. Assume that Jeremy drives Anita's car with her permission and negligently injures another person while driving Anita's car. Jeremy has an automobile liability insurance contract with basic liability limits of $100,000 per person for bodily injury liability. Anita has a similar policy with liability limits of $50,000 per person.
   (1) If a court of law awards a liability judgment of $75,000 against Jeremy, how much will each insurer pay?
   (2) If the liability judgment is $200,000, how much will each insurer pay?

## SELECTED REFERENCES

Anderson, Buist M. *Anderson on Life Insurance.* Boston: Little, Brown, 1991, chapters 6–14. See also *Anderson on Life Insurance—1996 Supplement.*

Dobbyn, John F. *Insurance Law in a Nutshell,* 2nd ed. St. Paul, Minn.: West Publishing Company, 1989.

Crawford, Muriel L., and William T. Beadles. *Law and the Life Insurance Contract,* 6th ed. Homewood, Ill.: Richard D. Irwin, 1989.

## CASE APPLICATION

Joshua owns a motorboat that struck and damaged another boat anchored at a marina. When the accident occurred, Joshua's friend, Zoe, was operating the motorboat. The owner of the damaged boat has asked Zoe to pay for the damage. Joshua is listed as the named insured on the declarations page of a boatowners liability policy. Joshua's policy included the following provisions:

### What Is Covered

"We" will pay all sums which an "insured" becomes legally obligated to pay as damages due to bodily injury or property damage arising out of the ownership, maintenance, or use of the described vessel.

### What Is Not Covered

"We" do not cover liability arising from the ownership, maintenance, or use of the described vessel:

1. that results from an intentional act of an insured . . .
2. to persons while they are being towed by the described vessel as water skiers, aquaplaners, or similar water sports.

### Definitions

1. The words "you" and "your" mean the persons named on the Declarations.
2. The words "we," "us," and "our" mean the company providing this insurance.

3. "Bodily Injury" means bodily harm, sickness, or disease to a person.
4. "Insured" means "you" and:
   - "your" spouse;
   - "your" relatives if residents of your household;
   - persons under the age of 21 in "your" care;
   - a person who operates a covered vessel with "your" permission.
   - "Property damage" means an injury to or the destruction of property. This includes the loss of use.

a. The above provisions refer to a described vessel. Identify the section of the policy that would describe Joshua's motorboat.
b. Explain whether Joshua's policy would provide coverage for the claim against Zoe. Identify the policy provisions that would be relevant in this situation.
c. The owner of the damaged boat uses the boat to transport customers for deep sea fishing. The owner is also holding Zoe responsible for the loss of revenues while the boat is being repaired. Explain whether Joshua's policy would pay for the lost revenues.
d. Assume that a skier towed by Joshua's motorboat is injured because of Joshua's negligence. If the injured skier sued Joshua for the injury, would Joshua be covered under the policy? Explain.

Keeton, Robert E., and Alan I. Widiss. *Insurance Law: A Guide to Fundamental Principles, Legal Doctrines, and Commercial Practices*, Student edition. St. Paul, Minn.: West Publishing Company, 1988.

Lorimer, James J., et al. *The Legal Environment of Insurance*, 4th ed., vols. 1 and 2. Malvern, Pa.: American Institute for Property and Liability Underwriters, 1993.

Wiening, Eric A., and Donald S. Malecki. *Insurance Contract Analysis*. Malvern, Pa: American Institute for Chartered Property Casualty Underwriters, 1992.

**NOTES**

1. C. Arthur Williams, Jr., George L. Head, Ronald C. Horn, and G. William Glendenning, *Principles of Risk Management and Insurance*, 2nd ed., vol. 2 (Malvern, Pa.: American Institute for Chartered Property Casualty Underwriters, 1981), pp. 52–56.
2. Williams et al., pp. 60–61.
3. Ibid., p. 201.
4. Eric A. Wiening and Donald S. Malecki, *Insurance Contract Analysis* (Malvern, Pa.: American Institute for Chartered Property Casualty Underwriters, 1992), p. 294.

*Part Three*

# PERSONAL PROPERTY AND LIABILITY RISKS

On-Line Resources

The **Insurance Services Office (ISO)** maintains a World Wide Web site at:
http://www.iso.com/

The **Insurance Information Institute** is a nonprofit educational and communications organization sponsored by the auto, home, and business insurance industry. The III sponsors a site at:
http://www.iii.org/

Useful features include "Consumer Alerts," the text of the organization's most requested brochures.

The **Insurance News Network** provides consumers with information about how to choose home and auto insurance, among other insurance topics. Check out this interesting site at:
http://www.insure.com/

Another site with lots of useful information about home and auto insurance is the **Independent Insurance Network,** sponsored by the Independent Insurance Agents of America. The address is:
http://www.iiaa.iix.com/

With Quicken InsureMarket's Risk Evaluator, you can take a quiz to find out the level of risk associated with owning your car in your zip code area. Visit **Quicken InsureMarket** at:
http://www.insuremarket.com/

The **U.S. National Weather Service's Interactive Weather Information Network** posts active warnings for floods and storms around the nation, in addition to providing local weather reports and forecasts and other weather data. You can find the site at:
http://iwin.nws.noaa.gov/

The **U.S. National Highway Traffic Safety Administration** sets and enforces safety performance standards for motor vehicles and motor vehicle equipment. Get information on crash test results, among other topics, at NHTSA's site at:
http://www.nhtsa.dot.gov/

# Chapter 6

# THE LIABILITY RISK

> *"I'm not an ambulance chaser. I'm usually there before the ambulance."*
>
> *Melvin Belli*

## Student Learning Objectives

After studying this chapter, you should be able to:

■ Define a tort and explain the major classes of torts.

■ Explain the law of negligence and the elements of a negligent act.

■ Explain some legal defenses that can be used in a lawsuit.

■ Apply the law of negligence to specific liability situations.

■ Discuss the special problems of products liability and professional liability.

■ Explain the defects in the civil justice system and proposals for tort reform.

The number of liability lawsuits has increased substantially in recent decades. Owners and operators of automobiles are being sued for the negligent operation of their vehicles; business firms are being sued because of defective products that injure others; directors and officers of corporations are being sued because of financial loss to the stockholders; physicians, attorneys, accountants, engineers, and other professionals are being sued for malpractice, negligence, and incompetence. Even government and charitable institutions are being sued more often because they no longer enjoy complete immunity from lawsuits. Thus, the liability risk is extremely important to those who wish to avoid or minimize potential losses.

This chapter discusses the liability risk and legal system in the United States. This knowledge is important because it forms the foundation for an understanding of liability insurance discussed later in the text. Topics discussed include the law of negligence and elements of a negligent act, application of the law of negligence to specific liability situations, discussion of important tort liability problems, and defects in the American legal system and reform proposals.

## BASIS OF LEGAL LIABILITY

Each person has certain legal rights. A **legal wrong** *is a violation of a person's legal rights, or a failure to perform a legal duty owed to a certain person or to society as a whole.*

There are three broad classes of legal wrongs. A *crime* is a legal wrong against society that is punishable by fines, imprisonment, or death. A *breach of contract* is another class of legal wrongs. Finally, a *tort* is a legal wrong for which the law allows a remedy in the form of money damages. The person who is injured or harmed (called the *plaintiff* or claimant) by the actions of another person (called the *defendant* or tortfeasor) can sue for damages.

Torts generally can be classified into the following three categories:

- Intentional torts
- Absolute liability
- Negligence

## Intentional Torts

Legal liability can arise from an intentional act or omission that results in harm or injury to another person or damage to the person's property. Examples of intentional torts include assault, battery, trespass, false imprisonment, fraud, libel, slander, and patent or copyright infringement.

## Absolute Liability

Because the potential harm to an individual or society is so great, some people may be held liable for the harm or injury done to others even though negligence cannot be proven. **Absolute liability** *means that liability is imposed regardless of negligence or fault.* Absolute liability is also referred to as **strict liability**. Some common situations of absolute liability include the following:

- Occupational injury and disease of employees under a workers compensation law
- Blasting operations that injure another person
- Manufacturing of explosives, medicines, and food products
- Owning wild or dangerous animals
- Crop spraying by airplanes

## Negligence

Negligence is another type of tort that can result in substantial liability. Since negligence is so important in liability insurance, it merits special attention.

## LAW OF NEGLIGENCE

Negligence is a legal wrong or tort that results in harm or injury to another person. **Negligence** *typically is defined as the failure to exercise the standard of care required by law to protect others from an unreasonable risk of harm.* The meaning of the term *standard of care* is based on the care required of a reasonably prudent person. In other words, your actions are compared with the actions of a reasonably prudent person under the same circumstances. If your conduct and behavior are below the standard of care required of a reasonably prudent person, you may be found negligent.

The standard of care required by law is not the same for each wrongful act. Its meaning is complex and depends on the age and knowledge of the parties involved; court interpretations over time; skill, knowledge, and judgment of the claimant and tortfeasor; seriousness of the harm; and a host of additional factors.

## Elements of a Negligent Act

In order to collect damages, the injured person must show that the tortfeasor is guilty of negligence. There are four essential elements of a negligent act.

- Existence of a legal duty
- Failure to perform that duty
- Damages or injury to the claimant
- Proximate cause relationship between the negligent act and the infliction of damages

**Existence of a Legal Duty**    *The first requirement is the existence of a legal duty to protect others from harm.* For example, a motorist has a legal duty to stop at a red light and to drive an automobile safely within the speed limits. A manufacturer has a legal duty to produce a safe product. A physician has a legal duty to inquire about allergies before prescribing a drug.

If there is no legal duty imposed by law, you cannot be held liable. For example, you may be a champion swimmer, but you have no legal obligation to dive into a swimming pool to save a two-year-old child from drowning. Nor do you have a legal obligation to stop and pick up a hitchhiker at night when the temperature is 30 degrees below zero. To be guilty of negligence, there must first be a legal duty or obligation to protect others from harm.

**Failure to Perform That Duty**    *The second requirement is the failure to perform the legal duty required by law:* you fail to comply with the standard of care to protect others from harm. Your actions would be compared with the actions of a reasonably prudent person under similar circumstances. If your conduct falls short of this standard, the second requirement would be satisfied.

The defendant's conduct can be either a positive or negative act. A driver who speeds in a residential area or runs a red light is an example of a positive act that a reasonably prudent person would not do. A negative act is simply the failure to act: you fail to do something that a reasonably prudent person would have done. If you injure another person because you failed to repair the faulty brakes on your automobile, you could be found guilty of negligence.

**Damages or Injury**   *The third requirement is damages or injury to the claimant.* The injured person must show that he or she has suffered damages or injury as a result of the actions of the alleged tortfeasor. For example, a speeding motorist may run a red light, smash into your car, and seriously injure you. Since you are injured and your car is damaged, the third requirement of a negligent act has been satisfied.

The dollar amount of damages awarded in a judgment depends on several factors. There are three types of damage awards:

- Special damages
- General damages
- Punitive damages

*Special damages* are paid for losses that can be determined and documented, such as medical expenses, loss of earnings, or property damage. *General damages* are paid for losses that cannot be specifically measured or itemized, such as compensation for pain and suffering, disfigurement, or loss of companionship of a spouse. Finally, *punitive damages* are paid to punish people and organizations so that others are deterred from committing the same wrongful act. Contrary to common belief, punitive damage awards are generally modest and rare (see Insight 6.1).

**Proximate Cause Relationship**   The final requirement of a negligent act is that a proximate cause relationship must exist. A **proximate cause** *is that cause unbroken by any new and independent cause, which produces an event that otherwise would not have occurred.* This means there must be an unbroken chain of events between the negligent act and the infliction of damages. For example, a drunk driver who runs a red light and kills another motorist would meet the proximate cause requirement. So would the owner of a building if a sign falls from the building and injures a passing pedestrian.

## Defenses Against Negligence

There are certain legal defenses that can defeat a claim for damages. Some important legal defenses include the following:

- Contributory negligence
- Comparative negligence
- Last clear chance rule
- Assumption of risk

**Contributory Negligence**   A few states have contributory negligence laws. **Contributory negligence** *means that if the injured person's conduct falls below the standard of care required for his or her protection, and such conduct contributed to the injury, the injured person cannot collect damages.* Thus, under the strict common law, if you contributed in any way to your own injury, you cannot collect damages. For example, if a motorist on an expressway suddenly slows down without signaling and is rear-ended by another driver, the failure to signal could constitute contributory negligence. The first motorist cannot collect damages for injuries if contributory negligence is established.

**Comparative Negligence**   Because of the harshness of contributory negligence laws if strictly applied, most states have enacted some type of comparative negligence law. Such laws allow an injured person to recover damages even though he or she has contributed to the injury. Under a **comparative negligence law,** if both the plaintiff (injured person) and the defendant contribute to the plaintiff's injury, the financial burden of the injury is shared by both parties according to their respective degrees of fault.

Comparative negligence laws are not uniform among the states. The major types of comparative negligence laws can be classified as follows:[1]

- Pure rule
- 49 percent rule
- 50 percent rule

Under the *pure rule,* you can collect damages for your injury even if you are negligent, but your

## INSIGHT 6.1

## Punitive-Damage Awards Found To Be Generally Modest and Rare

Here is the latest stunning development about runaway punitive-damage awards: They may not be as common as you think.

That's the conclusion of a study by two Cornell University professors and the National Center for State Courts. Their verdict: *Punitive awards are generally modest, and meted out in only the most extreme circumstances.*

Juries aren't "pulling numbers out of the air," says Theodore Eisenberg, one of the authors.

According to the study, most punitive awards aren't random, as critics have argued, but instead are closely tailored to the amount of compensatory damages, such as medical expenses and lost wages. Punitive damages are designed to punish and deter bad conduct.

The study also found that punitive damages are seldom awarded in product-liability or medical-malpractice cases—areas that have received special attention from groups advocating an overhaul of the civil justice system. Such damages are far more likely in cases involving intentional misbehavior, such as assault or slander, and in employment disputes, the study says.

Business lobbyists have tried to focus attention on verdicts such as the now-famous $4 million punitive award against BMW of North America, a unit of Bayerische Motoren Werke AG of Germany. That amount was 1,000 times the $4,000 compensatory award in the case, which accused BMW of selling as new a car that had been retouched because of paint damage. The Alabama Supreme Court later sliced the punitive award to $2 million, and the U.S. Supreme Court threw out the reduced amount as unconstitutionally excessive.

Other high-profile awards include $100 million punitive verdict against General Motors Corp. in a suit by a man who was severely injured in a Chevrolet Blazer and a $400 million award last fall against a Canadian funeral-home chain in a case over an aborted merger.

But the Cornell study, which examined about 6,000 state-court trials in 45 populous counties over a one-year period, *suggests that such jaw-dropping verdicts are the exception and not the rule.* The BMW case in particular, says Prof. Eisenberg, "was off the charts."

The study found a much closer relationship between punitive and compensatory damages in most cases. Where compensatory damages were $10,000, punitives averaged around $10,860. Where compensatory damages were $100,000, punitives averaged around $65,720. And where compensatory damages were $1 million, punitives averaged $397,810.

The study, released at a University of Chicago Law School conference, carries extra weight because its main data were compiled by the National Center for State Courts, a Williamsburg, Va., think tank known for unusually thorough records of state lawsuits. Proponents of so-called tort reform have scorned similar studies in the past because they relied on incomplete data or were funded in part by trial lawyers. In this case, the center's data collection was sponsored by a grant from the U.S. Justice Department.

In addition, the authors backed up their findings by examining the relationship between compensatory and punitive damages in 24 years of trial results compiled by the Rand Institute for Civil Justice. The Rand data come from Cook County, Ill., and California.

Source: Adapted from Edward Felsenthal, "Punitive-Damage Awards Found To Be Generally Modest and Rare," *The Wall Street Journal,* June 17, 1996, p. B7.

damage award is reduced proportionately. For example, if you are 60 percent responsible for an auto accident and your actual damages are $10,000, your damage award is reduced to $4000.

Under the *49 percent rule,* you can recover reduced damages only if your negligence is less than the negligence of the other party. This means you can recover from the other party only if you are 49 percent or less at fault.

Under the *50 percent rule,* you can recover reduced damages only if your negligence is not greater than the negligence of the other party. This means you can recover only if you are not more than 50 percent at fault. You should not confuse the 50 percent law with the 49 percent law discussed earlier. Unlike the 49 percent law, the 50 percent law allows each party to recover damages when both parties are equally at fault. However, each party's recovery would be limited to 50 percent of the actual damages.

**Last Clear Chance Rule** The doctrine of last clear chance is another statutory modification of the contributory negligence doctrine. Under the **last clear chance rule,** *a plaintiff who is endangered by his or her own negligence can still recover damages from the defendant if the defendant has a last clear chance to avoid the accident but fails to do so.* For example, a jaywalker who walks against a red light is breaking the law. But if a motorist has a last clear chance to avoid hitting the jaywalker and fails to do so, the injured jaywalker can recover damages for the injury.

**Assumption of Risk** The **assumption of risk** doctrine is another defense that can be used to defeat a claim for damages. *Under this doctrine, a person who understands and recognizes the danger inherent in a particular activity cannot recover damages in the event of an injury.* In effect, the assumption of risk bars recovery for damages even though another person's negligence causes the injury. For example, assume that you are voluntarily teaching a friend to drive an automobile, and he negligently crashes into a telephone post and injures you. He could use the assumption of risk doctrine as a legal defense if you sue for damages.

## IMPUTED NEGLIGENCE

**Imputed negligence** *means that under certain conditions, the negligence of one person can be imputed to another.* Several examples can illustrate this principle. First, an *employer-employee relationship* may exist where the employee is acting on behalf of the employer. The negligent act of an employee can be imputed to the employer. Therefore, if you are driving a car to deliver a package for your employer and negligently injure another motorist, your employer could be held liable for your actions.

Second, many states have some type of **vicarious liability law,** by which the negligence of the driver of an automobile is imputed to its owner. Under these laws, if the owner of an automobile gives permission to a friend to drive the automobile, and the friend negligently causes an accident, the owner can be held liable. In addition, many states have passed laws with respect to the operation of an automobile by a family member. Under the **family purpose doctrine,** the owner of an automobile can be held liable for the negligent acts committed by immediate family members while they are operating the family car. Thus, if Shannon, age 16, negligently injures another motorist while driving her father's car and is sued for $100,000, her father could be held liable.

Third, imputed negligence may arise out of a *joint business venture.* For example, two brothers may be partners in a business. One brother may negligently injure a customer with a company car, and the partnership is then sued by the injured person. Both partners could be held liable for the injury.

A **dram shop law** is a final example of imputed negligence. Under such a law, a business that sells liquor can be held liable for damages that may result from the sale of liquor. For example, assume that a bar owner continues to serve a customer who is drunk, and that after the bar closes, the customer injures three people while driving home. The bar owner could be held legally liable for the injuries.

## RES IPSA LOQUITUR

An important modification of the law of negligence is the doctrine of *res ipsa loquitur,* meaning "the thing speaks for itself." *Under this doctrine, the very fact that the event occurs establishes a presumption of negligence on behalf of the defendant. It is then up to the defendant to rebut the presumption of negligence.* The accident or injury normally would not have occurred if the defendant had not been careless. Examples of the doctrine of *res ipsa loquitur* include the following:

- A dentist extracts the wrong tooth.
- A surgeon leaves a surgical sponge in the patient's abdomen.
- A surgical operation is performed on the wrong patient.

To apply the doctrine of *res ipsa loquitur,* the following requirements must be met:

- The event is one that normally does not occur in the absence of negligence.
- The defendant has exclusive control over the instrumentality causing the accident.
- The injured party has not contributed to the accident in any way.

## SPECIFIC APPLICATIONS OF THE LAW OF NEGLIGENCE

### Property Owners

Property owners have a legal obligation to protect others from harm. However, the standard of care owed to others depends upon the situation. Three groups traditionally have been recognized: (1) trespasser, (2) licensee, and (3) invitee.[2] However, as will be discussed later, a number of jurisdictions have abolished or modified these common law classifications.

**Trespasser**    A **trespasser** *is a person who enters or remains on the owner's property without the owner's consent.* In general, the trespasser takes the property as he or she finds it. The property owner does not have any obligation to the trespasser to keep the land in reasonably safe condition. However, the property owner cannot deliberately injure the trespasser or set a trap that would injure the trespasser. The duty to refrain from injuring the trespasser or from setting a trap to injure that person is sometimes referred to as the duty of slight care.

**Licensee**    A **licensee** *is someone who enters or remains on the premises with the occupant's expressed or implied permission.* Examples of licensees include door-to-door salespersons, solicitors for charitable or religious organizations, police officers and fire fighters when they are on the property to perform their duties, and social guests in almost all jurisdictions. A licensee takes the premises as he or she finds them. However, the property owner or occupant is required to warn the licensee of any unsafe condition or activity on the premises, but there is no obligation to inspect the premises for the benefit of the licensee.

**Invitee**    An **invitee** *is someone who is invited onto the premises for the benefit of the occupant.* Examples of invitees include business customers in a store, mail carriers, and garbage collectors. In addition to warning the invitee of any dangerous condition, the occupant has an obligation to inspect the premises and to eliminate any dangerous condition revealed by the inspection. For example, a store escalator may be faulty. The customers must be warned of the unsafe escalator (perhaps by a sign) and prevented from using the escalator. The faulty escalator must be repaired; otherwise customers in the store could be injured, and the owner would be liable.

Many jurisdictions have abolished either partly or completely the preceding common-law classifications with respect to the degree of care owed to visitors. According to the Nebraska Supreme Court, 36 states and the District of Columbia have reconsidered the traditional common-law classification scheme. Of the 37 jurisdictions, 23 have abolished either some or all or the categories.[3]

### Attractive Nuisance Doctrine

An **attractive nuisance** *is a condition that can attract and injure children.* Under the attractive nuisance doctrine, the occupants of land are liable for the injuries of children who may be attracted by some dangerous condition, feature, or article. This doctrine is based on the principles that children may not be able to recognize the danger involved and may be injured, and that it is in the best interest of society to protect them rather than protect the owner's right to the land. Children are considered to be licensees rather than trespassers under certain conditions. Thus, the possessor of the land must keep the premises in a safe condition and use ordinary care to protect the trespassing children from harm.[4]

Several examples can illustrate the attractive nuisance doctrine, by which the occupant or owner can be held liable:

- The gate to a swimming pool is left unlocked, and a three-year-old child drowns.
- A homeowner has a miniature house for the children. A neighbor's child enters through an unlocked window, which falls on her neck and strangles her.
- A building contractor carelessly leaves the keys in a tractor. While driving the tractor, two small boys are seriously injured when the tractor overturns.

## Owners and Operators of Automobiles

The owner of an automobile who drives in a careless and irresponsible manner can be held liable for property damage or bodily injury sustained by another person. There is no single rule of law that can be applied here. The legal liability of the owner who is also the operator has been modified over time by court decisions, comparative negligence laws, the last clear chance rule, no-fault automobile insurance laws (see Chapter 11), and a host of additional factors. However, the laws in all states clearly require the owner of an automobile to exercise reasonable care while operating the automobile.

With respect to the liability of the owner who is not the operator, the general rule is that the owner is not liable for the negligent acts of operators. But there are exceptions to this general principle. In all states the owner is liable for an operator's negligence if an *agency relationship* exists. Therefore, if your friend drives your car on a business errand for you and injures someone, you could be held liable. In addition, under the *family purpose doctrine* discussed earlier, the owner of an automobile can be held liable for the negligent operation of the vehicle by an immediate family member.

## Governmental Liability

Based on the common law, federal, state, and local governments could not be sued unless the government agreed to the suit. The immunity from lawsuits was based on the doctrine of **sovereign immunity** meaning that the king can do no wrong. This doctrine, however, has been significantly modified over time by both statutory law and court decisions. At present, government can be held liable if it is negligent in the performance of a **proprietary function.** Proprietary functions of government typically include the operation of water plants; electrical, transportation, and telephone systems; municipal auditoriums; and similar money-making activities. Thus, if some seats collapse at a rock concert in a city auditorium, the city can be held liable for injuries to spectators. With respect to **governmental functions**—for example, the regulation of traffic—municipalities are normally immune from liability lawsuits. Even this immunity has also been eroded. Since the distinction between a governmental and a proprietary function is often a fine line, many courts have tried to find exceptions to the doctrine of governmental immunity or have eliminated it entirely.[5]

## Charitable Institutions

At one time, charitable institutions were generally immune from lawsuits. This immunity has gradually been eliminated by state law and court decisions. The trend today is to hold charities responsible for acts of negligence. This is particularly true with respect to commercial activities. For example, a hospital operated by a religious order can be sued for malpractice, and a church sponsoring a dance, carnival, or bingo game can be held liable for injuries to customers.

## Employer and Employee Relationships

Under the doctrine of **respondeat superior,** an employer can be held liable for the negligent acts of employees who are acting on the employer's behalf. Thus, if a sales clerk in a sporting goods store carelessly drops a barbell set on a customer's toe, the owner of the store can be held liable.

In order for an employer to be held liable for the negligent acts of the employees, two requirements must be fulfilled. First, the worker's legal status must be that of an employee. A person typically is considered an employee if he or she is given detailed instructions on how to do a job, is furnished tools or supplies by the employer, and is paid a wage or salary at regular intervals. Second, the employee must be acting within the scope of employment. This means the employee must be engaged in the type of work that he or she is employed to perform. There is no simple test to determine if the tort is committed within the scope of employment. Numerous factors are considered, including whether the act is authorized by the employer, whether the act is one commonly performed by the employee, and whether the act is intended to advance the employer's interests.[6]

## Parents and Children

Under the common law, parents usually are not responsible for their children's torts. Children who reach the age of reason (typically age seven and older) are responsible for their own wrongful acts.

However, there are several exceptions to this general principle. *First, a parent can be held liable if a child uses a dangerous weapon, such as a gun or knife, to injure someone.* For example, if a ten-year-old child is permitted to play with a loaded revolver, and someone is thereby injured or killed, the parents can be held responsible. *Second, the parent may be legally liable if the child is acting as an agent for the parent.* For example, if a son or daughter is employed in the family business, the parents can be held liable for any injury to a customer caused by the child's actions. *Third, if a family car is operated by a minor child, the parents can be held liable under the family purpose doctrine discussed earlier.* In addition, property damage and vandalism by children have increased over time, especially by teenagers. *Most states have passed laws that hold the parents liable for the willful and malicious acts of children that result in property damage to others.* For example, Nebraska has a parental liability law that requires parents to pay up to $1000 if their children destroy property or injure someone.

## Animals

Owners of wild animals are held absolutely liable (strict liability) for the injuries of others even if the animals are domesticated. For example, an owner of an exotic pet such as a tiger or snake is absolutely liable if the pet escapes and injures someone even if the owner uses due care in keeping the animal restrained.

In addition, depending on the state, strict liability may also be imposed on the owners of ordinary house dogs. Until recently, dog owners were liable for dog bites and other injuries only if the injured person could prove that the owner knew the dog was dangerous. If the dog had never bitten anyone, the dog owner usually was not liable. *However, in about 30 states and the District of Columbia, the injured person only has to show that the dog caused the injury; in such cases, the dog owner is liable based on the doctrine of strict liability.*[7] The potential legal liability can be catastrophic if the dog owner owns several dogs who severely injure or kill someone (see Insight 6.2).

---

### INSIGHT 6.2

### Florida Boy Dies After Attack By Neighbor's Six Rottweilers

A 10-year-old Lake Wales, Florida, boy died after being mauled by six Rottweilers that escaped from a neighbor's fenced yard and attacked him without provocation, authorities said.

The 60- to 80-pound dogs, whose previous roaming had irked and frightened neighbors, attacked Corey Hines as he walked into the yard at his grandmother's house, where he lived next door to the dogs, police said.

The dogs bit the child severely on his face, head and neck.

Two city parks workers had to be counseled after pulling the animals off Corey and seeing the damage, Lake Wales Mayor Dixon Armstrong said. Police patrols were stepped up after the 9 a.m. attack because of fears of a possible disturbance, Armstrong said.

A man who lives on the street, Marvin Stokes, 64, said that shortly after the attack, several people broke the front windows of the house where the dogs lived as well as all the windows on a car parked outside.

While neighbors gathered during the day to discuss the tragedy and comfort Corey's family, the woman who owns the dogs, Tracy Parker, 27, and her family were apparently not home.

It's not clear whether Corey's grandmother, Murlene Bradley, was in the yard or the house when the dogs attacked. Afterward, her sobs could be heard throughout the neighborhood. Cory died at Lake Wales Hospital shortly after the attack.

The dogs usually stayed behind a 4-foot-high, chain-link fence that was electrified on top, neighbors said.

Police said the dogs dug under the fence to get out.

They were being held at the Polk County Animal Control shelter. Director Larry Alexander said officials will seek a court order to destroy them.

SOURCE: "Florida Boy Dies After Attack By Neighbor's Six Rottweilers," *Sunday World Herald.* November 3, 1996, p. 21-A.

## SPECIAL TORT LIABILITY PROBLEMS

Certain tort liability problems have emerged that have caused serious problems for risk managers, business firms, physicians and other professionals, government officials, liability insurers, and taxpayers. These problems center around the increased number of liability lawsuits in certain areas and the cost and availability of liability insurance.

### Products Liability

**Products liability** *refers to the legal liability of manufacturers, wholesalers, or retailers of products to persons who incur bodily injuries or property damage from a defective product.* A manufacturer or seller of a product can be held liable as a result of improper product design, improper assembly of the product, failure to test and inspect the product, failure to warn of inherently dangerous characteristics, deceptive advertising, and failure to foresee possible abuse or misuse of the product.

In many jurisdictions, the number of products liability lawsuits has increased substantially over time. This can be explained by several factors.[8] *First, the courts have gradually rejected the older* **privity of contract** *doctrine.* Under this doctrine, the original seller of the goods was not liable to anyone for a defective product except to the immediate buyer or one in privity with him. This meant that only the person who was a party to the contract could bring action against the manufacturer of a defective product. Because a manufacturer sells to wholesalers and retailers, the injured person had recourse only against the retailer. However, as a result of adverse court decisions, injured persons in most states can now directly sue the manufacturer of a defective product. *In addition, emphasis on consumerism and consumer legislation have encouraged individuals to sue because of injuries from defective products.* In particular, the Consumer Product and Safety Act of 1972 has been credited with stimulating an increase in products liability lawsuits. *Finally, the substantial number of new products has resulted in an increase in lawsuits from defective products that cause injury.*

**Solutions to the Problem**   Several solutions have been proposed or enacted to reduce the magnitude of the products liability problem. They include the following:

- *Shorter statute-of-limitations period.* The manufacturer or seller's liability for a defective product would be subject to a shorter statute of limitations after the product is purchased.
- *State-of-the-art defense.* If the product conformed to the prevailing state of the art at the time it was manufactured, it would not be considered a defective product today.
- *Alteration of the product defense.* The manufacturer would have a defense if the injury were produced by alteration, modification, or misuse of the product by the defendant.
- *Limitation on attorney's fees.* This would discourage some attorneys from attempting to persuade injured persons to bring suit.
- *Elimination of punitive damages.* This would reduce the magnitude of the damage award.
- *Proposed product liability legislation.* Proposals for a federal products liability law have been introduced in each session of Congress since the early 1980s. One recent proposal would place caps on punitive damage awards, exempt wholesalers and retailers from being named in lawsuits in most cases, and place limitations on awards for pain and suffering.

### Professional Liability

The number of liability lawsuits and jury awards against professionals has also increased.

**Medical Malpractice**   **Medical malpractice** *is defined as negligence in doing some act that a reasonable physician would not have done under the same circumstances, or as a failure to do something that a physician would have done.*[9] Stated simply, malpractice is improper or negligent medical treatment in the eyes of the law. For example, a surgeon who performs a surgical procedure incorrectly can be held legally liable if the patient is paralyzed after the operation.

Because of the fear of a malpractice suit, physicians are practicing defensive medicine that results in unnecessary diagnostic tests or longer-than-necessary hospital stays. The result is an increase in total health care costs.

Medical malpractice insurance premiums have also increased substantially over time. Premiums for high-risk medical specialties, such as neurosurgery and obstetrics, often exceed $50,000 annually. As a result of premium increases and fear of being sued, many physicians have abandoned certain high-risk areas, such as obstetrics. As a result, there is a shortage of physicians in certain geographical areas who will deliver babies and provide prenatal care.

In addition, patients are more willing to sue their physicians than in the past. This is true for several reasons.[10] First, according to experts who have studied the problem, *some physicians provide improper or negligent care.* All physicians do not provide high-quality medical care. In many cases, physicians attempt some medical procedure beyond their normal skills or make errors in judgment. As a result, the patient is harmed, and the physician is sued.

Second, many patients sue their physicians because of unrealistic expectations. Advances in medical science and medical technology often result in high medical expectations. When patient expectations are high, failure to fulfill them often leads to a lawsuit.

Third, some patients sue their physicians because of the philosophy of entitlement. This means that some Americans believe that somebody owes them something when things are not quite right. Jurors occasionally leave the impression that the key question is not whether negligence is present, but who is better able to bear the burden of loss. The real attitude is "someone is injured, and therefore someone should collect."

Finally, there has been a deterioration in the physician-patient relationship. The medical profession as a group no longer commands the prestige it once enjoyed. This is due partly to the sharp increase in the cost of medical care, partly to publicized fraud by some physicians under the Medicare and Medicaid programs, and partly to studies that suggest large numbers of unneeded medical procedures, especially surgery, are performed each year. The result is that patients are more willing to sue than formerly.

Several suggestions and approaches have been taken to solve the medical malpractice problem. They include the following:

- *Limit on damage awards.* Many states have enacted laws that limit damage awards.

- *Arbitration panels.* Many states have formed arbitration panels to resolve disputes between physicians and patients.
- *Attorney's fees.* Limitations would be placed on contingent fees charged by attorneys.
- *Statute of limitations.* The statute of limitations for filing lawsuits against physicians would be shortened.
- *More effective state medical review boards.* Monitoring activities of state review boards would be upgraded so that problem physicians could be identified more easily. In some cases, state medical review boards have not taken prompt action to revoke the licenses of problem physicians.
- *Retraining problem physicians.* Physicians cited by review boards would have to undergo retraining.
- *Joint underwriting associations.* **Joint underwriting associations (JUA)** have been formed that require liability insurers in the state to write their share of professional liability insurance.

**Legal Malpractice** Lawsuits against attorneys for legal malpractice have also increased for several reasons. *First, the standards for judging legal negligence have been broadened.* Earlier, only a blatant legal error or omission could produce a malpractice suit. Today, because of adverse court decisions, attorneys are held to a higher standard of care than in the past.

*Second, the old rule of privity, which made an attorney responsible only to his or her clients, has lost its former force.* An attorney today may be held liable by a party who may benefit from the attorney's performance but is not a client.

*Third, there has been an increased willingness on the part of attorneys to testify against each other and even sue each other.* Testimony by one attorney against another was uncommon until recently.

*Finally, because of an increase in the scope of government, there are more complex laws, rules, and regulations.* New laws with respect to pollution, ecology, consumerism, and privacy have produced an entirely new bundle of individual rights. Thus, the margin for legal errors or omissions has increased, which has resulted in additional lawsuits for legal malpractice.

Several solutions to the legal malpractice problem have been offered. They include the following.

- *Defensive practice of law.* Attorneys are now specializing in limited areas of law. Questionable matters of law in other areas are referred to other legal specialists.
- *Educational seminars.* Local bar associations are conducting seminars on complex government regulations. Classes are also held on how an attorney can avoid a legal malpractice lawsuit. Also, attorneys may be required to meet certain continuing education requirements to keep their state license.
- *Waiver of rights.* In some cases, clients are asked to waive certain rights if the attorney's legal work or advice is in error.

**Liability of Architects and Engineers**   The number of malpractice lawsuits against architects and engineers has also increased over time. The increased number of lawsuits in this professional area can be explained by several factors. First, the increase in malpractice suits against architects is partly due to a broader interpretation of liability by the courts. Architects and engineers are now held legally liable for injuries to the general public as well as to the building owners, and to workers injured by a hazardous condition on the construction site. Second, new building materials and techniques have also increased the risk of a lawsuit. Third, in some jurisdictions, the courts have interpreted the statute of limitations as starting when a construction defect is discovered, rather than when the building was first designed. The overall result is a substantial increase in the architect's or engineer's potential liability exposure. Finally, the substantial increase in building costs has also increased the size of claims. Multimillion-dollar judgments in the construction industry are not uncommon.

Two approaches are now used to control this enormous liability exposure. First, professional architectural and engineering societies have sponsored loss-control seminars through which loss frequency and loss severity can be reduced. Second, many architects and engineers are analyzing the financial feasibility of proposed projects more carefully, in order to avoid those projects where lawsuits may be brought for the purpose of eliminating or reducing their professional fees.

**Professional Liability in Other Fields**   Other professional groups are experiencing similar liability problems. Public accounting firms have experienced a substantial increase in both the number and size of claims. Pharmacists have been sued in large numbers. Insurance agents have experienced a substantial increase in lawsuits because of errors and omissions. Even education has come under the malpractice attack. In one case, a young woman sued a university for a tuition refund on the grounds that she learned nothing in a particular course because of poor teaching. In some states, parents have sued the school district because their children can barely read, even though they have received diplomas.

## Directors and Officers

*Directors and officers of corporations* have also experienced an increase in liability lawsuits. Because average claim settlements are high, many corporations have experienced a substantial increase in liability insurance premiums for directors and officers, higher deductibles, and reductions in the amount of available insurance. The majority of suits against directors and officers are filed by disgruntled stockholders because of financial losses. Lawsuits often result if the market price of the stock drops sharply because earnings expectations have not been realized.

## Other Problem Areas

Cities and other government units have experienced a sharp increase in lawsuits over time. Cities are sued because someone is injured in a public park or playground; police departments are sued because of brutality, false arrest, wrongful death, or civil rights violation. The state department of roads is sued when a motorist is seriously injured because of a road defect with inadequate warning. Also, reported cases of child abuse or sexual abuse of children have increased substantially. As a result, some day-care centers have experienced a substantial increase in liability premiums.

## REFORMING THE CIVIL JUSTICE SYSTEM

Many legal experts believe that the civil justice system in the United States is seriously flawed, and that defects in the present system have contributed greatly to the problems of increased cost and availability of liability insurance.

## Defects in the Civil Justice System

It is argued that the civil justice system must be reformed for the following reasons:[11]

- Increased number of lawsuits
- Uncertainty of legal outcomes
- Increased compensation awards
- Long delay in settling lawsuits
- Costly and inefficient system

**Increased Number of Lawsuits**    Critics argue that the current system must be reformed because of the substantial increase in the number of lawsuits over time. The number of lawsuits filed in federal courts has increased from approximately 90,000 in 1960 to more than 250,000 in 1990.[12]

Many experts believe that the increased number of lawsuits and high litigation costs are crippling the American economy and making it more difficult for American firms to compete globally. One study by Tillinghast-Towers Perrin showed that estimated tort costs in the United States totaled $152 billion in 1994, or 2.2 percent of the nation's gross domestic product. These costs exclude damage awards, legal defense and claims costs, and insurance company administrative overhead. Although the growth in tort costs has slowed in recent years, the same study concluded that the U.S. tort system is the most expensive in the world and is a highly inefficient way to compensate claimants.   Tort costs in the United States are two-and-half times higher than the average of 11 other countries.[13]

Legal experts disagree concerning whether or not there has been an explosion in litigation over time. Some legal scholars believe that the litigation explosion is a myth and that the increase in lawsuits can be largely explained by the increase in population. Part of the confusion, however, may be due to the mistaken notion that only a single and homogeneous tort liability system exists in the United States. A Rand Corporation study shows that three separate tort liability systems are in existence: (1) routine suits, (2) high-stake personal injury suits, and (3) mass latent injury suits. The Rand Study concluded that the increase in routine personal injury suits (such as automobile suits) can be explained largely by the increase in population over time. However, with respect to high-stake personal injury suits (such as products liability, medical malpractice, and business torts) and mass latent injury suits (such as asbestos liability and silicone breast implants), there indeed has been an explosion in such suits over time. The increase in high-stake personal injury suits and mass latent injury suits has outpaced increases in the population.[14]

**Uncertainty of Legal Outcomes**    Critics also argue that because of changing legal doctrines, there is considerable uncertainty in predicting legal outcomes. The result is considerable confusion for insurers, employers, professionals, government officials, and taxpayers.

For example, an injured party at one time had to prove that the other party was at fault in order to collect damages. Today, emphasis is on providing an injured party with some form of legal redress, regardless of blame. Thus, critics of the legal system argue that the ability to pay is more important today than determining who is at fault, and that the burden of paying injured persons falls heavily on insurers, wealthy persons, corporations, and others with "deep pockets."

As a result of the uncertainty in legal outcomes, property and liability insurers maintain they often must pay tort liability claims that they did not envision paying when the insurance was first written.

**Increased Compensation Awards**    Critics also argue that damage awards  in certain types of lawsuits have increased substantially over time. For example, according to Jury Verdict Research, the median amount awarded to plaintiffs for injuries in 1995 was $62,000, up 17 percent from the median award of $53,000 in 1994. Median medical malpractice awards increased 40 percent from $356,000 in 1994 to $500,000 in 1995. Median awards to paraplegics more than doubled from $2.4 million in 1994 to 6.5 million in 1995. And median sexual harassment awards increased 40 percent from $131,140 in 1994 to $183,984 in 1995.[15]

**Long Delay in Settling Lawsuits**    The civil justice system is also marred by long delays in settling lawsuits. Disposition of cases often takes months or even years to settle. The life of an average civil lawsuit in federal courts is 14 months from filing to completion.[16] Over 80 percent of the time and cost of a typical lawsuit involves a pretrial examination of the facts, such as interviews, depositions, and requests for documents. Repeated requests for documents can be time-consuming and expensive during the discovery stage of a suit. Moreover, attorneys frequently use delay tactics during the discovery stage as an economic weapon against opponents. The overall result is a substantial increase in costs.

**Costly and Inefficient System**    The civil justice system is also costly and inefficient. In particular, critics argue that the present tort system is extremely inefficient in compensating victims. *One study by Tillinghast-Towers Perrin showed that less than 50 percent of the amount paid out in claims in 1994 went to people the tort system is designed to compensate.*[17] The remainder is accounted for by legal defense costs, claims-handling costs, and insurance administrative (overhead) costs.

## Tort Reform

In view of the preceding defects, most states have enacted some type of tort-reform legislation in recent years. Some important tort reforms include the following:

- Regulation of attorney fees
- Limits on the maximum amounts paid as damages
- Penalties to deter frivolous suits and defenses
- Limiting or restricting punitive damage awards
- Caps on noneconomic damages, such as pain and suffering
- Modifying the collateral source rule
- Modifying the joint and several liability rule

The first five reforms are self-explanatory, but the latter two proposals require a brief explanation. Under the **collateral source rule,** *the defendant cannot introduce any evidence that shows the injured party has received compensation from other collateral sources.* For example, a delivery driver who is injured in a rear-end collision may be able to collect medical expenses from the negligent driver. However, job-related medical expenses are also covered under a state's workers compensation law. Therefore, the injured delivery driver is "double dipping" and receives a total amount that exceeds the medical bills. The collateral source rule would be modified to allow the recovery from other sources to be considered in determining the damage award.

Under the **joint and several liability rule,** *several people may be responsible for the injury, but a defendant who is only slightly responsible may be required to pay the full amount of damages.* This would be true if such defendant had substantial financial assets ("deep pockets") to pay damages to the injured party, and the other defendants had little or no assets. Under tort reform, the joint and several liability rule would be modified. For example, many states now prohibit application of the joint and several liability rule to noneconomic damages, such as pain and suffering.

In addition, **alternative dispute resolution (ADR) techniques** are also used to resolve legal disputes. *An ADR is a technique for resolving a legal dispute without litigation.* For example, *arbitration* can be used by which parties in the dispute agree to be bound by the decision of an independent third party. *Mediation* can also be used by which a neutral third party tries to arrange a settlement between the contending parties without resorting to litigation. To reduce lawsuits between insurers and consumers over claims, many states now use binding arbitration or formal mediation to resolve disputes between disgruntled consumers and insurers (see Insight 6.3).

There are other proposals for reducing litigation costs in the United States. One controversial proposal would require the loser to pay the legal fees of the winner (see Insight 6.4).

**Obstacles to Tort Reform by State Courts**
Although tort reform is alive and well in most states, it has been hampered by state courts that have struck down certain statutes as unconstitutional. In late 1996, an Illinois judge gutted most of the provisions in a law reforming the state's civil justice system. The court ruled that the $500,000 cap on pain and suffering and other provisions violated the state's constitution. In addition, courts in another 25 states have issued more than 70 decisions that have struck down statutes enacted since the mid-1980s that limit lawsuits. Nine states have thrown out statutes that place caps on pain and suffering. As a result, the liability laws now vary widely among the states. For

# INSIGHT 6.3

## Arbitration Comes to Insurance Disputes

State insurance departments have long mediated informally between insurance companies and consumers when a claim involving homeowners or auto insurance is in dispute. But complaint handlers often have to close the case unresolved when the facts are in question and neither side will budge. Then a lawsuit is the only recourse. *Now some states are going a step further, offering disgruntled consumers binding arbitration or formal mediation to resolve the dispute.*

Florida set up its formal mediation program, which is run by the American Arbitration Association, in the aftermath of Hurricane Andrew and credits the program with keeping some 8,000 Andrew-related cases out of the courts. State officials relied on the system a second time following the East Coast winter storm in March 1993. Mediation will soon be available for all auto-and homeowners-insurance disputes at no cost to consumers. Both sides make their cases without legal representation, and decisions are binding only on the insurance company. Hawaii established a similar mediation program through AAA after Hurricane Iniki but the state doesn't have any plans to extend it to other disputes.

In California, disputed claims worth $1,000 to $15,000 are eligible for binding arbitration through the state-sponsored Judicial Arbitration and Mediation Services. A hearing costs the consumer $50, and decisions are binding on both parties. However, the insurance company's participation is voluntary, and so far many carriers have refused to participate. "They're not cooperating with us because they don't like us," says Dave Stolls, Chief of the California Insurance Department's claims services bureau. The department has taken a tough, pro-consumer stance under insurance commissioner John Garamendi.

SOURCE: Jennifer Cliff O'Donnell, "Arbitration Comes to Insurance Disputes," *Kiplinger's Personal Finance Magazine,* Vol. 48, No. 6 (June 1994), pp. 38–39.

example, the cap on damages for pain and suffering from medical malpractice now varies from $250,000 in California to $500,000 in Louisiana to $1 million in Colorado. However, similar caps on pain and suffering in Alabama, Kansas, and Ohio have been ruled unconstitutional.[18]

## SUMMARY

- A tort is a legal wrong for which the law allows a remedy in the form of money damages. There are three categories of torts: intentional torts, absolute or strict liability, and negligence.

- Negligence is defined as the failure to exercise the standard of care required by law to protect others from an unreasonable risk of harm. There are four elements of a negligent act:

  Existence of a legal duty

  Failure to perform that duty

  Damages or injury to the claimant

  Proximate cause relationship

- *Contributory negligence* means that if the injured person's conduct falls below the standard of care required for his or her protection, and such conduct contributed to the injury, the injured person cannot collect damages. Under a *comparative negligence law,* the injured person could collect, but the damage award would be reduced. Under the *last clear chance rule,* the plaintiff who is endangered by his or her own negligence can still recover damages from the defendant if the defendant has a last clear chance to avoid the accident but fails to do so. Under the *assumption of risk* doctrine, a person who understands and recognizes the danger inherent in a particular activity cannot recover damages in the event of injury.

- Under certain conditions, the negligence of one person can be imputed to another. Imputed negligence may arise from an employer-employee relationship, vicarious liability law, family-purpose doctrine, joint business venture, or a dram shop law.

- Under the doctrine of *res ipsa loquitur* (the thing speaks for itself), the very fact that the event occurs establishes a presumption of negligence on behalf of the defendant.

# A WAY TO TRIM LITIGATION COSTS?
## "Loser-Pays" Rule Deters Unnecessary Lawsuits

One good way to start an argument is to bring up the legal notion of "loser-pays."

This simple concept—in lawsuits, losers pay court costs and legal fees of winners—has split the ranks of business, even tort reformers.

And of course trial lawyers hate it.

Its fans say loser-pays would cut back on needless lawsuits and reduce the cost of limitation. Foes counter that it would deny the poor access to court.

Supporters appear to have the evidence on their side.

Loser-pays is the standard in Britain, so it's office called the English rule. But it is common throughout Europe, says Walter Olson, senior fellow at the Manhattan Institute, a free-market think tank, and author of "The Litigation Explosion."

"It has prevailed in Europe for centuries," Olson said. "It developed early in Roman law and spread from there to the civil law systems that developed in France and Germany and other countries."

Supporters say that one of loser-pays' big virtues is fairness.

If someone drags you into court and loses his case, but costs you plenty in legal fees, why should he simply walk away? At the very least, he should have to pay your legal fees, advocates say.

America actually has some very limited forms of loser-pays. Congress has passed many laws to force losing defendants to pay plaintiffs' legal fees. However, these laws don't make plaintiffs pay when they lose.

This one-way loser-pays is especially common in civil rights and environmental suits.

If defendants must pay the other side's fees when they lose, supporters say, it is only fair that plaintiffs must pay when they lose.

When U.S. News and World Report asked people, "If you sue someone and lose the case, should you pay his costs," 44% responded yes. When the question was rephrased to, "If someone sues you and you win the case, should he pay your legal costs," 85% answered yes.

But most who support loser-pays do so because they say that it will cut the costs of litigation in America.

In dollar volume on a per-capita basis, U.S. tort claims are about 10 times that of Britain, and medical malpractice claims are 40 times that of Britain.

*The cost of liability insurance in the U.S. is three to eight times that of Western European nations.*

Obviously, foreign legal systems have aspects other than loser-pays that the U.S. does not. Britain, for example, does not allow contingency fees for lawyers. But loser-pays has an important effect on the costs of lawsuits in other countries.

First of all, supporters say, the rule acts to deter claims with little merit. Put another way, loser-pays would discourage playing "litigation lottery" in search of big damage awards.

It also ends the tactic of using the costs of defending a suit or the risk of a fluke judgment to strong-arm defendants into pretrial settlements.

On the other hand, loser-pays also keeps defendants with deep pockets from using the cost of litigation to deter suits.

"Valid legal claims are often paid earlier and more fully in Europe than here." Olson says.

### Cases Study
### State civil lawsuit filings

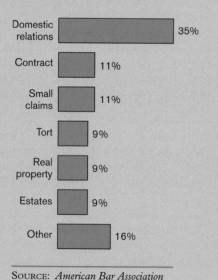

| | |
|---|---|
| Domestic relations | 35% |
| Contract | 11% |
| Small claims | 11% |
| Tort | 9% |
| Real property | 9% |
| Estates | 9% |
| Other | 16% |

Source: *American Bar Association*

SOURCE: Adapted from Charles Oliver, "A Way to Trim Litigation Costs? 'Loser-Pays' Rule Deters Unnecessary Lawsuits, *Investor's Business Daily,* June 9, 1995, pp. A1–A2.

- The standard of care required by law varies with the situation. Specific liability situations can involve property owners, an attractive nuisance, owners and operators of automobiles, governmental units and charitable institutions, employers and employees, parents and children, and the owners of animals.

- Products liability lawsuits have increased over time because of rejection of the privity of contract doctrine by the courts, increased emphasis on consumerism, new consumer protection laws, and the substantial number of new products that are produced each year. A person injured by a defective product can sue the manufacturer, wholesaler, or retailer.

- Large numbers of physicians have been sued for medical malpractice. Medical malpractice lawsuits have increased because of improper or negligent care by physicians, unrealistic patient expectations, the philosophy of entitlement, and a deterioration in the physician-patient relationship.

- Other professionals have been sued in large numbers, including attorneys, accountants, architects, engineers, and insurance agents.

- Many legal experts believe the civil justice system in the United States must be reformed because of the following defects:

  Increased number of lawsuits

  Uncertainty of legal outcomes

  Increased compensation awards

  Long delay in settling lawsuits

  Costly and inefficient system

- Tort-reform provisions include regulating attorney fees, placing limits on the maximum amount paid as damages, penalizing frivolous lawsuits and defenses, limiting or restricting punitive damage awards, placing caps on noneconomic damages, modifying the collateral source rule, and modifying the joint and several liability rule.

## KEY CONCEPTS AND TERMS

Absolute (strict) liability
Alternative dispute resolution (ADR) techniques
Arbitration
Assumption of risk
Attractive nuisance
Collateral source rule
Comparative negligence law

Contributory negligence law
Dram shop law
Elements of negligent act
Family purpose doctrine
General damages
Governmental function
Imputed negligence
Invitee

Joint and several liability rule
Joint underwriting association (JUA)
Last clear chance rule
Licensee
Mediation
Negligence
Philosophy of entitlement
Plaintiff
Privity of contract
Products liability

Proprietary function
Proximate cause
Punitive damages
*Res ipsa loquitur*
Respondeat superior
Sovereign immunity
Special damages
Tort
Tortfeasor
Trespasser
Vicarious liability

## QUESTIONS FOR REVIEW

1. Define the meaning of a tort and list the three broad classes of torts.

2. Define negligence. What are the essential elements of a negligent act?

3. Describe some legal defenses that can be used if a person is sued.

4. How does comparative negligence differ from contributory negligence?

5. Explain the meaning of imputed negligence.

6. What is a vicarious liability law?

7. Explain the meaning of *res ipsa loquitur*.

8. Briefly describe the standard of care to protect others from harm for each of the following liability situations:
   a. Property owners
   b. An attractive nuisance
   c. Owners and operators of automobiles
   d. Governmental units and charitable institutions
   e. Employers and employees
   f. Parents and children
   g. Owners of animals

9. Why have products liability and professional liability lawsuits increased substantially over time?

10. Explain some defects in the civil justice system in the United States.

## QUESTIONS FOR DISCUSSION

1. Smith Construction is building a warehouse for Ramon. The construction firm routinely leaves certain construction machinery at the building site overnight and on weekends. Late one night, Fred, age 10, began playing on some of Smith's construction equipment. Fred accidentally released the brakes of a

tractor on which he was playing, and the tractor rolled down a hill and smashed into the building under construction. Fred was severely injured in the accident. Fred's parents sue both Smith Construction and Ramon for the injury.

a. Based on the elements of a negligent act, describe the requirements that must be met for Smith Construction to be held liable for negligence.

b. Describe the various classes of persons that are recognized by the law with respect to entering upon the property of another. In which class of persons would Fred belong?

c. What other legal doctrine is applicable in this case because of Fred's age? Explain your answer.

2. a. Parkway Distributors is a wholesale firm that employs several outside salespersons. Alma, a salesperson employed by Parkway Distributors, was involved in an automobile accident with another motorist while she was using her automobile in making regular sales calls for Parkway Distributors. Alma and the motorist are seriously injured in the accident. The motorist sues both Alma and Parkway Distributors for the injury based on negligence.

(1) Describe the requirements that the motorist must establish to show that Alma is guilty of negligence.

(2) On what legal basis might Parkway Distributors be held legally liable for the injury to the motorist? Explain your answer.

b. Tom asks his girlfriend, LaToya, to go to a supermarket and purchase some steaks for dinner. While driving Tom's car to the supermarket, LaToya runs a stop sign and seriously injures a pedestrian. Does Tom have any legal liability for the injury? Explain your answer.

3. Whirlwind Mowers manufactures and sells power lawn mowers to the public and distributes the products through its own dealers. Uri is a homeowner who has purchased a power mower from an authorized dealer on the basis of the dealer's recommendation that "the mower is the best one available to do the job." Uri was cutting his lawn when the mower blade flew off and seriously injured his leg.

a. Uri sues Whirlwind Mowers and asks damages based on negligence in producing the power motor. Is Whirlwind Mowers guilty of negligence? Explain your answer.

b. The doctrine of *res ipsa loquitur* can often be applied to cases of this type. Show how this doctrine can be applied to this case. Your answer must include a discussion of *res ipsa loquitur*.

c. Explain the various types of damage awards that Uri might receive if Whirlwind Mowers is found guilty of negligence.

4. a. The number of products liability lawsuits has increased substantially over time, and the dollar amount of the damage awards has also increased.

(1) Explain the factors that have caused products liability lawsuits to increase over time.

(2) Discuss some possible solutions for reducing the magnitude of this problem.

b. Medical malpractice lawsuits have increased over time. How do you explain the substantial increase in the number of malpractice lawsuits against physicians?

c. Explain the various types of tort-reform legislation to correct the deficiencies in the civil justice system.

## CASE APPLICATION

Raphael went deer hunting with Ed. After seeing bushes move, Raphael quickly fired his rifle at what he thought to be a deer. However, Ed caused the movement in the bushes and was seriously injured by the bullet. Ed survived and later sued Raphael on the ground that "Raphael's negligence was the proximate cause of the injury."

a. Based on the above facts, is Raphael guilty of negligence? Your answer must include a definition of negligence and the essential elements of a negligent act.

b. Raphael's attorney believes that if contributory negligence could be established, it would greatly influence the outcome of the case. Do you agree with Raphael's attorney? Your answer must include a definition of contributory negligence.

c. If Raphael can establish comparative negligence on the part of Ed, would the outcome of the case be changed? Explain your answer.

d. Assume that Raphael and Ed are hunting on farmland without obtaining permission from the owner. If Raphael fell into a marshy pond covered by weeds and injured his back, would the property owner be liable for damages? Explain your answer.

## SELECTED REFERENCES

Carroll, Stephen J., with Nicholas Pace. *Assessing the Effects of Tort Reform.* Santa Monica, Calif.: Rand Corporation, 1987.

Hirsch, Donald J., and James H. Donaldson. *Casualty Claim Practice,* 5th ed. Homewood, IL.: Richard D. Irwin, 1992, chapters 3–5.

Kalfayan, Elise, ed. "What's Going On in the Tort System . . . You Need to Look Behind the Statistics." *Rand Checklist* (Rand Corporation), no. 370 (May 1988): 1–10.

Lorimer, James J., et al. *The Legal Environment of Insurance,* 4th ed., vol. 2. Malvern, Pa.: American Institute for Property and Liability Underwriters, 1993.

Pfennigstorf, Werner, et al. *A Comparative Study of Liability Law and Compensation Schemes in Ten Countries and the United States.* Oak Brook, Ill.: Insurance Research Council, 1991.

President's Council on Competitiveness. A Report from the President's Council on Competitiveness, *Agenda for Civil Justice Reform in America.* Washington, D.C.: U.S. Government Printing Office, 1991.

"Symposium: The Economics of Liability." *Journal of Economic Perspectives,* 5, no. 3 (September 1991): 3–136.

Winkler, Daniel T., George B. Flanigan, and Joseph E Johnson. "Cost Effects of Comparative Negligence: Tort Reform in Reverse." *CPCU Journal,* 44, no. 2 (June 1991): 114–123.

## NOTES

1. James J. Lorimer et al. *The Legal Environment of Insurance,* 3rd ed., vol. 2 (Malvern, Pa.: America Institute for Property and Liability Underwriters, 1987), pp. 196–97.

2. This section is based on Donald J. Hirsch and James H. Donaldson, *Casualty Claim Practice,* 5th ed. (Homewood, Ill.: Richard D. Irwin, 1992), pp. 61–65.

3. *Opinion of the Supreme Court of Nebraska, Case Title, Roger W. Heins, Appellant, v. Webster County, Nebraska, doing business as Webster County Hospital, Appellee.* Filed August 23, 1996, No. S-94-713.

4. Lorimer et al., pp. 148–49.

5. Ibid., p. 236.

6. Lorimer et al., Vol. 1, p. 319.

7. Northeast Louisiana Chapter of the Society of CPCU, "Liability Concerns of Dog Owners and Their Insurers," *CPCU Journal,* Vol. 45, No. 3 (September 1992), p. 184.

8. Barry B. Schweig, "Products Liability Problems," *Annals of the American Academy of Political and Social Science,* 443 (May 1979): 94–103.

9. Charles P. Hall, Jr., "Medical Malpractice Problem," *Annals of the American Academy of Political and Social Science,* 443 (May 1979): 84.

10. Hall, pp. 82–93.

11. *Insurance Facts, 1986–87 Property/Casualty Fact Book* (New York: Insurance Information Institute), pp. 55–59.

12. President's Council on Competitiveness, *Agenda for Civil Justice Reform in America* (Washington, D.C.: U.S. Government Printing Office, 1991), p. 1.

13. Susanne Sclafane, "Tort Cost Growth Levels Off, But '94 Price Tag Hits $152B," *National Underwriter,* Property & Casualty/Risk & Benefits Management Edition, November 13, 1995, pp. 2, 44.

14. Elsa Kalfayan, ed., "What's Going On in the Tort System . . . You Need to Look Behind the Statistics," *Rand Checklist,* no. 370 (May 1988): 1.

15. Edward Felsenthal, "Increase in Size of Jury Awards May Spur Efforts to Alter System," *The Wall Street Journal,* January 5, 1996, p. B2.

16. *Agenda for Civil Justice Reform in America,* p. 4.

17. Sclafane, p. 2.

18. Milo Geyelin, "Liability Limits Hit Roadblocks in State Courts," *The Wall Street Journal,* December 10, 1996, pp. B1, B12.

# Chapter 7

# Homeowners Insurance, Section I

*"There's no place like home, after the other places close.""*

*English Proverb*

## Student Learning Objectives

After studying this chapter, you should be able to:

■ Identify the major homeowners policies that are used today by homeowners, condominium owners, and renters.

■ Explain the major provisions in the Homeowners 3 policy, including:

Section I property coverages

Section I perils insured against

Section I exclusions.

■ Given a specific loss situation, explain whether the Homeowners 3 policy would cover the loss.

■ Explain the insured's duties after a loss occurs.

■ Explain and give an illustration of the replacement cost provision in the Homeowners 3 policy.

■ Explain how the mortgage clause protects the insurable interest of the mortgagee.

In this chapter, the popular homeowners policies that are widely used to insure homes, condominiums, and personal property are discussed in some detail. Each homeowners policy is divided into two major sections. Section I covers the property of the insured, which can include a home or condominium, other structures, and personal property. Section II provides personal liability insurance to the named insured and family members. It also covers the medical expenses of others who may be injured by an insured or an animal of the insured.

This chapter discusses only the Section I provisions in the homeowners policies. The Section II provisions are discussed in Chapter 8. This chapter provides an overview of the different homeowners policies, examines the Section I coverages in the Homeowners 3 policy, and discusses certain endorsements that broaden the Section I coverages.

## ISO HOMEOWNERS PROGRAM

Homeowner contracts were introduced in the 1950s. Since that time, they have been revised several times. The following section is based on the 1991 edition of the homeowners forms and 1994 coverage modifications drafted by the Insurance Services Office (ISO).[1] The ISO forms are widely used throughout the United States. Some insurers, however, have designed their own homeowner forms that may vary slightly from the ISO forms.

### Package Policy

Homeowners insurance is a **package policy** *that combines two or more separate coverages into one policy.* Prior to the introduction of homeowners insurance in the 1950s, property insurance on a private dwelling and personal property, theft coverage, and personal liability insurance could not be obtained in one policy. However, with the enactment of multiple-line laws, insurers were allowed to combine these coverages into one policy. As a result, the total premium is less than if separate policies had been purchased; there are fewer gaps in coverage; the major insurance needs of property owners are more easily met in one contract; and the insured deals with only one insurer. The majority of eligible private dwellings are now insured under some type of homeowners policy.

### Eligible Dwellings

The eligibility requirements for a homeowners policy are fairly strict. A homeowners policy on a private dwelling can be written only on an owner-occupied dwelling that does not contain more than two families (three or four families in some states). Each family is limited to a maximum of two boarders or roomers. Separate homeowners forms are written for renters and condominium owners.

### Overview of Homeowners Policies

The following forms are widely used in the present ISO homeowners program:

- HO-2 (broad form)
- HO-3 (special form)
- HO-4 (contents broad form)
- HO-6 (unit-owners form)
- HO-8 (modified coverage form)

In addition to the above, there is also an HO-1 policy (basic form). However, because of its relatively narrow coverage, it is seldom used.

**Homeowners 2 (Broad Form)** **Homeowners 2** *is a named-perils policy that insures the dwelling, other structures, and personal property against loss from certain listed perils.* Covered perils include fire, lightning, windstorm, hail, explosion, and other perils. A complete list of covered perils can be found in Exhibit 7.1 on pages 114–115. HO-2 also covers the additional living expenses or fair rental value in the event a covered loss makes the dwelling uninhabitable.

**Homeowners 3 (Special Form)** **Homeowners 3** *insures the dwelling and other structures against risk of direct loss to property.* This means that all direct physical losses to the dwelling and other structures are covered, except certain losses specifically excluded. Losses to the dwelling and other structures are paid on the basis of full replacement cost with no deduction for depreciation if certain conditions are met (discussed later).

Personal property is covered for the same *broad form perils* listed in HO-2. Homeowners 3 is a popular and widely used form that is discussed in greater detail later in this chapter.

**Homeowners 4 (Contents Broad Form)** **Homeowners 4** *is designed for tenants who rent apartments, houses, or rooms.* Homeowners 4 covers the tenant's personal property against loss or damage and also provides personal liability insurance. Personal property is covered for the same named perils listed in Homeowners 2. In addition, up to 10 percent of the insurance on personal property can be applied to cover any additions or alterations to the building made by the insured. Most renters need a homeowners policy (see Insight 7.1).

**Homeowners 6 (Unit-Owners Form)** **Homeowners 6** *is designed for the owners of condominium units and cooperative apartments.* The condominium association carries insurance on the building and other property owned in common by the owners of the different units. Homeowners 6 also covers the personal property of the unit owner for the same named perils listed in Homeowners 2. In addition,

## INSIGHT 7.1

### Renters Also Need Homeowners Insurance

Karen and Chris graduated from a large midwestern university, married, and moved to Dallas, Texas. Shortly after they moved into a rented apartment, a burglar broke into the apartment and stole a television set, stereo, camera, jewelry, and their silverware collection. The loss totaled $4500. The couple had no insurance. Chris tried to collect from the landlord, but he refused to pay. When the couple sued the landlord on the grounds that a security guard was negligent, a judge ruled that the landlord was not liable. In short, Karen and Chris had to eat the loss.

Each year thousands of renters experience similar uninsured losses. Renters also need homeowners insurance. Homeowners 4 (contents broad form) is designed for renters and covers the furniture, clothes, and most other personal property. The policy also provides a limited amount of insurance for building additions or alterations, such as new wallpaper in the kitchen. Coverage applies both on and off the premises. Personal property is insured for numerous perils, including fire and lightning, windstorm or hail, explosion, riot, vandalism or malicious mischief, theft, falling objects, and damage from the weight of ice, snow, or sleet. Under most circumstances, the policy also covers damage caused by water, steam, freezing of pipes, and electricity. Even loss from a volcanic eruption is covered. The policy, however, does not cover the building, since the owner is responsible for insurance on the building.

If the apartment cannot be lived in because of a covered loss, such as fire, the policy pays for the additional living expense of living temporarily in a hotel, motel, another apartment, or house. The policy also provides a minimum of $100,000 of personal liability insurance that covers the tenant and spouse if either is sued because of property damage or bodily injury to another person. Coverage is broad. With the major exceptions of business and professional liability, and liability arising out of the operation or ownership of an automobile, most personal acts are covered. Thus, if Karen's dog bites someone or she injures someone while playing golf, any resulting liability claim is covered.

Renters insurance is moderately priced. In most areas, a Homeowners 4 policy costs less than $200 annually for $6000 of property insurance and $100,000 of personal liability insurance. Most renters need homeowners insurance.

there is a minimum of $1000 of insurance on the condominium unit that covers certain property, such as built-in appliances, carpets, additional kitchen cabinets, and wallpaper. Finally, the policy pays a loss assessment charge of up to $1000 if the insured is assessed for a loss not covered by the condominium association's insurance.

### Homeowners 8 (Modified Coverage Form)

**Homeowners 8** *is a modified coverage form that covers loss to the dwelling and other structures based on the amount required to repair or replace using common construction materials and methods.* In some states, actual cash value is used as the basis of settlement. Thus, payment is not based on replacement cost.

The policy provides limited coverage for the theft of personal property. Theft coverage is limited to a maximum of $1000 per occurrence and applies only to losses that occur on the residence premises or in a bank or public warehouse.

The HO-8 form is designed for an older home whose replacement cost exceeds its market value. For example, under on HO-2 or HO-3 policy, a home with a market value of $100,000 may have a replacement cost of $150,000. To be indemnified on the basis of replacement cost, the homeowner must carry insurance at least equal to 80 percent of the replacement cost. However, a homeowner may be reluctant to insure a house for $120,000 (80% × $150,000) when its current market value is only $100,000. Likewise, an insurer will not insure a house for $120,000 under a homeowners policy when its current market value is substantially lower. Thus, to make homeowners coverage available on older homes and to reduce moral hazard, the HO-8 form has been developed.

Exhibit 7.1 compares the various homeowners forms, basic coverages, and insured perils.

## ANALYSIS OF HOMEOWNERS 3 POLICY (SPECIAL FORM)

In the remainder of this chapter, we examine the major provisions that appear in Section I in the Homeowners 3 policy (special form). As you study this section, you may find it helpful to refer to the Homeowners 3 policy in Appendix A at the end of the text.

### Persons Insured Under Section I

The definitions page in the homeowners policy defines the meaning of an insured. The following persons are insured under the Section I coverages:

- *Named insured and spouse.* The named insured and spouse if a resident of the named insured's household are both covered.
- *Family members.* Relatives residing in the named insured's household are also covered. If the children are attending college and are temporarily away from home, they are still insured under their parent's policy.
- *Other persons under age 21.* Other persons under age 21 who are in the care of an insured are covered. This can include a foster child, a ward of the court, or a foreign exchange student.

## SECTION I COVERAGES

There are four basic coverages and several additional coverages in Section I of the Homeowners 3 policy. They are as follows:

- Coverage A: Dwelling
- Coverage B: Other structures
- Coverage C: Personal property
- Coverage D: Loss of use
- Additional coverages

### Coverage A: Dwelling

Coverage A covers the dwelling on the residence premises as well as any structure attached to the dwelling. Thus, the home and an attached garage or carport would be insured under this section. Materials and supplies intended for construction or repair of the dwelling or other structures are also covered here.

Coverage A specifically excludes land. Thus, if the land on which the dwelling is located is damaged from an insured peril—such as from an airplane crash—the land is not covered.

### Coverage B: Other Structures

Coverage B insures other structures on the residence premises that are separated from the dwelling by clear space. This includes a detached garage, tool shed, or horse stable. Structures connected to the dwelling only by a fence, utility line, or other similar connection are considered to be other structures.

The amount of insurance under Coverage B is based on the amount of insurance on the dwelling (Coverage A). Under the HO-3 policy, 10 percent of the insurance on the dwelling applies as additional insurance to the other structures. For example, if the home is insured for $100,000, the other structures are covered for $10,000.

Coverage B has three major exclusions. First, the coverage does not apply to land, which includes land on which the other structures are located. Second, there is no coverage if the structure is used for business purposes. For example, if Charles operates an automobile repair business in a detached garage, there is no coverage if the garage burns in a fire.

Finally, with the exception of a private garage, there is no coverage if the other structure is rented to someone who is not a tenant of the dwelling. For example, assume that Sam owns and occupies a house that has a horse stable on the premises. If Sam rents the horse stable to another person, he would have no coverage under his homeowners policy if the stable is damaged by fire.

### Coverage C: Personal Property

Personal property owned or used by an insured is covered anywhere in the world. This also includes borrowed property. In addition, the insurance can be extended to cover the personal property of a guest or resident employee while the property is in any residence occupied by an insured. For example, if you invite a guest to dinner and the guest's coat burns in a fire, the loss can be covered under your policy.

## Exhibit 7.1

## Comparison of ISO Homeowners Coverages

| Coverage | HO-2 (broad form) | HO-3 (special form) |
|---|---|---|
| *Section I Coverages* | | |
| A. Dwelling | Minimum amount varies by company. | Minimum amount varies by company. |
| B. Other structures | 10% of A | 10% of A |
| C. Personal property | 50% of A | 50% of A |
| D. Loss of use | 20% of A | 20% of A |
| Covered perils | Fire or lightning<br>Windstorm or hail<br>Explosion<br>Riot or civil commotion<br>Aircraft<br>Vehicles<br>Smoke<br>Vandalism or malicious mischief<br>Theft<br>Falling objects<br>Weight of ice, snow, or sleet<br>Accidental discharge or overflow of water or steam<br>Sudden and accidental tearing apart, cracking, burning, or bulging of a steam, hot water, air conditioning, or automatic fire protective sprinkler system, or from within a household appliance<br>Freezing of a plumbing, heating, air conditioning, or automatic fire sprinkler system, or of a household appliance<br>Sudden and accidental damage from artificially generated electrical current<br>Volcanic eruption | Dwelling and other structures are covered against risk of direct loss to property. All losses are covered except certain losses specifically excluded.<br><br>Personal property is covered for the same perils as HO-2. |
| *Section II Coverages*[a] | | |
| E. Personal liability | $100,000 | $100,000 |
| F. Medical payments to others | $1,000 per person | $1,000 per person |

[a]Minimum amounts can be increased.

The amount of insurance on personal property is equal to 50 percent of the insurance on the dwelling. That amount can be increased. For example, if Eric's home is insured for $100,000, an additional $50,000 of insurance applies to personal property. The full amount of insurance on personal property applies both on and off the premises anywhere in the world. One exception is that if personal property is usually located at another residence of the insured, such as a cabin or vacation home, the off-premises coverage is limited to 10 percent of Coverage C, or $1000, whichever is

| HO-4 _(contents broad form)_ | HO-6 _(unit-owners form)_ | HO-8 _(modified coverage form)_ |
|---|---|---|
| | _Section I Coverages_ | |
| Not applicable | $1000 minimum on the unit | Minimum amount varies by company. |
| Not applicable | Included in coverage A | 10% of A |
| Minimum varies by company. | Minimum varies by company. | 50% of A |
| 20% of C | 40% of C | 10% of A |
| Same perils as HO-2 for personal property | Same perils as HO-2 for personal property | Fire or lightning |
| | | Windstorm or hail |
| | | Explosion |
| | | Riot or civil commotion |
| | | Aircraft |
| | | Vehicles |
| | | Smoke |
| | | Vandalism or malicious mischief |
| | | Theft (applies only to loss on the residence premises or in a bank or public warehouse up to a maximum of $1000) |
| | | Volcanic eruption |
| | _Section II Coverages[a]_ | |
| $100,000 | $100,000 | $100,000 |
| $1,000 per person | $1,000 per person | $1,000 per person |

[a]Minimum amounts can be increased.

greater. For example, assume that Eric has $50,000 of insurance on his personal property. He could take that property on an extended trip to Europe and have coverage up to a maximum of $50,000 while it is off the premises. Assume by contrast that Eric owns a cabin or summer home on a river, and that furniture and fishing gear are normally kept there the entire year. In this case, a maximum of $5000 would apply to the loss of the property because it is personal property normally located at that location (10 percent of $50,000 or $1000, whichever is greater).

If the insured moves personal property to a newly acquired principal residence, the property is not subject to the preceding limitation for 30 days after the move begins. This means that the insured's personal property is covered for the perils insured against while the property is being moved to the new location, as well as at the new principal residence itself. The insurer must be notified within 30 days for full protection to continue.

**Special Limits of Liability**    Because of moral hazard and loss-adjustment problems, and a desire by the insurer to limit its liability, certain types of property have maximum dollar limits on the amount paid for any loss (see Exhibit 7.2). The special limits can be increased by an endorsement or by scheduling.

The $200 limit on money includes coin collections. If you have a valuable coin collection, it should be scheduled and insured for a specific amount of insurance. A **schedule** *is a list of covered property with specific amounts of insurance.* A valuable stamp collection should also be specifically insured since there is a $1000 limit on stamps.

Boats have limited coverage under the homeowners policy. Coverage on boats is limited to $1000, including trailers, furnishings, equipment, and outboard motors. A boat with a value in excess of this limit should be specifically insured.

The theft of jewelry and furs is limited to a maximum of $1000. Expensive jewelry and furs should be scheduled and specifically insured. In addition, there is a $2000 limit on the theft of firearms and a $2500 limit on the theft of silverware, goldware, and pewterware. Thus, a valuable gun or silverware collection should be specifically insured based on the current value of the collection. Note that the limits on jewelry and furs, guns, silverware, and goldware apply only to the theft peril.

EXHIBIT 7.2

**Special Limits of Liability**

| Type of property | Amount |
|---|---|
| 1. Money, bank notes, bullion, gold, silver, platinum, coins, and medals | $200 |
| 2. Securities, valuable papers, manuscripts, personal records, passports, tickets, and stamps | $1000 |
| 3. Boats, trailers, and equipment | $1000 |
| 4. Other trailers not used with boats | $1000 |
| 5. Theft of jewelry, watches, furs, and precious and semiprecious stones | $1000 |
| 6. Theft of firearms | $2000 |
| 7. Theft of silverware, goldware, and pewterware | $2500 |
| 8. Property on the residence premises that is used for any business purpose | $2500 |
| 9. Property away from the residence premises that is used for any business purpose (except adaptable electronic equipment described in 10 and 11 below) | $250 |
| 10. Electronic apparatus, while in or upon a motor vehicle, if the electronic apparatus can be operated by the electrical system of the vehicle, or can be operated by other sources of power | $1000 |
| 11. Electronic apparatus, while *not in* or upon a motor vehicle, if the electronic apparatus can be operated by the electrical system of the vehicle or can be operated by other sources of power, and is *used for business purposes away from the premises* | $1000 |

The full amount of insurance applies to losses from other covered perils.

Property used for any business purpose is limited to $2500 on the premises and $250 away from the premises. However, the $250 limit does not apply to adaptable electronic apparatus as described in special limits of liability 10 and 11.

The homeowners policy also provides $1000 of coverage on portable electronic apparatus used in autos that can also be operated from other power sources—such as a cellular phone, portable television set, fax machine, or lap-top computer. *The coverage applies when the electronic apparatus is in or upon a motor vehicle and is used either for personal or business purposes.* For example, the theft of a portable cellular phone from a locked car is covered up to $1000. Higher limits can be obtained by an endorsement.

Finally, there is a similar $1000 limit on portable electronic apparatus that applies *when the electronic apparatus is not in or upon a motor vehicle, is away from the residence premises, and is used solely for business purposes.* For example, a lap-top computer used solely for business purposes is covered up to $1000 if it is stolen from your office at work. Higher limits are available by endorsement.

**Property Not Covered** Certain types of property are excluded under Coverage C. The following property is not covered.

1. *Articles separately described and specifically insured.* Coverage C does not cover articles separately described and specifically insured under either the homeowners policy or some other policy. The intent here is to avoid duplicate coverage. Thus, if jewelry or furs are specifically insured, the homeowners policy will not contribute toward the loss.

2. *Animals, birds, and fish.* Pets are excluded because they are difficult to value. Specialized coverages can be used to insure valuable animals, such as thoroughbred horses and pedigreed dogs.

3. *Motor vehicles and motorized land conveyances.* Motor vehicles and motorized land vehicles are specifically excluded. Thus, cars, motorcycles, and motorscooters are excluded under the policy. These vehicles can be covered by an auto insurance policy.

The exclusion also applies to the equipment and accessories of motor vehicles while in or on the car. Thus, the theft of a car jack or hub caps from the car would not be covered. Likewise, the exclusion applies to electronic apparatus including accessories, antennas, tapes, wires, records, or discs, which are designed to be operated solely by power from the electrical system of a motor vehicle, while in or upon the vehicle. Thus, loss to stereo tape players, stereo tapes, CB radios, and similar property is excluded from coverage. You should remember that the exclusion applies only while the property is in or upon the vehicle. A stereo tape or CB radio that is removed from a car and taken into the house would be covered under the homeowners policy. Likewise, snow tires stored in the garage during the summer would also be covered.

Finally, vehicles or conveyances not subject to motor vehicle registration that are used to service the insured residence or designed to assist the handicapped are exempt from the exclusion. Thus, a garden tractor, riding lawn mower, or electric wheelchair would be covered under the policy.

4. *Aircraft and parts.* Aircraft and parts are specifically excluded. However, hobby or model aircraft not used or designed for carrying people or cargo in flight are not subject to the exclusion.

5. *Property of roomers, boarders, and other tenants.* The property of roomers and boarders who are not related to an insured is excluded. Thus, if the insured rents a room to a student, the student's property is not covered under the insured's homeowners policy. However, the property of roomers, boarders, and tenants related to an insured is covered.

6. *Property in a regularly rented apartment.* Property in an apartment regularly rented or being held for rental to others by an insured is specifically excluded. However, as discussed later, the homeowners policy provides some coverage for landlord's furnishings in an apartment on the residence premises that is regularly rented or held for rental.

7. *Property rented or held for rental to others off the residence premises.* Property away from the

residence premises that is rented to others is specifically excluded. For example, if Jennifer owns a bike rental business and rents a bicycle to a customer, the bicycle is not covered under Jennifer's homeowners policy.

8. *Business records.* The homeowners policy excludes books of account, drawings or other paper records, and electronic data processing tapes, wires, records, discs, or other software media that contain business data. The overall effect of this exclusion is to eliminate coverage for the expense of reproducing business records.

## Coverage D: Loss of Use

Coverage D provides protection when the residence premises cannot be used because of a covered loss. The amount of additional insurance under this coverage is 20 percent of the amount of insurance on the dwelling (Coverage A). Three benefits are provided: *additional living expense, fair rental value, and prohibited use.*

**Additional Living Expense**   If a covered loss makes the residence premises not fit to live in, the company pays the additional living expenses that the insured may incur as a result of the loss. **Additional living expense** *is the increase in living expenses actually incurred by the insured to maintain the family's normal standard of living.* For example, assume that Heather's home is damaged by a fire. If she rents a furnished apartment for three months at $800 per month, the additional living expense of $2400 would be covered.

**Fair Rental Value**   The fair rental value is also paid when part of the premises is rented to others. **Fair rental value** *means the rental value of that part of the residence premises rented to others or held for rental less any expenses that do not continue while the premises are not fit to live in.* For example, Heather may rent a room to a student for a monthly rent of $200. If the home is uninhabitable after a fire, and it takes three months to rebuild, Heather would receive $600 for the loss of rents (less any expenses that do not continue). This payment would be in addition to their payment under the additional living expense coverage described earlier.

**Prohibited Use**   Loss-of-use coverage also includes prohibited use losses. Even if the covered home is not damaged, if a civil authority prohibits the insured from using the premises because of direct damage to a neighboring premises from a peril insured against in the insured's policy, the additional living expenses and fair rental value can be paid for up to two weeks. For example, Hillary may be ordered out of her home by a fire marshal because the house next door is unstable after an explosion occurred. Her additional living expenses or fair rental value loss would be covered for up to two weeks.

## Additional Coverages

In addition to basic Coverages A, B, C, and D, the HO-3 policy provides several additional coverages.

**Debris Removal**   The homeowners policy pays the reasonable expense of removing the debris of covered property damaged from an insured peril. Debris removal also pays the cost of removing volcanic ash, dust, or particles from a volcanic eruption that causes a direct loss to a building or property inside a building. Coverage also applies to the expense of removing a tree owned by the named insured that falls on a covered structure because of windstorm or hail, or because of the weight of ice, snow, or sleet. Finally, coverage applies to the expense of removing a neighbor's tree that falls on a covered structure from a peril insured against under Coverage C. The maximum paid for tree removal is $500 regardless of the number of trees.

The cost of removing debris is included in the policy limit that applies to the damaged property. However, if the actual damage plus the cost of removal exceeds the policy limit, an additional 5 percent of the amount of insurance is available for debris removal. For example, assume that a detached garage is covered for $20,000, and a total loss from a fire occurs. If the entire $20,000 is needed to rebuild the garage, up to $1000 is available for debris removal.

**Reasonable Repairs**   The policy pays the reasonable cost of necessary repairs incurred by the insured to protect the property from further damage after a covered loss occurs. For example, a broken picture window may have to be temporarily boarded up immediately after a severe windstorm to protect personal property from further damage.

**Trees, Shrubs, and Other Plants**  The homeowners policy covers trees, shrubs, plants, or lawns on the residence premises against loss from a limited number of perils. *Coverage is provided only for fire, lightning, explosion, riot, civil commotion, aircraft, vehicles not owned or operated by a resident of the premises, vandalism, malicious mischief, or theft.* Note that *windstorm* is not listed. Therefore, wind damage is not covered. If an expensive tree is blown over in a severe windstorm, the cost of replacing the tree is not covered. However, if the fallen tree damages a covered structure, such as the dwelling, the cost of removing the tree is covered under debris removal. Damage to the house from the tree is also covered.

The maximum limit for a loss under this coverage is 5 percent of the insurance that covers the dwelling. However, no more than $500 of that limit can be applied to any single tree, plant, or shrub (but not lawns).

**Fire Department Service Charge**  The policy pays up to $500 if the named insured is liable by a contract or agreement for a fire department charge when firefighters are called to protect covered property from an insured peril. However, coverage does not apply if the property is located within the governmental unit or district that provides the fire department protection.

**Property Removal**  If property is removed from the premises because it is endangered by an insured peril, direct loss from any cause is covered for a maximum of 30 days while the property is removed. Thus, furniture being moved and stored in a public warehouse because of a fire in the home is covered for a direct loss from any cause for a maximum of 30 days. For example, if an earthquake occurred and damaged the furniture in the warehouse, the loss caused by this otherwise excluded peril would be covered.

**Credit Card, ATM Card, Forgery, and Counterfeit Money**  Under federal law, there is a maximum liability of $50 per card if a credit card is stolen or lost and is used by someone else. However, a wallet or purse containing several credit cards may be stolen or lost. If credit cards are stolen or lost and used in an unauthorized manner, any loss to the insured is covered up to a maximum of $500. Likewise, loss that results from the theft or unauthorized use of an insured's ATM card is covered. If a forged or altered check results in a loss to the insured, it is also covered. If the insured accepts counterfeit money in good faith, that loss is covered, too.

**Loss Assessment**  The policy pays up to $1000 for any loss assessment charged against the named insured by a corporation or association of property owners because of the direct loss to property collectively owned by all members. However, the loss to the property owned collectively must be caused by a peril insured against in Coverage A (other than by an earthquake or land shock waves from a volcanic eruption).

**Collapse**  Collapse of a building (or any part of a building) is covered only if the loss is caused by any of the following:

1. Perils insured against in Coverage C

2. Hidden decay

3. Hidden insects or vermin damage

4. Weight of contents, equipment, animals, or people

5. Weight of rain that collects on a roof

6. Use of defective materials or methods in construction, remodeling, or renovation if the collapse occurs during the course of construction, remodeling, or renovation

Two exclusions apply to the collapse coverage. First, loss to an awning, fence, patio, pavement, swimming pool, underground pipes, and certain other property is not covered unless the loss is the direct result of the collapse of a building. Second, collapse does not include settling, cracking, shrinking, bulging, or expansion.

**Glass or Safety Glazing Material**  The policy covers the breakage of glass or safety glazing material that is part of a covered building, storm door, or storm window. Damage to covered property from the glass or safety glazing material is also covered. For example, if a baseball breaks a storm window, the glass damage is covered. If the shattering of glass also causes damage to a lamp near the window, the lamp damage would also be covered.

**Landlord's Furnishings**   The homeowners policy will pay up to $2500 for loss to the named insured's appliances, carpets, and other household furnishings in an apartment on the residence premises that is regularly rented out or held for rental by an insured. The coverage applies to all losses caused by the perils insured against (Coverage C perils), with the exception of theft. For example, Susan has a furnished apartment on the second floor of her house that is rented to students. The appliances, carpets, and furniture inside the apartment are covered up to $2500.

**Ordinance or Law**   Many communities have building codes that may increase the cost of repairing or reconstructing a damaged building. For example, a new ordinance may require the use of copper plumbing rather than galvanized or plastic plumbing when the plumbing must be replaced after a loss. However, an October 1994 endorsement by the Insurance Services Office added an additional benefit that will cover the increase in construction costs up to certain limits because of an ordinance or law. The named insured can now apply up to 10 percent of the amount of insurance on Coverage A to cover the increased costs of construction or repair because of some ordinance or law. If higher amounts of insurance are desired, an endorsement can be added to the policy. The coverage provided is additional insurance.

**Deductible**   A deductible of $250 applies to each covered loss. However, for an additional premium, the insured can reduce the deductible amount to $100. The deductible can be increased to reduce premiums. The deductible does not apply to a fire department service charge or to losses involving credit cards, ATM cards, forgery, or counterfeit money.

## SECTION I PERILS INSURED AGAINST

In this section, we discuss the various perils, or causes of loss, to covered property.

## Dwelling and Other Structures

The dwelling and other structures are insured against "risk of direct loss to property." *This means that all direct physical losses are covered except certain losses specifically excluded.* If a loss to the dwelling or other structure is not excluded, then it is covered under the policy.

**Excluded Losses**   Certain types of losses to the dwelling and other structures, however, are specifically excluded. They include the following:

1. *Collapse.* Losses involving collapse are specifically excluded, except those collapse losses covered under "additional coverages."

2. *Freezing.* Freezing of a plumbing, heating, air conditioning, or automatic fire protection sprinkler system, or household appliance, or the discharge, leakage, or overflow from within the system or appliance is not covered while the building is vacant or unoccupied, unless heat is maintained in the building, or the water supply is shut off and drained.

3. *Fences, pavement, patio, and similar structures.* Damage to a fence, pavement, patio, swimming pool, foundation, retaining wall, and similar structures is not covered if the damage is caused by freezing and thawing, or from the pressure of weight of water or ice.

4. *Dwelling under construction.* Theft in or to a dwelling under construction, or of materials and supplies used in construction, is not covered until the dwelling is both completed and occupied.

5. *Vandalism and malicious mischief.* Damage from vandalism, malicious mischief, or the breakage of glass and safety glazing materials is not covered if the dwelling is vacant for more than 30 consecutive days prior to the loss.

6. *Other exclusions.* The following losses are also excluded:
   - Wear and tear, marring, deterioration
   - Inherent vice (tendency of property to decompose), latent defect, mechanical breakdown
   - Smog, rust or other corrosion, mold, wet or dry rot
   - Smoke from agricultural smudging or industrial operations

- Release, discharge, seepage, or release or escape of pollutants unless the discharge or release is caused by a Coverage C peril
- Settling, cracking, shrinking, bulging, or expansion of pavements, patios, foundations, walls, floors, roofs, or ceilings
- Birds, vermin, rodents, or insects
- Animals owned or kept by an insured

7. *Losses excluded under Section I: Exclusions.* Certain additional losses to the dwelling and other structures are also excluded under Section I Exclusions (discussed later). Thus, with the exception of losses caused by the preceding perils and those listed in the Section I Exclusions, all other losses to the dwelling and other structures are covered.

## Personal Property

Personal property (Coverage C) is covered on a named-perils basis. The policy pays for a direct physical loss to personal property from the perils discussed in the following section.

**Fire or Lightning**  The homeowners policy covers a direct physical loss to property from fire or lightning. A direct physical loss means that fire or lightning is the proximate cause of the loss. **Proximate cause** *means there is an unbroken chain of events between the occurrence of a covered peril and damage or destruction of the property.* For example, assume that a fire starts in the bedroom of your home. Also assume that firefighters spray the other rooms to keep the fire from spreading, and that the water causes considerable damage to your books, furniture, and drapes. The entire loss is covered, including the water damage, since fire is the proximate cause of loss.

What is a fire? The homeowners policy does not define a fire; however, various court decisions have clarified its meaning. Two requirements must be fulfilled for a fire to be covered by the homeowners policy. *First, there must be combustion or rapid oxidation that causes a flame or at least a glow.* Thus, scorching, heating, and charring that occur without a flame or glow are not covered. For example, a garment accidentally scorched by an iron is not covered since there is no flame or glow.

*Second, the fire must also be hostile or unfriendly.* A hostile fire is outside its normal confines. A friendly fire is intentionally started and is exactly where it is supposed to be. For example, the glow at the end of a lit cigar would be a friendly fire. However, if the burning ashes fell on a couch causing a fire, the fire would be hostile, and the loss would be covered.

The homeowners policy also covers the peril of lightning. For example, the cost of rebuilding a chimney damaged by lightning would be covered, even if no fire occurs.

**Windstorm or Hail**  Windstorm or hail damage is also covered. However, damage to the interior of the building and its contents because of rain, snow, sand, or dust is not covered unless there is an opening in the roof or wall caused by wind or hail that then allows the elements to enter. For example, if a window is left open, rain damage to a sofa is not covered. But if the wind or hail should break the window, allowing rain to enter through the opening, the water damage to personal property inside the room would be covered.

An important exclusion applies to boats. Boats and related equipment are covered only while inside a fully enclosed building. For example, if a boat is stored in the driveway of the home and is damaged by a windstorm, the loss is not covered.

**Explosion**  Broad coverage is provided for damage caused by an explosion. Any type of explosion loss is covered, such as a furnace explosion that damages personal property.

**Riot or Civil Commotion**  Damage to personal property from a riot or civil commotion is covered. Each state defines the meaning of a riot. It is usually defined as an assembly of three or more persons who commit a lawful or unlawful act in a violent or tumultuous manner, to the terror or disturbance of others. Civil commotion is a large or sustained riot that involves an uprising of the citizens.

**Aircraft**  Aircraft damage, including damage from self-propelled missiles and spacecraft, is covered. For example, if a commercial jet crashes into your residential area, damage to your personal property is covered. Likewise, if a self-propelled missile from a nearby military base goes astray, the property is covered against loss.

**Vehicles**  Property damage from vehicles is covered. For example, if your suitcase, clothes, and camera are damaged in an auto accident, the loss is covered. Likewise, if you carelessly back out of the garage and run over your bicycle, the loss is covered.

**Smoke**  Sudden and accidental damage from smoke is covered. This includes smoke damage from a fireplace. For example, if the fireplace malfunctions and smoke pours into the living room, any smoke damage to the furniture, rugs, or drapes is covered. However, smoke damage from agricultural smudging or industrial operations is specifically excluded.

**Vandalism or Malicious Mischief**  If someone enters your home and damages any personal property, the loss is covered.

**Theft**  Theft losses are covered, including the attempted theft and the loss of property when it is likely that the property has been stolen.

Although coverage of theft is fairly broad, there are several exclusions. They include the following:

1. *Theft by an insured is excluded.* For example, if Wanda, age 16, steals $100 from her mother's purse before running away from home, the theft is not covered.
2. *Theft in or to a dwelling under construction,* or of materials and supplies used in the construction of a dwelling, is not covered until the dwelling is completed and occupied.
3. *Theft from any part of the premises rented to someone other than an insured is not covered.* For example, if the insured rents a room to a student, the theft of a radio owned by the insured and located inside the room would not be covered.

Several important exclusions also apply when the theft occurs away from the residence premises. They include the following:

1. *Secondary residence.* If property is located at any other residence owned, rented to, or occupied

by an insured, the loss is not covered unless an insured is temporarily residing there. For example, Sam owns a cabin on the river. Theft of property inside the cabin is not covered unless Sam is temporarily residing there. He is not required to be physically present in the residence at the time of loss, but he must be temporarily living or residing there. For example, if he is fishing at the river when the theft occurs, the loss would be covered.

In addition, *theft of personal property of a student while at a residence away from home is covered if the student has been there any time during the 45 days immediately preceding the loss.* For example, assume you are attending college and are temporarily living away from home. If your television set is stolen from your college residence, the loss is covered by your parent's HO-3 policy if you have been there any time during the 45-day period preceding the loss.

2. *Watercraft.* Theft of a boat, its furnishings, equipment, and outboard motor is excluded if the theft occurs away from the premises.

3. *Trailers and campers.* Theft of trailers or campers away from the premises is not covered. Trailers and campers can be covered under the personal auto policy, which is discussed in Chapter 10.

**Falling Objects**  Damage to personal property from falling objects is covered. However, loss to property inside the building is not covered unless the roof or outside wall of the building is first damaged by the falling object. For example, if a hand mirror falls off its stand and breaks, the loss is not covered. But if the mirror falls and breaks because the exterior of the dwelling is first damaged by a falling tree, the loss would be covered.

**Weight of Ice, Snow, or Sleet**  Damage to indoor personal property resulting from the weight of ice, snow, or sleet is also covered. For example, if the heavy weight of snow causes the roof to collapse, damage to the personal property inside the dwelling would be covered.

**Accidental Discharge or Overflow of Water or Steam**  If loss results from an accidental discharge or overflow of water or steam from a plumbing, heating, air conditioning, or automatic fire protective sprinkler system, or from a household appliance, the property damage is covered. For example, if an automatic dishwasher malfunctions and floods the kitchen, water damage to personal property, such as an area rug, would be covered. However, the cost of repairing the system or appliance from which the water or steam escapes is not covered.

**Sudden and Accidental Tearing Apart, Cracking, Burning, or Bulging of a Steam, Hot Water, Air Conditioning, or Automatic Fire Protective Sprinkler System, or Appliance for Heating Water**   If any of these perils cause damage to personal property, the loss is covered. For example, damage to personal property from a hot water heater that suddenly cracks is covered.

**Freezing of a Plumbing, Heating, Air Conditioning, or Automatic Fire Protective Sprinkler System, or Household Appliance** Freezing is not covered if the dwelling is unoccupied, unless the insured attempted to heat the building, or the water supply is shut off and the system is drained.

**Sudden and Accidental Damage from an Artificially Generated Electrical Current**   For example, an electrical power surge that causes an electric dryer to burn out would be covered. However, loss to tubes, transistors, or similar electronic components is specifically excluded. Thus, a television picture tube that burns out is not covered.

**Volcanic Eruption**   Loss resulting from a volcanic eruption is also covered. However, losses caused by earthquakes, land shock waves, or tremors are excluded.

## SECTION I EXCLUSIONS

In addition to the specific exclusions previously discussed, several general exclusions appear in the policy.

## Ordinance or Law

With the exception of the ordinance or law coverage described earlier under the additional coverages

section, and glass replacement as required by law, the policy excludes loss due to any ordinance or law. However, as we noted earlier, if the amount of insurance provided under the additional coverages section is inadequate, higher amounts can be obtained by an endorsement to the policy.

## Earth Movement

Property damage from earth movement is excluded. This includes damage from an earthquake, shock waves from a volcanic eruption, landslide, mine subsidence, mudflow, or earth sinking or shifting. However, ensuing loss by fire, explosion, or glass breakage, part of a building, storm door, resulting from the earth movement, is covered. An earthquake endorsement can be added to the policy.

## Water Damage

Property damage from certain water losses is specifically excluded. The following types of water damage losses are not covered:

- Floods, surface water, waves, tidal water, and overflow or spray from a body of water
- Water that backs up through sewers or drains or overflows from a sump
- Water below the surface of the ground that exerts pressure on or seeps through a building, sidewalk, driveway, foundation, swimming pool, or other structure

## Power Failure

There is no coverage for loss caused by the failure of power or other utility service if the failure takes place off the residence premises. For example, if the contents of a freezer thaw and spoil because you lose electric power during a storm, the loss is not covered. However, if the power failure is caused by an insured peril on the residence premises, any resulting loss is covered. Thus, if lightning strikes the home and power is interrupted on the premises, the spoilage of food in a freezer is covered.

## Neglect

If the insured neglects to use all reasonable means to save and preserve the property at or after the time of loss, the loss is not covered.

## War

Property damage from war is specifically excluded. War is commonly excluded in property insurance contracts.

## Nuclear Hazard

Nuclear hazard losses are excluded, including nuclear reaction, radiation, or radioactive contamination. For example, if a radiation leak from a nuclear power plant contaminates your property, the loss is not covered.

## Intentional Loss

An intentional loss that results from an intentional act committed by or at the direction of an insured is specifically excluded. The primary purpose of this exclusion is to discourage arson committed by an insured. For example, if a husband in a rage deliberately burns the home in which he and his wife are living, his innocent wife could not collect for the loss.

## Weather Conditions

This exclusion applies only to weather conditions that contribute to a loss that would otherwise be excluded. For example, landslide damage caused by excessive rain and heavy winds is excluded under this provision. Likewise, flooding or earth movement caused by excessive rain is excluded. However, damage to a house caused solely by windstorm or hail would be covered.

## Acts or Decisions

This exclusion applies to losses that result from the failure to act by any person, group, organization, or government body. For example, if a governmental unit fails to develop a plan to control flood losses, property damage from a flood that resulted from failure to develop a plan would not be covered.

## Faulty, Inadequate, or Defective Planning and Design

Also excluded are losses that result from faulty or defective planning, zoning, design, workmanship, materials, or maintenance. For example, a completed house that pulls away from the foundation because of faulty design or poor construction would not be covered.

## SECTION I CONDITIONS

Section I in the homeowners policy also contains numerous conditions. The most important include the following:

### Insurable Interest and Limit of Liability

If more than one person has an insurable interest in the property, the insurer's liability for any one loss is limited to the insured's insurable interest at the time of loss but not to exceed the maximum amount of insurance.

### Duties After a Loss

The insured must perform certain duties after a loss occurs. They include the following:

- *Give immediate notice.* The insured must give immediate notice to the insurer or an agent of the insurer. In case of a theft, the police must also be notified. The credit card company must also be notified in case of loss or theft of a credit or ATM card.
- *Protect the property.* The insured must protect the property from further damage, make reasonable and necessary repairs to protect the property, and keep an accurate record of the repair expenses.
- *Prepare an inventory of damaged personal property.* The inventory must show in detail the quantity, description, actual cash value, and the amount of loss. An inventory of your property before a loss occurs is highly advisable (see Insight 7.2).
- *Exhibit the damaged property.* The insured may be required to show the damaged property to the insurer as often as is reasonably required. The insured may also be required to submit to questions under oath without any other insured being present and sign a sworn statement.
- *File a proof of loss within 60 days after the insurer's request.* The proof of loss must include the time and cause of loss, interest of the insured and all others in the property, all liens on the property, other insurance covering the loss, and other relevant information.

## INSIGHT 7.2

### Don't Rely on Your Memory After a Loss Occurs

Can you close your eyes and remember every item in your house? If a hurricane, tornado, or fire destroys your home, clothes, furniture, jewelry, and other personal property, could you recall the exact property that is damaged or destroyed? Few people have complete records of the property in their homes.

Since memory is unreliable for keeping track of property and its value, an inventory of household items is highly advisable. Insurance agents offer the following tips:

1. The ideal inventory combines words and pictures. Take photos of every room in the house from several different angles.
2. Open the closet doors and photograph the contents. Take pictures of valuables in drawers and cabinets, especially jewelry and silverware. Close-ups are especially helpful.
3. The inventory can be easily accomplished by videotaping the household contents. If you own or rent a video camera, you can tape and describe the items and even discuss their value as you go along.
4. Make certain also to photograph the outside of the house, including the landscaping. It is difficult to rebuild a home from memory.
5. Some items may be overlooked. Be certain to include books, clocks, curtains and draperies, lamps, mirrors, tapes, records, audio and video equipment, pots and pans, and sporting equipment.
6. Record the cost and year of purchase of all major items. If an original bill is not available, estimate the cost of the article.
7. Do not keep the inventory in the home. Keep it in a safety deposit box or give it to a family member who lives elsewhere.

SOURCE: Adapted from Chris Olson, "Household Inventory Is Advised," *Sunday Omaha World Herald,* December 6, 1992, p. F1.

## Loss Settlement

Covered losses to *personal property* are paid on the basis of *actual cash value* at the time of loss but not to exceed the amount necessary to repair or replace the property. However, it is possible to add an endorsement to the policy that covers personal property on the basis of replacement cost. This endorsement is discussed later in the chapter.

Carpets, domestic appliances, awnings, outdoor antennas, and outdoor equipment, whether attached to the dwelling or not, are also indemnified on the basis of actual cash value.

Covered losses to the *dwelling and other structures* are paid on the basis of *replacement cost* with no deduction for depreciation. Replacement cost insurance on the dwelling is one of the most valuable features of the homeowner policies. If the amount of insurance carried is equal to at least 80 percent of the replacement cost of the damaged building at the time of loss, full replacement cost is paid with no deduction for depreciation up to the limits of the policy. **Replacement cost** *is the amount necessary to repair or replace the dwelling with material of like kind and quality at current prices.* For example, assume that a home has a current replacement value of $100,000 and is insured for $80,000. If the home is damaged by a tornado, and repairs cost $20,000, the full $20,000 is paid with no deduction for depreciation. If the home is totally destroyed, however, the maximum amount paid is the face amount of the policy—in this case, $80,000.

A different set of rules applies if the amount of insurance is less than 80 percent of the replacement cost at the time of loss. Stated simply, if the insurance carried is less than 80 percent of the replacement cost, the insured receives the *larger* of the following two amounts:

(1) Actual cash value of that part of the building damaged

or

(2) $\dfrac{\text{Amount of insurance carried}}{80\% \times \text{Replacement cost}} \times \text{Loss}$

For example, assume that a dwelling has a replacement cost of $100,000, but is insured for only $60,000. The roof of the house is 10 years old and has a useful life of 20 years, so it is 50 percent depreciated. Assume that the roof is severely damaged by a tornado, and the replacement cost of a new roof is $20,000. Ignoring the deductible, the insured receives the larger of:

(1) Actual cash value = $20,000 − $10,000
$$= \$10,000$$

(2) $\dfrac{\$60,000}{80\% \times \$100,000} \times \$20,000 = \$15,000$

The insured receives $15,000 for the loss. The entire loss would have been paid if the insured had carried at least $80,000 of insurance.

With the exception of losses that are both less than 5 percent of the amount of insurance and less than $2500, the insured must actually repair or replace the property to receive full replacement cost. Otherwise, the loss is paid on the basis of actual cash value. However, the insured can submit a claim for the actual cash value and then collect an additional amount when the actual repair or replacement is completed, provided the additional claim is made within 180 days after the loss.

Many insurers now offer a **guaranteed replacement cost** endorsement by which the insured agrees to insure the home to 100 percent of its estimated replacement cost rather than 80 percent. *In the event of a total loss, the insurer agrees to replace the home exactly as it was before the loss even though the replacement cost exceeds the amount of insurance stated in the policy.* Coverage is typically restricted to homes that are less than 25 years old. Homes that are of unique or unusual construction are ineligible.

## Loss to a Pair or Set

In the event of **loss to a pair or set,** *the insurer can elect either to repair or replace any part of the pair or set, or pay the difference between the actual cash value of the property before and after the loss.* For example, assume that Brandi has a set of three matching wall decorations hanging on the wall in her living room, and one of the decorations is badly damaged in a fire. The insurer can elect either to replace or repair the damaged wall decoration or pay the difference in the cash value of the set before and after the loss.

## Glass Replacement

To promote safety, many communities have laws that require broken glass doors, storm doors, shower doors, and similar glass to be replaced with safety glazing materials. Damage to glass from an insured peril will be settled on the basis of replacement with safety glazing materials when required by an ordinance or law.

## Appraisal Clause

An **appraisal clause** *is used when the insured and insurer agree that the loss is covered, but the amount of the loss is in dispute.* Either party can demand that the dispute be resolved by an appraisal. Each party selects a competent and disinterested appraiser. The appraisers then select an umpire. If they cannot agree on an umpire after 15 days, a judge in a court of record will appoint one. If the appraisers fail to agree on the amount of the loss, only their differences are submitted to the umpire. An agreement in writing by any two of the three is then binding on both parties. Each party pays the fee of his or her appraiser, and the umpire's fee is shared equally by both parties.

## Other Insurance

If other insurance covers a Section I loss, the insurer will pay only the proportion of the loss that its limit of liability bears to the total amount of insurance covering the loss. This is the pro rata liability clause that was explained in Chapter 5, and additional discussion is not needed here.

## Suit Against the Insurer

No legal action can be brought against the insurer unless all policy provisions have been complied with, and legal action is started within one year after the loss occurs.

## Insurer's Option

After giving written notice to the insured, the insurer has the right to repair or replace any part of the damaged property with like property. For example, assume that a television set is stolen. By giving written notice, the insurer can replace the stolen TV with a similar item rather than paying cash. Insurers often can purchase television sets, stereos, and other types of property from wholesale distributors at a lower cost than the insured would pay in the retail market. By exercising the replacement option, an insurer can meet its contractual obligation for a covered loss, but its loss settlement costs can be reduced.

## Loss Payment

The insurer is required to make a loss payment directly to the insured unless some other person is named in the policy or is legally entitled to receive the loss payment. In many homeowner contracts, a mortgagee (lender) is frequently named in the policy, which allows the mortgagee to receive a loss payment to the extent of its insurable interest (see below). A legal representative of the insured is also entitled to receive a loss payment. For example, if Angela dies before receiving payment for a covered loss, the loss payment is made to the executor of her estate.

## Abandonment of Property

The insurer is not obligated to accept any property abandoned by the insured after a loss occurs. The insurer has the option of paying for the damaged property in full and then taking the damaged property as salvage, or the insurer can elect to have the property repaired. However, the decision to exercise these options belongs to the insurer. For example, assume that your personal property is insured for $50,000. A fire occurs, and the salvage value of the property after the loss is $10,000. The insurer can pay you $40,000, or it can take all the damaged property and pay you $50,000. However, you cannot abandon the property to the insurer and demand payment of $50,000.

## Mortgage Clause

The **mortgage clause** is designed to protect the mortgagee's insurable interest. The mortgagee usually is a savings and loan institution, commercial bank, or other lending institution that makes a loan to the mortgagor so that the property can be purchased. The property serves as collateral for the mortgage. If the property is damaged or destroyed, the collateral securing the loan is impaired, and the mortgagee may not be repaid.

The mortgagee's insurable interest in the property can be protected by the mortgage clause that is part of the homeowner's policy. *Under this provision, if the mortgagee is named in the policy, the mortgagee is entitled to receive a loss payment from the insurer to the extent of its interest regardless of any policy violation by the insured.* For example, if Troy intentionally sets fire to his house, his loss is not covered because the fire is intentional. However, the mortgagee's insurable interest in the property is still protected. The loss payment would be paid to the mortgagee to the extent of the mortgagee's interest. The mortgagee is also entitled to a 10-day cancellation notice if the insurer decides to cancel.

In exchange for the guarantee of payment, the mortgage clause imposes certain obligations on the mortgagee. They are as follows:

- To notify the insurer of any change in ownership, occupancy, or substantial change in risk of which the mortgagee is aware
- To pay any premium due if the insured neglects to pay the premium
- To provide a proof-of-loss form if the insured fails to do so
- To give subrogation rights to the insurer in those cases where the insurer denies liability to the insured but must make a loss payment to the mortgagee

## SECTION I AND II CONDITIONS

The homeowners policy contains several common conditions that apply to both Section I and Section II. They are summarized as follows:

- *Policy Period.* The policy period begins and ends at 12:01 A.M. Only losses that occur within the policy period are covered.
- *Concealment or Fraud.* There is no coverage if an insured intentionally conceals or misrepresents any material fact, makes false statements, or engages in fraudulent conduct relating to the insurance.
- *Liberalization Clause.* If the insurer broadens the coverage it offers without an additional premium within 60 days before inception of the policy or during the policy period, the broadened coverage applies immediately to the present policy.
- *Waiver or Change of Policy Provisions.* A waiver or change in any policy provision must be approved in writing by the insurer to be valid. For

example, an agent cannot orally waive any policy provision in the homeowners policy.

- *Cancellation.* The insured can cancel at any time by returning the policy or by notifying the insurer in writing when the cancellation is to become effective.

    The insurer can cancel under the following conditions:

    1. The premium is not paid. The insured must be given at least 10 days written notice of cancellation.
    2. A new policy can be canceled for any reason if it has been in force for less than 60 days and is not a renewal policy. The insured must be given at least 10 days notice of cancellation.
    3. If the policy has been in force for 60 or more days or is a renewal policy, the insurer can cancel if there is a material misrepresentation of fact that would have caused the insurer not to issue the policy, or the risk has increased substantially after the policy was issued.
    4. If the policy is written for a period longer than one year, it can be canceled for any reason on the anniversary date by giving the insured at least 30 days notice of cancellation.

- *Nonrenewal of the Policy.* The insurer has the right not to renew the policy when it expires. The insured must be given at least 30 days notice before the expiration date if the policy is not renewed.
- *Assignment of the Policy.* The homeowners policy cannot be assigned to another party without the insurer's written consent. Thus, if Richard sells his home to Michelle, he cannot validly assign his homeowners policy to Michelle. The homeowners policy is a personal contract between the insured and insurer. The assignment provision allows the insurer to select its own insureds and provides some protection against moral hazard and adverse selection. However, after a loss occurs, the loss payment can be freely assigned to another party without the insurer's consent. The party who receives the payment does not become a new insured, and the risk to the insurer is not increased.
- *Subrogation.* A general principle is that an insured cannot unilaterally waive the insurer's right of subrogation against a third party who caused the loss without jeopardizing coverage under the policy, However, the homeowners policy contains an important exception to this general principle. The subrogation clause allows the insured to waive in writing before a loss occurs all rights of recovery against any person. For example, assume that Jerome lives in one unit of a duplex and rents out the other unit. The lease may state that Jerome as landlord waives his right of recovery against the tenant if the tenant should negligently cause a loss (such as a fire). The waiver would protect the tenant against a subrogation recovery by Jerome's insurer if the tenant should cause a loss. To be effective, however, the waiver must be in writing before a loss occurs.

    If the right of recovery is not waived, the insurer may require the insured to assign all rights of recovery against a third party to the extent of the loss payment. This allows the insurer to exercise its subrogation rights against a negligent third party who caused the loss.

- *Death of Named Insured or Spouse.* If the named insured or resident spouse dies, coverage is extended to the legal representative of the deceased but only with respect to the premises and property of the deceased. Coverage also continues for resident relatives who are insured under the policy at the time of the named insured or spouse's death.

## SECTION I ENDORSEMENTS

The final part of this chapter discusses several endorsements that modify the Section I coverages. Some property owners have special needs or desire broader coverage than that provided by a standard homeowners policy. Several endorsements can broaden the Section I coverages. They include the following:

- Inflation-guard endorsement
- Earthquake endorsement
- Personal property replacement cost endorsement
- Scheduled personal property endorsement
- Special personal property coverage endorsement

## Inflation-Guard Endorsement

Some homeowners are underinsured because of inflation. If a loss occurs and you do not carry insurance at least equal to 80 percent of the replacement cost of the dwelling, you will be penalized since the full replacement cost will not be paid.

To deal with inflation, you should add an **inflation-guard endorsement** to your homeowners policy if it is not included by your insurer. The inflation-guard endorsement is designed for use with the ISO homeowner forms and provides for an annual pro rata increase in the limits of liability under Coverages A, B, C, and D. The percentage increase is selected by the insured, such as 4 percent or 6 percent. For example, if the policyowner selects a 6 percent inflation-guard endorsement, the various limits are increased by 6 percent annually. This specified annual percentage increase is prorated throughout the policy year. Thus, a house originally insured for $100,000 would be covered for $103,000 at the end of six months.

## Earthquake Endorsement

An **earthquake endorsement** can be added that covers earthquakes, landslides, volcanic eruption, and earth movement. A single earthquake is defined as all earthquake shocks that occur within a 72-hour period. A 5 percent deductible must be satisfied based on the June 1994 edition of the ISO earthquake endorsement. The base deductible is 5 percent of the limit of liability that applies *either* to the dwelling (Coverage A) or to personal property (Coverage C), whichever is greater. There is a minimum deductible of $250. The deductible can be increased with a reduction in premiums. There is no other deductible that applies to an earthquake loss. The deductible does not apply to Coverage D (loss of use) and to Additional Coverages.

Although earthquakes have the potential for causing a catastrophic loss, most homeowners in earthquake zones do not have this coverage. All insurers in California selling homeowners insurance are required to offer earthquake insurance on new policies. However, the majority of homeowners in California have no coverage for earthquakes. The major reasons for the lack of coverage are cost, a higher 10 percent deductible, and a mistaken belief that earthquakes will not occur. Also, many property owners believe the federal government will provide disaster relief if an earthquake occurs.

## Personal Property Replacement-Cost Endorsement

As stated earlier, losses to personal property are indemnified on the basis of actual cash value. However, a **personal property replacement-cost endorsement** can be added to a homeowners policy to provide replacement cost coverage on personal property, awnings, carpets, domestic appliances, and outdoor equipment. With replacement cost coverage, there is no deduction for depreciation.

The replacement-cost endorsement for personal property has several important limitations. The amount paid is limited to the *smallest* of the following amounts:

- Replacement cost at the time of loss
- Full repair cost
- Coverage C amount if applicable
- Any special dollar limits in the policy (such as limits on jewelry, furs, and silverware)
- The limit that applies to any property separately described and specifically insured

If the replacement cost of the loss exceeds $500, the property must actually be repaired or replaced to receive replacement cost. Otherwise, only the cash value is paid.

The replacement-cost endorsement also excludes certain types of property, such as antiques, fine arts, and similar property; collector's items and souvenirs; property that is not in good or workable condition; and obsolete property stored or not used.

As a general rule, you should consider adding the replacement-cost endorsement for personal property to your homeowners policy. Because of depreciation, the amount paid for a loss under an actual cash value policy is substantially less than that payable under a replacement cost policy. Most insureds typically are unaware of the big gap between replacement cost and actual cash value (see Insight 7.3).

## Scheduled Personal Property Endorsement

If you have valuable jewelry, furs, silverware, cameras, musical instruments, fine arts, antiques, or

## INSIGHT 7.3

### Actual Cash Value Coverage On Personal Property Can Cost You a Bundle

If you own personal property, you should consider the big gap between replacement cost and actual cash value. *You stand to pay a large amount out of pocket because of depreciation if the loss payment is based on actual cash value.* The table below, based on the depre-

ciation schedule of a large property and liability insurer, shows that the insured would receive $7790 (less the deductible) based on *replacement cost* compared with only $3967 based on *actual cash value.* Actual cash value is replacement cost less depreciation.

| Item | Age | Replacement cost | Depreciation | Actual cash value |
|------|-----|------------------|--------------|-------------------|
| Television set | 5 years | $900 | $450 | $450 |
| Sofa | 4 years | 1500 | 600 | 900 |
| Draperies | 2 years | 2000 | 400 | 1600 |
| 5 women's dresses | 4 years | 500 | 400 | 100 |
| 3 men's shoes | 2 years | 200 | 133 | 67 |
| 3 end tables | 15 years | 1200 | 900 | 300 |
| Refrigerator | 10 years | 800 | 560 | 240 |
| Area rug | New | 200 | 0 | 200 |
| Cosmetics | 6 months | 200 | 180 | 20 |
| Kitchen dishes | 4 years | 250 | 200 | 50 |
| 30 cans food | New | 40 | 0 | 40 |
| *Total* | | *$7790* | *$3823* | *$3967* |

NOTE: The above hypothetical losses show the effect of depreciation, which is based on age and condittion of the property; the older the item, the greater is the amount of depreciation.

stamp or coin collections, the *scheduled personal property endorsement* can be added to the policy to provide broader coverage. All direct physical losses to the scheduled items are covered except certain losses specifically excluded.

## Special Personal Property Coverage Endorsement

Personal property in an unendorsed HO-3 policy is covered on a named-perils basis. Insureds sometimes desire coverage of personal property on an "all-risks" basis. This can be accomplished by adding the **special personal property coverage endorsement** to the HO-3 policy. The endorsement *changes*

*the coverage of personal property from a named-perils basis to a risk-of-direct-physical loss basis.* All direct physical losses to personal property are covered except those losses specifically excluded.

### SUMMARY

- The homeowners policy is a package policy that can be used to cover the dwelling, other structures, personal property, additional living expenses, and personal liability lawsuits.

- Section I provides coverage on the dwelling, other structures, personal property, loss-of-use benefits, and additional coverages. Section II provides personal liability insurance to the insured and also covers the medical expenses of others who may be injured while on the insured premises or by some act of the insured or by an animal owned by the insured.

- The HO-2 policy (broad form) covers the dwelling, other structures, and personal property against loss on a named-perils basis.

- The HO-3 policy (special form) covers the dwelling and other structures against risk of direct physical loss to the described property. This means that all losses to the dwelling and other structures are covered except those losses specifically excluded. However, personal property is covered only on a named-perils basis.

- The HO-4 policy (contents broad form) is designed for renters. HO-4 covers the personal property of tenants on a named-perils basis and also provides personal liability insurance.

- The HO-6 policy (unit-owners form) is designed for condominium owners. HO-6 covers the personal property of the insured on a named-perils basis. There is also a minimum of $1000 insurance on the condominium unit that covers certain property, such as alterations, fixtures, and improvements.

- The HO-8 policy (modified coverage form) is designed for older homes. Losses to the dwelling and other structures are indemnified on the basis of the amount required to repair or replace the property using common construction materials and methods. Losses are not indemnified based on replacement cost.

- The conditions section imposes certain duties on the insured after a loss to covered property occurs. The insured must give immediate notice of the loss; the property must be protected from further damage; the insured must prepare an inventory of the damaged personal property and may be required to show the damaged property to the insurer as often as is reasonably required; and proof of loss must be filed within 60 days after the insurer's request.

- The replacement-cost provision is one of the most valuable features of the homeowners policy. Losses to the dwelling and other structures are paid on the basis of replacement cost if the insured carries insurance at least equal to 80 percent of the replacement cost at the time of loss. Losses to personal property are paid on the basis of actual cash value. However, an endorsement can be added that covers personal property on a replacement-cost basis.

- The appraisal provision is designed to resolve disputes over the amount paid. Each party selects its own appraiser. The appraisers then select an umpire. An agreement by any two is binding on all parties.

- The mortgage clause provides protection to the mortgagee. The mortgagee is entitled to receive a loss payment from the insurer regardless of any policy violation by the insured.

- Certain endorsements can be added to the homeowners policy that modify the Section I coverages, including the following:

> Inflation-guard endorsement
>
> Earthquake endorsement
>
> Personal property replacement cost endorsement
>
> Scheduled personal property endorsement
>
> Special personal property coverage endorsement

## KEY CONCEPTS AND TERMS

| | |
|---|---|
| Additional living expense | Loss to pair or set clause |
| Appraisal clause | Mortgage clause |
| Earthquake endorsement | Package policy |
| Fair rental value | Personal property |
| Guaranteed replacement cost | replacement-cost endorsement |
| Homeowners 2 (broad form) | Proximate cause |
| Homeowners 3 (special form) | Replacement-cost insurance on the dwelling |
| Homeowners 4 (contents broad form) | Schedule |
| Homeowners 6 (unit-owners form) | Scheduled personal property endorsement |
| Homeowners 8 (modified coverage form) | Special personal property coverage endorsement |
| Inflation-guard endorsement | |

## QUESTIONS FOR REVIEW

1. Explain the advantages of a package policy to the insured.

2. Identify the basic types of homeowner policies and indicate the groups for which each form is designed.

3. Identify the basic coverages that are provided in Section I of the homeowners policy.

4. What additional coverages are provided in Section I of the homeowners policy?

5. Explain the special limits of liability that apply to certain types of property. Why are these limits used?

6. Describe the various exclusions that are found in Section I of the Homeowners 3 policy.

7. Explain the duties imposed on the insured after a loss.

8. Explain the replacement cost provisions of the home-owners policy and give an example.

9. Explain how the appraisal clause can be used to re-solve disputes.

10. Explain briefly how the mortgage clause protects the mortgagee's insurable interest.

## QUESTIONS FOR DISCUSSION

1. Amber has her home and personal property insured under a Homeowners 3 (special form) policy. Indicate whether or not each of the following losses is covered. If the loss is not covered, explain why it is not covered.

   a. Amber carelessly spills a can of black enamel paint while painting a bedroom. A white wall-to-wall carpet that is part of the bedroom is badly dam-aged and must be replaced.

   b. Water backs up from a clogged drainpipe, floods the basement, and damages some books stored in a box.

   c. Amber's house is totally destroyed in a tornado. Her valuable Doberman pinscher attack dog is killed in the tornado.

   d. Smoke from a nearby industrial plant damages Amber's freshly painted house.

   e. Amber is on vacation, and a thief breaks into her hotel and steals a suitcase containing jewelry, money, clothes, and an airline ticket.

   f. Amber's son is playing baseball in the yard. A line drive breaks the living room window.

   g. A garbage truck accidentally backs into the garage door and shatters it.

   h. Defective wiring causes a fire in the attic. Damage to the house is extensive. Amber is forced to move to a furnished apartment for three months while the house is being rebuilt.

   i. Amber's son is attending college but is home for Christmas vacation. A stereo set is stolen from his dormitory room during his absence.

   j. During the winter, heavy snow damages part of the front lawn, and the sod must be replaced.

   k. During a windstorm, a picket fence and an elm tree are blown over.

   l. Carpeting is damaged from the overflow of water from a bathtub because the insured left the water running while answering the telephone.

   m. The home is badly damaged in a severe earth-quake. As a result of the earthquake, the front lawn has a three-foot crack and is now uneven.

   n. An icemaker in the refrigerator breaks and water seeps into the flooring and carpets, causing consid-erable damage to the dwelling.

2. James has his home and personal property insured under a Homeowners 3 (special form) policy. The dwelling is insured for $60,000. The replacement cost of the home is $100,000. Indicate the extent to which each of the following losses would be covered under James's Homeowners 3 policy. (Ignore the de-ductible.)

   a. Lightning strikes the roof of the house and severely damages it. The actual cash value of the damaged roof is $10,000, and it will cost $16,000 to replace the damaged portion.

   b. A living room window is broken in a hailstorm. The drapes are water stained and must be re-placed. The actual cash value of the damaged drapes is $200. Replacement cost is $300.

   c. The hot water heater explodes and damages some household contents. The actual cash value of the damaged property is $1000, and the cost of replac-ing the property is $1600.

3. Sarah owns a valuable diamond ring that has been in her family for generations. She is told by an ap-praiser that the ring has a current market value of $20,000. She feels that the ring is adequately insured since she owns a Homeowners 3 (special form) pol-icy. Is Sarah correct in her thinking? If not, how would you advise her concerning proper protection of the ring?

4. Paul has his home and its contents insured under a Homeowners 3 (special form) policy. He carries $80,000 of insurance on the home, which has a re-placement cost of $100,000. Explain the extent to which each of the following losses is covered. (Assume there is no deductible.) If Paul's policy does not cover the loss, or inadequately covers any of these losses, show how full coverage can be obtained.

   a. Paul's coin collection, which is valued at $5000, is stolen from his home.

   b. Teenage vandals break into Paul's home and rip up a painting owned by Paul's wife. The painting is valued at $1000.

   c. A motorboat stored in the driveway of Paul's home is badly damaged during a hailstorm. The actual cash value of the damaged portion is $1000, and its replacement cost is $1500.

5. Pierre owns a home with an actual cash value of $200,000 that is subject to a $100,000 mortgage held by First Federal as the mortgagee. Pierre has

## CASE APPLICATION

Arturo and Phoebe are married and own a home insured for $150,000 under the HO-3 policy. The replacement cost of the home is $250,000. Personal property is insured for $75,000. Phoebe has jewelry and furs valued at $10,000. Arturo has a coin collection valued at $15,000 and a high-speed motorboat valued at $20,000.

a. Assume you are a risk management consultant who is asked to evaluate the above HO-3 policy. Based on the above facts, do you believe that their present coverages are adequate? If not, make several recommendations for improving the coverage.

b. A fire damaged one bedroom. The actual cash value of the loss is $10,000. The cost of repairs is $16,000. How much will the insurer pay for the loss?

c. A burglar broke into the home and stole a wide-screen television set, a VCR, and several paintings. The actual cash value of the stolen property is $4000. The cost of replacing the property is $9000. In addition, a stamp collection valued at $5000 was also taken. Indicate the extent, if any, to which an unendorsed HO-3 policy will cover the preceding losses.

d. Assume that Arturo and Phoebe have a disagreement with their insurer concerning the value of the above losses. How would the dispute be resolved under their HO-3 policy?

e. Assume that Phoebe operates an accounting business from her home. Her home business office contains a computer used solely for business, office furniture, file cabinets, and other business personal property. Explain whether her HO-3 policy would cover business personal property used in a home business.

the home insured for $160,000 under the HO-3 policy, and First Federal is named as mortgagee under the Mortgage Clause. Assume there is a covered fire loss to the dwelling in the amount of $50,000. To whom would the loss be paid? Explain your answer.

## SELECTED REFERENCES

*Fire, Casualty & Surety Bulletins,* Personal Lines Volume. Dwelling Section. Cincinnati: National Underwriter Company. The bulletins are published monthly.

Hamilton, Karen L., and Donald S. Malecki. *Personal Insurance: Property and Liability,* First edition. Malvern, Pa: American Institute for Chartered Property Casualty Underwriters, 1994, chapter 2.

"Homeowners Insurance," *Consumer Reports,* 58, no. 10 (October 1993): pp. 627–35.

*Policy Form & Manual Analysis Service.* Property Coverages, vol. 1. Homeowners Policy Program Section. Indianapolis: Rough Notes Company. The bulletins are published monthly.

Rejda, George E., Constance M. Luthardt, Cheryl L. Ferguson, and Donald R. Oakes. *Personal Insurance,* 3rd ed. Malvern, PA.: Insurance Institute of America, 1997.

## NOTES

1. The discussion of homeowners insurance in this chapter is based on the *Fire, Casualty & Surety Bulletins,* Personal Lines Volume, Dwelling Section (Cincinnati: National Underwriter Company); and the 1991 copyrighted homeowners forms and subsequent coverage modifications drafted by the Insurance Services Office (ISO). The ISO forms and various policy provisions are used with the permission of ISO.

# Chapter 8

# HOMEOWNERS INSURANCE, SECTION II

> *How to win in court: If the law is on your side, pound on the law; if the facts are on your side, pound on the facts; if neither is on your side, pound on the table.*
>
> *Unknown*

## Student Learning Objectives

After studying this chapter, you should be able to:

■ Identify the persons who are covered for personal liability insurance under Section II of the homeowners policy.

■ Explain the personal liability coverage found in Section II of the homeowners policy.

■ Explain the medical-payments-to-others coverage found in Section II of the homeowners policy.

■ Identify the major exclusions that apply to the Section II coverages in the homeowners policy.

■ Describe several liability endorsements that can be added to Section II of the homeowners policy.

■ Explain the important rules that consumers should follow when shopping for a homeowners policy.

This chapter continues the discussion of homeowners insurance by examining the important coverages that appear in Section II of the homeowners policy. Section II provides personal liability insurance to the named insured and family members and also covers the medical expenses of others who may be injured by some act of the insured or by an animal owned by the insured. Personal liability insurance is extremely important in a personal risk management program because a liability judgment for damages could result in a catastrophic loss. Also, legal defense costs can be enormous. With the major exceptions of legal liability arising out of the negligent operation of an automobile and business and professional liability, personal liability insurance will pay a liability judgment up to the policy limit. The policy also covers the cost of a legal defense.

This chapter clarifies the meaning of an insured under Section II; discusses the major coverages provided by personal liability insurance and medical-payments-to-others insurance; examines several optional endorsements that broaden the Section II coverages; and presents some important rules consumers should follow when shopping for a homeowners policy.

## PERSONAL LIABILITY INSURANCE

Personal liability insurance protects the named insured and family members for legal liability arising out of their personal acts. The insurer will provide a legal defense and pay out those sums the insured is legally obligated to pay up to the policy limits.[1]

### Persons Insured

Numerous persons are insured for personal liability under a homeowners policy. The policy covers the *named insured and spouse* if a resident of the same household. The policy also covers *family members* residing in the named insured's household. Children attending college who are temporarily away from home are insured under their parents' policy; other relatives must reside in the same household to be covered. *Other persons under age 21 in the care of an insured* are also covered if they reside in the same household, such as a foreign exchange student, a foster child, or a ward of the court. However, overnight guests are not covered.

The policy also covers *any person or organization legally responsible for covered animals or watercraft.* Thus, if you go on vacation and leave your dog with a neighbor, the neighbor is covered if your dog bites someone. However, the policy excludes coverage for a person or organization having custody of animals or watercraft for business purposes, such as an operator of a dog kennel or boat marina.

Finally, *with respect to any vehicle to which the insurance applies, employees of the insured are covered while working for the insured.* Thus, if a hired gardener injures someone while operating a tractor or riding mower, he or she is covered under the insured's policy.

### Insuring Agreements

The Section II liability coverages in the homeowners policy provide the following two coverages:

- Coverage E: Personal liability, $100,000 per occurrence
- Coverage F: Medical payments to others, $1000 per person

Higher limits are available with the payment of a small additional premium.

**Coverage E: Personal Liability** **Personal liability** *insurance protects the insured when a claim or suit for damages is brought because of bodily injury or property damage caused by the insured's negligence.* This means that if you are liable for damages, the insurer will pay up to the policy limits those sums that you are legally obligated to pay. Damages also include any prejudgment interest awarded against you.

The minimum amount of liability insurance is $100,000 for each occurrence. The insurance amount is a single limit that applies to both bodily injury and property damage liability on a per-occurrence basis. **Occurrence** *is defined as an accident, including continuous or repeated exposure to substantially the same general harmful conditions, which results in bodily injury or property damage during the policy period.* An occurrence can be a sudden accident, or it can be a gradual series of incidents that occur over time.

The insurer also agrees to provide a legal defense even if the suit is groundless, false, or fraudulent. The insurer has the right to investigate and settle the claim or suit by either defending you in a court of law or by settling out of court. As a practical matter, most personal liability suits are settled out of court. However, the insurer's obligation to defend you ends when the amount paid for damages from the occurrence equals the policy limits.

Personal liability coverage is broad. The liability insurance provided covers the personal activities of an insured anywhere in the world. The following examples illustrate the types of losses covered:

- While burning leaves in the yard, you accidentally set fire to your neighbor's house.
- You are playing golf and accidentally hit another golfer in the head with a golf ball.

- You are renting a motel room while on vacation and accidentally break a lamp.
- You carelessly run over another student with your ten-speed bicycle.
- A guest in your home trips on a torn carpet and sues you for bodily injury.
- You are shopping in an antique shop and carelessly break an expensive Chinese vase.

Personal liability insurance in Coverage E is based on legal liability and the law of negligence. Before the insurer will pay any sums for damages, you must be legally liable. In contrast, the next coverage discussed is not based on negligence and legal liability.

### Coverage F: Medical Payments to Others

This coverage is a mini-accident policy that is part of a homeowners policy. **Medical payments to others** *pays up to $1000 per person for the reasonable medical expenses of another person who is accidentally injured on an insured location, or by the activities of an insured, resident employee, or animal owned by or in the care of an insured.* This coverage can be illustrated by the following examples:

- A guest slips in your home and breaks an arm. Reasonable medical expenses are paid up to the policy limits.
- A neighbor's child falls off a swing in your backyard and is injured. The child's medical expenses are covered.
- Your dog bites a neighbor. The neighbor's medical expenses are paid up to the policy limits.

The insurer will pay all necessary medical expenses incurred or medically ascertained within three years from the date of the accident. The medical expenses covered are the reasonable charges for medical and surgical procedures, X-rays, dental care, ambulances, hospital stays, professional nursing, prosthetic devices, and funeral services.

Second, *medical payments coverage does not apply to you or to regular residents of your household, other than a residence employee.* For example, a swing set in your backyard may collapse, and your daughter and a neighbor's child are injured. Only the medical expenses of the neighbor's child are covered. An exception is a **residence employee** who is injured on the premises. For example, a baby sitter may burn her hand while cooking lunch for the

children. Her medical expenses would be covered under the policy.

Finally, *with respect to the medical expenses of others, the policy states the situations under which the benefits are paid.* Coverage F applies only to the following persons and situations:

- To a person on the insured location with the permission of an insured
- To a person off the insured location, if the bodily injury (a) arises out of a condition on the insured location or the ways immediately adjoining; (b) is caused by the activities of an insured; (c) is caused by a residence employee in the course of the residence employee's employment by an insured; or (d) is caused by an animal owned by or in the care of an insured

Medical payments to others covers the medical expenses of a person who is accidentally injured while on an insured location with the permission of an insured. Insured locations are defined in the policy and include the following:

- Residence premises shown in the declarations
- Any other residence acquired during the policy period, such as a summer home
- Nonowned premises where the insured is temporarily residing, such as a motel room
- Vacant land other than farmland
- Land owned or rented by an insured on which a residence is being built for an insured
- Cemetery plots or burial vaults
- Part of a premises occasionally rented to an insured for nonbusiness purposes, such as a hall rented for a wedding reception

Several important points are worth noting. *First, medical payments to others are not based on negligence and legal liability.* However, the insured is still protected if a lawsuit arises out of the injury. Thus, if your dog bites a child and $1000 of medical expenses are paid by your insurer, you are still insured under Coverage E if a lawsuit later results from the injury.

Second, medical payments to others covers injuries away from an insured location if the injury is caused by the activities of an insured, by a residence employee in the course of employment by an insured, or by an animal owned by or in the care of an insured. Thus, if you are playing recreational basketball and accidentally injure another player, the injured person's medical expenses would be paid by your policy up to the policy limit.

Finally, as noted earlier, liability loss exposures arising out of the personal activities of an insured are covered anywhere in the world under Coverage E and not just at an insured location. However, the meaning of an "insured location" becomes significant in determining whether medical payments to others are payable under Coverage F, and also in defining excluded activities at an insured location.

## SECTION II EXCLUSIONS

Three groups of exclusions appear in Section II. The first group applies to both personal liability and medical payments to others. The second group applies only to personal liability, while the third group applies only to medical payments to others.

### Personal Liability and Medical Payments Exclusions

Several exclusions apply to both personal liability (Coverage E) and medical payments to others (Coverage F).

**Intentional Injury** Bodily injury and property damage expected or intended by one or more insureds is excluded. For the exclusion to apply, the majority of courts have ruled that injury or damage must be expected or intended. Even though the act that causes injury or damage may be intentional, there must also be an intent to cause injury or damage, or an expectation that the act is likely to result in injury or damage. For example, if a softball player intentionally hits the umpire with a bat, it is clear that the player intended to injure the umpire. Thus, any claim or suit for damages would not be covered. Likewise, if you give your German shepherd dog a command to attack someone, coverage does not apply. Intentional acts that cause bodily injury or property damage are against the public interest and hence are properly excluded.

**Business Activities** Liability arising out of or in connection with a business activity engaged in by the insured is also excluded. For example, if you operate a beauty shop in your home and carelessly burn a customer with a hair dryer, a lawsuit by the customer is not covered. However, garage sales not conducted as a regular business are covered. Business activities, however, are clearly excluded (see Insight 8.1).

Legal liability arising out of the rental of any part of the premises is also excluded. For example, if you own a twelveplex apartment house that is rented to students, liability claims arising out of ownership of the apartment are not covered.

There are several exceptions to the preceding exclusion. First, if a house is occasionally rented and used only as a residence, coverage applies. For example, if a professor rents his or her home while on sabbatical leave, the liability coverages will still apply.

Coverage also applies if part of the residence is rented to others. For example, assume that you live in a duplex and rent the other unit to a single family. Liability coverage still applies if the renting family does not take in more than two roomers or boarders.

Coverage also applies if part of the insured residence is rented and used as an office, school, studio, or private garage. For example, if a room above a garage is rented to an artist who uses the room as a studio, the insured still has coverage for claims arising out of the rental.

**Professional Services** Legal liability arising out of professional services is excluded. Physicians and dentists are not covered for acts of malpractice under the homeowners policy. Also, attorneys, accountants, nurses, architects, engineers, and other professionals are not covered for legal liability for rendering or failing to render professional services. The loss exposures involving professional activities are substantially different from those faced by the typical homeowner. For this reason, a professional liability policy is necessary to cover professional activities. Professional liability insurance is examined in greater detail in Chapter 13.

**Uninsured Locations** Liability arising out of the ownership or rental of a premises that is not an "insured location" is also excluded. The meaning of an "insured location" has already been explained. Examples of uninsured locations would be farmland owned or rented by an insured, a principal or secondary residence owned by an insured other than the named insured or spouse, and land owned by the insured on which a fourplex is being built.

## INSIGHT 8.1

## Are You Insured If You Run a Business Out of Your Home?

Are you insured if you run a business out of your home? The homeowners policy clearly excludes liability arising out of business activity. But what exactly is a business activity? Despite the large number of court decisions, the legal opinions are not consistent. However, many courts generally agree that two criteria must be satisfied for the exclusion to apply: (1) continuity of the activity, and (2) monetary gain, or at least the hope of monetary gain in some courts. Courts that apply these two tests generally find that if the activity meets both requirements, it is a business activity even though it may not be the insured's full-time occupation. However, not all courts follow these two general rules.

- *Business in the home.* Many insureds operate a full-time business out of their homes, such as selling real estate, raising dogs, babysitting for pay, telephone solicitation, haircutting, or cosmetology. Liability exposures arising out of these business operations generally are not covered since the two tests referred to earlier are usually met. Also professional liability is excluded. Thus, physicians, dentists, attorneys, and other professionals who operate out of their homes are not covered for professional liability.
- *Hobbies.* Many insureds have hobbies that gradually evolve into a business liability exposure. These hobbies include photography, music, painting, ceramics, woodworking, or other activities. The insured may sell hobby items on a regular basis with the expectation of earning a profit or may receive income or fees from paid instruction on a regular

basis. Once again, the two tests of profit and continuity can be applied. If both tests are met, the business exclusion applies.

- *Youth employment.* Many youths work part time and earn income by delivering newspapers, babysitting, mowing lawns, shoveling snow, or other activities. Does the business exclusion apply to these activities? Once again, the various court decisions are inconsistent with respect to the business exclusion. As a general principle, part-time or casual work by youths would not be considered a business and, therefore, coverage would apply. Thus, if a teenager accidentally breaks a window while delivering newspapers, the loss would be covered. However, the part-time activity could become so extensive that it is considered a business. In one case, the court ruled that the business exclusion applied to a 15-year-old boy who operated a lawn-care business, devoted 20 to 25 hours a week to the business, adopted a trade name that was advertised in the local newspaper, and purchased several pieces of lawn-care equipment.[1] Thus, because of conflicting court decisions, you should check with your agent to determine if a particular business activity is likely to be excluded under a homeowners policy.

[1]*Hanover Insurance Co.* v. *Ransom,* 448 A.2d 399 (1982).

Source: Adapted from "The Business Pursuits Exclusion," Dwellings Section of *FC&S Bulletins,* Personal Lines volume, January 1996. Reprinted by permission of the National Underwriter Company.

**Motor Vehicles**    Liability arising out of the insured's ownership, maintenance, use, loading, or unloading of motor vehicles, motorized land conveyances, and trailers is also excluded. *Thus, liability arising from automobiles, trucks, motorcycles, mopeds, and motorbikes is not covered.* In addition, if you are towing a boat trailer, horse trailer, or rental trailer,

coverage does not apply. Coverage can be obtained by purchasing an auto insurance policy.

There is no coverage for liability arising out of the entrustment of an excluded vehicle or motorized land conveyance to any person. Finally, there is no coverage for vicarious parental liability, whether or not statutorily imposed, for the actions of a child or minor using an excluded motor vehicle or other motorized land vehicle.

The exclusion of motor vehicles and motorized land conveyances, however, does not apply to the following:

- *A trailer not being towed by or carried on a motorized land conveyance is covered.* For example, a utility trailer parked in the insured's driveway would be covered if it rolled into the street and injured someone.
- *A motorized land conveyance designed for recreational use off public roads and not subject to motor vehicle registration is covered if (a) it is not owned by an insured or (b) it is owned by the insured and on an insured location.* Thus, property damage caused by the insured while operating a rented snowmobile would be covered. Also, a snowmobile owned by the insured and used on an insured location would also be covered. An endorsement can be added to cover an owned snowmobile that is used away from an insured location.
- *A motorized golf cart when used to play golf on a golf course is also covered.* Thus, if you accidentally run over a golfer on the golf course, coverage applies. But if you live near a golf course and use the golf cart for transportation to the course, you are not covered if you injure someone.
- *A vehicle or conveyance not subject to motor vehicle registration is also covered if it is (a) used to service an insured residence, (b) designed for assisting the handicapped, or (c) in dead storage.* Thus, if you injure someone with a riding mower, the coverage applies. Also, if an insured injures someone while operating a motorized wheelchair, coverage applies. Likewise, a liability claim arising out of the dead storage of a car on an insured location is covered if the car is not subject to motor vehicle registration.

**Watercraft**   Section II coverages exclude liability arising out of the ownership, maintenance, use, loading, or unloading of certain watercraft and boats. The homeowners policy defines excluded watercraft by a generic exclusion, which is then followed by certain exceptions. Excluded watercraft are those principally designed to be propelled by engine power or electric motor, or are sailing vessels, whether owned by or rented to an insured. However, certain boats are exceptions to the preceding exclusion, and therefore, coverage applies.

The following boats, if not sailing vessels, are covered for both personal liability and medical payments to others:

- Boats not owned by an insured, with an inboard or inboard-outdrive engine or motor of 50 horsepower or less
- Boats not owned by or rented to an insured, with an inboard or inboard-outdrive engine or motor of more than 50 horsepower
- Boats with one or more outboard engines or motors of 25 total horsepower or less
- Boats with one or more outboard engines or motors of more than 25 horsepower, if the outboard engine or motor is not owned by an insured
- Boats with outboard engines or motors of more than 25 total horsepower if the insured (a) acquires them prior to the policy period and declares them at the policy inception, or (b) reports to the insurer within 45 days after acquiring the outboard engines or motors

The Section II coverages also apply to the following sailing vessels, with or without auxiliary power:

- Sail boats less than 26 feet in length
- Sail boats 26 feet or more in length not owned by or rented to an insured

**Aircraft**   Liability arising out of the ownership, maintenance, use, loading, or unloading of an aircraft is not covered. An aircraft is any device used or designed to carry people or cargo in flight, such as an airplane, helicopter, glider, or balloon. However, model or hobby aircraft not used or designed to carry people or cargo are not subject to the aircraft exclusion.

**War**   Section II coverages exclude war, undeclared war, civil war, insurrection, rebellion, and other hostile military acts. The homeowners contracts also exclude liability arising out of the discharge of a nuclear weapon even if accidental.

**Communicable Disease Exclusion**   Liability arising out of the transmission of a communicable disease by an insured is excluded under both personal liability insurance and medical payments to others. This exclusion is in response to the increased number of lawsuits by persons who claim they were infected with the AIDS or herpes virus as a result of sexual relations with the insured. However, the exclusion applies to all communicable diseases and is not limited only to sexually transmitted diseases.

**Sexual Molestation, Corporal Punishment, and Abuse Exclusion**    The homeowners policy excludes bodily injury or property damage liability arising out of sexual molestation, corporal punishment, or physical or mental abuse. For example, if an insured is sued because of bodily injury to a neighbor's child allegedly caused by sexual molestation, the suit would not be covered.

**Illegal Drugs Exclusion**    Liability arising out of the use, sale, manufacture, delivery, transfer, or possession of a controlled substance is specifically excluded. A controlled substance includes cocaine, LSD, marijuana, and all narcotic drugs. However, the exclusion does not apply to the legitimate use of prescription drugs by a person who is following the orders of a licensed physician.

## Personal Liability Exclusions

The second group of exclusions applies only to personal liability (Coverage E).

**Contractual Liability**    **Contractual liability** *means that you agree to assume the legal liability of another party by a written or oral contract.* The policy excludes the following contractual liability exposures:

- *Liability of an insured for any loss assessment* charged against the insured as a member of any association, corporation, or community of property owners. However, an additional coverage (discussed later) provides $1000 of coverage for a loss assessment if certain conditions are met.
- *Liability under any contract or agreement is excluded.* However, the exclusion does not apply to written contracts (a) that directly relate to the ownership, maintenance, or use of an insured location, or (b) where the liability of others is assumed by the insured prior to an occurrence.

Thus, there would be coverage for liability assumed under a written lease, an equipment rental agreement if the equipment is used to maintain the residence premises, an easement, and other written contracts where legal liability of a nonbusiness nature is assumed by an insured prior to an occurrence.

**Property Owned by the Insured**    *Property damage to property owned by the insured is also excluded.* Keep in mind that the definition of an insured excludes coverage not only for the named insured and spouse, but also for relatives residing in the household, and anyone under age 21 in the care of any insured. Thus, if a teenage son accidentally breaks some furniture, the parents' claim for damages against their son would not be covered.

**Property in the Care of the Insured**    *Damage to property rented to, occupied or used by, or in the care of the insured is not covered.* For example, if you rent a motel room and damage the furniture, your liability for the property damage is not covered.

The exclusion does not apply to property damage caused by fire, smoke, or explosion. For example, if you rent an apartment and carelessly start a fire, you can be held liable for the damage. In such a case the homeowners policy would cover the property damage to the apartment up to the policy limit.

**Workers Compensation**    *There is no coverage for bodily injury to any person who is eligible to receive benefits provided by the named insured under a workers compensation, nonoccupational disability, or occupational disease law.* This is true if the workers compensation benefits are either mandatory or voluntary. In some states, domestic workers must be covered for workers compensation benefits by their employers, while in other states, the coverage is voluntary.

**Nuclear Energy**    *The homeowners policy excludes liability arising out of nuclear energy.* If any insured is involved in a nuclear incident, any resulting liability is not covered by the homeowners policy.

**Body Injury to an Insured**    *There is no coverage for bodily injury to the named insured or to any resident of the household who is a relative or under age 21* *and in the care of an insured.* For example, if one spouse accidentally trips and injures the other spouse, the injured spouse cannot collect damages.

## Medical Payments Exclusions

The third group of exclusions under Section II applies only to medical payments to others (Coverage F).

**Injury to a Resident Employee Off an Insured Location**    *If an injury to a resident employee occurs off an insured location and does not arise out of or in the course of employment by an insured, medical payments coverage does not apply.* For example, if Tanya is employed by the insured as a babysitter and is injured on her way home, her medical expenses are not covered.

**Workers Compensation**    This is similar to the workers compensation exclusion discussed earlier under personal liability insurance. *Medical payments coverage does not apply to any person who is eligible to receive benefits provided by the named insured under a workers compensation, nonoccupational disability, or occupational disease law.* The injured employee's medical expenses should be covered by workers compensation insurance.

**Nuclear Energy**    Medical payments coverage does not cover any person for bodily injury that results from nuclear reaction, radiation, or radioactive contamination.

**Persons Regularly Residing on the Insured Location**    *Medical payments coverage does not cover injury to any person (other than a residence employee of an insured) who regularly resides on any part of the insured location.* Thus, a tenant injured in a household accident cannot receive payment for medical expenses. The intent here is to minimize collusion among household members.

## SECTION II ADDITIONAL COVERAGES

A homeowners policy also provides several additional coverages. They include coverage for claim expenses, first-aid expenses, damage to the property of others, and loss assessment charges.

## Claim Expenses

**Claim expenses** are paid as an additional coverage. The insurer pays the court costs, attorney fees, and other legal expenses incurred in providing a legal defense. The claim expenses are paid in addition to the policy limits for liability damages.

The insurer also pays the premiums on bonds required in a suit defended by the insurer. For example, a judgment may be appealed, and if an appeal bond is required, the insurer pays the premium.

Reasonable expenses incurred by the insured at the insurer's request to assist in the investigation and defense of a claim or suit are also paid. This obligation includes payment for the actual loss of earnings up to $50 per day. Finally, interest on a judgment that accrues after the judgment is awarded, but before payment is made, is also paid by the insurer.

## First-Aid Expenses

The insurer also pays any **first-aid expenses** incurred by the insured for bodily injury covered under the policy. For example, a guest may slip in your home and break a leg. If you call an ambulance to take the injured person to the hospital and are later billed for $300 by the ambulance company, this amount would be paid as a first-aid expense.

## Damage to Property of Others

**Damage to property of others** *pays up to $500 per occurrence for property damage caused by an insured.* The damaged property is valued on the basis of replacement cost. This coverage can be illustrated by the following examples:

- A son, age 10, accidentally breaks a neighbor's window while playing softball.
- At a party, you carelessly burn a hole in the owner's carpet with your cigarette.
- You borrow your neighbor's lawn mower and accidentally damage the blade by striking a rock.

The law of negligence does not apply to this coverage. Payment is made even though there is no legal obligation to do so. The purpose of this coverage is to preserve personal friendships and keep peace in the neighborhood. Also, in many states, the parents are held responsible for the property damage caused by a young child. If this coverage were not provided, the person whose property is damaged would have to file a claim for damages against the insured who caused the damage. Only a maximum of $500 is paid under this coverage. Amounts in excess of this limit are paid only by proving negligence and legal liability by the person who caused the damage.

Damage to property of others also contains a unique set of exclusions. The major exclusions are summarized as follows:

- *Property Covered Under Section I.* Property damage is excluded to the extent of any amount recoverable under Section I of the policy. The Section II coverages are coordinated with the Section I coverages so that they complement each other. For example, assume that you borrow an expensive camera, which has a replacement cost of $1500 and an actual cash value of $1250. If the camera is destroyed in a fire caused by your carelessness, the insurer would pay under Section I the actual cash value of $1250 less the $250 deductible, or $1000. Damage to the property of others under Section II would pay $500. Thus, the combination of both coverages would pay the full replacement cost of the destroyed camera, with no deductible.
- *Intentional Property Damage by an Insured, Age 13 or Older.* If the property damage is intentionally caused by an insured, age 13 or older, coverage does not apply. This exclusion is extremely relevant to teenage vandalism, which is a serious national problem. Thus, if a teenager damages a plate-glass window with a sling shot, deliberately knocks over a mailbox, or maliciously damages a tree, the parents' policy will not cover the property damage.
- *Property Owned by an Insured.* Property damage to property owned by an insured is also excluded. For example, if a son damages some power tools owned by his parents, the damage would not be covered. However, coverage does apply if the property is rented. Thus, if you rent a portable television set and accidentally drop it, the damage is covered. Likewise, if you rent a golf cart and damage it, the loss is covered.
- *Property Owned by or Rented to a Tenant.* Coverage does not apply to property owned by or rented to a tenant of an insured or to a resident in the named insured's household.
- *Business Liability.* Property damage arising out of a business engaged in by an insured is excluded. Thus, if you operate a lawn-maintenance business and accidentally cut down a shrub while mowing a customer's lawn, the damage is not covered.
- *Property Damage Due to an Act or Omission.* Property damage caused by an act or omission in connection with a premises owned, rented, or controlled by the insured, other than an insured location, is not covered. For example, without an endorsement, farmland owned by the insured is not covered under the homeowners policy. Thus, if the insured should accidentally damage the tractor of the tenant who is farming the land, the coverage does not apply.
- *Motor Vehicles, Aircraft, or Watercraft.* Property damage that results from the ownership, maintenance, or use of a motor vehicle, aircraft, or watercraft is not covered. For example, if you run over a neighbor's ten-speed bicycle with your automobile, the loss is not covered.

## Loss Assessment

The homeowners policy also provides coverage of $1000 for certain loss assessments. Higher limits are available by endorsement. For example, assume that you belong to a homeowners association that rents a hall for a monthly meeting. Someone is injured at one of the meetings, and is awarded a judgment of $110,000. If the association's liability policy has policy limits of only $100,000, the $10,000 balance will be split among the association members and each member would be assessed a portion of the $10,000 balance. The homeowners policy would pay your loss assessment charge up to $1000.

## ENDORSEMENTS TO SECTION II COVERAGES

Numerous endorsements can be added to a homeowners policy to broaden the Section II coverages. They include endorsements to cover business pursuits, personal injury, and watercraft and recreational vehicles.

## Business Pursuits

A **business pursuits endorsement** can be added to the homeowners policy to cover legal liability as a result of business activities in certain occupations. The endorsement is designed for office employees, sales representatives, messengers, collectors, and teachers. If an insured is engaged in any of these occupations and desires liability insurance covering business activities, the endorsement can be added to the policy.

## Personal Injury

The homeowners policy only covers legal liability arising out of bodily injury or property damage to someone else. Personal injury coverage, which should not be confused with bodily injury, can be added to the homeowners policy as an endorsement.

    **Personal injury** means legal liability arising out of the following:

- False arrest, detention or imprisonment, or malicious prosecution
- Libel, slander, or defamation of character
- Invasion of privacy, wrongful eviction, or wrongful entry

    For example, if you have a person arrested who is later found innocent, or if you make false statements that damage a person's reputation, you may be liable for damages. These losses are not covered under the homeowners policy but would be covered by the personal injury endorsement.

## Watercraft and Recreational Vehicles

As noted earlier, boats and recreational vehicles such as snowmobiles have specific limitations and exclusions under Section II of the homeowners policy. Separate endorsements can be added to provide additional liability coverages on boats and recreational vehicles.

- *Watercraft*. The **watercraft endorsement** covers watercraft otherwise excluded under the homeowners policy. The endorsement provides liability and medical payments coverage on any inboard or inboard-outdrive powered watercraft; sailing vessels 26 feet or more in length; and watercraft powered by one or more outboard motors exceeding 25 total horsepower.

- *Snowmobiles*. Snowmobiles owned by an insured are covered only while on an insured location. The **snowmobile endorsement** provides personal liability coverage and medical payments to owned snowmobiles away from an insured location. For example, if your snowmobile strikes and injures another person on a snowmobile trail in a public park, the loss would be covered.

## SHOPPING FOR A HOMEOWNERS POLICY

As an informed consumer, you should understand how the cost of a homeowners policy is determined. In addition, certain suggestions should be followed to make you a better-informed insurance consumer.

## Cost of Homeowners Insurance

Homeowner premiums are based on a number of factors, which include the following:

- Construction
- Location
- Fire-protection class
- Age of home
- Construction costs
- Type of policy
- Deductible amount
- Insurer

    First, *construction* of the home is extremely important in determining the rate paid. The more fire-resistant the home is, the lower the rate. Thus wooden homes generally cost 5 to 10 percent more to insure than brick homes. However, earthquake insurance costs are substantially less for wooden homes.

    Second, *location* of the home is another important rating factor. For rating purposes, the loss experience of each territory is determined. Insureds who reside in territories with high losses from fires, crime, or natural disasters must pay higher rates than insureds who reside in low-loss territories.

    Third, the *fire-protection class* affects the rates charged. The Insurance Services Office rates the quality of public fire departments from one to ten. The lower the score, the better the fire department and the lower the rate. Accessibility of the home to the fire department and water supply and hydrants are also important. Homes in rural areas generally have higher rates than homes in large cities.

In addition, *construction costs* have a significant impact on rates. The costs of labor and materials vary widely in the United States. The higher the cost of repairing or rebuilding your home, the higher your premium is likely to be.

The *age of the home* also affects the rates charged. Insurers may charge up to 20 percent less to insure newer homes than older ones, which are more susceptible to damage from fire and storms. Also, old wiring and outdated building code standards can make older homes more susceptible to loss.

The preceding rating factors deal with the home itself, which generally are outside of the insured's control. However, the remaining three factors—type of policy, deductible amount, and insurer—are important cost factors within the insured's control.

The *type of policy* is extremely important in determining the total premium. The Homeowners 3 policy (special form) is more expensive than the Homeowners 2 policy (broad form) because it provides broader coverage.

The *deductible amount* has an important impact on cost. The higher the deductible, the lower the premium. A flat $250 deductible now applies to all covered losses. The deductible can be increased with a reduction in premiums. The deductible does not apply to a fire department service charge, coverage for credit or ATM cards, scheduled property that is specifically insured, and the personal liability coverages under Section II.

Finally, the homeowner's *insurer* has a significant impact on the total premium. There is considerable price variation among property insurers, depending on loss experience, underwriting standards, and geographical area.

## Suggestions for Buying a Homeowners Policy

As a careful insurance consumer, you should remember the following suggestions when a homeowners policy is purchased:

- Carry adequate insurance.
- Add necessary endorsements.
- Shop around for a homeowners policy.
- Consider a higher deductible.
- Take advantage of discounts.
- Don't ignore natural disaster perils.
- Consider purchasing a personal umbrella policy for additional protection.

**Carry Adequate Insurance**   The first suggestion is to carry adequate amounts of property insurance on both your home and personal property. This is particularly important if a room is added or home improvements are made, since the value of the home may be substantially increased. The home must be insured to at least 80 percent of its replacement cost to avoid a penalty if a loss occurs. *However, you should seriously consider insuring your home to 100 percent of replacement cost.* Few homeowners can afford an additional 20 percent payment out of pocket if a total loss occurs. By adding the guaranteed replacement cost endorsement to the policy if it is available, full replacement cost will be paid even if the actual cost exceeds the policy limit.

**Add Necessary Endorsements**   Certain endorsements may be necessary depending on your needs, local property conditions, or high values for certain types of personal property. To deal with inflation, you should add an *inflation guard endorsement* to your homeowners policy if it is not included by your insurer. An *earthquake endorsement* is desirable if you live in an earthquake zone. The *personal property replacement cost endorsement* is also desirable because you are indemnified on the basis of replacement cost with no deduction for depreciation; the replacement cost endorsement provides for a more adequate loss payment if your personal property is damaged or stolen. In addition, if you own valuable property, such as jewelry, furs, fine art, or a valuable coin or stamp collection, you should add the *scheduled personal property endorsement* to your policy. Each item is listed and specifically insured for a certain amount.

**Shop Around for a Homeowners Policy**   Another important suggestion is to shop around for a homeowners policy. As we noted earlier, there is considerable price variation among insurers. *You can reduce your homeowners premium by shopping around.* Consequently, it pays to get a price quote from several insurers before you buy a homeowners policy. Some states publish shoppers' guides to assist consumers who purchase homeowners policies. These guides indicate wide variation in premiums charged by insurers. For example, Exhibit 8.1 shows the five lowest- and five highest-cost policies in Phoenix, Arizona as a result of a survey of 48 insurers by the Arizona Department of Insurance.

### Exhibit 8.1

## Homeowners 3 Premiums for Phoenix, Arizona

| | | Annual premium | |
|---|---|---|---|
| Rank | Name | Masonry | Frame |
| *Five lowest-cost policies* | | | |
| 1. Unisun Insurance Co. | | $328 | $328 |
| 2. United Services Automobile Assn. | | 335 | 372 |
| 3. Hartford Insurance Co. of the Midwest | | 363 | 386 |
| 4. Federated Mutual Insurance Co. | | 373 | 393 |
| 5. Bankers Standard Insurance Co. | | 379 | 399 |
| *Five highest-cost policies* | | | |
| 44. American Economy Insurance Co. | | $650 | $656 |
| 45. Grain Dealers Mutual Insurance Co. | | 684 | 684 |
| 46. American Spirit Insurance Co. | | 769 | 769 |
| 47. Sentry Ins. A Mutual Co. | | 781 | 805 |
| 48. Metropolitan Prop. & Cas. Insurance Co. | | 789 | 789 |

NOTE: Premiums are annual premiums based on the rates in effect 10/1/95. The hypothetical house is a one-story, single-family dwelling with 2200 square feet. The insurance limits are $115,000 on the dwelling, $57,500 on the contents, $11,500 for additional living expenses, $100,000 personal liability coverage, $2000 medical payments coverage, and a flat $250 deductible.

SOURCE: Arizona Department of Insurance.

**Consider a Higher Deductible** Another suggestion for reducing premiums is to purchase the policy with a higher deductible. The standard homeowners deductible is $250. *However, a higher deductible can substantially reduce your premiums.* You can usually get a discount of 10 percent with a $500 deductible and a 20 to 30 percent discount with a $1000 deductible. For example, Tom Beam has a $1000 deductible in his homeowners policy instead of the standard $250, which saves him $180 annually. In other words, Tom saves $180 each year but loses only $750 in coverage. That additional $750 is very expensive coverage.

**Take Advantage of Discounts** When you shop for a homeowners policy, you should inquire whether you are eligible for any discounts or credits, which can further reduce your premiums. Insurers offer a wide variety of discounts based on numerous factors, including age of the home, fire and smoke alarms, sprinkler system, deadbolt locks, and fire extinguishers (see Insight 8.2).

**Don't Ignore Natural Disaster Perils** Earthquakes, hurricanes, tornadoes, floods, and forest and grass fires can result in billions of dollars in property damage and thousands of deaths. In 1996, Hurricane Fran caused almost $1 billion in property damage in North Carolina, South Carolina, Virginia, and Maryland. In 1992, Hurricane Andrew caused billions of dollars in property damage and widespread personal hardship in South Florida and several other states. In 1995, severe floods in various parts of the United States caused substantial property damage to homes and other property. In early 1994, a severe earthquake in Northridge, California caused billions of property damage and the loss of numerous lives.

The homeowners policy covers hurricanes, tornadoes, windstorm, and fire losses. *However, earthquakes and floods are specifically excluded.* Although federal flood insurance is available, and an earthquake endorsement can be added to the homeowners policy, most property owners are not insured against these two perils. The major reasons for being uninsured are the high cost of coverage in high-risk areas, imposition of a substantial deductible, misperception by policyowners of the true probability of loss, and a mistaken belief that a loss will not occur. Although federal assistance is typically available after a natural disaster occurs, many property owners do not qualify for aid, or financial assistance is limited. If you reside in a flood or earthquake zone, you should seriously consider covering such perils in your personal risk management program.

**Consider Purchasing a Personal Umbrella Policy for Additional Protection**  A homeowners policy with minimum limits provides only $100,000 of personal liability insurance, which is insufficient in the event of a catastrophic liability loss. A **personal umbrella policy** can be purchased, which provides an additional $1 to $10 million of liability insurance after the underlying liability coverage under the homeowners policy is exhausted. A personal umbrella policy also covers liability arising out of personal injury, which includes coverage for libel, slander, and defamation of character. The homeowners policy does not cover this exposure without an endorsement. The personal umbrella policy also provides excess liability insurance on your cars, boats, and recreational vehicles. The personal umbrella is discussed in greater detail in Chapter 9.

Finally, in addition to cost, other factors should be considered when you buy a homeowners policy. These factors include the financial strength and reputation of the insurer, quality of the agent and services provided, policy limitations, and the claim practices of an insurer. With respect to the claim practices by insurers, a Consumers Union study of homeowners insurance can help you select the right insurer.[2] However, all other factors being equal, a low-cost policy is preferable to a high-cost policy.

## SUMMARY

- Section II of the homeowners policy protects the named insured, resident relatives, and other persons for legal liability arising out of their personal acts.

- Several groups of persons are insured under Section II of the homeowners policy. These include the named insured and spouse if a resident of the same household, resident relatives, other persons under age 21 in the care of an insured, persons or organizations responsible for the insured's animals or watercraft, and employees of an insured while operating a vehicle to which the insurance applies.

- Insured locations include the residence premises described in the declarations, other residences acquired during the policy period, a residence where the insured is temporarily residing, vacant land other than farmland, cemetery or burial plots, land on which a residence is being built, and occasional rental of a premise for other than business purposes.

- Personal liability insurance (Coverage E) protects the insured against a claim or suit for damages because of bodily injury or property damage caused by the insured's negligence. The company will defend the insured and pay out those sums that the insured is legally obligated to pay up to the policy limits.

- Medical payments to others (Coverage F) pays the reasonable medical expenses of another person who may be accidentally injured on the premises, or by the activities of an insured, resident employee, or animal owned by or in the care of an insured. It is not necessary to prove negligence and establish legal liability before the medical expenses are paid. The coverage does not apply to injuries of the named insured and regular residents of the household, other than residence employees.

- Section II also provides four additional coverages: (1) claim expenses, (2) first-aid expenses, (3) damage to property of others, and (4) coverage for a loss assessment charge.

- Several liability endorsements can be added to the homeowners policy that modify the Section II coverages. They include coverage for business activities, for personal injury, and for watercraft and recreational vehicles.

- The cost of a homeowners policy depends on numerous factors. These factors include construction, location, fire-protection class, age of the home, construction costs, type of policy, deductible amount, and insurer.

- Certain suggestions should be followed when shopping for a homeowners policy:

    Carry adequate insurance.

    Add necessary endorsements.

    Shop around for a homeowners policy.

Consider a higher deductible.

Take advantage of discounts.

Don't ignore natural disaster perils.

Consider purchasing a personal umbrella policy.

## KEY CONCEPTS AND TERMS

Business activities
Business pursuits
   endorsement
Claim expenses
Contractual liability
Damage to property of
   others
First-aid expenses
Intentional injury

Medical payments to
   others
Occurrence
Personal injury
Personal liability
Personal umbrella policy
Residence employee
Snowmobile endorsement
Watercraft endorsement

## QUESTIONS FOR REVIEW

1. Identify the people who can be an insured under Section II of the homeowners policy.

2. Does the homeowners policy provide personal liability coverage only at the residence described in the declarations? Explain.

3. Describe the coverage for personal liability (Coverage E) in Section II of the homeowners policy.

4. Describe the coverage for medical payments to others (Coverage F) in Section II of the homeowners policy.

5. Who are the persons covered for medical payments to others (Coverage F) in the homeowners policy?

6. List the exclusions that apply to the Section II coverages in the homeowners policy.

7. In addition to coverage for personal liability (Coverage E) and medical payments to others (Coverage F), several additional coverages are provided in Section II of the homeowners policy. Identify the additional coverages that are found in Section II.

8. Describe three endorsements that can be added to the Section II coverages in the homeowners policy.

9. Identify the major factors that determine the cost of a homeowners policy.

10. Explain briefly the suggestions that consumers should follow when shopping for a homeowners policy.

## QUESTIONS FOR DISCUSSION

1. Indicate whether the following losses are covered under Section II in the homeowners policy. Assume there are no special endorsements. Give reasons for your answers.

   a. The insured's dog bites a neighbor's child and also chews up the neighbor's coat.

   b. The insured accidentally injures another player while playing softball.

   c. A guest slips on a waxed kitchen floor and breaks an arm.

   d. A neighbor's child falls off a swing in the insured's yard and breaks an arm.

   e. The insured accidentally falls on an icy sidewalk and breaks a leg.

   f. The insured rents a lawnmower and damages the mower because of carelessness.

   g. While driving to the supermarket, the insured strikes another motorist with the automobile.

   h. A ward of the court, age 10, in the care of the insured, deliberately breaks a neighbor's window.

   i. The insured paints houses for a living. A can of paint accidentally falls on a customer's roof and discolors it.

   j. The insured falls asleep while smoking a cigarette, and a rented apartment is badly damaged by the fire.

   k. The insured borrows a camera, and it is stolen from a motel room while the insured is on vacation.

2. Joseph is the named insured under a Homeowners 3 policy (special form) with a liability limit of $100,000 per occurrence and $1000 medical payments. For each of the following situations, explain whether the loss is covered under Section II of Joseph's homeowners policy.

   a. Joseph is a self-employed accountant who works in his home. One of Joseph's clients sues him for negligence in preparing an incorrect financial statement and recovers a $3000 judgment against him.

   b. A maid who works for Joseph's wife falls from a ladder in the home and is injured. The maid incurs medical expenses of $1000. The maid sues Joseph for $10,000 alleging that his wife was negligent. The employer does not have workers compensation insurance.

   c. Joseph's 25-year-old son, who recently married and now lives in his own apartment, negligently killed another hunter in a hunting accident. The son is sued for $1 million in a wrongful-death accident.

3. Martha rents an apartment and is the named insured under a Homeowners 4 policy (contents broad form) with a liability limit of $100,000 per occurrence and $1000 medical payments. For each of the following situations, indicate to what extent, if any, the loss is

## CASE APPLICATION

Lucia and her husband, Geraldo, recently purchased a new home for $250,000. The home is insured under an HO-3 policy for $250,000 with no special endorsements attached. The home is located in an area where property values have increased steadily over the years. Lucia collects antiques for a hobby. Geraldo has a stamp collection that contains several rare stamps. The couple also owns a 30-foot sailboat that is used on weekends.

a. Assume you are a risk management consultant who has been asked to evaluate the couple's HO-3 policy. Identify three endorsements that Lucia and Geraldo may wish to purchase to modify their HO-3 policy.

b. Explain how the above HO-3 policy would be modified by each endorsement identified in your answer to (a) above.

c. For each of the following losses, indicate whether Section II of the homeowners policy would provide full coverage for the loss. If full coverage would not be provided, explain why.

1. Lucia entertained members of a local garden club in her home and served the guests a buffet luncheon. Two guests became seriously ill and sued Lucia, alleging she had served them contaminated food. The court awarded each guest damages of $60,000.

2. Geraldo is an architect. The roof of a new addition to a client's home collapsed. The client alleges that the roof collapsed because of Geraldo's faulty design. The cost of rebuilding is $40,000. The client seeks to recover that amount from Geraldo.

3. During a visit to a friend's home, Lucia accidentally broke a figurine that she picked up to admire. The figurine had a value of $475. The friend is seeking payment from Lucia.

covered under Section II of Martha's homeowners policy. Assume there are no special endorsements, and each situation is an independent event.

a. Martha is at a party at a friend's house. She accidentally burns a hole in the living room couch with her cigarette. It will cost $500 to repair the damaged couch.

b. Martha rents a snowmobile at a ski resort and accidentally collides with a skier. Martha is sued for $200,000 by the injured skier.

4. Personal liability insurance in a homeowners policy is written on an occurrence basis. Explain the meaning of an occurrence and give an illustration in your answer.

5. Explain whether each of the following losses would be covered under Section II in the homeowners policy. If the exposure is not covered, explain how coverage can be obtained.

a. The insured owns a restaurant in a large city. The insured is sued by several customers who allege they became seriously ill from a contaminated banana cream pie.

b. While operating a 30-foot sailboat, the insured injured a swimmer.

c. The insured's son, age 12, deliberately broke the windshield wiper on a neighbor's car.

d. The insured is sued by his ex-wife, who alleges her reputation has been ruined because the insured lied about her relationship with another man.

## SELECTED REFERENCES

*Fire, Casualty & Surety Bulletins.* Personal Lines volume. Dwelling section. Cincinnati, Ohio: National Underwriter Company. The bulletins are published monthly.

Hamilton, Karen L., and Donald S. Malecki. *Personal Insurance: Property and Liability,* First edition. Malvern, Pa: American Institute for Chartered Property Casualty Underwriters, 1994, Chapter 3.

"Homeowners Insurance." *Consumer Reports,* 58, no. 10 (October 1993): 627–35.

*Policy, Form & Manual Analysis Service.* Casualty Coverages volume, liability section. Indianapolis:

Rough Notes Company. The bulletins are published monthly.

Rejda, George E., Constance M. Luthardt, Cheryl L. Ferguson, and Donald R. Oakes. *Personal Insurance,* 3rd ed. Malvern, PA.: Insurance Institute of America, 1997.

## NOTES

1. The discussion of Section II liability coverages in this chapter is based largely on the *Fire, Casualty & Surety Bulletins,* Personal Lines volume, Dwelling section (Cincinnati: National Underwriter Company); and the 1991 copyrighted HO-3 policy and subsequent coverage modifications drafted by the Insurance Services Office (ISO). The HO-3 policy and various policy provisions are used with the permission of ISO.

2. "Homeowners Insurance," *Consumer Reports,* 58, no. 10 (October 1993): 627–35.

# Chapter 9

# OTHER PERSONAL PROPERTY AND LIABILITY COVERAGES

> " *Variety is the very spice of life.* "
>
> *William Cowper,*
> Olney Hymns *(1779)*

## Student Learning Objectives

After studying this chapter, you should be able to:

■ Describe the major forms that are used in the ISO dwelling program.

■ Explain how a mobilehome can be insured.

■ Identify the types of property that can be insured under the Personal Articles Floater.

■ Explain how recreational boats can be insured.

■ Explain the major provisions of the following government insurance programs:

    federal flood insurance

    FAIR plans

    federal crop insurance

■ Describe the basic characteristics of title insurance.

■ Explain the major characteristics of a personal umbrella policy.

In this chapter, we continue our discussion of property and liability insurance by examining several additional coverages that meet specific needs. The chapter emphasizes five major areas. The first part of the chapter discusses the Insurance Services Office (ISO) dwelling program, which is designed for dwellings that are ineligible for a homeowners policy and for property owners who do not want a homeowners policy. The second part discusses the coverages on mobile homes, recreational boats, and valuable personal property, such as jewelry and furs. The third part discusses certain government insurance programs, including flood insurance, FAIR plans, and crop insurance. The chapter also examines the basic characteristics of title insurance that protects property owners against loss because of a defective title. Finally, the chapter concludes with a discussion of the personal umbrella policy that provides considerable protection against a catastrophic personal liability lawsuit.

## ISO DWELLING PROGRAM

Although the majority of homeowners are insured under a homeowners policy, certain dwellings are ineligible for coverage under a homeowners policy. For example, if the home is not occupied by the owner but is rented to a tenant, the property owner is ineligible for a homeowners policy. Also, some property owners do not need a homeowners policy, or want a less costly policy. Most of these homes can be insured under a dwelling policy drafted by the Insurance Services Office (ISO).

The ISO dwelling forms are narrower in coverage than the current homeowners forms. One major difference is that the dwelling forms do not include coverage for theft or for personal liability insurance without appropriate endorsements. In contrast, the homeowners forms automatically include theft coverage and personal liability insurance as part of a package policy.

Three major dwelling forms are now used in the ISO dwelling program.[1]

- Dwelling Property 1 (basic form)
- Dwelling Property 2 (broad form)
- Dwelling Property 3 (special form)

### Dwelling Property 1 (Basic Form)

**Dwelling property 1 (basic form)** provides coverages similar to the homeowners policies discussed in Chapter 7. Coverage A insures the *dwelling* and structures attached to the dwelling. Loss to the dwelling is indemnified on a replacement cost basis.

Coverage B provides insurance on *other structures,* such as a detached garage or tool shed.

Coverage C insures *personal property* owned or used by the insured and residing family members; up to 10 percent of the insurance can be applied to cover personal property anywhere in the world.

Coverage D covers the *fair rental value* if a loss makes part of the dwelling rented to others or held for rental unfit for normal use. A maximum of 10 percent of the insurance on the dwelling can be applied to cover the loss of rents, subject to a maximum monthly limit of 1/12 of that 10 percent. For example, if the dwelling is insured for $60,000, a total of $6000 can be applied to cover the loss of rents, with a maximum monthly limit of $500.

Finally, Coverage E provides *additional living expense* coverage, which pays for the necessary increase in living expenses incurred by the named insured so that the household can maintain its normal standard of living.

The basic form provides coverage only for a limited number of perils that apply to both the dwelling and personal property. Coverage for the perils of fire, lightning, and internal explosion can be purchased alone. Coverage for vandalism and malicious mischief and the extended coverage perils can be added by payment of an additional premium. The *extended coverage perils* are windstorm or hail, explosion, riot or civil commotion, aircraft, vehicles, smoke, and volcanic eruption.

### Dwelling Property 2 (Broad Form)

**Dwelling property 2 (broad form)** provides broader coverage than the basic form. The broad form includes all of the perils listed in the basic form and adds additional perils. The additional perils are damage from burglars; falling objects; weight of ice, snow, or sleet; accidental discharge or overflow of water or steam; explosion of a steam or hot water heating system, air conditioning or automatic fire protective sprinkler system, or approved appliance for heating water; freezing of a plumbing, heating, air conditioning, or automatic fire protective system or household appliance; and sudden and accidental damage from an artificially generated electrical current.

### Dwelling Property 3 (Special Form)

**Dwelling property 3 (special form)** insures the dwelling and other structures against "risk of direct loss to property." All direct physical losses are covered except certain losses specifically excluded. However, personal property is covered for the same named perils found in the broad form discussed earlier.

### Endorsements to the Dwelling Program

Several endorsements can be added to a dwelling form, depending on the needs and desires of the property owner. They include *theft coverage,* which can be written on a limited or broad basis by an endorsement. Personal liability insurance is also available by adding a *personal liability supplement* to the policy, which provides personal liability insurance similar to the liability coverages found in the homeowners policy.

## MOBILEHOME INSURANCE

Many low-income and middle-income families cannot afford conventional housing. Thus, there is considerable interest in the less expensive forms of housing, such as mobilehomes.

Under the ISO program, **mobilehome insurance** is written by adding an endorsement to either a Homeowners 2 or Homeowners 3 policy, which tailors the homeowners policy to meet the special characteristics of mobilehomes. A number of specialty insurers also write a mobilehome insurance based on their own forms tailored to the mobilehome exposures. The following discussion of mobilehome insurance is based on the ISO program.[2]

### Eligibility

The mobilehome must be at least 10 feet wide and 40 feet long, be capable of being towed on its own chassis, and must be designed for year-round living. These requirements are imposed to eliminate coverage for camper trailers pulled by automobiles and insured under an automobile policy.

### Coverages

Coverages on a mobilehome are similar to those found in a homeowners policy. Coverage A insures mobilehomes on a *replacement cost basis*. Coverage A also insures floor coverings, household appliances, dressers, cabinets, and other built-in furniture when installed on a permanent basis. The policy also covers utility tanks and other structures attached to the mobilehome such as a carport or small storage shed.

Some mobilehomes have depreciated to the point where replacement cost coverage is inappropriate. In such cases, an optional actual cash value endorsement can be added. Under this endorsement, the insurer has the option of (1) paying the cost of repairs, (2) replacing the damaged property with similar property, but not necessarily from the same manufacturer, or (3) paying the amount in money. If paid in money, the insurer pays the lower of the difference in actual cash value before and after the loss or the cost to replace the property with similar property.

Coverage B insures other structures and is 10 percent of Coverage A, with a minimum limit of $2000. Coverage C insures unscheduled personal property and is limited to 40 percent of Coverage A. Coverage D provides for loss-of-use coverage and is 20 percent of the Coverage A limit.

An additional coverage pays up to $500 for the cost incurred in transporting the mobilehome to a safe place to avoid damage when it is endangered from a covered peril. No deductible applies to this coverage. The $500 limit can be increased to a higher limit by an endorsement.

Finally, Coverages E and F provide for comprehensive personal liability insurance and medical payments to others. This coverage is similar to the coverage provided in the homeowner contracts.

## INLAND MARINE FLOATERS

Many people own certain types of valuable personal property—such as jewelry, furs, and cameras—that are frequently moved from one location to another. This property can be insured by an appropriate inland marine floater. An **inland marine floater** *is a policy that provides broad and comprehensive protection on property that is frequently moved from one location to another.*

### Basic Characteristics of Inland Marine Floaters

Although inland marine floaters are not uniform, they have certain common characteristics:[3]

- *Coverage can be tailored to the specific type of personal property to be insured.* For example, under the personal articles floater, several types of property can be insured, such as jewelry, coins, or stamps. The insured can select the appropriate coverage needed.
- *Desired amounts of insurance can be selected.* The homeowners policy has several limits on personal

property. There is a $200 limit on money and coins, a $1000 limit on stamp collections, and a $2500 limit for the theft of silverware or goldware. Higher limits are available through a floater policy.

- *Broader and more comprehensive coverage can be obtained.* For example, the personal articles floater insures against risks of direct physical loss to covered property. This means that all direct physical losses are covered except those losses specifically excluded.
- *Most floaters cover insured property anywhere in the world.* However, fine arts usually are covered only within the United States.

## Personal Articles Floater

The **personal articles floater (PAF)** is the principal contract now used to provide comprehensive protection on valuable personal property.[4] The coverage also can be added as an endorsement to a homeowners policy. When written as a separate contract, the PAF insures certain optional classes of personal property on an "all-risks" basis. *All direct physical losses are covered except certain losses specifically excluded.*

The classes of personal property that can be covered include the following:

- *Jewelry.* Because of moral hazard, insurance on jewelry is carefully underwritten. Each item is described with a specific amount of insurance.
- *Furs.* Each item is listed separately with a specific amount of insurance.
- *Cameras.* Most photographic equipment can be covered under the PAF. Each item must be individually described and valued.
- *Musical instruments.* Musical instruments, cases, amplifying equipment, and similar articles can also be covered. Instruments played for pay are not covered unless an endorsement is added to the policy.
- *Silverware.* The PAF can also be written to cover silverware and goldware.
- *Golfer's equipment.* Golf clubs and equipment are covered anywhere in the world. Golfer's clothes in a locker are also covered when the insured is playing golf.
- *Fine arts.* Fine arts include paintings, etchings, lithographs, antique furniture, rare books, rare glass, bric-a-brac, and manuscripts. Coverage of fine arts is on a valued basis. The amount of insurance listed in the schedule for that item is the amount paid for a loss.
- *Stamp and coin collections.* Stamp and coin collections can be insured on a *blanket basis;* the stamps or coins are not described, and the insurance applies to the entire collection. The amount paid is the cash market value at the time of loss, with a $1000 maximum limit on any unscheduled coin collection and a $250 maximum limit on any single stamp or coin. However, if the stamps or coins are valuable, they can be individually *scheduled.* In case of loss to a scheduled item, the amount paid is the lowest of actual cash value, reasonable cost of repairs, replacement cost, or amount of insurance.

## Scheduled Personal Property Endorsement

Coverage provided by a personal articles floater can be added to a homeowners policy by use of the **scheduled personal property endorsement (HO-61).** The endorsement provides essentially the same coverages provided by the free-standing personal articles floater.

## INSURANCE ON PLEASURE BOATS

Millions of Americans own or operate boats for pleasure and recreation. However, the homeowners policy provides only limited coverage of boats. Coverage on a boat, its equipment, and boat trailer is limited to $1000. Direct loss from windstorm or hail is covered only if the boat is inside a fully enclosed building. Theft of the boat or its equipment away from the premises is excluded. Also, boats are covered only against a limited number of named perils (broad form perils), and more comprehensive protection may be desired. Finally, legal liability arising out of the operation on ownership of larger boats is not covered under the homeowners policy. For these reasons, boat owners often purchase separate insurance contracts that provide broader protection.[5]

Insurance on recreational boats generally can be divided into two categories:

- Boat owners package policy
- Yacht insurance

## Boat Owners Package Policy

Many insurers have designed a **boat owners package policy** that combines physical damage insurance on the boat, medical expense insurance, liability insurance, and other coverages into one policy. Although the package policies are not uniform, they have certain common characteristics.

**Physical Damage Coverage**   A boat owners policy provides physical damage insurance on the boat on an "all-risks" basis. All direct physical losses are covered except certain losses specifically excluded. Thus, if the boat collides with another boat, is stranded on a reef, or is damaged by heavy winds, the loss is covered. Certain exclusions apply, including wear and tear, gradual deterioration, mechanical breakdown, using the boat for commercial purposes, and using the boat (except sailboats in some policies) in any race or speed contest.

**Liability Coverage**   The insured is covered for property damage and bodily injury liability arising out of the negligent ownership or operation of the boat. For example, if an operator carelessly damages another boat, swamps another boat, or accidentally injures some swimmers, the loss is covered. Certain exclusions apply, including intentional injury, using the boat for commercial purposes, and using the boat (sailboats sometimes excepted) in any race or speed test.

**Medical Expense Coverage**   This coverage is similar to that found in auto insurance contracts. The coverage pays the reasonable and necessary medical expenses of a covered person who is injured while in the boat or while boarding or leaving the boat. Most policies impose a time limit of one to three years during which time the medical expenses must be incurred. In addition, many boat owners policies also cover the medical expenses of waterskiers who are injured while being towed. If not covered, coverage can be obtained by an endorsement to the policy.

**Uninsured Boaters Coverage**   Some boat owners policies have an optional uninsured boaters coverage for bodily injury caused by an uninsured boater, which is similar to the uninsured motorists coverage in auto insurance.

## Yacht Insurance

**Yacht insurance** is designed for larger boats, such as cabin cruisers, inboard motorboats, and sailboats over 26 feet in length. Yacht policies are not standard, but certain coverages typically appear in all policies. The following section summarizes the major provisions of a yacht policy of one insurer.

**Property Damage**   This coverage insures the yacht and its equipment for property damage on an "all-risks" basis. The policy covers accidental direct physical loss or damage to the yacht except certain losses specifically excluded. Coverage applies to the yacht, spars, sails, machinery, furniture, dinghies, outboard motors, and other equipment. Thus, if the yacht is damaged or sinks because of heavy seas, high winds, or collision with another vessel, the loss is covered. Exclusions include wear and tear; weathering; damage from insects, mold, animals, and marine life; marring, scratching, denting, and blistering; and manufacturer's defects. A deductible applies to property damage losses.

**Liability Coverage**   Liability coverage insures the legal liability of an insured arising out of the ownership, operation, or maintenance of the yacht. For example, collision with another boat or damage to a dock or marina would be covered. The coverage also includes the cost of raising, removing, or destroying a sunken or wrecked yacht. In addition, legal liability to a paid crew as defined in the Jones Act or under general Maritime law is also covered.

**Medical Payments Coverage**   This coverage pays for necessary and reasonable medical expenses because of accidental bodily injury. Covered expenses include medical, hospital, ambulance, professional nursing, and funeral costs incurred within one year of the accident. Coverage applies only to people who are injured while in or upon the yacht or while boarding or leaving the yacht. Employees are not covered.

**Uninsured Boater**   This coverage pays the bodily injury damages up to the policy limit that the insured is legally entitled to recover from an uninsured owner or operator of another yacht.

**Other Coverages** Other available coverages include possible legal liability incurred by the insured to maritime workers covered under the United States Longshoremen and Harbor Workers Compensation Act who are injured in the course of employment; physical damage insurance on a yacht trailer listed in the declarations; and coverage for personal property while aboard the yacht.

## FEDERAL PROPERTY INSURANCE PROGRAMS

Federal insurance programs are often necessary because certain perils are difficult to insure privately, and coverage may not be available at affordable premiums from private insurers. Three government insurance programs merit a brief discussion:

- Federal flood insurance
- FAIR plans
- Federal crop insurance

### Federal Flood Insurance

Buildings in flood zones are difficult to insure privately because the requirements of an insurable risk discussed in Chapter 2 are not easily met. The exposure units in flood zones are not independent of each other, and the potential for a catastrophic loss is present. Thus, premiums for property insurance in flood-prone areas would be too high for most insureds to pay. Also, adverse selection is a problem since only property owners in flood zones are likely to seek protection. For these reasons, financial assistance from the federal government is needed.

The **National Flood Insurance Program** was created by the National Flood Insurance Act of 1968.[6] *The purpose of the act is to provide flood insurance at subsidized rates to persons in flood zones.* Flood insurance is now available in all states, the District of Columbia, Puerto Rico, and the Virgin Islands. Flood insurance can be purchased from agents and brokers who represent private insurers. Agents or brokers who are not affiliated with private insurers can write federal flood insurance directly with the National Flood Insurance Program (NFIP).

Federal law requires individuals to purchase flood insurance if they have federal guaranteed financing to build, buy, refinance, or repair structures located in special flood zones in the participating community. This includes FHA and VA loans as well as most conventional mortgage loans.

**Write-Your-Own Program** In 1983, the federal government enacted a *write-your-own program* to encourage private insurers to write flood insurance with financial assistance from the federal government. Under the write-your-own program, private insurers sell federal flood insurance under their own names, collect the premiums, retain a specified percentage for operating expenses and commissions, and invest the remainder. The insurers service the policies and pay all claims. If the insurers' losses exceed premiums and investment income, they are reimbursed by the federal government for the difference. However, any profits go to the federal government.

**Eligibility Requirements** Most buildings and their contents can be covered by flood insurance if the community agrees to adopt and enforce sound flood control and land use measures.

When a community joins the program, it is provided with a flood hazard boundary map that shows the general area of flood losses, and residents are allowed to purchase limited amounts of insurance at subsidized rates under the emergency portion of the program.

A flood insurance rate map is then prepared that divides the community into specific zones to determine the probability of flooding in each zone. When this map is prepared, and the community agrees to adopt more stringent flood control and land use measures, the community enters the regular phase of the program. Higher amounts of flood insurance can then be purchased.

**Definition of Flood** **Flood** is defined as a general and temporary condition of partial or complete inundation of normally dry areas from (1) the overflow of inland or tidal waters, (2) the unusual and rapid accumulation of runoff or surface waters from any source, and (3) mudslides that are proximately caused by flooding. Thus, flood damage caused by an overflow of rivers, streams, or other bodies of water, by abnormally high waves, or by severe storms is covered. Mudslide damage is also covered if the mudslide is caused by the accumulation of water on the earth's surface or under the ground.

**Amounts of Insurance**  Under the *emergency program,* maximum coverage on single-family dwellings is limited to $35,000 on the building and $10,000 on the contents. For other residential and non-residential buildings, maximum coverage is limited to $100,000 on the building and $100,000 on the contents (see Exhibit 9.1).

Under the *regular* program, maximum coverage on single-family dwellings is limited to $250,000 on the building and $100,000 on the contents. Commercial structures can be insured up to a limit of $500,000 on the building and $500,000 on the contents (see Exhibit 9.2).

The insured is required to carry insurance equal to 80 percent of the replacement cost of the dwelling or the maximum amount of insurance available, whichever is less. If this requirement is met, the cost to replace or repair the property is paid up to the policy limit with no deduction for depreciation.

**Deductible**  A $500 deductible applies separately to both the building and contents. Higher deductibles up to $5000 are available with a saving in premiums.

**Premiums**  Because the rates are subsidized, the cost of the protection is relatively low. In low- to moderate-risk areas, coverage is available for as little as $85 per year. In high-risk areas, the average premium is about $300 per year.

The public is often confused about the availability of federal flood insurance and coverages under the program. Insight 9.1 discusses some common myths about the program.

## FAIR Plans

During the 1960s, major riots occurred in many cities in the United States, resulting in millions of dollars in property damage. Subsequently, many property owners in riot-prone areas were unable to obtain property insurance at affordable premiums. This problem resulted in the creation of **FAIR plans** (Fair Access to Insurance Requirements), which were enacted into law as a result of the Urban Property and Reinsurance Act of 1968. *The basic purpose of a FAIR plan is to make property insurance available to urban property owners who are unable to obtain coverage in the normal markets.* FAIR plans

**EXHIBIT 9.1**

**Emergency Program Flood Insurance Coverages**

**Buildings**

| | |
|---|---|
| Single Family | $ 35,000 |
| Other Residential | 100,000 |
| Non-residential | 100,000 |

**Contents**

| | |
|---|---|
| Residential | $ 10,000 |
| Non-residential | 100,000 |

SOURCE: Federal Emergency Management Agency.

typically provide coverage for fire and extended-coverage insurance, vandalism, malicious mischief, and, in a few states, crime insurance and sprinkler leakage. FAIR plans have been established in 31 states and the District of Columbia. In addition, beach and windstorm plans operate in seven states along the Atlantic and Gulf Coast seaboard where property is highly vulnerable to damage from severe windstorms and hurricanes.[7]

Each state with a FAIR plan has a pool or syndicate that provides basic property insurance to persons who cannot obtain insurance in the regular markets. The pools or syndicates are operated by private insurers. Each insurer in the pool or syndicate is assessed its proportionate share of losses and expenses based on the proportion of property insurance premiums written in the state.

Before a building can be insured, it must first be inspected. If it meets certain underwriting standards, a policy is issued. If the building is substandard, it may still be insurable at substantially higher premiums. In some cases, certain improvements to the building must be made before the policy is issued. Finally, insurance may be denied if the condition of the building makes it uninsurable. If the insurance is denied, the applicant must be informed of the reasons the property cannot be insured.

FAIR plans are highly controversial. Critics argue FAIR plans are no longer needed and should be phased out, since the social threat of widespread riot losses has subsided. Also, some critics charge that property insurers have used the FAIR plans to rid themselves of undesirable business, such as bowling alleys, bars, restaurants, and property subject to brush fires in certain areas, such as California.

EXHIBIT 9.2

**Regular Program Flood Insurance Coverages**

| | Basic insurance limits | Additional insurance limits | Total insurance available |
|---|---|---|---|
| **Building Coverage** | | | |
| Single Family Dwelling | $ 50,000 / | $200,000 | $250,000 |
| 2–4 Family Dwelling | $ 50,000 / | $200,000 | $250,000 |
| Other Residential | $135,000 / | $115,000 | $250,000 |
| Non-residential or Small Business | $135,000 / | $365,000 | $500,000 |
| **Contents Coverage (per unit)** | | | |
| Residential | $ 15,000 / | $ 85,000 | $100,000 |
| Non-residential or Small Business | $115,000 / | $385,000 | $500,000 |

SOURCE: Federal Emergency Management Agency.

Critics also argue that the subsidized rates under California's FAIR plan encourage property owners to buy expensive homes in areas where brush fires frequently occur. As a result, the taxpayers must pay the cost of bailing out wealthy people whose homes are damaged or destroyed by brush fires. In rebuttal, property insurers maintain that FAIR plan premiums are inadequate, that sizeable underwriting losses have been incurred since the plans began operating, and that arson-for-profit claims have increased.

## Federal Crop Insurance

Many farmers desire crop insurance that provides protection against adverse weather conditions and other perils that damage crops. Federal crop insurance provides coverage for unavoidable crop losses, such as hail, wind, excessive rain, drought, and plant disease.

Congress has changed the federal crop insurance program several times over the years. The most recent change resulted in enactment of the Federal Crop Insurance Reform Act of 1994. Two basic coverages are presently available: (1) catastrophic crop insurance, and (2) multiple peril crop insurance.

Federal law requires farmers who wish to be eligible for federal farm benefits to purchase catastrophic crop insurance. The insurance provides producers with a financial safety net against the risk of a major crop loss. **Catastrophic crop insurance** *guarantees 50 percent of the producer's average yield for each insured crop; the indemnity payment is 60 percent of the expected market price for that crop.* If a producer has production records for the most recent four or more years, the yield guarantee will be 50 percent of the simple average yield for those years.

Example: The producer's average corn yield is 100 bushels per acre. The yield guarantee is 50 bushels per acre, and the expected market price for corn is $2.50 a bushel. Assume that the actual yield is 30 bushels per acre. The indemnity payment for the loss of 20 bushels per acre is $30 per acre (60% × $2.50 × 20).

The cost to the producer for catastrophic crop insurance is an annual processing fee of $50 per crop per county, up to a maximum of $200 per county.

Producers can obtain additional protection by purchasing a multiple-peril crop insurance policy from private insurers that *includes and adds* to the coverage provided by catastrophic insurance. **Multiple-peril crop insurance** *offers producers a choice of a 65 percent or a 75 percent yield guarantee, and producers can elect to be paid up to 100 percent of the expected market price.* Producers who purchase a multiple peril policy with a 65 percent or 75 percent yield guarantee are not required to buy a separate catastrophic crop insurance policy.

## INSIGHT 9.1

## Myths About the National Flood Insurance Program

To clear up misconceptions about Federal flood insurance, the National Flood Insurance Program (NFIP) has compiled the following list of common myths about the program.

1. **Myth: You can't buy flood insurance if you are located in a high-risk flood area.**

   **Fact:** You can buy Federal flood insurance no matter where you live if your community belongs to the NFIP, except in Coastal Barrier Resources System (CBRS) areas. The Program was created in 1968 to provide affordable flood insurance to people who live in areas with the greatest risk of flooding, called Special Flood Hazard Areas (SFHAs). In fact, under the National Flood Insurance Act, lenders must require borrowers whose property is located within an SFHA to purchase flood insurance as a condition of receiving a Federally backed mortgage loan. There is an exemption for conventional loans on properties within CBRS areas.

2. **Myth: You can't buy flood insurance immediately before or during a flood.**

   **Fact:** You can purchase flood coverage at any time. There is a 30-day waiting period after you've applied and paid the premium before the policy is effective, with the following exceptions: 1) If the initial purchase of flood insurance is in connection with the making, increasing, extending or renewing of a loan, there is no waiting period. The coverage becomes effective at the time of the loan, provided application and presentment of premium is made at or prior to loan closing. 2) If the initial purchase of flood insurance is made during the 13-month period following the effective date of a revised flood map for a community, there is a one-day waiting period.

   The policy does not cover a "loss in progress," defined by the NFIP as a loss occurring as of 12:01 a.m. on the first day of the policy term. In addition, you cannot increase the amount of insurance coverage you have during a loss in progress.

3. **Myth: Flood insurance is only available for homeowners.**

   **Fact:** Flood insurance is available to protect homes, condominiums, apartments and nonresidential buildings, including commercial structures.

4. **Myth: You can't buy flood insurance if your property has been flooded.**

   Fact: It doesn't matter how many times your home, apartment or business has flooded. You are still eligible to purchase flood insurance, provided that your community is participating in the NFIP.

5. **Myth: Only residents of high-risk flood zones need to insure their property.**

   **Fact:** Even if you live in an area that is not flood-prone, it's advisable to have flood insurance. Between 25 percent and 30 percent of NFIP's claims come from outside high-risk flood areas. The NFIP's low-cost policy, available for as little as $85 per year, is designed for residential properties located in low- to moderate-flood risk zones.

6. **Myth: The NFIP does not offer any type of basement coverage.**

   **Fact:** Yes it does. The NFIP defines a basement as any area of a building with a floor that is subgrade, or below ground level on all sides. Under NFIP building coverage, basements are insured for cleanup and items used to service the building, such as furnaces, hot-water heaters, air conditioners, utility connections, circuit breaker boxes, pumps and tanks used in solar energy systems, as well as the repair of structural damage to basement walls. Items in basements insured under NFIP contents coverage include clothes washers and dryers, and food freezers and the food in them. Improve-

*Continued*

## TITLE INSURANCE

Discussion of property insurance coverages would not be complete without a brief description of title insurance on the home. **Title insurance** *protects the owner of property or the lender of money against any*

*unknown defects in the title to the property under consideration.*[8] Defects to a clear title can result from an invalid will, incorrect description of the property, defective probate of a will, undisclosed liens, easements, and numerous other legal defects that occurred sometime in the past. In particular, the

ments to a basement, such as finished walls, floors, or ceilings, as well as personal belongings located in a basement, are not covered in either NFIP building or contents coverage.

7. **Myth: Federal disaster assistance will pay for flood damage.**

   **Fact:** Federal disaster assistance declarations are awarded in less than 50 percent of flooding incidents. The premium for an NFIP policy, averaging about $300 a year, is less expensive than interest on Federal disaster loans, even though they are always granted on favorable terms.

   Furthermore, if you are uninsured and receive Federal disaster assistance after a flood, you must purchase flood insurance to receive disaster relief in the future.

8. **Myth: The NFIP encourages coastal development.**

   **Fact:** One of the NFIP's primary objectives is to guide development away from high-risk flood areas. NFIP regulations minimize the impact of structures that are built in SFHAs by requiring them not to cause obstructions to the natural flow of floodwaters. Also, as a condition of community participation in the NFIP, those structures built within SFHAs must adhere to strict floodplain management regulations.

   In addition, the Coastal Barrier Resources Act (CBRA) of 1982 relies on the NFIP to discourage building in the fragile coastal areas covered by CBRA by prohibiting the sale of flood insurance in designated CBRA areas. These laws do not prohibit property owners from building along coastal areas; however, they do transfer the financial risk of such building from federal taxpayers to those who choose to live or invest in these areas.

9. **Myth: The NFIP does not cover flooding resulting from hurricanes or the overflow of rivers or tidal waters.**

   **Fact:** The NFIP defines covered flooding as a general and temporary condition during which the surface of normally dry land is partially or completely inundated. Two adjacent properties or two or more acres must be affected. Flooding can be caused by any one of the following:
   - The overflow of inland or tidal waters.
   - The unusual and rapid accumulation or runoff of surface waters from any source, such as heavy rainfall.
   - The incidence of mudslides or mudflows, caused by flooding, which are comparable to a river of liquid and flowing mud.
   - The collapse or destabilization of land along the shore of a lake or other body of water, resulting from erosion or the effect of waves, or water currents exceeding normal cyclical levels.

10. **Myth: Wind-driven rain is considered flooding.**

    **Fact:** No it isn't. Rain entering through wind-damaged windows, doors or a hole in a wall or the roof, resulting in standing water or puddles, is considered windstorm, rather than flood damage. Federal flood insurance only covers damage caused by the general condition of flooding (defined above), typically caused by storm surge, wave wash, tidal waves, or the overflow of any body of water above normal, cyclical levels. Buildings that sustain this type of damage usually have a watermark, showing how high the water has risen before it subsides. Although the Standard Flood Insurance Policy (SFIP) specifically excludes wind and hail coverage, most homeowners' policies provide coverage.

SOURCE: Adaptation of "Myths and Facts About the NFIP," National Flood Insurance Program, Federal Emergency Management Agency, May 1996.

problem of a forged title has increased in recent years. Without a clear title, the owner could lose the property to someone with a superior claim, or incur other losses because of an unknown lien, unmarketability of the title, and attorney expenses. Title insurance is designed to provide protection against these losses.

Any liens, encumbrances, or easements against real estate are normally recorded in a courthouse in the area where the property is located. This information is recorded in a legal document known as an abstract, which is a history of ownership and title to the property. When real estate is purchased, the purchaser may hire an attorney to search the abstract to determine if there are any defects to a clear title to the property. However, the purchaser is not fully protected by this method, since there may be an unknown lien, encumbrance, or other title defect not recorded in the abstract. The owner could still incur a loss despite a diligent and careful title search. Thus, the owner needs a stronger guarantee that he or she will be indemnified if a loss occurs. Title insurance can provide that guarantee (see Insight 9.2).

Title insurance policies have certain characteristics that distinguish them from other contracts.

- *The policy provides protection against title defects that have occurred in the past, prior to the effective date of the policy.*
- *The policy is written by the insurer based on the assumption that no losses will occur.* Any known title defects or facts that have a bearing on the title are listed in the policy and excluded from coverage.
- *The premium is paid only once when the policy is issued.* No additional premiums are required even though the policy term runs indefinitely in the future.
- *The policy term runs indefinitely in the future.* As long as the title defect occurred before the issue date of the policy, any insured loss is covered no matter when it is discovered in the future.
- *If a loss occurs, the insured is indemnified in dollar amounts up to the policy limits.* The policy does not guarantee possession by the owner, removal of any title defects, or a legal remedy against known defects.

In addition, the policy limit is usually the purchase price of the house. If the house appreciates in value over the years, the homeowner could be underinsured at the time of loss. This is especially true in those areas where inflation in housing prices is occurring.

## PERSONAL UMBRELLA POLICY

Personal liability claims occasionally reach catastrophic levels and exceed the liability limits of the basic contracts (homeowners and automobile insurance). After these basic limits are exhausted, you may be required to pay thousands of dollars from your personal assets. This is particularly important for insureds who have accumulated sizable amounts of financial assets. However, you should not assume that only wealthy people need protection against catastrophic lawsuits. Because of the increased frequency and severity of lawsuits, most people also need catastrophic protection. For example, some common occurrences that can result in a catastrophic judgment include a chain-reaction collision accident on an icy highway where several people are injured or killed; a boating accident in which a boat is swamped by another boat and several people are injured or drown; or a defamation of character lawsuit by someone who alleges that his or her reputation is ruined.

The **personal umbrella policy** *is designed to provide protection against a catastrophic lawsuit or judgment.* Most insurers write this coverage in amounts ranging from $1 million to $10 million. Coverage is broad and typically includes coverage for catastrophic liability exposures associated with the home, boats, cars, recreational vehicles, and sports.

## Basic Characteristics

Although personal umbrella policies are not standard contracts, they contain several common characteristics, summarized as follows:[9]

- The umbrella policy provides excess liability insurance over basic underlying contracts.
- Coverage is broad and includes protection against certain losses not covered by the underlying contracts.
- A self-insured retention must be met for certain losses covered by the umbrella policy but not covered by any underlying contract.
- The umbrella policy is reasonable in cost.

**Excess Liability Insurance** *The personal umbrella policy provides excess insurance over any basic underlying insurance that may apply.* The umbrella policy pays only after the basic limits of the underlying contracts are exhausted. The insured is required to carry certain minimum amounts of liability insurance on the underlying contracts. Although the required amounts of underlying insurance vary among insurers, the amounts shown in Exhibit 9.3 are typical. If the required amounts of underlying

## INSIGHT 9.2

# How Much Do You Know About Title Insurance?

Title insurance protects rights that homeowners may not know they have, title insurance companies say.

While a home may be the biggest investment many people make, some don't realize the extent of their rights as homeowners.

Title insurance, issued after an investigation of the property's previous ownership, protects the current owner's legal rights to a home in much the same way that homeowner's insurance protects the property and its contents, experts said.

Although lenders require both homeowner's and title insurance to protect their interests when a home is purchased, a home sale not involving a lender can be made without title insurance. However, examples are rare.

"Title insurance is issued for 97 percent to 98 percent of homes sold," said Pat Mealey, escrow closer for Classic Title & Escrow Co. in Omaha. "I've only had one home in the past two years that has sold without title insurance."

Title insurance can be purchased in Nebraska for any property. Title insurance can be purchased for property in Iowa, but state law prevents it from being sold in Iowa. As a result, title insurance for property in Iowa is purchased from companies in other states.

The cost of title insurance for lender and homeowner is about $290 for a $50,000 home and $440 for a $100,000 home. Those amounts cover both lender and homeowner.

### How Much Do You Know About Title Insurance?

The following quiz is designed to test your awareness of what could be lost if your home does not have title insurance.

1. Lenders protect their financial interests by making title insurance a loan policy to home buyers. This policy . . .
   A. Fully covers the home purchaser's interest.
   B. Covers one-half of the home purchaser's interest.
   C. Covers an amount of the home purchaser's interest that is negotiated by the lender and purchaser.
   D. Does not cover any part of the home purchaser's interest or equity.
2. If a homeowner does not have title insurance, what does he stand to lose financially and legally?
   A. Half of the down payment.
   B. Half of any legal costs that result from defending the property interests.
   C. All of the down payment, any legal costs that result from defending the property interests and the property's title.
   D. Half of the down payment, plus the property's title.
3. If you lose your property because someone else successfully claims rights to it, you still owe the remaining balance on your mortgage. True or False.
4. Your equity in a property cannot be affected by being without title insurance. True or False.
5. If you buy title insurance, it guarantees that . . .
   A. No other individuals can claim any right to your home.
   B. The title insurer will defend any lawsuit attacking your title as insured.
   C. The title insurer will clear up title problems but not pay the insured's losses.
   D. All of the above.
6. Of the following, which is *not* a possible reason why a person can lose title to his home?
   A. Mistakes in recording legal documents.
   B. Forged deeds, releases or wills.
   C. Instruments executed under valid power of attorney.
   D. Misinterpretations of wills.
7. The property of current owners may be sold to satisfy estate taxes that were owed by previous owners. True or False.
8. Title insurance coverage . . .
   A. Costs one-fourth of the home's price.
   B. Costs up to one-half of the home's price.

*Continued*

C. Varies from state to state.

D. None of the above.

9. Payments for title insurance are typically made . . .

A. Over a 10- to 12-year period.

B. On a case by case basis.

C. In a lump sum when the home is purchased.

D. In a lump sum after the mortgage has been fully paid.

10. Title insurance coverage lasts . . .

A. Five, 10 or 15 years, depending upon the type of coverage purchased.

B. As long as the home is owned by the title holder.

C. Throughout the life of the mortgage.

D. For one year, renewable every year.

### The Answers

1. D.

2. C.

3. True. "It occasionally happens that someone owns a property that is sold for unpaid taxes," said Alan Prince, executive vice president of Chicago Title and Trust Family of Insurers in Chicago. "The title passes to someone else, but that doesn't relieve the previous owner from his mortgage. It's like being required to pay for a car that is demolished. Without title insurance, the owner is not covered. With title insurance, the company pays the lender if someone else claims rights to the home."

4. False, "Without title insurance, the owner loses all investment in the home if someone else claims rights to it," Prince said.

5. B.

6. C. "A valid power of attorney would always act in the interest of the homeowner," Prince said. "Title insurance would protect the homeowner against the other possibilities."

7. True.

8. C. "Title insurance is not sold at a nationwide flat fee," Prince said. "It's based on the price of the home but varies from state to state."

9. C.

10. B.

### How to tally your score:

- Eight to 10 correct answers. You know your homeowner's rights and would be prepared if someone challenged your claims to your property.

- Seven to five correct answers. You have a good sense of what your rights as a homeowner are under the law but could benefit from learning a few more facts.

- Three of four correct answers. You are likely to wind up on the losing end if someone successfully fought your ownership rights.

- Less than three correct answers. You stand to lose every right to your home if you don't learn about title insurance protection.

SOURCE: Adaptation of Chris Olson, "Title Insurance Protects Homeowner's Rights," *Sunday World Herald*, July 31, 1994, pp. 1-F; 2-F.

insurance are not maintained, the umbrella insurer pays only that amount it would have been required to pay if the underlying insurance had been kept in force.

**Broad Coverage**    *The personal umbrella policy provides broad coverage of personal liability loss exposures.* In addition to excess liability insurance, the personal umbrella policy also covers certain losses not covered by any underlying contract after a self-insured retention or deductible is met.

The insuring agreement provides coverage for both personal injury and property damage liability. Personal injury is broadly defined to include bodily injury, libel, slander, defamation of character, invasion of privacy, wrongful eviction or detention,

---

### Exhibit 9.3

**Typical Underlying Coverage Amounts Required to Qualify for a Personal Umbrella Policy**

| | |
|---|---|
| Automobile liability insurance | $250,000/$500,000/$50,000 or $500,000 single limit |
| Comprehensive personal liability insurance (separate contract or homeowners policy) | $100,000 |
| Large watercraft | $300,000 or higher |
| Employers liability insurance (where required or permitted by law) | $100,000 |

---

false arrest or false imprisonment, and malicious prosecution.

The umbrella policy also covers liability for property damage. Property damage is defined as physical injury to tangible property and includes loss of use of the damaged property.

The umbrella insurer agrees to pay for personal injury or property damage losses that exceed the liability limits for the underlying coverages, or for loss that exceeds a self-insured retention (deductible) if the loss is not covered by any underlying insurance. In addition to the policy limits, umbrella policies will also pay the legal defense costs.

**Self-Insured Retention**    If a loss is covered by the umbrella policy but not by any underlying insurance, the insured must satisfy a **self-insured retention.** The self-insured retention is usually $250 per occurrence ($1000 in North Carolina and Texas). Examples of claims not covered by underlying contracts but insured under the umbrella policy include libel, slander, defamation of character, contractual liability, and a wide variety of additional claims (see Insight 9.3 ).

Several examples can illustrate how the personal umbrella policy works. Assume that Tyrone has a $1 million personal umbrella policy. He also has an automobile insurance liability policy with limits of $250,000/$500,000/$50,000, and personal liability insurance of $100,000 under the homeowners policy.[10] If Tyrone injures another motorist in an auto accident and incurs a $650,000 judgment, the underlying auto insurance policy pays the first $250,000. The personal umbrella policy pays the

remaining $400,000, because the underlying limits of $250,000 per person under the auto policy have been exhausted.

If Tyrone's German shepherd bites and mauls a neighbor's child, and Tyrone incurs a judgment of $150,000, the homeowners policy would pay $100,000 and the umbrella policy would pay $50,000.

Finally, assume that Tyrone is sued by his ex-wife for defamation of character and must pay damages of $10,000. If there is no underlying coverage and the self-insured retention is $250, the umbrella policy would pay $9750.

**Reasonable Cost**    *The personal umbrella policy is also reasonable in cost.* The actual cost depends on several variables, including the number of cars, boats, and motorcycles to be covered. However, for most families, protection can be obtained by an annual premium of less than $250 for a $1 million policy. Payment of a relatively modest premium will provide you with a greater peace of mind, since you are covered for a catastrophic lawsuit involving personal liability.

### Umbrella Liability Exclusions

Personal umbrella policies also contain certain exclusions. Some common exclusions include the following:[11]

- Any obligation under a workers compensation, disability benefits, or similar law
- Damage to property owned by a covered person

## INSIGHT 9.3

## The Perils an Umbrella Policy Can Protect Against

AUTO ACCIDENTS cause most of the personal injuries that result in huge monetary settlements paid by umbrella liability insurance. But there are plenty of other calamities that can put your assets at serious risk. Consider these recent real-life cases:

- You know the game: One person kneels behind another and a third pushes the "victim" over. In a case settled last year, three 10-year-olds were the players. One child broke his arm and the other two were sued. The case cost the kneeling boy $100,000 and the one who did the pushing $195,000.
- A 40-year-old window washer broke his heel in a fall after a downspout he was holding onto broke away from the house on which he was working. Although the worker was found partially responsible, the fall cost the homeowner $1.2 million.
- A 22-year-old suffered permanent eye damage when he was struck by a golf ball. He sued, claiming that the golfer who hit the ball had failed to look out for other players. The errant shot cost the golfer $160,000.

- A professional dancer suffered permanent knee damage—and an end to her career—when she was knocked down on a beginner's ski slope. She offered to settle for the $300,000 covered by the defendant's insurance, but was rebuffed. The case went to trial, where it cost the defendant $2.2 million.
- A woman suffered severe cuts when her leg was hit by the propeller of a boat she was attempting to board. She sued, claiming that the boat began to move before she was safely aboard. The injury cost the boat owner $175,000.
- At an end-of-school swim party, a 16-year-old dove and hit his head on the bottom of the pool. He became a quadriplegic, and the case resulted in a $1.5-million settlement against the homeowner.
- A 5-year-old suffered brain damage when a dinner bell at his grandfather's home fell and struck him in the head. A lawsuit against the grandfather led to a $500,000 settlement.

SOURCE: *Kiplinger's Personal Finance Magazine,* Vol. 49, No. 7 (July 1995), p. 82.

---

- Personal injury or property damage that is insured under a nuclear energy liability policy
- An act committed or directed by a covered person with the intention to cause injury or property damage
- Aircraft
- Watercraft. The exclusion does not apply to boats with inboard motors of 50 horsepower or less, outboard motors of 25 horsepower or less, or to sailing vessels less than 26 feet long.
- Business activity or business property. The exclusion does not apply to your use or to a family member's use of a private passenger auto.
- Performance or lack of performance of a professional service
- An act or failure to act as an officer, trustee, or director of a corporation or association. The

exclusion does not apply to a nonprofit corporation or association.

### SUMMARY

- The ISO dwelling program is designed for dwellings that are ineligible for coverage under the homeowner contracts and for persons who do not want or need a homeowners policy.
- The *Dwelling Property 1 policy* is a basic form that provides fire and extended-coverage insurance and coverage for vandalism or malicious mischief. The *Dwelling Property 2 policy* is a broad form that includes all perils covered under the basic form and adds additional perils. The *Dwelling Property 3 policy* is a special form that covers the dwelling and other structures against risks of direct loss to property. All direct physical losses are covered except for those

losses specifically excluded; personal property is covered on a named-perils basis.

- A mobilehome can be insured by an endorsement to Homeowners 2 or Homeowners 3. Thus, the coverages on a mobilehome are similar to those found in homeowner contracts.

- An *inland marine floater* provides broad and comprehensive protection on personal property that is frequently moved from one location to another. Although inland marine floaters are not uniform, they have certain common characteristics. Insurance can be tailored to the specific types of personal property to be insured; desired amounts of insurance and type of coverage can be selected; broader and more comprehensive coverage can be obtained; and most floaters cover insured property anywhere in the world.

- The *personal articles floater (PAF)* insures certain optional classes of personal property on an "all-risks" basis. All direct physical losses are covered except certain losses specifically excluded. The classes are jewelry, furs, cameras, musical instruments, silverware, golfer's equipment, fine arts, postage stamps, and rare and current coins. Individual items are listed and insured for specific amounts.

- The *scheduled personal property endorsement* is an endorsement that can be added to the homeowners policy that provides essentially the same coverages provided by the personal articles floater.

- Insurance on pleasure or recreational boats generally can be divided into two categories. A *boat owners package policy* combines physical damage insurance, medical expense insurance, liability insurance, and other coverages into one contract. A *yacht policy* is designed for larger boats such as cabin cruisers and inboard motorboats. The yacht policy provides physical damage insurance on the boat and equipment, liability insurance, medical payments insurance, and other coverages on a broad and comprehensive basis.

- The flood peril is difficult to insure privately because of the problems of a catastrophic loss, prohibitively high premiums, and adverse selection. Federal flood insurance is available at subsidized rates to cover buildings and personal property in flood zones.

- Under the *write-your-own program,* private insurers write flood insurance, collect premiums, and pay claims. The insurers are reimbursed for any losses by the federal government.

- *FAIR plans* provide basic property insurance to individuals who are unable to obtain coverage in the normal markets. The property must be inspected before the policy is issued. If the property meets certain underwriting standards, it can be insured at standard or surcharged rates. In some cases, the owner may be required to make certain improvements in the property before the policy is issued. If the insurance is denied, the applicant must be informed of the reasons why the property cannot be insured.

- The current federal crop insurance program requires producers who wish to be eligible for federal farm benefits to purchase *catastrophic crop insurance*. Additional protection can be obtained by purchasing *multiple peril crop insurance* from private insurers.

- *Title insurance* protects the owner of property or lender of money against any unknown defects in the title to the property.

- The *personal umbrella policy* is designed to provide protection against a catastrophic lawsuit or judgment. The major features of the personal umbrella policy are as follows:

    The policy provides excess liability insurance over basic underlying insurance contracts.

    Coverage is broad and includes protection against certain losses not covered by the underlying contracts.

    A self-insured retention must be met for certain losses covered by the umbrella policy but not by any underlying contract.

    The umbrella policy is reasonable in cost.

## KEY CONCEPTS AND TERMS

| | |
|---|---|
| Boat owner's package policy | Multiple-peril crop insurance |
| Catastrophic crop insurance | National Flood Insurance Program |
| Dwelling Property 1 (basic form) | Personal Articles Floater (PAF) |
| Dwelling Property 2 (broad form) | Personal liability supplement |
| Dwelling Property 3 (special form) | Personal umbrella policy |
| Extended-coverage perils | Physical damage coverage |
| FAIR plan | Self-insured retention |
| Flood | Title insurance |
| Inland marine floater | Uninsured boater coverage |
| Liability coverage | Yacht insurance |
| Medical expense coverage | |
| Mobilehome insurance | |

## QUESTIONS FOR REVIEW

1. Describe briefly the major forms that are now used in the dwelling program.

2. Identify the basic coverages in a policy covering mobilehomes.

3. Show how the personal articles floater can be used to cover a valuable silverware, coin, or stamp collection.

4. Identify the coverages found in a typical boat owners package policy.

5. Describe the major coverages in a yacht policy.

6. Why is the flood peril difficult to insure privately?

7. Describe briefly the major provisions of the federal flood insurance program.

8. What is the purpose of a FAIR plan?

9. Describe the basic characteristics of title insurance.

10. Explain the major characteristics of the personal umbrella policy.

## QUESTIONS FOR DISCUSSION

1. Fernando owns a fourplex and lives in one unit. The building is insured under the Dwelling Property 1 (basic form) policy for $160,000. The replacement cost of the building is $200,000. Explain to what extent, if any, Fernando will recover for the following losses:

   a. A fire occurs in one of the apartments because of defective wiring. The actual cash value of the damage is $10,000, and the replacement cost is $12,000.

   b. The tenants move out because the apartment is unfit for normal living. It will take three months to restore the apartment to its former condition. The apartment is rented for $600 monthly.

   c. A tenant's personal property is damaged in the fire. The actual cash value of the damaged property is $5000, and its replacement cost is $7000.

2. Marcie owns a mobile home that is insured by an endorsement to a Homeowners 3 policy. Explain to what extent, if at all, this policy would pay for each of the following losses:

   a. A severe windstorm damages the roof of the mobilehome.

   b. A built-in range and oven are also damaged in the storm.

   c. A window air conditioner is badly damaged in the storm.

   d. Marcie must move to a furnished apartment for three months while the mobilehome is being repaired.

3. Morgan has an outboard motorboat insured under a boat owners package policy. Indicate whether each of the following losses would be covered under Morgan's policy. If the loss is not covered, or not completely covered, explain why.

   a. Morgan's boat was badly damaged when it struck a log floating in the water.

   b. An occupant in Morgan's boat was injured and incurred medical expenses when the boat struck a concrete abutment.

   c. The motor was stolen when the boat was docked at a marina.

   d. A small child in Morgan's boat was not wearing a life jacket. The child fell overboard and drowned. The child's parents have sued Morgan.

4. Jann has a personal umbrella policy in the amount of $1 million. The self-insured retention is $250. Jann has the following liability limits under his homeowners and automobile insurance contracts:

   > Homeowners policy $100,000
   >
   > Personal auto policy $500,000 single limit

   Indicate whether each of the following losses would be covered under Jann's personal umbrella policy. If the loss is not covered, or not covered fully, explain why.

   a. Jann coaches a Little League baseball team. A team member sitting behind third base was struck in the face by a line drive and lost the sight in one eye. Jann is sued by the parents, who allege that Jann's coaching is inadequate. The team member is awarded damages of $1 million.

   b. Jann is a member of the board of directors for the local Young Men's Christian Association (YMCA). Jann is sued by a YMCA member who was seriously injured when a trampoline collapsed. The injured member is awarded damages of $500,000.

   c. Jann accuses a male teenager, age 14, of stealing his racing bike valued at $2000. The police arrest the youth and book him. The police later arrested the actual thief and recovered the bicycle. Jann is sued by the youth's parents for the false arrest. The teenager is awarded damages of $100,000.

d. Jann failed to stop at a red light, and his car struck another motorist. The injured motorist is awarded damages of $200,000.

## SELECTED REFERENCES

Chesebrough, John R., and George E. Rejda. "Personal Umbrella Liability Insurance—A Critical Analysis," *CPCU Journal,* Vol. 48, No. 2 (June 1995), pp. 98–104.

*Fire, Casualty & Surety Bulletins.* Fire and Marine volume and Casualty and Surety volume. Cincinnati: National Underwriter Company. See also the Personal Lines volume. The bulletins are published monthly.

Hamilton, Karen L., and Donald S. Malecki. *Personal Insurance: Property and Liability,* First edition. Malvern, Pa: American Institute for CPCU, 1994, chapter 6.

*Policy, Form & Manual Analysis Service.* Property Coverages volume. Inland Marine Section. Indianapolis: Rough Notes Company. The bulletins are published monthly.

Rejda, George E., Constance M. Luthardt, Cheryl L. Ferguson, and Donald R. Oakes. *Personal Insurance,* 3rd ed. Malvern, PA.: Insurance Institute of America, 1997.

## NOTES

1. The ISO dwelling program is described in detail in *Fire, Casualty & Surety Bulletins,* Personal Lines volume, Dwelling section. The dwelling property forms by the Insurance Services Office were also used by the author in preparing this section.
2. For a detailed explanation of mobilehomes, see "Mobilehome Insurance," *Fire, Casualty & Surety Bulletins,* Personal Lines volume, Dwelling section.
3. J. J. Launie, George E. Rejda, and Donald R. Oakes, *Personal Insurance,* 2nd ed., (Malvern, Pa: Insurance Institute of America, 1991), chapter 6.
4. Discussion of the personal articles floater is based on Launie et al., chapter 6; *Fire, Casualty, & Surety Bulletins,* Personal Lines volume, Misc. Personal section; and Insurance Services Office, Personal Articles Floater (IPA 06 01).

## CASE APPLICATION

Jesse is a former zookeeper who retired early because of poor health. He recently purchased a small cottage near a river for $60,000 that will be his major residence. The river occasionally overflows during heavy rainstorms, which has caused damage to several homes in the area. Jesse lives alone. However, he has two dogs, a cat, a parrot, and a domesticated wild tiger as pets. He also owns a small 15-horsepower runabout boat that is used to cross the river to buy groceries and supplies from a convenience store.

An insurance agent has informed Jesse that an HO-3 policy cannot be obtained on the cottage since the underwriter would not approve the application. However, the agent stated he would try to get the underwriter to issue a dwelling DP-3 policy. If that policy cannot be obtained, the agent would try to get a DP-1 policy. As a last resort, the agent stated that coverage could be obtained through the state's FAIR plan.

a. Assume you are a risk management consultant. Identify the major loss exposures that Jesse faces.
b. Explain the major differences among the HO-3, DP-3, and DP-1 policies discussed by the agent.
c. To what extent will each of the coverage alternatives discussed by the agent cover the loss exposures identified in (a) above?
d. Assume that Jesse obtains a DP-3 policy. Do you recommend that he also purchase the personal liability supplement? Explain.
e. Assume that Jesse obtains a DP-1 policy. Do you recommend that he also purchase flood insurance through the federal flood insurance program? Explain.

5. Insurance on pleasure boats is based on Launie et al., chapter 6; *Fire, Casualty & Surety Bulletins,* Companies and Coverages volume, Aircraft-Marine section; and the boatowner policy discussed in the *CPCU Handbook of Insurance Policies,* First edition (Malvern, Pa.: American Institute for CPCU and Insurance Institute of America, 1994), pp. 86–91.

6. Current details of the federal flood insurance program can be found in the *Fire, Casualty & Surety Bulletins,* Fire and Marine volume, Catastrophe section.

7. FAIR plans exist in Arkansas (rural), California, Connecticut, Delaware, District of Columbia, Florida (joint underwriting association), Georgia, Hawaii, Illinois, Indiana, Iowa, Kansas, Kentucky, Louisiana, Maryland, Massachusetts, Michigan, Minnesota, Mississippi (rural), Missouri, New Jersey, New Mexico, New York, North Carolina, Ohio, Oregon, Pennsylvania, Rhode Island, Virginia, Washington, West Virginia, and Wisconsin. Beach and windstorm plans exist in Alabama, Florida, Louisiana, Mississippi, North Carolina, South Carolina, and Texas.

8. A complete description of title insurance can be found in S. S. Huebner, Kenneth Black, Jr., and Bernard L. Webb, *Property and Liability Insurance,* 4th ed. (Englewood Cliffs, N.J.: Prentice Hall, 1996), chapter 23.

9. Discussion of the personal umbrella policy is based on John R. Chesebrough and George E. Rejda, "Personal Umbrella Liability Insurance—A Critical Analysis," *CPCU Journal,* Vol. 48, No. 2 (June 1995), pp. 98–104; "Personal Umbrella Liability Insurance," in *Fire, Casualty & Surety Bulletins,* Companies and Coverage volume, Personal Packages section (Cincinnati: National Underwriter Company); and "Your Personal Excess Liability Policy," *The CPCU Handbook of Insurance Policies,* First edition (Malvern, Pa.: American Institute for CPCU/Insurance Institute of America, 1994), pp. 109–15.

10. The figures $250,000/$500,000 refer to a limit of $250,000 per person and $500,000 per accident for bodily injury liability. The $50,000 figure is the limit for property damage liability.

11. "Personal Umbrella Policy," *1993–1994 Policy Kit for Insurance Professionals* (Schaumburg, Ill.: Alliance of American Insurers), p. 53.

# Chapter 10

# AUTOMOBILE INSURANCE

*" If you can't pay, you can lose your driving privileges. "*

*Consumer Shopping Guide for*
*Automobile Insurance, State of Missouri*

## Student Learning Objectives

After studying this chapter, you should be able to:

■ Identify the persons who are insured for liability coverage under the Personal Auto Policy (PAP).

■ Describe the liability coverage in the PAP.

■ Explain the medical payments coverage in the PAP.

■ Describe the uninsured motorists coverage in the PAP.

■ Explain the coverage that insures your automobile against physical damage or losses.

■ Explain the duties imposed on the insured after an accident or loss.

In 1994, about 34 million motor vehicle accidents occurred, and 43,000 persons were killed in these accidents. The economic cost is staggering. In 1994, automobile accidents resulted in an estimated economic loss of almost $111 billion.[1] These costs include property damage; medical, hospital, and legal expenses; administrative costs of insurance; and numerous other costs.

Automobile accidents can cause great financial insecurity to individuals and families. Legal liability arising out of the negligent operation of an automobile can reach catastrophic levels. Medical expenses, pain and suffering, the unexpected death of a family member, and the damage or loss of an expensive automobile can have a traumatic financial impact on the individual or family. Shock and grief are additional costs that cannot be quantified.

Automobile insurance is the major technique for dealing with the loss exposures described above. In this chapter, the major provisions of the **Personal Auto Policy (PAP)**—drafted by the Insurance Services Office (ISO) and widely used throughout the United States—are discussed in some detail. Some insurers, such as State Farm and Allstate, have designed their own forms that differ somewhat from the PAP form, but the differences are relatively minor.

### OVERVIEW OF PERSONAL AUTO POLICY

The Pap was introduced in 1977 and has been revised several times since then. The following discussion is based on the current (1994) edition of the PAP.[2]

## Eligible Vehicles

Only certain types of vehicles are eligible for coverage under the PAP. An eligible vehicle is a four-wheel motor vehicle owned by the insured or leased by the insured for at least six continuous months. Thus, a private passenger automobile, station wagon, or jeep owned by the insured is eligible for coverage.

A pickup truck or van is eligible for coverage if the vehicle has a gross vehicle weight of less than 10,000 pounds and is not used to transport goods and materials. Pickups or vans used to transport goods and materials may be covered if (1) their use is incidental to the insured's business of installing, maintaining, or repairing furnishings or equipment, or (2) they are used in farming or ranching.

A private passenger automobile owned by two or more resident relatives (such as father and daughter) or by two or more unrelated individuals living together can also be insured by adding a *micellaneous-type vehicle endorsement* to the policy. This miscellaneous-type vehicle endorsement is discussed later in the chapter.

## Your Covered Auto

An extremely important definition with respect to the PAP coverages is the definition of **your covered auto.** Four classes of vehicles are considered to be covered autos:

- Any vehicle shown in the declarations
- Newly acquired vehicles
- Trailer owned by the insured
- Temporary substitute auto

*First, any vehicle listed in the declarations is a covered auto.* Covered autos include a private passenger auto, station wagon, jeep, pickup, or van owned by the named insured. A private passenger automobile leased for at least six months can also be listed as a covered auto.

*Second, a newly acquired private passenger auto, pickup, or van is a covered auto if the vehicle is acquired by the named insured during the policy period.* As we noted earlier, a pickup or van must have a gross vehicle weight of less than 10,000 pounds and must not be used to transport business materials unless the materials are incidental to the named insured's

business, and that business is installing, maintaining, or repairing furnishings or equipment, or farming or ranching.

- *Additional vehicle.* If the newly acquired vehicle is an *additional vehicle,* you are automatically insured from the date of acquisition provided you notify the insurer within 30 days after you become the owner and ask the insurer to insure it. For example, if you own one car and purchase a second car, you are automatically covered when you drive away from the lot. An additional premium must be paid for the newly acquired vehicle. In addition, if the newly acquired vehicle is an *additional vehicle,* you have the broadest coverage shown for any vehicle listed in the declarations. For example, if two cars are listed in the declarations, and only one car has collision coverage, the additional vehicle is insured for a collision loss.
- *Replacement vehicle.* If the newly acquired vehicle *replaces* one shown in the declarations, the new vehicle automatically has the same coverage as the vehicle it replaced. You must report a replacement vehicle to the insurer within 30 days of acquisition only if you wish to add or continue physical damage insurance (Part D) on the replacement vehicle. For example, if you have collision insurance on a 1993 Ford that is traded in for a new Ford, you have 30 days to notify your insurer that you want to continue the collision insurance on the new car. If you forget to notify the insurer, and six weeks later you are involved in an accident, the physical damage loss to the new car is not covered.

*Third, a trailer owned by the named insured is a covered auto.* A trailer is a vehicle designed to be pulled by a private passenger auto, pickup, or van and also includes a farm wagon or farm implement while being towed by such vehicles. For example, you may be pulling a boat trailer that upsets and injures another motorist. The liability section of the PAP would cover the loss.

*Finally, a* **temporary substitute vehicle** *is a covered auto.* A temporary substitute auto is a **nonowned auto** or trailer you are temporarily using because of mechanical breakdown, repair, servicing, loss, or destruction of a covered vehicle. Thus, if you drive a loaner car while your car is in the garage for repairs, your PAP covers the vehicle.

## Summary of PAP Coverages

The PAP consists of a declarations page, a definitions page, and the following six parts:

Part A: Liability Coverage
Part B: Medical Payments Coverage
Part C: Uninsured Motorists Coverage
Part D: Coverage for Damage to Your Auto
Part E: Duties after an Accident or Loss
Part F: General Provisions

## PART A: LIABILITY COVERAGE

**Liability coverage (Part A)** is the most important part of the PAP. It protects a covered person against a suit or claim arising out of the negligent ownership or operation of an automobile.

### Insuring Agreement

In the Part A insuring agreement, the insurer agrees to pay any damages for bodily injury or property damage for which an insured is legally responsible because of an auto accident. Liability coverage can be written with a **single limit** that applies to both bodily injury and property damage liability. *This means that the total amount of insurance applies to the entire accident without a separate limit for each person.* For example, a single limit of $500,000 would apply to both bodily injury and property damage liability.

The PAP policy can also be written with split limits. **Split limits** *mean the amounts of insurance for bodily injury liability and property damage liability are stated separately.* For example, split limits of $250,000/ $500,000/$100,000 mean you have bodily injury liability coverage of $250,000 for each person and $500,000 for each accident. You also have $100,000 of property damage liability coverage.

The amount paid as damages includes any prejudgment interest awarded against the insured. Many states now allow plaintiffs (injured persons) to receive interest on the judgment from the time the suit is entered to the time the judgment is handed down. Any prejudgment interest is considered part of the damage award and is subject to the policy

limit of liability. For example, assume you are liable for a $50,000 judgment and $5000 of prejudgment interest. If your policy has adequate liability limits, the liability payment is $55,000.

In addition to the payment for damages, the insurer agrees to defend you and pays all legal defense costs. The defense costs are paid in addition to the policy limits. *However, the insurer's duty to settle or defend the claim ends when the limit of liability has been exhausted.* Thus, once the policy limits are paid out (including any prejudgment interest), the insurer has no further obligation to defend you. The insurer also has no obligation to defend any claim not covered under the policy. For example, if you intentionally cause bodily injury or property damage and are sued, the insurer has no obligation to defend you since intentional acts are specifically excluded.

Finally, all states have financial responsibility or compulsory insurance laws that require motorists to carry a minimum amount of liability insurance or to post a bond at the time of an accident. The minimum liability limits per person for bodily injury range from $10,000 to $50,000 and are woefully inadequate in view of the high damage awards in recent years. If you have a good driving record, the minimum liability limits can be substantially increased with a relatively small increase in premiums.

### Insured Persons

The following four groups are insured under the liability section of the PAP:

- Named insured and any family member
- Any person using the named insured's covered auto
- Any person or organization, but only for liability arising out of an insured person's use of a covered auto on behalf of that person or organization
- Any person or organization legally responsible for the named insured's or family members' use of any automobile or trailer (other than a covered auto or one owned by that person or organization)

*First, the named insured and family members are insured for liability coverage.* The named insured also includes a spouse if a resident of the same household. A family member is a person related to the named insured by blood, marriage, or adoption who resides in the same household, including a ward or foster child. Thus, the husband, wife, and children are covered while using any automobile, owned or nonowned. If the children are attending college and are temporarily away from home, they are still insured under their parents' policy.

*Second, any other person using the named insured's covered auto is also insured provided that person can establish a reasonable belief that permission to use the covered auto exists.* For example, Roger may have permitted his girlfriend, Tina, to drive his car several times over the past six months. If Tina takes Roger's car without his express permission, she is covered under his policy as long as she can show a reasonable belief that Roger would have given her permission.

*Third, any person or organization legally responsible for the acts of a covered person while using a covered auto is also insured.* For example, if Claude drives his car on an errand for his employer, and he injures someone, the employer is covered for any suit or claim.

*Finally, coverage applies to any person or organization legally responsible for the named insured's or family members' use of any automobile or trailer (other than a covered auto or one owned by the person or organization).* For example, Claude may borrow the car of a fellow worker to mail a package for his employer. If Claude injures someone while driving that car, the employer is also covered for any suit or claim. However, the PAP does not extend coverage to the employer when the named insured is using an automobile owned by the employer. So if Claude is driving to the post office in a company car, the employer is not insured under Claude's PAP.

## Supplementary Payments

In addition to the policy limits and a legal defense, certain supplementary payments can also be paid.

- Up to $250 for the cost of a bail bond
- Premiums on appeal bonds and bonds to release attachments
- Interest accruing after a judgment
- Up to $50 daily for the loss of earnings
- Other reasonable expenses

Premiums on a bail bond can be paid up to $250 because of an automobile accident that results in property damage or bodily injury. However, payment is not made for a traffic violation such as a speeding ticket except if an accident occurs. For example, assume Henry is drunk and injures another motorist in an accident. If he is arrested, and bail is set at $2500, the company will pay the bail bond premium up to a maximum of $250.

Premiums on an appeal bond and a bond to release an attachment of property in any suit defended by the insurer are also paid as supplementary payments. If interest accrues after a judgment is awarded, the interest is also paid as a supplementary payment. Any prejudgment interest, however, is part of the liability limits.

The insurer will also pay up to $50 daily for the loss of earnings (but not other income) due to attendance at a hearing or trial at the company's request.

Finally, other reasonable expenses incurred at the insurer's request are paid. For example, you may be a defendant in a trial and be requested to testify. If you have meal or transportation expenses, they would be paid as a supplemental payment.

## Exclusions

A lengthy list of exclusions applies to the liability coverage under the PAP. They are summarized as follows:

1. *Intentional injury or damage.* Intentional bodily injury or property damage is specifically excluded.

2. *Property owned or transported.* Liability coverage is not provided to any person for damage to property owned or being transported by that person. For example, the suitcase and camera belonging to a friend may be damaged in an automobile accident while you and your friend are on vacation together. The damage would not be covered.

3. *Property rented, used, or in the insured's care.* Damage to property rented to, used by, or in the care of the insured is not covered. For example, if you rent some skis that are damaged in an automobile accident, the property damage is not covered. The exclusion, however, does not ap-

ply to property damage to a residence or private garage. For example, if you rent a house and carelessly back into a partly opened garage door, the property damage would be covered.

4. *Bodily injury to an employee.* Bodily injury to an employee of the insured who is injured during the course of employment is also excluded. The intent here is to cover the employee's injury under a workers compensation law. However, a domestic employee injured during the course of employment would be covered if workers compensation benefits are not required or available.

5. *Use as a public or livery conveyance.* There is no liability coverage on a vehicle while it is being used as a public or livery conveyance. The intent here is to exclude coverage if the insured makes the vehicle available for hire to the general public. However, the exclusion does not apply to share-the-expense carpools.

6. *Vehicles used in the automobile business.* If a person is employed or engaged in the automobile business, liability arising out of the operation of vehicles in the automobile business is excluded. The automobile business refers to the selling, repairing, servicing, storing, or parking of vehicles designed for use mainly on public highways. This also includes road testing and delivery. For example, assume you take your car to a garage for repairs. If an automobile mechanic has an accident and injures someone while road testing your car, your PAP liability coverage does not protect the mechanic. (However, if you are sued because you are the car owner, you are covered.) The intent of this exclusion is to exclude loss exposures that should be covered under the auto repair firm's liability policy, such as a garage policy.

The preceding exclusion does not apply to the operation, ownership, or use of a covered auto by the named insured, family member, or any partner, agent, or employee of the named insured or family member. For example, if an auto mechanic has an accident while driving his or her car to pick up a part, the mechanic's PAP would cover the loss.

7. *Other business vehicles.* Liability coverage does not apply to any vehicle maintained or used in any other business (other than farming or ranching). This exclusion is similar to the preceding automobile business exclusion except it applies to all other business use with certain exceptions. The intent here is to exclude liability coverage for commercial vehicles and trucks that are used in a business. For example, if you drive a city bus or operate a large cement truck, your PAP liability coverage does not apply.

The exclusion does not apply to a private passenger auto, pickup, or van owned by the insured, or to a nonowned vehicle used as a temporary substitute because a covered auto has broken down or is being repaired or serviced. Thus, you are covered if you drive your car on company business.

8. *Using a vehicle without reasonable belief of permission.* If a person uses a vehicle without a reasonable belief that he or she has permission to do so, the liability coverage does not apply.

9. *Nuclear energy exclusion.* Liability of insureds who are covered under special nuclear energy contracts is also excluded.

10. *Vehicle with fewer than four wheels.* Liability coverage does not apply to any vehicle that has fewer than four wheels or is designed for use mainly off public roads. Thus, motorcycles, mopeds, motorscooters, minibikes, and trail bikes are excluded. However, these vehicles can be covered by adding a miscellaneous-type vehicle endorsement to the policy.

11. *Vehicle furnished or made available for the named insured's regular use.* Liability coverage excludes a vehicle other than a covered auto that is owned by, furnished, or made available for the named insured's regular use. You can occasionally drive another person's car and still have coverage under your policy. *However, if the nonowned automobile is driven regularly or is furnished or made available for your regular use, your PAP liability coverage does not apply.* For example, if your employer furnishes you with a car, or a car is available for your regular use in a company carpool, the liability coverage does not apply. The key point is not how frequently you drive someone else's car, but whether it is furnished or made available for your regular use.

For an additional premium, the **extended nonowned coverage endorsement** can be added to the PAP that covers the insured while operating a nonowned auto on a regular basis.

12. *Vehicle owned by, furnished, or made available for the regular use of any family member.* This exclusion is similar to the preceding exclusion. However, the exclusion does not apply to the named insured and spouse. For example, if the mother occasionally drives a car owned by her daughter, the mother's PAP provides coverage while driving the daughter's car. Without this exception, the named insured and spouse would not have any liability coverage under their PAP while driving a car owned by or furnished for the regular use of any family member.

13. *Racing vehicle.* Liability coverage does not apply to any vehicle while it is located inside a racing facility for the purpose of competing in or preparing for a prearranged racing or speed contest.

## Limit of Liability

The insurer's maximum limit of liability from any single automobile accident is the amount stated in the declarations. This is true regardless of the number of insureds, claims made, vehicles or premiums shown in the declarations, or vehicles involved in the auto accident.

## Out-of-State Coverage

An important feature applies if the accident occurs in a state other than where the covered auto is principally garaged. If the accident occurs in a state that has a financial responsibility law with higher liability limits than the limits shown in the declarations, the PAP automatically provides the higher specified limits.

In addition, if the state has a compulsory insurance or similar law that requires a nonresident to have insurance whenever he or she uses a vehicle in that state, the PAP also provides the required minimum amounts and types of coverage. This provision insures compliance with an out-of-state no-fault law and the payment of required benefits. No-fault automobile insurance laws are discussed in Chapter 11.

EXHIBIT 10.1

Marina carelessly injures another motorist while driving her own car and must pay damages of $30,000. If two automobile liability policies cover the loss, each insurer pays its pro rata share of the loss. Assume that Marina is insured for $50,000 in Company A and $100,000 in Company B. Company A pays $10,000 and Company B pays $20,000. This can be illustrated by the following.

Company A

$$\frac{\$50,000}{\$150,000} \times \$30,000 = \$10,000$$

Company B

$$\frac{\$100,000}{\$150,000} \times \$30,000 = \$20,000$$

$$\text{Total} \qquad \$30,000$$

Leon is the named insured and borrows Marina's car with her permission. Both policies will cover any loss. Leon has $50,000 of liability insurance and Marina has $100,000. Leon negligently injures another motorist and must pay damages of $125,000. *The rule is that insurance on the borrowed car is primary, and other insurance is excess.* Each company pays as follows:

| | |
|---|---|
| Marina's insurer (primary) | $100,000 |
| Leon's insurer (excess) | 25,000 |
| Total | $125,000 |

Marina's insurer pays $100,000 while Leon's insurer pays the remaining $25,000.

## Other Insurance

In some cases, more than one automobile liability policy covers a loss. The PAP has a provision for determining the amount and priority of payments. If other applicable liability insurance applies to an *owned vehicle,* the insurer pays only its pro rata share of the loss. The insurer's share is the proportion that its limit of liability bears to the total applicable limits of liability under all policies. However, if the insurance applies to a *nonowned vehicle,* the insurer's insurance is excess over any other collectible insurance (see Exhibit 10.1).

## PART B: MEDICAL PAYMENTS COVERAGE

**Medical payments coverage** is an accident benefit that is frequently included in the PAP. Benefits are paid without regard to fault.

## Insuring Agreement

Under this provision, the company will pay all reasonable medical and funeral expenses incurred by an insured for services rendered within three years from the date of the accident. Covered expenses include medical, surgical, X-ray, dental, and funeral services. The benefit limits typically range from $1000 to $10,000 per person and apply to each insured who is injured in the accident.

Medical payments coverage is not based on fault. Thus, if you are injured in an automobile accident and you are at fault, medical payments can still be paid to you and to other injured passengers in the car.

## Insured Persons

Two groups are insured for medical payments coverage:

- Named insured and family members
- Other persons while occupying a covered auto

*The named insured and family members are covered if they are injured while occupying any motor vehicle or are injured as pedestrians when struck by a motor vehicle designed for use mainly on public roads.* For example, if the parents and children are hurt in a car accident while on vacation, their medical expenses are covered up to the policy limits. If the named insured or any family member is struck by a motor vehicle or trailer while walking, their medical expenses are also paid. However if you are injured by a farm tractor, snowmobile, or bulldozer, your injury is not covered, since these vehicles are not designed for use mainly on public roads.

*Other persons are also covered for their medical expenses while occupying a covered auto.* For example, if you own your car and are the named insured, all passengers in your car are covered for their medical expenses under your policy. However, if you are operating a *nonowned vehicle,* other passengers in the car (other than family members) are not covered for their medical expenses under your policy. The intent here is to have other passengers in the nonowned vehicle seek protection under their own insurance or under the medical expense coverage that applies to the nonowned vehicle.

## Exclusions

Medical payments coverage has numerous exclusions. They are summarized as follows:

1. *Motorized vehicle with fewer than four wheels.* Bodily injury while occupying a motorized vehicle with fewer than four wheels is excluded.

2. *Public or livery conveyance.* If a covered auto is used as a public or livery conveyance, the medical payments coverage does not apply. The exclusion does not apply to a share-the-expense carpool.

3. *Using the vehicle as a residence.* Coverage does not apply if the injury occurs while the vehicle is being used as a residence or premises. For example, if you own and occupy a camper trailer as a residence in a campground while on vacation, medical expense coverage does not apply if you burn yourself while cooking on a stove in the trailer.

4. *Injury occurring during course of employment.* Coverage does not apply if the injury occurs during the course of employment, and workers compensation benefits are required or available.

5. *Vehicle furnished or made available for the named insured's regular use.* Coverage does not apply to any injury sustained while occupying or when struck by a vehicle (other than a covered auto) that is owned by the named insured or is furnished or made available for the named insured's regular use. The intent here is to avoid providing "free" medical payments coverage on an owned or regularly used car not described in the policy.

6. *Vehicle furnished or made available for the regular use of any family member.* A similar exclusion applies to any vehicle (other than a covered auto) that is owned by any family member or is furnished or made available for the regular use of any family member. The exclusion does not apply to the named insured and spouse. For example, if a son living at home owns a car that is not insured for medical payments coverage, and the parents are injured while occupying the son's car, the parent's medical expenses would be covered under their policy.

7. *Using a vehicle without a reasonable belief.* Coverage does not apply if the injury occurs

while occupying a vehicle without a reasonable belief of being entitled to do so.

8. *Vehicle used in the business of an insured.* Coverage does not apply to any injury sustained while occupying a vehicle when it is being used in the business of an insured. The intent here is to exclude medical payments coverage for nonowned trucks and commercial vehicles used in the business of an insured person. The exclusion does not apply to a private passenger auto (owned or nonowned), an owned pickup or van, or trailer used with any of the preceding vehicles.

9. *Nuclear weapon, radiation, or war.* Bodily injury from a nuclear weapon, nuclear radiation, or war is not covered.

10. *Racing vehicle.* Coverage does not apply to a bodily injury sustained while occupying a vehicle located inside a racing facility for the purpose of competing in or preparing for a prearranged racing or speed contest.

## Other Insurance

If other automobile medical payments insurance applies to an *owned vehicle,* the insurer pays its pro rata share of the loss based on the proportion that its limits bear to the total applicable limits.

However, medical payments coverage is excess with respect to a *nonowned vehicle.* For example, assume that Kim is driving her car and picks up Sydney for lunch. Kim loses control of the car and hits a tree, and Sydney is injured. Sydney's medical bills are $6000. Kim has $2000 of medical expenses coverage, and Sydney has $5000. Kim's insurer pays the first $2000 as primary insurer, and Sydney's insurer pays the remaining $4000 as excess insurance.

## PART C: UNINSURED MOTORISTS COVERAGE

Some persons are irresponsible and drive without liability insurance. The **uninsured motorists coverage** pays for the bodily injury (and property damage in some states) caused by an uninsured motorist, by a hit-and-run driver, or by a negligent driver whose insurance company is insolvent.

## Insuring Agreement

The insurer agrees to pay compensatory damages that an insured is legally entitled to receive from the owner or operator of an uninsured motor vehicle because of bodily injury caused by an accident. Damages include medical bills, lost wages, and compensation for a permanent disfigurement resulting from the accident. Several important points must be emphasized with respect to this coverage.

1. *The coverage applies only if the uninsured motorist is legally liable.* If the uninsured motorist is not liable, the insurer will not pay for the bodily injury.

2. *The insurer's maximum limit of liability for any single accident is the amount shown in the declarations.* You cannot receive duplicate payments for the same elements of loss under the uninsured motorists coverage and Part A or Part B of the policy, or any underinsured motorists coverage provided by the policy. Also, you cannot receive a duplicate payment for any element of loss for which payment has been made by or on behalf of persons or organizations legally responsible for the accident. Finally, the insurer will not pay you for any part of a loss if you are entitled to be paid for that part of the loss under a workers compensation or disability benefits law.

3. *The claim is subject to arbitration if the insured and insurer disagree over the amount of damages or whether the insured is entitled to receive any damages.* Under this provision, each party selects an arbitrator. The two arbitrators select a third arbitrator. A decision by two of the three arbitrators is binding on all parties. However, the decision is binding only if the damage award does not exceed the state's minimum financial responsibility law limits.

4. *Many states also include coverage for property damage from an uninsured motorist in their uninsured motorists law.* In these states, if an uninsured driver runs a red light and smashes into your car, the property damage to the car would be covered under the uninsured motorists coverage, subject to any applicable deductible.

There is considerable variation among the states that include property damage coverage in their uninsured motorists law. In some states, property damage coverage is an optional coverage that is purchased separately from the regular uninsured motorists coverage. In other states, both bodily injury and property damage coverages are included together in the uninsured motorists coverage; however, the insured has the option of waiving the coverage if it is not desired. In some states, both bodily injury and property damage coverage are mandatory under the state's uninsured motorists law. Finally, the property damage is subject to a deductible, such as $200 or $300 (or some other stated amount).

## Insured Persons

Three groups are insured under the uninsured motorists coverage.

- Named insured and family members
- Any other person while occupying a covered auto
- Any person legally entitled to recover damages

First, the named insured and family members are covered if they are injured by an uninsured motorist. Second, any other person who is injured while occupying a covered auto is also insured; the coverage applies only if the individual is occupying a covered auto. Finally, any person legally entitled to recover damages is also insured. An individual may not be physically involved in the accident but may be entitled to recover damages from the person or organization legally responsible for the bodily injury of the insured person. For example, if the named insured is killed by an uninsured motorist, the surviving spouse could still collect damages under the uninsured motorists coverage.

## Uninsured Vehicles

An extremely important provision defines an uninsured motor vehicle. Four groups of vehicles are considered to be uninsured vehicles:

1. An uninsured vehicle is a motor vehicle or trailer for which no bodily injury liability insurance policy or bond applies at the time of the accident.

2. A bodily injury liability policy or bond may be in force on a vehicle. However, the amount of insurance on that vehicle may be less than the amount required by the state's financial responsibility law in the state where the named insured's covered auto is principally garaged. This vehicle is also considered to be an uninsured motor vehicle.

3. A hit-and-run vehicle is also considered to be an uninsured vehicle. Thus, if the named insured or any family member is struck by a hit-and-run driver while occupying a covered auto or a nonowned auto, or while walking, the uninsured motorists coverage will pay for the injury.

4. Another uninsured vehicle is one to which a bodily injury liability policy applies at the time of the accident, but the insurer or bonding company denies coverage or becomes insolvent. For example, if you have a valid claim against a negligent driver, but his or her insurer becomes insolvent before the claim is paid, your uninsured motorists coverage would pay the claim.

Certain vehicles are not considered to be an uninsured motor vehicle. An uninsured motor vehicle does not include any of the following:

1. Any vehicle owned by or furnished for the regular use of the named insured or any family member

2. Any vehicle owned or operated by a qualified self-insurer (except a self-insurer that is or becomes insolvent)

3. Any vehicle owned by a governmental unit or agency

4. Any vehicle operated on rails or crawler treads

5. Any vehicle designed mainly for use off public roads, while not on a public road

6. Any vehicle used as a residence or premises

## Exclusions

The uninsured motorists coverage has several general exclusions, summarized as follows:

1. *No uninsured motorists coverage on vehicle.* Coverage does not apply to an insured while

occupying or when struck by a motor vehicle, owned by that insured, which is not insured for coverage under this policy.

2. *Family members.* Family members are not covered while they are occupying a vehicle owned by the named insured that is insured for uninsured motorists coverage on a primary basis under any other policy. The intent is to have such family members seek protection under the policy insuring the vehicle they are occupying.

3. *Settling without the insurer's consent.* If an insured or legal representative settles a bodily injury claim without the insurer's consent, coverage does not apply. The purpose of this exclusion is to protect the insurer's interest in the claim.

4. *Using the vehicle as a public or livery conveyance.* If an insured occupies a covered auto when it is being used as a public or livery conveyance, coverage does not apply. The exclusion does not apply to a share-the-expense carpool.

5. *No reasonable belief of permission.* Coverage does not apply to any insured who is using a vehicle without a reasonable belief that he or she is entitled to do so.

6. *No benefit to workers compensation insurer.* The uninsured motorists coverage cannot directly or indirectly benefit a workers compensation insurer or self-insurer. A workers compensation insurer may have a legal right of action against a third party who has injured an employee. If an uninsured driver injures an employee who receives workers compensation benefits, the workers compensation insurer could sue the uninsured driver or attempt to make a claim under the injured employee's uninsured motorists coverage. This exclusion prevents the uninsured motorists coverage from providing benefits to the workers compensation insurer.

7. *No punitive damages.* The PAP excludes payment for punitive or exemplary damages under the uninsured motorists coverage.

## Other Insurance

If other insurance applies to the loss, recovery for damages under all such policies may equal but not exceed the highest applicable limit on any one vehicle under any policy providing protection on either a primary or excess basis. Thus, you can collect in total an amount equal to the highest limit of all policies that apply to you.

In addition, if the insurer provides uninsured motorists coverage on a *vehicle not owned by the named insured,* the insurance provided is excess over any collectible insurance providing coverage on a primary basis.

Finally, if one or more policies provide uninsured motorists coverage, the insured's policy will pay only its pro rata share of the loss, which is the proportion that the insurer's limit of liability bears to the total of all applicable limits provided. The pro rata rule applies regardless of whether the coverage is on a primary basis or excess basis.

## Underinsured Motorists Coverage

The **underinsured motorists coverage** can be added to the PAP to provide more complete protection. The underinsured motorists coverage applies when a negligent driver carries liability insurance, but the limits carried are less than the insured's actual bodily injury.

An underinsured vehicle is defined as a vehicle to which a liability policy or bond applies at the time of the accident, but the liability limits carried are less than the limits provided by the insured's underinsured motorists coverage. The maximum amount paid for the bodily injury under the coverage varies among the states. *In general, the maximum amount paid is the underinsured motorist's limit less the amount paid by the negligent driver's insurer.* For example, assume that Nadia adds the underinsured motorists coverage to her policy in the amount of $100,000. She is injured by a negligent driver who has liability limits of $25,000/$50,000, which satisfy the state's minimum required limits. If her bodily injury damages are $100,000, she would receive only $25,000 from the negligent driver's insurer, since that is the applicable limit of liability. However, she would receive another $75,000 from her insurer under the underinsured motorists coverage.

However, assume that Nadia's bodily injury damages are $125,000. The maximum amount she would collect under the underinsured motorists coverage is still only $75,000, which is the difference between the $100,000 limit under her underinsured motorists coverage and the $25,000 collected from the negligent driver's insurer (see preceding rule). To collect the full amount of her injury, Nadia should have carried limits of at least $125,000.

You should not confuse the underinsured motorists coverage with the uninsured motorists coverage. The two coverages are mutually exclusive. You can collect under one coverage or the other, depending on the situation, but not both. The uninsured motorists coverage applies when the bodily injury (or property damage in some states) is caused by an uninsured motorist, by a hit-and-run driver, or by a driver whose insurer is insolvent. In contrast, the underinsured motorists coverage is applicable only when the other driver has automobile liability insurance, but the liability limits carried are less than the limit provided by the underinsured motorists coverage.

## PART D: COVERAGE FOR DAMAGE TO YOUR AUTO

Part D **(coverage for damage to your auto)** provides coverage for the damage or theft of an automobile.

### Insuring Agreement

The insurer agrees to pay for any direct and accidental loss to a covered auto or nonowned auto, including its equipment, less any deductible. If two autos insured under the same policy are damaged in the same accident, only one deductible must be met. If the deductible amounts are different, the higher deductible will apply. *Two optional coverages are available: (1) collision and (2) other than collision (also called comprehensive).* A collision loss is covered only if the declarations page indicates that collision coverage is provided for that auto. Likewise, coverage for an other-than-collision loss is in force only if the declarations page indicates that other-than-collision coverage is provided for that auto.

The physical damage coverages under Part D also apply to a newly acquired private passenger auto, pickup, van, camper body, or trailer provided the named insured requests coverage within 30 days after becoming the owner. *In addition, the Part D coverages apply to a nonowned auto and temporary substitute auto on an excess basis.* For example, if you rent a car on a vacation, your Part D coverages apply to that car. However, if an accident occurs, you will be responsible for paying the deductible just as if the loss had occurred to your own car, because rental companies typically do not carry collision insurance on their own cars.

As mentioned earlier, the Part D coverages on your car also apply to rental cars. However, there may be some restrictions on the Part D coverages when a car is rented, such as a limit on the number of days of coverage in a year when a car is rented. In addition, many insurers have discontinued providing liability and collision coverage on rental cars used for business purposes without payment of an extra premium. Thus, before you rent a car, you should check with your agent to determine the extent to which your present coverages apply to a rental car. This information is especially important in determining whether you should purchase the "collision damage waiver," which covers physical damage to the rental car if you have an accident.

**Collision Loss**   **Collision** *is defined as the upset of your covered auto or nonowned auto or its impact with another vehicle or object.* The following are examples of a collision loss:

- Your car hits another car, a telephone pole, a tree, or a building.
- Your car is parked, and you find the rear fender dented when you return.
- You open the car door in a parking lot, and the door is damaged when it hits the vehicle parked next to you.

Collision losses are paid regardless of fault. If you cause the accident, your insurer will pay for the damage to your car, less any deductible. If some other driver damages your car, you can either collect from the negligent driver (or from his or her insurer), or look to your insurer to pay the claim. If you collect from your own insurer, you must give up subrogation rights to your insurer, who will then attempt to collect from the negligent driver who caused the accident. If the entire amount of the loss is recovered, your insurer will refund the deductible.

However, insurers take three different approaches when only *part* of the total loss payment is recovered. First, the insurer may reimburse the insured for the deductible amount and then retain the balance of the subrogation recovery. Second, the insurer may split the recovery with the insured on a pro rata basis. Finally, the insurer may retain an amount equal to the loss payment with any balance paid to the insured. Because subrogation practices differ among insurers, it is important to know how a subrogation recovery will be handled before seeking payment under your own policy or from the insurer covering the at-fault driver.

**Other-Than-Collision Loss**    The PAP can be written to cover an **other-than-collision loss.** The PAP distinguishes between a collision and an other-than-collision loss. The distinction is important because some car owners do not desire collision coverage on their cars. Also, the deductibles under the two coverages may be different. Other-than-collision coverage is frequently written with a lower deductible.

Loss from any of the following perils is considered to be an other-than-collision loss:

- Missiles or falling objects
- Fire
- Theft or larceny
- Explosion or earthquake
- Windstorm
- Hail, water, or flood
- Malicious mischief or vandalism
- Riot or civil commotion
- Contact with a bird or animal
- Glass breakage

These losses are self-explanatory, but a few comments are in order. Remember that colliding with a bird or animal is not a collision loss. Thus, if you hit a bird or a deer with your car, the physical damage to the car is considered to be an other-than-collision loss. In addition, if glass breakage is caused by a collision, you can elect to have it covered as a collision loss. This distinction is important because both coverages (collision loss and other-than-collision loss) may be written with deductibles. Without this qualification, you would have to pay two de-

ductibles if the car has both body damage and glass breakage in the same accident (assuming both coverages are elected). By treating glass breakage as part of the collision loss, only one deductible has to be satisfied.

Finally, although motor vehicle thefts have increased over time, they have declined in recent years (see Exhibit 10.2). However, you are less likely to recover your vehicle if it is stolen because high-tech thieves and car rings have made auto thefts a big business operation. The decline in auto theft rates, however, has been offset by large increases in loss payments for the stolen vehicles.[3]

**Nonowned Auto**    The Part D coverages also apply to a nonowned auto. A **nonowned auto** *is a private passenger auto, pickup, van, or trailer not owned by or furnished or made available for the regular use of the named insured or family member, while it is in the custody of or is being operated by the named insured or family member.* In addition, a nonowned auto includes a temporary substitute vehicle. For example, if Megan borrows Mike's car, Megan's collision coverage and other-than-collision coverage on her car apply to the borrowed car. However, Megan's insurance is excess over any physical damage insurance on the borrowed car.

The Part D coverages apply only if the nonowned auto is not furnished or made available for the regular use of the named insured or family member. You can occasionally drive a borrowed automobile, and your physical damage insurance will cover the borrowed vehicle. *However, if the vehicle is driven on a regular basis or is furnished or made available for your regular use, the Part D coverages do not apply.* The key point here is not how frequently you drive a nonowned auto, but whether the vehicle is furnished or made available for your regular use.

*A temporary substitute vehicle is also considered to be a nonowned auto.* A temporary substitute vehicle is a nonowned auto or trailer that is used as a temporary replacement for a covered auto that is out of normal use because of its breakdown, repair, servicing, loss, or destruction. *Thus, the Part D coverages that apply to a covered auto also apply to a temporary substitute vehicle for that auto.* Hence, if your car is in the shop for repairs, and you are furnished a loaner

EXHIBIT **10.2**

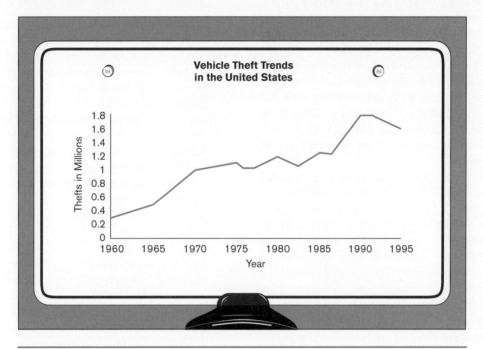

SOURCE: "Driving Down Your Insurance Costs," *USAA Magazine,* Vol. 27, No. 1 (Feb/Mar 1996), p. 13.

car, your physical damage insurance also applies to the loaner car.

If you have an accident while operating a nonowned auto, the PAP provides the broadest coverage applicable to any covered auto shown in the declarations. For example, assume that you own two cars. One vehicle is insured for both a collision loss and an other-than-collision loss, while the second vehicle is insured only for an other-than-collision loss. If you drive a nonowned auto, the borrowed vehicle is covered for both collision and other-than-collision losses.

**Deductible**  The collision coverage is typically written with a straight deductible of $250, or some higher amount. Some insurers offer this coverage with a $100 deductible but at a higher cost. Coverage for other-than-collision losses is also normally written with a deductible. Deductibles are designed to reduce small claims, hold down premiums, and encourage the insured to be careful in protecting the car from damage or theft.

## Transportation Expenses

Part D also provides a supplementary payment for temporary transportation expenses. The insurer will pay, without application of a deductible, up to $15 daily to a maximum of $450 for temporary transportation expenses incurred by the insured because of loss to a covered auto. Payments can be made for a train, bus, taxi, rental car, or other transportation expense. *Payments are made for other-than-collision losses only if the declarations indicate that other-than-collision coverage is provided on that auto. Likewise, payments are made for collision losses only if the declarations indicate that collision coverage is provided for that auto.*

The coverage also includes payment of any loss-of-use expenses for which the insured is legally responsible because of loss to a nonowned auto, such as the loss of daily rent on a rental car. However, loss-of-use expenses are paid for other-than-collision losses or for collision losses only if the declarations indicate that such coverages are in effect.

Finally, if the loss is caused by the total theft of a covered auto or nonowned auto, expenses incurred during the first 48 hours after the theft occurred are not covered. If the loss is caused by other than theft, expenses incurred during the first 24 hours after the auto has been withdrawn from use are not covered.

Coverage for *towing and labor costs* can be added by an endorsement. This coverage pays for towing and labor costs if a covered auto or nonowned auto breaks down, provided the labor is performed at the place of breakdown. The maximum amount paid is $25, $50, or $75 for each breakdown depending on the amount of insurance purchased. For example, if you call a repair truck because your car fails to start, the labor costs and any tow-in costs will be paid up to the policy limits. Labor costs, however, are covered only for work done at the place of the breakdown. The cost of repairs at a service station or garage is not covered.

## Exclusions

Numerous exclusions apply to the Part D coverages, summarized as follows:

1. *Use as a public or livery conveyance.* Loss to a covered auto or any nonowned auto is excluded if the vehicle is being used as a public or livery conveyance. Again, the exclusion does not apply to a share-the-expense carpool.

2. *Damage from wear and tear, freezing, and mechanical or electrical breakdown.* There is no coverage for any damage due to wear and tear, freezing, mechanical or electrical breakdown, or road damages to tires. The intent is to exclude the normal maintenance cost of operating an automobile and to cover tire defects under the tire manufacturer's warranty. However, the exclusion does not apply to the total theft of a covered auto or any nonowned auto. For example, if a stolen car is recovered but the electrical system is damaged by a thief who hot-wired the car, the loss is covered.

3. *Radioactive contamination or war.* Damage from radioactive contamination or war is excluded.

4. *Electronic equipment.* Electronic equipment designed for the reproduction of sound is excluded, such as a stereo set and tape decks. Other electronic equipment that receives or transmits audio, visual, or data signals is also excluded, such as a citizens' band radio, car telephone, or personal computer. Tapes, records, discs, or other accessories are also excluded. Coverage of excluded equipment can be obtained by an endorsement to the policy.

The preceding exclusion does not apply to equipment designed for the reproduction of sound and accessories if the equipment is permanently installed in a covered auto or nonowned auto. The exclusion also does not apply if the equipment can be removed from a housing unit permanently installed in the auto, is designed to be operated solely by power from the auto's electrical system, and is in or upon a covered auto or nonowned auto at the time of loss. For example, a removable stereo that is stolen from the trunk of your car would be covered. The exclusion also does not apply to electronic equipment necessary for the normal operation of the auto or the monitoring of its systems.

Finally, please note that the PAP excludes telephones, which include cellular phones that many motorists use while driving. The use of cellular phones while driving is highly controversial. Some safety experts believe that using a cellular phone while driving can be extremely dangerous (see Insight 10.1).

5. *Government destruction or confiscation.* The PAP also excludes the total loss to a covered auto or nonowned auto due to the destruction or confiscation by a governmental or civil authority. For example, if a drug dealer's car is confiscated by a federal drug agency, the loss would not be covered.

6. *Loss to a camper body or trailer not shown in the declarations.* The exclusion does not apply to a newly acquired camper body or trailer acquired during the policy period provided you ask the

## INSIGHT 10.1

## Using Phone at Wheel Labeled as Dangerous as Drunk Driving

Talking on a cellular telephone while driving quadruples the risk of having an accident, making it as dangerous as driving while drunk, Canadian scientists say.

The first large study of the wireless phones, which now number 34 million in the United States, also indicated to the authors' surprise that so-called hands-free phones are no safer than conventional hand-held phones.

"This may indicate that the main factor . . . is a driver's limitations in attention rather than dexterity," said Dr. Donald Redelmeier of the University of Toronto.

Surprisingly, the authors of a report on the study, which appeared in the New England Journal of Medicine, are not recommending bans on using the phones while driving.

"Our study is not about the role of regulation, but about the role of individual responsibility," Dr. Redelmeier said. "Our role is to inform the debate (over cell phone safety), not to dominate the discussion."

"No insurance company would be surprised by (the findings)," said Steven Goldstein, director of public relations for the Insurance Information Institute, which represents several large insurance companies. "Hand-held cell phones should not be used while you are driving any more than you should turn around while you are on the Interstate to reprimand your child in the back seat," he said.

A spokesman for the Cellular Telecommunications Industry Association cautioned, however, that the study indicated only an association between talking on the phone and accidents, not that talking on the phone actually causes accidents. But even CTIA cautioned against using the phones while driving.

"When you are behind the wheel, your most important responsibility is safe driving. Period." said CTIA's Tim Ayers. "It is not using a phone, or drinking coffee, or reading a map or combing your hair."

Dr. Redelmeier and statistician Robert Tibshirani studied 699 accidents in Toronto over a 14-month period in 1994 and 1995. None of the accidents involved serious injuries. In each case, they used telephone company records to determine whether the driver was using a cellular phone during or immediately before the accident.

For controls, they used the same drivers, examining their phone records from the day preceding the accident. This type of "crossover study" is the scientific way of asking: "Did anything unusual happen to you immediately before the event being studied?" in this case, the collision.

Ayers and Dr. Redelmeier said cellular phone service providers helped researchers by giving them 100 consecutive days of billing records for each of the 699 drivers in the study.

That allowed Dr. Redelmeier and Tibshirani, a statistics professor at the University of Toronto, to examine 26,798 telephone calls. They then attached a value to the number of calls in which an accident was involved and compared those to the calls where there was no crash.

The trade association and a federal official cautioned that the study had one weakness: It did not determine that the drivers were actually on the phone when the accident occurred. However, it did establish a 10-minute window in which a call was made and the accident happened.

Because few drivers would admit they were on the phone at the time of an accident for liability reasons, the billing records could only be used to confirm that 10-minute window.

Overall, the researchers found that people using a cellular phone were 4.3 times as likely to have an accident as other drivers. Those using hands-free phones were 5.9 times as likely to have an accident, but the number of such drivers was too small for the difference between accident rates using hands-free and hand-held phones to be statistically significant. The researchers did not examine other potential causes of inattention.

For comparison, Dr. Redelmeier noted that driving with a blood alcohol level at the legal limit also causes a fourfold increase in risk. But a blood alcohol level 50 percent above the legal limit gives a tenfold increase.

The use of phones while driving has been controversial ever since they were introduced. Both simulations and real driving experiments have shown that such calls slow reaction times by a halfsecond or more.

SOURCE: Adapted from "Using Phone at Wheel Labeled as Dangerous as Drunk Driving," *Omaha World Herald*, February 13, 1997, pp. 1–2.

insurer to insure it within 30 days after you become the owner.

7. *Loss to a nonowned auto used without reasonable belief of permission.* Loss to a nonowned auto is not covered when it is used by the named insured or family member without a reasonable belief of permission.

8. *Awnings or cabanas.* Loss to awnings, cabanas, or equipment designed to create additional living facilities is also excluded. An endorsement can be added to cover such property.

9. *Radar detection equipment.* Loss to equipment for the detection or location of radar or laser is also excluded. The exclusion is justified since radar detection equipment is designed to circumvent enforcement of state and federal speed laws.

10. *Custom furnishings or equipment.* Loss to any custom furnishings or equipment in or upon a pickup or van is not covered. For example, loss to custom furnishings or equipment in a van such as carpeting, furniture, bars, cooking and sleeping facilities, height-extending roofs, and custom murals or paintings is specifically excluded. However, a special customized equipment endorsement can be added that covers the excluded furnishings or equipment.

11. *Nonowned auto maintained or used in the automobile business.* Loss to a nonowned auto maintained or used by someone employed in the automobile business is specifically excluded. For example, if you are a mechanic and damage a customer's car while road testing it, the physical damage loss is not covered under your PAP. This is a business loss exposure that should be covered under a commercial garage policy.

12. *Nonowned auto maintained or used in any other business.* A nonowned auto maintained or used in any other business not otherwise described in exclusion 11 is also excluded. However, the exclusion does not apply to a nonowned auto that is a private passenger auto or trailer.

13. *Racing vehicle.* Loss to a covered auto or nonowned auto is not covered while it is located inside of a racing facility for the purpose of competing in or preparing for a prearranged racing or speed contest.

14. *Rental car.* Loss to, or loss of use of, a vehicle rented by the named insured or family member is not covered if a state law or rental agreement precludes the car rental agency from recovering from the named insured or family member.

## Limit of Liability

The amount paid for a physical damage loss is the lower of the actual cash value of the damaged or stolen property or the amount necessary to repair or replace the property with other property of like kind and quality. If the cost of repairs exceeds the vehicle's actual cash value, the vehicle may be declared a total loss, and the amount paid is the actual cash value less any deductible. For a partial loss (such as a smashed fender), only the amount necessary to repair or replace the damaged property with property of like kind and quality will be paid. If the value of the vehicle is increased after the repairs are completed (such as repainting the entire car when only one fender is damaged), the insurer will not pay for the betterment or increase in value. Finally, loss to a nonowned trailer is limited to $500.

## Payment of Loss

The insurer has the option of paying for a physical damage loss in money (including any sales tax), or it can repair or replace the damaged or stolen property. If the car or its equipment is stolen, the insurer will pay the expense of returning the stolen car to the named insured and will also pay for any damage resulting from the theft. The insurer also has the right to keep all or part of the recovered stolen property at an agreed or appraised value.

To hold down the cost of collision claims to damaged vehicles, many insurers are now using a network of repair shops, which some refer to as "managed care" for body shops. Motorists whose cars are damaged in auto accidents are required to use a body shop that is part of the network (see Insight 10.2).

## INSIGHT 10.2

# Auto Insurers Are Trying Out Managed Care

A patient is injured. An insurance company mandates where the patient is treated and then tells the provider how much to spend to make the patient well.

Sound familiar?

Here's the twist: The patient is a car.

The industry that brought HMOs is now considering CMOs—Car Maintenance Organizations. Insurers already are using the concept in Florida, California and Colorado, and they have plans to make it more widely available.

Managed care for cars has been so obviously cribbed from the health-care industry that describing it is easy: Explain a standard HMO arrangement, then substitute "car" for patient, "collision repairer" for doctor and "body shop" for hospital.

"It actually makes much more sense for vehicles than it does for humans," said Michael York, chief executive of Carnet Holding Corp., which started the first CMO in 1988 in Los Angeles and has 50,000 cars in the program. "With people you never know when to stop spending money to save them. With cars, when the cost of repairs exceeds 75 percent of the value of the vehicle, the patient is dead."

Given their similarities, it's not surprising that CMOs have sparked bitter fights between carriers and body shops that mirror the brawls between carriers and doctors over HMOs.

Insurers argue that CMOs bring efficiency and lower premiums to a system badly in need of greater price discipline. Body shops and lobbyists object to CMOs in terms usually reserved for medieval plagues.

"We view this approach as Armageddon," said Edward Kizenberger, director of the New York State Auto Collision Technicians Association, which helped defeat CMO efforts there. "It could wipe out about 50 percent of all body shops." Kizenberger and others say CMOs could bankrupt many shops and lead to corner-cutting as insurers ratchet down reimbursements.

The system works like this: Instead of getting estimates at a handful of body shops, drivers who have been in accidents are required by insurers to pick garages from a network. Insurers negotiate group discounts with body shops, which allows them to offer lower premiums to consumers.

Garages on insurers' lists get a steady flow of business. Carriers get tighter control over repairs, because they contract with the shops and can monitor prices and procedures. Drivers face limited choices, but save money and know exactly where to go.

Three years ago, when Progressive Insurance Group offered a 10 percent discount for auto managed care in Colorado, about one in five drivers signed up.

Major players in the insurance industry are studying CMOs. Significant obstacles loom, however. *Twenty-six states have anti-steering laws, which prohibit carriers from dictating where consumers take damaged cars.* The auto body lobby fought for those laws and won't let them be scrapped without a fight.

That's what Infinity Insurance Co. discovered when it tried to introduce a CMO in Maryland in September. The Collision Auto Repair Specialists of Maryland, a body shop association, got wind of Infinity's plan, informed regulators about it and pointed out it violated state anti-steering laws.

"We were there when the bell rang and we shot it down," said George Martin, the body shop association president.

Infinity dropped its plans, and its officials would not comment.

CMOs are a reaction to a variety of market characteristics nearly identical to those that produced HMOs. Chief among these is soaring costs. According to the American Insurance Association, the price of settling collision claims rose about 65 percent between 1985 and 1994 in many states, nearly twice the rate of inflation. As with health care, technological advances are what's driving up these numbers.

"New cars have a lot more sophisticated engineering, and many have computers in them," said David Snyder, assistant general counsel at the insurance association. "That makes them far more expensive to buy and far more expensive to fix."

Just as it did for hospitals, managed care for cars is expected to transform the body shop industry by increasing pressure to become more cost-effective.

SOURCE: David Segal, "Auto Insurers Are Trying Out Managed Care," *Omaha World Herald*, December 9, 1995, pp. 27, 30.

## Other Sources of Recovery

If other insurance covers a physical damage loss, the insurer pays only its pro rata share of the loss. The insurer's share is the proportion that its limit of liability bears to the total of all applicable limits.

With respect to a nonowned auto (including a temporary substitute), the Part D coverages are excess over any other collectible source of recovery. *This means that any physical damage insurance on the borrowed car is primary, and your physical damage insurance is excess.* Thus, if you borrow a car and damage it, the owner's physical damage insurance (if any) applies first, and your collision insurance is excess, subject to any deductible. For example, assume that you borrow a friend's car and damage it in an accident. The owner's collision deductible is $500, and your collision deductible is $250. If damages to the borrowed car are $2000, the owner's PAP pays $1500 ($2000 − $500), and your PAP pays $250 ($500 − $250). The remaining $250 of loss would have to be paid either by the owner or by you. In short, if the owner's collision deductible is larger than your deductible, your insurer pays the difference between the two deductibles.

## Appraisal Provision

The PAP contains an appraisal provision for handling disputes over the amount of a physical damage loss. This is particularly important in the case of damage to a low-mileage car or to a car that is above average in condition. The insured may claim that the car is worth more than the amount stated in the various publications of car prices that automobile dealers use. To resolve the dispute, either party can demand an appraisal of the loss. Each party selects an appraiser. The two appraisers then select an umpire. Each appraiser states separately the actual cash value of the car and the amount of the loss. If the appraisers fail to agree, they submit their differences to the umpire. A decision by any two parties is binding on all. Each party pays his or her appraiser, and the umpire's expenses are shared equally. Finally, by agreeing to an appraisal, the insurer does not waive any rights under the policy.

## PART E: DUTIES AFTER AN ACCIDENT OR LOSS

You should know what to do if you have an accident or loss. Some obligations are based on common sense, while others are required by law and by the provisions of the PAP. You should first determine if anyone is hurt. If someone is injured, an ambulance should be called. If there are bodily injuries, or the property damage exceeds a certain amount (such as $200), you must notify the police in most jurisdictions. You should give the other driver your name, address, and the name of your agent and insurer and request the same information from him or her. Under no circumstances should you admit that you caused the accident. The question of negligence and legal liability will be resolved by the insurers involved (or court of law if necessary) and not by you. If you admit that you are responsible for the accident, you prejudice your insurer's obligation and ability to defend you and jeopardize your insurance coverage.

Your agent should be promptly notified of the accident, even if there are no injuries or property damage. Failure to report the accident promptly to your insurer could jeopardize your coverage if you are later sued by the other driver.

After the accident occurs, a number of duties are imposed on you. You must cooperate with the insurer in the investigation and settlement of a claim. You must send to the insurer copies of any legal papers or notices received in connection with the accident. If you are claiming benefits under the uninsured motorists, underinsured motorists, or medical payments coverages, you may be required to take a physical examination at the insurer's expense. You must also authorize your insurer to obtain medical reports and other pertinent records. Finally, you must submit a proof of loss at the insurer's request (see Insight 10.3).

Some additional duties are imposed on you if you are seeking benefits under the uninsured motorists coverage. The police must be notified if a hit-and-run driver is involved. Also, if you bring a lawsuit against the uninsured driver, you must send copies of the legal papers to your insurer.

## INSIGHT 10.3

# How to File an Auto Insurance Claim

### Auto Insurance Claims

Taking the time **now** to review the steps you should follow after an auto accident will help reduce the anxiety surrounding the incident and avoid costly and time-consuming mistakes.

### Before You Have a Claim

Be sure you know the answers to these questions before you have to file a claim:

- How much liability insurance do you have? This coverage pays for damage you cause to another vehicle or injuries to other people.
- Does your state have no-fault insurance? What coverages does it provide?
- If you have collision and/or comprehensive coverage, what is your deductible (the amount you've agreed to pay out of your own pocket if you suffer a loss)?

### At the Scene

- Stop your car and get help for the injured.
  Have someone call the police or highway patrol. Tell them how many people were injured and the types of injuries. The police can then notify the nearest medical unit. Give whatever help you can to the injured but avoid moving anyone so you don't aggravate the injury. Covering an injured person with a blanket and making that person comfortable usually is as much as you can do.
- Provide the police with whatever information they require.
  Ask the investigating officer where you can obtain a copy of the police report, which you may need to support any claim you submit to your insurance company.
- Try to protect the accident scene.
  Take reasonable steps to protect your car from further damage, such as setting up flares, getting the car off the road and calling a tow truck. If necessary, have the car towed to a repair shop. But remember, your insurance company probably will want to have an adjuster inspect it and appraise the damage before you order repair work done.

- Make notes.
  Keep a pad and pencil in your glove compartment. Write down the names and addresses of all drivers and passengers involved in the accident. Also note the license number, make and model of each car involved and record the driver's license number and insurance identification of each driver. Record the names and addresses of as many witnesses as possible, as well as the names and badge numbers of police officers or other emergency personnel. If you run into an unattended vehicle or object, try to find the owner. If you can't, leave a note containing your name, address and phone number.

### Filing Your Claim

If your car is involved in an accident, if it is damaged by fire, flood or vandalism, or if it is stolen, put your insurance to work for you by following these steps in filing your claim:

- Phone your insurance agent or a local company representative.
  Do it as soon as possible even if you're far from home and even if someone else caused the accident. Ask your agent how to proceed and what forms or documents will be needed to support your claim. Your company may require a "proof of loss" form, as well as documents relating to your claim, such as medical and auto repair bills and a copy of the police report.
- Supply the information your insurer needs.
  Cooperate with your insurance company in its investigation, settlement or defense of any claim, and turn over to the company immediately copies of any legal papers you receive in connection with your loss. Your insurer will represent you if a claim is brought against you and defend you if you are sued.
- Keep records of your expenses.
  Expenses you incur as a result of an automobile accident may be reimbursed under your policy. Remember, for example, that your no-fault insurer usually will pay your medical and hospital expenses, and possibly such other costs as lost wages and at least part of your costs if you have to hire a temporary housekeeper.
- Keep copies of your paper work.
  Store copies of all paper work in your own files. You may need to refer to it later.

Source:  Insurance Information Institute.

If your car is damaged, and you are seeking indemnification under Coverage D, other duties are imposed on you. You must take reasonable steps to protect the vehicle from further damage; your insurer will pay for any expense involved. You must also permit the insurer to inspect and appraise the car before it is repaired. If you and the insurer cannot agree on the amount of the physical damage loss, you can demand an appraisal.

## PART F: GENERAL PROVISIONS

This section contains eight general provisions. Only two of them are discussed here.

### Policy Period and Territory

The PAP provides coverage only in the United States, its territories or possessions, Puerto Rico, and Canada. The policy also provides coverage while a covered auto is being transported between the ports of the United States, Puerto Rico, or Canada. For example, if you rent a car while vacationing in England, Germany, or Mexico, you are not covered. Additional automobile insurance must be purchased to be covered while driving in foreign countries. If you intend to drive in Mexico, you should first obtain liability insurance from a Mexican insurer. A motorist from the United States who has not purchased insurance from a Mexican insurer could be detained in jail after an accident, have his or her automobile impounded, and be subject to other penalties as well.

### Termination

An important provision applies to termination of the insurance by either the insured or insurer. There are four parts to this provision:

- Cancellation
- Nonrenewal
- Automatic termination
- Other termination provisions

**Cancellation**   The named insured can cancel at any time by returning the policy to the insurer or by giving advance written notice of the effective date of **cancellation.**

The insurer also has the right of cancellation. If the policy has been in force for *less than 60 days,* the insurer can cancel by sending a cancellation notice to the named insured. At least 10 days' notice must be given if the cancellation is for nonpayment of premiums and at least 20 days notice in all other cases. Thus, the insurer has 60 days to investigate a new insured to determine if he or she is acceptable.

After the policy has been in force for 60 days, or if it is a renewal or continuation policy, the insurer can cancel for only three reasons: (1) the premium has not been paid, (2) the driver's license of any insured has been suspended or revoked during the policy period, or (3) the policy was obtained through material misrepresentation (see Insight 10.4).

**Nonrenewal**   The insurer may decide not to renew the policy when it comes up for renewal. If the insurer decides not to renew the policy, the named insured must be given at least 20 days' notice before the end of the policy period. If the policy period is less than six months, the insurer has the right not to renew the policy every six months after its original effective date. If the policy period is one year or longer, the insurer has the right of nonrenewal at each anniversary date.

**Automatic Termination**   If the insurer decides to renew the policy, an automatic termination provision becomes effective. This means that if the named insured does not accept the insurer's offer to renew, the policy automatically terminates at the end of the current policy period. Thus, once the insurer bills the named insured for another period, the insured must pay the premium, or the policy automatically terminates on its expiration date. However, some insurers may provide a short grace period to pay the renewal premium.

Finally, if other insurance is obtained on a covered auto, the PAP insurance on that auto automatically terminates on the day the other insurance becomes effective.

**Other Termination Provisions**   Many states place additional restrictions on the insurer's right to cancel or not renew. If state law requires a longer pe-

## INSIGHT 10.4

## Can I Be Canceled?

Most states give insurers a specified number of days in which to consider your renewal application for coverage. During that time, a company may decide to cancel your coverage. (Many states also have rules limiting the grounds on which a company can do this, and spelling out the notification it must give you.)

But after this period is up, it's much more difficult for the insurer to cancel you. *Most states permit cancellation of coverage only for a few specified reasons, such as the policyholder's failure to pay the premiums, fraud, suspension or revocation of his or her driver's license, or significant misrepresentation on the application (such as failing to mention that your three teenage sons live with you and regularly drive your car).*

The company must notify you of its decision to cancel your coverage, and it must return the unused portion of your premium. This is rather like cancelling a magazine subscription before it's up. If you paid an annual premium and your coverage was canceled after three months, the company would refund nine months' worth of premium. You also get back part of the premium if *you* cancel your coverage. Unlike the insurer, you don't need any grounds for canceling.

Most states permit an insurer to refuse to renew your policy if your driving record gets markedly worse. Nonrenewal is different from cancellation. Again, different insurers have different rules about what constitutes an unacceptably bad driving record. But some accidents—those caused by drunk driving, for instance—will probably trigger a nonrenewal from virtually every company.

SOURCE: Barbara Taylor, *How to Get Your Money's Worth in Home and Auto Insurance* (New York: Insurance Information Institute, 1991), p. 55. Copyright © 1991 by McGraw-Hill, Inc. Reprinted by permission of McGraw-Hill, Inc.

riod of advance notice to the named insured, or modifies any termination provision, the PAP is modified to comply with those requirements. Also, if the policy is canceled, the named insured is entitled to any premium refund; however, making or offering to make a premium refund is not a condition for cancellation. Finally, the effective date of cancellation stated in the cancellation notice is the end of the policy period.

## INSURING MOTORCYCLES AND OTHER VEHICLES

The PAP excludes coverage for motorcycles, mopeds, and similar vehicles. However, a miscellaneous-type vehicle endorsement can be added to the PAP to insure motorcycles, mopeds, motorscooters, golf carts, motor homes, dune buggies, and similar vehicles. One exception is a snowmobile, which requires a separate endorsement to the PAP. The miscellaneous-type vehicle endorsement can be used to provide the same coverages found in the PAP.

You should be aware of several points if the miscellaneous-type vehicle endorsement is added to the PAP. First, the liability coverage does not apply to a nonowned vehicle. Although other persons are covered while operating your motorcycle with your permission, the liability coverage does not apply if you operate a nonowned motorcycle (other than as a temporary substitute vehicle).

Second, a passenger hazard exclusion can be elected, which excludes liability for bodily injury to any passenger on the motorcycle. When the exclusion is used, the insured pays a lower premium. For example, if a passenger on your motorcycle is thrown off and is injured, the liability coverage on the motorcycle does not apply.

Finally, the amount paid for any physical damage losses to the motorcycle is limited to the lowest of (1) the stated amount shown in the endorsement, (2) the actual cash value, or (3) the amount necessary to repair or replace the property (less any deductible).

## SUMMARY

- The personal auto policy (PAP) consists of a declarations page, a definitions page, and six major parts:

  Part A: Liability Coverage

  Part B: Medical Payments Coverage

  Part C: Uninsured Motorists Coverage

  Part D: Coverage for Damage to Your Auto

  Part E: Duties After an Accident or Loss

  Part F: General Provisions

- Liability coverage protects the insured from bodily injury and property damage liability arising out of the negligent operation of an automobile or trailer. A single limit of liability applies to both bodily injury and property damage. The coverage can also be written with split limits.

- A covered auto includes any vehicle shown in the declarations; newly acquired vehicles; a trailer owned by the insured; and a temporary substitute auto.

- Insured persons include the named insured and spouse, family members, other persons using a covered auto if there is a reasonable belief that permission to use the vehicle exists, and any person or organization legally responsible for the acts of a covered person.

- Medical payments coverage pays all reasonable medical, dental, and funeral expenses incurred by an insured person for services rendered within three years from the date of the accident.

- Uninsured motorists coverage pays for the bodily injury of a covered person caused by an uninsured motorist, a hit-and-run driver, or by a negligent driver whose insurer is insolvent.

- Underinsured motorists coverage can be added as an endorsement to the PAP. The coverage applies when a negligent driver carries liability insurance, but the liability limits carried are less than the limit provided by the underinsured motorists coverage.

- Coverage for damage to your auto pays for any direct physical loss to a covered auto or nonowned auto less any deductible. A collision loss is covered only if the declarations page indicates that collision coverage is in effect.

- Certain duties are imposed on the insured after an accident occurs. A person seeking coverage must cooperate with the insurer in the investigation and settlement of a claim and send to the insurer copies of any legal papers or notices received in connection with the accident.

- After the policy has been in force for 60 days, or it is a renewal or continuation policy, the insurer can cancel the policy only if the premium has not been paid, the driver's license of an insured has been suspended or revoked during the policy period, or the policy was obtained through material misrepresentation. However, if the insurer decides not to renew the policy when it comes up for renewal, the named insured must be given at least 20 days' notice before the end of the policy period.

- Motorcycles and mopeds can be insured by adding the miscellaneous-type vehicle endorsement to the personal auto policy.

## KEY CONCEPTS AND TERMS

Cancellation

Collision

Coverage for damage to your auto

Liability coverage

Medical payments coverage

Miscellaneous-type vehicle endorsement

Nonowned auto

Nonrenewal

Other-than-collision loss

Personal auto policy (PAP)

Single limit

Split limits

Supplementary payments

Temporary substitute auto

Underinsured motorists coverage

Uninsured motorists coverage

Your covered auto

## QUESTIONS FOR REVIEW

1. Describe the major coverages that are found in the personal auto policy.

2. Indicate the types of vehicles that are eligible for coverage under the personal auto policy.

3. Who are the persons insured for liability coverage under the personal auto policy?

4. Describe the supplementary payments that can be paid under the liability section of the personal auto policy.

5. If you drive a borrowed automobile and damage it, will your personal auto policy pay for the damage? Explain.

6. Who are the persons insured for medical payments coverage under the personal auto policy?

7. Explain the major features of the uninsured motorists coverage in the personal auto policy.

8. Describe the insuring agreement under coverage for damage to your auto in the personal auto policy.

9. Explain the duties imposed on the insured after an accident or loss occurs.

10. How can motorcycles and mopeds be insured?

## QUESTIONS FOR DISCUSSION

1. Fred has a personal auto policy that provides the following coverages: $300,000 liability coverage, $5000 medical payments coverage, $25,000 uninsured motorists coverage, $250 deductible for a collision loss, and a $100 deductible for an other-than-collision loss. With respect to each of the following situations, indicate whether or not the losses are covered. Assume that each situation is a separate event.

   a. Fred's son, age 16, is driving a family car and kills a pedestrian in a drag racing contest. The heirs of the deceased pedestrian sue for $100,000.

   b. Fred borrows a friend's car to go to the supermarket. He fails to stop at a red light and negligently smashes into another motorist. The other driver's car, valued at $5000, is totally destroyed. In addition, damages to the friend's car are $1000.

   c. Fred's daughter, Myra, attends college in another state and drives a family automobile. Fred tells her that no other person is to drive the family car. Myra lets her boyfriend drive the car, and he negligently injures another motorist. The boyfriend is sued for $10,000.

   d. Fred's wife is driving a family car in a snowstorm. She loses control of the car on an icy street and smashes into the foundation of a house. The property damage to the house is $20,000. Damages to the family car are $5000. Fred's wife has medical expenses of $3000.

   e. Fred is walking across a street and is struck by a motorist who fails to stop. He has bodily injuries in the amount of $15,000.

   f. Fred's car is being repaired for faulty brakes. While road testing the car, a mechanic injures another motorist and is sued for $50,000.

   g. Fred's car hits a cow crossing a highway. The cost of repairing the car is $700.

   h. A thief breaks a car window and steals a camera and golf clubs locked in the car. It will cost $200 to replace the damaged window. The stolen property is valued at $500.

   i. Fred's wife goes shopping at a supermarket. When she returns, she finds that the left rear fender has been damaged by another driver who did not leave a name. The cost of repairing the car is $500.

   j. Fred works for a construction company. While driving a large cement truck, he negligently injures another motorist. The injured motorist sues Fred for $20,000.

   k. Fred's son drives a family car on a date. He gets drunk, and his girlfriend drives him home. The girlfriend negligently injures another motorist who has bodily injuries in the amount of $10,000.

   l. Several stereo tapes valued at $200 are stolen from Fred's car. The car was locked when the theft occurred.

   m. A video cassette recorder (VCR) and personal laptop computer are stolen from Fred's car. The value of the stolen property is $2500.

2. Louise is the named insured under a personal auto policy that provides coverage for bodily injury and property damage liability, medical payments, and the uninsured motorists coverage. For each of the following situations, briefly explain whether the claim is covered by Louise's personal auto policy.

   a. Louise ran into a telephone pole and submitted a medical expense claim for Jason, a passenger in Louise's car at the time of the accident.

   b. Louise loaned her car to Bianca. While operating Louise's car, Bianca damaged Gray's car in an accident caused by Bianca's negligence. Bianca is sued by Gray for damages.

   c. Louise's husband ran over a bicycle while driving the car of a friend. The owner of the bicycle demands that Louise's husband pay for the damage.

   d. In a fit of anger, Louise deliberately ran over the wagon of a neighbor's child that had been left in Louise's driveway after repeated requests that the wagon be left elsewhere. The child's parents seek reimbursement.

3. Clarice has a PAP with the following coverages:
   Liability coverage $300,000 single limit
   Medical payment coverage $5,000 each person
   Uninsured motorists coverage $25,000 each person
   Collision loss $250 deductible
   Other-than-collision loss $100 deductible
   Towing and labor cost coverage $25 each disablement

To what extent, if any, is each of the following losses covered under Clarice's PAP? Treat each event separately.

a. Clarice rents a car while on vacation. She is involved in an accident with another motorist when she failed to yield the right of way. The injured motorist is awarded a judgment of $250,000. The rental agency carries only liability limits of $30,000 on the rental car. The rental agency carries no collision insurance on its cars and is seeking $15,000 from Clarice for repairs to the rental car.

b. Clarice borrows her friend's car with permission. She is in an accident with another motorist in which she is at fault. The cost of repairing the friend's car is $2000. The friend has a $500 deductible for collision losses and $100 for other-than-collision losses.

c. Clarice is employed as a salesperson and is furnished a company car. She is involved in an accident with another motorist while driving the company car during business hours. The injured motorist claims Clarice is at fault and sues her for $10,000. Damages to the company car are $2500.

d. Clarice's car will not start because of a defective battery. A wrecker tows the car to a service station where the battery is replaced. Towing charges are $60. The cost of replacing the battery is $100.

4. Gilbert was driving a neighbor's pickup truck to get a load of firewood. A child darted out between two parked cars and ran into the street in front of the truck. In an unsuccessful attempt to avoid hitting the child, Gilbert lost control of the vehicle and hit a telephone pole. The child was critically injured, the pickup truck was badly damaged, and the telephone pole collapsed. Gilbert has liability coverage and collision coverage under his personal auto policy. The neighbor also has a personal auto policy with liability coverage and collision coverage on the pickup.

a. If Gilbert is found guilty of negligence, which insurer will pay first for the bodily injuries to the child and the property damage to the telephone pole? Explain.

b. Which insurer will pay for the physical damage to the neighbor's pickup? Explain.

5. Pablo traded in his 1988 Ford for a new Ford. Two weeks later, he hit an oily spot in the road on his way to work and skidded into a parked car. The 1988 Ford was insured under the personal auto policy with full coverage, including a $250 deductible for a collision loss. At the time of the accident, Pablo had not notified his insurer of the trade-in. The physical damage to the parked car was $5000. Damage to Pablo's car was $3000. Will Pablo's personal auto policy cover either or both of these losses? Explain.

## SELECTED REFERENCES

"A Guide to Auto Insurance," *Consumer Reports,* 60 (October 1995): 638–45.

"Auto Insurance: How to Choose the Right Company," *Consumer Reports,* 57 (August 1992): 489–500.

*Fire, Casualty & Surety Bulletins.* Personal Lines volume, Personal Auto section. Cincinnati: National Underwriter Company. The bulletins are published monthly. Up-to-date information on the personal auto policy can be found in the Personal Lines volume, Personal Auto section.

Hamilton, Karen L., and Donald S. Malecki. *Personal Insurance: Property and Liability,* First edition. Malvern, Pa: American Institute for CPCU, 1994, Chapter 4.

*Policy, Form & Manual Analysis Service.* Casualty Coverages volume. Indianapolis: Rough Notes Company. See "Personal Auto Policy" in the Automobile Liability Section. The bulletins are published monthly.

Rejda, George E., Constance M. Luthardt, Cheryl L. Ferguson, and Donald R. Oakes. *Personal Insurance,* 3rd ed. Malvern, Pa.: Insurance Institute of America, 1997.

## NOTES

1. *The Fact Book 1996, Property/Casualty Insurance Facts* (New York: Insurance Information Institute, 1996), p. 84.

2. The material in this chapter is based on J. J. Launie, George E. Rejda, and Donald R. Oakes, *Personal Insurance,* 2nd ed. (Malvern, Pa.: Insurance Institute of America 1992), chapters 7 and 8; *Fire, Casualty & Surety Bulletins,* Personal Lines volume, Personal Auto section (Cincinnati: National Underwriter Company); and the June 1994 edition of the Personal Auto Policy (copyrighted) by the Insurance Services Office. The Personal Auto Policy is used with the permission of the Insurance Services Office.

3. "Driving Down Your Insurance Costs," *USAA Magazine,* Vol. 27, No. 1 (Feb/Mar 1996), p. 13.

# CASE APPLICATION

Kim, age 20, is a college student who recently purchased her first car from a friend who had financial problems. The vehicle is a high mileage 1985 Toyota Tercel with a current market value of $1000. Assume you are a risk management consultant and Kim asks your advice concerning the various coverages in the PAP.

a. Briefly describe the major coverages that are available in the PAP.

b. Which of the available coverages in (a) above should Kim purchase? Justify your answer.

c. Which of the available coverages in (a) above should Kim not purchase? Justify your answer.

d. Assume that Kim purchases the PAP coverages that you have recommended. To what extent, if any, would Kim's insurance cover the following situations?

    1. Danielle, Kim's roommate, borrows Kim's car with her permission and injures another motorist. Danielle is at fault.

    2. Kim is driving under the influence of alcohol and is involved in an accident where another motorist is seriously injured.

    3. During the football season, Kim charges a fee to transport fans from a local bar to the football stadium. Several passengers are injured when Kim suddenly changed lanes without signaling.

    4. Kim drives her boyfriend's car on a regular basis. While driving the boyfriend's car, she is involved in an accident in which another motorist is injured. Kim is at fault.

    5. Kim rents a car in England where she is participating in a summer study program. The car is stolen from a dormitory parking lot.

e. Kim also owns a motorcycle. To what extent, if any, does Kim's PAP cover the motorcycle?

# Chapter 11

# AUTOMOBILE INSURANCE AND SOCIETY

> *" The basic difficulty with the automobile insurance system is that the insured event is too complicated. "*
>
> *Jeffrey O'Connell,*
> *The Injury Industry and the Remedy of No-Fault Insurance*

## Student Learning Objectives

After studying this chapter, you should be able to:

■ Describe the various approaches for compensating innocent automobile accident victims.

■ Explain the meaning of no-fault automobile insurance laws and the arguments for and against such laws.

■ Identify the methods for providing automobile insurance to high-risk drivers.

■ Identify the major factors that determine the cost of automobile insurance.

■ Explain the rules that should be followed in shopping for automobile insurance.

Millions of motorists are killed or injured each year in automobile accidents. Society is then faced with the problem of compensating automobile accident victims for their bodily injuries and property damage caused by negligent drivers. Society also has the problem of providing automobile insurance to irresponsible drivers, including drunk drivers, high-risk drivers, and drivers who habitually break traffic laws. Also, some drivers cannot afford automobile insurance and so drive uninsured. Society must then compensate innocent accident victims who are injured by the uninsured drivers. In addition, critics argue that the present tort liability system for compensating accident victims is inefficient, expensive, inequitable, and slow and should be replaced by an alternative system called no-fault insurance. Finally, automobile insurance rates have increased substantially over time, which has angered consumers and caused them to seek ways to reduce their premiums.

This chapter continues the discussion of auto insurance by examining the above problems. Four major areas are emphasized. First, the various approaches for compensating automobile accident victims are discussed, including financial responsibility laws, compulsory insurance laws, unsatisfied judgment funds, and the uninsured motorists coverage. Second, no-fault automobile insurance as an alternative approach for compensating automobile accident victims is considered. Third, the various methods for providing automobile insurance to high-risk drivers are explored, including automobile insurance plans, joint underwriting associations (JUAs), reinsurance facilities, the Maryland Automobile Insurance Fund, and specialty automobile insurers. Finally, the chapter concludes with a discussion of the cost of auto insurance and offers suggestions for buying auto insurance.

## APPROACHES FOR COMPENSATING AUTOMOBILE ACCIDENT VICTIMS

In many cases, innocent persons who are injured in auto accidents are unable to recover financial damages from the negligent motorists. Although accident victims have bodily injuries or suffer property damage, they may recover nothing or receive less than full indemnification from the negligent drivers who caused the accident. To deal with this problem, the states use a number of approaches to provide some protection to accident victims from irresponsible and reckless drivers. They include the following:[1]

- Financial responsibility laws
- Compulsory insurance laws
- Unsatisfied judgment funds
- Uninsured motorists coverage
- No-fault automobile insurance

### Financial Responsibility Laws

All states have enacted some type of financial responsibility law or compulsory insurance law requiring motorists to furnish proof of financial responsibility up to certain minimum dollar limits. A **financial responsibility law** *does not require proof of financial responsibility until after the driver has his or her first accident or until after conviction for certain offenses, such as driving under the influence of alcohol.* Proof of financial responsibility is typically required under the following circumstances:

- After an accident involving bodily injury or property damage over a certain amount

- Failure to pay a final judgment resulting from an automobile accident
- Conviction for certain offenses, such as drunk driving or reckless driving

Under these conditions, if a motorist does not meet the state's financial responsibility law requirements, the state can revoke or suspend the motorist's driving privileges.

Evidence of financial responsibility can be provided by producing an automobile liability policy with at least certain minimum limits, such as $25,000/$50,000/$25,000.[2] Other ways in which the financial responsibility law can be satisfied are by posting a bond, depositing securities or money in the amount required by law, or by showing that the person is a qualified self-insurer. Exhibit 11.1 shows the minimum liability insurance requirements in the various states and Canadian provinces.

Although financial responsibility laws provide some protection against irresponsible motorists, they have two major defects:

- *There is no guarantee that all accident victims will be paid.* Financial responsibility laws normally have no penalties other than the loss of driving privileges. Thus, the accident victim may not be paid if he or she is injured by an uninsured driver, hit-and-run driver, or driver of a stolen car. An irresponsible motorist often drives without a license, so the law fails to achieve the objective of getting the irresponsible driver off the road.
- *Accident victims may not be fully indemnified for their injuries.* Most financial responsibility laws require only minimum liability insurance limits, which are relatively low. If the bodily injury exceeds the minimum limit, the accident victim may not be fully compensated.

### Compulsory Insurance Laws

Most jurisdictions have enacted some type of compulsory automobile liability insurance law as a condition for driving within the state. A **compulsory insurance law** *requires the owners and operators of motor vehicles to carry liability insurance at least equal to a certain minimum amount before the vehicle can be registered or licensed.* The law can also be satisfied by posting a bond that guarantees financial responsibility or

Exhibit 11.1
## Financial Responsibility and Compulsory Automobile Insurance Laws

| State | Liability limits[a] | State | Liability limits[a] |
|---|---|---|---|
| Alabama | 20/40/10 | Montana | 25/50/10 |
| Alaska | 50/110/25 | Nebraska | 25/50/25 |
| Arizona | 15/30/10 | Nevada | 15/30/10 |
| Arkansas | 25/50/15 | New Hampshire | 25/50/25 |
| California | 15/30/5 | New Jersey | 15/30/5 |
| Colorado | 25/50/15 | New Mexico | 25/50/10 |
| Connecticut | 20/40/10 | New York | 25/50/10[b] |
| Delaware | 15/30/10 | North Carolina | 25/50/15 |
| D.C. | 25/50/10 | North Dakota | 25/50/25 |
| Florida | 10/20/10 | Ohio | 12.5/25/7.5 |
| Georgia | 15/30/10 | Oklahoma | 10/20/10 |
| Hawaii | 25/10/25 | Oregon | 25/50/10 |
| Idaho | 25/50/15 | Pennsylvania | 15/30/5 |
| Illinois | 20/40/15 | Rhode Island | 25/50/25 |
| Indiana | 25/50/10 | South Carolina | 15/30/5 |
| Iowa | 20/40/15 | South Dakota | 25/50/25 |
| Kansas | 25/50/10 | Tennessee | 25/50/10 |
| Kentucky | 25/50/10 | Texas | 20/40/15 |
| Louisiana | 10/20/10 | Utah | 25/50/15 |
| Maine | 20/40/10 | Vermont | 20/40/10 |
| Maryland | 20/40/10 | Virginia | 25/50/20 |
| Massachusetts | 20/40/5 | Washington | 25/50/10 |
| Michigan | 20/40/10 | West Virginia | 20/40/10 |
| Minnesota | 30/60/10 | Wisconsin | 25/50/10 |
| Mississippi | 10/20/5 | Wyoming | 25/50/20 |
| Missouri | 25/50/10 | | |

### Canada[c]

| Province | Liability limit | Province | Liability limit |
|---|---|---|---|
| Alberta | $200,000 | Nova Scotia | 200,000 |
| British Columbia | 200,000 | Ontario | 200,000 |
| Manitoba | 200,000 | Prince Edward Is. | 200,000 |
| New Brunswick | 200,000 | Quebec | 50,000 |
| Newfoundland | 200,000 | Saskatchewan | 200,000 |
| Northwest Terrs. | 200,000 | Yukon | 200,000 |

[a]The first two figures refer to bodily injury liability limits and the third figure to property damage liability. For example, 20/40/10 means coverage up to $40,000 for all persons injured in an accident, subject to a limit of $20,000 for one individual, and $10,000 coverage for property damage.

[b]50/100 if injury results in death.

[c]In all Canadian provinces except Quebec, the amount of liability insurance shown is available to settle either bodily injury or property damage claims—or both. When a claim involving both bodily injury and property damage reaches this "inclusive" limit, payment for property damages is limited to $20,000 in Manitoba, New Brunswick, Newfoundland, and Yukon and to $10,000 in the other provinces and territories having "inclusive" limits. Quebec laws provide that people injured in accidents in Quebec be compensated by a government fund. Benefits paid to non-residents are scaled down in proportion to their degree of fault. The $50,000 limit relates to liability for damage to property in Quebec and to liability for bodily injury and property damage outside Quebec.

SOURCE: *The Fact Book 1996, Property/Casualty Insurance Facts* (New York: Insurance Information Institute), pp. 115–16.

by depositing money or other valuable securities that can satisfy a judgment.

Compulsory insurance laws have both desirable and undesirable features. These laws are considered superior to financial responsibility laws because they provide a stronger guarantee of protection to the public against loss. Supporters of compulsory insurance laws also argue that many registered vehicles are uninsured in those states with financial responsibility laws. Thus, compulsory laws are necessary.

Critics of compulsory insurance laws, however, point out the following defects:[3]

- *The number of uninsured motorists may not be reduced by a compulsory insurance law.* Some drivers may not license their vehicles because they cannot afford the insurance. Other drivers may drop their insurance after the vehicle is licensed.
- *Compulsory laws do not provide complete protection.* The laws require only a minimum amount of liability insurance, which is relatively low. As a result, some accident victims may not be fully compensated for their injuries.
- *Payment to all injured persons is not guaranteed.* Some injured victims may not be compensated because they are injured by hit-and-run drivers, by drivers whose insurance has lapsed, by drivers of stolen cars, and by out-of-state drivers.
- *Compulsory laws do not prevent or reduce the number of automobile accidents,* which is the heart of the automobile accident problem.

## Unsatisfied Judgment Funds

Five states—Maryland, Michigan, New Jersey, New York, and North Dakota—have established unsatisfied judgment funds for compensating innocent accident victims. An **unsatisfied judgment fund** *is a fund established by the state to compensate accident victims who have exhausted all other means of recovery.* These funds have certain common characteristics.[4]

*First, the accident victim must obtain a judgment against the negligent motorist who caused the accident and must show that the judgment cannot be collected.* Thus, there must be an unsatisfied judgment.

*Second, the maximum amount paid generally is limited to the state's financial responsibility law limit.* The amount paid may also be reduced by collateral sources of recovery, such as benefits from a workers compensation law.

*Finally, the method of financing benefits varies among the states.* Funds can be obtained by assessing the uninsured motorists in the state, by charging each motorist a fee, or by assessing insurers according to the amount of automobile liability premiums written in the state.

The major advantage of an unsatisfied judgment fund is that innocent accident victims have some protection against irresponsible motorists. However, there are several disadvantages. The innocent accident victim must still get a judgment against the negligent driver; administration of the funds is cumbersome and slow; and unsatisfied judgment funds have experienced financial problems in recent years.

## Uninsured Motorists Coverage

In many cities and states, large numbers of drivers are uninsured. An estimated 9 percent of the vehicles nationally are uninsured, but the percentage of uninsured vehicles is considerably higher in certain states, such as 23 percent in Florida.[5] Although all states have financial responsibility or compulsory insurance laws, these laws generally have proven ineffective in getting uninsured drivers off the road. Thus, other methods are needed to have protection from an uninsured driver.

**Uninsured motorists coverage** is another approach for compensating injured automobile accident victims. The insurer agrees to pay the accident victim who has a bodily injury (or property damage in some states) caused by an uninsured motorist, by a hit-and-run driver, or by a negligent driver whose insurer is insolvent.

Uninsured motorists coverage has several advantages.

- *Motorists have some protection against an uninsured driver.* Many states require the coverage to be mandatorily included in all automobile liability insurance policies sold within the state. In other states, coverage is included in the policy unless the insured voluntarily declines the protection by signing a written waiver.
- *The coverage is relatively inexpensive in the majority of states.*

- *Finally, claim settlement is faster and more efficient than a tort liability lawsuit.* Although the accident victim must establish negligence by the uninsured driver, it is not necessary to sue the negligent driver and win a judgment.

Uninsured motorist's coverage, however, has several defects as a technique for compensating injured automobile accident victims. They include the following:[6]

- *Unless higher limits are purchased, the maximum amount paid is limited to the state's financial responsibility or compulsory insurance law requirement.* The minimum limits are relatively low. Thus, the accident victim may not be fully compensated for his or her loss.
- *The injured person must establish that the uninsured motorist is legally liable for the accident.* This may be difficult in some cases and expensive if an attorney must be hired.
- *Property damage is not covered in many states.* Thus, unless you have collision coverage, you would collect nothing for any property damage caused by an uninsured motorist in those states.

## No-Fault Automobile Insurance

No-fault automobile insurance is another method for compensating injured accident victims. Because of dissatisfaction and defects in the traditional tort liability system, about half of the states, the District of Columbia, and Puerto Rico currently have no-fault laws in effect. Although no-fault laws vary among the states, certain common characteristics are present.

**Definition of No-Fault Insurance**   **No-fault insurance** *means that after an automobile accident involving a bodily injury, each party collects from his or her insurer regardless of fault.* It is not necessary to determine who is at fault and prove negligence before a loss payment is made. Regardless of who caused the accident, each party collects from his or her insurer.

In addition, a true no-fault law places some restriction on the right to sue the negligent driver who caused the accident. If the claim is below a certain **monetary threshold** (such as $2000), an injured motorist would not be permitted to sue but instead would collect from his or her insurer. However, if the bodily injury claim exceeds the threshold amount, the injured person has the right to sue the negligent driver for damages. In three states, a verbal rather than monetary threshold is used. A **verbal threshold** *means that a suit for damages is allowed only in serious cases, such as those involving death, dismemberment, disfigurement, or permanent loss of a bodily member or function.* Thus, if the injured person has a less severe injury than those listed, the injured person would not be permitted to sue but instead would collect from his or her insurer.

**Basic Characteristics of No-Fault Plans** No-fault plans vary widely among the states with respect to type of law, benefits provided, and restrictions on the right to sue.[7]

1. *Types of no-fault plans.* There are several types of no-fault plans. Under a **pure no-fault plan,** *the injured person cannot sue at all, regardless of the seriousness of the claim, and no payments are made for pain and suffering.* In effect, the tort liability system for a bodily injury is abolished, since the accident victim cannot sue for damages. Instead, the injured person would receive unlimited benefits from his or her insurer for medical expenses and the loss of wages. No state has enacted a pure no-fault plan at this time, but Michigan's law comes closest to this concept.

   Under a **modified no-fault plan,** *an injured person has the right to sue a negligent driver only if the bodily injury claim exceeds the dollar or verbal threshold.* Otherwise, the accident victim collects from his or her insurer. Thus, modified no-fault plans only partially restrict the right to sue.

   An **add-on plan** *pays benefits to an accident victim without regard to fault, but the injured person still has the right to sue the negligent driver who caused the accident.* This also includes the right to sue for pain and suffering (general damages). Hence the name: the law adds benefits but takes nothing away. Since the injured person still retains the right to sue, add-on plans are not true no-fault laws.

   Finally, three states (Kentucky, New Jersey, and Pennsylvania) have **choice no-fault plans.** Under such laws, motorists can elect to be covered under the state's no-fault law with lower premiums or can retain the right to sue under the tort liability system with higher premiums.

Slightly more than half of the jurisdictions with no-fault laws have modified plans where restrictions are placed on the right to sue. The remainder have add-on plans in which the insured person receives additional benefits from his or her insurer but still retains the right to sue. As noted earlier, no state has enacted a pure no-fault plan, and three states have choice no-fault laws.

2. *No-fault benefits.* No-fault benefits are provided by adding an endorsement to the automobile insurance policy. The endorsement is typically called "basic reparations benefits coverage" or "personal injury protection coverage," which describes the no-fault benefits. Benefits are restricted to the injured person's *economic loss,* such as medical expenses, a percentage of lost wages, and certain other expenses. The injured person can sue for *noneconomic loss* (such as pain and suffering and inconvenience) only if the dollar threshold is exceeded or the verbal threshold is met.

The following benefits are typically provided:

- Medical expenses
- Loss of earnings
- Essential services expenses
- Funeral expenses
- Survivors' loss benefits

*Medical expenses are paid usually up to some maximum limit.* Rehabilitation expenses incurred by an injured accident victim are also paid.

*Payments are made for the loss of earnings.* The no-fault benefits are typically limited to a stated percentage of the disabled person's weekly or monthly earnings, with a maximum limit in terms of dollar amount and duration.

*Benefits are paid for* **essential services expenses** *ordinarily performed by the injured person.* Examples are housework, cooking, lawn mowing, and house repairs.

*Funeral expenses are paid up to some dollar limit.* In some states, funeral expenses are included as part of the medical expense limit. In other states, funeral expenses are a separate benefit.

**Survivors' loss benefits** *are also payable to eligible survivors, such as a surviving spouse and dependent children.* The survivors typically receive periodic income payments or a lump sum to compensate them for the death of a covered person.

A number of states also require that **optional no-fault benefits** above the prescribed minimums be made available. Many states also require insurers to offer **optional deductibles** that may be used to restrict or eliminate certain no-fault coverages.

3. *Right to sue.* In those states with add-on plans, there are no restrictions on the right to sue. The accident victim can receive first-party no-fault benefits from his or her insurer and still retain the right to sue the negligent driver for damages.

All states permit a lawsuit in the event of a serious injury. A serious injury typically is a personal injury that results in death, dismemberment, disfigurement, bone fracture, permanent loss of a bodily function or organ, or permanent disability. Under these circumstances, the injured person can sue for damages, including payment for pain and suffering.

In those states with modified no-fault laws, the right to sue is restricted. In general, the accident victim can sue the negligent driver for general damages, including pain and suffering, only if the dollar threshold for medical expenses exceeds a certain amount, or the injury is serious.

Finally, the three states with choice no-fault laws allow motorists to elect coverage under the state's no-fault law with lower premiums and restrictions on lawsuits, or alternatively, to retain the right to sue under the tort liability system with higher premiums.

4. *Exclusion of property damage.* With the exception of Michigan, no-fault laws cover only bodily injury and exclude property damage. Thus, if a negligent driver smashed into your automobile, you would still be permitted to sue for the property damage to your car. It is argued that the defects inherent in the tort liability system with respect to bodily injuries are not normally

present to the same degree in property damage claims; thus, a lawsuit for property damage does not normally result in long court delays, expensive legal fees, and similar defects now found in bodily injury lawsuits.[8]

**Arguments for No-Fault Laws**    Proponents of no-fault laws argue that an alternative system is needed because of defects in the present tort liability system. Defects in the present system include the following:

- *Difficulty of determining fault.* Critics argue that automobile accidents occur suddenly and unexpectedly, and that determination of fault is often difficult. In contrast, under a no-fault law, it is not necessary to determine fault. Each party collects from his or her insurer if the bodily injury claim does not exceed the dollar threshold or does not meet the description of a verbal threshold.
- *Limited scope of reparations system.* Another shortcoming is that the present tort liability system is deficient in its scope of reparations. An earlier Department of Transportation (DOT) study found that only 45 percent of the seriously injured or the beneficiaries of those killed benefited in any way from the tort liability system.[9] One in ten victims received no compensation from any source whatsoever.
- *Inequities in claim payments.* In the present system, smaller claims often are overpaid, while serious claims may be underpaid. The DOT study showed that, for small claims with an economic loss of $500 or less, the average settlement was four and one-half times the actual economic loss. For seriously or fatally injured accident victims with an economic loss of $25,000 or more, only about one-third was recovered.
- *Large proportion of liability premium dollar used to pay legal costs.* A large percentage of each liability premium dollar is used to pay lawyers, claims investigators, and other costs of determining blame. The DOT study showed that only 44 cents on the dollar went to automobile accident victims to compensate them for their losses.
- *Delay in payments.* Large numbers of claims are not paid promptly because of investigation, negotiation, and waiting for a court date. The

DOT study showed that only about half of the claims were settled in six months or less.

**Arguments Against No-Fault Laws**    Supporters of the present system argue that no-fault laws are also defective. Major arguments against no-fault laws include the following.[10]

- *Defects of the negligence system are exaggerated.* Generations of judges, lawyers, and juries have successfully applied negligence concepts to automobile accidents. A large proportion of fatal crashes and serious accidents involve alcohol where fault can usually be determined without difficulty. Also, the fact that most claims are settled out of court suggests the present system is working fairly well.
- *Claims of efficiency and premium savings are exaggerated.* Predictions of greater efficiency and premium savings from no-fault laws are exaggerated and unreliable. In some states with no-fault laws, premiums have increased more rapidly than in tort liability states.
- *Court delay is not universal.* Court delay because of congestion is a problem only in certain large metropolitan areas, and this delay can be reduced by providing for more adequate courts and improved procedures. Also, court delay is a separate problem and should be attacked as such rather than used as an argument for a no-fault system. The courts are burdened because of an increase in the number of divorce cases, drug and other criminal cases, and other types of civil suits.
- *Safe drivers may be penalized.* A no-fault plan may penalize safe drivers and provide a bonus for irresponsible motorists who cause the accidents. The rating system may inequitably allocate the accident costs to the drivers who are not at fault, and their premiums may go up as a result.
- *There is no payment for pain and suffering.* Plaintiff attorneys argue that the true cost to the accident victim cannot be measured only by the actual dollar amount of medical expenses and loss of wages. Pain and suffering should also be considered in determining the amount of damages.
- *The present system just needs to be reformed.* This could be done by increasing the number of judges and courtrooms, limiting the fees of

attorneys, and using arbitration rather than the courts to settle small cases. Rather than replacing the old system with a new system of no-fault, the present system needs only to be reformed, not abandoned.

**How Effective Are No-Fault Laws?**    A few states have repealed their no-fault laws, partly because of low dollar thresholds that resulted in additional lawsuits. However, in those states that have relatively high dollar thresholds or verbal thresholds, no-fault laws appear to be working fairly well. A study of no-fault plans by the Institute for Civil Justice provides valuable information concerning the effectiveness of present no-fault plans. The major conclusions are as follows:[11]

- *No-fault plans reduce transaction costs (attorney fees and claim processing costs).* All no-fault plans reduce transaction costs. However, a no-fault plan that absolutely banned compensation for noneconomic loss would eliminate about three-fourths of the transaction costs. Alternative plans that allow some access to the liability system would reduce transaction costs by 20 to 40 percent, depending on plan design.
- *No-fault plans match the compensation received for an injury more closely with the economic loss sustained.* No-fault plans increase the fraction of economic loss that is compensated and reduce the amount paid for noneconomic loss. Economic loss includes medical bills, lost wages, and other losses measured in monetary terms. Injured people with smaller claims tend to recover amounts that approximate their medical costs and lost wages. However, seriously injured people whose compensation is capped by policy limits recover a larger share of their economic loss because they can collect both no-fault benefits and liability compensation.
- *No-fault plans eliminate compensation for noneconomic loss for injured people below the threshold with less serious injuries.* Noneconomic losses include pain and suffering, disfigurement, and other losses not measured in monetary terms.
- *No-fault plans generally pay benefits faster.* On average, no-fault plans pay benefits to injured people about two months faster than under the traditional system.

*No-fault plans can yield substantial savings over the traditional system, or such plans can increase costs depending on plan design.* Under different no-fault alternatives, total injury coverage costs may decrease. Such costs, however, may be higher under no-fault, depending on the threshold and level of no-fault benefits. This is especially true in states that have relatively low dollar thresholds. Whether a particular no-fault plan will reduce total injury coverage costs will depend on the provisions in the plan.

## AUTOMOBILE INSURANCE FOR HIGH-RISK DRIVERS

Some drivers have difficulty obtaining automobile insurance through normal market channels. This is especially true of younger drivers, who account for a disproportionate number of automobile accidents, drivers who have poor driving records, and drunk drivers. These drivers can obtain automobile insurance in the **shared market** (also called the **residual market**). The shared market refers to plans in which automobile insurers participate to make insurance available to drivers who are unable to obtain coverage in the standard markets.

High-risk drivers who have difficulty in obtaining automobile insurance in the standard markets can purchase automobile insurance from a number of sources. They include the following:

- Automobile insurance plans
- Joint underwriting associations (JUAs)
- Reinsurance facilities
- Maryland Automobile Insurance Fund
- Specialty automobile insurers

### Automobile Insurance Plans

Each state has an *automobile insurance plan* (formerly called an assigned risk plan) or some other method for providing automobile insurance to persons who are unable to get protection in the voluntary market. Under this arrangement, all automobile insurers in the state are assigned their proportionate share of high-risk drivers based on the total volume of automobile business written in the state. However, the premiums charged are substantially higher than insurance obtained in the voluntary markets. It is not uncommon for high-risk drivers to pay two or three times the standard premium.

The major advantage of automobile insurance plans is that a high-risk driver generally has at least one source for obtaining liability insurance. Thus, the social objective of protecting innocent accident victims is at least partially met. However, such plans have several disadvantages, which include the following:

- *Despite higher premiums paid by high-risk drivers, automobile insurance plans have incurred substantial underwriting losses.* Thus, good drivers in the voluntary markets are subsidizing the substandard drivers.
- *High premiums may cause many high-risk drivers to go uninsured.* This produces the exact opposite of what the plans are intended to accomplish.
- *Many drivers who are "clean risks" with no driving convictions are arbitrarily placed in the plans.* This can happen when poor loss experience or inadequate rate increases by regulatory officials cause insurers to restrict the writing of automobile insurance in a given territory.
- *The driver does not have a choice of insurers.* Thus, freedom of choice is reduced.

## Joint Underwriting Associations

Four states (Florida, Hawaii, Mississippi, and Missouri) have established joint underwriting associations to make automobile insurance available to high-risk drivers. A **joint underwriting association** (JUA) is an organization of automobile insurers operating in the state in which high-risk business is placed in a common pool, and each company pays its pro rata share of pool losses and expenses. The JUA influences the design of the high-risk automobile policy and sets the rates that are charged. All underwriting losses are proportionately shared by the companies on the basis of premiums written in the state.

A limited number of companies are designated as servicing insurers to service the high-risk JUA business. Each agent or broker is assigned a company that provides claim services and other services to the policyowners. Although only a limited number of large insurers are servicing insurers, all companies share in the underwriting losses as noted earlier.

Joint underwriting associations have been criticized in recent years because of substantial underwriting deficits and the high proportion of drivers who are placed in these plans. Critics argue that large numbers of drivers with spotless records are placed in pools originally designed for high-risk drivers. In rebuttal, insurers maintain that automobile rates are inadequate, especially for younger drivers, which has forced insurers to place a large proportion of motorists in a JUA.

## Reinsurance Facilities

Four states (Massachusetts, New Hampshire, North Carolina, and South Carolina) have established a **reinsurance facility** or pool for placing high-risk automobile drivers. Under this arrangement, the company must accept all applicants for insurance, both good and bad drivers. If the applicant is considered a high-risk driver, the insurer has the option of placing the driver in the reinsurance pool. Although the high-risk driver is in the reinsurance pool, the original insurer services the policy. Underwriting losses in the reinsurance facility are shared by all automobile insurers in the state. In recent years, the reinsurance facilities have also experienced substantial underwriting losses. The result is that good drivers are heavily subsidizing the poor drivers in the plans.

## Maryland Automobile Insurance Fund

The **Maryland Automobile Insurance Fund** is a state fund that makes auto insurance available to motorists in Maryland who are unable to obtain insurance in the voluntary markets. The state fund came into existence because of high rates charged by private insurers, large numbers of motorists who had been placed in the assigned risk plan, and difficulties experienced by high-risk drivers in obtaining insurance. The fund limits the insurance to drivers who have been canceled or refused insurance by private insurers.

## Specialty Automobile Insurers

**Specialty automobile insurers** are insurers that specialize in insuring motorists with poor driving records. These insurers typically insure drivers who have been canceled or refused insurance, teenage drivers, and drunk drivers. The premiums are substantially higher than premiums paid in the normal or standard markets. The actual premium paid is based on the individual's driving record, typically over the past three years. The higher the number of chargeable accidents or moving vehicle traffic violations, the higher the premium charged. The liability insurance limits are at least equal to the financial responsibility law requirement in the state, and many companies offer higher limits on an optional basis. In addition, because the drivers have a high probability of being involved in an accident, medical payments coverage is often limited to $1000 per person, and collision insurance may require a $250 or higher deductible.

Some insurers have driver incentive plans to encourage safe driving: premiums are periodically reduced, say 5 percent each quarter, if the insured has had no chargeable offenses against him or her. However, if another accident or traffic violation occurs during the policy period, the driver typically is surcharged and must pay higher premiums.

## COST OF AUTOMOBILE INSURANCE

Automobile insurance is a costly and necessary coverage. Payment of automobile insurance premiums can quickly deplete a modest checking account. Depending on where you live, your age, driving experience, and other factors, the annual cost of insuring your car can range from several hundred dollars to several thousand dollars. You should have some knowledge of the factors that determine your automobile insurance premiums and what you can do to reduce the premiums. This section discusses the major factors that determine the cost of automobile insurance. Discussion is limited to liability insurance and physical damage insurance on the car, since these two coverages account for a large proportion of the total annual premium. Medical payments coverage and the uninsured motorists coverage are relatively low-cost items in the total premium.

The major rating factors for determining private passenger automobile premiums are as follows:[12]

- Territory
- Age, gender, and marital status
- Use of the automobile
- Driver education
- Good student discount
- Number and types of automobiles
- Individual driving record

### Territory

A base rate for liability insurance is first established, determined largely by the territory where the automobile is principally used and garaged. Each state is divided into rating territories—for example, a large city, a part of a city, a suburb, or a rural area. Claims data are compiled for each territory in determining the basic rate. Thus, a city driver normally pays a higher rate than a rural driver because of the higher number of automobile accidents in congested cities. In addition, because of higher claim costs, large numbers of vehicles, and traffic congestion, average annual auto insurance premiums are substantially higher in certain states (see Exhibit 11.2).

After the base rate is determined, it is modified by other rating factors. These factors are discussed in the following section.

### Age, Gender, and Marital Status

Age, gender, and marital status are important in determining the total premium. Most states permit these factors to be used in determining premiums.

Age is an extremely important rating factor, since young drivers account for a disproportionate number of accidents. In 1994, drivers under age 25 accounted for about 15 percent of all licensed drivers; however, this group accounted for 28 percent of the drivers in all accidents and 26 percent of all fatal accidents.[13] Older drivers over age 65 are also involved in a high percentage of fatal accidents (see Exhibit 11.3).

Gender is also important. In recent years, female drivers have experienced higher accident rates than male drivers. However, male drivers are involved in a higher proportion of accidents where someone is killed.[14] Although insurers generally charge female drivers lower rates than males, the rate gap is narrowing, especially at the younger ages (see Insight 11.1, p. 206).

Insurers typically use several rating classes for rating young drivers under age 30, such as under age 20, ages 20 and 21; ages 22 through 24, and ages 25 through 29.

---

EXHIBIT 11.2

## Auto Insurance Premiums Vary Widely Among the States

**Average Annual Premiums**

The following table lists the 10 highest and lowest average annual auto insurance premiums in the United States, according to the National Association of Insurance Commissioners:

| | *Highest* | | | *Lowest* | |
|---|---|---|---|---|---|
| *Rank* | *State* | *Amount* | *Rank* | *State* | *Amount* |
| 1. | New Jersey | $1,106.21 | 1. | North Dakota | $467.15 |
| 2. | Hawaii | 1,090.32 | 2. | Iowa | 484.89 |
| 3. | Rhode Island | 1,033.52 | 3. | South Dakota | 516.18 |
| 4. | District of Columbia | 1,033.11 | 4. | Nebraska | 526.21 |
| 5. | New York | 1,029.09 | 5. | Idaho | 533.21 |
| 6. | Massachusetts | 1,025.47 | 6. | North Carolina | 547.08 |
| 7. | Connecticut | 943.38 | 7. | Maine | 547.51 |
| 8. | California | 887.33 | 8. | Wyoming | 549.72 |
| 9. | Nevada | 881.52 | 9. | Wisconsin | 555.20 |
| 10. | Louisiana | 876.70 | 10. | Kansas | 561.74 |

NOTE:  Rank is based on premiums paid in 1994, the latest year for which figures are available.

SOURCE: *Sunday World Herald,* February 11, 1996, p. 2-M.

---

Marital status is also important since young married male drivers tend to have relatively fewer accidents than unmarried male drivers in the same age category.

Certain credits and rate discounts may be allowed with respect to the rating factor of age. A premium credit may be given if a youthful driver of a family car is attending a school or college more than 100 miles away from home and does not have a car at school. Also, female drivers ages 30 through 64 may be eligible for a rate discount if they are the only drivers in their households. Older drivers are also eligible for rate discounts from many insurers.

## Use of the Automobile

Use of the automobile is another important rating factor. Insurers classify automobiles on the basis of how the car is driven, such as the following:

- Pleasure use—not used in business or customarily driven to work, unless the one-way mileage to work is under 3 miles.
- Drive to work—not used in business, but is driven 15 or more miles each way.

- Business use—customarily used in business or professional pursuits.
- Farm use—principally garaged on a farm or ranch, and not used in any other business or driven to school or work.

A car classified for farm use has the lowest rating factor, followed next by pleasure use of the car. Driving the car to work or using it for business purposes requires a higher rating factor.

## Driver Education

If a youthful operator successfully completes an approved driver education course, he or she can receive a driver training credit, such as 10 or 15 percent. The rate credit is based on the premise that driver education courses for teenage drivers can reduce accidents and hold down insurance rates.

## Good Student Discount

A **good student discount** is available in many states. The cost reduction is based on the premise that good students are better drivers. The psychological

## Exhibit 11.3

### The Odds of Dying

Even though their crash rate is substantially lower than teenagers', older drivers have a slightly higher involvement rate in *fatal* crashes, as shown here. Drivers age 80 and older have nearly 20 fatal crashes for every 100 million miles they drive; 16-year-olds have 17 fatal accidents for every 100 million miles.

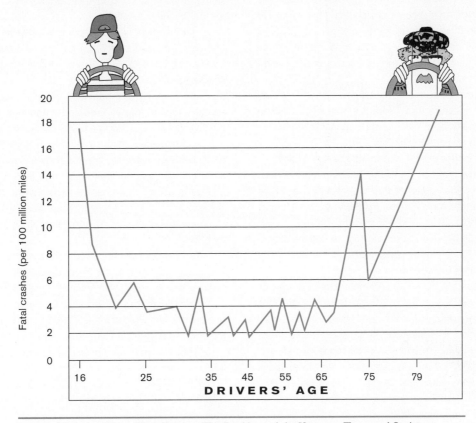

Source: Excerpted from "Safe Driving, The Rookies and the Veterans, Teens and Seniors at Greatest Risk on Nation's Roadways," *USAA Magazine,* Vol. 26, No. 2 (April 1995), p. 13.

makeup and intellectual capacity of the superior student also contribute to the safer operation of an automobile. Also, a superior student will probably spend more time studying and less time driving the family car. However, most insurers have not found a strong statistical relationship between good grades and superior driving to support the discount.[15]

To qualify for the discount, the individual must be a full-time student in high school or college, be at least age 16, and meet one of the following:

- Rank in the upper 20 percent of the class

- Have a B average, or the equivalent
- Have at least a 3.0 average
- Be on the Dean's List or honor roll

A school official must sign a form indicating that the student has met one of the scholastic requirements.

### Number and Types of Automobiles

A **multicar discount** is also available if the insured owns two or more automobiles. This discount is based on the assumption that two cars owned by the

## INSIGHT 11.1

### Auto Insurance Rate Gap Narrows for Youthful Male and Female Drivers

All things being equal, Casey and Carla Allender are.

Born one minute apart, the 18-year-old, opposite-sex twins share a lot in common, including the same ZIP code, pickup truck and driving record.

So why would Casey be quoted as much as $300 more than his sister for six months of auto insurance?

"Because he's a boy," said their mother, Vicki Allender of Gilbert, Ariz. "And it's not fair. . . . Even though they say boys are more irresponsible and drive more than girls, I don't think that's true."

Mrs. Allender is right, insurance specialists say.

And car-insurance premiums have begun to reflect a change in the long-standing discrepancy between rates for youthful male drivers and those for their female counterparts.

"The gap between boys and girls is definitely closing," said Carrie Rosen, media-relations specialist for CNA Insurance Companies in Chicago.

The rates are based on what insurance companies pay out in losses.

"The general trend in the last decade is that more young females are involved in crashes," said Allan Williams of the Insurance Institute for Highway Safety in Arlington, Va. "And they're catching up to the males in the number of crashes they cause."

Therefore, their insurance premiums have been catching up to the boys.

Insurance Services Office Inc., which analyzes insurance losses industrywide, recently recommended higher rates for youthful females and slightly lower ones for males. Many insurance companies use ISO figures to set their premiums.

Previously, ISO recommended that youthful males pay 78 percent more than young females for identical coverage.

"But the middle of last year, July of 1995, we reviewed our data," said George Meno, regional director for ISO in San Francisco.

*The latest recommendations are that the male rate should be only 45 percent more than for females, with male rates going down 3 percent while female rates increase 19 percent.*

The findings were based on the rate classification of youthful drivers as principal operators without driver-training discount and with a clean driving record.

Williams said the increase in female crashes "is partly because more are likely to be licensed drivers than there used to be. But there are other factors, too, such as they're driving more aggressively now or driving more like males."

Law-enforcement officers are well aware that there's been a change.

"It's been gradual," said motorcycle officer Kenny Blanchard of the Phoenix Police Department. "It hasn't been all of a sudden."

Young male drivers still have a propensity to speed, but it's the females who are causing more and more of the accidents, Blanchard said.

"They're worse than males when it comes to wrecks because they just don't pay attention," the officer said. "They're playing with their hair or the radio, and the skid marks are like zero so you know they didn't see it coming."

He thinks part of the problems with females is inexperience. To prove his point, Blanchard cited an accident involving a close friend.

"My buddy just got hit by a 16-year-old girl, and she'd only had her license for two days," he said. "A lot I write up for accidents only have their temporary licenses."

Source: Adapted from Linda Helser, "Insurance Gap Narrows for Boy, Girls," *Omaha World Herald*, March 30, 1996, pp. 29–30.

same person will not be driven as frequently as only one car owned by that person.

The year, make, and model of the automobile also affect the cost of physical damage insurance on the car. Premiums on a new car will be considerably higher than premiums on a car several years old. As the car gets older, the collision premiums decline.

Also, the damageability and repairability of the car are important rating factors for physical damage insurance. New cars are now rated based on susceptibility to damage and cost of repairs. Cars that are damage-resistant and relatively easy to repair generally have lower rates.

### Individual Driving Record

Many companies have **safe driver plans** where the premiums paid are based on the individual driving record of the insured and operators who live with the insured. The insured who has a clean driving record qualifies for a lower rate than drivers who have poor records. A clean driving record means the driver has not been involved in any accident where he or she is at fault and has not been convicted of a serious traffic violation in the last three years. A driver without a clean record must pay higher premiums.

Accident points are assessed for accidents and traffic violations, and rate surcharges are applied accordingly. Points are charged for a conviction of drunk driving, failure to stop and report an accident, homicide or assault involving an automobile, driving on a suspended or revoked driver's license, and other offenses. The actual premium paid is based on the total number of accumulated points.

Most insurers impose a surcharge for a chargeable accident that exceeds a given amount, such as $500. The surcharge generally lasts three years. For example, the base premium may be surcharged 10 percent for the first accident and 25 percent for the second.

The preceding discussion has focused on the major cost factors in automobile insurance. However, the cost of automobile insurance also has important political implications and has become a political issue in many states. Motorists generally believe they are being overcharged and "ripped off" by automobile insurers because of excessively high premiums. For

example, in the Los Angeles area, it is common for high-risk drivers to pay $3000 or more annually for their automobile insurance. In rebuttal, automobile insurers maintain that the business is generally unprofitable or marginally profitable because of the increased number of automobile accidents, rising medical and auto repair costs, excessive jury awards, and fraudulent claims. As a result, several large automobile insurers have attempted to withdraw from states where the business generally has been unprofitable.

## SHOPPING FOR AUTOMOBILE INSURANCE

As a careful insurance consumer, you should remember the following suggestions when an auto insurance policy is purchased:

- Have adequate liability insurance.
- Carry higher deductibles.
- Drop collision insurance on an older vehicle.
- Shop around for automobile insurance.
- Take advantage of discounts.
- Improve your driving record.

### Have Adequate Liability Insurance

Adequate liability insurance is the most important consideration in automobile insurance. Damage awards have soared in recent years because of inflation, higher hospital and medical costs, higher wage losses, changing concepts of damages, and more liberal juries. A negligent driver who is underinsured could have a deficiency judgment filed against him or her, whereby both present and future income and assets can be attached to satisfy the judgment. This can be avoided by adequate liability limits.

For standard drivers, substantial amounts of liability insurance can be purchased without a proportionate increase in the premium. Liability premiums do not increase proportionately with higher limits because the probability of a large claim is significantly lower than the probability of a smaller claim. For example, there are relatively fewer claims exceeding $500,000 than claims under $25,000.

You should also consider purchasing a personal umbrella policy, which will provide an additional $1 to $10 million of liability insurance on your car on an excess basis after the underlying coverage is exhausted. However, you must increase the underlying liability coverage on your car to certain specified limits before the umbrella policy applies. Otherwise, you will have a substantial gap in coverage.

## Carry Higher Deductibles

Another important recommendation is to carry higher deductibles on collision and comprehensive insurance. Some insureds have deductibles as low as $100, which is too low in view of the rapid inflation in car prices over time. A deductible of $100 made sense years ago, when car prices were considerably lower—but not today. Increasing the deductible to $250 or $500 will reduce the collision insurance premium from most insurers by at least 10 to 20 percent.

## Drop Collision Insurance on an Older Vehicle

You should consider dropping collision insurance on your car if it is an older model with a low market value. The cost of repairs after an accident will often exceed the value of an older car, but the insurer will pay no more than its current market value (less the deductible). One rough rule of thumb is that when a standard-size automobile (such as a Chevrolet, Ford, or Dodge) is over six years old, the physical damage insurance on the car should be dropped.

## Shop Around for Automobile Insurance

Another important principle is to shop carefully for automobile insurance. Several agents should be contacted so that premiums can be compared. There is intense price competition among automobile insurers, and considerable variation in underwriting standards, loss experience, and claim practices. All insurers do not charge the same premium for comparable coverages. Several states have prepared shoppers' guides to help insurance consumers make a better decision when automobile insurance is purchased. Exhibit 11.4, for example, lists the five

---

EXHIBIT 11.4

### Automobile Insurance Premiums for Phoenix, Arizona (six-month premiums)

| Rank | Names | Premiums[a] |
|------|-------|-------------|
| | *Five lowest-price policies* | |
| 1. | AIU Insurance Company | $505.66 |
| 2. | Amex AC | 509.60 |
| 3. | United Services Auto. Assoc. | 510.56 |
| 4. | Teachers Insurance Company | 526.80 |
| 5. | Liberty Mutual Fire Ins. Co. | 567.00 |
| | *Five highest-price policies* | |
| 53. | Milwaukee Safeguard Insurance Company | $1338.00 |
| 54. | Phoenix Indemnity Insurance Company | 1371.51 |
| 55. | Leader National Insurance Company | 1385.00 |
| 56. | Atlantic Casualty Company | 1462.00 |
| 57. | Acceptance Insurance Company | 1541.47 |

NOTE: The premiums shown are for six months based on the rates in effect as of February 29, 1996. The hypothetical driver is a married male, age 48, who drives 15 miles each way to work (30 miles round-trip). He drives a 1993 Ford Taurus LX, 4-door sedan with an automatic shift and has a clean driving record for the last three years.

[a]The coverages are bodily injury liability, $100,000/$300,000 or a single limit of $300,000; property damage liability, $50,000; medical payments, $5000; uninsured motorist (same limits as liability); collision, $200 deductible; and comprehensive, $100 deductible.

SOURCE: Department of Insurance, State of Arizona, *Automobile Premium Comparison Survey,* Edition 1, April 1996.

## INSIGHT 11.2

## Firm Unites Auto Insurers On the Internet

Think of it as a drive-through window serving up auto insurance—on-line.

**Strategic Concepts** Corp., an Internet start-up, plans to unveil today a one-stop service to shop for insurance over the Internet's World Wide Web, which is becoming the multimedia business district in cyberspace. The Burlingame, Calif., company's service will allow users to draw from a database of insurance products and regulatory issues, submit an electronic application for insurance and compare quotes from a variety of insurance companies. InsWeb plans to go beyond auto insurance and introduce a full menu of insurance products year end.

Some 15 companies plan to participate in the launch of InsWeb including **Kemper** Corp.'s Kemper Life Insurance Co. unit, **Fremont General** Group, and various offerings from affiliates of **Xerox** Corp.'s Talegen insurance unit.

"It's the first time that you will be able to purchase insurance sitting at your desk and at your convenience," said Hussein Enan, chairman and chief executive of Strategic Concepts. Mr. Enan predicted that the service will have as many as 70 companies on board by the end of the year. Though consumers may enter into binding agreements to purchase insurance, they won't yet be able to pay for it on-line. And regulations in some states, such as California, wouldn't allow on-line purchasing.

Strategic Concepts will draw two revenue streams from participating insurance companies—rented space on Strategic Concepts' Web site and a fee each time a consumer submits an application. Applicants won't pay a fee.

While various insurance resources exist on the Internet, InsWeb is believed to be among the first to organize a central clearinghouse of insurers for consumers to do comparison shopping.

That feature may make some insurance companies uneasy. "Why on earth would lots of companies want to show up at the same place where customers would bid them against each other?" asks Jerry Michalski, editor of Release 1.0, a technology newsletter.

"Everyone is uncomfortable with the potential to have their business commoditized and that's what I suppose might happen," said Thomas H. Walker, senior vice president at **American Re** Corp., a reinsurer. Still, he adds, the technology could help firms to better distinguish their offerings despite the "auction market" that could arise on-line.

Strategic Concepts' Mr. Enan acknowledges that some companies won't want to be shopped based on prices alone and therefore will not publish them. But he added, the service could help any of the 2,000 insurance companies and their 700,000 agents cut the costs of distributing product information. "We think there will be tremendous cost savings because the medium is so much more efficient," he said.

SOURCE: Adapted from Jared Sandberg, "Firm Unites Auto Insurers on the Internet," *The Wall Street Journal,* October 23, 1995, p. B-8.

lowest- and five highest-cost auto insurance policies in Phoenix, as reported in a survey by the Arizona Department of Insurance. As this table shows, there is wide variation among insurers for the same coverages.

In addition, some insurers are now providing rate quotes and electronic applications over the Internet's World Wide Web. As a result, consumers who are computer literate have a convenient central clearing house to do effective comparison shopping (see Insight 11.2).

It should be stressed that price should not be the only consideration in selecting an automobile insurer. Other important factors include company claim practices, services provided by agents and insurers, and the financial strength of the insurer.

In addition, when shopping for auto insurance, you should not falsify or conceal a poor driving record or where the car is garaged. Insurers are now using sophisticated computer systems to check on driving records. If your driving record is falsified or

## INSIGHT 11.3

### Insurers End Discounts for Anti-Lock Brakes

Auto insurers are starting to eliminate discounts for cars equipped with anti-lock brakes after concluding the devices don't significantly reduce accident claims.

USAA, the nation's fifth-largest auto insurer, has notified 2.5 million customers that it is ending the discounts because, it said, there is virtually no difference in the claims experience between vehicles equipped with anti-lock brakes and those with standard brakes. The Allstate Corp., the second-largest auto insurer, is considering ending its discounts.

Auto-safety experts say anti-lock brakes haven't lived up to their billing because human nature has defeated technology. But the experts disagree whether it is the fault of the engineers who designed the systems or of the drivers who use them improperly.

Conventional brakes, when pressed and held, lock the wheels, which can make a vehicle spin or skid out of control. Even without a skid, steering becomes difficult or impossible.

Anti-lock braking systems use a computer chip that directs sensors to apply pressure with a pumping action to slow the wheels without locking them. Drivers also can steer around obstacles while braking.

But the computer-directed pumping causes a vibration that usually can be felt as a pulsing in the brake pedal. Some drivers, believing their brakes are failing, react by pumping the pedal, which increases the stopping distance. Other drivers, who were taught to pump brakes to avoid a skid, continue to pump anti-lock brakes, although they shouldn't.

And some people drive faster and take more risks because they believe anti-lock brakes will stop them sooner, insurers say.

The result, insurer say, is that the anti-lock brakes aren't reducing accident claims.

"We see no justification for continuing our discounts for anti-lock brakes in states where we are not legally required to do so," said John Wolmsley, spokesman for USAA. The 5 percent to 10 percent discounts will be available only in the three states—New York, New Jersey and Florida—that require them.

State Farm Mutual Automobile Insurance, which has been America's largest auto insurer for 50 years, has offered discounts for anti-lock brakes only in the three states where it is required.

"There is no evidence that anti-lock brakes reduce claims payments. Therefore, we see no reason to voluntarily offer discounts for the device," said State Farm spokesman Dave Hurst.

SOURCE: Adapted from "Insurers End Discounts for ABS, Brakes Not Living Up to Billing, They Say," *Sunday World Herald*, December 17, 1995, p. 15-A.

---

incomplete, your policy could be canceled or premiums increased.

## Take Advantage of Discounts

When you shop for auto insurance, you should determine whether you are eligible for one or more discounts. All insurers do not offer the same discounts, and certain discounts are not available in all states. However, some common discounts include the following:

- **Multicar discount**—10 to 25 percent
- **No accidents in three years**—5 to 10 percent
- **Drivers over age 50**—5 to 15 percent
- **Defensive driving course**—5 to 10 percent
- **Anti-theft device**—5 to 50 percent discount for comprehensive
- **Automatic seat belt and air bag**—20 to 60 percent for medical payments
- **Good student discount**—5 to 25 percent
- **Auto and HO policy with same insurer**—5 to 15 percent
- **College student away from home without a car**—10 to 40 percent

Many insurers have eliminated the discount previously given for anti-lock brakes after concluding such brakes do not significantly reduce auto accidents (see Insight 11.3).

## INSIGHT 11.4

## Cut Your Car Insurance Premiums
## By As Much As 20%

Want to trim the cost of your auto insurance by one-fifth? Smart, aggressive shopping will do it. Indeed, Americans are now so savvy about shopping for policies that auto premium increases have eased nationwide. According to a recent study by the Consumer Federation of America, since 1989 the cost of car insurance has accelerated by an average of only 3% a year—down from the 10% annual hikes of the '80s. Today's average annual premium: $800. "Consumers have switched to lower-cost, more efficient insurers by shopping around," says Robert Hunter, CFA's director of insurance. Experts recommend these steps to shave 10% to 20% from policy costs:

**Get price quotes.** To find the least expensive insurer, call your state insurance department for a free guide that ranks insurers by price—some states have them. After selecting for price, make sure the company is considered financially sound by rating agencies like A.M. Best. You'll find its guide in most large libraries.

**Check out commission-free insurers.** Direct writers do not charge commissions, because they sell to consumers directly over the phone. Such insurers can cut 5% to 15% off your premium. Two direct writers with

top reputations are Amica (800-622-6422) and Geico (800-841-3000).

**Ask about discounts.** You probably know that air bags and antitheft devices will reduce your premiums 10% to 20%. But most drivers don't realize they can also qualify for lower rates if they are over 50, take a safe-driving course or have driving-age kids whose average school grade is B or better.

**And ask about group member discounts.** If you belong to an organization such as the American Legion, a credit union or an auto club, you may be able to garner discounts of 5% to 10%.

**Buy only what you need.** Raising your car insurance deductible from $250 to $500 will cut your collision premium 15% to 30%. Generally, collision insurance wastes your money if your car is older than five years and the premium exceeds 10% of the car's resale value. You can find the resale value in the Blue Book, the official used-car guide available in public libraries and at most banks. Cancel your collision coverage, and you might cut your premium by 25%.

SOURCE: Adapted from Sheryl Nance-Nash, "Cut Your Car Insurance Premiums By As Much As 20%," *Money* (February 1996), p. 17.

### Improve Your Driving Record

If you are a high-risk driver and are paying exorbitant premiums, a clean driving record over a three-year period will substantially reduce your premiums. Meanwhile, other alternatives should be considered. While physical damage insurance on a late-model car can easily double the premiums for a high-risk driver, an older-model car can be driven with no collision insurance. You might also consider riding a motorcycle or bicycle, or using mass transit. However, there is no substitute for a good driving record.

Finally, you should not drive when you are drinking. Drunk drivers account for a relatively high proportion of automobile accidents in which someone is seriously injured or killed. A conviction for driving under the influence (DUI) can result in a

substantial fine, loss of your driver's license, and possible imprisonment. In addition to the legal and moral implications of a DUI conviction, your automobile insurance premiums could increase substantially. Premiums can easily double or triple after a DUI conviction.

Insight 11.4 presents some additional suggestions for reducing auto insurance premiums.

### SUMMARY

- Financial responsibility laws require motorists to show proof of financial responsibility at the time of an accident involving bodily injury or property damage over a certain amount, for conviction of certain offenses, and for failure to pay a final judgment resulting from an automobile accident. Most motorists meet the financial responsibility law requirements by carrying automobile liability insurance limits of a certain amount.

- Compulsory insurance laws require the owners and operators of automobiles to carry automobile liability insurance at least equal to a certain amount before the automobile can be registered or licensed.
- Five states have unsatisfied judgment funds to compensate accident victims who have exhausted all other means of recovery. The accident victim must obtain a judgment against the negligent driver who caused the accident and show that the judgment cannot be collected.
- Uninsured motorists coverage is another approach for compensating automobile accident victims. Uninsured motorists coverage compensates the accident victim who has bodily injuries caused by an uninsured motorist, by a hit-and-run driver, or by a negligent driver whose company is insolvent.
- No-fault automobile insurance means that after an automobile accident involving a bodily injury, each party collects from his or her own insurer, regardless of fault. There are several types of no-fault plans:

  Pure no-fault plan

  Modified no-fault plan

  Add-on plan

  Choice no-fault plan
- The arguments for no-fault automobile insurance laws are summarized as follows:

  Difficulty of determining fault

  Limited scope of the reparations system

  Inequities in claim payments

  High costs and inefficiency

  Delay in payments
- The arguments against no-fault automobile insurance laws are summarized as follows:

  The defects of the negligence system are exaggerated.

  Claims of efficiency and premium savings are exaggerated.

  Court delays are not universal.

  Safe drivers may be penalized.

  There is no payment for pain and suffering.

  The present system needs only to be reformed.
- Several approaches are used to provide automobile insurance to high-risk drivers:

  Automobile insurance plans

  Joint underwriting association (JUAs)

  Reinsurance facilities

  Maryland Automobile Insurance Fund

  Specialty automobile insurers
- The premium charged for automobile insurance is a function of numerous variables, including territory; age, gender, and marital status; use of the automobile; driver education; good student discount; number and types of automobiles; and the insured's driving record.
- Consumer experts suggest several rules to follow when shopping for automobile insurance:

  Have adequate liability insurance.

  Carry higher deductibles.

  Drop collision insurance on an older vehicle.

  Shop around for insurance.

  Take advantage of discounts.

  Improve your driving record.

## KEY CONCEPTS AND TERMS

| | |
|---|---|
| Add-on plan | Optional deductibles |
| Automobile insurance plan | Optional no-fault benefits |
| Compulsory insurance law | Pure no-fault plan |
| Essential services expenses | Rating factors |
| Financial responsibility law | Reinsurance facility (or pool) |
| Good student discount | Safe driver plans |
| Joint underwriting association (JUA) | Servicing insurer |
| Maryland Automobile Insurance Fund | Shared market (residual market) |
| Modified no-fault plan | Specialty automobile insurers |
| Monetary threshold | Survivors' loss benefits |
| Multicar discount | Uninsured motorists coverage |
| No-fault automobile insurance | Unsatisfied judgment fund |
| | Verbal threshold |

## QUESTIONS FOR REVIEW

1. What is a financial responsibility law?
2. Explain the meaning of a compulsory insurance law.
3. What is an unsatisfied judgment fund? How do these funds work?
4. Explain the meaning of no-fault automobile insurance. Describe the major types of no-fault laws.
5. List the arguments for and against no-fault automobile insurance.

6. Explain the nature and purpose of an automobile insurance plan.

7. What is a joint underwriting association (JUA)?

8. How does a reinsurance facility work?

9. What factors determine the premium charged for automobile liability and physical damage insurance?

10. Explain the suggestions that a person should follow when shopping for automobile insurance.

## QUESTIONS FOR DISCUSSION

1. All states have passed some type of financial responsibility or compulsory insurance law to compensate accident victims.

   a. Describe how a financial responsibility law functions. In your answer, indicate the various ways in which proof of financial responsibility can be satisfied.

   b. Does a compulsory automobile liability insurance law adequately protect innocent accident victims? In your answer, state the arguments for and against compulsory insurance laws.

2. Unsatisfied judgment funds are used in some states to compensate accident victims.

   a. Describe the major features of an unsatisfied judgment fund.

   b. How effective are unsatisfied judgment funds in meeting the problem of compensating innocent accident victims?

3. Many states have passed some type of no-fault automobile insurance law to compensate accident victims.

   a. Describe the benefits that are typically paid under a no-fault law.

   b. Explain the rationale for enactment of a no-fault automobile insurance law.

   c. What is a "threshold" in a no-fault automobile insurance law?

## CASE APPLICATION

Paige, age 22, recently graduated from college and has purchased a new Taurus sedan. She has a clean driving record. Collision coverage on the car in the midwestern city where she lives would cost approximately $315 annually with a $100 deductible, $283 with a $250 deductible, $246 with a $500 deductible, and $184 with a $1000 deductible. The state has a compulsory insurance law that requires minimum liability limits of $25,000/$50,000/$10,000. Paige would like to purchase collision insurance with a $100 deductible because the out-of-pocket cost to repair her car in an accident where she is at fault would be relatively small. She also would like to purchase only minimum liability limits, since she has few financial assets to protect. Paige is also concerned that she might be seriously injured by a driver who has no insurance.

Assume you are a risk management consultant and that Paige asks your advice concerning her automobile insurance coverages. Based on the above facts, answer the following questions.

a. Paige wants to know why automobile insurance costs so much. Explain to her the factors that determine automobile insurance rates.

b. Do you recommend that Paige purchase collision insurance with a $100 deductible? Explain your answer.

c. Do you agree with Paige that only minimum liability limits should be purchased because she has few financial assets to protect? Explain your answer.

d. Assume that Paige adds the uninsured motorist coverage to her policy. Would she be completely protected against the financial consequences of a bodily injury caused by an uninsured driver? Explain your answer.

e. Paige would like to reduce her automobile premiums since her monthly car payments are high. Explain to Paige the various methods for reducing automobile insurance premiums.

d. How well have no-fault automobile insurance laws worked? Explain your answer.

4. Automobile insurance plans (assigned risk plans) are used in most states to meet the problem of providing automobile insurance to high-risk drivers.

   a. Describe the eligibility requirements for obtaining insurance from an automobile insurance plan.

   b. Explain the process for assigning high-risk drivers to individual insurers.

   c. Are the automobile insurance plans financially self-supporting? Explain your answer.

5. Several states have established a reinsurance facility or a joint underwriting association (JUA) for providing automobile insurance to high-risk drivers.

   a. Describe how a reinsurance facility works.

   b. Describe how a joint underwriting association (JUA) functions.

   c. Is the problem of providing automobile insurance to high-risk drivers adequately met by these approaches? Explain your answer.

## SELECTED REFERENCES

"A Guide to Auto Insurance," *Consumer Reports,* 60 (October 1995): 638–45.

"Auto Insurance: How to Choose the Right Company," *Consumer Reports,* 57 (August 1992), pp. 489–500.

Carrol, Stephen J., and James S. Kakalik. "No-Fault Approaches to Compensating Auto Accident Victims," *Journal of Risk and Insurance,* 60, no. 11 (June 1993): 265–87.

———. *No-Fault Automobile Insurance: A Policy Perspective.* Santa Monica, Calif.: Rand, Institute for Civil Justice, 1991.

Carrol, Stephen J., James S. Kakalik, Nicholas M. Pace, and John L. Adams. *No-Fault Approaches to Compensating People Injured in Automobile Accidents.* Santa Monica, Calif.: Rand, Institute for Civil Justice, 1991.

Cummins, J. David, and Sharon Tennyson. "Controlling Automobile Insurance Costs," *Journal of Economic Perspectives,* 6, no. 2 (Spring 1992): 95–115.

*Fire, Casualty & Surety Bulletins.* Cincinnati: National Underwriter Company. The bulletins are published monthly. Detailed information on the material discussed in this chapter can be found in the Personal Lines volume.

Hamilton, Karen L., and Donald S. Malecki. *Personal Insurance: Property and Liability,* First edition. Malvern, Pa.: American Institute for Chartered Property Casualty Underwriter, 1994, Chapter 5.

Harrington, Scott. E. "State Decisions to Limit Tort Liability: An Empirical Analysis of No-Fault Automobile Insurance Laws." *Journal of Risk and Insurance,* 61 (June 1994), pp. 276–94.

Johnson, Joseph E., George B. Flanigan, and Daniel T. Winkler. "Cost Implications of No-Fault Automobile Insurance." *Journal of Risk and Insurance,* 59 (March 1992): 116–23.

O'Connell, Jeffrey. "No-Fault Insurance: What, Why, and Where?" *Annals of the American Academy of Political and Social Science,* 443 (May 1979).

Rejda, George E., Constance M. Luthardt, Cheryl L. Ferguson, and Donald R. Oakes. *Personal Insurance,* 3rd ed. Malvern, PA.: Insurance Institute of America, 1997.

U.S. Department of Transportation. *Compensating Auto Accident Victims: A Followup on No-Fault Auto Insurance Experiences.* Washington, D.C.: U.S. Government Printing Office, 1985.

## NOTES

1. A complete discussion of these laws can be found in *Fire, Casualty & Surety Bulletins,* Personal Lines volume, Personal Auto section (Cincinnati: National Underwriter Company). Discussion of financial responsibility laws is based on this source.

2. The first two figures refer to bodily injury liability limits and the third figure refers to property damage liability.

3. David L. Bickelhaupt, *General Insurance,* 11th ed. (Homewood, Ill.: Richard D. Irvin, 1983), pp. 587–89. See also, J. J. Launie, George E. Rejda, and Donald R. Oakes, *Personal Insurance,* 2nd ed. (Malvern, Pa.: Insurance Institute of America, 1991), p. 201.

4. Karen L. Hamilton and Donald S. Malecki. *Personal Insurance: Property and Liability,* First edition (Malvern, Pa.: American Institute for Chartered Property Casualty Underwriter, 1994), pp. 209–10; see also Launie et al, pp. 202–03.

5. "Business Bulletin," *The Wall Street Journal,* May 2, 1996, p. A1.

6. Launie, et al, pp. 203–04.

7. This discussion is based on "No-Fault Automobile Insurance," in *Fire, Casualty & Surety Bulletins,* Personal Lines volume, Personal Auto section (Cincinnati: National Underwriter Company).

8. Robert I. Mehr and Gary W. Eldred. "Should the No-Fault Concept Be Applied to Property

Damage?" *Journal of Risk and Insurance*, 42 (March 1975): 17.

9. U.S. Department of Transportation, *Major Vehicle Crash Losses and Their Compensation in the United States: A Report to Congress and the President* (Washington, D.C.: U.S. Government Printing Office, 1971), pp. 15–100. The statistics cited in this section are based on this source.

10. Robert E. Keeton. "The Impact of Insurance on Trends in Tort Law," in John D. Long, ed., *Issues in Insurance,* vol. 1 (Malvern, Pa.: American Institute for Property and Liability Underwriters, 1978), pp. 196–97.

11. Stephen J. Carroll et al. *No-Fault Approaches to Compensating People Injured in Automobile Accidents* (Santa Monica, Calif.: Rand, Institute for Civil Justice, 1991), pp. xvi, 43.

12. A detailed explanation of these rating factors can be found in Launie et al., chapter 9.

13. *The Fact Book 1996: Property/Casualty Insurance Facts* (New York: Insurance Information Institute ), p. 8.

14. Ibid, p. 87.

15. Hamilton and Malecki, p. 249.

# Part Four

# COMMERCIAL PROPERTY AND LIABILITY RISKS

On-Line Resources

Several sites listed in the On-Line Resources for Part 3 also contain information on commercial insurance. For example, see the Insurance Services Office (ISO) site at

http://www.iso.com/

and the Insurance Information Institute site at:

http://www.iii.org/

The Associated Aviation Underwriters (AAU) maintains a site at:

http://www.aau.com/

For a sampling of the many companies that describe their commercial insurance offerings on-line, see:

http://www.yahoo.com/business_and_economy/companies/
financial_services/insurance/commercial/

The Federal Bureau of Investigation gives current crime statistics, along with other interesting information, at its site:

http://www.fbi.gov/

# Chapter 12

# COMMERCIAL PROPERTY INSURANCE

*“Knowledge of commercial property insurance is absolutely essential to a successful risk management program.”*

*Connie Luthardt,*
*American Institute for Chartered Property Casualty Underwriters*

## Student Learning Objectives

After studying this chapter, you should be able to:

■ Identify the major documents that form a commercial package policy.

■ Explain the major provisions of the building and personal property coverage form.

■ Describe the major coverages for insuring a business income loss, including the business income coverage form and extra expense insurance.

■ Explain the major provisions of builders risk insurance, glass insurance, and boiler and machinery insurance.

■ Identity the major types of ocean marine and inland marine insurance.

■ Describe the major features of the businessowners program for small- to medium-sized business firms.

Business firms own valuable commercial real estate and business personal property, such as office furniture, computers, supplies, machinery, and inventories of finished products. Firms may also have in their possession the property of customers, which can be damaged or destroyed from a direct physical damage loss. In addition, there may be a substantial loss of business income or extra expenses incurred because of a direct physical damage loss to covered property.

This chapter discusses commercial property insurance, with special emphasis on the commercial insurance program developed by the Insurance Services Office (ISO). More specifically, the chapter discusses the components of a commercial package policy, the building and personal property coverage form, business income insurance, builders risk insurance, glass insurance, and boiler and machinery insurance. In addition, ocean marine and inland marine coverages are examined. The chapter con-

cludes with a discussion of the businessowners policy designed for owners of small- to medium-sized
business firms.

## OVERVIEW OF COMMERCIAL PACKAGE POLICY

A **package policy** *is one that combines two or more
ISO coverages into a single policy.* If both property and
liability insurance lines are combined into a single
policy, it is also known as a *multiple-line policy.* The
following section discusses the general format and
structure of the **commercial package policy
(CPP)** that is widely used by business firms.

The CPP can be used to insure motels, hotels,
apartment houses, office buildings, retail stores, institutions such as churches and schools, processing
firms such as dry cleaners, manufacturing firms, and
similar commercial firms. The CPP can also be tailored to cover most commercial property and liability loss exposures in a single policy, with the major
exceptions of workers compensation and surety
bonds.

By use of a package policy, the firm has fewer
gaps in protection, relatively lower premiums because individual policies are not purchased, and the
convenience of a single policy. Insurers and producers also benefit from packaging (see Insight 12.1).

### Policy Format

Under the ISO program, each commercial package
policy contains (1) *a common policy declarations page,*
(2) *a common policy conditions page, and* (3) *two or
more coverage parts.*[1] Exhibit 12.1 shows in greater
detail the various parts of a commercial package
policy.

**Common Policy Declarations**  Each commercial package policy contains a *common policy declarations page* that shows the name and address of the
insured, policy period, description of the insured
property, coverage parts that apply, and the premium paid.

**Common Policy Conditions**  Each commercial package policy also contains a *common policy*

*conditions page* that applies to all commercial lines of
insurance. The common conditions are summarized
as follows:

- *Cancellation.* Either party can cancel by giving
  the other party advance notice. The insurer can
  cancel by giving notice of cancellation for nonpayment of premiums at least 10 days in advance and 30 days in advance for any other
  reason. If the insurer cancels, a pro rata refund
  of the premium is made. If the insured cancels,
  the refund may be less than pro rata.
- *Changes.* Any changes in the policy can only be
  made by an endorsement issued by the insurer.
- *Examination of books and records.* The insurer has
  the right to audit the insured's books and
  records any time during the policy period and
  up to three years after the policy period ends.
- *Inspections and surveys.* The insurer has the right
  to make inspections and surveys that relate to
  insurability of the property and premiums to be
  charged.
- *Premiums.* More than one party may be named
  as an insured in the declarations page. The first
  named insured in the declarations is the party
  responsible for the payment of premiums.
- *Transfer of rights and duties.* The insured's rights
  and duties under the policy cannot be transferred without the insurer's written consent.
  One exception is that the rights and duties can
  be transferred to a legal representative if an individual named insured should die.

**Coverage Parts**  Each commercial package
policy also contains two or more *coverage parts,*
which can include the following:

- Commercial property coverage forms
- Commercial general liability coverage forms
- Commercial crime coverage forms
- Boiler and machinery coverage forms
- Inland marine coverage forms
- Commercial auto coverage forms
- Farm coverage forms

Each coverage part, in turn, contains (1) its
own declarations page that applies to that coverage, (2) the specific conditions that apply to that

## INSIGHT 12.1

### Don't Ignore the Advantages of a Package Policy

The ISO commercial package policy is the industry standard for commercial package policies. As such it has advantages to insurers, insureds, and producers (insurance agents, brokers, or sales employees).

**Insurer advantages**

For the insurance company, one advantage of packaging is reduced administrative expense. It costs the insurer less to underwrite and issue one package policy instead of two or more monoline policies for the same insured. Also, an insurer will increase its premium volume if it can write a package policy covering a number of an insured's exposures instead of writing a monoline policy. Package policies can also help insurers avoid adverse selection. If an insured has one particularly hazardous exposure, the higher likelihood of a loss resulting from that exposure can be mitigated to some degree by the insurer's obtaining a premium for other exposures of the insured that are less likely to result in loss.

**Insured's advantages**    For the insured, an advantage of packaging is that there are fewer policies to buy and maintain. Packaging reduces the chance of delay in loss settlement due to disputes between different insurers. For example, losses involving loading of automobiles sometimes fall in a "gray area" between auto liability and general liability. If one insurer provides both coverages, payment of a claim will not be delayed as it might be if each coverage were written by a separate insurer and each insurer felt the claim was covered under the other's policy. Finally, insureds, like insurers, benefit from reduced administrative expense in writing package policies.

**Producer advantages**    Packaging is advantageous to producers for two reasons. First, the availability of packages facilitates account selling, or obtaining a customer's entire account instead of only a piece of it. Second, some packages are more easily sold and rated than separate monoline policies. This allows the producer to provide quotes more quickly for prospective customers, and it increases the producer's efficiency.

SOURCE: Adapted from Bernard L. Webb, Arthur L. Flitner, and Jerome Trupin, *Commercial Insurance*, 3rd ed. (Malvern, Pa.: Insurance Institute of America, 1996), pp. 9–10.

coverage part, (3) coverage forms that describe the various coverages provided, and (4) a causes-of-loss form that describes the various perils that are covered.

**Rate Discount**    The insured receives a rate discount if the CPP contains both commercial property and liability coverages. The rate discount is determined by applying an appropriate *package modification factor* to the various coverage parts. The rate discounts vary by state and by insurer. For example, a factor of 0.75 means that the premium for that coverage part is 75 percent of the premium that would apply if the policy were written as a monoline policy.[2]

## BUILDING AND PERSONAL PROPERTY COVERAGE FORM

The building and personal property coverage form is one of several property forms that are used in the ISO program. This form is widely used to cover a direct physical damage loss to commercial buildings and business personal property. The following section discusses the 1995 edition of the ISO form.

### Covered Property

The insured can select the property to be covered. Covered property can include (1) the building, (2) business personal property of the insured, and

Eₓₕᵢᵦᵢₜ 12.1

## Components of the Commercial Package Policy (CPP)

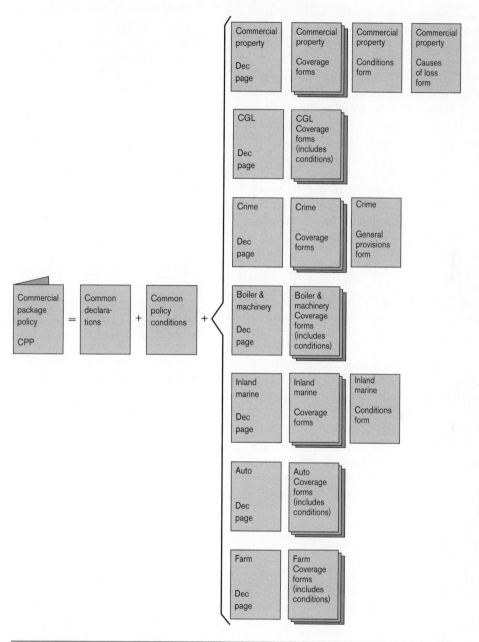

SOURCE:  Bernard L. Webb, Arthur L. Flitner, and Jerome Trupin, *Commercial Insurance,* 3rd ed. (Malvern, Pa.: Insurance Institute of America, 1996), Exhibit 1-1, p. 11.

(3) personal property of others in the care, custody, or control of the insured.

**Building**   The form covers the building described in the declarations and includes any completed additions and fixtures, machinery, and equipment that are permanently installed. Certain outdoor fixtures are also covered, such as light poles, flag poles, and mailboxes. Finally, equipment used to maintain or service the building (such as fire-extinguishing equipment, appliances for cooking and dishwashing, floor buffers, and vacuum cleaners) is also covered.

**Business Personal Property of the Insured**
Business personal property of the insured inside or on the building or within 100 feet of the premises is also covered. Business personal property includes furniture and fixtures; machinery and equipment; stock or inventory; and all other personal property owned by the insured and used in the insured's business. In addition, the insured's interest in the personal property of others is covered to the extent of labor, materials, and other charges. For example, a machine shop may repair a piece of machinery owned by a customer. If parts and labor are $1000 and the machinery is damaged from an insured peril before it is delivered to the customer, the insured's interest of $1000 is covered.

The insured's use interest in improvements and betterments as a tenant is also covered as business personal property. Improvements and betterments are fixtures, alterations, installations, or additions that are made part of the building at the insured's expense and cannot be removed legally. An example of an improvement is the installation of a new air conditioning unit by an insured who leases a building to open a new bar and restaurant.

Finally, business personal property includes leased personal property for which the insured has a contractual obligation to insure. An example would be leased computer equipment, for which the insured is required to provide insurance.

**Personal Property of Others**   Personal property of others in the care, custody, or control of the insured is also covered. For example, if a tornado destroys a machine shop and equipment belonging to customers are damaged, the loss would be covered.

**Additional Coverages**   Four additional coverages are provided, summarized as follows:

1. *Debris removal.* The additional coverage is limited to 25 percent of the amount paid for a direct physical damage loss to covered property plus the deductible that applies to that loss. For example, for a $4000 physical damage loss and a $250 deductible, the policy would pay $1250 for debris removal. However, if the cost of debris removal exceeds that limit, an additional $10,000 is available under the "limits of insurance" provision in the policy.

   The additional coverage does not apply to the cost of extracting pollutants from land or water or to the cost of removing, restoring, or replacing polluted land or water.

2. *Preservation of property.* If property is moved to another location for safekeeping because of a covered loss, any direct physical damage or loss to the property while being moved or while stored at the other location is covered. Coverage applies only if the loss or damage occurs within 30 days after the property is first moved.

3. *Fire department service charge.* A maximum of $1000 can be paid for a fire department service charge. No deductible applies to this coverage.

4. *Pollutant clean up and removal.* The insurer also pays the cost to clean up and remove pollutants from land or water at the described premises if the release or discharge of the pollutants results from a covered cause of loss. The maximum paid is limited to $10,000 during each separate 12-month policy period.

**Extensions of Coverage**   If a coinsurance requirement of 80 percent or higher is shown in the declarations, or a value reporting period symbol is shown on the declarations page, the insurance can be extended to cover other property. Each extension is an additional amount of insurance. The extensions of coverage are summarized as follows:

1. *Newly acquired or constructed property.* Insurance on the building is extended to cover new buildings while being built on the described premises and to newly acquired buildings at other locations. The insurance applies for a maximum

period of 30 days and is limited to a maximum of $250,000 for each building. In addition, the insurance on business personal property ($100,000 maximum) can be applied to business personal property at newly acquired locations. This insurance also applies for a maximum period of 30 days.

2. *Personal effects and property of others.* Insurance on business personal property can be extended to cover the personal effects of the named insured, officers, partners, or employees. However, the extension does not apply to theft. The extension also applies to personal property of others in the named insured's care, custody, or control. The maximum paid is limited to $2500.

3. *Valuable papers and records.* Insurance on business personal property can also be extended to cover the costs of researching, replacing, or restoring lost information on lost or damaged valuable papers and records. The maximum paid is limited to $2500.

4. *Property off premises.* Covered property (other than stock) that is temporarily at a location not owned, leased, or operated by the insured is covered up to $10,000. However, the extension does not apply to covered property in or on a vehicle, property in the care, custody, or control of salespersons, or property at a fair or exhibition. Coverage does apply, however, to property off the premises for repair, tools and equipment on a job site, and property loaned to others by the insured.

5. *Outdoor property.* Outdoor fences, radio and television antennas, detached signs, and trees, plants, and shrubs are covered up to a maximum of $1000, but not more than $250 for any single tree, shrub, or plant. The insurance applies only to losses caused by fire, lightning, explosion, riot or civil commotion, or aircraft.

## Other Provisions

Numerous additional provisions are included in the building and personal property coverage form, but it is beyond the scope of this text to discuss each of them. Several important provisions, however, are summarized here.

**Deductible**   A standard deductible of $250 applies to each occurrence. Higher deductible amounts are available. Only one deductible has to be satisfied if several buildings or different types of business personal property are damaged in the same occurrence.

**Coinsurance**   If a coinsurance percentage is stated in the declarations, the coinsurance requirement must be met to avoid a coinsurance penalty. To reduce misunderstanding and confusion, the form contains several excellent examples of how coinsurance works.

**Valuation Provision**   A valuation provision states the rules for establishing the value of covered property at the time of loss. Except for certain losses (see Exhibit 12.2), insured property is valued at its actual cash value. The form does not define actual cash value, but it is interpreted to mean replacement cost less depreciation.

**Optional Coverages**   Three optional coverages are also available, which eliminates the need for a separate endorsement.

1. *Agreed value.* This option suspends the coinsurance clause and substitutes a new agreement that covers any loss in the same proportion that the limit of insurance bears to the agreed value shown in the declarations. For example, if the agreed value for an item is $100,000, and the limit of insurance is $100,000, then any loss is covered at a rate of 100 percent.

2. *Inflation guard.* This option automatically increases the amount of insurance by an annual percentage shown in the declarations.

3. *Replacement cost.* Under the replacement cost option, there is no deduction for depreciation if a loss occurs. However, this option does not apply to the property of others; contents of a residence; manuscripts; works of art, antiques, and similar property; stock (unless designated in the declarations); and any increase in the cost of repair or replacement attributable to a building ordinance or similar law. Replacement cost insurance generally is recommended when buildings and their contents are insured. Otherwise, the loss is paid on an actual cash value basis.

EXHIBIT 12.2

**Valuation of Property—Building and Personal Property Coverage Form**

| Property type | Valuation basis |
|---|---|
| Property other than that specifically listed | Actual cash value |
| Building damage of $2500 or less | Replacement cost except for some personal property items considered part of a building |
| Stock sold but not delivered | Selling price less discounts and unincurred costs |
| Glass | Replacement cost for safety glazing if required by law |
| Improvements and betterments: | |
| (a) replaced by other than the insured | Not covered |
| (b) replaced by insured | Actual cash value |
| (c) not replaced | Percentage of cost based on remaining life of lease |
| Valuable papers and records | Cost of blank media plus cost of transaction or copying ($2500 research cost as coverage extension) |

SOURCE: Bernard L. Webb, Arthur L. Flitner, and Jerome Trupin, *Commercial Insurance,* 3rd ed. (Malvern, Pa.: Insurance Institute of America, 1996), Exhibit 2-4, p. 36.

## CAUSES-OF-LOSS FORMS

A *causes-of-loss form* must be added to the policy to have a complete contract. There are four causes-of-loss forms:

- Causes-of-loss basic form
- Causes-of-loss broad form
- Causes-of-loss special form
- Causes-of-loss earthquake form

The earthquake form can be used with any of the three causes-of-loss forms, or it can be used separately to provide earthquake and volcanic eruption insurance.

### Causes-of-Loss Basic Form

The **causes-of-loss basic form** provides coverage for the following perils: fire, lightning, explosion, windstorm or hail, smoke, aircraft or vehicles, riot or civil commotion, vandalism, sprinkler leakage, sinkhole collapse, and volcanic action.

These perils are self-explanatory, but two comments are in order. *Sprinkler leakage* provides coverage for the accidental leakage or discharge of any substance from an automatic sprinkler system. For example, if the sprinkler system in a department store accidentally leaks water that damages the stock, the loss is covered.

*Sinkhole collapse* means the sinking or collapse in underground empty spaces created by the action of water on limestone or dolomite rock formations. Although damage caused by the sinkhole collapse is covered, the cost of filling the sinkhole is specifically excluded.

### Causes-of-Loss Broad Form

The **causes-of-loss broad form** includes all causes of loss covered by the basic form plus the following additional causes:

- Breakage of glass (maximum of $100 per plate and $500 per occurrence)
- Falling objects

- Weight of snow, ice, or sleet
- Water damage

In addition, collapse is covered as an additional coverage and not as a cause of loss. Collapse is covered only if caused by the following:

- Any broad form peril
- Hidden decay
- Hidden insect or vermin damage
- Weight of people or personal property
- Weight of rain that collects on a roof
- Use of defective materials or methods in construction or remodeling if collapse occurs during the course of construction or remodeling.

## Causes-of-Loss Special Form

The **causes-of-loss special form** insures against "risks of direct physical loss" (formerly called "all-risks"). This means that all direct physical damage losses to insured property are covered unless specifically excluded or limited in the form itself. The burden of proof falls on the insurer to show that the loss is not covered because of a specific exclusion or limitation that applies. In addition, collapse is included as an additional coverage.

The special form also provides for two additional extensions of coverage. First, property in transit is covered for certain perils up to $1000 while the property is in or on a motor vehicle owned, leased, or operated by the insured. Second, if a covered water damage loss occurs, the cost of tearing out and replacing part of the building or structure to repair the leaking water system or appliance is also covered. However, the cost of repairing or replacing the system or appliance itself is not covered.

## Causes-of-Loss Earthquake Form

Damage from earthquakes can be covered by adding the **causes-of-loss earthquake form** to a commercial property policy. All earthquake shocks or volcanic eruptions that occur within a 168-hour period are considered to be a single event. Consequently, the policy limit applies to all damage that occurs during this period.

A percentage deductible is stated in the declarations and is usually two to five percent of the value of the insured property. In some areas where earthquakes are more likely to occur, the percentage deductible can be as high as 10 percent.

## REPORTING FORMS

A firm may have sharp fluctuations in its inventories throughout the year. A **reporting form** requires the insured to report periodically the value of the insured inventory. As long as the report is accurate, the amount of insurance on the inventory is automatically adjusted based on the amount of insured values.

Under the ISO commercial property program, the *value reporting form* is used to insure fluctuations in inventory. An advanced premium is paid at the inception of the policy based on the limit of insurance. The final premium is determined at the end of the policy period based on the values reported. The insured has the option of reporting daily, weekly, monthly, quarterly, or at the end of the policy year. As long as the insured reports the correct values, the full amount of the loss is covered up to the policy limits. For example, assume that the insured correctly reports an inventory of $1 million at the last reporting date, and the inventory is increased to $5 million before the next reporting date. If a total loss occurs, the entire inventory of $5 million would be covered (less the deductible).

However, the value reporting form contains a *full reporting clause* (honesty clause) that requires the insured to report honestly. If the insured is dishonest and underreports, he or she will be penalized if a loss occurs. *If the insured underreports the property values at a location, and a loss occurs at that location, recovery is limited to the proportion that the last value reported bears to the correct value that should have been reported.* For example, if the actual inventory on hand is $500,000, and the insured reports only $400,000, only four-fifths of any loss will be paid (less the deductible).

## BUSINESS INCOME INSURANCE

Business firms often experience a consequential, or indirect, loss as a result of a direct physical damage loss to covered property, such as the loss of profits, rents, or extra expenses. **Business income** insurance (formerly called business interruption insurance) is designed to cover the loss of business income, expenses that continue during the shutdown period, and extra expenses because of a direct physical loss to insured property.

Two basic ISO forms are used to insure business income losses: (1) business income (and extra expense) coverage form and (2) extra expense coverage form.[3]

## Business Income Coverage Form

The **business income (and extra expense) coverage form** is used to cover the loss of business income regardless of whether the income is derived from retail or service operations, manufacturing, or rents. When a firm has a business income loss, profits are lost, and certain expenses may still continue, such as rent, interest, insurance premiums, and officers' salaries. The present form covers both the loss of business income and extra expenses that result from a physical damage loss to covered property.

**Loss of Business Income**   The business income (and extra expense) coverage form covers the loss of business income due to the suspension of operations during the period of restoration. The suspension of operations must result from the direct physical loss or damage to property caused by an insured peril at the described premises. The insured perils are listed in the causes-of-loss form attached to the policy. *Business income is defined as the net profit or loss (before income taxes) that would have been earned plus continuing normal operating expenses, including payroll.* In effect, the amount paid represents the profit (or loss) that would have occurred if the suspension of operations had not occurred, plus expenses that continue during the period of suspension. For example, assume that a retail shoe store has a fire and must suspend operations for six months. All regular employees are laid off during the shutdown period. Assume also that the firm's estimated sales and expenses for the 12 months of the policy period are as shown in Exhibit 12.3.

Assuming that income is earned equally over the period, the store's normal net income for 12 months is estimated to be $50,000. Thus, if the store is shut down for only six months, it will lose net income of $25,000. During the shutdown period, the firm

EXHIBIT 12.3

### Estimated Sales and Expenses for the 12 Months of the Policy Period

| | |
|---|---:|
| Sales | $400,000 |
| Less cost of goods sold | −200,000 |
| Gross income | $200,000 |
| Less expenses | −150,000 |
| Net income before taxes | $50,000 |

also had continuing expenses of $10,000, such as payment of rent, interest, utilities, and other expenses. Thus, the total loss payment would be $35,000. This can be summarized as follows.

| | |
|---|---:|
| Net income lost during the period of suspension | $25,000 |
| Continuing expenses during the period of suspension | +10,000 |
| Amount paid | $35,000 |

The loss payment of $35,000 represents the loss of net income plus an amount for continuing expenses.

**Additional Coverages**   The business income form automatically provides several additional coverages, summarized as follows:

1. *Extra expenses.* Extra expenses are the necessary expenses incurred by the firm during a period of restoration that would not have been incurred if the loss had not taken place. Examples of covered extra expenses are the cost of relocating temporarily, increased rent at another location, and the rental of substitute equipment.

2. *Action of civil authority.* Loss of business income and extra expenses caused by action of a civil authority that prohibits access to the described premises because of a covered cause of loss are also paid. The coverage for business income begins 72 hours after the time of that action and continues for up to three consecutive weeks after the coverage begins.

3. *Alterations and new buildings.* The loss of business income as a result of a direct physical damage loss to a new building on the premises

(whether completed or under construction) is also covered. The loss of business income because of alterations or additions to existing buildings is covered as well.

4. *Extended business income.* A business that reopens may experience reduced earnings after the repairs are completed, and additional time may be needed to recapture old customers. For example, a restaurant that reopens after a fire may need time to attract former customers. The extended business income provision covers the reduction in earnings for a limited period after the business reopens. The extended period begins on the date the property is repaired and operations are resumed and ends after 30 consecutive days or when business income returns to normal, whichever occurs first.

Coinsurance    The business income coverage form can be purchased with a coinsurance requirement of 50, 60, 70, 80, 90, 100, or 125 percent. This latter percentage can be used if the business expects to be shut down for more than one year. *The basis for coinsurance is the sum of net income and all operating expenses, including payroll, that would have been earned (if the loss had not occurred) for the 12 months following inception of the policy or the last anniversary date, whichever is later.* This sum is then multiplied by the coinsurance percentage to determine the required amount of insurance. For example, assume that net income and operating expenses for the 12 months of the current policy term are $400,000, and that the coinsurance percentage is 50 percent; the required amount of insurance would be $200,000.

The actual coinsurance percentage selected depends on the length of time it takes to resume operations, and also on the period of time during which most of the business is done. If the firm expects to be shut down for more than one year, the 125 percent option should be selected. If the firm expects to be shut down for no more than six months and business is uniform throughout the year, a coinsurance percentage of 50 percent should be selected. However, when seasonal peak periods are considered, this percentage may be inadequate, since 50 percent of the firm's business may not occur within a consecutive six-month period. Thus, when business income is seasonal or has peak periods, a coinsurance

percentage higher than 50 percent is advisable to provide greater protection during a prolonged shutdown period that continues during the peak period.

Ordinary payroll is covered under the business income coverage form unless it is excluded by an endorsement to the policy. The endorsement can exclude ordinary payroll, or it can be covered for a limited period, such as 90 days. Limiting or excluding ordinary payroll reduces the premium.

Optional Coverages    The business income form also has coverages that can be activated by an appropriate entry on the declarations page. The optional coverages are summarized as follows:

1. *Maximum period of indemnity.* This optional coverage eliminates coinsurance and pays for the loss of business income for a maximum period of 120 days. The amount paid cannot exceed the policy limit. This option can be used by smaller firms that will not be shut down for more than 120 days if a loss occurs.

2. *Monthly limit of indemnity.* This optional coverage eliminates coinsurance and limits the maximum monthly amount that will be paid for each consecutive 30-day period to a fraction of the policy limit. The fractions are one-third, one-fourth, and one-sixth. For example, if the fraction selected is one-third, and the policy limit is $120,000, the maximum paid for each consecutive 30-day period is $40,000.

3. *Agreed value.* This option suspends the coinsurance clause and places no limit on the monthly amount paid, provided the agreed amount of business income insurance is carried. The agreed amount is the coinsurance percentage (50 percent or higher) multiplied by an estimate of net income and operating expenses for the 12 months of the policy period.

4. *Extended period of indemnity.* This option extends the recovery period following completion of repairs from 30 days to a longer period stated in the declarations. The extended period of indemnity can be 60, 90, 120, 150, 180, 270, or 360 days. This option is advantageous for those firms that need a longer recovery period to recapture old business and resume normal operations.

## Extra Expense Coverage Form

Certain firms such as banks, newspapers, and bakeries must continue to operate after a loss occurs; otherwise, customers will be lost to competitors. The **extra expense coverage form** is a separate form that can be used to cover the extra expenses incurred by the firm to continue operations during a period of restoration. Loss of profits is not covered, since the firm will still be operating. However, the additional expenses to continue operating are covered, subject to certain limits stated in the declarations on the amount of insurance that can be used. A common limitation is that up to 40 percent of the insurance can be used during the first month following the loss, up to 80 percent for two months, and up to 100 percent when the restoration period exceeds two months.

## Business Income from Dependent Properties

Some firms depend on a single supplier for raw materials and supplies or on a single customer to purchase most or all of the firm's products. The insured's business may incur a loss because of property damage incurred by the sole supplier or customer. An appropriate endorsement can be added to a business income policy that covers loss of income at the insured's location that results from direct damage to property at other locations.

There are four types of dependent properties situations for which this coverage may be needed.[4]

- *Contributing location.* A *contributing location* is a location that furnishes materials or services to the insured. For example, the insured may depend on one supplier for raw materials. If the supplier's factory is damaged, the insured's business may be forced to shut down.
- *Recipient location.* A *recipient location* is a location that purchases the insured's products or services. For example, a specialized cheese manufacturer may sell most of its cheese production to a resort hotel. If the hotel is closed because of fire, the cheese factory may have to shut down.
- *Manufacturing location.* A *manufacturing location* is a location that manufactures products for delivery to the insured's customers. If the manufacturer's plant is damaged, the products cannot be delivered, and the insured would incur a loss.
- *Leader location.* A *leader location* is a location that attracts customers to the insured's place of business. For example, a major department store in a shopping center may have a fire. As a result, smaller stores in the shopping center may experience a decline in sales.

## Leasehold Interest Insurance

The **leasehold interest coverage form** is designed to cover the loss that may result from the cancellation of a valuable lease when the building is damaged by a covered cause of loss. The amount paid for the loss is the present value of the leasehold interest for the remaining months of the lease. In determining the leasehold interest, an interest rate ranging from 5 to 15 percent can be used. For example, assume that Oscar has signed a long-term lease that has four years left to run. The lease requires a monthly rent of $2500. However, if the lease is canceled because of a fire, and Oscar must now pay a monthly rent of $3500 at a comparable new location, he would receive the present value of $1000 monthly (at 6 percent discount), payable at the beginning of the month for 48 months, or $42,793.

## Miscellaneous Business Income Coverages

Several specialized coverages are also available that cover the loss of business income or extra income. These coverages include *tuition fees insurance* that covers the loss of tuition if a school or college has a loss and *weather insurance* that covers losses due to weather conditions, such as excessive rain or snow (see Insight 12.2).

## OTHER COMMERCIAL COVERAGES

The building and personal property coverage form discussed earlier is designed to meet the commercial property and liability insurance needs of most business firms. However, many firms have certain needs that require the use of specialized coverages, which include the following:

- Builders risk insurance
- Condominium insurance
- Glass insurance
- Boiler and machinery insurance
- Credit insurance
- Difference in conditions (DIC) insurance

## INSIGHT 12.2

### Forecast for Winter: Insurance Against Snow

Leave it to the insurance industry to find yet another way to profit from rotten weather: Snow insurance.

Eager insurance agents are out trying to convince shopping centers, condominiums, cities and even cemeteries that they can limit their snow removal costs by buying insurance.

Laurie Tillman, president of Good Weather Insurance Agency in Salem, said she wrote one snow removal policy two years ago and 10 last year. This year, she expects to write 1,000.

Logan Airport last year bought a $300,000 insurance policy that promised the airport $50,000 for every inch of snow that fell beyond the expected 44 inches for the season.

The airport was simply trying to bring some predictability to its snow removal costs. But when the actual snowfall hit 100 inches, the airport cleaned up.

Logan's windfall notwithstanding, snow insurance doesn't save money over the long haul. For every snowy winter, there will be a relatively mild one—and insurers could not make money unless premiums in the dry years covered costs in the wet ones. But insurance smooths out the hills and valleys. It guarantees there won't be one catastrophic year that will bust the budget or put a company out of business.

In an effort to take the concept one step further, Frederick Penn Insurance Agency in Needham has created a product called "income guarantee insurance." In English, it means that when it snows heavily and a restaurant or a retailer loses business for the day, an insurance policy will kick in and reimburse the firm for a portion of the lost income.

"I was talking to a client, a restaurant owner, and he told me he got killed last winter with all the snow," said Richard Penn, president of the agency. "I said, there's got to be a way to protect him for that."

Snow insurance is a variation on an old theme. Farmers long have been able to buy insurance to protect them in years when the weather destroyed their crops. Promoters of fairs and outdoor concerts have also been able to buy weather insurance.

In a sense, weather insurance is a lot like life insurance. "Life insurers have detailed statistics about when people will die. We have detailed statistics going back years on weather conditions," said Tillman.

SOURCE: "Forecast for winter: Insurance against snow," *Lincoln Journal Star*, October 13, 1996, p. 3D.

## Builders Risk Insurance

A new building under construction is exposed to numerous perils, especially the peril of fire. Under the simplified commercial property program by ISO, the **builders risk coverage form** can be used to insure buildings under construction. This form can be used to cover the insurable interest of a general contractor, subcontractor, or building owner.

Under the builders risk coverage form, insurance is purchased equal to the *full value* of the completed building. Since the building is substantially overinsured during the initial stages of construction, the rate charged is adjusted to reflect the average value exposed.

If desired, a *builders risk reporting form* can be attached as an endorsement, which requires the builder to report monthly the value of the building under construction. The initial premium reflects the value of the building at the inception of the policy period and not on the completed value of the building. However, as construction progresses, the amount of insurance on the building is increased based on the reported values. The final premium paid is based on the actual values reported.

The reporting form is used to cover high-value buildings under construction (such as a high-rise office building) where the value of the building is relatively low during the initial period of construction when the foundation is being built. The value of the building then accelerates as additional stories are added.[5]

## Condominium Association Coverage Form

Owners of individual condominium units have a common interest in the building, which includes the exterior walls, the roof, and the plumbing, heating, and air conditioning systems. However, property insurance on the building and other condominium property is purchased in the name of the condominium owners association.

The **condominium association coverage form** provides insurance on the building and equipment to maintain or service the building. If required by the condominium association agreement, the form also covers fixtures, improvements, alterations that are part of the building, and appliances within the individual units (such as a refrigerator, stove, or dishwasher). In addition, the association form covers business personal property, such as outdoor furniture and a riding lawn mower. However, personal property of the individual unit owners is specifically excluded. The unit-owner's personal property (such as furniture, clothes, and household contents) is normally insured under the Homeowners 6 policy (unit-owners form).

## Condominium Commercial Unit-Owners Coverage Form

Business or professional firms may own individual units in a commercial condominium. For example, a physician or business firm may own individual office space in a commercial office building that is legally organized as a condominium.

The **condominium commercial unit-owners coverage form** covers the unit owner's business personal property, which includes furniture; fixtures and improvements that are part of the building and owned by the unit owner; machinery and equipment; stock; personal property used in the business; and personal property of others in the care, control, and custody of the insured.

The commercial form does not cover the building since insurance on the building is purchased by the condominium owners association. In addition, the commercial form also excludes fixtures and improvements that are part of the building and appliances within a unit (such as a refrigerator, stove, or

dishwasher) if the association agreement requires the association to insure such property.

## Glass Insurance

Because of architectural and decorative considerations, the use of glass in building construction has increased. However, under the broad and special causes-of-loss forms discussed earlier, breakage of building glass is limited to $100 per plate and $500 per occurrence. Under the commercial property insurance program of the ISO, the basic form for writing glass insurance is the **glass coverage form**. This form can be used in combination with other coverages, or it can be used to form a separate glass insurance policy.

To be covered, the glass must be scheduled either in the declarations or in a glass coverage schedule. Coverage is broad and comprehensive. Glass breakage from any cause is covered (except by fire, nuclear hazard, or war and military action). Lettering and ornamentation are also covered if separately described. Glass damage from the accidental or malicious application of chemicals is also covered.

The insurer has four options for paying a glass claim:

- Pay the actual value of the lost or damaged property.
- Pay the cost of repairing or replacing the property.
- Take the property at an agreed or appraised value.
- Repair or replace the property with property of like kind and quality.

The insurer must let the insured know of its settlement intention within 30 days after a sworn statement of loss.

In addition, certain other items are also paid, including the expense of (1) debris removal, (2) installing temporary plates or boarding up openings, (3) repairing or replacing frames, and (4) removing or repairing any obstructions to repair the broken glass.

Finally, the glass insurance is suspended if the building is vacant for 60 consecutive days unless the insurer is notified and an additional premium is paid.

## Boiler and Machinery Insurance

A boiler explosion can cause substantial property damage to the firm and may also cause damage to the property of others. Boiler and machinery insurance can be used to insure boilers, machinery, and other equipment for both direct and indirect loss. Business firms often purchase boiler and machinery insurance for the extensive loss prevention services that insurers provide. Safety engineers will periodically inspect the boiler and other machinery for structural defects and other weaknesses that can cause a loss. Thus, there is great emphasis on loss prevention in the interest of safety.

The **boiler and machinery coverage form** is used to insure boilers and machinery against loss from an explosion or from other covered causes. Boiler and machinery insurance can be written separately as a monoline policy, or it can be part of a commercial package policy.

**Coverage Provided**    The insurer agrees to pay for direct damage to covered property from a covered cause of loss. *Covered property* is property owned by the insured or property in the insured's care, custody, or control for which the insured is legally liable. A *covered cause of loss* is defined as an accident to an object listed in the declarations. An *object* refers to the boiler, machinery, or equipment described in the declarations. An *accident* is a sudden and accidental breakdown of an object or part of an object, such as an explosion, bursting flywheel, or electrical short circuit. At the time the breakdown occurs, there must be physical damage to the object that requires repair or replacement.

**Extension of Coverage**    The boiler and machinery coverage form has four extensions of coverage, summarized as follows:

1. *Expediting expenses.* The insurance can be applied to cover the reasonable extra cost of making temporary repairs, expediting permanent repairs, or expediting permanent replacement of damaged property. For example, overtime wages and extra transportation charges to speed up delivery of a replacement part are examples of covered expenses. The maximum amount paid for expediting expenses is the lower of $25,000 or what is left of the limit of insurance after the insurer pays for a loss to covered property.

2. *Automatic coverage for newly acquired property.* Newly acquired objects similar to the boiler and machinery described in the declarations are automatically covered. The insured must notify the insurer within 90 days and pay an additional premium.

3. *Legal defense.* The policy also provides a legal defense if the insured is sued because of an insured accident that causes damage to the property of another in the insured's care, custody, or control. The insurer either settles the suit or claim, or defends the insured. However, the insurer reserves the right to settle the suit or claim at any point.

4. *Supplementary payments.* Supplementary payments are also paid by the insurer for costs associated with any suit it defends. These include defense costs; cost of bonds to release attachments; reasonable expenses incurred at the insurer's request; loss of earnings up to $100 daily because of time off from work; court costs assessed against the insured; prejudgment interest; and interest on the original judgment.

**Indirect Losses**    Indirect, or consequential, losses can also be covered by an appropriate endorsement, including the following.

1. *Business income insurance* can be added to cover the loss of business income from an insured loss. Under a *valued form,* a specified daily amount is paid for each day of total shutdown regardless of the firm's actual loss of earnings. If the firm is partially shut down, a proportionate part of the daily indemnity is paid. Under an *actual loss sustained form,* the amount paid for a loss is the loss of net profits that would have been earned plus continuing expenses.

2. *Extra expense insurance* covers the extra expense of maintaining operations after an accident to an insured object until the firm can resume its normal operations. The extra expense endorsement excludes the loss of income. For example, a firm may have its own power plant to produce electricity and have an emergency standby connection with an outside public utility firm in case power is interrupted. If an accident occurs and

### INSIGHT 12.3

## Example of a Boiler and Machinery Loss

A steam boiler explosion in Acme Manufacturing Company's factory damaged Acme's building and personal property, property in Acme's custody that belonged to one of Acme's customers, and the building of a neighboring firm. In addition, the explosion injured several Acme employees as well as a customer who was on Acme's premises. In addition to its own property losses, Acme's customer, its neighbor, and its own employees made liability claims against Acme for their property damage and bodily injury. The claims were covered as shown below.

　　Covered by Acme's boiler and machinery insurance:

* Destruction of Acme's steam boiler
* Damage to Acme's building
* Damage to Acme's business personal property
* Customer's liability claim for damage to goods in Acme's custody

Not covered by boiler and machinery insurance but covered by Acme's commercial general liability insurance:

* Neighboring firm's liability claim against Acme for damage to its building
* Customer's liability claim for bodily injury

Not covered by boiler and machinery insurance but covered by Acme's workers compensation insurance:

* Acme employees' claim against Acme for their bodily injuries

SOURCE: Bernard L. Webb, Arthur L. Flitner, and Jerome Trupin, *Commercial Insurance*, 3rd ed. (Malvern, Pa.: Insurance Institute of America, 1996), p. 145.

the power is interrupted, the extra costs of the outside power would be covered.

3. *Consequential damage insurance* covers the spoilage of specified property from the lack of power, light, heat, steam, or refrigeration if an accident occurs to an insured object. For example, the loss of refrigeration in a meat packing plant results in the spoilage of meat. The spoilage loss would be covered by this endorsement.

Insight 12.3 provides an example of a boiler and machinery loss to a manufacturing plant because of a steam boiler explosion.

### Credit Insurance

**Credit insurance** protects a firm against abnormal credit losses because of customer insolvency or past due accounts when they are filed for collection within a specified time stated in the policy. Credit insurance is written only for manufacturers, wholesalers, and service organizations. Retail firms are ineligible for coverage. Only abnormal credit losses are covered; normal credit losses (called the primary loss) are

seldom covered. Credit insurance is designed to cover only those losses that exceed the firm's normal credit losses in the regular course of business. There usually is a limit on the amount paid on any one account, which is based on the debtor's credit rating. There is also a maximum limit on total losses paid during the policy term.

Credit losses generally are subject to two deductibles. First, credit losses are reduced by the *primary loss amount,* which reflects the firm's normal credit losses. The primary loss amount for a firm is a percentage of the firm's net annual sales based on the bad-debt experience of similar firms, or the firm's actual loss experience. If normal credit losses were covered, the premiums for credit insurance would be considerably higher.

Second, the insured is expected to bear a portion of any credit loss by a *coinsurance percentage* that acts as a deductible. The coinsurance percentage typically is 10 to 20 percent and applies to each covered loss. The purpose of this deductible is to encourage the insured to be careful in the granting of credit, especially to firms with marginal credit ratings.

## Difference in Conditions Insurance

**Difference in conditions (DIC) insurance** is an "all-risks" policy that covers other perils not insured by basic property insurance contracts.[6] DIC insurance is written as a separate contract to supplement the coverage provided by the underlying contracts. As such, it excludes perils covered by the underlying contracts (such as fire and extended coverage perils, vandalism and malicious mischief, and sprinkler leakage). However, most other insurable perils are covered. The policy can also be written to cover flood, earthquake, and building collapse. However, a substantial deductible must be satisfied for losses not covered by the underlying contracts.

DIC insurance has two major advantages. First, it can be used to fill gaps in coverage. Many large multinational corporations use a DIC policy to insure their overseas property. Many foreign countries require property insurance to be purchased locally; if the local coverage is inadequate, a DIC policy can fill the gap in coverage.

Second, DIC insurance can be used to insure unusual and catastrophic exposures that are not covered by the underlying contracts. Some unusual losses that have been paid include the following:

- An accident caused molasses to spill into a machine. The cost to clean the machine was $38,000.
- Dust collection on a roof solidified and the weight caused the roof to collapse.
- A city water main broke, which flooded the basement of an industrial plant, causing hundreds of thousands of dollars of damage.

Finally, DIC is less expensive than the purchase of separate contracts for flood and earthquake. It costs less because it is excess over the underlying coverages, and it does not require either coinsurance or insurance to full value.

## TRANSPORTATION INSURANCE

Billions of dollars of goods are shipped by business firms each year. These goods are exposed to damage or loss from numerous transportation perils. The goods can be protected by ocean marine and inland marine contracts. **Ocean marine insurance** *provides protection for goods transported over water.* All types of ocean-going vessels and their cargo can be insured by ocean marine contracts; the legal liability of ship owners and cargo owners can also be insured.

**Inland marine insurance** *provides protection for goods shipped on land.* This includes insurance on imports and exports, domestic shipments, and means of transportation such as bridges and tunnels. In addition, inland marine insurance can be used to insure fine art, jewelry, furs, and other property.[7]

## Ocean Marine Insurance

Ocean marine insurance is one of the oldest forms of transportation insurance. The ocean marine contracts are incredibly complex, reflecting basic marine law, trade, customs, and court interpretations of the various policy provisions.

Ocean marine insurance can be divided into four major classes to reflect the various insurable interests:

- **Hull insurance** *covers physical damage to the ship or vessel.* It is similar to automobile collision insurance that covers physical damage to an automobile caused by a collision. Hull insurance is always written with a deductible. In addition, hull insurance contains a *collision liability clause* (also called a running down clause) that covers the owner's legal liability if the ship collides with another vessel or damages its cargo. However, the running down clause does not cover legal liability arising out of injury or death to other persons, damage to piers and docks, and personal injury and death of crew members.
- **Cargo insurance** *covers the shipper of the goods if the goods are damaged or lost.* The policy can be written to cover a single shipment. If regular shipments are made, an *open-cargo policy* can be used that insures the goods automatically when a shipment is made. The shipper is required to report periodically the number of shipments that are made. The open-cargo policy has no expiration date and is in force until it is canceled.
- **Protection and indemnity (P&I) insurance** *is usually written as a separate contract that provides comprehensive liability insurance for property damage or bodily injury to third parties.* P&I insurance protects the ship owner for damage caused

by the ship to piers, docks, and harbor installations, damage to the ship's cargo, illness or injury to the passengers or crew, and fines and penalties.

- **Freight insurance** *indemnifies the ship owner for the loss of earnings if the goods are damaged or lost and are not delivered.*

## Basic Concepts in Ocean Marine Insurance

Ocean marine insurance is based on certain fundamental concepts. The following section discusses these concepts and related contractual provisions.

**Implied Warranties**   Ocean marine contracts contain three **implied warranties:** (1) seaworthy vessel, (2) no deviation from course, and (3) legal purpose. The ship owner implicitly warrants that the vessel is *seaworthy,* which means that the ship is properly constructed, maintained, and equipped for the voyage to be undertaken. The warranty of *no deviation* means that the ship cannot deviate from its original course, no matter how slight the deviation. However, an intentional deviation is permitted in the event of an unavoidable accident, to avoid bad weather, to save the life of an individual on board, or to rescue persons from some other vessel. The warranty of *legal purpose* means that the voyage should not be for some illegal venture, such as smuggling drugs into a country.

The implied warranties are based on court decisions, and they are just as binding as any expressed warranty stated in the contract. A violation of an implied warranty, such as an unexcused deviation, permits the insurer to deny liability for the loss. The implied warranties are strictly enforced, since a breach of them would cause an increase in hazard to the insurer.

**Covered Perils**   An ocean marine policy provides broad coverage for certain specified perils, including **perils of the sea,** such as damage or loss from bad weather, high waves, collision, sinking, and stranding. Other covered perils include loss from fire, enemies, pirates, thieves, jettison (throwing goods overboard to save the ship), barratry (fraud by the master or crew at the expense of the ship or cargo owners), and similar perils.

Ocean marine insurance can also be written on an "all-risks" basis. All unexpected and fortuitous losses are covered except those losses specifically excluded. Common exclusions are losses due to delay, war, inherent vice (tendency of certain types of property to decompose), and strikes, riots, or civil commotion.

**Particular Average**   In marine insurance, the word *average* refers to a partial loss. A **particular average** *is a loss that falls entirely on a particular interest,* as contrasted with a general average, a loss that falls on all parties to the voyage. Under the *free-of-particular-average clause* (FPA), partial losses are not covered unless the loss is caused by certain perils, such as stranding, sinking, burning, or collision of the vessel.

The FPA clause is often written as a franchise deductible, where the franchise amount is stated as a percentage of the insured property. Thus, an FPA clause of 3 percent means that a covered loss under 3 percent falls entirely on the insured; but if the loss is 3 percent or more the insurer pays the loss in full.

**General Average**   A **general average** *is a loss incurred for the common good and consequently is shared by all parties to the venture.* For example, if a ship damaged by heavy waves is in danger of sinking, part of the cargo may have to be jettisoned to save the ship. The loss falls on all parties to the voyage: the ship owner, cargo owners, and freight interests. Each party must pay its share of the loss based on the proportion that its interest bears to the total value in the venture. For example, assume that the captain must jettison $1 million of steel to save the ship. Also assume that the various interests are as follows:

| | |
|---|---:|
| Value of steel | $ 2 million |
| Value of other cargo | 3 million |
| Value of ship and freight | 15 million |
| Total | $20 million |

The owner of the steel would absorb 2/20 of the loss, or $100,000. The owners of the other cargo would pay 3/20 of the loss or, $150,000. Finally, the ship and freight interests would pay 15/20 of the loss, or $750,000.

Four conditions must be satisfied to have a general average loss.[8]

- *Necessary.* The sacrifice is necessary to protect all interests in the venture—ship, cargo, and freight.

- *Voluntary*. The sacrifice must be voluntary.
- *Successful*. The effort must be successful. At least part of the value must be saved.
- *Free from fault*. Any party that claims a general average contribution from other interests in the voyage must be free from fault with respect to the risk that threatens the venture.

**Coinsurance**   Although an ocean marine policy does not contain a specific coinsurance clause, losses are settled as if there is a 100 percent coinsurance clause. An ocean marine policy is a valued contract, by which the face amount is paid if a total loss occurs. If the insurance carried does not equal the full value of the goods at the time of loss, the insured must share in the loss. Thus, if $50,000 of cargo insurance is carried on goods worth $100,000, only one-half of any partial loss will be paid. The policy face is paid in the event of a total loss.

## Inland Marine Insurance

Inland marine insurance grew out of ocean marine insurance. Ocean marine insurance first covered property from the point of embarkation to the place where the goods landed. As commerce and trade developed, the goods had to be shipped over land as well. Inland marine insurance developed in the 1920s to cover property being transported over land, means of transportation such as bridges and tunnels, and property of a mobile nature.

## Nationwide Marine Definition

As inland marine insurance developed, conflicts arose between fire insurers and marine insurers. To resolve the confusion and conflict, the companies drafted a nationwide marine definition in 1933 to define the property that marine insurers could write. The definition was approved by the National Association of Insurance Commissioners (NAIC) and was later revised and broadened in 1953. In 1976, the NAIC drafted a new definition of marine insurance that has been adopted by most states. At present, marine insurers can write insurance on the following types of property:

- Imports
- Exports
- Domestic shipments
- Means of transportation and communication

- Personal property floater risks
- Commercial property floater risks

## Major Classes of Inland Marine Insurance

Commercial property that can be insured by inland marine contracts can be conveniently classified into the following five categories.[9]

- Domestic goods in transit
- Property held by bailees
- Mobile equipment and property
- Property of certain dealers
- Means of transportation and communication

**Domestic Goods in Transit**   The goods may be shipped by a common carrier, such as a trucking company, railroad, airline, or by the company's own trucks. The goods can be damaged because of fire, lightning, flood, earthquake, or from other perils. The goods can also be damaged from the collision, derailment, or overturn of the transportation vehicle. These losses can be insured by an inland marine policy.

Although a common carrier is legally liable for safe delivery of the goods, liability does not extend to all losses. For example, a common carrier is not responsible for losses due to acts of God (such as lightning), acts of public authority, acts of public enemies (war), improper packaging by the shipper, and inherent vice.

In addition, shipping charges are reduced if the shipper agrees to limit the carrier's liability for the goods at less than their full value (called a released bill of lading). Consequently, the shipper can save money by agreeing to a released bill of lading and then purchase insurance to cover the shipment.

**Property Held by Bailees**   Inland marine insurance can be used to insure property held by a bailee. A **bailee** *is someone who has temporary possession of property that belongs to another*. Examples of bailees are dry cleaners, laundries, and television repair shops. Under common law, bailees are legally liable for damage to customers' property only if they or their employees are negligent. However, to ensure customer good will, many bailees purchase bailee's customer insurance to cover the damage or loss to customers' property while in the bailee's possession regardless of fault, normally from named perils.

**Mobile Equipment and Property** Inland marine property floaters can be used to cover property that is frequently moved from one location to another, such as a tractor, crane, or bulldozer. Also, plumbing, heating, or air conditioning equipment can be covered while being transported to a job site or while being installed.

In addition, a property floater policy can be used to insure certain other types of property, such as fine art, livestock, theatrical property, computers, and signs.

**Property of Certain Dealers** Inland marine insurance is also used to insure the property of certain dealers. Specialized inland marine policies or inland marine "block" policies are used to insure the property of jewelers, furriers, and dealers in diamonds, fine art, cameras, and musical instruments, and other dealers. Most policies provide coverage on an "all-risks" loss.

**Means of Transportation and Communication** *Means of transportation and communication refers to property at a fixed location that is used in transportation or communication.* Inland marine insurance can be used to cover bridges, tunnels, piers, docks, wharves, pipelines, power transmission lines, radio and television towers, outdoor cranes, and similar equipment for loading, unloading, or transporting. For example, a bridge may be damaged by a flood or ice jam, or by a ship that collides with the bridge; a television tower or power line may be blown over in a windstorm; or a fire may start in a tunnel when a gasoline truck overturns and explodes. These losses can be insured under inland marine contracts.

The commercial property loss exposures just described can be insured by a wide variety of inland marine contracts. For purpose of regulation, inland marine contracts are divided into two categories: (1) filed forms and (2) nonfiled forms. Filed forms mean that the policy forms and rates are filed with the state insurance department. Filed forms are typically used in situations where there are a large number of potential insureds, and the loss exposures are reasonably homogeneous.

In contrast, nonfiled forms refer to policy forms and rates that are not filed with the state insurance department. Nonfiled forms are used in situations where the insured has specialized or unique needs, the number of potential insureds is relatively small, and the loss exposures are diverse.[10]

## Filed Inland Marine Forms

Under the ISO simplified commercial inland marine program, the various policy forms and rates are filed with the state insurance department.

Numerous forms can be used in the ISO commercial inland marine insurance program. The major forms are summarized here:

- The **accounts receivable coverage form** indemnifies the firm if it is unable to collect outstanding customer balances because of damage or destruction of the records. A firm may incur a sizeable loss if its accounts receivable records are destroyed by a fire, theft, or other peril, and the amount owned by customers cannot be collected.
- The **camera and musical instrument dealers coverage form** is used to cover stock in trade consisting principally of cameras or musical instruments and related equipment and accessories. The property of others in the insured's care, custody, or control is also covered.
- The **commercial articles coverage form** covers photographic equipment and musical instruments that are used commercially by photographers, professional musicians, motion picture producers, production companies, and other persons.
- The **equipment dealers coverage form** covers the stock in trade of dealers in agricultural implements and construction equipment. The form can also be extended to cover furniture, fixtures, office supplies, and machinery used in the business.
- The **film coverage form** covers exposed motion picture film as well as magnetic or video tapes.
- The **floor plan coverage form** refers to a financing plan in which the dealer borrows money to buy merchandise to display and sell, but the title is held by the lending institution or manufacturer. For example, a firm selling television sets, refrigerators, and home appliances could insure merchandise under this form.
- The **jewelers block coverage form** covers jewelry, watches, and precious stones of retail and wholesale jewelers, jewelry manufacturers, and diamond wholesalers.

- The **mail coverage form** covers securities in transit by first-class mail, registered or certified mail, or express mail. It is designed for stock brokerage firms, banks, and other financial institutions that ship securities by mail.

- The **physicians and surgeons equipment coverage form** covers the medical, surgical, or dental equipment of physicians and dentists, including furniture, fixtures, and improvements.

- The **signs coverage form** covers neon, mechanical, and electrical signs. Each covered sign must be scheduled.

- The **theatrical property coverage form** covers costumes, stage scenery, and similar property used in theatrical productions. For example, a New York play may be presented in another city, which requires the shipment of stage props and scenery to that city. The theatrical property can be covered under this form.

- The **valuable papers and records coverage form** covers loss to valuable papers and records, such as student transcripts in a university, plans and blueprints of an architectural firm, and prescription records in a drugstore. The form covers the cost of reconstructing the damaged or destroyed records. The form can also be used to insure the loss of irreplaceable records, such as a rare manuscript. However, each item must be scheduled with a specified amount of insurance.

## Nonfiled Inland Marine Forms

A wide variety of nonfiled forms are available to meet the specialized or unique needs of commercial firms. Only a few of them are discussed here.

**Shipment of Goods**    We noted earlier that inland marine insurance can be used to cover the domestic shipment of goods. An **annual transit policy** can be used by manufacturers, wholesalers, and retailers to cover the shipment of goods on public trucks, railroads, and coastal vessels. Both outgoing and incoming shipments can be insured. These forms are not standardized, but they have similar characteristics. They can be written either on an "all-risks" or named-perils basis.

Although a transit policy provides broad coverage, certain exclusions are present. The policy can be written to cover the theft of an entire shipment, but pilferage of the goods generally is not covered. Other common exclusions are losses from strikes, riots, or civil commotion, leakage and breakage (unless caused by an insured peril), marring, scratching, dampness, molding, and rotting.

A **trip transit policy** is used by firms and individuals to cover a single shipment. For example, an electrical transformer worth several thousand dollars that is shipped from an eastern factory to the West coast, or the household goods of executives who are transferred, can be insured under a variation of the trip transit policy.

**Bailee Forms**    As stated earlier, a bailee is someone who has temporary possession of property that belongs to others. A *bailee's liability policy* can be used to cover the firm's liability to the property of customers, such as clothes in a laundry. A bailee's liability policy, however, covers the loss only if the firm is legally liable. In contrast, a *bailee's customer policy* can be used to cover the loss or damage to the property of others regardless of legal liability. A bailee's customer policy generally is designed for firms that hold the property of others that have high values, such as fur coats. A covered loss is paid regardless of legal liability, and the goodwill of customers is maintained.

**Business Floaters**    A **business floater** is an inland marine policy that covers property that frequently moves (floats) from one location to another. Numerous business floaters are available. For example, a *contractors equipment floater* can be used to insure the property of contractors, such as bulldozers, tractors, cranes, earth movers, and scaffolding equipment. An *installation floater* covers equipment and machinery while the property is in transit for installation and also while the property is being installed. And a *salespersons floater* covers damage or loss to samples used by salespersons in their business.

**Means of Transportation and Communication**    Inland marine contracts can be used to cover bridges, tunnels, towers, pipelines, power lines, and similar property. This type of property can be insured either on a risks-of-direct-physical-loss basis or on a named-perils basis, depending on the specific needs of the insured. For example, a toll bridge can lose revenues because a ship ran into a bridge pylon, forcing the bridge to close. A business income policy can be written to cover the loss of income.

## BUSINESSOWNERS POLICY (BOP)

The **businessowners policy (BOP)** is a package policy specifically designed for small- to medium-sized retail stores, office buildings, apartment buildings, and similar firms. The following discussion is based on the 1996 edition of the businessowners policy drafted by the ISO.[11]

### Eligible Firms

In 1996, the ISO broadened the eligibility requirements for its BOP program. As a result, additional business firms are now eligible for a BOP. The BOP can be written to cover buildings and business personal property of the owners of apartments and residential condominium associations; office and office condominium associations; retail establishments; and eligible mercantile, service, or processing firms such as appliance firms, beauty parlors, and photocopy services.

Apartment buildings cannot exceed six stories in height and are limited to a maximum of 60 dwelling units. Office buildings are limited to a maximum of six stories or a maximum area of 100,000 square feet in total floor area. Buildings used primarily for certain eligible mercantile, service, or processing occupancies cannot exceed 25,000 square feet in total floor area, and annual gross sales for eligible classes cannot exceed $3 million at any insured location.

Certain business firms are ineligible for a BOP because the loss exposures are outside that contemplated for the average small- to medium-sized firm. They include automobile repair or service stations; dealers in automobiles, motorcycles, or mobile homes; parking lots; bars; places of amusement such as a bowling alley; and banks and financial institutions.

### BOP Coverages

The BOP is designed to meet the property insurance needs of most small- to medium-sized firms in one contract. The following is a summary of the basic characteristics of the BOP.

1. *Buildings* The BOP covers the buildings described in the declarations, which also includes completed additions, fixtures, and outdoor fixtures. The building coverage also includes personal property in apartments or rooms furnished by the named insured as a landlord, and personal property owned by the named insured to maintain or service the premises, such as fire extinguishing equipment and refrigerating and dishwashing appliances. The limit of insurance on the building is automatically increased by a stated percentage each year to keep pace with inflation.

2. *Business personal property.* Business personal property is also covered. This includes property owned by the named insured used in the business; property of others in the insured's care, custody, and control for which the insured is legally liable; tenant's improvements and betterments; and leased personal property for which the named insured has a contractual responsibility to insure. A peak season provision provides for a temporary increase of 25 percent of the amount of insurance when inventory values are at their peak.

   In addition, personal property at newly acquired locations is covered for a maximum of $10,000 for 30 days. This provision provides automatic protection until the BOP can be endorsed to cover the new location. Personal property in transit or temporarily away from the store is covered up to a maximum of $5000.

3. *Covered perils.* Two property forms are used under the BOP. The *standard property coverage form* provides coverage on a named-perils basis. Covered perils are fire, lightning, explosion, windstorm or hail, smoke, aircraft or vehicles, riot or civil commotion, vandalism, sprinkler leakage, sinkhole collapse, volcanic action, and certain transportation perils. The *special property coverage form* insures against "risks of direct physical loss." All direct physical losses are covered unless specifically excluded or limited in the form itself.

4. *Additional coverages.* The BOP also provides several additional coverages needed by the typical businessowner:
   - Debris removal

- Preservation of property coverage after a loss occurs
- Fire department service charge
- Business income, extended business income, and extra expense
- Pollutant cleanup and removal
- Loss of business income because of action by a civil authority
- Money order and counterfeit paper currency losses ($1000 maximum)
- Forgery and alteration losses ($2500 maximum).

5. *Optional coverages.* The BOP can also be used to provide several optional coverages to meet the specialized needs of businessowners:
- Outdoor signs
- Exterior glass
- Interior glass
- Burglary and robbery
- Employee dishonesty
- Mechanical breakdown

6. *Deductible.* A standard deductible of $250 per occurrence applies to all property coverages. However, a proposed 1997 change by ISO would increase the basic deductible on property coverage to $500. Higher deductibles are available if desired. The deductible does not apply, however, to the fire department service charge, business income losses, extra expenses, and action by a civil authority.

7. *Business liability insurance.* The businessowner is insured for bodily injury and property damage liability and advertising and personal injury liability. Medical expense coverage is also provided. These liability loss exposures are discussed in Chapter 13.

## SUMMARY

- Under the ISO commercial property insurance program, a commercial package policy contains a common declarations page, a common policy conditions page, and two or more coverage parts. Each coverage part, in turn, has its own declarations page, policy conditions, coverage forms, and a causes-of-loss form.
- A *commercial package policy* is one that combines two or more ISO coverage parts into a single policy. A package policy has fewer gaps in coverage, relatively lower premiums since individual policies are not purchased, and the convenience of a single policy.

- The coverage parts under the ISO commercial insurance program include the following:

  Commercial property coverage

  Commercial general liability coverage

  Crime coverage

  Inland marine coverage

  Boiler and machinery coverage

  Commercial auto coverage

  Farm coverage

- The *building and personal property coverage form* can be used to insure the commercial building, business personal property, and personal property of others in the care and custody of the insured.

- Under the ISO commercial property insurance program, a causes-of-loss form must be added to a commercial policy to form a complete contract. There are four causes-of-loss forms:

  Causes-of-loss basic form

  Causes-of-loss broad form

  Causes-of-loss special form

  Causes-of-loss earthquake form

- The *business income coverage form* covers the loss of business income due to the suspension of business operations because of a covered loss. Business income is the net profit or loss before income taxes that would have been earned if the loss had not occurred, plus normal operating expenses, including payroll. Extra expenses incurred as a result of a loss are also covered.

- The *extra expense coverage form* covers only the extra expenses incurred by the firm to continue operations during the period of restoration. Loss of profits is not covered, since the firm will still be operating.

- Certain miscellaneous commercial coverages are important to business firms that have unique or specialized needs, including builders risk insurance, condominium insurance, glass insurance, boiler and machinery insurance, and difference in conditions insurance.

- Ocean marine insurance can be divided into four categories that reflect the various insurable interests:

  Hull insurance

  Cargo insurance

  Protection and Indemnity insurance

  Freight insurance

- A particular average loss in marine insurance is a loss that falls entirely on a particular interest as contrasted with a general average loss that falls on all parties to the voyage.

- Inland marine contracts are used to insure the following classes of commercial property:

    Domestic goods in transit

    Property held by bailees

    Mobile equipment and property

    Property of certain dealers

    Means of transportation and communication

- For purposes of regulation, inland marine contracts are divided into filed forms and nonfiled firms. Filed forms are policy forms and rates that are filed with the state insurance department. Nonfiled forms are not filed with the state insurance department.

- Filed inland marine forms include the following:

    Accounts receivable coverage form

    Camera and musical instrument dealers coverage form

    Commercial articles coverage form

    Equipment dealers coverage form

    Film coverage form

    Floor plan coverage form

    Jewelers block coverage form

    Mail coverage form

    Physicians and surgeons equipment coverage form

    Signs coverage form

    Theatrical property coverage form

    Valuable papers and records coverage form

- Nonfiled inland marine forms include the following:

    Annual transit policy

    Trip transit policy

    Bailee forms

    Business floaters

    Insurance on means of transportation and communication

- The *businessowners policy* is a package policy for small- to medium-sized business firms. It covers the building, business personal property, loss of business income, extra expenses, and business liability exposures. Optional coverages are available for outdoor signs, exterior glass, interior glass, burglary and robbery, employee dishonesty, and mechanical breakdown.

## KEY CONCEPTS AND TERMS

Annual transit policy

Bailee

Boiler and machinery coverage form

Builders risk coverage form

Building and personal property coverage form

Business floater

Business income (and extra expense) coverage form

Business income insurance

Businessowners policy (BOP)

Cargo insurance

Causes-of-loss forms (basic, broad, special, earthquake)

Collision liability clause (running down clause)

Commercial package policy (CPP)

Condominium association coverage form

Condominium commercial unit-owners coverage form

Credit insurance

Difference in conditions insurance (DIC)

Extra expense coverage form

Franchise deductible

Free-of-particular-average clause (FPA)

Freight insurance

General average

Glass coverage form

Hull insurance

Implied warranties

Inland marine insurance

Leasehold interest coverage form

Means of transportation and communication

Monoline policy

Nationwide marine definition

Ocean marine insurance

Open-cargo policy

Package policy

Particular average

Perils of the sea

Protection and Indemnity insurance (P&I)

Reporting form

Trip transit policy

## QUESTIONS FOR REVIEW

1. Identify the major documents that are used to form a commercial package policy.

2. Briefly explain the advantages of a package policy to insureds, insurers, and producers.

3. Describe the major provisions of the building and personal property coverage form.

4. Explain the major provisions in the business income coverage form.

5. Identify the major coverages under a boiler and machinery insurance policy.

6. Describe each of the major classes of ocean marine insurance.

7. What is the difference between a particular average loss and general average loss in ocean marine insurance? What conditions must be fulfilled in order to have a general average loss?

8. Identify the major classes of commercial property that can be insured under an inland marine insurance policy.

9. Describe briefly several inland marine forms that are filed with state insurance departments.

10. Briefly describe the major coverages under the businessowners policy.

## QUESTIONS FOR DISCUSSION

1. a. Describe briefly how the causes-of-loss broad form differs from the causes-of-loss special form.

   b. Alicia owns a television repair shop that is insured under a commercial property insurance policy. The policy includes the building and personal property coverage form and the causes-of-loss broad form. Indicate whether the following losses would be covered under her policy. If not, why not?

      (1) A fire occurs on the premises, and the building is badly damaged.

      (2) Television sets owned by customers are damaged by vandals who broke into the shop after business hours.

      (3) A burglar stole some money and securities from an unlocked safe.

2. Issac owns a retail shoe store. The store is insured for $90,000 under the business income coverage form with a 50 percent coinsurance provision. Because of an explosion, Issac was forced to close the store for one month before it could be reopened. If the explosion had not occurred, Issac's estimated net profits and operating expenses for the 12-month period after the policy's inception date would have been $180,000. However, for the one-month period that the store was closed, Issac had a business income loss of $12,000 (loss of net income plus continuing operating expenses).

   a. How much will Issac recover for the business income loss? Show your calculations.

   b. How does the business income coverage form differ from the extra expense coverage form?

3. Carlos rents an office in a desirable city office building under a long-term lease. The rental is $2000 monthly. Carlos's lease has 10 more years to run and states that if the premises are damaged by a fire and are rendered untenantable, either Carlos or the landlord can cancel the lease by giving 30 days notice to the other party. Carlos has been advised by a rental agent that a comparable office would cost $3000 per month to rent today.

   a. What type of insurance would you recommend to Carlos in this situation?

   b. Explain how the recommended coverage would cover Carlos's loss exposure.

4. a. The Mary Queen, an ocean-going oil tanker, negligently collided with a large freighter. The Mary Queen is insured by an ocean marine hull insurance policy with a collision or running down clause included in the policy. For each of the following

losses, explain whether the ocean marine coverage would apply to the loss.

   (1) Damage to the Mary Queen

   (2) Damage to the freighter

   (3) Death or injury to the crew members on the freighter

### CASE APPLICATION

a. Kimberly owns and operates a tennis shop in a resort area. The business is seasonal. A large part of the annual revenues are due to sales in June, July, and August. Kimberly keeps the shop open during the remaining months of the year, but the inventory carried during those months is reduced. During the summer months, the amount of inventory on hand is substantially increased. Kimberly has the business insured under the standard businessowners policy (BOP) with no special endorsements attached.

   1. Assume you are a risk management consultant. Identify the major loss exposures that Kimberly faces.

   2. Assume that a covered loss occurs in July, which damages part of the inventory. Does the BOP provide any protection for the increase in inventory during the summer months? Explain your answer.

   3. Kimberly plans to hire an additional employee during the summer months when sales are increasing. She is concerned about possible employee theft and dishonesty. Explain to Kimberly how this loss exposure can be handled under the BOP.

b. Assume you are a risk management consultant. Identify the type of inland marine policy that could be purchased to protect the following types of property. Indicate whether the policy form would be filed or nonfiled.

   1. Property of customers in a dry cleaning establishment

   2. Scenery, props, and costumes used by a local theatrical group

   3. Cameras and equipment owned by a professional photographer

b. Briefly explain each of the following ocean marine terms or provisions.

(1) Free-of-particular average

(2) General average

(3) Open cargo policy

## SELECTED REFERENCES

*Fire, Casualty & Surety Bulletins.* Fire and Marine volume and Casualty-Surety volume. Cincinnati: National Underwriter Company. The bulletins are published monthly and provide detailed information on all commercial property insurance lines.

Kensicki, Peter R., Robert S. Smith, Thomas S. Marshall, Seeman Waranch, and Darwin B. Close. *Principles of Insurance Production,* 2nd ed., vol. 2. Malvern Pa.: Insurance Institute of America, 1986, Chapters 9–11.

*Policy, Form & Manual Analysis Service.* Property Coverages volume. Indianapolis: Rough Notes Company. The reference materials are published monthly and provide detailed information on commercial property insurance coverages.

Rodda, William H., James S. Trieschmann, Eric A. Wiening, and Bob A. Hedges. *Commercial Property Risk Management and Insurance,* 3rd ed., vols. 1 and 2. Malvern, Pa.: American Institute for Property and Liability Underwriters, 1988.

Webb, Bernard L., Arthur L. Flitner and Jerome Trupin. *Commercial Insurance,* 3rd ed. Malvern, Pa.: Insurance Institute of America, 1996.

## NOTES

1. Discussion of commercial property insurance in this chapter is based on Bernard L. Webb, Arthur L. Flitner, and Jerome Trupin, *Commercial Insurance,* 3rd ed. (Malvern, Pa.: Insurance Institute of America, 1996); and *Fire, Casualty & Surety Bulletins,* Fire and Marine volume, Commercial Property section (Cincinnati: National Underwriter Company). The author also drew on the various commercial property forms of the Insurance Services Office (copyrighted) that appeared in the *CPCU Handbook of Insurance Policies,* First Edition (Malvern, Pa.: American Institute for CPCU/Insurance Institute of America, 1994).

2. Webb et al., p. 15.

3. This section is based on the *Fire, Casualty & Surety Bulletins,* Fire and Marine volume, Business Income Section; *Fire, Casualty & Surety Bulletins,* Guide to Policies 1 Volume, Business Income section; and Webb et al., pp. 89–113.

4. Webb et al., p 110.

5. Peter R. Kensicki, et al., *Principles of Insurance Production,* 2nd. ed., vol. 2. (Malvern, Pa.: Insurance Institute of America, 1986), p. 158.

6. This section is based on William H. Rodda, James S. Trieschmann, Eric A. Wiening, and Bob A. Hedges, *Commercial Property Risk Management and Insurance,* 2nd ed., vol. 1 (Malvern, Pa.: American Institute for Property and Liability Underwriters, 1983), pp. 216–223.

7. Transportation insurance is discussed in detail in *Fire, Casualty & Surety Bulletins,* Fire and Marine volume, Inland Marine section (Cincinnati: National Underwriter Company); Webb et al., chapter 7; Rodda et al., vols. 1 and 2; and Philip Gordis, *Property and Casualty Insurance,* 31st ed. (Indianapolis: Rough Notes Company, 1988). The author drew on these sources in preparing this section.

8. Gordis, pp. 329–30.

9. Webb et al., pp. 156–60.

10. Ibid., p. 162.

11. A detailed explanation of the businessowners policy can be found in *Fire, Casualty & Surety Bulletins,* Fire and Marine volume, Commercial Property section (Cincinnati: National Underwriter Company); and Webb et al., chapter 11.

# Chapter 13

# COMMERCIAL LIABILITY INSURANCE

> " *If a firm wants to survive in this jungle, it must have protection against catastrophic legal liability lawsuits.* "
>
> *Jack Willhoft, President,*
> *Spartan Arch Skate Company*

## Student Learning Objectives

After studying this chapter, you should be able to:

■ Identify the important general liability loss exposures of business firms.

■ Describe the basic coverages provided by the commercial general liability policy (CGL).

■ Explain the coverage provided by a workers compensation policy.

■ Describe the basic characteristics of other general liability policies, including the business auto coverage form, bailee's customer form, and commercial umbrella policy.

■ Identify the liability coverages provided by the businessowners policy (BOP).

■ Describe the basic characteristics of a medical malpractice liability policy.

B usiness firms operate in an intense, competitive environment where liability suits are routine. Firms are sued because of defective products, injuries to customers or employees, property damage, pollution of the environment, sexual harassment, and numerous other reasons. This chapter discusses the major general liability loss exposures faced by business firms and the major commercial liability coverages for insuring those exposures. The coverages discussed include the commercial general liability policy, workers compensation and employers liability insurance, commercial automobile liability

insurance, aviation insurance, bailee's liability insurance, and the commercial umbrella liability policy. The chapter concludes with a discussion of professional liability insurance.

## GENERAL LIABILITY LOSS EXPOSURES

General liability refers to the legal liability arising out of business operations other than automobile or aviation accidents or employee injuries. The major general liability loss exposures of business firms include the following:

- Premises and operations
- Products liability
- Completed operations
- Contractual liability
- Contingent liability

## Premises and Operations

Legal liability can arise out of the *ownership and maintenance of the premises* where the firm does business. Firms are legally required to maintain the premises in a safe condition and are also responsible for the actions of their employees. Customers in a store fall into the legal category of *invitees,* and the highest degree of care is owed to them. The customers must be warned and protected against any dangerous condition on the premises. For example, a firm can be held liable if a customer trips on a torn carpet and breaks a leg, or if a ceiling collapses and injures a customer.

Legal liability can also arise out of the firm's operations, either on or off the premises. For example, employees unloading lumber in a lumberyard may accidentally damage a customer's truck; or a construction worker on a high-rise building may carelessly drop a tool that injures a pedestrian.

## Products Liability

**Products liability** *refers to the legal liability of manufacturers, wholesalers, and retailers to persons who are injured or incur property damage from defective products.* As noted in Chapter 6, the number of products liability lawsuits and the size of the damage awards have increased substantially over time. Firms can be successfully sued on the basis of negligence, breach of warranty, and strict liability. These topics were discussed earlier in Chapter 6, and additional treatment is not needed here.

## Completed Operations

**Completed operations** *refers to liability arising out of faulty work performed away from the premises after the work or operation is completed.* Contractors, plumbers, electricians, repair shops, and similar firms are liable for bodily injuries and property damage to others after their work is completed. When the work is in progress, it is part of the operations exposure. However, after the work is completed, it is a completed-operations exposure. For example, a hot water tank may explode if it is improperly installed; or ductwork in a supermarket may collapse and injure a customer because of improper installation.

A general liability policy provides coverage for both products liability and completed operations. Both products liability and completed-operations loss exposures are now included in a definition called **products-completed operations hazard.** *The policy covers liability losses that occur away from the premises and arise out of the insured's product or work after the insured has relinquished possession of the product, or the work has been completed.* For example, assume that a gas furnace is improperly installed and explodes one month later. The loss is covered under the products-completed operations hazard.

## Contractual Liability

**Contractual liability** *means that the business firm agrees to assume the legal liability of another party by a written or oral contract.* For example, a manufacturing firm may rent a building, and the lease specifies that the building owner is to be held harmless for any liability arising out of use of the building. Thus, by a written lease, the manufacturing firm is assuming some potential legal liability that ordinarily would be the owner's responsibility.

## Contingent Liability

**Contingent liability** *refers to liability arising out of work done by independent contractors.* As a general rule, business firms are not legally liable for work done by independent contractors. However, under certain conditions, a firm can be held liable for work performed by independent contractors. A firm can be held liable if (1) the activity is illegal, (2) the situation or type of work does not permit delegation of authority, or (3) the work done by the independent contractor is inherently dangerous.[1] For example, a general contractor may hire a subcontractor to perform a blasting operation. If someone is injured in the blast, the general contractor can be held liable even though the subcontractor is primarily responsible.

## Other General Liability Loss Exposures

Business firms are often exposed to other important general liability loss exposures, as summarized here.

- *Environmental pollution.* Chemical, manufacturing, and other firms may pollute the environment by smoke, fumes, acids, toxic chemicals, waste materials, and other pollutants. In addition, leaking underground storage tanks are currently a major liability exposure for many firms.
- *Fire legal liability.* Another important loss exposure is **fire legal liability.** A firm may rent or use property such as a building that belongs to another party. If a fire occurs because of the negligence of the firm or its employees, the firm can be held legally liable for the loss.
- *Liquor liability.* Under a **liquor liability law** (also called a dramshop law), bars, restaurants, taverns, and other establishments that sell liquor can be held legally liable for injuries caused by intoxicated customers. However, general liability policies typically exclude liquor liability coverage for firms in the business of manufacturing, selling, distributing, or serving of alcoholic beverages.
- *Directors and officers liability.* An increasing number of officers and directors of business firms have been sued in recent years by stockholders, competing firms, government agencies, and other parties. Numerous lawsuits are initiated by angry stockholders who claim that they have incurred financial loss because of mismanagement by officers and directors. A **directors and officers liability policy** can be used to cover the legal liability of directors and officers.
- *Personal injury.* In addition to bodily injury and property damage liability, a business firm may be sued for personal injury. **Personal injury** *refers to false arrest, detention or imprisonment, malicious prosecution, libel, slander, defamation of character, violation of the right of privacy, and unlawful entry or eviction.* For example, a department store may be successfully sued by an innocent customer who is erroneously arrested for shoplifting.
- *Property in the insured's care, custody, or control.* Liability can also arise out of damage to property in the insured's care, custody, or control. General liability policies usually exclude coverage for this exposure. This can be a problem for firms that work on the property of others, such as an automobile repair garage or a television repair shop. In some cases, a bailee's liability policy can be used to cover liability for damage to personal property in the care, custody, or control of the insured.
- *Sexual harassment.* Employers increasingly are being sued by employees on the grounds of sexual harassment. Such suits are expensive to defend. To reduce the possibility of a sexual harassment suit, many employers have adopted strict policies that prohibit certain actions, such as lewd and suggestive language.

## COMMERCIAL GENERAL LIABILITY POLICY (CGL)

The **commercial general liability (CGL) policy** is widely used by business firms to cover their general liability loss exposures. The CGL policy has two coverage forms: an occurrence form and a claim-made form. The following section discusses both forms, based on the 1996 edition of the CGL policy drafted by the Insurance Services Office (ISO).[2]

### Overview of the CGL Occurrence Policy

The CGL occurrence policy can be written alone or as part of a commercial package policy. The complete contract consists of a common policy declarations page, common policy conditions page, CGL declarations page, CGL coverage form, and applicable endorsements.

The occurrence form contains five major sections:

- Section I: Coverages
  Coverage A: Bodily injury and property damage liability
  Coverage B: Personal and advertising injury liability
  Coverage C: Medical payments
  Supplementary payments: Coverages A and B
- Section II: Who Is an Insured?
- Section III: Limits of Insurance
- Section IV: Commercial General Liability Conditions
- Section V: Definitions

## Section I: Coverages

Section I provides coverage for bodily injury and property damage liability, personal and advertising injury liability, medical payments, and certain supplementary payments.

### Coverage A: Bodily Injury and Property Damage Liability

The insurer agrees to pay on behalf of the insured all sums up to the policy limits that the insured is legally obligated to pay because of **bodily injury or property damage** to which the insurance applies. The bodily injury or property damage must be caused by an occurrence. An **occurrence** *is defined as an accident, including continuous or repeated exposure to substantially the same general harmful conditions.* For example, an explosion occurs in a store, and several customers are injured; or a drug company manufactures a defective batch of flu vaccine, and over a period of time, several persons become violently ill. These incidents would be considered occurrences and would be covered by the CGL.

### Defense Costs

The insurer also provides a legal defense. The insurer has the right to investigate a claim or suit and settle it at its discretion. The insurer's duty to defend ends when the applicable limits of insurance are paid out. The legal defense costs are paid in addition to the policy limits.

### Exclusions

A lengthy list of exclusions applies to both bodily injury and property damage liability. The major exclusions are summarized here.

- *Expected or intended injury.* Bodily injury or property damage that is expected or intended by the insured is not covered. However, the exclusion does not apply to bodily injury that results from the use of reasonable force to protect persons or property.
- *Contractual liability.* The policy excludes liability assumed by a contract or agreement. However, the exclusion does not apply to liability assumed by an *insured contract* or to liability that the insured would have in the absence of the contract or agreement. An insured contract refers to a lease of the premises, a sidetrack agreement, an easement agreement required by a municipality, an elevator maintenance agreement, or tort liability assumption (liability imposed by law in the absence of any contract or agreement).
- *Liquor liability.* The exclusion applies only to firms in the business of manufacturing, distributing, selling, serving, or furnishing alcohol. For example, if a bartender continues to serve a drunk customer who injures another person, the bar owner is not covered for any claim or suit. However, the liquor exclusion does not apply to firms that are not in the liquor business. For example, an insured that serves drinks at a company-sponsored party would be covered. Coverage can be obtained by adding the liquor liability coverage form to the policy.
- *Workers compensation.* Any legal obligation of the insured to pay benefits under a workers compensation law or similar law is excluded.
- *Employers liability.* The policy excludes liability for bodily injury to an employee arising out of and in the course of employment. The policy also excludes a claim by a spouse or close relative who is seeking damages as a result of a job-related injury by an employee of the insured. For example, a suit by a spouse who seeks damages for the loss of consortium (loss of companionship, affection, and comfort) following a work-related injury is not covered.
- *Pollution exclusion.* Pollution and contamination claims are also excluded. The exclusion also applies to cleanup costs that are incurred as a result of a government order. Coverage can be obtained by a pollution endorsement or by adding a separate pollution liability coverage form to the policy.
- *Aircraft, auto, and watercraft exclusion.* Liability arising out of the ownership or operation of aircraft, autos, and watercraft is specifically excluded. The intent here is to exclude legal liability covered by other policies. The exclusion does not apply to watercraft while ashore on premises owned or rented by the insured and to nonowned watercraft less than 26 feet in length and not used to carry people or property for a fee. In addition, the exclusion does not apply to bodily injury to customers resulting from parking automobiles on the premises or next to the premises, which is important for firms that park the cars of customers. However, physical damage to the car being parked is not covered

because of the care, custody, or control exclusion (discussed later).

- *Mobile equipment.* Mobile equipment is not covered when the equipment is (a) being transported by an auto or (b) used in or in preparation for any racing, speed, or demolition contest, or in any stunting activity. For example, a bulldozer is excluded while being transported to a job site by an auto. However, coverage can be added by an endorsement to the policy.
- *War.* Bodily injury or property damage due to war is specifically excluded. War is defined to include civil war, insurrection, rebellion, or revolution. The exclusion applies only to liability assumed by a contract or agreement.
- *Care, custody, or control exclusion.* The **care, custody, or control exclusion** excludes property owned, rented, or occupied by the insured, premises that the insured sells or abandons, property loaned to the named insured, and personal property in the insured's care, custody, or control. Other excluded losses are property damage to that particular part of real property on which the insured, contractors, or subcontractors are working and part of any property that must be restored, repaired, or replaced because the insured's work is incorrectly performed.
- *Property damage to the insured's product.* The policy excludes **property damage to the insured's product** if the damage results from a defect in the product. For example, a defective hot water tank may explode. The damage to the tank itself is not covered. However, property damage from the explosion would be covered under the manufacturer's liability policy.
- *Property damage to the insured's work.* The policy also excludes **property damage to insured's work** that is included in the "products-completed operations hazard." The insured's work refers to the work or operations of the insured as well as material, parts, and equipment used in the work. For example, an employee of a heating contractor may improperly install a gas furnace that later explodes after it was installed. Although the property damage to the customer's building is covered, the value of the employee's work is specifically excluded. The exclusion does not apply if the work is performed by a subcontractor on behalf of the insured.

- *Property damage to impaired property.* The policy also excludes **property damage to impaired property** that is not physically damaged. If property is impaired because of a defect in the insured's product or work, or failure to perform, the loss is not covered. Impaired property is tangible property that cannot be used or is less useful because (1) it incorporates the insured's product or work, or (2) the insured fails to perform the terms of a contract or agreement, and (3) the property can be restored to use by correction of the insured's product or work or fulfillment of the contract. For example, assume that the insured manufactures airplane parts, and a faulty part causes several jets to be grounded. The planes are considered impaired property. The loss of use of the jets is not covered by the insured's CGL policy.
- *Recall of products.* Damages and expenses arising out of the recall of defective products are also excluded. In recent years, firms have incurred substantial losses in recalling defective products such as automobiles, drugs, or food products. The CGL specifically excludes such losses. Coverage can be obtained, however, by an endorsement to the policy.

In addition to the preceding exclusions, CGL policies do not cover claims involving suits by aggrieved employees against their employers because of sexual harassment, wrongful discharge, failure to promote, and similar employment practices. Specific coverage for these loss exposures must be purchased (see Insight 13.1).

**Coverage B: Personal and Advertising Injury Liability**  Under this coverage, the insurer agrees to pay those sums that the insured is legally obligated to pay because of personal injury or advertising injury. Personal injury is an injury (other than bodily injury) that results from any of the following:

- False arrest, detention, or imprisonment
- Malicious prosecution
- Wrongful eviction or entry
- Libel or slander
- Publication of material that violates a person's right to privacy

## INSIGHT 13.1

### How Can Employers Deal with Sexual Harassment, Failure to Promote, and Similar Employment Practices Loss Exposures?

The CGL policy specifically excludes coverage for employment-related claims, such as sexual harassment, failure to promote or hire, and wrongful termination. To deal with these loss exposures, some insurers make available **employment practices liability (EPL) insurance.** Although the various policies are not standard, they have similar characteristics.

The policies do not cover all employment practices but specify the exact types of claims covered. *Covered events typically include discrimination, sexual harassment, and wrongful termination. Some policies also cover the failure to employ or promote, wrongful discipline, and breach of an employment contract. Most*

*policies also cover "back pay" for the wages and salaries lost by discharged employees who are successful in their suit against the employer.*

The policy is sold with a deductible, ranging from $1000 to $250,000. The insured must also participate in the payment of losses exceeding the deductible, such as 5 to 10 percent, but the deductible could be as high as 25 percent.

SOURCE: Adapted from "Employment Practices Liability Insurance," in Bernard L. Webb, Arthur L. Flitner, and Jerome Trupin, *Commercial Insurance*, 3rd ed. (Malvern, Pa.: Insurance Institute of America, 1996), pp. 335–36.

For example, if a customer is falsely arrested for shoplifting, the firm is covered if the customer sues.

The policy also covers **advertising injury,** which is an injury due to the following:

- Oral statement or written publication of material that slanders or libels
- Publication of material that results in a violation of a person's right to privacy
- Misappropriation of advertising ideas
- Infringement of a copyright, title, or slogan

For example, if a textbook publisher uses copyrighted material without permission and is sued, the CGL would cover the suit.

**Coverage C: Medical Payments**    **Medical payments** cover the medical expenses of persons who are injured in an accident on the premises or on ways next to the premises, or as a result of the insured's operations. The medical expenses must be incurred within one year of the accident and are paid without regard to legal liability. For example, if a customer falls on a slippery floor in a supermarket, the medical expenses are covered up to the policy limits.

**Supplementary Payments: Coverages A and B**    Certain supplementary payments are included under Coverages A and B in addition to the policy limits:

- All expenses incurred by the insurer
- Up to $250 for the cost of a bail bond because of an accident or traffic violation arising out of the use of a vehicle to which the insurance applies
- Cost of bonds to release attachments
- Actual loss of earnings by the insured up to $250 a day because of time off from work
- All costs taxed against the insured in the suit
- Prejudgment interest and interest that accrues after entry of the judgment

### Section II: Who Is an Insured?

The named insured stated in the declarations includes the proprietor and spouse if a sole proprietorship; partners, members, and their spouses if a partnership; members and managers if a limited liability company; and officers, directors, and stockholders if a corporation.

In addition, the following are insureds: employees acting within the scope of their employment, any real estate managers of the insured, a temporary representative if the insured should die, a legal representative if the insured should die, drivers of mobile equipment owned by the insured, and newly acquired or formed organizations.

## Section III: Limits of Insurance

The limits of insurance state the maximum amount the insurer will pay regardless of the number of insureds, claims made or suits brought, or persons or organization making such claims or bringing suits. There are six limits that apply (see Exhibit 13.1).

1. *General aggregate limit*. The **general aggregate limit** is the maximum amount the insurer will pay for the sum of the following: damages under Coverage A, except injury and damages included in the "products-completed operations hazard," damages under Coverage B, and medical expenses under Coverage C.

2. *Products-completed operations aggregate limit*. The **products-completed operations aggregate limit** is the maximum amount the insurer will pay under Coverage A because of injury and

damage included in the "products-completed operations hazard."

3. *Personal and advertising injury limit*. This is the maximum amount the insurer will pay under Coverage B for personal injury and advertising injury.

4. *Each-occurrence limit*. The **each-occurrence limit** is the maximum amount the insurer will pay for the sum of all damages under Coverage A and the medical expenses under Coverage C arising out of any one occurrence.

5. *Fire damage limit*. This is the maximum amount the insurer will pay under Coverage A for property damage to rented premises from a single fire.

6. *Medical expense limit*. This is the maximum amount the insurer will pay under medical expenses because of a bodily injury sustained by any one person.

## Section IV: Commercial General Liability Conditions

This section states the various conditions that apply to the general liability coverage form. The conditions

---

EXHIBIT 13.1

**Illustration of the CGL Limits of Insurance**

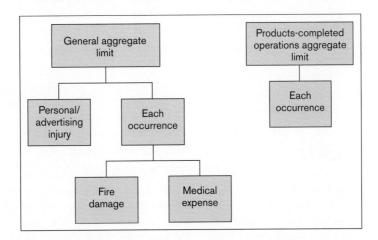

SOURCE: Bernard L. Webb, Arthur L. Flitner, and Jerome Trupin, *Commerical Insurance*, 3rd ed. (Malvern, Pa.: Insurance Institute of America, 1996); Exhibit 9-1, p. 215.

include provisions dealing with bankruptcy; duties in the event of an occurrence, claim, or suit; legal action against the insurer; other insurance; premium audit; and numerous additional conditions.

## Section V: Definitions

This section in the CGL policy defines more precisely the various terms used in the policy. Fifteen definitions are stated in some detail. However, space limitations preclude a discussion of these definitions here.

## Overview of the CGL Claims-Made Policy

The Insurance Services Office (ISO) also offers a claims-made policy, which is similar to the occurrence policy with the major exceptions of payment of claims on a claims-made basis, inclusion of an extended reporting period (Section V), and moving the definitions to Section VI.

**Meaning of "Claims Made"** An **occurrence policy** is one that covers claims arising out of occurrences that take place during the policy period, regardless of when the claim is made. In contrast, the **claims-made policy** *only covers claims that are first reported during the policy period, provided the event occurred after the retroactive date (if any) stated in the policy.* The retroactive date is an extremely important concept that is discussed later.

To illustrate the difference between the two concepts, assume that a building contractor replaces an occurrence policy with a claims-made policy. If the contractor is sued because of a defect in a building constructed five years earlier, the occurrence policy would defend the claim. However, assuming no retroactive coverage, the claims-made policy would not cover the loss since the loss occurred before the inception date of the policy.

**Rationale for Claims-Made Policies** Insurers have resorted to claims-made policies because of the problem of **long-tail** losses. The long-tail refers to a relatively small number of claims that are reported years after the policy was first written. Under an occurrence policy, the insurer that provided coverage when the incident occurred is responsible for the claim. Consequently, insurers found themselves paying claims on policies that had expired

years earlier. As a result, insurers found it extremely difficult to estimate accurately the correct premiums to charge and also the correct loss reserve to establish for claims incurred but not yet reported (IBNR). Under a claims-made policy, premiums, losses, and loss reserves can be estimated with greater accuracy.

**Retroactive Date** A claims-made policy can be written to cover events that occur prior to the inception of the policy. Coverage will depend on the retroactive date, if any, inserted in the policy. To be covered, the occurrence must take place after the retroactive date, and the claim must be reported during the current policy term. If the occurrence takes place before the retroactive date, the claims-made policy will not respond.

For example, assume that the retroactive date is the date of the original claims-made policy. The issue date of the original claims-made policy is January 1, 1995. The most recent claims-made policy is issued on January 1, 1997. The insured would be covered for all occurrences that take place after January 1, 1995, and are reported during the current policy period.

**Extended Reporting Periods** The claims-made policy also contains a provision that extends the period for reporting claims. *The purpose of the extended reporting period is to provide coverage under an expired claims-made policy when the claim is first reported after the policy expires.*

The **basic extended reporting period** is automatically provided without an extra charge whenever one of the following occurs:

- The policy is canceled or not renewed.
- The insurer renews or replaces the policy with a retroactive date that is later than the retroactive date in the original policy.
- The claims-made policy is replaced with an occurrence policy.

The basic extended reporting period provides for two separate reporting periods or "tails." The first tail is a five-year period after the policy expires, and the second tail is a 60-day period after the expiration date. For example, assume that a customer in a supermarket slips and falls on a wet floor during the policy period. The insured reports the occurrence promptly to the company, but no actual claim is made against the insured during the policy period. Any resulting claim arising out of that reported occurrence is covered by the expired policy if the claim is made before the end of the five-year period.

The second tail of 60 days applies to all other claims; these are claims that result from occurrences that take place during the policy period (or after the retroactive date), but are not reported to the insurer during the policy period. Coverage applies if the occurrence is reported to the insurer within 60 days after the policy expires. For example, referring back to our illustration, the insured may have been unaware that the customer fell, so the incident was not reported to the company. However, if a claim is made against the insured after the policy expires, coverage applies if the occurrence is reported to the insurer within 60 days after the expiration date.

If the insured wants a longer reporting period after the policy expires, the supplemental extended reporting period can be added by an endorsement and payment of an additional premium. The insured must request the endorsement in writing within 60 days after the policy expires.

## WORKERS COMPENSATION AND EMPLOYERS LIABILITY INSURANCE

All states have workers compensation laws that require most employers to provide workers compensation benefits to employees who have a job-related injury or an occupational disease. Exhibit 13.2 shows some typical workers compensation claims reported by employers in a 1996 survey. Employers can meet their legal obligation to injured employees by buying a workers compensation policy from a private insurer.

The following section discusses the current version of the workers compensation policy introduced by the Insurance Services Office (ISO) in 1992.[3] The historical development of workers compensation as a form of social insurance is treated in Chapter 23.

The workers compensation and employers liability policy provides the following coverages:

- Part One: Workers Compensation Insurance
- Part Two: Employers Liability Insurance
- Part Three: Other-States Insurance

### Part One: Workers Compensation Insurance

Part One refers to **workers compensation insurance.** Under this section, the insurer agrees to pay all workers compensation benefits and other benefits that the employer must legally provide to covered employees who have a job-related injury or an occupational disease. There are no policy limits for part one. The insurer instead pays all benefits required by the workers compensation law of any state listed in the declarations. In recent years, occupational disease has become increasingly more important in the payment of workers compensation claims.

Under certain conditions, the employer can be held responsible for payments made by the insurer that exceed regular workers compensation benefits. The employer is responsible for any payments in excess of the benefits regularly provided by the workers compensation law because of serious and willful misconduct; knowingly employing workers in violation of the law; failing to comply with a health or safety regulation; or discharging, coercing, or discriminating against any employee in violation of the workers compensation law. The employer must reimburse the insurer for any payments that exceed regular workers compensation benefits.

### Part Two: Employers Liability Insurance

Part Two refers to **employers liability insurance** that covers employers against lawsuits by employees who are injured in the course of employment, but whose injuries (or disease) are not compensable under the state's workers compensation law. This part is similar to other liability insurance policies where negligence must be established before the insurer is legally obligated to pay.

Employers liability insurance is needed for several reasons. First, a few states do not require workers compensation insurance with smaller employers with fewer than a certain number of employees, such as three or less. In such cases, an employer is covered under the employers liability section if an employee with a work-related injury or disease sues for damages.

Second, an injury or disease that occurs on the job may not be considered to be work related, and, therefore, it would not be covered under the state's workers compensation law. However, the injured employee may still believe that the employer should

EXHIBIT 13.2

**Types of Workers Compensation Claims**

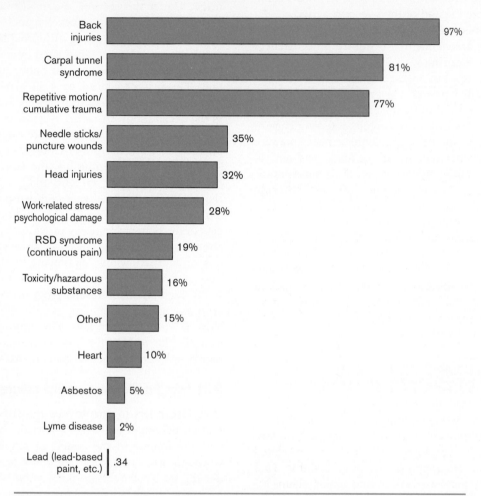

SOURCE: *Risk & Insurance,* Vol. 7, No. 7 (November 1996), p. 21. Data are based on the 4th annual Workers' Compensation Survey conducted jointly by *Risk & Insurance* and *Human Resource Executive* magazines.

be held accountable, and the employer would be covered if sued.

Third, some state workers compensation laws permit lawsuits by spouses and dependents for the *loss of consortium.* The employer would be covered under Part Two in such a case.

Finally, in a growing number of cases, employers are confronted with lawsuits because of *third-party over cases.* An injured employee may sue a negligent third party, and the third party, in turn, sues the employer for contributory negligence. The lawsuit

would be covered under Part Two (unless the employer assumed the liability of the third party). For example, assume that a machine is defective, and its operator is injured. In addition to payment of workers compensation benefits, the state may allow the injured employee to sue the negligent third party. If the injured employee sues the manufacturer of the defective machine, the manufacturer, in turn, could sue the employer for failure to provide proper operating instructions, or for failure to enforce safety rules. The employer would be covered in such cases.

The employers liability section of the policy also contains several exclusions. Major exclusions include liability assumed under contract, punitive damages, bodily injury to an employee employed in violation of the law, workers compensation claims (covered under Part One), intentional injury, bodily injury outside the United States or Canada, and damages arising out of coercion, demotion, evaluation, reassignment, harassment, discrimination, or termination of any employee.

### Part Three: Other-States Insurance

Part Three of the workers compensation and employers liability policy provides **other-states insurance**. Workers compensation coverage (Part One) applies only to those states listed on the information page (declarations page) of the policy. However, the employer may be faced with a workers compensation claim under the law of another state. This possibility could arise if an employee is injured while on a business trip in a state that was not considered at all when the workers compensation policy was first written, or if the law of a particular state is broadened so that employees are now covered under that state's workers compensation law. Also, the employer's operations may be expanded in a particular state, which brings the employees under the state's workers compensation law.

Other-states insurance applies only if one or more states are shown on the information page of the policy. The information page is the equivalent of a declarations page (see Exhibit 13.3). In such cases, if the employer begins work in any of the states listed, the policy applies as if that state were listed in the policy for workers compensation purposes. Thus, the employer has coverage for any workers compensation benefits that it may have to make under that state's workers compensation law.

### Voluntary Compensation Coverage

Some employers wish to provide workers compensation benefits to employees even though they are not required by law to do so. A **voluntary compensation endorsement** can be added to the policy by which the insurer agrees to pay workers compensation benefits to employees not covered under the law.

## COMMERCIAL AUTOMOBILE INSURANCE

Legal liability arising out of the ownership and use of cars, trucks, and trailers is another important loss exposure for many firms. The following section examines several commercial auto coverages that can be used to meet this exposure.[4]

### Business Auto Coverage Form

The ISO business auto coverage form is widely used by business firms to insure their commercial auto exposures. Firms have considerable flexibility with respect to the autos that can be covered. There are nine numerical classifications, and each has a numbered symbol:

1. Any auto
2. Owned autos only
3. Owned private passenger autos only
4. Owned autos other than private passenger autos only
5. Owned autos subject to no-fault
6. Owned autos subject to a compulsory uninsured motorists law
7. Specifically described autos
8. Hired autos only
9. Nonowned autos only

If any one or more of the symbols 1 through 6 are selected, there is automatic coverage on any new owned autos that the firm acquires during the policy period. If symbol 7 is used, new cars are covered only if two conditions are met: (1) the company must already insure all autos that the insured owns for the coverage provided, or the new auto replaces one that the insured previously owned that had such coverage, and (2) the firm informs the company within 30 days after acquisition that it wants the auto insured for that coverage.

**Liability Insurance Coverage**  The insured is covered for a bodily injury or property damage claim arising out of an accident caused by the ownership, maintenance, or use of a covered auto. The insurer also agrees to defend the insured and pay all legal defense costs.

Exhibit 13.3

# Workers Compensation and Employers Liability Insurance Policy Information Page

**WORKERS COMPENSATION AND EMPLOYERS LIABILITY INSURANCE POLICY**

**INFORMATION PAGE**

**insurer:**

**P O L I C Y   N O .**

1.  The Insured:  AMR Corporation          ___ Individual          ___ Partnership
    Mailing address:  2000 Industrial Highway      _X_ Corporation or  _____
                      Workintown, PA 19000

    Other workplaces not shown above:

2.  The policy period is from      10/1/96    to    10/1/97    at the insured's mailing address.

3.  A.  Workers Compensation Insurance;  Part One of the policy applies to the Workers Compensation Law of the states listed here;    PA

    B.  Employers Liability Insurance: Part One of the policy applies to work in each state listed in item 3.A. The limits of our liability under part two are;

    |  |  |  |
    |---|---|---|
    | Bodily Injury by Accident | $ __100,000__ | each accident |
    | Bodily Injury by Disease | $ __500,000__ | Policy limit |
    | Bodily Injury by Disease | $ __100,000__ | each employee |

    C.  Other States Insurance:  Part Three of the policy applies to the states, if any listed here:

    All except those listed in Item 3A and ME, NV, ND, OH, WA, WV, WY, and OR

    D.  This policy Includes these endorsements and schedules:

    See Schedule

4.  The premium for this policy will be determined by our Manuals of Rules, Classifications, Rates and Rating Plans. All information required below is subject to verication and change by audit.

    | Classfications | Code No. | Premium Basis Total estimated Annual Remuneration | Rate Per $100 of Remuneration | Estimated Annual Premium |
    |---|---|---|---|---|
    | Sheet Metal Shop | 0454 | 300,000 | 11.53 | 34,590 |
    | Clerical Office | 0953 | 275,000 | .49 | 1,348 |
    |  |  | Experience Modification of 1.382 Applied |  | 13,728 |
    |  |  | Experience Premium Discount |  | (4,869) |
    |  |  | Total Estimated Annual Premium  $ |  | 44,797 |

    Minimum Premium  $   1,273          Expense Constant $          140

    Countersigned by  _____

WC 00 00 01 A
© 1987 National Council on Compensation Insurance.

SOURCE: Bernard L. Webb, Arthur L. Flitner, and Jerome Trupin, *Commercial Insurance,* 3rd ed. (Malvern, Pa.: Insurance Institute of America, 1996), Exhibit 12-2, p. 310.

When liability insurance is provided, there is also automatic coverage on all trailers that have a load capacity of 2000 pounds or less and are designed primarily for travel on public roads. Also, mobile equipment, such as a bulldozer, grader, or scraper, is covered while being carried or towed by a covered auto. Liability coverage also applies to a temporary substitute auto that is used because a covered auto is out of service because of breakdown, service, or damage.

**Physical Damage Insurance** The insured has a choice of physical damage coverages that can be used to insure covered autos against damage or loss. Several physical damage coverages are available, summarized as follows:

- *Comprehensive coverage.* The insurer will pay for loss to a covered auto or its equipment from any cause except the covered auto's collision with another object or its overturn.
- *Specified causes-of-loss coverage.* Only losses from specified perils are covered: fire, lightning, or explosion; theft; windstorm, hail, or earthquake; flood; mischief or vandalism; and the sinking, burning, collision, or derailment of any conveyance transporting the covered auto.
- *Collision coverage.* Loss caused by the covered auto's collision with another object or its overturn is covered under this provision.

Coverage for towing and labor costs can also be added. The company will pay up to the limit shown in the declarations for towing and labor costs incurred each time a covered auto of the private passenger type is disabled. However, the labor must be performed at the place of disablement.

In addition, the insurer will pay up to $15 per day (after 48 hours) up to a maximum of $450 for transportation expenses incurred by the insured because of the theft of a covered auto of the private passenger type. The coverage applies only to covered autos that are insured for either comprehensive or specified causes-of-loss coverage.

## Nonownership Liability Coverage

Salespersons, repair and maintenance employees, employees who make deliveries, inspection personnel, and other employees frequently drive their automobiles on company business. A business firm can be held legally liable for damages caused by employees while they are using their own cars on company business. If the employee carries liability insurance on his or her car, the firm is also protected as an additional insured. But the liability limits may be inadequate, or the policy may have lapsed. The firm may also be exposed to liability claims arising from the operation of other nonowned automobiles—for example, a restaurant or hotel that parks cars for the guests. These nonownership exposures can also be insured by selecting the appropriate covered auto designation symbol or combination of symbols.

## Garage Coverage Form

The **garage coverage form** is a specialized form designed to meet the insurance needs of "garages," which include service stations, parking garages, automobile dealerships, repair shops, and similar businesses. The major coverages include liability coverage, garagekeepers coverage, and physical damage coverage.

**Liability Coverage** The liability section of the garage coverage form is broad and comprehensive. The company agrees to pay all sums that the insured must legally pay as damages because of bodily injury or property damage caused by an accident in the course of garage operations. *Garage operations* are defined to include automobiles, business premises, and business activities. As such, the liability section automatically includes premises and operations liability coverage, products and completed operations coverage, and incidental contractual liability, as well as automobile liability insurance.

The insured has a choice of autos that can be covered, and numerical symbols are used to denote the covered autos (symbols 21–31), an approach similar to the business auto policy.

The liability section of the garage policy contains numerous exclusions. Only two of them are discussed here. *First, damage to the property of others in the insured's care, custody, or control is excluded.* Thus, damage to a customer's car on an automobile servicing hoist, or damage to a customer's car while it is being road tested by a mechanic would not be covered. These common exposures can be covered by adding garagekeepers coverage to the policy.

*Second, there is no coverage for property damage to any of the insured's products if the product is defective at the time it is sold.* This exclusion is important for firms that sell automobiles, gasoline, parts, tires, batteries, or other products. For example, assume that a tire dealer sells a tire that has a hidden defect. The defective tire later blows out, and the car is damaged in a collision loss. This exclusion eliminates coverage for the defective tire, but the property damage caused by the defective tire would be covered. The intent of this exclusion is to cover property damage or bodily injury caused by a defective product but not any damage to the product itself.

**Garagekeepers Coverage**  The owner of a parking lot, auto repair shop, or storage garage who keeps a customer's car for storage or repair and receives compensation is legally considered a bailee for hire. Regardless of signs to the contrary posted on the premises, the garage owner can be held legally liable for the loss or damage to a customer's car because of the failure to exercise ordinary care. As noted earlier, the garage coverage form excludes coverage for property of others in the care, custody, or control of the insured. This exclusion can be eliminated by adding garagekeepers coverage to the policy. Under this coverage, the insurer agrees to pay all sums that the insured legally must pay as damages for loss to customers' autos while in the garage owner's care for service, repairs, parking, or storage. Three coverages are available: (1) comprehensive coverage, (2) specified causes-of-loss coverage, and (3) collision coverage. These coverages are based on the legal liability of the insured. For example, if a customer's car is stolen because the garage owner carelessly left the garage door unlocked, the loss would be covered. It is possible, however, to broaden the coverage on customers' automobiles without regard to legal liability by the payment of an additional premium.

**Physical Damage Coverage**  Physical damage insurance on covered autos can also be included in the garage policy. The following three coverages are available:

- *Comprehensive coverage.* The company will pay for a loss from any cause except for the covered auto's collision with another object or its overturn.

- *Specified causes-of-loss coverage.* Covered perils are fire, lightning, explosion, theft, windstorm, hail, earthquake, flood, mischief, vandalism, and the sinking, burning, collision, or derailment of any conveyance transporting the covered auto.
- *Collision coverage.* Loss caused by the covered auto's collision with another object or its overturn is covered under this provision.

## AIRCRAFT INSURANCE

Major commercial airlines own fleets of expensive jets, and the liability exposure is enormous. Occasionally, a commercial jet will crash, killing hundreds of passengers and causing extensive property damage to surrounding buildings. Legal liability arising out of the crash of a fully loaded jet airliner can be catastrophic. In addition, some firms own aircraft used on company business. Company planes often crash, resulting in death or bodily injury to the passengers, as well as death or injury to people on the ground and substantial property damage to surrounding buildings where the crash occurs. Finally, thousands of Americans own or operate small planes, which often crash because of pilot error or inexperience.

Most states apply the common-law rules of negligence to aviation accidents. However, some states have absolute or strict liability laws that hold the owners or operators of aircraft absolutely liable for certain aviation accidents. As a result of international treaties and agreements among countries, absolute liability is also imposed on commercial airlines for aviation accidents that occur during international flights.

### Aviation Insurers

Aviation insurance is a highly specialized market that is underwritten by a relatively small number of insurer organizations. Most of the domestic aviation market is accounted for by two multicompany aviation pools: United States Aircraft Insurance Group (USAIG) and Associated Aviation Underwriters (AAU). Both pools underwrite and manage aviation insurance on behalf of the individual insurers that belong to the pool. Both pools account for most of the aviation insurance that is written for commercial airlines, aircraft manufacturers, and large domestic airports.

## Aviation Insurance for Private Business and Pleasure Aircraft

Associated Aviation Underwriters, a major aviation pool, offers a policy designed for the owners and operators of private business and pleasure aircraft. The policy provides physical damage coverage for damage to the aircraft, liability coverage for injury to passengers and people on the ground, and medical expense coverage for passengers.[5]

**Physical Damage Coverage**  A plane on the ground can be damaged from fire, collapse, theft, vandalism, or other perils. While taxiing, the plane can collide with vehicles, buildings, or other aircraft. But the most severe exposure is present when the plane is in flight. A plane can collide with another aircraft; it can be struck by lightning or be damaged by turbulent winds; it can also experience mechanical difficulties from a fire or explosion.

Physical damage insurance provides coverage for direct damage to the aircraft. The insured has a choice of physical damage coverages. There are three insuring agreements for physical damage to the aircraft:

- *"All-risks" basis.* All physical damage losses to the aircraft, including disappearance, are covered except those losses excluded.
- *"All-risks" basis, not in flight.* The aircraft is covered on an "all-risks" basis only when it is on the ground and not in flight. However, fire or explosion following a crash is not covered.
- *"All-risks" basis, not in motion.* The aircraft is covered on an "all-risks" basis only when it is standing still. However, fire or explosion after a crash is not covered.

Although aircraft can be covered on an "all-risks" basis, certain exclusions apply. Excluded losses include damage to tires (unless caused by fire, theft, or vandalism), wear and tear, deterioration, mechanical or electrical breakdown, and failure of installed equipment. However, these exclusions do not apply if a covered loss occurs.

**Liability Coverage**  Liability coverage pays for bodily injury or property damage arising out of the insured's ownership, maintenance, or use of the insured aircraft. Coverage also applies to bodily injury arising out of the premises where the aircraft is stored.

Liability coverage contains several important exclusions. Excluded losses are liability assumed in a contract, workers compensation, and damage to property in the insured's care, custody, and control (except personal effects of passengers up to $250 and damage to an aircraft hangar or its contents up to $5,000). Also excluded are damage or injury from noise, such as sonic boom, interference with the quiet enjoyment of property, and pollution losses.

**Medical Payments to Passengers**  The policy also provides medical payments coverage to passengers, which includes hospital, ambulance, nursing, and funeral services. Crew members can also be covered for an additional premium.

## BAILEE'S CUSTOMER INSURANCE

A bailee is someone who has temporary possession of property that belongs to another party. Bailees—such as a laundry or dry cleaner, for example—are legally liable for damage to the customers' goods only if they or their employees are guilty of negligence. However, the customers expect to be paid for the loss or damage to their goods regardless of who is at fault. If the customers are not reimbursed, the bailee may lose future business. In the case of a destructive fire or tornado, the business may be financially ruined if the customers are not reimbursed for their damaged property.

A bailee's customer policy is a generic name for a policy that covers loss or damage to the property of customers regardless of the bailee's legal liability. Although the polices are not standard, they can be written to meet the needs of a particular bailee, including laundries and dry cleaners, tailors, television repair shops, and upholsterers.

A bailee's customer policy can be illustrated by an analysis of the **bailee coverage named-perils policy** drafted by the American Association of Insurance Services (AAIS).[6] The policy is written on a named-perils basis. The perils covered are fire; lightning; windstorm; hail; explosion; strike; riot or civil commotion; damage from aircraft, spacecraft, or self-propelled missiles; damage from physical contact with vehicles; collision, derailment, upset, or overturn of a transporting land vehicle; vandalism; and theft. For example, if a suit or dress is damaged in a fire or tornado, or if the garment is damaged when a delivery truck overturns in a collision, the loss would be covered.

The above policy contains numerous exclusions. Excluded are those losses that result from dishonest or illegal acts; voluntary parting with the title or possession of covered property if the insured is induced to do so by trickery or fraud; mysterious disappearance; any cause when the only proof is an inventory shortage; theft of property left overnight in or on delivery vehicles (unless the vehicle is locked in a private garage or building occupied by the insured); breaking of fragile items or marring, scratching, tearing, or ripping (unless caused by a covered peril); a process performed on the covered property (except if a fire or explosion results); explosion or implosion inside a boiler; and misdelivery. For example, if a garment is damaged by cleaning fluid or shrinks in the cleaning process, the loss is not covered.

## COMMERCIAL UMBRELLA POLICY

Because firms are frequently sued for large amounts, they seek protection against catastrophic liability judgments not adequately insured under a standard liability policy. The commercial umbrella policy can provide protection against catastrophic liability judgments that may bankrupt a firm. The amount of insurance is frequently written for $5 million, $10 million, or higher limits.

### Basic Characteristics

Although commercial umbrella policies are not standard, they have certain basic characteristics that are discussed in the following section.[7]

**Excess Liability Insurance**   The liability insurance is excess over any basic underlying limits that may apply. The umbrella policy pays only after the basic limits of the underlying coverages are exhausted. *The insured is indemnified for the ultimate net loss in excess of the applicable underlying limit.* **Ultimate net loss** is the total amount that the insured is legally obligated to pay. (Legal defense costs may or may not be included.) The *applicable underlying limit* is either (1) the amount recoverable under the underlying insurance contract, or (2) the retained limit if the loss is not covered by the underlying insurance.

The umbrella policy may cover certain losses that are excluded by the underlying contracts. If the loss is covered by the commercial umbrella policy but not by any underlying contract, a **retained limit** (also known as a SIR, or self-insured retention) must be satisfied. Commercial umbrella policies typically require a retained limit of $10,000 to $25,000 or even higher, depending on the underwriter's requirement.

**Required Underlying Coverages**   The insured is required to carry certain minimum amounts of liability insurance before the company assumes the umbrella liability exposures. Umbrella insurers may require the insured to have the following underlying coverages and limits. [8]

*Commercial general liability insurance*

   $1,000,000 (each occurrence)

   $2,000,000 (general aggregate)

   $2,000,000 (completed operations aggregate)

*Business auto liability insurance*

   $1,000,000 (combined single limit)

*Employer liability insurance*

   $100,000 (bodily injury per accident)

   $100,000 (bodily injury by disease per employee)

   $500,000 (disease aggregate)

The commercial umbrella liability applies when the loss exceeds the underlying limits.

**Liability Coverages**   The commercial umbrella policy typically indemnifies the insured for the following types of liability losses.

*Bodily injury liability* covers losses that result from bodily injury, shock, fright, mental injury and mental anguish, humiliation, sickness or disease sustained by a person, and death that may result from any of the preceding.

*Property damage liability* covers losses that result from physical injury to tangible property, including the loss of use of that property. In addition, loss that results from the loss of use of tangible property not physically injured is also covered.

*Personal injury* covers losses that result from false arrest and imprisonment, malicious prosecution, wrongful entry or eviction, libel, slander, defamation of character, violation of privacy, and discrimination because of race, religion, sex, or physical disability.

*Advertising injury* covers losses that arise out of the insured's advertising activities, including libel, slander, defamation of character, violation of privacy, misappropriation of advertising ideas or style, and infringement of a copyright, title or slogan.

## Exclusions

Some important exclusions are typically found in the commercial umbrella liability policy, including the following:

- Bodily injury or property damage expected or intended by the insured
- Bodily injury consisting of humiliation or mental injury or anguish related to the employment of any person by the insured
- Obligations of the insured under a workers compensation or similar law
- Liability arising out of any aircraft, or watercraft over a certain length
- Pollution losses
- Property damage to the insured's products, or work performed by one on behalf of the insured
- Expenses in recalling defective products
- Failure of the insured's products or work to meet the standards warranted or represented by the insured
- Under advertising liability, breach of contract, incorrect description of an item, and mistake in an advertised price
- Personal injury consisting of discrimination related to the employment or prospective employment of any person by the insured

Finally, if the commercial umbrella liability policy contains an exclusion that is also present in an underlying contract, the firm has no coverage under either contract for the loss.

## LIABILITY INSURANCE, BUSINESS OWNERS POLICY

The businessowners policy (BOP) discussed in Chapter 12 also contains a business liability coverage form that provides general liability insurance to business firms. The liability coverage is written only on an occurrence basis, and with some minor exceptions, it is similar to the commercial general liability coverage form discussed earlier.[9]

### Basic Coverages

The BOP liability form has two basic coverages: (1) business liability coverage and (2) medical expenses coverage. Business liability includes both bodily injury and property damage liability, and advertising and personal injury liability. Coverage for medical expenses is also provided. Thus, if a customer in a retail shoe store falls and breaks an arm, the customer's medical expenses would be paid without regard to legal liability.

### Amount of Insurance

The minimum amount of insurance provided for liability and medical expenses is $300,000 for each occurrence, which can be increased to $500,000 or $1 million. This limit is the maximum the insurer will pay for both liability and medical expense losses.

The BOP has a medical expense limit of $5000 per person and a fire legal liability limit of $50,000. Higher fire legal liability limits are available.

In addition, the BOP has two aggregate limits on the total amounts of covered claims that can be paid during the policy period. *The first aggregate limit applies to products and completed operations losses and is equal to the liability and medical expense limit discussed earlier.*

*The second aggregate limit applies to all other covered losses (including medical expenses) and is equal to twice the liability and medical expense limit.* However, fire legal liability is an exception. Fire legal liability losses are subject only to the fire legal liability limit and do not reduce the aggregate limit.

### Legal Defense

The insurer pays the legal costs of defending the insured. The legal costs are in addition to the amount that the insurer is legally obligated to pay because of the insured's negligence.

The definition of an insured also includes employees while acting within the scope of their activities. This feature protects a negligent employee who might be named in the lawsuit along with the employer.

## Exclusions

In general, the liability form excludes claims involving pollution, automobiles, aircraft, watercraft, workers compensation, and professional services. However, druggists liability insurance is automatically included in the present form, but an additional premium is required if the insured is a retail drug store. In addition, liability coverage for hired and nonowned autos can be added as an endorsement to the policy. This latter coverage is especially important if the firm has employees who park the cars of customers. Finally, the policy contains the usual liquor liability exclusion discussed earlier, but there is an important exception. *Liability coverage* is provided if alcohol is served at functions incidental to the insured's business. Thus, if the company has a Christmas party, and an intoxicated employee injures someone, the firm is covered if a lawsuit ensues.

## PROFESSIONAL LIABILITY INSURANCE

Chapter 6 examined the problem of professional liability and the increased number of lawsuits against physicians, surgeons, attorneys, accountants, professors, and other professionals. This section briefly discusses some professional liability insurance coverages that provide protection against a malpractice lawsuit or lawsuit involving a substantial error or omission.

### Malpractice Liability Insurance

Physicians, surgeons, dentists, and hospitals require substantial amounts of **malpractice liability insurance** that covers acts of malpractice resulting in harm or injury to patients. The *physicians, surgeons, and dentist professional liability coverage part* drafted by the ISO covers acts of malpractice by physicians and surgeons. This policy has the following characteristics:[10]

- Broad coverage is provided.
- Liability is not restricted to accidental acts.
- The insured's liability for the negligent acts of employees is also covered.
- There is a maximum limit per medical incident and an aggregate limit for each coverage.

- Professional liability insurance is not a substitute for general liability insurance.
- The current forms may permit the insurer to settle a claim without the insured physician's or surgeon's consent.
- An extended reporting period can be added.

*The insuring agreement provides broad coverage.* The insurer agrees to pay all sums that the insured is legally obligated to pay as damages because of injury caused by a medical incident. A *medical incident* is any act or omission in the furnishing of professional medical or dental services by the insured, an employee of the insured, or any person acting under the personal direction or supervision of the insured. Since *injury* is not defined, it includes bodily injury, property damage, and also intangible damages such as mental suffering, humiliation, undue familiarity, invasion of privacy, libel, and slander, if such acts arise out of professional services. For example, if Dr. Jones operates on a patient and the patient is paralyzed after the operation, Dr. Jones would be covered for a malpractice lawsuit.

*Liability is not restricted to accidental acts of the physician or surgeon.* In many cases, the physician or surgeon deliberately intends to do a certain act; however, the professional diagnosis or the performance of the act may be faulty, and the patient is injured. For example, Dr. Jones may intend to operate on a patient by using a certain surgical procedure. If the patient is harmed or injured by the operation, Dr. Jones would still be covered for his willful, intentional act to operate in a certain way.

*The policy covers the physician for liability arising out of the negligent acts of an employee;* however, a nurse typically is not included as an insured under the physician's policy but must secure his or her own professional liability policy. For example, if the office nurse gives a wrong shot to a patient, and the patient is harmed, the physician has liability coverage for the incident. However, the nurse is not covered under the physician's policy for the incident. If desired, coverage for employees can be provided by an endorsement to the policy.

*There is a maximum limit per medical incident and an aggregate limit for each coverage.* For example, a patient and the patient's family may file separate claims against a physician for damages arising out of the same medical incident. Under current forms, the per-medical-incident limit is the maximum that

## INSIGHT 13.2

## Doctors Who Rush with Patients May Be Sued More

*Primary-care doctors who rush their patients through are more likely to be accused of malpractice than those who take more time, encourage people to talk and inject a little humor, a study suggests.*

The study, which used audiotapes to record how doctors acted, is important in light of pressure on managed-care organizations to curb costs by shortening patient visits.

"When faced with a bad outcome, patients and families are more likely to sue a physician if they feel the physician is not caring and compassionate," said Dr. Wendy Levinson, a University of Chicago medical professor and co-author of the report, which appears today in the Journal of the American Medical Association.

A medical consumer advocate, Dr. Sidney Wolfe of the Public Citizen Health Research Group, said the findings should be a warning to health maintenance organizations.

"The focus in the HMO industry has been profit," Dr. Wolfe said, "and HMOs should pay attention to this study because they are heading for trouble."

In the federally financed study, researchers audiotaped 10 patient visits each with 59 primary-care physicians and 65 general and orthopedic surgeons.

In analyzing the tapes, the researchers focused on four factors: the length of the visits, doctors' explanations to patients, whether they encouraged patients to talk about their problems and whether they injected humor and warmth.

Doctors who had been contacted two or more times by patients or their lawyers wanting malpractice compensation—even if no suit was eventually filed—average 15 minutes for office visits. Those who had been contacted fewer than twice had an average visit length of 18.3 minutes.

Dr. Levinson said that by listening to the tapes and scoring doctors on how they interacted, researchers were able to pinpoint with 75 percent accuracy those who were more likely to face malpractice claims, and with 84 percent accuracy those who weren't.

SOURCE: "Doctors Who Rush with Patients May Be Sued More," *Omaha World Herald*, February 19, 1997.

---

would be paid for both claims. The aggregate limit is the maximum amount that would be paid as damages during any policy year.

*Professional liability insurance is not a substitute for other necessary forms of liability insurance.* General liability insurance is also needed that covers liability arising out of a hazardous condition on the premises or acts of the insured that are not professional in nature. For example, a patient may trip on a torn carpet in the doctor's office and break an arm. The professional liability policy would not cover this event.

*Current forms permit the insurer to settle the claim without the physician's or surgeon's consent.* Payment of a claim could be viewed as an admission of guilt. Older forms required the insurer to obtain the physician's consent before a claim could be settled. However, current forms permit the insurer to settle without the physician's consent since an occasional

claim against a physician in certain high-risk categories is not viewed as being overly detrimental to his or her character.

*Finally, an extended reporting period endorsement can be added.* A physician with a claims-made policy may retire, change insurers, or drop the malpractice insurance. To protect the physician, an extended reporting period endorsement can be added, which covers future claims arising out of incidents that occurred during the period the claims-made policy was in force.

In summary, a professional liability policy for physicians and surgeons provides considerable protection. But the insurance is expensive. Malpractice insurance covering certain high-risk specialities can cost $75,000 or more each year in certain parts of the country. Physicians have responded to the medical malpractice problem by practicing defensive medicine, by abandoning high-risk specialities such as obstetrics and neurosurgery, and by pushing for legislation to limit malpractice awards.

Finally, the amount of time physicians spend with their patients appears to be an important factor in determining whether a physician will be sued for malpractice (see Insight 13.2).

## Errors And Omissions Insurance

**Errors and omissions insurance** provides protection against loss incurred by a client because of some negligent act, error, or omission by the insured. Professionals who need errors and omission insurance include insurance agents and brokers, travel agents, real estate agents, stockbrokers, attorneys, consultants, engineers, architects, and other individuals who give advice to clients. The errors and omissions coverage is designed to meet the needs of each profession.

This type of coverage can be illustrated by the *insurance agents and brokers errors and omissions policy*. The policy has a number of provisions. First, the insurer agrees to pay all sums that the insured is legally obligated to pay because of any negligent act, error, or omission by the insured (or by any other person for whose acts the insured is legally liable) in the conduct of business as general agents, insurance agents, or insurance brokers. For example, assume that Mark is an independent agent who fails to renew a property insurance policy for a client. The policy lapses, and a subsequent loss is not covered. If the client sues for damages, Mark would be covered for the omission.

The policy is normally sold with a sizable deductible. A $1000 deductible is common. An insurer may require a higher deductible so that the agent has an incentive to minimize mistakes and errors.

Errors and omissions policies are generally issued on a claims-made basis covering claims made against the agent or broker only because of errors during the current policy period (or after the retroactive date).

Finally, the policy contains relatively few exclusions. However, claims that result from dishonest, fraudulent, criminal, or malicious acts by the insured, libel and slander, bodily injury, or destruction of tangible property are specifically excluded.

## SUMMARY

- General liability refers to the legal liability of business firms arising out of business operations other than liability for automobile or aviation accidents or employee injuries. The most important general liability loss exposures are as follows:

  Premises and operations

  Products liability

  Completed operations

  Contractual liability

  Contingent liability

- Legal liability can arise out of the *ownership and maintenance of the premises* where the firm does business. *Products liability* means the firm can be held liable for property damage or bodily injury arising out of a defective product. *Completed operations* refers to liability arising out of faulty work performed away from the premises after the work is completed. *Contractual liability* means the business firm agrees to assume the legal liability of another party by a written or oral contract. *Contingent liability* means the firm can be held liable for work by independent contractors.

- Other important general liability loss exposures include environmental pollution; property in the insured's care, custody, or control; fire legal liability; liability arising out of a liquor or dramshop law; directors and officers liability; and personal injury.

- The *commercial general liability policy (CGL)* can be used to cover most general liability loss exposures of business firms. The CGL provides coverage for the following:

  Bodily injury and property damage liability

  Personal and advertising injury liability

  Medical payments

  Supplementary payments

- An *occurrence policy* is one that covers liability claims arising out of occurrences that take place during the policy period, regardless of when the claim is made.

- A *claims-made policy* covers only claims that are first reported during the policy period or extended reporting period, provided the event occurred after the retroactive date, if any, stated in the policy.

- Insurers have resorted to claims-made policies because of the problem of the *long tail*. The long tail refers to the relatively small number of claims that are reported years after the policy is first written. As a result, it is difficult to estimate premiums, losses, and loss reserves accurately. A claims-made policy enables an insurer to estimate premiums and losses more accurately.

- All states have workers compensation laws that require covered employers to provide workers compensation benefits to employees who are disabled from work-related accidents or occupational disease. The workers compensation insurer pays all benefits that the employer must legally provide to employees who are occupationally disabled.

- The *business auto coverage form* can be used by business firms to insure the liability exposures from automobiles. The employer can select those autos to be covered under the policy.

- The *garage coverage form* is designed to meet the insurance needs of service stations, parking garages, repair shops, and similar firms. The major coverages include liability insurance, garagekeepers insurance, and physical damage insurance. *Garagekeepers insurance* covers the garage owner's liability for damage to customers' automobiles while in the garage owner's care for service or repairs.

- Aviation insurance covering private business and pleasure aircraft provides physical damage coverage on the aircraft, liability coverage for injury to passengers and people on the ground, and medical expense coverage for passengers.

- The *bailee coverage named-perils policy* can be used to cover the loss or damage to the property of customers regardless of the bailee's legal liability.

- The *commercial umbrella policy* provides protection to firms against a catastrophic judgment that may bankrupt the firm. The umbrella policy is excess insurance over the underlying coverages.

- Section II of the businessowners policy provides business liability coverage and medical expense coverage to small- to medium-sized business firms. The insured's employees are also covered for their negligent acts while acting within the scope of their employment.

- Medical malpractice liability insurance is designed to cover professional liability arising out of a medical incident. Medical malpractice insurance has several important features:

    Coverage is broad.

    Liability is not restricted to accidental acts.

    The insured is protected against the negligent acts of employees.

    There is a maximum limit for each medical incident and an aggregate limit for each coverage.

    Current forms permit the company to settle a claim without the physician's or surgeon's consent.

## KEY CONCEPTS AND TERMS

Advertising injury
Aircraft insurance
Bailee coverage named-perils policy
Basic extended reporting period
Bodily injury and property damage liability
Business auto coverage form
Business liability coverage form
Care, custody, or control exclusion
Claims-made policy
Commercial general liability policy (CGL)
Commercial umbrella policy
Completed operations
Contingent liability
Contractual liability
Each-occurrence limit
Employers liability insurance
Employment practices liability insurance (EPL)
Errors and omissions insurance
Fire legal liability
Garage coverage form
General aggregate limit
Liquor liability law (dramshop law)
Long tail
Malpractice liability insurance
Medical payments
Occurrence
Occurrence policy
Other-states insurance
Personal injury
Products-completed operations aggregate limit
Products-completed operations hazard
Products liability
Property damage to the impaired property
Property damage to the insured's product
Property damage to the insured's work
Retained limit
Retroactive date
Supplemental extended reporting period
Ultimate net loss
Workers compensation insurance
Voluntary compensation endorsement

## QUESTIONS FOR REVIEW

1. Identify the major general liability loss exposures of business firms.

2. Define each of the following:
   a. Products liability
   b. Completed operations
   c. Contractual liability
   d. Contingent liability

3. Briefly describe the meaning of "products and completed operations hazard."

4. Briefly explain the major coverages in the commercial general liability policy.

5. Explain the difference between an occurrence policy and a claims-made policy.

6. Describe the three coverages in the insuring agreements of a workers compensation policy. Why is coverage for employers liability (Part Two) needed?

7. Describe the major features of the business auto coverage form and garage coverage form.

8. Briefly explain the major coverages that are used to insure aircraft.

9. Why is liability insurance needed by a bailee? In your answer, give a brief description of the bailee coverage named-perils policy.

10. Briefly describe the major features of the commercial umbrella policy.

11. Explain the major characteristics of a professional liability policy.

## QUESTIONS FOR DISCUSSION

1. Mario owns an appliance and furniture store and is insured under a commercial general liability policy with an occurrence form. Explain whether Mario's CGL policy would provide coverage for each of the following situations:

   a. Mario forcibly detained a customer whom he erroneously accused of shoplifting. Eight months later, after the policy had expired, the customer sued Mario for defamation of character.

   b. Mario's employees were delivering a large desk to a customer's house. The customer's front door and the desk were scratched and damaged when the desk hit the door. The customer immediately filed a claim for the damage to the door and the desk.

   c. An advertising firm sues Mario for using copyrighted material without permission when the material first appears in a special holiday ad. Mario maintains that the ad material is original and belongs to him.

   d. Unknown to Mario, an automatic dishwasher had a defective part. One week after the dishwasher was installed in a customer's house, it malfunctioned and caused considerable water damage to the kitchen carpet. The homeowner holds Mario responsible for the damage.

   e. An employee accidentally knocked over a heavy lamp that injured a customer's foot. The customer later presents a bill for medical expenses to Mario for payment.

2. Carla operates a sporting goods store in a rented location at a shopping mall. She is insured under a commercial general liability policy (CGL) with the following limits:

| | |
|---|---|
| General aggregate limit | $1,000,000 |
| Products-completed operations aggregate limit | 1,000,000 |
| Personal and advertising injury limit | 250,000 |
| Each-occurrence limit | 300,000 |
| Fire damage limit (any one fire) | 100,000 |
| Medical expense limit (any one person) | 5,000 |

The propane tank that Carla kept in the store exploded. Indicate the dollar amount, if any, that Carla's insurer will pay for each of the following losses:

   a. Three customers were injured by flying debris with medical expenses of $6000, $7500, and $5000, respectively.

   b. A fire resulted from the explosion. Damages are $50,000.

   c. The store had to suspend operations for three months. Carla's lost profits are estimated to total $20,000. She also had continuing expenses of $10,000 during the period of suspension.

3. Joanna owns and operates a small retail food store in a suburban shopping center. The store is insured for liability coverage under a businessowners policy. Indicate with reasons whether or not the following situations are covered under Joanna's businessowners policy. Treat each situation separately.

   a. A clerk accidentally injures a customer with a shopping cart. Both Joanna and the clerk are sued.

   b. A customer slips on a wet floor and breaks a leg.

   c. Joanna has a customer arrested for shoplifting. The customer is innocent and sues for damages.

   d. A woman returns a spoiled package of gourmet cheese and demands her money back.

   e. Joanna has a Christmas party for her employees after the store closes. One employee gets drunk and injures another motorist while driving home. The injured motorist sues both Joanna and the employee.

4. A surgeon is insured under a physicians, surgeons, and dentists professional liability policy. Indicate with reasons whether or not the following situations are covered by the professional liability policy. Treat each situation separately.

   a. An office nurse gives a patient a wrong drug. Both the physician and the nurse are sued.

   b. The surgeon sets the broken arm of a patient. The patient sues because the arm becomes deformed and crooked.

   c. A patient waiting to see the doctor is injured when the legs of an office chair collapse.

## CASE APPLICATION

a. Lastovica Construction is insured under a commercial general liability (CGL) policy. The firm agreed to build a new plant for the Smith Corporation. A heavy machine used by Lastovica Construction accidentally fell from the roof of the partially completed plant. Mike, an employee of the firm, was severely injured when the falling machine crushed his foot. Tara, a pedestrian, was also injured by the machine while walking on a public sidewalk in front of the building.

   1. Tara sued both Lastovica Construction and the Smith Corporation for her injury. Indicate the extent, if any, of the CGL insurer's obligation to provide a legal defense to Lastovica Construction.

   2. What legal defense could the Smith Corporation use to counter Tara's claim based on the nature of its relationship with Lastovica Construction? Explain your answer.

   3. Does Lastovica Construction have any responsibility for Mike's medical expenses and lost wages? Explain.

b. Jacques owns a restaurant that is insured under a claims-made commercial general liability policy. The policy term is January 1, 1996, through December 31, 1996. On December 15, 1996, a customer became violently ill from eating a piece of banana cream pie that had become contaminated. On February 1, 1997, the customer made a claim against Jacques for the illness. Jacques had no prior notice that the customer had become ill. Explain with reasons whether or not Jacques's policy will cover the loss.

## SELECTED REFERENCES

*Fire, Casualty & Surety Bulletins.* Casualty and Surety volume. Cincinnati: National Underwriter Company. The bulletins are published monthly. Detailed information on all forms of commercial liability insurance can be found in this volume.

Huebner, S.S., Kenneth Black, Jr., and Bernard L. Webb. *Property and Liability Insurance,* 4th ed. Upper Saddle River, N.J.: Prentice Hall, 1996.

Kensicki, Peter R., Robert S. Smith, Thomas S. Marshall, Seeman Waranch, and Darwin B. Close. *Principles of Insurance Production,* 2nd ed., vol. 2. Malvern, Pa.: Insurance Institute of America, 1986.

Malecki, Donald S., Ronald C. Horn, Eric A. Wiening, and James H. Donaldson. *Commercial Liability Risk Management and Insurance,* 2nd ed., vols. 1 and 2. Malvern, Pa.: American Institute for Property and Liability Underwriters, 1986.

*Policy, Form & Manual Analysis Service.* Casualty Coverages volume. Indianapolis: Rough Notes Company. The reference materials are published monthly and provide detailed information on commercial liability insurance coverages.

Webb, Bernard L., Arthur L. Flitner, and Jerome Trupin. *Commercial Insurance.* 3rd ed. Malvern, Pa.: Insurance Institute of America, 1996.

Wells, Alexander T., and Bruce D. Chadbourne, *Aviation Insurance and Risk Management.* Malabar, Fl.: Krieger Publishing Company, 1992.

## NOTES

1. Emmett J. Vaughan, and Therese M. Vaughan, *Fundamentals of Risk and Insurance,* 7th ed. (New York: Wiley, 1996), p. 586.

2. This section is based on *Fire, Casualty & Surety Bulletins,* Casualty and Surety volume (Cincinnati: National Underwriter Company); Peter R. Kensicki, Robert S. Smith, Thomas S. Marshall, Seeman Waranch, and Darwin B. Close, *Principles of Insurance Production,* 2nd ed., vol. 2 (Malvern, Pa.: Insurance Institute of America, 1986); and Bernard L. Webb, Arthur L. Flitner, and Jerome Trupin, *Commercial Insurance,* 3rd ed. (Malvern, Pa.: Insurance Institute of America, 1996). The author also drew on the various commercial general liability forms of the Insurance Services Office (copyrighted) that appeared in the *CPCU Handbook of Insurance Policies,* First edition (Malvern, Pa.: American Institute for CPCU/Insurance Institute of America, 1994). The author drew heavily on these sources in the preparation of this chapter.

3. The workers compensation and employers liability policy is discussed in detail in *Fire, Casualty & Surety Bulletins,* Casualty and Surety volume, Workers Compensation section (Cincinnati: National Underwriter Company).

4. This section is based on the *Fire, Casualty & Surety Bulletins,* Casualty and Surety volume, Auto section (Cincinnati: National Underwriter Company), and

the business auto coverage form and garage coverage form found in the *CPCU Handbook of Insurance Policies*, pp. 305–30.

5. Aircraft insurance is discussed in *Fire, Casualty & Surety Bulletins*, Companies & Coverages volume, Aircraft-Marine Section (Cincinnati, Ohio: The National Underwriter Company).

6. *1993–1994 Policy Kit for Insurance Professionals* (Schaumburg, Ill.: Alliance of American Insurers, 1993–94), pp. 356–58.

7. A detailed discussion of the commercial umbrella policy can be found in Webb, et al, pp. 34–50. See also the *1993–1994 Policy Kit for Insurance Professionals* (Schaumburg, Ill.: Alliance of American Insurers, 1993–94), pp. 399–411.

8. Webb et al., p. 346.

9. A detailed discussion of the businessowners policy can be found in *Fire, Casualty & Surety Bulletins*, Fire and Marine volume, Commercial Property section (Cincinnati: National Underwriter Company).

10. Professional liability insurance for physicians is discussed in *Fire, Casualty & Surety Bulletins*, Casualty and Surety volume, Public Liability section (Cincinnati: National Underwriter Company).

# Chapter 14

# CRIME INSURANCE AND SURETY BONDS

*"A crime policy containing employee dishonesty coverage should be considered by any business."*

*FC & S Bulletins*

## Student Learning Objectives

After studying this chapter, you should be able to:

■ Define burglary, robbery, and theft.

■ Explain the coverage provided under the employee dishonesty coverage form.

■ For a given crime coverage form, describe the coverage provided with respect to the property covered and insured perils.

■ Explain the three parties to a bond and show how surety bonds differ from insurance.

■ Identify the major types of surety bonds and give an example where each can be used.

The annual cost of crime to business firms is enormous. Business firms each year experience billions of dollars of losses because of crimes against property by robbery, burglary, larceny, motor vehicle theft, and employee dishonesty. "White collar" crimes such as embezzlement, fraud, and illegal activities have also increased in recent years. Moreover, since many crimes are not reported, the true cost of crime is substantially understated.

This chapter discusses the Insurance Services Office (ISO) commercial crime insurance program that protects employers against robbery, burglary, theft, employee dishonesty, and numerous other crime perils. Without crime insurance, many business firms that experience a financially damaging theft or burglary would be forced out of business. In addition,

the chapter discusses surety bonds that provide indemnification to an injured party if the bonded party fails to perform.

## COMMERCIAL CRIME INSURANCE PROGRAM

In 1986, the ISO introduced a simplified-language commercial crime program to replace the older commercial crime insurance forms. The commercial crime program was again modified in 1990. The general format is similar to the commercial package policy discussed in Chapter 12.

### Basic Definitions

Most property crimes against business firms are due to burglary, robbery, or theft. For purposes of insurance, **burglary** is defined as the taking of property from inside the premises by someone who unlawfully enters or leaves the premises, and there are marks of forcible entry or exit. **Robbery** is defined as the taking of property from a person by someone who has (1) caused or threatens to cause bodily harm to that person, or (2) committed an obviously unlawful act that is witnessed by that person. **Theft** is a much broader term and is defined as any act of stealing. It includes burglary and robbery, as well as shoplifting and employee theft.

## Common Crime Insurance Provisions

Under the ISO program, a *crime general provisions form* is included in most crime policies. The general provisions form contains common crime insurance provisions that apply to most crime coverages. It is beyond the scope of this text to discuss each provision in detail. However, certain common provisions are extremely important in understanding commercial crime insurance. They include the following:

- Dishonest acts committed by the insured
- Indirect loss
- Discovery period for a loss
- Loss sustained during prior insurance
- Noncumulation of limit of insurance

**Dishonest Acts Committed by the Insured** Loss that results from any dishonest or criminal act committed by the insured or by any partners of the insured is specifically excluded.

**Indirect Loss**   Any indirect loss that results from a covered loss is specifically excluded. For example, if the business is temporarily closed because of property damage by a burglar, the business income loss is not covered.

**Discovery Period for a Loss**   The **discovery period** means that the insurer will pay for a covered loss that occurs during the policy period if the loss is discovered no later than one year after the policy period ends. *The purpose of this provision is to provide coverage for a loss that occurs during the policy period but is not discovered until after the policy expires.* For example, if a $10,000 loss is discovered during the discovery period and traced to an employee who stole the money before the policy expired, the loss would be covered up to the limit of insurance.

**Loss Sustained During Prior Insurance** Another important provision is titled **loss sustained during prior insurance.** *Under this provision, the current policy provides coverage for a loss that occurred during the term of the prior policy but was discovered only after the discovery period under the prior policy had expired.*

The purpose of this provision is to enable an employer to change insurers without penalty. This provision applies only if there is no break in the continuity of coverage under both policies. The current policy must become effective at the time of cancellation or termination of the previous policy. In addition, the loss must be covered by the current policy had it been in effect when the prior loss occurred.

The maximum recovery under this provision is limited to the policy limit under the previous policy, or the limit of insurance under the current policy, whichever is less (see Insight 14.1).

---

### INSIGHT 14.1

### Which Insurer Pays an Embezzlement Loss?

Shin Electric carried insurance covering the dishonest acts of employees in the amount of $20,000 with Insurer A. The coverage was replaced with Insurer B in the amount of $30,000. Three years after the change of insurers, Mr. Shin discovered that a dishonest accountant had embezzled $25,000 while Insurer A's coverage was in force. Since the discovery period had run out, Insurer A pays nothing. Since Insurer B's coverage had been in force continuously since the previous insurance was terminated, Insurer B is responsible for the loss. However, Insurer B will pay only $20,000 and not the full loss since that amount is the limit under the previous policy.

---

EXHIBIT 14.1

## Crime Coverage Forms

---

Form A    Employee Dishonesty (Blanket)

Form A    Employee Dishonesty (Schedule)

Form B    Forgery or Alteration

Form C    Theft, Disappearance, and Destruction

Form D    Robbery and Safe Burglary—Property Other Than Money and Securities

Form E    Premises Burglary

Form F    Computer Fraud

Form G    Extortion

Form H    Premises Theft and Robbery Outside the Premises—Property Other Than Money and Securities

Form I     Lessees of Safe Deposit Boxes

Form J     Securities Deposited with Others

Form K    Liability for Guests' Property—Safe Deposit Box

Form L    Liability for Guests' Property—Premises

Form M   Safe Depository Liability

Form N    Safe Depository Direct Loss

Form O    Public Employee Dishonesty (Per Loss)

Form P    Public Employee Dishonesty (Per Employee)

Form Q    Robbery and Safe Burglary—Money and Securities

Form R    Money Orders and Counterfeit Paper Currency

---

SOURCE: Bernard L. Webb, Arthur L. Flitner, and Jerome Trupin, *Commercial Insurance*, 3rd ed. (Malvern, Pa.: Insurance Institute of America, 1996), Exhibit 5-1, p. 119.

---

**Noncumulation of Insurance Limits** Another common provision is referred to as *noncumulation of limit of insurance*. The limit of insurance stated in the policy is not cumulative. This means that regardless of the number of years the insurance is in force, the limit of insurance is not cumulative from year to year. For example, if the limit of insurance is $10,000, and a dishonest treasurer embezzles $50,000 over a five-year period, the maximum amount paid for the loss is $10,000.

## Commercial Crime Coverage Forms

Numerous crime coverage forms are currently used.[1] Each form is designated by a letter (see Exhibit 14.1). Forms A, B, O, and P have been developed by the Surety Association of America. The remaining forms are designed by the ISO. The crime coverage forms can be issued separately as a monoline policy or as part of a commercial package policy.

**Form A. Employee Dishonesty** This form covers the loss of money, securities, and property other than money and securities that result from the dishonest acts of employees. **Employee dishonesty** *is defined to mean dishonest acts committed by an employee alone, or in collusion with others, that result in loss to the insured or financial benefit to the employee.* Examples of covered losses include embezzlement of funds by the company's treasurer; stealing by a cashier; theft of goods by a factory worker; and even unauthorized discounts to friends by a salesperson.

There are two employee dishonesty coverage forms. One form provides *blanket coverage* that covers all employees for their dishonest acts. The other form provides *scheduled coverage* in which individual employees or positions are identified. Scheduled coverage, in turn, is written on a *name schedule* or *position schedule* basis. Under a name schedule, the names of covered employees are listed in a schedule, and the limit of insurance that applies to each employee is also stated. Under a position schedule, the schedule identifies the covered positions, location of the positions, and the number of employees occupying each position.

The blanket form provides coverage on a *per-loss basis,* which means the maximum amount paid for any one occurrence is the limit of insurance stated in the declarations. *An occurrence is a loss involving one or more employees, whether the result of a single act or series of acts.* Thus, the maximum insurance limit applies in the event of collusion by two or more employees. For example, assume that the limit of insurance is $20,000 and that two cashiers acting together over a period of months have embezzled $40,000. This is considered one occurrence, and only $20,000 will be paid.

In contrast, under the scheduled form, coverage applies on a *per-employee basis. In this form, an occurrence is defined as loss caused by each employee, whether the result of a single act or series of acts.* The most the insurer is obligated to pay for any loss is the limit of insurance shown in the schedule for each employee. Referring back to our earlier example, if both employees in the theft are named in the schedule or occupy a covered position, there would be two occurrences. Assuming the limit of insurance on each employee is $20,000, the maximum paid would be $40,000.

Employee dishonesty insurance also contains several important exclusions and limitations, including the following:

- *Employee canceled under prior insurance.* There is no coverage for any loss caused by an employee for whom coverage has been canceled under a previous policy and not reinstated since the last cancellation.
- *Inventory shortages.* There is no coverage for any loss if proof of loss depends on an inventory computation or on a profit and loss computation. The intent here is to exclude inventory losses, such as errors in record keeping, that may not be due to employee dishonesty.
- *Cancellation as to any employee.* The insured must notify the insurer of any dishonest act even though the loss does not exceed the deductible. The insurance coverage ceases immediately on that employee involved in the dishonest act. The firm could encounter some serious coverage problems if a minor loss by a dishonest employee

is not reported. If that employee later became involved in another loss, and the insurer became aware of the earlier loss, the insured would have no coverage.

Employee thefts cause billions of dollars of losses each year to business firms. An employer's worst nightmare is to hire a dishonest employee. Many firms are now using a wide variety of background checks to weed out dishonest employees (see Insight 14.2).

**Form B. Forgery or Alteration**   This form provides coverage against loss that results from the forgery or alteration of checks, drafts, bills of exchange, promissory notes, and similar instruments. For example, a cashier in a supermarket may cash a payroll check for $500 forged by a customer. This loss would be covered. Loss caused by the insured's employees, officers, and directors is specifically excluded. These groups are covered for dishonest acts under Form A, discussed earlier.

**Form C. Theft, Disappearance, and Destruction**   This form covers the theft, disappearance, or destruction of money and securities *inside the premises.* Containers of covered property such as a cash register, safe, vault, or cash box are also covered. For example, a bank may be held up; money may be destroyed in a fire or a tornado; or a cash register or safe may be damaged in a burglary. These losses would be covered.

The form also provides coverage *outside the premises* while the property is in the care and custody of a messenger. A messenger is defined as the named insured, any partner, or any employee who has custody of the money or securities outside the premises. For example, the owner of a retail store may be robbed of the day's receipts while taking the money to a bank. In addition, the loss of money or securities in the custody of an armored-car company is covered. The amount payable is limited only to the amount of loss that cannot be recovered from the armored-car company.

**Form D. Robbery and Safe Burglary— Property Other Than Money and Securities**   This form covers the robbery of property inside the premises other than money and securities while in the care of a custodian. A custodian is defined as the named insured, any partner, or any employee who has custody of the property inside the premises with

## INSIGHT 14.2

### An Employer's Nightmare: Hiring Dishonest Employees

**Background Checks**

It's a manager's worst nightmare: bringing in a new employee only to find out the hard way that the new hire has a record of theft, drug abuse, or other serious problems.

Employee theft alone costs companies an estimated $40 billion annually. And besides the direct costs of on-the-job crimes, there are legal liability issues. Lately, courts are holding some companies responsible for harm done if well-established job screening tests would have revealed the risks.

Employers thus would be smart to consider more sophisticated pre-employment screening, writes Small Business Reports (November). Here are some of the basics:

**Criminal record scans**  You can check with private security firms or public agencies to find out if the applicant has ever been convicted of a crime. But always consider whether a particular crime has any bearing on the job.

**Drug tests**  These tests have become pretty common, but they need to be part of a formal policy against hiring someone who tests positive to avoid discrimination charges.

**Credit checks**  You may want to contact a credit service to check on an employee who would have important financial duties. Just remember that you'll need his or her permission to get a credit history.

SOURCE: Excerpted from Christine Shenot, "CEO Briefing on Human Resources," *Investor's Business Daily*, November 23, 1993, p. 4. Reprinted with permission of *Investor's Business Daily*.

the exception of a watchperson or janitor. For example, if the owner of an art shop is robbed of several valuable paintings, the loss would be covered.

The form also covers the loss of property other than money and securities from *safe burglary inside the premises.* Damage to the premises, safe, or vault is covered if the insured owns the property or is legally liable for damages. For example, a burglar may break into a safe inside the premises. The loss of property inside the safe, other than money and securities, and damage to the building and safe are all covered.

The form also covers *robbery outside the premises* if the property is in the care of a messenger. A messenger is defined as the named insured, any partner, or any employee who has custody of the property outside the premises. For example, a garment shop employee may be pushing a cart of clothes to a parking lot for a special sale. If someone grabs an expensive coat and runs away, the loss is covered even though no threats are made. (Remember the definition of robbery also includes the witnessing of an unlawful act.)

**Form E. Premises Burglary**  This form provides coverage for premises burglary and robbery of a watchperson. Covered property is property inside the premises other than money or securities. For example, if a retail television store is burglarized and several sets are stolen, the loss would be covered. *To be a covered burglary loss, there must be marks of forcible entry or exit.* Damage to the premises is also covered. For example, if a thief cuts a hole in the roof to gain entry, the damage to the roof is covered if the insured owns the building or is legally liable for damages.

Robbery of a watchperson is also covered. If property inside the premises is stolen by violence or threat of violence to a security guard on duty, the loss would be covered.

**Form F. Computer Fraud**  This form covers the theft of money, securities, and property by computer fraud. For example, a personal computer may be used to gain access to a business computer. The business computer may be instructed to issue a check to a fictitious person. If the check is issued and cashed, the theft loss would be covered.

Computer crimes are widespread, and most major corporations are victims of computer-related crimes. These crimes include credit card fraud,

## INSIGHT 14.3

### Computer Crime Called "Extraordinarily Widespread"

Nearly every major corporation that responded to a nationwide survey said it had been a victim of cybercrime ranging from employees snooping through confidential files to criminal theft of trade secrets.

"*It's extraordinarily widespread,*" David Carter, a criminal justice professor at Michigan State University in East Lansing who conducted the survey, said in an interview Tuesday.

The mail survey of 500 corporate security directors of major corporations was conducted from June through August. Of the 150 that responded, 148—or 98.6 percent—said their companies had been victims of computer-related crimes. Of those, 43.3 percent said they had been victims at least 25 times.

Release of the study comes as more companies are exploiting cyberspace for commercial purposes. Businesses ranging from Hollywood studios to hardware stores are advertising on the World Wide Web portion of the Internet. Banks are devising ways for consumers to transact business on-line. One Monday, an alliance of 13 companies announced a venture that would enable television broadcasters to transmit data to home computers.

*The most common crimes and misdeeds reported in the survey were credit card fraud, telecommunications fraud, employee use of computers for personal reasons, unauthorized access to confidential files and unlawful copying of copyrighted or licensed software.*

Computer security consultant Patricia Fisher of Janus Associates in Stamford, Conn., said the findings were in line with what she has seen in ferreting out abuse of corporate computer systems.

"What we're seeing is it's such a riskless crime," she said. "If you're computer literate, you can find ways to steal or misuse information without being caught."

While problems with hackers breaking into computers from outside a company appear to be on the rise, most computer crimes are committed by staff and contract workers, the survey indicated.

Companies mistakenly think that hackers are their biggest threat because of the extensive news coverage they have received, Ms. Fisher said.

"Seventy-five to 80 percent of everything happens from inside. There's more opportunity because you're right there on the site. And there may be more motivation if you're unhappy with what's going on."

Steven Bellovin, a network security researcher for AT&T, said corporations should not only worry about employee-caused cybercrime. There also have been cases of corporate computer professionals stealing confidential information from competitors' computers.

*Continued*

unauthorized access to confidential files, telecommunication fraud, and unlawful copying of computer software programs (see Insight 14.3).

**Form G. Extortion**   This form covers extortion losses. **Extortion** *is the surrender of property away from the premises as a result of a threat to do bodily harm to the named insured, relative, or invitee who is being held captive.* For example, if Fred arrives at work and receives a phone call that his wife is being held captive and will be harmed unless $100,000 is delivered to a location away from the premises, the loss is potentially recoverable. However, the loss is excluded if the property is surrendered before making a reasonable effort to report the extortionist's demands to the FBI, local authorities, or an associate of the named insured.

**Form H. Premises Theft and Robbery Outside the Premises—Property Other Than Money and Securities**   This form covers the theft of property, other than money and securities, inside the premises and robbery outside the premises while in the care and custody of a custodian. The property is covered against actual or attempted theft, which is defined as any act of stealing. This form can be used by a firm that wants the broader coverage provided by the theft peril rather than the narrower perils of burglary and robbery.

**Form I. Lessees of Safe Deposit Boxes**   This form covers the theft of securities, and burglary and robbery of property other than money and securities, while inside a safe deposit box or during the course of deposit or removal from the box. Section 1 of the

"When I see how easy it is for hackers to get into many computer systems, I have to assume professionals can do just as well," he said.

Carter said 96.6 percent of the corporations reported problems with telecommunications fraud.

"We're seeing everything from simply stealing telephone credit-card numbers to entry into computers and manipulating billing," he said.

Credit-card numbers, for company telephone or banking accounts, often are stolen and sold to someone outside the company.

Ms. Fisher said employees of a large corporation were running their own telecommunications business with the company computer. They were only discovered when the company noticed unusually large phone bills.

Cellular phones also are a big source of corporate security headaches, Carter said. The phones emit a signal containing the billing code, which can be picked up with computer-driven sensory equipment.

The survey indicated that the largest reported increases, in addition to cellular fraud, were in theft or attempted theft of confidential client information, trade secrets, new product plans and descriptions and product pricing information. Also more computer "viruses" were introduced.

Carter said a surprising indication was the extent of reported computer misuse by employees seeking to gain an advantage over coworkers through sexual harassment, threats and political maneuvering.

For example, security directors reported cases of employees sending phony computer messages directing coworkers to do unnecessary tasks, thereby diverting them from work that might impress the boss.

---

### Cyberabuses

Most common computer-related abuses reported by security directors of 120 major American corporations, and percentage who reported problems, according to a Michigan State University survey:

- Credit-card fraud, 96.6.
- Telecommunications fraud, 96.6.
- Employees' personal use of company computers, 96.
- Unauthorized access to confidential files, 95.1.
- Cellular phone fraud, 94.5.
- Unlawful copying of software, 91.2.

SOURCE: "Computer Crime Called 'Extraordinarily Widespread,'" *Omaha World Herald,* October 25, 1995, p, 22.

---

form covers securities against loss by theft, disappearance, or destruction. Section 2 of the form covers property other than money and securities against loss by burglary, robbery, and vandalism. For example, if a burglar breaks into a safe deposit box and steals some securities and jewelry, the loss is covered.

**Form J. Securities Deposited with Others** This form covers the theft, disappearance, or destruction of securities deposited with others, such as with a bank or stock brokerage firm. For example, if shares of common stock are deposited in a bank as collateral for a loan, and the securities disappear or are stolen, the loss would be covered.

**Form K. Liability for Guests' Property— Safe Deposit Box** This form covers the legal liability of the insured for loss or damage to the property of guests while in a safe deposit box on the premises. The policy is based on legal liability. Loss to the property of guests is not covered unless the insured is legally liable. For example, if a guest's jewelry is deposited in a hotel's safe deposit box and is stolen, the loss would be covered.

**Form L. Liability for Guests' Property— Premises** This form covers the legal liability of the insured arising out of the property of guests inside the premises and in the insured's possession. The form excludes coverage for loss to vehicles and their equipment, property inside the vehicle, and samples or articles held for sale or delivery. For example, if a motel carelessly damages the luggage of a guest, the loss would be covered.

**Form M. Safe Depository Liability** This form covers the insured's legal liability arising out of loss or damage to the property of customers while inside a safe deposit box, vault, or temporarily elsewhere on the premises while in the course of deposit or removal from the box or vault. Customers' property is defined as money, securities, and property other than money and securities.

The form is designed for insureds, other than financial institutions, that provide safe deposit facilities. There are hundreds of private safe deposit companies operating in the United States at the present time. Financial institutions, however, such as banks and savings and loans institutions, are ineligible for coverage. Financial institutions can obtain coverage under a bankers blanket bond or other financial institution bond.

**Form N. Safe Depository Direct Loss** This form provides coverage for direct damage to the property of customers while inside a safe deposit box, vault, or temporarily elsewhere on the premises in the course of deposit or removal from the safe or vault. The covered causes of loss are actual or attempted robbery or burglary, destruction, and damage.

**Form O. Public Employee Dishonesty—Per Loss** This form is designed to cover employee dishonesty for government entities. The form covers the loss of money, securities, and property other than money and securities against dishonest acts by employees. The limit of insurance applies to each loss. In Form O, an occurrence is defined to mean all loss caused by one or more employees in a single act or series of acts.

**Form P. Public Employee Dishonesty—Per Employee** This form is similar to Form O except the limit of insurance applies to each employee. Occurrence is defined to mean all loss caused by each employee in a single act or series of acts.

**Form Q. Robbery and Safe Burglary—Money and Securities** This form covers the robbery of a custodian inside the premises, safe burglary inside the premises, and robbery of a messenger outside the premises. The form covers only money and securities.

**Form R. Money Orders and Counterfeit Paper Currency** This form covers losses due to money orders that are not paid upon presentation and counterfeit paper currency. For example, if a supermarket accepts a stolen American Express money order in the amount of $250, the loss would be covered.

## ISO Crime Coverage Plans

The various crime coverage forms just discussed can be combined to meet the specialized needs of business firms and also to approximate the protection provided under the previous crime insurance program. The ISO has numerous crime coverage plans, which describe the different ways the crime coverage forms can be combined to obtain the desired protection.

It is beyond the scope of this text to discuss each crime coverage plan in detail. However, **Plan 1, Commercial Crime,** can be used as an illustration. Plan 1 permits the use of any combination of coverage forms A through J, as well as Q, to meet the crime insurance needs of a particular firm. For example, Heavenly Hamburgers, a fast-food chain, may want protection against employee dishonesty (Form A), robbery and safe burglary (Form D), and coverage for the theft, disappearance, and destruction of money and securities (Form C). This combination will meet most commercial crime exposures faced by the firm.

Finally, in addition to the crime coverages just discussed, a few insurers offer highly specialized coverages for certain loss exposures such as the kidnap and ransom of wealthy individuals and celebrities (see Insight 14.4).

## SURETY BONDS

An analysis of crime insurance would not be complete without a discussion of surety bonds. A **surety bond** *is a bond that provides monetary compensation if the bonded party fails to perform certain acts.* For example, a contractor may be financially overextended and is unable to complete a building project. A public official may embezzle public funds, or the executor of an estate may illegally convert part of the estate assets to his or her own use. Surety bonds can be used to meet these loss exposures.[2]

### Parties to a Surety Bond

There are always three parties to a surety bond:

- Principal
- Obligee
- Surety

## INSIGHT 14.4

## Kidnap and Ransom Insurance Targets Growing Market

A woman and her male accomplice were arrested for allegedly trying to extort $24 million from entertainer-comedian Bill Cosby. Meanwhile, Boulder, Colo. police are still grappling with the murder mystery of child beauty-pageant participant JonBenet Ramsey and the puzzle of an accompanying ransom note.

*These two high-profile cases are among the latest highlighting the need for wealthy, influential and popular individuals to secure kidnapping, ransom and extortion insurance*, one of the more secretive, yet flourishing coverages in the industry, insurance officials say.

"I think the potential is well into the hundreds of millions in terms of premiums, industrywide, in the United States," said John Kozero, public relations director for the Novato, Calif.-based Fireman's Fund.

There are an estimated 8,000 kidnappings a year, about 6,000 of which occur in Latin America, according to Kroll Associates, a New York-based international crisis management and investigative consulting firm.

Hot spots are Colombia, Mexico, Brazil, the Philippines, Ecuador, Guatemala, Algeria, Russia and Turkey. "In the United States, there is less a kidnapping problem than there is elsewhere in the world," said Jean McDermott-Lucey, vice president of American International Underwriter (AIU) Crisis Management Division. "There's a tremendous opportunity to sell this insurance product in Latin America."

In addition to Fireman's Fund and AIU, the kidnap, ransom and extortion insurance—commonly referred to as K&R—is offered by syndicates at Lloyd's of London and the Chubb Group of Insurance Companies.

AIU and Fireman's Fund are among the K&R providers who offer crisis response services. Crisis response services can include negotiating ransoms and the release of kidnap victims.

Fireman's Fund has offered the coverage for the past two years.

"We've been very satisfied with the trend in sales," Mr. Kozero said.

Limits range from $1 million to $30 million, with premiums starting at $1,000, according to the insurer.

AIU's kidnap and ransom/extortion insurance offers a capacity limit of $50 million, with an average North American premium of $1,500–$3,000, according to Ms. McDermott-Lucey. In Latin America, the low premium ranges from $4,000–$5,000, with a high of $20,000–$30,000, she noted.

AIU recently changed some language in its kidnap policy to cover what it calls "personal extortion"—incidents in which an extortionist threatens to divulge some sort of personal information, as with the young woman who allegedly threatened to tell supermarket tabloids that she was Bill Cosby's illegitimate daughter. That incident would have been covered under the company's revised policy wording, Ms. McDermott-Lucey said.

"We're clarifying in our language that there doesn't have to be the threat of injury or bodily injury," she noted.

Industry officials agree this coverage is among the least talked-about.

"Confidentiality is important, especially, to the client," Mr. Kozero noted. "It's the core of this type of insurance, because if people know you have it, you might find that people may think you an easier target."

This secretiveness is manifest in a contractual confidentiality clause, prohibiting insureds from divulging knowledge of the coverage.

SOURCE: Adapted from Stephanie D. Esters, "Kidnap & Ransom Ins. Targets Growing Market," *National Underwriter*, Property & Casualty/Risk & Benefits Management Edition, February 3, 1997, pp. 33, 40.

---

The **principal** is *the party who agrees to perform certain acts or fulfill certain obligations.* For example, Lastovica Construction may agree to build an office building for the city of Omaha. If the company is required to obtain a performance bond before the contract is awarded, Lastovica Construction would be known as the principal.

The **obligee** is *the party who is reimbursed for damages if the principal fails to perform.* Thus, the city of Omaha would be reimbursed for damages if Lastovica Construction failed to complete the building on time or according to contract specifications.

The surety is the final party to a bond. The **surety** is *the party who agrees to answer for the debt,*

EXHIBIT 14.2

**Comparison of Insurance and Surety Bonds**

| *Insurance* | *Surety bonds* |
|---|---|
| 1. There are two parties to an insurance contract. | 1. There are three parties to a bond. |
| 2. The insurer expects to pay losses. The premium reflects expected loss costs. | 2. The surety theoretically expects no losses to occur. The premium is viewed as a service fee, by which the surety's credit is substituted for that of the principal. |
| 3. The insurer normally does not have the right to recover a loss payment from the insured. | 3. The surety has the legal right to recover a loss payment from the defaulting principal. |
| 4. Insurance is designed to cover unintentional losses that ideally are outside of the insured's control. | 4. The surety guarantees the principal's character, honesty, integrity, and ability to perform. These qualities are within the insured's control. |

*default, or obligation of another.* For example, Lastovica Construction may purchase a performance bond from United Fidelity. If Lastovica Construction (principal) fails to perform, the city of Omaha (obligee) would be reimbursed for any loss by United Fidelity.

## Comparison of Surety Bonds and Insurance

Surety bonds are similar to insurance contracts since both provide protection against specified losses. However, there are some important differences between them. The major differences are listed in Exhibit 14.2.

## Types of Surety Bonds

Different types of surety bonds can be used to meet specific needs and situations. Although surety bonds are not uniform and have different characteristics, they can generally be grouped into the following categories:

- Contract bonds
  bid bond
  performance bond
  payment bond
  maintenance bond
- License and permit bonds
- Public official bonds
- Judicial bonds
  fiduciary bond
  court bond
- Federal surety bonds
- Miscellaneous surety bonds

**Contract Bonds**    A **contract bond** *guarantees that the principal will fulfill all contractual obligations.* There are several types of contract bonds. Under a *bid bond,* the owner (obligee) is guaranteed that the party awarded a bid on a project will sign a contract and furnish a performance bond. Under a *performance bond,* the owner is guaranteed that work will be completed according to the contract specifications. For example, if a building is not completed on time, the surety is responsible for completion of the project and the extra expense in hiring another contractor.

A *payment bond* guarantees that the bills for labor and materials used in building the project will be paid by the contractor when the bills are due. A *maintenance bond* guarantees that poor workmanship by the principal will be corrected, or defective materials will be replaced. This maintenance guarantee is often included in a performance bond for one year without additional charge.

**License and Permit Bonds**    These types of bonds are commonly required of persons who must obtain a license or permit from a city or town before they can engage in certain activities. A **license and permit bond** *guarantees that the person bonded will comply with all laws and regulations that govern his or her activities.* For example, a liquor store owner may post a bond guaranteeing that liquor will be sold according to the law. A plumber or electrician may post a bond guaranteeing that the work performed will comply with the local building code.

**Public Official Bonds**    This type of bond is usually required by law for public officials who are elected or appointed to public office. A **public official bond** *guarantees that public officials will faithfully perform their duties for the protection of the public.* For example, a state treasurer must comply with state law governing the deposit of public funds.

**Judicial Bonds**    **Judicial bonds** *guarantee that the party bonded will fulfill certain obligations specified by law.* There are two classes of judicial bonds. First, a *fiduciary bond* guarantees that the person responsible for the property of another will faithfully exercise his or her duties, give an accounting of all property received, and make up any deficiency for which the courts hold the fiduciary liable. For example, administrators of estates, receivers or liquidators, or guardians of minor children may be required to post a bond guaranteeing their performance.

The second type of judicial bond is a court bond. A *court bond* is designed to protect one person (obligee) against loss in the event that the person bonded does not prove that he or she is legally entitled to the remedy sought against the obligee. For example, an *attachment bond* guarantees that if the court rules against the plaintiff who has attached the property of the defendant in a lawsuit, the defendant will be reimbursed for damages as a result of having the property attached.

Finally, a *bail bond* is another type of court bond. If the bonded person fails to appear in court at the appointed time, the entire bond may be forfeited.

**Federal Surety Bonds**    These bonds are required by federal agencies that regulate the actions of business firms such as manufacturers, wholesalers, and large import firms. A **federal surety bond** *guarantees that the bonded party will comply with federal standards.* The bond also guarantees the payment of taxes or duties that accrue if the bonded party fails to pay.

**Miscellaneous Surety Bonds**    This category consists of bonds that cannot be classified in any other group. For example, an *auctioneer's bond* guarantees the faithful accounting of sales proceeds by an auctioneer; a *lost-instrument bond* guarantees the obligee against loss if the original instrument (such as a lost stock certificate) turns up in the possession of another party; and an *insurance agent bond* indemnifies an insurer for any penalties that may result from the unlawful acts of agents.

## SUMMARY

- *Burglary* is the taking of property from inside the premises by someone who unlawfully enters or leaves the premises, and there are marks of forcible entry or exit.

- *Robbery* is the taking of property from a person by someone who has caused or threatens to cause bodily harm to that person or has committed an obviously unlawful act that is witnessed by that person.

- *Theft* is any act of stealing.

- There are a wide variety of crime coverage forms in the commercial crime program by the Insurance Services Office. The coverage forms are designed to meet the commercial crime exposures of business firms.

- The *employee dishonesty coverage form (Form A)* covers the loss of money, securities, and property other than money and securities that results from the dishonest acts of employees.

- Several exclusions and limitations apply to the employee dishonesty coverage form, including the following:

  Loss caused by an employee who has been canceled under a previous policy and has not been reinstated is specifically excluded.

  There is no coverage for an inventory shortage if proof of loss depends on an inventory computation or on a profit or loss computation.

  The insured is required to notify the insurer of any dishonest act. Coverage ceases immediately on the employee involved in the dishonest act.

- The various crime coverage forms can be combined to meet the specialized needs of business firms. The Insurance Services Office has a number of plans that combine the various crime coverage forms and endorsements.

- There are three parties to a surety bond. The *principal* is the party who agrees to perform certain obligations. The *obligee* is the party who is reimbursed for damages if the principal fails to perform. The *surety* is the party who agrees to answer for the debt, default, or obligation of another.

- Surety bonds are similar to insurance contracts since losses are expected. However, there are several major differences between surety bonds and insurance.

There are two parties to an insurance contract; there are three parties to a bond.

The insurer expects to pay losses; the surety theoretically expects no losses to occur.

The insurer normally does not have the right to recover a loss payment from the insured; the surety has the right to recover from a defaulting principal.

Insurance covers unintentional losses outside of the insured's control; the surety guarantees the principal's character and ability to perform, which are within the insured's control.

- Surety bonds guarantee the performance of the principal. Surety bonds include various contract bonds, license and permit bonds, public official bonds, judicial bonds, federal surety bonds, and miscellaneous surety bonds.

## KEY CONCEPTS AND TERMS

Blanket coverage
Burglary
Commercial crime policy
Contract bond
Discovery period
Employee dishonesty
Employee dishonesty
  coverage form (Form A)
Extortion
Federal surety bond
Forgery or alteration
  coverage form (Form B)
Inside the premises
ISO crime coverage plans
Judicial bond
License and permit bond
Loss sustained during
  prior insurance
Name schedule
Noncumulation of limit of
  insurance
Obligee

Outside the premises
Position schedule
Premises burglary
  coverage form (Form E)
Principal
Public official bond
Robbery
Robbery and safe burglary
  coverage form (Form D)
Robbery inside the
  premises
Robbery outside the
  premises
Safe burglary
Scheduled coverage
Surety
Surety bond
Theft
Theft, disappearance, and
  destruction coverage
  form (Form C)

## QUESTIONS FOR REVIEW

1. Define burglary, robbery, and theft.

2. Briefly describe some common policy provisions that apply to most commercial crime coverages.

3. Briefly describe the various documents that form a complete commercial crime policy under the crime insurance program by the Insurance Services Office.

4. Briefly describe the coverage provided by the employee dishonesty coverage form.

5. Briefly explain the exclusions and limitations under the employee dishonesty coverage form.

6. Identify three other crime coverage forms and give an example where each can be used.

7. Describe the three parties to a bond.

8. How do surety bonds differ from insurance contracts?

9. Identify three surety bonds and give an example where each can be used.

## QUESTIONS FOR DISCUSSION

1. Southeast Community College is insured under a theft, disappearance, and destruction coverage form with an insurance limit of $25,000. What dollar amount, if any, will the insurer pay for the following losses that resulted from a single theft in the business office? If the loss is not covered, or not fully covered, explain why not.

   a. $2000 damage to the building when a thief broke into the business office

   b. $3000 to replace student records taken from a file cabinet

   c. $15,000 in cash taken from a locked cash box that was pried open

   d. $10,000 in negotiable bonds that were stolen from a safe in the business office

2. Carmine owns several retail stores. The employees are insured under the employee dishonesty coverage form with an insurance limit of $10,000. Carmine discovered that Iris, a long-time accountant, had embezzled $3000 from the firm in order to pay the gambling debts of her son, who had been threatened with bodily harm. Iris agreed to repay the firm, and the embezzlement was not reported to the insurer. Several months later, Iris stole $2000 from the company's cash receipts and then disappeared. What is the liability of the insurer, if any, for the loss? Explain your answer.

3. Clocktower Super Market is insured under an employee dishonesty coverage form that was issued on January 1, 1996. The coverage is written on a *blanket basis,* and the limit of insurance is $10,000. The coverage terminated on January 1, 1997, and was replaced with a new policy by another insurer on the same date with a policy term of one year. What dollar amount, if any, will each insurer pay for the following losses?

   a. An embezzlement of $5000 by a single employee occurred in 1996. The loss is not discovered until July 1997.

   b. Three cashiers acting together stole $15,000 in early 1997. The loss is discovered in December 1997.

c. Would your answer to part (b) be the same or different if this coverage is written on a name schedule basis with a limit of insurance of $10,000 on each named employee? Explain your answer.

4. Vasquez Construction has been awarded a contract by a school board to build a new public school and must provide a performance bond.

   a. With respect to the performance bond, identify the principal, surety, and obligee.

   b. If Vasquez Construction fails to complete the building according to the terms of the contract, what would be the surety's obligation?

## CASE APPLICATION

Numerous crime coverage forms can be used to insure specific crime exposures. Assume that you are a risk management consultant. For each of the following losses, identify an appropriate crime coverage form that could be used to insure the loss.

a. Camille owns a liquor store and is taking the day's receipts to the bank. She is confronted by a person with a gun and is told to hand over the money. Fearing for her life, she surrenders the money.

b. Travis owns a supermarket. When the store was closed, a burglar broke into a locked safe, and stole several thousand dollars.

c. Isabel is a bank teller. Just before the bank closed, a customer she was waiting on pulled out a gun and held up the bank. The robber ordered her to put the cash in her register into a brown paper bag. An undisclosed amount of cash was stolen.

d. Barry is the president of a stock brokerage firm. He received a phone call telling him that his wife was being held hostage and would not be released until he placed a sum of money under a bush in the city park.

e. Elliott owns a sporting goods store. A thief hid in the store until closing and removed merchandise from the store shelves. The thief then broke a window to get out and escaped with the merchandise.

c. Does the surety have any recourse against Vasquez Construction in this example? Explain your answer.

## SELECTED REFERENCES

*Fire, Casualty & Surety Bulletins*. Casualty and Surety volume, Crime section and Surety section. Cincinnati: National Underwriter Company. The bulletins are published monthly. Detailed information on commercial crime insurance and surety bonds can be found in this volume.

Huebner, S.S., Kenneth Black, Jr., and Bernard L. Webb. *Property and Liability Insurance*, 4th ed. Upper Saddle River, N.J.: Prentice Hall, 1996.

*Policy, Form & Manual Analysis Service*. Casualty Coverages volume. Indianapolis: Rough Notes Company. The reference materials are published monthly and provide detailed information on commercial crime coverages.

Webb, Bernard L., Arthur L. Flitner, and Jerome Trupin. *Commercial Insurance*, 3rd ed. Malvern, Pa.: Insurance Institute of America, 1996, chapter 5.

## NOTES

1. The commercial crime coverage forms discussed in this section are based on *Fire, Casualty & Surety Bulletins*, Casualty and Surety volume, Crime section (Cincinnati: National Underwriter Company); *Policy, Form & Manual Analysis Service*. Casualty Coverages volume, Crime insurance section (Indianapolis: Rough Notes Company); and Bernard L. Webb, Arthur L. Flitner, and Jerome Trupin, *Commercial Insurance*, 3rd ed. (Malvern, Pa.: Insurance Institute of America, 1996), Chapter 5. The author also drew on the various (copyrighted) commercial crime coverage forms and documents of the Insurance Services Office that appeared in the *CPCU Handbook of Insurance Policies*, First edition (Malvern, Pa.: American Institute for CPCU/Insurance Institute of America, 1994). The author drew heavily on these sources in the preparation of this chapter.

2. The discussion of surety bonds is based on *Fire, Casualty & Surety Bulletins*, Casualty and Surety volume, Surety section (Cincinnati: National Underwriter Company).

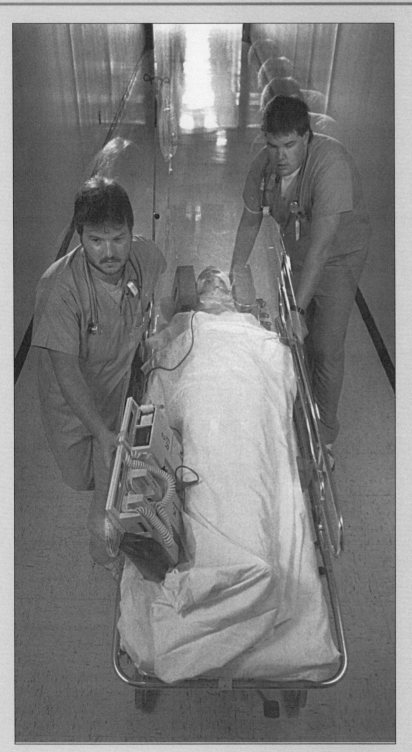

# Part Five

# LIFE AND HEALTH RISKS

Information on life insurance and annuities is available at many sites on the World Wide Web. For example, see LifeNet at:

http://www.lifenet.com/

and InsWeb at:

http://www.insweb.com/

Insight 18.1, in Chapter 18 of this text, lists some sources of on-line term life insurance quotes.

Insurance and Risk Management Central provides information on insurance-related topics at:

http://www.irmcentral.com/

Go to the "Shopping for Personal Insurance" page to access information on life insurance and health and disability insurance.

Get up-to-date vital statistics on the U.S. population from the Bureau of the Census at:

http://www.census.gov/

An extensive list of links to Web sites on estate planning is provided by FindLaw Internet Legal Resources at:

http://www.findlaw.com/

Go to "Legal Subject Index" and then to "Probate, Trusts & Estates."

The Pension and Welfare Benefits Administration is an agency within the U.S. Department of Labor that "protects the integrity of pensions, health plans, and other employee benefits." Find out more about the agency at:

http://www.dol.gov/dol/pwba/

Information on Medicare and Medicaid is available from the U.S. Health Care Financing Administration at:

http://www.hcfa.gov/

Social Security Online provides information about benefits at:

http://www.ssa.gov/

# Chapter 15

# FUNDAMENTALS OF LIFE INSURANCE

*" The human life value, expressed in dollars, should be carefully appraised for life and health purposes. "*

*S.S. Huebner*
The Economics of Life Insurance

## Student Learning Objectives

After studying this chapter, you should be able to:

■ Explain the meaning of premature death and identify the costs associated with premature death.

■ Describe the financial impact of premature death on the different types of families in the United States.

■ Describe the basic methods for estimating the amount of insurance to own, including the human life value approach, needs approach, and capital retention approach.

■ Explain the yearly renewable term method for providing life insurance protection to an individual.

■ Show how the level-premium method can provide lifetime insurance protection to an individual.

■ Explain the purpose of the legal reserve.

In a personal risk management program, the risk of premature death must be given high priority. If a family head dies prematurely, the surviving family members can experience considerable financial insecurity. A woman earning $60,000 annually, for example, may be the sole support of her disabled husband and three small children. During the course of her lifetime, she manages to save $30,000. She has only $50,000 of life insurance. If she died suddenly at age 39, could her family survive on the $80,000 left to them? Although Social Security survivor benefits may be payable, there are other financial factors to consider, including a college education for the children. It is clear that $80,000 will not go far. Her premature death has created financial insecurity for the surviving family members. The family's share of her earnings is lost forever.

This chapter discusses the risk of premature death and how life insurance can be used to alleviate the financial consequences of premature death. The major areas discussed include the meaning of premature death, the financial impact of premature death on the different types of families in the United States, and an analysis of the various methods of estimating the amount of life insurance to own. The chapter concludes with a discussion of the basic methods for providing life insurance to an individual, which include the yearly renewable term method and the level-premium method.

## PREMATURE DEATH

### Meaning of Premature Death

**Premature death** *can be defined as the death of a family head with outstanding unfulfilled financial obligations,* such as dependents to support, children to educate, a mortgage to be paid off, and car payments or other installment debts. Premature death can cause serious financial problems to the surviving family members since their share of the deceased breadwinner's earnings is lost forever. If replacement income from other sources is inadequate, or if the accumulated financial assets available to the family are also inadequate, the surviving family members will be exposed to great financial insecurity.

### Costs of Premature Death

As stated in Chapter 1, there are certain costs associated with premature death. These costs are worth repeating. First, the deceased breadwinner's income is terminated, and the family's share of that income is lost forever. Second, additional expenses are incurred because of funeral expenses, uninsured medical bills, probate and estate settlement costs, and federal estate taxes for large estates. Third, because of insufficient income, some families will experience a reduction in their standard of living. Finally, certain noneconomic costs are incurred, such as emotional grief, loss of a role model, and counseling and guidance for the children.

### Chances of Dying Prematurely

The problem of premature death has declined over time due to significant breakthroughs in medical science, improvements in health because of economic growth and higher real incomes, and improvements in public health and sanitation. In 1995, life expectancy at birth was 79.2 years for females and 72.3 years for males.[1] Although life expectancy has increased over time, large numbers of Americans die each year from the three major causes of death—heart disease, cancer, and stroke. Although AIDS is still a leading cause of death for Americans ages 25–45, newer data suggest that AIDS deaths are declining (see Insight 15.1).

Exhibit 15.1 indicates the chances of dying *before age 65* for selected ages. Roughly one in five people now age 20 will die before age 65.

### Economic Justification of Life Insurance

Life insurance can be used to alleviate the financial consequences of premature death. The purchase of life insurance is economically justified if the insured earns an income, and others are dependent on that earning capacity for at least part of their financial support. If the breadwinner dies prematurely, life insurance can be used to restore the family's share of the deceased breadwinner's earnings.

It should be noted that a life insurance policy is a *valued policy* that pays a stated sum to a named beneficiary and is not a contract of indemnity. *The insured event is the uncertainty of the time of death.* We must all die, but the time of death is uncertain.

As stated earlier, a family head may die with outstanding financial obligations and dependents to support, which may result in financial insecurity for the surviving dependents. However, the financial impact of premature death on the family is not uniform and depends on the type of family in which the breadwinner dies.

## FINANCIAL IMPACT OF PREMATURE DEATH ON DIFFERENT TYPES OF FAMILIES

The composition of the family has changed significantly over time. As a result, premature death has a more severe financial impact on certain types of

# INSIGHT 15.1

## AIDS Deaths Take Notable Dip in U.S.

For the first time since the AIDS epidemic began in the United States 16 years ago, deaths from the disease have declined nationwide, federal health officials reported.

In a sign that the trend will continue, the encouraging numbers do not significantly reflect the growing use by AIDS patients of powerful new drug combinations that include protease inhibitors, which probably will further extend survival.

*Deaths among people with AIDS dropped 13 percent during the first six months of 1996, from 24,900 to 22,000,* compared with the same period the previous year, according to the Federal Centers for Disease Control.

Health officials attributed the reduction to increased resources devoted to treatment and prevention, particularly in improved therapies designed to stave off often life-threatening AIDS-related infections.

The news was not entirely unexpected. During a major AIDS meeting, New York City health officials reported a substantial and unprecedented drop of almost 30 percent in AIDS deaths there, and federal officials predicted this was a harbinger of a national trend that would soon become apparent when the latest figures became available in late February.

The federal officials stressed that the trends should not cause complacency among the public.

"We're finally seeing deaths go down, but it's not good enough," said Health and Human Services Secretary Donna Shalala. "Too many people are still dying, and too many people are still getting infected. The new drugs don't work for everyone. We must still focus on prevention."

While the overall numbers were upbeat, the patterns varied among gender, racial groups and risk groups, with some not faring as well as others. "The numbers are shifting to our most vulnerable people," Ms. Shalala said.

For example, while the number of AIDS deaths declined 15 percent among men, deaths among women were up 3 percent. Also, deaths declined 18 percent among gay men and 6 percent among intravenous drug users, but they increased 3 percent among those who had become infected through heterosexual contact.

"We have made a great deal of progress in both prevention and treatment of AIDS, but declines have not yet been seen in all people," said Dr. David Satcher, the director of CDC. "We must ensure we reach women and minority communities with effective prevention programs and provide access to quality care."

Also, HHS said it would release an additional $202 million in funds under the Ryan White Comprehensive AIDS Resources Emergency Act, which provides resources for treatment of people with HIV and AIDS.

Many local health officials have credited the drop in AIDS deaths to funding increases in this program that have made therapy and health-care services more accessible.

The CDC reported that AIDS deaths increased steadily through 1994 but increased only slightly in 1995, which was viewed as a leveling off when adjusted for increases in the population.

In more good news, the CDC reported that while the number of people diagnosed with AIDS continued to grow, the rate of growth has slowed in recent years. From 1994 to 1995, the number of people diagnosed increased 2 percent from 61,200 to 62,200. From 1993 to 1994, the growth rate was 5 percent.

If these trends continue, "hopefully, with a combined strategy to prevent new infections and to provide early diagnosis and treatment for people who are infected, AIDS incidence will soon begin to decline," CDC said.

But, as with deaths, the incidence numbers were not all positive. In 1996, for the first time, blacks accounted for a larger proportion of AIDS cases (41 percent) than whites, and the proportion of female AIDS cases continued to increase. In 1996, women made up one-fifth of the newly reported cases of AIDS.

SOURCE: Adapted from "AIDS Deaths Take Notable Dip in U.S.," *Omaha World Herald,* February 28, 1997, pp. 1, 10.

EXHIBIT 15.1
**Probability of Death Prior to Age 65**

| Age | Within a year | Prior to age 65 | Age | Within a year | Prior to age 65 |
|-----|---------------|-----------------|-----|---------------|-----------------|
| 0   | 0.0100        | 0.21            | 35  | 0.0017        | 0.18            |
| 5   | 0.0003        | 0.20            | 40  | 0.0022        | 0.17            |
| 10  | 0.0002        | 0.20            | 45  | 0.0032        | 0.16            |
| 15  | 0.0006        | 0.20            | 50  | 0.0050        | 0.14            |
| 20  | 0.0011        | 0.19            | 55  | 0.0081        | 0.12            |
| 25  | 0.0012        | 0.19            | 60  | 0.0126        | 0.07            |
| 30  | 0.0014        | 0.18            |     |               |                 |

SOURCE: Kenneth Black, Jr., and Harold D. Skipper, Jr, *Life Insurance,* 12th ed. (Englewood Cliffs, N.J.: Prentice-Hall, 1994), Table 1–1, p. 7.

families than on others. The following section examines the financial impact of premature death on the different types of families and their need for life insurance. In general, the different types of families in the United States can be classified as follows:[2]

- Single people
- Single-parent families
- Two-income earners
- Traditional families
- Blended families
- Sandwiched families

## Single People

The number of single people has increased in recent years. Younger adults are postponing marriage, and many young and middle-aged adults are single because of divorce. Also, many older adults are single once again because of the death of their spouse.

*In general, the premature death of a single person who has no dependents to support or outstanding financial obligations is not likely to create a financial problem for others.* Other than a modest amount of life insurance for burial purposes and for uninsured medical bills, large amounts of life insurance are not needed by this group.

## Single-Parent Families

The number of single-parent families with children under age 18 has increased sharply in recent years because of the large number of children born outside

of marriage, widespread divorce and legal separation, death, and imprisonment. Premature death of a family head in a single-parent family can cause great financial insecurity for the surviving children. *The need for large amounts of life insurance on the family head is great.* However, many single-parent families are living in poverty, and their ability to purchase large amounts of life insurance is limited. In 1992, 47 percent of the female-headed families with children and no husband present were poor, compared with 9 percent of the male-present families.[3] These families are simply too poor to purchase large amounts of life insurance.

## Two-Income Earners

The traditional family in which only one spouse works outside the home has been largely replaced by families in which both spouses work. In 1993, about 68 percent of the married couples with children under age 18 were in the labor force.[4] *In two-income families with children, the death of one income earner can cause considerable financial insecurity for the surviving family members since both incomes are normally needed to maintain the family's standard of living. Family heads need substantial amounts of life insurance.* Life insurance can replace the income that is lost because of premature death, and the family can maintain its previous standard of living.

*In contrast, in the case of a married working couple without children, premature death of one income earner is not as likely to cause serious financial problems for the surviving spouse.* The surviving spouse is already in the labor force and is supporting herself or himself. Moreover, career couples without children do not have to pay college education costs for the children, and child-care costs are not incurred. Thus, the need for large amounts of life insurance by income earners within this group is reduced considerably.

## Traditional Families

The traditional family—in which only one parent is in the labor force and the other parent stays home to care for the children—has declined in relative importance in recent years. In traditional families, the father typically has a job outside the home, and the mother stays at home to take care of the children. In 1947, it was unusual to find working mothers with a preschool-age child (only about 12 percent of the mothers with a child under age six were in the labor force at that time). In 1993, nearly 60 percent of mothers with preschool-age children were in the labor force, a rate nearly five times higher than in 1947.[5] *However, in traditional families with children in which only one parent works outside the home, premature death can cause great financial insecurity. Family heads need large amounts of life insurance.*

In most traditional families, the husband usually dies first. Because of a longer life expectancy, the majority of married women with children who are not in the labor force will survive their husbands by several years. Unfortunately, most husbands fail to keep their life insurance up to date. They may die with an insufficient amount of life insurance and with sizable outstanding debts and financial obligations. As a result, some families may be forced to adjust their standard of living downward if the husband dies prematurely. In addition, many older widows under age 60 whose children are grown have been out of the labor force for several years. Some older widows may also be exposed to severe financial insecurity if their husbands should die because of an insufficient amount of life insurance proceeds. These widows generally are ineligible for Social Security survivor benefits because they are under age 60 and have no eligible children under age 16 in their care.

## Blended Families

A blended family is one in which a divorced spouse with children remarries, and the new spouse also has children. *Premature death of a working spouse in a blended family can cause great financial insecurity. Family heads in this group need substantial amounts of life insurance.* Both spouses may be in the labor force at the time of remarriage, and the death of one spouse may result in a reduction in the family's standard of living since the family's share of that income is lost. Also, in many blended families, older children are present from the previous marriage, and additional children are born out of the new marriage. As a result, expensive child-care costs are incurred over a longer period, and funds for the children's education and the parents' retirement may be limited. In addition, the impact of premature death can actually affect two separate households if the deceased parent did not have custody of the dependent children.

## Sandwiched Families

A sandwiched family is one in which a son or daughter with children is also supporting an aged parent or parents. Thus, the son or daughter is "sandwiched" between the younger and older generations.

*Premature death of a working spouse in a sandwiched family can cause considerable financial insecurity to the surviving family members, and the need for life insurance is great.* Premature death can result in a loss of financial support to both the surviving children and parent(s). Life insurance is needed to replace the loss of income to the surviving family members.

## AMOUNT OF LIFE INSURANCE TO OWN

In a personal risk management program, life insurance is an important technique for alleviating the financial consequences of premature death. In 1995, the average amount of life insurance in force per household in the United States was only $124,100, which represents less than 28 months of disposable income per household.[6] The correct amount of life insurance to own, however, is an individual matter, since family needs and financial goals vary widely among families. In the past, some life insurers and financial planners have proposed certain arbitrary rules for determining the amount of life insurance to own, such as six to ten times annual earnings. These rules, however, are meaningless because they do not consider that family size, needs, and financial goals vary from family to family.

Three approaches can be used to estimate the amount of life insurance to own:

- Human life value approach
- Needs approach
- Capital retention approach

## Human Life Value Approach

As noted earlier, the family's share of the deceased breadwinner's earnings is lost forever if the family head dies prematurely. This loss is called the human life value. **Human life value** *can be defined as the present value of the family's share of the deceased breadwinner's future earnings.* It can be calculated by the following steps:

1. Estimate the individual's average annual earnings over his or her productive lifetime.

2. Deduct federal and state income taxes, Social Security taxes, life and health insurance premiums, and the costs of self-maintenance. The remaining amount is used to support the family.

3. Determine the number of years from the person's present age to the contemplated age of retirement.

4. Using a reasonable discount rate, determine the present value of the family's share of earnings for the period determined in step 3.

For example, assume that Francisco, age 25, is married and has two children. He earns $25,000 annually and plans to retire at age 65. (For the sake of simplicity, we will assume that his earnings will remain constant.) Of this amount, $10,000 is used for federal and state taxes, life and health insurance, and Francisco's personal needs. The remaining $15,000 is used to support his family. This stream of future income is then discounted back to the present to determine Francisco's human life value. Using a reasonable discount rate of 6 percent, the present value of $1 payable annually for 40 years is $15.05. Therefore, Francisco has a human life value of $225,750 ($15,000 × $15.05 = $225,750). This sum represents the present value of the family's share of Francisco's earnings that would be lost if he should die prematurely. As you can see, the human life has an enormous economic value when earning capacity is considered. The major advantage of the human life value concept is that it crudely measures the economic value of a human life.

However, the human life value approach has several defects that limit its usefulness in trying to measure accurately the correct amount of life insurance to own. *First, other sources of income are not considered,* such as Social Security survivor benefits.

*Second, in its simplest form, work earnings and expenses are assumed to remain constant.* This assumption is clearly unrealistic. Moreover, it is difficult to estimate accurately the future increase in earnings.

*Third, the amount of income allocated to the family is a critical factor in determining the human life value.* This amount can quickly change depending on several factors, such as divorce, birth, or death in the family.

*In addition, the long-run discount rate is critical.* The human life value can be substantially increased merely by assuming a lower discount rate.

*Finally, the effects of inflation on earnings and expenses are ignored.* Inflation can quickly erode the real purchasing power of the policy proceeds.

## Needs Approach

The second method for estimating the amount of life insurance to own is the **needs approach.** Under this method, the various family needs that must be met if the family head should die are analyzed, and the amount of money needed to meet these needs is determined. The amount of existing life insurance and financial assets is then subtracted from the total amount needed. The difference, if any, is the amount of new life insurance that should be purchased (see Insight 15.2). The most important family needs are the following:

- Estate clearance fund
- Income during the readjustment period
- Income during the dependency period
- Life income to the surviving spouse
- Special needs
    Mortgage redemption fund
    Educational fund
    Emergency fund
- Retirement needs

**Estate Clearance Fund** An **estate clearance fund** or cleanup fund is immediately needed when the family head dies. Cash is needed for burial expenses, expenses of last illness, installment debts,

## INSIGHT 15.2

## Life Insurance: Three Families' Needs

Life insurance needs vary depending on individual and family situations. The amount of life insurance needed can be determined by the needs approach. First, you estimate what your future financial needs would be less any Social Security benefits you expect. (Contact your local Social Security office for more information.) Second, you determine what current assets you have, including your present life insurance, to meet these needs. (Omit assets like automobiles and your personal residence that would not likely be sold by your family.) Third, subtract your assets from your needs to determine the amount of additional life insurance you should have, if any. (While certain assets will generate investment income, it has been assumed that all such income will be offset by the effects of inflation.)

The needs approach tailors your life insurance protection to your individual needs. Three hypothetical family situations are described below to illustrate how the needs approach identifies the type and amount of financial security different members require.

### Chris Swift

Chris Swift is 39 and earns $60,000 a year. He has a wife and two children ages 12 and 6. He has four primary financial needs: (1) to provide income to support his family for 12 years until the younger child is 18, (b) to build a 20-year retirement fund for his wife, (c) to establish a college education fund for his children, and (d) to provide for other miscellaneous expenses (for example, emergencies, funeral, and so on). He calculated his total financial needs, taking into account the Social Security benefits his family would receive if he died. In spite of these benefits and his current assets, his present insurance provides only part of what he needs. He needs an additional $606,000 of insurance.

1. Financial needs
   a. Family living expenses $360,000
   b. Retirement fund for wife 200,000
   c. College education 200,000
   d. Other (emergency, final expenses) 32,000
   Total financial needs $792,000

2. Current assets
   a. Cash and savings $ 26,000
   b. Mutual funds 50,000
   c. Life insurance 110,000
   Less: Current assets −$186,000

3. Additional life insurance needed $606,000

### Kim Lukens

Kim Lukens is married, 51 years old, and earns $75,000 a year. She has two grown children who are out of college, so she has no education or family living expense needs. (She assumes her husband could support himself

*Continued*

estate administration expenses, and estate, inheritance, and income taxes.

**Income During the Readjustment Period** The **readjustment period** is a one- or two-year period following the breadwinner's death. During this period, the family should receive approximately the same amount of income it received while the family head was alive. The purpose of the readjustment period is to give the family time to adjust its

until age 62 if she died.) Kim has two primary financial needs: (a) to establish a 20-year retirement fund beyond what Social Security will provide, and (b) to provide an estate clearance fund. She needs an additional $102,000 of insurance.

| | | |
|---|---|---|
| 1. Financial needs | | |
|    a. Retirement fund | $400,000 | |
|    b. Estate clearance fund | 32,000 | |
|    Total financial needs | | $432,000 |
| 2. Current assets | | |
|    a. Cash and savings | $ 55,000 | |
|    b. Mutual funds and securities | 125,000 | |
|    c. Life insurance | 150,000 | |
|    Less: Current assets | | −$330,000 |
| 3. Additional life insurance needed | | $102,000 |

**Stephanie Hauser**

Stephanie Hauser is single, 29 years of age, and earns $28,000 a year. She rents an apartment but has investment real estate holdings. She provides a modest amount of financial support for her 62-year-old disabled mother. However, if Stephanie should die, she would like to provide $7500 a year to support her mother for the rest of her life. Stephanie has two primary financial needs: (a) to provide income to support her mother, and (b) to provide for other miscellaneous expenses that might occur. Stephanie can insure her mother's financial support for life by $90,000 of additional life insurance with her mother as beneficiary.

| | | |
|---|---|---|
| 1. Financial needs | | |
|    a. Dependent support | $165,000 | |
|    b. Other (emergency, final expenses) | 17,000 | |
|    Total financial needs | | $182,000 |
| 2. Current assets | | |
|    a. Cash, savings, and securities | $ 6,000 | |
|    b. Equity in real estate, excluding home | 36,000 | |
|    c. Life insurance | 50,000 | |
|    Less: Current assets | | −$ 92,000 |
| 3. Additional life insurance needed | | $ 90,000 |

living standard to a different level. There is normally an emotional shock and considerable grief when the family head dies, especially if the death is unexpected. Providing an equivalent amount of income to the family during this period can prevent a financial shock that would only compound the family's grief.

**Income During the Dependency Period**
The **dependency period** follows the readjustment

period. It is the period until the youngest child reaches age 18. The family should receive income during this period so that the surviving spouse can remain at home, if necessary, to care for the children during their critical formative years. The amount of income needed during the dependency period is substantially reduced if the surviving spouse is already in the labor force at the time the family head dies, and she or he plans to continue working.

**Life Income to the Surviving Spouse**    Some surviving spouses have been out of the labor force for several years. When the children are grown, the surviving spouse may be middle-aged. The occupational skills that the spouse possesses may be obsolete, and it may be difficult to find a job that will pay an adequate salary. Thus, it is often desirable to plan for a life income to the surviving spouse.

There are two income periods to consider: (1) income during the blackout period, and (2) income to supplement Social Security benefits after the blackout period. The **blackout period** refers to the period from the time Social Security benefits to a surviving spouse terminate to the time they are resumed. Social Security benefits terminate when the youngest child reaches age 16 and are resumed at when the spouse reaches age 60. Thus, it is desirable to provide income during the blackout period and also to supplement Social Security benefits at retirement.

If a surviving spouse has a career and is already in the labor force, the need for a life income is greatly reduced. However, this is clearly not true of an older spouse under age 60 who has been out of the labor force for years, and the children are grown. The need for income during the blackout period is especially important for this group.

**Special Needs**    Certain special needs must also be considered. These needs include a mortgage redemption fund, educational fund, and emergency fund.

1. *Mortgage redemption fund.* It is often desirable to provide the family with funds to pay off the mortgage. The amount of monthly income needed is greatly reduced when monthly mortgage payments or rent payments are not required.

2. *Educational fund.* The family head may wish to provide an educational fund for the children. If

the child intends to go to a private college or university, the costs will be considerably higher than at a public institution.

3. *Emergency fund.* An emergency fund should also be provided. An unexpected event may occur, such as the need for a new furnace, major dental work, or a new car.

**Retirement Needs**    The family head may survive to retirement, so the need for an adequate retirement income must also be considered. In most cases, the typical wage earner is eligible for Social Security retirement benefits, and may also be eligible for private pension benefits from an employer. If retirement income from these sources is inadequate, it may be necessary to supplement the Social Security benefits from other sources. Additional income can be obtained from cash-value life insurance, individual investments, a retirement annuity, an individual retirement account, or a 401 (k) plan. Failure to plan for retirement could result in serious financial hardship because of inadequate income during old age.

**Advantages and Disadvantages of the Needs Approach**    The major advantage of the needs approach is that it is a reasonably accurate method for determining the amount of life insurance to own when specific family needs and objectives are recognized. The needs approach also considers other sources of income and financial assets in determining the amount of life insurance to own. If present life insurance and financial assets are insufficient for meeting these needs, the inadequacy is quickly recognized. Finally, the needs approach can also be used to recognize needs during a period of disability or retirement.

The needs approach, however, has several disadvantages.[7] First, future projections over the insured's lifetime require numerous assumptions and the use of a computer. Dynamic programming models with changing assumptions can be complex and usually are not needed by the typical insured.

Second, family needs must be periodically evaluated to determine if they are still appropriate as circumstances change. The need for life insurance can quickly change if there is a divorce, birth, or death of a family member.

In addition, in its simplest form, the needs approach ignores inflation, which can result in a substantial understatement of the amount of life insurance to own. However, the effects of inflation can be incorporated in a dynamic programming model, which requires the use of a computer.

Finally, the needs approach ignores the preservation of estate assets for the heirs, such as the children.

## Capital Retention Approach

The **capital retention approach** (also called capital needs analysis) is another method for estimating the amount of life insurance to own. Unlike the needs approach, which assumes liquidation of the life insurance proceeds, the capital retention approach preserves the capital needed to provide income to the family. The income-producing assets are then available for distribution later to the heirs.

The amount of life insurance needed based on the capital retention approach can be determined by the following steps:

- Prepare a personal balance sheet.
- Determine the amount of income-producing capital.
- Determine the amount of additional capital needed (if any).

**Prepare a Personal Balance Sheet**    The first step is to prepare a personal balance sheet that lists all assets and liabilities. The balance sheet should include all death benefits from life insurance and from other sources. For example, Enrique, age 35, has a wife and two children, ages three and five. Enrique earns $60,000 annually. If he should die, he wants his family to receive $30,000 annually. He also wants to establish an emergency fund and educational fund, and pay off the mortgage. Enrique's personal balance sheet, including death benefits from life insurance and his pension plan, is as follows:

*Assets*

| | |
|---|---|
| House | $125,000 |
| Automobiles | 15,000 |
| Personal and household property | 45,000 |
| Securities and investments | 28,000 |
| Checking account | 2,000 |
| Individual and group life insurance | 100,000 |
| Private pension death benefit | 20,000 |
| Total | $335,000 |

*Liabilities*

| | |
|---|---|
| Mortgage | $100,000 |
| Auto loan | 10,000 |
| Charge accounts and other bills | 5,000 |
| Total | $115,000 |

**Determine the Amount of Income-Producing Capital**    The next step is to determine the amount of income-producing assets that can provide income to the family. This step is performed by subtracting the liabilities, cash needs, and nonincome-producing capital from total assets. Enrique has $55,000 of capital that can produce income for the family. This is illustrated as follows:

| | | |
|---|---|---|
| Total assets | | $335,000 |
| Less: | | |
|   Mortgage | $100,000 | |
|   Other liabilities | 15,000 | |
|   Final expenses | 10,000 | |
|   Emergency fund | 10,000 | |
|   Educational fund | 60,000 | |
|   Nonincome-producing capital (automobiles, personal and household property, equity in home) | 85,000 | |
| Total deductions | | −280,000 |
| Capital now available for income | | $ 55,000 |

You should note that in the preceding illustration, equity in the home ($25,000) is not an income-producing asset. Unless the house is sold or rented, equity in the home ordinarily does not produce cash income for the family. Thus, equity in the home is considered to be part of *nonincome-producing capital* that is subtracted from total assets to arrive at the amount of liquid assets that can produce income for the family.

**Determine the Amount of Additional Capital Needed**    The final step is to determine the amount of additional capital (if any) that is needed. This step involves a comparison of the income objective with other sources of income, such as Social Security survivor benefits. In Enrique's case, his family would have an income shortage of $14,700 annually based on his present financial situation.

Assuming the liquid assets and life insurance proceeds can be invested to earn 6 percent annually, Enrique needs an additional $245,000 of life insurance to meet his financial goals. This is illustrated as follows:

| | |
|---|---|
| Income objective for family | $30,000 |
| Less: | |
|    Capital now available for income | −3,300 |
|    ($55,000 × 6%) | |
| Social Security survivor benefits | −12,000 |
| Income shortage | $14,700 |
| Total new capital required | |
|    ($14,700/0.06) | $245,000 |

The capital retention approach has the advantages of simplicity, ease of understanding, and preservation of capital. In addition, investment income on the emergency and educational funds can be used as a partial hedge against inflation, or can be accumulated to offset rising educational costs. The major disadvantage, however, is that a larger amount of life insurance is required to produce a given amount of income.

## METHODS FOR PROVIDING LIFE INSURANCE PROTECTION

Two basic methods can be used to provide life insurance to individuals: yearly renewable term method and level-premium method.[8]

### Yearly Renewable Term Method

**Yearly renewable term insurance** *provides life insurance protection for only one year.* The insured is permitted to renew the policy for successive one-year periods with no evidence of insurability. This means that evidence of good health or a physical examination is not required when the policy is renewed.

The pure premium for yearly renewable term insurance is determined by the death rate at each attained age. For the sake of simplicity, interest and operating expenses of the insurer are ignored in this discussion. The insurance protection is only for one year, and individuals within the group must pay their pro rata share of death claims. Based on the Commissioners 1980 Standard Ordinary Table of Mortality, the death rate for males at age 30 is 1.73 for each 1000 lives. If 100,000 males, age 30, are

insured for $1000 for one year, the insurance company must pay 173 death claims, or $173,000. If interest and expenses are ignored, each insured must pay a premium of $1.73 ($173,000/100,000 = $1.73). You will notice that the $1.73 in premiums is the same as the death rate at age 30. At age 31, the male death rate is 1.78 per 1000 lives. If the 99,827 survivors want the protection for another year, the insurer must pay 178 death claims, or $178,000. Each of the 99,827 insureds must pay their pro rata share of the death claims, or $1.78 ($178,000/99,827 = $1.78). Finally, if the 99,649 survivors wish to insure their lives for another year, the insurer must pay $183,000 in death claims. Each insured's share of the total death claims would be $1.83 ($183,000/99,649 = 1.83).

You can see that the yearly renewable term insurance premium increases as the individual gets older. *The premium increase is gradual during the early years, but it rises sharply during the later years.* The following illustration shows the pure premiums for $1000 of yearly renewable term insurance for males at various attained ages. (Interest and expenses are again ignored.)

| | |
|---|---|
| Age 30 | $1.73 |
| Age 40 | $3.02 |
| Age 50 | $6.71 |
| Age 60 | $16.08 |
| Age 70 | $39.51 |
| Age 80 | $98.84 |
| Age 90 | $221.77 |
| Age 98 | $657.98 |
| Age 99 | $1000.00 |

Because premiums increase with age, yearly renewable term insurance premiums eventually become prohibitive in cost, so some insureds may drop their insurance. The healthier members may drop their life insurance as the premiums increase, but the unhealthy persons will continue to renew their policies despite the premium increase. This leads to adverse selection against the insurer. The insurer may then have a disproportionate number of impaired lives in the group, which drives the death rate up even more.

You can see that under the yearly renewable method, the premiums are substantial at the older ages. Therefore, if the insured wants lifetime protection, the yearly renewable term method is impractical because the premiums are prohibitive in cost at the older ages. Some other method must be used to provide lifetime protection. This method is called the level-premium method.

## Level-Premium Method

Under the *level-premium method,* premiums do not increase from year to year but remain level throughout the premium paying period, and the insured has lifetime protection to age 100. Under this method, premiums paid during the early years of the policy are higher than is necessary to pay current death claims, while those paid in the later years are inadequate for paying death claims. The redundant or excess premiums paid during the early years are invested at compound interest, and the accumulated funds are then used to supplement the inadequate premiums paid during the later years of the policy. Since the method of investing and accumulating the fund is regulated by state law, it is referred to as a **legal reserve**. The legal reserve technically is a composite liability account of the insurer and should

not be allocated to individual contracts. However, for our purposes, we can view the legal reserve as the aggregate of the individual accounts established for the individual policyowners.[9]

As stated earlier, under the level-premium method, premiums do not increase with age. *A level premium is possible since the excess premiums are invested at compound interest and are used to supplement the deficiency in premiums during the later years.* In contrast, under the yearly renewable term method, the premiums are very low during the early years but gradually increase to a point where they become prohibitive in cost. For this reason, lifetime protection cannot be provided to most insureds under the yearly renewable term method.

**Fundamental Purpose of the Legal Reserve**
The excess premiums paid during the early years are reflected in a legal reserve. The concept of a legal reserve can be illustrated in greater detail by Exhibit 15.2, which represents the legal reserve under an ordinary life policy. The legal reserve steadily

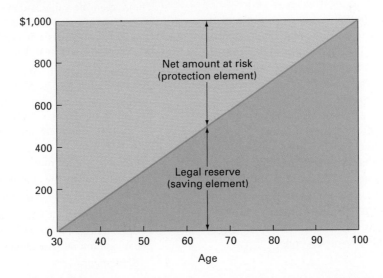

EXHIBIT 15.2

**Proportion of Protection and Savings Elements**
**$1000 Ordinary Life Contract, Issued to a Male Age 30;**
**1980 C.S.O. Table, 5 Percent Interest**

SOURCE: Adapted from Kenneth Black, Jr. and Harold Skipper, Jr., *Life Insurance,* 12th ed., © 1994, p. 34. Reprinted by permission of Prentice-Hall, Inc., Englewood Cliffs, NJ.

increases over time and is equal to the face amount of the policy at age 100. If the insured is still alive at age 100, the face amount of the policy is paid at that time. *The difference between the face amount of the policy and the legal reserve is called the* **net amount at risk**. The net amount at risk represents the pure insurance portion of the policy. It declines over time as the legal reserve increases. Thus, from a conceptual standpoint the death claim can be viewed as consisting of two elements: a legal reserve (saving element) and the net amount at risk (protection element).[10] As the legal reserve increases, the net amount at risk declines. *It follows that the fundamental purpose of the legal reserve is to provide lifetime protection.* As the death rate increases with age, the legal reserve also increases, and the net amount at risk declines, which produces a cost of insurance within practical limits.[11] Therefore, by the level premium method, the insurer can provide the insured with lifetime protection.

**Cash Values**    **Cash values** should not be confused with the legal reserve. Under the level-premium method, a legal reserve results. Because of the legal reserve, cash values become available. The policyowner may no longer want the insurance, and the policy can be surrendered for its cash surrender value. However, cash values and the legal reserve are not the same thing and are computed separately. The cash values are below the legal reserve for several years, but after the policy has been in force over an extended period, such as 15 years, the cash surrender value will equal the full reserve. The various cash surrender options are examined in Chapter 17.

*You should also remember that cash values are the by-product of the level-premium method, not the purpose of it.* The fundamental purpose of the level-premium method is to provide lifetime protection and not to build up a savings account in the form of cash values. This is not to say that an individual cannot save by purchasing cash-value life insurance. Indeed, in the aggregate, large amounts are annually saved by policyowners in the form of accumulated cash values. However, the savings feature is incidental to the fundamental goal of lifetime protection.

## SUMMARY

- Premature death means that a family head dies with outstanding unfulfilled financial obligations, such as dependents to support, children to educate, or a mortgage to be paid off. Great financial insecurity may result if a family head dies prematurely.

- There are at least four costs associated with premature death.

    There is the loss of the human life value. The family's share of the deceased breadwinner's earned income is lost forever.

    Additional expenses may be incurred, such as burial costs, expenses of the last illness, and probate and estate settlement costs.

    Because of insufficient income, some families may experience a reduction in their standard of living.

    Noneconomic costs are also incurred, such as the emotional grief of the surviving dependents and loss of a role model and guidance for the children.

- The purpose of life insurance can be economically justified if a person has an earning capacity, and someone is dependent on those earnings for at least part of his or her financial support.

- The financial impact of premature death on the family varies by family type. Premature death can cause considerable economic insecurity if a family head dies in a single-parent family, in a family with two-income earners with children, or in a traditional, blended, or sandwich family. In contrast, if a single person without dependents or an income earner in a two-income family without children dies, financial problems for others are unlikely.

- The human life value is defined as the present value of the family's share of the deceased breadwinner's earnings. This approach crudely measures the economic value of a human life.

- The needs approach can be used to determine the amount of life insurance to own. After considering other sources of income and financial assets, the various family needs are converted into specific amounts of life insurance. The most important family needs are as follows:

    Estate clearance fund

    Income during the readjustment period

    Income during the dependency period

    Life income to the surviving spouse

    Special needs: mortgage redemption fund, education fund, emergency fund

    Retirement needs

- The capital retention approach for estimating the amount of life insurance to own is based on the assumption that income-producing capital will be preserved and not liquidated.

- Under the yearly renewable term method, life insurance protection is provided for only one year. The policy can be renewed for successive one-year periods with no evidence of insurability. The method is not suitable for lifetime protection because premiums increase with age until they reach prohibitively high levels.

- Under the level-premium method, premiums do not increase from year to year but remain level throughout the premium-paying period. The insured has lifetime protection to age 100. Under this method, premiums paid during the early years are higher than is necessary to pay current death claims. The excess premiums paid during the early years are invested and used to supplement the inadequate premiums paid during the later years.

- The legal reserve is a liability item that reflects the excess premiums paid during the early years of the policy. It steadily increases until it reaches the face amount of the policy by age 100. The fundamental purpose of the legal reserve is to provide lifetime protection.

- Because a legal reserve is necessary for lifetime protection, cash values become available. However, cash values are the by-product of the level-premium method, not the purpose of it. Since the insured has paid more than is actuarially necessary during the early years of the policy, he or she should receive something back if the policy is surrendered.

## KEY CONCEPTS AND TERMS

| | |
|---|---|
| Blackout period | Level-premium method |
| Capital retention approach | Needs approach |
| | Net amount at risk |
| Cash values | Premature death |
| Dependency period | Readjustment period |
| Estate clearance fund | Yearly renewable term insurance |
| Human life value | |
| Legal reserve | |

## QUESTIONS FOR REVIEW

1. Explain the meaning of premature death and costs associated with premature death.

2. Explain the economic justification for the purchase of life insurance.

3. Define the human life value. How is the human life value measured?

4. Describe the needs approach for determining the amount of life insurance to own.

5. Describe the capital retention approach for determining the amount of life insurance to own.

6. Explain the yearly renewable term method for providing life insurance to individuals.

7. Is the yearly renewable term method suitable for lifetime protection?

8. Explain the level-premium method for providing life insurance to individuals.

9. Describe the purpose of the legal reserve in cash value life insurance.

10. Why does a level-premium whole life policy provide cash values?

## QUESTIONS FOR DISCUSSION

1. "The financial impact of premature death is uniform for all families." Do you agree or disagree with this statement? Explain your answer.

2. The human life value concept provides a method for estimating the amount of life insurance to own.
   a. Describe the steps in the calculation of an individual's human life value.
   b. All other factors unchanged, explain the effect, if any, of a reduction in the interest rate used to calculate the individual's human life value.
   c. Explain the defects in the human life value approach as a technique for determining the amount of life insurance to own.

3. José, age 30, is married and has one child. He has been told that he should purchase life insurance to protect his family.
   a. Describe each of the basic family needs for which José may need life insurance.
   b. Explain the limitations in the needs approach as a method for determining the amount of life insurance to own.

4. A significant aspect of a whole life policy is the fact that the net amount at risk decreases over the duration of the contract.
   a. What is the net amount at risk?
   b. Explain why the net amount at risk in a whole life policy decreases over the duration of the contract.
   c. What is the significance of a decreasing net amount at risk in a whole life insurance policy?

5. An agent remarked that "the fundamental purpose of the legal reserve is to accumulate cash values and provide a means of saving money." Do you agree or disagree with this statement? Explain your answer.

## SELECTED REFERENCES

Belth, Joseph M. *Life Insurance: A Consumer's Handbook*, 2nd ed. Bloomington: Indiana University Press, 1985.

Black, Kenneth, Jr., and Harold D. Skipper, Jr. *Life Insurance*, 12th ed. Englewood Cliffs, N.J.: Prentice-Hall, 1994.

Dorfman, Mark S., and Saul W. Adelman. *Life Insurance: A Financial Planning Approach*, 2nd ed. Chicago: Dearborn Financial Publishing, 1992.

Graves, Edward E., ed. *McGill's Life Insurance*. Bryn Mawr, Pa.: The American College, 1994.

Mehr, Robert I., and Sandra G. Gustavson. *Life Insurance: Theory and Practice*, 4th ed. Plano, Tex.: Business Publications, 1987.

Rejda, George E., Constance M. Luthardt, Cheryl L. Ferguson, and Donald R. Oakes. *Personal Insurance*, 3rd ed. Malvern, Pa.: Insurance Institute of America, 1997.

## NOTES

1. *The 1996 Annual Report of the Board of Trustees of the Federal Old-Age and Survivors Insurance and Disability Insurance Trust Funds* (Washington, D.C.: U.S. Government Printing Office, 1996), p. 61.
2. This section is based on George E. Rejda, *Social Insurance and Economic Security*, 5th ed. (Englewood Cliffs, N.J.: Prentice-Hall, 1994), Chapter 3.
3. U.S. Congress, House, Committee on Ways and Means, *Overview of Entitlement Programs, 1994 Green Book*, Background Material and Data on Programs Within the Jurisdiction of the Committee on Ways and Means (Washington, D.C.: U.S. Government Printing Office, 1994), p. 1159.
4. Ibid., p. 535.
5. Ibid., p. 532.
6. *1996 Life Insurance Fact Book* (Washington, D.C.: American Council of Life Insurance, 1996), p. 22.
7. Glenn L. Wood, Claude C. Lilly III, Donald S. Malecki, Edward E. Graves, and Jerry S. Rosenbloom, *Personal Risk Management and Insurance*, 4th ed., vol. 2 (Malvern, Pa.: American Institute for Property and Liability Underwriters, 1989), p. 241.
8. Edward E. Graves, ed., *McGill's Life Insurance* (Bryn Mawr, Pa.: The American College, 1994), pp. 19–31.
9. Graves, p. 25. The legal reserve technically is a liability item that must be offset by sufficient assets. Otherwise, regulatory authorities may declare the insurer to be insolvent.
10. This is only a concept. In practice, the death claim paid by the insurer does not consist of two separate benefits that equal the face value of the policy. An or-

dinary life insurance policy is an undivided contract, and the death benefit is the face amount of insurance.

11. The cost of insurance is a technical term and is obtained by multiplying the net amount at risk by the death rate at the insured's attained age. Under the level-premium method, the cost of insurance can be kept within reasonable bounds at all ages.

## CASE APPLICATION

Althea, age 35, is a registered nurse who earns $40,000 annually. She is married and has two children, ages two and five. If she should die, she wants her family to receive $20,000 annually. She also wants to set up a final expense fund of $10,000, establish an educational fund of $100,000, and pay off the mortgage, automobile loan, and outstanding credit card balances. Her husband, Nicholas, is capable of supporting himself if she should die. Althea's personal balance sheet, including life insurance and a pension death benefit, is as follows:

*Assets*

| | |
|---|---|
| Condominium | $150,000 |
| Personal property | 40,000 |
| Two automobiles | 18,000 |
| Mutual funds | 30,000 |
| Checking account | 2,000 |
| Individual and group life insurance | 80,000 |
| Pension death benefit | 15,000 |
| Total | $335,000 |

*Liabilities*

| | |
|---|---|
| Mortgage | $125,000 |
| Auto loan | 8,000 |
| Credit card balance | 2,000 |
| Total | $135,000 |

Estimated Social Security survivor benefits are $12,080 annually. Assume that the life insurance proceeds and liquid funds can earn 6 percent annually. Using the capital retention method, calculate the amount of additional life insurance that Althea should purchase to attain her financial goals.

# Chapter 16

# Types of Life Insurance and Annuities

> *"The life insurance needs of virtually any buyer can be met satisfactorily with just two policy forms—straight life and five-year renewable term."*
>
> *Joseph M. Belth*
> Life Insurance: A Consumer's Handbook

## Student Learning Objectives

After studying this chapter, you should be able to:

■ Describe the major characteristics of term insurance.

■ Explain the essential features of ordinary life insurance.

■ Explain the basic characteristics of variable life insurance, universal life insurance, and variable universal life insurance.

■ Describe the basic characteristics of current assumption whole life insurance.

■ Show how an annuity differs from life insurance.

■ Identify the major types of individual annuities that are sold today.

In a personal risk management program, life insurance is an important technique for alleviating the financial consequences of premature death. Life insurance death benefits can restore, either partly or completely, the family's share of the deceased breadwinner's earnings. There are numerous life insurance policies on the market today. Because these policies are complex, consumers can become confused about the best type of life insurance to buy.

This chapter discusses the major types of individual life insurance policies sold today. Four principal areas are emphasized. The chapter begins with a discussion of the traditional forms of life insurance—term, whole life, and endowment insurance.

Variations of whole life insurance contracts are also analyzed, including variable life insurance, universal life insurance, and variable universal life insurance. Life insurance policies that meet special needs or have unique features are also examined. Finally, the chapter concludes with a discussion of the major types of individual annuities sold today.

## TYPES OF LIFE INSURANCE

From a generic viewpoint, life insurance policies can be classified as either **term insurance** or **cash-value life insurance.** Term insurance provides temporary protection, while cash value life insurance has a savings component and builds cash values. Numerous variations and combinations of these two types of life insurance are available today.

## Term Insurance

Term insurance has several basic characteristics.[1] First, the period of protection is temporary, such as one, five, ten, or twenty years. Unless the policy is renewed, the protection expires at the end of the period.

Most term insurance policies are *renewable*, which means the policy can be renewed for additional periods without evidence of insurability. The premium is increased at each renewal and is based on the insured's attained age. The purpose of the renewal provision is to protect the insurability of the insured. However, this results in adverse selection against the insurer. Since premiums increase with age, insureds in good health tend to drop their insurance, while those in poor health will continue to renew, regardless of the premium increase. To minimize adverse selection, many insurers have an age limitation beyond which renewal is not allowed, such as age 70 or 80. Some insurers, however, permit term policies to be renewed to age 100.

Most term insurance policies are also *convertible*, which means the term policy can be exchanged for a cash value policy without evidence of insurability. There are two methods for converting a term policy. Under the *attained-age method*, the premium charged is based on the insured's attained age at the time of conversion. Under the *original-age method*, the premium charged is based on the insured's original age. Most insurers offering the original-age method require the conversion to take place within five years of the issue date of the term policy. The policyowner must also pay the difference between the premiums paid on the term policy and those that would have been paid on the new policy, with interest on the difference at a specified rate.[2] The purpose of the financial adjustment is to place the insurer in the same financial position it would have achieved if the policy had been issued at the original age. Because of the financial adjustment required, few term insurance policies are converted based on the original-age method.

Finally, term insurance policies have no cash value or savings element. Although some long-term policies develop a small reserve, it is used up by the contract expiration date.

**Types of Term Insurance**   A wide variety of term insurance products are sold today. They include the following:

- Yearly renewable term
- Five, ten, fifteen, or twenty-year term
- Term to age 65
- Decreasing term
- Reentry term

*Yearly renewable term insurance* is issued for a one-year period, and the policyowner can renew for successive one-year periods to some stated age without evidence of insurability. Premiums increase with age at each renewal date. Most yearly renewable term policies also allow the policyowner to convert to a cash value policy.

Term insurance can also be issued for *five, ten, fifteen, or twenty years, or for longer periods*. The premiums paid during the term period are level, but they increase when the policy is renewed.

A *term to age 65 policy* provides protection to age 65, at which time the policy expires. The policy can be converted to a permanent plan of insurance, but the decision to convert must be exercised before age 65. For example, the insurer may require conversion to a permanent policy before age 60. Since premiums are level, the policy develops a small reserve that is used up by the end of the period.

*Decreasing term insurance* is a form of term insurance where the face amount gradually declines each year. Although the face amount declines over time, the premium is level throughout the period. In some policies, the premiums are structured so that the policy is fully paid for a few years before the coverage expires. For example, a 20-year decreasing term policy may require premium payments for 17 years. This is to avoid paying a relatively large premium for only a small amount of insurance near the end of the term period. Finally, decreasing term insurance can be written as a separate policy, or it can be added as a rider to an existing contract.

*Reentry term* (also called revertible term) is another important term insurance product. Under a reentry term policy, renewal premiums are based on select (lower) mortality rates if the insured can periodically demonstrate acceptable evidence of insurability. Select mortality rates are based on the mortality experience of recently insured lives. However, to remain on the low-rate schedule, the insured must periodically show that he or she is in good health and is still insurable. The rates are substantially increased if the insured cannot provide satisfactory evidence of insurability.

**Uses of Term Insurance**    Term insurance is appropriate in three situations. *First, if the amount of income that can be spent on life insurance is limited, term insurance can be effectively used.* Because of mortality improvements and keen price competition, term insurance rates have declined sharply in recent years. Substantial amounts of life insurance can be purchased for a relatively modest annual premium outlay. Exhibit 16.1 shows the best buys for $500,000 of term life insurance for males as of January 1997 based on a survey of 140 life insurers. Because of a longer life expectancy, premiums for females would be substantially lower.

*Term insurance is also appropriate if the need for protection is temporary.* For example, decreasing term insurance can be effectively used to pay off the mortgage if the family head dies prematurely.

*Finally, term insurance can be used to guarantee future insurability.* A person may desire large amounts of permanent insurance, but may be financially unable to purchase the needed protection today. Inexpensive term insurance can be purchased, which can be converted later into a permanent insurance policy without evidence of insurability.

**Limitations of Term Insurance**    Term insurance has two major limitations. *First, term insurance premiums increase with age and eventually reach prohibitive levels.* Thus, term insurance is not suitable for individuals who need large amounts of life insurance beyond age 65 or 70. For example, based on the rates of one insurer, the premium for a $500,000 annually renewable term policy for a male nonsmoker, age 25, is $353. The premium increases to $2914 at age 65 and $9805 at age 75.

*Second, term insurance is inappropriate if you wish to save money for a specific need.* Term insurance policies do not accumulate cash values. Thus, if you wish to save money for a child's college education or accumulate a fund for retirement, term insurance is inappropriate.

Decreasing term insurance also has several disadvantages and should not be used to meet all of your insurance needs. If you become uninsurable, you must convert the remaining insurance to a permanent plan in order to freeze the insurance at its present level. If the policy is not converted, the insurance protection continues to decline even though you are uninsurable. Moreover, decreasing term insurance does not provide for changing needs, such as a birth or adoption of a child. Nor does it provide an effective hedge against inflation. Because of inflation, the amount of life insurance in most families should be periodically increased just to maintain the real purchasing power of the original policy.

Despite these limitations, term insurance can play an important role in the insurance programs of most people. However, buying term insurance is no simple task but requires consideration of several important factors (see Insight 16.1).

---

EXHIBIT 16.1

**Best Buys in Term Life Insurance, $500,000 (January 1997)**

| Age | Ten-year level | Fifteen-year level | Twenty-year level |
|-----|----------------|--------------------|--------------------|
| 35 | $   280 | $   320 | $     420 |
| 40 | $   375 | $   440 | $     565 |
| 45 | $   585 | $   700 | $     900 |
| 50 | $   910 | $1,115 | $  1,370 |
| 55 | $1,345 | $1,675 | $  1,800 |
| 60 | $2,185 | $2,709 | $  3,560 |
| 65 | $3,779 | $4,437 | $  6,235 |
| 70 | $6,470 | $9,330 | $11,304 |

NOTE: The premiums shown are guaranteed annual premiums for males, no tobacco, and are based on a market survey of 445 policies offered by 140 insurers as of December 31, 1996.

SOURCE: Quotesmith Corporation.

# INSIGHT 16.1

## Buying Term Insurance
## Is No Simple Task

Selecting a term policy "is relatively simple, but not as simple as it seems at first glance," says New York insurance consultant Glenn S. Daily.

Here's a guide to get the job done.

### How Long a Need?

Most people buy life insurance to provide for family needs if they were to die tomorrow. But if you don't die tomorrow, how long will coverage be needed? The answer determines the types of policies to consider.

To beef up coverage for only a year or two, look at "annual renewable term" or ART. Prices start low, but go up each year as the odds of imminent death increase.

If the need is longer—but has a predictable end, such as your child's college graduation—a cheaper choice may be a term policy whose annual cost will stay the same for five, 10, 15, even 20 years. To boost coverage until college graduation in 13 years, for instance, compare ART and a 15-year plan.

### Care to Convert?

If you may need coverage for more than 20 years, a term policy may not be the best choice. While most policies are guaranteed renewable for decades, they can become unaffordable in later life.

Consider cash-value policies, where the premiums initially are much higher but usually are designed to remain level for life. Or select a term policy now with the thought of "converting" to cash-value later.

Most term policies give holders the right to switch to a cash-value plan at the same insurer, regardless of health. But while many policies are convertible at least to age 60, some cheap term policies restrict conversion to the first several years.

Also consider how attractive a particular insurer's cash-value products might be. Atlanta financial adviser Elliot S. Lipson suggests looking at term policies from **USAA Life Insurance Co.,** San Antonio, which sells direct to consumers, and **Northwestern Mutual Life Insurance Co.,** a Milwaukee insurer that sells through agents. Both companies have highly regarded cash-value products and decent—although not bargain-basement—ART rates.

### Call for Quotes

A few phone calls is all it takes to get a batch of term-insurance proposals headed to your mailbox. Mr. Daily suggests calling the following four sources:

- Quotesmith Corp., a Darien, Ill., firm that maintains a database of term products and acts as an agent (800-556-9393). At no cost, Quotesmith will supply a long list of prices and rank policies by their guaranteed cost over periods of one, five, 10, 15 or 20 years.
- A local agent for Northwestern Mutual.
- USAA (800-531-8000).
- Wholesale Insurance Network, which represents several insurers other than USAA that sell direct to consumers (800-808-5810). The absence of agent commissions doesn't affect term prices much, but it can boost the investment return if you convert to a cash value plan.

### Rather Meet Face-to-Face?

Besides contacting a Northwestern representative, who sells primarily for that company, look for an agent who sells term from multiple insurers. Keep in mind, though, that agents usually make far more money selling a cash-value policy than a term one.

To locate an agent active in term, consider calling Quotesmith or Compulife Software Inc., Amherst, N.Y. (800-567-8376) for the names of local agents who use those companies' term-comparison software.

*Continued*

## Take a Level-Headed Look

Proceed with care if you have one or more proposals for level-premium coverage, the hot-selling plans that are the subject of the current fire-sale pitch. There's a big plus and a big negative for buyers to weigh.

Premiums on these plans are often guaranteed by the insurer for the entire initial period. That means you can lock in your cost if you've got a finite need. (On many ART plans, in contrast, charges are guaranteed for just one year and merely projected beyond that.)

But level-premium buyers take a big financial risk if they might want to continue coverage beyond the initial period. At that time, holders in good health can typically "re-enter" the coverage at a new set of favorable rates. Others who can't pass a physical exam can see their premiums soar several-fold.

Watch out for insurance proposals showing later-year premiums that assume you re-enter. Make sure you also see the much-higher costs you might pay if you don't re-enter. Mr. Lipson suggests consumers avoid the re-entry plans unless they are "absolutely certain" they won't need coverage beyond the initial period.

## Add It All Up

If you expect to need coverage for 10 years, add up the 10-year costs for various plans. For a more refined calculation, use a calculator or computer to figure the "present value" of those payments.

Also consider what the costs might be if you decide to keep the coverage longer. If the policy provides for re-entry, assume you don't make the cut.

## Prefer to be 'Preferred'

Insurers give their lowest rates to very healthy nonsmokers who qualify as "preferred." After asking a few questions about smoking and general health, many insurance sellers supply proposals that assume you make the grade.

As you narrow your choice of companies, ask the agent or insurer about the specific criteria for preferred status. Even if you're in great shape, for instance, you might be disqualified if a parent died of heart disease before age 60. You might ask to see some non-preferred "standard" rates.

Rates are significantly higher for smokers. Some companies divide smokers into preferred and standard groups; others don't.

## Other Options to Explore

Compare the proposals you've received with any supplemental group coverage offered by an employer. Also consider term plans offered to members of professional associations or other groups.

Such plans are occasionally a good deal, although often not. If a group plan has a single rate for everyone, that's probably a good deal for older workers and smokers but a lousy choice for young nonsmokers.

Another possibility for people in New York, Connecticut and Massachusetts: reasonably priced Savings Bank Life Insurance.

CHECK RATINGS: Picking a company with high ratings is slightly less important on term policies than on cash value, insurance specialists say. When insurers fail, policy cash values are sometimes tied up for years. But death benefits have usually been paid on time.

Still, there's no reason to look at low-rated insurers when lots of high-rated ones offer good rates.

Term buyers probably should rule out companies not rated single-A, single-A-plus or the top single-A-double-plus from rating service A.M. Best Co., Oldwick, N.J., says Chicago agent Ted S. Bernstein. Be extra picky if you think you might convert.

SOURCE: Adapted from Karen Damato, "Buying Term Life Insurance Is No Simple Task," *The Wall Street Journal*, March 31, 1995, pp. C1, C15.

## Whole Life Insurance

In contrast to term insurance, which provides short-term protection, **whole life insurance** *is a cash-value policy that provides lifetime protection.* From a historical or traditional perspective, the following two types of whole life insurance merit some discussion:

- Ordinary life insurance
- Limited-payment life insurance

**Ordinary Life Insurance**　**Ordinary life insurance** (also called straight life and continuous premium whole life) provides lifetime protection to age 100, and the death claim is a certainty. If the insured is still alive at age 100, the face amount of insurance is paid to the policyowner at that time.

In addition, premiums do not increase from year to year but remain level throughout the premium paying period. Under an ordinary life policy, the policyowner is overcharged for the insurance protection during the early years and undercharged during the later years when premiums are inadequate to pay death claims. As stated in Chapter 15, the excess premiums are reflected in a liability item known as a legal reserve. The legal reserve makes it possible to provide lifetime protection.

Ordinary life insurance also has an investment or saving element called a cash surrender value. The cash values are due to the overpayment of insurance premiums during the early years. As a result, the policyowner builds a cash equity in the policy. The policy may be surrendered for its cash value, or the cash value may be borrowed under a loan provision. The cash values are relatively small during the early years, but increase over time. For example, in many ordinary life policies, a $100,000 policy issued at age 20 would have at least $50,000 of cash value at age 65.

Finally, ordinary life insurance contains cash surrender or nonforfeiture options, dividend options (if participating), and settlement options that can be used to meet a wide variety of financial needs and objectives. These options are discussed in Chapter 17.

**Uses of Ordinary Life Insurance**　Ordinary life insurance is appropriate in two general situations: (1) when lifetime protection is needed, and (2) when additional savings are desired.

*An ordinary life policy is appropriate when lifetime protection is needed.* This means that the need for life insurance will continue beyond age 65 or 70. Some financial planners and consumer experts point out that the average person does not need large amounts of life insurance beyond age 65, since the need for life insurance declines with age. This view is an oversimplification of a complex issue and can be misleading. Some persons may need substantial amounts of life insurance beyond age 65. For example, an estate clearance fund is still needed at the older ages; there may be a sizable federal estate tax problem if the estate is large, so substantial amounts of life insurance may be needed for estate liquidity; a divorce settlement may require the purchase and maintenance of a life insurance policy on a divorced spouse, regardless of age; and the policyowner may wish to leave a sizable bequest to a surviving spouse, children, or charity, regardless of when death occurs. Since an ordinary life policy can provide lifetime protection, these objectives can be realized even though the insured dies at an advanced age.

*Ordinary life insurance can also be used to save money.* Some insureds wish to meet their protection and savings needs by an ordinary life policy. As stated earlier, ordinary life insurance builds cash values that can be obtained by surrendering the policy or by borrowing the cash value. Life insurance as a method of saving is discussed in Chapter 18.

**Limitation of Ordinary Life Insurance**　*The major limitation of ordinary life insurance is that some persons are still underinsured after the policy is purchased.* Because of the savings feature, some persons may voluntarily purchase or else be persuaded by a life insurance agent to purchase an ordinary life policy when term insurance would be a better choice. For example, assume that Mark, age 30, is a married graduate student with two dependents to support. He estimates that he can spend only $500 annually on life insurance. This premium would purchase about $56,000 of ordinary life insurance. The same premium would purchase about $500,000 of yearly renewable term insurance from many insurers. It is difficult to justify the purchase of an ordinary life insurance policy if it leaves the insured inadequately covered.

**Limited-payment Life Insurance**　A **limited-payment policy** is another type of traditional whole life insurance. The insurance is permanent, and the insured has lifetime protection. The premiums are level, but they are paid only for a certain period. For example, Shannon, age 35, may purchase a

20-year limited payment policy in the amount of $25,000. After 20 years, the policy is completely paid up, and no additional premiums are required. A paid-up policy should not be confused with one that *matures*. A policy matures when the face amount is paid as a death claim or as an endowment. A policy is *paid up* when no additional premium payments are required.

The most common limited-payment policies are for 10, 20, 25, or 30 years. A policy paid up at age 65 or 70 is another form of limited-payment insurance. An extreme form of limited-payment life insurance is **single-premium whole life insurance,** which provides lifetime protection with a single premium. Since the premiums under a limited-payment policy are higher than under an ordinary life policy, the cash values are also higher.

A limited-payment policy should be used with caution. It is extremely difficult for a person with a modest income to insure his or her life adequately with a limited-payment policy. Because of relatively high premiums, the amount of permanent life insurance that can be purchased is substantially lower than if an ordinary life policy were purchased. If permanent life insurance is desired, most persons will find that their need for permanent protection can be met more adequately by an ordinary life policy.

### Endowment Insurance

**Endowment insurance** is another traditional form of life insurance. An endowment policy pays the face amount of insurance if the insured dies within a specified period; if the insured survives to the end of the endowment period, the face amount is paid to the policyowner at that time. For example, if Stephanie, age 35, purchased a 20-year endowment policy and died any time within the 20-year period, the face amount would be paid to her beneficiary. If she survives to the end of the period, the face amount is paid to her.

At the present time, endowment insurance is relatively unimportant in terms of total life insurance in force. In 1993, endowment insurance accounted for less than one-half of one percent of the life insurance in force. Because of the Deficit Reduction Act of 1984 (DEFRA), most new endowment policies cannot meet the tax definition of life insurance. If this definition is not met, the investment income credited to the cash surrender value is subject to current taxation. Thus, adverse tax consequences have discouraged the purchase of new endowment policies, and most life insurers have discontinued the sale of new endowment policies. Even so, many older endowment policies are still in force, and some contracts are still used in tax-qualified retirement plans. Although endowment policies are no longer readily available in the United States, they remain popular in many foreign countries.

## VARIATIONS OF WHOLE LIFE INSURANCE

Traditional whole life policies have been criticized because the rate of return on the savings component is relatively low and is not disclosed to the policyowner. As a result, many policyowners have replaced their older life insurance policies with life insurance products that offer higher returns. Also, life insurers have experienced keen competition in recent years from mutual funds, commercial banks, and other financial institutions. To become more competitive and to overcome the criticisms of traditional cash value policies, insurers have developed a wide variety of whole life products that combine insurance protection with an investment element. Some important variations of whole life insurance include the following:

- Variable life
- Universal life
- Variable universal life
- Current assumption whole life
- Indeterminate-premium whole life insurance

### Variable Life Insurance

**Variable life insurance** *can be defined as a fixed premium policy in which the death benefit and cash surrender values vary according to the investment experience of a separate account maintained by the insurer.* The amount of life insurance and cash surrender value may increase or decrease with the investment experience of the separate account.

Although there are different policy designs, variable life policies have certain common features. *First, a variable life policy is a permanent whole life contract with a fixed premium.* The premium is level and is guaranteed not to increase.

*Second, the entire reserve is held in a separate account and is invested in equities or other investments.* The policyowner generally has the option of investing the cash values in a variety of investments, such as a common stock fund, bond fund, balanced fund, money market fund, or international fund. If the investment experience is favorable, the face amount of insurance is increased. If the investment experience is poor, the amount of insurance could be reduced, but it can never fall below the original face amount.

*Finally, cash surrender values are not guaranteed, and there are no minimum guaranteed cash values.* The actual cash values depend on the investment experience. Thus, although the risk of excessive mortality and expenses is borne by the insurer, the investment risk is retained entirely by the policyowner.

## Universal Life Insurance

Universal life insurance is another important variation of whole life insurance. A considerable amount of universal life is sold today as an investment rather than as protection.

**Basic Characteristics** **Universal life insurance** *can be defined as a flexible premium policy that provides lifetime protection under a contract that unbundles the protection and saving components.* The policyowner determines the amount and frequency of the premium payments, which can be monthly, quarterly, semiannually, annually, or a single payment. The premiums, less any explicit expense charges, are credited to a cash value account from which monthly mortality charges are deducted and to which monthly interest is credited based on current rates that may change over time. In addition, many universal life policies also have a monthly deduction for administrative expenses.

Universal life insurance has certain characteristics that distinguish it from traditional cash value contracts, including the following:[3]

- Unbundling of component parts
- Two forms of universal life
- Considerable flexibility
- Cash withdrawals permitted
- Favorable income-tax treatment

**Unbundling of Component Parts** A distinct characteristic of universal life insurance is the separation or unbundling of three components: protection component, saving component, and expense component.[4] The separation of these parts is reported

annually to the policyowner in a disclosure statement covering the previous year. The annual disclosure statement shows the premiums paid, death benefit, and cash surrender value. The statement also shows the mortality charge for the cost of insurance, expense charge for sales and administrative expenses, and interest credited to the cash value account.

1. *Mortality charge.* A monthly mortality charge is deducted from the cash-value account for the cost of the insurance protection. The cost of insurance is determined by multiplying the applicable monthly rate by the net amount at risk (difference between the current death benefit and cash value).

   The policy contains a table that shows the maximum rate per $1000 of insurance that the company can charge for the cost of the insurance protection. The maximum guaranteed rate is based either on the 1958 CSO mortality table or, for policies issued after 1989, on the newer 1980 CSO tables for male and female lives. These tables are conservative and overstate the actual death rates. Most insurers charge less than the contractually guaranteed maximum rate. However, the insurer has the right to increase the current mortality charge up to the maximum guaranteed rate stated in the policy.

   In addition, the monthly rate for the cost of insurance is usually lower if the insured is a nonsmoker and meets certain other requirements that relate to smoking habits.

2. *Expense charges.* When a life insurance policy is sold, the insurer incurs relatively high first-year acquisition expenses because of commissions, sales, and administrative expenses. Thus, the premium charged must include a loading for expenses.

   The expense charges in a universal life policy can be in the form of a (1) front-end load, (2) back-end load, or (3) both. If the policy has a *front-end load,* insurers typically deduct 5 to 10 percent of each premium for expenses. Some insurers also charge a first-year policy fee, such as $250. Many insurers also charge a monthly fee for administrative expenses, such as $4 or $5 monthly. There may be a special fee for each partial cash withdrawal, such as $25.

   If the policy has only a *back-end load,* the entire premium is credited to the cash-value account and earns interest at the quoted rate. In such a case, how does the insurer recover its acquisition and renewal expenses? There are at least three sources of income available for expenses. *First, the insurer can credit the cash-value account with a lower interest rate than is actually earned on the invested assets.* The difference is available for expenses.

*Second, the mortality charge may include a margin for expenses.* The actual mortality charge assessed against the policy may be increased, which provides additional income for expenses.

*Third, a back-end loaded policy typically has a relatively high back-end surrender charge that applies if the policy is surrendered during the early years.* The surrender charge can be as high as 150 percent of the first-year premium,[5] which means that the policyowner can lose a substantial amount of money if the policy is surrendered during the early years. The surrender charge is graded downward and usually disappears after a period of time, such as 10, 15, or 20 years.

3. *Interest rate.* The saving component or cash value is also shown separately. The interest earnings on the cash value depend on the interest rate. Two rates of interest are stated. The cash value is credited with a contractually *guaranteed minimum interest rate,* such as 4 or 4 1/2 percent. However, the cash value earns a much higher rate of return based on the *current interest rate* declared by the company. The current interest rate is not guaranteed for life but changes periodically depending on market conditions and company experience.

If the policyowner borrows the cash value, the amount borrowed is normally credited with a lower rate of interest. The cash value representing the amount borrowed is credited with either the guaranteed minimum interest rate or a rate 1 or 2 percent below the policy loan rate.

To illustrate the interaction of the three components, consider a simple example. Assume that Jacob, age 25, buys a universal life policy with a face amount of $100,000. The planned annual premium is $497, which can be changed. For sake of simplicity, assume that the mortality charge, expense charge, and the crediting of interest are made annually. (However, in practice, universal life policies have a monthly mortality and expense charge and monthly crediting of interest.)

Each premium is subject to a 5 percent expense charge. The policy also has a monthly administrative charge of $2.50. The policy provides for a maximum mortality charge, but the current mortality charge is only about two-thirds the maximum rate. The policy has a guaranteed interest rate of 4 percent and a current interest rate of 6 1/2 percent that is not guaranteed.

When Jacob pays the first premium of $497, there is an expense charge of approximately $25 (5 percent of $497). There is also an administrative charge of $30 ($2.50 monthly). The first-year mortality charge is $119 ($1.19 per $1000 of the specified $100,000 death benefit). The remaining $323 is credited with $21 of interest (6.5 percent on $323). Thus, the cash value account at the end of the first year is $344. This can be summarized as follows:

Annual premium ($497) − Expense and administrative charges ($55) − Mortality charge ($119) + Interest ($21) = Cash value account at end of year ($344)

However, if Jacob surrenders the policy at the end of the first year, the surrender value is zero because of the surrender charge. A declining surrender charge applies if the policy is terminated within 19 years after the issue date. Exhibit 16.2 shows in greater detail the cash value accumulation based on the guaranteed and current interest rates.

**Two Forms of Universal Life Insurance**
Another characteristic is that universal life insurance is available in two forms. This can be illustrated by Exhibit 16.3. *Option A pays a level death benefit during the early policy years.* As the cash value increases over time, the amount of pure insurance protection declines. However, the death benefit increases during the later years of the policy. If the death benefit did not increase, the policy would effectively become an endowment contract and would not meet the current definition of life insurance by the Internal Revenue Service. Thus, the policy would not qualify for favorable income tax treatment.

*Option B provides for an increasing death benefit.* The death benefit is equal to a specified amount of insurance plus the accumulated cash value. Thus, as the cash value increases over time, the death benefit

EXHIBIT 16.2

**$100,000 Universal Life Policy, Male Age 25, Nonsmoker, 6½ Percent Assumed Interest**

| | | End of Year | | | | | | |
| | | Guaranteed[a] | | | Assumed[b] | | | |
| Year | Planned annual premium | Death benefit | Cash value | Surrender value | Death benefit | Cash value | Surrender value | Age |
|---|---|---|---|---|---|---|---|---|
| 1 | $497.00 | $100,000 | $ 291 | $ 0 | $100,000 | $ 344 | $ 0 | 26 |
| 2 | 497.00 | 100,000 | 595 | 0 | 100,000 | 723 | 21 | 27 |
| 3 | 497.00 | 100,000 | 912 | 210 | 100,000 | 1,122 | 420 | 28 |
| 4 | 497.00 | 100,000 | 1,242 | 540 | 100,000 | 1,546 | 844 | 29 |
| 5 | 497.00 | 100,000 | 1,585 | 930 | 100,000 | 1,999 | 1,344 | 30 |
| 6 | 497.00 | 100,000 | 1,943 | 1,335 | 100,000 | 2,481 | 1,873 | 31 |
| 7 | 497.00 | 100,000 | 2,315 | 1,753 | 100,000 | 2,995 | 2,433 | 32 |
| 8 | 497.00 | 100,000 | 2,703 | 2,188 | 100,000 | 3,531 | 3,016 | 33 |
| 9 | 497.00 | 100,000 | 3,095 | 2,627 | 100,000 | 4,103 | 3,635 | 34 |
| 10 | 497.00 | 100,000 | 3,504 | 3,083 | 100,000 | 4,712 | 4,291 | 35 |
| 11 | 497.00 | 100,000 | 3,942 | 3,568 | 100,000 | 5,387 | 5,013 | 36 |
| 12 | 497.00 | 100,000 | 4,387 | 4,059 | 100,000 | 6,095 | 5,767 | 37 |
| 13 | 497.00 | 100,000 | 4,839 | 4,558 | 100,000 | 6,849 | 6,568 | 38 |
| 14 | 497.00 | 100,000 | 5,298 | 5,064 | 100,000 | 7,642 | 7,408 | 39 |
| 15 | 497.00 | 100,000 | 5,765 | 5,578 | 100,000 | 8,508 | 8,321 | 40 |
| 16 | 497.00 | 100,000 | 6,241 | 6,101 | 100,000 | 9,423 | 9,283 | 41 |
| 17 | 497.00 | 100,000 | 6,714 | 6,620 | 100,000 | 10,389 | 10,295 | 42 |
| 18 | 497.00 | 100,000 | 7,195 | 7,148 | 100,000 | 11,411 | 11,364 | 43 |
| 19 | 497.00 | 100,000 | 7,675 | 7,675 | 100,000 | 12,493 | 12,493 | 44 |
| 20 | 497.00 | 100,000 | 8,153 | 8,153 | 100,000 | 13,672 | 13,672 | 45 |
| 40 | 497.00 | 100,000 | 9,944 | 9,944 | 100,000 | 60,197 | 60,197 | 65 |

[a] The guaranteed values are based on a 4 percent guaranteed interest rate.

[b] The assumed values are based on an assumed interest rate of 6½ percent and are not guaranteed.

also increases. Option B is more expensive since the insurer must pay a higher death benefit.

**Considerable Flexibility**  Universal life insurance also has several desirable features that provide considerable flexibility. They include the following:

- Premiums can be increased or decreased, and the frequency of payments can be varied.
- Premium payments can be any amount as long as there is sufficient cash value to cover mortality costs and expenses.
- The death benefit can be increased or decreased. (Evidence of insurability is required to increase the amount of insurance.)
- The policy can be changed from a level death benefit to a death benefit equal to a specified face amount plus the policy cash value (with evidence of insurability).
- The policyowner can add to the cash value at any time, subject to maximum guideline limits that govern the relationship of the cash value to the death benefit.
- A partial cash withdrawal (not a loan) can be made without terminating the policy.
- Policy loans are also permitted at competitive interest rates.
- If the policy permits, additional insureds can be added to the policy.

EXHIBIT 16.3

**Universal Life Insurance Death Benefits**

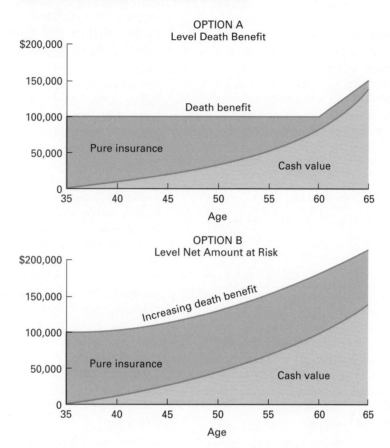

SOURCE: Kenneth Black, Jr. and Harold D. Skipper, Jr., *Life Insurance*, 12th ed., © 1994, p. 131. Reprinted by permission of Prentice-Hall, Inc., Englewood Cliffs, NJ.

**Cash Withdrawals Permitted**   Part or all of the cash value can also be withdrawn. Interest is not charged on the amounts withdrawn, but the death benefit is reduced by the amount of the withdrawal. Most insurers also charge a surrender fee for each cash withdrawal.

Policy loans are also permitted. As stated earlier, the cash value borrowed is usually credited with only the lower guaranteed rate of interest or is credited with a rate that is below the current rate paid on nonborrowed funds.

**Favorable Income-tax Treatment**   At present, universal life insurance enjoys the same favorable federal income-tax advantages as traditional cash-value policies. The death benefit paid to a named beneficiary is normally received income-tax free. Interest credited to the cash value is not taxable to the policyowner in the year credited.

**Limitations of Universal Life Insurance**   Although universal life insurance is superior to traditional cash-value policies in many respects, it has several limitations. Financial planners and consumer experts point out the following defects in present universal life insurance contracts.[6]

1. *Misleading rates of return.* Advertised rates of return on most universal life insurance contracts currently range from about 5 1/2 to 6 1/2 percent, depending on the insurer. *However, the rates advertised are gross rates of return and not net*

*rates.* The advertised rates do not reflect sales commissions, expenses, and the cost of the insurance protection. After these deductions, the effective yearly returns are substantially lower than the advertised rates and are often negative for several years after the policy is purchased. For example, a 1986 study by the National Insurance Consumer Organization of four universal life policies for a 40-year-old nonsmoking male, based on a $250,000 death benefit and $2,500 annual premium, showed the following:[7]

| Company | Quoted interest rate on saving portion | Net Rate of Return | | |
|---|---|---|---|---|
| | | 5 years | 10 years | 20 years |
| Jefferson Standard | 10.75% | −19.1% | 5.0% | 9.0% |
| Life of Virginia | 10.25 | 8.9 | 9.4 | 9.9 |
| Massachusetts Mutual | 9.70 | −11.7 | 2.9 | 7.5 |
| USAA | 10.25 | 6.8 | 8.6 | 9.8 |

The above calculations were based on the insurers' current interest rates and expense charges but assumed insurance rates for the least costly term policies available. As you can see, the advertised gross rates overstate the net rate of return on the saving component since they do not reflect charges for sales commissions, expenses, and the cost of insurance.

2. *Incomplete disclosure.* As stated earlier, the protection, saving, and expense components in a universal life policy are unbundled or separated. *However, this disclosure is incomplete and not rigorous, since the policyowner is not given information on how the expenses are allocated between the protection and saving components in the policy.* Professor Joseph Belth, a widely respected consumer insurance expert, maintains that the cost of the insurance protection and the yearly rate of return on the saving component cannot be accurately determined without making some assumptions concerning the allocation of expenses between the protection and saving components.[8] The early rates of return will vary widely depending on how the expenses are allocated between the protection and saving components. Professor Belth argues that the advertising of universal life insurance policies is often misleading and deceptive because the ads quote a high gross return on the saving component and may also quote a low cost for the protection component, but neither figure includes an allocation of the expense charges. Thus, he argues that net rates of return rather than gross rates should be disclosed to the policyowners.

3. *Decline in interest rates.* Many earlier sales presentations showed sizable cash values at some future date based on relatively high interest rates. The sales illustrations also showed that premium payments would vanish after a relatively short period, such as 10 years. *However, interest rates have declined sharply in recent years. As a result, the cash value and premium-payment projections based on higher interest rates are misleading and invalid.* Because of the sharp decline in interest rates, many policyowners have become disenchanted with universal life insurance and have surrendered or lapsed their policies. In particular, policyowners who expected premium payments to vanish after a relatively short period are angry because the premiums have not vanished according to the schedule furnished them when the policy was first purchased.

In addition, the sales illustrations of many companies are often based on dubious assumptions that are designed to enhance the cash value. Some common enhancements include the following:[9]

- *Persistency bonus.* Some policies pay additional interest at the end of 10, 15, or 20 years, which inflates the cash surrender value. You will not receive the bonus if the policy is lapsed or surrendered before the bonus date.
- *Lapse-supported pricing.* This enhancement is based on the assumption that a certain number of policyowners will lapse their policies, and their loss will be your gain. A **lapsed policy** is one that is not in force because premiums have not been paid. However, if the assumption concerning lapsed policies is wrong, your return will be less than illustrated.
- *Expected improvements in mortality.* If the mortality improvement is not realized, your return will be less than illustrated.

To deal with the above deceptive sales illustrations, the National Association of Insurance Commissioner (NAIC) has drafted a Life Insurance Policy Illustration Model Regulation, which will apply to all policies sold after January 1, 1997, or later, if changed by the adopting state. If adopted by the states, insurers would be prohibited from using mortality gains and lapse-support pricing in their sales illustrations. The NAIC model law will be discussed in greater detail in Chapter 18.

4. *Right to increase mortality charge.* Another limitation is that the insurer has the right to increase the current mortality charge up to the maximum limit. Thus, other expenses can be hidden in the mortality charge. If the insurer's expenses increase, the mortality charge could be increased to recoup these costs. The increase may not be noticed or questioned since the insured may believe that the increase is justified because he or she is getting older.[10]

5. *Lack of firm commitment to pay premiums.* Another limitation is that the policyowner often lacks a firm commitment to pay premiums. As a result, the policy may lapse because of nonpayment of premiums. As stated earlier, under a universal life policy, premiums can be reduced or skipped. However, at some point, money may have to be added to the account, or the policy may lapse. Many insurers have experienced a substantial increase in lapsed universal life policies, which is partly due to the lack of a firm commitment by policyowners to make fixed and regular premium payments.

## Variable Universal Life Insurance

Variable universal life insurance (also called universal life II and flexible-premium variable life insurance) is another interest-sensitive product. This policy is similar to the universal life policy but with two major exceptions:

- The policyowner has a variety of investment options for investment of the cash values.
- There is no minimum guaranteed rate of interest.

A variable universal life policy allows the policyowner to invest the cash values in a wide variety of investments. For example, the insurer may have an aggressive stock fund, bond fund, balanced fund, global fund, real estate fund, and money market fund. Depending on the policyowner's investment goals and objectives and tolerance for risk, the funds can be invested accordingly.

*In addition, a variable universal life policy has no minimum guaranteed rate of interest, and the principal is not guaranteed.* If the investment experience is poor, cash values can decline to zero. Thus, the investment risk falls entirely on the policyowner. There is wide variation in the investment returns, depending on how the funds are invested. For this reason, financial planners recommend caution in the purchase of a variable universal life policy.

## Current Assumption Whole Life Insurance

**Current assumption whole life insurance** (also called interest-sensitive whole life) is a nonparticipating whole life policy in which the cash values are based on the insurer's current mortality, investment, and expense experience. A nonparticipating policy is a policy that does not pay dividends.

**Common Features** Although current assumption whole life products vary among insurers, there are some common features, summarized as follows:[11]

1. *An accumulation account is used to reflect the value of the account.* The accumulation account is credited with the premiums paid less expenses and mortality charges plus interest based on current rates.

2. *If the policy is surrendered, a surrender charge is deducted from accumulation account.* A surrender charge that declines over time, such as 10 to 20 years, is deducted from the accumulation account to determine the net cash surrender value.

3. *A guaranteed interest rate and current interest rate are used to determine cash values.* The minimum cash values are based on the guaranteed interest rate, such as 4 or 4 1/2 percent. However, the accumulation account is credited with a higher interest rate based on current market conditions and company experience.

4. *A fixed death benefit and maximum premium level at the time of issue are stated in the policy.* (However, under the low-premium version discussed next, both are subject to change.)

In addition to the preceding characteristics, current assumption whole life products generally can be classified into two categories: (1) low-premium products, and (2) high-premium products.

**Low-Premium Products** Under the low-premium version, the initial premium is substantially lower than the premium paid for a regular, nonparticipating whole life policy. The low premium is initially guaranteed only for a certain period, such as two years. However, after the initial guaranteed period expires, a *redetermination provision* allows the insurer to recalculate the premium based on the same or different actuarial assumptions with respect to mortality, interest, and expenses (hence, the name "current assumption whole life"). However, if the new premium is higher than the initial premium, the policyowner generally has the option of paying the higher premium and maintaining the same death benefit. Alternatively, the policyowner can continue to pay the lower premium, but the death benefit is reduced.

**High-Premium Products** Although premiums are higher under the second category, these policies typically contain a *vanishing premium provision* in which the premiums vanish after a certain time period, such as ten years. The premium vanishes when the accumulation account exceeds the net single premium needed to pay up the contract based on current interest and mortality costs.[12] *However, the policy remains paid up only if current interest and mortality experience remain unchanged or are more favorable than initially assumed.* If the accumulation account falls below the minimum cash surrender value, additional premiums are required, or the standard nonforfeiture options apply.

### Indeterminate-Premium Whole Life Insurance

An **indeterminate-premium whole life policy** *is a generic name for a nonparticipating policy that permits the insurer to adjust premiums based on anticipated future experience.* The maximum premium that can be charged is stated in the policy. The actual premium paid when the policy is issued is considerably lower and may be guaranteed for some initial period, such as two to three years. The intent is to have the actual premium paid reflect current market conditions. After the initial guaranteed period expires, the insurer can increase premiums up to the maximum limit if future anticipated experience with respect to mortality, investments, and expenses is expected to worsen. However, the premiums may not change if future experience is expected to be similar to past

experience. Conversely, if future experience is expected to improve, then the insurer can further reduce the premiums if it desires to do so.

Exhibit 16.4 summarizes the basic characteristics of the major forms of life insurance. This chart helps to clarify the major types of life insurance and how they differ.

## OTHER TYPES OF LIFE INSURANCE

A wide variety of additional life insurance products are sold today. Some policies are designed to meet special needs or have unique features. Others combine term insurance and cash-value life insurance to meet these needs.

### Modified Life Insurance

A **modified life policy** is a whole life policy in which premiums are lower for the first three to five years and are higher thereafter. The initial premium is slightly higher than for term insurance, but considerably lower than an ordinary life policy issued at the same age.

There are several variations of the modified life policy. Under one version, the premium increases only once at the end of three or five years, and a dividend is paid that can be used to offset most or all of the premium increase. Under another version, the premiums gradually increase each year for five years and remain level thereafter. Finally, term insurance can be used for the first three to five years, which automatically converts into an ordinary life policy at a slightly higher premium than a regular ordinary life policy issued at the same age.

The major advantage of a modified life policy is that insureds can purchase permanent insurance immediately even though they cannot afford the higher premiums for a regular policy. Modified life insurance is particularly attractive to persons who expect that their incomes will increase in the future and that higher premiums will not be financially burdensome.

### Family Income Policy

The **family income policy** is a combination of decreasing term and whole life insurance. It pays a monthly income of $10 for each $1000 of life

**EXHIBIT 16.4**

**Life Insurance Comparison Chart**

|  | Term | Ordinary life | Variable life | Universal life | Variable universal life | Current assumption whole life |
|---|---|---|---|---|---|---|
| Death benefit | Level or decreasing | Fixed level | Guaranteed minimum death benefit + increases from investments | Either level or increasing amount | Either level or increasing amount | Fixed level |
| Cash value | None | Guaranteed cash values | Depends on investment performance (not guaranteed) | Guaranteed minimum cash value + excess interest | Depends on investment performance (not guaranteed) | Guaranteed minimum cash value + excess interest |
| Premium | Increases at each renewal | Level premiums | Fixed level | Flexible premiums | Flexible premiums | May vary based on experience; guaranteed maximum premium |
| Policy loans | No | Yes | Yes | Yes Loans affect interest rate credited to cash value | Yes | Yes |
| Partial withdrawal of cash value | No | No | No | Yes | Yes | Yes |
| Surrender charge | No | No | Yes | Yes | Yes | Yes |

SOURCE: Adapted from Glenn L. Wood, Claude C. Lilly III, Donald S. Malecki, Edward E. Graves, and Jerry S. Rosenbloom, *Personal Risk Management and Insurance*, 4th ed., vol. 2 (Malvern, Pa.: American Institute for Property and Liability Underwriters, 1989), p. 259. Copyright © 1989 by the American Institute for Property and Liability Underwriters. Reprinted by permission of the American Institute for Property and Liability Underwriters.

insurance if the insured dies within the family income period. The family income period is the period during which income payments are made. The monthly income is paid to the end of the family income period, at which time the face amount of insurance is paid.

For example, assume that a $50,000, 20-year family income policy is purchased. If the insured dies five years after the policy is issued, the beneficiary receives $500 monthly for the next 15 years, at which time the face amount of $50,000 is paid. If the insured dies after the family income period expires, only the face amount of insurance is paid.

## Preferred Risks

Many life insurers sell policies at lower rates to individuals known as **preferred risks.** These are individuals whose mortality experience is expected to be lower than average. The policy is carefully underwritten and is sold only to individuals whose health history, weight, occupation, and habits indicate more favorable mortality than the average. The insurer may also require the purchase of a minimum amount of insurance, such as $100,000. If an individual qualifies for a preferred rate, substantial savings are possible.

A discount for nonsmokers is a current example of a preferred risk policy. Most insurers offer substantially lower rates to nonsmokers in recognition of the more favorable mortality that can be expected of this group.

## Second-to-Die Life Insurance

**Second-to-die life insurance** (also called survivorship life) is a form of life insurance that insures two or more lives and pays the death benefit upon the death of the second or last insured. The insurance usually is whole life, but it can be term. Since the death proceeds are paid only upon the death of the second or last insured, the premiums are substantially lower than if two individual policies were issued.

Second-to-die life insurance is widely used at the present time in estate planning. As a result of an unlimited marital deduction, the deceased's entire estate can be left to a surviving spouse free of any federal estate tax. However, when the surviving spouse dies, a sizable federal estate tax may be payable. A second-to-die policy would provide the cash to pay the estate taxes.

## "Vanishing-Premium Policy"

A **"vanishing-premium policy"** is a form of participating whole life insurance in which the premiums are paid by policyowner dividends after a relatively short period, such as nine or ten years. Under such a policy, the dividends are accumulated at interest or used to purchase paid-up additions to the policy. After a number of years, the accumulated dividends plus future dividends are used to pay future premiums. Alternatively, the cash value of the paid-up additions can be periodically liquidated as needed and, along with future dividends, used to pay all future premiums. As a result, the premium "vanishes" at the end of some time period.

It should be noted, however, that dividends are not guaranteed. The actual dividends paid may fall short of projected dividends and thus may be inadequate for covering all premiums beyond the projected vanishing date. In recent years, numerous life insurers have reduced their dividends because of falling interest rates. As a result, premiums under many policies have not vanished according to the original schedule, and policyowners have been forced to pay premiums out of pocket beyond the projected vanishing date (see Insight 16.2).

Because policyowners have been misled, the National Association of Insurance Commissioners (NAIC) has drafted a new model law on sales presentations. If adopted by the states, the model law would prohibit insurers from using the term "vanishing premium" in their sales presentations.

## Juvenile Insurance

**Juvenile insurance** refers to life insurance purchased by a parent or adult on the lives of children under a certain age, such as age 14 or 15. Insurers generally require the child to be at least one month old before he or she can be insured. Some insurers, however, will insure a child as young as one day old.

*The major disadvantage in insuring children is that the family head may be inadequately insured.* Scarce premium dollars that could be used to increase the life insurance on the family head are instead diverted to the children.

Other arguments for life insurance on children are not convincing. One argument is that insurance on children is less expensive because it is purchased at a younger age. This argument is deceptive.

---

## INSIGHT 16.2

### The Rip-Off: "Vanishing Premium" Life

For over a decade life insurers have been using a gimmick called a vanishing premium to sell some whole life policies. The pitch: Instead of buying cheap term insurance that pays off only when you die, or a traditional whole life policy that requires decades of premium payments, you invest two, three, even five times the annual premium for term insurance in a whole life policy that will be paid off in only eight to 10 years. By that time, the agent may explain, your policy will be generating enough in dividends to pay the premiums on its own. You still have life insurance but no pesky premium bills. Meanwhile, your cash value grows and grows, making the policy an ideal way to save for financial goals, such as retirement or college tuition.

Unfortunately, the only people whose financial goals are well served by vanishing premium policies are the insurers and their sales agents. The agent, for example, pockets a commission equal to 55% or more of the first-year premium plus another 5% to 8% of subsequent annual premiums. *What's worse, the premiums may never "vanish." That's largely because the*

*rosy investment returns rarely come to pass.* Indeed, dividends may be so low that policyholders will still be paying premiums out of their own pockets years later. Buyers who catch on and drop their policies within three to four years have typically wasted about $2,000 in premiums.

THE REMEDY: Never buy a whole life policy if the agent can't—or won't—explain the assumptions behind any projected investment returns. And think twice before buying insurance as an "investment" to begin with. Instead, stick to mutual funds and other vehicles in which expenses are lower and reasonably visible.

If you already own a vanishing-premium policy and wonder whether it's worth keeping, consider having it independently evaluated. For $40, the Consumer Federation of America (202-387-6121) will analyze the fine print and tell you if the policy lives up to the agent's promises.

SOURCE: Adapted from Lani Luciano, "The Rip-Off: 'Vanishing Premium' Life, Typical Tab: $2,000," *Money*, Vol. 24, No. 8 (August 1995), p. 144.

---

Although insurance premiums on children are lower, they are paid over a much longer time period. Premiums at the older ages are higher, but they are paid for shorter periods of time. Moreover, when present values are taken into account, the child's policy can be more expensive. One study indicated that the present value of the premiums for a $20,000 life-paid-up-at-age-65 policy issued by one insurer on a child at age 15 is $5584 at a 4 percent discount rate. However, the present value of the premiums for the same type of policy issued by the same insurer at age 35 is only $3905.[13] In short, a juvenile insurance policy may be no bargain when it comes to cost.

Another argument is that life insurance should be purchased to guarantee the future insurability of the children. This argument has slightly greater validity, but only if the husband and wife are adequately insured. Unfortunately, a guaranteed insurability option cannot be purchased separately but must be added to the permanent life insurance policy. Even if future insurability cannot be guaranteed, the odds are

that the children will still be able to purchase insurance in the future. More than 90 percent of all new policies sold are issued at standard rates. However, despite the disadvantages of insuring children, juvenile insurance is widely sold at the present time (see Insight 16.3).

### Savings Bank Life Insurance

**Savings bank life insurance** (SBLI) is a type of life insurance sold in mutual savings banks of three states—Massachusetts, New York, and Connecticut. To be eligible, a person must either reside or regularly work in the state where the insurance is sold. The insurance is sold over the counter, so soliciting agents are not used. The objective is to avoid the substantial acquisition expenses incurred by commercial insurers when life insurance is initially sold.

The amount of savings bank life insurance is limited by law. In Connecticut, the maximum limit

# INSIGHT 16.3

## 'Kiddie' Life Insurance
## Stirs Skepticism

So-called juvenile policies are a huge business for the insurance industry. One in every four cash-value insurance policies sold each year covers the lives of children under age 18, according to Limra International, a Windsor, Conn. life-insurance research firm.

[T]he decision to insure a child's life is controversial. If life insurance is meant to be used to protect one's dependents, why should a parent need or want to own coverage on a child?

Insurance companies say there are many reasons why someone should consider buying a juvenile policy.

For one thing, children's policies cost less than comparable coverage on adults. And getting coverage for children guarantees they will always have some life insurance, even if they later become uninsurable.

"Most adults will need life insurance at some point in their lives," says Hughes "Pete" Perry Jr., assistant vice president for marketing support at Mutual Life Insurance Co. of New York. "What better time to buy it than when a child is young and the cost of insurance is low?"

Then there's the investment feature of cash-value policies, a deal-clincher for many parents and grandparents. With a typical "variable universal life" policy, for example, a portion of the premiums policy-holders pay is deposited in a separate tax-deferred portfolio of stocks, bonds and money-market instruments. The child can borrow part of the policy's cash value and use it toward college tuition bills or other big-ticket expenses.

This feature makes a juvenile policy an "extremely attractive gift," Mr. Perry says. "It can give a child financial freedom during adulthood."

Yet critics of juvenile coverage argue that it is excessive and expensive.

"Life insurance should be used only to cover true economic risk," says Bert Whitehead Sr., a financial planner at Cambridge Associates in Franklin, Mich. "If you'd be better off financially if someone were dead, then you own too much."

They also point out that there are less costly ways to achieve the same results:

**Invest elsewhere.** Life insurance comes with extra costs that lower returns. For instance, part of a policy's premiums pay an agent's commissions, and ongoing fees are deducted from its cash value or premiums to cover the cost of the insurance protection. As a result, a low-cost mutual fund is often a better investment over a period of many years.

"You're dramatically better off investing for investment's sake," concludes Ray Martin, vice president of client relations for Ayco Co., a financial planning firm in Albany, N.Y.

He says a $150,000 variable universal policy purchased for a one-year-old could amass a cash value of $13,200 by the time the infant reaches age 18. That assumes annual premiums are $500 and the policy's investment accounts earn an average of 10% a year after expenses. But parents who invested $500 a year in a typical stock-market index fund earning 10% would end up with roughly $20,000 after paying capital gains taxes of 28%, Mr. Martin says.

By choosing investments that pay out little or no taxable income, parents can imitate the tax-deferred growth of an insurance policy's cash value, Mr. Martin says. He suggests growth-stock mutual funds that pay little or no dividends.

**Self-insure.** Parents who dutifully set aside some money in an account for their children's future shouldn't need the financial protection a juvenile insurance policy offers, says Joseph Belth, a former insurance professor at Indiana University in Bloomington, Ind.

[T]he expenses that arise from a child's death are limited and can be offset with any unneeded balance in a college education account.

**Explore riders.** Parents who buy a life insurance policy on themselves often have the option of adding a "rider" to cover children or a spouse.

A typical children's rider offering $10,000 coverage on all of a parent's dependent kids should add no more than $100 to his or her annual premiums, Louisville, Ky., financial planner David Bohannon says.

SOURCE: Adapted from Vanessa O'Connell, "Kiddie Life Insurance Stirs Skepticism," *The Wall Street Journal,* January 29, 1996, pp. C1, C20.

is $100,000 for an individual policy and $200,000 for group term coverage if the individual has an account in a savings bank in the state. In Massachusetts, the maximum limit on individual coverage is $500,000 ($350,000 for group term insurance). In New York, the maximum limit on individual coverage is $50,000 ($500,000 for group term insurance).[14]

Savings bank life insurance is low-cost life insurance. Thus, there are some substantial price advantages for thrifty insurance consumers who reside or work in the three states where the insurance is sold. Based on the interest-adjusted cost method, (discussed in Chapter 18), the net cost of the life insurance is often lower than policies sold by commercial life insurers. This is partly due to the method of selling. The insurance is sold only to walk-ins, so there are no overhead expenses for a field force of agents.

## Industrial Life Insurance

**Industrial life insurance** is a class of insurance in which the policy face amount is relatively small, and the premiums are collected by an insurance agent (called a **debit agent**) at the policyowner's home. More than nine out of ten policies are cash-value policies.

Industrial life insurance rates are substantially higher than rates charged for ordinary insurance, for three reasons. First, mortality costs are relatively higher since the policies are typically written on low-income persons without a medical examination. Second, selling and administrative costs are relatively higher because the premiums are collected at the policyowners' homes. Third, lapse rates are much higher than other forms of life insurance.

Finally, industrial life insurance and monthly debit ordinary insurance are also known as **home service life insurance.** Both types of insurance are serviced by agents who collect the premiums at the policyowners' homes. The amount of life insurance per policy generally ranges from $5000 to $25,000. Home service life insurance is relatively unimportant and accounted for only 0.2 percent of all legal reserve life insurance in force at the end of 1995.[15]

## Group Life Insurance

**Group life insurance** is important in that it provides life insurance on a number of persons in a single master contract. Physical examinations are not required, and certificates of insurance are issued to members of the group as evidence of insurance.

Group life insurance is important in terms of total life insurance in force. In 1995, group life insurance accounted for 38 percent of all life insurance in force in the United States.[16] It is an important employee benefit provided by employers, and will be discussed in greater detail in Chapter 21.

## ANNUITIES

Annuities are designed to provide retirement income to individuals. They can greatly enhance the financial security of individuals during their old age.

### Annuity Concept

An **annuity** *can be defined as a periodic payment to an individual that continues for a fixed period or for the duration of a designated life or lives.* The person who receives the periodic payments or whose life governs the duration of payment is known as the **annuitant.**

An annuity is the opposite of life insurance. Life insurance creates an immediate estate and provides protection against dying too soon before financial assets can be accumulated. *The fundamental purpose of a life annuity is to provide a lifetime income that cannot be outlived to an individual.* An annuity is designed to liquidate a principal sum and provides protection against living too long. It provides protection against the loss of income because of excessive longevity and the exhaustion of one's savings.

Annuities are possible because the risk of excessive longevity is pooled by the group. Individuals acting alone cannot be certain that their savings will be sufficient during retirement. Some persons may die early before exhausting their savings, while others will still be alive after their principal is exhausted. These persons can come together as a group, deposit their savings with an insurance company, and receive a guarantee of a lifetime income. Although the insurer cannot predict how long an individual member of the group will live, the insurer can determine the approximate number of annuitants who will be alive at the end of each successive year. Thus, the insurer can calculate the amount that each person must contribute to the pool. Interest can be earned on the funds before they are paid out. Also, some annuitants will die early, and their unliquidated principal can be used to provide additional payments to those annuitants who survive beyond their life expectancy. Thus, the annuity payments consist of three sources: premium payments, interest earnings, and the unliquidated principal of annuitants who die early. By pooling the risk of excessive longevity, annuitants can be provided with a periodic income that they cannot outlive.

Annuitants tend to be healthy individuals who live longer than most persons. In recognition of their increased life expectancy, special annuity tables are used to compute the premium payments.

## Types of Annuities

A wide variety of annuities are presently sold by insurers. For the sake of convenience, the different types of annuities can be classified as follows:

1. Time when payments begin
   - Immediate annuity
   - Deferred annuity
2. Nature of the insurer's obligation
   - Life annuity (no refund)
   - Life annuity with guaranteed payments
   - Installment or cash refund annuity
   - Joint-and-survivor annuity
3. Fixed or variable benefits
   - Fixed annuity
   - Variable annuity

**Time When Payments Begin**    Annuities can be classified according to the time the payments begin. The annuity payments can be made monthly, quarterly, semiannually, or annually. The payments can start immediately or be deferred until some later date.

1. *Immediate annuity.* An **immediate annuity** *is one where the first payment is due one payment interval from the date of purchase.* If the income is paid monthly, the first payment starts one month from the purchase date, or one year from the purchase date if the income is paid annually.

   Immediate annuities are typically purchased in a lump sum by people near retirement. Financial planners recommend that consumers shop around for an immediate annuity because of the wide variation in monthly payments.

2. *Deferred annuity.* A **deferred annuity** *provides an income at some future date.* Several types of deferred annuities are sold today. A popular form of deferred annuity is the *retirement annuity,* which is essentially a plan for accumulating a sum of money for retirement purposes. The premiums are accumulated at interest (less expenses) prior to retirement. At the maturity date, the annuitant can elect to have the accumulated sum applied under one of the annuity options stated in the contract. Typical options include a life annuity with no refund feature; life income with five, ten, fifteen, or twenty years of guaranteed payments; installment refund; and cash refund options. The cash option is also available, by which cash is elected rather than the annuity. But this leads to adverse selection since those in poor health will elect to take the cash rather than the annuity.

   If the annuitant dies during the period prior to retirement (called the *accumulation period*), the death benefit paid is typically equal to the sum of the premiums paid, or the cash value, if higher. If the annuitant dies during the liquidation period, any death benefit paid will depend on the annuity option selected. For example, if a life annuity option is selected, nothing is paid. If a life income with 10 years of guaranteed payments is selected, payments continue to the beneficiary if fewer than 10 years of payments have been received.

   The **retirement income policy** (often called a retirement endowment) is similar to the retirement annuity discussed earlier, except that it provides a substantial amount of life insurance equal to $1000 for each $10 of monthly retirement income, or the cash value, if higher. For example, a $500 monthly retirement income policy would initially provide $50,000 of life insurance. The cash value in the policy will eventually exceed the face amount of insurance, and it then becomes the death benefit paid prior to retirement. Any death benefit after retirement will depend on the annuity option selected by the annuity owner.

   A deferred annuity can be purchased with a lump sum, or the contract may permit flexible premiums and installment payments. A deferred annuity purchased with a lump sum is called a **single-premium deferred annuity.** Because of relatively high investment returns and tax-free buildup during the accumulation period, single-premium deferred annuities have been increasingly popular with investors in recent years.

An equity-indexed annuity is a newer type of single-premium deferred annuity that is rapidly growing in importance. An **equity-indexed annuity** can be defined as a single-premium fixed annuity that offers the opportunity for growth based on the performance of the stock market. Interest is credited to the annuity based on the growth in the S & P 500 stock index. However, the principal is guaranteed against loss if the annuity is held for a specified term, such as seven years.

A deferred annuity can also be purchased with flexible premiums. A **flexible-premium annuity** is a contract that permits the annuity owner to vary the premium deposits. There is no requirement that a specified amount must be deposited each year. Thus, the annuity owner has considerable flexibility in the payment of premiums. The amount of retirement income will depend on the accumulated sum in the annuity at retirement.

**Nature of the Insurer's Obligation**    Annuities can also be classified in terms of the insurer's obligation under the contract. Payments may be made only during the lifetime of the annuitant, or the annuity may guarantee a certain number of payments. In addition, the annuity payments may be based on two or more lives.

A **life annuity** (no refund) provides a lifetime income to the annuitant only while he or she is alive. No further payments are made after the annuitant dies. A life annuity with no refund feature pays the highest amount of lifetime income for each dollar spent. It is suitable for a person who needs maximum lifetime income and has no dependents or has provided for them through other means.

A **life annuity with guaranteed payments** is one that pays a life income to the annuitant with a certain number of guaranteed payments. If the annuitant dies before receiving the guaranteed number of payments, the remaining payments are paid to a designated beneficiary. This option can be used by someone who needs lifetime income and also wishes to provide income to the beneficiary in the event of an early death. Due to the guaranteed payments, the income paid is relatively less than the income paid by a pure life annuity.

An **installment refund annuity** pays the annuitant a lifetime income. However, if the annuitant dies before receiving total payments equal to the purchase price of the annuity, the income payments continue to the beneficiary until they equal the purchase price. Another version of this option is the **cash refund annuity.** If the annuitant dies before receiving total payments equal to the purchase price of the annuity, the balance is paid in one lump sum to the beneficiary.

A **joint-and-survivor annuity** is based on the lives of two or more annuitants, such as a husband and wife or brother and sister. The annuity income is paid until the death of the last annuitant. Some contracts pay the full amount of original income until the last survivor dies. Other plans pay only two-thirds or one-half of the original income when the first annuitant dies.

**Fixed or Variable Benefits**    Annuities can also be classified in terms of fixed or variable benefits. Under a **fixed annuity,** the periodic payment is a guaranteed fixed amount; during the accumulation period, the premiums are invested in bonds, mortgages, and other fixed income securities with a guaranteed return.

In contrast, a **variable annuity** is an annuity that provides a lifetime income, but the periodic income payments will vary depending on the level of common stock prices. *The fundamental purpose of a variable annuity is to provide an inflation hedge by maintaining the real purchasing power of the periodic payments during retirement.* It is based on the assumption that a long-run correlation exists between the cost of living and common stock prices.

**Basic Characteristics of a Variable Annuity** Premiums are invested in a portfolio of common stocks or other investments that presumably will increase in value during a period of inflation. The premiums are used to purchase **accumulation units** during the period prior to retirement, and the value of each accumulation unit varies depending on common stock prices. For example, assume that the accumulation unit is initially valued at $1, and the annuitant makes a monthly premium payment of

**E XHIBIT 16.5**

## Annuity Funds' Average Performance and Fees
### Returns for periods ended March 31, 1997

| Type of fund | Average fund expense | Average total expense | 1st-Qtr total return | One-year total return | Three-year annualized return | Five-year annualized return |
|---|---|---|---|---|---|---|
| Aggressive Growth | 0.95% | 2.21% | −7.78% | −0.23% | 12.35% | 12.13% |
| Balanced | 0.84 | 2.12 | −0.41 | 9.42 | 10.58 | 9.21 |
| Corporate Bond | 0.69 | 1.94 | −0.72 | 4.20 | 5.39 | 5.89 |
| Government Bond General | 0.64 | 1.90 | −0.95 | 3.01 | 4.80 | 5.54 |
| Growth | 0.86 | 2.12 | −2.41 | 8.12 | 14.68 | 11.97 |
| Growth & Income | 0.67 | 1.94 | 1.39 | 14.48 | 18.13 | 14.52 |
| High-Yield Bond | 0.80 | 2.09 | 0.25 | 10.09 | 8.92 | 10.21 |
| International Bond | 1.12 | 2.42 | −2.69 | 5.60 | 4.92 | 4.88 |
| International Stock | 1.15 | 2.42 | 1.78 | 9.92 | 8.54 | 10.02 |
| Money Market | 0.52 | 1.79 | 0.85 | 3.69 | 3.73 | 2.97 |
| Specialty Fund | 1.05 | 2.34 | −2.07 | 11.66 | 9.79 | 10.55 |
| U.S. Diversified Equity Average | 0.82 | 2.09 | −2.47 | 8.25 | 15.34 | 12.80 |
| Fixed-Income Average | 0.74 | 2.00 | −1.08 | 4.08 | 5.19 | 5.70 |

SOURCE: Morningstar Inc.

SOURCE: Excerpted from Bridget O'Brien, "Despite Annuities' High Expenses, Low-Fee Choices Aren't Pursued," *The Wall Street Journal*, April 4, 1997, p. R10.

$100. During the first month, 100 accumulation units are purchased.[17] If common stock prices increase during the second month, and the accumulation unit rises to $1.10, about 91 accumulation units can be purchased. If the stock market declines during the third month, and the accumulation unit declines to $0.90, about 111 accumulation units can be purchased. Thus, accumulation units are purchased over a long period of time in both rising and falling markets.

At retirement, the accumulation units are then converted into **annuity units.** The number of annuity units remains constant during the liquidation period, but the value of each unit will change each month or year depending on the level of common stock prices. For example, at retirement, assume that the annuitant has 10,000 accumulation units that have a current market value of $60,000. Assume that the accumulation units are converted into 100 annuity units.[18] As stated earlier, the number of annuity units remains constant, but the value of each unit will change over time. Assume that the annuity unit is initially valued at $5 when the annuitant retires. A monthly income of $500 will be paid. During the second month, if the annuity unit increases in value to $5.10, the monthly income also increases to $510. During the third month, if the annuity units decline to $4.90 because of a stock market decline, the monthly income is reduced to $490. Thus, the monthly income depends on the level of common stock prices.

**Investment Performance of Variable Annuities** In general, variable annuities are effective in maintaining purchasing power. A study by Morningstar showed that over a 10-year period ending May 1993, diversified U.S. equity variable annuities earned an average annual total return of 11.35 percent. During the same period, the average annual inflation rate was only 3.8 percent.[19] Thus, variable annuities provided an effective inflation hedge during that period.

The investment performance, however, of variable annuities varies widely, depending on the insurer and type of investment (see Exhibit 16.5 and Insight 16.4).

## INSIGHT 16.4

## Variable Annuities: Here's to the
## Winners, and Losers

With the markets leaping about like fleas, it is an opportune moment to take a look at which variable annuities have provided the calmest rides over time.

The bafflingly named variable annuity is essentially a bunch of mutual funds in a tax-deferred wrapper. It is called variable because the value of the investment zigzags up and down, just as it does in mutual funds.

Variable annuities are supposed to be long-term investments. So, if you put money into one of these deals—which usually impose stiff surrender penalties—you had better be happy with the handful of fund choices allowed.

It is a positive sign if lots of the funds wrapped up in the variable-annuity package are beating their peers, that is, if the growth fund is doing better than the average growth fund. And if you are not a fan of high risk, you might want to stick with funds that have proven over five years that they can deliver the goods consistently.

With that in mind, we asked Morningstar Inc., a Chicago firm that tracks variable-annuity funds, to sift through the offerings and come up with some that fit the bill.

[T]he criteria are the same ones we have used in the past: Because investors put most of their money into core stock and bond funds, Morningstar excluded exotic offerings such as science and technology funds, international stock or bond funds, high-yield bond funds, and stock funds that invest in companies with a market size of less than $1 billion.

### Top and Bottom of the Heap

*Best-Performing Variable Annuities*

Contracts with at least one stock,[1] one bond,[2] and one balanced fund that beat the average for its category in at least 10 quarters over the last 20. Funds must have lower-than-average risk.

| Name of variable annuity | No. funds in contract[3] | No. of funds with five-year records | Total no. winning funds |
|---|---|---|---|
| Aetna Marathon Plus | 33 | 10 | 5 |
| American Capital/Nationwide | 8 | 4 | 3 |
| American General Variety Plus | 13 | 6 | 3 |
| Bankers Security USA Plan (Q) | 17 | 8 | 5 |
| Hartford Deferred Comp (Q) | 11 | 6 | 3 |
| John Hancock Accom. | 18 | 4 | 3 |
| Life of Virginia Commonwealth | 33 | 13 | 7 |
| MassMutual Life Trust | 13 | 6 | 3 |
| MetLife Preference Plus | 7 | 5 | 3 |
| Phoenix Big Edge Choice/Plus/Strat | 10 | 3 | 3 |
| Pru. Disc. Plus | 14 | 7 | 4 |
| TIAA-CREF (Q) | 7 | 3 | 3 |
| Vanguard Variable Annuity Plan | 9 | 3 | 3 |

*Continued*

*Worst-Performing Variable Annuities*

In at least 10 quarters out of the past 20 quarters, no stock[1] or balanced fund beat its objective.

| Name of variable annuity | No. Funds in gontract[3] | No. of funds with five-year records | No. funds that beat objective |
|---|---|---|---|
| Dreyfus/Transam. Triple Adv. | 13 | 4 | 2 |
| First Variable Capital Five/Vista II | 9 | 3 | 0 |
| Franklin Valuemark | 23 | 8 | 3 |
| Golden Amer. GoldenSelect | 13 | 4 | 0 |
| IDS Flexible Annuity | 6 | 3 | 1 |
| Manulife Acct 2 Annuity/Lifestyle | 8 | 3 | 0 |
| Merrill Lynch Retirement Plus | 17 | 4 | 0 |
| Minn. Mut. Multioption Select/A | 14 | 6 | 2 |
| MONY Keynote (Q) | 7 | 6 | 1 |
| PaineWebber Advantage | 7 | 3 | 0 |
| Union Central Life Carillon | 10 | 4 | 1 |

[1]Excludes international and aggressive growth funds.

[2]Excludes high-yield and global bond funds.

[3]Excluding money market funds.

NOTE: All figures are as of 6/29/96. Q= "qualified" i.e. available only in retirement plans

SOURCE: Morningstar

To qualify, the winning funds had to have five-year track records. They also had to have beaten the average for their category in at least 10 of the 20 quarters through midyear. (Winning funds also had to have a five-year Morningstar risk score that was at most 10% above the average for their category.)

Morningstar also eliminated variable annuities that are available only in a single state and stripped out money-market funds.

Finally, at least half the funds in the winning variable annuities had to have five-year records that met the above criteria (high performance, low risk). That left out **Best of America IV/Nationwide.** True, it has one winning stock fund, one winning bond fund and one winning balanced fund. But it has a total of 12 funds with five-year records—so just a quarter of its funds look good by our measures.

In contrast, **Vanguard Variable Annuity Plan, TIAA-CREF** (for teachers) and **Phoenix Big Edge** have only three winning funds with five year-records—but 100% of their funds with five-year records are winners.

If a variable annuity has tons of funds, odds are that some won't flop. But it helps the investor if the variable annuity has made an effort to pack in winning funds. Best of America's Vision annuity has 30 funds, but only nine have five-year records, and only three of them are winners.

What the losers have in common is that none have stock or balanced funds with five-year records that beat their objectives. Similarly, you will find some scary funds in the winning annuities. So use this exercise as a starting place, not as a shopping list.

SOURCE: Adopted from Ellen E. Schultz, "Variable Annuities: Here's to the Winners, and Losers," *The Wall Street Journal*, July 21, 1996, pp. C1, C23.

**Variable Annuity Expenses**  Some variable annuities have relatively high annual expense rates, which can be a costly drag on investment performance if the wrong annuity is purchased. Annual charges include a mortality and expense risk charge that compensates the insurer for assuming certain risks, a charge for administrative expenses, an investment manager's fee, a surrender charge that declines over time, and an annual contract fee of $25 to $50. Total charges and fees can be 2 percent or more of the total assets in many variable annuities (see Exhibit 16.5).

In summary, variable annuities can be attractive to certain investors who wish to save for retirement on a tax-deferred basis. However, variable annuities are not for everyone; they are long-term investments and should not be purchased if the funds will be needed in the near-term future. A surrender penalty may be imposed for five to ten years after the purchase date, and withdrawal of funds prior to age 59 1/2 will result in a tax penalty.

## SUMMARY

- Term insurance provides temporary protection and is typically renewable and convertible without evidence of insurability. Term insurance is appropriate when income is limited, or there are temporary needs. However, since term insurance usually has no cash values, it cannot be used for retirement or savings purposes.

- There are several traditional forms of whole life insurance. *Ordinary life insurance* is a form of whole life insurance that provides lifetime protection to age 100. The premiums are level and are payable for life. The policy develops an investment or saving element called a cash surrender value, which results from the overpayment of premiums during the early years. An ordinary life policy is appropriate when lifetime protection is desired or additional savings are desired.

- A *limited-payment policy* is another traditional form of whole life insurance. The insured also has lifetime protection. However, the premiums are paid only for a limited period, such as 10, 20, or 30 years, or until age 65.

- An *endowment policy* pays the face amount of insurance if the insured dies within a specified period. If the insured survives to the end of the endowment period, the face amount of insurance is paid to the policy-owner at that time.

- *Variable life insurance* is a fixed premium policy in which the death benefit and cash surrender value vary according to the investment experience of a separate account maintained by the insurer. The entire reserve is held in a separate account and is invested in equities or other investments. The cash surrender values are not guaranteed.

- *Universal life insurance* is another variation of whole life insurance. Conceptually, universal life can be viewed as a flexible-premium policy that provides lifetime protection under a contract that separates the protection and saving components. Universal life insurance has the following features:

    Unbundling of protection, savings, and expense components

    Two forms of universal life insurance

    Considerable flexibility

    Cash withdrawals permitted

    Favorable income-tax treatment

- *Variable universal life insurance* is similar to universal life insurance with two major exceptions. First, the cash values can be invested in a wide variety of investments. Second, there is no minimum guaranteed interest rate, and the investment risk falls entirely on the policyowner.

- *Current assumption whole life insurance* is a nonparticipating whole life policy in which the cash values are based on the insurer's current mortality, investment, and expense experience. An accumulation account is credited with a current interest rate that changes over time.

- An *indeterminate premium whole life policy* is a nonparticipating policy that permits the insurer to adjust premiums based on anticipated future experience. The initial premiums are guaranteed for a certain time period and can then be increased up to some maximum limit.

- A *modified life policy* is a whole life policy in which premiums are lower for the first three to five years and are higher thereafter.

- The *family income policy* is a combination of decreasing term and whole life insurance. It pays a monthly income of $10 for each $1000 of life insurance if the insured dies within the family income period. The monthly income is paid to the end of the period, at which time the face amount of insurance is paid.

- Many insurers sell policies with lower rates to preferred risks. The policies are carefully underwritten and sold only to individuals whose health history, weight, occupation, and habits indicate more favorable mortality than average. Minimum amounts of insurance must be purchased.

- *Second-to-die life insurance (survivorship life)* insures two or more lives and pays the death benefit upon the death of the second or last insured.

- A *vanishing-premium policy* is a form of participating whole life insurance in which out-of-pocket payments for the premiums are intended to vanish after a certain time period. This is accomplished by the appropriate use of the dividends, which accumulate at interest or are used to buy paid-up additions that are used later to pay future premiums.

- *Juvenile insurance* refers to life insurance purchased by a parent or other adult on the lives of children under a certain age, such as age 15 or 16.

- *Savings bank life insurance* is sold in mutual savings banks of three states—Massachusetts, New York, and Connecticut.

- *Industrial life insurance* is a type of insurance in which the policies are sold in small amounts, and the premiums are paid to an agent at the policyowner's home.

- *Group life insurance* provides life insurance on persons in a group under a single master contract.

- An *annuity* provides periodic payments to an individual, which continue for a fixed period or for the duration of a designated life or lives. The fundamental purpose of a life annuity is to provide a lifetime income to an individual.

- Annuities can be classified in terms of the following:

  Time when payments begin
    Immediate annuity
    Deferred annuity
  Nature of the insurer's obligation
    Life annuity (no refund)
    Life annuity with guaranteed payments
    Installment or cash refund annuity
    Joint-and-survivor annuity
  Fixed or variable benefits
    Fixed annuity
    Variable annuity

## KEY CONCEPTS AND TERMS

| | |
|---|---|
| Accumulation unit | Debit agent |
| Annuitant | Deferred annuity |
| Annuity | Endowment insurance |
| Annuity unit | Equity-indexed annuity |
| Cash surrender value | Family income policy |
| Convertible | Fixed annuity |
| Current assumption whole life insurance | Flexible-premium annuity |

| | |
|---|---|
| Group life insurance | Renewable |
| Home service life insurance | Retirement income policy |
| | Retroactive method |
| Immediate annuity | Savings bank life insurance |
| Indeterminate-premium whole life policy | Second-to-die life insurance |
| Industrial life insurance | Single-premium deferred annuity |
| Installment refund annuity | Single-premium whole life insurance |
| Joint-and-survivor annuity | |
| Juvenile insurance | Term insurance |
| Lapsed policy | Universal life insurance |
| Life annuity | Vanishing-premium policy |
| Life annuity with guaranteed payments | Variable annuity |
| Limited-payment policy | Variable life insurance |
| Modified life policy | Variable universal life insurance |
| Ordinary life insurance | Whole life insurance |
| Preferred risk policy | |
| Reentry term | |

## QUESTIONS FOR REVIEW

1. Describe the basic characteristics of term insurance.

2. When is the use of term insurance appropriate?

3. Describe the basic characteristics of ordinary life insurance.

4. Under what situations can an ordinary life policy be used?

5. Describe the basic features of a variable life insurance policy.

6. Explain the major characteristics of universal life insurance.

7. Describe the basic characteristics of a *preferred risk policy*.

8. Should life insurance be purchased on the lives of children? Explain.

9. What is the fundamental objective of an annuity?

10. Identify the basic types of individual annuities sold today.

## QUESTIONS FOR DISCUSSION

1. Mark, age 32, wants to purchase a five-year term insurance policy in the amount of $100,000. The policy is both renewable and convertible.

   a. Describe the situations under which term insurance can be used.

   b. What rights does Mark have because the policy is renewable and convertible? Explain your answer.

c. If Mark wishes to save money for retirement purposes, do you recommend purchase of this contract?

d. Explain to Mark the advantages and disadvantages of a reentry term policy.

2. Kelly, age 35, is considering the purchase of the following individual life insurance policies with a face amount of $100,000.

(1) Five-year renewable and convertible term policy (renewable until age 65)

(2) Ordinary life policy

(3) Twenty-payment life policy

(4) Life-paid-up-at-age-65 policy

a. Which of these contracts requires the highest and lowest current annual premium outlay?

b. If Kelly intends to keep the insurance until age 65, under which of these contracts will the annual premium increase?

c. Which of these contracts will allow Kelly to continue her life insurance beyond age 65? Explain your answer.

3. For each of the following situations, describe a life insurance policy that can be used to meet the situation. Treat each item separately.

a. An increasing face amount of life insurance to offset inflation

b. Monthly income to the family if the insured dies prematurely at a young age

c. Insuring the human life value of an individual, age 30, at the lowest possible annual premium

d. Life insurance that is paid up when the insured retires at age 65

e. A policy that permits the cash value to be invested in stocks, bonds, or other investments

f. A policy that provides flexibility as financial circumstances change

g. Insurance that is sold over the counter

h. A policy designed to pay estate taxes upon the death of a surviving spouse

4. a. How is universal life insurance similar to traditional cash value policies?

b. How does universal life insurance differ from traditional cash value policies?

c. Explain the major differences between universal life and variable universal life insurance.

d. Describe the major features of each of the following:

(1) Current assumption whole life insurance

(2) Indeterminate premium whole life insurance

(3) Vanishing premium policy

## CASE APPLICATION

Sharon, age 28, is a single parent who earns $22,000 annually as a secretary at a local university. She is the sole support of her son, age 3. Sharon is concerned about the financial well-being of her son if she should die. Although she finds it difficult to save, she would like to start a savings program to send her son to college. She is presently renting an apartment but would like to own her home someday. A friend has informed her that life insurance might be useful in her present situation. Sharon knows nothing about life insurance, and the amount of income available for life insurance is limited. Assume you are a financial planner who is asked to make recommendations concerning the type of life insurance that Sharon should buy. The following types of life insurance policies are available:

- Five-year renewable and convertible term
- Life paid up at age 65
- Ordinary life insurance
- Universal life insurance

a. Which of the above policies best meets the need for protection of Sharon's son if she should die prematurely? Explain your answer.

b. Which of the above policies best meets the need to accumulate a college retirement fund for Sharon's son? Explain your answer.

c. Which of the above policies best meets the need to accumulate money for a down payment on a home? Explain your answer.

d. What major obstacle does Sharon face if she tries to meet all of her financial needs by purchasing cash value life insurance?

e. Sharon decides to purchase the 5-year term policy in the amount of $300,000. The policy has no cash value. Identify a basic characteristic of a typical term insurance policy that would help Sharon accumulate a fund for retirement.

5. Although annuities and life insurance are based on the principles of pooling and compound interest, there are some important differences between them.

   a. Describe the major differences between life insurance and annuities.

   b. Explain briefly each of the following types of individual annuities:

      (1) Retirement income policy

      (2) Variable annuity

   c. Describe the investment characteristics of an equity indexed annuity.

## SELECTED REFERENCES

Belth, Joseph M. *Life Insurance: A Consumer's Handbook,* 2nd ed. Bloomington: Indiana University Press, 1985.

Black, Kenneth, Jr., and Harold D. Skipper, Jr. *Life Insurance,* 12th ed. Englewood Cliffs, N.J.: Prentice-Hall, 1994.

Dorfman, Mark S., and Saul W. Adelman. *Life Insurance: A Financial Planning Approach,* 2nd ed. Chicago: Dearborn Financial Publishing, 1992.

Graves, Edward E., ed. *McGill's Life Insurance.* Bryn Mawr, Pa.: The American College, 1994.

Holson, Laura M. and Liz Comte Reisman, "Lessons in Life," *Smart Money,* Vol. 3, No. 12 (December 1994), pp. 130–139.

Longo, Tracey, "There is No Free Insurance," *Kiplinger's Personal Finance Magazine,* Vol. 49, No. 10 (October 1995), pp. 97–101.

Mehr, Robert I., and Sandra G. Gustavson. *Life Insurance: Theory and Practice,* 4th ed. Plano, Tex.: Business Publications, 1987.

Rejda, George E., Constance M. Luthardt, Cheryl L. Ferguson, and Donald R. Oakes. *Personal Insurance,* 3rd ed. Malvern, Pa.: Insurance Institute of America, 1997.

"When It's Time to Buy Life Insurance, How Much Coverage Do You Need?" *Consumer Reports,* 58 (July 1993): 431–50. See also "Life Insurance, Part 2: Choosing a Universal-Life Policy," *Consumer Reports,* 58 (August 1993): 525–39.

## NOTES

1. These characteristics are discussed in greater detail in Kenneth Black, Jr., and Harold D. Skipper, Jr., *Life Insurance,* 12th ed. (Englewood Cliffs, N.J.: Prentice-Hall, 1994), chapter 4.

2. Ibid., pp. 86–87.

3. This section is based on Black and Skipper, pp. 126–42; *Consumer Reports,* 51 (August 1986), pp. 515–29; and Joseph M. Belth, ed., "The War Over Universal Life—Part 1," *Insurance Forum,* 8, no. 11 (November 1981): 137–40.

4. Belth, ed., "The War Over Universal Life—Part 1," pp. 137–40.

5. *Consumer Reports,* 51 (August 1986), p. 516.

6. The limitations of universal life are discussed in considerable detail in Belth, ed., "The War Over Universal Life—Part 1," pp. 137–40, and Belth, ed., "The War Over Universal Life—Part 2," *Insurance Forum,* 8, no. 12 (December 1981): 141–44. See also Joseph M. Belth, ed., *The Insurance Forum,* 19, (March 1992), pp. 11–13; and "Universal Life Insurance," *Consumer Reports,* 47 (January 1982), pp. 42–44.

7. Karen Slater, "Return on Universal Life Insurance Can Be a Lot Less Than Expected," *The Wall Street Journal,* February 11, 1986.

8. See Belth, ed., "The War Over Universal Life—Part 1," pp. 137–40.

9. Kristin Davis, "Making Life Insurance Easier to Swallow," *Kiplinger's Personal Finance Magazine,* 47, No. 8 (August 1993): 48.

10. *Consumer Reports* (August 1986), p. 518.

11. This section is based on Black and Skipper, pp. 109–13.

12. Ibid., p. 112.

13. Glenn L. Wood, Claude C. Lilly III, Donald S. Malecki, Edward E. Graves, and Jerry S. Rosenbloom, *Personal Risk Management and Insurance,* 4th ed., vol. 2 (Malvern, Pa.: American Institute for Property and Liability Underwriters, 1989), p. 29.

14. *1996 Life Insurance Fact Book,* p. 122.

15. *1996 Life Insurance Fact Book,* p. 32.

16. *1996 Life Insurance Fact Book,* p. 17.

17. We will ignore any deduction for administrative and sales expenses. Some individual variable annuity contracts have a front-end load.

18. The actual number of annuity units will depend on the age of the annuitant, the number of guaranteed payments, the conversion rates, the assumed investment return, and other factors.

19. *Morningstar Variable Annuity/Life Performance Report* (June 1993), p. A10.

# Chapter 17

# LIFE INSURANCE CONTRACTUAL PROVISIONS

> *"Nearly every family buys life insurance; yet few policyholders ever read a life contract with any effort to understand its provisions."*
>
> Mehr and Gustavson,
> Life Insurance: Theory and Practice, 4th ed.

## Student Learning Objectives

After studying this chapter, you should be able to:

■ Describe the incontestable clause, suicide clause, and grace period provision.

■ Identify the dividend options that are found in participating policies.

■ Explain the nonforfeiture options that are found in cash-value policies.

■ Describe the various settlement options for the payment of life insurance proceeds.

■ Describe the waiver of premium benefit and accelerated death benefits rider that can be added to a life insurance policy.

In a personal risk management program, life insurance is an important technique for attaining financial and economic security. Although most people own life insurance, they seldom read their policies and therefore do not understand the basic provisions and additional benefits that the policy may contain. As a result, they do not attain the maximum financial advantages from their policies. Moreover, family needs, financial goals, and circumstances change over time. A life insurance policy should be periodically evaluated to determine if the present coverage is adequate. This evaluation requires reading and understanding the policy.

The law requires a life insurance policy to include certain provisions. Other contractual provisions are optional. This chapter discusses some common life insurance policy provisions and is divided into three major parts. The first part discusses the important life insurance contractual provisions that have an impact on consumers. The second part analyzes the basic options that frequently appear in life insurance policies, including dividend options, nonforfeiture options, and settlement options. The final part explores several optional benefits and riders that can be added to a life insurance policy.

## LIFE INSURANCE CONTRACTUAL PROVISIONS

Life insurance policies contain numerous contractual provisions, some more important than others. The following section discusses the major contractual provisions that life insurance consumers should understand.

### Ownership Clause

The owner of a life insurance policy can be the insured, the beneficiary, or another party. In most cases, the applicant, insured, and owner are the same person. Under the **ownership clause,** *the policyowner possesses all contractual rights in the policy while the insured is living.* These rights include naming and changing the beneficiary, surrendering the policy for its cash value, borrowing the cash value, receiving dividends, and electing settlement options. These rights generally can be exercised without the beneficiary's consent.

The policy also provides for a change of ownership. The policyowner can designate a new owner by filing an appropriate form with the company. The insurer may require the policy to be endorsed to show the new owner.

### Entire-Contract Clause

*The* **entire-contract clause** *states that the life insurance policy and attached application constitute the entire contract between the parties.* All statements in the application are considered to be representations rather than warranties. No statement can be used by the insurer to void the policy unless it is a material misrepresentation and is part of the application. In addition, no officer of the insurer can change the policy terms unless the policyowner consents to the change.

There are two basic purposes of the entire contract clause. It prevents the insurer from modifying the policy without the knowledge or consent of the owner by changing its charter or bylaws. It also protects the beneficiary, since a statement made in connection with the application cannot be used by the insurer to deny a claim unless the statement is a material misrepresentation and is part of the application.

### Incontestable Clause

*The* **incontestable clause** *states that the insurer cannot contest the policy after it has been in force two years during the insured's lifetime.* This means that after the policy has been in force for two years during the insured's lifetime, the insurer cannot later contest a death claim on the basis of material misrepresentation, concealment, or fraud when the policy was first issued. The insurer has two years in which to discover any irregularities in the contract. With few exceptions, if the insured dies, the death claim must be paid after the contestable period expires. For example, if Charles, age 40, applies for a life insurance policy, conceals the fact that he has high blood pressure, and dies within the two-year period, the insurer could contest the claim on the basis of a material concealment. But if he dies *after* expiration of the period, the insurer must pay the claim.

The purpose of the incontestable clause is to protect the beneficiary from financial hardship if the insurer tries to deny payment of the claim years after the policy was first issued. Since the insured is dead, he or she cannot refute the insurer's allegations. As a result, the beneficiary could be financially harmed if the claim is denied on the grounds of a material misrepresentation or concealment.

The incontestable clause is normally effective against fraud. If the insured makes a fraudulent misstatement to obtain the insurance, the company has two years to detect the fraud. Otherwise, the death claim must be paid. However, there are certain situations where the fraud is so outrageous that payment of the death claim would be against the public interest. In these cases, the insurer can contest the claim after the contestable period runs out. They include the following:[1]

- The beneficiary takes out a policy with the intent of murdering the insured.
- The applicant for insurance has someone else take a medical examination.
- An insurable interest does not exist at the inception of the policy.

### Suicide Clause

Most life insurance policies contain a suicide clause. *The* **suicide clause** *states that if the insured*

## INSIGHT 17.1

### Is This Death a Suicide?

**Facts**

A 20-year-old Marine served in a fighter squadron as a radar technician. He was familiar with .45 caliber automatic pistols and had given instructions on their use. The Marine was a happy-go-lucky, cheerful person who sometimes tried to "shake up" his friends by placing a .45 to his head and pulling the trigger. One day when the Marine was apparently in good spirits, he suddenly put a pistol to his head, said "Here's to it" to a friend, and pulled the trigger. The gun fired, killing the Marine. The insurance company that insured him claimed this was a suicide.

**Decision**

The death is not a suicide.

**Reasoning**

The company must prove that the death was intentional. The burden of proof was not met here.

*Angelus v. Government Personnel Life Ins. Co.,* 321 P.2d 545 (Wash. 1958).

SOURCE: Joseph L. Frascona, *Business Law, Text and Cases,* 3rd ed. (Dubuque, Iowa: William C. Brown, 1987), p. 1014. Reprinted by permission of Prentice-Hall.

---

*commits suicide within two years after the policy is issued, the face amount of insurance will not be paid; there is only a refund of the premiums paid.* In some life insurance policies, suicide is excluded for only one year. If the insured commits suicide after the period expires, the policy proceeds are paid just like any other claim.

In legal terms, death is normally considered an unintentional act because of the strong instinct of self-preservation. Thus, there is a presumption against suicide. Consequently, the burden of proving suicide always rests on the insurer. In order to deny payment of the claim, the insurer must prove conclusively that the insured has committed suicide (see Insight 17.1).

The purpose of the suicide clause is to reduce adverse selection against the insurer. By having a suicide clause, the insurer has some protection against the individual who wishes to purchase life insurance with the intention of committing suicide.

### Grace Period

*A life insurance policy also contains a* **grace period** *during which the policyowner has a period of 31 days to pay an overdue premium.* However, universal life and other flexible-premium policies usually have a longer grace period, such as 61 days. The insurance remains in force during the grace period. If the insured dies within the grace period, the overdue premium is deducted from the policy proceeds.

The purpose of the grace period is to prevent the policy from lapsing by giving the policyowner additional time to pay an overdue premium. The policyowner may be temporarily short of funds or may have forgotten to pay the premium. In such cases, the grace period provides considerable financial flexibility.

### Reinstatement Clause

A policy may lapse if the premium has not been paid by the end of the grace period, or if an automatic premium loan provision is not in effect. *The* **reinstatement provision** *permits the owner to reinstate a lapsed policy.* The following requirements must be fulfilled to reinstate a lapsed policy.

- Evidence of insurability is required.
- All overdue premiums plus interest must be paid from their respective due dates.
- Any policy loan must be repaid or reinstated, with interest from the due date of the overdue premium.

- The policy must not have been surrendered for its cash value.
- The policy must be reinstated within a certain period, typically three or five years from the date of lapse.

It may be advantageous for a policyowner to reinstate a lapsed policy rather than purchase a new one. First, the premium is lower since the reinstated policy was issued at an earlier age. Second, the acquisition expenses incurred in issuing the policy must be paid again under a new policy. Third, cash values and dividends are usually higher under the reinstated policy; the new policy may not develop any cash values until the end of the third year. Fourth, the incontestable period and suicide period under the old policy may have expired. Reinstatement of a lapsed policy does not reopen the suicide period, and a new incontestable period generally applies only to statements contained in the application for reinstatement. Statements contained in the original application cannot be contested after the original incontestable period expires. Finally, the reinstated policy may contain more favorable policy provisions, such as a 5 or 6 percent policy loan rate in an older policy.

A major disadvantage of reinstating a lapsed policy is that a substantial cash outlay is required if the policy lapsed several years earlier. Also, most life insurers have reduced their rates over time and have developed new products. As a result, it may be less expensive to purchase a new policy rather than reinstate a lapsed policy even though the insured is older when the new purchase is made. As a practical matter, most lapsed policies are not reinstated because of the required cash outlay.

## Misstatement of Age or Sex Clause

Under the **misstatement of age or sex clause,** *if the insured's age or sex is misstated, the amount payable is the amount that the premiums paid would have purchased at the correct age and sex.* For example, assume that Troy, age 35, applies for a $20,000 ordinary life policy, but his age is incorrectly stated as age 34. If the premium is $20 per $1000 at age 35 and $19 per $1000 at age 34, the insurer will pay only 19/20 of the death proceeds. Thus, only $19,000 would be paid (19/20 × $20,000 = $19,000).

## Beneficiary Designation

*The beneficiary is the party named in the policy to receive the policy proceeds.* The principal types of beneficiary designations are as follows:

- Primary and contingent beneficiary
- Revocable and irrevocable beneficiary
- Specific and class beneficiary

**Primary and Contingent Beneficiary** A **primary beneficiary** *is the beneficiary who is first entitled to receive the policy proceeds on the insured's death.* A **contingent beneficiary** *is entitled to the proceeds if the primary beneficiary dies before the insured.* If the primary beneficiary dies before receiving the guaranteed number of payments under an installment settlement option, the remaining payments are paid to the contingent beneficiary.

In many families, the husband will name his wife primary beneficiary (and vice versa), and the children will be named as contingent beneficiaries. The legal problem in naming *minor children* as beneficiaries is that they lack the legal capacity to receive the policy proceeds directly. Most insurers will not pay the death proceeds directly to minor children.[2] Instead, they will require a guardian to receive the proceeds on the minor's behalf. If a court of law appoints a guardian, payment of the proceeds may be delayed and legal expenses will be incurred. One solution is to have a *guardian* named in the will who can legally receive the proceeds on the children's behalf. Another approach is to pay the proceeds to a *trustee* (such as a commercial bank with a trust department) which has the discretion and authority to use the funds for the children's welfare.

The insured's estate can be named as primary or contingent beneficiary. However, many financial planners do not recommend designation of the estate as beneficiary. The death proceeds may be subject to attorney fees and other probate expenses, state inheritance taxes, and claims of creditors. Payment of the proceeds may also be delayed until the estate is settled.

**Revocable and Irrevocable Beneficiary** Most beneficiary designations are revocable. A **revocable beneficiary** *means that the policyowner reserves the right to change the beneficiary designation* *without the beneficiary's consent.* The revocable beneficiary has only the expectation of benefits, and the policyowner can change the beneficiary whenever desired. All policy rights under the contract can be exercised without the consent of the revocable beneficiary.

In contrast, an **irrevocable beneficiary** *is one that cannot be changed without the beneficiary's consent.* If the policyowner wishes to change the beneficiary designation, the irrevocable beneficiary must consent to the change. However, most policies today provide that the interest of a beneficiary, even an irrevocable beneficiary, terminates if the beneficiary dies before the insured. Thus, if the irrevocable beneficiary dies before the insured, all rights to the policy proceeds revert to the policyowner who can then name a new beneficiary.[3]

**Specific and Class Beneficiary**    A **specific beneficiary** means the beneficiary is specifically named and identified. In contrast, under a **class beneficiary,** a specific person is not named but is a member of a group designated as beneficiary, such as children of the insured. A class designation is appropriate whenever the insured wishes to divide the policy proceeds equally among members of a particular group.

Most insurers restrict the use of a class designation because of the problem of identifying members of the class. Although all insurers permit the designation of children as a class, they will not permit this designation to be used when the class members cannot be identified, or the relationship to the insured is remote. For example, the class designation "my children" means that all children of the insured share in the policy proceeds, whether legitimate, illegitimate, or adopted. But if "children of the insured" is used as the designation, the insured's children by any marriage would be included, but the spouse's children by a former marriage would be excluded. Thus, a class designation must be used with great care.

## Change of Plan Provision

Life insurance policies usually contain a **change-of-plan provision** that allows policyowners to exchange their present policies for different contracts. The purpose of this provision is to provide flexibility to the policyowner. The original policy may no longer be appropriate if family needs and financial objectives change.

If the change is to a *higher premium policy,* such as changing from an ordinary life to a limited-payment policy, the policyowner must pay the difference in cash values between the two policies plus interest at a stipulated rate. Evidence of insurability is not required, since the pure insurance protection (net amount at risk) is reduced.

In addition, based on company practice, the policyowner may be allowed to change to a *lower-premium policy,* such as changing from a limited-payment policy to an ordinary life policy. In such a case, the insurer refunds the difference in cash values under the two policies to the policyowner. Evidence of insurability is required in this type of change, since the pure insurance protection is increased (higher net amount at risk).

## Exclusions and Restrictions

A life insurance policy contains remarkably few exclusions and restrictions. *Suicide* is excluded only for the first two years. During a period of war, some insurers may insert a **war clause** in their policies, which excludes payment if the insured dies as a direct result of war. The purpose of the war clause is to reduce adverse selection against the insurer when large numbers of new insureds may be exposed to death during war time.

In addition, **aviation exclusions** may be present in some policies. Most newly issued policies do not contain any exclusions with respect to aviation deaths, and aviation death claims are paid like any other claim. However, some insurers exclude aviation deaths other than as a fare-paying passenger on a regularly scheduled airline. Military aviation may also be excluded, or be covered only by payment of an extra premium. In addition, a private pilot who does not meet certain flight standards may have an aviation exclusion rider inserted in the policy, or be charged a higher premium.

During the initial underwriting of the policy, the insurer may discover *certain undesirable activities or hobbies* of the insured. These activities may be excluded or covered only by payment of an extra premium. Some excluded activities are automobile racing, sky diving, scuba diving, flying a hang glider, and travel or residence in a dangerous country.

## Payment of Premiums

Life insurance premiums can be paid annually, semiannually, quarterly, or monthly. If the premium is paid other than annually, the policyowner must pay a carrying charge, which can be relatively expensive when the true rate of interest is calculated. For example, the semiannual premium may be 52 percent of the annual premium and so could be viewed as a carrying charge of only 4 percent. However, the actual charge is 16.7 percent. Assume that your annual premium is $100. You pay the semiannual premium of $52 and defer payment of $48. Six months later, the $48 and $4 carrying charge are due. This means that you are paying $4 for the use of $48 for six months, which is the equivalent of an annual charge of 16.7 percent.[4]

## Assignment Clause

A life insurance policy is freely assignable to another party. There are two types of assignments. *Under an* **absolute assignment,** *all ownership rights in the policy are transferred to a new owner.* For example, the policyowner may wish to donate a life insurance policy to a church, charity, or educational institution. This can be accomplished by an absolute assignment. The new owner can then exercise the ownership rights in the policy.

*Under a* **collateral assignment,** *the policyowner assigns a life insurance policy as collateral for a loan.* The assignment form used is typically the American Bankers Association's assignment form. *Under this form, only certain rights are transferred to the creditor to protect its interest, and the policyowner retains the remaining rights.* The party to whom the policy is assigned can receive the policy proceeds only to the extent of the loan; the balance of the proceeds is paid to the beneficiary.

The purpose of the assignment clause is to protect the insurer from paying the policy proceeds twice if an unrecorded assignment is presented to the insurer after the death claim is paid to the beneficiary. If the insurer is not notified of the assignment, the proceeds are paid to the named beneficiary when the policy matures as a death claim or endowment. Under general rules of law, the insurer is relieved of any further obligation under the policy, even though a valid assignment is in existence at the insured's death. However, if the insurer is notified of the assignment, a new contract exists between the insurer and assignee (one who receives the assignment, such as a bank), and the insurer then recognizes the assignee's rights as being superior to the beneficiary's rights.

## Policy Loan Provision

Cash value life insurance contains a **policy loan provision** that allows the policyowner to borrow the cash value. The interest rate is stated in the policy. Older policies typically have a 5 or 6 percent loan rate. Newer policies typically have an 8 percent loan rate. However, all states permit insurers to charge a variable policy loan interest rate based on the National Association of Insurance Commissioner's model bill. If a variable rate is used, there are limits on the maximum rate that can be charged. The maximum interest rate is the greater of Moody's Composite Yield on seasoned corporate bonds two months prior to the determination date or the interest rate credited to the cash value plus one percent.[5] The policy loan rate can be revised as often as every three months. Many insurers pay higher dividends to policyholders who have their old policies endorsed to provide for a flexible loan rate.

On newly issued participating contracts, many insurers will reduce the dividend based on the amount of cash value borrowed. This has the effect of indirectly increasing the effective interest rate on the policy loan. For example, one insurer would have paid a dividend of $313.70 on a $10,000 policy issued to a male age 30 with no outstanding policy loans. However, since the individual had borrowed $5,300, the dividend was reduced to $107.20, a reduction of almost two-thirds.[6] Moreover, under interest-sensitive policies, such as universal life and variable universal life, the current interest rate credited to the cash values that are borrowed is typically reduced, which again increases the effective interest rate on the loan.

Interest on a policy loan must either be paid annually, or it is added to the outstanding loan if not paid. If the loan is not repaid by the time the policy matures as a death claim or endowment, the face amount of the policy is reduced by the amount of indebtedness. With the exception of a policy loan to pay a premium, the insurer can defer granting the loan for up to six months, but this is rarely done.

Persons who borrow their cash values often believe that they are paying interest on their own money. *This view is clearly incorrect. The cash legally belongs to the insurer.* Although you have the contractual right to surrender or borrow the cash value, the cash legally belongs to the insurer. Interest must be paid on the loan because the insurer assumes a certain interest rate when premiums, legal reserves, dividends, and surrender values are calculated. The insurer's assets must be invested in interest-bearing securities and other investments so that the contractual obligations can be met. *A policyowner must pay interest on the loan to offset the loss of interest to the insurer.* If the loan had not been granted, the insurer could have earned interest on the funds.

Notice, too, that policy loan provisions make it necessary for the insurer to keep some assets in lower-yielding, liquid investments to meet the demand for policy loans. Since these funds could have been invested in higher-yielding investments, policyowners who borrow should pay interest because higher yields must be forsaken.

**Advantages of Policy Loans**  The major advantage of a policy loan is the relatively low rate of interest that is paid. This is especially true for older contracts. The low policy loan rates of 5, 6, or 8 percent are substantially lower than the rates charged by banks. There is also no credit check on the policyowner's ability to repay the loan; there is no fixed repayment schedule; and the policyowner has complete financial flexibility in determining the amount and frequency of loan repayments.

**Disadvantages of Policy Loans**  The major disadvantage is that the policyowner is not legally required to repay the loan, and the policy could lapse if the total indebtedness exceeds the available cash value. Rather than repay the loan, the policyowner may let the policy lapse or may surrender the policy for any remaining cash value. Finally, if the loan has not been repaid by the time the policy matures, the face amount of insurance is reduced by the amount of the debt.

## Automatic Premium Loan

The automatic premium loan provision can be added to most cash value policies. *Under the* **automatic premium loan provision,** *an overdue premium is automatically borrowed from the cash value after the grace period expires, provided the policy has a loan value sufficient to pay the premium.* The policy continues in force just as before but a premium loan is now outstanding. Interest is charged on the premium loan at the stated contractual rate. Premium payments can be resumed at any time without evidence of insurability.

The basic purpose of an automatic premium loan is to prevent the policy from lapsing because of nonpayment of premiums. The policyowner may be temporarily short of funds, or may forget to pay the premium. Thus, the automatic premium loan provides considerable financial flexibility to the policyowner.

The automatic premium loan provision, however, has two major disadvantages. First, it may be overused. The policyowner may get into the habit of using the automatic premium loan provision too frequently. If the cash values are relatively modest, and are habitually borrowed over an extended period, the cash values could eventually be exhausted, and the contract would terminate. A second disadvantage is that the policy proceeds will be reduced if the premium loans are not repaid by the time the policy matures.

## DIVIDEND OPTIONS

Life insurance policies frequently contain dividend options. If the policy pays dividends, it is known as a **participating policy.** Both stock and mutual insurers issue participating policies; the policyowner has the right to share in the divisible surplus of the insurer. The dividend represents largely a refund of part of the gross premium if the insurer has favorable experience with respect to mortality, interest, and expenses. In contrast, a policy that does not pay dividends is known as a **nonparticipating policy.**

Policy dividends are generally derived from three sources: (1) the difference between expected and actual mortality experience; (2) excess interest earnings on the assets required to maintain legal reserves; and (3) the difference between expected and actual operating expenses. Since the dividends paid are determined by the insurer's actual operating experience, they cannot be guaranteed.

There are several ways in which dividends can be taken:

- Cash
- Reduction of premiums
- Accumulate at interest
- Paid-up additions
- Term insurance (fifth dividend option)

## Cash

A dividend is usually payable after the policy has been in force for a stated period, typically one or two years. The policyowner receives a check equal to the dividend, usually on the anniversary date of the policy.

## Reduction of Premiums

The dividend can be used to reduce the next premium coming due. The dividend notice will indicate the amount of the dividend, and the policyowner must then remit the difference between the premium and actual dividend paid. This option is appropriate whenever premium payments become financially burdensome. It can also be used if the policyowner has a substantial reduction in income and expenses must be reduced.

## Accumulate at Interest

The dividend can be retained by the insurer and accumulated at interest. The policy guarantees a minimum interest rate such as 3 percent, but a higher rate may be paid based on current market conditions. The accumulated dividends generally can be withdrawn at any time. If not withdrawn, they are added to the amount paid when the policy matures, or the contract is surrendered for its cash value. The dividend itself is not taxable for income-tax purposes. However, the interest income on the accumulated dividends is taxable income and must be reported annually for federal and state income tax purposes. Thus, the interest option may be undesirable for policyowners who wish to minimize income taxes.

## Paid-up Additions

Under the paid-up additions option, the dividend is used to purchase a reduced amount of paid-up whole life insurance. For example, assume that Paige, age 20, owns an ordinary life policy. If a dividend of $50

were paid, about $200 of paid-up whole life insurance could be purchased.

The paid-up additions option has some favorable features. *First, the paid-up additions are purchased at net rates, not gross rates;* there is no loading for expenses. *A second advantage is that evidence of insurability is not required.* Thus, if the insured is substandard in health or is uninsurable, this option may be appealing, since additional amounts of life insurance can be purchased.

However, the paid-up additions option also has some unfavorable features. *First, in some policies, the paid-up increments of insurance may be overpriced.* The frequently advanced argument that paid-up additions are relatively inexpensive since they are purchased at net rates is somewhat misleading. In a careful price analysis of paid-up additions, Professor Joseph Belth found that the paid-up additions purchased in some policies were indeed low-priced, but in other policies, they were high-priced increments of life insurance.[7]

*A second disadvantage is that reduced paid-up insurance is a form of single-premium whole life insurance.* Consumer experts point out that rarely is a single-premium policy appropriate for most insureds. For example, if $100,000 of ordinary life insurance is desired, the insured normally does not pay a single premium of $40,000 to obtain the protection. Why, then, should a $40 dividend be used to buy a $100 paid-up addition? Since most persons are underinsured, a better approach would be to use the dividends to purchase another policy, assuming, of course, that the person is insurable.[8]

## Term Insurance (Fifth Dividend Option)

Some insurers have a fifth dividend option by which the dividend is used to purchase term insurance. Two forms of this option are typically used. *The dividend can be used to purchase one-year term insurance equal to the cash value of the basic policy, and the remainder of the dividend is then used to buy paid-up additions or is accumulated at interest.* This option may be appropriate if the policyowner regularly borrows the cash value. The face amount of the policy would not be reduced by the amount of any outstanding loans at the time of death.

*A second form of this option is to use the dividend to purchase yearly renewable term insurance.* The actual

## INSIGHT 17.2

### Which Dividend Option Is Best?

There is no one best dividend option. *The best dividend option is the one that is best for you in terms of your financial circumstances, needs, and objectives.* If your income is limited or if premium payments are financially burdensome, the dividend can be paid in cash or used to reduce the next premium. If you are substandard in health or uninsurable, then the paid-up additions option is appropriate. If income tax considerations are important, you should not use the interest option since the interest is taxable. Instead, the paid-up additions option

would be more appropriate, since the dividend becomes the legal reserve under the paid-up addition, and interest accumulations on the legal reserve are not taxed as current income to the policyowner. If your objective is to have a paid-up policy at retirement, then the paid-up additions option is desirable. If you need additional life insurance, the fifth dividend option can be used if it is available. In short, no single dividend option is best for all insureds. Each insured must choose an option suited to his or her situation.

amount of term insurance purchased depends on the amount of the dividend, the insured's attained age, and the insurer's term insurance rates. However, it is not uncommon for a $40 dividend to purchase $10,000 or more yearly renewable term insurance under this option. Unfortunately, this desirable option is offered by only a small proportion of companies.

### Other Uses of Dividends

The dividends can also be used to convert a policy into a *paid-up contract*. If the paid-up option is used, the policy becomes paid-up whenever the reserve value under the basic contract plus the reserve value of the paid-up additions or deposits equal the net single premium for a paid-up policy at the insured's attained age. For example, an ordinary life policy issued at age 25 could be paid up by age 48 by using this option.

The dividend can also be used to *mature a policy as an endowment.* When the reserve value under the basic policy plus the reserve value of the paid-up additions or deposits equal the face amount of insurance, the policy matures as an endowment. For example, a $50,000 ordinary life policy issued at age 25 would mature as an endowment at age 58 by using this option.[9]

Finally, keep in mind that the use of dividend options will vary among insureds. There is no best

dividend option. The best option to use is the one that best meets your financial goals and objectives (see Insight 17.2).

## NONFORFEITURE OPTIONS

If a cash-value policy is purchased, the policyowner pays more than is actuarially necessary for the life insurance protection. Thus, the policyowner should get something back if the policy is surrendered. The payment to a withdrawing policyowner is known as a nonforfeiture value or cash surrender value.

All states have standard **nonforfeiture laws** that require insurers to provide at least a minimum nonforfeiture value to policyowners who surrender their policies. There are three **nonforfeiture options** or cash surrender options:

- Cash value
- Reduced paid-up insurance
- Extended term insurance

### Cash Value

*The policy can be surrendered for its cash value, at which time all benefits under the policy cease.* A policy normally does not build any cash value until the end of the second or third year, although some policies have a small cash value at the end of the first year.

The cash values are small during the early years because the relatively high first-year acquisition expenses incurred by the insurer in selling the policy have not yet been recovered. However, over a long period, the cash values accumulate to substantial amounts.

The insurer can delay payment of the cash value for six months if the policy is surrendered. This provision is required by law and is a carryover from the Great Depression of the 1930s, when cash demands on life insurers were excessive. Insurers generally do not delay payment of the cash value because of fear that confidence in the company will be undermined.

The cash surrender option can be used if the insured no longer needs life insurance. Although it is usually not advisable to surrender a policy for cash since other options may be more appropriate, there are circumstances where the cash surrender option can be used. For example, if an insured is retired and no longer has any dependents to support, the need for substantial amounts of life insurance may be reduced. In such a case, the cash surrender option could be used.

## Reduced Paid-up Insurance

Under the **reduced paid-up insurance** *option, the cash surrender value is applied as a net single premium to purchase a reduced paid-up policy.* The amount of insurance purchased depends on the insured's attained age, the cash surrender value, and the mortality and interest assumptions stated in the original contract. The reduced paid-up policy is the same as the original policy, but the face amount of insurance is reduced. An ordinary life or limited-payment policy would be converted to a reduced paid-up policy. An endowment policy would mature at the same date but for a reduced amount. If the original policy is participating, the reduced paid-up policy also pays dividends.

The reduced paid-up insurance option is appropriate if life insurance is still needed, but the policyowner does not wish to pay premiums. For example, assume that Sean has a $100,000 ordinary life policy that he purchased at age 21. He is now age 65 and wants to retire, but he does not want to pay premiums after retirement. The cash surrender value can be used to purchased a reduced paid-up policy of about $83,000.

## Extended Term Insurance

Under the **extended term insurance** *option, the net cash surrender value is used as a net single premium to extend the full face amount of the policy (less any indebtedness) into the future as term insurance for a certain number of years and days.* In effect, the cash value is used to purchase a paid-up term insurance policy equal to the original face amount (less any indebtedness) for a limited period. The length of the term insurance protection is determined by the insured's attained age when the option is exercised, the net cash surrender value, and the company's premium rates for extended term insurance. For example, in our earlier illustration, if Sean stopped paying premiums at age 65, the cash value would be sufficient to keep the $100,000 policy in force for another 15 years and 272 days. If he is still alive after that time, the policy is no longer in force.

If the policy lapses for nonpayment of premiums, and the policyowner has not elected another option, the extended term option automatically goes into effect in most policies. This means that many policies are still in force even though the policyowners mistakenly believe the policy is not in force because of nonpayment of premiums. However, if the automatic premium loan provision has been added to the policy, it has priority over the extended term option.

A whole life or endowment policy contains a table of nonforfeiture values that indicates the benefits under the three options at various ages. Exhibit 17.1 illustrates the nonforfeiture values for an ordinary life policy issued at age 21.

## SETTLEMENT OPTIONS

**Settlement options,** or *optional methods of settlement,* refer to the various ways that the policy proceeds can be paid other than in a lump sum. The policyowner may elect the settlement option prior to the insured's death, or the beneficiary may be granted the right. In addition, most policies permit the cash surrender value to be paid under the settlement options if the policy is surrendered. The most common settlement options are as follows:

- Interest option
- Fixed-period option
- Fixed-amount option
- Life income options

EXHIBIT 17.1

**Nonforfeiture Options (Dollar Amount for Each $1000 of Ordinary Life Insurance Issued at Age 21)**

| End of policy year | Cash or loan value | Paid-up insurance | Extended Term Insurance | |
|---|---|---|---|---|
| | | | *Years* | *Days* |
| 1 | $   0.00 | $   0 | 0 | 0 |
| 2 | 0.00 | 0 | 0 | 0 |
| 3 | 4.79 | 15 | 1 | 315 |
| 4 | 16.21 | 48 | 6 | 161 |
| 5 | 27.91 | 81 | 11 | 15 |
| 6 | 39.91 | 113 | 14 | 275 |
| 7 | 52.20 | 145 | 17 | 158 |
| 8 | 64.78 | 176 | 19 | 157 |
| 9 | 77.66 | 206 | 20 | 342 |
| 10 | 90.84 | 236 | 22 | 29 |
| 11 | 104.33 | 265 | 22 | 351 |
| 12 | 118.13 | 294 | 23 | 231 |
| 13 | 132.25 | 322 | 24 | 54 |
| 14 | 146.69 | 350 | 24 | 191 |
| 15 | 161.43 | 377 | 24 | 290 |
| 16 | 176.47 | 403 | 24 | 356 |
| 17 | 191.79 | 429 | 25 | 28 |
| 18 | 207.38 | 454 | 25 | 42 |
| 19 | 223.22 | 478 | 25 | 36 |
| 20 | 239.29 | 502 | 25 | 13 |
| Age 60 | 563.42 | 806 | 17 | 26 |
| Age 65 | 608.49 | 833 | 15 | 272 |

## Interest Option

*Under the* **interest option**, *the policy proceeds are retained by the insurer, and interest is periodically paid to the beneficiary.* The interest can be paid monthly, quarterly, semiannually, or annually. Most insurers guarantee a minimum interest rate on the policy proceeds retained under the interest option. If the policy is participating, a higher rate of interest is paid based on excess interest earnings. For example, an insurer may pay 5 1/2 percent on the proceeds even though the contractual rate is only 3 percent.

The beneficiary can be given withdrawal rights, by which part or all of the proceeds can be withdrawn. The beneficiary may also be given the right to change to another settlement option.

The interest option provides considerable flexibility, and it can be used in a wide variety of circumstances. In particular, it can be effectively used if the funds will not be needed until some later date. For example, educational funds could be retained at interest until the children are ready for college. Meanwhile, the interest income can supplement the family's income.

## Fixed-Period Option

Under the **fixed-period** or **installment-time option,** *the policy proceeds are paid to a beneficiary over some fixed period of time.* Payments can be made monthly, quarterly, semiannually, or annually. Both principal and interest are systematically liquidated

EXHIBIT 17.2

**Fixed-Period Option (Minimum Monthly Income Payments per $1000 Proceeds, 3 Percent Interest)**

| Period (years) | Monthly payment | Period (years) | Monthly payment | Period (years) | Monthly payment |
|---|---|---|---|---|---|
| 1 | $84.50 | 11 | $8.86 | 21 | $5.32 |
| 2 | 42.87 | 12 | 8.24 | 22 | 5.15 |
| 3 | 29.00 | 13 | 7.71 | 23 | 4.99 |
| 4 | 22.07 | 14 | 7.26 | 24 | 4.84 |
| 5 | 17.91 | 15 | 6.87 | 25 | 4.71 |
| 6 | 15.14 | 16 | 6.53 | 26 | 4.59 |
| 7 | 13.17 | 17 | 6.23 | 27 | 4.48 |
| 8 | 11.69 | 18 | 5.96 | 28 | 4.37 |
| 9 | 10.54 | 19 | 5.73 | 29 | 4.27 |
| 10 | 9.62 | 20 | 5.51 | 30 | 4.18 |

under this option. If the primary beneficiary dies before receiving all payments, the remaining payments will be paid to a contingent beneficiary or to the primary beneficiary's estate.

Exhibit 17.2 illustrates the fixed-period option of one insurer for each $1000 of proceeds at a guaranteed interest rate of 3 percent. The length of the period determines the amount of each payment. If the fixed period is five years, a $50,000 policy would provide a monthly income of $895.50. However, the monthly benefit would be only $481 if a ten-year period is elected.

The fixed-period option can be used in those situations where income is needed for a definite time period, such as during the readjustment, dependency, and blackout periods. The fixed-period option, however, should be used with caution. It is extremely inflexible. Partial withdrawals by the beneficiary normally are not allowed because of the administrative expense of recomputing the amount of the payment during the fixed period. However, many insurers will permit the beneficiary to withdraw the commuted value of the remaining payments in a lump sum.

## Fixed-Amount Option

Under the **fixed-amount** or **installment-amount option,** *a fixed amount is periodically paid to the beneficiary.* The payments are made until both the

principal and interest are exhausted. If excess interest is paid, the period is lengthened, but the amount of each payment is unchanged.

For example, assume that the death benefit is $100,000, the credited interest rate is 4 1/2 percent, and the desired monthly benefit is $1000. The actual monthly payout schedule would be calculated by the insurer. In this case, the beneficiary would receive $1000 monthly for 125 months and a final payment of about $570. At that time, the principal and interest would be exhausted.

The fixed amount option provides considerable flexibility. The beneficiary can be given limited or unlimited withdrawal rights, and also the right to switch the unpaid proceeds to another option. The beneficiary may also be allowed to increase or decrease the fixed amount. It is also possible to arrange a settlement agreement, by which the periodic payments can be increased at certain times, such as when grown children start college. Unless there is some compelling reason for using the fixed-period option, the fixed-amount option is recommended because of its flexibility.

## Life Income Options

Death benefits can also be paid to the beneficiary under a **life income option.** The cash surrender value can also be disbursed under a life income option. The major life income options are as follows.

**Life Income**    *Under this option, installment payments are paid only while the beneficiary is alive and cease on the beneficiary's death.* Although this option provides the highest amount of installment income, there may be a substantial forfeiture of the proceeds if the beneficiary dies shortly after the payments start. Since there is no refund feature or guarantee of payments, other life income options are usually more desirable.

**Life Income with Period Certain**    *Under this option, a life income is paid to the beneficiary with a certain number of guaranteed payments.* If the primary beneficiary dies before receiving the guaranteed number of payments, the remaining payments are paid to a contingent beneficiary. For example, assume that Megan is receiving $600 monthly under a life income option with 10 years certain. If she dies after receiving only one year of payments, the remaining nine years of payments will be paid to a contingent beneficiary or to her estate.

**Life Income with Refund**    Under this option, a lifetime income is paid to the beneficiary. *If the beneficiary dies before receiving payments equal to the amount of insurance, the difference is refunded in installments or in a lump sum to another beneficiary.* For example, assume that Paige has $50,000 of life insurance paid to her under a refund annuity. If she dies after receiving payments of only $10,000, the remaining $40,000 is paid to another beneficiary or to her estate.

**Joint-and-Survivor Income**    *Under this option, income payments are paid to two persons during their lifetimes, such as a husband and wife.* For example, Richard and Margo may be receiving $600 monthly under a joint-and-survivor income annuity. If Richard dies, Margo continues to receive $600 monthly during her lifetime. There are also variations of this option, such as a joint-and-two-thirds annuity or joint-and-one-half annuity. Thus, the monthly income of $600 would be reduced to $400 or $300 on the death of the first person.

Various life income options for single lives are illustrated in Exhibit17.3, which shows the amount of monthly income paid by one insurer for each $1000 of insurance, and the guaranteed interest rate is 3 percent.

Females usually receive lower periodic payments under the life income options than males because of a longer life expectancy. For example, if the proceeds are $50,000, a female beneficiary, age 65, would receive $285 monthly under the life income option with 10 years certain, while the male beneficiary the same age would receive $322.50.

Exhibit 17.4 illustrates the joint-and-survivor income option of one insurer at various ages for each $1000 of insurance and the guaranteed interest rate is 3 percent. For example, an ordinary life policy may have a cash value of $50,000. If the cash is paid out under the joint-and-survivor income option, a monthly income of $256.50 would be paid during the lifetime of both persons, age 65.

## Advantages of Settlement Options

The major advantages are summarized as follows:

1. *Periodic income is paid to the family.* Settlement options can restore part or all of the family's share of the deceased breadwinner's earnings. The financial security of the family can then be maintained.

2. *Principal and interest are guaranteed.* The insurance company guarantees both principal and interest. There are no investment worries and administrative problems, since the funds are invested by the insurer.

3. *Settlement options can be used in life insurance planning.* Life insurance can be programmed to meet the policyowner's needs and objectives.

4. *An insurance windfall can create problems for the beneficiary.* The funds may be spent unwisely; bad investments may be made; and others may try to get the funds. Many insurers now offer money market accounts for investment of the death proceeds so that beneficiaries are not forced to make immediate decisions concerning disposition of the funds.

## Disadvantages of Settlement Options

The major disadvantages are summarized as follows:

1. *Higher yields often can be obtained elsewhere.* Interest rates offered by other financial institutions may be considerably higher.

<small>EXHIBIT 17.3</small>

## Life Income Options (Minimum Monthly Income Payments per $1000 Proceeds, 3 Percent Interest)

| Adjusted Age | | Certain Period | | | |
|---|---|---|---|---|---|
| Male | Female | None | 10 Years | 20 Years | Refund |
| 50 | 55 | $ 4.62 | $4.56 | $4.34 | $4.36 |
| 51 | 56 | 4.72 | 4.65 | 4.40 | 4.44 |
| 52 | 57 | 4.83 | 4.75 | 4.46 | 4.52 |
| 53 | 58 | 4.94 | 4.85 | 4.53 | 4.61 |
| 54 | 59 | 5.07 | 4.96 | 4.59 | 4.69 |
| 55 | 60 | 5.20 | 5.07 | 4.66 | 4.79 |
| 56 | 61 | 5.33 | 5.19 | 4.72 | 4.88 |
| 57 | 62 | 5.48 | 5.31 | 4.78 | 4.99 |
| 58 | 63 | 5.64 | 5.43 | 4.84 | 5.09 |
| 59 | 64 | 5.80 | 5.57 | 4.90 | 5.20 |
| 60 | 65 | 5.98 | 5.70 | 4.96 | 5.32 |
| 61 | 66 | 6.16 | 5.85 | 5.02 | 5.44 |
| 62 | 67 | 6.36 | 5.99 | 5.07 | 5.57 |
| 63 | 68 | 6.57 | 6.14 | 5.13 | 5.71 |
| 64 | 69 | 6.79 | 6.30 | 5.17 | 5.85 |
| 65 | 70 | 7.03 | 6.45 | 5.22 | 6.00 |
| 66 | 71 | 7.28 | 6.62 | 5.26 | 6.15 |
| 67 | 72 | 7.54 | 6.78 | 5.30 | 6.31 |
| 68 | 73 | 7.83 | 6.95 | 5.33 | 6.48 |
| 69 | 74 | 8.13 | 7.11 | 5.36 | 6.66 |
| 70 | 75 | 8.45 | 7.28 | 5.39 | 6.85 |
| 71 | 76 | 8.79 | 7.45 | 5.41 | 7.05 |
| 72 | 77 | 9.16 | 7.62 | 5.43 | 7.26 |
| 73 | 78 | 9.55 | 7.79 | 5.45 | 7.48 |
| 74 | 79 | 9.96 | 7.95 | 5.46 | 7.71 |
| 75 | 80 | 10.41 | 8.11 | 5.48 | 7.95 |

2. *The settlement agreement may be inflexible and restrictive.* The policyowner may have a settlement agreement that is too restrictive. The beneficiary may not have withdrawal rights or the right to change options. For example, the funds may be paid over a 20-year period under the fixed period option with no right of withdrawal. An emergency may arise, but the beneficiary could not withdraw the funds.

3. *Life income options have limited usefulness at the younger ages.* Life income options should rarely be used before age 65 or 70, which restricts their usefulness at the younger ages. If a life income option is elected at a young age, the income payments are substantially reduced. Also, using a life income option is the equivalent of purchasing a single-premium life annuity, which may be purchased more cheaply from another insurer.

Exhibit 17.4

## Joint-and-Survivor Life Income Option (Minimum Monthly Income Payments per $1000 Proceeds, 3 Percent Interest)

| Adjusted Age | | Joint Payee Adjusted Age | | | | | | |
|---|---|---|---|---|---|---|---|---|
| Male | | 45 | 50 | 55 | 60 | 65 | 70 | 75 |
| | Female | 50 | 55 | 60 | 65 | 70 | 75 | 80 |
| 45 | 50 | $3.68 | $3.80 | $3.90 | $3.97 | $4.02 | $4.06 | $4.10 |
| 50 | 55 | 3.80 | 3.97 | 4.13 | 4.25 | 4.34 | 4.41 | 4.46 |
| 55 | 60 | 3.90 | 4.13 | 4.35 | 4.56 | 4.72 | 4.84 | 4.92 |
| 60 | 65 | 3.97 | 4.25 | 4.56 | 4.86 | 5.13 | 5.33 | 5.48 |
| 65 | 70 | 4.02 | 4.34 | 4.72 | 5.13 | 5.51 | 5.85 | 6.10 |
| 70 | 75 | 4.06 | 4.41 | 4.84 | 5.33 | 5.85 | 6.33 | 6.73 |
| 75 | 80 | 4.10 | 4.46 | 4.92 | 5.48 | 6.10 | 6.73 | 7.28 |

## Use of a Trust

The policy proceeds can also be paid to a trustee, such as the trust department of a commercial bank. Under certain circumstances, it may be desirable to have the policy proceeds paid to a trustee rather than disbursed under the settlement options. This would be the case if the amount of insurance is substantial; if considerable flexibility and discretion in the amount and timing of payments are needed; if there are minor children or mentally handicapped adults who cannot manage their own financial affairs; or if the amounts paid must be periodically changed as the beneficiary's needs and desires change. These advantages are partly offset by the payment of a trustee's fee, and the investment results cannot be guaranteed.

## ADDITIONAL LIFE INSURANCE BENEFITS

Other benefits can often be added to a life insurance policy by the payment of an additional premium. These additional benefits provide valuable protection to the policyowner.

## Waiver-of-Premium Provision

A **waiver-of-premium provision** can be added to a life insurance policy. In some policies, the waiver-of-premium is automatically included. Under this provision, if the insured becomes totally disabled from bodily injury or disease before some stated age, all premiums coming due during the period of disability are waived. During the period of disability, death benefits, cash values, and dividends continue as if the premiums had been paid.

Before any premiums are waived, the insured must meet the following requirements:

- Become disabled before some stated age, such as before age 60 or 65.
- Be continuously disabled for six months. (Some insurers have a waiting period of four months.)
- Satisfy the definition of total disability.
- Furnish proof of disability satisfactory to the insurer.

There is a retroactive refund of premiums paid by the policyowner during the first six months of disability if all premiums are being waived under the contract. Newer waiver-of-premium provisions, however, may not provide a retroactive refund.

The insured must also satisfy the definition of disability stated in the policy. The most common definitions of disability are as follows:

- The insured cannot engage in *any occupation* for which he or she is reasonably fitted by education, training, and experience.

- During the first two years, total disability means that the insured cannot perform all duties of *his or her occupation*. After the initial period, total disability means that the insured cannot engage in any occupation reasonably fitted by education, training, and experience.
- Total disability is the entire and irrecoverable loss of sight of both eyes, or the use of both hands or both feet, or one hand and one foot.

The first definition of total disability appears in many older life insurance policies. *Under this definition, the insured is considered totally disabled if he or she cannot work in any occupation reasonably fitted by education, training, and experience.* For example, assume that Dr. Brown is a chemistry professor who has throat cancer and cannot teach. If he can find some other job for which he is reasonably fitted by training and education, such as a research scientist for a chemical firm, he would not be considered disabled. However, if he cannot work in any occupation reasonably fitted by his education, training, and experience, then he would be considered totally disabled.

The second definition of total disability is more liberal and is found in many newer life insurance policies. *For the first two years of disability (in some companies five years), total disability means the insured cannot perform all the duties of his or her own occupation.* After the initial period expires, the definition becomes stricter. *The insured is considered totally disabled only if he or she cannot engage in any occupation reasonably fitted by education, training, and experience.* For example, assume that Dr. Pudwill is a dentist whose hand is severely injured in a hunting accident. For the first two years, he would be considered totally disabled, since he is unable to perform all duties of his occupation. Premiums during this initial period would be waived. However, after the initial period expires, if he could work in any occupation for which he is reasonably fitted by his education and training, he would not be considered totally disabled. Thus, if he could get a job as a research scientist, or as a professor in a dental school, he would not be considered disabled. He would then have to resume premium payments.

*Total disability can also be defined in terms of the loss of use of bodily members.* For example, if Geoffrey loses his eyesight in an explosion, or if both legs are paralyzed from some crippling disease, he would be considered totally disabled.

Before any premiums are waived, the insured must furnish satisfactory proof of disability to the insurer. The insurer may also require continuing proof of disability once each year. If satisfactory proof of disability is not furnished, no further premiums will be waived.

If you have adequate amounts of disability-income insurance, the waiver-of-premium rider is not needed. If you become disabled, the life insurance premiums could be treated like any other type of monthly expense that must be paid, such as housing, utilities, and food. However, most breadwinners are underinsured against the risk of long-term disability. Thus, many financial planners recommend adding this provision to a life insurance policy, especially if the face amount of life insurance is large. During a period of long-term disability, premium payments can be financially burdensome. Since most persons are underinsured for disability-income benefits, waiver of premiums during a period in which income is reduced is highly desirable.

## Guaranteed Purchase Option

The **guaranteed purchase option** *permits the insured to purchase additional amounts of life insurance at specified times in the future without evidence of insurability.* The purpose of the option is to guarantee the insured's future insurability. Additional amounts of life insurance may be needed in the future, or the insured may be unable to afford additional amounts of life insurance today. The guaranteed purchase option guarantees the ability to purchase additional amounts of life insurance at standard rates, even though the insured may be substandard in health or be uninsurable.

**Amount of Insurance** The typical option permits additional amounts of life insurance to be purchased with no evidence of insurability when the insured attains ages 25, 28, 31, 34, 37, and 40. The option usually is not available after age 40. However, some insurers permit an option to be exercised beyond age 40 up to age 65.

The amount of life insurance that can be purchased at each option date is limited to the face amount of the basic policy subject to some minimum and maximum amount. The minimum amount of each additional policy is $5000 or $10,000, and the maximum amount is stated in the rider. With some insurers, the additional policy is limited to a maximum of $25,000. For example, assume that Saul, age 22, purchases a $25,000 ordinary life policy with a guaranteed purchase option and becomes uninsurable after the policy is issued. Assuming that he elects to exercise each option, he would have the following amount of insurance:

| | |
|---|---|
| Age 22 | $25,000 (basic policy) |
| | + |
| Age 25 | $25,000 |
| Age 28 | 25,000 |
| Age 31 | 25,000 |
| Age 34 | 25,000 |
| Age 37 | 25,000 |
| Age 40 | 25,000 |
| Total insurance at age 40 | $175,000 |

Although uninsurable, Saul has increased his insurance coverage from $25,000 to $175,000.

**Advanced Purchase Privilege**  Most insurers have some type of advance purchase privilege, by which an option can be immediately exercised on the occurrence of some event. If the insured marries, has a birth in the family, or legally adopts a child, an option can be immediately exercised prior to the next option due date. Some insurers will provide automatic term insurance for 90 days if the insured marries or a child is born. The insurance expires after 90 days unless the guaranteed insurability option is exercised.

If an option is exercised under the advance purchase privilege, the number of total options is not increased. If an option is exercised early, each new purchase eliminates the next regular option date. Finally, the policyowner typically has only 30 to 60 days to exercise an option. If the option expires without being used, it cannot be exercised at some later date. In some insurers, failure to exercise an option may terminate all subsequent options. This is to protect the insurer from adverse selection.

**Other Considerations**  Four additional points should be noted concerning the guaranteed purchase option. One important consideration is whether the waiver-of-premium rider can be added to the new policy without furnishing evidence of insurability. Insurer practices vary in this regard. The most liberal provision permits the waiver-of-premium rider to be added to the new policy if the original policy contains such a provision. If the premiums are waived under the basic policy, they are also waived under the new policy. Thus, in our earlier example, if premiums are being waived under Saul's original policy of $25,000 because he is totally disabled, the premiums for each new policy will also be waived as long as he remains disabled. A less liberal approach is to permit the disabled insured to purchase a new policy with no evidence of insurability, but not to waive the new premiums under the waiver-of-premium rider.

Second, the guaranteed purchase option usually cannot be added to a term insurance policy. It is restricted to ordinary life, limited-payment, or endowment policies.

Third, when an option is exercised, the premium is based on the insured's attained age. As each option is exercised, the premium rate increases because the insured is older. However, even though the insured may be substandard in health or uninsurable, the premium rate is a standard rate based on the insured's attained age.

Finally, the incontestable clause in each additional policy is effective from the date of issue of the basic policy. If the incontestable period under the basic policy has expired, a new incontestable period does not apply to each additional policy. However, suicide is treated differently. The suicide provision in each additional policy is effective from the date of issue of the additional policy.

## Accidental Death Benefit Rider

The **accidental death benefit rider** (also known as **double indemnity**) *doubles the face amount of life insurance if death occurs as a result of an accident.* In some policies, the face amount is tripled. The cost of the rider is relatively low. For example, at one insurer, the rider costs $69 annually when added to a $100,000 policy issued to a male age 35. Thus, if the insured dies as a result of an accident, $200,000 will be paid.

**Requirements for Collecting Benefits**  Before a double indemnity benefit is paid, several requirements must be satisfied:

- Death must be caused directly and independently of any other cause by accidental bodily injury.
- Death must occur within 90 days of the accident.
- Death must occur before some specified age, such as age 60, 65, or 70.

*The first requirement is that accidental injury must be the direct cause of death.* If death occurs from some other cause, such as disease, the double indemnity benefit is not paid. For example, assume that Sam is painting his two-story house. If the scaffold collapses, and Sam is killed, a double indemnity benefit would be paid because the direct cause of death is an accidental bodily injury. However, if Sam died from a heart attack and fell from the scaffold, the double payment would not be made. In this case, heart disease is the direct cause of death, not accidental bodily injury.

*A second requirement is that death must occur within 90 days of the accident.* The purpose of this requirement is to establish the fact that accidental bodily injury is the proximate cause of death. However, since modern medical technology can prolong life for extended periods, many insurers are using longer time periods, such as 120 or 180 days.

*Finally, the accidental death must occur before some specified age.* In order to limit their liability, insurers typically impose some age limitation. Although some policies provide lifetime accidental death benefits, coverage usually terminates on the policy anniversary date just after the insured reaches a certain age, such as age 70.

Financial planners generally do not recommend purchase of the double indemnity rider. Although the cost is relatively low, there are three major objections to the rider. *First, the economic value of a human life is not doubled or tripled if death occurs from an accident.* Therefore, it is economically unsound to insure an accidental death more heavily than death from disease. *Second, most persons will die as a result of a disease and not from an accident.* Since most persons are underinsured, the premiums for the double indemnity rider could be better used to purchase an additional amount of life insurance, which would cover both accidental death and death from disease.

*Finally, the insured may be deceived and believe that he or she has more insurance than is actually the case.* For example, a person with a $50,000 policy may believe that he or she has $100,000 of life insurance.

## Cost-of-Living Rider

The **cost-of-living rider** *allows the policyowner to purchase one-year term insurance equal to the percentage change in the consumer price index with no evidence of insurability.* The amount of term insurance changes each year and reflects the cumulative change in the Consumer Price Index (CPI) from the issue date of the policy. However, insurers may limit the amount of insurance that can be purchased each year, such as a maximum of 10 percent of the policy face value. The policyowner pays the entire premium for the term insurance.

For example, assume that Luis, age 28, buys a $100,000 ordinary life insurance policy and that the CPI increases 5 percent during the first year. He would be allowed to purchase $5000 of one-year term insurance, and the total amount of insurance in force would be $105,000. The term insurance can be converted to a cash value policy with no evidence of insurability.

## Accelerated Death Benefits Rider

Many insurers now make available a living benefits rider that can be added to a life insurance policy. The **accelerated death benefits rider** *allows insureds who are terminally ill or who suffer from certain catastrophic diseases to collect part or all of their life insurance benefits before they die, primarily to pay for the medical care they require.* Benefits may also be payable if the insured is receiving long-term care in a nursing home or hospital.

Although accelerated death benefits riders are not uniform, they generally can be classified as follows:

- Terminal illness rider
- Catastrophic illness rider
- Long-term care rider

The *terminal illness rider* allows terminally ill insureds with a life expectancy of six months or a year to receive part or all of the policy proceeds. Many insurers allow the rider to be added without an extra premium, but any lump sums advanced are discounted for interest to reflect the time value of money. The face amount of insurance, cash values if any, and premiums are reduced after the payment is made. For example, based on the rider of one insurer, Harry Crockett, age 59, who is terminally ill with cancer, requests 50 percent of his $100,000 term insurance policy. After the benefit is discounted for interest, he receives $46,296. After the payment is made, premiums are reduced 50 percent, and the face amount is reduced to $50,000.

The *catastrophic illness rider* allows insureds who have certain catastrophic diseases to collect part or all of the policy face amount. Covered diseases typically include AIDS, life-threatening cancer, coronary artery disease, kidney failure, and similar types of catastrophic diseases.

The *long-term care rider* allows insureds who require long-term care to collect part of their life insurance prior to death. The rider may cover care in a skilled nursing facility, intermediate care facility, or custodial care facility. Some riders also cover certain types of home care. To illustrate, based on the rider of one insurer, a monthly benefit can be paid equal to 2 percent of the face amount of insurance up to a maximum of 50 percent of the face amount. Thus, if the face amount is $200,000, a monthly benefit of $4000 could be paid up to 25 months.

As an alternative, terminally ill insureds may be able to sell their policies to private firms. A number of firms will buy the life insurance policies of terminally ill insureds at a discount (called a viatical settlement), especially policies owned by AIDS patients. The cash enables AIDS victims to pay their medical bills and other expenses. However, critics argue that the states do not adequately regulate such purchases, and that there is potential for abuse.

Finally, as a result of new federal legislation in 1996, accelerated death benefits and viatical settlements paid to terminally ill and chronically ill individuals now receive favorable income tax treatment (see Insight 17.3).

## INSIGHT 17.3

### Accelerated Death Benefits and Viatical Settlements Now Receive Favorable Income Tax Treatment

The **Health Insurance Portability and Accountability Act of 1996** states that accelerated death benefits and viatical settlements paid to the terminally ill and chronically ill are income-tax free under certain conditions.

- **Terminally ill.** A terminally ill individual is an individual who has been certified by a physician as having an illness or physical condition that is reasonably expected to result in death within 24 months of the certification. The amounts paid to a terminally ill individual as an accelerated death benefit or viatical settlement are excludable from gross income.
- **Chronically ill.** The policy proceeds can also be paid to a chronically ill individual who is not terminally ill. A chronically ill individual is someone who has been certified by a licensed health care practitioner within the preceding 12 months as (1) being unable to perform at least two activities of daily living without substantial assistance, such as eating, bathing, or going to the toilet, because of a loss of functional capacity or (2) requiring substantial supervision because of a severe cognitive impairment. *However, to be excluded from income, the amount received generally must be used to pay for the expenses of qualified long-term care services. Alternatively, payments can be received periodically without regard to the actual long-term care expenses incurred, but there is a dollar cap on the amount excludable from income. The maximum amount of excludable payments is $175 daily, or the equivalent amount in the case of payments received on a different periodic basis. After 1997, the maximum amount will be adjusted for inflation.*

SOURCE: Adapted from *1996 Tax Legislation: Law and Explanation* (CCH Incorporated: Chicago, Ill., 1996), pp. 177–178.

## SUMMARY

- The *incontestable clause* states that the company cannot contest the policy after it has been in force two years during the insured's lifetime.

- The *suicide clause* states that if the insured commits suicide within two years after the policy is issued, the face amount is not paid. There is only a refund of the premiums paid.

- The *grace period* allows the policyowner a period of 31 days to pay an overdue premium. Universal life and other flexible premium policies usually have a longer grace period, such as 61 days. The insurance remains in force during the grace period.

- There are several types of beneficiary designations. A *primary beneficiary* is the party who is first entitled to receive the policy proceeds upon the insured's death. A *contingent beneficiary* is entitled to the proceeds if the primary beneficiary dies before the insured or dies before receiving the guaranteed number of payments under an installment settlement option. A *revocable beneficiary* designation means that the policyowner can change the beneficiary without the beneficiary's consent. An *irrevocable beneficiary* designation is one that cannot be changed without the beneficiary's consent.

- A *dividend* represents a refund of part of the gross premium if the experience of the company is favorable. Dividends paid to policyowners are not taxable and can be taken in several ways:

  Cash

  Reduction of premiums

  Accumulate at interest

  Paid-up additions

  Term insurance (in some companies)

- There are three *nonforfeiture* or cash surrender options:

  Cash value

  Reduced paid-up insurance

  Extended term insurance

- The cash value can be borrowed under the policy loan provision. An automatic premium loan provision can also be added to the policy, by which an overdue premium is automatically borrowed from the cash value.

- *Settlement options* are the various ways that the policy proceeds can be paid other than in a lump sum. The most common settlement options are as follows:

  Interest option

  Fixed-period option

  Fixed-amount option

  Life income options

- A *waiver-of-premium provision* can be added to a life insurance policy, by which all premiums coming due during a period of total disability are waived. Before any premiums are waived, the insured must meet the following requirements:

  Become disabled before some stated age, such as age 60 or 65

  Be continuously disabled for six months

  Satisfy the definition of total disability

  Furnish proof of disability satisfactory to the insurer

- The *guaranteed purchase option* permits the policyowner to purchase additional amounts of life insurance at specified times in the future without evidence of insurability. The purpose of the option is to guarantee the insured's future insurability.

- The *accidental death benefit rider (double indemnity rider)* doubles the face amount of life insurance if death occurs as a result of an accident. Consumer experts generally do not recommend purchase of the double indemnity rider.

- The *cost-of-living rider* allows the policyowner to purchase one-year term insurance equal to the percentage change in the Consumer Price Index with no evidence of insurability.

- The *accelerated death benefits rider* pays part of the life insurance death benefit to a terminally ill insured before death occurs to help pay for medical and other expenses.

## KEY CONCEPTS AND TERMS

Absolute assignment
Accelerated death benefits rider
Accidental death benefit rider (double indemnity)
Automatic premium loan provision
Aviation exclusions
Change-of-plan provision
Class beneficiary
Collateral assignment
Contingent beneficiary
Cost-of-living rider
Entire-contract clause
Extended term insurance
Fixed-amount option
Fixed-period option
Grace period
Guaranteed purchase option
Incontestable clause
Interest option
Irrevocable beneficiary
Life income option
Misstatement of age or sex clause
Nonforfeiture laws
Nonforfeiture options
Nonparticipating policy
Ownership clause
Participating policy
Policy loan provision
Primary beneficiary
Reduced paid-up insurance
Reinstatement provision
Revocable beneficiary
Settlement options
Specific beneficiary
Suicide clause
Waiver-of-premium provision
War clause

## QUESTIONS FOR REVIEW

1. Briefly explain the ownership clause and entire contract clause in a life insurance contract.

2. Describe the incontestable clause and explain why it appears in a life insurance policy.

3. Explain the requirements for reinstating a lapsed policy.

4. If the insured's age is misstated, can the company refuse to pay the policy proceeds? Explain.

5. Describe the various beneficiary designations in life insurance.

6. Can a life insurance policy be assigned to another party? Explain.

7. Are dividends guaranteed? Explain.

8. Explain the nonforfeiture or cash surrender options that are found in cash value life insurance.

9. Identify the various settlement options for the payment of life insurance proceeds.

10. Explain the definition of total disability that is found in a typical waiver-of-premium provision.

## QUESTIONS FOR DISCUSSION

1. A policy that pays dividends is known as a participating policy. The dividends can be paid several ways.
   a. Explain the nature of a life insurance dividend.
   b. Describe the dividend options that are typically found in participating life insurance policies.
   c. For each of the options described in part (b), indicate an appropriate situation where it can be used.

2. Life insurance proceeds can be paid under the fixed-period or fixed-amount settlement options. Compare the fixed-period option and the fixed-amount option with respect to the degree of flexibility that can be obtained if they are used in a settlement plan or agreement.

3. Jim, age 32, purchased a $300,000 five-year renewable and convertible term insurance policy. In answering the health questions, Jim told the agent that he had not visited a doctor within the last five years. However, he had visited the doctor two months earlier. The doctor told Jim that he had a serious heart disease. Jim did not reveal this information to the agent when he applied for life insurance. Jim died

## CASE APPLICATION

Sonja, age 25, recently purchased a $50,000 ordinary life insurance policy. The waiver-of-premium rider and guaranteed purchase option are attached to the policy. For each of the following situations, indicate the extent of the insurer's obligation, if any, to Sonja or to Sonja's beneficiary. Identify the appropriate policy provision or rider that applies in each case. Treat each event separately.

a. Sonja fails to pay the second annual premium due on January 1. She dies 15 days later.

b. Sonja commits suicide three years after the policy was purchased.

c. At Sonja's death, the life insurer discovers that Sonja deliberately lied about her age. Instead of being 25 years old, as she indicated, she was actually 26 years old at the time the policy was purchased.

d. Two years after the policy was purchased, Sonja is told that she has leukemia. She is uninsurable but would like to obtain additional life insurance.

e. Sonja is seriously injured in an automobile accident. After six months, she is still unable to return to work. She has no income from her job, and the insurance premium payments are financially burdensome.

f. Sonja has a mentally disabled son. She wants to make certain that her son will have a continuous income after her death.

g. Sonja lets her policy lapse. After four years, she wants to get the policy reinstated. Her health is fine. Point out to Sonja how she can get her life insurance back.

h. Sonja wants to retire and does not wish to pay the premiums on her policy. Indicate the various options that are available to her.

i. Ten years after the policy was purchased, Sonja is fired from her job. She is unemployed and is in desperate need of cash.

j. When Sonja applied for life insurance, she concealed the fact that she had high blood pressure. She died five years later.

three years after the policy was purchased. At that time, the life insurer discovered the heart ailment. Explain the extent of the insurer's obligation, if any, with respect to payment of the death claim.

4. Additional riders and benefits often can be added to a life insurance policy to provide greater protection to the insured. Describe each of the following riders and options:

a. Waiver-of-premium rider

b. Guaranteed purchase option

c. Double indemnity rider

d. Cost-of-living rider

e. Accelerated death benefits rider

## SELECTED REFERENCES

Anderson, Buist M. *Anderson on Life Insurance.* Boston: Little, Brown, 1991, chapters 15–22.

Belth, Joseph M. *Life Insurance: A Consumer's Handbook,* 2nd ed. Bloomington: Indiana University Press, 1985.

Black, Kenneth, Jr., and Harold D. Skipper, Jr. *Life Insurance,* 12th ed. Englewood Cliffs, N.J.: Prentice-Hall, 1994.

Crawford, Muriel L., and William T. Beadles. *Law and the Life Insurance Contract,* 6th ed. Homewood, Ill: Richard D. Irwin, 1989.

Dorfman, Mark S., and Saul W. Adelman. *Life Insurance: A Financial Planning Approach,* 2nd ed. Chicago: Dearborn Financial Publishing, 1992.

Graves, Edward E., ed. *McGill's Life Insurance.* Bryn Mawr, Pa.: The American College, 1994, chapters 34–44.

Mehr, Robert I., and Sandra G. Gustavson. *Life Insurance: Theory and Practice,* 4th ed. Plano, Tex: Business Publications, 1987.

Rejda, George E., Constance M. Luthardt, Cheryl L. Ferguson, and Donald R. Oakes. *Personal Insurance,* 3rd ed. Malvern, Pa.: Insurance Institute of America, 1997.

Thornton, John H., and Kennes C. Huntley. "A Survey of Life Insurance Policy Provisions." *Journal of the American Society of CLU and ChFC,* 44, no. 3 (May 1990): 72–84.

## NOTES

1. Edward E. Graves, ed., *McGill's Life Insurance* (Bryn Mawr, Pa.: The American College, 1994), p. 819.

2. There are some exceptions. In some states, minors can receive a limited amount of proceeds.

3. Graves, p. 838.

4. Joseph M. Belth, *Life Insurance: A Consumer's Handbook,* 2nd ed. (Bloomington: Indiana University Press, 1985), pp. 152–53.

5. Black, Kenneth, Jr., and Harold D. Skipper, Jr. *Life Insurance,* 12th ed. (Englewood Cliffs, N.J.: Prentice-Hall, 1994), p. 225.

6. *Life Insurance: How to Buy the Right Policy from the Right Company at the Right Price* (Mount Vernon, N.Y.: Consumers Union, 1988), p. 69.

7. Belth, pp. 108–9.

8. A qualification is necessary here. If the insured is substandard or uninsurable, then the paid-up additions option makes sense. However, if a person is insurable, a reasonable approach would be to let the dividends accumulate either at interest or under the paid-up additions option for several years. The accumulated cash could then be used to purchase a new policy. If the new policy is participating, the dividends from both contracts could pay a large portion of the annual premium under the new policy.

9. Robert I. Mehr and Sandra G. Gustavson, *Life Insurance: Theory and Practice,* 4th ed. (Plano, Tex.: Business Publications, Inc., 1987), p. 206.

# Chapter 18

# Buying Life Insurance

> *Insurance companies often succeed in making consumers believe that one policy is much like another.*
>
> *Consumers Union*

## Student Learning Objectives

After studying this chapter, you should be able to:

■ Explain the defects in the traditional net cost method for determining the cost of life insurance.

■ Explain the interest-adjusted surrender cost index and net payment cost index for determining the cost of life insurance.

■ Explain the methods that can be used to determine the rates of return on the saving component of a cash-value policy.

■ Explain the rules that should be followed when life insurance is purchased.

Most people buy life insurance without much thought. They are often unaware of the huge cost variations among insurers and frequently purchase insurance from the first agent who persuades them to buy. The result is that many insureds pay far more than is necessary for the insurance protection they receive. As will be pointed out later, if you make a mistake and purchase a high-cost policy rather than a low-cost policy, this mistake can cost you thousands of dollars over your lifetime.

This chapter discusses the fundamentals of life insurance buying. Specific topics discussed include the various methods for determining the cost of life insurance, the rate of return earned on the saving component of a cash value policy, and suggested rules to follow when buying life insurance.

## DETERMINING THE COST OF LIFE INSURANCE

The cost of life insurance is a complex subject. In general, cost can be viewed as the difference between what you pay for a life insurance policy and what you get back. If you pay premiums and get nothing back, the cost of the insurance equals the premiums paid. However, if you pay premiums and later get something back, such as cash values and dividends, your cost will be reduced. Thus, in determining the cost of life insurance, four major cost factors must be considered: (1) annual premiums, (2) cash values, (3) dividends, and (4) time value of money. Two widely used cost methods that consider some or all of the preceding factors are the *traditional net cost method* and *interest-adjusted cost method.* Although the following discussion is based on cash-value life insurance, the same cost methods can be used to determine the cost of term insurance.

## Traditional Net Cost Method

From an historical perspective, life insurers earlier used the **traditional net cost method** to illustrate the net cost of life insurance. Under this method, the annual premiums for some time period are added together. Total dividends to be received during the same period and the cash value at the end of the period are then subtracted from the total premiums to determine the net cost of life insurance. For example, assume that the annual premium for a $10,000 ordinary life insurance policy issued to a female, age 20, is $132.10. Estimated dividends over a 20-year period are $599, and the cash surrender value at the end of the twentieth year is $2294 (see Exhibit 18.1). The average cost per year is a minus $12.55 (−$1.26 per $1000).

The traditional net cost method has several defects and is misleading. The most glaring defects are as follows:

- *The time value of money is ignored.* Interest that the policyowner could have earned on the premiums by investing them elsewhere is ignored.
- *The insurance is often shown to be free.* This is contrary to common sense, since no life insurer can provide free life insurance to the public and remain in business.
- *The steepness of the dividend scale is ignored.* Some insurers pay small dividends at first and then pay ballooning dividends in later years. The timing and amount of each dividend are ignored.
- *The dividend scale is assumed to remain unchanged.* In most insurers, dividends will change over time.
- *The net cost is based on the assumption that the policy will be surrendered.* The assumption that the policyowner will keep the insurance exactly 20 years (or some other period) and then surrender the policy is questionable.

## Interest-Adjusted Method

The **interest-adjusted method** developed by the National Association of Insurance Commissioners is a more accurate measure of life insurance costs.

### EXHIBIT 18.1
### Traditional Net Cost Method

| | |
|---|---|
| Total premiums for 20 years | $2642 |
| Subtract dividends for 20 years | −599 |
| Net premiums for 20 years | $2043 |
| Subtract the cash value at the end of 20 years | −2294 |
| Insurance cost for 20 years | −$251 |
| Net cost per year (−$251 ÷ 20) | −$12.55 |
| Net cost per $1000 per year (−$12.55 ÷ 10) | −$1.26 |

*Under this method, the time value of money is taken into consideration by applying an interest factor to each element of cost.*

There are two principal types of interest adjusted cost indexes, the *surrender cost index* and the *net payment cost index.* The surrender cost index is useful if you believe you may surrender the policy at the end of 10 or 20 years, or some other time period. The net payment cost index is useful if you intend to keep your policy in force, and cash values are of secondary importance to you.

**Surrender Cost Index**    The **surrender cost index** *measures the cost of life insurance if you surrender the policy at the end of some time period, such as 10 or 20 years* (see Exhibit 18.2).

The annual premiums are accumulated at 5 percent interest, which recognizes the fact that the policyowner could have invested the premiums elsewhere. Dividends are also accumulated at 5 percent interest, which considers interest earnings on the dividends as well as the amount and timing of each dividend. The accumulated net premiums for 20 years are $3762.

The next step is to subtract the cash value at the end of 20 years from the net premiums, which results in a total insurance cost of $1468. This is the amount the policyowner pays for the insurance protection for 20 years, after considering the time value of money.

The final step is to convert the total interest-adjusted cost for 20 years into an annual cost. This is done by dividing the total interest-adjusted cost by an *annuity due* factor of 34.719. This factor means that a $1 deposit at the *beginning* of each year at

## EXHIBIT 18.2
### Surrender Cost Index

| | |
|---|---:|
| Total premiums for 20 years, each accumulated at 5% | $4586 |
| Subtract dividends for 20 years, each accumulated at 5% | −824 |
| Net premiums for 20 years | $3762 |
| Subtract the cash value at the end of 20 years | −2294 |
| Insurance cost for 20 years | $1468 |
| Amount to which $1 deposited annually at the beginning of each year will accumulate to in 20 years at 5% | $34.719 |
| Interest-adjusted cost per year ($1468 ÷ $34.719) | $42.28 |
| Cost per $1000 per year ($42.28 ÷ 10) | $4.23 |

## EXHIBIT 18.3
### Net Payment Cost Index

| | |
|---|---:|
| Total premiums for 20 years, each accumulated at 5% | $4586 |
| Subtract dividends for 20 years, each accumulated at 5% | −824 |
| Insurance cost for 20 years | $3762 |
| Amount to which $1 deposited annually at the beginning of each year will accumulate to in 20 years at 5% | $34.719 |
| Interest-adjusted cost per year ($3762 ÷ $34.719) | $108.36 |
| Cost per $1000 per year ($108.36 ÷ 10) | $10.84 |

5 percent interest will accumulate to $34.719 at the end of 20 years. By dividing the total interest-adjusted cost of $1468 by $34.719, you end up with an annual interest-adjusted cost of $42.28, or $4.23 for each $1000 of insurance. As you can see, the interest-adjusted cost is positive, which means that it costs something to own life insurance when foregone interest is considered. In this case, the average annual cost is $42.28 if the policy is surrendered after 20 years.

**Net Payment Cost Index**    The **net payment cost index** *measures the relative cost of a policy if death occurs at the end of some specified time period, such as 10 or 20 years.* It is based on the assumption that you will not surrender the policy. Therefore, it is the appropriate cost index to use if you intend to keep your life insurance in force.

The net payment cost index is calculated in a manner similar to the surrender index except that the cash value is not subtracted (see Exhibit 18.3).

If the policy is kept in force for 20 years, the policy has an annual cost of $108.36 ($10.84 per $1000) after interest is considered.

### Substantial Cost Variation among Insurers

There are enormous cost variations in cash value life insurance based on the interest-adjusted cost indexes. Exhibit 18.4 shows the policy summary and

interest-adjusted cost data at the end of 20 years for participating whole life policies in the amount of $250,000, for a male, age 35. *A low index number is preferable to a high index number.* For example, Central Life Assurance had the lowest surrender cost index at the end of the 20-year period (−$1.84 per $1000). In contrast, the Knights of Columbus and Woodmen of the World had the highest surrender cost index ($2.69 per $1000). *This wide variation in costs highlights the point stated earlier—you can save thousands of dollars over a long period by paying careful attention to the cost index when you shop for life insurance.*

Unfortunately, most consumers do not use interest-adjusted cost data when buying a life insurance policy. Instead, they use premiums as a basis for comparing costs. However, using premiums alone to compare the cost of the various policies provides only an incomplete comparison. The interest-adjusted cost indexes will provide more accurate information concerning the expected cost of a policy.

### Obtaining Cost Information

If you are approached to buy life insurance, you can ask the life insurance agent to give you interest-adjusted cost data on the policy. In addition, certain states, such as New York, have issued *shoppers guides* that provide cost data on life insurance. Cost data can be easily obtained by calling certain price-quoting services toll free for information on low-cost

**Exhibit 18.4**

## Participating Whole Life Policies of Select Leading Writers—$250,000, Male, Age 35, Nonsmoker

| Company | Policy name | Initial premium | Total premiums | Total cash divs. | Total face amount | Total cash value | Guar. cash value | Payments index | Surrender cost index |
|---|---|---|---|---|---|---|---|---|---|
| | | | | | Summary—20 Policy Years | | | | |
| Aid Assoc. for Lutherans | QUALITY Life | $2,740 | $54,800 | $28,365 | $345,036 | $111,715 | $68,750 | $6.72 | $ −1.20 |
| American National Life | PAR 100 | 2,985 | 59,700 | 26,448 | 351,185 | 89,365 | 54,250 | 6.14 | −0.11 |
| Berkshire Life | Ordinary Life | 3,213 | 64,260 | 40,567 | 417,974 | 122,472 | 59,675 | 6.67 | −0.21 |
| Central Life Assurance | Heritage Extra | 3,175 | 63,500 | 38,633 | 384,283 | 135,666 | 69,967 | 6.86 | −1.84 |
| Century Life | Pro Fit Whole Life | 3,055 | 61,100 | 42,170 | 473,456 | 133,099 | 60,237 | 5.73 | −1.21 |
| Connecticut Mutual Life | CM 2000 | 2,555 | 51,100 | 12,815 | 300,934 | 78,304 | 57,895 | 8.10 | 1.43 |
| Country Life | Executive Whole Life | 2,878 | 57,550 | 31,525 | 380,145 | 115,695 | 63,213 | 6.39 | −1.26 |
| Equitable Life Assurance | Whole Life | 2,973 | 59,460 | 35,565 | 378,995 | 118,607 | 62,500 | 6.47 | −1.02 |
| Franklin Life | Presidential Plus | 2,727 | 54,540 | 24,466 | 322,628 | 95,250 | 62,305 | 7.43 | 0.25 |
| General American Life | Whole Life 98 | 4,790 | 95,800 | 52,438 | 487,291 | 170,373 | 67,338 | 9.78 | 2.02 |
| Great-West Life | Fee Based Whole Life | 2,530 | 50,600 | 19,495 | 337,267 | 80,462 | 53,778 | 6.99 | 0.79 |
| Guardian Life | Whole Life 100 | 2,848 | 56,950 | 20,000 | 309,377 | 99,931 | 69,900 | 8.49 | 0.44 |
| Ind. Order of Foresters | Forester Advantage | 2,670 | 53,400 | 12,896 | 364,500 | 107,750 | 61,000 | 8.60 | 1.57 |
| Indianapolis Life | Executive Whole Life | 2,940 | 58,800 | 31,218 | 373,770 | 125,358 | 69,250 | 6.93 | −1.25 |
| John Hancock Mutual Life | Mod. Premium Whole Life | 2,535 | 60,000 | 35,535 | 386,516 | 120,246 | 57,625 | 6.15 | −0.82 |
| Knights of Columbus | Whole Life | 3,155 | 63,100 | 32,674 | 369,569 | 114,885 | 63,490 | 7.62 | 2.69 |
| Lincoln National Life | Whole Life Plus IV | 2,753 | 55,050 | 17,413 | 305,589 | 88,877 | 64,235 | 8.48 | 1.08 |
| Lutheran Brotherhood Life | Presidential Life (96) | 3,233 | 64,650 | 28,583 | 340,822 | 116,256 | 73,250 | 8.60 | 0.17 |
| Manulife Financial | Premier Whole Life | 2,580 | 51,600 | 18,425 | 321,507 | 78,535 | 54,610 | 7.70 | 1.41 |
| Massachusetts Mutual Life | Whole Life | 2,780 | 55,600 | 23,678 | 340,795 | 100,950 | 62,430 | 7.71 | 0.04 |
| Metropolitan Life | Life at 98 | 2,725 | 54,500 | 24,675 | 331,043 | 110,125 | 71,750 | 7.08 | −1.19 |
| Mutual Life of New York | MONY Premier Plus | 2,930 | 58,600 | 21,187 | 336,564 | 99,006 | 62,500 | 7.98 | 0.78 |
| National Life (VT) | Pace | 2,305 | 57,375 | 23,583 | 346,977 | 88,058 | 46,613 | 7.09 | 1.15 |

*(Continued)*

EXHIBIT 18.4 (Continued)

## Participating Whole Life Policies of Select Leading Writers $250,000, Male, Age 35, Nonsmoker

| Company | Policy name | Initial premium | Total premiums | Total cash divs. | Total face amount | Total cash value | Guar. cash value | Payments index | Surrender cost index |
|---|---|---|---|---|---|---|---|---|---|
| | | | | | Summary—20 Policy Years | | | | |
| Nationwide Life | Equity Plus | $3,138 | $62,760 | $18,216 | $308,970 | $88,643 | $64,213 | $9.71 | $2.31 |
| New England Mutual Life | Ordinary Life Vanguard 7 | 3,110 | 62,200 | 19,773 | 326,427 | 97,227 | 62,483 | 9.49 | 1.63 |
| New York Life | Whole Life | 2,945 | 58,900 | 25,969 | 341,255 | 103,267 | 62,500 | 7.77 | 0.57 |
| Northwestern Mutual Life | Select 100 | 3,333 | 66,650 | 30,540 | 356,640 | 128,912 | 79,107 | 8.52 | −0.59 |
| Penn Mutual Life | Traditional Life | 3,210 | 64,200 | 35,723 | 380,727 | 122,463 | 66,250 | 7.41 | −0.22 |
| Phoenix Home Life | Whole Life | 3,045 | 60,900 | 25,735 | 352,019 | 112,800 | 66,053 | 8.19 | −0.01 |
| Principal Mutual Life | Century 250 | 2,713 | 54,250 | 19,773 | 332,203 | 85,274 | 56,750 | 7.81 | 1.27 |
| Provident Mutual Life | Whole Life II | 2,878 | 57,550 | 16,682 | 303,752 | 91,473 | 67,500 | 9.11 | 1.34 |
| Prudential Insurance | Legacy Select 200 | 3,080 | 61,600 | 32,820 | 380,872 | 115,175 | 57,440 | 7.20 | −0.09 |
| Security Mutual Life (NY) | Customizer 3 | 3,640 | 72,800 | 28,358 | 361,701 | 121,644 | 78,279 | 10.14 | 1.12 |
| Southern Farm Bureau Life | Whole Life 1000 | 3,263 | 65,250 | 26,108 | 358,452 | 100,536 | 60,750 | 8.97 | 1.97 |
| State Farm Life | Estate Protector | 3,058 | 61,150 | 24,995 | 348,402 | 105,187 | 63,600 | 8.39 | 0.69 |
| Sun Financial | Sun Permanent Life | 3,358 | 67,160 | 39,916 | 465,189 | 129,910 | 58,760 | 7.08 | −0.36 |
| Union Central Life | LFP 100 | 3,525 | 70,500 | 26,438 | 342,988 | 118,655 | 71,750 | 10.03 | 1.76 |
| USAA Life | Whole Life | 2,890 | 57,800 | 34,268 | 404,888 | 127,325 | 64,572 | 5.99 | −1.44 |
| Western & Southern Life | Economy Life | 2,765 | 55,300 | 25,571 | 337,775 | 111,140 | 68,500 | 7.15 | −0.98 |
| Woodmen of the World | Whole Life | 3,118 | 62,360 | 18,317 | 318,000 | 88,356 | 60,933 | 9.71 | 2.69 |
| Median Values | | $2,959 | $59,580 | $26,039 | $347,690 | $110,633 | $62,857 | $7.70 | $0.35 |

SOURCE: Adapted from Andrew D. Gold, "Whole Life Policy Survey," *Best's Review, Life/Health* (April 1994), p. 38.

## INSIGHT 18.1

### Term-Insurance Quotes: Online vs. By Mail

HERE ARE THE RESULTS of our online shopping for the lowest annual premiums on $200,000, 15-year term policies for healthy, nonsmoking, 45-year-old women and men.

| Quote Service/ Web Address | Instant Quote? | Best Rates For Women And Men | Premiums |
|---|---|---|---|
| **Insurance Quote Services** (http://www.iquote.com) 800-972-1104 | No | **W:** Old Republic Life Insurance Co. **M:** CNA Insurance Cos. | $246 $309 |
| **MasterQuote** (http://www.masterquote.com) 800-337-5433 | No | **W:** First Penn-Pacific Life Insurance Co. **M:** First Penn-Pacific Life | $280 $350 |
| **QuickQuote** (http://www.quickQuote.com) 800-867-2404 | Yes | **W:** Old Republic Life **M:** Lincoln Benefit Life Co. | $306 $381 |
| **Quotesmith** (http://www.quotesmith.com) 800-431-1147 | Yes | **W:** First Penn-Pacific Life/ Lincoln Benefit Life **M:** First Penn-Pacific Life/ Lincoln Benefit Life | $280 $350 |
| **Term Quote** (http://www.rcinet.com/~ termquote) 800-444-8376 | No | **W:** First Penn-Pacific Life **M:** First Penn-Pacific Life | $280 $350 |

SOURCE: Excerpted from "Insurance online: Faster, not cheaper," *Kiplinger's Personal Finance Magazine* (October 1996), p. 90.

---

policies. The same information is available on the internet (see Insight 18.1). Finally, most policy illustrations include interest-adjusted cost data.

However, if you use interest-adjusted cost data, keep in mind the following points:

- *Shop for a policy and not an insurer.* Some insurers have excellent low-cost policies at certain ages and amounts, but they are not as competitive when other ages and amounts are considered.
- *Compare only similar plans of insurance.* You should compare policies of the same type with the same benefits. Otherwise, the comparison can be misleading.

- *Ignore small variations in the cost index numbers.* Small cost differences can be offset by other policy features or by services that you can expect to get from an agent or insurer.
- *Cost indexes apply only to a new policy.* The cost data should not be used to determine whether to *replace* an existing policy with a new one. Other factors should be considered as well (see Insight 18.2).
- *The type of policy you buy should not be based solely on a cost index.* You should buy the right type of policy that meets your needs, such as term, whole life, or some combination. Once you have decided on the type of policy, then compare costs.

## INSIGHT 18.2

### The Replacement Problem

If you already own a life insurance policy, a health insurance policy, or an annuity contract, you should be careful if you consider replacing it. Although the relative financial strength of the original company and the replacing company is an important factor in your decision, you should consider other factors as well. Some of those additional factors are described briefly in the following paragraphs.

*If you consider replacing life or health insurance, your state of health and other items affecting your eligibility should be reviewed.* You may not qualify for new insurance or you may qualify only at high rates.

*You should determine the cost of getting out of the original policy.* Many policies contain substantial surrender charges.

*You should determine the cost of getting into the replacement policy.* Many policies involve substantial front-end expenses.

*You should determine whether the cost of continuing the original policy is reasonable.* If the cost is reasonable, there may be little if any reason to replace it. (A procedure for making such a determination is described in the appendix to this chapter.)

*You should consider the tax implications of a replacement.* In some situations, the termination of a life insurance policy or an annuity contract may trigger an income tax liability. You may be able to defer the tax, but you should consult your tax adviser.

*You should consider the incontestability clause.* For example, if a life insurance policy is more than two years old, the company usually is barred from alleging that the policy is void because of false statements you made in the application. Thus the original policy may not be contestable, while the replacement policy may be contestable for two years.

*You should also be aware of the suicide clause.* Suicide is commonly excluded during the first two years of a life insurance policy. Thus the original policy may currently cover suicide, while the replacement policy may not cover suicide for two years.

*If someone recommends replacement, you should try to determine the amount of compensation the person making the recommendation will receive if you follow the advice.* Some who recommend replacement are motivated by a genuine desire to help you reduce your expenses or avoid the problems that may arise if your original company gets into financial trouble. However, in the current environment of public concern about the financial strength of insurance companies, some persons may descend on the policyowners of a troubled company like sharks who detect blood in the water. The fact that a person receives a commission does not necessarily mean he or she is giving bad advice, but you should be on guard.

SOURCE: Adapted from Joseph M. Belth, ed., *The Insurance Forum*, 23, (September 1996), p. 92.

## New NAIC Policy Illustration Model Regulation

Our discussion of life insurance costs would not be complete without a brief discussion of the new Life Insurance Policy Illustration Model Regulation drafted by the National Association of Insurance Commissioners (NAIC). The model act would apply to new policies sold on or after January 1, 1997, or later, if changed by an adopting state.

If adopted by the states, the new model act will have a dramatic and sweeping impact on the way policy illustrations are calculated and presented. Certain deceptive sales practices are prohibited in the illustration of policy values. Insurers are prohibited from using anticipated gains from improvements in mortality in the sales illustration; the term "vanishing premium" cannot be used; the applicant and agent must sign the illustration and indicate they have discussed and understand that the "nonguaranteed elements" in the policy are subject to change and can be lower or higher; and the values shown in the illustration must be supportable by a self-support test. For example, lapse-supported pricing cannot be used. The self-support test requires that assumptions concerning lapses must be limited to actual experience for the first five years and zero lapses for the remaining life of the block of policies.

Finally, the insurer must provide an annual report on the policy and notify the policyowners when a change occurs in the dividend scale or individual pricing elements that would negatively affect the policy values. When fully implemented, the proposed model regulation should reduce misunderstanding of policy values by policyowners and reduce deceptive sales practices by agents.

## RATE OF RETURN ON SAVING COMPONENT

Another important consideration is the rate of return earned on the saving component in a traditional whole life insurance policy. Consumers normally do not know the annual rate of return they earn on the savings component in their policies. A consumer who buys a traditional cash-value policy with a low return can lose a considerable amount of money over the life of the policy. Thus, the annual rate of return you earn on the saving component is critical if you intend to save money over a long period of time.

### Linton Yield

The **Linton yield** is one method that can be used to determine the rate of return on the saving portion of a cash-value policy. It was developed by M. Albert Linton, a well-known life insurance actuary. In essence, the Linton yield is the average annual rate of return on a cash-value policy if it is held for a specified number of years. It is based on the assumption that a cash-value policy can be viewed as a combination of insurance protection and a savings fund. To determine the average annual rate of return for a given period, it is first necessary to determine that part of the annual premium that is deposited in the savings fund. This can be determined by subtracting the cost of the insurance protection for that year from the annual premium (less any dividend). The balance of the premium is the amount that can be deposited into the savings fund. Thus, the average annual rate of return is the compound interest rate that is required to make the savings deposits equal the guaranteed cash value in the policy at the end of a specified period.

Unfortunately, current rates of return based on the Linton yield are not readily available to insurance

consumers. An earlier study by Consumers Union provided annual rates of return on certain whole life policies at the end of 5, 10, and 20 years based on the Linton yield. *The study showed that as of 1985 the annual rates of return for a participating whole life policy in the amount of $50,000 issued to a male age 25 ranged from −63.44 percent to 5.27 percent at the end of 5 years; from −5.23 percent to 10.72 percent at the end of 10 years; and from 4.47 percent to 11.91 percent at the end of 20 years.*[1] Most policies had annual returns of 7 to 10 percent, up significantly from the 2 to 6 percent yields reported in an earlier 1980 study by Consumers Union.

Similar data are also available for a small number of *nonparticipating* whole life policies. In general, the annual rates of return are much lower for nonparticipating policies. *The Consumers Union study showed that as of 1985 the annual rates of return for a nonparticipating whole life policy in the amount of $50,000 issued to a male age 25 ranged from −77.49 percent to −1.63 percent at the end of 5 years; from −19.31 percent to 8.59 percent at the end of 10 years; and from −3.26 percent to 10.97 percent at the end of 20 years.*

The negative returns during the early years are explained by the heavy first-year acquisition and administrative expenses that are incurred when the policy is first sold. An agent receives a commission equal to at least one-half of the first year's premium. There may be a medical examiner's fee, an inspection report, and other expenses in issuing the policy. In recognition of these first-year expenses, most cash-value policies do not have any cash value at the end of the first year, and the cash values are relatively low in the first few years of the policy. Thus, if you surrender or lapse the policy during the early years of the policy, you will lose a substantial amount of money.

The preceding data should be used with caution. The rates of return cited in the earlier Consumers Union study should not be viewed as the rates of return available today. Interest rates have declined sharply since 1985, and if current rates of return based on the Linton yield were available, they undoubtedly would be much lower today. Unfortunately for consumers, a more recent study of life insurance costs by Consumers Union did not provide rates of return based on the Linton yield.[2] Consumer advocates have recommended that annual rates-of-return data on the savings component should be furnished to the purchasers of traditional whole life policies. However, the life insurance industry has vigorously opposed this recommendation, arguing that it is actuarially improper to separate the savings and protection components of a traditional whole life policy since it is an undivided contract and thus rates of return on the savings component should not be provided.

## Yearly Rate-of-Return Method

Professor Joseph M. Belth has developed a simple method for calculating the **yearly rate of return** on the savings component of a cash value policy.[3] The yearly rate of return is based on the following formula:

$$i = \frac{(CV + D) + (YPT)(DB - CV)(.001)}{(P + CVP)} - 1$$

where

$i$ = yearly rate of return on the savings component, expressed as a decimal

$CV$ = cash value at end of policy year

$D$ = annual dividend

$YPT$ = assumed yearly price per $1000 of protection (see benchmark prices in Exhibit 18.5)

$DB$ = death benefit

$P$ = annual premium

$CVP$ = cash value at end of preceding policy year

The first expression in the numerator of the formula is the amount available in the policy at the end of the policy year. The second expression in the numerator is the assumed price of the protection component, which is determined by multiplying the amount of protection by an assumed price per $1000 of protection. Assumed prices per $1000 of protection for various ages are benchmarks derived from certain United States population death rates (see Exhibit 18.5). Finally, the expression in the denominator of the formula is the amount available in the policy at the beginning of the policy year.

For example, assume that Mark purchased a $100,000 participating ordinary life policy at age 35. He is now aged 42 at the beginning of the eighth policy year. He would like to know the yearly rate of return on the savings component for the eighth year of the policy. The annual premium is $1500. The cash value in the policy is $7800 at the end of the seventh policy year and $9200 at the end

### Exhibit 18.5
### Benchmark Prices

| Age | Benchmark price |
|---|---|
| Under 30 | $1.50 |
| 30–34 | 2.00 |
| 35–39 | 3.00 |
| 40–44 | 4.00 |
| 45–49 | 6.50 |
| 50–54 | 10.00 |
| 55–59 | 15.00 |
| 60–64 | 25.00 |
| 65–69 | 35.00 |
| 70–74 | 50.00 |
| 75–79 | 80.00 |
| 80–84 | 125.00 |

NOTE: *The benchmark prices were derived from certain United States population death rates. The benchmark figure for each five-year age bracket is close to the death rate per $1000 at the highest age in that bracket.*

SOURCE: Adapted from Joseph M. Belth, *Life Insurance: A Consumer's Handbook,* 2nd ed. (Bloomington: Indiana University Press, 1985), Table 9, p. 84. Reprinted by permission of the author.

of the eighth policy year. The eighth-year dividend is $400. Since Mark is aged 42 at the beginning of the eighth policy year, the benchmark price is $4.00 (see Exhibit 18.5).

Based on the preceding information, the yearly rate of return for the eighth policy year is calculated as follows:

$$i = \frac{(9,200 + 400) + (4)(100,000 - 9,200)(.001)}{(1,500 + 7,800)} - 1$$

$$= \frac{(9,600) + (4)(90,800)(.001)}{(9,300)} - 1$$

$$= \frac{9,600 + 363}{9,300} - 1$$

$$= \frac{9,963}{9,300} - 1 = 1.071 - 1 = .071 = 7.1\%$$

The yearly rate of return for the eighth policy year is 7.1 percent, assuming that the yearly price per $1000 of protection is $4.

The major advantage of Belth's method is simplicity—you do not need a computer. The information needed can be obtained by referring to your policy and premium notice, or by contacting your agent or insurer. The same methodology can be used to evaluate an existing life insurance policy. (See the appendix at the end of the chapter.)

## SHOPPING FOR LIFE INSURANCE

You should consider several important factors when thinking about purchasing life insurance. They include the following:

- Determine if you need life insurance.
- Estimate the amount of life insurance needed.
- Decide on the best type of life insurance for you.
- Decide whether you want a policy that pays dividends.
- Shop around for a low-cost policy.
- Consider the financial strength of the insurer.
- Deal with a competent agent.

### Determine If You Need Life Insurance

The first step is to determine if you need life insurance. If you are married or single with one or more dependents to support, you may need a substantial amount of life insurance. You may also need life insurance if you have a temporary need, such as paying off the mortgage on your home. In addition, if you have accumulated substantial assets, large amounts of life insurance may be needed to provide estate liquidity and to pay federal estate taxes that are due within nine months of your death.

*However, if you are single and no one is presently dependent on you for financial support, you do not need life insurance, other than a modest amount for burial purposes.* The arguments for buying life insurance when you are young and insurable are not compelling. Even if your situation should change and you need life insurance in the future, *more than nine out of ten applicants for life insurance are accepted at standard rates.* Thus, it is a waste of money to buy life insurance when it is not needed.

### Estimate the Amount of Life Insurance Needed

The needs approach and capital retention approach are practical methods for determining the amount of life insurance needed. Persons with dependents often need surprisingly large amounts of life insurance. In

determining the amount needed, you must consider your family's present and future financial needs, potential survivor benefits from Social Security, and the financial assets currently owned. These factors are discussed in greater detail in Chapter 19.

If you carry a sufficient amount of life insurance, it is unnecessary to purchase additional life insurance as supplemental coverage. These coverages include accidental life insurance policies from life insurers, accidental death and dismemberment insurance offered by commercial banks, credit life insurance on consumer loans, and life insurance sold by mail. In addition, flight insurance sold at airports is a bad buy for most consumers because commercial jets rarely crash (see Insight 18.3).

### Decide on the Best Type of Life Insurance for You

The next step is to select the best type of life insurance policy for you. *The best policy is one that best meets your financial needs.* If the amount of money you can spend on life insurance is limited, or if you have a temporary need, consider only term insurance. If you need lifetime protection, consider ordinary life insurance or universal life insurance. If you believe that you cannot save money without being forced to do so, also consider ordinary life insurance or universal life insurance as a savings vehicle. However, remember that the annual rates of return on cash-value policies can vary enormously.

Also, avoid purchasing a policy that you cannot afford. A large percentage of new life insurance policies lapse for nonpayment of premiums during the first two years. The lapse rate for policies in force for less than two years was 17 percent in 1995.[4] *If you drop the policy after a few months or years, you will lose a substantial sum of money. Be sure you can afford the premium.*

### Decide Whether You Want a Policy that Pays Dividends

In recent decades, participating life insurance policies that pay dividends generally have been better buys than nonparticipating policies because of high interest rates that permitted insurers to raise their dividends. However, interest rates have declined sharply in recent years, and many insurers have substantially reduced their dividends because excess interest earnings have declined. Thus, if you believe

---

## INSIGHT 18.3

### Skip the Flight Insurance at Airports

FLIGHT INSURANCE. This hardy perennial pays off if you die in a plane crash. American Express, for example sells cardholders $1 million of coverage for $14 per trip. Sure, plane crashes are high-impact news events that get people worried about safety. But think a minute. You already have adequate comprehensive life insurance, right? Why would your family need more money if you died in a crash than if you were run over by a cab at the airport? And don't forget that American Express automatically gives you $100,000 of coverage free when you charge your ticket on Amex's green and gold cards.

*Finally, your chances of dying in a crash are wildly improbable.* If every passenger on every scheduled U.S. commercial flight had paid $14 for a $1-million policy in 1995, and a $1-million claim was paid for every victim that year, the result would be a $7.4-billion profit to the insurer.

*Suggestion: Skip the insurance and the airplane food, and buy a good lunch.*

SOURCE: Excerpted from William Giese, "Insurance You Can Do Without," *Kiplinger's Personal Finance Magazine* (February 1997), p. 72.

---

that interest rates will be higher in the future, you should consider a participating policy because excess interest has a powerful impact on dividends. However, if you believe that interest rates will continue to fall and will remain at lower levels in the future, then consider a nonparticipating policy. Policies that do not pay dividends generally require a lower initial premium outlay.

### Shop Around for a Low-Cost Policy

One of the most important suggestions is to shop carefully for a low-cost policy. There is enormous variation in the cost of life insurance. You should not purchase a life insurance policy from the first agent who approaches you. *Instead, you should compare the interest-adjusted cost of similar policies from several insurers before you buy.* Otherwise, you may be overpaying for the insurance protection. If you make a mistake and purchase a high-cost policy, this mistake can cost you thousands of dollars over your lifetime.

When you shop for a low-cost policy, you should also consider **low-load life insurance.** A small number of life insurers sell insurance directly to the public by using telephone representatives or fee-only financial planners. The major advantage is that marketing expenses account for only 10 to 25 percent of the first year's premium rather than 90 to 125 percent on policies sold by agents. Two major low-load insurers that sell policies by phone are Veritas (800-552-3553) and USAA (800-531-8000).

### Consider the Financial Strength of the Insurer

In addition to cost, you should consider the financial strength of the insurer issuing the policy. Some life insurers have become insolvent and have gone out of business. Although all states have state guaranty funds that pay the claims of insolvent life insurers, there are limits on the amount guaranteed. Although death claims are paid promptly, you may have to wait years before you can borrow or withdraw your cash value. Thus, it is important to buy life insurance only from insurers that are financially sound.

A number of rating organizations periodically grade and rate life insurers on their financial strength (see Exhibit 18.6). The companies are rated based on the amount of their capital and surplus, legal reserves, quality of investments, past profitability, competency of management, and numerous other factors. However, the various ratings are not always a reliable guide for consumers and can be confusing. There are wide variations in the grades given by the different rating agencies. A grade of A is the third-highest grade from A.M. Best, while for Standard & Poor's and Duff & Phelps, a grade of A is the sixth-highest grade. A grade of A is only the second-highest grade from Weiss. Thus, you should be careful and conservative when you are evaluating the financial strength of an insurer. Joseph M. Belth, a nationally known consumer expert in life insurance, recommends that an insurer should receive a high rating from at least two of the following four rating

EXHIBIT 18.6

**The Rating Categories***

| Rank number | Ratings | | | | |
|---|---|---|---|---|---|
| | Standard & Poor's | Moody's | Duff & Phelps | Weiss # | A.M. Best |
| 1 | AAA, AAAq | Aaa | AAA | A+ | A++ |
| 2 | AA+ | Aa1 | AA+ | A | A+ |
| 3 | AA, AAq | Aa2 | AA | A– | A |
| 4 | AA– | Aa3 | AA– | B+ | A– |
| 5 | A+ | A1 | A+ | B | B++ |
| 6 | A, Aq | A2 | A | B– | B+ |
| 7 | A– | A3 | A– | C+ | B |
| 8 | BBB+ | Baa1 | BBB+ | C | B– |
| 9 | BBB, BBq | Baa2 | BBB | C– | C++ |
| 10 | BBB– | Baa3 | BBB– | D+ | C+ |
| 11 | BB+ | Ba1 | BB+ | D | C |
| 12 | BB, BBq | Ba2 | BB | D– | C– |
| 13 | BB– | Ba3 | BB– | E+ | D |
| 14 | B+ | B1 | B+ | E | E |
| 15 | B, Bq | B2 | B | E– | F |
| 16 | B– | B3 | B– | F | |
| 17 | CCC, CCCq | Caa | CCC | | |
| 18 | R | Ca | DD | | |
| 19 | | C | | | |

*The ratings in a given rank are not necessarily equivalent to one another.

#Weiss designates small companies by the letter "S" immediately preceding the rating.

SOURCE: Joseph M. Belth, ed., *The Insurance Forum,* 23, (September 1996), p. 87.

agencies before a policy is purchased. The following are considered high ratings for someone who is *conservative*:[5]

**Standard & Poor's:  AAA, AAAq, AA+, AA, AAq, AA –**
**Moody's: Aaa, Aa1, Aa2, Aa3, A1**
**Duff & Phelps: AAA, AA+, AA**
**Weiss: A+, A, A–, B+, B, B–**

## Deal with a Competent Agent

You should also deal with a competent agent when you buy life insurance. Selling life insurance is a tough job, and only a relatively small proportion of new life insurance agents are successful. The industry turnover rate is high; the four-year retention rate is only 17 percent.[6]

Most new agents receive only a minimum amount of training before they are licensed to sell life insurance. New agents also are often placed under intense pressure to sell life insurance. Even mature agents are expected to sell a certain amount of insurance. As a result, some agents have engaged in deceptive sales practices by misrepresenting the insurance to clients or by recommending policies that maximize commissions rather than meeting the client's needs. Because of deceptive sales practices by agents, several major life insurers have been subject to heavy fines by state insurance departments and class action litigation by angry policyowners. Insight 18.4 highlights the deceptive sales practices by one major life insurer.

To reduce the possibility of receiving bad advice or being sold the wrong policy, you should consider the professional qualifications of the agent. An agent

# INSIGHT 18.4

## Life Insurers Sidestep Sales-Fraud Taint

When a Prudential agent came unannounced to Mrs. Trerice's mobile home in Holiday, Fla. in 1982, she let him in. The agent reminded her that her husband had a $6,000 Prudential life insurance policy, and she had one for $1,000. Both were paid up.

"He advised me to take out a (new), $5,000 policy, and I wouldn't have to pay any premiums, because the premiums and the interest on the first policies would pay it," Mrs. Trerice recalls. So she bought two policies for a total of $10,000 coverage.

Mrs. Trerice assumed that if her husband died, she would be paid $10,000 for the new policies plus $6,000 for the original two, and that they wouldn't have to pay a dime in premiums.

But in 1987 the Trerice's began receiving bills from Prudential. Upon inquiring with the local office, she was told that not only would she have to begin paying Prudential more than $700 per year to keep the new policies in force, the older policies were completely drained of any cash value and were worthless.

The Trerices and scores of other people, mostly senior citizens, have sued Prudential charging they were subjected to deceptive sales pitches.

After admitting to fraudulent sales practices, Prudential Insurance Co. of America is settling the class action, defending the additional lawsuits, contending with charges that it destroyed damaging documents and trying to repair its image with industry regulators, analysts and the public.

"We are learning these lessons," said Prudential spokesman Bob DeFillippo. "They've cost us a lot, and they've cost us our reputation."

Prudential, the nation's largest life insurance company, isn't the first to admit such charges. But some doubt whether the Prudential penalties under discussion, or any penalties other companies have paid, are sufficient incentive for the industry to reform itself.

"A lot of people are trying very hard to do something about this, but the ways they're trying to do it do not get into disclosing the vital information," said Joseph Belth, professor emeritus of insurance at Indiana University.

"I wonder if it can ever really be cleaned up, unless you have an alteration of this nondisclosure environment."

Prudential has agreed to spend at least $410 million to reimburse up to 10.7 million people who bought policies from 1982 to 1995. Accountants at Arthur Andersen & Co. said it could cost up to $2 billion.

### Steering Clear of a Scam

The Prudential Insurance Co. of America is being sued by customers who charge they were the victims of deceptive sales practices by Prudential agents. The company has admitted that some of its agents did make improper pitches. Some tips for avoiding insurance scams:

1  As with buying anything, if something sounds too good to be true, it probably is. If someone offers to sell you something for nothing, walk away.

2  If someone offers to replace your outstanding policy, or use proceeds from one policy to pay premiums for another, be suspicious and get a second opinion.

3  Cash-value products such as whole life, universal life and variable life insurance may not be the right choice for most people. Instead, consider term life, which is simply insurance against premature death.

4  Cash-value policies, which combine life insurance with a savings or investment feature and can be borrowed against tax-free, are only appropriate for high-income people, and only if they are kept at least 10 years.

5  Ask the agent, and get an answer you understand: What is your commission the first year, over five years, over 10 years? The industry average is 65 percent of the first year's premium, and commissions vary from 50 percent to 75 percent.

SOURCE: Robert Hunter. Consumer Federation of America

*Continued*

*Prudential was accused of churning, or selling to previous policyholders more expensive policies that are paid for with dividends earned on the first. The tactic stripped value from the old policies and drained customer savings, regulators said.*

*Some agents used a vanishing premiums pitch, in which policyholders are told they will only have to pay premiums for a few years. But premium billings do not stop on the anticipated date.*

*Other accusations included payout projections that assumed unrealistically high interest rates, and sales of life insurance products disguised as investments.*

The practices created a flurry of activity by the industry and regulators. The firms said that they are more selective in hiring agents, and that they train them better and check up on them by having non-commissioned agents call customers shortly after the sales close.

Industry groups are considering industrywide marketing standards. And state insurance regulators are considering model state regulations designed to stop the practices.

One idea under consideration is to spread commissions out over several years instead of paying them all up front, which some argue encourages churning.

Source: Adapted from "Life Insurers Sidestep Sales-Fraud Taint," Sunday World Herald, February 9, 1997, p. 3-M.

who is a **Chartered Life Underwriter (CLU), Chartered Financial Consultant (ChFC),** or **Certified Financial Planner (CFP)** should be technically competent to give proper advice. More importantly, agents who hold the preceding professional designations are expected to abide by a code of ethics that places their clients' interests ahead of their own. Agents who are currently studying for these professional designations should also be considered.

## SUMMARY

- There are enormous cost variations among similar life insurance policies. Purchase of a high-cost policy can cost thousands of dollars over the insured's lifetime for the same amount of insurance protection.

- The traditional net cost method to illustrate the cost of life insurance has several defects:

  The time value of money is ignored.

  The insurance is often shown to be free.

  The steepness of the dividend scale is ignored.

  The dividend scale is assumed to remain unchanged.

  The net cost is based on the assumption that the policy will be surrendered.

- The interest-adjusted method is a more accurate measure of life insurance costs. The time value of money is taken into consideration by applying an interest factor to each element of cost. If you are interested in surrendering the policy at the end of a certain period, the surrender cost index is the appropriate cost index to use. If you intend to keep your policy in force, the net payment cost index should be used.

- Annual rates-of-return data on the saving component in traditional cash-value life insurance policies are not readily available to consumers. However, the yearly-rate-of-return method by Professor Joseph Belth can be helpful in this regard.

- Life insurance experts typically recommend several rules to follow when shopping for life insurance:

  Determine if you need life insurance.

  Estimate the amount of life insurance needed.

  Decide on the best type of insurance for you.

  Decide whether you want a policy that pays dividends.

  Shop around for a low cost policy.

  Consider the financial strength of the insurer.

  Deal with a competent agent.

## KEY CONCEPTS AND TERMS

Benchmark net cost indexes
Certified Financial Planner (CFP)
Chartered Financial Consultant (ChFC)
Chartered Life Underwriter (CLU)
Interest-adjusted method
Linton yield
Low-load life insurance
Net payment cost index
Surrender cost index
Traditional net cost method
Yearly rate-of-return method

## QUESTIONS FOR REVIEW

1. Describe the traditional net cost method for determining the cost of life insurance.

2. Explain the defects of the traditional net cost method.

3. Explain the surrender cost index and net payment cost index. How are these indexes an improvement over the traditional net cost method?

4. Where can interest-adjusted cost information be obtained?

5. List the rules that should be followed if interest-adjusted data are used.

6. Why are the rates of return on the saving element in most cash-value policies negative during the early years?

7. Briefly explain the yearly rate-of-return method that can be used to determine the rate of return on the saving component of a cash-value policy.

8. Describe the rules that should be followed when shopping for life insurance.

9. Is it desirable to replace an older life insurance policy with a new policy? Explain.

10. Should cost be the only factor to consider when a life insurance policy is purchased? Explain.

## QUESTIONS FOR DISCUSSION

1. A life insurance agent remarked that "most life insurance policies cost about the same, and it really is not necessary to be concerned about cost." Do you agree or disagree with the agent's remarks? Explain.

2. A friend remarked that "cash-value life insurance is a good place to save money, since the annual return is reasonable and the money is safe." Do you agree or disagree with this statement? Explain your answer.

3. You have been asked for some advice on how to buy life insurance. What suggestions can you give?

4. Contrast the Linton yield and the yearly-rate-of-return method as techniques for determining the rates of return on the saving component of a cash-value policy.

## SELECTED REFERENCES

Belth, Joseph M. *Life Insurance: A Consumer's Handbook,* 2nd ed. Bloomington: Indiana University Press, 1985.

Black, Kenneth, Jr., and Harold D. Skipper, Jr. *Life Insurance,* 12th ed. Englewood Cliffs, N.J.: Prentice-Hall, 1994.

Dorfman, Mark S., and Saul W. Adelman. *Life Insurance: A Financial Planning Approach,* 2nd ed. Chicago: Dearborn Financial Publishing, 1992.

## CASE APPLICATION

A participating ordinary life policy in the amount of $10,000 is issued to an individual, age 35. The following cost data are given:

| | |
|---|---|
| Annual premium | $230 |
| Total dividends for 20 years | $1613 |
| Cash value at end of 20 years | $3620 |
| Accumulated value of the annual premiums at 5 percent for 20 years | $7985 |
| Accumulated value of the dividends at 5 percent for 20 years | $2352 |
| Amount to which $1 deposited annually at the beginning of each year will accumulate in 20 years at 5 percent | $34.719 |

a. Based on the above information, compute the annual net cost for each $1000 of life insurance at the end of 20 years using the *traditional net cost method.*

b. Compute the annual *surrender cost index* for each $1000 life insurance at the end of 20 years.

c. Compute the annual *net payment cost index* for each $1000 of life insurance at the end of 20 years.

Graves, Edward E., ed. *McGill's Life Insurance.* Bryn Mawr, Pa.: The American College, 1994.

Holson, Laura M. and Liz Comte Reisman, "Lessons in Life," *Smart Money,* Vol 3, No. 12 (December 1994), pp. 130–39.

Longo, Tracey. "There is No Free Insurance," *Kiplinger's Personal Finance Magazine,* Vol. 49, No. 10 (October 1995), pp. 97–101.

Miller, Walter N. "The Problem with Sales Illustrations: Why It Exists and How It Should Be Addressed," *Journal of the American Society of CLU and ChFC,* 47, no. 3 (May 1993): 64–71.

Mehr, Robert I., and Sandra G. Gustavson. *Life Insurance: Theory and Practice,* 4th ed. Plano, Tex.: Business Publications, 1987.

Rejda, George E., Constance M. Luthardt, Cheryl L. Ferguson, and Donald R. Oakes. *Personal Insurance,* 3rd ed. Malvern, Pa.: Insurance Institute of America, 1997.

"When It's Time to Buy Life Insurance, How Much Coverage Do You Need?" *Consumer Reports,* 58 (July 1993): 431–50. See also "Life Insurance—Part 2: Choosing a Universal-Life Policy," *Consumer Reports,* 58 (August 1993): 525–39; and "Life Insurance—Part 3: Should You Buy A Whole-Life Policy?" *Consumer Reports,* 58 (September 1993): 595–603.

## NOTES

1. "Life Insurance: How to Protect Your Family: Whole Life Insurance," *Consumer Reports,* 51 (July 1986): 458.

2. "When It's Time to Buy Life Insurance," *Consumer Reports,* 58 (July 1993): 431–50. See also *Consumer Reports,* 58 (August 1993): 525–39, and *Consumer Reports,* 58 (September 1993): 595–603, for the complete study.

3. This section is based on Joseph M. Belth, *Life Insurance: A Consumer's Handbook,* 2nd ed. (Bloomington: Indiana University Press, 1985), pp. 89–91, 208–9.

4. *1996 Life Insurance Fact Book* (Washington, D.C.: American Council of Life Insurance, 1996), p. 67.

5. Joseph M. Belth, ed., *The Insurance Forum,* 23, (September 1996), p. 88.

6. *1995 Agent Production and Survival—Ordinary Agents in the United States.* (Hartford, CT.: LIMRA International, Inc., 1996), p. 1.

# IS YOUR LIFE INSURANCE REASONABLY PRICED? (HOW TO EVALUATE AN EXISTING LIFE INSURANCE POLICY)

If you own a life insurance policy on which you have paid premiums for some years, and if you are wondering whether you are receiving fair value for your money, this article is aimed at you.

## THE PLAYERS

Many of those in the life insurance business are legitimate and ethical salespeople; however, the business is plagued by a significant number of replacement artists and conservation artists. A replacement artist is a person who uses dubious methods to convince you—the owner of an existing life insurance policy—to replace your policy with a new one. Some replacement artists attempt to discredit the agent and the company from whom you bought your existing policy. Some of what replacement artists say may be accurate, but some of it may be deceptive or even false. The problem is that most policyowners cannot determine what is accurate and what is not.

A conservation artist, on the other hand, is a person who uses dubious methods to convince you—the owner of an existing life insurance policy— that your policy should not be replaced. Some conservation artists attempt to discredit the replacement artist. Some of what conservation artists say may be accurate, but some of it may be deceptive or even false. The problem is that most policyowners cannot determine what is accurate and what is not.

In short, a war is going on between replacement artists and conservation artists. As the owner of an existing life insurance policy, you are caught in the middle. You probably do not know enough about life insurance to be able to distinguish accurate information from inaccurate information, and you probably do not know whom to believe. The purpose of this article is to arm you with the ability to find out for yourself whether the life insurance protection you own is reasonably priced.

## THE GENERAL APPROACH

This article describes three steps you must follow in order to determine whether the life insurance protection you own is reasonably priced: (1) gather certain information about each policy you wish to evaluate; (2) perform certain calculations using the information gathered in the first step; and (3) compare the results of your calculations with certain benchmarks.

### Gathering Information

The most difficult step is not the arithmetic, but rather assembling the necessary information. Some of what you need is in the policy itself, but you may find the information difficult to extract. And some of what you need may not be in the policy. It is suggested that you obtain the information by writing a carefully worded letter to the president of the life insurance company that issued the policy. A suggested letter is shown after the explanatory appendix.

You may find the address of the company on the policy itself, on a recent premium notice, or by calling your local library. You may find the policy number on the policy itself or on a recent premium notice. Your letter should request the following items of information:

1. The amount that the insurance company would have paid to your beneficiary if you had died at the end of the most recently completed policy year. This is the death benefit (*DB*) of your policy.

2. The amount that the insurance company would have paid to you if you had surrendered your policy at the end of the most recently completed policy year. This is the cash value (*CV*) of your policy. (Some policies do not have cash values, so the amount here could be zero.)

3. The amount that the insurance company would have paid to you if you had surrendered your policy at the end of the year preceding the most recently completed policy year. This (*CVP*) corresponds to item 2, but for one year earlier.

4. The premium (*P*) for the most recently completed policy year. (Policies that are "paid up" require no further premiums, so the amount here could be zero.)

5. The dividend (*D*) for the most recently completed policy year. (Some policies do not pay dividends, so the amount here could be zero.)

6. The date on which the most recently completed policy year began.

7. Your insurance age, in accordance with the company's method of determining age, on the date referred to in item 6 above.

It is recommended that you word the letter exactly as illustrated, and that you keep a copy of the letter. If you receive no response, or if you receive an inadequate response, you should file a written complaint with your state insurance commissioner. You may obtain the address of your state insurance commissioner from your local library.

## The Calculations

Once you have acquired the information listed in the preceding section, you are ready to perform certain calculations, except for the choice of an interest rate (*i*). It is suggested that you use an interest rate of 6 percent (0.06) in your calculations. (For comments concerning the interest rate, see the explanatory appendix.)

Now you are ready to perform certain calculations in order to arrive at a yearly price per $1000 of protection for the most recently completed policy year. The formula is as follows:

$$\frac{(P + CVP)(1 + i) - (CV + D)}{(DB - CV)(0.001)}$$

To illustrate, suppose the response to your letter provided the following information:

1. Death benefit (*DB*): $25,000

2. Cash value at end of most recently completed policy year (*CV*): $10,450

3. Cash value at end of year preceding most recently completed policy year (*CVP*): $10,000

4. Premium (*P*): $550

5. Dividend (*D*): $400

6. Date on which most recently completed policy year began: March 10, 1994.

7. Your insurance age on March 10, 1994: 56

Your next step is to plug these figures into the formula. The calculations are as follows.

$$\frac{(550 + 10,000)(1 + 0.06) - (10,450 + 400)}{(25,000 - 10,450)(0.001)}$$

$$= \frac{(10,550)(1.06) - 10,850}{(14,550)(0.001)}$$

$$= \frac{11,183 - 10,850}{14.550}$$

$$= \frac{333}{14.550} = 22.89$$

In other words, the yearly price per $1000 of protection in the most recently completed policy year (which began on March 10, 1994) is $22.89, assuming 6 percent interest.

## The Comparison

The benchmarks against which to compare yearly prices per $1000 of protection are shown in the box below. The suggested interpretations of the benchmark figures are as follows:

1. If the yearly price per $1000 of protection is less than the benchmark figure, the price of your protection is low, and you should not consider replacing your policy.

2. If the yearly price per $1000 of protection is more than the benchmark figure but less than double that figure, the price of your protection is moderate, and again you should not consider replacing your policy.

3. If the yearly price per $1000 of protection is more than double the benchmark figure, the price of your protection is high, and you should consider replacing your policy.

To illustrate, the benchmark figure for age 56 is $15, and the yearly price per $1000 of protection that came out of your calculations is $22.89. Since the latter is more than the benchmark figure but less than double that figure, the price of your protection is moderate, and you should not consider replacing your policy.

**Benchmarks**

| Age | Price |
| --- | --- |
| Under 30 | $1.50 |
| 30–34 | 2.00 |
| 35–39 | 3.00 |
| 40–44 | 4.00 |
| 45–49 | 6.50 |
| 50–54 | 10.00 |
| 55–59 | 15.00 |
| 60–64 | 25.00 |
| 65–69 | 35.00 |
| 70–74 | 50.00 |
| 75–79 | 80.00 |
| 80–84 | 125.00 |

## SEVERAL WARNINGS

Life insurance policies are complex financial instruments. In this article, we have tried to simplify the subject so that you can find out for yourself whether your life insurance protection is reasonably priced. The simplification process, however, makes it necessary to voice warnings in several areas.

1. If your policy carries an extra premium because of a health impairment or other problem, the analysis of such a policy is beyond the scope of this article.

2. If your policy covers more than one life, the analysis of such a policy is also beyond the scope of this article. Examples are family policies (in which husband, wife, and children are covered in one policy) and joint life policies (which cover two lives and pay the face amount on the first death).

3. It is possible that the year for which you perform the calculations—the most recently completed policy year—is not representative of other policy years. For example, the price of the protection in the first one or two policy years is often quite high, reflecting sales commissions and other expenses associated with the issuance of a life insurance policy. As another example, the price in a single isolated year may be quite low or quite high because of certain structural characteristics of the policy. For these reasons, you might wish to gather the information and perform the calculations for a few other years, especially if the figure for the most recently completed policy year is either very low or very high. The postscript of the suggested letter is optional; it is designed to help you obtain the information for a few other years, should you wish to perform the calculations.

4. You may obtain a negative result. This may arise because of an unusual year, as mentioned in the preceding paragraph, or because the price of the protection in your policy is extremely low. A negative figure does not mean the company is crazy—remember that you are using a modest interest rate of 6 percent in your calculations.

5. If the amount payable on surrender of your policy is equal to the amount payable on death, you have no life insurance protection, and the yearly price per $1000 of protection is without meaning. Under these circumstances, you should view your policy as a savings account. Calculate the yearly rate of return (expressed as a decimal) with the following formula:

$$\frac{CV + D}{P + CVP} - 1$$

You can then judge your policy by comparing the yearly rate of return with what you can earn in a savings bank, savings and loan association, or credit union. In making such a comparison, however, you should consider the income tax situation, as discussed in the explanatory appendix below.

6. If the amount payable on surrender of your policy is only slightly smaller than the amount payable on the death (less than, say, 5 percent below the amount payable on death), you have very little life insurance protection, and the yearly price per $1000 of protection has very little meaning. Under these circumstances, you should view your policy as essentially a savings account. Use the above formula to approximate the yearly rate of return.

7. If yours is a small policy—less than, say, $3000 in face amount—the yearly price per $1000 of protection may be high because of the expenses associated with the maintenance of a small policy. It may not be worth the bother to replace a small policy; indeed, a small policy may not be worth keeping unless you have some emotional attachment to it.

8. We were careful to say that, if the price of the protection in your policy is high, you should *consider* replacing your policy. We did *not* say you should necessarily replace your policy. There are several reasons for you to proceed with caution: a replacement necessarily involves the purchase of a new policy, and the purchase of a new policy requires care if you wish to acquire low-priced protection; surrendering an existing policy may involve the sacrifice of certain valu-

able policy provisions; surrendering an existing policy may involve certain income tax considerations; purchasing a new policy may involve significant expenses in the first one or two years, as mentioned earlier; and because of a health impairment or other problem, you may find it difficult to qualify for a new policy.

## AN EXPLANATORY APPENDIX

Instead of following the suggestions in this article blindly, you may prefer to acquire some understanding of the formula and the benchmarks. The purpose of this appendix is to provide a brief explanation.

Let's consider the numerator of the formula. The first parenthetical expression $(P + CVP)$ is the amount that you would have had available to put into some other savings vehicle if you had decided to surrender the policy at the end of the year preceding the most recently completed policy year. You would have received the cash value ($CVP$) and you would have been relieved of the premium ($P$).

Multiplying the above expression by $(1 + i)$ tells you what you would have had in that other savings vehicle by the end of the most recently completed policy year if you had invested the $(P + CVP)$ at an annual interest rate of $i$. This leads us to a discussion of the interest rate.

The interest rate you choose is not important if your policy has little or no cash value. However, the interest rate you choose is quite important if your policy has a substantial cash value. If your policy has a cash value, it probably has a loan clause that permits you to borrow against the policy up to approximately the cash value at a fixed interest rate of 5 to 8 percent or at a variable interest rate. If you believe you could put the money in some other savings vehicle at a much higher interest rate and with a high degree of safety, and if the amount available is substantial, you should consider borrowing against your policy and investing the proceeds of the loan. Bear in mind, however, that the savings vehicle you are thinking about may produce interest income that is subject to current income tax, and that the interest you pay on the policy loan is not deductible. The interest earnings built into cash-value life insurance, on the other hand, are income-tax deferred and eventually will be either partially or fully income-tax exempt. For simplicity, we suggested you use an interest rate of 6 percent in the calculations.

The last parenthetical expression in the numerator of the formula $(CV + D)$ is the amount that you had available, at the end of the most recently completed policy year, having continued the policy for that year. The difference between the product of the first two expressions ($11,183 in the example) and the last expression ($10,850) is the price you paid ($333) for the life insurance protection in that year (assuming 6 percent interest).

Now let's consider the denominator of the formula. The cash value is the savings component of the policy, and is an asset from your point of view. Therefore, the life insurance protection you had ($14,550) is the difference between the death benefit ($25,000) and the cash value ($10,450). The other expression in the denominator moves the decimal point three places to the left, so that the denominator represents the amount of life insurance protection in thousands of dollars (14.550).

Since the price you paid for the protection (assuming 6 percent) was $333, and since the amount of protection in thousands of dollars was 14.550, the yearly price per $1000 of protection (assuming 6 percent) was $22.89.

Finally, the benchmarks were derived from certain United States population death rates. The benchmark figure for each five-year age bracket is slightly above the death rate per 1000 at the highest age in that bracket. What we are saying is that, if the price of your life insurance protection per $1000 is in the vicinity of the "raw material cost" (that is, the amount needed just to pay death claims based on population death rates), your life insurance protection is reasonably priced.

## SUGGESTED LETTER

President
XYZ Life Insurance Company
Post Office Box 245
Ellettsville, IN 47429

Dear President:

Please furnish me with the following information concerning my policy number 1 234 567.

1. The amount that you would have paid in a single sum to my beneficiary if I had died at the end of the most recently completed policy year, including any supplemental term life insurance benefits. Please disregard any accidental death benefits, any dividends, and any loan against the policy.

2. The amount that you would have paid in a single sum to me if I had surrendered the policy at the end of the most recently completed policy year. Please disregard any dividends and any loan against the policy.

3. The amount that you would have paid in a single sum to me if I had surrendered the policy at the end of the year preceding the most recently completed policy year. Please disregard any dividends and any loan against the policy.

4. The premium for the most recently completed policy year, including the premiums for any supplemental term life insurance benefits. Please exclude the premiums for any accidental death benefits, disability benefits, or guaranteed insurability benefits. Please exclude the interest on any loan against the policy, and assume I paid the year's premium in full at the beginning of the year.

5. The dividend for the most recently completed policy year, including the dividends for any supplemental term life insurance benefits. Please exclude any dividends for any accidental death benefits or disability benefits. Please exclude any dividends credited to dividend accumulations or additions.

6. The date on which the most recently completed policy year began.

7. My age, according to your records, when the most recently completed policy year began.

Thank you for providing the information that I have requested.

Sincerely yours,

[*Editor's note:* The following postscript is optional. See the third point in the section entitled "Several Warnings."]

P.S.: Also, please furnish the above information for the two policy years preceding the most recently completed policy year, and for the two policy years following the most recently completed policy year. In the case of amounts payable in future years, please identify any nonguaranteed amounts and base the figures on your company's current scale.

[1] The material in this appendix was written by Joseph M. Belth, Ph. D., professor emeritus of insurance in the School of Business at Indiana University (Bloomington), and author of *Life Insurance: A Consumer's Handbook* (1985). It was first published in the June 1982 issue of *The Insurance Forum,* of which Professor Belth is the editor, and was modified slightly for the purposes of this appendix. Copyright © 1982 by Insurance Forum, Inc., P.O. Box 245, Ellettsville, IN 47429. Used by permission.

# Chapter 19

# Life Insurance Planning and Estate Planning

*" The primary question to answer is: How much money would my dependents need if I died tomorrow? "*

Consumer Reports

## Student Learning Objectives

After studying this chapter, you should be able to:

■ Describe the four steps in the life insurance planning process.

■ Determine the amount of life insurance needed to attain your financial goals and objectives.

■ Explain the approaches that can reduce the adverse effects of inflation on a life insurance program.

■ Describe the general objectives of estate planning and the basic steps in the estate planning process.

■ Identify the major estate planning tools used in estate planning.

■ Explain the special advantages of life insurance in estate planning, and indicate how life insurance is taxed.

Life insurance is designed to replace the family's share of the deceased breadwinner's earnings and provide the funds needed to attain certain financial goals and objectives. A basic question to answer is whether existing life insurance and financial assets are sufficient to attain the insured's financial goals and objectives. Life insurance planning involves an analysis of the insured's financial goals and the amount of life insurance needed to attain these goals.

Estate planning is also part of the overall planning process, since it involves the distribution of property to family members for their financial well-being after the insured dies. Estate planning is used to distribute property to the heirs according to the decedent's wishes, to conserve estate assets, to minimize estate taxes, and to meet other financial goals and objectives as well. As will be pointed out later, life insurance can play an important role in the estate planning process.

This chapter discusses the fundamentals of life insurance planning, which is a method for determining the family's financial requirements and the amount of life insurance needed to satisfy them. The chapter also examines the fundamentals of estate planning, which is a systematic process for the conservation of estate assets and the orderly distribution of estate property.

## LIFE INSURANCE PLANNING

**Life insurance planning** *is a systematic method for determining the insured's financial goals and the total amount needed to attain these goals; present life insurance and financial assets are subtracted from the amount needed to determine the additional amount of life insurance, if any, for attaining these goals.*

Life insurance planning involves four basic steps:

- Determining the insured's financial goals
- Comparing present life insurance and financial assets with the amount needed for attaining these goals
- Determining the amount of new life insurance needed
- Reviewing the program periodically

### Determining the Insured's Financial Goals

The first step is to determine the insured's financial goals. A life insurance agent can determine the client's financial goals after a detailed interview. As stated in Chapter 15, there are several basic needs that should be considered in determining the amount of life insurance to own:

- Estate clearance fund
- Income during the readjustment period
- Income during the dependency period
- Life income to surviving spouse
- Special needs
    - Mortgage redemption
    - Educational fund
    - Emergency fund
- Retirement needs

For example, Patti and Tim are married and have a son, age three. Patti, age 30, is a registered nurse in a community hospital and earns $38,000 annually. She plans to continue working if Tim should die. Tim, age 33, is an accountant who earns $35,000 annually. Because women have a longer life expectancy, we will assume that Tim dies first. If he should die, he estimates that his family will need $20,000 for funeral expenses, probate costs, installment debts, and unin-

sured medical costs; $80,000 to pay off the mortgage; $25,000 for an emergency fund; and $100,000 for an educational fund for his son.

Tim also wants his family to have a monthly income of $3000 during the readjustment and dependency periods and $2000 during the blackout period. He also wants to establish a fund to provide retirement income to his wife for 20 years. The retirement fund is designed to supplement Patti's estimated private pension benefit ($700 monthly) and her estimated Social Security widow's benefit ($800 monthly). Tim's cash needs and future income needs are summarized as follows:

*Cash Needs*

| | |
|---|---|
| Estate clearance fund | $ 20,000 |
| Mortgage redemption fund | 80,000 |
| Emergency fund | 25,000 |
| Educational fund | 100,000 |

*Income Needs*

| | |
|---|---|
| Readjustment and dependency periods | $3000 monthly for 15 years |
| Blackout period | 2000 monthly for 15 years |
| Retirement fund for Patti | 500 monthly for 20 years |

### Comparing Present Life Insurance and Assets with the Amount Needed

The second step is to compare Tim's present life insurance and financial assets with the amount needed to attain his financial goals. In most cases, substantial amounts of life insurance must be purchased to achieve these goals.

Tim is insured for $40,000 under a group life insurance plan and also owns $50,000 of individual life insurance. A private pension death benefit of $10,000 is also payable upon his death. Tim owns several mutual funds and a savings account in the amount of $20,000 and has $4745 in a checking account. In addition, his wife and son are entitled to Social Security survivor benefits if he should die. Patti's OASDI survivor benefits are payable until her son reaches age 16. The son's OASDI benefits are payable until age 18. Patti is also entitled to a OASDI widow's benefit beginning at age 60.

In this example, we assume that only the son will receive OASDI survivor benefits. The son's benefit is estimated to be $500 monthly. Since Patti's earned income will exceed the maximum annual limit allowed under the Social Security earnings test ($8640 in 1997 for beneficiaries under age 65), she will lose all of her monthly survivor benefits. Thus, OASDI benefits payable to a surviving spouse with an eligible child are ignored in our example. The earnings test is discussed in greater detail in Chapter 23.

As a starting point, a needs analysis chart should be prepared. Exhibit 19.1 illustrates Tim's financial needs and present financial resources. It is clear that Tim cannot attain his financial goals based on his present program. His cash needs alone exceed his present insurance coverages and financial assets by $100,000.

---

### Exhibit 19.1

### Tim's Life Insurance Needs and Present Coverages and Resources

| Cash needs | | Present insurance and financial assets | |
|---|---|---|---|
| Estate clearance | $ 20,000 | OASDI lump sum death benefit | $     255 |
| Mortgage redemption | 80,000 | Group life insurance | 40,000 |
| Emergency fund | 25,000 | Individual life insurance | 50,000 |
| Educational fund | 100,000 | Private pension death benefit | 10,000 |
| | $225,000 | Mutual funds and savings account | 20,000 |
| | | Checking account | 4,745 |
| | | | $125,000 |

| Income needs | |
|---|---|
| Readjustment period | $3,000 monthly for  2 years |
| Dependency period | 3,000 monthly for 13 years |
| Blackout period | 2,000 monthly for 15 years |
| Retirement fund for Patti | 500 monthly for 20 years |

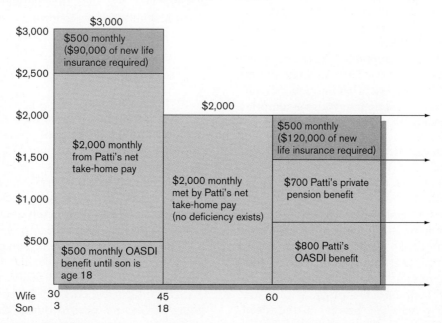

The income needs also cannot be met. An additional $500 monthly is needed until the son reaches age 18. An additional $500 monthly is also required to provide supplemental retirement income to Patti for 20 years starting at age 60. In short, additional life insurance is needed to fill these gaps.

## Determining the Amount of New Life Insurance Needed

The third step is to determine the amount of new life insurance needed. The amount needed is based on the following assumptions:

- *Tim dies immediately.* Since the time of death is uncertain, the only safe assumption is that the various needs must be met immediately.
- *Patti continues to work if Tim should die.* The amount of life insurance is reduced significantly if the surviving spouse is in the labor force and continues to work after the other spouse dies.
- *OASDI survivor benefits are payable only to the son until age 18.* Patti will lose all of her monthly survivor benefits because of the OASDI earnings test. Thus, the OASDI survivor benefits that otherwise would have been paid to Patti will be ignored.
- *The life insurance proceeds are invested at an interest rate equal to the rate of inflation.* Such an assumption builds into the program an automatic hedge against inflation that preserves the real purchasing power of the proceeds. In addition, the calculations are simplified, and the use of present value tables and assumptions concerning future inflation rates are unnecessary. Although this assumption overstates somewhat the amount of life insurance needed, it is a conservative assumption that adds a margin of safety to the program.

Tim has total cash needs of $225,000. However, present insurance and financial assets total only $125,000. Therefore, an additional $100,000 of life insurance is required.

Tim also has several income needs. As noted earlier, in determining the amount of life insurance needed, we assume that the death proceeds are invested at a rate of interest equal to the rate of inflation. By ignoring interest, a desirable inflation hedge is automatically built into the program that preserves the real purchasing power of the death

proceeds. In this case, an additional $500 monthly for 20 years, or $120,000 of life insurance, will be needed to supplement Patti's estimated private pension and OASDI survivor benefits starting at age 60.

Additional life insurance will not be needed to provide income during the blackout period. Since Patti will continue working after Tim's death, her net take-home pay will be sufficient to provide income during this period. However, if a surviving spouse does not work or works only part-time during the blackout period, then additional life insurance is needed to fill this need.

The final need is to provide $3000 monthly during the readjustment and dependency periods. The son's OASDI survivor benefit is $500 monthly, and Patti's net take-home pay is $2000 monthly. The additional $500 monthly can be provided by $90,000 of life insurance.

In summary, Tim needs an additional $310,000 of life insurance to accomplish his goals. The new life insurance plus his present financial assets and life insurance should enable him to meet all of the cash and income needs discussed earlier. The complete program for Tim is illustrated in Exhibit 19.2.

**What Happens If Patti Dies First?**  A complete program must also consider Tim's cash and income needs if Patti should die first. Ignoring his present savings and the OASDI lump sum death benefit, Tim estimates that he will need an additional $200,000 for the following cash needs:

| | |
|---|---|
| Estate clearance | $ 20,000 |
| Mortgage redemption | 80,000 |
| Education fund | 100,000 |
| Total | $200,000 |

Patti is presently insured for $40,000 under her employer's group life insurance plan. She also has an individual policy in the amount of $10,000 that her parents purchased for her as a child. Thus, an additional $150,000 of life insurance is needed to meet the cash needs. Patti decides to purchase an inexpensive term insurance policy in the amount of $150,000 to provide the necessary cash if she should die first.

The final consideration is Tim's need for additional income if Patti should die. In this case, he believes that his present salary plus his son's OASDI survivor benefits will be sufficient for providing the income needed during the readjustment

## Exhibit 19.2

### Tim's Additional Life Insurance Requirements

| Cash needs | | Present insurance and financial assets | |
|---|---|---|---|
| Estate clearance | $ 20,000 | OASDI lump sum death benefit | $     255 |
| Mortgage redemption | 80,000 | Group life insurance | 40,000 |
| Emergency fund | 25,000 | Individual life insurance | 50,000 |
| Educational fund | 100,000 | Private pension death benefit | 10,000 |
| | $225,000 | Mutual funds and savings account | 20,000 |
| | | Checking account | 4,745 |
| | | | $125,000 |

| Income needs | |
|---|---|
| Readjustment period | $3,000 monthly for   2 years |
| Dependency period | 3,000 monthly for 13 years |
| Blackout period | 2,000 monthly for 15 years |
| Retirement fund for Patti | 500 monthly for 20 years |

Amount of new life insurance required = $100,000 (cash needs) + $210,000 (income needs) = $310,000

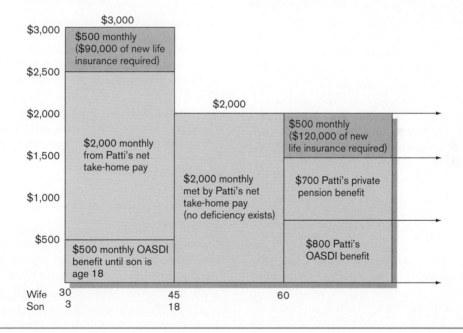

and dependency periods. Thus, new life insurance to provide additional income is not needed.

### Reviewing the Program Periodically

The final step in life insurance planning is a periodic review of the program. Cash and income needs can quickly change depending on circumstances. A birth, death, adoption, disability, divorce, legal separation, remarriage, or early retirement can affect the amount of life insurance needed. At a minimum, a life insurance plan should be periodically reviewed every three years. If the insured's financial goals and circumstances change dramatically, a new plan may be necessary.

## Effect of Inflation on Life Insurance Planning

An increase in consumer prices over time can seriously erode the purchasing power of the life insurance proceeds. For example, if prices double, the purchasing power of the life insurance proceeds is reduced by one half. Although inflation is not a serious threat at the present time, it is still prudent to consider the impact of inflation on a life insurance program.

There is no perfect solution to the problem of inflation. However, several approaches can reduce the adverse effects of inflation on life insurance benefits. *First, Social Security monthly income benefits are automatically adjusted each year for inflation.* Whenever the Consumer Price Index increases during the measurement period, Social Security benefits are correspondingly increased by the same percentage. Since Social Security survivor benefits provide a relatively large proportion of the income needed during the readjustment, dependency, and life income periods, the benefits paid are an effective inflation hedge during these periods. However, Social Security benefits are not paid during the blackout period, which is a critical income period for many surviving spouses.

*A second approach is to assume that the policy proceeds are invested at a rate of interest equal to the rate of inflation.* This approach assumes that the investment income on the policy proceeds is offset completely by the effects of inflation and overstates somewhat the amount of life insurance needed. However, the real purchasing power of the proceeds is maintained. This approach was used in our earlier illustration.

*A third approach is to assume a relatively low interest rate in determining the amount of interest earned on the life insurance proceeds.* The policy proceeds can usually be invested at a rate of interest that exceeds the rate of inflation. The excess interest earned can be considered in determining the amount of new life insurance needed. For example, if the policy proceeds are invested at 6 percent and the inflation rate is 4 percent, the amount of new life insurance needed should be based only on an interest assumption of 2 percent. Such an approach requires the use of present value discount tables to determine the required amount of life insurance.

*Another approach is to purchase additional life insurance as an inflation fund.* Life insurance proceeds can be periodically withdrawn to supplement the monthly income payments, depending on the rate of inflation.

*Finally, a variable life or universal life insurance policy (option B) can be purchased as an inflation hedge.* As an alternative, *a cost-of-living rider* can be added to the policy that increases the face amount of insurance during the period of inflation. The dividends paid under a participating policy can help pay the cost of the rider.

## ESTATE PLANNING

**Estate planning** *is a process for the conservation and distribution of a person's property and wealth.* It is another part of a total financial plan because it provides for the distribution of your property to your heirs and other groups.

### Objectives of Estate Planning

The general objectives of estate planning are to (1) conserve estate assets both before and after death, (2) distribute property according to the individual's wishes, (3) minimize federal estate and state inheritance taxes, (4) provide estate liquidity to meet the costs of estate settlement, and (5) provide for the family's financial needs.[1] A properly designed estate plan will accomplish all of the preceding objectives and provide other benefits as well (see Exhibit 19.3).

### Problem of Estate Shrinkage

**Estate shrinkage** *refers to the decline in the value of an estate after an individual dies because of failure to develop an effective estate plan.* As a result, surviving family members and other heirs receive substantially reduced amounts when the property is actually distributed. Estate planners can cite numerous examples of substantial estate shrinkage because of lack of an estate plan or because of an improperly designed plan. Even the estates of famous people can experience substantial shrinkage after the celebrity dies (see Exhibit 19.4).

Estates can shrink because of the costs associated with the death itself, such as funeral expenses and uninsured medical expenses. There may also be outstanding installment debts, mortgage debt, and

EXHIBIT 19.3

## Six Reasons to Plan Your Estate

Estate planning is an easy thing to put off. Maybe you think it's too early; maybe you think your estate is too small. Here are six good reasons why you should plan your estate now:

| *With a plan* | *Without a plan* |
|---|---|
| 1. You decide who receives a share of your assets. | State laws determine who inherits your assets—they could pass to an estranged relative. |
| 2. You decide how and when your beneficiaries will receive their inheritance. | The terms and timing are set by law. Your children could be left unfettered control of a sizable estate. |
| 3. You decide who'll manage your estate (executor, trustee, etc.) | The court appoints administrators—administrators whose ideas may not be compatible with your own. |
| 4. You can reduce estate taxes and administrative expenses. | Costs are usually greater, due to required administrative expenses and unnecessary taxes. |
| 5. You select a guardian for your child. | The court appoints a guardian for your child. |
| 6. You can provide for the orderly continuance or sale of a family business. | Financial loss and family hardships may result from an untimely forced sale. |

SOURCE: Practice Development Institute. Reprinted with permission.

business claims against the estate that must be paid. The estate can also shrink because of legal costs of settling the estate, including attorney fees, administrator and executor fees, appraisal fees, court costs, and bond costs. The fees are substantially higher if the estate is complex, or an attorney must defend the estate in a contested claim.

Forced liquidation of property can also reduce the value of the estate. The estate may lack liquidity to pay federal and state death taxes, so property may have to be liquidated at reduced prices to obtain the needed cash. A profitable business may have to be sold as well to obtain the necessary cash. Finally, payment of the federal estate tax and state death taxes can substantially reduce the size of the estate before the property is distributed to the heirs.

## Federal Estate and Gift Taxes

We noted earlier that an important objective of estate planning is to reduce or eliminate estate taxes and death taxes. These taxes include the federal estate tax and federal gift tax.

**Federal Estate Tax** A federal estate tax is payable if the decedent's taxable estate exceeds $600,000. The federal estate tax starts at 37 percent on estates exceeding $600,000 and progressively in-

creases to 55 percent on estates of $3 million or higher.[2]

The **gross estate** includes the value of the property that you own when you die. The gross estate also includes one half of the value of property owned jointly with your spouse, life insurance death proceeds in which the insured has any incidents of ownership at the time of death, and certain other items. Incidents of ownership in life insurance include the right to change the beneficiary, the right to borrow the cash value, and the right to select a settlement option.

The gross estate can be reduced by certain deductions in determining the **taxable estate.** Allowable deductions include funeral and administrative expenses, claims against the estate, debts owed at the time of death, casualty and theft losses that occur during the settlement of the estate, and contributions to charities. A marital deduction (discussed later) is also allowed and can result in a substantial reduction or elimination of the taxable estate.

A unified tax credit can be used to reduce any federal estate or gift tax that is payable. The **unified tax credit** *is a tax credit that reduces dollar-for-dollar any federal estate or gift tax due.* The maximum tax credit is currently $192,800. For example, assume that Pedro dies and has a gross estate of $700,000. Allowable deductions are $100,000. The

EXHIBIT 19.4

**Estates of Famous Persons**

| Name | Gross estate | Settlement costs | Net estate | Percent shrinkage |
|---|---|---|---|---|
| Stan Laurel | $    91,562 | $     8,381 | $    83,181 | 9% |
| William Frawley | 92,446 | 45,814 | 46,632 | 49% |
| "Gabby" Hayes | 111,327 | 21,963 | 89,364 | 20% |
| Hedda Hopper | 472,661 | 165,982 | 306,679 | 35% |
| Nelson Eddy | 472,715 | 109,990 | 362,725 | 23% |
| Marilyn Monroe | 819,176 | 448,750 | 370,426 | 55% |
| W. C. Fields | 884,680 | 329,793 | 554,887 | 37% |
| Humphrey Bogart | 910,146 | 274,234 | 635,912 | 30% |
| Dixie Crosby | 1,332,571 | 781,953 | 550,618 | 59% |
| Erle Stanley Gardner | 1,795,092 | 636,705 | 1,158,387 | 35% |
| Franklin D. Roosevelt | 1,940,999 | 574,867 | 1,366,132 | 30% |
| Clark Gable | 2,806,526 | 1,101,038 | 1,705,488 | 30% |
| Cecil B. DeMille | 4,043,607 | 1,396,064 | 2,647,543 | 35% |
| Al Jolson | 4,385,143 | 1,349,066 | 3,036,077 | 31% |
| Gary Cooper | 4,984,985 | 1,530,454 | 3,454,531 | 31% |
| Henry J. Kaiser, Sr. | 5,597,772 | 2,488,364 | 3,109,408 | 44% |
| Harry M. Warner | 8,946,618 | 2,308,444 | 6,638,174 | 26% |
| Elvis Presley | 10,165,434 | 7,374,635 | 2,790,799 | 73% |
| Alwin C. Ernst, CPA | 12,642,431 | 7,124,112 | 5,518,319 | 56% |
| J. P. Morgan | 17,121,482 | 11,893,691 | 5,227,791 | 69% |
| William E. Boeing | 22,386,158 | 10,589,748 | 11,796,410 | 47% |
| Walt Disney | 23,004,851 | 6,811,943 | 16,192,908 | 30% |
| John D. Rockefeller, Sr. | 26,905,182 | 17,124,988 | 9,780,194 | 64% |
| Frederick Vanderbilt | 76,838,530 | 42,846,112 | 33,992,418 | 56% |

SOURCE: Barry Kaye, *Save a Fortune on Your Estate Taxes: Wealth Creation and Preservation* (Homewood, Ill.: Business One Irwin, 1993), p. 24.

federal estate tax on a taxable estate of $600,000 is $192,800. However, as a result of the unified tax credit of $192,800, the estate tax is zero.

Exhibit 19.5 shows the federal and gift tax rates that apply at the time of this writing.

The federal estate tax must be paid within nine months of the deceased's death unless an extension of time for filing has been granted. For this reason, liquidity is extremely important in estate planning, because cash must be available to pay estate taxes.

**Federal Gift Tax**   A federal gift tax is payable if the gift exceeds a certain amount. However, the unified tax credit discussed earlier can be used to reduce the amount of the tax. Under present law, you can give a maximum gift of $10,000 annually to as many persons as you desire without incurring a federal gift tax on the transfer. If the spouse joins in the gift, a total of $20,000 can be given annually to each person.

Certain gifts are not taxable gifts. They include gifts of $10,000 or less to any one person during a calendar year, payment of tuition or medical expenses, gifts to a spouse, gifts to charities, and certain other exceptions.

## Steps in Estate Planning

Estate planning is a process that involves certain steps. An estate attorney or financial planner typically

EXHIBIT 19.5

**Federal Estates and Gift Tax Rates (1993 and Beyond)**

| If your tax base is over | But not over | Your tax is | + | % | On excess over |
|---|---|---|---|---|---|
| $        0 | $     10,000 | $          0 | | 18 | $          0 |
| 10,000 | 20,000 | 1,800 | | 20 | 10,000 |
| 20,000 | 40,000 | 3,800 | | 22 | 20,000 |
| 40,000 | 60,000 | 8,200 | | 24 | 40,000 |
| 60,000 | 80,000 | 13,000 | | 26 | 60,000 |
| 80,000 | 100,000 | 18,200 | | 28 | 80,000 |
| 100,000 | 150,000 | 23,800 | | 30 | 100,000 |
| 150,000 | 250,000 | 38,300 | | 32 | 150,000 |
| 250,000 | 500,000 | 70,800 | | 34 | 250,000 |
| 500,000 | 750,000 | 155,800 | | 37 | 500,000 |
| 750,000 | 1,000,000 | 248,300 | | 39 | 750,000 |
| 1,000,000 | 1,250,000 | 345,800 | | 41 | 1,000,000 |
| 1,250,000 | 1,500,000 | 448,300 | | 43 | 1,250,000 |
| 1,500,000 | 2,000,000 | 555,800 | | 45 | 1,500,000 |
| 2,000,000 | 2,500,000 | 780,800 | | 49 | 2,000,000 |
| 2,500,000 | 3,000,000 | 1,025,800 | | 53 | 2,500,000 |
| 3,000,000 | 10,000,000 | 1,290,800 | | 55 | 3,000,000 |
| 10,000,000 | 21,040,000 | 5,140,800 | | 60 | 10,000,000 |
| 21,040,000 | | 11,764,800 | | 55 | 21,040,000 |

NOTE:  All rates are before the application of the $600,000 unified credit or exemption equivalent. The actual tax credit for each unified credit is $192,800.

SOURCE:  David T. Phillips & Bill S. Wolfkiel, *Estate Planning Made Easy* (Chicago, Ill.: Dearborn Publishing, Inc., 1994), Figure 8.1, p. 47.

performs the following steps:

- Obtain facts about the estate.
- Evaluate potential claims against the estate.
- Design an appropriate estate plan.
- Prepare the necessary legal documents.
- Periodically review and revise the plan.

*The first step is to obtain relevant facts about the individual's estate.* A detailed questionnaire must be filled out that shows the financial assets and real estate owned, names of family members, whether or not a will is in existence, business interests, estate plan objectives of the individual, the current estate plan, and other relevant information.

*The second step is to evaluate potential claims against the estate.* This includes an estimate of funeral and last illness expenses, attorney fees and probate expenses, the amount of federal estate and state gift taxes that may have to be paid, unpaid federal income taxes at the time of death, and other expenses that will be charged to the estate.

*The third step is to design an appropriate plan.* The estate attorney or financial planner designs a plan to meet the objectives of the individual and family. The plan design includes the judicious selection of various estate planning tools, such as a will, marital deduction, gifts, trusts, and life insurance. These tools are explained in greater detail later in the chapter.

*The fourth step is preparation of the required legal documents by a competent attorney.* An attorney usually drafts the legal documents such as a will or trust. The legal documents are complex and often include specific clauses and provisions to reflect the individual's estate-planning objectives. Thus, use of a do-it-yourself legal documents kit sold in bookstores is not advised.

*Finally, the estate plan should be periodically reviewed and revised when necessary.* The plan should be revised if there is a marriage or divorce; a child is born; a spouse or family member dies; a new business is acquired or an existing business is sold; the individual's financial position changes significantly; the individual moves to another state with a different estate tax; or the federal estate tax law is changed.

When an estate plan is drafted, certain pitfalls and mistakes should be avoided. Insight 19.1 points out ten pitfalls to avoid.

## Tools of Estate Planning

An effective estate plan requires the use of certain estate planning tools. They include the following:

- Will
- Marital deduction
- Gifts
- Trusts
- Life insurance

**Will**    A will is a key tool in estate planning. A **will** *is a legal instrument by which property is disposed of in accordance with the individual's wishes.* It provides certain advantages in estate planning. A properly drafted will should accomplish the following:

- minimize legal and financial obstacles in distributing property to the heirs
- speed up the estate settlement process
- reduce family disputes among the heirs with respect to the distribution of valuable property, such as antiques and family heirlooms
- name a guardian for any minor children
- name a personal representative or executor to settle the estate
- provide for the creation of trusts to attain your estate objectives
- substantially reduce federal estate taxes and state death taxes

Many people die without a will. This is known as **dying intestate.** The property is then distributed according to the intestate provisions of state law where the individual lived. Dying intestate often results in property being distributed to people whom the deceased would not have wanted to receive the property. For example, in many states, if an individual with children dies without a will, the surviving spouse receives only one-third of the estate property, and the other two-thirds goes to the children. The deceased may have intended that the surviving spouse should receive all of the property. In addition, if there are no children, part of the estate may pass to the parents. Thus, the surviving spouse may be deprived of needed financial assets for self-support.

**Marital Deduction**    The marital deduction is a powerful estate planning tool that can substantially reduce federal estate taxes. It applies when property is left to a surviving spouse. The **marital deduction** *is a deduction of the value of the property that is included in the gross estate but is passed on to the surviving spouse.* For example, assume that Richard dies and has a gross estate valued at $1,300,000. He leaves only $600,000 of property outright to his wife. In this case, the marital deduction is $600,000. Debts, administrative costs, and funeral expenses total $100,000. The taxable estate is $600,000 and the tentative federal estate tax is $192,800. However, as a result of the unified credit of $192,800, the federal estate tax is zero (see Exhibit 19.6).

If the estate is large, estate planners generally do not recommend leaving the entire estate outright to the surviving spouse by use of an unlimited marital deduction. Although all property would pass free of federal estate taxes to the surviving spouse, it would be subject to the federal estate tax when the surviving spouse dies. The federal estate tax payable at that time on the second estate generally is higher than that paid on the first, since the second estate does not qualify for the marital deduction (unless the surviving spouse remarries). This can result in higher federal estate taxes and a shrinkage in the estate property that can be passed on to the heirs, such as children.

**Gifts**    Gifts can also reduce the amount of the taxable estate. An individual can give a maximum of $10,000 annually to as many persons as desired without incurring a federal gift tax on the transfer. If the spouse joins in the gift, a total of $20,000 can be given annually to each person.

Gifts can be effectively used as an estate planning tool, since they can reduce the size of the taxable estate. However, a gift tax may have to be paid if the value of the gift exceeds $10,000 annually

## INSIGHT 19.1

# The Ten Pitfalls of Estate Planning

All estate plans should be checked against the following ten "pitfalls." Although there are more than ten pitfalls to avoid, it is doubtful that any others could do more damage.

1. **Failure to Make a Proper Will and Revise it Periodically**

   By failing to prepare a will, a decedent surrenders the right to distribute his or her property and allows the state to take over that task. Even after a will has been prepared, it may be seriously outmoded at death unless reviewed periodically.

2. **Lack of Flexibility in Planning**

   A will must be drafted with enough flexibility to permit heirs and beneficiaries to meet emergencies or changing needs. Ideally, a will should take into account not only current family requirements but also future needs. Planning for the future, however, should not override basic necessities. For example, a decedent may provide for a child's college education without permitting proceeds to be diverted for any other purposes. At death, the will may prevent the family from using the proceeds for any purpose other than college, although the money is desperately needed for food and shelter.

3. **Not Enough Liquidity at Death**

   If an estate plan does not provide enough cash to cover final expenses, valuable assets may have to be sold immediately, frequently at a fraction of their value. Thus, estate shrinkage must be taken into account when preparing an estate plan. One solution is life insurance, which will automatically provide the required liquidity at death.

4. **Failure to Plan for Disposal of Business Interest**

   Intelligent planning can provide a guaranteed buyer for a business interest at a guaranteed sales price with assurance that money will be on hand instantly when death occurs. Another option is for heirs to continue the business. Advance planning will give them the best possible chance of succeeding.

5. **Failure to Arrange and Integrate Life Insurance with Other Assets**

   Life insurance policies should be checked periodically and integrated with other assets, such as Social Security and stocks and bonds, to form a cohesive plan. Policy settlement options should be considered, thereby permitting proceeds to be paid in monthly installments.

6. **Failure to Take Advantage of Tax Saving Mechanisms**

   Estate plans should be reviewed annually to make sure that any tax law changes are reflected in the plan and to take advantage of any new tax savings method. In fact, any properly drafted estate plan will strive for the greatest tax savings possible. Every dollar that escapes tax results in an additional dollar for estate beneficiaries.

7. **Failure to Plan for Retirement**

   Retirement plans and goals must be specifically identified. Unless such plans are known, an estate planner cannot determine whether sufficient funds are available to accommodate retirement desires. Retirement planning and the next pitfall are interrelated.

8. **Overdependence on Government and Business Insurance and Pension Plans**

   Social Security and pension benefits may be considerable. But overreliance on them can be disastrous. For example, if an individual changes jobs and fails to convert group insurance coverage in time, he or she may become uninsurable and die grossly underinsured. In another case, an individual may decide to return to work after retiring. If so, he or she may lose most Social Security benefits because of regulations governing earnings.

9. **Failure to Apportion Funds Sensibly**

   Funds should be allocated first to stable investments. This means that life insurance and an emergency savings account take precedence over other investments. Only excess funds should be available for high-risk investments.

10. **Failure to Prepare an Estate Plan and Review it Periodically**

    This is an all-inclusive category and perhaps the most important: With proper planning and periodic reviews, no estate planning pitfalls exist.

SOURCE: *Estate Planning*, 4th ed. (Chicago, Ill.: Dearborn, R&R Newkirk, 1993), pp. 16–17.

## EXHIBIT 19.6

### Calculating Federal Estate Taxes

| | | |
|---|---:|---:|
| Gross estate | | $1,300,000 |
| Less: | | |
|   Debts | $60,000 | |
|   Administrative costs | 35,000 | |
|   Funeral expenses | 5,000 | |
| | | −100,000 |
| Adjusted gross estate | | $1,200,000 |
| Less: | | |
|   Marital deduction | | −600,000 |
| Taxable estate | | $ 600,000 |
| Tentative tax | | $ 192,800 |
| Less: | | |
|   Unified credit | | −192,800 |
| Federal estate tax | | $ 0 |

($20,000 if the spouse joins in the gift). If a federal gift tax is payable, part or all of the unified tax credit can be used to defray the gift tax. However, any portion of the unified tax credit that is used to defray gift taxes is no longer available for reducing federal estate taxes.

**Trusts**    Trusts are widely used in estate planning. A **trust** *is an arrangement in which property is legally transferred to a trustee, who manages the property for the benefit of named beneficiaries.* A trustee can be a bank, trust company, or an adult. A trust can provide security to the beneficiaries and insure competent management of estate property after the individual dies. Certain types of trusts can also reduce estate taxes and administrative costs in settling an estate. The savings in estate taxes are often substantial.

There are two broad categories of trusts: (1) living, or *inter vivos* trust, and (2) testamentary trust.

1. Living trust   In a **living trust (*inter vivos* trust),** property is placed in the trust while the individual is still alive. If the creator of the trust has the right to revoke the trust and receive the property back, the trust is known as a **revocable living trust.** A revocable living trust can be used to reduce probate costs and provide privacy if the trust is still in existence at the

creator's death. In recent years, revocable living trusts have become increasingly popular as an estate planning tool.

If the creator of the trust gives up the right to receive the property back, the trust is known as an **irrevocable trust**. An irrevocable trust can reduce estate taxes, since property is taken out of the estate. Probate costs are also reduced.

A credit shelter trust is a popular type of irrevocable trust that has great potential in reducing federal estate taxes. A **credit shelter trust** (also called a bypass trust) *is an irrevocable trust designed to make use of the $600,000 lifetime exemption that could be lost when the first spouse dies and the unlimited marital deduction is used (see Insight 19.2).* It is widely used in estate planning at the present time.

2. Testamentary trust   A second broad category of trusts is a **testamentary trust.** A testamentary trust is provided for in the will and is not established until the creator dies. The testamentary trust can be used to protect minors, handicapped family members, or spendthrift heirs who have problems managing money. This type of trust adds flexibility to the estate plan, since the trustee can be granted discretionary powers to deal with the beneficiary's problems and needs as they arise.

**Life Insurance**    Life insurance is a widely used estate planning tool. In particular, a second-to-die policy is often used in estate planning to provide funds to pay the federal estate tax. A **second-to-die policy** *insures the lives of two people, such as a married couple, and the death proceeds are paid only upon the death of the second spouse.* The death proceeds provide the necessary liquidity to the estate for payment of estate taxes. The cost of a second-to-die policy is substantially lower than two separate policies.

Life insurance has several advantages as an estate planning tool. First, it provides estate liquidity. Cash is immediately available for funeral expenses, estate clearance costs, and death taxes. Thus, if the amount of life insurance is adequate, forced liquidation of property to raise the needed cash is unnecessary.

Second, life insurance proceeds paid to a named beneficiary are not subject to probate costs. The proceeds are paid immediately to the heirs without first having to go into a probate court.

## INSIGHT 19.2

### How to Reduce Federal Estate Taxes with a Credit-Shelter Trust

Scott and Jennifer are married and have adult children. Scott dies and has a taxable estate of $2 million. Because of the marital deduction, Jennifer receives $2 million, and Scott's taxable estate is zero. Shortly thereafter, Jennifer dies, leaving a taxable estate of $2 million. The first $600,000 is exempt from the federal estate tax because of the unified credit, but the remaining $1.4 million is subject to taxes of $588,000. *The problem is that the couple took advantage of the $600,000 lifetime exemption for only one estate, but not both.* This is summarized as follows:

| No Estate Plan | |
|---|---|
| Scott and Jennifer's Assets Total $2 Million. | |
| **SCOTT DIES** | |
| Leaves everything to Jennifer | $2,000,000 |
| Estate tax after marital deduction | -0- |
| **JENNIFER DIES** | |
| Leaves everything to her children | $2,000,000 |
| Taxable estate | 2,000,000 |
| Tentative tax | 780,800 |
| Less: Unified credit | 192,800 |
| Estate tax | $ 588,000 |

Now consider a more effective strategy. Both Scott and Jennifer establish credit-shelter trusts. Assume that Scott dies, and $600,000 goes into his credit-shelter trust. Jennifer receives income from the trust during her lifetime and has the right to withdraw limited amounts of principal. Because the trust does not qualify for the

marital deduction, $600,000 is included in Scott's taxable estate. However, because of the unified credit, the estate tax on that amount is zero. The remaining $1.4 million goes to Jennifer under the marital deduction. When she dies, her taxable estate is only $1.4 million. The $600,000 credit-shelter trust is not included in the estate because she does not own it. Thus, her estate is taxed only on $800,000 ($1,400,000 less $600,000), which creates an estate tax of $320,000. Thus, the credit-shelter trust saves $268,000 in federal estate taxes ($588,000 less $320,000). This is summarized as follows:

| With Credit-Shelter Trust | |
|---|---|
| Scott and Jennifer's Assets Total $2 Million. | |
| **SCOTT DIES** | |
| Tentative tax on $600,000 in credit-shelter trust | $192,800 |
| Less: Unified credit | 192,800 |
| Tax on credit-shelter trust | -0- |
| Tax on $1.4 million passed to Jennifer | -0- |
| **JENNIFER DIES** | |
| Credit-shelter assets go to children. | $600,000 |
| Tax on credit-shelter assets | -0- |
| Estate of $1.4 million goes to children. | 1,400,000 |
| Tentative tax on $1.4 million | 512,800 |
| Less: Unified credit | 192,800 |
| Estate tax | 320,000 |
| Estate tax saving | $ 268,000 |

Finally, life insurance can provide for the equitable treatment of heirs. For example, assume that a farmer has two daughters, and that one daughter helps manage the farm. The farm is valued at $500,000 and is left to that daughter in the farmer's will. The farmer can then purchase a $500,000 life insurance policy and name the other daughter owner and beneficiary. Both children would be treated equally when the farmer dies.

### Taxation of Life Insurance

The advantages of life insurance as an estate planning tool can be negated by unfavorable tax treatment if not properly planned. The following section discusses briefly the taxation of life insurance.

**Federal Estate Tax**    If the insured has any **incidents of ownership** in a life insurance policy at the time of death, the entire proceeds are included in

INSIGHT 19.3

## Dear Mom and Dad: Here's Something That's Easier to Read Than to Discuss

My brothers and I recently discussed what would happen if either of our parents fell ill or died.

We agreed that we should talk to our folks about their wishes concerning things like nursing homes, life-support machines and funeral arrangements. We also agreed that we should push them to get some critical legal documents drawn up, including living wills and durable powers of attorney.

In fact, we agreed on a lot of things—everything, that is, except who is going to pick up the phone and have the big discussion. We still haven't agreed on that one.

Just how do you get the ball rolling? I put that question to Richard Kohan, an estate-planning expert at Price Waterhouse.

"Ask your parents what they would like to accomplish with their estate," he suggested. For instance, he said, there might be needy friends, political causes or favorite charities that your parents would like to benefit.

"If you put it in that context, it makes estate planning less morbid and it makes parents realize the importance of doing estate planning."

And just what does estate planning involve? At a minimum, each parent should have a will, a durable power of attorney and a medical power of attorney. A medical power of attorney designates somebody to make healthcare decisions for your parents, should they become too ill to do so themselves, while a durable power of attorney designates someone to handle their finances. Your parents may also want to draw up living wills, which state their wishes concerning life-prolonging medical procedures.

Even if your folks already have wills, they may need to update them—especially if they have moved to a different state, if there's been a change in federal or state tax law or if there's been a big change in the value of their estate. Also, encourage both of your parents to draw up a letter of instructions, which specifies who should receive their personal belongings.

Next, ask your parents whether their estate, including the value of their home and all investments, is likely to top $600,000. How come? Your parents can pass on their assets to one another without paying any federal estate taxes. But if either of them leaves more than $600,000 to their children, grandchildren and anybody else, federal estate taxes kick in at rates that start at 37% and rise rapidly.

What should parents do? A good estate-planning lawyer can suggest a variety of ways to save on estate

*Continued*

the deceased's estate for federal estate tax purposes. As stated earlier, incidents of ownership include the right to change the beneficiary, the right to borrow the cash value or surrender the policy, and the right to select a settlement option. The proceeds are also included in the insured's gross estate if they are payable to the estate. They can be removed from the gross estate if the policyowner makes an *absolute assignment* of the policy to someone else and has no incidents of ownership in the policy at the time of death. However, if the assignment is made within three years of death, the policy proceeds will be included in the deceased's gross estate for federal estate tax purposes. Life insurance proceeds can also be removed from the gross estate by establishing an irrevocable life insurance trust.

**Federal Income Tax**   Life insurance proceeds paid in a lump sum are generally received income-tax-free by the beneficiary. If the proceeds are periodically liquidated under the settlement options, the payments consist of both principal and interest. The principal is received income-tax-free, but the interest is taxable as ordinary income.

Premiums paid for individual life insurance policies generally are not deductible for income-tax purposes. Dividends on life insurance policies are received income-tax-free. However, interest on dividends retained under the interest option is taxable to the policyowner. If the dividends are used to buy paid-up additions to the policy, the cash value of the paid-up additions accumulates income-tax-free. Thus, compared with the interest option, the

taxes. But for starters, you might mention a couple of popular strategies.

Your parents may want to use a bypass trust, which would allow both of them to make full use of the $600,000 federal estate tax exemption. Here's how it might work. When the first parent dies, $600,000 goes into a trust earmarked for the kids, but the surviving spouse continues to get the income kicked off by the trust. That ensures that the first parent's $600,000 exemption gets used. On the death of the second parent, another $600,000 will be exempt, thereby sheltering a full $1.2 million from federal estate taxes.

Both of your parents could also shrink their estates by taking advantage of the annual $10,000 gift-tax exclusion. Every year, they could give a combined gift of $20,000 to each of their children, without triggering the gift tax.

Moreover, if your parents want to help with medical bills or a grandchild's college tuition, these gifts aren't counted toward the $10,000 annual exclusion, so long as the money is paid directly to the medical provider or college.

Of course, all these clever arrangements can be thrown into disarray if kids don't know where to find their parents' key documents. "You want to know the whereabouts of all estate-planning documents, all insur-ance policies, all collectibles, all brokerage accounts," said San Francisco investment adviser Malcolm Gissen. "You also want to know whether they're owed money or whether they owe it."

Mr. Gissen advises asking your parents what they plan to do if maintaining their home becomes too burden-some. They may be able to hire somebody to help with chores, or they could take in a lodger who does house-work in lieu of rent. "But if you need somebody to look after your parents around the clock, it can get very ex-pensive," Mr. Gissen said. The alternative? "There's a range of options, from senior housing to nursing homes to living with the children."

And if you've worked your way through all the other issues, you might as well finish the job. So go ahead, ask about funeral arrangements.

But it sure isn't easy to ask your parents whether they want to be buried or cremated. As a cop-out, you could simply send them this article. That's what my brothers and I plan to do.

SOURCE: Jonathan Clements, "Dear Mom and Dad: Here's Something That's Easier to Read Than to Discuss," *The Wall Street Journal,* April 11, 1995, p. C1.

paid-up additions option provides a small tax advantage.

In addition, the annual increase in cash value under a permanent life insurance policy is presently income-tax-free. However, if the policy is surrendered for its cash value, any gain is taxable as ordinary income. If the cash value exceeds the premiums paid less any dividends, the excess is taxable as ordinary income.

Estate planning is a complex process. We have only touched the basic principles of estate planning in this chapter, and actual case situations can be extremely complicated. For this reason, estate planning is not a do-it-yourself activity, and a team of highly competent professionals is required. A *Chartered Life Underwriter (CLU), Chartered Financial Consultant (ChFC),* or *Certified Financial Planner (CFP)* can make valuable suggestions but cannot give legal advice. Therefore, a competent *attorney* who can give legal advice and draw up the necessary legal documents is also necessary. A *tax accountant* may also be needed, especially if there are complex business interests that must be considered. If a trust is required, a *trust officer* of a commercial bank or trust company can provide valuable advice on the conservation and investment of estate assets.

Finally, adult children should have a frank discussion with their parents concerning their financial affairs. This includes such things as a will, location and list of financial assets, durable power of attorney, health-care proxy, and funeral arrangements (see Insight 19.3).

## SUMMARY

- Life insurance planning is a systematic plan for determining the insured's financial goals, which are then translated into specific amounts of life insurance.
- There are four steps in life insurance planning:

    Determining the insured's financial goals

    Comparing present life insurance and financial assets with the amount needed for attaining these goals

    Determining the amount of new life insurance needed

    Reviewing the program periodically

- Inflation can seriously erode the purchasing power of life insurance. Several approaches can be used to reduce the adverse effects of inflation:

    Social Security survivor benefits are automatically adjusted each year for inflation.

    The policy proceeds can be assumed to be invested at a rate of interest equal to the rate of inflation.

    A relatively low interest rate can be assumed in determining the amount of interest that can be earned on the life insurance proceeds. The excess interest earned can be considered in determining the amount of required life insurance.

    Additional life insurance can be purchased and used as an inflation fund.

    A variable life or universal life insurance policy can be purchased, or a cost-of-living rider can be used to increase the face amount of insurance during a period of inflation.

- Estate planning is a system for the conservation and distribution of a person's property and wealth. Without a proper estate plan, the value of an estate may be substantially reduced after an individual dies.
- There are five basic steps in the estate-planning process:

    Obtain facts about the estate.

    Evaluate potential claims against the estate.

    Design an appropriate estate plan.

    Prepare the necessary legal documents.

    Periodically review and revise the plan.

- Several estate planning tools can be used in the estate-planning process:

    Will

    Marital deduction

    Gifts

    Trusts

    Life insurance

## KEY CONCEPTS AND TERMS

Credit shelter trust (bypass trust)
Dying intestate
Estate planning
Estate shrinkage
Federal estate and gift taxes
Gross estate
Incidents of ownership
Irrevocable trust
Life insurance planning
Living trust (*inter vivos* trust)
Marital deduction
Revocable trust
Second-to-die policy
Taxable estate
Testamentary trust
Trust
Unified tax credit
Will

## QUESTIONS FOR REVIEW

1. Explain the four steps in life insurance planning.
2. In determining the amount of new life insurance needed, certain assumptions must be made. Explain these assumptions.
3. To what extent should Social Security benefits be considered in life insurance planning?
4. Why is it necessary to review a life insurance program periodically?
5. Explain the general objectives of estate planning.
6. Describe the factors that may contribute to shrinkage of the estate after an individual dies.
7. Briefly describe the unified tax credit that applies to both the federal estate and federal gift tax.
8. Explain the five basic steps in the estate-planning process.
9. Briefly describe how the following can be effectively used in estate planning:
    a. Will
    b. Marital deduction
    c. Gifts
    d. Trusts
    e. Life insurance
10. With respect to the federal estate tax and the federal income tax, briefly explain how life insurance is taxed.

## QUESTIONS FOR DISCUSSION

1. A life insurance agent remarked that "life insurance planning offers several advantages to the insured, but certain precautions should be observed."
    a. Explain the advantages of life insurance planning.
    b. What precautions should be followed if your life insurance is planned?

## CASE APPLICATIONS

### Case 1

Scott, age 28, and Brenda, age 25, are married and have a daughter, age three. Scott has the following cash and income needs:

| *Cash needs* | |
|---|---|
| Estate clearance | $20,000 |
| Mortgage redemption | 90,000 |
| Emergency fund | 20,000 |
| Education fund | 50,000 |

| *Income needs* | |
|---|---|
| Readjustment period | $2000 monthly |
| Dependency period | 2000 monthly |
| Blackout period | 1000 monthly |

Brenda is employed outside the home. Her monthly net take-home pay is $1500 after taxes and other deductions. She plans to continue working if Scott should die. Based on the assumption that the life insurance proceeds can be invested at a rate of interest equal to the rate of inflation, answer the following questions:

a. How much additional life insurance, if any, is needed to meet Scott's cash needs if his present life insurance and financial assets total $100,000?

b. Ignoring the availability of OASDI survivor benefits, how much additional life insurance, if any, is needed to provide the desired amount of income during the readjustment and dependency periods?

c. In the above example, how much additional life insurance, if any, is needed if OASDI survivor benefits of $500 monthly are paid to the child until age 18?

d. How much additional life insurance, if any, is needed to provide the desired amount of income during the blackout period if Brenda does not work outside the home?

### Case 2

Sam and Kathy, both age 60, are married and have adult children. They own the following assets and life insurance.

| *Joint ownership* | |
|---|---|
| Residence | $150,000 |
| Mutual funds, securities, and cash | 650,000 |

| *Sam's Property* | |
|---|---|
| Private pension plan | 700,000 |
| Individual retirement account (IRA) | 300,000 |
| Life insurance | 600,000 |

| *Kathy's Property* | |
|---|---|
| Private pension plan | 100,000 |
| Individual retirement account (IRA) | 50,000 |
| Life insurance | 250,000 |

Sam and Kathy have separate wills. In his will, Sam bequeaths all of his property to Kathy if she is living and to the children if Kathy dies first. Kathy is the beneficiary of Sam's retirement plans and life insurance. The couple would like to update their estate plan so that federal estate taxes are minimized.

Based on the above information, answer the following questions.

a. Assume Sam dies first. Administrative expenses, funeral expenses, and probate costs are $100,000. What is the amount of Sam's *gross estate*?

b. In the above example, does Sam's estate have any federal estate tax liability? Explain your answer.

c. What fundamental error in estate planning did Sam commit by leaving all of his property outright to Kathy?

d. Explain how a credit-shelter trust (bypass trust) would avoid the error identified in (c) above.

2. A life insurance author remarked that "rapid inflation can complicate the life insurance planning process."

   a. Explain how inflation can complicate the life insurance planning process.

   b. Describe the various approaches that can reduce the adverse impact of inflation on a life insurance program.

3. One important objective of estate planning is to minimize the federal estate tax. Explain how the following estate planning tools can reduce federal estate taxes:

   a. Gifts

   b. Marital deduction

   c. Credit shelter trust

4. An attorney who specializes in estate planning stated that "life insurance can be an effective estate planning tool if properly used."

   a. Explain how the payment of life insurance proceeds can be arranged to reduce the federal estate tax.

   b. Are there any advantages of having the life insurance proceeds paid to a named beneficiary rather than to the insured's estate? Explain.

## SELECTED REFERENCES

Kaye, Barry. *Save a Fortune On Your Estates Taxes, Wealth Creation and Preservation.* Homewood, Ill.: Business One Irwin, 1993.

Leimberg, Stephan R. et al. *The Tools and Techniques of Estate Planning,* 10th ed. Cincinnati: National Underwriter Company, 1995.

Phillips, David T, and Bill S. Wolfkiel. *Estate Planning Made Easy.* Chicago, Ill.: Dearborn Financial Publishing, Inc., 1994.

Roha, Ronaleen R. "An Estate-Planning Kit for Dawdlers," *Kiplinger's Personal Finance Magazine,* 49 (June 1995): 71–76.

## NOTES

1. For additional information, see Stephan R. Leimberg et al., *The Tools and Techniques of Estate Planning,* 10th ed. (Cincinnati: National Underwriter Company, 1995); and Lawrence J. Ackerman, "Estate Planning Principles" in Davis W. Gregg and Vane B. Lucas, eds., *Life and Health Insurance Handbook,* 3rd ed. (Homewood, Ill.: Richard D. Irwin, 1973), chapter 55.

2. The marginal tax rate is 55 percent on taxable estates over $3 million to $10 million, 60 percent on taxable estates over $10 million to $21,040,000, and 55 percent on taxable estates over $21,040,000.

# Chapter 20

# INDIVIDUAL HEALTH INSURANCE

> *"This health-care system of ours is badly broken, and it is time to fix it."*
>
> President Clinton's health-care address to Congress

## Student Learning Objectives

After studying this chapter, you should be able to:

■ Explain the major health care problems in the United States.

■ Describe the individual medical expense coverages, including hospital insurance and surgical expense insurance.

■ Explain the basic characteristics of major medical insurance.

■ Describe the major characteristics of long-term care insurance.

■ Explain the major characteristics of individual disability-income contracts.

■ Discuss the rules that should be followed when individual health insurance is purchased.

In a personal risk management program, the risk of poor health should receive high priority. Millions of Americans are sick or injured each year, which often results in great financial insecurity. Two major problems are encountered if the sickness or injury is severe—payment of medical bills and the loss of earned income. A serious illness or injury can result in the payment of catastrophic medical bills, and a lengthy disability can result in the loss of thousands of dollars of earned income. Without proper protection, you may have to pay thousands of dollars out of your own pocket. For example, Mark, age 32, is a hotel waiter who had a brain tumor that required immediate surgery. The surgeon's fee, hospital expenses, and related medical bills totaled $140,000. He had no health insurance. In addition, he was off work for more than one year and did not have any disability income insurance to restore his lost earnings. In short, because of the lack of health insurance, Mark experienced serious financial insecurity and eventually had to declare bankruptcy.

This chapter is the first of two chapters dealing with private health insurance. Discussion here is limited largely to individual health insurance; the following chapter discusses group health insurance coverages provided by employers as an employee benefit. Although the various group plans account for more than 90 percent of the total medical expense insurance premiums paid, a considerable amount of individual insurance is still being sold. Individual coverages are especially important to individuals and families who are not covered by any group plan.

This chapter discusses the problems of health care in the United States, individual medical expense coverages, major medical insurance, long-term-care insurance, disability income insurance, and important health insurance contractual provisions. The chapter concludes with a discussion of important rules to follow when individual health insurance is purchased.

## HEALTH-CARE PROBLEMS IN THE UNITED STATES

Although the health of Americans has improved remarkably over time and life expectancy has increased, there is considerable dissatisfaction with the present health-care system in the United States. The present system has four major problems:[1]

- Soaring health-care costs
- Inadequate access to medical care
- Uneven quality of medical care
- Waste and inefficiency

### Soaring Health-Care Costs

Health-care expenditures in the United States have soared in recent years. The United States spends more on health care than any other nation in the world. In 1995, national health expenditures totaled $989 billion, or 13.6 percent of the gross domestic product (see Exhibit 20.1). If present trends continue, in the year 2000, projected national health expenditures will total $1.5 trillion, or about 16 percent of the gross domestic product.[2]

Numerous factors have been identified that explain the rise in health care expenditures. They

EXHIBIT 20.1

**National Health Insurance Expenditures as a Percent of Gross Domestic Product**

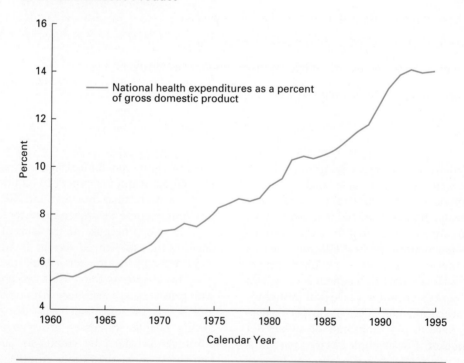

SOURCE: Katharine R. Levit et al, "National Health Expenditures, 1995," *Health Care Financing Review,* 18 (Fall 1996): 176.

include population growth that increases the demand for medical care, general price inflation and medical care inflation, new and expensive technology, aging of the population, cost shifting by Medicare and Medicaid to private health insurers, and state-mandated health insurance benefits. The growth in private health insurance has also contributed to the problem, since health insurance removes a financial barrier to care and increases the demand for medical care. Finally, the tax subsidy of health insurance has also contributed to the problem. Health insurance contributions by employers are income-tax deductible and are not taxable to employees. As a result, the tax subsidy has encouraged the growth of expensive group health insurance plans that are more likely to be used.

## Inadequate Access to Medical Care

Another problem is that certain groups have inadequate access to medical care. *First, millions of Americans have no health insurance.* The March, 1996, Current Population Survey shows that despite low unemployment, the percentage of the nonelderly population without health insurance remains stubbornly high. *In 1995, 40.3 million people, or 17.4 percent of the nonelderly population, were not covered by health insurance, up from 39.4 million or 17.1 percent of the nonelderly population in 1994.*[3] People likely to be uninsured include employees working for smaller employers that cannot afford health insurance, low-income families who cannot qualify for government health insurance programs, individuals of Hispanic origin, illegal and legal immigrants, and single people under age 25. Some states have a high proportion of uninsured residents, including Arizona, California, New Mexico, and Texas.

*Second, some welfare recipients find it difficult to find a physician who will treat them promptly because of inadequate reimbursement rates.* This limited access to health care is especially detrimental to women with high-risk pregnancies who delay receiving prenatal care.

*Finally, residents of small rural communities often have an access problem* because of the shortage of physicians in many rural areas.

## Uneven Quality of Medical Care

In addition, the quality of medical care is uneven and varies widely, depending on physician specialty and geographic location. One study showed that residents of New Haven, Conn. are twice as likely to undergo coronary artery bypass surgery than are residents of Boston, Mass.[4] The increase in medical malpractice suits over time is another indication that some physicians at times provide low-quality medical care.

## Waste and Inefficiency

A final problem is the waste and inefficiency in the present system. The administrative costs of delivering health insurance benefits are excessively high; there is excessive paperwork by both health-care providers and insurers; claim forms are not uniform nationally; a considerable amount of medical care provided by physicians is considered inappropriate; defensive medicine by physicians often results in unnecessary tests and procedures; there is duplication of expensive technology in many cities; and fraud and abuse by health-care providers are widespread.

## TYPES OF INDIVIDUAL HEALTH INSURANCE COVERAGES

Health insurers sell a wide variety of individual health insurance coverages. The quality of the coverage varies widely. Some plans provide broad and comprehensive protection, while others are limited with numerous exclusions.

The most important individual coverages include the following:

- Hospital-surgical insurance
- Major medical insurance
- Long-term care insurance
- Disability income insurance

## HOSPITAL-SURGICAL INSURANCE

Insurers sell a variety of individual **hospital-surgical insurance plans.** These plans are also called basic plans since they cover routine medical expenses and generally are not designed to cover catastrophic losses. The types of covered medical expenses vary widely among insurers. The most complete plans cover the following:

- Hospital expenses
- Surgical expenses

- Outpatient diagnostic X-rays and lab expenses
- Physician's in-hospital expense benefit
- Maternity expenses

## Hospital Expenses

An individual hospital-surgical policy covers medical expenses incurred while in a hospital. A typical policy provides benefits for (1) daily room and board charges and (2) miscellaneous hospital expenses incurred during the hospital stay.

There are two basic approaches for paying *daily room and board charges.* Under an **indemnity plan,** actual room and board charges are paid up to some maximum daily limit, such as up to $400 daily for 120 days. Under a plan that provides **service benefits,** the full cost of a semi-private room is paid up to a maximum number of days. Newer plans typically provide service benefits for hospital care.

Individual hospital-surgical plans also cover *miscellaneous hospital expenses,* such as X-rays, drugs, laboratory fees, and other ancillary charges. Depending on the plan, part or all of the miscellaneous expenses are paid up to some maximum limit. For example, the plan may pay a maximum benefit for miscellaneous expenses that is some multiple of the daily room and board benefit, such as 10, 15, or 20 times the daily benefit.

## Surgical Expenses

Individual hospital-surgical plans also include coverage for surgical expenses. Several methods are used to compensate surgeons. Older plans use a **schedule approach** by which the various surgical operations are listed in a schedule, and a maximum dollar amount is paid for each procedure, such as $400 for an appendectomy and $2000 for a valve replacement in the heart.

A **relative-value schedule** is a variation of the schedule approach in which units or points are attached to each operation based on the degree of difficulty. A conversion factor is then used to convert the relative value of the operation into a dollar amount that is paid to the physician. One advantage of a relative-value schedule is that it can be adapted to differences in the cost of living and in surgeons' fees in different geographical areas.

Newer plans typically reimburse surgeons on the basis of their **usual, reasonable, and customary charges.** Under this approach, surgeons are reimbursed based on their usual fees as long as the fee is reasonable and customary. Many insurers consider a fee to be reasonable and customary if it does not exceed the 80th or 90th percentile for a similar medical procedure performed by other surgeons in the same area. The policy pays the reasonable and customary fee, subject to any deductible or coinsurance requirements. The insured must pay that portion of the fee that exceeds the upper limit. Because insurers differ in how usual and customary fees are calculated, some insureds may have to pay substantial amounts out-of-pocket for that portion of the fee that exceeds the allowable upper limit.

## Outpatient Diagnostic X-ray and Lab Expenses

Many hospital-surgical plans cover *outpatient diagnostic X-rays and lab expenses.* Many physicians have well-equipped offices for routine X-rays and laboratory tests for diagnosing the medical problems of patients. The maximum amount paid is limited to a stated dollar amount, such as $200 or $500 for any single illness or injury. However, some plans provide for maximum higher limits of several thousands of dollars.

## Physician's In-Hospital Benefit

Many plans provide a *physician's in-hospital benefit.* This benefit pays for *nonsurgical treatment* provided by a physician to a patient while in the hospital. The policies limit the maximum amount paid for each visit and also usually limit the number of visits during any single hospital stay.

## Maternity Expenses

Individual hospital-surgical policies may cover part of the insured's maternity expenses. Some policies include maternity benefits while others offer the coverage as an optional benefit. A maternity benefits rider can be added to the policy by payment of an additional premium. The rider is relatively expensive, and the amount paid is limited and below the actual cost of childbirth.

The maternity rider results in strong adverse selection because women who are likely to become pregnant will add the rider to their individual policies.

Adverse selection is controlled by high premiums, by limits on the amount paid, and by a lengthy elimination period of ten months. Because of cost, many financial planners do not recommend purchase of the rider.

## MAJOR MEDICAL INSURANCE

Insureds often desire broader coverage than that provided by the basic coverages just discussed. **Major medical insurance** is designed to pay a high proportion of the covered expenses of a catastrophic illness or injury. A typical individual major medical policy has the following characteristics:

- Broad coverage
- High maximum limits
- Benefit period
- Deductible
- Coinsurance
- Exclusions

### Broad Coverage

Major medical insurance provides broad coverage of all reasonable and necessary medical expenses and other related expenses from a covered illness or injury. The policy covers eligible expenses incurred while in the hospital, in the doctor's office, or at home. Eligible medical expenses include hospital room and board charges, miscellaneous hospital services and supplies, treatment by licensed physicians and surgeons, prescription drugs, durable medical equipment, and numerous other expenses.

### High Maximum Limits

Major medical policies are also written with high lifetime limits of $500,000, $1 million, or some higher amount. Some plans have no maximum limits. High limits are necessary to meet the crushing financial burden of a major catastrophic illness or injury.

### Benefit Period

The maximum amount paid under a major medical policy depends partly on the length of the benefit period. A **benefit period,** *such as three years, refers to the length of time that major medical benefits will be paid*

*after the deductible is satisfied.* When the benefit period ends, the insured must then satisfy a new deductible in order to establish a new benefit period. For example, assume that Jennifer has a $1 million major medical expense policy with a $500 deductible and a three-year benefit period. Assume that she is severely injured in an auto accident and satisfies the deductible on the first day of her injury. A three-year benefit period for that illness is then established. At the end of three years, Jennifer must again satisfy a new deductible if the maximum amount of $1 million has not been paid.

The purpose of the benefit period is to provide a definite time period within which eligible medical expenses for a specific disease or injury must be incurred in order to be reimbursed under the policy.

### Deductible

A major medical policy normally contains a deductible that must be satisfied before benefits are paid. The purpose of the deductible is to eliminate payment of small claims and the relatively high administrative expenses of processing small claims. By eliminating small claims, the insurer can provide high policy limits and still keep the premiums reasonable.

Several types of deductible provisions are found in individual major medical policies, including the following:

- Each-illness deductible
- Calendar-year deductible
- Family deductible
- Common-accident provision

An **each-illness deductible** *means that a separate deductible applies to each covered illness or injury.* (This type of deductible is also called a "per cause" deductible.) Under this type of deductible, only the medical expenses relating to a specific illness or injury can be accumulated to satisfy the deductible. Medical expenses must be incurred by the insured within a certain time period, such as 90 or 120 days. The important point to remember is that the deductible must be satisfied for each separate illness or injury before major medical benefits are payable.

A **calendar-year deductible** means *the deductible has to be satisfied only once during the calendar year.* All covered medical expenses incurred by the insured during the calendar year can be applied toward the deductible. Once the deductible is met, no additional deductible has to be satisfied during the calendar year. To avoid paying for two deductibles in a short period, most plans have a carryover provision. This means that unreimbursed medical expenses incurred during the last three months of the calendar year that are applied to this year's deductible can also be carried over and applied to next year's deductible.

The **family deductible** *specifies that medical expenses for all family members are accumulated for purposes of satisfying the deductible.* The accumulation period typically is one month, but a longer period could be used. For example, a $100 monthly deductible may be used. If medical expenses for the entire family exceed $100 during the month, the major medical policy starts to pay.

Individual major medical policies also contain a **common-accident provision.** *This means that only one deductible has to be satisfied if two or more family members are injured in a common accident, such as an automobile accident.*

## Coinsurance

Major medical policies contain a **coinsurance provision** *that requires the insured to pay a certain percentage of eligible medical expenses in excess of the deductible.* (Coinsurance is also called a percentage participation clause.) A typical plan requires the insured to pay 20 percent or 25 percent of covered expenses in excess of the deductible. For example, assume that Megan has covered medical expenses in the amount of $10,500. She has a $1 million major medical policy with a $500 deductible and an 80-20 coinsurance provision. The insurer will pay $8,000 of the total bill, and Megan will pay $2000 (plus the deductible). This is summarized as follows:

| | |
|---|---|
| Covered expenses | $10,500 |
| Less the deductible | −500 |
| Remaining expenses | $10,000 |
| 80% paid by insurer | 8,000 |
| 20% paid by Megan | $ 2,000 |

*The purposes of the coinsurance clause are to reduce premiums and prevent overutilization of policy benefits.* Since the insured pays part of the cost, premiums are reduced. It is also argued that the patient will not

demand the most expensive medical services if he or she pays part of the cost, and that physicians and other health care providers will be more restrained in setting their fees if the patient pays part of the cost.

Major medical policies also contain a **stop-loss limit** by which 100 percent of the eligible medical expenses are paid after the insured incurs a certain amount of out-of-pocket expenses, such as $2000. *The purpose of the stop-loss limit is to reduce the financial burden of a catastrophic loss.* For example, if Megan's covered medical expenses in excess of the deductible are $100,000 and the stop-limit is $2000, her major medical policy would pay $98,000. She would pay only $2000 (plus the deductible). Without the stop-limit, Megan would have to pay $20,000 (plus the deductible).

## Exclusions

All major medical policies contain exclusions. Some common exclusions include the following:

- Expenses caused by war or military conflict
- Elective cosmetic surgery
- Dental care except as a result of an accident
- Eye and hearing examinations, eyeglasses, and hearing aids
- Pregnancy and childbirth, except complications of pregnancy
- Expenses covered by workers compensation and similar laws
- Services furnished by governmental agencies unless the patient has an obligation to pay
- Experimental surgery

In addition, major medical plans typically contain **internal limits** for certain types of expenses, to control cost. There may be annual or lifetime limits on the amount paid for certain diseases, such as alcoholism and drug addiction. For example, one plan limits inpatient coverage for alcoholism and drug addiction to no more than 45 days of treatment during any successive 12-month period.

## LONG-TERM CARE INSURANCE

Long-term care insurance is another coverage that is rapidly growing in popularity. **Long-term care insurance** pays a daily or monthly benefit for medical

EXHIBIT **20.2**

## The Cost of Long-Term Care Can Be Staggering

**At one time, long-term care may have been affordable.
But times have changed . . . as you can see in the chart below . . .**

In 1965, the average cost in the U.S. for one year of nursing home care was $2,900. Today, it's more than 12 times that much. And by 2001, the average cost for one year of nursing home care is projected to be $48,200.\*

**Will you be able to afford this if you need long-term care?**

\*Source of costs cited from 1965–1984 are based on unpublished data from the *Office of National Health Statistics, Health Care Financing Administration, Office of the Actuary.* Cost cited for 2001 is based on a conservative 5% annual increase over 1995 cost of $36,000 per year.

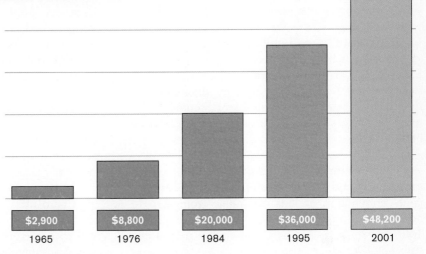

| $2,900 | $8,800 | $20,000 | $36,000 | $48,200 |
| 1965 | 1976 | 1984 | 1995 | 2001 |

SOURCE: Teachers Insurance and Annuity Association.

or custodial care received in a nursing facility, hospital, or at home.

## Chance of Entering a Nursing Home

Many older Americans will spend some time in a nursing home. One study showed that 40 to 45 percent of the persons attaining age 65 in 1990 will stay in a nursing home at least once during their lifetime. About half of the patients admitted to nursing homes will stay less than six months. However, one in five will stay one year or more, and one in 10 will stay three or more years.[5]

The cost of long-term care in a nursing home is staggering. Many long-term facilities charge $36,000 or more annually (see Exhibit 20.2). The Medicare program does not cover long-term care in a nursing facility, and custodial care is excluded altogether. In addition, most elderly are not initially eligible for long-term care under the Medicaid program, which is a welfare program that imposes strict eligibility requirements and a stringent means test. As a result, many older Americans have purchased long-term care policies to meet the crushing financial burden of an extended stay in a nursing facility.

## Basic Characteristics

More than 130 insurers sell long-term care policies. The policies sold currently usually have certain generic characteristics.[6]

**Type of Care Provided**    The policies typically cover skilled nursing care, intermediate nursing care, and custodial care. *Skilled nursing care* is medical care provided by skilled medical personnel 24 hours a day under the supervision of a physician, such as care provided by a registered nurse or physical therapist. *Intermediate nursing care* is medical care for a stable condition that requires daily but not continuous 24-hour nursing supervision. The care is ordered by a physician and is supervised by registered nurses. It is less specialized than skilled nursing care and often involves more personal care. *Custodial care* is care that helps the patient with daily living activities, such as assistance in bathing, eating, dressing, and using the toilet; this type of care is also called personal care.

Many policies also cover *home health care.* Some plans cover only skilled nursing care provided in the home by registered nurses, licensed practical nurses, and physical, occupational, or speech therapists. Other policies are broader and also cover the services of home health aides from licensed agencies who provide patients with personal or custodial care. However, few policies pay for someone to come into your home and cook meals or run errands.

**Aggregate Benefits**    Purchasers have a choice of benefits, such as daily benefits of $80, $100, or $120, which are paid over a maximum period of two, three, or four years, or over the insured's lifetime. Other plans have a choice of lifetime maximum benefits, such as $120 daily and a $250,000 lifetime limit.

**Elimination Period**    An elimination period is a waiting period during which time benefits are not paid. Elimination periods can range from zero to 365 days. Common elimination periods are 30, 60, 100, or 180 days. A longer elimination period can substantially reduce premiums.

**Eligibility for Benefits**    All policies have one or more **gatekeeper provisions,** which determine if the insured is eligible to receive benefits. One common gatekeeper provision requires the insured to be unable to perform a certain number of **activities of daily living,** commonly called ADLs. Examples include walking, bathing, dressing, eating, getting into and out of bed, and using the toilet. Benefits are paid if the insured cannot perform a certain number of ADLs listed in the policy without assistance from another person, such as two out of five ADLs.

**Inflation Protection**    Protection against inflation is usually made available as an optional benefit. For example, based on an inflation rate of 5 percent annually, a daily charge of $86 will increase to $228 in 20 years.[7] Protection against inflation is especially important if the policy is purchased at a younger age.

Two methods are used to provide protection against inflation. One method allows the insured to purchase additional amounts of insurance in the future without evidence of insurability. For example, one insurer allows the insured to exercise four options, one every five years, to increase his or her coverage 20 percent each time an option is exercised.

A second method provides for an automatic benefit increase by which the daily benefit is increased by a fixed percentage, such as 5 percent for the next 10 or 20 years. The dollar amount of the annual increase will depend on whether the inflation adjustment is based on simple or compound interest. A daily benefit of $80 will increase to $160 in 20 years based on 5 percent simple interest; however, if the benefit is compounded, it will increase to $212. Also, adding an automatic benefit increase to the policy is expensive and could double the amount of the annual premium in some cases.

**Guaranteed Renewable**    The policies sold currently are guaranteed renewable. Once issued, the policy cannot be canceled. However, rates can be increased for the underwriting class in which the insured is placed.

**Premiums**    Coverage is expensive. For example, one insurer charges $740 annually for a policy sold to a person age 60 with a $100 daily benefit, four-year maximum limit per confinement, and a seven-day elimination period. That same policy sold to a person at age 79 would cost $5190 annually.

**Taxation of Long-Term Care Insurance**    Long-term care insurance now receives favorable income tax treatment as a result of the Health Insurance Portability and Accountability Act of 1996. A long-term care policy that meets certain requirements is treated as an accident and health insurance contract. The long-term care coverage can be an individual or group plan. Premiums are deductible by the employer under a group plan and are not taxable to the employee.

Annual premiums are deductible as medical expenses under an individual plan if the premiums plus other unreimbursed medical expenses exceed $7\frac{1}{2}$ percent of the individual's adjusted gross income. However, certain annual limits apply. For 1997, the maximum annual deduction for long-term care premiums ranges from $200 for people age 40 or below to $2500 for people age 71 or older. These limits are indexed for inflation.

If the policy is a *per diem policy* that pays a specific daily amount, the maximum daily benefit excludable from income is limited to $175 (indexed for inflation). Finally, long-term care insurance cannot be made available to employees in a cafeteria plan or flexible spending account.

In recent years, health insurers have upgraded their individual long-term care contracts. However, there is still considerable variation among the various policies with respect to daily benefits, home care services, exclusions, elimination periods, and similar provisions. Insight 20.1 discusses some key factors to consider when you are shopping for a long-term care policy.

## DISABILITY-INCOME INSURANCE

Disability-income insurance is another important form of individual health insurance. A serious disability can result in a substantial loss of work earnings. Unless you have replacement income from disability-income insurance, or income from other sources, you may be financially insecure. Many

---

### INSIGHT 20.1

## What to Look for When You Pick a Policy

LONG-TERM-CARE POLICIES are more inclusive than they used to be. They routinely cover so-called functional infirmities (such as needing help to bathe and dress), physical impairment (such as stroke), and cognitive impairment (such as Alzheimer's disease). Avoid buying a policy that requires a hospital stay before you can collect benefits.

The younger you are, the lower the premiums. Premiums are fixed when you sign on, but they can be raised later for a whole class of policies (that's what insurer CNA did last year). Extra features add to the cost.

When you buy a policy you'll select some key features:

- **Daily benefit.** That's the amount you want to receive daily for nursing-home and home-care coverage. Benefits of $100 a day are common but you can select $200 or more. Don't feel obliged to cover the full cost of care. If charges in your area are running about $120 a day, you can select benefits of $100 and pay the rest out of pocket.
- **Home care.** This benefit typically covers skilled care from nurses and therapists, as well as personal care from health aides and others. Policies may include home-care benefits at half the daily benefit of nursing-home coverage, but planners increasingly recommend buying the same daily benefit for both.
- **Benefit period.** Payments continue for the period you choose, typically from two to five years, but in many cases for a lifetime. A period of two or three years ought to be enough for most people, says

John Haslett, a long-term-care specialist in Reston, Va., because few people spend longer than that in a nursing home.

- **Elimination period.** This is the deductible period during which you must pay for care out of your own pocket before benefits kick in. The longer you're willing to wait, the lower your premiums.
- **Inflation protection.** Companies often offer inflation-protection riders that increase the daily benefit amount. The best protection, especially for younger buyers in their sixties, is 5% a year compounded, beginning the year after you buy the policy. Simple inflation adjustments of 5% annually may be fine for older buyers in their seventies if such adjustments are offered in your state.

### Comparing Coverage

About 120 companies offer long-term-care insurance. Choose a company with a history of refining and updating policies. Look for a financially solid insurer rated A or better by A.M. Best Co., Moody's Investors Service or Standard & Poor's Corp.

The table below illustrates premiums for roughly similar policies from six major insurers, issued to buyers at ages 60, 65 and 70. Features include a daily benefit of $100 for both nursing-home and home care; a 90- or 100-day waiting period; a three-year benefit period; and a 5% compound inflation adjustment. Policyholders can qualify for benefits if they need assistance in performing two or more activities of daily living. They don't have to be hospitalized before qualifying.

*Continued*

## Sizing up the Candidates

| Company | 800 number | Annual Premium | | |
| | | At age 60 | At age 65 | At age 70 |
| --- | --- | --- | --- | --- |
| Amex | 456-3399 | $1,260 | $1,720 | $2,460 |
| CNA | 775-1541 | 856 | 1,168 | 1,696 |
| Fortis-Time* | 800-1212 | 1,170 | 1,420 | 2,100 |
| John Hancock | 543-6415 | 1,310 | 1,765 | 2,507 |
| Travelers | 842-7794 | 1,095 | 1,436 | 2,162 |
| Unum* | 331-1538 | 892 | 1,255 | 1,796 |

*Standard rates; some people may qualify for lower rates.

Premiums are for individual policies, and men and women of the same age pay the same premium. Amex gives no discount if both spouses buy policies, but Travelers gives a 15% discount and the others 10%.

Don't buy any policy on price alone. Although comparing policies has become easier, the policies are not standardized and details vary. For example, John Hancock permits policyholders to, in effect, automatically convert some or all of their nursing-home coverage to additional home-care benefits. If you use the Amex patient-care coordinator, the policy pays 100% of home care charges and eliminates the 100-day waiting period.

For help evaluating policies, find the nearest health-insurance counseling and advocacy program by calling your area agency on aging or your state insurance department. For a free *Guide to Long-Term Care Insurance,* write to the Health Insurance Industry Association, c/o Publications Office, 555 13th St., N.W., Suite 600 East, Washington, DC 20004, or call 202-824-1600.

SOURCE: Ronaleen R. Roha, "Considering Long-Term Care," *Kiplinger's Personal Finance Magazine,* 50 (March 1996):112.

workers seldom think about the financial consequences of a long-term disability. However, the probability of becoming disabled before age 65 is much higher than is commonly believed, especially at the younger ages. For example, *the probability that a person age 25 will be totally disabled for at least 90 days prior to age 65 is 54 percent* (see Exhibit 20.3).

The financial loss to the family from long-term total and permanent disability can be substantially greater than the financial loss that results from premature death at the same age. In the case of premature death, the family loses its share of the deceased family head's future earnings, and funeral expenses

are also incurred. However, in the case of long-term total and permanent disability, earned income is lost; medical bills are being incurred; savings are reduced or depleted; employee benefits may be lost; and additional expenses are incurred, such as getting someone to care for the disabled person. It is clear that disability income insurance should be a high priority in a personal risk management program.

**Disability-income insurance** provides income payments when the insured is unable to work because of sickness or injury. An individual policy pays monthly income benefits to an insured who becomes totally disabled from a sickness or accident. The

## Exhibit 20.3

### Probability of Becoming Disabled for at least 90 Days before Age 65

| Age | |
|-----|-----|
| 25 | 54% |
| 30 | 52 |
| 35 | 50 |
| 40 | 48 |
| 45 | 44 |
| 50 | 39 |
| 55 | 32 |
| 60 | 9 |

Based on 1985 Commissioners Disability Table.

Source: Adapted from Edward E. Graves, ed., *McGill's Life Insurance* (Bryn Mawr, Pa: The American College, 1994), Table 7-2, p. 141.

amount of disability insurance you can buy is related to your earnings. To prevent overinsurance and to reduce moral hazard and malingering, most insurers limit the amount of disability income to no more than 60 to 80 percent of your gross earnings.

## Meaning of Total Disability

The most important policy provision in a disability income policy is the meaning of total disability. Most policies require the worker to be totally disabled to receive benefits.

**Definitions of Total Disability** There are several definitions of total disability. The most important include the following:

- Inability to perform all duties of the insured's own occupation
- Inability to perform the duties of any occupation for which the insured is reasonably fitted by education, training, and experience
- Inability to perform the duties of any gainful occupation
- Loss-of-income test

The most liberal definition defines total disability in terms of your own occupation. **Total disability** *is the complete inability of the insured to perform each and every duty of his or her own occupation.* An example would be a surgeon whose hand is blown off in a

hunting accident. The surgeon could no longer perform surgery and would be totally disabled under this definition.

The second definition is more restrictive. In this case, *total disability is the complete inability to perform the duties of any occupation for which the insured is reasonably fitted by education, training, and experience.* Thus, if the surgeon who lost a hand in a hunting accident could get a job as a professor in a medical school or as a research scientist, he or she would not be considered disabled because these occupations are consistent with the surgeon's training and experience.

The third definition is the most restrictive and is commonly used for hazardous occupations where a disability is likely to occur. *Total disability is defined as the inability to perform the duties of any gainful occupation.* The courts generally have interpreted this definition to mean that the person is totally disabled if he or she cannot work in any gainful occupation reasonably fitted by education, training, and experience.

Finally, some insurers use a loss-of-income test to determine if the insured is disabled. *You are considered disabled if your income is reduced as a result of a sickness or accident.* A disability-income policy containing this definition typically pays a percentage of the maximum monthly benefit equal to the percentage of earned income that is lost. For example, assume that Stanley earns $5000 monthly and has a disability-income contract with a maximum monthly benefit of $3000. If Stanley's work earnings are reduced to $2500 monthly because of the disability (50 percent), the policy pays $1500 monthly (50 percent of $3000).

Many insurers now combine the first two definitions. *For the initial period of disability—typically two years—total disability is defined in terms of the insured's own occupation. After the initial period of disability expires, the second definition is applied.* For example, Dr. Myron Pudwill is a dentist who can no longer practice because of arthritis in his hands. For the first two years, he would be considered totally disabled. However, after two years, if he could work as a dental supply representative or even as a professor in a dental school, he would no longer be considered disabled because he is reasonably fitted for these occupations by his education and training.

Finally, the policy may also contain a definition of *presumptive disability.* A total disability is presumed to exist if the insured suffers the total and irrecoverable loss of sight in both eyes, or the total loss or use of both hands, both feet, or one hand and one foot.

**Partial Disability** Some disability-income policies also pay partial disability benefits. **Partial disability** *is defined as the inability of the insured to perform one or more important duties of his or her occupation.* Partial disability benefits are paid at a reduced rate for a shorter period. For example, a person may be totally disabled from an automobile accident. If the person recovers and goes back to work on a part-time basis to see if recovery is complete, partial disability benefits may be paid.

**Residual Disability** Newer policies frequently include a residual disability benefit, or it can be added as an additional benefit. **Residual disability** *means that a pro rata disability benefit is paid to an insured whose earned income is reduced because of an accident or sickness.* The typical residual disability provision has a time and duties test that considers both income and occupation. One common residual disability provision is as follows:[8]

1. You are not able to do one or more of your important daily business duties, or you are not able to do your usual daily business duties for as much time as it would normally take for you to do them.

2. Your loss of monthly income is at least 25 percent of your prior monthly income.

3. You are under the care and attendance of a physician.

However, some insurers use an alternative definition of residual disability that considers only the loss of earned income: **Residual disability** *means that you are engaged in your regular or another occupation, and your income is reduced because of an accident or sickness by at least 20 percent of your prior income.*

Finally, most insurers consider a loss of earned income in excess of 75 or 80 percent to be a loss of 100 percent, in which case the full monthly benefit for total disability is paid.

One major advantage of the residual disability definition is the payment of a partial benefit if the insured returns to work but earnings are reduced. For example, Chris is a salesperson who earns $4000 monthly. He is seriously injured in an auto accident. When he returns to work, his earnings are only $3000 monthly, or a reduction of 25 percent. If his disability income policy pays a monthly benefit of $2000 for total disability, a residual benefit of $500 is paid, and his total monthly income is $3500.

## Benefit Period

The **benefit period** is the length of time that disability benefits are payable after the elimination period is met. The insured has a choice of benefit periods, such as 2, 5, or 10 years, or up to age 65.

Most disabilities are relatively short. About 98 percent of all disability claimants recover within the first year of disability.[9] However, this does not mean that a one-year benefit period is adequate. The longer the disability lasts, the less likely the disabled person will recover. For example, a person who became disabled at age 22 and remains disabled for one year has a 32 percent chance of remaining disabled for at least five more years.[10] Thus, because of uncertainty concerning the duration of disability, you should elect a longer benefit period—ideally, one that pays benefits to age 65.

Exhibit 20.4 contains a convenient worksheet that can help you estimate the amount of disability income needed. The worksheet takes into consideration other sources of income, such as investment income and disability benefits from your employer.

## Elimination Period

Individual policies normally contain an **elimination period** (waiting period), during which time benefits are not paid. Insurers offer a range of elimination periods, such as 30, 60, 90, 180, or 365 days. Most insurers have stopped offering elimination periods that are shorter than 14 days, and elimination periods of 30 or more days are now the rule.

High-quality disability income policies are expensive and can cost as much as 2 to 3 percent of your annual earnings. Increasing the elimination period from 30 to 90 days can substantially reduce the premiums. For example, in one plan, a male accountant who purchases a monthly benefit of $4250 to age 65 will pay $4036 annually for a policy with a 30-day elimination period. However, if he elects a 90-day elimination period, the annual premium would be about $1888, or 53 percent less. The majority of employers have sick leave or short-term disability plans that would provide some income during the longer elimination period.

---

Exhibit 20.4

## How Much Disability Income Insurance Do You Need?

---

### 1. ESTIMATED MONTHLY EXPENSES

Mortgage/Rent                                                    _____

Utilities                                                       _____

Miscellaneous home expenses                                     _____

Loan payments                                                   _____

Food                                                            _____

Clothing                                                        _____

Insurance payments/expenses                                     _____

Medical and dental expenses                                     _____

Miscellaneous (vacation, entertainment, etc.)                   _____

Education                                                       _____

Transportation                                                  _____

TOTAL                                                           _____

### 2. ESTIMATED MONTHLY INCOME

**If you are single:**

Current monthly take-home pay                                   _____

Subtract investment income                                      _____

TOTAL                                                           _____

**If you are married[1]**

Current monthly take-home pay                                   _____

Subtract investment income                                      _____

Subtract spouse's pay                                           _____

TOTAL                                                           _____

### 3. EXISTING BENEFITS

Social Security/Workers compensation                            _____

Other government insurance                                      _____

Group disability income insurance                               _____

Individual disability income insurance                          _____

TOTAL

### 4. THE AMOUNT OF DISABILITY INSURANCE YOU NEED

If the total from 3 is greater than the total from 2, you probably have adequate coverage. But if the total from 3 is less than the total in 2, subtract total 3 from total 2. This is the amount of additional monthly coverage you need.

### 5. HOW MANY MONTHS CAN YOU AFFORD TO LIVE WITHOUT YOUR SALARY?

$$\frac{\text{Amount from savings accounts that you would feel comfortable spending}}{\text{Total expenses} - \text{short-term disability benefits provided by your employer}} = \begin{array}{l}\text{The number of} \\ \text{months you can get} \\ \text{by without long-term} \\ \text{disability coverage.}\end{array}$$

---

[1]This worksheet should be completed for each spouse.

One disadvantage, however, is that a group disability income plan is usually not convertible into an individual policy if the worker becomes unemployed. Thus, group insurance is not a satisfactory substitute for a high-quality disability-income policy.

Finally, to make disability-income insurance more affordable, *some insurers sell policies with initially lower rates that gradually increase with age.* This approach is similar to term life insurance rates that increase as the insured gets older.

## Waiver of Premium

A **waiver-of-premium** provision is built into the policy, which states that if the insured is totally disabled for 90 days, future premiums will be waived as long as the insured remains disabled. In addition, there is a refund of the premiums paid during the initial 90-day period. If the insured recovers from the disability, premium payments must be resumed.

## Rehabilitation Provision

Disability-income policies typically include a rehabilitation provision. The insurer and insured may agree on a vocational rehabilitation program. To encourage rehabilitation, part or all of the disability-income benefits are paid during the training period. At the end of training, if the insured is still totally disabled, the benefits continue as before. But if the individual is fully rehabilitated and is capable of returning to work, the benefits will terminate. The costs of rehabilitation are usually paid by the company.

## Accidental Death, Dismemberment, and Loss-of-Sight Benefits

Some disability-income policies pay accidental death, dismemberment, and loss-of-sight benefits in the event of an accident. The maximum amount paid, known as the principal sum, is based on a schedule. For example, the principal sum is paid for loss of both hands or both feet or sight of both eyes.

## Optional Disability-Income Benefits

Several optional benefits can be added to a disability income policy. They including the following:

1. *Cost-of-living rider* Under this option, the disability benefits are periodically adjusted for increases in the cost of living, usually measured by the Consumer Price Index. Two limitations generally apply to the cost-of-living adjustment. First, the annual increase in benefits may be limited to a certain maximum percentage (such as 5 percent per year); second, there may be a maximum limit on the overall increase in benefits (such as a 100 percent maximum increase in benefits). The rider is expensive and can increase the basic premium by 25 to 40 percent.

2. *Option to purchase additional insurance.* Your income may increase, and you may need additional disability-income benefits. Under this option, the insured has the right to purchase additional disability-income benefits at specified times in the future with no evidence of insurability. The premium is generally based on the insured's age at the time the additional benefits are purchased.

3. *Social Security substitute* Social Security disability benefits are difficult to obtain because of a strict definition of disability and stringent eligibility requirements. The Social Security substitute option pays you an additional amount if you are turned down for Social Security disability benefits.

4. *Return of premium* This rider pays back some of the premiums paid into the policy. For example, after 10 years, you would receive 80 percent of the premiums paid, less any claims. The option is controversial and has little to recommend it. Disability-income insurance is designed to provide income protection and should not be viewed as being similar to cash-value life insurance. The option is also expensive and can increase the already high cost of a policy by 30 to 100 percent.

## Tighter Disability-Income Market

Although disability-income insurance is important, it is becoming more difficult to obtain. Disability-income insurers have experienced an explosion of claims and high underwriting losses in recent years. As a result, the market for disability income insurance has tightened and is more restrictive. The underwriting losses are due to several factors. They include an excessive number of claims by physicians with noncancellable policies that could not be repriced; a substantial increase in claims for alcohol and drug abuse and emotional disorders; liberal

---

### INSIGHT 20.2

## Disability Insurers Are Tightening Up

Stunned by an explosion in the number and cost of claims, disability insurers are redesigning their policies, limiting the amount of benefits they'll pay on individual policies and requiring longer waiting periods before they'll pay anything at all.

A few years ago, agents routinely recommended "own-occupation" coverage that would pay off as long as you were unable to work at your own job—regardless of whether you were capable of holding another one. What's more, your premium was guaranteed never to go up. *Now a growing number of policies limit own-occupation coverage to two years, and premiums could increase over the life of the policy.*

Many of the changes are a result of abuses by workers with a "Lotto mentality," says John Ryan, a Denver insurance broker who specializes in disability coverage. Facing a layoff, for example, a worker with a bad back could claim that he couldn't do his job anymore and cash in on a generous own-occupation policy. Last year, for the second year in a row, disability insurers paid out half a billion dollars more in benefits than they collected in premiums.

On the plus side, premiums for the revamped policies are 15% to 30% lower than the old policies. "Companies are becoming more realistic in the policy design, and at the very least they're more affordable for consumers," says Larry Schneider, a disability insurance specialist in Falls Church, Va.

Individual policies are also starting to incorporate some of the back-to-work benefits that are characteristic of group policies, such as coverage for physical therapy, job training and job-search assistance.

SOURCE: "Insurance: Disability insurers are tightening up," *Kiplinger's Personal Finance Magazine,* 50 (August 1996): 16.

---

policy provisions; inadequate rates; excessive issue limits; payment of lifetime benefits; and liberal claims treatment of physicians and attorneys.

Some insurers have withdrawn from the disability income market, while others have redesigned their policies. The UNUM Corp., a major disability insurer, will no longer sell individual policies with level premiums and lifetime benefits. Disability insurers have also reduced the maximum benefit period available under the own-occupation definition of disability; issue limits have been cut back from a maximum of 80 percent of income to 60 or 65 percent; new policies sold to physicians do not pay lifetime benefits, and monthly payments are capped; elimination periods have been increased; and underwriting standards have tightened (see Insight 20.2).

### INDIVIDUAL MEDICAL EXPENSE CONTRACTUAL PROVISIONS

All states have laws that require certain contractual provisions to appear in individual medical expenses insurance contracts, while other provisions are optional. It is beyond the scope of this text to analyze in detail all contractual provisions. Instead, attention is focused on those provisions that are commonly found in newly issued individual medical expense contracts and are relevant to insurance consumers.

### Renewal Provisions

A renewal provision refers to the length of time that an individual medical expense policy can remain in force. The principal renewal provisions used currently are the following:[11]

- Optionally renewable
- Nonrenewable for stated reasons only
- Guaranteed renewable
- Noncancellable

**Optionally Renewable** This provision gives the insured the least protection with respect to continuation of coverage. Under an **optionally renewable policy,** *the insurer has the right to terminate a policy on any anniversary date, or in some cases, on a premium date.* The policy is renewable only with the consent of the insurer. Instead of nonrenewal, the insurer may specify the conditions that must be met before the policy is renewed. These conditions could include a policy amendment that excludes certain types of losses or injuries to certain parts of the body, or coverage for certain occurrences may be limited.

**Nonrenewable for Stated Reasons Only** This type of renewal provision provides greater protection than a policy renewable solely at the option of the insurer. Under this provision, *the insurer can refuse to renew the policy only for certain stated reasons.* These reasons can include the following: (1) the insured reaches a certain age, (2) the insured ceases to be employed, and (3) the insurer refuses to renew all policies bearing the same form number as the insured's policy.

**Guaranteed Renewable** This type of renewal provision provides considerable protection to the insured. A **guaranteed renewable policy** *is one in which the insurer guarantees to renew the policy to some stated age. However, the insurer has the right to increase premium rates for the underwriting class in which the insured is placed.* The policy cannot be canceled, and renewal of the policy is at the insured's sole discretion.

**Noncancellable** A noncancellable policy provides the greatest protection to the insured. A **noncancellable policy** *is one that cannot be canceled: the insurer guarantees renewal of the policy to some stated age, and the premiums are guaranteed and cannot be increased during that period.* A noncancellable medical expense policy allows the insured to keep the insurance in force by the timely payment of premiums until at least age 50, or if the policy is issued after age 44, for at least five years from the issue date. Provided the insured pays the premiums on time, the insurer cannot cancel, refuse to renew, or increase premium rates stated in the policy, or unilaterally make any changes in the policy provisions.

## Preexisting-Conditions Clause

To control adverse selection, individual health insurance contracts may contain a **preexisting-conditions clause.** A preexisting condition is a physical or mental condition of the insured that existed during a specified period—such as three to six months—prior to the effective date of the policy. Preexisting conditions are not covered until the pol-

icy has been in force for a specified period, generally one or two years. For example, an insured may have been treated for alcoholism six months prior to issuance of the policy. If that condition is not excluded, it is covered only after the policy has been in force for a specific period, such as one year.

## Notice of Ten-Day Right to Examine Policy

If you are not satisfied with the policy, you have 10 days to send it back after receiving it. The entire premium will be refunded, and the policy will be void.

## Claims

A number of important provisions in an individual medical expense policy deal with claims. Under the *notice of claim provision* you are required to give written notice to the insurer within 20 days after a covered loss occurs or as soon as is reasonably possible. Under the *claims forms provison,* the insurer is required to send you a claim form within 15 days after notice is received. Finally, under the *proof of loss provision* you must send written proof of loss to the insurer within 90 days after a covered loss occurs. If it is not reasonably possible to provide proof of loss within 90 days, your claim will not be affected if the proof is sent as soon as possible. However, in any event, you must provide proof of loss within one year unless you are legally incapable of doing so.

## Grace Period

A grace period is a required provision. The **grace period** *is a 31-day period after the premium due date to pay an overdue premium.* If the premium is paid after the due date but within the grace period, coverage is still in force.

## Reinstatement

If the premium is not paid within the grace period, the health insurance policy lapses. The **reinstatement provision** *permits the insured to reinstate a lapsed policy.* If the insured pays the premium to the insurance company or agent, and an application is not required, the policy is reinstated. However, if an application for reinstatement is required, the policy is reinstated only when the insurer approves the application. If the insurer has not previously notified the insured that the application for reinstatement has been denied, the policy is then automatically reinstated on the 45th day following the date of the conditional receipt. The reinstated policy is subject to a ten-day waiting period for sickness, but accidents are covered immediately.

## Time Limit on Certain Defenses

The time limit on certain defenses is a required provision and has the same effect as the incontestable clause in life insurance. The **time limit on certain defenses** *states that after the policy has been in force for three years, the insurer cannot void the policy or deny a claim on the basis of misstatements in the application, except for fraudulent misstatements.* (Some insurers use a two-year period.) After three years, the insurer could deny a claim if it could prove that the insured made a fraudulent misstatement when the policy was first issued.

## SHOPPING FOR HEALTH INSURANCE

High quality health insurance is expensive. You should not waste money buying policies that do not provide meaningful protection. Certain rules should be followed when you are shopping for an individual policy:

- Insure for the catastrophic loss.
- Consider group health insurance first.
- Don't ignore disability income insurance.
- Avoid limited policies.
- Watch out for restrictive policy provisions and exclusions.
- Use deductibles and elimination periods to reduce premiums.
- Deal with a reputable insurer.
- Shop around for health insurance.

### Insure for the Catastrophic Loss

The most important rule to follow is to have protection against a catastrophic loss that can destroy you financially. The cost of a serious illness or injury can be ruinous. Open heart surgery can cost more than $75,000; a heart transplant can cost more than $200,000; and the cost of a crippling automobile accident requiring several major operations, plastic surgery, and rehabilitation can exceed $250,000. Unless you have adequate health insurance or financial assets to meet these expenditures, you will be financially insecure. The inability to pay for cata-

strophic medical bills is a major cause of personal bankruptcy. *Thus, you should purchase a high quality individual major medical policy* (or, alternatively, have coverage under a group major medical plan). To limit out-of-pocket expenses, make certain the major medical policy has a stop-loss limit that requires the insurer to pay 100 percent of all covered expenses in excess of the stop-loss limit.

### Consider Group Health Insurance First

In a personal risk management program, you should first determine whether group health insurance is available. You may be eligible to participate in a group health insurance plan sponsored by your employer, professional association, or some other group.

Group health insurance is preferable to individual insurance for several reasons. First, employers frequently offer a number of group health insurance plans to their employees, ranging from traditional fee-for-service group indemnity plans to managed care plans, such as health maintenance organizations (HMOs) and preferred provider organizations (PPOs). Depending on your financial circumstances and need for protection, you can choose the plan that best meets your needs and ability to pay. HMOs and PPOs are discussed in Chapter 21.

Second, group health coverages typically are broader in coverage than individual protection with fewer exclusions and restrictions.

Third, employers usually pay a large part of the monthly premiums, which makes the plan financially attractive to the employees and their families. Some employers pay the entire cost.

Finally, there are substantial tax advantages to employees under present law. The employer's contributions do not result in taxable income to the employee, and the employee's contributions can often be made with *before-tax dollars*. These tax advantages should not be ignored in a group health insurance plan.

### Don't Ignore Disability Income Insurance

Don't ignore the importance of disability income insurance in your personal risk management program. A substantial amount of earned income is lost each year because of sickness and injury, which is not replaced by disability income and sick leave benefits. Data show clearly that many workers are paying insufficient attention to the risk of disability in their personal insurance programs. For example, in 1992 alone, the income lost from temporary nonoccupational disabilities of six months or less, as well as the income lost during the first six months of a long-term disability, totaled about $74 billion. However, individual and group benefits to workers in private employment, sick leave for government employees, and Social Security benefits for the sixth month of disability totaled only about $35 billion. *Insurance and sick leave benefits replaced only 47 percent of the income lost.*[12] The proportion of income replaced during a long-term disability would be even less. Thus, it is clear that most workers are underinsured with respect to both short-term and long-term disability.

You should consider purchasing an individual guaranteed renewable or noncancellable disability income policy that will pay at least two-thirds of your earnings up to age 65 with an elimination period of 30 to 90 days. Even if you are covered under a group disability income plan, an individual policy should still be considered. As stated earlier, if you lose your job, group disability income benefits generally cannot be converted to an individual policy.

## Avoid Limited Policies

A **limited policy** is one that covers only certain specified diseases or accidents, or pays limited benefits or places serious restrictions on the right to receive them. A **hospital indemnity policy** is one example of a limited policy. It pays a fixed daily, weekly, or monthly benefit during a hospital stay. The amount paid is on an unallocated basis without regard to the actual expenses of hospital confinement. For example, the policy may promise to pay $3000 monthly ($100 daily) for five years if you are hospitalized, no health questions are asked, and the first month's premium is only $1. It sounds like a good deal, but in health insurance, there is no such thing as a "free lunch." The policy is limited. Few persons will ever collect benefits for an extended period. The average hospital stay for persons under age 65 is under six days. If you are confined for only six days, the total benefit paid would be only $600. During that time, you may have incurred several thousands of dollars of medical bills, but only a small amount would be paid by the hospital indemnity policy. Also, the policy covers you only while in the hospital. If you recover at home, no payment is made. Finally, the application contains a preexisting-

conditions clause that excludes coverage for a preexisting condition for one year.

A **dread-disease policy** is another limited contract. It provides high maximum limits for a single disease or for certain specified diseases, such as cancer, encephalitis, or spinal meningitis. A **cancer policy** is an example of a dread-disease policy. If you have a major medical insurance policy, cancer insurance is unnecessary. It is illogical to insure yourself more heavily against only one disease because you do not know how you will become disabled. Consumer groups generally are opposed to limited policies and dread-disease policies (see Insight 20.3).

Finally, **accident-only policies** should be avoided because they are limited in coverage and benefits. A list of these policies is endless and includes accident insurance offered by sponsors of credit cards, travel accident policies that cover you while on vacation, and airline accident policies sold over the counter or from vending machines in airports.

## Watch Out for Restrictive Policy Provisions and Exclusions

If you are shopping for an individual policy, you should be aware of any restrictions on coverage that might apply. Two common restrictions are a **preexisting-conditions clause** and an **exclusionary rider.** An individual policy with a preexisting conditions clause longer than one year should not be purchased. If possible, you should also avoid purchasing an individual policy in which an exclusionary rider appears. If you have been treated for certain diseases, such as cancer or heart disease, the insurer may add a rider to the policy that excludes the condition.

Finally, as a last resort, if you are uninsurable and cannot obtain either individual or group coverage, you may be eligible for coverage from a state high risk pool for the uninsurable. More than half the states have high risk pools. Information on enrolling is available from your state insurance department.

## Use Deductibles and Elimination Periods to Reduce Premiums

High-quality health insurance is expensive. A comprehensive major medical policy that covers the entire family can easily cost more than $4000

## Consumer Groups Have Doubts About Dreaded-Disease Policies

Avnet Inc., an electronic component distributor in Culver City, Calif., has a payroll-deduction program that allows employees to buy homeowners, auto and extra life insurance.

But the option that is most popular with Avnet's 7,500 domestic employees is cancer insurance. About one-fifth pay anywhere from $16 to $27 a month for the coverage.

Once the province of agents hawking door to door, cancer insurance and other "limited-benefit" medical policies are a hot new offering in employee-pay-all benefit programs at many small and midsize companies. Such insurance, usually offered as a supplement to an employer's comprehensive health plan, includes policies for cancer, heart disease and hospital stays.

Insurers say these limited-benefit policies offer important protection at a cheap price. *But, while hospital-stay policies can be helpful in certain situations, cancer insurance and other "dreaded-disease" policies generally are a bad deal, consumer advocates say.*

"When you insure your auto, you insure the whole thing, not just the right front fender," says James H. Hunt, a consultant for the Consumer Federation of America.

About 10.6 million people had cancer or other specific-disease policies in 1994, while about 3.5 million had a supplemental hospital policy, according to the most recent data from the Health Insurance Association of America.

Insurers acknowledge that supplemental policies, which largely faded when comprehensive coverage came on the scene, are no substitute for a major medical plan. Still, as employers raise deductibles and coinsurance on comprehensive plans, such policies can be a valuable safety net for employees who could be on the hook for several thousand dollars a year or more if illness strikes, insurers say.

"To sustain their family's routine in the face of illness, people may need more than major medical," says Kathelen Spencer, a senior vice president for **Aflac** Inc.'s American Family Life Assurance Co., of Columbus, Ga.

Aflac, which offers four cancer policies, sends a payment of $1,500 to $5,000 once a person is diagnosed with any cancer except skin cancer. The insurance then offers limited payment—usually in the form of cash paid to the policyholder—for such expenses as hospitalization, radiation and chemotherapy, surgery, and physician fees. It also has an allowance for treatment-related transportation and lodging. Aflac also sells plans that pay a daily benefit for time spent in the hospital or intensive-care unit.

Companies that offer similar insurance include Colonial Life & Accident Insurance Co., a subsidiary of **UNUM** Corp., and **Mutual of Omaha** Cos. Such policies usually pay benefits regardless of any comprehensive coverage.

*Consumer advocates say cancer and other dreaded-disease policies are like insuring your house against an earthquake, but not buying coverage for fires, floods and other catastrophes.*

"What happens if you get hit by a truck?" says Bob Hunter, director of insurance for the Consumer Federation of America.

If you're worried that the deductible on your comprehensive health coverage is too high, you may want to pay more for richer coverage or just stash some money away to cover the gap. Dreaded-disease policies may look cheap, but high distribution costs tend to eat up a large chunk of your premium dollars while offering relatively meager benefits in return, says Lawrence Singer, a senior vice president at Segal Co., a benefits-consulting firm in New York.

Insurers sometimes argue that limited-benefit policies offer some freedom to members of managed-care plans, who may want to go outside their plan's approved network of doctors. But, such policies would likely cover only a fraction of the cost of outside treatment and many managed-care plans already offer some coverage for out-of-network care.

Besides, "if you wouldn't want to use your health plan when you get really sick, you probably shouldn't be in it," Mr. Hunter says.

Cancer insurance has a history of abusive sales tactics, consumer advocates say. In the 1970s and 1980s, seniors often were sold multiple policies with redundant benefits. A few states, including New York, New Jersey and Connecticut, ban sales of specific-disease policies altogether.

SOURCE: Adapted from Nancy Ann Jeffrey, "Consumer Groups Have Doubts About Dreaded-Disease Policies," *The Wall Street Journal,* February 21, 1996, pp. C1, C15.

EXHIBIT 20.5

## Have You Chosen The Best Health Plan? Use This Checklist to Compare

|  | Plan A | Plan B | Plan C |
|---|---|---|---|
| **What it costs:** | | | |
| Premium (your cost)................................................................ | _____ | _____ | _____ |
| Deductible (what you pay before your health plan pays)..................... | _____ | _____ | _____ |
| Doctor Visit (% you pay)............................................................ | _____ | _____ | _____ |
| Pharmacy (per prescription)....................................................... | _____ | _____ | _____ |
| Vision.................................................................................. | _____ | _____ | _____ |
| Emergency (% you pay).............................................................. | _____ | _____ | _____ |
| Out-of Area (% you pay or if covered at all)..................................... | _____ | _____ | |
| **What it covers:** | | | |
| Doctor Visits......................................................................... | _____ | _____ | _____ |
| Outpatient Tests & Procedures.................................................... | _____ | _____ | _____ |
| Preventive Care (help control blood pressure, cholesterol, etc.).................................................................... | _____ | _____ | _____ |
| Women's Preventive Care (Pap smear, mammography)...................... | _____ | _____ | _____ |
| Maternity............................................................................. | _____ | _____ | _____ |
| Well Baby Care....................................................................... | _____ | _____ | _____ |
| Physicals (annual).................................................................. | _____ | _____ | _____ |
| Hospitalization...................................................................... | _____ | _____ | _____ |
| Emergency or Urgent Care......................................................... | _____ | _____ | _____ |
| Mental Health........................................................................ | _____ | _____ | _____ |
| **Is It convenient?** | | | |
| Do I have to file claim forms?..................................................... | _____ | _____ | _____ |
| Is there toll-free access to a customer service representative?.............. | _____ | _____ | _____ |
| Does the plan limit access to specialists?...................................... | _____ | _____ | _____ |
| Can I use a specialist as a primary care physician (i.e. OB/GYN)?..................................................................... | _____ | _____ | _____ |

SOURCE: *Sunday World Herald,* October 13, 1996, p. 21-A.

annually. Premiums can be reduced by purchasing the policy with a substantial deductible. If you can afford it, an annual deductible of $500 or $1000 will substantially reduce your premiums. Likewise, premiums for a disability income policy can be substantially reduced by buying the policy with a 90-day elimination period.

## Deal with a Reputable Insurer

You should deal with a reputable insurer that will pay your claims and not fight them. The payoff under a health insurance policy occurs when a claim is paid. A reputable insurer will have a fair and courteous claims policy. Unfortunately, some insurers do not fit this category.

It is difficult for the average insured to know the claims practices of health insurers. One suggestion is to contact the complaint division of your state insurance department and inquire about the company. If a large number of complaints are filed against a particular company, you may want to find another company. Another suggestion is to ask a friend or acquaintance who may be a policyowner in the company how fairly he or she has been treated. In any event, a company with a legalistic, narrow, or restrictive claims policy should be avoided.

In addition, you should deal only with a financially strong insurer. A liberal claims policy is of little value if the insurer is broke when you file a claim. You should insure with insurers that receive a high financial rating from at least two rating services.

## Shop Around for Health Insurance

You should contact more than one insurer before a policy is purchased. Although price is important, it is not the only consideration. A low-premium policy may contain restrictive provisions or pay limited benefits, or may reflect a restrictive claims policy. Exhibit 20.5 contains a convenient worksheet that will enable you to compare the various policies.

## SUMMARY

- Individual health insurance policies can generally be classified into the following categories:

  Hospital-surgical insurance

  Major medical insurance

  Long-term care insurance

  Disability-income insurance

- Individual hospital-surgical policies typically cover hospital expenses, surgical expenses, outpatient diagnostic X-rays and lab expenses, and physician's in-hospital expenses. Some policies also cover the partial cost of a pregnancy, or maternity benefits can be added as an optional benefit.

- Major medical insurance is designed to cover the expenses of a catastrophic illness or injury. A typical major medical plan has certain characteristics:

  Broad coverage

  High maximum limits

  Benefit period

  Deductible

  Coinsurance

  Exclusions

- Long-term care insurance pays a daily or monthly benefit for medical or custodial care in a nursing facility or at home.

- Disability-income policies provide for the periodic payment of income to an individual who is totally disabled. The benefits are paid after an elimination period is satisfied. The insured generally has a choice of benefit periods. In addition, after 90 days, all premiums are waived if the insured is totally disabled.

- The definition of disability is stated in a disability-income policy. For the first two years, total disability is typically defined as the inability to perform all duties of the insured's own occupation. After that time, total disability is defined as the inability to perform the duties of any occupation for which the insured is reasonably fitted by education, training, and experience.

- A renewal provision refers to the length of time that an individual medical expense policy can remain in force. The principal types of renewal provisions used currently are as follows:

  Optionally renewable

  Nonrenewable for stated reasons only

  Guaranteed renewable

  Noncancellable

- Health insurance policies contain certain contractual provisions. Some provisions are required by state law, while others are optional.

- Consumer experts recommend certain rules to follow when health insurance is purchased:

  Insure for the catastrophic loss.

  Consider group insurance first.

  Don't ignore disability income insurance.

  Avoid limited policies.

  Watch out for restrictive policy provisions and exclusions.

  Use deductibles and elimination periods to reduce premiums.

  Deal with a reputable insurer.

  Shop around for health insurance.

## KEY CONCEPTS AND TERMS

| | |
|---|---|
| Accident only policy | Internal limits |
| Activities of daily living (ADLs) | Limited policy |
| | Long-term-care insurance |
| Benefit period | Major medical insurance |
| Calendar-year deductible | Noncancellable |
| Cancer policy | Nonrenewable for stated |
| Coinsurance | reasons only |
| Common-accident provision | Optionally renewable |
| Disability-income insurance | Partial disability |
| Dread-disease policy | Physician's in-hospital |
| Each-illness deductible | benefit |
| Elimination period | Preexisting-conditions |
| Exclusionary rider | clause |
| Gatekeeper provisions | Reasonable and |
| Guaranteed renewable | customary charges |
| Hospital indemnity policy | Reinstatement provision |
| Hospital-surgical insurance | Relative-value schedule |
| Indemnity plan | Residual disability |

Service benefits
Stop-loss limit
Surgical schedule
Time limit on certain
   defenses provision
Total disability

Usual, reasonable, and
   customary charges
Waiver of premium

## QUESTIONS FOR REVIEW

1. Describe the benefits that are typically included in a hospital-surgical insurance policy.

2. Explain the basic characteristics of a major medical policy. Why are deductibles and coinsurance used in a major medical policy?

3. Describe the various types of deductibles that may be found in major medical policies.

4. Briefly describe the characteristics of long-term care insurance.

5. Explain the major features of a disability-income policy.

6. Explain the various definitions of total disability that are found in individual disability-income contracts.

7. Explain the meaning of partial disability and residual disability in a disability-income policy.

8. Explain the options that can be added to a disability-income policy.

9. Identify the basic types of renewal provisions in individual health insurance policies.

10. Briefly describe the following clauses:
    a. Preexisting conditions
    b. Time limit on certain defenses

## QUESTIONS FOR DISCUSSION

1. Explain the major differences between a typical individual hospital-surgical insurance policy and an individual major medical policy with respect to each of the following:
    a. Use of a surgical schedule
    b. Use of deductibles
    c. Benefit limits

2. George and Lu Sercl and their two daughters, Noreen and Karen, are insured under an individual major medical policy. The policy contains a $300 deductible that applies to each covered person, a common accident provision, and an 80 percent coinsurance provision.

a. Lu had gallbladder surgery and incurred covered medical expenses of $9300. How much of the loss will be paid by the insurance company? Show your calculations.

b. George, Noreen, and Karen were injured in the same bobsledding accident. Covered medical expenses were $600 for George, $450 for Noreen, and $375 for Karen. How much of the total loss will be paid by the insurance company? Show your calculations.

3. Mark is insured under an individual major medical insurance policy. The plan has a calendar-year deductible of $300, 80-20 percent coinsurance, and a stop limit of $2000. Mark recently had an appendectomy operation and incurred the following medical expenses:

| | |
|---|---:|
| Outpatient diagnostic tests | $   700 |
| Hospital expenses | 18,000 |
| Surgeon's fee | 1,500 |
| Prescription drugs outside of the hospital | 100 |

In addition, Mark could not work for four weeks and lost $2000 in earnings.

a. Based on the above information, how much of the loss will be paid by the insurance company? Show your calculations.

b. If Mark's policy did not have a stop-loss limit, how much would the insurance company pay? Show your calculations.

4. If you are shopping for an individual health insurance policy, what important factors should you consider? Explain your answer.

## SELECTED REFERENCES

Black, Kenneth, Jr., and Harold D. Skipper, Jr. *Life Insurance,* 12th ed. Englewood Cliffs, N.J.: Prentice-Hall, 1994, chapters 16–17.

Consumers Union. "Health Care in Crisis, The Search for Solutions: Does Canada Have the Answer?" *Consumer Reports,* 57, no. 9 (September 1992): 579–92.

———. "Health Care in Crisis: Are HMOs the Answer?" *Consumer Reports,* 57, no. 8 (August 1992): 519–31.

———. "Wasted Health Care Dollars." *Consumer Reports,* 57, no. 7 (July 1992): 435–48.

Health Insurance Association of America. *Fundamentals of Health Insurance, Part A.* Washington, D.C.: Health Insurance Association of America, 1997.

Rejda, George E., Constance M. Luthardt, Cheryl L. Ferguson, and Donald P. Oakes. *Personal Insurance.* 3rd ed. Malvern, Pa.: Insurance Institute of America, 1997.

Rejda, George E. "Problem of Poor Health," in *Social Insurance and Economic Security,* 5th ed. Englewood Cliffs, N.J.: Prentice-Hall, 1994, pp. 187–223.

Sadler, Jeff. *Disability Income: The Sale, the Product, the Market,* 2nd ed. Cincinnati: National Underwriter Company, 1995.

Soule, Charles E. "Individual Disability Income Insurance: A New Look at the Next Millennium." *Journal of the American Society of CLU & ChFC,* 50 (September 1996): 60–69.

## NOTES

1. This section is based on George E. Rejda, *Social Insurance and Economic Security,* 5th ed. (Englewood Cliffs, N.J.: Prentice-Hall, 1994), pp. 191–205.

2. Catherine R. Levit, et al, "National Health Expenditures, 1995," *Health Care Financing Review,* 18 (Fall 1996), pp. 175–77; and Salley T. Burner and Daniel R. Waldo, *Health Care Financing Review,* 16 (Summer 1995), p. 221.

3. Employee Benefit Research Institute, *Sources of Health Insurance and Characteristics of the Uninsured, Analysis of the March 1996 Current Population Survey,* EBRI Issue Brief Number 179 (November 1996), p. 1.

4. Rejda, *Social Insurance and Economic Security,* 5th ed., p. 204.

5. U.S. Department of Health and Human Services, Health Care Financing Administration, *Guide to Choosing a Nursing Home,* Pub. No. HCFA-02174, p. 2.

6. This section is based on *A Shopper's Guide to Long-Term Care Insurance* (Kansas City, Mo.: National Association of Insurance Commissioners, 1993).

7. Ibid, p. 14.

8. Kenneth Black, Jr., and Harold D. Skipper, Jr., *Life Insurance,* 12th ed. (Englewood Cliffs, N.J.: Prentice-Hall, 1994), pp. 503–4.

9. Jeff Saddler, *Disability Income: The Sale, The Product, The Market,* 2nd ed. (Cincinnati, Ohio: The National Underwriter Company, 1995), p. 157.

10. Edward E. Graves, ed., *McGill's Life Insurance* (Bryn, Mawr, PA.: The American College, 1994), p. 143.

11. *Fundamentals of Health Insurance, Part A* (Washington, D.C.: Health Insurance Association of America, 1997), pp. 111–112.

12. U.S. Bureau of the Census, *Statistical Abstract of the United States: 1995* (115th edition.) Washington, DC, 1995, Table 608, p. 386.

## CASE APPLICATION

Lorri, age 28, is a registered nurse who earns $3000 monthly in a hospital. She is seriously injured in an automobile accident in which she is at fault and is expected to be off work for at least one year. She has a guaranteed renewable disability-income policy that pays $1800 monthly up to age 65 for accidents and sickness after a 90-day elimination period. A residual disability benefit is included in the policy. Lorri's policy contains the following provisions:

Total disability means: (a) your inability during the first 24 months to perform substantially all of the important duties of your occupation; and you are not working at any gainful occupation; (b) After the first 24 months that benefits are payable, it means your inability to engage in any gainful occupation.

Gainful occupation means: Any occupation or employment for wage or profit which is reasonably consistent with your education, training, and experience.

a. If Lorri is off work for one year because of the accident, indicate the extent, if any, of the insurer's obligation to pay disability benefits.

b. Assume that Lorri is disabled for one year, recovers, and returns to work part time. If she earns $1500 monthly, indicate the extent, if any, of the insurer's obligation to pay her disability benefits.

c. Assume that after two years, Lorri is unable to return to work as a full-time hospital nurse. A drug manufacturer offers her a job as a lab technician, which she accepts. Indicate the extent, if any, of the insurer's obligation to pay her disability benefits.

d. Following the accident, could Lorri's insurer cancel her policy or increase her premiums? Explain your answer.

# Chapter 21

# EMPLOYEE BENEFITS: GROUP LIFE AND HEALTH INSURANCE

*"There's safety and savings in numbers. Try to get group coverage."*

*Herbert S. Denenberg,*
The Shopper's Guidebook

## Student Learning Objectives

After studying this chapter, you should be able to:

■ Explain the important underwriting principles followed in group insurance.

■ Describe the basic characteristics of group term life insurance.

■ Identify the major providers of group health insurance coverages.

■ Explain the major characteristics of the following group health insurance coverages:

> basic medical expense insurance
>
> major medical insurance
>
> dental insurance
>
> short-term disability income
>
> long-term disability income

■ Explain the meaning of the term "managed care" in a group health insurance plan.

■ Describe the important characteristics of the following types of managed care plans:

> health maintenance organizations (HMOs)
>
> preferred provider organizations (PPOs)

■ Show how cafeteria plans can benefit employees.

In a personal risk management program, you should consider the availability of employee benefits. Employee benefit plans are employer-sponsored plans that pay benefits if a worker dies, becomes sick or disabled, retires, or is unemployed. Most large employers have a wide variety of employee benefit plans that provide considerable financial security to employees and their dependents.

Employee benefits are very important in total employee compensation. Although a starting salary may be relatively low, exceptional employee benefits can substantially increase the total compensation package. For example, one employer pays an annual salary of $18,500 for an entry-level position, which is a relatively modest salary. When employer contributions for health and dental insurance, life insurance, and other benefits are added, total annual compensation is increased to approximately $23,000, an increase of 24 percent.

This is the first of two chapters dealing with employee benefit plans. This chapter is limited largely to group life and health insurance plans, since most employers make these plans available to employees. Private pensions and other retirement plans are discussed in Chapter 22. The topics discussed in this chapter include group life insurance, group medical expense insurance, group dental insurance, group disability income insurance, and the important provisions of the new Health Insurance Portability and Accountability Act of 1996. The chapter concludes with a discussion of cafeteria plans.

## GROUP INSURANCE

Group insurance differs from individual insurance in several respects. A distinctive characteristic of group insurance is the coverage of many persons under one contract. A **master contract** is formed between the insurer and group policyowner for the benefit of the individual members. In most plans, the group policyowner is the employer. Employees receive a certificate of insurance that shows they are insured.

A second characteristic is that group insurance may be relatively lower in cost than comparable insurance purchased individually. Employers usually pay part or all of the cost, which reduces or eliminates premium payments by the employees. In addition, administrative and marketing expenses are reduced as a result of mass distribution methods.

Another characteristic is that individual evidence of insurability is usually not required. Group selection of risks is used, not individual selection. The insurance company is concerned with the insurability of the group as a whole rather than with the insurability of any single member within the group.

Finally, **experience rating** is used in group insurance plans. If the group is sufficiently large, the actual loss experience is a major factor in determining the premiums that are charged.

### Basic Underwriting Principles

Since individual evidence of insurability is usually not required, group insurers must observe certain underwriting principles so that the loss experience of the group is favorable. These principles are as follows:[1]

- Insurance incidental to the group
- Flow of persons through the group
- Automatic determination of benefits
- Minimum participation requirements
- Third-party sharing of cost
- Simple and efficient administration

**Insurance Incidental to the Group** Insurance must be incidental to the group; that is, the group should not be formed for the sole purpose of obtaining insurance. This requirement is necessary to reduce adverse selection against the insurer. If the group is formed for the specific purpose of obtaining insurance, a disproportionate number of unhealthy persons would join the group to obtain low-cost insurance, and the loss experience would be unfavorable.

**Flow of Persons Through the Group** Ideally, there should be a flow of younger persons into the group and a flow of older persons out of the group. Without a flow of younger persons into the group, the average age of the group will increase, and premium rates will likewise increase. The higher premiums may cause some younger and healthier members to drop out of the plan, while the older and unhealthy members will still remain, which would lead to still higher rates. However, turnover of employees should not be so significant that administrative costs are high.

**Automatic Determination of Benefits**    The benefits should be automatically determined by some formula that precludes the individual selection of insurance amounts by either the employer or the employees. The amount of insurance can be based on earnings, position, length of service, or some combination of these factors. The purpose of this requirement is to reduce adverse selection against the insurer. If individual members were permitted to select the amount of insurance, unhealthy persons would select larger amounts, while healthier persons would be likely to select smaller amounts. The result would be a disproportionate amount of insurance on the impaired lives. However, many group insurance plans allow employees to select their own benefit levels up to certain maximum limits. If additional amounts of insurance are desired above the maximum allowed, evidence of insurability is usually required.

**Minimum Participation Requirements**    A minimum percentage of the eligible employees must participate in the plan. If the plan is a **noncontributory plan,** the premiums are paid entirely by the employer, and 100 percent of the eligible employees must be covered. If the plan is **contributory,** the employee pays part of the cost and a large proportion of the eligible employees must elect to participate in the plan. In a contributory plan, it may be difficult to get 100 percent participation, so a lower percentage such as 50 to 75 percent is typically required.

There are two reasons for the minimum participation requirement. First, if a large proportion of eligible employees participate, adverse selection is reduced, since the possibility of insuring a large proportion of unhealthy lives is reduced. Second, if a high proportion of eligible members participate, the expense rate per insured member or per unit of insurance can be reduced.

**Third-Party Sharing of Cost**    Ideally, individual members should not pay the entire cost of their protection. In most groups, the employer pays part of the cost. A third-party sharing of cost avoids the problem of a substantial increase in premiums for older members. In a plan in which the members pay the entire cost, younger persons help pay for the insurance provided to older persons. Once they become aware of this, some younger persons may drop out of the plan and obtain their insurance more cheaply elsewhere. Older unhealthy members will still remain, causing premiums to increase even more. However, if the employer absorbs any increase in premiums because of adverse mortality experience, premiums paid by the employees can be kept fairly stable. In addition, a third-party sharing of cost makes the plan more attractive to individual members and encourages greater participation in the plan.

**Simple and Efficient Administration**    The group plan should be simple and should be efficiently administered. Premiums are collected from the employees by payroll deduction and remitted to the insurer. Payroll deduction reduces the insurer's administrative expenses and tends to keep participation in the plan high.

## Eligibility Requirements in Group Insurance

Insurers typically require that certain eligibility requirements must be satisfied before the insurance is in force. The eligibility requirements generally are designed to reduce adverse selection against the insurer.

**Eligible Groups**    Types of groups eligible for group insurance are determined by insurance company policy and state law. Eligible groups include individual employer groups, multiple-employer groups, labor unions, creditor-debtor groups, and miscellaneous groups, such as fraternities and sororities.

Group insurers usually require the group to be a certain size before the group is insured. Traditionally, this was ten lives, but some insurers now insure groups with as few as two or three members. There are two reasons for a minimum-size requirement. First, the insurer has some protection against insuring a group that consists largely of substandard individuals, so that the financial impact of one impaired life on the loss experience of the group is reduced. Second, certain fixed expenses must be met regardless of the size of the group. The larger the group, the broader is the base over which these expenses can be spread, and the lower is the expense rate per unit of insurance.

**Eligibility Requirements**   Before employees can participate in a group insurance plan, they must meet certain eligibility requirements, including the following:

- Be full-time employees
- Satisfy a probationary period
- Apply for insurance during the eligibility period
- Be actively at work

Employers generally require the workers to be employed full time before they can participate in the plan. A **full-time worker** is one who works the required number of hours established by the employer as a normal work week, which must be at least 30 hours. However, some group plans permit part-time workers to be covered. In some group insurance plans, new employees may have to satisfy a **probationary period,** which is a period of one to six months, before he or she can participate in the plan. The purpose of the probationary period is to eliminate transient workers who will be with the firm for only a short period. It is administratively expensive to maintain records and insure workers who will not be working permanently for the firm.

After the probationary period (if any) expires, the employee is eligible to participate in the plan. However, if the plan is contributory, the employee must request coverage either before or during the eligibility period. The **eligibility period** is a period of time—typically 31 days—during which the employee can sign up for the insurance without furnishing evidence of insurability.

Finally, the employee must be **actively at work** on the day the insurance becomes effective. The employee who is actively at work is presumably meeting certain minimum health standards, which also gives the insurer some protection against adverse selection.

## GROUP LIFE INSURANCE PLANS

Group life insurance is a popular and relatively inexpensive employee benefit. In 1995, about $4.8 trillion of group life insurance was in force, which accounted for 38 percent of the total life insurance in force in the United States.[2]

The major types of group life insurance plans currently used are the following:

- Group term life insurance
- Group accidental death and dismemberment insurance (AD&D)
- Group universal life insurance

### Group Term Life Insurance

**Group term life insurance** is the most important form of group life insurance in existence today. More than 99 percent of the group life insurance in force is group term life insurance. The insurance provided is **yearly renewable term insurance,** which provides low-cost protection to the employees during their working careers.

The amount of term insurance on the employee's life is typically one to five times the annual salary or earnings. The term insurance remains in force as long as the employee is part of the group. If the employee quits or is laid off, he or she has the right to convert the group term insurance to an individual cash value policy within 31 days without evidence of insurability. However, the group term insurance normally cannot be converted into an individual term insurance policy.[3] As a practical matter, relatively few employees convert their group insurance because of the problem of cost and because group insurance will probably be provided by another employer. Those employees who do convert are usually substandard in health or uninsurable, which results in strong adverse selection against the insurer.

Most group plans allow a modest amount of life insurance to be written on the employee's spouse and dependent children. Because of state law and tax considerations, the amount of dependent life insurance is relatively low. The insurance on the spouse's life can be converted to an individual cash value policy. Some states also require that the conversion option should apply to the insurance on the children.

Most employers provide a reduced amount of term insurance on retired employees. The amount of insurance may be a flat amount, such as $10,000, or it may be a percentage of the amount of insurance at the date of retirement, such as 50 percent.

Group term insurance has the major advantage of providing low-cost protection to employees that can be used to supplement individual life insurance policies. However, it has two major disadvantages. First, the insurance is temporary and terminates when the individual is no longer part of the group. Second, it is expensive for an older worker to convert to an individual policy after retirement.

Finally, group term life insurance is used by commercial banks and other lending institutions to insure the lives of debtors. Credit life insurance provides for the cancellation of any outstanding debt if the borrower dies. The lending institution is both the policyowner and beneficiary. The unpaid balance of the loan is paid to the creditor at the debtor's death. Many financial planners do not recommend the purchase of credit life insurance because of excessive rates. Although the rates are regulated by the states, some debtors are overcharged for their protection, since term insurance can often be purchased more cheaply on an individual basis.

## Group Accidental Death and Dismemberment Insurance

Many group life insurance plans also provide **group accidental death and dismemberment (AD&D) insurance** that pays additional benefits if the employee dies in an accident or incurs certain types of bodily injury. The AD&D benefit is some multiple of the group life insurance benefit, such as one or two times the insurance on the employee's life. The full AD&D benefit is called the **principal sum,** which is paid if the employee dies in an accident. In addition, a percentage of the principal sum is paid for certain types of dismemberments, such as one-half the principal sum for the loss of a hand, foot, or eye because of accidental bodily injury.

Many plans also make available **voluntary accidental death and dismemberment insurance** in which employees can voluntarily purchase additional amounts of AD&D insurance. The employees normally pay the entire cost of the voluntary coverage.

## Group Universal Life Insurance

In addition to group term insurance, some employers make available **group universal life insurance** for their employees. These plans are similar to individual universal life insurance policies, but there are some important differences. The major characteristics

of group universal life plans are summarized as follows:[4]

1. *Plan design.* Two approaches are used in the plan design. Under the first approach, there is only one plan. The employee who wants only term insurance pays only the mortality and expense charges. The employee who wants to accumulate cash values must pay higher premiums. Under the second approach, two plans are used—term insurance and universal life insurance. The employee who wants only term insurance pays into the term insurance plan. The employee who wants universal life insurance must pay higher premiums so that cash values are accumulated. The employee may be required to pay initial premiums equal to two or three times the cost of the pure insurance protection.

2. *Amount of insurance.* Universal life insurance is issued on a guaranteed basis up to certain limits with no evidence of insurability. Employees generally select the amount of guaranteed coverage equal to some multiple of their salaries, such as one to five times annual salary. Higher amounts of insurance require evidence of insurability, usually based on a simplified medical questionnaire.

3. *Mortality and expense charges.* Most group universal life plans have guaranteed mortality charges for three years; after that time, the group is experience-rated. Expense charges must also be paid. These charges are generally lower than the expenses assessed against individual policies. Finally, there is a minimum interest rate guarantee on the cash values, such as 4 or 4 1/2 percent; higher current rates are paid that change over time, such as 5 1/2 or 6 percent.

4. *Premium flexibility.* Premiums can be reduced, increased, or even eliminated if the cash value is sufficient to pay current mortality and expense charges.

5. *Loans and withdrawals.* Employees can make policy loans and withdrawals. The loan or withdrawal amount must be at least equal to a certain minimum amount, such as $250 or $500. The policy loan rate usually is based on some index, such as Moody's composite bond yield. Interest

credited to the cash values on the amounts borrowed is also reduced, such as 2 percent less than Moody's composite bond yield.

6. *Options at retirement.* The retired employee has the option of continuing the universal life coverage, and the insurer bills the retired employee directly. The employee also has the option of terminating the coverage and withdrawing the cash value; electing a settlement option for liquidation of the cash value in the form of annuity income; or decreasing the amount of pure insurance so that the cash value is sufficient to keep the policy in force with no additional premiums required.

7. *Dependent coverage.* A term insurance rider can be added to cover dependents, such as $10,000 to $50,000 on the spouse and $5000 to $10,000 on each child.

## GROUP MEDICAL EXPENSE INSURANCE

**Group medical expense insurance** is an employee benefit that pays the cost of hospital care, physicians' and surgeons' fees, and related medical expenses. These plans are extremely important in providing financial security to employees and their families. Group plans currently account for more than 90 percent of the total premiums paid for medical expense insurance.

Group medical expense insurance is available from a number of sources. Major sources include the following:

- Commercial insurers
- Blue Cross and Blue Shield plans
- Health maintenance organizations (HMOs)
- Self-insured plans by employers

### Commercial Insurers

Commercial life and health insurers sell both individual and group medical expense plans. Some property and casualty insurers also sell medical expense coverages. Most individuals and families insured by commercial insurers are covered under group plans. The business is highly concentrated. Fewer than 100 insurers write most of the business; about 30 insurers write over half of the business.[5]

Commercial insurers also sponsor managed care plans that provide benefits to members in a cost effective manner, including health maintenance organizations (HMOs) and preferred provider organizations (PPOs). Managed care plans are discussed in greater detail later in the chapter.

### Blue Cross and Blue Shield Plans

**Blue Cross and Blue Shield plans** are medical expense plans that cover hospital expenses, physician and surgeon fees, ancillary charges, and other medical expenses. Major medical insurance is also available. The various plans sell individual, family, and group coverages. Most insureds are covered by group plans.

**Blue Cross plans** cover hospital expenses and other related expenses. The plans typically provide **service benefits** rather than cash benefits to the insured. Blue Cross plans typically pay the full cost of a semiprivate room, and payment is made directly to the hospital rather than to the insured.

**Blue Shield plans** cover physicians' and surgeons' fees and related medical expenses. Most plans today write both Blue Cross and Blue Shield coverages. In early 1997, 49 joint plans were in existence that wrote both Blue Cross and Blue Shield coverages. Six separate Blue Cross plans and four separate Blue Shield plans were also in existence. The joint plans offer both basic medical expense benefits and major medical insurance. Finally, like commercial insurers, Blue Cross and Blue Shield plans also sponsor managed care plans, including HMOs and PPOs.

In the majority of states, Blue Cross and Blue Shield plans are nonprofit organizations that receive favorable tax treatment and are regulated under special legislation. However, in order to raise capital and become more competitive, a few Blue Cross and Blue Shield plans have recently converted to a for-profit status with stockholders and a board of directors. In addition, many nonprofit plans own profit-seeking affiliates. Blue Cross and Blue Shield plans are discussed in greater detail in Chapter 24.

### Health Maintenance Organizations (HMOs)

**Health maintenance organizations (HMOs)** are managed care plans that provide broad, comprehensive health-care services to the members for a fixed prepaid fee. There is heavy emphasis on controlling cost, and the care provided by physicians is carefully monitored. HMOs are discussed in greater detail later in the chapter.

## Self-insured Plans by Employers

Many employers self-insure part or all of the health insurance benefits provided to their employees. **Self-insurance (also called self-funding)** *means that the employer pays part or all of the cost of providing health insurance to the employees.*

Self-insured plans are usually established with stop-loss insurance and an administrative services only (ASO) contract. **Stop-loss insurance** *means that a commercial insurer will pay claims that exceed a certain dollar amount up to some maximum limit.* The insurer pays the amount of claims in excess of the stop limit up to some specified maximum limit. An **ASO contract** *is a contract between an employer and commercial insurer (or other third party) in which the insurer provides only administrative services.* These services can include plan design, claims processing, actuarial support, and record keeping.

Employers self-insure their medical expense plans for several reasons, including the following:

- Under the Employee Retirement Income Security Act of 1974 (ERISA), self-insured plans generally are not subject to state regulation. Thus, a national employer does not have to comply with 51 separate state laws.
- Costs may be reduced or increase less rapidly because of savings in state premium taxes, commissions, and the insurer's profit.
- The employer retains part or all of the funds needed to pay claims and earns interest until the claims are paid.
- Self-insured plans are exempt from state laws that require insured plans to offer certain state-mandated benefits.

Although self-insured plans are widespread, a recent study by KPMG Peat Marwick for the Henry J. Kaiser Family Foundation suggests that self-insured plans subject to ERISA may be declining in relative importance. Overall, from 1993 to 1995, the study showed that the percentage of workers with health insurance that were covered by a fully self-insured or partly self-insured health plan (regardless of the type of plan) declined from 60 percent to 51 percent.[6] The decline was attributed to the growth of managed care plans (discussed later) that attempt to control health-care costs for employers in a cost-effective manner.

## TYPES OF GROUP MEDICAL EXPENSE PLANS

Group medical expense plans have changed rapidly over time. Older plans were often called **traditional group indemnity plans** or fee-for-service plans. These plans permitted insureds considerable freedom in selecting their own physicians and other health-care providers; the plans paid cash indemnity benefits for covered services up to certain maximum limits, and cost containment was not heavily stressed. It should be noted, however, that newer group indemnity plans have several cost containment provisions, such as preadmission certification by which a covered person is approved for admission into a hospital and second surgical opinions.

Two types of traditional group indemnity plans that merit some discussion are (1) basic medical expense insurance and (2) major medical insurance.

### Basic Medical Expense Insurance

**Basic medical expense insurance** *is a generic name for group plans that provide only basic benefits.* The benefits are sufficient to pay routine medical expenses but generally are not designed to cover a catastrophic loss. Group basic medical expense plans typically provide the following benefits:

- Hospital expense insurance
- Surgical expense insurance
- Physicians' visits
- Miscellaneous benefits

**Hospital expense insurance** covers medical expenses incurred while in a hospital. Some older indemnity plans pay actual room and board charges up to some stated maximum, such as $500 per day. New plans typically pay **service benefits** in which the full cost of a semiprivate room is paid if the employee is hospitalized. In addition to daily room and board benefits, most new plans provide full payment (generally up to some maximum dollar amount) for miscellaneous hospital charges, such as drugs, X rays, and operating room charges.

**Surgical expense insurance** is usually included in a basic plan to help pay surgeons' and physicians' fees for surgical operations. Several methods are used to compensate physicians. Older plans may use a **schedule approach** in which the various surgical operations are listed in a schedule, and a maximum dollar amount is specified for each procedure. A variation of the schedule approach is a **relative-value schedule** in which units or points are assigned to each operation based on the degree of difficulty. A conversion factor is then used to convert the relative value of the operation into a specific dollar amount paid to the physician.

Newer plans typically reimburse physicians on the basis of their **usual, reasonable, and customary charges.** A physician is paid his or her usual fee as long as it is considered reasonable and customary. Many insurers consider a fee to be reasonable and customary if it does not exceed the 85th or 90th percentile amount for a similar medical procedure performed by other physicians in the same area. However, insurers differ in how usual and customary fees are calculated. As a result, patients often must pay substantial amounts out-of-pocket because of "balance billing" by physicians for the remainder of the fee not paid by insurance (see Insight 21.1).

Group basic medical expense plans also provide benefits for **physicians' visits** other than for surgery. Most plans cover physicians' visits only while the employee is hospitalized, but some plans cover office or home visits as well. The amount paid can be a fixed amount, or it can be based on the physician's reasonable and customary charges.

Finally, basic plans provide a wide variety of miscellaneous benefits. Depending on the plan, basic benefits may cover home health care visits by medical specialists, extended care facility benefits, radiation therapy, diagnostic X rays, CAT scans and magnetic resonance imaging (MRI), and supplemental accident benefits.

## Major Medical Insurance

Many employers also provide major medical insurance for their employees. Major medical insurance can be written as a supplement to a basic medical expense plan, or it can be combined with a basic plan to form a comprehensive major medical policy.

**Supplemental Major Medical Insurance**
**Supplemental major medical insurance** *is designed to supplement the benefits provided by a basic plan.* Some medical expenses are not covered under a basic plan, or the benefits paid may be exhausted. Medical expenses not covered under a basic plan may be eligible for reimbursement under the supplemental major medical plan.

Supplemental major medical insurance plans have characteristics similar to the individual major medical policies described in Chapter 20, but the benefits have much higher limits and are more comprehensive.

Most supplemental major medical plans have high lifetime limits that typically range from $250,000 to $1 million. A few plans have no limits. These high limits reflect the rapid increase in medical costs over time.

A **coinsurance provision** of 80 percent is typically found in supplemental major medical plans. However, the coinsurance provision is modified by a **stop-loss limit,** which places a dollar limit on the maximum amount that an individual must pay. Under a stop-loss provision, once the individual's out-of-pocket expenses exceed a certain amount, such as $2000, all remaining eligible medical expenses are paid in full.

A corridor deductible is often used to integrate a basic medical expense plan with a supplemental major medical plan. Before the supplemental major medical plan pays any benefits, a corridor deductible must be met. A **corridor deductible** *is one that applies only to eligible medical expenses not covered by the basic medical expense plan.* As noted earlier, some medical expenses are not covered under a basic plan, or the expenses may be covered but the benefits paid by the basic plan are exhausted. These expenses may be eligible for reimbursement under the supplemental major medical plan, subject to a corridor deductible. This type of deductible can be illustrated by the following example:

| | |
|---|---|
| Total medical expenses | $30,000 |
| Paid by basic medical expense plan | 20,000 |
| Remaining medical expenses | $10,000 |
| Corridor deductible paid by the insured | 200 |
| Balance of medical expenses to be paid | $9,800 |
| 80 percent paid by supplemental major medical plan | 7,840 |
| 20 percent paid by the insured | $1,960 |

## INSIGHT 21.1

### Doctors Can Leave You on Hook as Insurers Cut Back

When Sid Marshall had gall bladder surgery, he figured his health insurance would cover the cost.

But the insurer determined Mr. Marshall's surgeon was more expensive than others in the area, and paid only $3,800 of the doctor's $4,500 fee. Several weeks later, the surgeon billed Mr. Marshall for $700.

"I was totally surprised," says Mr. Marshall, 59 years old, who lives in Neptune, N.J., and is insured through his wife's employer-sponsored health plan. "We pay so much for our medical insurance that we ought to be covered."

Typically, employees with traditional health plans that let them pick their own doctors have had to pay a deductible before the coverage kicks in, then come up with a co-insurance payment that generally amounts to 20% of eligible charges.

*But in an effort to control costs, insurers have been scaling back what they consider eligible, or "reasonable and customary," charges.* That's putting new pressure on physicians to try to bill patients for the remainder, a practice called "balance billing."

Many doctors refrain from balance billing because they don't want to lose patients, says Dr. Nancy Dickey, chairman of the American Medical Association. Still, she acknowledges, "the temptation is certainly there."

Health-maintenance organizations, which limit people to the plan's panel of doctors, usually don't allow physicians to charge patients more than a co-payment of $5 to $15. But point-of-service plans—new breeds of managed-care plans that pay some of the costs of doctors outside the plan's network—also can leave patients on the hook for a big piece of the tab.

If you want to avoid or at least reduce such bills, you should understand how your insurance works and be ready to ask your doctor some pointed questions, consumer advocates say.

Insurers set "reasonable and customary" rates for thousands of medical procedures. Using their own data, and often information from the Health Insurance Association of America, a trade association, insurers decide what's the most they'll pay for a medical service in a metropolitan area or other region.

For example, the insurer might draw the line at the 85th percentile of fees they've examined. That means doctors who charge at or below that point would be considered eligible for full reimbursement. *Doctors who charge above that level generally will be denied payment for any excess charges.*

In general, most doctors who take Blue Cross & Blue Shield insurance agree not to charge more than what those plans pay. But many doctors have no such understanding with commercial insurers.

To cut costs, some of those insurers have reduced eligible rates in recent years, says Michelle Hansen, a

*Continued*

**Comprehensive Major Medical Insurance** Many employers have comprehensive major medical plans for their employees. **Comprehensive major medical insurance** *is a combination of basic benefits and major medical insurance in one policy.* This type of plan is widely used by employers who want both basic benefits and major medical protection in a single policy. This type of plan is characterized by a deductible, such as $200 or $300 per year, by high maximum limits of $250,000 to $1 million, and by coinsurance. In addition, the deductible and coinsurance provisions may not be applied to certain medical expenses. For example, in one plan, the deductible does not apply to hospital expenses. The first $3000 of covered hospital expenses are paid in full, and a coinsurance rate of 80 percent is applied to the remaining hospital expenses.

A **calendar-year deductible** is widely used in comprehensive major medical plans. The deductible has to be met only once during the calendar year. All covered medical expenses incurred by the insured during the year can be used to satisfy the deductible.

The deductible applies separately to the employee and each family member. However, to minimize the financial impact on the family, the major

consultant for Towers Perrin, a New York benefits-consulting firm.

One such company is **Prudential Insurance Co. of America's** Prudential HealthCare Group unit, which has lowered eligible rates to the 80th from the 90th percentile during the past decade, says Eduard Pfister, director for health-care operations.

For their part, many doctors feel increasingly squeezed—on one side by discounts demanded by HMOs and large employers and on the other by reduced payments from Medicare and Medicaid. For some, there's only one golden goose left.

"If doctors can't make money on other patients, they're going to try to get it from indemnity patients," says Mary Case, a principal at benefits-consultant Kwasha Lipton in Fort Lee, N.J.

Patients with traditional insurance should ask doctors how much they charge for any planned procedure and find out whether the doctor's fees are fully eligible, says Geraldine Dallek, health-policy director for Families USA, a consumer advocacy group in Washington.

Preferred-provider organizations and point-of-service plans usually offer to pay 70% for doctors who aren't in the plan's network. But be aware that they're talking about eligible fees, so if your doctor charges above the reasonable and customary rate, you might have to pay a lot more than you thought, says Arthur

Drechsler, a senior vice president for Segal Co., a benefits-consulting firm in New York.

Many people automatically pay any bills they get from their doctor. But, if you ask, your doctor may be willing to waive or at least reduce a balance bill, says Martin Schneider, editor and publisher of Health Pages, a quarterly consumer health magazine in New York. "Doctors aren't in business to make you unhappy," Mr. Schneider says. "Usually, there's room for negotiating."

Mr. Marshall had no chance to negotiate when he was rushed to the hospital with his gall bladder problem. But, after receiving the doctor's bill, Mr. Marshall called several other surgeons and learned they'd have taken his insurance with no additional fee. Mr. Marshall convinced his doctor to let him pay the $700 over a year and says he might ask the surgeon to settle for $300. In an emergency, people often think, "I don't care what the price is," Mr. Marshall says. "The fact of the matter is, ultimately, you do care."

SOURCE: Adapted from Nancy Ann Jeffrey, "Doctors Can Leave You on Hook as Insurers Cut Back," *The Wall Street Journal,* January 26, 1996, p. C1.

medical plan may contain a **family deductible provision.** Under this provision, additional deductibles for family members are waived if two or three separate deductibles have been satisfied by individual family members during the year.

## MANAGED CARE PLANS

Traditional group indemnity plans have declined in importance because of the rapid growth in managed care plans. Employers and insurers have designed new types of managed care plans to hold down the

escalation in health care costs. **Managed care** *is a generic name for medical expense plans that provide covered services to the members in a cost-effective manner.* Under such plans, the employees' choice of physicians and hospitals may be limited to certain health-care providers; cost control and reduction are heavily emphasized; utilization review is done at all levels; the quality of the care provided by physicians is carefully monitored and evaluated; health-care providers share in the financial results through various risk-sharing techniques; and preventive care and healthy life styles are emphasized. Managed-care plans have grown rapidly over time. In 1994, 70 percent of the people covered by employer-sponsored plans were enrolled in managed care plans.[7] In particular, the growth in Blue Cross and Blue Shield managed care plans is impressive and now exceeds enrollments in the traditional fee-for-service plans (see Exhibit 21.1).

There are several types of managed care plans. The most important include the following:

- Health maintenance organizations (HMOs)
- Preferred provider organizations (PPOs)
- Exclusive provider organizations (EPOs)
- Point-of-service (POS) plans

## Health Maintenance Organizations (HMOs)

A **health maintenance organization (HMO)** *is an organized system of health care that provides comprehensive services to its members for a fixed prepaid fee.* Almost one in four workers in employer-sponsored health plans was enrolled in an HMO in 1995 (see Exhibit 21.2).

**Basic Characteristics**    HMOs have a number of basic characteristics.[8] *First, the HMO has the responsibility for organizing and delivering comprehensive health services to its members.* The HMO owns or leases medical facilities, enters into agreements with hospitals and physicians to provide medical services, hires ancillary personnel, and has general managerial control over the various services provided.

*Second, an HMO provides broad comprehensive health services to the members.* Most services are covered in full, with relatively few maximum limits on individual services. However, many HMOs will limit the amount paid for the treatment of alcoholism and drug addiction. Covered services typically include the full cost of hospital care, surgeons' and physicians' fees, maternity care, laboratory and X-ray services, outpatient services, special-duty nursing, and numerous other services. Office visits to HMO physicians are also covered, either in full or at a nominal charge for each visit.

*Third, selection of a physician is usually limited to physicians who are affiliated with the HMO.* However, as will be discussed later, some newer HMOs allow insureds to select any physician at higher out-of-pocket costs. In addition, because HMOs operate in a limited geographical area, there may be limited coverage for treatment received outside of the area. HMOs typically provide only emergency medical treatment received outside of the geographical area of the HMO.

EXHIBIT 21.1

**Blues' Managed Care Enrollment Surpasses Fee-For-Service**

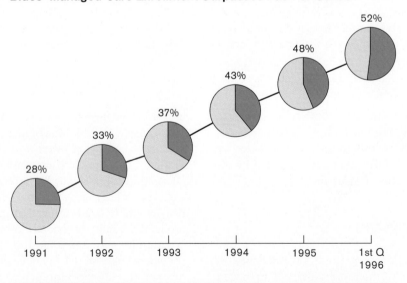

SOURCE: *National Underwriter,* Life & Health/Financial Services Edition, September 2, 1996, p. 1.

## Exhibit 21.2

**Nationwide Employer-Sponsored Health Plan Enrollment in 1995**

**Percent of Employees in Each Type of Plan**

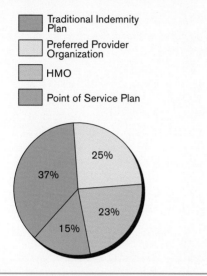

- ■ Traditional Indemnity Plan
- ☐ Preferred Provider Organization
- ▨ HMO
- ▨ Point of Service Plan

SOURCE: Foster Higgins, *Highlights, A Monthly Summary of Benefit News* (February 1995), p. 2.

*Fourth, HMO members pay a fixed prepaid fee (usually paid monthly) for the medical services provided.* High deductibles and coinsurance requirements are usually not emphasized. However, many HMOs now require copayments for certain diseases, such as alcoholism or drug addiction. There may also be a nominal fee for certain services, such as $10 for an office visit or $10 for a prescription drug.

*In addition, there is heavy emphasis on controlling costs.* Some HMO physicians are paid a salary, which holds down costs since the provider has no financial incentive to provide unnecessary services. HMOs also enter into contracts with specialists and providers to provide certain services at negotiated fees. Many HMOs pay physicians or medical groups a **capitation fee,** which is a fixed annual amount for each plan member regardless of the number of services provided. In addition, access to an expensive specialist is controlled by a gatekeeper physician. A **gatekeeper physician** is a primary care physician who determines if medical care from a specialist is necessary. However, some HMOs now allow patients to bypass the primary care physician and see a

specialist directly (see Insight 21.2). Finally, HMOs emphasize preventive care and healthy life styles, which also hold down costs.

**Types of HMOs**  There are several types of HMOs. Under a **staff model,** physicians are employees of the HMO and are paid a salary and possibly an incentive bonus to hold down costs.

Under a **group model,** physicians are employees of another group that has a contract with the HMO to provide medical services to its members. The HMO pays the group of physicians a monthly or annual capitation fee for each member. As stated earlier, a capitation fee is a fixed amount for each member regardless of the number of services provided. In return, the group agrees to provide all covered services to the members during the year. The group model typically has a closed panel of physicians that requires members to select physicians affiliated with the HMO.

Under a **network model,** the HMO contracts with two or more independent group practices to provide medical services to covered members. The HMO pays a fixed monthly fee for each member to the medical group. The medical group then decides how the fees are distributed among the individual physicians.

A final type of HMO is an **individual practice association plan (IPA).** An IPA is an open panel of physicians who work out of their own offices and treat patients on a fee-for-service basis. However, the individual physicians agree to treat HMO members at reduced fees. Physicians may be paid a capitation fee for each member or may be paid a reduced fee. For example, physicians may be paid only 90 percent of their usual fee for an office visit. In addition, to encourage cost containment, most IPAs have risk-sharing agreements with the participating physicians. Payments may be reduced if the plan experience is poor. A bonus is paid if the plan experience is better than expected.

## Preferred Provider Organizations (PPOs)

A **preferred provider organization (PPO)** is a plan that contracts with health care providers to provide medical services to the members at reduced fees. The employer, insurer, or other group negotiates contracts with physicians, hospitals, and other

## INSIGHT 21.2

### Some HMOs Are Loosening Their Gatekeeper Restrictions

They are known as gatekeepers, and they are what many Americans dislike most about their health-maintenance organizations. They are the primary-care doctors who must say yes before a patient can see a specialist.

Mike Shoemaker, a Phoenix businessman, hated the requirement. He remembers when his wife was advised to consult a series of stomach specialists but had to go back to a primary-care doctor each time for permission.

Shoemaker recently switched his company's 28 employees to an HMO that allows visits to specialists without such approval. "Now we have the flexibility and freedom to go to anybody we want," he said.

Many other Americans are demanding the same freedom, and they are getting it from a growing number of HMOs.

Even HMOs that still require permission are trying to simplify and speed up the process. A number of plans let members get approval by telephone, and then the green light can be given not only by the primary-care doctor but also by another HMO doctor or a nurse. In other HMOs, a member can bring a magnetic identification card to the primary doctor's office, where an aide will quickly put through a routine referral by swiping the card's data into a computer system.

But, as with many things in life, freedom can have its price. Although many experts say the jury is still out on whether easier access to specialists will necessarily be followed by higher costs, *some HMOs are taking no chances and are charging more for plans that allow visits to specialists without prior permission.* In some cases, monthly premiums might rise 15 percent; in others, the patient might pay an extra fee, say $30, each time the option is used.

And some HMOs have merely moved the responsibility for permission to another party: the specialist. In those cases, the patient may freely visit the specialist, but that doctor must then call a company nurse or medical director for approval to proceed further, even to order tests.

"It's a backdoor kind of gatekeeper," said Rich Sinni, a benefits expert with Back Consultants.

Backdoor or not, some HMOs take patient empowerment a step beyond another popular group of managed health plans, those that permit members to go to specialists of their choice even if they are outside a prescribed network of doctors.

Under those plans, the patient typically must still get permission from a primary-care doctor to go outside the network. The patient also pays extra for the privilege, usually the first few hundred dollars of fees plus 20 or 30 percent of anything beyond that.

Easing restrictions on seeing specialists results in fewer complaints from HMO members, saves time for patients and doctors alike and eliminates a mountain of costly paperwork, managed-care experts say. Blue Shield of California said that complaints about access to specialists had fallen by 30 percent after it introduced a plan last summer that permits members to go directly to doctors in some high-demand fields, like sports medicine.

Health-maintenance organizations originally installed gatekeepers, a concept popularized by U.S. Healthcare Corp. in the early 1980s, to save money and to improve care. The idea was to reduce the number of unnecessary consultations with specialists, as well as the accompanying procedures and tests, and to raise the quality of care by coordinating the actions of various doctors.

But whether the gatekeeper actually does all that is a matter of much debate.

Managed-care experts say HMO members normally go to their primary care physicians for 80 to 90 percent of their medical needs anyway. And while many patients complain that they have been denied access to special-

*Continued*

providers of care to provide certain medical services to the plan members at discounted fees. To encourage patients to use PPO providers, deductibles and copayment charges are reduced. In addition, the patient may be charged a lower fee for certain routine

treatments, or offered increased benefits such as preventive health care services.

PPOs should not be confused with HMOs. There are two important differences.[9] First, PPO providers typically do not provide medical care on a

ized care, the HMOs say that requests to see specialists are nearly always approved.

"I'm not sure, when you look at the administrative cost, whether in fact the gatekeeper saves any money," said John Erb, a health-care consultant with the Foster Higgins benefits consulting firm.

Indeed, there has been a backlash. In the last two years, at least 17 states have ordered health plans to provide direct access to certain specialists, like obstetricians.

But the plans themselves are coming to see the value of looser rules.

"As managed care gets to be a bigger and bigger percentage of the market, we need to make it more and more acceptable to more people," said Margaret Stanley, a health-care executive with the California Public Employees Retirement System, which recently began offering the Blue Shield HMO that allows direct access to some specialists.

United Healthcare Corp., which pioneered HMOs in Minneapolis in the 1970s without gatekeepers, said such plans are among its fastest growing. One of the biggest managed-care companies, United Healthcare already covers 1.7 million people in 18 states in HMOs without gatekeepers and says it is planning to introduce similar plans this year in California and seven other states.

The approach has also attracted interest in New York, where Physicians Health Services said it had added 75,000 "open access" members in the last 18 months, and in Florida, where several thousand employees of the Dade County school board recently joined such an HMO.

Many other big health insurers, including Prudential Healthcare, Aetna, U.S. Healthcare and Health Systems International, also are looking at offering HMOs without gatekeepers.

"Our feedback from both members and doctors is that the whole referral-to-specialist process is an area that merits attention and deserves to be improved," said Dr. William Roper, a senior vice president at Prudential Healthcare.

In a 27-city survey of 85,000 health-plan members last year, 30 percent of those who responded said they were not satisfied with the referral process, according to Sachs/Scarborough, health-care market researchers.

By contrast, James Carlson, executive vice president of United Healthcare, said a group of potential customers in Arizona recently erupted in "a standing ovation" after an HMO executive explained how a no-gatekeeper plan works.

And in Minneapolis, Steve Wetzell, executive director of the Buyers Health Care Action Group, a Minnesota-based organization of big employers, said that "virtually every care system that we contracted with has created a looser set of rules."

Just how those rules are loosened varies from plan to plan.

Kaiser Permanente, the California-based HMO, permits direct access to specialists for allergies, certain vision problems and drug and alcohol problems, and in some regions for sports medicine, dermatology and podiatry, said Dan Danzig, a Kaiser spokesman. But Kaiser expects the specialist to report back to the primary physician, who remains responsible for the patient's overall care.

In Minneapolis, where HMOs are deeply entrenched, Medica Health Plans says it has seen no substantive difference in costs or frequency of visits to hospitals and doctors between plans that have gatekeepers and plans that do not.

SOURCE: "Some HMOs are Loosening Their Gatekeeper Restrictions," *Sunday World Herald,* February 2, 1997, p. 5-A.

prepaid basis, but are paid on a fee-for-service basis as their services are used. However, as stated earlier, the fees charged are below the provider's regular fee. Second, unlike an HMO, patients are not required to use a preferred provider but have freedom of choice every time they need care. However, the patients have a financial incentive to use a preferred provider because the deductible and copayment charges are reduced.

PPOs have the major advantage of controlling

health-care costs because provider fees are negotiated at a discount. PPOs also help physicians to build up their practice. Patients also benefit because they pay less for their medical care.

## Exclusive Provider Organizations (EPOs)

An **exclusive provider organization (EPO)** is a plan that does not cover medical care received outside of a network of preferred providers. If patients receive medical care outside the network, they must pay the entire cost themselves. The preferred providers who are in the network are reimbursed on a fee-for-service basis based on a schedule of negotiated fees.

## Point-of-Service Plans (POS)

A **point-of-service plan (POS)** is a newer form of managed care that is rapidly growing in importance. A point-of-service plan is also known as an open-ended HMO or hybrid plan that combines the characteristics of HMOs and PPOs.

The POS plan establishes a network of preferred providers. If patients see providers who are in the network, they pay little or nothing out of pocket, which is similar to an HMO. However, if the patients receive care from providers outside the network, the care is covered, but the patients must pay substantially higher deductibles and copayments. For example, a patient who sees a physician outside the network may be required to pay a $500 annual deductible and a coinsurance charge of 30 percent. If the patient sees a participating physician within the network, there is no additional charge.

The POS plan has the major advantage of preserving freedom of choice for plan members; it also eliminates the fear that plan members will not be able to see a physician or specialist of their choice. The major disadvantage is the substantially higher cost that a member must pay to see a provider outside the network.

## Advantages of Managed Care Plans

Managed care plans have a number of advantages for employers, employees, and health insurers. One major advantage is that the rate of increase in health insurance premiums has been reduced over time because of the heavy emphasis on cost control. However, HMO rates are beginning to rise because

EXHIBIT 21.3

**Reported Annual HMO Premium Rate Changes (Straight Averages), 1991 to 1995**

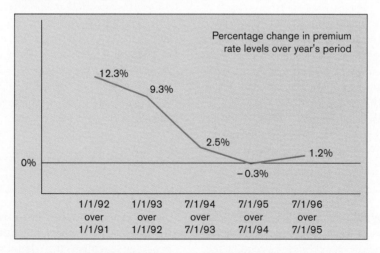

SOURCE: "HMO rates: watch them rise," *On Managed Care*, Vol. 2, No. 1 (January 1997), Figure 1, p.1.

of disappointing earnings by large HMO chains (see Exhibit 21.3).

Other advantages are that managed-care plans generally have lower hospital and surgical utilization rates than traditional group indemnity plans; plan members pay little or nothing out of pocket if they utilize network providers; and employees do not have to file claim forms.

## Disadvantages of Managed Care Plans

*According to many critics, the major disadvantage of managed care plans is that the quality of care is being reduced because of the heavy emphasis on cost control.* Critics argue that access to specialists may be delayed because some gatekeeper physicians do not promptly refer sick patients to specialists because of the additional cost to the plan; some patients who should be hospitalized are not admitted into a hospital; and certain diagnostic tests are not performed.

Many physicians criticize managed care plans because of restrictions placed on their freedom to treat patients. HMO physicians must often obtain approval from plan administrators or insurers before certain diagnostic tests or procedures can be given; physicians may have to argue for additional days of hospital coverage for patients who are too sick to be released; referral to a specialist may be denied or delayed; and prescription drugs may be limited only to certain drugs on an approved list. In addition, physicians argue that some HMOs impose a "gag rule" on the right of the doctor to discuss with patients alternative methods of treatment not approved by the HMO. Thus, many plan physicians believe the traditional doctor-patient relationship is being seriously compromised by outside third parties.

In addition, managed care plans commonly provide financial incentives to health-care providers to hold down costs, such as an incentive bonus based on the profitability of the plan. Critics argue that network physicians often have a financial conflict-of-interest between providing the highest quality medical care to their patients and holding down costs to increase plan profits and the amount of their bonus.

Finally, many workers are unaware of the various restrictions and limitations in managed care plans, and state regulation of HMOs varies widely. As an informed health consumer, you should be aware of the limitations that apply and know how to protect yourself from bad HMO practices even if you have no state protection (see Insight 21.3).

## GROUP MEDICAL EXPENSE CONTRACTUAL PROVISIONS

Group medical expense insurance plans contain numerous contractual provisions that can have a significant financial impact on the insured. Three important provisions deal with (1) preexisting conditions, (2) coordination of benefits, and (3) continuation of group health insurance.

### Preexisting Conditions

Group medical expense plans typically contain a **preexisting conditions provision** that excludes coverage for a medical condition for a limited *period* after the worker enters the plan. The purposes of this provision are to reduce adverse selection against the insurer and to control employer costs.

In 1996, Congress enacted the **Health Insurance Portability and Accountability Act,** which places limits on the right of insurers and employers to deny or limit coverage for preexisting conditions. Group health plans must comply with all nondiscrimination, preexisting conditions, and crediting requirements at the beginning of their first plan year starting after June 30, 1997.

Most employees who change or lose jobs will now have access to group health insurance coverage. Employers and insurers that offer health insurance plans are prohibited from dropping people because they are sick, or from imposing waiting periods for preexisting conditions for more than 12 months (18 months for late enrollees). Employers and health insurers must also give credit for previous coverage so that workers who maintain continuous health insurance coverage (without a gap of 63 days) can never be excluded because of a preexisting condition.

The following discussion summarizes the major provisions of the new law dealing with preexisting conditions:

- Employer-sponsored group health insurance plans cannot exclude or limit coverage for a preexisting condition for more than 12 months (18 months for late enrollees). A **preexisting condition** *is defined as a medical condition diagnosed or*

## INSIGHT 21.3

### Protect Yourself From Bad HMO Practices Even If Your State Doesn't

How much protection you get from shabby HMO practices depends largely on where you live. As the table shows, states vary widely in the way they regulate managed-care providers. Five states—California, Colorado, Georgia, Maryland and New York—shield health consumers in each of the five key measures listed in the table, while Hawaii, Idaho, Kentucky and New Jersey have no such protections.

Simply put, a lack of safeguards can be harmful to your health. Just ask Judy Loesch of Trenton. In 1995, Loesch, 48, started getting severe back pains and was sent by her doctor to a nearby hospital emergency room. Hospital staffers did a few preliminary tests, but although Loesch could barely walk, they could not admit her to the hospital until her HMO, Blue Choice, gave approval. That took more than six hours. Loesch was eventually admitted, and subsequent testing revealed a bulging disk. Blue Choice says the holdup was because it didn't consider the situation an emergency.

Protect yourself against HMO woes by learning about the following five key protections for health consumers and what to do if your state doesn't offer them:

* **Access to specialists for primary care.** Before an HMO will pay for nonemergency treatment by a specialist, a member must get a referral from his or her primary-care physician (PCP). This can be a burden for women, the disabled and chronically ill patients who need regular access to specialized care. As a result, 21 states now require HMOs to let women choose a network obstetrician-gynecologist as their PCP, be treated by one without a referral or to give patients access to other specialty care.

    **If you have no state protection:** Your PCP may be able to provide a fixed number of pre-authorized referrals if you need frequent access to specialist. If not, take your case to the plan medical director.
* **The right to full disclosure from your physician.** So-called gag rules at some HMOs prevent doctors from discussing financial incentives they receive to limit care or from telling patients about treatments that aren't likely to approved by the plan. Eighteen states believe patients have a right to know about these issues.

    **If you have no state protection:** Ask your doctor about his or her compensation plan and restrictions on treatment options anyway. Gag rules are loosely enforced, if at all.
* **Authorization for emergency services whenever—and wherever—you need them.** Patients can be frustrated when help is delayed while an emergency room seeks payment approval. That's why 16 states now make it easier for HMO patients to receive treatment in an emergency even from an out-of-network hospital.

    **If you have no state protection:** Call your HMO customer service number to ask which hospitals are in the HMO's network and how a plan defines an emergency. Find out which options it offers for after-hours care.
* **Help with filing complaints.** All states require HMOs to address complaints or permit appeals related to treatment or payment. But just 34 of them stipulate specific grievance protections for consumers, such as setting a time limit for resolving disputes.

    **If you have no state protection:** Whenever you feel you aren't getting a fair hearing from your HMO, write or call the agency that oversees HMOs in your state. That could be the state insurance department, the office of consumer protection or the attorney general's office.
* **Quality assurance.** The federal government requires most HMOs to compile information on their medical quality, such as their standards for making treatment decisions and which quality management strategies they employ. But only 31 have agencies that formally oversee HMO quality.

    **If you have no state protection:** Check with the National Committee for Quality Assurance, which accredits HMOs and, increasingly, issues summaries

*Continued*

of their performance in reports (800-839-6487) or at its Website (http://www.ncqa.org). Just remember:

With consumer health-care protections spotty at best, it pays to take intensive care of yourself.

## Only five states shield members across the board

California, Colorado, Georgia, Maryland and New York have all five HMO protections. A ✓ means the state restricts harmful HMO practices. An ✗ indicates no protection exists.

| State | Direct access to specialists | Gag rules | Easier access to emergency care | Improved grievance procedures[1] | Quality controls[1] | State | Direct access to specialists | Gag rules | Easier access to emergency care | Improved grievance procedures[1] | Quality controls[1] |
|---|---|---|---|---|---|---|---|---|---|---|---|
| Alabama | ✓ | ✗ | ✗ | ✓ | ✓ | Montana | ✗ | ✗ | ✗ | ✓ | ✗ |
| Alaska | ✗ | ✗ | ✗ | ✗ | ✓ | Nebraska | ✓ | ✗ | ✗ | ✗ | ✓ |
| Arizona | ✗ | ✗ | ✓ | ✗ | ✗ | Nevada | ✗ | ✗ | ✗ | ✓ | ✓ |
| Arkansas | ✓ | ✗ | ✓ | ✓ | ✓ | New Hampshire | ✗ | ✓ | ✗ | ✗ | ✗ |
| California | ✓ | ✓ | ✓ | ✓ | ✓ | New Jersey | ✗ | ✗ | ✗ | ✗ | ✗ |
| Colorado | ✓ | ✓ | ✓ | ✓ | ✓ | New Mexico | ✗ | ✗ | ✗ | ✓ | ✗ |
| Connecticut | ✓ | ✗ | ✓ | ✗ | ✗ | New York | ✓ | ✓ | ✓ | ✓ | ✓ |
| Delaware | ✗ | ✓ | ✗ | ✓ | ✓ | North Carolina | ✓ | ✗ | ✗ | ✓ | ✗ |
| Florida | ✓ | ✗ | ✓ | ✓ | ✓ | North Dakota | ✗ | ✗ | ✗ | ✓ | ✗ |
| Georgia | ✓ | ✓ | ✓ | ✓ | ✓ | Ohio | ✗ | ✗ | ✗ | ✓ | ✓ |
| Hawaii | ✗ | ✗ | ✗ | ✗ | ✗ | Oklahoma | ✗ | ✗ | ✗ | ✓ | ✓ |
| Idaho | ✗ | ✗ | ✗ | ✗ | ✗ | Oregon | ✓ | ✗ | ✗ | ✓ | ✗ |
| Illinois | ✓ | ✗ | ✗ | ✓ | ✓ | Pennsylvania | ✗ | ✓ | ✓ | ✓ | ✓ |
| Indiana | ✓ | ✓ | ✗ | ✗ | ✓ | Rhode Island | ✗ | ✓ | ✗ | ✓ | ✓ |
| Iowa | ✗ | ✗ | ✗ | ✓ | ✓ | South Carolina | ✗ | ✗ | ✗ | ✗ | ✗ |
| Kansas | ✗ | ✗ | ✓ | ✓ | ✓ | South Dakota | ✗ | ✗ | ✗ | ✓ | ✓ |
| Kentucky | ✗ | ✗ | ✗ | ✗ | ✗ | Tennessee | ✗ | ✓ | ✗ | ✗ | ✗ |
| Lousiana | ✓ | ✗ | ✓ | ✗ | ✓ | Texas | ✗ | ✓ | ✓ | ✓ | ✓ |
| Maine | ✓ | ✓ | ✗ | ✓ | ✓ | Utah | ✓ | ✗ | ✗ | ✓ | ✓ |
| Maryland | ✓ | ✓ | ✓ | ✓ | ✓ | Vermont | ✗ | ✓ | ✗ | ✓ | ✓ |
| Massachussetts | ✗ | ✓ | ✗ | ✗ | ✗ | Virginia | ✓ | ✓ | ✓ | ✓ | ✗ |
| Michigan | ✗ | ✗ | ✗ | ✓ | ✓ | Washington | ✓ | ✓ | ✗ | ✗ | ✗ |
| Minnesota | ✗ | ✗ | ✓ | ✓ | ✓ | West Virginia | ✓ | ✗ | ✓ | ✗ | ✓ |
| Mississippi | ✓ | ✗ | ✗ | ✗ | ✗ | Wisconsin | ✗ | ✓ | ✗ | ✓ | ✗ |
| Missouri | ✗ | ✗ | ✗ | ✓ | ✗ | Wyoming | ✗ | ✗ | ✗ | ✓ | ✓ |

NOTE: [1] As of July 1

SOURCE: Adapted from Karen Cheny and Luis Fernando Llosa, "Protect yourself from bad HMO practices even if your state doesn't," *Money*, Vol. 25, No. 12 (December 1996), pp. 25–27.

*treated during the previous six months.* A preexisting condition exclusion cannot be applied to pregnancy, newly born children, or adopted children.

- After the initial 12-month period expires, no new preexisting condition period may ever be imposed on workers who maintain continuous coverage, with no more than a 63-day gap in coverage, even if the workers should change jobs or health plans.
- *Insurers and employers must give credit for previous coverage of less than 12 months with respect to any preexisting condition exclusion found in the new health plan.* For example, a worker with a preexisting condition who was previously insured for eight months under a group plan when he or she changes jobs or health plans would face a maximum additional exclusion of four months for a preexisting condition, rather than the normal 12 months.
- Discrimination based on health status is prohibited. Employers that offer health insurance to employees and dependents cannot exclude, drop from coverage, or charge higher premiums based on health status. Health status is broadly defined to include the individual's medical condition; physical and mental illness; medical history; claims experience; evidence of insurability, including conditions arising out of acts of domestic violence; genetic information; and disability.
- The new law guarantees the availability of group health insurance to small employers. Commercial insurers, HMOs, and other groups issuing health insurance coverages are prohibited from denying coverage to firms that employ between two and 50 employees.

Because of limits on preexisting conditions and credit for previous and continuous coverage, employees will no longer be afraid to change jobs for fear of losing their group health insurance protection. As a result, they can change jobs and still be assured of health insurance coverage. Thus, the new law makes the health insurance protection "portable."

However, portability does not mean that employees can take their present group health insurance benefits with them when they change jobs. **Portability** *means that when employees change jobs, the new employer or health plan must give them credit for previous and continuous health insurance coverage.* When the employees leave their present job, the insurer or employer must provide information show-

ing how long they were covered while working at that job. The worker then presents this documentation to the new employer or health plan. If a worker has been covered for 12 months or more by a previous employer or health plan and does not have a gap in coverage of more than 63 days, the worker is eligible for coverage under the new employer's plan even though he or she has a preexisting condition.

The new law also includes a demonstration project to evaluate the effectiveness of medical savings accounts (MSAs). A **medical savings account** *is a high-deductible major medical policy that allows the insured to pay premiums with before-tax dollars.* Money in the account earns interest free of taxation, and funds withdrawn to pay medical bills are not taxed unless the funds are used for nonmedical purposes. Money in the account at the end of the year can be rolled over to the next year, but there are limits on how much money can go into the account each year (see Insight 21.4).

Medical savings accounts are controversial. Proponents argue that insureds with medical savings accounts will be more sensitive to the cost of medical care and will shop around for low-cost providers. Opponents argue that only healthy insureds will elect MSAs to save money, which will drive up costs for other insureds who are covered under group indemnity or managed care plans.

## Coordination of Benefits

Group medical insurance plans typically contain a **coordination-of-benefits** provision, which specifies the order of payment when an insured is covered under two or more group health insurance plans. Total recovery under all plans is limited to 100 percent of covered expenses. The purpose is to prevent overinsurance and duplication of benefits if an insured is covered by more than one plan.

The coordination-of-benefit provisions in most group plans are based on rules developed by the National Association of Insurance Commissioners (NAIC). These rules are complex and are beyond the scope of this text to discuss in detail. The following summarizes the major provisions based on the latest NAIC rules.

1. *Coverage as an employee is usually primary to coverage as a dependent.* For example, Karen and Chris Swift both work, and each is insured as a

## INSIGHT 21.4

### Medical Savings Accounts: A New Tax Break for Medical Costs

Tax-free medical savings accounts (MSAs) permit a limited number of self-employed people and small businesses with 50 or fewer employees to set up such accounts this year [1997]. But the experiment could turn out to be more than Congress bargained for.

*An MSA works like this: You (or your employer) buy a catastrophic-care health insurance policy with a high deductible (between $1,500 and $2,250 for an individual and $3,000 to $4,500 for a family). Then you put 65% to 75% of the insurance deductible into the MSA, where it earns interest tax-free and is excluded from your taxable income.*

*You tap the account as needed to pay out-of-pocket medical costs with tax-free dollars. Whatever you don't spend grows over time, tax-deferred, into a kind of IRA.*

If you're self-employed, you should jump at the chance to open an MSA because you probably already have a high-deductible policy. MSAs will also be attractive to small firms with employees who are mostly young, healthy and willing to gamble on a high-deductible policy.

By law, the number of MSAs is capped at 750,000 accounts. But in practice, the IRS won't close the window until September 1 [1997] by which time far more than 750,000 accounts may have been set up. Proponents of MSAs are hoping that the cap will be exceeded so that Congress will remove it altogether. But once you've established an MSA, you can keep it for life.

Check with your current insurer to see if it will be offering MSAs. If not, contact a trade or professional organization you belong to, or call one of the companies listed here.

**MSAs: Who's selling them**

GOLDEN RULE INSURANCE CO.   888-672-0829
Account balances earn 5% interest, guaranteed for one year; $3 monthly account fee

TIME INSURANCE CO.   888-846-3672
4.5% interest rate on balances over $750; no account or transaction fees

SOURCE: Adapted from "Insurance: A new tax break for medical costs," *Kiplinger's Personal Finance Magazine* (January 1997), p. 18.

dependent under the other's group medical insurance plan. If Karen incurs covered medical expenses, her plan pays first. She then submits any unreimbursed expenses (such as the deductible and coinsurance payments) to Chris' insurer for payment. No more than 100 percent of the eligible medical expenses are paid under both plans.

2. With respect to dependent children, if the parents are married or are not separated (regardless of whether they have ever been married), *the plan or the parent whose birthday occurs first during the year is primary; the plan of the parent with the later birthday is secondary.* For example, if Karen's birthday is in January and Chris' birthday is in July, Karen's plan would pay first if her son is hospitalized. Chris' plan would be secondary.

3. If the parents of dependent children are not married, or are separated (regardless of whether they have ever been married), or are divorced, and if there is no court decree specifying who is responsible for the child's health-care expenses, the following rules apply:
   - The plan of the parent who is awarded custody pays first.
   - The plan of the stepparent who is the spouse of the parent awarded custody pays second.
   - The plan of the parent without custody pays third.
   - The plan of the stepparent who is the spouse of the parent without custody pays last.

## Continuation of Group Health Insurance

Employees often quit their jobs, are laid off, or fired. If a qualifying event occurs that results in a loss of coverage, employees and covered dependents can elect to remain in the employer's plan for a limited period under the Consolidated Omnibus Budget Reconciliation Act of 1985 (also known as CO-BRA). The COBRA law applies to firms with 20 or more employees. A qualifying event includes termination of employment for any reason (except gross misconduct), divorce or legal separation, death of the employee, and attainment of a maximum age by dependent children. If the worker loses his or her job or no longer works the required number of hours, the terminated worker and covered dependents can elect to remain in the employer's plan for up to 18 months. However, they must pay 102 percent of the group rate. If the worker dies or is divorced or legally separated or has a child who is no longer eligible for coverage, covered dependents have the right to remain in the group plan for up to three years.

After the period of protection under COBRA expires, some workers with preexisting conditions may be unable to obtain individual health insurance. The new Health Insurance Portability and Accountability Act guarantees individual health insurance to eligible persons with no evidence of insurability if certain conditions are met. Eligible persons with health problems are guaranteed individual health insurance if they can meet the following requirements: (1) have employment-based health insurance for at least 18 months, (2) are ineligible for COBRA or have exhausted their COBRA coverage, and (3) are ineligible for coverage under any other employment-based health plan. The insurance provided is a guaranteed renewable policy.

## GROUP DENTAL INSURANCE

**Group dental insurance** helps pay the cost of normal dental care as well as damage to teeth from an accident. Dental insurance has the principal advantage of helping employees meet the costs of regular dental care. It also encourages insureds to see their dentists on a regular basis, thereby preventing or detecting dental problems before they become serious.

### Types of Plans

There are two basic types of group dental insurance plans.[10] Under a **scheduled plan,** the various dental services are listed in a schedule, and a flat dollar amount is paid for each service. If the dentist charges more than the specified amount, the patient must pay the difference.

Under a **nonscheduled plan** (also called **comprehensive dental insurance**), most dental services are covered, including oral examinations, X rays, cleaning, fillings, extractions, inlays, bridgework and dentures, oral surgery, root canals, and orthodontia. Dentists are reimbursed on the basis of their reasonable and customary charges subject to any limitations on benefits stated in the plan.

### Cost Controls

To control costs and reduce adverse selection against the insurer when the plan is initially installed, several cost controls are used. They include the following:[11]

- Deductibles and coinsurance
- Maximum limit on benefits
- Waiting periods
- Exclusions
- Predetermination-of-benefits provision

Most dental insurance plans use **deductibles** and **coinsurance** to control costs. The coinsurance percentage may vary depending on the type of service. To encourage regular visits to a dentist, many plans do not impose any coinsurance requirements for one or two routine dental examinations each year. However, fillings and oral surgery may be paid only at a rate of 80 percent, while the cost of orthodontia or dentures is typically paid at a lower rate of 50 percent.

**Maximum limits on benefits** are also used to control costs. There may be a maximum annual limit on the amount paid, such as $2000 during the calendar year. Another approach is to impose a lifetime maximum on certain types of dental services, such as a lifetime maximum of $2000 for dentures.

**Waiting periods** for certain types of services are also used to control costs. For example, some plans do not cover dentures until the employee is insured for at least one year, and there may be only one replacement of dentures for each five-year period.

Certain **exclusions** are used to reduce costs. Common exclusions include cosmetic dental work, such as capping a tooth; replacement of lost or stolen dental devices, such as dentures or a space retainer; and benefits provided under a workers compensation or similar law.

Finally, a **predetermination-of-benefits provision** is used to control costs. Under this provision, if the cost of dental treatment exceeds a certain amount, such as $200, the dentist submits a plan of treatment to the insurer. The insurer then specifies the services covered and how much the plan will pay. The employee is informed of the amount the plan will pay and then makes a rational decision on whether or not to proceed with the proposed plan of treatment.

## GROUP DISABILITY-INCOME INSURANCE

**Group disability-income insurance** pays weekly or monthly cash payments to employees who are disabled from accidents or illness. There are two basic types of plans: (1) short-term plans, and (2) long-term plans.

### Short-Term Plans

Many employers have short-term plans that pay disability benefits for relatively short periods ranging from 13 weeks to two years. The majority of short-term plans sold today pay benefits for a maximum period of 26 weeks. In addition, most plans have a short elimination period of one to seven days for sickness, while accidents are typically covered from the first day of disability. The elimination period reduces nuisance claims, holds down costs, and discourages malingering and excessive absenteeism.

More short-term plans cover only **nonoccupational disability,** which means that an accident or illness must occur off the job. *Disability is usually defined in terms of the worker's own occupation. You are considered totally disabled if you are unable to perform all of the duties of your own occupation.* Partial disability is seldom covered under a group short-term plan; you must be totally disabled to qualify.

The amount of disability-income benefits is related to the worker's normal earnings and is typically equal to some percentage of weekly earnings, such as 50 to 70 percent. Thus, if Amy's weekly earnings are $600, she could collect a maximum weekly benefit of $420 if she becomes disabled.

In addition, short-term plans have relatively few exclusions. As noted earlier, a disability that occurs on the job is usually not covered, since occupational disability is covered under a workers compensation law. Also, except for very small groups, preexisting conditions are immediately covered. Most plans also cover alcoholism, drug addiction, and nervous and mental disorders.

### Long-Term Plans

Many employers also have long-term plans that pay benefits for longer periods, typically ranging from two years to age 65. However, if the disability occurs beyond age 65, benefits are paid for a limited period. For example, under the plan of one disability insurer, if the worker is under age 60 at the time of disability, the maximum benefit period is to age 65. However, if a worker age 66 becomes disabled, the maximum benefit period is only 21 months.

A dual definition of disability is typically used to determine if a worker is totally disabled. *For the first two years, you are considered disabled if you are unable to perform all of the duties of your own occupation. After two years, you are still considered disabled if you are unable to work in any occupation for which you are reasonably fitted by education, training, and experience.* In addition, in contrast to short-term plans, long-term plans typically cover both occupational and nonoccupational disability.

The disability-income benefits are usually paid monthly, and the maximum monthly benefits are substantially higher than the short-term plans. The maximum monthly benefit is generally limited to 50 to 65 percent of the employee's normal earnings. Most plans commonly pay maximum monthly benefits of $2000, $3000, $4000, or even higher amounts. A waiting period of three to six months is typically required before the benefits are payable.

To reduce malingering and moral hazard, other disability-income benefits paid for by the employer are taken into consideration. If the disabled worker is also receiving Social Security or workers compensation benefits, the long-term disability benefit is reduced accordingly. However, many plans limit the reduction only to the amount of the initial Social Security disability benefit. Thus, if Social Security disability benefits are increased because of increases in the cost of living, the long-term disability-income benefit is not reduced further.

Some long-term plans have additional supplemental benefits. Under the **cost-of-living adjustment,** benefits paid to disabled employees are adjusted annually for increases in the cost of living. However, there may be a maximum limit on the percentage increase in benefits.

Under the **pension accrual benefit,** the plan makes a pension contribution so that the disabled employee's pension benefit remains intact. For example, if both Carlos and his employer contribute 6 percent of his salary into a pension plan, and he becomes disabled, the plan would pay an amount equal to 12 percent of his monthly salary into the company's pension plan for as long as he remains disabled. Thus, Carlos would still receive his pension at the normal retirement age.

Finally, if the disabled worker dies, the plan may pay monthly **survivor income benefits** to an eligible surviving spouse or children for a limited period following the disabled worker's death, such as two years.

## CAFETERIA PLANS

The final part of this chapter deals with cafeteria plans. **Cafeteria plans** *allow employees to select those employee benefits that best meet their specific needs.* Instead of a single benefits package that applies to all employees, cafeteria plans allow employees to select among the various group life, medical expense, disability, dental, and other plans that are offered. Cafeteria plans also allow employers to introduce new benefits to meet the specific needs of certain employees.

Although cafeteria plans vary among employers, they have certain common characteristics. First, in many plans, the employer gives each employee a certain number of dollars or credits that can be spent on the different benefits or taken as cash. If taken as cash, the employer's credits are taxed as income to the employee.

Second, cafeteria plans typically allow employees to establish a flexible spending account. A **flexible spending account** *is an arrangement by which the employee agrees to a salary reduction, which can be used to pay for plan benefits, unreimbursed medical and dental expenses, dependent care expenses, and other expenses permitted by the Internal Revenue Code.* In effect, the worker pays for the benefits with before-tax dollars.

Finally, if the cafeteria plan meets certain requirements specified in the Internal Revenue Code, the employer's credits are not currently taxable to the employee. Also, any additional amounts spent by the employee on the various benefits are generally paid with before-tax dollars, which provides a significant tax advantage.

Cafeteria plans have certain advantages, including the following:

- Employees can select those benefits that best meet their specific needs.
- Employee appreciation of the benefit package may increase since employees have a greater awareness of the cost of the benefits selected.
- Employees generally pay their share of the cost of benefits with before-tax dollars, which reduces taxes and increases take-home pay.
- Employers can more easily control rising employee benefit costs. For example, an employer may limit the number of benefit dollars or credits given to each employee, or offer the employees a medical expense plan with a higher deductible.

Cafeteria plans also have certain disadvantages, including the following:

- The employer may incur higher initial development and administrative costs in establishing a cafeteria plan rather than a traditional benefits plan.
- Labor union attitudes may be negative. The labor union may believe that a cafeteria plan is contrary to the practice of bargaining for the best benefit package for all employees.
- Administrative complexity is increased. The employee benefits manager must have knowledge of the details of a large number of plans and must be able to answer the specific questions of employees concerning these plans.

## SUMMARY

- Group insurance provides benefits to a number of persons under a single master contract. Low-cost protection is provided, since the employer pays part or all of the premiums. Evidence of insurability is usually not required. Larger groups are subject to experience rating, by which the group's loss experience determines the premiums charged.
- Certain underwriting principles are followed in group insurance to obtain favorable loss experience:

  Insurance must be incidental to the group.

There should be a flow of persons through the group.

The benefits should be determined by some formula that precludes individual selection of insurance amounts.

A minimum percentage of eligible employees must participate in the plan.

There should be a third-party sharing of costs.

There should be simple and efficient administration.

- Most groups today are eligible for group insurance benefits. However, employees must meet certain eligibility requirements:

  Be full-time employees

  Satisfy a probationary period in some plans

  Apply for insurance during the eligibility period

  Be actively at work

- There are several types of group life insurance plans:

  Group term life insurance

  Group accidental death and dismemberment insurance (AD&D)

  Group universal life insurance

- Group medical expense plans are available from a number of sources, including:

  Commercial insurers

  Blue Cross and Blue Shield

  Health maintenance organizations (HMOs)

  Self-insured plans by employers

- Group basic medical expense insurance provides only basic benefits, which typically include:

  Hospital expense insurance

  Surgical expense insurance

  Physicians' visits insurance

  Coverage for miscellaneous benefits

- Group major medical insurance is designed to cover catastrophic losses. There are two basic types of group major medical plans:

  Supplemental major medical insurance

  Comprehensive major medical insurance

- Managed care is a generic name for a medical expense plan that provides necessary medical care in a cost-effective manner.

- A health maintenance organization (HMO) is a managed care plan that provides broad, comprehensive services to the members for a fixed, prepaid fee. A typical HMO has the following characteristics:

  Organized plan to deliver health services to the members

  Broad comprehensive health services

  Fixed prepaid fee

  Emphasis on cost containment

- A preferred provider organization (PPO) is a plan that contracts with health care providers to provide certain medical services to the members at discounted fees. Member pay lower deductibles and coinsurance charges if preferred providers are used.

- An exclusive provider organization (EPO) is a managed care plan that does not cover medical care received outside the network of preferred providers.

- A point-of-service plan (POS) is a managed care plan that allows members to receive medical care outside the network of preferred providers. However, the patient must pay higher deductible and copayment charges.

- Group medical expense plans contain certain contractual provisions that may have a financial impact on the insured. Major provisions include:

  Preexisting conditions provision

  Coordination of benefits provision

  Continuation of group health insurance under the COBRA law

- There are two basic types of group dental insurance plans:

  Scheduled plans

  Nonscheduled plans (comprehensive plans)

- Many employers provide disability income benefits to covered employees. There are two basic types of plans:

  Short-term disability income plans

  Long-term disability income plans

- Cafeteria plans allow employees to select those benefits that best meet their specific needs. Flexible spending accounts in a cafeteria plan allow employees to pay for the benefits with before-tax dollars.

## KEY CONCEPTS AND TERMS

Blue Cross and Blue Shield plans
Cafeteria plans
Calendar-year deductible
Coinsurance
Comprehensive major medical insurance
Contributory plan
Coordination-of-benefits provision
Corridor deductible
Cost-of-living adjustment
Eligibility period

Exclusive provider organization (EPO)
Experience rating
Family deductible provision
Flexible spending account
Group accidental death and dismemberment insurance (AD&D)
Group term life insurance
Group universal life insurance
Health maintenance organization (HMO)

Managed care plans
Master contract
Noncontributory plan
Nonoccupational
   disability
Nonscheduled dental
   insurance plan
   (comprehensive
   insurance)
Pension accrual benefit
Point-of-service plan
   (POS)
Predetermination-of-
   benefits provision
Preferred provider
   organization (PPO)

Probationary period
Relative-value schedule
Scheduled dental
   insurance plan
Self-insured plans
Stop-loss limit
Supplemental major
   medical insurance
Traditional group
   indemnity plans
Usual, customary, and
   reasonable (UCR)
   charges
Voluntary accidental death
   and dismemberment
   insurance

## QUESTIONS FOR REVIEW

1. Describe the nature of group insurance plans and show how group insurance differs from individual insurance.

2. Describe the underwriting principles that are followed in group insurance.

3. Explain the eligibility requirements that are commonly required in group insurance plans.

4. Describe the major forms of group life insurance.

5. Identify the benefits commonly found in group basic medical expense plans.

6. Explain the two basic types of group major medical insurance.

7. What is a managed care plan? Identify the major types of managed care plans.

8. Briefly explain each of the following group provisions:
   a. preexisting conditions
   b. coordination of benefits
   c. continuation of group health insurance under the COBRA law

9. Describe the two types of group dental insurance plans.

10. Explain the characteristics of group short-term and long-term disability-income plans.

11. Explain the characteristics of cafeteria plans.

## QUESTIONS FOR DISCUSSION

1. Although individual underwriting and evidence of insurability are not usually required in group life insurance, there are several factors inherent in the group approach that result in favorable plan experience. Explain these factors.

2. Compare group term life insurance with group universal life insurance with respect to the following:
   a. Continuation of coverage after leaving this group
   b. Use of employer contributions
   c. Right to convert the coverage

## CASE APPLICATION

Nancy Olson is president of a consulting firm that has 10 employees. The only employee benefit provided by the firm is a paid two-week vacation for employees with one or more years of service. The firm's profits have substantially increased, and Nancy would like to provide some additional benefits to the employees. Nancy would like advice concerning the types of benefits to provide. Assume you are an employee benefits consultant. Based on the following considerations, answer the following questions:

a. Nancy would like to provide life insurance for the employees equal to two times salary. What type of life insurance do you recommend?

b. Several employees have expressed an interest in having some life insurance in force on their lives after retirement. Explain to Nancy how employees can have life insurance on their lives after retirement.

c. Nancy would also like to provide health insurance benefits to the employees. Identify the major types of group health insurance plans that she might consider.

d. Assume that Nancy decides to offer both a traditional group indemnity health insurance plan and a point-of-service HMO option to the employees. Explain the major differences between these two plans to Nancy.

e. Are there any other group insurance benefits that Nancy should consider? Explain your answer.

f. Nancy would like to give the employees a choice of benefit plans. Explain to Nancy how this can be accomplished.

3. Compare group short-term disability-income plans with long-term disability-income plans with respect to each of the following:

   a. Benefit period

   b. Definition of disability

   c. Consideration of other benefits

4. Compare a supplemental group major medical plan with a comprehensive major medical plan with respect to each of the following:

   a. Use of deductibles

   b. Use of coinsurance

   c. Use of a stop-loss limit

5. When group dental insurance plans are initially installed, the insurer is exposed to a high degree of adverse selection. Describe several features that are incorporated into group dental insurance plans to make this coverage feasible despite the possibility of adverse selection.

6. a. Health maintenance organizations (HMOs) can be viewed as an acceptable alternative to the traditional group indemnity plans for consumers.

   a. Describe the basic characteristics of HMOs.

   b. Explain the major characteristics of preferred provider organizations (PPOs).

   c. How does a preferred provider organization (PPO) differ from a health maintenance organization (HMO)?

   d. What are the advantages and disadvantages of managed care plans?

## SELECTED REFERENCES

Beam, Burton T., Jr., and John J. McFadden. *Employee Benefits*, 4th ed. Chicago: Dearborn Financial Publishing, 1996.

Consumers Union. "Can HMOs Help Solve the Health-Care Crisis?" *Consumer Reports*, 61, no. 10 (October 1996): 28–35.

———. "How Good Is Your Health Plan?" *Consumer Reports*, 61, no. 8 (August 1996): 28–42.

Hall, Charles P., Jr. "The Environment of Health Plans in the 1990s." In Jerry S. Rosenbloom, ed., *The Handbook of Employee Benefits: Design, Funding, and Administration.* 4th ed. Burr Ridge, Ill.: Irwin Professional Publishing, 1996, pp. 75–99.

Rosenbloom, Jerry S., ed., *The Handbook of Employee Benefits: Design, Funding, and Administration,* 4th ed. Burr Ridge, Ill.: Irwin Professional Publishing, 1996.

*Source Book of Health Insurance Data, 1996.* Washington, D.C.: Health Insurance Association of America, 1997.

## NOTES

1. Burton Beam, Jr., and John J. McFadden, *Employee Benefits*, 4th ed., revised. (Chicago: Dearborn Financial Publishing, 1996), pp. 81–87. See also Davis W. Gregg and Vane B. Lucas, eds., *Life and Health Insurance Handbook,* 3rd ed. (Homewood, Ill.: Richard D. Irwin, 1973), pp. 360–63.

2. *1996 Life Insurance Fact Book* (Washington, D.C.: American Council of Life Insurance, 1996), p. 17.

3. In a few states, the terminating employee is allowed to purchase term insurance for a limited period (such as one year), after which he or she must convert to some form of cash-value life insurance.

4. Beam and McFadden, pp. 143–49.

5. Kenneth Black, Jr., and Harold D. Skipper, Jr., *Life Insurance,* 12th ed. (Englewood Cliffs, N.J.: Prentice-Hall, 1994), p. 757.

6. Derek Liston and Martha Priddy Patterson, *Analysis of the Number of Workers Covered By Self-Insured Health Plans Under The Employee Retirement Income Security Act of 1974–1993 and 1995* (Menlo Park, CA.: Henry J. Kaiser Family Foundation, 1996), p. 6.

7. *Source Book of Health Insurance Data, 1996* (Washington, D.C.: Health Insurance Association of America, 1997), p. 33.

8. Beam and McFadden, pp. 255–59.

9. Ibid, p. 263.

10. Ibid, pp. 302–305.

11. Ibid, pp. 300–305.

# Chapter 22

# EMPLOYEE BENEFITS: RETIREMENT PLANS

*" As the population of the country matures, several strains will be placed on our already burdened retirement system. "*

*President's Commission on Pension Policy,*
Coming of Age: Toward a National
Retirement Income Policy

## Student Learning Objectives

After studying this chapter, you should be able to:

■ Explain the basic features of private retirement plans, including minimum age and service requirements, retirement ages, and vesting rules.

■ Distinguish between defined contribution and defined benefit retirement plans.

■ Identify the major types of funding instruments that can be used to fund a pension plan.

■ Describe the basic characteristics of Section 401(k) plans.

■ Explain the major features of retirement plans for the self-employed (Keogh plans).

■ Describe the basic characteristics of an Individual Retirement Account (IRA).

■ Explain the major features of Simplified Employee Pension plans (SEPs).

Americans are living longer and are spending a relatively longer period of their adult lifetime in retirement. On average, males age 65 can expect to live another 15 years, while females the same age can expect to live another 19 years. The major risk for many retired persons is insufficient income, so this risk should receive high priority in your personal risk management program. The earlier you start preparing for retirement, the better off financially you will be. For example, an individual age 26 who contributes $2000 annually into a tax-deferred retirement plan earning a total return of 10 percent annually will have $973,704 at age 65. Since Social Security retirement benefits provide only a minimum floor of income, the additional income from a tax-deferred retirement plan can mean the difference between a high standard of living and a much lower standard of living during your retirement years.

This chapter discusses the major types of private retirement plans. Topics include the fundamentals of private pensions, Section 401(k) plans, retirement plans for the self-employed (Keogh plans), individual retirement accounts (IRAs), and simplified employee pension plans (SEPs).

## FUNDAMENTALS OF PRIVATE PENSION PLANS

Millions of workers are covered by private retirement plans. These plans have an enormous social and economic impact on the nation. Substantial amounts of retirement income are paid to retired workers and their dependents, which increases their financial security during retirement. Pension plans are also an important source of capital funds in the financial markets. These funds are invested in housing developments, shopping centers, new plants, machinery and equipment, and other worthwhile economic investments.

The development and growth of private pension plans has been greatly influenced by federal legislation and the Internal Revenue Code. **The Employee Retirement Income Security Act of 1974 (ERISA)** established minimum pension standards to protect the rights of participating employees. Since that time, numerous changes in the tax code have had a significant impact on private retirement plans. The most recent change was enactment of the **Small Business Job Protection Act** in 1996, which provided for a new SIMPLE retirement plan (discussed later) for small employers. In addition, the Internal Revenue Service (IRS) has issued numerous and complex regulations concerning private pension plans. The following discussion is based on current requirements of the Internal Revenue Code.[1]

### Favorable Income Tax Treatment

Private retirement plans that meet certain IRS requirements are called **qualified plans** and receive favorable income tax treatment. The employer's contributions are tax deductible up to certain limits as an ordinary business expense; the employer's contributions are not considered taxable income to the employees; the investment earnings on plan assets accumulate on a tax-deferred basis; and the pension benefits attributable to the employer's contributions are not taxed until the employee retires or receives the funds. The tax advantages to employees are substantial (see Exhibit 22.1).

### Minimum Coverage Requirements

A qualified plan must benefit workers in general and not only **highly compensated employees.**[2] Certain **minimum coverage requirements** must be satisfied to receive favorable tax treatment. The coverage rules are complex and beyond the scope of the text to discuss in detail. However, to reduce discrimination in favor of highly compensated employees, a qualified retirement plan must meet one of the following tests:

1. **Ratio percentage test.** The plan must benefit a percentage of employees that is at least 70 percent of the highly compensated employees covered by the plan. Thus, if a plan covers 100 percent of the highly compensated employees, it must also cover at least 70 percent of the nonhighly compensated employees. Likewise, if the plan covers only 50 percent of the highly compensated employees, it must also cover at least 35 percent (50% × 70%) of the nonhighly compensated employees.

2. **Average benefits test.** Under this test, two requirements must be met: (1) the plan must benefit a reasonable classification of employees and must not discriminate in favor of highly compensated employees, and (2) the average benefit must be at least 70 percent of the average benefit provided to all highly compensated employees.

For example, Ajax Manufacturing has 1000 eligible employees, and 100 employees are highly compensated. Assume that 100 percent of the highly compensated employees (100) are covered by the plan. The ratio percentage test is satisfied if at least 70 percent of the nonhighly compensated

EXHIBIT 22.1

## The Advantage of a Tax-Deferred Retirement Plan

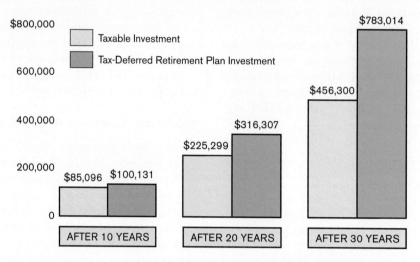

This hypothetical example assures a $10,000 annual investment, an 8% annual rate of return, and a 36% federal tax bracket. The taxable investments are invested after-tax, and their earnings are taxed every year, and the tax liability is deducted from the balance. The tax-deferred retirement plan investments are invested pre-tax, and their earnings grow tax-deferred until they are withdrawn at the end of each specified period, when they are each taxed at a rate of 36%.

*Source:* Fidelity Investments

employees, or 630 employees, are also covered by the plan.

## Minimum Age and Service Requirements

Most pension plans have a **minimum age and service requirement** before employees can participate in the plan. *Under present law, all eligible employees who have attained age 21 and have completed one year of service must be allowed to participate in the plan.* One exception is that the plan can require two years of service if there is 100 percent immediate vesting (discussed later) upon entry into the plan.

For purposes of determining eligibility, a year of service is a 12-month period during which the employee works at least 1000 hours.

## Retirement Ages

A typical pension plan has three retirement ages:

- Normal retirement age
- Early retirement age
- Late retirement age

**Normal Retirement Age**    The **normal retirement age** is the age that a worker can retire and receive a full, unreduced benefit. Age 65 is the normal retirement age in most plans. However, as a result of an amendment to the Age Discrimination Act, most employees cannot be forced to retire at some stated mandatory retirement age. To remain qualified, a private pension plan cannot impose a mandatory retirement age.

### Early Retirement Age

An **early retirement age** is the earliest age that workers can retire and receive a retirement benefit. The majority of employees currently retire before age 65. For example, a typical plan may permit a worker with 10 years of service to retire at age 55.

In a defined benefit plan (discussed later), the retirement benefit is actuarially reduced for early retirement. The actuarial reduction is necessary for three reasons: (1) the worker's full benefit will not have accrued by the early retirement date; (2) the retirement benefit is paid over a longer period of time; and (3) early retirement benefits are paid to some workers who would have died before reaching the normal retirement age.

### Late Retirement Age

The **late retirement age** is any age beyond the normal retirement age. A relatively small number of older employees continue working beyond the normal retirement age. However, under current law with certain exceptions, workers can defer retiring with no maximum age limit as long as they can do their jobs.

Pension plans are required by law to recognize earnings and/or service after the normal retirement age for purposes of determining contributions and benefits. Under a defined-contribution plan, older workers must be treated the same as younger workers, and employers must continue their contributions into the plan. Under a defined-benefit plan, benefits continue to accrue for employees working beyond the normal retirement age. However, one exception is that a defined-benefit plan can stop the accrual of benefits after a specified number of years if the plan so allows. For example, the plan may provide that after an employee has 25 years of service, there is no further accrual of benefits. This is not considered age discrimination.

## Types of Pension Plans

There are two basic types of pension plans:

- Defined-contribution plan
- Defined-benefit plan

A **defined-contribution plan** *is a plan in which the contribution rate is fixed, but the retirement benefit is variable.* For example, both the employer and employee may contribute 6 percent of pay into the plan. Although the contribution rate is known, the retirement benefit will vary depending on the worker's age, earnings, contribution rate, investment return, and normal retirement age.

Defined-contribution plans are widely used by business firms and by nonprofit organizations and state and local governments, in which pension costs must be budgeted as a percentage of payroll. However, from the employee's viewpoint, a defined-contribution plan has several disadvantages. Retirement benefits can only be estimated, and the formula may produce an inadequate benefit if the worker enters the plan at an advanced age. Another disadvantage is that employees must make decisions on how to invest the funds. Many employees are ignorant of the factors to consider in choosing a particular investment, such as a stock fund, bond fund, money market fund, and other investment options.

A defined-benefit plan is the second basic type of pension plan. A **defined-benefit plan** *is a plan in which the retirement benefit is known, but the contributions will vary depending on the amount necessary to fund the desired benefit.* For example, a worker age 50 may be entitled to a retirement benefit at the normal retirement age equal to 50 percent of the his or her highest five years of earnings. An actuary then determines the amount that must be contributed to the plan to produce the desired benefit. Defined-benefit plans favor older workers who enter the plan at the older ages since the employer must contribute a relatively larger amount for these workers than for younger workers.

## Amount of Retirement Benefits

Most private pension plans are typically designed to pay retirement benefits, which, together with Social Security benefits, will restore about 50 to 75 percent of the worker's earnings prior to retirement. The actual benefit payable is based on a benefit formula.

## Benefit Formulas

In a defined-contribution plan, a money purchase formula is typically used to determine the retirement contributions. A **money purchase formula** *is a* *percentage of the worker's pay that is paid into the plan.* For example, both the employee and employer may contribute 6 percent of salary into the plan. Each employee has an account, and the actual retirement benefit will depend on the value of the employee's account at retirement.

In a defined-benefit plan, the benefit amount can be based on **career-average earnings,** which is an average of the worker's earnings while participating in the plan, or it can be based on an average of **final pay,** which generally is an average of the worker's earnings over a three- to five-year period prior to retirement.

When a new defined-benefit pension plan is installed, some older workers may be close to retirement. In order to pay more adequate retirement benefits, defined-benefit plans may give credit for service with the firm prior to the installation of the plan. The **past-service credits** provide additional pension benefits. The actual amount paid, however, will depend on the benefit formula used to determine benefits.

In a defined-benefit plan, numerous formulas can be used to determine the retirement benefit. They include the following:[3]

1. *Flat dollar amount for all employees.* This formula is sometimes used in collective bargaining plans by which a flat dollar amount is paid to all employees regardless of their earnings or years of service. Thus, the plan may pay $300 monthly to each worker who retires.

2. *Flat percentage of annual earnings.* Under this formula, the retirement benefit is a fixed percentage of the worker's earnings, such as 25 to 50 percent. The benefit may be based on career-average earnings or on an average of final pay.

3. *Flat dollar amount for each year of service.* Under this formula, a flat dollar amount is paid for each year of credited service. For example, the plan may pay $20 monthly at the normal retirement age for each year of credited service. If the employee has 30 years of credited service, the monthly pension is $600.

   Years of service are extremely important in determining the total pension benefit. Frequent job changes and withdrawal from the labor force for extended periods can significantly reduce the size of the pension benefit. This is especially true for women who may have prolonged breaks in employment due to family considerations.

4. *Unit-credit formula.* The unit-credit formula is widely used at the present time. Under this formula, both earnings and years of service are considered. For example, the plan may pay a retirement benefit equal to 1 percent of the worker's final average pay multiplied by the number of years of service. Thus, a worker with a final average monthly salary of $2000 and 30 years of service would receive a monthly retirement benefit of $600.

## Vesting Provisions

**Vesting** *refers to the employee's right to the benefits attributable to the employer's contributions if employment terminates prior to retirement.* The employee is always entitled to a refund of his or her contributions plus any investment earnings on the account upon termination of employment. However, the right to the employer's contribution, or benefits attributable to the contributions, depends on the extent to which vesting has been attained.

A qualified plan must meet one of the following **minimum vesting standards:**

- *Cliff vesting.* Under this rule, the worker must be 100 percent vested after five years of service.
- *Graded vesting.* Under this rule, the rate of vesting must meet the following minimum standard:

| Years of service | Percentage vested |
|---|---|
| 3 | 20% |
| 4 | 40 |
| 5 | 60 |
| 6 | 80 |
| 7 | 100 |

From the employer's viewpoint, the basic purpose of vesting is to reduce labor turnover. Employees have an incentive to remain with the firm until a vested status has been attained. In a defined-benefit plan, if employees terminate their employment before full vesting is attained, the forfeitures generally are used to reduce the employer's future pension contributions. However, in a defined contribution plan, forfeitures can either be reallocated to the accounts of the remaining participants or used to reduce future employer contributions.

## Limits on Contributions and Benefits

For 1997, under a *defined-contribution plan,* the maximum annual addition that can be made to an employee's account is limited to 25 percent of compensation, or $30,000, whichever is lower. The $30,000 figure is indexed for inflation.[4]

For 1997, *under a defined-benefit plan,* the maximum annual benefit is limited to 100 percent of the worker's average compensation for the three highest consecutive years of compensation, or $125,000, whichever is lower. This latter figure is indexed for inflation.

There is also a maximum limit on the annual compensation that can be counted when determining benefits and contributions under all plans. For 1997, the maximum annual compensation that can be counted in the contribution or benefit formula is $160,000 (indexed for inflation).

Participants in defined-benefit plans are protected against the loss of pension benefits up to certain limits if the pension plan should terminate. The **Pension Benefit Guaranty Corporation (PBGC)** is a federal corporation that guarantees the payment of vested or nonforfeitable benefits up to certain limits if a private pension plan is terminated. For 1997, the maximum monthly guarantee is $2761.36.

## Early Distribution Penalty

There is a 10 percent tax penalty if funds are withdrawn before age 59½. The 10 percent tax applies to the amount included in gross income. However, the early distribution penalty does not apply to distributions that are:

- Made after age 59½
- Made after the death or total and permanent disability of the employee
- Made after attaining age 55 and separation from service

- Made as part of a series of substantially equal payments paid over the worker's life expectancy or joint life expectancy of the worker and beneficiary after separation from service
- Distributions that do not exceed deductible medical expenses under the Internal Revenue Code (medical expenses that exceed 7½ percent of adjusted gross income)
- Payments to an alternate payee as a result of a qualified domestic relations order
- Payments made in connection with certain employee stock ownership plans (ESOPs)

The pension contributions, however, cannot remain in the plan indefinitely. Plan distributions must start no later than April 1 of the calendar year following the year in which the individual attains age 70½. However, beginning in 1997, participants older than 70½ who are still working can delay receiving minimum distributions from a qualified retirement plan. Under the new tax law, the required beginning date of a participant who is still employed after age 70½ is April 1 of the calendar year that follows the calendar year in which he or she retires. *The new tax change does not apply to IRAs.*

## Funding of Pension Benefits

Qualified private pension plans use advance funding to fund the pension benefits. **Advance funding** *means the employer systematically and periodically sets aside funds prior to the employee's retirement.* This type of funding increases the security of benefits for the active employees because funds are periodically set aside prior to retirement, and the contributions and investment income receive favorable income-tax treatment.

A qualified plan must meet certain minimum funding standards. In a defined-benefit plan, the employer must make an annual contribution at least equal to the normal cost of the plan, plus an amount sufficient to amortize any unfunded liabilities over a period of years, which can range from 5 to 40 years depending on the liability and when it occurred.[5] **Normal cost** is the amount necessary to fund the pension costs attributable to the current year's operation of the plan. Liabilities under the plan may arise because of an unfunded initial past service liability,

## INSIGHT 22.1

### The Pension Eraser:
### 'Integrating' Social Security Can Cut Benefits

Mary Jane Forbush looked forward to a pension *and* Social Security when she retired.

But she didn't realize that one benefit was erasing the other. Her employer of 13 years, **J. C. Penney Co.**, subtracted her projected Social Security payments from her pension, which left her with zero pension. "I wasn't expecting much," says the Paradise, Calif., retiree, now 76. "But I didn't expect nothing."

How can someone qualify for a pension and then not receive it? The answer can be found in the little-noticed way that many companies "integrate" their pensions or profit-sharing plans with Social Security benefits.

Because employers contribute the equivalent of 6.2% of workers' pay up to a maximum of $65,400 to fund Social Security benefits (the employee also contributes 6.2% of his or her pay), many attempt to recover the cost of those benefits by reducing the benefits paid by the company.

#### Concept Spreads

Such integration formulas affect more than half of the 30 million Americans covered by pensions in the private sector. In recent years, the formulas have spread to profit-sharing, cash-balance and other employer-sponsored savings plans.

The impact of pension integration is controversial because it affects the companies' lowest-paid employees, who may suddenly see their pension benefits slashed in half. At the same time, the formulas increase the benefits of the higher-paid. "This is the Social Security crisis no one is talking about," says David

Certner, legislative counsel at the American Association of Retired Persons, in Washington.

The subject is sensitive. Although Shell Oil Co., **Kimberly-Clark Corp.** and **Travelers Group Inc.** all acknowledge using such integration formulas, none of those companies would discuss the subject. Rita Metras, director of benefits policy at **Eastman Kodak Co.**, explains that by integrating its benefits, Kodak can reverse Social Security's tilt toward the lower-paid. "Social Security replaces a much higher percentage of pay at the lower salary level, and we're trying to even out the benefit" for the higher-paid, she says.

However, Karen Ferguson, director of the Pension Rights Center, a nonprofit group in Washington, calls it unfair to lower-paid employees to consider their Social Security benefits without also considering the many benefits available to the higher-paid, including stock options, bonuses and additional executive "nonqualified" pension plans.

#### Effect on Savings Plans

The issue is also attracting more attention because of the spread beyond traditional pension plans into employer-sponsored savings plans. (It doesn't directly affect 401(k) retirement plans, but the presence of a 401(k) is often used by employers to reduce the combined Social Security and pension target amount they think a person should receive in retirement.) Integration can also affect middle-income workers, not just the lowest-paid.

Valerie Chasin was making $49,700 as a programmer at **Factory Mutual** in Norwood, Mass. When she was laid off in 1994 after 11 years, her employer

*Continued*

changes in actuarial assumptions, and experience gains and losses. If the employer fails to meet the minimum funding standard, a tax penalty is imposed.[6]

The minimum funding standard technically applies to defined contribution pension plans. However, because there is no past-service liability, the minimum funding standard is met provided the employer makes the required contribution each year based on the plan's contribution formula.[7]

## Integration with Social Security

Private pension benefits are frequently reduced because of Social Security benefits. Because employers pay one-half of the total OASDI payroll tax, they argue that OASDI retirement benefits should be considered in the calculation of pension benefits. The Internal Revenue Service has prescribed complex integration rules that must be followed when a retirement plan is integrated with OASDI.

estimated that 49-year-old Ms. Chasin would receive $1,139 a month from Social Security when she retires at age 65. So it subtracted $569 a month from her pension. She will receive $461 a month when she turns 65.

While the methods vary from company to company, here's how integration works: Some companies, such as **Mobil Corp.** and **Sears, Roebuck & Co.,** estimate what workers will receive from Social Security in retirement, and subtract some of that from their pensions.

### Retiree's Complaint

Elwood Vaughn, 69, a supervisor who was laid off after 18 years at Marion Power Shovel, in Marion, Ohio, says the company explained to him that because he would receive $603.86 a month from Social Security, the company would subtract half of that, or $301.93, from his pension, since it had paid half of his Social Security tax. "I can't believe this is legal," he complains. A spokesman for **Global Industrial Technologies Inc.,** which now owns Marion Power Shovel, says the company was using a standard formula.

Many companies use a less-obvious plan of integration called the "excess" method. Instead of subtracting Social Security benefits from pensions, employers simply add extra contributions for the higher paid.

For instance, pension plans at **General Electric Co.** and **Prudential Insurance Co. of America** and profit-sharing plans at **Merck & Co.** and **Dow Jones & Co.** (publisher of The Wall Street Journal) provide one level of retirement contribution on all salary, and an additional, "excess," contribution, typically 5.7%, for salary above $65,400.

That additional contribution can result in higher-paid employees' getting a much larger contribution as a percentage of their pay. For instance, at Penney, someone earning $20,000 and retiring at age 65 after 35 years will receive a pension equal to 28.75% of pay. An employee with the same age and service but earning $100,000 will receive 41%. (Mrs. Forbush received nothing because Penney was using an older formula and miscalculated her benefits.)

Proponents of Social Security integration say employers are only trying to be fair to the higher-paid by "evening out" the progressive nature of Social Security, which provides a higher percentage of income replacement at the lowest wage levels. For someone who works 35 years and earns $15,000, Social Security will replace about 50% of preretirement pay, compared with about 25% for someone with income close to $64,500. People don't pay in to Social Security above that ceiling, and therefore don't receive a benefit on that higher portion of their pay. As a result, someone making $100,000 gets only 16% of his or her salary replaced by Social Security, says Kodak's Ms. Metras.

But Steven Fuchs, an independent actuary in Glen Carbon, Ill., points out that the person making $100,000 isn't having FICA taxes taken out of income above $64,500. That FICA savings is money he or she can save and invest. If on top of that, the employer gives back the equivalent of the FICA tax, the employee gets a boost of roughly 12% on pay above $64,500.

SOURCE: Excerpted from Ellen E. Schultz, "The Pension Eraser: 'Integrating' Social Security Can Cut Benefits," *The Wall Street Journal,* March 12, 1997, pp. C1, C24.

Only one of them is discussed here. Under the *offset plan,* the maximum reduction in total benefits in a defined benefit retirement plan is 0.75 percent of the worker's final average compensation times the number of years of service, but not to exceed 35 years; moreover the maximum offset cannot reduce the original pension benefit by more than one half.

*Example:* Ben retires after 30 years of service with his employer. His final average compensation is $30,000. The maximum pension reduction because of Social Security is $6,750 (.0075 × $30,000 × 30). If the defined benefit formula produced a benefit of $15,000, the pension could be reduced by $6,750. Ben's pension would be $8,250.

Millions of workers are in integrated plans. The integration formulas do not affect all employees uniformly. Low-income workers are hit especially hard by the reduction in pension benefits, while upper-income workers often benefit (see Insight 22.1).

## Top-Heavy Plans

Special rules apply to top-heavy plans. A **top-heavy plan** generally is a retirement plan in which more than 60 percent of the benefits or contributions are for key employees. A plan is considered top-heavy if the present value of the cumulative accrued benefits for the key employees exceeds 60 percent of the present value of the cumulative accrued benefits under the plan for all covered employees. (Accrued benefits are measured in terms of benefits for defined-benefit plans and account balances for defined contribution plans.)

A top-heavy plan must meet certain additional requirements to retain its qualified status. These requirements include the following:

- A special rapid vesting schedule must be used for nonkey employees (100 percent vesting after three years, or 20 percent after two years and 20 percent for each year thereafter).
- Certain minimum benefits or contributions must be provided for nonkey employees.
- There is a reduced limit on aggregate benefits and contributions for key employees covered by both a defined-benefit and a defined-contribution plan.

## FUNDING AGENCY AND FUNDING INSTRUMENTS

An employer must select a funding agency when a pension plan is established. A **funding agency** *is a financial institution or individual that provides for the accumulation or administration of the funds that will be used to pay pension benefits.* If the funding agency is a commercial bank or individual trustee, the plan is called a *trust-fund plan.* If the funding agency is a life insurer, the plan is called an *insured plan.* If both funding agencies are used, the plan is called a *combination plan.*

The employer must select a funding instrument to fund the pension plan. A **funding instrument** *is a trust agreement or insurance contract that states the terms under which the funding agency will accumulate, administer, and disburse the pension funds.* The major funding instruments are as follows:[8]

- Trust-fund plan
- Deposit-administration plan
- Immediate-participation guarantee (IPG) plan
- Group deferred annuity
- Guaranteed investment contract (GIC)

## Trust-Fund Plan

About two-thirds of all pension assets are in trust fund plans.[9] Under a **trust-fund plan,** all contributions are deposited with a trustee, who invests the funds according to the trust agreement between the employer and trustee. The trustee can be a commercial bank or individual trustee. Annuities are not usually purchased when the employees retire, and the pension benefits are paid directly out of the fund. The trustee does not guarantee the adequacy of the fund, nor are there any guarantees of principal and interest rates. A consulting actuary periodically determines the adequacy of the fund.

## Deposit-Administration Plan

A **deposit-administration plan** is an insured plan. All pension contributions are deposited in an unallocated fund. When the worker retires, an immediate annuity is purchased out of the plan's assets.

A **separate account** is a variation of the deposit-administration plan. Under a separate account, the pension funds are segregated, so that the account assets are not commingled with the insurer's general assets. The pension funds can be invested in an equity account or fixed-income account.

## Immediate-Participation Guarantee Plan

An **immediate-participation guarantee plan (IPG)** is another insured plan. All pension contributions are deposited in an unallocated fund. The fund immediately reflects any unfavorable plan experience with respect to mortality, investments, and expenses. Annuities generally are not purchased when the workers retire; the pension benefits are paid directly out of the plan's assets. The insurer does not guarantee the adequacy of the fund. However, the insurer periodically evaluates the fund to determine if it is sufficient to continue paying the promised benefits to the retired workers. If the fund declines to a level that is inadequate for paying full benefits to the retired workers, annuities would then be purchased for them.

## Group Deferred Annuity

A group deferred annuity is an insured plan that has declined in importance in recent years. Under a **group deferred annuity,** a single-premium deferred annuity is purchased each year equal to the retirement benefit earned for that year. For example, under a defined-benefit pension plan, the worker may earn for the current year a monthly retirement benefit of $25 starting at age 65. A benefit equal to that amount would be purchased for that year. The benefit amount paid at retirement is the sum of the benefits payable under all deferred-annuity contracts that have been purchased on the worker's behalf.

Group deferred annuities are not widely used today because newer and more flexible pension products have been developed. Most plans have changed to other methods of funding, but older deferred annuities purchased before the change still remain in force.[10]

## Guaranteed Investment Contract

A **guaranteed investment contract (GIC)** is an arrangement in which the insurer guarantees a relatively high interest rate for a number of years on a lump sum deposit. Guaranteed investment contracts have been extremely popular with employers in recent years because of the relatively high interest rate guarantee by the insurer. In addition, the principal is guaranteed against loss. Finally, most guaranteed investment contracts make annuity options or other payment options available, but the employer is not required to use these options.

In summary, qualified retirement plans are extremely important for a comfortable retirement. Unfortunately, some workers do not participate in the employer's plan or do not make the maximum contribution available to them. The result is insufficient income during retirement. Most workers underestimate considerably the amount of money needed for a comfortable retirement. Insight 22.2 should help you determine if you are on the right track for a comfortable retirement.

## SECTION 401 (K) PLANS

Section 401(k) plans are becoming increasingly popular among employees as a tax-deferred savings plan. A **Section 401(k) plan** *is a qualified cash or deferred arrangement (CODA) that allows eligible employees the option of putting money into the plan or receiving the funds as cash.* A Section 401(k) plan can be a qualified profit-sharing plan, saving or thrift plan, or stock bonus plan. A plan can be established that involves only employer contributions, both employer and employee contributions, or only employee contributions.

In a typical plan, both the employer and employees contribute, and the employer matches part or all of the employee's contributions. Most plans allow the employees to determine how the funds are invested. Employees typically have a choice of investments, such as a common stock fund, bond fund, fixed income, and other funds. Many plans also allow the contributions to be invested in company stock. However, it is risky to invest a large proportion of the funds in the company's stock (see Insight 22.3).

## Annual Limit on Elective Deferrals

Eligible employees can voluntarily elect to have their salaries reduced if they participate in a Section 401(k) plan. For 1997, the maximum salary reduction is $9500 (indexed for inflation). The amount of salary deferred is then invested in the employer's Section 401(k) plan. The amounts deferred are not subject to the federal income tax until the funds are withdrawn. However, Social Security taxes must be paid on the contributions to the plan.

## Actual Deferral Percentage Test

To prevent discrimination in favor of highly compensated employees in a Section 401(k) plan, an **actual deferral percentage (ADP) test** must be satisfied. This means that the actual percentage of

## INSIGHT 22.2

# Retirement Honing: How Much Should You Have Saved for a Comfortable Life?

Readers ask me all kinds of intriguing questions. But no inquiry is more popular than this: Am I on track to retire in comfort?

Unfortunately, there is no quick and easy answer, and only an idiot would offer one. But that didn't deter me.

I asked T. Rowe Price Associates, the Baltimore mutual fund company, to put together the table below. It shows the amount you should have saved as a percent of your current annual salary—depending on how far you are from retirement and how aggressively you invest.

The table, for instance, indicates that aggressive investors who are 15 years from retirement should have socked away an amount equal to just over three times their pretax salary, while more conservative investors should have a tad more than five times their salary saved.

The table, I believe, will give you some sense for whether you have put away enough money for retirement so far. But before you read too much into the numbers, be aware of the table's limitations.

A fistful of assumptions underlie the numbers. Investors are assumed to save 8% of their pretax salary every year between now and retirement, after which they withdraw an annual amount equal to 75% of their preretirement income.

This 75% wouldn't all be spending money; taxes would have to be paid out of this sum. T. Rowe Price's calculations are based on investors living 25 years in retirement, at which point their savings are exhausted.

What about returns? Aggressive investors are assumed to hold a mix of 80% stocks and 20% bonds before retirement and a combination of 65% stocks and 35% bonds after retirement.

Moderate-risk investors, meanwhile, split their money between 65% stocks and 35% bonds until they quit the work force, at which point they switch to a mix of

### Enough Already?

Are you on track to retire? Figure out how much you have saved for retirement as a percent of your current annual salary, then compare this number to the appropriate figure in the table. For instance, if you are a conservative investor with 20 years to retirement, you should have amassed a retirement kitty equal to 369% of your salary.

| Investment Strategy | Years to Retirement | | | | | | | |
| --- | --- | --- | --- | --- | --- | --- | --- | --- |
| | 0 | 5 | 10 | 15 | 20 | 25 | 30 | 35 |
| Aggressive | 957% | 675% | 463% | 307% | 193% | 109% | 48% | 3% |
| Moderate | 1,046 | 773 | 558 | 393 | 268 | 172 | 98 | 42 |
| Conservative | 1,148 | 890 | 676 | 505 | 369 | 261 | 174 | 105 |

SOURCE: T. Rowe Price Associates

*Continued*

salary deferred for highly compensated employees is subject to certain limitations. In general, the eligible employees are divided into two groups: (1) highly compensated employees, and (2) other eligible employees. The percentage of salary deferred for each employee is totaled and then averaged to get an actual deferral percentage (ADP) for each group. The ADPs of both groups are then compared. The rules for calculating the ADPs are complex and beyond the scope of this text to discuss in detail. However, Exhibit 22.2 shows the permissible ADPs for highly compensated employees based on these rules. For example, if the nonhighly compensated group has an ADP of 6 percent, the ADP for the

50% stocks and 50% bonds. As for conservative investors, they maintain a portfolio of 50% stocks and 50% bonds until they retire; thereafter, they hold 35% stocks and 65% bonds.

For stock and bond performance numbers, T. Rowe Price tapped the Ibbotson Associates database to get the average returns over the past 50 years for Standard & Poor's 500-stock index and intermediate-term government bonds. T. Rowe Price further assumed that the salary earned, the amount saved each year and the annual amount withdrawn in retirement all rise with inflation, which ran at just over 4% a year during the past five decades.

Seem like reasonable assumptions? The amount shown for current savings still could prove too high or too low. Suppose your salary rises much faster than inflation and, thus, so does your desired retirement lifestyle. To compensate, you would need either to have more money than the table indicates or to salt away more than the assumed 8% savings rate.

On the other hand, if Social Security will make a significant contribution to your retirement income or if you expect a traditional company pension, you probably don't need a nest egg big enough to replace 75% of your salary. For you, the amounts shown in the table will be too high.

"Even if you don't think the assumptions apply to you, the table points up the virtues of starting to save early and investing aggressively," notes Steven Norwitz, a T. Rowe Price vice president. "If you delay saving for retirement until the last 10 or 15 years, you've really dug yourself into a hole."

T. Rowe Price's figures are based on projected returns over long periods. To give you a sense for just how iffy such forecasts can be, Minneapolis financial planner Ross Levin ran a "Monte Carlo analysis" focusing on the projected 4% inflation rate.

Let's say you are an aggressive investor who is 20 years from retirement. The table suggests you should have 193% of salary saved. But if the average annual inflation rate turns out to be only modestly higher or lower, the right figure might be as much as 258% or as little as 95%.

Because returns and inflation may not match your forecasts, "you should look at your portfolio every year," Mr. Levin advises. "You want to monitor your results to make sure you're on track to meet your goal."

What if you seem to have too little currently saved? To catch up, all you may need is a modest boost in your annual savings rate, especially if you are 20 or more years from retirement. Alternatively, you can greatly increase your retirement nest egg by delaying retirement. That has the triple benefit of increasing the time you have to save, lengthening the time over which your nest egg will grow and shortening the time spent in retirement.

You could also, of course, invest more aggressively. Indeed, it is tempting to assume that you will invest heavily in stocks, so that you can then judge yourself by the smaller sums shown in the table for aggressive investors.

"Maybe these people are investing too conservatively," Mr. Norwitz says. "But you don't want people to rush out and take more risk than they can live with."

SOURCE: Jonathan Clements, "Retirement Honing: How Much Should You Have Saved for a Comfortable Life?", *The Wall Street Journal*, January 28, 1997, p. C1.

highly compensated group is limited to 8 percent for favorable tax treatment.

## Limitations on Distributions

The tax law also places limitations on the distribution of funds under a 401(k) plan. A 10 percent tax penalty applies to any distribution of funds before age 59½ except for death or disability of the employee, payments that are part of a life or joint life annuity payout, separation from service after age 55, payments for medical expenses deductible under the Internal Revenue Code, and payments to a qualified payee under a qualified domestic relations order.

## INSIGHT 22.3

# 401(k) Nest Egg Can Be Fragile

### Concern Grows Over Heavy Investment in Company Stock

Edith Thomson found out the hard way that a 401(k) plan isn't necessarily a safe nest egg for retirement.

The 41-year employee of San Francisco's Emporium department store had a 401(k) account worth $84,000 by 1989—much of it invested in the store's parent company, Carter Hawley Hale. When the company hit financial problems, it encouraged Mrs. Thomson and others to shift money from a limited-risk account to even more Carter Hawley shares.

"That was my biggest mistake," said Mrs. Thomson, now 68.

When Carter Hawley sought bankruptcy protection in 1991, all but $8,000 of Mrs. Thomson's nest egg disappeared.

The case is by no means unique. Financial advisers and government officials warn that such a risk is possible with many 401(k)s, which are free to invest heavily in company stock or in a few cases in real estate. It is becoming a growing concern as more Americans depend on the accounts.

About 23 percent of the money invested in 401(k) plans nationwide, or roughly $150 billion, is invested in the employers' own stock, according to Access Research Inc., a Windsor, Conn., consulting firm.

Unlike traditional pension plans, 401(k) plans lack the insurance and other safeguards provided by the Employment Retirement Income Security Act, or ERISA.

"Employees should be careful what they do with their money," said Sean Hanna, of the Institute of Management & Administration, based in New York. "When you invest it in a 401(k), you shouldn't invest out of loyalty for the company. You should have a cold-hearted, green eyeshade view."

About 22 million Americans have money in 401(k) plans, which allow people to build retirement savings, tax-deferred, through paycheck deductions.

While many workers consider 401(k) plans the equivalent of a pension, they are very different from defined-benefit pensions, the traditional plans offered by large firms that provide a monthly check.

Besides insurance, defined benefit plans are covered by strict rules that prevent companies from putting more than 10 percent of their stock in the plans. No such 401(k) protection exists.

Workers at the home-decorating business Color Tile Inc. found that out too late. The company's investment of 401(k) money into its stores—perfectly legal—turned sour when it field for bankruptcy protection this year.

Among others with high own-stock concentrations in 401(k) plans: Wal-Mart Stores Inc., with 85 percent of its assets in Wal-Mart stock, and Cooper Tire & Rubber Co. with 77 percent, the Institute on Management and Administration says.

A bill sponsored by Sen. Barbara Boxer, D-Calif., would extend the 10 percent restriction to 401(k) plans. Sen. Boxer calls the lack of such rules "an unintended consequence, a quirk of history."

When Congress passed ERISA in 1974, Section 401(k) wasn't on the books. It was added four years later to the law governing profit-sharing plans—not pension plans. Profit-sharing plans allow companies to distribute some profits to workers, typically through stock.

The close relation of 401(k) and profit sharing plans makes a regulatory fix tricky, said Labor Secretary Robert Reich.

"We don't want to deter or undermine profit-sharing plans," said Reich, whose agency polices pensions. "But at the same time, we want to make sure that there's adequate diversification in 401(k) plans."

The Labor Department and other pension experts emphasize that while concentration of company stock is a concern, 401(k) plans are just one piece of a worker's retirement plan that also includes Social Security and, in some cases, a traditional pension plan as well.

Others warn that the problem could get worse as companies structure plans to channel workers into company stock.

Many companies offer to match the money that employees contribute to 401(k) plans. In 20 percent of cases, the matching contribution is done at least partly in company stock, the institute said.

Source: Excerpted from "401(k) Nest Egg Can Be Fragile: Concern Grows Over Heavy Investment in Company Stock," *Omaha World Herald*, August 16, 1996, p. 7.

## Exhibit 22.2

### Permissible Actual Deferral Percentages (ADPs) for Highly Compensated Employees

| ADP for Non-HCE | ADP for HCE |
|---|---|
| 1% | 2  % |
| 2 | 4 |
| 3 | 5 |
| 4 | 6 |
| 5 | 7 |
| 6 | 8 |
| 7 | 9 |
| 8 | 10 |
| 9 | 11.25 |
| 10 | 12.50 |
| 11 | 13.75 |
| 12 | 13 |

Source: Nicholas Kaster, et al, *1997 U.S. Master Pension Guide* (Chicago, IL.: CCH INCORPORATED, 1997), p. 727.

The plan may permit the withdrawal of funds for a financial hardship, but the 10 percent penalty tax still applies to the withdrawal (other than for disability or medical expenses as discussed earlier) if the employee is under age 59½. Thus, if a worker withdraws funds to build a house or to pay for the college education of the children, the penalty tax still applies. However, 401(k) plans typically have a **loan provision** that allows funds to be borrowed without a tax penalty (see Insight 22.4 ).

Despite the tax penalties for a premature distribution (see Exhibit 22.3), many employees are now using their 401(k) funds and other retirement funds for purposes other than retirement, such as spending the funds outright, paying off debts, or buying a home. This is particularly true for older workers who change jobs. *A 1993 U. S. Department of Labor survey showed that only 34 percent of the workers age 45–54 rolled a lump sum 401 (k) distribution into another retirement plan.*[11] Employees who take money out of their retirement plans early will receive a substantially lower amount of income during retirement. As a result, they may be exposed to serious financial insecurity during retirement.

## RETIREMENT PLANS FOR THE SELF-EMPLOYED

Sole proprietors and partners can establish qualified retirement plans and enjoy most of the favorable tax advantages now available to participants in qualified corporate pension plans. Retirement plans for the owners of unincorporated business firms are commonly called **Keogh plans** or HR-10 plans. The contributions to the plan are income-tax deductible up to certain limits, and the investment income accumulates on a tax-deferred basis. The amounts deposited and the investment earnings are not taxed until the funds are distributed.

With some exceptions, the same rules that apply to qualified corporate pension plans now apply to retirement plans for the self-employed.

### Limits on Contributions and Benefits

For 1997, if the Keogh plan is a defined-contribution plan, the maximum annual contribution is limited to 25 percent of compensation or $30,000, whichever is lower. However, for purposes of determining the amount that can be contributed, self-employment net earnings must be reduced by (1) one-half of the Social Security self-employment tax and (2) the actual contributions into the plan. This latter adjustment presents a problem because the amount of the Keogh deduction and the amount of net earnings are dependent on each other. Fortunately, the Internal Revenue Service has prepared a worksheet to help you make the correct calculation. *However, for our purposes, the maximum annual contribution into a defined contribution Keogh plan is limited to 20 percent of net earnings after subtracting one-half of the Social Security self-employment tax.* If the 20 percent figure is used, the resulting amount is exactly equal to 25 percent of compensation after the two adjustments are made.

For example, after deducting one-half of the Social Security payroll tax, Shannon has net self-employment earnings of $50,000. She can make a maximum tax-deductible contribution of $10,000 into the plan, which reduces her taxable earnings to $40,000. This amount is exactly equal to 25 percent of her net income after the contribution is made ($10,000/$40,000 = 25%).

## INSIGHT 22.4

# Borrowing From 401(k) Can Be Good Move

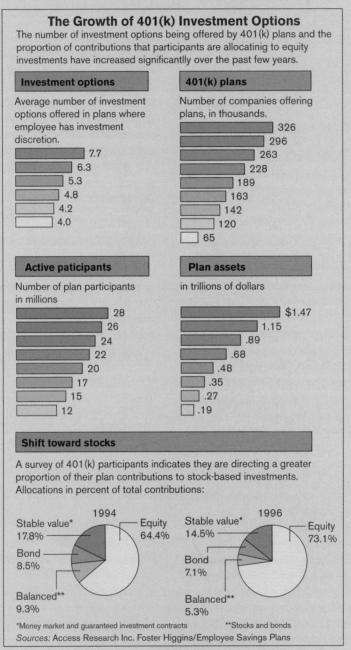

### The Growth of 401(k) Investment Options

The number of investment options being offered by 401(k) plans and the proportion of contributions that participants are allocatinig to equity investments have increased significantlly over the past few years.

**Investment options**

Average number of investment options offered in plans where employee has investment discretion.

- 7.7
- 6.3
- 5.3
- 4.8
- 4.2
- 4.0

**401(k) plans**

Number of companies offering plans, in thousands.

- 326
- 296
- 263
- 228
- 189
- 163
- 142
- 120
- 65

**Active paticipants**

Number of plan participants in millions

- 28
- 26
- 24
- 22
- 20
- 17
- 15
- 12

**Plan assets**

in trillions of dollars

- $1.47
- 1.15
- .89
- .68
- .48
- .35
- .27
- .19

**Shift toward stocks**

A survey of 401(k) participants indicates they are directing a greater proportion of their plan contributions to stock-based investments. Allocations in percent of total contributions:

**1994**
Stable value* 17.8%
Equity 64.4%
Bond 8.5%
Balanced** 9.3%

**1996**
Stable value* 14.5%
Equity 73.1%
Bond 7.1%
Balanced** 5.3%

*Money market and guaranteed investment contracts  **Stocks and bonds

*Sources:* Access Research Inc. Foster Higgins/Employee Savings Plans

KNIGHT-RIDDER TRIBUNE

*Continued*

Millions of Americans are pouring money into tax-deferred 401(k) retirement plans, but many others are scared off by the hefty 10 percent penalty on any money you take out before you are 59½.

The simple solution has been to "borrow" from your 401(k) rather than withdraw. You have to pay the money back, with interest, but the interest goes into your 401(k) account rather than to a bank or some other lender. You pay the interest to "yourself," making the loan, in effect, interest free.

It's tempting and certainly is preferable to paying the early-withdrawal penalty. But there is a risk to consider first—lost investment earnings.

When you borrow from your 401(k), you are not, as many people suppose, borrowing against 401(k) assets that remain intact and growing. In fact, you are selling some of your 401(k) assets to raise cash. As you repay the loan, the money is reinvested as if it were a new contribution. So there are no investment earnings on borrowed money until it's restored.

Suppose, for example, that at the beginning of this year you'd borrowed $5,000 from a 401(k) account that was then worth $25,000. If the $20,000 remaining in the account had been invested in a stock mutual fund that mirrored the performance of the Standard & Poor's 500 index, it would have earned about 14 percent and grown to $22,800.

If you hadn't borrowed the $5,000, your $25,000 account would have grown to $28,500. That extra $5,000 would have earned $700—earnings you gave up by taking out the loan.

This doesn't mean borrowing from a 401(k) is always a bad move. If the stock fund lost a lot of value, for instance, you'd be better off having pulled money out of it.

Still, it's important to compare the real cost of borrowing from your 401(k) with the cost, in fees and interest, that you'd pay with some other type of loan. You might, for example, get a home-equity loan that would only cost 6 or 7 percent once you account for the tax deduction on the interest payments.

If you can borrow elsewhere at an interest rate that's lower than the rate of return you expect from your 401(k), you're probably better off doing so.

But if the decision is a close call, look at a couple of other factors.

Obviously, the earnings lost on money borrowed from a 401(k) are less significant if you repay the loan quickly. If you just need a short-term loan, it might be simpler to borrow from your 401(k) than to go through the hassle of getting approval from an outside lender.

On the other hand, if you're looking for a long-term loan, the lost investment earnings would probably make it less desirable to give up your potential 401(k) earnings on the borrowed amount. Since those earnings would be tax deferred, they could grow substantially if left to compound year after year.

Next, consider how the application fees, when viewed as a percentage of the loan amount, affect your borrowing costs for a non-401(k) loan. The shorter the term and the smaller the amount borrowed, the greater their impact.

Suppose, for example, you'd be charged $250 to have your home appraised as part of a home-equity loan application. If you were borrowing only $5,000, the appraisal would equal 5 percent of the loan—on top of the interest you'd pay on the loan itself.

If you're going to pay the loan off over five or 10 years, this one-time fee doesn't have too much effect on your annual overall borrowing costs. But if you're borrowing for one year or less, the $250 fee, once added to the regular interest charges, could push your borrowing costs up to the range you'd pay on a credit card.

Finality, consider your tax bracket. The higher it is, the more you benefit by having the taxes on your 401(k) earnings deferred. People in high tax brackets, thus, pay a higher price for borrowing from their 401(k)s.

SOURCE: Jeff Brown, "Borrowing From 401(k) Can Be Good Move," *Sunday World Herald*, January 26, 1997, p. 66-R.

EXHIBIT 22.3

## The Tax Consequences of Taking a 401(k) Distribution

| | |
|---|---:|
| Amount withdrawn from 401(k) distribution. . . | $ 30,000 |
| The immediate withholding of 20% of the assets by the employer as required by law. . . | 6,000* |
| A 10% tax penalty based on the amount withdrawn. . . | − 3,000 |
| Plus, income tax based on tax bracket (36%) on the amount withdrawn. . . | − 10,800 |
| Remaining balance after income taxes and penalties. . . | = 16,200 |

*This withholding can be recovered by reporting it on Form 1040 at tax time and counts toward the penalty and taxes noted earlier.

SOURCE: *The Scudder Investor Series: Retirement Bulletin* (May 1996).

For 1997, if the Keogh plan is a *defined-benefit plan,* a self-employed individual can fund for a maximum annual benefit equal to 100 percent of average compensation for the three highest consecutive years of compensation, or $125,000, whichever is lower. This latter figure is indexed for inflation.

For example, assume that Nancy, age 50, establishes a defined-benefit plan that will provide a retirement benefit equal to 50 percent of her net income at age 65. If average net income for the three highest consecutive years is $50,000, she can fund for a maximum annual benefit of $25,000. An actuary then determines the amount that she can contribute annually into the plan to reach that goal. In this case, based on 7 percent interest and certain actuarial assumptions, Nancy could contribute $10,847 annually into the plan.

### Other Requirements

Certain other requirements must also be met, including the following:

- All employees at least age 21 and with one year of service must be included in the plan. A two-year waiting period can be required if the plan provides for full and immediate vesting upon entry.
- Certain annual reports must be filed with the Internal Revenue Service.
- A 10 percent tax penalty applies to the withdrawal of funds prior to age 59½ (except for certain distributions as noted earlier).
- Plan distributions must start no later than April 1 of the year following the calendar year

in which the self-employed person attains age 70½ (unless the worker is employed beyond age 70½).
- If the plan is top-heavy, the special top-heavy rules discussed earlier must also be met.

## INDIVIDUAL RETIREMENT ACCOUNT (IRA)

Persons with earned income can establish an Individual Retirement Account (IRA) to provide supplementary income during retirement. An **individual retirement account (IRA)** allows workers with taxable compensation to make annual contributions to a retirement plan up to certain limits and receive favorable tax treatment.

### Eligibility Requirements

There are two basic eligibility requirements for establishing an IRA plan. First, the participant must have taxable compensation during the year. Taxable compensation includes wages and salaries, bonuses, commissions, self-employment income, and taxable alimony and separate maintenance payments. Investment income does not qualify. Second, the participant must be under age 70½. No IRA contributions are allowed for the tax year in which the participant attains age 70 ½ or any later year.

### Limits on Contributions

The maximum annual tax-deductible contribution is limited to $2000 or 100 percent of taxable compensation, whichever is less. An IRA plan can also be established for a *nonworking spouse* **(spousal IRA).** If a nonworking spouse is included, the individual can contribute annually a maximum of 100 percent of compensation up to $4000 (formerly $2250). *Beginning in 1997, the annual spousal IRA limit is increased from $2250 to $4000.* The higher limit can substantially increase the amount of assets at retirement (see Exhibit 22.4). The contributions can be divided between the two accounts in any amount, provided no more than $2000 is contributed to the account of either spouse.

## Tax Deduction of IRA Contributions

The tax law creates three categories of workers with respect to the deduction of IRA contributions. Workers with taxable compensation may be allowed (1) a full deduction, (2) partial deduction, or (3) no deduction.

**Full Deduction**  A full deduction is allowed in only two general situations. *First, workers who are not active participants in an employer-sponsored retirement plan can make fully deductible IRA contributions up to the maximum annual limit of $2000 ($4000 for a spousal IRA).* The worker is considered an active participant in a retirement plan if the employer or union has a retirement plan in which money is added to the worker's account, or the worker is eligible for retirement credits. The worker is considered an active participant even if vesting has not been attained.

*Second, even if the worker is covered by an employer-sponsored retirement plan, a full deduction is allowed if the worker's annual adjusted gross income is $25,000 or less ($40,000 or less for married couples filing jointly).* If the worker's adjusted gross income exceeds the maximum allowed, he or she may still be eligible for a partial deduction.

**Partial Deduction**  Workers who are covered by a retirement plan and have an adjusted gross income between $25,000 and $35,000 annually (between $40,000 and $50,000 for married couples) can receive a partial IRA deduction. The partial deduction declines and is phased out as the worker's adjusted gross income (AGI) increases.

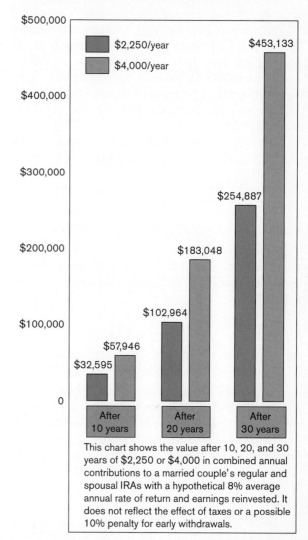

**EXHIBIT 22.4**

**Potential Benefit of the New Spousal IRA Limit**

Legend:
- $2,250/year
- $4,000/year

After 10 years: $32,595 / $57,946
After 20 years: $102,964 / $183,048
After 30 years: $254,887 / $453,133

This chart shows the value after 10, 20, and 30 years of $2,250 or $4,000 in combined annual contributions to a married couple's regular and spousal IRAs with a hypothetical 8% average annual rate of return and earnings reinvested. It does not reflect the effect of taxes or a possible 10% penalty for early withdrawals.

Source: *Fidelity Investments*

The partial deduction is based on the following formula:

$$\frac{\$10,000 - \text{excess AGI}}{\$10,000} \times \begin{array}{c} \text{Maximum IRA} \\ \text{contribution} \end{array}$$

$$= \begin{array}{c} \text{IRA deduction} \\ \text{limit} \end{array}$$

*The excess AGI is the amount of the worker's adjusted gross income in excess of the threshold amount.* The threshold amounts are $25,000 for single workers, $40,000 for married couples filing jointly, and $0 for married persons filing separate tax returns. There is a $200 floor under this formula. If the result is less than $200, the worker can contribute and deduct $200. However, if the deduction is completely phased out (is zero), no deduction is allowed. The formula can be made clearer by the following examples:

*Example 1.* Lorri has an adjusted gross income of $30,000. She can deduct a maximum of $1000.

$$\frac{\$10,000 - \$5000}{\$10,000} \times \$2000$$

$$= \$1000 \text{ IRA deduction limit}$$

*Example 2.* Nicole and Jason both work, have an adjusted gross income of $44,000, and file a joint return. The maximum IRA deduction for each person is $1200.

$$\frac{\$10,000 - \$4000}{\$10,000} \times \$2000$$

$$= \$1200 \text{ IRA deduction limit}$$

In the preceding examples, each person would also be allowed to make an additional *nondeductible contribution* (see below). Thus, Lorri would be allowed to make an additional nondeductible contribution of $1000. Nicole and Jason could each make a nondeductible contribution of $800 into their IRA plans.

**No Deduction**   Workers with an annual adjusted gross income of $35,000 or more ($50,000 or more for married couples) are allowed to make annual contributions into an IRA plan up to the maximum limits but cannot deduct the amounts contributed. However, the investment income accumulates income-tax free until withdrawn, which can be a financial advantage.

If a taxpayer has made both deductible and nondeductible IRA contributions, part of any distribution of funds is treated as a tax-free return of the nondeductible contributions (since they have already been taxed). The Internal Revenue Service has prepared a complex worksheet for determining how much of the total distribution is income-tax free. The remaining part of the distribution must be included in taxable income.

In summary, depending on whether the worker is an active participant in a retirement plan and the amount of earned income, IRA contributions can be fully deductible, partially deductible, or not deductible at all.

## Withdrawal of Funds

Amounts deposited into an IRA generally cannot be withdrawn before age 59½ without incurring a substantial tax penalty. A 10 percent penalty tax must be paid on the amount of the distribution included in gross income. However, the penalty tax does not apply to distributions that result from any of the following:

- Death of the individual
- Disability of the individual
- Substantially equal payments paid over the life expectancy of the individual or individual and beneficiary
- Portions of any distributions treated as a return of nondeductible contributions

Beginning in 1997, there are two additional situations in which IRA assets can be withdrawn prior to age 59½ without paying a tax penalty:

- Distributions used to pay for unreimbursed medical expenses in excess of 7½ percent of adjusted gross income
- Distributions used to pay medical insurance premiums for the worker, worker's spouse, and dependents if the worker has received unemployment compensation benefits for 12 consecutive weeks

The distribution must start no later than April 1 of the year following the calendar year in which the individual attains age 70½. The funds can be withdrawn as a lump sum or in installments. If taken as installment payments, a minimum annual distribution requirement must be met. The minimum annual payments are based on the life expectancy of the individual or joint life expectancy of the individual and beneficiary. If the IRA funds actually paid out are less than the amount required by law, there is a 50 percent excise tax on the excess accumulation. The purpose of this requirement is to force IRA participants to have the funds paid out over a reasonable period so that the federal government can collect taxes on the amounts that are tax-deferred.

## Taxation of Distributions

All distributions are taxed as ordinary income except for any nondeductible contributions that are received income-tax free. As we noted earlier, if there are any nontaxable contributions, part of the distribution is considered a *nontaxable return* of the nondeductible contributions. The other part is taxable and must be included in the taxpayer's income. A complex formula is used to compute the nontaxable and taxable portions of each distribution.

## Funding an IRA Plan

There are two principal types of IRA plans:

* Individual retirement account
* Individual retirement annuity

**Individual Retirement Account**  The individual can establish an individual retirement account, which must be either a trust account or custodial account. An IRA can be established with a bank, insured credit union, savings and loan institution, mutual fund, stock brokerage firm, or a person who is eligible to be a trustee or custodian. No more than $2000 can be deposited annually on behalf of any individual, and all contributions must be made in cash. No part of the funds can be used to purchase a life insurance policy.

In addition, gold and silver coins issued by the federal government can be used to fund an IRA plan. Some financial planners recommend that a small percentage of IRA funds be invested in gold and silver coins as an inflation hedge.

**Individual Retirement Annuity**  An individual retirement annuity can also be used to fund an IRA plan. The annuity must be purchased from a life insurer and meet certain requirements. The contract must be nontransferable by the owner. The

annuity must also permit flexible premiums so that if the worker's earnings change, the IRA contributions can also be changed.

**IRA Rollover Account**  If you receive a lump-sum pension distribution from your employer, the funds can be rolled over into an **IRA rollover account**. If the funds are received directly, the employer must deduct 20 percent for federal income taxes. The tax is deferred if the employer transfers the funds directly into an individual retirement account.

The assets in the IRA rollover account can be paid out as income when the worker retires. Exhibit 22.5 shows how long the payments will last given certain rates of return and withdrawal rates.

In summary, an IRA provides substantial tax advantages, and regular contributions can substantially increase the amount of retirement income. IRA contributions can accumulate to sizeable amounts, especially if the plan is started at an early age. Even high school students with part-time jobs can benefit from an IRA. Exhibit 22.6 shows the powerful effect of starting an IRA at an early age.

## Exhibit 22.5

### How Long Will Your Retirement Assets Last?

| Annual Withdrawal Rate | Average Annual Total Return | | | | | | |
|---|---|---|---|---|---|---|---|
| | 4% | 5% | 6% | 7% | 8% | 9% | 10% |
| **15%** | 7 | 8 | 8 | 9 | 9 | 10 | 11 |
| **14** | 8 | 9 | 9 | 10 | 11 | 11 | 13 |
| **13** | 9 | 9 | 10 | 11 | 12 | 13 | 15 |
| **12** | 10 | 11 | 11 | 12 | 14 | 16 | 18 |
| **11** | 11 | 12 | 13 | 14 | 16 | 19 | 25 |
| **10** | 13 | 14 | 15 | 17 | 20 | 26 | |
| **9** | 14 | 16 | 18 | 22 | 28 | | |
| **8** | 17 | 20 | 23 | 30 | | | |
| **7** | 21 | 25 | 33 | | | | |
| **6** | 28 | 36 | | | | | |

*Years Your Assets Will Last*

Source: Excerpted from "How Much Can You Take From Your Retirement Assets," *In The Vanguard* (Winter 1997).

**EXHIBIT 22.6**

## Early-Start IRAs Pay Big Dividends

| Age | Investor A | | Investor B | | Investor C | |
|---|---|---|---|---|---|---|
| | Contribution | Year-end-value | Contribution | Year-end-value | Contribution | Year-end-value |
| 8 | 0 | 0 | 0 | 0 | 0 | 0 |
| 9 | 0 | 0 | 0 | 0 | 0 | 0 |
| 10 | 0 | 0 | 0 | 0 | 0 | 0 |
| 11 | 0 | 0 | 0 | 0 | 0 | 0 |
| 12 | 0 | 0 | 0 | 0 | 0 | 0 |
| 13 | 0 | 0 | 0 | 0 | 0 | 0 |
| 14 | 0 | 0 | 0 | 0 | $2,000 | $ 2,200 |
| 15 | 0 | 0 | 0 | 0 | 2,000 | 4,620 |
| 16 | 0 | 0 | 0 | 0 | 2,000 | 7,282 |
| 17 | 0 | 0 | 0 | 0 | 2,000 | 10,210 |
| 18 | 0 | 0 | 0 | 0 | 2,000 | 13,431 |
| 19 | 0 | 0 | $2,000 | $ 2,200 | 0 | 14,774 |
| 20 | 0 | 0 | 2,000 | 4,620 | 0 | 16,252 |
| 21 | 0 | 0 | 2,000 | 7,282 | 0 | 17,877 |
| 22 | 0 | 0 | 2,000 | 10,210 | 0 | 19,665 |
| 23 | 0 | 0 | 2,000 | 13,431 | 0 | 21,631 |
| 24 | 0 | 0 | 2,000 | 16,974 | 0 | 23,794 |
| 25 | 0 | 0 | 2,000 | 20,872 | 0 | 26,174 |
| 26 | $2,000 | $2,200 | 0 | 22,959 | 0 | 28,791 |
| 27 | 2,000 | 4,620 | 0 | 25,255 | 0 | 31,670 |
| 28 | 2,000 | 7,282 | 0 | 27,780 | 0 | 34,837 |
| 29 | 2,000 | 10,210 | 0 | 30,558 | 0 | 38,321 |
| 30 | 2,000 | 13,431 | 0 | 33,614 | 0 | 42,153 |
| 31 | 2,000 | 16,974 | 0 | 36,976 | 0 | 46,368 |
| 32 | 2,000 | 20,872 | 0 | 40,673 | 0 | 51,005 |
| 33 | 2,000 | 25,159 | 0 | 44,741 | 0 | 56,106 |
| 34 | 2,000 | 29,875 | 0 | 49,215 | 0 | 61,716 |
| 35 | 2,000 | 35,062 | 0 | 54,136 | 0 | 67,888 |
| 36 | 2,000 | 40,769 | 0 | 59,550 | 0 | 74,676 |
| 37 | 2,000 | 47,045 | 0 | 65,505 | 0 | 82,144 |
| 38 | 2,000 | 53,950 | 0 | 72,055 | 0 | 90,359 |
| 39 | 2,000 | 61,545 | 0 | 79,261 | 0 | 99,394 |
| 40 | 2,000 | 69,899 | 0 | 87,187 | 0 | 109,334 |
| 41 | 2,000 | 79,089 | 0 | 95,905 | 0 | 120,267 |
| 42 | 2,000 | 89,198 | 0 | 105,496 | 0 | 132,294 |
| 43 | 2,000 | 100,318 | 0 | 116,045 | 0 | 145,523 |
| 44 | 2,000 | 112,550 | 0 | 127,650 | 0 | 160,076 |
| 45 | 2,000 | 126,005 | 0 | 140,415 | 0 | 176,083 |
| 46 | 2,000 | 140,805 | 0 | 154,456 | 0 | 193,692 |

*(Continued)*

EXHIBIT 22.6    *(Continued)*

## Early-Start IRAs Pay Big Dividends

| | Investor A | | Investor B | | Investor C | |
|---|---|---|---|---|---|---|
| Age | Contribution | Year-end-value | Contribution | Year-end-value | Contribution | Year-end-value |
| 47 | 2,000 | 157,086 | 0 | 169,902 | 0 | 213,061 |
| 48 | 2,000 | 174,995 | 0 | 186,892 | 0 | 234,367 |
| 49 | 2,000 | 194,694 | 0 | 205,581 | 0 | 257,803 |
| 50 | 2,000 | 216,364 | 0 | 226,140 | 0 | 283,358 |
| 51 | 2,000 | 240,200 | 0 | 248,754 | 0 | 311,942 |
| 52 | 2,000 | 266,420 | 0 | 273,629 | 0 | 343,136 |
| 53 | 2,000 | 295,262 | 0 | 300,992 | 0 | 377,450 |
| 54 | 2,000 | 326,988 | 0 | 331,091 | 0 | 415,195 |
| 55 | 2,000 | 361,887 | 0 | 364,200 | 0 | 456,715 |
| 56 | 2,000 | 400,276 | 0 | 400,620 | 0 | 502,386 |
| 57 | 2,000 | 442,503 | 0 | 440,682 | 0 | 552,625 |
| 58 | 2,000 | 488,953 | 0 | 484,750 | 0 | 607,887 |
| 59 | 2,000 | 540,049 | 0 | 533,225 | 0 | 668,676 |
| 60 | 2,000 | 596,254 | 0 | 586,548 | 0 | 735,543 |
| 61 | 2,000 | 658,079 | 0 | 645,203 | 0 | 809,098 |
| 62 | 2,000 | 726,087 | 0 | 709,723 | 0 | 890,007 |
| 63 | 2,000 | 800,896 | 0 | 780,695 | 0 | 979,008 |
| 64 | 2,000 | 883,815 | 0 | 858,765 | 0 | 1,076,909 |
| 65 | 2,000 | 973,704 | 0 | 944,641 | 0 | 1,184,600 |
| Less Total Invested: | | (80,000) | | (14,000) | | (10,000) |
| Equals Net Earnings: | | 893,704 | | 930,641 | | 1,174,600 |
| Money Grew: | | 11-fold | | 66-fold | | 117-fold |

NOTE: Interest assumption is 10 percent.

SOURCE: Excerpted from *Mutual Funds Magazine* (April 1995), p. 42.

## SIMPLIFIED EMPLOYEE PENSION (SEP)

A **simplified employee pension (SEP)** is a retirement plan in which the employer contributes to an individual retirement account (IRA) established for each eligible employee; however, the annual contribution limits are substantially higher. SEP plans are popular with smaller employers because the amount of required paperwork is minimal.

One type of plan is called a **SEP-IRA** in which the employer contributes to an individual retirement account owned by each employee. The SEP-IRA must cover all qualifying employees who are at least age 21 and have worked for the employer in at least three of the immediately preceding five years and have received at least $400 from the employer in compensation during the tax year.

*For 1997, the maximum annual tax-deductible employer contribution to a SEP-IRA is limited to 15 percent of the employee's compensation, or $24,000, whichever is less.* There is full and immediate vesting of all employer contributions under the plan.

Another type of SEP is a salary reduction plan (also called a SARSEP). However, as a result of federal legislation enacted in 1996, new SARSEP plans cannot be established. Existing SARSEP plans established before 1997 can still continue to receive plan contributions, but new plans cannot be created. Instead, small employers have the option of establishing a new simplified pension plan known as a SIMPLE plan.

## SIMPLE RETIREMENT P.LANS

Beginning in 1997, smaller employers are eligible to establish a Savings Incentive Match Plan for Employees, or SIMPLE for short. The **SIMPLE retirement plan** is limited to employers who employ 100 or fewer eligible employees and do not maintain another qualified plan. Under a SIMPLE plan, employers are exempt from most nondiscrimination and administrative rules that apply to qualified plans. By simplifying the pension rules, Congress believes that smaller employers will be encouraged to establish pension plans for their employees.

A SIMPLE plan can be structured either as an individual retirement account (IRA) or as a 401 (k) plan. Only the IRA arrangement is discussed here.

---

EXHIBIT 22.7

**SIMPLE Retirement Plan Contribution Methods**

**Comparing Employer Contribution Methods**

**To illustrate the differences between these two contribution methods, let's look at hypothetical funding requirements for an employee making $30,000 a year.**

| | If the employer chooses the 3% matching contribution | If the employer chooses the 2% non-elective contribution |
|---|---|---|
| *Example A*  *The employee contributes 5% of salary ($30,000) or $1,500.* | | |
| | Employer matches employee's contribution on a dollar-for-dollar basis, up to 3% of the employee's compensation **(3% × $30,000 = $900)**. Of course, in any two years in a five-year period, the employer has the flexibility to reduce his match to 1% of the employee's compensation **(1% × $30,000 = $300)**. | Employer contributes 2% of the employee's compensation **(2% × $30,000 = $600)**. |
| *Example B*  *The employee contributes 2.5% of salary ($30,000) or $750.* | | |
| | Employer matches the employee's contribution on a dollar-for-dollar basis, up to 3% of his compensation. Since the employee only chose to contribute 2.5% of his compensation which is $750, the employer would only have to match **$750**. In any two years in a five-year period, the employer could reduce his match to **1% or $300**. | Employer contributes 2% of the employee's compensation **(2% × $30,000 = $600)**. |
| *Example C*  *The employee decides not to contribute anything.* | | |
| | The employer is not required to contribute anything because there's no salary reduction contribution for the employer to match. | The employer is required to contribute 2% of the employee's compensation **(2% × $30,000 = $600)**. |

SOURCE: *Fidelity Investments.*

Under a SIMPLE plan, eligible employees can elect to contribute a percentage of salary up to $6,000 annually. *The employer has the option of either (1) matching the employee's contributions on a dollar-for-dollar basis up to 3 percent of salary, or (2) making a nonelective contribution of 2 percent of salary for all eligible employees.* If employers are strapped for cash during lean years, they can reduce the matching contribution to 1 percent of salary provided the employees are notified, and the employer has made a 3 percent matching contribution for three out of the last five years. The $6,000 annual contribution is indexed for inflation in increments of $500. Exhibit 22.7 illustrates the difference between the two contribution methods.

All employees who have received at least $5,000 from the employer during any two previous years and are reasonably expected to receive at least $5,000 in compensation during the current year must be allowed to participate in a SIMPLE plan. Self-employed individuals can also participate. All contributions go into an IRA account and are fully and immediately vested. Withdrawal of funds by SIMPLE participants under age 59½ are subject to a 10 percent tax penalty; however, withdrawals during the first two years of participation are subject to a stiff 25 percent tax penalty.

## SUMMARY

- Under the tax law, qualified pension plans must meet certain *minimum coverage requirements,* which are designed to reduce discrimination in favor of highly compensated employees.
- To meet the minimum coverage requirement, a retirement plan must satisfy one of the following tests:

    Ratio percentage test
    Average benefits test

- All employees who are at least age 21 and have one year of service must be allowed to participate in a qualified retirement plan.

- A retirement plan has a normal retirement age, an early retirement age, and a late retirement age. Most employees cannot be forced to retire at some mandatory retirement age. Benefits generally continue to accrue for employees who work beyond the normal retirement age.

- There are two basic types of pension plans.

    Under a *defined-contribution plan,* the contribution rate is fixed, but the retirement benefit is variable.

    Under a *defined-benefit plan,* the retirement benefit is known in advance, but the contributions needed to fund the benefit will vary.

- A *money purchase* benefit formula is commonly used in a defined-contribution plan.

- The benefits in a defined-benefit plan are typically based on the following benefit formulas:

    Flat dollar amount for all employees
    Flat percentage of annual earnings
    Flat dollar amount for each year of service
    Unit-benefit formula

- A qualified private pension plan must meet one of the following minimum vesting standards:

    Cliff vesting
    Graded vesting

- For 1997, under a defined-contribution plan, the maximum annual addition that can be made to an employee's account is limited to 25 percent of compensation, or $30,000, whichever is lower.

- For 1997, *under a defined-benefit plan,* the maximum annual benefit is limited to 100 percent of the worker's average compensation for the three highest consecutive years of compensation, or $125,000, whichever is lower.

- The major types of funding instruments to fund a pension plan are as follows:

    Trust-fund plan
    Deposit-administration plan
    Immediate-participation guarantee (IPG) plan
    Guaranteed investment contract
    Group deferred annuity

- A *Section 401(k) plan* is a qualified cash or deferred arrangement (CODA) that allows eligible employees the option of putting money into the plan or receiving the funds as cash. The employee typically agrees to a salary reduction, which reduces the employee's taxable income. For 1997, the maximum salary reduction is limited to $9500 (indexed for inflation). The contributions deposited in the plan accumulate income-tax free until the funds are withdrawn.

- A self-employed individual can establish a *Keogh plan* for the self-employed (HR-10 plan) and receive favorable federal income-tax treatment. The contributions to the plan are income-tax deductible, and the investment income accumulates on a tax-deferred basis. The maximum annual contribution to a defined contribution Keogh plan is limited to 20 percent of net income (after subtracting one-half of the Social Security self-employment tax) or $30,000, whichever is lower.

- The maximum annual contribution to an *individual retirement account (IRA)* is the lower of $2000 or 100 percent of compensation. The maximum is increased to $4000 for a spousal IRA.

- The full IRA deduction is available only for persons who are not active participants in an employer-sponsored retirement plan, or whose adjusted gross income is $25,000 or less ($40,000 or less for married couples filing jointly).

- A partial IRA deduction may be allowed depending on the amount of annual earnings.

- A *simplified employee pension (SEP)* is a retirement plan in which the employer contributes to an individual retirement account (IRA) established for each eligible employee. For 1997, the maximum annual tax-deductible employer contribution to a SEP-IRA is limited to 15 percent of the employee's compensation, or $24,000, whichever is less. There is full and immediate vesting of all employer contributions under the plan.

- Under a *SIMPLE plan,* eligible employees can elect to contribute a percentage of salary up to $6,000 annually. The employer has the option of either matching the employee's contributions on a dollar-for-dollar basis up to 3 percent of salary, or making a nonelective contribution of 2 percent of salary for all eligible employees.

## KEY CONCEPTS AND TERMS

Actual deferral percentage (ADP)
Advance funding
Average benefits test
Career-average earnings
Defined-benefit plan
Defined-contribution plan
Deposit-administration plan
Early distribution penalty
Early retirement age
Employee Retirement Income Security Act of 1974 (ERISA)
Final pay
Funding agency
Funding instrument
Group deferred annuity
Guaranteed investment contract (GIC)
Highly compensated employees
Immediate-participation guarantee plan (IPG)
Individual Retirement Account (IRA)
Initial past-service liability
Keogh plans for the self-employed (HR-10 plans)
Late retirement age
Minimum coverage requirements
Minimum participation requirements
Minimum vesting standards
Money purchase formula
Normal cost
Normal retirement age
Past-service credits
Pension Benefit Guaranty Corporation (PBGC)
Qualified plan
Ratio percentage test
Salary-reduction SEP plan
Section 401(k) plan
Separate account
SIMPLE retirement plan
Simplified Employee Pension (SEP)
Spousal IRA
Top-heavy plan
Trust-fund plans
Vesting

## QUESTIONS FOR REVIEW

1. Describe the favorable federal income-tax advantages to the employer and employees from a qualified corporate pension plan.

2. Explain the minimum coverage requirements that an employer must meet to have a qualified private pension plan.

3. Explain the three retirement ages normally found in private pension plans.

4. What is a defined-contribution plan? What is a defined-benefit plan?

5. Explain the advantages of advance funding of pension benefits.

6. Briefly identify the major funding instruments that can be used to fund a pension plan.

7. Explain the basic features of a retirement plan for the self-employed (HR-10 plan).

8. Describe the basic characteristics of the Individual Retirement Account (IRA).

9. Explain the major characteristics of the new SIMPLE retirement plan.

10. Explain the basic characteristics of a Section 401(k) plan.

## QUESTIONS FOR DISCUSSION

1. Qualified corporate private pension plans must meet certain requirements to receive favorable federal income tax treatment. Explain briefly each of the following:
   a. Minimum age and service requirements
   b. Minimum vesting standards
   c. Limitations on contributions and benefits
   d. Limitations on the withdrawal of pension funds

2. a. What is a funding agency?
   b. Briefly describe the basic characteristics of each of the following funding instruments:
      (1) Trust-fund plan
      (2) Deposit-administration plan
      (3) Immediate-participation guarantee plan (IPG)
   c. What is a guaranteed investment contract (GIC)?

3. Self-employed persons can establish a qualified retirement plan (Keogh plan) and receive favorable income-tax treatment. Explain briefly each of the following:
   a. Limitations on contributions and benefits
   b. Employees who must be included in the plan
   c. Income tax advantages of a qualified Keogh plan

4. a. Explain the basic characteristics of a Simplified Employee Pension (SEP) plan.
   b. Briefly describe the basic characteristics of a Section 401(k) plan.
   c. Explain the purpose of the actual deferral percentage (ADP) rules in a Section 401(k) plan.
   d. When can Section 401(k) funds be withdrawn? Explain your answer.

## SELECTED REFERENCES

Allen, Everett T. Jr., Joseph J. Melone, Jerry S. Rosenbloom, and Jack VanDerhei. *PENSION PLANNING: Pension, Profit Sharing, and Other Deferred Compensation Plans*, 8th ed. Burr Ridge, Ill.: McGraw-Hill Companies, 1997.

Beam, Burton T., Jr., and John J. McFadden. *Employee Benefits*, 4th ed. Chicago, Ill.: Dearborn Financial Publishing, 1996.

Commerce Clearing House. *1996 Tax Legislation: Law and Explanation* Chicago, Ill.: CCH INCORPORATED, 1997.

Kaster, Nicholas, et al. *1997 U.S. Master Pension Guide.* Chicago, IL.: CCH INCORPORATED, 1997.

McGill, Dan M., et al. *Fundamentals of Private Pensions*, 7th ed. Philadelphia, PA.: University of Pennsylvania Press, 1996.

Rosenbloom, Jerry S., ed., *The Handbook of Employee Benefits, Design, Funding, Administration*. Burr Ridge, Ill.: Irwin Professional Publishing, 1996.

## NOTES

1. This chapter is based on Nicholas Kaster et al, *1997 U.S. Master Pension Guide* (Chicago, Ill.: CCH INCORPORATED, 1997); *1996 Tax Legislation: Law and Explanation* (Chicago, Ill.: CCH INCORPORATED, 1997); Burton T. Beam, Jr., and John J. McFadden, *Employee Benefits*, 4th ed.(Chicago: Dearborn Financial Publishing, 1996); Everett T. Allen, Jr., Joseph J. Melone, Jerry S. Rosenbloom, and Jack L. VanDerhei, *Pension Planning*, 7th ed. (Homewood, Ill.: Richard D. Irwin, 1992); and Jerry S. Rosenbloom and G. Victor

### CASE APPLICATION

Arthur, age 25, recently accepted a job in marketing research with a major corporation, at an annual salary of $24,000. He would like to set up a savings plan and has heard that an Individual Retirement Account (IRA) may be a good way to save money. Assume that you are a financial planner and that Arthur comes to you for advice. Answer each the following questions based on the following situations. Treat each situation separately.

a. Is Arthur eligible to set up an IRA ? Explain your answer.

b. Assume that Arthur receives a salary increase and now earns $26,000 annually. What is the maximum annual tax-deductible contribution he can make to an IRA plan?

c. Arthur believes that an IRA would be a good way to save money for a down payment on a house because the investment income receives favorable tax treatment. If he needs the funds in five years, do you recommend that he set up an IRA? Explain your answer.

d. Arthur would like to invest the IRA contributions in fixed-income investments because he is risk-adverse. How would you advise him with respect to the investment of IRA contributions?

e. Arthur would like to retire before age 59 ½ but is told he will have to pay a 10 percent tax penalty on the amount withdrawn and included in gross income. Can you suggest one way that he might receive the IRA funds as retirement income before age 59 ½ without a tax penalty?

Hallman, *Employee Benefit Planning*, 3rd ed. (Englewood Cliffs, N. J.: Prentice-Hall, 1991). Current IRS tax documents for taxpayers were also extensively used.

2. For 1997, highly compensated employees are employees who (1) owned 5 percent of the company at

any time during the year or preceding year, or (2) had compensation from the employer in excess of $80,000 (indexed for inflation).

3. Rosenbloom and Hallman, pp. 250–52.

4. An inflation increase that is not a multiple of $5000 is rounded down to the next lowest multiple of $5000. For 1997, the maximum limit is $30,000.

5. Vincent Amoroso, "Costing and Funding Retirement Benefits," in Jerry S. Rosenbloom, ed., *The Handbook of Employee Benefits, Design, Funding, Administration* (Burr Ridge, Ill.: Irwin Professional Publishing, 1996), p. 987.

6. There is an initial tax of 5 percent on the accumulated funding deficiency, with an additional 100 percent tax if not corrected within 90 days after notice from the IRS.

7. Beam and McFadden, p. 520.

8. Amoroso, pp. 959–66.

9. Amoroso, p. 959.

10. Amoroso, p. 964.

11. *The Scudder Investor Series Retirement Bulletin* (May 1996).

# Chapter 23

# SOCIAL INSURANCE

> *"Social security programs have been designed to aid people in their quest for economic security.""*
>
> Robert J. Myers, Social Security, 4th ed.

## Student Learning Objectives

After studying this chapter, you should be able to:

■ Explain the reasons for social insurance programs.

■ Describe the basic characteristics of social insurance.

■ Explain the major provisions of the Old-Age, Survivors, Disability, and Health Insurance (OASDHI) program.

■ Describe the basic objectives and important provisions of state unemployment insurance programs.

■ Explain the basic objectives and major provisions of workers compensation insurance.

Social insurance programs are compulsory government insurance programs with certain characteristics that distinguish them from private insurance and other government insurance programs. Social insurance programs are extremely important in a personal risk management program. They provide a safety net against financial insecurity that can result from premature death, unemployment, poor health, job-related disabilities, and old age. Social insurance programs are especially valuable to individuals and families who have limited incomes. For example, Stephanie is a single parent, age 30, who became totally and permanently disabled in an auto accident in 1997. She is the sole support of her son, age 3. Assume she is eligible for Social Security disability benefits. If her annual earnings are $15,000 in 1997, she and her son would receive monthly disability benefits of approximately $952 ($11,424 annually),[1] which would enable her to maintain at least a minimum standard of living.

This chapter discusses the major social insurance programs in the United States. Topics discussed include the basic characteristics of social insurance programs, the Old-Age, Survivors, Disability, and Health Insurance (OASDHI) program, and state unemployment insurance and workers compensation programs.

# SOCIAL INSURANCE

## Reasons for Social Insurance

Although the United States has a highly developed system of private insurance, social insurance programs are necessary for three reasons. *First, social insurance programs are enacted in order to solve complex social problems.* A social problem affects most or all of society and is so serious that direct government intervention is necessary. For example, the Social Security program came into existence because of the Great Depression of the 1930s, when massive unemployment required a direct government attack on economic insecurity.

*Social insurance programs are also necessary because certain risks are difficult to insure privately.* For example, unemployment is difficult to insure privately because it does not completely meet the requirements of an insurable risk. However, the risk of unemployment can be insured by state unemployment insurance programs.

*Finally, social insurance programs provide a base of economic security to the population.* Social insurance programs provide a layer of financial protection to most persons against the long-term financial consequences of premature death, old age, occupational and nonoccupational disability, and unemployment.

## Basic Characteristics of Social Insurance

Social insurance programs in the United States have certain characteristics that distinguish them from other government insurance programs:[2]

- Compulsory programs
- Floor of income
- Emphasis on social adequacy rather than individual equity
- Benefits loosely related to earnings
- Benefits prescribed by law
- No means test
- Full funding unnecessary
- Financially self-supporting

**Compulsory Programs** With few exceptions, social insurance programs are compulsory. A compulsory program has two major advantages. First, the goal of providing a floor of income to the population can be achieved more easily. Second, adverse selection is reduced, since both healthy and unhealthy lives are covered.

**Floor of Income** Social insurance programs are generally designed to provide only a floor of income with respect to the risks that are covered. Most persons are expected to supplement social insurance benefits with their own personal program of savings, investments, and private insurance.

The concept of a floor of income is difficult to define precisely. One extreme view is that the floor of income should be so low as to be virtually nonexistent. Another extreme view is that the social insurance benefit by itself should be high enough to provide a comfortable standard of living, so that private insurance benefits would be unnecessary. A more realistic view is that social insurance benefits, when combined with other income and financial assets, should be sufficient for most persons to maintain a reasonable standard of living. Any group whose basic needs are still unmet would be provided for by supplemental public assistance benefits.

**Social Adequacy Rather Than Individual Equity** Social insurance programs pay benefits based largely on social adequacy rather than on individual equity. **Social adequacy** *means that the benefits paid should provide a certain standard of living to all contributors. This means that the benefits paid are heavily weighted in favor of certain groups, such as low-income persons, large families, and the presently retired aged.* In technical terms, the actuarial value of the benefits received by these groups exceeds the actuarial value of their contributions. In contrast, the individual equity principle is followed in private insurance. **Individual equity** *means that contributors receive benefits directly related to their contributions; the actuarial value of the benefits is closely related to the actuarial value of the contributions.*

The basic purpose of the social adequacy principle is to provide a floor of income to all covered persons. If low-income persons received social insurance benefits actuarially equal to the value of their tax contributions (individual equity principle), the benefits paid would be so low that the basic objective of providing a floor of income to everyone would not be achieved.

**Benefits Loosely Related to Earnings**
Social insurance benefits are related to the worker's earnings. The higher the worker's covered earnings, the greater will be the benefits. The relationship between higher earnings and higher benefits is loose and disproportionate, but it does exist. Thus, some consideration is given to individual equity.

**Benefits Prescribed by Law** Social insurance programs are prescribed by law. The benefits or benefit formulas, as well as the eligibility requirements, are established by law. In addition, the administration or supervision of the program is performed by government.

**No Means Test** Social insurance benefits are paid as a matter of right without any demonstration of need. A formal means test is not required. A **means test** is used in public assistance—welfare applicants must show that their income and financial assets are below certain levels. By contrast, applicants for social insurance benefits have a statutory right to the benefits if they fulfill certain eligibility requirements.

**Full Funding Unnecessary** It is unnecessary for social insurance programs to be fully funded. For example, a **fully funded program** under Social Security means that the accumulated assets plus the present value of future contributions with respect to persons now age 15 or over will be sufficient to discharge all liabilities for benefits payable over the next 75 years. The OASDI trust-fund balance totaled $550 billion on September 30, 1996. To be fully funded, a trust-fund balance of $9.4 trillion would have been required.[3]

A fully funded Social Security program is unnecessary for several reasons. First, because the program will operate indefinitely and not terminate in the predictable future, full funding is unnecessary. Second, because the Social Security program is compulsory, new workers will always enter the program and pay taxes to support it. Third, the federal government can use its taxing and borrowing powers to raise additional revenues if the program has financial problems. Finally, from an economic viewpoint, full funding would require substantially higher Social Security taxes, which would be deflationary and cause substantial unemployment. In contrast,

private pension plans must emphasize full funding, since private pension plans can terminate.

**Financially Self-supporting** Social insurance programs in the United States are designed to be financially self-supporting. This means the programs should be almost completely financed from the earmarked contributions of covered employees, employers, and the self-employed, and interest on the trust-fund investments.

## OLD-AGE, SURVIVORS, DISABILITY, AND HEALTH INSURANCE (OASDHI)

The Old-Age, Survivors, Disability, and Health Insurance (OASDHI) program, commonly known as Social Security, is the most important social insurance program in the United States. Social Security was enacted into law as a result of the Social Security Act of 1935. More than nine out of ten workers are working in occupations covered by Social Security, and about one in six persons receives a monthly cash benefit.[4]

### Covered Occupations

The following groups are covered under the Social Security program:

1. *Employees in private firms.* Virtually all private sector employees are covered under the program at the present time.

2. *Federal civilian employees.* Federal civilian employees hired after 1983 are covered on a compulsory basis. However, federal civilian employees hired before 1984 are covered only for Hospital Insurance under Medicare but not OASDI.

3. *State and local government employees.* State and local government employees can be covered by a voluntary agreement between the state and the federal government. About 80 percent are now covered. However, state and local government employees hired after March 1986 are covered for Hospital Insurance under the Medicare program and must pay the Hospital Insurance tax.

After July 1, 1991, all state and local government employees who are not participating in a public retirement system are covered on a compulsory basis. However, students employed in public schools, colleges and, universities can be excluded.

4. *Employees of nonprofit organizations.* All employees of nonprofit charitable, educational, and religious organizations are covered if they are paid at least $100 during the year.

5. *Self-employment.* Self-employed persons are covered if their net annual earnings are $400 or more.

6. *Other groups.* Ministers are covered on a self-employment basis unless they elect out because of conscience or religious principles. U.S. military personnel are covered on a compulsory basis. Finally, railroad workers subject to the Railroad Retirement Act are not required to pay OASDI taxes directly. However, because of certain coordinating provisions, railroad employees are, in reality, covered compulsorily for OASDI and Hospital Insurance (HI).

## Determination of Insured Status

Before you or your family can receive benefits, you must have credit for a certain amount of work in covered employment. For 1997, you receive one **credit** (also called a **quarter of coverage**) for each $670 of covered earnings. A maximum of four credits can be earned each year. The amount of covered earnings required to earn one credit will automatically increase each year as average wages in the national economy rise.

To become eligible for the various benefits, you must attain an insured status. There are three types of insured status: (1) fully insured, (2) currently insured, and (3) disability-insured. Retirement benefits require a fully insured status; survivor benefits require either a fully insured or currently insured status; however, certain survivor benefits require a fully insured status. Disability benefits require a disability-insured status.

**Fully Insured**    To be eligible for retirement benefits, you must be fully insured. You are **fully insured** for retirement benefits if you have 40

credits. However, for people born before 1929, fewer credits are required as shown below:

| Year of birth | Credits needed |
|---|---|
| 1929 or later | 40 |
| 1928 | 39 |
| 1927 | 38 |
| 1926 | 37 |
| 1925 | 36 |
| 1924 | 35 |

Persons born on January 1 are considered to have been born in the previous year.

**Currently Insured**    You are **currently insured** if you have earned at least six credits during the last 13 calendar quarters ending with the quarter of death, disability, or entitlement to retirement benefits.

**Disability Insured**    The number of credits required to be **disability insured** depends on your age when you become disabled. If you are *age 31 or older*, you must have earned a certain number of credits as shown by the following:

| Disabled at age | Credits needed |
|---|---|
| 31 through 42 | 20 |
| 43 | 21 |
| 44 | 22 |
| 45 | 23 |
| 46 | 24 |
| 47 | 25 |
| 48 | 26 |
| 49 | 27 |
| 50 | 28 |
| 51 | 29 |
| 52 | 30 |
| 53 | 31 |
| 54 | 32 |
| 55 | 33 |
| 56 | 34 |
| 57 | 35 |
| 58 | 36 |
| 59 | 37 |
| 60 | 38 |
| 61 | 39 |
| 62 or older | 40 |

In addition, at least 20 of the credits must be earned during the past 10 years immediately before you became disabled.

Younger workers under age 31 can acquire a disability-insured status with fewer credits. For *ages 24 through 30,* you must have worked half the time between age 21 and the time you become disabled. For example, a worker disabled at age 27 needs credit for three years of work out of the past six years.

If you become *disabled before age 24,* you must have earned six credits during the three-year period ending when your disability begins. Finally, blind persons are required only to have a fully insured status. They are not required to meet the recent-work test requirement that applies to other disability applicants.

## OASDHI BENEFITS

It is customary to refer to the Social Security program as OASDI when only the monthly cash benefits are considered. When Medicare is also included, the program is called OASDHI. The OASDHI program has four principal benefits:

- Retirement benefits
- Survivor benefits
- Disability benefits
- Medicare benefits

## Retirement Benefits

Social Security retirement benefits are an important source of income to most retired workers. Without these benefits, poverty and economic insecurity among the aged would be substantially increased.

**Full Retirement Age**   The **full retirement age** (also called the normal retirement age) for full benefits is currently age 65. However, the full retirement age will gradually increase in the future to age 67 to improve the financial solvency of the OASDI program and allow for the increase in life expectancy.

Exhibit 23.1 shows the increase in the full retirement age. For persons attaining age 62 in 2000, the normal retirement age will be increased to age 65

### Exhibit 23.1
**Future Increases in the OASDI Normal Retirement Age**

| *Year of birth* | *Year of attainment of age 62* | *Normal retirement age* |
| --- | --- | --- |
| 1937 and before | 1999 and before | 65 |
| 1938 | 2000 | 65, 2 mo. |
| 1939 | 2001 | 65, 4 mo. |
| 1940 | 2002 | 65, 6 mo. |
| 1941 | 2003 | 65, 8 mo. |
| 1942 | 2004 | 65, 10 mo. |
| 1943–54 | 2005–16 | 66 |
| 1955 | 2017 | 66, 2 mo. |
| 1956 | 2018 | 66, 4 mo. |
| 1957 | 2019 | 66, 6 mo. |
| 1958 | 2020 | 66, 8 mo. |
| 1959 | 2021 | 66, 10 mo. |
| 1960 and later | 2022 and later | 67 |

## INSIGHT 23.1

## Delaying Social Security Benefits May Not Be as Smart as You Think

If you plan to retire early, you've no doubt heard that it's always best to delay taking Social Security.

That's the conventional wisdom. It can also be terrible advice.

Many retirees hold out for full Social Security benefits starting at age 65, rather than settle for 80% of benefits beginning at age 62. For some, that's the right choice. But for many, it's a big mistake.

What's the best decision for you? Let's look at the trade-off. If you retire at age 62 but don't take Social Security until age 65, you'll have to use a big chunk of savings to finance your first three years of retirement. The reward is higher benefits starting at age 65. But it takes a long time for those higher benefits to compensate for the savings used up during those initial retirement years.

For proof, consider some numbers crunched by Harold Evensky, an investment adviser in Coral Gables, Fla. Mr. Evensky starts by assuming that inflation is running at 3% and that your savings earn an 8% annual return, which should be possible with a balanced portfolio that's split between stocks and bonds.

Based on those two assumptions, Mr. Evensky figures it's worth delaying Social Security until age 65, rather than starting at 62, only if you live to at least age

84. If you die before then, the government wins at the expense of your heirs, who will inherit less than if you had taken Social Security early.

What are the chances that you will live to age 84? About half of 62-year-olds will manage that feat, Mr. Evensky says, with the odds stacked in favor of women, because they tend to live longer. Thus, despite the widespread belief that you are always better off taking Social Security at age 65 rather 62, in truth it's pretty much a toss-up.

So how do you decide when to take Social Security? Ask yourself five questions.

- **How will you pay for your initial retirement years?** If you can fund your early retirement years without tapping your retirement accounts, it may be worth delaying Social Security, Mr. Evensky says.

  But he thinks delaying benefits would be a mistake if you have to start yanking big wads of money out of retirement accounts, and thus give up years of tax-deferred growth.

  Pulling money out of retirement accounts, rather than taking Social Security, will also mean a bigger tax bill. Your Social Security benefits may be partly taxable. But paying tax on 50% or 85% of

*Continued*

and two months. In each succeeding year, the full retirement age will be increased by two additional months until it reaches age 66 for persons attaining age 62 in 2005. The full retirement age will then be maintained at age 66 through 2016. Beginning in 2017, for persons attaining age 62, the full retirement age will again be increased two months each year until it reaches age 67 for persons attaining age 62 in 2022 and later.

**Early Retirement Age**   Workers and their spouses can retire as early as age 62 with actuarially reduced benefits. The benefit payable at age 65 is

reduced 5/9 of 1 percent per month for each of the first 36 months that the person is below the normal retirement age at the time of retirement, and by 5/12 of 1 percent for additional months as the retirement age increases. Thus, at present, when the full retirement age is 65, a worker retiring at age 62 has a 20 percent reduction in benefits.

The actuarial reduction in benefits for early retirement at age 62 will gradually increase to 30 percent in the future when the new higher full retirement age provisions become fully effective.

The decision to delay receiving benefits until the full retirement age or to take them early depends

your benefits is better than paying tax on 100% of your retirement-account withdrawals.

- **What sort of investor are you?** If your idea of a good long-term investment is a five-year certificate of deposit, you might as well put off Social Security and run down your savings, because the benefits boost you'll get by delaying will probably be worth more than the investment gains you'll earn with your savings.

  Conversely, if you're a savvy investor who is willing to hold a hefty amount of stocks even in retirement, it's worthwhile taking Social Security early so that you won't have to tap your savings so soon.

- **What's your family health history?** If your parents lived well into their 80s and you're in good health, you should probably delay Social Security. But if longevity isn't on your side, go ahead and apply for benefits as soon as you retire.

- **Is your spouse much younger?** If you've been the family's main breadwinner and your spouse is younger, you may want to put off taking Social Security, says, J. Robert Treanor, a Social Security expert with benefits consultants William M. Mercer Inc.

How come? If you take Social Security early, not only will you get reduced benefits, but your spouse will also receive a reduced survivor benefit upon your death.

- **Do you foresee working again?** If you retire and then decide to go back to work, your Social Security benefits will get trimmed, which can involve some irritating paperwork. Those under 65 lose $1 of Social Security benefits for every $2 of earned income above the annual exempt amount. For those between 65 and 69, the haircut is $1 of benefits for every $3 of earnings above the annual exempt amount.

  Although this is a hassle, the financial loss shouldn't be permanent, Mr. Treanor notes. Suppose, for instance, that you apply for Social Security at 62 and later decide to go back to work for a year, which prompts the government to limit your benefits. Once you turn 65, the government will bump up your monthly check to compensate for the loss.

SOURCE: Adapted from Jonathan Clements, "Delaying Social Security Benefits May Not Be as Smart as You Think," *The Wall Street Journal,* April 18, 1995, p. C1.

on a number of factors. In some cases, delaying Social Security benefits may not be advisable (see Insight 23.1).

**Monthly Retirement Benefits** Monthly retirement benefits can be paid to retired workers and their dependents. Eligible persons include the following:

1. *Retired worker.* Monthly retirement benefits can be paid at the full retirement age (currently age 65) to a fully insured worker. Reduced benefits can be paid as early as age 62.

2. *Spouse of retired worker.* The spouse of a retired worker can also receive monthly benefits if she or he is at least age 62 and has been married to the retired worker for at least one year. A divorced spouse is also eligible for benefits based on the retired worker's earnings if she or he is at least age 62, and the marriage lasted at least 10 years.

3. *Unmarried children under age 18.* Monthly benefits can also be paid to unmarried children of a retired worker who are under age 18 (or under 19 if full-time elementary or high school students).

4. *Unmarried disabled children.* Unmarried disabled children age 18 or over are also eligible for benefits based on the retired worker's earnings if they were severely disabled before age 22 and continue to remain disabled.

5. *Spouse with dependent children under age 16.* A spouse at any age can receive a monthly benefit if the spouse is caring for an eligible child under age 16 (or is caring for a child of any age who was disabled before age 22) who is receiving a benefit based on the retired worker's earnings. The mother's or father's benefit terminates when the youngest child attains age 16 (unless the mother or father is caring for a child disabled before age 22).

**Retirement Benefit Amount**   The monthly retirement benefit is based on the worker's **primary insurance amount (PIA),** which is the monthly amount paid to a retired worker at the full retirement age (currently age 65) or to a disabled worker. The PIA, in turn, is based on the worker's **average indexed monthly earnings (AIME),** which is a method that updates the worker's earnings based on increases in the average wage in the national economy. The indexing of covered wages results in a relatively constant replacement rate so that workers retiring today and in the future will have about the same proportion of their work earnings replaced by Social Security benefits.

Earnings are indexed by taking into account changes in average wages in the national economy since the worker actually earned the money. The indexing year is the second year before the worker reaches age 62, becomes disabled, or dies, whichever occurs first. For example, assume that Vicki is a registered nurse who retired at age 62 in 1997. The critical year for setting the index factor is the second year before she attained age 62 (1995). To illustrate the method for one year, assume that Vicki's earnings in 1970 were $7800. If her actual earnings in 1970 are multiplied by the index factor for that year (3.99365), her indexed earnings are $31,150.47. This procedure is carried out for each year during the measurement period, which begins with 1951, except that actual dollar amounts are counted for and after the indexing year. The index factors change each year as average wages in the national economy change.

For persons born after 1928, the highest 35 years of indexed earnings are used to calculate the worker's AIME for retirement benefits. (For those born earlier, few years are counted.) The AIME is then used to determine the worker's primary insurance amount. A weighted benefit formula is used, which reflects the social adequacy principle discussed earlier.

Exhibit 23.2 provides examples of monthly OASDI retirement benefits for selected beneficiary designations.

**Delayed Retirement Credit**   To encourage working beyond the full retirement age, a delayed retirement credit is available. The delayed retirement credit applies to the period beyond the full retirement age and up to age 70. For people attaining age 65 in 1997, the primary insurance amount is increased 5 percent for each year of delayed retirement (prorated monthly). The credit will gradually increase to a maximum of 8 percent in the future for workers who were born in 1943 or later.

**Automatic Cost-of-living Adjustment**   The monthly cash benefits are automatically adjusted each year for changes in the cost of living, which maintains the real purchasing power of the benefits during periods of inflation. Whenever the consumer price index for all urban wage earners and clerical workers on a quarterly basis increases from the third quarter of the previous year to the third quarter of the present year, the benefits are automatically increased by the same percentage for the December benefits (payable in early January). The cost-of-living increase for benefits payable in January 1997 was 2.9 percent.

**Earnings Test**   The Social Security program has an **earnings test (retirement test)** that may result in a loss of monthly cash benefits. If a beneficiary has earnings in excess of certain limits, he or she will lose part or all of the benefits. *The purposes of the earnings test are to restrict monthly cash benefits only to those persons who have lost their earned income and to hold down the costs of the program.*

For 1997, beneficiaries ages 65 through 69 can earn a maximum of $13,500 with no loss of monthly benefits. Benefits are reduced $1 for each $3 of earnings in excess of the annual exempt amount. The

## Exhibit 23.2

The following table shows approximate monthly benefits at age 65 for you and your spouse. It is assumed that you have worked steadily and received pay raises at a rate equal to the U.S. average throughout your working career. It is also assumed that your earnings, and the general level of wages and salaries in the country, will stay the same until you retire. This way, **the table shows the value of your benefits in today's dollars.**

Your spouse may qualify for a higher retirement benefit based on her or his own work record.

## Monthly Benefits at Age 65

| Your age in 1997 | Who receives benefits | Your Present Annual Earnings | | | | |
|---|---|---|---|---|---|---|
| | | $15,000 | $24,000 | $36,000 | $48,000 | $65,400 and up |
| 65 | You | $640 | $864 | $1,147 | $1,236 | $1,326 |
| | Spouse | 320 | 432 | 573 | 618 | 663 |
| 64 | You | 629 | 850 | 1,129 | 1,220 | 1,315 |
| | Spouse | 314 | 425 | 564 | 610 | 657 |
| 63 | You | 629 | 851 | 1,131 | 1,225 | 1,326 |
| | Spouse | 314 | 425 | 565 | 612 | 663 |
| 62 | You | 636 | 859 | 1,144 | 1,243 | 1,350 |
| | Spouse | 318 | 429 | 572 | 621 | 675 |
| 61 | You | 637 | 861 | 1,146 | 1,249 | 1,363 |
| | Spouse | 318 | 430 | 573 | 624 | 681 |
| 55* | You | 606 | 821 | 1,091 | 1,213 | 1,355 |
| | Spouse | 298 | 404 | 537 | 597 | 667 |
| 50* | You | 603 | 817 | 1,083 | 1,215 | 1,384 |
| | Spouse | 296 | 401 | 531 | 596 | 679 |
| 45* | You | 607 | 824 | 1,087 | 1,223 | 1,414 |
| | Spouse | 298 | 404 | 534 | 600 | 694 |
| 40* | You | 589 | 801 | 1,053 | 1,185 | 1,377 |
| | Spouse | 286 | 389 | 512 | 576 | 669 |
| 35* | You | 571 | 777 | 1,018 | 1,147 | 1,335 |
| | Spouse | 274 | 373 | 489 | 551 | 641 |
| 30* | You | 575 | 783 | 1,022 | 1,152 | 1,340 |
| | Spouse | 276 | 376 | 491 | 554 | 644 |

*These amounts are reduced for retirement at age 65 because the normal retirement age is higher for these persons.

SOURCE: *1997 Guide to Social Security and Medicare* (Louisville, KY.: William M. Mercer, November 1996), p. 11.

annual exempt amount for beneficiaries ages 65–69 will increase in the future based on the following schedule:

| | | | |
|---|---|---|---|
| 1998 | $14,500 | 2001 | $25,000 |
| 1999 | $15,500 | 2002 | $30,000 |
| 2000 | $17,000 | | |

Beginning in 2003, the earnings limit for ages 65–69 will be increased based on increases in average wages in the national economy.

A more stringent earnings test applies to beneficiaries under age 65. For 1997, the annual exempt amount for beneficiaries under age 65 is $8640. Benefits are reduced $1 for each $2 of earnings in excess of the annual exempt amount. The annual exempt amount for beneficiaries under age 65 is increased each year based on increases in average wages in the national economy.

The earnings test has three major exceptions. First, persons age 70 and older can earn any amount and receive full benefits. Second, the earnings test does not apply to investment income, dividends, interest, rents, or annuity payments. The purpose of this exception is to encourage private savings and investments to supplement the Social Security benefits. *Finally, a special monthly earnings test is used for the initial year of retirement if it produces a more favorable result than the annual test.* Under this special test, the monthly exempt amount is one-twelfth of the annual exempt amount. For the initial year of retirement, regardless of total earnings for the year, full benefits are paid to a beneficiary who neither earns more than the monthly exempt amount nor performs substantial services in self-employment. The purpose of the special monthly test is to pay full retirement benefits, starting with the first month of retirement, to the worker who retires generally in or after the middle of the year. Otherwise, the worker would lose some or all of the benefits if he or she retires after earning more than the maximum allowed under the annual test.

## Survivor Benefits

Survivor benefits can be paid to the dependents of a deceased worker who is either fully or currently insured. For certain survivor benefits, a fully insured status is required.

1. *Unmarried children under age 18.* Survivor benefits can be paid to unmarried children under age 18 (under 19 if full-time elementary or high school students).

2. *Unmarried disabled children.* Unmarried children age 18 or over who become severely disabled before age 22 are eligible for survivor benefits based on the deceased parent's earnings.

3. *Surviving spouse with children under age 16.* A widow, widower, or surviving divorced spouse is entitled to a monthly benefit if she or he is caring for an eligible child who is under age 16 (or who is disabled) and is receiving a benefit based on the deceased worker's earnings. The benefits terminate for the surviving spouse when the youngest child reaches age 16 or the disabled child dies, marries, or is no longer disabled.

4. *Surviving spouse age 60 or over.* A surviving spouse age 60 or over is also eligible for survivor benefits. The deceased worker must be fully insured. A surviving divorced spouse age 60 or older is also eligible for survivor benefits if the marriage lasted at least 10 years.

5. *Disabled widow or widower, ages 50 through 59.* A disabled widow, widower, or surviving divorced spouse who is age 50 or older can receive survivor benefits under certain conditions. The person must be disabled at the time of the worker's death or become disabled no later than seven years after the mother's or father's benefits end. The deceased must be fully insured.

6. *Dependent parents.* Dependent parents age 62 and over can also receive survivor benefits based on the deceased's earnings. The deceased worker must be fully insured.

7. *Lump-sum death benefit.* A lump-sum death benefit of $255 can be paid when a worker dies. The benefit, however, can only be paid if there is an eligible surviving widow, widower, or entitled child.

The value of Social Security survivor benefits is substantial. For an average wage earner who dies and leaves a spouse and two children, the value of the survivor benefits is equivalent to about $300,000 of private life insurance.[5] The benefits, however, are paid monthly and not in a lump sum.

## Disability Benefits

Disability-income benefits can be paid to disabled workers who meet certain eligibility requirements, including the following:

- Be disability-insured
- Meet a five-month waiting period
- Satisfy the definition of disability

A disabled worker must be disability-insured and must also meet a five-month waiting period. Benefits begin after a waiting period of five full calendar months. Therefore, the first payment is for the sixth full month of disability.

The definition of disability stated in the law must also be met. A strict definition of disability is used in the program: *The worker must have a physical or mental condition that prevents him or her from doing any substantial gainful work and is expected to last (or has lasted) at least 12 months or is expected to result in earlier death.* The impairment must be so severe that the worker is prevented from doing any substantial gainful work in the national economy. In determining whether a person can do substantial gainful work, his or her age, education, training, and work experience can be taken into consideration. If the disabled person cannot work at his or her own occupation but can engage in other substantial gainful work, the disability claim will not be allowed.[6]

The major groups eligible to receive OASDI disability-income benefits are as follows:[7]

1. *Disabled worker.* A disabled worker under the full retirement age receives a benefit equal to 100 percent of the primary insurance amount. The worker must meet the definition of disability, be disability-insured, and satisfy a full five-month waiting period.

2. *Spouse of a disabled worker.* Benefits can be paid to the spouse of a disabled worker at any age if she or he is caring for a child under age 16 or one who became disabled before age 22 and is receiving benefits based on the disabled worker's earnings. If no eligible children are present, the spouse must be at least age 62 to receive benefits.

3. *Unmarried children under age 18.* Disability benefits can be paid to unmarried children under age 18 (or under 19 if a full-time elementary or high school student).

4. *Unmarried disabled children.* Unmarried children age 18 or over who became severely disabled before age 22 are also eligible for benefits, based on the disabled worker's earnings.

## Medicare Benefits

The fourth principal benefit is Medicare. **Medicare** covers the medical expenses of almost all persons age 65 and older. Medicare also covers disabled persons under age 65 who have been entitled to disability benefits for at least 24 months (they need not be continuous). In addition, the program covers persons under age 65 who need long-term kidney dialysis treatment or a kidney transplant.

Medicare consists of two parts: **Hospital Insurance (Part A)** and **Supplementary Medical Insurance (Part B).**

**Hospital Insurance (Part A)**  *Inpatient hospital care* is covered for up to 90 days for each benefit period. A benefit period starts when the patient first enters the hospital and ends when the patient has been out of the hospital or skilled nursing facility for 60 consecutive days. For the first 60 days, Medicare pays all covered costs except for an initial hospital deductible ($760 in 1997). The deductible is paid only once during the benefit period no matter how many times the patient goes to a hospital. For the 61st through 90th day, Medicare pays all covered costs except for a daily coinsurance charge ($190 in 1997). If the patient is still in the hospital after 90 days, a *lifetime reserve* of 60 additional days can be used. Lifetime reserve days are subject to a daily coinsurance charge ($380 in 1997). The hospital deductible and coinsurance charges are adjusted each year to reflect changes in hospital costs.

Inpatient care in a *skilled nursing facility* is also covered up to a maximum of 100 days in a benefit period. The first 20 days of covered services are paid in full. For the next 80 days, the patient must pay a daily coinsurance insurance charge ($95 in 1997). To be eligible for coverage, the patient must be hospitalized first for at least three days and must require skilled nursing care. Intermediate care and custodial care are not covered.

*Home health care services* in the patient's home are covered if the patient requires skilled care for an injury or illness. The number of visits is unlimited if certain conditions are met. Prior hospitalization is not required, and a deductible is not required for home health services.

Part A pays for part-time or intermittent skilled nursing care, home health aides, medical social workers, and different types of therapists. In addition, the home health benefit covers the full cost of some medical supplies and equipment and 80 percent of the approved amount for durable medical equipment, such as wheel chairs and hospital beds.

*Hospice care* for terminally ill beneficiaries is covered for up to 210 days if the care is provided by a hospice certified by Medicare. Hospice care beyond 210 days is covered if a physician certifies that the beneficiary is still terminally ill. A hospice program is a program that provides inpatient, outpatient, and home care services to terminally ill patients, such as cancer patients.

Finally, Part A pays for the cost of inpatient *blood transfusions* furnished by a hospital or skilled nursing facility during a covered stay, except for the first three pints of blood per year. However, the patient cannot be charged for the first three pints if the blood is replaced, or the cost of the blood is covered under Part B.

Hospitals are reimbursed for inpatient services provided to Medicare beneficiaries under a prospective payment system. Under this system, hospital care is classified into **diagnosis-related groups (DRGs),** and a flat amount is paid for each type of care depending on the diagnosis group in which the case is placed. Thus, a flat, uniform amount is paid to each hospital for the same type of care or treatment. However, the amount paid varies among different geographical locations and by urban and rural facilities.

The purpose of the DRG system is to create a financial incentive to encourage hospitals to operate more efficiently. Hospitals are allowed to keep payment amounts that exceed their costs, but they must absorb any costs in excess of the DRG flat amounts.

**Supplementary Medical Insurance (Part B)**
Part B of Medicare is a voluntary program that covers physician's fees and other related medical services. Persons covered under Part A on the basis of covered earnings are automatically covered under Part B unless they voluntarily decline the coverage.

Part B pays for several types of services that are medically necessary. *Physician's services* are covered in the doctor's office, hospital, or elsewhere. Medical supplies furnished by a doctor in the office, services of the office nurse, and drugs administered by a doctor are also covered.

*Outpatient hospital services* for diagnosis and treatment are covered, such as care in an emergency room or outpatient clinic in a hospital. Laboratory tests, X rays, and diagnostic hospital services as an outpatient are also covered.

An unlimited number of *home health-care visits* is also provided under Part B if the beneficiary is not

covered under Part A. Such visits are the same as those provided by Part A.

Finally, *other medical and health care services* are covered, including diagnostic tests, X rays and radiation treatment, limited ambulance services, prosthetic devices, physical therapy and speech pathology services, hospital equipment and other durable medical equipment used at home, and supplies for fractures.

Part B excludes numerous medical services and items, including routine physicals, most dental care, dentures, routine foot care, hearing aids, and most prescription drugs. Eye glasses are covered only if the patient needs corrective lenses after a cataract operation.

*Part B pays 80 percent of the approved charges for covered medical services after the beneficiary pays a calendar-year deductible of $100.* However, beneficiaries may have to pay more than 20 percent of the Medicare-approved amount for certain services. If a hospital provides outpatient hospital services, the beneficiary must pay 20 percent of the amount the hospital actually charges, and not 20 percent of the Medicare-approved amount. Also, if the beneficiary receives outpatient mental services, only 50 percent of the Medicare-approved amount is paid.

The 20 percent coinsurance charge does not apply to home health visits, pneumococcal vacine and flu shots, and outpatient clinical diagnostic laboratory tests (except in Maryland).

REIMBURSEMENT OF PHYSICIANS   As stated earlier, Part B generally pays only 80 percent of the Medicare-approved amount, which is usually less than the physician's actual fee. The approved amount is based on a complex relative-value fee schedule that determines payment based on the time, skill, and intensity of the services provided; the cost of practicing medicine; and medical malpractice costs. Geographical variations in the cost of practicing medicine are also considered.

Medicare payments to physicians are made on an assigned or nonassigned basis. By accepting an assignment, a physician agrees to accept the Medicare-approved amount as payment in full. The patient is not liable for any additional out-of-pocket costs other than the calendar-year deductible and coinsurance payments. However, physicians who do not accept an assignment of a Medicare claim cannot charge more than 115 percent of the Medicare allowable fee for such physicians.

PART B MONTHLY PREMIUM    Part B beneficiaries must pay a monthly premium for the benefits provided ($43.80 in 1997), which is supplemented by the federal government out of general revenues. In 1996, general revenues accounted for about 74 percent of all Part B income; enrollee premiums accounted for 24 percent, while interest income on the trust fund assets accounted for 2 percent.[8]

### Medicare and Managed Care    The law allows Medicare beneficiaries to elect coverage under either a fee-for-service arrangement or a managed care plan. Under *fee-for-service,* beneficiaries can select any physician or health care provider who charges fees for the services provided. Medicare pays its share of the approved charges, and the beneficiary pays the remainder. Most Medicare beneficiaries are currently enrolled under fee-for-service.

As an alternative to fee-for-service, Medicare beneficiaries have the option of enrolling in a *managed care plan,* such as a Health Maintenance Organization (HMO). In a typical HMO plan, beneficiaries must usually receive all covered services from health-care providers that are part of the network. Depending on the plan, beneficiaries may have to pay a fixed monthly premium and a copayment charge every time a service is used. In addition, beneficiaries must continue to pay Part B premiums, but they do not have to pay any Medicare deductibles or coinsurance charges.

Managed care plans have several advantages. First, in addition to Medicare benefits, the plan may provide extra benefits, such as prescription drugs, eye examinations, routine physicals, and hearing aids. Second, except for a possible small copayment fee, there are usually no additional charges no matter how many times a beneficiary sees a physician, is hospitalized, or uses other covered services; thus, medical costs are more predictable than under fee-for-service. Finally, a medigap policy is not needed.

### Medigap Insurance    Because of numerous exclusions, deductibles, cost-sharing provisions, and limitations on approved charges, Medicare does not pay all medical expenses. As a result, most Medicare beneficiaries either have post-retirement health benefits from their former employers or have purchased a **Medigap policy** or Medicare supplement policy that pays part or all of the covered charges not paid by Medicare.

Medigap policies are sold by private insurers and are strictly regulated by federal law. There are 10 standard policies, and each policy offers a different combination of benefits. The basic policy has a core package of benefits. The remaining policies have a different combination of benefits, but they all include the core package. Each policy has a letter designation ranging from A through J. Insurers are not allowed to change the various combination of benefits or the letter designations.

Insurers must provide an open enrollment period of six months from the date the applicant first enrolls in Medicare Part B and is age 65 or older. Applicants cannot be turned down or charged higher premiums because of poor health if they buy a policy during that period. Once the Medigap open enrollment period ends, beneficiaries may not be able to buy a policy of their choice but may have to accept whatever an insurer is willing to provide.

Insurers and agents are subject to criminal charges and fines if they engage in deceptive sales practices. Certain practices are forbidden, including the sale of a policy that duplicates Medicare coverage, selling a policy that is not an approved standard policy, and making a false statement that the policy meets legal standards when it does not.

## Financing Social Security Benefits

OASDI benefits are financed by a payroll tax paid by employees, employers, and the self-employed; interest income on the trust-fund investments; and revenues derived from taxation of part of the monthly cash benefits.

In 1997, the worker paid a tax contribution rate of 7.65 percent on a maximum taxable earnings base of $65,400, and 1.45 percent on all earned income in excess of that amount. The employee's contribution is matched by an identical contribution from the employer. The self-employed pay a tax rate of 15.3 percent on the same earnings base, and 2.9 percent on all earnings in excess of that amount. However, the self-employed are allowed certain deductions, which reduce the effective tax rate.[9] The maximum taxable earnings base will automatically increase in the future if average wages in the national economy increase.

Hospital Insurance (Part A) of Medicare is financed largely by a payroll tax of 1.45 percent on all earned income, including earnings in excess of the OASDI taxable earnings base. (The 1.45 percent is part of the 7.65 percent mentioned earlier.) The self-employed pay 2.9 percent on all earned income. Finally, as noted earlier, Supplementary Medical Insurance (Part B) is financed by monthly premiums and by general revenues of the federal government.

## Taxation of Benefits

About 20 percent of the beneficiaries who receive monthly cash benefits must pay an income tax on part of the benefits. The amount of benefits subject to taxation depends on your total combined income. *Combined income* includes earnings, pension income, dividends, and taxable interest from investments and other sources *plus* tax-exempt interest *plus* one-half of your Social Security benefits. If you file a federal tax return as an individual and your combined income is between $25,000 and $34,000, up to 50 percent of your benefits is subject to taxation. If your combined income exceeds $34,000, up to 85 percent of your benefits is subject to taxation.

If you file a joint return and if you and your spouse have a combined income between $32,000 and $44,000, up to 50 percent of the benefits are subject to taxation. If your combined income exceeds $44,000, up to 85 percent of the benefits are subject to taxation.

At the end of each year, you will receive a form from the Social Security Administration that shows the amount of Social Security benefits received. The Internal Revenue Service has prepared a detailed worksheet to determine the amount of the benefits, if any, to include in your taxable income.

## OASDHI PROBLEMS AND ISSUES

The Social Security program is controversial. Numerous problems and issues are associated with the program. Some timely issues include the proposed privatization of Social Security, the Medicare financial crisis, and the earnings test.

1. *Privatization of Social Security.* A highly controversial issue is the proposed privatization of Social Security. Because of likely serious problems in the present OASDI program, several proposals have been made to privatize part of the present program.

   In a recent report, the Advisory Council on Social Security identified four major problems in the OASDI program:[10]

   - *Long term deficit.* Based on the 1995 Board of Trustees report and the intermediate cost assumptions, the Social Security trust funds will experience serious financial problems in the future. Beginning in 2012, the trust funds will pay out more in annual benefits than they collect from payroll and income taxes. Interest on the trust fund investments will keep the balance positive until 2020. After that time, the trust fund balances will start to decline, and in the absence of any changes, full benefits could not be paid on time beginning in 2030. In addition, the long-term deficit over a 75-year projection period is estimated to be 2.17 percent of taxable payroll. Little support exists today, however, for increasing payroll tax rates by 2.17 percentage points to eliminate the deficit.

   - *Deterioration in the long-range balance because of the passage of time.* Because of the aging of the U.S. population, whenever the program is brought into 75-year balance under a stable tax rate, the simple passage of time will put the system again into deficit. The reason is that expensive years previously beyond the forecasting horizon, with more beneficiaries getting higher real benefits, are then brought into the forecast period. The Advisory Council believes the long-term actuarial deficit will continue to increase beyond the traditional 75-year projection period.

   - *Money's worth issue.* The third area of concern is that under present law, many younger workers and future workers will be paying employee and employer taxes over their working lifetimes that substantially exceed the present value of their anticipated benefits. The Advisory Council believes that the program should provide a reasonable money's worth return on the contributions of younger

## Exhibit 23.3

### Internal Real Rates of Return on Single Worker's Accumulated Lifetime OASDI Payroll Taxes under Current Law, by Worker's Year of Birth

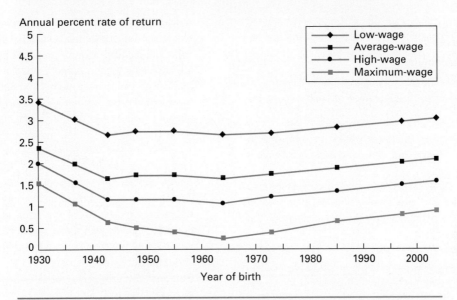

SOURCE: *Report of the 1994–1996 Advisory Council on Social Security, Volume I: Findings and Recommendations* (Washington, D.C.: 1994–1996 Advisory Council on Social Security, 1997), p. 41.

workers and future generations, while still taking into account the redistributive nature of the Social Security program.

The Advisory Council calculated the internal real rates of return (IRR) that single workers with different lifetime earnings could expect to receive from Social Security under present law. The IRR is the rate of return at which the present discounted value of future benefits is equal to the present discounted value of the taxes paid. *Note that the IRR is in real terms,* which is the return after the effects of projected inflation are removed. *Based on present law, most average and upper-income single workers will receive an internal real rate of return (IRR) that is less than 2 percent* (see Exhibit 23.3). The projected rates of return are relatively low when compared to other investments in the economy. For example, in its calculations, the Council assumed that the long-term rate of return on government bonds is 2.3 percentage points higher than the future expected inflation rate. In contrast,

the expected rates of return on stocks are between 4½ and 5 percentage points higher than the expected rate of return on government bonds.[11] Thus, with the exception of low-wage earners, younger workers, on average, could expect to receive higher real returns by investing the tax contributions in common stocks.

- *Public confidence.* The final issue involves public confidence in the program. Polling data suggest that younger people have little confidence in the program, and that they believe Social Security benefits will not be available for them when they retire. Polling data also suggest some erosion in public confidence in Social Security over time.

The Advisory Council could not agree on the best way to deal with the preceding problems. A deeply divided council presented three proposals that would dramatically change the character of the present program. The proposals are highly controversial and are summarized in Insight 23.2.

## INSIGHT 23.2

## Proposals for Reforming Social Security

The Advisory Council on Social Security presented three competing plans to eliminate the long-term deficit.

### Points of Agreement

The following individual proposals generally have majority support since each appears in at least two of the three plans.

- Social Security coverage would be extended to cover all newly hired state and local government employees.
- The Consumer Price Index would be changed to correct for the overstatement of inflation, which would reduce future benefit increases based on the automatic cost-of-living provisions.
- The number of years of earnings used to determine benefits would be increased from 35 to 38.
- Social Security benefits would be taxed to the extent they exceed what the worker has paid in, similar to defined-benefit pension plans.
- The increase in the normal retirement age for full benefits would be accelerated so that it would reach age 67 in 2011. After that time, the retirement age would increase with longevity.

The five changes would reduce the long-term deficit from 2.17 percent to 0.64 percent of taxable payroll, or more than two-thirds, and would shift the trust fund exhaustion date from 2030 to 2052.

### Three Competing Plans

- **Maintain benefits (MB).** This plan would maintain existing benefits and would incorporate the first four points listed above. Beginning in 2010, income from the taxation of Social Security benefits would be redirected from the Hospital Insurance trust fund to the OASDI trust funds. *In addition, a controversial proposal would allow the trust funds to invest up to 40 percent of trust fund assets in a common stock index fund.* The investments would be passively managed by an independent board and would reflect a broad market average. Finally, in 2045, the payroll tax would be increased 0.8 percent for both employees and employers.

- **Individual account (IA).** In addition to the five changes listed above, the plan would create individual accounts. The federal government would hold the accounts, but the workers could choose among a specified set of investments. The funds could not be withdrawn before retirement. At retirement, the account value would be converted into an indexed life annuity for the worker and spouse. *To finance contributions into individual accounts, the tax contribution rate would be increased 1.6 percentage points only for the employees.* Finally, the existing Social Security tax rate would be maintained, but future benefits would be cut back to a level that could be funded with those revenues. The reduction in future benefits would affect primarily middle- and upper-income workers.

- **Personal Security Account (PSA).** In addition to changes one, two, and five above, the plan would create a two-tier system. *The first tier would be a flat monthly benefit of $410 in 1996 dollars (indexed for increases in national average wages). The second tier would be a personal security account.* Workers could direct 5 percentage points of their current payroll tax into a personal security account, which would be privately managed and invested in a variety of financial instruments. The balance of the employee's payroll tax plus the employer's tax would be used to finance the flat basic benefit. At retirement, the workers would receive (1) the flat benefit and (2) the proceeds from their personal security account. *To finance the transition costs of moving to the new system, the payroll tax would be increased 1.52 percentage points plus additional government borrowing.*

The three proposals are highly controversial. Taxes would be increased, which is politically unpopular; part of the tax contributions would be invested in common stocks with possible greater risk to the workers; and the present system would be dramatically changed.

Source: Adaptation of National Academy of Social Insurance, *Advisory Council on Social Security Plans,* Washington, D.C. (December 1996).

2. *Medicare financial crisis.* Part A of Medicare is experiencing a serious financial crisis at the present time. *Based on the 1996 Board of Trustees report, the Hospital Insurance (HI) trust fund will be exhausted in 2001. In addition, the HI trust fund is severely out of actuarial balance over the next 75 years.*[12] As a result, the HI trust fund will face a serious cash flow problem in the near-term future.

The cash flow problem is due to a number of factors, including an increase in the number of aged and disabled Medicare beneficiaries, inflation in hospital costs that have exceeded the overall rate of inflation, fraud and abuse by health-care providers, and a fee-for-service method of reimbursement that some experts believe is inefficient and inflationary.

In addition, the growth in Supplementary Medical Insurance (SMI) has exceeded the growth in hospital insurance in recent years. SMI expenditures have been increasing rapidly for many years and are projected to nearly triple as a percent of gross domestic product by 2020. General revenues of the federal government, which paid about 70 percent of SMI costs from 1990–1995, are projected to increase to 84 percent of SMI costs by 2005 and will continue to increase after that time.[13] The federal government has no general revenues by itself, and the critical public policy question is how additional general revenues for SMI payments will be obtained in the future.

In recent years, Congress has enacted numerous cost-containment measures to control Medicare spending, including reducing payments to physicians and hospitals, placing spending limits on specific medical services, limiting fees of physicians who refuse assignment, implementing the diagnosis-related group method for reimbursing hospitals, and enacting a resource-based relative value scale for paying physicians. In addition, it has been proposed that Part B premiums should be income tested; that is, upper income beneficiaries should pay higher Part B premiums based on their incomes.

The Board of Trustees has notified Congress of the potential cash flow problem of HI and has recommended that Congress take prompt action to control Medicare spending for both HI and SMI through specific legislation and as part of comprehensive health-care reform.

3. *Earnings Test.* Another controversial issue is the OASDI earnings test.[14] As stated earlier, monthly cash benefits are reduced or eliminated if earned income exceeds certain maximum annual limits. For beneficiaries under age 65, benefits are reduced $1 for each $2 of earnings above the annual exempt amount. For beneficiaries ages 65–69, benefits are reduced $1 for each $3 of earnings above the annual exempt amount. Critics of the earnings test argue that the current test is inequitable and unfair and should be eliminated or substantially modified. The major arguments against the earnings test are summarized as follows:

- The earnings test is an oppressive tax on earnings above the annual exempt amount.
- Work incentives are reduced.
- Earned income is discriminated against in favor of investment income.
- The earnings test is complex and costly to administer.

The principal argument against the earnings test is that it results in an oppressive tax on work earnings above the annual exempt amount. The loss of benefits can be viewed as a tax. In addition, a beneficiary who works must pay a Social Security tax and federal and state income taxes. Thus, when the loss of benefits from the earnings test and the payment of taxes are considered, the marginal tax rate on earnings above the exempt amount is prohibitively high. For example, assume that a beneficiary earns $1000 above the maximum annual exempt amount and is in the 28 percent federal and 5 percent state income tax brackets. *A beneficiary under age 65 would net only $93.50, which is equivalent to a marginal tax rate of about 91 percent. A beneficiary age 65–69 would net only $260.17, which is equivalent to a marginal tax rate of about 74 percent (see Exhibit 23.4).*

The marginal tax rates shown for beneficiaries under age 65 do not take into consideration the recalculation of benefits at age 65 to reflect the withholding of benefits because of the earnings test. The marginal tax rates shown also do not reflect the increase in benefits because of the delayed retirement credit for beneficiaries age 65 or older who work

EXHIBIT 23.4

|  | OASDI beneficiaries under age 65 | OASDI beneficiaries ages 65–69 |
|---|---|---|
| Earnings above the exempt amount | $1,000.00 | $1,000.00 |
| Loss of OASDI benefits because of the earnings test | −500.00 | −333.33 |
| Social Security tax | −76.50 | −76.50 |
| Federal income tax | −280.00 | −280.00 |
| State income tax | −50.00 | −50.00 |
| Net earnings = | $   93.50 | $   260.17 |
| Marginal tax rate = | 90.65% | 73.98% |

beyond the normal retirement age. Consideration of such factors would lower the marginal tax rates shown. However, since most beneficiaries do not consider these factors in their decision to work, they are ignored in the illustration.

In addition, critics argue that work incentives are reduced by the earnings test because of high and oppressive marginal tax rates on earnings above the exempt amount. Some research studies, however, suggest that the reduction in work incentives from the earnings test is relatively small.[15]

It is also argued that the earnings test is unfair since it discriminates against earned income in favor of investment income. Investment income is not subject to the earnings test, and unlimited amounts of investment income can be received with no loss of benefits. However, work earnings above the exempt amount will result in a reduction or complete loss of benefits.

Finally, the earnings test is complex and costly to administer, and encourages some beneficiaries to cheat.

Certain groups, however, are opposed to the elimination of the earnings test. The following arguments are presented for retention of the earnings test:

- The cost of the OASDI program initially would be substantially increased if the test were eliminated.
- Additional benefits would go largely to upper-income workers who have not yet retired.
- Relatively few persons are actually affected by the earnings test.
- It is illogical to pay full OASDI benefits to workers who have not yet retired.

## UNEMPLOYMENT INSURANCE

Unemployment insurance programs are federal-state programs that pay weekly cash benefits to workers who are involuntarily unemployed. Each state has its own unemployment insurance program. The various state programs arose out of the unemployment insurance provisions of the Social Security Act of 1935.

Unemployment insurance has several basic objectives:[16]

- Provide cash income during involuntary unemployment
- Help unemployed workers find jobs
- Encourage employers to stabilize employment
- Help stabilize the economy

Weekly cash benefits are paid to unemployed workers during periods of **short-term involuntary unemployment,** thus helping unemployed workers maintain their economic security. A second objective is to help unemployed workers find jobs; applicants for benefits must register for work at local employment offices, and officials provide assistance in finding suitable jobs. A third objective is to encourage employers to stabilize their employment through experience rating (discussed later). Finally, unemployment benefits help stabilize the economy during recessionary periods.

### Coverage

Most private firms, state and local governments, and nonprofit organizations are covered for unemployment benefits. A *private firm* is subject to the federal unemployment tax if it employs one or more employees in each of at least 20 weeks during the calendar year (or preceding calendar year), or it pays wages of $1500 or more during a calendar quarter of either year. Most jobs in *state and local government* are also covered for unemployment insurance benefits. However, state and local governments are not required to pay the federal unemployment tax but instead may elect to reimburse the system for the benefits paid to government employees. In addition, *nonprofit charitable, educational or religious organizations* are covered if they employ four or more workers for at least one day in each of 20 different weeks during the current or prior year. The nonprofit organization has the right either to pay the unemployment tax or reimburse the states for the benefits paid.

*Agricultural firms* are covered if they have a quarterly payroll of at least $20,000 or employ 10 or more workers in at least 20 weeks during the current or prior year. *Domestic employment* in a private household is covered if the employer pays domestic wages of $1000 or more in a calendar quarter during the current or prior year.

### Eligibility Requirements

An unemployed worker must meet the following eligibility requirements:

- Have qualifying wages and employment during the base year
- Be able and available for work
- Actively seek work
- Be free from disqualification
- Serve a one-week waiting period

*The applicant must earn qualifying wages of a specified amount during his or her base year.* In most states, the base year is the first four of the last five calendar quarters preceding the unemployed worker's claim for benefits. Most states also require employment in at least two calendar quarters during the base year. The purpose of this requirement is to limit benefits to workers with a current attachment to the labor force.

*The applicant must also be physically and mentally capable of working and must be available for work.* The claimant must register for work at a public employment office and actively seek work.

*In addition, the applicant must not be disqualified from receiving benefits.* Disqualifying acts include voluntarily quitting his or her job without good cause, direct participation in a labor dispute, being discharged for misconduct, or refusing suitable work.

*Finally, a one-week waiting period must be satisfied in most states.* The waiting period eliminates short-term claims, holds down costs, and provides time to obtain the claimant's wage record and process the claim.

### Benefits

A weekly cash benefit is paid for each week of total unemployment. The benefit paid varies with the worker's past wages, within certain minimum and maximum dollar amounts. Most states use a formula that pays weekly benefits based on a fraction of the worker's high quarter wages. For example, a fraction of $\frac{1}{26}$ results in the payment of benefits equal to 50 percent of the worker's full-time wage in the highest quarter (subject to minimum and maximum amounts). For instance, assume that Jennifer earns $400 weekly or $5200 during her highest quarter. Applying the fraction of $\frac{1}{26}$ to this amount produces a weekly unemployment benefit of $200, or 50 percent of her full-time weekly wage. Several states also pay a dependent's allowance for certain dependents.

As of July 1995, maximum weekly unemployment benefits ranged from $175 in Missouri to $354 in New Jersey.[17] In virtually all jurisdictions, the maximum duration of regular benefits is limited to 26 weeks. Massachusetts has a maximum duration of 30 weeks.

During periods of high unemployment, some workers exhaust their regular unemployment benefits. A permanent federal-state program of extended benefits pays additional benefits to unemployed workers who exhaust their regular benefits during periods of high unemployment in individual states. Under the **extended-benefits program,** claimants can receive up to 13 additional weeks of benefits or one-half the total amount of regular benefits, whichever is less. There is an overall limit of 39 weeks for both regular and extended benefits. The costs of the extended benefits are shared equally by the federal government and the states.

### Financing

State unemployment insurance programs are financed largely by payroll taxes paid by employers on the covered wages of employees. A few states also require the employees to contribute. All tax contributions are deposited in the Federal Unemployment Trust Fund. Each state has a separate account, which is credited with the unemployment-tax contributions and the state's share of investment income. Unemployment benefits are paid out of each state's account.

For 1997, covered employers paid a federal payroll tax of 6.2 percent on the first $7000 of annual wages paid to each covered employee. Employers can credit toward the federal tax any contributions paid under an approved unemployment insurance program and any tax savings under an approved experience-rating plan. The total employer credit is limited to a maximum of 5.4 percent. The remaining 0.8 percent is paid to the federal government and used for state and federal administrative expenses, for financing the federal government's share of the extended benefits program, and for maintaining a loan fund from which states can temporarily borrow when their accounts are depleted.

Because of a desire to strengthen their unemployment reserves and maintain fund solvency, the majority of states have a taxable wage base that exceeds $7000.

**Experience rating** is also used, by which firms with favorable employment records pay reduced tax rates. The major argument in support of experience rating is that firms have a financial incentive to stabilize their employment. However, some cyclical and seasonal firms have little control over their employment, and experience rating provides little financial incentive for them to stabilize employment. Also, labor unions are opposed to experience rating, since some business firms resist benefit increases and contest some valid claims.

## Problems and Issues

State unemployment insurance programs have numerous problems. Some important problems are summarized as follows:

1. *Decline in the proportion of unemployed who receive benefits.* Only a relatively small proportion of the total unemployed at any time receive unemployment benefits. On average, only 48 percent of unemployed workers received unemployment insurance benefits in 1993. This compares with a peak of 81 percent of the unemployed who received benefits in April 1975 and a low point of 26 percent in October 1987.[18]

   Four factors have been identified that help explain the long-term decline in the proportion of unemployed who receive benefits: (1) stricter eligibility requirements and more restrictive policy changes at the state and federal level, (2) a decline in the percentage of unionized workers where unemployment insurance claims have been historically high, (3) a decline in the proportion of workers employed in the manufacturing sector where unemployment claim rates also have been high; and (4) the increasing percentage of the unemployed who live in states in which the receipt of unemployment benefits is below the national average.[19]

2. *Inadequate benefits.* Another serious problem is that weekly unemployment insurance benefits are inadequate in many states, especially for average and upper-income workers. One measure of benefit adequacy is a 50 percent replacement rate. The ratio of pretax weekly unemployment benefits to pretax wages over some time period should be at least 50 percent for most workers. This standard is being met for low-income workers in most states. In 1994, 52 jurisdictions paid weekly benefits that met the 50 percent standard for single, full-time workers who earned the federal minimum wage of $4.25 per hour. *However, for average- and upper-income workers, the 50 percent standard is not being met in many states.* In 1994, 15 jurisdictions did not meet the 50 percent standard for full-time workers who earned a more adequate wage of $10 per hour.[20]

   Another measure of benefit adequacy is to determine whether the weekly benefits are sufficiently high to pay the recurring and necessary expenses of unemployed workers. The Advisory Council on Unemployment Compensation has prepared low and high estimates of the amounts needed to pay the necessary and recurring expenses of unemployment insurance recipients based on the 1992 Consumer Expenditures Survey.[21] In 1992, for workers with pretax incomes between $10,000 and $14,999, only three states met the low estimate standard. For workers earning between $15,000 and $19,999, only 15 states met the low estimate standard. For workers earning between $20,000 and $29,000, only 38 states met that standard; and for workers earning between $30,000 and $39,000, only 30 states met the low estimate standard. In addition, the vast majority of states did not meet the high estimate standard at all income levels.[22]

Based on the preceding data, unemployment benefits are inadequate for many unemployed workers, especially for average- and upper-income workers. As a result, during periods of extended unemployment many unemployed workers will either deplete their savings or be forced into debt despite receiving unemployment benefits.

3. *Inadequate financing.* Many state unemployment insurance programs are inadequately financed, and their reserve accounts are relatively low. During previous recessions, many states found their reserve funds inadequate for meeting the increased cost of benefits due to high unemployment and a longer duration of payments. States are permitted to borrow from the federal unemployment account if their accounts decline to a level where benefit obligations cannot be met.

One widely used measure to estimate the adequacy of a state's unemployment reserve account is known as the "high-cost multiple."[23] A value of one means that the state's current reserve account could pay 12 months of unemployment benefits at the highest unemployment rate historically experienced. The Interstate Commission of Employment Security Administrators has recommended a high-cost multiple of 1.5, which would enable the state to pay benefits for 18 months during a recession without borrowing. However, in 1993, only five states had a high-cost multiple of 1.5 or higher, and only 19 jurisdictions had a high-cost multiple of one or higher.[24]

In the past, many states with high-cost multiples below one have experienced serious financial problems during recessions. Thus, if the U.S. economy should experience a severe recession, many states once again will exhaust their unemployment reserves and be forced to borrow from the federal government to pay benefits.

## WORKERS COMPENSATION

Millions of workers are injured or sick each year because of job-related activities. According to the Bureau of Labor Statistics, 6.6 million workplace injuries and illnesses occurred in 1995, or 8.1 cases for every 100 full-time workers.[25] In addition to pain and suffering, disabled workers must deal with the loss of earned income, payment of medical bills, partial or permanent loss of bodily functions or limbs, and job separation.

**Workers compensation** is a social insurance program that provides medical care, cash benefits, and rehabilitation services to workers who are disabled from job-related accidents or disease. The benefits are extremely important in reducing economic insecurity that may result from a job-related disability.[26]

### Development of Workers Compensation

Under the *common law of industrial accidents,* dating back to 1837, workers injured on the job had to sue their employers and prove negligence before they could collect damages. However, an employer could use three common law defenses to block lawsuits from injured workers:

- Contributory negligence doctrine
- Fellow-servant doctrine
- Assumption-of-risk doctrine

Under the contributory negligence doctrine, an injured worker could not collect damages if he or she contributed in any way to the injury. Under the *fellow-servant doctrine,* the injured worker could not collect if the injury resulted from the negligence of a fellow worker. And under the *assumption-of-risk doctrine,* the injured worker could not collect if he or she had advance knowledge of the dangers inherent in a particular occupation. As a result of the harsh common law, relatively few disabled workers collected adequate amounts for their injuries.

The enactment of *employer liability laws* between 1885 and 1910 was the next step in the development of workers compensation. These laws reduced the effectiveness of the common law defenses, improved the legal position of injured workers, and required employers to provide safe working conditions for their employees. However, injured workers were still required to sue their employers and prove negligence before they could collect for their injuries.

Finally, the states passed *workers compensation laws* as a solution to the growing problem of work-related accidents. In 1908, the federal government passed a workers compensation law covering certain federal employees, and by 1920, all but six states had passed similar laws. All states today have workers compensation laws.

Workers compensation is based on the fundamental principle of **liability without fault.** *The employer is held absolutely liable for job-related injuries or disease suffered by the workers, regardless of who is at fault.* Disabled workers are paid for their injuries according to a schedule of benefits established by law. The workers are not required to sue their employers to collect benefits. The laws provide for the prompt payment of benefits to disabled workers regardless of fault and with a minimum of legal formality. The costs of workers compensation benefits are therefore considered to be a normal cost of production, which is included in the price of the product.

## Objectives of Workers Compensation

State workers compensation laws have several basic objectives:[27]

- Broad coverage of employees for job-related accidents and disease
- Substantial protection against the loss of income
- Provide sufficient medical care and rehabilitation services
- Encouragement of safety
- Reduction in litigation

*A fundamental objective is to provide broad coverage of employees for job-related accidents and disease.* This objective has largely been met. In 1990, workers compensation laws covered about 87 percent of all wage and salaried workers.

*A second objective is to provide substantial protection against the loss of income.* The cash benefits are designed to restore a substantial proportion of the disabled worker's lost earnings, so that the disabled worker's previous standard of living can be maintained.

*A third objective is to provide sufficient medical care and rehabilitation services to injured workers.* Workers compensation laws require employers to pay hospital, surgical, and other medical costs incurred by injured workers. Also, the laws provide for rehabilitation services to disabled employees so they can be restored to productive employment.

*Another objective is to encourage firms to reduce job-related accidents and to develop effective safety programs.* Experience rating is used to encourage firms to reduce job-related accidents and disease, since firms with superior accident records pay relatively lower workers compensation premiums.

*Finally, workers compensation laws are designed to reduce litigation.* The benefits are paid promptly to disabled workers without requiring them to sue their employers. The objective is to reduce or eliminate the payment of legal fees to attorneys, and time-consuming and expensive trials and appeals.

## Types of Laws

State workers compensation laws are either compulsory or elective. Almost all states have compulsory laws that require covered employers to provide specified benefits to workers who are disabled from a job-related accident or disease.

Three states (New Jersey, South Carolina, and Texas) have elective laws that permit employers either to elect or reject the workers compensation law. If the employer rejects the law and the injured employee sues for damages based on the employer's negligence, the employer is deprived of the three common-law defenses. In such a case, the injured worker has only to establish the employer's negligence to collect damages.

## Complying with the Law

Employers can comply with state law by purchasing a workers compensation policy, by self-insuring, or by obtaining insurance from a monopoly or competitive state fund.

Most firms purchase a workers compensation policy from a private insurer. The policy pays the benefits that the employer must legally provide to workers who have a job-related accident or disease.

Self-insurance is allowed in most states. Many large firms self-insure their workers compensation losses to save money. In addition, group self-insurance is often available to smaller firms that pool their risks and liabilities.

Finally, workers compensation insurance can be purchased from a state fund in certain states. In six states, covered employers must purchase workers compensation insurance from a *monopoly state fund.* (Four of the six states, however, allow employers to self-insure.) Nineteen states have *competitive state funds* that compete with private insurers.[28]

## Covered Occupations

Most occupations are covered by workers compensation laws. However, certain occupations are excluded, or coverage is incomplete. Because of the nature of the work, most states exclude or provide incomplete coverage for farm workers, domestic servants, and casual employees. Some states have numerical exemptions, by which small firms with fewer than a specified number of employees (typically three to five) are not required to provide workers compensation benefits. However, employers can voluntarily cover employees in an exempted class.

## Eligibility Requirements

Two principal eligibility requirements must be met to receive workers compensation benefits.[29] First, the disabled person must work in a covered occupation. Second, the worker must have a job-related accident or disease. *This means the injury or disease must arise out of and in the course of employment.* The courts have gradually broadened the meaning of this term over time. The following situations are usually covered under a typical workers compensation law:

- An employee who travels is injured while engaging in activities that benefit the employer.
- The employee is injured while performing specified duties at a specified location.
- The employee is on the premises and is injured going to the work area.
- The employee has a heart attack while lifting some heavy materials.

## Workers Compensation Benefits

Workers compensation laws provide four principal benefits:

- Unlimited medical care
- Disability income
- Death benefits
- Rehabilitation services

**Unlimited Medical Care**   Medical care generally is covered in full in all states. However, 30 states have medical fee schedules that limit the amounts paid for certain medical procedures.

Medical care is expensive and presently accounts for 45 to 50 percent of total workers compensation costs.[30] To hold down medical costs, many states allow employers to use managed care plans to treat injured employees. The use of health maintenance organizations (HMOs) and preferred provider organizations (PPOs) has increased dramatically over time. As of 1995, 29 states allow *managed care arrangements* to be used in providing medical care to injured workers.[31]

**Disability Income**   Disability-income benefits can be paid after the disabled worker satisfies a waiting period that usually ranges from three to seven days. If the injured worker is still disabled after a certain number of days or weeks, most states pay disability benefits retroactively to the date of injury.

The weekly cash benefit is based on a percentage of the injured worker's average weekly wage, typically two-thirds, and is subject to minimum and maximum payments. There are four classifications of disability: (1) temporary total, (2) permanent total, (3) temporary partial, and (4) permanent partial.

Temporary total disability claims are the most common and account for about three-fourths of all cash claims. For example, a worker in Nebraska may break a leg and be totally disabled for three months. After a one-week waiting period, the disabled worker would receive two-thirds of his or her average weekly wage up to a maximum of $427 weekly.

**Death Benefits**    Death benefits can be paid to eligible survivors if the worker dies as a result of a job-related accident or disease. Two types of benefits are paid. First, a burial allowance is paid. Second, weekly income benefits can be paid to eligible surviving dependents. The weekly benefit is based on a proportion of the deceased worker's wages (typically two-thirds) and is usually paid to a surviving spouse for life or until she or he remarries. Upon remarriage, the widow or widower typically gets one or two years of payments in a lump sum. A weekly benefit can also be paid to each dependent child until a specified age, such as age 18 or later.

**Rehabilitation Services**    All states provide rehabilitation services to restore disabled workers to productive employment. In addition to weekly disability benefits, workers who are being rehabilitated are compensated for board and room, travel, books, and equipment. Training allowances may also be paid in some states.

## Second-Injury Funds

Workers compensation laws typically have provisions for a **second-injury fund.** The purpose is to encourage employers to hire handicapped workers. If a second-injury fund did not exist, employers would be reluctant to hire handicapped workers because of the higher benefits that might have to be paid if a second injury occurs.

For example, assume that a worker with a pre-existing injury or handicap is injured in a job-related accident. When combined with the first injury, the second injury produces a disability more severe than that caused by the second injury alone. Thus, the workers compensation benefits that must be paid are higher than if only the second injury had occurred. The employer pays only for the second injury, and

the second-injury fund pays the additional benefits that are required.

## Problems and Issues

Numerous problems and issues are associated with current workers compensation programs. Some important problems are summarized as follows.

1. *Compensation for occupational disease.* An important issue is the compensation of workers who are disabled by an occupational disease. Thousands of workers are disabled each year because of exposure to asbestos, cotton dust, radiation, hazardous waste materials, or other dangerous chemicals and substances. Some workers are not even aware they have been exposed or they have a disease.

   The problem of compensating workers with an occupational disease is difficult because of three factors:

   • *There is often a long latency period before the disease is detected.* It can take years for an occupational disease to manifest itself because of an earlier exposure to some dangerous substance, such as asbestos fibers.

   • *The problem of causality is also present.* The worker must show that the cause of the disease is job-related. For example, lung cancer is caused by exposure to asbestos, but it is also caused by heavy smoking off the job.

   • *There are often barriers to recovery under a workers compensation law.* For example, the law may require that a claim must be filed within a certain period after the last workplace exposure to the disease. There is also the problem of determining when the employee first became exposed to or contracted the disease, and which employer or insurer is responsible for the claim. This can be a major problem if the employee has worked for several employers with different workers compensation insurers.

   Proposed solutions to the problem include a federal compensation fund, an asbestos claim facility to settle asbestos claims outside of court, and amending workers compensation laws to eliminate barriers to recovery. In addition, special occupational disease funds exist in some jurisdictions to pay claims.

2. *Cumulative trauma disorders.* Another important problem is the substantial increase in cumulative trauma disorder claims. *Cumulative trauma disorders* are a form of occupational disease that results from repeated motions in the hand, wrist, and arm, such as highly repetitive motions used by workers in meat-packing plants. Carpal tunnel syndrome is an example of a cumulative trauma disorder that can cause serious nerve damage and a crippling of hands, arms, and wrists. Jobs that make workers highly susceptible to carpal tunnel syndrome are in meat-packing, product fabrication, food preparation, construction, mining, and clerical fields, such as typing at a computer terminal.

Employers are now using a number of approaches to reduce carpal tunnel claims. They include a redesign of work stations and special chairs for computer operators to reduce stress, instruction on the correct use of tools, and improved work habits.

3. *Increased litigation.* Although a fundamental objective of workers compensation is to reduce lawsuits, attorneys are involved in a substantial percentage of claims, especially high-cost claims. A study of claims by the National Council on Compensation Insurance revealed that 80 to 90 percent of the high-cost claims involved attorneys. High-cost claims included permanent total disability cases, permanent partial disability cases, and negotiated awards.[32]

The increased litigation is due to (1) suits by injured workers who are dissatisfied with their workers compensation awards and then sue for higher amounts; (2) denial of claims by some employers, which results in lawsuits by the injured workers; and (3) court decisions that have eroded the **exclusive remedy doctrine.** This doctrine states that workers compensation benefits should be the sole and exclusive remedy for injured workers; workers have a statutory right to receive benefits without proving negligence, but in turn, they give up the right to sue the employer. This doctrine has been eroded by court decisions in recent years. As a result, injured employees often can receive both workers compensation benefits and a tort damage award based on negligence.

## SUMMARY

- Social insurance programs are compulsory insurance programs with certain characteristics that distinguish them from other government insurance programs. Social insurance programs in the United States have the following characteristics:

  Compulsory programs

  Floor of income

  Emphasis on social adequacy rather than individual equity

  Benefits loosely related to earnings

  Benefits prescribed by law

  No means test

  Full funding unnecessary

  Financially self-supporting

- The Social Security program (OASDHI) is the most important social insurance program in the United States. Four major benefits are provided:

  Retirement benefits

  Survivor benefits

  Disability benefits

  Medicare benefits

- Unemployment insurance programs are federal-state programs that pay weekly cash benefits to workers who are involuntarily unemployed. Unemployment programs have several objectives:

  Provide cash income to unemployed workers during periods of involuntary unemployment

  Help unemployed workers find jobs

  Encourage employers to stabilize employment

  Help stabilize the economy

- Unemployed workers must meet certain eligibility requirements to receive weekly cash benefits:

  Have qualifying wages and employment during the base year

  Be able and available for work

  Actively seek work

  Be free from disqualification

  Serve a one-week waiting period in most states

- Workers compensation is a social insurance program that provides medical care, cash benefits, and rehabilitation services to workers who are disabled from job-related accidents or disease. Workers compensation laws have the following objectives:

  Broad coverage of employees for job-related injuries and disease

  Substantial protection against the loss of income

Sufficient medical care and rehabilitation services

Encouragement of safety

Reduction in litigation

- State workers compensation laws typically pay the following benefits:

Unlimited medical care

Weekly disability-income benefits

Death benefits to survivors

Rehabilitation services

## KEY CONCEPTS AND TERMS

Assumption-of-risk
  doctrine
Average indexed monthly
  earnings (AIME)
Competitive state fund
Credit (quarter of
  coverage)
Contributory negligence
  doctrine
Currently insured
Diagnosis-related groups
  (DRGs)
Disability insured
Earnings test (retirement
  test)
Experience rating
Extended-benefits
  program
Fellow-servant doctrine
Fully funded program
Fully insured

Hospital Insurance
  (Part A)
Individual equity
Liability without fault
Means test
Monopoly state fund
Primary insurance amount
  (PIA)
Resource-based relative-
  value scale
Second-injury fund
Short-term involuntary
  unemployment
Social adequacy
Social Security
  (OASDHI)
Supplementary Medical
  Insurance (Part B)
Unemployment insurance
Workers compensation

## QUESTIONS FOR REVIEW

1. Why are social insurance programs necessary?

2. Describe the basic characteristics of social insurance programs.

3. Explain the meaning of fully insured, currently insured, and disability insured under the OASDI program.

4. Describe briefly the major benefits under the Social Security program.

5. Why are wages indexed for purposes of determining monthly cash income benefits under the OASDI program?

6. Explain the definition of disability used in the OASDI program.

7. Describe the basic objectives of unemployment insurance programs.

8. Explain the eligibility requirements for receiving unemployment insurance benefits.

9. Describe the basic objectives of workers compensation laws.

10. Identify the major benefits under a typical workers compensation law.

## QUESTIONS FOR DISCUSSION

1. Critics of the OASDI program believe the program should be partially or totally privatized to eliminate the financial problems that OASDI may experience in the future.

   a. Identify the major problems in the present OASDI program.

   b. Describe the major proposals for privatizing the OASDI program.

2. Critics argue that Medicare must be reformed because of the current financial crisis in the HI program.

   a. Why is the HI trust fund expected to be exhausted in the near-term future if the financing is not changed?

   b. Describe several approaches for holding down increases in Medicare spending.

   c. Does the Supplementary Medical Insurance (SMI) program contribute to the financial problems of Medicare? Explain your answer.

3. The earnings (retirement) test is one of the most controversial issues in the OASDI program.

   a. Describe the major characteristics of the earnings test.

   b. Explain the purposes of the earnings test.

   c. Why should the earnings test be abolished?

   d. Why should the earnings test be retained?

4. A critic of unemployment insurance stated that "unemployment insurance programs are designed to maintain the economic security of unemployed workers, but several critical problems must be resolved."

   a. Are all types of unemployment covered under the state unemployment insurance programs? Explain.

   b. Describe some situations that may disqualify a worker for unemployment benefits.

   c. Are all unemployed persons receiving unemployment insurance benefits at the present time? Explain your answer.

5. Workers compensation laws provide considerable financial protection to workers who have a job-related injury or disease.

   a. Explain the fundamental principle on which workers compensation laws are based.

   b. Explain the eligibility requirements for collecting workers compensation benefits.

   c. Explain the problem of compensating workers who have an occupational disease.

   d. Explain the problem of cumulative trauma disorders in workers compensation insurance.

## SELECTED REFERENCES

Advisory Council on Social Security. *Report of the 1994–1996 Advisory Council on Social Security,* Vol. I and II. Washington, D.C.: U.S. Government Printing Office, 1997.

Advisory Council on Unemployment Compensation. *Reports and Recommendations.* Washington, D.C.: Advisory Council on Unemployment Compensation, 1994.

———. *Unemployment Insurance in the United States: Benefits, Financing, Coverage.* Washington, D.C.: Advisory Council on Unemployment Compensation, 1995.

———. *Collected Findings and Recommendations: 1994–1996.* Washington, D.C.: Advisory Council on Unemployment Compensation, 1996.

———. *Defining Federal and State Roles in Unemployment Insurance.* Washington, D.C.: Advisory Council on Unemployment Compensation, 1996.

*John Burton's Workers' Compensation Monitor.* This important periodical is published six times annually and analyzes all aspects of workers' compensation insurance.

Myers, Robert J. *Social Security.* 4th ed. Philadelphia: Pension Research Council and University of Pennsylvania Press, 1993.

———. "Privatization of Social Security: A Good Idea?" *Journal of the American Society of CLU and ChFC,* Vol. 50, No. 4 (July 1996), pp. 42–46.

## CASE APPLICATION

Simon, age 35, and Andrea, age 33, are married and have a son, age one. Simon is employed as an accountant and earns $40,000 annually. Andrea is an associate professor of finance at a local university and earns $70,000 annually. Both are currently and fully insured under the OASDI program. Assume you are a financial planner who is asked to give advice concerning OASDI and other social insurance programs. Answer each of the following questions based on the following situations. Treat each situation separately.

a. Simon is killed in an automobile accident. To what extent, if any, would the surviving family members be eligible to receive OASDI survivor benefits?

b. Andrea has laryngitis that damaged her vocal cords. As a result, she can no longer teach. She is offered a research position in the business research bureau of the university where she is employed. To what extent, if any, would Andrea be eligible to receive OASDI disability benefits?

c. A deranged student fired a handgun at Andrea because she gave him a grade of D+. As a result, Andrea was seriously injured and is expected to be off work for at least one year while she is recovering. To what extent, if any, would existing social insurance programs in the United States provide income during the period of temporary disability?

d. Simon would like to retire at age 62 and still work part-time as an accountant. He has been informed that the OASDI earnings test would be relevant in his case. Explain how the earnings test might affect his decision to work part-time after retirement.

e. Simon resigned from his job to find a higher-paying position. Explain whether or not Simon could receive unemployment insurance benefits during the period of temporary unemployment before he finds a new job.

*1996 Analysis of Workers Compensation Laws.* Washington, D.C.: U.S. Chamber of Commerce, 1996.

Rejda, George E. *Social Insurance and Economic Security,* 5th ed. Englewood Cliffs, New Jersey: Prentice-Hall, Inc., 1994.

———— "Unemployment Compensation Programs," in Jerry D. Rosenbloom, ed., 4th ed. *The Handbook of Employee Benefits, Design, Funding, Administration.* Burr Ridge, IL.: Irwin Professional Publishing, 1996, chapter 28.

Robertson, A. Haeworth. *Social Security: What Every Taxpayer Should Know.* Charlotte, N.C.: Retirement Policy Institute, 1992.

Worrall, John D., and David L. Durbin. "Workers Compensation Insurance," in Jerry D. Rosenbloom, ed., 4th ed. *The Handbook of Employee Benefits, Design, Funding, Administration.* Burr Ridge, IL.: Irwin Professional Publishing, 1996, chapter 27.

## NOTES

1. *1997 Guide to Social Security and Medicare* (Louisville, Ky.: William M. Mercer, November, 1996), p. 23.

2. George E. Rejda, *Social Insurance and Economic Security,* 5th ed. (Englewood Cliffs, N.J.: Prentice-Hall, 1994), pp. 22–30.

3. Social Security Administration.

4. See Rejda, chapters 5 and 6, for a complete discussion of the Social Security program. This section is based largely on this source.

5. Social Security Administration, *Basic Facts About Social Security,* SSA Publication No. 05-10080 (August 1995), p. 2.

6. A more liberal rule applies to blind workers. A blind worker age 55 or older must be unable to perform work that requires skills or abilities comparable to those required by the work that he or she did regularly before age 55 (or before he or she became blind, if later than age 55).

7. Rejda, pp. 252–53.

8. *1996 Annual Report of the Board of Trustees of the Federal Supplementary Medical Insurance Trust Fund* (June 1996), p. 36.

9. The self-employed are allowed two deductions that reduce the effective tax rate. First, net earnings from self-employment are reduced by an amount approximately equal to one-half of the total self-employment tax. This reflects the fact that the employer's share of the total Social Security tax is not considered taxable income to the employee. Second, for income-tax purposes, half of the self-employment tax is deductible as a business expense, which reflects the fact that employers are allowed to deduct the Social Security taxes paid on behalf of their employees.

10. *Report of the 1994–1996 Advisory Council on Social Security, Volume I: Findings and Recommendations* (Washington, D.C.: 1994–1996 Advisory Council on Social Security, 1997), pp. 11–14.

11. Ibid, p. 41.

12. Social Security and Medicare Boards of Trustees, *Status of the Social Security and Medicare Programs, A Summary of the 1996 Annual Reports* (June 1996), p. 11.

13. Ibid, p. 12.

14. This discussion is based on Rejda, pp. 138–45.

15. For example, see Michael D. Packard, "The Earnings Test and the Short-Run Work Response to Its Elimination," *Social Security Bulletin,* 53, no. 9 (September 1990): 2–16.

16. The material on unemployment insurance in this chapter is based on Rejda, chapters 14 and 15.

17. Employment and Training Administration, U.S. Department of Labor, *Significant Provisions of State Unemployment Insurance Laws* (July 5, 1995).

18. Committee on Ways and Means, U.S. House of Representatives, *1994 Green Book, Background Material and Data on Programs Within the Jurisdiction of the Committee on Ways and Means* (Washington, D.C.: U.S. Government Printing Office, 1994), p. 267.

19. Advisory Council on Unemployment Compensation, *Report and Recommendations* (Washington, D.C.: Advisory Council on Unemployment Compensation, 1994), pp. 31–32.

20. Advisory Council on Unemployment Compensation, *Unemployment Insurance in the United States: Benefits, Financing, Coverage* (Washington, D.C.: Advisory Council on Unemployment Compensation, 1995), Table C-1, pp. 242–43.

21. The low estimate is based on the 1992 Consumer Expenditure Survey and includes housing, utilities, health care, some transportation, and debt payments. The high estimate includes housing, utilities, health care, transportation, debt payments, insurance, regular services, and support payments.

22. *Unemployment Insurance in the United States: Benefits, Financing, Coverage,* Table 9-2, p. 133.

23. The "high-cost multiple" is calculated by dividing a state's reserve ratio by the highest cost rate (highest ratio of benefits paid divided by total covered wages) incurred during any 12-month period.

24. *Unemployment Insurance in the United States: Benefits, Financing, Coverage,* Table 5-1, p. 56.

25. Bureau of Labor Statistics as reported in *The Wall Street Journal,* March 25, 1997, p. A1.

26. The material on workers compensation in this section is based on Rejda, chapter 12.

27. Rejda, pp. 307–10.

28. Monopoly state funds exist in Nevada, North Dakota, Ohio, Washington, West Virginia, and Wyoming. States that have a competitive state fund are Arizona, California, Colorado, Hawaii, Idaho, Kentucky, Louisiana, Maine, Maryland, Michigan, Minnesota, Montana, New York, Oklahoma, Oregon, Pennsylvania, Tennessee, Texas, and Utah.

29. Rejda, p. 314.

30. John D. Worrall, and David L. Durbin, "Workers Compensation Insurance," in Jerry D. Rosenbloom, ed., 4th ed. *The Handbook of Employee Benefits, Design, Funding, Administration* (Burr Ridge, IL.: Irwin Professional Publishing, 1996), p. 590.

31. Ibid, p. 594.

32. Angela Calise Dauer, "'Stunning' Attorney Involvement Revealed in WC," *National Underwriter,* Property & Casualty/Risk & Benefits Management Edition, October 1995, p. 3.

# Part Six

# THE INSURANCE INDUSTRY

Many insurance industry associations have established World Wide Web sites. Some of these associations were listed in the On-Line Resources for Part One. Others include the following:

The American Institute for Chartered Property Casualty Underwriters and Insurance Institute of America at:

> http://www.aicpcu.org

The Casualty Actuarial Society at:

> http://www.casact.org/

The National Association of Insurance Women at:

> http://www.naiw.org/

The American Insurance Association at:

> http://www.aiadc.org/

The American Association of Independent Insurance Agents at:

> http://www.iiaa.iix.com/

The National Association of Insurance Brokers at:

> www.naib.org/

The Professional Insurance Agents Association at:

> www.pianet.com/

The National Association of Mutual Insurance Companies at:

> http://www.namic.org/

Still others, such as that of the Society of Certified Insurance Counselors, can be found at the Insurance Association Center at:

> http://connectyou.com/ins/

Several Web sites feature information about careers in insurance. For example, see the Insurance Career Center at:

> http://connectyou.com/talent/

For information about regulation of the insurance industry, visit the site of the National Association of Insurance Commissioners at:

> http://www.naic.org/

The map of insurance regulators features links to regulators' sites in various states.

# Chapter 24

# Types of Insurers and Marketing Systems

*"A good agent or broker is worth his [or her] weight in gold; a bad one can be a disaster."*

Herbert S. Denenberg,
The Shopper's Guidebook

## Student Learning Objectives

After studying this chapter, you should be able to:

■ Describe the major types of private insurers in the United States, including

stock insurers

mutual insurers

reciprocal exchanges

Lloyd's Associations

Blue Cross and Blue Shield plans

Health maintenances organizations (HMOs).

■ Explain the legal distinction between agents and brokers.

■ Describe the basic marketing systems for selling life insurance, including

general agency system

managerial (branch office) system

direct response system.

■ Describe the different marketing systems for selling property and liability insurance, including

independent agency system

exclusive agency system

direct writing

direct response.

■ Describe the major characteristics of mass merchandising plans.

There are thousands of life and health insurers and property and liability insurers doing business in the United States today. The private insurance industry has a profound impact on the American economy. The industry controls some $2.7 trillion in financial assets and provides more than 2.2 million jobs. The industry also is an important source of capital to the business community. In addition, private insurers make available insurance contracts and financial products that enable individuals and families to attain a high degree of financial security. Finally, indemnification for losses is one of the most important economic functions of private insurance; insureds are restored partly or completely to their previous financial position, thereby maintaining their economic security.

This chapter discusses the basic characteristics of the private insurance industry, including the major types of private insurers, the various methods for marketing insurance, and the role of agents and brokers in the sales process.

## TYPES OF PRIVATE INSURERS

A large number of private insurers are currently doing business in the United States. In mid-1995, 1736 U.S. life insurers were operating in various states. These insurers make available a wide variety of life and health products, private pension plans, and related financial products. In addition, at the end of 1993, 3346 property and liability insurers were doing business in the United States.[1] These insurers sell some form of property and liability insurance and related lines, including inland marine coverages and surety and fidelity bonds.

In terms of legal organization and ownership, the major types of private insurers can be classified as follows:

- Stock insurers
- Mutual insurers
- Reciprocal exchanges
- Lloyd's Associations
- Blue Cross and Blue Shield plans
- Health maintenance organizations (HMOs)

### Stock Insurers

A **stock insurer** *is a corporation owned by stockholders who participate in the profits and losses of the insurer.*

The stockholders elect a board of directors who appoint executive officers to manage the corporation. The board of directors has the ultimate responsibility for the corporation's financial success.

The types of insurance that a stock insurer can write are determined by its charter. In property and liability insurance, the majority of stock insurers are multiple-line insurers that write most types of insurance, with the exception of life and health insurance. Some states also permit the writing of life and health insurance.

A stock insurer cannot issue an assessable policy. As assessable policy permits the insurer to assess the policyowners additional premiums if losses are excessive. Instead, the stockholders must bear all losses. But they also share in the profits: if the business is profitable, dividends can be declared and paid to the stockholders based on the amount of common stock ownership.

Stock insurers predominate in the property and liability insurance industry, especially with respect to commercial lines of insurance. Stock insurers account for a large proportion of the property and liability premiums written by private insurers and typically market their insurance by using the independent agency system (discussed later).

### Mutual Insurers

A **mutual insurer** *is a corporation owned by the policyowners.* The policyowners elect the board of directors, which appoints the executives who manage the corporation. Since relatively few policyowners bother to vote, the board of directors has effective management control of the company.

A mutual insurer may pay a dividend or give a rate reduction in advance. In life insurance, a dividend is largely a refund of a redundant premium that can be paid if the mortality, investment, and operating experience is favorable. However, since the mortality and investment experience cannot be guaranteed, the dividends legally cannot be guaranteed by insurers.

There are several types of mutual insurers, including the following:

- Assessment mutual
- Advance premium mutual
- Factory mutual
- Fraternal insurer

**Assessment Mutual**    An **assessment mutual** *is an insurer that has the right to assess policy-owners an additional amount if the experience is unfavorable.* Relatively few assessment mutuals are in existence today, partly because of the practical problem of collecting the assessments. Those insurers still doing business are smaller insurers that operate in limited geographical areas and write only a limited number of lines of insurance.

**Advance Premium Mutual**    An **advance premium mutual** *is owned by the policyowners, but it does not issue an assessable policy.* Once the insurer's surplus exceeds a certain amount (difference between assets and liabilities), the states will not permit a mutual insurer to issue an assessable policy. The advance premium mutual is generally larger and financially stronger than the assessment mutual described earlier. The premiums charged are expected to be sufficient to pay all claims and expenses. Any additional costs because of poor experience are paid out of the company's surplus.

In life insurance, most mutual insurers pay dividends annually to the policyowners. In property and liability insurance, dividends to policyowners are not paid on a regular basis. Property and liability insurers instead charge lower initial premiums that are closer to the actual amount needed for claims and expenses.

**Factory Mutual**    A **factory mutual** *is a specialized insurer that insures only superior properties.* There is great emphasis on loss prevention, and before a factory can be insured, it must meet stringent underwriting standards. The factory typically must be of superior construction, have an approved sprinkler system, and meet other requirements.

A factory mutual provides periodic inspection and engineering services to its insureds. Since the costs of these loss-control services are high, only the larger risks are eligible for the insurance. The insurance contracts provide broad coverage, and coinsurance normally is not used.

A distinct characteristic of factory mutual insurance is a relatively high initial premium. The premium paid will substantially exceed the amounts needed for claims and expenses. At the end of the period, a large percentage of the initial premium—typically 65 percent or more—is refunded as a dividend to the policyowner. As a result, the insureds receive their protection at relatively low cost because of the great emphasis on loss prevention.

**Fraternal Insurer**    A **fraternal insurer** *is a mutual insurer that provides life and health insurance to members of a social or religious organization.* To qualify as a fraternal insurer under a state's insurance code, the insurer must have some type of social or religious organization in existence, such as a lodge or a religious, charitable, or benevolent society. Examples of fraternals are the Knights of Columbus, Catholic Workmen, and Aid Association for Lutherans.

Fraternal insurers sell only life and health insurance to their members. The assessment principle was originally used to pay death claims. Today, most fraternals operate on the basis of the level premium and legal reserve system that is used by commercial life insurers. Fraternal insurers also sell term life insurance.

Since fraternals are nonprofit or charitable organizations they receive favorable tax treatment.

**Changing Corporate Structure of Mutual Insurers**    The corporate form of a mutual insurer owned solely by policyowners is gradually changing. Two changes are noteworthy. First, a number of advanced premium mutuals have converted to stock insurers in recent years. The major reason for such demutualization is the need for additional capital to remain competitive.

Converting from a mutual to a stock insurer, however, is cumbersome, slow, and expensive. The second change involves creation of a mutual holding company as an alternative to demutualization. *A number of states have recently enacted legislation that would allow mutual insurers to sell stock to the public by reorganizing as a mutual holding company.* A new mutual holding company would be created and controlled by the policyowners. The mutual holding company would have a minimum of 51 percent ownership in a stock subsidiary company or operating unit. This latter entity would sell stock to the public to raise the capital needed to expand or remain competitive (see Insight 24.1).

## Reciprocal Exchanges

A **reciprocal exchange** *can be defined as an unincorporated mutual.* A reciprocal insurer has several

# INSIGHT 24.1

## Mutual Insurers Consider New Means of Going Public

### A Look at Mutual Insurers

**Biggest Mutual insurers**
Ranked by policyholder surplus
as of Dec 31, 1996

| COMPANY | AMOUNT (billions) |
|---|---|
| State Farm, Bloomington, Ill. | $30.05 |
| Prudential, Newark, N.J. | 9.37 |
| Metropolitan Life, New York | 7.15 |
| Liberty Mutual, Boston | 4.87 |
| Nationwide, Columbus, Ohio | 4.64 |
| New York Life, New York | 4.01 |
| Northwestern, Milwaukee | 3.51 |

NOTE: Listed are companies that sell to the general public. Coverages sold include any or all of the following: life, health, home, auto and business insurance

*Source:* A.M. Best Co.

**A shrinking Universe**
Mergers, insolvencies and demutualizations have already decreased the ranks steadily. Chart shows number of mutual insurers.

As the insurance industry consolidates and becomes more competitive, mutuals find they are in danger of being left behind by bigger and better-capitalized publicly owned insurers. As a result, some of the nation's biggest mutuals are considering going public themselves.

Converting from a mutual to a shareholder-owned company is both cumbersome and costly, however. *To make the process easier, mutuals are pushing states to adopt legislation allowing them to create special operating units that could issue stock, while the parent company remains under the ownership of policyholders.*

### Push for Hybrid Structure

So far, about 10 states have approved this hybrid-type of company, and about a dozen others—including Massachusetts and New York—are debating it. Although states traditionally have discouraged conversions by mutuals out of concern for policyholder interests, many have been swayed recently by the mutuals' argument that shareholder-owned companies have a big competitive advantage because they can raise capital more easily.

For policyholders, one benefit of such a conversion is that their policies would in most instances be backed by a bigger, stronger company that would be less likely to suffer a ratings downgrade because it is losing competitive ground. *But consumer activists fret that mutual policyholders would be gaining some things they won't like, such as competing demands for capital within the company.* For example, policyholders who desire higher dividends to be paid on policies or improved claims service would be up against shareholders who favor higher stock dividends and earnings.

### Backed by Leading Mutuals

In Massachusetts, three powerhouses—**John Hancock Mutual Life Insurance** Co., **Liberty Mutual Insurance**

*Continued*

Co. and **Massachusetts Mutual Life Insurance** Co.—are backers of a pending state bill to allow the hybrid mutuals. One of the newest states to take up the matter is New York. **Metropolitan Life Insurance** Co., **New York Life Insurance** Co. and several other prominent New York mutuals are part of a group lobbying for a recently introduced bill.

Elsewhere, two Midwestern mutuals, **AmerUs Life Holdings** Inc., Des Moines, Iowa, and **General American Life Insurance** Co., St Louis, have converted to the hybrid form; Washington, D.C.-based **Acacia Mutual Life Insurance** Co. is deep into the process; and **Pacific Mutual Life Insurance** Co. announced that it is seeking approval from California regulators to begin conversion to a hybrid.

Mutuals have long had the option of converting to stock ownership through a process known as "demutualization." But it is a costly, cumbersome and controversial route because many state laws require mutuals converting to shareholder ownership to compensate their policyholders, who, by long tradition, have been defined as the owners. Demonstrating to regulators that policyholders are equitably compensated—with cash, stock or policy enhancements—leads to big bills for consultants, actuaries, accountants and lawyers. But no such demonstration is generally necessary under the hybrid form, analysts say.

### Policyholders' Interests

The concept is borrowed from the savings-and-loan industry, says Moody's Investors Service analyst Joel Salomon. It involves creation of a "mutual holding company." Many historical rights of mutual policyholders—such as the right to vote for board members—are transferred to the holding company from the long-standing mutual operating business. Policyholders' contractual rights—matters related to premiums and benefits, for instance—continue with the operating unit.

It is this operating unit, or an intermediate holding company above it, that has the ability to sell a public stake.

To be sure, the hybrid-company form isn't without controversy of its own. Jason Adkins, executive director of the Center for Insurance Research, a policyholder-rights organization based in Cambridge, Mass., calls much of the legislation—both approved and proposed—"grossly anticonsumer." He argues that some versions "substantially alter the legal rights and protections formerly available to mutual policyholders" and introduce "obvious conflicts of interest." For example, directors of a mutual holding company, he says, would no longer owe a fiduciary duty solely to policyholders, as they have historically.

"In a gust of greed," he contends, some mutual-insurance managers are promoting the hybrid form because they can obtain, sooner or later, "sizable stock options" and other financial incentives customary at publicly owned companies.

### Advantages for Management

But Stephen Brown, John Hancock's chairman, says the criticism "is not valid." He contends that ample regulatory and other safeguards exist to protect policyholders' interests, and he believes policyholders, who must approve the conversions, gain by becoming part of a "stronger and sounder" company.

Certain aspects of the hybrid form clearly favor management. The permanent 51% policyholder stake virtually eliminates the threat of a hostile takeover—and the loss of managers' jobs, analysts note. But a conversion isn't without its downside. Investors' permanent minority status could lead to a stock-trading discount relative to other insurers.

Source: Excerpted from Leslie Scism, "Mutual Insurers Consider New Means of Going Public," *The Wall Street Journal*, April 28, 1997, p. B8.

distinct characteristics. *First, in its purest form, insurance is exchanged among the members; each member of the reciprocal insurers the other members and, in turn, is insured by them.* Thus, there is an exchange of insurance promises—hence the name reciprocal exchange.

*Second, a reciprocal is managed by an attorney-in-fact.* The attorney-in-fact is usually a corporation that is authorized by the subscribers to seek new members, pay losses, collect premiums, handle reinsurance arrangements, invest the funds, and perform other administrative duties. However, the attorney-in-fact is not personally liable for the payment of claims and is not the insurer. The reciprocal exchange is the insurer.

*Third, from an historical perspective, reciprocals can be classified as pure or modified.* Historically, the reciprocals that operated earlier were of the pure type. A separate account was kept for each member. The account was credited with the member's premiums and share of investment earnings and debited for the member's share of losses and expenses. The balance in the account could be paid to a terminating member. Thus, in its purest form, insurance was provided "at cost" to the member.

Most reciprocals today are of the modified type. In the modified form, a reciprocal is similar to an advance premium mutual. Individual accounts are not set up for each member to reflect the profit or losses of the reciprocal. In effect, the financial operations of the reciprocal are similar to a mutual insurer, with the exception of management by an attorney-in-fact.[2]

Most reciprocals are relatively small and account for only a small percentage of the total property and liability insurance premiums written. In addition, most reciprocals specialize in a limited number of lines of insurance. However, a few reciprocals are multiple-line insurers and can be large.

## Lloyd's Associations

Insurance can also be purchased from a Lloyd's Association. There are two basic types of **Lloyd's Associations:** (1) Lloyd's of London, and (2) American Lloyds.

**Lloyd's of London** **Lloyd's of London** is a major worldwide ocean marine insurer that writes a wide variety of risks and is extremely important as a professional reinsurer. Lloyd's is also famous for writing insurance on diverse exposure units such as a pianist's fingers, a Kentucky Derby winner's legs, and a hole-in-one at a professional golf tournament.

Lloyd's of London has several important characteristics. *First, Lloyd's technically is not an insurance company, but is an association that provides physical facilities and services to the members for selling insurance.* Lloyd's by itself does not write insurance; the insurance is written by the syndicates that belong to Lloyd's. In this respect, Lloyd's is similar to the New York Stock Exchange, which does not buy or sell securities, but provides a marketplace and other services to the members.

*Second, the insurance is actually written by the various syndicates that belong to Lloyd's.* The syndicates are managed by an underwriting agent who is responsible for appointing a professional underwriter for each major type of business. The syndicates tend to specialize in marine, aviation, automobile, and other property and liability insurance lines. The unusual exposure units that have made Lloyd's famous account for only a small part of the total business. Likewise, life insurance accounts only for a small fraction of the total business and is limited to short-term contracts.

*Third, the individual members (called Names) who belong to the various syndicates have unlimited liability with respect to insurance written as individuals.* Some 34,000 Names are members of Lloyd's of London, of which 2700 are Americans.[3] Names pledge their personal fortunes to pay their agreed-upon share of the insurance written as individuals and have unlimited liability.

Prior to 1993, Lloyd's experienced severe underwriting losses. These losses were due largely to natural disasters, asbestos liability claims, and mismanagement. Because of unlimited liability, many individual Names could not pay their share of claims and were financially ruined.

*Another characteristic is that corporations with limited liability can join Lloyd's of London.* Because of the underwriting losses mentioned earlier and the need to raise new capital, corporations are now permitted to join Lloyd's of London. Unlike the individual Names, however, corporations have limited liability. The infusion of new capital from corporations has substantially increased the ability of Lloyd's to write new business.

*Individual members must also meet stringent financial requirements.* Each member must make a substantial underwriting deposit. All premiums are deposited into a premium trust fund, and withdrawals are allowed only for claims and expenses. A central guarantee fund pays the loss if an individual member is financially insolvent.

*Finally, Lloyd's is licensed only in a small number of jurisdictions in the United States.* In the other states, Lloyd's must operate as a nonadmitted insurer. This means that a surplus lines broker or agent can place business with Lloyd's, but only if the insurance cannot be obtained from an admitted insurer in the state. Despite the lack of licensing, Lloyd's does a considerable amount of business in the United States. In particular, Lloyd's of London reinsures a large number of American insurers and is an important professional reinsurer.

In conclusion, the financial situation of Lloyd's is improving. After five years of losses, Lloyd's reported a profit in 1993 (the books are audited every three years). Despite the return to profitability, conflict remains. Litigation by some Names against Lloyd's over their share of pre-1993 underwriting losses continues. Another heated issue is the competing financial interests of individual Names who have unlimited liability, versus corporate members, who have limited liability.[4]

**American Lloyds**  Private underwriters in the United States have formed associations similar to Lloyd's of London. The American Lloyds associations, however, differ from Lloyd's of London in many respects. First, the number of individual underwriters is smaller. Second, the liability of an individual underwriter is limited. Each underwriter is responsible only for his or her share of the loss and not that of any insolvent member. Third, the personal net worth and financial strength of an underwriter are considerably lower than that of a Lloyd's of London member. Fourth, an American Lloyd's association does not operate through a syndicate, but is managed by an attorney-in-fact. Finally, the financial reputation of an American Lloyds association is not as good as Lloyd's of London. Several associations have failed, and some states, such as New York, forbid the formation of new associations.

**Insurance Exchanges**  Several states earlier passed legislation that allowed **insurance exchanges**

to be organized to provide a market for large and unusual domestic and foreign risks that were difficult to insure in the normal markets. These exchanges included the New York Insurance Exchange; the Insurance Exchange of the Americas in Miami, Florida; and the Illinois Insurance Exchange. The exchanges were organized as syndicates with broker members who provided direct insurance and reinsurance on a basis similar to that provided by the syndicates of Lloyd's of London. Because of heavy financial losses, the New York and Miami exchanges have discontinued operations. The Illinois Exchange, however, continues to operate.

## Blue Cross and Blue Shield Plans

Blue Cross and Blue Shield plans are another type of insurer organization. In most states, Blue Cross plans typically are organized as nonprofit, community-oriented prepayment plans that provide coverage primarily for hospital services. Blue Shield plans generally are nonprofit, prepayment plans that provide payment for physicians' and surgeons' fees and other medical services. In recent years, the majority of Blue Cross and Blue Shield plans have merged into single entities. In early 1997, 49 plans jointly wrote Blue Cross and Blue Shield benefits. However, six separate Blue Cross plans and four Blue Shield plans were in operation.

Although most members are insured through group plans, individual and family coverages are also available. Blue Cross and Blue Shield plans also sponsor health maintenance organizations (HMOs) and preferred provider organizations (PPOs).

In the majority of states, Blue Cross and Blue Shield plans are nonprofit organizations that receive favorable tax treatment and are regulated under special legislation. However, in order to raise capital and become more competitive, a few Blue Cross and Blue Shield plans have recently converted to a for-profit status with stockholders and a board of directors. In addition, many nonprofit Blue Cross and Blue Shield plans own profit-seeking affiliates.

## Health Maintenance Organizations (HMOs)

Health maintenance organizations (HMOs) are organized plans of health care that provide broad, comprehensive health-care services to the members for a fixed prepaid fee. Almost one in four workers in employer-sponsored health plans was enrolled in an HMO in 1995. HMOs provide broad health-care services to a specified group for a fixed prepaid fee; cost control is emphasized; choice of health-care providers may be restricted; and less costly forms of treatment are often provided. The characteristics of HMOs have already been discussed in Chapter 21, so additional treatment is not needed here.

## AGENTS AND BROKERS

A successful sales force is the key to the company's financial success. Most policies today are sold by agents and brokers.

### Agents

An **agent** *is someone who legally represents the insurer and has the authority to act on the insurer's behalf.* As we noted in Chapter 4, an agent can bind the principal by expressed powers, by implied powers, and by apparent authority. If you buy insurance, you will probably purchase the insurance from an agent. However, there is an important difference between a life insurance agent and a property and liability insurance agent. A life insurance agent usually does not have the authority to bind the company. He or she is merely a soliciting agent who induces persons to apply for life insurance. The applicant for life insurance must be approved by the company before the insurance becomes effective.

In contrast, a property and liability insurance agent typically has the power to bind the company immediately with respect to certain types of coverage. *This is normally done by a binder, which is temporary evidence of insurance until the policy is actually issued.* Binders can be oral or written. For example, if you telephone an agent and request insurance on your motorcycle, the insurance can become effective immediately.

### Brokers

*In contrast to an agent who represents the insurer, a* **broker** *is someone who legally represents the insured.* A broker legally does not have the authority to bind the insurer. Instead, the broker can solicit or accept applications for insurance and then attempt to place the coverage with an appropriate insurer. But the insurance is not in force until the insurer accepts the business.

A broker is paid a commission from the insurers where the business is placed. Many brokers are also licensed as agents, so that they have the authority to bind their companies as agents.

Brokers are extremely important in property and liability insurance at the present time. Large brokerage firms have knowledge of highly specialized insurance markets, provide risk management and loss control services, and control the accounts of large corporate insurance buyers.

Brokers are also important in the surplus line markets. *Surplus lines refer to any type of insurance for which there is no available market within the state, and the coverage must be placed with a nonadmitted insurer.* A **nonadmitted insurer** *is an insurer not licensed to do business in the state.* A **surplus lines broker** *is a special type of broker who is licensed to place business with a nonadmitted insurer.* An individual may be unable to obtain the coverage from an admitted insurer because the loss exposure is too great, or the required amount of insurance is too large. A surplus lines broker has the authority to place the business with a surplus lines insurer if the coverage cannot be obtained in the state from an admitted company.

Finally, brokers are also important in the area of employee benefits, especially for larger employers. Large employers often obtain their group life and medical expense coverages through brokers.

## TYPES OF MARKETING SYSTEMS

Marketing systems refer to the various methods for selling insurance. Insurers employ actuaries, claims adjusters, underwriters, and other home office personnel, but unless insurance policies are profitably sold, the insurer's financial survival is unlikely. Thus, an efficient marketing system is essential to an insurance company's survival.

### Life Insurance Marketing Systems

Several basic marketing methods are used by life and health insurers:

- General agency system
- Managerial (branch office) system
- Direct-response system

**General Agency System**    Under the **general agency system,** the general agent is an independent businessperson who represents only one insurer.

## INSIGHT 24.2

### How About Life Insurance Selling As a Career?

Selling life insurance is a tough job, and only a relatively small number of new life insurance agents are successful. The four-year retention rate for the industry is 17 percent.

Most insurers use various psychological and aptitude tests to select potentially successful agents. The tests are imperfect tools at best, but two traits of a successful life insurance agent have been identified. One is empathy, which enables an agent to "read" a client's feelings and attitudes. The other is the agent's ego; the fear of rejection does not bother the successful agent. The most successful agents are not easily discouraged and will work harder at making a sale if the prospect initially says no.

Insurers typically finance new agents for an initial period in the form of a guaranteed draw. A successful new agent can expect to earn $25,000–$30,000 for the first year and $50,000–$70,000 after five years. However, the highly successful agents who belong to the elite Million Dollar Round Table (MDRT) earn considerably higher incomes. This is an organization of members who consistently sell large amounts of insurance annually. However, membership in the MDRT is no longer based on the amount of life insurance sold but on first-year commissions. In 1997, the requirement for membership was at least $53,000 in first-year commissions. Members of the MDRT typically earn $100,000 or more annually.

Most agents in the life insurance industry will earn incomes that fall below the MDRT figures. However, for the serious, highly talented agent, the financial rewards can be great.

---

The general agent is in charge of a territory and is responsible for hiring, training, and motivating new agents (see Insight 24.2). The general agent receives a commission based on the amount of business produced.

Most insurers provide some financial assistance to the general agent. The insurer pays all or part of the expenses of hiring and training new agents and thus has considerable control over the selection of agents and their training. The insurer may also provide an allowance for agency office expenses and other expenses.

A considerable amount of new life insurance is sold currently by personal-producing general agents. A **personal-producing general agent** is a variation of the agency system by which an experienced agent is hired primarily to sell insurance under a contract that provides both direct and overriding commissions. A personal-producing general agent typically is an above-average salesperson with a proven sales record. The agent is hired primarily to sell insurance and not to recruit and train new agents. The personal-producing general agent usually receives higher commissions than a typical

agent. In return, the agent may be expected to sell a certain amount of insurance for a particular insurer. In addition, the personal-producing general agent may have contracts with more than one insurer. Finally, the personal-producing general agent usually pays his or her expenses but may receive a higher overriding commission to help pay expenses.

**Managerial (Branch Office) System**   The **managerial system** (also called the **branch office system**) is another distribution system for selling life insurance, especially by larger insurers. Under this system, branch offices are established in various areas. The branch manager has the responsibility for hiring and training new agents. However, the branch manager is considered an employee of the insurer, who typically is paid a salary and a bonus based on the volume and quality of the insurance sold and the number of new productive agents added. Under this system, the insurer pays the expenses of the branch office, including the financing of new agents.

**Direct-Response System**   The direct-response is a marketing system where life and health insurance is sold without the services of an agent. Potential customers are solicited by advertising in the mail, newspapers, magazines, television, radio, and other media. Some insurers also use *telemarketing* and the telephone and internet to sell insurance. The life and health insurance products that are promoted usually are easy to understand and require relatively low premium outlays. These products include accident policies, hospital indemnity policies, credit life insurance, and basic forms of term insurance.

The major advantages of the direct-response system are that advertising can be specifically directed toward selected markets, acquisition costs can be held down, and new markets can be penetrated. The disadvantages, however, are that complex products cannot be easily sold by this method since an agent's services may be required, the advertising promoting the product may be misleading or deceptive, and the products generally are supplemental in nature and may not be designed as a basic coverage.[5]

Finally, substantial amounts of new individual life insurance, annuities, long-term care insurance, and other insurance and financial products are now being sold in group insurance plans by convenient payroll deduction plans (see Insight 24.3).

## Property and Liability Insurance Marketing Systems

There are four basic systems for marketing property and liability insurance:

- Independent agency system
- Exclusive agency system
- Direct writer
- Direct-response system

**Independent Agency System**    The **independent agency system,** which is sometimes called the American agency system, has several basic characteristics. First, *the independent agency is a firm that usually represents several unrelated insurers.* Agents are authorized to write business on behalf of these insurers and in turn are paid a commission based on the amount of business produced.

Second, the agency owns the *expirations or renewal rights to the business.* If a policy comes up for renewal, the agency can place the business with another insurer if it chooses to do so. Likewise, if the

contract with an insurer is terminated, the agency can place the business with other insurers.

Third, the independent agent is *compensated by commissions that vary by line of insurance.* The commission rate on renewal business typically is the same as new business. If a lower renewal rate is paid, the insurer would lose business, since the agent would place the insurance with another insurer. A second commission called a *contingent or profit-sharing commission* (also called a bonus) may also be paid to the agent based on a favorable loss ratio.

The commission method of compensating agents has been criticized on two grounds:[6]

- *It creates a conflict of interest.* When the agent places the business with the lowest-cost company, the client benefits, but the agent's commission is lower.
- *The commission is not necessarily related to the service provided.* A high-premium policy results in a high commission even though it may require little effort by the agent.

To correct for these defects, a negotiated fee system is sometimes used. The company quotes a premium net of commissions, and the agent then negotiates a fee with the insured based on the amount of effort required.

Independent agents perform several functions. They are frequently authorized to adjust small claims. The larger agencies may also provide loss control services to the insureds, such as accident prevention and fire control engineers. Also, for some lines, the agency may bill the policyowners and collect the premiums. However, most insurers have resorted to *direct billing,* by which the policyowner is billed directly by the insurer and then remits the premium to the company. This is particularly true of personal lines of insurance, such as auto and homeowners.

**Exclusive Agency System**    Under the **exclusive agency system,** *the agent represents only one insurer or group of insurers under common ownership.* The agent is generally prohibited by contract from representing other insurers.

Agents under the exclusive agency system do not usually own the expirations or renewal rights to the policies. There is some variation, however, in this regard. Some insurers do not give their agents

# INSIGHT 24.3

## Payroll Deductions for Insurance Proliferate

It's becoming one of the easiest and most common ways to buy life insurance, disability coverage, long-term care policies and other kinds of insurance.

It's called "payroll-deduction sales," and unless you work in a barn, it's probably taking place in a workplace near you. Instead of buying an insurance policy at home, on the phone or by mail, you merely check off some boxes on forms your employer distributes. Premiums are deducted automatically from each paycheck.

For instance, employees at Duke University in Durham, N.C., can buy homeowners insurance, auto coverage, annuities, several kinds of life insurance, disability coverage and long-term care from a handful of different companies.

But while buying insurance at work may be convenient, it isn't always a good idea. *Just because the products are available for sale through payroll deduction doesn't mean they're screened or endorsed by your employer, or that you're getting a good policy at a good price.*

In recent years, however, as employers cut back on benefits they provide, they've found that payroll-deduction products are an inexpensive way to pad "options" onto a benefits plan. The most common additions: universal life, long-term care and long-term disability insurance.

Further, cutbacks in medical coverage have coincided with a rapid rise in optional, quasimedical policies employees can buy through payroll deduction, including cancer and dread-disease coverage, dental, vision, nursing-home and supplemental medical coverage.

Although employees pay the premiums themselves, they nevertheless perceive the sale as a "benefit," because they think they're getting a special price, which may or may not be the case.

The trend is welcomed by insurers, who have a cost-efficient way to sell small policies to large numbers of people at once. Indeed, payroll-deduction products are one of the fastest-growing areas of sales to individuals.

However, don't assume that your employer has scrutinized the insurance products for quality, says Jack Bruner, benefits-practice leader for Hewitt Associates, a benefits consulting firm based in Lincolnshire, Ill. "The employee assumes there's a due-diligence review, but unfortunately, many employers offer these things willy-nilly."

---

**One-Stop Shopping**

What employees are buying through payroll deductions:

*Insurance*

- Life (universal, variable, term)
- Accidental death and dismemberment
- Disability
- Dental
- Vision
- Supplemental medical
- Long-term care
- Cancer

*Other*

- Annuities
- Mutual funds

---

Toby Kahr, associate vice president of human resources at Duke University, says he's aware that employees perceive that there's an implicit stamp of approval on the products in the plan, which is why he tries to screen the companies that "continually" approach him, and he gets help from consulting firms.

### Unnecessary Policies

Still, he acknowledges that not all employers bother to hire consultants, which is an extra expense. And even with guidance from experts, he sometimes has to drop vendors when it turns out that employees complain about the service and problems getting claims paid.

What's more, even when the insurance companies pass muster, in terms of quality, they often pressure employees to buy things they don't need. "Some companies imply a need for insurance when there isn't a need, and they advertise the premiums as being the best, when they're not," Mr. Kahr says.

Avoid problems by following a few simple guidelines. *Before signing on the dotted line, ask yourself whether you need the coverage. Some insurance, like dread disease coverage, is considered marginal and a poor use of your dollars. Then check around to make sure you're getting a good price.* For example, you might be paying higher rates for life insurance if you buy it in the workplace if the insurer is charging the same rate for all ages.

SOURCE: Adapted from Ellen E. Schultz, "Payroll Deductions for Insurance Proliferate," *The Wall Street Journal*, April 15, 1995, pp. C1, C10.

any ownership rights in the expirations. Other insurers may grant limited ownership of expirations while the agency contract is in force, but this interest terminates when the agency contract is terminated.[7] In contrast, under the independent agency system, the agency has complete ownership of the expirations.

Another difference is the payment of commissions. Exclusive agency insurers generally pay a lower commission rate on renewal business than on new business. This results in a strong financial incentive for the agent to write new business and is one factor that helps explain the rapid growth of exclusive agency insurers. In contrast, as noted earlier, insurers using the independent agency system typically pay the same commission rate on new and renewal business.

Also, exclusive agency insurers provide strong supportive services to the new agent. The new agent usually starts as an employee during a training period to learn the business. After the training period, the agent becomes an independent contractor who is then paid on a commission basis.

The functions performed by exclusive agents vary among insurers. Some insurers limit exclusive agents to selling insurance, while others permit them to adjust small first-party claims as well. Virtually all exclusive agency insurers use the direct billing method and are responsible for issuance of the policy.

**Direct Writer**    A direct writer is often erroneously confused with an exclusive agency insurer. A **direct writer** *is an insurer in which the salesperson is an employee, not an independent contractor.* The insurer pays all the selling expenses, including the employee's salary and Social Security taxes. Similar to exclusive agents, an employee of a direct writer represents only one insurer.

Employees of direct writers are usually compensated on a "salary plus" arrangement. Some companies pay a basic salary plus a commission directly related to the amount of insurance sold. Others pay a salary and a bonus that represent both selling and service activities of the employee.

**Direct-Response System**    A **direct-response insurer** *is an insurer that sells through the mails or other mass media,* such as newspapers and magazines, radio, or television. No agents are used to sell the insurance.

The direct-response system has several advantages to property and liability insurers. Lower selling expenses are incurred because market segmentation can be more precise, and underwriting can be more selective. Mailing lists can be prepared to identify groups that are likely to have fewer claims than average. However, the major disadvantage is that the insurance sold must be limited to the simple lines of insurance, such as auto and homeowners insurance.[8]

**Mixed Systems**    The distinction between the traditional marketing systems is breaking down as insurers search for new ways to market their products. Many property and liability insurers currently use more than one marketing system. These systems are referred to as **mixed systems.** For example, exclusive agency companies and direct writers have entered the rural markets and smaller towns by contracting with independent agencies in those areas. The independent agencies are already established, which minimizes the heavy start-up costs of financing new agents in those areas. Some insurers using the independent agency system also use the direct response system to reach additional customers.

As the evolution in insurance marketing continues, insurers continue to seek new and innovative ways to market their products. In particular, providing product information to consumers on the internet is likely to receive greater emphasis (see Insight 24.4).

**Market Shares**    In recent years, independent agency companies have experienced a substantial decline in their share of the personal lines property and liability insurance market. In contrast, exclusive agency insurers, direct writers, and direct response insurers as a group have experienced an increase in their share of premiums written in the personal lines market.

There are three major reasons for the strong growth in the personal lines market.[9] *First, these companies as a group tend to have lower total expense ratios than the independent agency companies.* Part of this is due to differences in commission rates. As noted earlier, exclusive agency insurers have lower commission rates on renewal business than the independent agency insurers.

## INSIGHT 24.4

## Webpages Can Be Revolutionary Tools for Insurers

The Internet audience is huge—30 million users today and probably double that in 18 months. It constitutes a relatively affluent and knowledgeable group connected to each other and the businesses that serve them.

The Internet market is too large, too sophisticated and has too much momentum to ignore. Insurance companies that disregard the tremendous potential of this medium are ignoring what is clearly the most efficient mechanism for explaining products and delivering fundamental information to customers and prospects.

Here are some of the most important benefits to insurance companies, agents and potential prospects offered by the Internet:

- **Access to information.** Without the Internet, it isn't possible to create a central repository of insurance information available to users as well as insurance professionals.

   Regulatory information is in the library, but financial reports for the companies are not. Agent locations are in the Yellow Pages, but claims locations often require a phone call to the company to determine hours and procedures. Consumers bent on due diligence have to be dedicated to ferreting out information.

   On the Internet, all of these information sources can be linked together as if they were in one place. The user can access all aspects of information about insurance companies, from product lines and regulations to answers to frequently asked questions and sales information, from a single source in an easy-to-use format.
- **Convenience of information.** Many consumers will want to do their insurance shopping when it is convenient for them. The Internet never closes.
- **Depth of information.** Presenting information in summary form, along with an easy way to get to the level of detail users need, is an ideal way to make information meaningful and accessible. Progressive disclosure of detail allows consumers to digest information at their own pace and is ideally suited to a complex, sophisticated product like insurance.

- **Timeliness of information.** Printed information must be finalized before it can reach a consumer. Information on the Internet is available in real time. Indeed, a product sheet updated in Milwaukee can be displayed on a San Diego user's screen within seconds.
- **Accuracy of information.** Not only does the insurance company providing information on the Net directly control its content, the company can also control the method of presentation and ensure that the consumer receives consistent and accurate messages.
- **Productivity.** Agents and sales-people spend significant time qualifying prospects. On the Internet, prospects qualify themselves prior to contacting the agent or company. Furthermore, the Web will become a producer's best friend—an instant source of information and training.
- **Efficiency.** Marketing materials, latest policy information and other materials are expensive for companies to produce and time-consuming for them to deliver to their distribution forces. Publishing on the Internet is inexpensive, and permits rapid-turn-around updates.
- **Interactivity.** Publishers of insurance marketing materials can take advantage of interactivity by collecting marketing information via on-line surveys, and even tailoring responses to an individual customer's questions in real time.
- **Elasticity.** Insurance industry information—particularly marketing materials—is static and limited in its visual appeal. Space on a printed page is at a premium and the graphics must often be limited. On the Web, however, you get unlimited space to convey your message.

Source: Excerpted from Darrell J. Ticehurst, "Webpages Can Be Revolutionary Tools for Insurers," *National Underwriter,* Life & Health/Financial Services Edition, January 22, 1996, pp. 7, 10, 11, 20.

*Second, such insurers were among the first to use direct billing, mechanization of policy writing, and other internal service functions.* This has enabled them to reduce their expenses and prices.

*Third, the combined effect of a large automobile insurance market and the relative simplicity of the market have enabled such insurers to build up large agency forces with a minimum of delay and financial expense.* Exclusive agency insurers, direct writers, and mail order insurers initially concentrated on automobile insurance. This line of insurance is relatively simple to sell and service when compared with the commercial lines market. As a result of their initial success with automobile insurance, these insurers also sold homeowners insurance to the same customers, since homeowners insurance possessed many of the marketing characteristics of automobile insurance. This has resulted in additional growth in the personal lines market.

In contrast, independent agency insurers dominate the commercial lines market and account for most of the premiums written in this market. The commercial lines markets are highly specialized markets that require a great deal of skill and knowledge in providing proper insurance coverages and risk management services to business firms. Independent agency insurers have highly specialized agents and loss control specialists to service this market effectively. Although exclusive agency insurers and direct writers have made some inroads into the commercial lines market, the independent agency insurers as a group still continue to dominate this market.

## MASS MERCHANDISING

Some property and liability insurers use mass merchandising to market their insurance. **Mass merchandising** *is a plan for insuring individuals in a group under a single program of insurance at reduced premiums.* Property and liability insurance is sold on a group basis to employers, labor unions, trade associations, and other groups.

Mass merchandising plans have several distinct characteristics. First, property and liability insurance is solid to individual members of a group; auto and homeowners insurance are popular lines that have been used in mass merchandising plans. Second, individual underwriting is used; individuals applying for coverage must meet the insurer's underwriting

standards. Third, rate reductions of 5 to 15 percent are typically given because of a lower commission scale for agents and savings in administrative expenses. In addition, premiums are paid by payroll deduction. Finally, employers usually do not contribute to the plans; any employer contributions result in taxable income to the employees.

Mass merchandising plans have the advantages of possibly lower premiums to insureds, convenience of payroll deduction, and the availability of insurance counseling. However, despite these advantages, mass merchandising is not widely used to market personal lines of insurance. One estimate is that mass merchandising plans account for less than 1 percent of the personal lines of insurance sold.[10] The slow growth is due to adverse tax consequences to employees, lack of enthusiasm by employers, and a reduced potential for cost savings.

## SUMMARY

- There are several basic types of insurers:

    Stock insurers

    Mutual insurers

    Reciprocal exchanges

    Lloyd's Associations

    Blue Cross and Blue Shield Plans

    Health maintenance organizations (HMOs)

- An agent is someone who legally represents the insurer and has the authority to act on the insurer's behalf. In contrast, a broker is someone who legally represents the insured.

- *Surplus lines* refer to any type of insurance for which there is no available market within the state, and the coverage must be placed with a nonadmitted insurer. A *nonadmitted insurer* is a company not licensed to do business in the state. *A surplus lines broker* is a special type of broker who is licensed to place business with a nonadmitted insurer.

- In life insurance, several basic marketing methods are used:

    General agency system

    Managerial (branch office) system

    Direct response system

- In property and liability insurance, there are four basic marketing systems:

    Independent agency system

    Exclusive agency system

    Direct writer

    Direct response system

- Mass merchandising is a plan by which property and liability insurance is sold on a group basis. Individual members of a group are insured under a single program of insurance at reduced permiums. There is, however, individual underwriting.

## KEY CONCEPTS AND TERMS

Advance premium mutual
Agent
Assessment mutual
Broker
Contingent or profit-
  sharing commission
Direct-response system
Direct writer
Exclusive agency system
Expirations or renewal
  rights to business
Fraternal insurer
Factory mutual
Farm mutual
General agency system

Independent agency
  system
Insurance exchange
Lloyd's of London
Managerial (branch office)
  system
Mass merchandising
Mutual insurer
Nonadmitted insurer
Personal-producing
  general agent
Reciprocal exchange
Stock insurer
Surplus line broker

## QUESTIONS FOR REVIEW

1. Explain the major characteristics of a stock insurer.

2. Describe the major features of a mutual insurer. Identify the basic types of mutual insurers.

3. Describe the major features of Lloyd's of London.

4. Describe the basic characteristics of a reciprocal exchange.

5. What is a fraternal insurer? Explain your answer.

6. What is the legal distinction between an agent and a broker?

7. Explain briefly the basic characteristics of the following marketing systems in life and health insurance:
   a. General agency system
   b. Managerial (branch office) system
   c. Direct response system

8. Explain briefly the basic characteristics of the following marketing systems in property and liability insurance:
   a. Independent agency system
   b. Exclusive agency system
   c. Direct writer
   d. Direct-response system

9. Who owns the policy expirations or renewal rights to the business under the independent agency system?

10. Describe the characteristics of a mass merchandising plan in property and liability insurance.

## QUESTIONS FOR DISCUSSION

1. Compare a stock insurer with a mutual insurer with respect to each of the following:
   a. Legal ownership of the company
   b. Right to assess policyowners
   c. Payment of dividends

2. An insurance author stated that "Lloyd's of London is an association that provides physical facilities and services to the members for selling insurance. The insurance is underwritten by the various syndicates who belong to Lloyds." Describe Lloyd's of London with respect to each of the following:
   a. Nature of the operation
   b. Types of insurance written
   c. Financial safeguards to protect insureds

3. Property and liability insurance can be marketed under different marketing systems. Compare the independent agency system with the exclusive agency system with respect to each of the following:
   a. Legal status of the agents
   b. Number of insurers represented
   c. Ownership of policy expirations

4. Market share is extremely important in the profitability of insurers. Independent agency companies tend to dominate the commercial lines market, while exclusive agency companies account for a relatively large share of the personal lines market.
   a. Explain the factors that account for the relatively high market share of the personal lines market by exclusive agency companies.
   b. Why do independent agency companies continue to dominate the commercial lines market?

## SELECTED REFERENCES

Barrese, James, and Jack M. Nelson. "Independent and Exclusive Agency Insurers: A Reexamination of the Cost Differential." *Journal of Risk and Insurance,* 59, no. 3 (September 1992): 375–97.

Black, Kenneth, Jr., and Harold D. Skipper, Jr. *Life Insurance,* 12th ed. Englewood Cliffs, N.J.: Prentice, Hall, 1994, chapter 33.

> ## CASE APPLICATION
>
> Acme Insurance is a medium-sized stock property and liability insurer that specializes in the writing of commercial lines of insurance. The board of directors has appointed a committee to determine the feasibility of forming a new subsidiary insurer that would sell only personal lines of insurance, primarily homeowners and automobile insurance. The new insurance company would have to meet certain management objectives. One member of the board of directors believes the new insurer should be legally organized as a mutual insurer. Assume you are an insurance consultant who is asked to serve on the committee. To what extent, if any, would each of the following objectives of the board of directors be met by a mutual property and liability insurer? Treat each objective separately.
>
> a. Acme Insurance must legally own the new insurer.
>
> b. The new insurer must be able to raise additional capital for expansion in the future.
>
> c. The policies sold should pay dividends to the policyowners.
>
> d. The new insurer should be licensed to do business in all states.

McNamara, Michael J. "An Examination of the Relative Efficiency of Mutual and Stock Life Insurance Companies." *Journal of Insurance Issues*, 14, no. 1 (January 1991): 13–30.

Shapiro, Robert D., and Sidney A. LeBlanc, "The Merger of Mutual Life Insurance Companies: A Possible Answer to the Demands of the 1990s." *Journal of the American Society of CLU & ChFC*, 46, no. 6 (November 1992): 78–82.

Webb, Bernard L., Connor M. Harrison, and James J. Markham. *Insurance Operations.* vol. 1. Malvern, Pa.: American Institute for Chartered Property Casualty Underwriters, 1992, chapters 1–3.

## NOTES

1. *1996 Life Insurance Fact Book* (Washington, D.C.: American Council of Life Insurance), p. 109; *The Fact Book 1996, Property/Casualty Insurance Facts* (New York: Insurance Information Institute), p. 7.

2. Barry D. Smith, et al., *Property and Liability Insurance Principles,* 2nd ed. (Malvern, Pa.: Insurance Institute of America, 1994), pp. 28–29.

3. Nicholas Bray, "Lloyd's of London Isn't Out of Woods Yet," *The Wall Street Journal*, August 29, 1996, p. A6.

4. Lisa S. Howard, "Skirmishes Continuing Over Lloyd's Future." *National Underwriter*, Property & Casualty/Risk & Benefits Management Edition, March 31, 1997, pp. 35, 38.

5. Kenneth Black, Jr. and Harold D. Skipper, Jr., *Life Insurance,* 12th ed. (Englewood Cliffs, N.J.: Prentice-Hall, Inc., 1994), pp. 950–52.

6. Bernard L. Webb et al., *Insurance Company Operations,* 3rd ed., vol. 1 (Malvern, Pa.: American Institute for Property and Liability Underwriters, 1984), p. 62.

7. Webb et al., pp. 64–65.

8. Webb et al., pp. 66–67.

9. Bernard L. Webb, Connor M. Harrison, and James J. Markham, *Insurance Operations,* vol. I (American Institute for Chartered Property Casualty Underwriters, 1992), p. 116–17.

10. Ibid, p. 104.

# Chapter 25

# INSURANCE COMPANY OPERATIONS

> "People who work for insurance companies do a lot more than sell insurance."
>
> *Insurance Information Institute*

## Student Learning Objectives

After studying this chapter, you should be able to:

■ Explain the rate-making function.

■ Define underwriting and explain the steps in the underwriting process.

■ Explain the meaning of "production."

■ Describe the objectives of claim settlement and the various steps in the settlement of a claim.

■ Explain the reasons for reinsurance and the different types of reinsurance treaties.

■ Explain the importance of insurance company investments and describe the different types of investments.

People buy property and liability insurance and life and health insurance to provide protection against certain pure risks that can result in great financial insecurity. In order to make insurance available to the public, insurers must engage in a wide variety of specialized functions or activities. This chapter discusses the major functional operations of insurers, including rate making, underwriting, production, claim settlement, reinsurance, investments, and other functional operations.

## INSURANCE COMPANY OPERATIONS

The most important insurance company operations consist of the following:
- Rate making
- Underwriting
- Production
- Claim settlement
- Reinsurance
- Investments

Insurers also engage in other operations, such as accounting, legal services, loss control, and data processing.

## Rate Making

**Rate making** refers to the pricing of insurance. Insurance pricing differs considerably from the pricing of other products. When other products are sold, the company generally knows in advance what its costs of production are, so that a price can be established to cover all costs and yield a profit. However, the insurance company does not know in advance what its actual costs are going to be. The premium charged for the insurance may be inadequate for paying all claims and expenses during the policy period, because it is only after the period of protection has expired that the company can determine its actual losses and expenses. Of course, the insurer hopes that the premium paid in advance will be sufficient to pay all claims and expenses and yield a profit.

The person who determines the rates is known as an **actuary.** An actuary is a highly skilled mathematician who is involved in all phases of insurance company operations, including planning, pricing, and research. In life insurance, the actuary studies important statistical data on births, deaths, marriages, disease, employment, retirement, and accidents. Based on this information, the actuary determines the rates for life and health insurance policies. The objectives are to calculate premiums that will make the business profitable, enable it to compete effectively with other insurers, and allow it to pay claims and expenses as they occur. A life insurance actuary must also determine the legal reserves a company needs for future obligations.[1]

Professional certification as an actuary is attained by passing a series of examinations administered by the Society of Actuaries, which qualifies the actuary as a Fellow of the Society of Actuaries.

In property and liability insurance, actuaries also determine the rates for different lines of insurance. Rates are determined by the company's past loss experience and by industry statistics. Statistics on hurricanes, tornadoes, fires, diseases, crime rates, traffic accidents, and the cost of living are also carefully analyzed. Many companies use their own loss data in establishing the rates. Other companies obtain loss data from **insurance advisory organizations.** These organizations calculate historical or prospective loss costs that individual companies can use in calculating their rates. Companies add a loading for expenses to the prospective loss costs in determining the actual rates charged.

Actuaries in property and liability insurance also determine the adequacy of loss reserves,[2] allocate expenses, and compile statistics for company management and for state regulatory officials. Also, actuaries help resolve management problems in underwriting, sales, claims, and product development.

To become a certified actuary in property and liability insurance, the individual must pass a series of examinations administered by the Casualty Actuarial Society. Successful completion of the examinations enables the actuary to become a Fellow of the Casualty Actuarial Society.

## Underwriting

**Underwriting** *refers to the process of selecting and classifying applicants for insurance.* The underwriter is the person who decides to accept or reject an application. The fundamental objective of underwriting is to produce a profitable book of business. The underwriter constantly strives to select certain types of applicants and to reject others in order to obtain a profitable portfolio.

**Statement of Underwriting Policy**  Underwriting starts with a clear statement of underwriting policy. An insurer must establish underwriting policy that is consistent with company objectives. The objective may be a large volume of business with low unit profits or a smaller volume at a larger unit of profit. Classes of business that are acceptable, borderline, or prohibited must be clearly stated. The amounts of insurance that can be written on acceptable and borderline business must also be determined.

The insurer's underwriting policy is determined by top-level management in charge of underwriting. The *line underwriters*—persons who make daily decisions concerning the acceptance or rejection of business—are expected to follow official company policy. The underwriting policy is stated in detail in an *underwriting guide* that specifies the lines of insurance to be written; territories to be developed; forms and rating plans to be used; acceptable, borderline, and prohibited business; amounts of insurance to be written; business that requires approval by a senior underwriter; and other underwriting details.

**Basic Underwriting Principles**   As noted earlier, the goal of underwriting is to produce a profitable volume of business. To achieve this goal, certain underwriting principles are followed. Three important principles are as follows:

- Selection of insureds according to the company's underwriting standards
- Proper balance within each rate classification
- Equity among policyowners

*The first principle is that the underwriter must select prospective insureds according to the company's underwriting standards.* This means that the underwriters should select only those insureds whose actual loss experience will not exceed the loss experience assumed in the rating structure. For example, a factory mutual may wish to insure only high-grade factories, and expects that its actual loss experience will be well below average. Underwriting standards are established with respect to eligible factories, and a rate is established based on a relatively low loss ratio.[3] Assume that the expected loss ratio is established at 30 percent, and the rate is set accordingly. The underwriters ideally should insure only those factories that can meet the stringent underwriting requirements, so that the actual loss ratio for the group will not exceed 30 percent.

The purpose of the underwriting standards is to reduce adverse selection against the insurer. There is an old saying in underwriting, "select or be selected against." Adverse selection is the tendency of people with a higher-than-average chance of loss to seek insurance at standard (average) rates, which if not controlled by underwriting will result in higher-than-expected loss levels.

*The second underwriting principle is to have a proper balance within each rate classification.* This means that a below-average insured in an underwriting class should be offset by an above-average insured, so that on balance, the class or manual rate for the group as a whole will be adequate for paying all claims and expenses. For example, much of the underwriting today is class underwriting, especially for personal lines of insurance. Exposure units with similar loss-producing characteristics are grouped together and placed in the same underwriting class. Each exposure unit within the class is charged the same rate. However, all exposure units are not completely identical. Some will be above average for the class as a whole, while others will be below average. The underwriter must select a proper balance of insureds so that the class rate (average rate) will be adequate for paying all claims and expenses.

*A final underwriting principle is equity among the policyowners.* This means that equitable rates should be charged, and that each group of policyowners should pay its own way in terms of losses and expenses. Stated differently, one group of policyowners should not unduly subsidize another group. For example, a group of 20-year-old persons and a group of 80-year-old persons should not pay the same premium rate for individual life insurance. If identical rates were charged to both groups, younger persons would be subsidizing older persons. This would be inequitable. Once the younger persons became aware that they were being overcharged, they would seek other insurers whose classification systems are more equitable. The first insurer would then end up with a disproportionate number of older, unhealthy persons, and the underwriting results would be unprofitable. Thus, because of competition, there must be rate equity among the policyowners.

**Steps in Underwriting**   After the insurer's underwriting policy is established, it must be communicated to the sales force. Initial underwriting starts with the agent in the field.

Agent as First Underwriter   This is often called field underwriting. The agent is told what types of applicants are acceptable, borderline, or prohibited. For example, in auto insurance, an agent may be told not to solicit applicants who have been convicted for drunk driving, who are single drivers under age 21, or who are young drivers who own high-powered sports cars. In property insurance, certain exposures, such as bowling alleys and restaurants, may have to be submitted to a company underwriter for approval.

In property and liability insurance, the agent often has authority to bind the company immediately, subject to subsequent disapproval of the application and cancellation by a company underwriter. Thus, it is important that the agent follow company policy when soliciting applicants for insurance. To encourage a submission of only profitable business, a *contingent or profit-sharing commission* is often paid based on the agent's favorable loss experience.

In life insurance, the agent must also solicit applicants in accordance with the company's underwriting policy. The agent may be told not to solicit applicants who are drug addicts, active alcoholics, or persons who work in hazardous occupations.

SOURCES OF UNDERWRITING INFORMATION The underwriter requires certain types of information in deciding whether to accept or reject an applicant for insurance. The type of information varies by type of insurance. In property insurance, both the physical features of the property and personal characteristics of the applicant must be considered. Physical features include the type of construction, occupancy of the building, quality of fire protection, water supply, and exposure from surrounding buildings.

With respect to personal characteristics of the applicant, information that reveals the presence of *moral hazard* is particularly important. The underwriter wants to screen out applicants who may intentionally cause a loss or inflate a claim beyond its actual value. Thus, the applicant's present financial condition, past loss record, living habits, and moral character are especially important in the underwriting process.

Underwriting information can be obtained from a wide variety of sources. The most important sources include the following:

- Application
- Agent's report
- Inspection report
- Physical inspection
- Physical examination and attending physician's report
- Medical Information Bureau (MIB)

The **application** is a basic source of underwriting information. The application varies depending on the type of insurance. For example, in life insurance, the application will show the individual's age, sex, weight, occupation, personal and family health history, and any hazardous hobbies, such as sky diving.

An **agent's report** is another source of information. Most companies require the agent to give an evaluation of the prospective insured. For example,

in life insurance, the agent may be asked to state how long he or she has known the applicant, to estimate the applicant's annual income and net worth, to judge whether the applicant plans to lapse or surrender existing life insurance, and to determine whether the application is the result of the agent's solicitation.

An **inspection report** may be required, especially if the underwriter suspects moral hazard. An outside firm investigates the applicant for insurance and makes a detailed report to the company. The report may include the applicant's present financial condition, drinking habits, marital status, amount of outstanding debts, delinquent bills, policy record, felony convictions, and additional information, such as whether the applicant has ever declared bankruptcy.

A **physical inspection** may also be required before an application for property and liability insurance is approved. The agent or company representative may physically inspect the building or plant to be insured, and submit a report to the underwriter. For example, in workers compensation insurance, an inspection may reveal unsafe working conditions, such as dangerous machinery; violation of safety rules, such as not wearing goggles when a grinding machine is used; and an excessively dusty or toxic plant.

Especially important for life insurance, a physical examination will reveal whether the applicant is overweight, has high blood pressure, or has any abnormalities in the heart, respiratory system, urinary system, or other parts of the body. An **attending physician's report** may also be required, which is a report from a physician who has treated the applicant in the past.

A final source of underwriting information in life insurance is a **Medical Information Bureau (MIB) report.** Companies that belong to the bureau report any health impairments, which are then recorded and made available to member companies. For example, if an applicant for life insurance has high blood pressure, this information would be recorded in the MIB files, which are coded and do not reveal the decision made by the submitting company.

MAKING AN UNDERWRITING DECISION After the underwriter evaluates the information, an underwriting decision must be made. There are three basic underwriting decisions with respect to an initial application for insurance:

- Accept the application
- Accept the application subject to certain restrictions or modifications
- Reject the application

The underwriter can accept the application and recommend that the policy be issued. A second option is to accept the application subject to certain restrictions or modifications. Several examples illustrate this second type of decision. Before a crime insurance policy is issued, the applicant may be required to place iron bars on windows or install an approved central station burglar alarm system; the applicant may be refused a homeowners policy and offered a more limited dwelling and contents policy; a large deductible may be inserted in a property insurance policy; or a higher rate for life insurance may be charged if the applicant is substandard in health. If the applicant agrees to the modifications or restrictions, the policy is then issued.

The third decision is to reject the application. However, excessive and unjustified rejection of applications reduces the insurer's profitability and alienates the agents who solicited the business. If an application is rejected, the rejection should be based on a clear failure to meet the insurer's underwriting standards.

Many insurers now use computerized underwriting for certain personal lines of insurance that can be standardized, such as automobile and homeowners insurance. As a result, underwriting decisions can be expedited.

**Other Underwriting Considerations**    Other factors are also considered in underwriting. They include the following:

1. *Rate adequacy and underwriting.* When rates are considered adequate for a class, insurers are more willing to underwrite new business. However, if rates are inadequate, prudent underwriting requires a more conservative approach to the acceptance of new business. If moral hazard is excessive, the business generally cannot be insured at any rate.

    In addition, in commercial property and liability insurance, the underwriters have a considerable impact on the price of the product. A great deal of negotiation over price takes place

between the line underwriter and the agent concerning the proper pricing of a commercial risk.

Finally, the critical relationship between adequate rates and underwriting profits or losses results in periodic underwriting cycles in certain lines of insurance, such as commercial general liability and commercial multiperil insurance. If rates are adequate, underwriting profits are higher, and underwriting is more liberal. Conversely, when rates are inadequate, underwriting losses occur, and underwriting becomes more restrictive (see Insight 25.1).

2. *Reinsurance and underwriting.* Availability of reinsurance facilities may result in more liberal underwriting. However, if reinsurance cannot be obtained on favorable terms, the underwriting may be more restrictive.

3. *Renewal underwriting.* In life insurance, policies are not cancelable. In property and liability insurance, most policies can be canceled or not renewed. If the loss experience is unfavorable, the insurer may either cancel or not renew the policy. Most states have placed restrictions on the insurer's right to cancel.

## Production

The term **production** refers to the sales and marketing activities of insurers. Agents who sell insurance are frequently referred to as **producers.** This word is used because an insurance company can be legally chartered, personnel can be hired, and policy forms printed, but nothing is produced until a policy is sold. The key to the insurer's financial success is an effective sales force.

**Agency Department**    Life insurers have an agency or sales department. This department is responsible for recruiting and training new agents and for the supervision of general agents, branch office managers, and local agents.

Property and liability insurers have marketing departments. To assist agents in the field, special agents may also be appointed. A *special agent* is a highly specialized technician who provides local agents in the field with technical help and assistance with their marketing problems. For example, a special agent may explain a new policy form or a special rating plan to agents in the field.

## INSIGHT 25.1

## How Underwriting Cycles in Insurance Work

Underwriting cycles in property and liability insurance are of perennial interest both inside and outside the insurance industry, especially when the cycle is on the downside. There are two key cycles in insurance markets. One cycle is regulatory in nature, while the other is economic.

### Regulatory Cycle

The first type of cycle—fluctuations in pricing and profits caused by regulatory forces—is very common in insurance and other regulated industries. During periods of adequate profitability, regulators tend to hold prices steady, delay rate increases, or allow only limited rate increases.

The following scenario is familiar in the insurance industry. As regulators delay rate increases, companies shift from a position of adequate profitability to a point where profits are minimal, or nonexistent, and rates tend to be depressed relative to costs. Eventually, companies start to withdraw from the unprofitable business and the regulator, faced with a reduced availability of insurance, allows the rates to rise. This action restores profitability to the insurers, thus setting the stage for a replay of the same events.

### Economic Cycle

The second type of insurance cycle, the economic type, is more complex. Basically, a purely economic cycle is rooted in two factors: a high level of competition among suppliers (insurance companies) and a high degree of insensitivity to price changes on the demand or consumer side. In economic jargon, this latter factor is referred to as price inelasticity. Insurance is a virtual necessity for most businesses and coverage will continue to be bought even if prices go up. If prices come down, however, businesses will not buy two policies, although in some cases they may increase their coverage.

In an economic cycle, during periods when profits are at least adequate, insurance companies have an incentive to expand their business. To attract new policyholders they reduce rates. As soon as some companies begin to cut rates, other companies follow suit. Often rates are slashed to levels that are below the initial round of cuts.

Since consumer demand for insurance products is inelastic, this pricing strategy does not lead to expansion through added buying. The net result is a decline in both premiums and profits for all carriers.

This decline continues until companies reach the "can't take it any more" stage. At this point, a change in market psychology occurs. Rates start to go up. Since the financial base of some companies has eroded significantly, fewer policies are issued, limiting the overall availability of insurance. Eventually, profitability is restored and insurance again becomes widely available, which in turn leads to a new cycle.

SOURCE: Adapted from Sean Mooney, "How Insurance Cycles Work," *Insurance Review*, 51 no. 1 (January 1990): 31–32. Reprinted by permission of Insurance Information Institute.

---

In addition to development of an effective sales force, an insurance company engages in a wide variety of marketing activities. These activities include the development of marketing philosophy and the company's perception of its role in the marketplace; identification of short-run and long-run production goals; marketing research; development of new products to meet the changing needs of consumers and business firms; developing new marketing strategies; and advertising the insurer's products.

**Professionalism in Selling**    The marketing of insurance has been characterized by a distinct trend toward professionalism in recent years. This means that the modern agent should be a competent professional who has a high degree of technical knowledge in a particular area of insurance and who also places the needs of his or her clients first. The professional agent identifies potential insureds, analyzes their insurance needs, and recommends the best solution to the problem. After the sale, the agent has the responsibility of providing follow-up service to clients to keep their insurance programs up to date. Finally, a professional agent abides by a code of ethics.

Several organizations have developed professional programs for agents and ot her personnel in the insurance industry. In life and health insurance, the American College has established the **Chartered Life Underwriter (CLU)** program. An individual must pass ten professional examinations to receive the CLU designation. A minimum of three years' experience in life or health insurance is also required.

The American College also awards the **Chartered Financial Consultant (ChFC)** designation for professionals who are working in the financial services industry. To earn the ChFC designation, students must pass 10 professional examinations.

A similar professional program exists in property and liability insurance. The American Institute for Chartered Property Casualty Underwriters has established the **Chartered Property Casualty Underwriter (CPCU)** program. The CPCU program requires an individual to pass 10 examinations.

Other professionals are also important in the insurance industry. Many financial planners are also licensed as insurance agents. The **Certified Financial Planner (CFP)** designation is awarded by the International Board of Standards and Practices for Certified Financial Planners (IBCFP). Many agents in property and liability insurance have been awarded the **Certified Insurance Counselor (CIC)** sponsored by the Society of Certified Insurance Counselors.

## Claim Settlement

Every insurance company has a claims division or department for settling claims. This section examines the basic objectives in settling claims, the different types of claim adjusters, and the various steps in the claim-settlement process.

**Basic Objectives in Claim Settlement**
From the insurer's viewpoint, there are several basic objectives in settling claims.[4]

- Verification of a covered loss
- Fair and prompt payment of claims
- Personal assistance to the insured

*The first objective in settling claims is to verify that a covered loss has occurred.* This involves determining whether a specific person or property is covered under the policy, and the extent of the coverage. This objective is discussed in greater detail later in the chapter.

*The second objective is the fair and prompt payment of claims.* If a valid claim is denied, the fundamental social and contractual purpose of protecting the insured is defeated. Also, the insurer's reputation may be harmed, and the sales of new policies may be adversely affected. Fair payment means that the insurer should avoid excessive claim settlements and should resist the payment of fraudulent claims, since they will ultimately result in higher premiums. If the insurer follows a liberal claims policy, all policyowners will suffer because a rate increase will become necessary.

Most states have passed laws that prohibit unfair claim practices. These laws are patterned after the National Association of Insurance Commissioners' Model act. Some unfair claim practices prohibited by these laws include the following:[5]

1. Refusing to pay claims without conducting a reasonable investigation based on all available information.

2. Not attempting in good faith to effect prompt, fair, and equitable settlements of claims in which liability has become reasonably clear.

3. Compelling insureds to institute litigation to recover amounts due under an insurance policy by offering substantially less than the amounts ultimately recovered in actions brought by such insureds.

*A third objective is to provide personal assistance to the insured after a covered loss occurs.* Aside from any contractual obligations, the insurer should also provide personal assistance after a loss occurs. For example, the claims adjustor could assist the agent in helping a family find temporary housing after a fire occurs.

**Types of Claims Adjustors**    The person who adjusts a claim is known as a **claims adjustor**. The major types of adjustors include the following:

- Agent
- Company adjustor

- Independent adjustor
- Adjustment bureau
- Public adjustor

An **agent** often has authority to settle small first-party claims up to some maximum limit.[6] The insured submits the claim directly to the agent, who has the authority to pay up to some specified amount. This approach to claim settlement has three advantages: it is speedy, it reduces adjustment expenses, and it preserves the policyowner's good will.

A **company adjustor** can settle a claim. The adjustor is usually a salaried employee who represents only one company. After notice of the loss is received, the company adjustor will investigate the claim, determine the amount of loss, and arrange for payment (see Insight 25.2).

An **independent adjustor** can also be used to settle claims. An independent adjustor is a person who offers his or her services to insurance companies and is compensated by a fee. The company may use an independent adjustor in certain geographical areas where the volume of claims is too low to justify a branch office with a staff of fulltime adjustors. An independent adjustor may also be used in highly specialized areas where a company adjustor with the necessary technical skills and knowledge is not available.

An **adjustment bureau** can be used to settle claims. An adjustment bureau is an organization for adjusting claims that is supported by insurers that use its services. Claims personnel employed by an adjustment bureau are highly trained individuals who adjust claims on a full-time basis. An adjustment bureau is frequently used when a catastrophic loss, such as a hurricane, occurs in a given geographical area, and a large number of claims are submitted at the same time.

A **public adjustor** can be involved in settling a claim. *A public adjustor, however, represents the insured rather than the insurance company and is paid a fee based on the amount of the claim settlement.* A public adjustor may be employed by the insured if a complex loss situation occurs and technical assistance is needed, and also in those cases where the insured and insurer cannot resolve a dispute over a claim.

**Steps in Settlement of a Claim**    There are several important steps in settling a claim:

- Notice of loss must be given.
- The claim is investigated.
- A proof of loss may be required.
- A decision is made concerning payment.

NOTICE OF LOSS    The first step is to notify the insurer of a loss. A provision concerning notice of loss is usually stated in the policy. A typical provision requires the insured to give notice immediately or as soon as possible after the loss has occurred. For example, the homeowners policy requires the insured to give immediate notice; a medical expense policy may require the insured to give notice within 30 days after the occurrence of a loss, or as soon afterward as is reasonably possible; and the personal auto policy requires that the insurer must be notified promptly of how, when, and where the accident or loss happened. The notice must also include the names and addresses of any injured persons and of witnesses.

INVESTIGATION OF THE CLAIM    After notice is received, the next step is to investigate the claim. An adjustor must determine that a covered loss has occurred and must also determine the amount of the loss. A series of questions must be answered before the claim is approved. The most important questions include the following:[7]

- Did the loss occur while the policy was in force?
- Does the policy cover the peril that caused the loss?
- Does the policy cover the property destroyed or damaged in the loss?
- Is the claimant entitled to recover?
- Did the loss occur at an insured location?
- Is the type of loss covered?
- Is the claim fraudulent?

The last question dealing with fraudulent claims is especially important. Insurance fraud is widespread, especially in auto and health insurance. Dishonest people frequently submit claims for bodily injuries that have never occurred.

FILING A PROOF OF LOSS    A proof of loss may be required before the claim is paid. A proof of loss is a sworn statement by the insured that substantiates

## INSIGHT 25.2

### Twisted Gutters, Leaky Roofs Fill Adjuster's Day

Guy Fuscardo is running late. An elderly woman and her son-in-law are waiting impatiently by their kitchen door.

"You took so long the damage got worse," the son-in-law grumbles as Mr. Fuscardo comes up the walk.

Mr. Fuscardo, an insurance adjuster with **Nationwide Insurance Enterprise,** apologizes profusely, hoping to clear the air. But the woman is ornery, her son-in-law caustic, as they detail damage from the recent winter storms. "There was ice this thick" on the roof, she says, her arms a foot apart. Water poured through the attic, stained two bedroom ceilings and carpets, and dripped into the living room. "I was up in the attic every half-hour, checking on it," she complains. "Oh, my poor legs."

In the four weeks after Christmas, some 4,500 claims were filed with Nationwide in western Pennsylvania, nearly six times the norm. During January, Mr. Fuscardo made twice as many visits to homeowners as usual, looking at damage, reviewing contractors' estimates and calculating how much Nationwide, a private, multiline insurer based in Columbus, Ohio, will pay. In his 25 years as an adjuster, he says only the winter of 1994 was worse.

An early riser, Mr. Fuscardo was out handing one homeowner a check at 7:30 this morning in Pittsburgh before driving an hour east to mostly rural Westmoreland County. In the car, a Ford Taurus owned by Nationwide, the paperwork for his cases is stacked in a leather binder. His cellular phone is often to his ear, his pager on his belt. On the seat beside him are a 30-foot tape measure and a camera (he goes through four rolls of film a week taking pictures of damage). The trunk holds overalls and steel-toed boots in case he has to go to a fire scene.

Though there are tough days, Mr. Fuscardo generally loves his job visiting homes and businesses to assess property damage. Many homeowners assume he's out to short change them, but Mr. Fuscardo says his philosophy is: *"I'm going to pay what I owe. I'm not going to pay you more. I'm not going to pay you less."*

His second call, just after 9:30 a.m., takes him to Sarah Portser's house. The big January blizzard left a gaping hole in her bedroom ceiling, exposing the attic above and forcing her to move her bed to the hallway, safe from falling plaster. Upsetting to her, it is routine damage to Mr. Fuscardo. In a few minutes, he measures the bedroom, makes some rapid calculations and reviews her contractor's estimate. He gives her an extra $100 because the stenciling she did around one doorway will probably be obliterated by workmen, and then writes out a check for $468.

In the car, Mr. Fuscardo explains that he appreciated her honesty when he noticed some stains on one wall. Mrs. Portser told him they were from another incident. "Nine out of 10 people would have tried to claim that," he says.

Mr. Fuscardo estimates that 85% of his cases this winter have involved roof claims. Some are more offbeat.

*Continued*

the loss. For example, under the homeowners policy, the insured may be required to file a proof of loss that indicates the time and cause of the loss, interest of the insured and others in the damaged property, other insurance that may cover the loss, and any change in title or occupancy of the property during the term of the policy.

DECISION CONCERNING PAYMENT    After the claim is investigated, the adjustor must make a decision concerning payment. There are three possible decisions. *The claim can be paid.* In most cases, the claim is paid promptly according to the terms of the policy. *The claim can be denied.* The adjustor may believe that the policy does not cover the loss, or that the claim is fraudulent. Finally, the claim may be valid, but there may be a dispute between the insured and insurer over the amount to be paid. *In the case of a dispute, a policy provision may specify how the dispute is to be resolved.* For example, if a dispute arises under the homeowners policy, both the insured and insurer select an independent appraiser.

In the afternoon, Mr. Fuscardo goes to look at Elmer Dick's storm-damaged chicken coops. Mr. Fuscardo knows Mr. Dick, a truck driver from prior claims.

During the blizzard, Mr. Dick claims, snow, wind and ice destroyed his chicken pens and killed some birds. He has a contractor's estimate for the damage: nearly $6,000.

But Mr. Fuscardo is convinced that Mr. Dick's policy doesn't cover the pens, which are essentially stakes pounded in the ground covered with mesh wire. The policy applies only to "structures," like garages. The two men stand in a bone-chilling wind in Mr. Dick's backyard, arguing as chickens cluck around their feet.

"I don't see how they can cover that, Elmer," Mr. Fuscardo says. "That is not a structure."

"Oh, come on," says Mr. Dick.

"I don't lie to you. To me that is not a structure."

"Hey, it looked better before," Mr. Dick points out.

After some back-and-forth, the two agree that a shaky wooden shed, which Mr. Fuscardo hadn't noticed before, qualifies for coverage. But Mr. Fuscardo shakes his head and laughs as he adds up the cost of materials and labor on the shed, coming up with a total that's about one-fifth of the contractor's estimate. "I think I'm overpaying this," he teases. "I got a soft heart."

"See, I'm fair," he says. Demands Mr. Dick: "How do I know if you're fair? I hear people say they got a bad hot water heater, and they get a whole new damn game room from their insurance company!"

Mr. Fuscardo is philosophical about such outbursts. "I see people at their worst," he notes. "As claims adjusters, people aren't happy when we get there because they've been through a catastrophe."

The elderly woman and her son-in-law are even more skeptical of the adjuster. The two lead Mr. Fuscardo on a tension-filled tour of the damage in their house. In the end, Mr. Fuscardo disappoints them. While the estimates for the interior work look OK, he's suspicious of one for more than $800 for the exterior cleaning. "It's too much money," he says. "I don't understand."

"What's there to understand?" the homeowner snaps back. To bolster her case, she pulls out an old bill for comparable work from several years back. Mr. Fuscardo examines the document and asks a few questions, realizing the prior workman charged her for work he didn't do.

The homeowner is deflated. "I never saw that," she says.

But he ends up writing a check for the bedroom work and promises to come back and look at a revised estimate for the house cleaning. He thinks "customer retention" is important and tries to mollify angry customers.

SOURCE: Excerpted from Matt Murray, "Twisted Gutters, Leaky Roofs Fill Adjuster's Day," *The Wall Street Journal,* February 5, 1996, pp. B1–B2.

The two appraisers select an umpire. If the appraisers cannot agree on an umpire, a court of law will appoint one. An agreement by any two of the three is then binding on all parties.

## Reinsurance

Reinsurance is another important insurance operation. This section discusses the meaning of reinsurance, the reasons for reinsurance, and the different types of reinsurance contracts.

**Definitions** **Reinsurance** *is the shifting of part or all of the insurance originally written by one insurer to another insurer.* The insurer that initially writes the business is called the **ceding company.** The insurer that accepts part or all of the insurance from the ceding company is called the **reinsurer.** The amount of insurance retained by the ceding company for its own account is called the **net retention** or **retention limit.** The amount of the insurance ceded to the reinsurer is known as the **cession.** Finally, the reinsurer in turn may obtain reinsurance from another insurer. This is known as a **retrocession.**

**Reasons for Reinsurance** Reinsurance is used for several reasons. The most important reasons include the following:

- Increase underwriting capacity
- Stabilize profits
- Reduce the unearned premium reserve
- Provide protection against a catastrophic loss

Reinsurance also enables an insurer to retire from a territory or class of business and to obtain underwriting advice from the reinsurer.

INCREASE UNDERWRITING CAPACITY Reinsurance can be used to increase the insurance company's underwriting capacity to write new business. The company may be asked to assume liability for losses in excess of its retention limit. Without reinsurance, the agent would have to place large amounts of insurance with several companies. This is awkward and may create ill will on behalf of the policyowner. Reinsurance permits the primary company to issue a single policy in excess of its retention limit for the full amount of insurance.

STABILIZE PROFITS Reinsurance can be used to stabilize profits. An insurer may wish to avoid large fluctuations in annual financial results. Loss experience can fluctuate widely because of social and economic conditions, natural disasters, and chance. Reinsurance can be used to level out the effects of poor loss experience. For example, reinsurance may be used to cover a large exposure. If a large, unexpected loss occurs, the reinsurer would pay the portion of the loss in excess of some specified limit. Another arrangement would be to have the reinsurer reimburse the ceding insurer for losses that exceed a specified loss ratio during a given year. For example, an insurer may wish to stabilize its loss ratio at 70 percent. The reinsurer then agrees to reimburse the ceding insurer for part or all the losses in excess of 70 percent up to some maximum limit.

REDUCE THE UNEARNED PREMIUM RESERVE Reinsurance can be used to reduce the unearned premium reserve. For some insurers, especially newer and smaller ones, the ability to write large amounts of new insurance may be restricted by the unearned premium reserve requirement. The **unearned premium reserve** *is a liability item on the insurer's balance sheet that represents the unearned portion of gross premiums on all outstanding policies at the time of valuation.* In effect, the unearned premium reserve reflects the fact that premiums are paid in advance, but the period of protection has not yet expired. As time goes on, part of the premium is considered earned, while the remainder is unearned. It is only after the period of protection has expired that the premium is fully earned.

As noted earlier, an insurer's ability to grow may be restricted by the unearned premium reserve requirement. This is because the entire gross premium must be placed in the unearned premium reserve when the policy is first written. The insurer also incurs relatively heavy first-year acquisition expenses in the form of commissions, state premium taxes, underwriting expenses, expenses in issuing the policy, and other expenses. In determining the size of the unearned premium reserve, there is no allowance for these first-year acquisition expenses, and the insurer must pay them out of its surplus. (Policyholders' surplus is the difference between assets and liabilities.[8]) For example, a one-year property insurance policy with an annual premium of $1200 may be written on January 1. The entire $1200 must be placed in the unearned premium reserve. At the end of each month, one-twelfth of the premium, or $100, is earned and the remainder is unearned. On December 31, the entire premium is fully earned. However, assume that first-year acquisition expenses are 30 percent of the gross premium, or $360. This amount will come out of the insurer's surplus. Thus, the more business it writes, the greater is the short-term drain on its surplus. A rapidly growing insurer's ability to write new business could eventually be impaired.

Reinsurance reduces the level of the unearned premium reserve required by law and temporarily increases the insurer's surplus position. As a result, the ratio of policyholders' surplus to net written premiums is improved, which permits the insurer to continue to grow.

PROVIDE PROTECTION AGAINST A CATASTROPHIC LOSS Reinsurance also provides financial protection against a catastrophic loss. Insurers experience catastrophic losses because of natural disasters, industrial explosions, commercial airline disasters, and similar events. Reinsurance can provide considerable protection to the ceding company that experiences a catastrophic loss. The reinsurer pays part or all of the losses that exceed the ceding company's retention up to some specified maximum limit.

OTHER REASONS FOR REINSURANCE    An insurer can use reinsurance to retire from the business or from a given line of insurance. Reinsurance permits the insurer's liabilities for existing insurance to be transferred to another carrier; thus, the policyowner's coverage remains undisturbed.

Finally, reinsurance can enable an insurer to obtain the underwriting advice and assistance of the reinsurer. An insurer may wish to write a new line of insurance, but it may have little experience with respect to underwriting the line. The reinsurer can often provide valuable assistance with respect to rating, retention limits, policy coverages, and other underwriting details.

Types of Reinsurance    There are two principal forms of reinsurance: (1) facultative and (2) treaty.

FACULTATIVE REINSURANCE    **Facultative reinsurance** *is an optional, case-by-case method that is used when the ceding company receives an application for insurance that exceeds its retention limit.* Before the policy is issued, the primary insurer shops around for reinsurance and contacts several reinsurers. The primary insurer is under no obligation to cede insurance, and the reinsurer is under no obligation to accept the insurance. But if a willing reinsurer can be found, the primary insurer and reinsurer can then enter into a valid contract.

Facultative reinsurance is frequently used when a large amount of insurance is desired. Before the application is accepted, the primary insurer determines if reinsurance can be obtained. If available, the policy can then be written.

Facultative reinsurance has the advantage of flexibility, since a reinsurance contract can be arranged to fit any kind of case. It can increase the insurer's capacity to write large amounts of insurance. The reinsurance tends to stabilize the insurer's operations by shifting large losses to the reinsurer.

The major disadvantage of facultative reinsurance is that it is uncertain. The ceding insurer does not know in advance if a reinsurer will accept any part of the insurance. There is also a further disadvantage of delay, since the policy will not be issued until reinsurance is obtained. In times of bad loss experience, the reinsurance market tends to dry up. Therefore, facultative reinsurance has the further disadvantage of being unreliable.

TREATY REINSURANCE    **Treaty reinsurance** *means the primary insurer has agreed to cede insurance to the reinsurer, and the reinsurer has agreed to accept the business.* All business that falls within the scope of the agreement is automatically reinsured according to the terms of the treaty.

Treaty reinsurance has several advantages to the primary insurer. It is automatic, and no uncertainty or delay is involved. It is also economical, since it is not necessary to shop around for reinsurance before the policy is written.

Treaty reinsurance could be unprofitable to the reinsurer. The reinsurer generally has no knowledge about the individual applicant and must rely on the underwriting judgment of the primary insurer. The primary insurer may write bad business and then reinsure it. Also, the premium received by the reinsurer may be inadequate. Thus, if the primary insurer has a poor selection of risks or charges inadequate rates, the reinsurer could incur a loss. However, if the primary insurer consistently cedes unprofitable business to its reinsurers, the ceding insurer will find it difficult to operate since reinsurers will not want to do business with them.

There are several types of reinsurance treaties and arrangements, including the following:

- Quota-share treaty
- Surplus-share treaty
- Excess-of-loss treaty
- Reinsurance pool

*Quota-Share Treaty*    Under a **quota-share treaty,** the ceding insurer and reinsurer agree to share premiums and losses based on some proportion. *The ceding insurer's retention limit is stated as a percentage rather than as a dollar amount.* For example, Apex Fire and Geneva Re may enter into a quota-share treaty by which premiums and losses are shared 50 percent and 50 percent. Thus, if a $12,000 loss occurs, Apex Fire pays $12,000 to the insured but is reimbursed by Geneva Re for $6000.

Premiums are also shared based on the same agreed-on percentages. However, the reinsurer pays a **ceding commission** to the primary insurer to help compensate for the expenses incurred in writing the business. Thus, in the previous example, Geneva Re would receive 50 percent of the premium less a ceding commission that is paid to Apex Fire.

The major advantage of quota-share reinsurance is that the unearned premium reserve is reduced. For smaller insurers and other insurers that wish to reduce a surplus drain, a quota-share treaty can be especially effective. The principal disadvantage is that a large share of potentially profitable business is ceded to the reinsurer.

*Surplus-Share Treaty* Under a **surplus-share treaty,** the reinsurer agrees to accept insurance in excess of the ceding insurer's retention limit, up to some maximum amount. *The retention limit is referred to as a line and is stated as a dollar amount.* If the amount of insurance on a given policy exceeds the retention limit, the excess insurance is ceded to the reinsurer up to some maximum limit. The primary insurer and reinsurer then share premiums and losses based on the fraction of total insurance retained by each party. Each party pays its respective share of any loss regardless of its size.

For example, assume that Apex Fire has a retention limit of $200,000 (called a line) for a single policy, and that four lines, or $800,000 are ceded to Geneva Re. Apex Fire now has a total underwriting capacity of $1 million on any single exposure. Assume that a $500,000 property insurance policy is issued. Apex Fire takes the first $200,000 of insurance, or two-fifths, and Geneva Re takes the remaining $300,000, or three-fifths. These fractions then determine the amount of loss paid by each party. If a $5000 loss occurs, Apex Fire pays $2000 (two-fifths), and Geneva Re pays the remaining $3000 (three-fifths). This can be summarized as follows:

| | | |
|---|---|---|
| **Apex Fire** | $   200,000 | (one line) |
| **Geneva Re** | 800,000 | (four lines) |
| Total underwriting capacity | $1,000,000 | |

*$500,000 policy*

| | |
|---|---|
| **Apex Fire** | $200,000 (2/5) |
| **Geneva Re** | $300,000 (3/5) |

*$5000 loss*

| | |
|---|---|
| **Apex Fire** | $2000 (2/5) |
| **Geneva Re** | $3000 (3/5) |

Under a surplus-share treaty, premiums are also shared based on the fraction of total insurance retained by each party. However, the reinsurer pays a ceding commission to the primary insurer to help compensate for the acquisition expenses.

The principal advantage of a surplus-share treaty is that the primary insurer's underwriting capacity is increased. The major disadvantage is the increase in administrative expenses. The surplus-share treaty is more complex and requires greater record-keeping.

*Excess-of-Loss Treaty* An **excess-of-loss treaty** is designed largely for catastrophic protection. Losses in excess of the retention limit are paid by the reinsurer up to some maximum limit. The excess-of-loss treaty can be written to cover (1) a single exposure, (2) a single occurrence, such as a catastrophic loss from a tornado, or (3) excess losses when the primary insurer's cumulative losses exceed a certain amount during some stated time period, such as a year. For example, assume that Apex Fire wants protection for all windstorm losses in excess of $1 million. Assume that an excess-of-loss treaty is written with Franklin Re to cover single occurrences during a specified time period. Franklin Re agrees to pay all losses exceeding $1 million but only to a maximum of $10 million. If a $5 million hurricane loss occurs, Franklin Re would pay $4 million.

*Reinsurance Pool* Reinsurance can also be provided by a reinsurance pool. A **reinsurance pool** *is an organization of insurers that underwrites insurance on a joint basis.* Reinsurance pools have been formed because a single insurer alone may not have the financial capacity to write large amounts of insurance, but the insurers as a group can combine their financial resources to obtain the necessary capacity. For example, the combined hull and liability loss exposures on a commercial jet can exceed $300 million if the jet should crash. Such high limits are usually beyond the financial capability of a single insurer. However, a reinsurance pool for aviation insurance can provide the necessary capacity. Reinsurance pools also exist for nuclear energy exposures, oil refineries, marine insurance, insurance in foreign countries, and numerous other types of exposures.

The method for sharing losses and premiums varies depending on the type of reinsurance pool. Pools work in two ways.[9] First, each pool member agrees to pay a certain percentage of every loss. For example, if one insurer has a policyowner that incurs a $100,000 loss, and there are 50 members in the pool, each insurer would pay 2 percent, or $2000 of the loss, depending on the agreement.

A second arrangement is similar to the excess-of-loss reinsurance treaty. Each pool member is responsible for its own losses below a certain amount. Losses exceeding that amount are shared by all members in the pool.

## Investments

The investment function is an extremely important function in the overall operations of insurance companies. Since premiums are paid in advance, they can be invested until needed to pay claims and expenses.

**Life Insurance Investments**   At the end of 1995, U.S. life insurers held assets of $2.14 trillion.[10] The funds available for investment are derived primarily from premium income, investment earnings, and maturing investments that must be reinvested.

Life insurance investments have an important economic and social impact on the nation. First, life insurance contracts are long-term in nature, and the liabilities of life insurers extend over long periods of time, such as 50 or 60 years. Most life insurance investments are therefore long-term in nature, and the primary investment objective is safety of principal. Thus, in 1995, 50 percent of the assets were invested in mortgages and corporate bonds, which are long-term investments. Government securities accounted for 19 percent of the total assets. Only 17 percent of the assets were invested in stocks, which fluctuate widely in value. The remaining assets were invested in real estate, policy loans, and miscellaneous assets.[11]

Investment income is extremely important in reducing the cost of insurance to policyowners since the premiums can be invested and earn interest. The interest earned on investments is reflected in the payment of dividends to policyowners, which reduces the cost of life insurance.

Finally, life insurance premiums are an important source of capital funds to the economy. These funds are invested in shopping centers, housing developments, office buildings, hospitals, new plants, and other economic and social ventures.

**Property and Liability Insurance Investments**   In 1994, property and liability insurers held assets of $704.6 billion, and net premiums written for all lines totaled nearly $251 billion.[12] Premiums are typically paid in advance, so they can be invested until needed for claims and expenses.

Two important points must be stressed when the investments of property and liability insurers are analyzed. *First, in contrast to life insurance, property and liability insurance contracts are short term in nature.* The policy period in most contracts is one year or less, and property claims are usually settled quickly. Also, in contrast to life insurance claims, which are generally fixed in amount, property and liability claim payments can vary widely depending on catastrophic losses, inflation, medical costs, construction costs, automobile repair costs, economic conditions, and changing value judgments by society. For these reasons, the investment objective of liquidity is extremely important to property and liability insurers.

*Second, investment income is extremely important in offsetting unfavorable underwriting experience.* The investment of capital and surplus funds, along with the funds set aside for loss reserves and the unearned premium reserve, generate investment earnings that usually permit an insurer to continue its insurance operations despite an underwriting deficit. For example, in 1994, property and liability insurers incurred an underwriting loss of $22.2 billion. However, investment income and realized capital gains totaled $35.4 billion. The combined net income after taxes was $10.9 billion.[13] Thus, despite a large underwriting loss, the business overall was still profitable.

## OTHER INSURANCE COMPANY FUNCTIONS

Insurers also perform other functions. They include accounting, legal, loss control services, and data processing.

### Accounting

The **accounting department** is responsible for the financial accounting operations of an insurer. Accountants prepare financial statements, develop budgets, analyze the company's financial operations, and keep track of the millions of dollars that flow into and out of a typical company each year. Periodic reports are prepared dealing with premium income, operating expenses, claims, investment income, and dividends to policyowners. Accountants also prepare state and federal income tax returns and file an annual convention statement for review by state regulatory officials.

### Legal Function

Another important function of insurance companies is the **legal function.** In life insurance, attorneys are widely used in advanced underwriting and estate planning. Attorneys also draft the legal language and policy provisions in insurance policies and review all new policies before they are marketed to the public. Other activities include legal assistance to actuarial personnel who testify at rate hearings; reviewing advertising and other published materials; providing general legal advice concerning taxation, marketing, investments, and insurance laws; and lobbying for legislation favorable to the insurance industry.

Finally, attorneys must keep abreast of the frequent changes in state and federal laws that affect the company and its policyowners. These include laws on consumerism, cost disclosure, affirmative action programs, truth in advertising, and similar legislation.

### Loss-Control Services

**Loss control** is an important part of risk management, and a typical property and liability insurer provides numerous loss control services. These services include advice on alarm systems, automatic sprinkler systems, fire prevention, occupational safety and health, prevention of boiler explosions, and other loss prevention activities. In addition, loss control specialists can provide valuable advice on the construction of a new building or plant to make it safer and more resistive to damage, which can result in a substantial rate reduction.

### Data Processing

Another important functional area is **data processing (EDP).** Use of the computer has revolutionized the insurance industry by speeding up the processing of information and by eliminating many routine tasks. The computer is now used in accounting, policy processing, premium notices, information retrieval, telecommunications, simulation studies, market analysis, training and education, sales, and policyowner services. Information can quickly be obtained on premium volume, claims, loss ratios, investments, and underwriting results.

### SUMMARY

- Rate making refers to the pricing of insurance. Insurance rates are determined by persons called actuaries.
- Underwriting refers to the process of selecting and classifying applicants for insurance. There are several important underwriting principles:

    Selection of insureds according to the company's underwriting standards

    Proper balance within each rate classification

    Equity among policyowners

- In determining whether to accept or reject an applicant for insurance, underwriters have several sources of information. They include the application, agent's report, inspection report, physical inspection, physical examination, attending physician's report, and the Medical Information Bureau.
- Production refers to the sales and marketing activities of insurers. Agents who sell insurance are called producers.
- From the insurer's viewpoint, there are several basic objectives in settling claims:

    Verification of a covered loss

    Fair and prompt payment of claims

    Personal assistance to the insured

- The person who adjusts a claim is known as a claims adjustor. The major types of adjustors are as follows:

    Agent

    Company adjustor

    Independent adjustor

    Adjustment bureau

    Public adjustor

- Several steps are involved in settling a claim:

  Notice of loss must be given to the company.

  The claim is investigated by the company.

  A proof of loss must be filed.

  A decision is made concerning payment.

- Reinsurance is the shifting of part or all of the insurance originally written by one insurer to another insurer. Reinsurance is used for several reasons:

  To increase the company's underwriting capacity

  To stabilize profits

  To reduce the unearned premium reserve

  To provide protection against a catastrophic loss

- Facultative reinsurance means the primary company shops around for reinsurance. The primary company is under no obligation to reinsure, and the reinsurer is under no obligation to accept the insurance. But if the primary company and reinsurer enter into a valid contract, it is known as a facultative treaty. In contrast, under treaty reinsurance, if the business falls within the scope of the agreement, the primary company must cede insurance to the reinsurer, and the reinsurer must accept.

- The most important types of automatic reinsurance treaties are as follows:

  Quota-share treaty

  Surplus-share treaty

  Excess-of-loss treaty

  Reinsurance pool

- Other important insurance company operations include investments, accounting, legal services, loss-control services, and data processing.

## KEY CONCEPTS AND TERMS

| | |
|---|---|
| Adjustment bureau | Class underwriting |
| Agent's report | Company adjustor |
| Ceding commission | Excess-of-loss treaty |
| Ceding company | Facultative reinsurance |
| Certified Financial Planner (CFP) | Independent adjustor |
| | Inspection report |
| Certified Insurance Counselor (CIC) | Line underwriter |
| | Medical Information |
| Cession | Bureau (MIB) report |
| Chartered Financial Consultant (ChFC) | Producers |
| | Public adjustor |
| Chartered Life Underwriter (CLU) | Quota-share treaty |
| | Rate making |
| Chartered Property Casualty Underwriter (CPCU) | Rating bureau |
| | Reinsurance |
| | Reinsurance pool |
| Claims adjustor | Retention limit |

Retrocession

Surplus-share treaty

Treaty reinsurance

Underwriting

Unearned premium reserve

## QUESTIONS FOR REVIEW

1. Briefly describe the rate-making function.

2. Define underwriting. Explain several important underwriting principles.

3. Describe the sources of information available to underwriters.

4. Explain the meaning of production.

5. What are the objectives in the settlement of claims?

6. Describe the steps in the claim settlement process.

7. Define reinsurance. Why is reinsurance used?

8. Distinguish between facultative reinsurance and treaty reinsurance.

9. Describe the following types of reinsurance treaties:
   a. Quota-share treaty
   b. Surplus-share treaty
   c. Excess-of-loss treaty
   d. Reinsurance pool

10. Briefly describe the following insurance company operations:
    a. Accounting
    b. Legal services
    c. Loss control
    d. Data processing

## QUESTIONS FOR DISCUSSION

1. a. The underwriting function is often misunderstood by the public. Explain the basic objectives of the underwriting function.

   b. How does the underwriting department handle the problem of adverse selection?

2. a. If loss occurs, the claims adjustor must determine if the loss is covered by the policy. Explain the items of coverage that the claims adjustor must check to determine if the loss is covered under the policy.

   b. Explain the difference between a public adjustor and claims adjustor employed by an insurance company.

3. a. Explain the nature and purpose of a special agent.

   b. Describe the various marketing activities of insurance companies.

4. Apex Fire enters into a first surplus-share reinsurance treaty with Geneva Re. Apex Fire has a retention limit

of $100,000 and four lines of insurance are ceded to Geneva Re. A building is insured with Apex Fire in the amount of $300,000. If a $30,000 loss occurs, how much will the ceding company and reinsurer pay? Explain your answer.

5. Explain the major differences between life insurance company investments and property and liability insurance company investments.

## SELECTED REFERENCES

Black Kenneth, Jr. and Harold D. Skipper, Jr. *Life Insurance,* 12th ed. Englewood Cliffs, N.J.: Prentice-Hall, Inc., 1994, chapters 23–24, 31, 33.

Graves, Edward E., ed. *McGill's Life Insurance.* Bryn Mawr, Pa.: The American College, 1994, chapters 21–22, 29, 32.

*Insurance Careers,* 1993 Edition. Vol. 21. Memphis, Tenn.: Wallace Witmer Company, 1993.

Smith, Barry et al. *Property and Liability Insurance Principles,* 2nd ed. Malvern, Pa.: Insurance Institute of America, 1994, chapters 3–6.

Webb, Bernard L., Connor M. Harrison, and James J. Markham. *Insurance Operations.* Vols. 1 and 2. Malvern, Pa.: American Institute for Chartered Property Casualty Underwriters, 1992.

## CASE APPLICATION

Reinsurance can be used by an insurer to solve several problems. Assume you are an insurance consultant who is asked to give recommendations concerning the type of reinsurance plan or arrangement to use. For each of the following situations, indicate the type of reinsurance plan or arrangement that the ceding insurer should use, and explain the reasons for your answer.

a. Company A is an established insurer and is primarily interested in having protection against a catastrophic loss arising out of a single occurrence.

b. Company B is rapidly growing and desires a plan of reinsurance that will reduce the drain on its surplus from writing a large volume of new business.

c. Company C has received an application to write a $25 million life insurance policy on the life of the chief executive officer of a major corporation. Before the policy is issued, the life insurer wants to make certain that adequate reinsurance is available.

d. Company D would like to increase its underwriting capacity to underwrite new business.

## NOTES

1. A legal reserve is a liability item on a company's balance sheet that measures the insurer's obligations to its policyowners. State laws require a company to maintain policy reserves at a level that is sufficient to pay all policy obligations as they fall due.

2. In property and liability insurance, a loss reserve is an estimated liability item that represents an amount for claims reported but not yet paid, claims in the process of settlement, and claims that have already occurred but have not been reported. See Chapter 26 for a further discussion of loss reserves.

3. A loss ratio is the ratio of incurred losses to earned premiums. For example, if incurred losses are $70 and earned premiums are $100, the loss ratio is 0.70, or 70 percent.

4. For additional information on claim settlement, see Bernard L. Webb, Connor M. Harrison, and James J. Markham, *Insurance Operations,* vol. I (American Institute for Chartered Property Casualty Underwriters, 1992), chapter 13.

5. Webb et al., pp. 205–06.

6. A first-party claim is a claim submitted by the insured to the insurer, such as fire damage to property owned by the insured.

7. Robert I. Mehr and Emerson Cammack, *Principles of Insurance,* 8th ed. (Homewood, Ill.: Richard D. Irwin, 1985), pp. 616–17.

8. Technically, for a stock insurer, policyholders' surplus is the sum of capital stock (value of the contributions of original stockholders), plus surplus (the amount paid in by the organizers in excess of the par value of the stock), plus any retained earnings. In the case of a mutual insurer, there is no capital account. Policyholders' surplus is the excess of assets over liabilities.

9 *Sharing the Risk,* 3rd ed. (New York: Insurance Information Institute, 1989), pp. 119–20.

10. *1996 Life Insurance Fact Book* (Washington, D.C.: American Council of Life Insurance), p. 84.

11. Ibid., p. 85.

12. *The Fact Book 1996 Property/Casualty Insurance Facts* (New York: Insurance Information Institute), pp. 20–21.

13. Ibid., p. 6.

# Chapter 26

# Insurance Pricing

*Actuaries hold an insurance company's profits in their hands.*

*Insurance Careers*

## Student Learning Objectives

After studying this chapter, you should be able to:

■ Explain the major objectives of rate making.

■ Describe the basic rate-making methods that are used in property and liability insurance, including judgment rating, class rating, and merit rating.

■ Explain how an underwriting profit or loss for a property and liability insurer is determined.

■ Explain the basic concepts of rate making that are used in life insurance, including net single premium, net level premium, and gross premium.

■ Describe the various reserves that insurers are required to maintain by law.

Insurance pricing, or rate making, is one of the most important functions of an insurance company. Actuaries hold the profits of an insurance company in their hands. They must determine the correct rates that an insurer should charge for the insurance offered, expenses that will be incurred, and whether a particular line of insurance should be offered. Actuaries must examine vast amounts of statistics and loss data to determine the correct rates to charge. The actual rates must be high enough to pay all losses and expenses and still earn a profit for the insurer. However, if the rates charged are too high, the insurer may find itself at a competitive disadvantage.

This chapter explores the fundamentals of rate making. The major areas discussed include the objectives of rate making, the basic rate-making methods used in property and liability and life insurance, and the various types of reserves that insurers must maintain by law.

## OBJECTIVES OF RATE MAKING

Rate making, or insurance pricing, has several basic objectives. Since insurance rates—primarily property and liability rates—are regulated by the states, certain statutory or regulatory requirements must be satisfied. Also, due to the overall goal of profitability, certain business objectives must be stressed in rate making. Thus, rate-making goals can be classified into two basic categories—regulatory objectives and business objectives.

## Regulatory Objectives

The goal of insurance regulation is to protect the public. The states have rating laws that require insurance rates to meet certain standards. In general, rates charged by insurers must be adequate, not excessive, and not unfairly discriminatory.

**Adequate Rates**    The first regulatory requirement is that rates must be adequate. *This means the rates charged by insurers should be high enough to pay all losses and expenses.* If rates are inadequate, an insurer may become insolvent and fail. As a result, policyowners, beneficiaries, and third-party claimants may be financially harmed if their claims are not paid. However, rate adequacy is complicated by the fact that the insurer does not know its actual costs when the policy is first sold. The premium is paid in advance, but it may not be sufficient to pay all claims and expenses during the policy period. It is only after the period of protection has expired that an insurer can determine its actual costs.

**Not Excessive**    The second regulatory requirement is that the rates must not be excessive. *This means that the rates should not be so high that policy-owners are paying more than the actual value of their protection.* Exorbitant prices are not in the public interest.

**Not Unfairly Discriminatory**    The third regulatory requirement is that the rates must not be unfairly discriminatory. *This means that exposures that are similar with respect to losses and expenses should not be charged substantially different rates.*[1] For example, if two healthy males, age 30, buy the same type and amount of life insurance from the same insurer, they should not be charged two different rates. However, if the loss exposures are substantially different, it is not unfair rate discrimination to charge different rates. Thus, if two males, age 30 and age 65, apply for the same type and amount of life insurance, it is not unfair to charge the older male a higher rate because of the higher probability of death.

## Business Objectives

Insurers are also guided by certain business objectives in designing a rating system. The rating system should also meet the following objectives:[2]

- Simplicity
- Stability
- Responsiveness
- Encouragement of loss control

**Simplicity**    The rating system should be easy to understand so that producers can quote premiums with a minimum amount of time and expense. This is especially important in the personal lines market, where the relatively small premiums do not justify a large amount of time and expense in the preparation of premium quotations. In addition, commercial insurance purchasers should understand how their premiums are determined so that they can take active steps to reduce their insurance costs.

**Stability**    Rates should be stable over short periods so that consumer satisfaction can be maintained. If rates change rapidly, insurance consumers may become irritated and dissatisfied. They may then look to government to control the rates or to enact a government insurance program.

**Responsiveness**    The rates should also be responsive over time to changing loss exposures and changing economic conditions. In order to meet the objective of rate adequacy, the rates should increase when loss exposures increase. For example, as a city grows, automobile insurance rates should increase to reflect the greater traffic and increased frequency of automobile accidents. Likewise, the rates should reflect changing economic conditions. Thus, if inflation causes liability awards to increase, liability insurance rates should be increased to reflect this trend.

**Encouragement of Loss Control**    The rating system should also encourage loss-control activities that reduce both loss frequency and severity. This is important since loss control tends to keep insurance affordable. Profits are also stabilized. As you will see later, certain rating systems provide a strong financial incentive to the insured to engage in loss control.

## BASIC DEFINITIONS OF RATE MAKING

Before proceeding, you should be familiar with some basic terms that are widely used in rate making. A **rate** is the price per unit of insurance. An **exposure**

**unit** is the unit of measurement used in insurance pricing. It varies by line of insurance. For example, in fire insurance, the exposure unit is $100 of coverage; in products liability insurance, it is $1000 of sales; and in automobile collision insurance, it is one car-year, which is one car insured for a year.

The **pure premium** refers to that portion of the rate needed to pay losses and loss-adjustment expenses. **Loading** refers to the amount that must be added to the pure premium for other expenses, profit, and a margin for contingencies. The **gross rate** consists of the pure premium and a loading element. Finally, the **gross premium** paid by the insured consists of the gross rate multiplied by the number of exposure units. Thus, if the gross rate is 10¢ per $100 of property insurance, the gross premium for a $500,000 building would be $500.

## RATE MAKING IN PROPERTY AND LIABILITY INSURANCE

There are three basic rate-making methods in property and liability insurance—judgment, class, and merit rating. Merit rating in turn can be broken down into schedule rating, experience rating, and retrospective rating. Thus, the basic rating methods can be conveniently classified as follows:[3]

- Judgment rating
- Class rating
- Merit rating
    Schedule rating
    Experience rating
    Retrospective rating

### Judgment Rating

**Judgment rating** *means that each exposure is individually evaluated, and the rate is determined largely by the underwriter's judgment.* This method is used when the loss exposures are so diverse that a class rate cannot be calculated, or when credible loss statistics are not available.

Judgment rating is widely used in ocean marine insurance and in some lines of inland marine insurance. Since the various ocean-going vessels, ports of destination, cargoes carried, and dangerous waters are so diverse, ocean marine rates are determined largely by judgment.

### Class Rating

The second type of rating method is class rating. Most rates used today are class rates. **Class rating** *means exposures with similar characteristics are placed in the same underwriting class, and each is charged the same rate.* The rate charged reflects the *average loss experience* for the class as a whole. Class rating is based on the assumption that future losses to insureds will be determined largely by the same set of factors. For example, major classification factors in life insurance include age, sex, health, and whether the applicant smokes or is a nonsmoker. Accordingly, healthy persons who are the same age and sex and do not smoke are placed in the same underwriting class and charged the same rate for life insurance. Smokers are placed in a different underwriting class and charged higher rates.

The major advantage of class rating is that it is simple to apply. Also, premium quotations can be quickly obtained. As such, it is ideal for the personal lines market.

Class rating is also called *manual rating,* since the various rates are published in a rating manual. Class rating is widely used in homeowners insurance, private passenger automobile insurance, workers compensation, and life and health insurance.

There are two basic methods for determining class rates: the pure premium and loss ratio methods.

As stated earlier, the pure premium is that portion of the gross rate needed to pay losses and loss-adjustment expenses. The **pure premium** *can be determined by dividing the dollar amount of incurred losses and loss-adjustment expenses by the number of exposure units.* Incurred losses include all losses paid during the accounting period, plus amounts held as reserves for the future payment of losses that have already occurred during the same period. Thus, incurred losses include all losses that occur during the accounting period whether or not they have been paid by the end of the period. Loss-adjustment expenses are the expenses incurred by the company in adjusting losses during the same accounting period.

To illustrate how a pure premium can be derived, assume that in automobile collision insurance, 500,000 automobiles in a given underwriting class generate incurred losses and loss-adjustment expenses of $30 million over a one-year period. The pure premium is $60. This can be illustrated by the following:

Pure premium =

$$\frac{\text{Incurred losses and loss-adjustment expenses}}{\text{Number of exposure units}}$$

$$= \frac{\$30,000,000}{500,000}$$

$$= \$60$$

The final step is to add a loading for expenses, underwriting profit, and a margin for contingencies. The expense loading is usually expressed as percentage of the gross rate and is called the expense ratio. The **expense ratio** *is that proportion of the gross rate available for expenses and profit.* The final gross rate can be determined by dividing the pure premium by 1 minus the expense ratio. For example, if expenses are 40 percent of the gross rate, the final gross rate is $100. This can be illustrated by the following:[4]

$$\text{Gross rate} = \frac{\text{Pure premium}}{1 - \text{Expense ratio}}$$

$$= \frac{\$60}{1 - 0.40}$$

$$= \$100$$

Under the loss ratio method, the actual loss ratio is compared with the expected loss ratio, and the rate is adjusted accordingly. The **actual loss ratio** *is the ratio of incurred losses and loss-adjustment expenses to* **earned premiums.**[5] The **expected loss ratio** *is the percentage of the premiums that is expected to be used to pay losses.* For example, assume that a line of insurance has incurred losses and loss-adjustment expenses in the amount of $800,000, and earned premiums are $1 million. The actual loss ratio is 0.80, or 80 percent. If the expected loss ratio is 0.70, or 70 percent, the rate must be increased 14.3 percent. This can be illustrated by the following:

$$\text{Rate change} = \frac{A - E}{E}$$

where
$$A = \text{Actual loss ratio}$$
$$E = \text{Expected loss ratio}$$

$$= \frac{0.80 - 0.70}{0.70}$$

$$= 0.143, \text{ or } 14.3\%$$

## Merit Rating

The third principal type of rating method is merit rating. **Merit rating** *is a rating plan by which class rates (manual rates) are adjusted upward or downward based on individual loss experience.* Merit rating is based on the assumption that the loss experience of a particular insured will differ substantially from the loss experience of other insureds. Thus, class rates are modified upward or downward depending on individual loss experience.

There are several different types of merit rating plans:

- Schedule rating
- Experience rating
- Retrospective rating

**Schedule Rating**    Under a **schedule rating** *plan, each exposure is individually rated. A basis rate is determined for each exposure, which is then modified by debits or credits for undesirable or desirable physical features.* Schedule rating is based on the assumption that certain physical characteristics of the insured's operations will influence the insured's future loss experience. Thus, the physical characteristics of the exposure to be insured are extremely important in schedule rating.

Schedule rating is used in commercial property insurance for large, complex buildings, such as an industrial plant. Each building is individually rated based on the following factors:

- Construction
- Occupancy
- Protection
- Exposure
- Maintenance

*Construction* refers to the physical characteristics of the building. A building may be constructed with frame, brick, fire-resistive, or fire-proof materials. A frame building is charged a higher rate than a brick or fire-resistive building. Also, tall buildings and buildings with large open areas may receive debits because of the greater difficulty of extinguishing or containing a fire.

*Occupancy* refers to use of the building. The probability of a fire is greatly influenced by its use. For example, open flame and sparks from torches and welding can quickly cause a fire. Also, if highly combustible materials or chemicals are stored in the building, the fire will be more difficult to contain.

*Protection* refers to the quality of the city's water supply and fire department. It also includes protective devices installed in the insured building. Rate credits are given for a fire alarm system, security guard, automatic sprinkler system, fire extinguishers, and similar protective devices.

*Exposure* refers to the possibility that the insured building will be damaged or destroyed from a fire that starts in an adjacent building and spreads to the insured building. The greater the exposure from surrounding buildings, the greater are the charges applied.

Finally, *maintenance* refers to the housekeeping and overall maintenance of the building. Debits are applied for poor housekeeping and maintenance. Thus, debits may be given if oily rags are scattered about.

**Experience Rating**    Experience rating is another form of merit rating. Under an **experience rating** *plan, the class, or manual, rate is adjusted upward or downward based on past loss experience.* The most distinctive characteristic of experience rating is that *the insured's past loss experience is used to determine the premium for the next policy period.* The loss experience over the past three years is typically used to determine the premium for the next policy year. If the insured's loss experience is better than the average for the class as a whole, the class rate is reduced. If the loss experience is worse than the class average, the rate is increased. In determining the magnitude of the rate change, the actual loss experience is modified by a *credibility factor*[6] based on the volume of experience.

For example, assume that a retail firm has a general liability insurance policy that is experienced rated. Annual premiums are \$30,000, and the expected loss ratio is 30 percent. If the actual loss ratio over the past three years is 20 percent, and the credibility factor (C) is 0.29, the firm will receive a premium reduction of 9.7 percent. This can be illustrated by the following:

$$\text{Premium change} = \frac{A-E}{E} \times C$$

$$= \frac{0.20 - 0.30}{0.30} \times 0.29$$

$$= -9.7\%$$

Thus, the new premium for the next policy period is \$27,090. As you can see, experience rating provides a financial incentive to reduce losses, since premiums can be reduced by favorable loss experience.

Experience rating is generally limited only to larger firms that generate a sufficiently high volume of premiums and more credible experience. Smaller firms are normally ineligible for experience rating. This rating system is frequently used in general liability insurance, workers compensation, commercial automobile liability insurance, and group health insurance.

**Retrospective Rating**    The final form of merit rating is retrospective rating. Under a **retrospective rating** *plan, the insured's loss experience during the current policy period determines the actual premium paid for that period.* Under this rating plan, the insured is charged a minimum and a maximum premium. If actual losses during the current policy period are small, the minimum premium is paid. If losses are large, the maximum premium is paid. The actual premium paid generally will fall somewhere between the minimum and maximum premium, depending on the insured's loss experience during the current policy period. Retrospective rating is widely used by large firms in workers compensation insurance, general liability insurance, automobile liability and physical damage insurance, and burglary and glass insurance.

## RATE MAKING IN LIFE INSURANCE

Our discussion of rate making so far has applied largely to property and liability insurance. This section briefly examines the fundamental of life insurance rate making.[7]

### Net Single Premium

Life insurance policies can be purchased with a single premium, or with annual, semiannual, quarterly, or monthly premiums. Although most policies are not purchased with a single premium, the net single premium forms the foundation for the calculation of all life insurance premiums.

The **net single premium (NSP)** *can be defined as the present value of the future death benefit.* It is that sum that, together with compound interest, will be sufficient to pay all death claims. In calculating the

EXHIBIT 26.1

## Commissioners 1980 Standard Ordinary Mortality Table, Male Lives

| Age at beginning of year | Number living at beginning of designated year | Number dying during designated year | Age at beginning of year | Number living at beginning of designated year | Number dying during designated year |
|---|---|---|---|---|---|
| 0 | 10,000,000 | 41,800 | 25 | 9,663,007 | 17,104 |
| 1 | 9,958,200 | 10,655 | 26 | 9,645,903 | 16,687 |
| 2 | 9,947,545 | 9,848 | 27 | 9,629,216 | 16,466 |
| 3 | 9,937,697 | 9,739 | 28 | 9,612,750 | 16,342 |
| 4 | 9,927,958 | 9,432 | 29 | 9,596,408 | 16,410 |
| 5 | 9,918,526 | 8,927 | 30 | 9,579,998 | 16,573 |
| 6 | 9,909,599 | 8,522 | 31 | 9,563,425 | 17,023 |
| 7 | 9,901,077 | 7,921 | 32 | 9,546,402 | 17,470 |
| 8 | 9,893,156 | 7,519 | 33 | 9,328,932 | 18,200 |
| 9 | 9,885,637 | 7,315 | 34 | 9,510,732 | 19,021 |
| 10 | 9,878,322 | 7,211 | 35 | 9,491,711 | 20,028 |
| 11 | 9,871,111 | 7,601 | 36 | 9,471,683 | 21,217 |
| 12 | 9,863,510 | 8,384 | 37 | 9,450,466 | 22,681 |
| 13 | 9,855,126 | 9,757 | 38 | 9,427,785 | 24,324 |
| 14 | 9,845,369 | 11,322 | 39 | 9,403,461 | 26,236 |
| 15 | 9,834,047 | 13,079 | 40 | 9,377,225 | 28,319 |
| 16 | 9,820,968 | 14,830 | 41 | 9,348,906 | 30,758 |
| 17 | 9,806,138 | 16,376 | 42 | 9,318,148 | 33,173 |
| 18 | 9,789,762 | 17,426 | 43 | 9,284,975 | 35,933 |
| 19 | 9,772,336 | 18,177 | 44 | 9,249,042 | 38,753 |
| 20 | 9,754,159 | 18,533 | 45 | 9,210,289 | 41,907 |
| 21 | 9,735,626 | 18,595 | 46 | 9,168,382 | 45,108 |
| 22 | 9,717,031 | 18,365 | 47 | 9,123,274 | 48,536 |
| 23 | 9,698,666 | 18,040 | 48 | 9,074,738 | 52,089 |
| 24 | 9,680,626 | 17,619 | 49 | 9,022,649 | 56,031 |

*Continued*

NSP, only mortality and investment income are considered. Insurance company expenses or the loading element are considered later, when the gross premium is calculated.

The NSP is based on three basic assumptions: (1) premiums are paid at the beginning of the policy year, (2) death claims are paid at the end of the policy year, and (3) the death rate is uniform throughout the year.

Certain assumptions must also be made concerning the probability of death at each attained age. Although life insurers generally develop their own mortality data, we will use the Commissioners 1980

Standard Ordinary Mortality Table in our illustrations (see Exhibit 26.1).

Also, since we are assuming that premiums are paid in advance, and that death claims are paid at the end of the policy year, the amount needed to pay death benefits is discounted for compound interest. It is assumed that the amounts needed for death claims can be discounted annually at 5 percent compound interest.

**Term Insurance**   The NSP for term insurance can be calculated easily. The period of protection is

| Age at beginning of year | Number living at beginning of designated year | Number dying during designated year | Age at beginning of year | Number living at beginning of designated year | Number dying during designated year |
|---|---|---|---|---|---|
| 50 | 8,966,618 | 60,166 | 75 | 4,898,907 | 314,461 |
| 51 | 8,906,452 | 65,017 | 76 | 4,584,446 | 323,341 |
| 52 | 8,841,435 | 70,378 | 77 | 4,261,105 | 328,616 |
| 53 | 8,771,057 | 76,396 | 78 | 3,932,489 | 329,936 |
| 54 | 8,694,661 | 83,121 | 79 | 3,602,553 | 328,012 |
| 55 | 8,611,540 | 90,163 | 80 | 3,274,541 | 323,656 |
| 56 | 8,521,377 | 97,655 | 81 | 2,950,885 | 317,161 |
| 57 | 8,423,722 | 105,212 | 82 | 2,633,724 | 308,804 |
| 58 | 8,318,510 | 113,049 | 83 | 2,324,920 | 298,194 |
| 59 | 8,205,461 | 121,195 | 84 | 2,026,726 | 284,248 |
| 60 | 8,084,266 | 129,995 | 85 | 1,742,478 | 266,512 |
| 61 | 7,954,271 | 139,518 | 86 | 1,475,966 | 245,143 |
| 62 | 7,814,753 | 149,965 | 87 | 1,230,823 | 220,994 |
| 63 | 7,664,788 | 161,420 | 88 | 1,009,829 | 195,170 |
| 64 | 7,503,368 | 173,628 | 89 | 814,659 | 168,871 |
| 65 | 7,329,740 | 186,322 | 90 | 645,788 | 143,216 |
| 66 | 7,143,418 | 198,944 | 91 | 502,572 | 119,110 |
| 67 | 6,944,474 | 211,390 | 92 | 383,472 | 97,191 |
| 68 | 6,773,084 | 223,471 | 93 | 286,281 | 77,900 |
| 69 | 6,509,613 | 235,453 | 94 | 208,381 | 61,660 |
| 70 | 6,274,160 | 247,892 | 95 | 146,721 | 48,412 |
| 71 | 6,026,268 | 260,937 | 96 | 98,309 | 37,805 |
| 72 | 5,765,331 | 274,718 | 97 | 60,504 | 29,054 |
| 73 | 5,490,613 | 289,026 | 98 | 31,450 | 20,693 |
| 74 | 5,201,587 | 302,680 | 99 | 10,757 | 10,757 |

SOURCE: Black/Skipper, *Life Insurance*, 12 ed., 1994, pp. 518–519. Reprinted by permission of Prentice-Hall, Inc., Englewood Cliffs, N.J.

only for a specified period or to a stated age. The face amount is paid if the insured dies within the specified period, but nothing is paid if the insured dies after the period of protection expires.

The NSP for *yearly renewable term insurance* is considered first. Assume that a $1000 yearly renewable term insurance policy is issued to a male age 45. *The cost of each year's insurance is determined by multiplying the probability of death by the amount of insurance multiplied by the present value of $1 for the time period the funds are held.* By referring to the 1980 CSO mortality chart in Exhibit 26.1, we see that out

of 10 million males alive at age zero, 9,210,289 are still alive at the beginning of age 45. Of this number, 41,907 persons will die during the year. Therefore, the probability that a person age 45 will die during the year is 41,907/9,210,289. This fraction is then multiplied by $1000 to determine the amount of money the insurer must have on hand from each policyowner at the end of the year to pay death claims. However, since premiums are paid in advance, and death claims are paid at the end of the year, the amount needed can be discounted for one year of interest. From Exhibit 26.2, we see that

## EXHIBIT 26.2

### Present Value of $1 at 5% Rate of Compound Interest

| Number of years | 5% | Number of years | 5% |
|---|---|---|---|
| 1 | 0.9524 | 21 | 0.3589 |
| 2 | 0.9070 | 22 | 0.3418 |
| 3 | 0.8638 | 23 | 0.3256 |
| 4 | 0.8227 | 24 | 0.3101 |
| 5 | 0.7835 | 25 | 0.2953 |
| 6 | 0.7462 | 26 | 0.2812 |
| 7 | 0.7107 | 27 | 0.2678 |
| 8 | 0.6768 | 28 | 0.2551 |
| 9 | 0.6446 | 29 | 0.2429 |
| 10 | 0.6139 | 30 | 0.2314 |
| 11 | 0.5847 | 35 | 0.1813 |
| 12 | 0.5568 | 40 | 0.1420 |
| 13 | 0.5303 | 45 | 0.1113 |
| 14 | 0.5051 | 50 | 0.0872 |
| 15 | 0.4810 | 53 | 0.0753 |
|  |  | 54 | 0.0717 |
| 16 | 0.4581 | 55 | 0.0683 |
| 17 | 0.4363 |  |  |
| 18 | 0.4155 |  |  |
| 19 | 0.3957 |  |  |
| 20 | 0.3769 |  |  |

SOURCE: Alan Gart and David J. Nye, "Present Value of $1" *Insurance Company Finance.* Copyright © 1986 Insurance Institute of America, Inc. Reprinted by permission.

the present value of $1 at 5 percent interest is 0.9524. Thus, if the probability of death at age 45 is multiplied by $1000, and the sum is discounted for one year's interest, the resulting net single premium is $4.33. This calculation is summarized as follows:

*Age 45, NSP*

$$\frac{41,907}{9,210,289} \times \$1000 \times 0.9524 = \$4.33$$

If $4.33 is collected in advance from each of the 9,210,289 persons who are alive at age 45, this amount together with compound interest will be sufficient to pay all death claims.

If the policy is renewed for another year, the NSP at age 46 would be calculated as follows:

*Age 46, NSP*

$$\frac{45,108}{9,168,382} \times \$1000 \times 0.9524 = \$4.69$$

The NSP for a yearly renewable term insurance policy issued at age 46 is $4.69. Premiums for subsequent years are calculated in the same manner.

Now consider the NSP for a *five-year term insurance policy* in the amount of $1000 issued to a person age 45. In this case, the company must pay the death claim if the insured dies any time within the five-year period. However, any death claims are paid at the end of the year in which they occur, not at the end of the five-year period. Consequently, the cost of each year's mortality must be computed separately and then added together to determine the net single premium.

The cost of insurance for the first year is determined exactly as before, when we calculated the net single premium for yearly renewable term insurance. Thus, we have the following equation:

*Age 45, first-year insurance cost*

$$\frac{41,907}{9,210,289} \times \$1000 \times 0.9524 = \$4.33$$

The next step is to determine the cost of insurance for the second year. Referring back to Exhibit 26.1, we see that at age 46, 45,108 people will die during the year. Thus, for the 9,210,289 persons who are alive at age 45, the probability of dying during age 46 is 45,108/9,210,289. Note that the denominator does not change but remains the same for each probability fraction. Since the amount needed to pay second-year death claims will not be needed for two years, it can be discounted for two years at 5 percent interest. Thus, for the second year, we have the following calculation:

*Age 46, second-year insurance cost*

$$\frac{45,108}{9,210,289} \times \$1000 \times 0.9070 = \$4.44$$

For each of the remaining three years, we follow the same procedure (see Exhibit 26.3). If the insurer collects $22.74 in a single premium from each of the 9,210,289 persons who are alive at

## EXHIBIT 26.3

### Figuring the NSP for a Five-Year Term Insurance Policy

| Age | Probability of death | | Amount of insurance | | Present value of $1 at 5 percent | | Cost of insurance |
|---|---|---|---|---|---|---|---|
| 45 | $\dfrac{41,907}{9,210,289}$ | × | $1000 | × | 0.9524 | = | $ 4.33 (year 1) |
| 46 | $\dfrac{45,108}{9,210,289}$ | × | $1000 | × | 0.9070 | = | 4.44 (year 2) |
| 47 | $\dfrac{48,536}{9,210,289}$ | × | $1000 | × | 0.8638 | = | 4.55 (year 3) |
| 48 | $\dfrac{52,089}{9,210,289}$ | × | $1000 | × | 0.8227 | = | 4.65 (year 4) |
| 49 | $\dfrac{56,031}{9,210,289}$ | × | $1000 | × | 0.7835 | = | 4.77 (year 5) |
| | | | | | | NSP = | $22.74 |

age 45, that sum together with compound interest will be sufficient to pay all death claims during the five-year period.

**Ordinary Life Insurance**   In calculating the NSP for an ordinary life policy, the same method described earlier for the five-year term policy is used except that the calculations are carried out to the end of the mortality table (age 99). Thus, in our illustration, the NSP for a $1000 ordinary life insurance policy issued at age 45 would be $270.84.

## Net Level Premium

Most life insurance policies are not purchased with a single premium because of the large amount of cash that is required. Consumers generally find it more convenient to pay for their insurance in installment payments. If premiums are paid annually, the net single premium must be converted into a net annual level premium, which must be the mathematical equivalent of the net single premium. The net annual level premium cannot be determined by simply dividing the net single premium by the number of years over which the premiums are to be paid. Such a division would produce an insufficient premium, for two reasons. First, the net single premium is based on the assumption that the entire premium is paid in advance at the beginning of the period. If premiums are paid in installments, and some persons die prematurely, the insurer would suffer the loss of future premiums.

Second, installment payments result in the loss of interest income because of the smaller amounts that are invested. Thus, the mathematical adjustment for the loss of premiums and interest is accomplished by dividing the net single premium by the present value of an appropriate life annuity due of $1. To be more precise, the **net annual level premium (NALP)** *is determined by dividing the net single premium by the present value of a life annuity due (PVLAD) of $1 for the premium-paying period.* Thus, we obtain the following:

$$\text{NALP} = \frac{\text{NSP}}{\text{PVLAD of \$1 for the premium-paying period}}$$

The concept of a life annuity due requires a brief explanation. The annual premium payments can be viewed as being similar to a life annuity, except that the payments flow from the insured to the insurer. Both life annuity payments and premium payments are similar in that both are paid during the lifetime of a specified individual, or for a stated period of time. Both cease on death (unless the annuity has a refund feature), and both are discounted for compound interest. The major exception is that the first premium is due immediately (since premiums are paid in advance), while the first annuity payment is due one payment interval from the date of purchase.[8] Thus, the annual payments are the equivalent of a regular life annuity plus one payment that is made immediately. However, in order to distinguish the premium payments from the annuity payments, we refer to the series of premium payments as a *life annuity due*. If the annual level premiums are to be paid for life—such as in an ordinary life policy—the premium is called a *whole life annuity due*. If the annual premiums are to be paid for only a temporary period—such as in the case of term insurance or limited payments policies—the premium is called a *temporary life annuity due*.[9]

**Term Insurance** Consider the net annual level premium for a five-year term insurance policy in the amount of $1000 issued at age 45. Recall that the net single premium for a five-year term insurance policy at age 45 is $22.74. This sum must be divided by the present value of a five-year *temporary life annuity due of $1*. For the first year, a $1 payment is due immediately. For the second year, the probability that a person age 45 will still be *alive* at age 46 to make the second payment of $1 must be determined. Referring back to Exhibit 26.1, 9,210,289 persons are alive at age 45. Of this number, 9,168,382 are still alive at age 46. Thus, the probability of survival is 9,168,382/9,210,289. This fraction is multiplied by $1, and the resulting sum is then discounted for one year's interest. Thus, the present value of the second payment is $0.948. Similar calculations are performed for the remaining three years. The various calculations are summarized as follows:

Age 45 $1 due immediately = $1.000

$$\text{Age 46 } \frac{9,168,382}{9,210,289} \times \$1 \times 0.9524 = 0.948$$

$$\text{Age 47 } \frac{9,123,274}{9,210,289} \times \$1 \times 0.9070 = 0.898$$

$$\text{Age 48 } \frac{9,074,738}{9,210,289} \times \$1 \times 0.8638 = 0.851$$

$$\text{Age 49 } \frac{9,022,649}{9,210,289} \times \$1 \times 0.8227 = \underline{0.826}$$

$$\text{PVLAD of \$1} = \$4.503$$

The present value of a five-year temporary life annuity due of $1 at age 45 is $4.50. If the net single

premium of $22.74 is divided by $4.50, the net annual level premium is $5.05.

$$\text{NALP} = \frac{\text{NSP}}{\text{PVLAD of \$1}} = \frac{\$22.74}{\$4.50} = \$5.05$$

**Ordinary Life Insurance** The net annual level premium for a $1000 ordinary life insurance policy issued at age 45 is calculated in a similar manner. The same procedure is used except that the calculations are extended to the end of the mortality table. Thus, the present value of a *whole life annuity due of $1* for ages 45 through 99 must be calculated. If the calculations are performed, the present value of a whole life annuity due of $1 at age 45 is $15.312. The net single premium ($270.84) is then divided by the present value of a whole life annuity due of $1 at age 45 ($15.312), and the net annual level premium is $17.69.

**Gross Premium** The gross premium is determined by adding a loading allowance to the net level premium. The loading must cover all operating expenses, provide a margin for contingencies, and in the case of stock life insurers, provide for a contribution to profits. If the policy is a participating policy, the loading must also reflect a margin for dividends.

Three major types of expenses are reflected in the loading allowance: (1) production expenses, (2) distribution expenses, and (3) maintenance expenses.[10] Production expenses are the expenses incurred before the agent delivers the policy, such as policy printing costs, underwriting expenses, and the cost of the medical examination. Distribution expenses are largely selling expenses, such as the first-year commission, advertising, and agency allowances. Maintenance expenses are the expenses incurred after the policy is issued, such as renewal commissions, costs of collecting renewal premiums, and state premium taxes.

## RESERVES IN PROPERTY AND LIABILITY INSURANCE

The remainder of this chapter focuses largely on the various financial reserves of insurance companies. Insurers are required by law to maintain minimum reserves on their balance sheets. Since premiums are paid in advance, but the period of protection extended into the future, insurers must establish certain reserves to assure that the premiums collected in advance will be available to pay future losses.

Property and liability insurers are required to maintain two principal types of financial reserves:

- Unearned premium reserve
- Loss reserves

## Unearned Premium Reserve

The unearned premium reserve is the principal liability item on the company's balance sheet. The **unearned premium reserve** *is a liability item that represents the unearned portion of gross premiums on all outstanding policies at the time of valuation.* An insurer is required by law to place the entire gross premium in the unearned premium reserve when the policy is first written, and renewal premiums must be placed in the same reserve.

**Reasons for the Unearned Premium Reserve** *The fundamental purpose of the unearned premium reserve is to pay for losses that occur during the policy period.* Premiums are paid in advance, but the period of protection extends into the future. To assure policyowners that future losses will be paid, the unearned premium reserve is required.

*The unearned premium reserve is also needed so that premium refunds can be paid to the policyowners in the event of cancellation.* If the insurer cancels, a full pro rata premium refund based on the unexpired portion of the policy term must be paid to the policyowner. Thus, the unearned premium reserve must be adequate so the premium refunds can be made in the event of cancellation.

*Finally, if the business is reinsured, the unearned premium reserve serves as the basis for determining the amount that must be paid to the reinsurer for carrying the reinsured policies to the end of their terms.* In practice, however, the amount paid to the reinsurer may be considerably less than the unearned premium reserve, since the reinsurer does not incur heavy first-year acquisition expenses in acquiring the reinsured policies.

**Methods of Calculation** Several methods can be used to calculate the unearned premium reserve. Only one of them is described here.[11] Under the *annual pro rata method,* it is assumed that the policies are written uniformly throughout the year. For purposes of determining the unearned premium reserve, it is assumed that all policies are issued on July 1, which is the average issue date. Therefore, on December 31, the unearned premium reserve for all one-year policies is one-half of the premium income attributable to these policies. For two-year policies, the unearned premium reserve is three-fourths of the premium income, and for three-year policies, it is five-sixths of the premium income.

**Equity in Unearned Premium Reserve** The law requires an insurer to place the entire gross premium in the unearned premium reserve. This results in a redundant or excessive reserve, since most of the expenses incurred in writing the business are incurred when the policy is first written. Relatively lower expenses are incurred after the policy is issued. However, because of emphasis on insurer solvency, the law prohibits an insurer from taking credit in advance for these prepaid expenses. Although the premium is being earned gradually over the policy period, the initial acquisition and underwriting expenses cannot be amortized over the same period. Instead, they are treated as cash expenses, to be charged off immediately. Therefore, since the unearned premium reserve must be established on the basis of a gross premium rather than a net premium, it is substantially overstated. *This overstatement or redundancy in the unearned premium reserve is called the* **equity in the unearned premium reserve.** Authorities estimate that the unearned premium reserve may be overstated by 20 to 40 percent, with 35 percent being a typical or average estimate of the equity in this reserve.

**Effect on Underwriting Profit or Loss** The equity in the unearned premium reserve is extremely important in determining the true underwriting profit or loss of a property-liability insurer. For example, assume that a new property insurance company begins operating on January 1. It plans to sell only one-year property insurance policies. In establishing the rates, the insurer has an expected loss ratio of 60 percent, an expected expense ratio of 35 percent, and expects to earn an underwriting profit of 5 percent.[12] Also assume that the business is written uniformly throughout the year, and the annual pro rata method is used to determine the unearned premium reserve. During the year, $10 million of property insurance premiums are written. Losses and loss adjustment expenses incurred total $3 million, and expenses incurred are $3.5 million.[13] On December 31, what is the insurer's underwriting profit or loss? The law requires the company to use a *statutory underwriting formula* to determine its underwriting results. Investment gains or losses are not considered in the formula. The statutory formula is as follows:

Statutory underwriting profit or loss =

$$\text{Earned premiums} - \frac{\text{Losses incurred and loss-adjustment expenses incurred}}{} - \text{Expenses incurred}$$

In our illustration, the company has a statutory underwriting loss of $1.5 million. This can be illustrated as follows:

*($000 omitted)*

| | |
|---|---:|
| Premiums written | $10,000 |
| Deduct unearned premiums | −5,000 |
| Earned premiums | $ 5,000 |
| Losses incurred | $3,000 |
| Expenses incurred | $3,500 |
| Total losses and expenses | −6,500 |
| Statutory underwriting loss | ($ 1,500) |

Although the insurer's actual loss and expense experience conforms exactly to the experience anticipated in the rating structure, it has a statutory underwriting loss rather than a 5 percent underwriting profit. This is due to the statutory method for determining a profit or loss. As noted earlier, the first-year acquisition expenses cannot be amortized over the policy term but must be immediately charged off as a cash expense. This produces a statutory underwriting loss in our example.

The statutory underwriting loss of $1.5 million is a charge against the insurer's surplus. Thus, a rapidly growing insurer will experience a surplus drain because of a continuous increase in the unearned premium reserve. The opposite is true for an insurer whose premium volume is declining. The insurer will have a gain in its surplus account as the business runs off the books. The equity in the unearned premium reserve will flow into the insurer's surplus with the passage of time as the policy terms run off. Thus, to correct for the distortion that may

result from the statutory formula, an *adjusted underwriting profit or loss* (called a trade profit or loss) is often used by financial analysts to determine the true underwriting results.

One method for determining the insurer's adjusted underwriting profit or loss is to consider the equity in the unearned premium reserve. The increased equity in the unearned premium reserve can be added to the statutory profit or loss to determine the adjusted underwriting profit or loss. In our earlier illustration, the insurer experienced an increase of $5 million in the unearned premium reserve. If an estimated equity of 35 percent in the unearned premium reserve is assumed, the insurer has an adjusted underwriting profit rather than a loss. This can be illustrated as follows.

*($000 omitted)*

| | |
|---|---:|
| Statutory underwriting loss | −1500 |
| Equity in the unearned premium reserve | 1750 |
| Adjusted underwriting profit | $ 250 |

After adjusting the statutory formula for the equity in the unearned premium reserve, the insurer has an adjusted underwriting profit of $250,000, which is exactly 5 percent of earned premiums.

Based on the statutory formula method for determining underwriting profits, the property and liability industry is not highly profitable. The return on net worth is generally lower than that recorded by other industries (see Insight 26.1).

## Loss Reserves

The loss reserve is another important liability reserve for property-liability insurers. A loss reserve is the estimated cost of settling claims that have already occurred but have not been paid as of the valuation date. More specifically, the **loss reserve** *is an estimated amount for (1) claims reported and adjusted but not yet paid, (2) claims reported and filed but not yet adjusted, and (3) claims incurred but not yet reported to the company.* The loss reserve is especially important to casualty insurers because bodily injury and property damage liability lawsuits may take a long time to settle—often several years. In contrast, property insurance claims, automobile collision and comprehensive losses, and other first party insurance claims are settled more quickly; hence loss reserves are relatively small for property insurers.

---

## INSIGHT 26.1

## How Profitable Is the Property and Liability Insurance Industry?

In 1994, the property/casualty insurance industry's rate of return, as computed by generally accepted accounting principles (GAAP), fell to 5.5 percent. The rate of return in statutory accounting terms fell to about half of what it had been in 1993. The GAAP figures are estimates because many insurance companies, particularly mutuals, do not report their data in GAAP terms. Generally, the return on net worth of the property/casualty insurance business has been considerably less stable over the years than that of other industries.

| | Annual Rate of Return: Net Income after Taxes as a % of Equity | | | | | |
|---|---|---|---|---|---|---|
| | Property/casualty ins. | | | Other industries | | |
| Year | Statutory accounting[1] | GAAP accounting[2] | Diversified financial[3] | Commercial banks | Utilities | Fortune 500[4] |
| 1985 | 2.8% | 4.0% | 9.4% | 13.0% | 13.0% | 11.6% |
| 1986 | 13.9 | 13.6 | 15.9 | 12.8 | 13.3 | 11.6 |
| 1987 | 13.2 | 15.8 | 16.3 | 11.1 | 12.8 | 14.4 |
| 1988 | 13.2 | 13.2 | 12.8 | 14.6 | 12.7 | 16.2 |
| 1989 | 9.1 | 9.9 | 13.0 | 13.6 | 12.4 | 15.0 |
| 1990 | 8.5 | 8.6 | 12.7 | 9.9 | 11.5 | 13.0 |
| 1991 | 8.9 | 9.2 | 13.9 | 11.9 | 11.5 | 10.2 |
| 1992 | 4.4 | 4.4 | 12.8 | 12.2 | 9.4 | 9.0 |
| Year | Statutory accounting[1] | GAAP accounting[2] | Diversified financial[3] | Commercial banks | Electric & gas utilities | Fortune 500 Combined industrial & services businesses[4] |
| 1993 | 10.6 | 10.4 | 17.1 | 14.9 | 11.1 | 11.9 |
| 1994 | 5.6 | 5.5 | 18.4 | 15.6 | 11.3 | 13.7 |

[1]Net income after taxes, divided by year-end policyholders' surplus. Calculated by the Insurance Information Institute from A.M. Best data.

[2]Return on year-end net worth, Insurance Services Office.

[3]Composed largely of companies engaged in property and casualty insurance with or without life insurance and other financial services.

[4]Median return on equity.

SOURCE: *The Fact Book, 1996 Property/Casualty Insurance Facts* (New York: Insurance Information Institute), p. 20.

---

There are four principal methods for estimating the size of the loss reserve for reported losses:[14]

- Individual estimate method
- Average value method
- Loss ratio method
- Tabular value method

Under the **individual estimate method,** a loss reserve is established for each claim. This method is used when a number of claims in a particular line of insurance is too small, or when the variation in claims is too large to assign an average value to each claim.

Under the **average value method,** an average value is assigned to each claim. This method is used when the number of claims is large, the average amount of each claim is relatively small, and the claims are quickly settled. For example, loss reserves for automobile physical damage claims are often based on this method.

Under the **loss ratio method,** a statutory formula based on the expected loss ratio is used to estimate the loss reserve. The expected loss ratio is multiplied by premiums earned during some time period. Losses and loss-adjustment expenses that have been paid to date are then subtracted from the ultimate loss figure to determine the current loss reserve. This method is required by law for certain lines of insurance, such as workers compensation and liability insurance claims.

The **tabular value method** is used to estimate loss reserves for certain claims for which the amounts paid will depend on the length of life, duration of disability, remarriage of the beneficiary, and similar factors. This method is often used to establish loss reserves involving total permanent disability, partial permanent disability, survivorship benefits, and similar claims. The loss reserve is called a *tabular reserve* because the duration of the benefit period is based on data derived from mortality, morbidity, and remarriage tables.

## LIFE INSURANCE POLICY RESERVES

Policy reserves are the major liability item of life insurers. This section briefly examines the nature, purposes, and types of life insurance policy reserves.[15]

### Nature of the Reserve

Under a level-premium plan of life insurance, the premiums paid during the early years of the contract are higher than is necessary to pay death claims, while those paid during the later years are insufficient to pay death claims. The excess or redundant premiums collected during the early years of the contract must be accounted for and held for future payment to the policyowners' beneficiary. The redundant premiums paid during the early years result in the creation of a policy reserve. *Policy reserves are a liability item on the company's balance sheet that must be offset by assets equal to that amount.* Policy reserves are considered a liability item because they represent an obligation by the insurer to pay future policy benefits to policyowners. The policy reserves held by the insurer plus future premiums and future interest earnings will enable the insurer to pay all future policy benefits if the actual experience conforms to

the actuarial assumptions used in calculating the reserve. Policy reserves are often called *legal reserves,* since state insurance laws specify the minimum basis for calculating them.

### Purposes of the Reserve

The policy reserve has two fundamental purposes. *First, it is a formal recognition of the insurer's obligation to pay future benefits.* The policy reserve plus future premiums and interest earnings must be sufficient to pay all future policy benefits.

*Second, the reserve is a legal test of the insurer's solvency.* The insurer must hold assets equal to its legal reserves and other liabilities. This is the legal test of the insurer's ability to meet its present and future obligations to its policyowners. Policy reserves should not, therefore, be viewed as a fund. Rather, they are a liability item that must be offset by "funds" or assets. About 80 percent of the insurer's assets are needed to offset its reserve liabilities.

### Definition of the Reserve

The **policy reserve** *can be defined as the difference between the present value of future benefits and the present value of future net premiums.* The net single premium is equal to the present value of future benefits. At the inception of the policy, the net single premium is also equal to the present value of future net premiums. The net single premium can be converted into a series of annual installment payments without changing this relationship. However, once the first installment premium payment is made, this is no longer true. The present value of future benefits and the present value of future net premiums are no longer equal to each other. The present value of future benefits will increase over time, since the date of death is drawing closer, while the present value of future net premiums will decline, since fewer premiums will be paid. Thus, the difference between the two is the policy reserve.

This is illustrated by Exhibit 26.4, which shows the prospective reserve (defined later) for an ordinary life policy issued at age 45. At the inception of the policy, the net single premium is equal to the present value of future benefits and the present value of future net premiums.

The present value of future benefits increases over time, while the present value of future net premiums declines, and the reserve is the difference

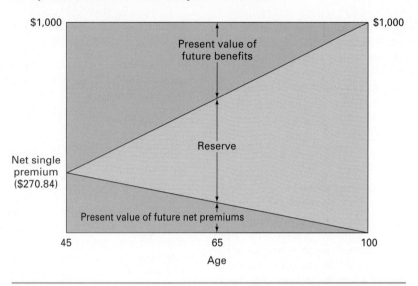

**Exhibit    26.4**

**Prospective Reserve—Ordinary Life Insurance**

between them. At age 100, the reserve is equal to the policy face amount. If the insured is still alive at that time, the face amount of insurance is paid to the policyowner.

## Types of Reserves

The reserve can be viewed either retrospectively or prospectively. If we refer to the past experience, the reserve is known as a retrospective reserve. The **retrospective reserve** *represents the net premiums collected by the insurer for a particular block of policies, plus interest earnings at an assumed rate, less the amounts paid out as death claims.*[16] Thus, the retrospective reserve is the excess of the net premiums accumulated at interest over the death claims paid out.

The reserve can also be viewed prospectively when we look to the future. The **prospective reserve** *is the difference between the present value of future benefits and the present value of future net premiums.* The retrospective and prospective methods are the mathematical equivalent of each other. Both methods will produce the same level of reserves at the end of any given year if the same set of actuarial assumptions is used.

Reserves can also be classified based on the time of valuation. At the time the reserves are valued, they can be classified as terminal, initial, and mean.

A **terminal reserve** *is the reserve at the end of any given policy year.* It is used by companies to determine cash surrender values and also to determine the net amount at risk for purposes of determining dividends. The **initial reserve** *is the reserve at the beginning of any policy year.* It is equal to the preceding terminal reserve plus the net level annual premium for the current year. The initial reserve is also used by insurers to determine dividends. Finally, the **mean reserve** *is the average of the terminal and initial reserves.* It is used to indicate the insurer's reserve liabilities on its annual statement.

## SUMMARY

- State rating laws require insurance rates to meet certain standards. The rates charged by insurers must be adequate, not excessive, and not unfairly discriminatory.

- The rating system should also meet certain business objectives. The rates should be simple, stable, responsive, and should encourage loss prevention.

- Three major rating methods are used in property and liability insurance: judgment, class, and merit rating.

- Judgment rating means that each exposure is individually evaluated, and the rate is determined largely by the underwriter's judgment.

- Class rating means that exposures with similar characteristics are placed in the same underwriting class, and each is charged the same rate. The rate charged reflects the average loss experience for the class as a whole. Most personal lines of insurance are class rated.

- Merit rating is a rating plan by which class rates are adjusted upward or downward based on individual loss experience. It is based on the assumption that the loss experience of a particular insured will differ substantially from the loss experience of other insureds.

- There are three principal types of merit rating plans:

  Schedule rating

  Experience rating

  Retrospective rating

- Under *schedule rating,* each exposure is individually rated, and debits and credits are applied based on the physical characteristics of the exposure to be insured.

- *Experience rating* means that the insured's past loss experience is used to determine the premium for the next policy period. *Retrospective rating* means the insured's loss experience during the current policy period determines the actual premium paid for that period.

- In life insurance rate making, the *net single premium* is the present value of the future death benefit. The *net annual level premium* must be the mathematical equivalent of the net single premium. The net annual level premium is determined by dividing the net single premium by the present value of a life annuity due to $1 for the premium-paying period. A loading for expenses must be added to the net annual level premium to determine the gross premium paid by the insured.

- The unearned premium reserve in property and liability insurance is a liability reserve that represents the unearned portion of gross premiums on all outstanding policies at the time of valuation. The fundamental purpose of the unearned premium reserve is to pay for losses that occur during the policy period.

- A loss reserve is the estimated cost of settling claims that have already occurred but have not been paid as of the valuation date. There are several methods for estimating the size of the loss reserve:

  Individual estimate method

  Average value method

  Loss ratio method

  Tabular value method

- In life insurance, a policy reserve is defined as the difference between the present value of future benefits and the present value of future net premiums. Policy reserves or legal reserves are a formal recognition of the insurer's obligation to pay future benefits. Also,

the reserve is a legal test of an insurer's solvency, since the insurer must hold assets equal to its legal reserves and other liabilities.

## KEY CONCEPTS AND TERMS

| | |
|---|---|
| Actual loss ratio | Mean reserve |
| Adjusted underwriting profit or loss | Merit rating |
| | Net annual level premium (NALP) |
| Annual pro rata method | |
| Class rating (manual rating) | Net single premium (NSP) |
| Earned premiums | Policy reserves |
| Equity in the unearned premium reserve | Prospective reserve |
| | Pure premium |
| Expected loss ratio | Rate |
| Expense ratio | Retrospective rating |
| Experience rating | Retrospective reserve |
| Exposure unit | Schedule rating |
| Gross premium | Temporary life annuity due |
| Gross rate | |
| Initial reserve | Terminal reserve |
| Judgment rating | Unearned premium reserve |
| Loading | |
| Loss reserve | Whole life annuity due |

## QUESTIONS FOR REVIEW

1. Describe the major objectives of rate making.

2. Explain the meaning of judgment rating.

3. What is class rating?

4. What is merit rating? Describe the three principal types of merit-rating plans.

5. Explain the concept of the net single premium in life insurance.

6. How is the net annual level premium computed?

7. What is the gross premium and how is it determined?

8. Explain the nature and purposes of unearned premium reserve in property and liability insurance.

9. What is a loss reserve? Describe the various types of loss reserves in property and liability insurance.

10. Describe the nature of a policy reserve (legal reserve) in life insurance.

## QUESTIONS FOR DISCUSSION

1. Class rates (manual rates) are widely used in personal lines of insurance.

   a. Briefly describe the principal methods of determining class rates.

   b. Explain the advantages of class rating to insurers.

2. Merit rating is used in property and liability insurance where the final premium paid depends at least partly on the loss experience of the individual insured. Describe the major features of each of the following types of merit-rating plans:

   a. Schedule rating

   b. Experience rating

   c. Retrospective rating

3. A property and liability insurer has a redundancy or equity in its unearned premium reserve.

   a. Explain the reasons for the unearned premium reserve in property and liability insurance.

   b. Explain how the redundancy or equity in the unearned premium reserve arises.

4. Property and liability insurers are required to maintain certain types of loss reserves.

   a. Explain the nature of a loss reserve in property and liability insurance.

   b. Briefly describe the following types of loss reserves:

      (1) Individual estimate method

      (2) Average value method

## CASE APPLICATION

Assume that you are asked to explain how premiums in a life insurance policy are calculated. Based on the following information, answer the questions below.

a. Compute the net single premium for a five-year term insurance policy in the amount of $1000 issued at age 40.

b. Compute the net annual level premium for the same policy as in part (a).

c. Is the net annual level premium the actual premium paid by the policyowner? Explain your answer.

| Age at beginning of year | Number living at beginning of designated year | Number dying during designated year | Present value of $1 at 5% | |
|---|---|---|---|---|
| | | | Year | Factor |
| 40 | 9,377,225 | 28,319 | 1 | 0.9524 |
| 41 | 9,348,906 | 30,758 | 2 | 0.9070 |
| 42 | 9,318,148 | 33,173 | 3 | 0.8638 |
| 43 | 9,284,975 | 35,933 | 4 | 0.8227 |
| 44 | 9,249,042 | 38,753 | 5 | 0.7835 |

### SELECTED REFERENCES

Black, Kenneth, Jr., and Harold D. Skipper, Jr. *Life Insurance*, 12th ed. (Englewood Cliffs, N.J.: Prentice-Hall, Inc., 1994), chapters 18–21.

Graves, Edward E., ed. *McGill's Life Insurance*. Bryn Mawr, Pa.: The American College, 1994, chapters 15–17.

Troxel, Terrie E., and George E. Bouchie. *Property-Liability Insurance Accounting and Finance*, 4th ed. Malvern, Pa.: American Institute for Chartered Property Casualty Underwriters, 1995.

Webb, Bernard L., Connor M. Harrison, and James J. Markham. *Insurance Operations*, Vols. 1 and 2. Malvern, Pa.: American Institute for Chartered Property Casualty Underwriters, 1992, chapters 10–12.

### NOTES

1. Robert J. Gibbons, George E. Rejda, and Michael W Elliott, *Insurance Perspectives* (Malvern, Pa.: American Institute for Chartered Property Casualty Underwriters, 1992), p. 119.

2. Bernard L. Webb, Conner M. Harrison, and James J. Markam, *Insurance Operations*, Vol. 2 (Malvern, Pa.: American Institute for Chartered Property Casualty Underwriters, 1992), pp. 97–98.

3. The basic rate-making methods are discussed in some detail in Webb et al., chapter 10. See also Bernard L. Webb, J. J. Launie, Willis Parks Rokes, and Norman A. Baglini, *Insurance Company Operations,* Vol. 1 (Malvern, Pa.: American Institute for Property and Liability Underwriters, 1978), chapters 8 and 9.

4. An equivalent method for determining the final rate is to divide the pure premium by the permissible loss ratio. The *permissible loss ratio* is the same as the expected loss ratio. If the expense ratio is 0.40, the permissible loss ratio is 1 – 0.40, or 0.60. Thus, if the pure premium of $60 is divided by the permissible loss ratio of 0.60, the resulting gross rate is also $100.

$$\text{Gross rate} = \frac{\text{Pure premium}}{\text{Permissible loss ratio}} = \frac{\$60}{0.60} = \$100$$

5. Earned premiums are the premiums actually earned by a company during the accounting period, rather than the premiums written during the same period.

6. The credibility factor (C) refers to the statistical reliability of the data. It ranges from a value of 0 to 1 and increases as the number of claims increases. If the actuary believes that the data are highly reliable and can accurately predict future losses, a credibility factor of 1 can be used. However, if the data are not completely reliable as a predictor of future losses, a credibility factor of less than 1 is used.

7. This section is based on Kenneth Black, Jr., and Harold D. Skipper, Jr., *Life Insurance,* 12th ed.

(Englewood Cliffs, N.J.: Prentice Hall, 1994), pp. 530–43 and pp. 552–54; and Dan M. McGill, *Life Insurance* (Homewood, Ill.: Richard D. Irwin, 1967), pp. 182–275. The author drew heavily on these sources in preparing this section.

8. For example, if an immediate life annuity is purchased with annual payments, the first payment would be due one year from the purchase date.

9. Black and Skipper, p. 553.

10. McGill, pp. 247–48.

11. For the various methods of calculating the unearned premium reserve, see Terrie E. Troxel and Cormick L. Breslin, *Property-Liability Insurance Accounting and Finance,* 2nd ed. (Malvern, Pa.: American Institute for Property and Liability Underwriters, 1983), pp. 133–37.

12. The loss ratio is the ratio of losses and loss-adjustment expenses to *earned premiums.* The expense ratio is the ratio of expenses incurred to *written premiums.*

13. Expenses incurred of $3.5 million are based on written premiums. Remember that the expense ratio is the ratio of expenses incurred to written premiums ($3,500,000/$10,000,000 = 35%).

14. Troxel and Breslin, pp. 108–10.

15. Life insurance reserves are discussed in greater detail in Black and Skipper, chapter 20, and McGill, pp. 218–45.

16. McGill, p. 219.

# Chapter 27

# GOVERNMENT REGULATION OF INSURANCE

*« There are serious shortcomings in state laws and regulatory activities with respect to protecting the interests of insurance consumers. »*

*General Accounting Office*

## Student Learning Objectives

After studying this chapter, you should be able to:

■ Explain the major reasons insurers are regulated.

■ Identify key legal cases and legislation that have had an important impact on insurance regulation.

■ Explain the various methods for regulating insurers.

■ Identify the areas that are regulated.

■ Explain the objectives of rate regulation and the different types of rating laws.

■ Explain the major arguments for and against state regulation of insurance.

The insurance industry is regulated by the states, and certain federal laws apply to private insurers. This chapter discusses the fundamentals of insurance regulation. Topics discussed include the reasons insurers are regulated, the various methods for regulating insurers, and the specific areas that are regulated. The chapter concludes with a discussion of current controversial issues in insurance regulation.

## REASONS FOR INSURANCE REGULATION

Insurers are regulated by the states for several reasons, including the following:

- Maintain insurer solvency
- Compensate for inadequate consumer knowledge
- Ensure reasonable rates
- Make insurance available

### Maintain Insurer Solvency

Insurance regulation is necessary to maintain the solvency of insurers. This goal is called **solidity,** by which regulation aims at preserving or enhancing the financial strength of insurers. Solvency is important for two reasons. First, premiums are paid in advance, but the period of protection extends into the future.

If an insurer goes bankrupt and a future claim is not paid, the insurance protection paid for in advance is worthless. Therefore, to ensure that claims will be paid during the policy period, the financial strength of insurers must be carefully monitored.

A second reason for stressing solvency is that individuals can be exposed to great financial insecurity if insurers fail and claims are not paid. For example, if the insured's home is totally destroyed by a tornado and the loss is not paid, he or she may be financially ruined. Thus, because of the possibility of great financial hardship to insureds, beneficiaries, and third-party claimants, regulation must stress insurer solvency.

Insurer solvency is an important issue that is discussed in greater detail later in the chapter.

## Compensate for Inadequate Consumer Knowledge

Regulation is also necessary because of inadequate consumer knowledge. Insurance contracts are technical, legal documents that contain complex clauses and provisions. Without regulation, an unscrupulous insurer could draft a contract so restrictive and legalistic that it would be worthless.

Also, most consumers do not have sufficient information for comparing and determining the monetary value of different insurance contracts. It is difficult to compare dissimilar policies with different premiums because the necessary price and policy information is not readily available. For example, individual health insurance policies vary widely by cost, coverages, and benefits. The average consumer would find it difficult to evaluate a particular policy based on the premium alone.

Without good information, consumers cannot select the best insurance product. This can reduce the impact that consumers have on insurance markets, and can also reduce the competitive incentive of insurers to improve product quality and lower price. Thus, regulation is needed to produce the same market effect that results from knowledgeable consumers who are purchasing products in highly competitive markets.

Finally, some agents are unethical, and state licensing requirements are minimal. Thus, regulation is needed to protect consumers against unscrupulous agents.

## Ensure Reasonable Rates

Regulation is also necessary to ensure reasonable rates. The rates should not be so high that consumers are exploited by being charged more than the value of the coverage. Nor should the rates be so low that the solvency of insurers is threatened. Whether a rate is too high or too low is often difficult for the regulators to determine. Rate regulation is an extremely complex issue. The various rating philosophies and different types of rating laws are discussed later in the chapter.

## Make Insurance Available

Another regulatory goal is to make insurance available to all persons who need it. Insurers are often unwilling to insure all applicants for a given type of insurance because of underwriting losses, inadequate rates, adverse selection, and a host of additional factors. However, the public interest may require regulators to take actions that expand private insurance markets to make insurance more readily available. If private insurers are unable or unwilling to supply the needed coverages, then government insurance programs may be necessary.

## HISTORICAL DEVELOPMENT OF INSURANCE REGULATION

In this section, the development of insurance regulation by the states is briefly reviewed. You should pay careful attention to certain landmark legal decisions and legislative acts that have had a profound impact on insurance regulation.

### Early Regulatory Efforts

Insurance regulation first began when state legislatures granted charters to new insurers, which authorized their formation and operation. The new insurers were initially subject to few regulatory controls. The charters required only that the companies issue periodic reports and provide public information concerning their financial conditions.

The creation of state insurance commissions was the next step in insurance regulation. In 1851, New Hampshire became the first state to create a separate insurance commission to regulate insurers.

Other states followed. In 1859, New York created a separate administrative agency headed by a single superintendent who was given broad licensing and investigative powers. Thus, initial insurance regulation developed under the jurisdiction and supervision of the states.

### Paul v. Virginia

The case of **Paul v. Virginia** in 1868 was a landmark legal decision that established the right of the states to regulate insurance.[1] Samuel Paul was an agent in Virginia who represented several New York insurers. Paul was fined for selling fire insurance in Virginia without a license. He appealed the case on the grounds that Virginia's law was unconstitutional. He argued that since insurance was interstate commerce, only the federal government had the right to regulate insurance under the commerce clause of the U.S. Constitution. The Supreme Court disagreed. The Court ruled that issuance of an insurance policy was not interstate commerce. Therefore, the insurance industry was not subject to the commerce clause of the Constitution. *Thus, the legal significance of Paul v. Virginia was that insurance was not interstate commerce, and that the states rather than the federal government had the right to regulate the insurance industry.*

### South-Eastern Underwriters Association Case

The precedent set in *Paul v. Virginia,* which held that insurance is not interstate commerce, was overturned by the Supreme Court in 1944. The **South-Eastern Underwriters Association (SEUA)** was a cooperative rating bureau that was found guilty of price fixing and other violations of the Sherman Antitrust Act. *In the SEUA case, the Supreme Court ruled that insurance was interstate commerce when conducted across state lines and was subject to federal regulation.*[2] The Court's decision that insurance was interstate commerce and subject to federal antitrust laws caused considerable turmoil for the industry and state regulators. The decision raised serious doubts concerning the legality of private rating bureaus, and the power of the states to regulate and tax the insurance industry.

### McCarran-Ferguson Act

To resolve the confusion and doubt that existed after the SEUA decision, Congress passed the **McCarran-**

**Ferguson Act** (Public Law 15) in 1945. *The McCarran Act states that continued regulation and taxation of the insurance industry by the states are in the public interest. It also states that federal antitrust laws apply to insurance only to the extent that the insurance industry is not regulated by state law.* Therefore, as long as state regulation is in effect, federal antitrust laws will not apply to insurance. However, the exemption from antitrust laws is not absolute. The Sherman Act forbids any acts or agreements to boycott, coerce, or intimidate. In these areas, insurers are still subject to federal law.

At present, the states still have the primary responsibility for regulating insurance. However, Congress can repeal the McCarran Act, which would then give the federal government primary authority over the insurance industry. There have been strong pressures from some politicians and consumer groups to repeal the McCarran Act, but Congress to date has not done so. This important issue is explained later in the chapter.

## METHODS FOR REGULATING INSURERS

Three principal methods are used to regulate insurers: legislation, courts, and state insurance departments.

### Legislation

All states have insurance laws that regulate the operations of insurers. These laws regulate (1) formation of insurance companies, (2) licensing of agents and brokers, (3) financial requirements for maintaining solvency, (4) insurance rates, (5) sales and claim practices, (6) taxation, and (7) rehabilitation or liquidation of insurers. Also, laws have been passed to protect the rights of consumers, such as laws restricting the right of insurers to cancel and laws making insurance more widely available.

Insurers are also subject to regulation by certain federal agencies and laws. Only a few are mentioned here. The Federal Trade Commission has authority to regulate mail-order insurers in those states where they are not licensed to do business. The Securities and Exchange Commission has regulations concerning the sale of variable annuities and has jurisdiction over the sale of insurance company securities to the public. The Employee Retirement Income Security Act of 1974 (ERISA) applies to the private pension plans of insurers.

## Courts

State and federal courts periodically hand down decisions concerning the constitutionality of state insurance laws, the interpretation of policy clauses and provisions, and the legality of administrative actions by state insurance departments. As such, the various court decisions can affect the market conduct and operations of insurers in an important way.

## State Insurance Departments

Each state and the District of Columbia have a separate insurance department or bureau. An insurance commissioner, who is elected or appointed by the governor, has the responsibility for administering state insurance laws. Through administrative rulings, the state insurance commissioner wields considerable power over insurers doing business in the state. The insurance commissioner has the power to hold hearings, issue cease-and-desist orders, and revoke or suspend an insurer's license to do business.

The state insurance commissioners belong to an important association known as the **National Association of Insurance Commissioners (NAIC).** The NAIC, founded in 1871, meets periodically to discuss industry problems that might require legislation or regulation. The NAIC has drafted model laws in various areas and has recommended adoption of these proposals by state legislatures. Although the NAIC has no legal authority to force the states to adopt the recommendations, most states have accepted all or part of them.

## WHAT AREAS ARE REGULATED?

Insurers are subject to numerous laws and regulations. The principal areas regulated include the following:

- Formation and licensing of insurers
- Financial regulation
- Rate regulation
- Policy forms
- Sales practices and consumer protection

## Formation and Licensing of Insurers

All states have requirements for the formation and licensing of insurers. A new insurer is typically formed by incorporation. The insurer receives a charter or certificate of incorporation from the state, which authorizes its formation and legal existence.

After being formed, insurers must be licensed before they can do business. The licensing requirements for insurers are more stringent than those imposed on other new firms. If the insurer is a capital stock insurer, it must meet certain minimum capital and surplus requirements, which vary by state and by line of insurance. A new mutual insurer must meet a minimum surplus requirement (rather than capital and surplus since there are no stockholders), and other requirements.

A license can be issued to a domestic, foreign, or alien insurer. A **domestic insurer** is an insurer domiciled in the state; it must be licensed in the state as well as in other states where it does business. A **foreign insurer** is an out-of-state insurer that is chartered by another state; it must be licensed to do business in the state. An **alien insurer** is an insurer chartered by a foreign country. It must also meet certain licensing requirements.

## Financial Regulation

In addition to minimum capital and surplus requirements, insurers are subject to other financial regulations. These financial regulations are designed to maintain solvency.

**Admitted Assets**   An insurer must have sufficient assets to offset its liabilities. Only admitted assets can be shown on the insurer's balance sheet. **Admitted assets** *are assets that an insurer can show on its statutory balance sheet in determining its financial condition.* All other assets are nonadmitted.

Most assets are classified as admitted assets. These include cash, bonds, common and preferred stocks, mortgages, real estate, and other legal investments. Nonadmitted assets include premiums overdue 90 or more days, office furniture and supplies, and certain investments or amounts that exceed statutory limits for certain types of securities. Nonadmitted assets are excluded because their liquidity is uncertain. As a result, policyholders' surplus is decreased by an increase in nonadmitted assets.

**Reserves**   **Reserves** *are liability items on an insurer's balance sheet and reflect obligations that must be met in the future.* The states have regulations for the calculation of reserves. The various methods for calculating reserves were discussed in Chapter 26.

**Surplus**   The surplus position is also carefully monitored. **Policyowners' surplus** is *the difference between an insurer's assets and its liabilities.* The surplus of a capital stock insurer consists of two items: (1) a capital stock account that represents the value of the shares issued to the stockholders, and (2) paid-in surplus that represents amounts paid in by stockholders in excess of the par value of the stock. Both items together represent policyowners' surplus. Since a mutual insurer has no stockholders, policyowners' surplus is simply the difference between assets and liabilities.

In property and liability insurance, policyowners' surplus is important for several reasons. First, the amount of new business an insurer can write is limited by the amount of policyowners' surplus. One conservative rule is the *Kenney rule,* by which a property insurer can safely write $2 of new net premiums for each $1 of policyowners' surplus.[3] Second, policyowners' surplus is necessary to offset any substantial underwriting or investment losses. Finally, policyowners' surplus is required to offset any deficiency in loss reserves that may occur over time.

In life insurance, policyowners' surplus is less important because of substantial safety margins in the calculation of premiums and dividends, conservative interest assumptions used in calculating legal reserves, conservative valuation of investments, greater stability in operations over time, and less likelihood of a catastrophic loss.

**Risk-based Capital**   To reduce the risk of insolvency, life and health insurers must meet certain risk-based capital standards based on a model law developed by the NAIC. The NAIC has drafted a similar model law for property and liability insurers. Only the standards for life and health insurers are discussed here.

**Risk-based capital** *means that insurers must have a certain amount of capital, depending on the riskiness of their investments and insurance operations. Insurers are graded by regulators based on how much capital they have relative to their risk-based capital*

*requirements.* For example, insurers that invest in less-than-investment grade corporate bonds ("junk bonds") must set aside more capital than if Treasury bonds were purchased.

The risk-based capital requirements are based on a formula that considers four types of risk—asset default risk, insurance risk, interest rate risk, and general business risk. Asset default risk is the risk of default of specific assets and a market decline in the insurer's investment portfolio. Insurance risk is the risk that premiums and reserves may be inadequate for paying benefits. Interest rate risk reflects possible losses due to changing interest rates. Examples include a decline in the market value of assets supporting contractual obligations and liquidity problems arising from disintermediation because of changing interest rates. Finally, business risk refers to other risks that insurers face, such as guaranty fund assessments and insolvency because of bad management.

The insurer's "total adjusted capital" is then compared with the amount of risk-based capital. (Total adjusted capital essentially is statutory capital and surplus with certain adjustments.) A ratio of 100 percent or above means that insurers have met or exceeded their minimum risk-based capital requirements. Insurers with ratios of at least 75 percent but under 100 percent would have to file a plan with regulators to increase their risk-based capital. Insurers with ratios of at least 50 percent but less than 75 percent would be ordered to take specific action. If the ratio falls below 50 percent, regulators have the authority to take control of the insurer and are required to do so if the ratio falls to 35 percent.

Exhibit 27.1 shows the distribution of risk-based capital ratios for 130 major life insurers that account for 85 percent of the life insurance industry assets. The vast majority of insurers have met the minimum risk-based capital requirements by a substantial margin.

The risk-based capital standards give regulators an early warning with respect to insurers with financial problems. The standards also discourage insurers from investing too heavily in risky investments. For example, a heavy concentration in junk bonds led to the collapse and seizure of the Executive Life Insurance Co. in April 1991 after the junk bond market collapsed.

EXHIBIT 27.1

## Distribution of Risk-Based Capital (RBC) Ratios for 130 Major U.S. Life Insurers

| RBC ratio | Number of Companies | | | | | |
|---|---|---|---|---|---|---|
| | 1991 | 1992 | 1993 | 1994 | 1995 | 1996 |
| >200% | 45 | 54 | 99 | 108 | 116 | 122 |
| 175%–200% | 19 | 27 | 16 | 9 | 8 | 3 |
| 150%–175% | 24 | 21 | 10 | 8 | 3 | 3 |
| 125%–150% | 22 | 17 | 4 | 3 | 2 | 1 |
| 100%–125% | 12 | 6 | 0 | 1 | 0 | 1 |
| <100% | 8 | 5 | 1 | 1 | 1 | 0 |
| | 130 | 130 | 130 | 130 | 130 | 130 |
| **Composite RBC Ratio for 130 U.S. Life Insurers**\*\* | 162.3% | 172.1% | 215.9% | 224.3% | 242.9% | 257.0% |

\*\*1991 and 1992 Composite RBC ratios are estimated.

SOURCE: Frederick S. Townsend, "Industry Passes 250 Percent of Required Capital," *National Underwriter,* Life & Health/Financial Service Edition, April 2, 1997, p. 1.

**Investments**    Insurance company investments are regulated with respect to types, quality, and percentage of total assets or surplus that can be invested in different investments. The basic purpose of these regulations is to prevent insurers from making unsound investments that could threaten the company's solvency and harm the policyowners.

Life insurers typically invest in common and preferred stocks, bonds, mortgages, real estate, and policy loans. The laws generally place maximum limits on each type of investment based on a percentage of assets or surplus. For example, a state may specify that common stock investments are limited to a maximum of 10 percent of total assets.

Property and liability insurers are subject to fewer restrictions in their investments than life insurers. The actual restrictions vary among the states, and only two general comments are made here.[4] First, with respect to minimum capital requirements, the funds must usually be invested in federal, state, or municipal bonds, or bonds and notes secured by mortgages and trust deeds on improved real estate. In some states, certain public utility or high-quality corporate bonds can be used to meet this requirement. In addition, assets equal to a specified percentage of the unearned premium and loss reserves must also be invested in restricted securities with the same high quality.

Second, any excess funds over the minimum capital requirements and reserve liabilities can be invested in the common stock of solvent corporations or in real estate the company can legally hold. There are restrictions, however, on the proportion of assets that can be invested in any single corporation.

**Limitations on Expenses**    In life insurance, a small number of states, including New York, place limitations on the amounts that can be spent in acquiring new business and maintaining old business. The laws are extremely complex, but in general, they limit the amounts that can be spent on acquisition expenses, commissions, bonuses, service fees, and other expenses. New York's law is far-reaching in this regard, since insurers doing business in New York must abide by the expense limitations on contracts written in other states.

The purpose of expense limitation laws is to prevent wasteful price competition that would result in life insurers competing with each other by offering higher commissions to agents. Thus, the laws are aimed at holding down the cost of life insurance to consumers.

**Dividend Policy** In life insurance, the annual gain from operations can be distributed in the form of dividends to policyowners, or it can be added to the insurer's surplus for present and future needs. Many states limit the amount of surplus a participating life insurer can accumulate to a maximum of 10 percent of policy reserves. The purpose of this limitation is to prevent life insurers from accumulating a substantial surplus at the expense of dividends to policyowners.

**Reports and Examinations** Annual reports and examinations are used to maintain insurer solvency. Each insurer must file an annual report with the state insurance department in states where it does business. The annual report provides detailed financial information to regulatory officials with respect to assets, liabilities, reserves, investments, claim payments, risk-based capital, and other information.

Insurance companies are also periodically examined by the states. Depending on the state, domestic insurers are examined every three to five years by the state insurance department. Licensed out-of-state insurers are also periodically examined.

**Liquidation of Insurers** If an insurer is technically insolvent, the state insurance department assumes control of the company. With proper management, the insurer may be successfully rehabilitated. If the insurer cannot be rehabilitated, it is liquidated according to the state's insurance code.

Most states have adopted the Insurers Supervision, Rehabilitation, and Liquidation Model Act drafted by the NAIC in 1977 or similar types of legislation. The Act is designed to achieve uniformity among the states in the liquidation of assets and payment of claims of a defunct insurer and provides for a comprehensive system for rehabilitation and liquidation.

If an insurer becomes insolvent, some claims may still be unpaid. All states have **insurance guaranty funds** that provide for the payment of unpaid claims of insolvent property and liability insurers. In life insurance, all states have enacted guaranty laws and guarantee associations to pay the claims of policyowners of insolvent life and health insurers.

The *assessment method* is the major method used to raise the necessary funds to pay unpaid claims. Insurers are generally assessed after an insolvency occurs. New York is an exception because it maintains a permanent preassessment solvency fund, which assesses property and liability insurers prior to any insolvency. Insurers can recoup part or all of the assessments paid by special state premium tax credits, refunds from the state guaranty funds, and higher insurance premiums. The result is that taxpayers and the general public indirectly pay the claims of insolvent insurers.

The guaranty funds limit the amount that policyowners can collect if an insurer goes broke. For example, in life insurance the guaranty funds typically place a limit of $100,000 on cash values and $300,000 on the combined benefits from all policies. Some state funds also do not protect out-of-state residents when an insurer domiciled in the state goes broke.

## Rate Regulation

All states except Illinois have rating laws that require property and liability insurance rates to meet certain statutory standards. As noted in Chapter 26, rates must be adequate, reasonable (not excessive), and not unfairly discriminatory. However, there are wide variations among states with respect to implementation of these objectives.

Rate regulation is far from uniform. Some states have more than one rating law, depending on the type of insurance. The principal types of rating laws are the following:

- Prior-approval laws
- File-and-use laws
- Open-competition laws
- Flex-rating laws

**Prior-Approval Laws** The majority of states have some type of prior approval law for regulating rates. Under a **prior-approval law,** rates must be filed and approved by the state insurance department before they can be used. In most states, if the rates are not disapproved within a certain period, such as 30 or 60 days., they are deemed to be approved.

Insurance companies have criticized prior approval laws on several grounds. There is often considerable delay in obtaining a needed rate increase, since state insurance departments are often understaffed. The rate increase that is granted may be inadequate, and needed rate increases can be denied for political purposes. In addition, the statistical data required by the state insurance department to support a rate increase may not be readily available.

**File-and-Use Laws**   This type of law is more liberal than the laws discussed earlier. Under a **file-and-use law,** insurers are required only to file the rates with the state insurance department, and the rates can be used immediately. Regulatory authorities have the authority to disapprove the rates later if they violate state law. This type of rating law overcomes the problem of delay that exists under a prior-approval law.

A variation of file and use is a *use-and-file* law. Under this law, insurers can put into effect rate changes, but the rates must be filed with the regulatory authorities within a certain period after first being used.

**Open-Competition Laws**   **Open-competition laws** (also called no-filing laws) are the most liberal of all rating laws. Under an open-competition law, insurers are not required to file their rates with the state insurance department. However, insurers may be required to furnish rate schedules and supporting data to state officials. The fundamental assumption underlying an open-competition law is that market forces will determine the price and availability of insurance rather than the discretionary acts of regulatory officials (see Insight 27.1).

**Flex-Rating Laws**   Some states have enacted an innovative rating law known as flex rating. Under a **flex-rating law,** prior approval of rates is required only if the rate increase or decrease exceeds a specific predetermined range. Margins of 5 or 10 percent are typically permitted without prior approval. The purpose of a flex-rating law is to allow insurers to make rate changes more rapidly in response to changing market conditions.

**Life Insurance Rate Regulation**   Life insurance rates are not directly regulated by the states.[5] Rate adequacy in life insurance is indirectly achieved by regulations that require legal reserves to be at least a minimum size. Minimum legal reserve requirements affect the rates that must be charged to pay death claims and expenses.

## Policy Forms

The regulation of new policy forms is another important area of insurance regulation. Because insurance contracts are technical and complex, the state insurance commissioner has the authority to approve or disapprove new policy forms before the contracts are sold to the public. The purpose is to protect the public from misleading, deceptive, and unfair provisions.

## Sales Practices and Consumer Protection

The sales practices of insurers are regulated by laws concerning the licensing of agents and brokers, and by laws prohibiting twisting, rebating, and unfair trade practices.

**Licensing of Agents and Brokers**   All states require agents and brokers to be licensed. Depending on the type of insurance sold, applicants must pass one or more written examinations. The purpose is to ensure that agents have knowledge of the state insurance laws and the contracts they intend to sell. If the agent is incompetent or dishonest, the state insurance commissioner has the authority to suspend or revoke the agent's license.

All states have legislation requiring the continuing education of agents. The continuing education requirements are designed to upgrade an agent's knowledge and skills.

**Twisting**   All states forbid twisting. **Twisting** *is the inducement of a policyowner to drop an existing policy in another company due to misrepresentation or incomplete information.* Twisting laws apply largely to life insurance policies; the objective here is to prevent policyowners from being financially harmed by replacing one life insurance policy with another.

All states have replacement regulations so that policyowners can make an informed decision concerning the replacement of an existing life insurance policy. These laws are based on the premise that replacement of an existing life insurance policy generally is not in the policyowner's best interest. For example, a new front-end load for commissions and expenses must be paid; a new incontestable clause and suicide clause must be satisfied; and higher premiums based on the policyowner's higher attained age may have to be paid. *However, in some cases, switching policies can be financially justified.* One earlier study of life insurance policy replacements found

## INSIGHT 27.1

## Is Strict Rate Regulation Desirable for Consumers?

Are prior-approval or open-competition rating laws better for consumers? More than 100 research studies have been published concerning the financial and economic effects of insurance regulation. A large number of studies compared states with regulated rates to states with unregulated rates. Statewide loss ratios (defined as the ratio of incurred losses to earned premiums for direct business) were commonly used to compare the states. In general, the higher the loss ratio, the lower the unit price of insurance (ratio of premiums to losses).

Three broad conclusions emerge from an analysis of the empirical studies concerning the impact of rate regulation on automobile insurance rates.

*A number of studies showed that states with regulated auto insurance rates had higher loss ratios (lower unit prices) than did states with competitive pricing.* Thus, strict rate regulation under prior-approval laws tends to increase loss ratios and lower unit prices. State regulatory officials may deliberately hold down rate increases to make auto insurance more affordable.

*However, strict rate regulation that keeps auto insurance rates down and below free-market levels may lead to an increase in the residual market.* The residual market refers to special plans that make auto insurance available to drivers who cannot obtain coverage in the standard markets, such as an automobile insurance

plan (assigned-risk plan) where rates are significantly higher. There is considerable evidence that in states with strict rate regulation, the proportion of drivers placed in residual market plans is much higher than in states with competitive rating laws. Since the rates are inadequate in the voluntary standard market, a higher proportion of drivers may be placed in a residual market plan where the rates are substantially higher. In contrast, under open-competition laws, most drivers can be insured in the voluntary standard market by paying market prices. In addition, in states with strict rate regulation, insurers often respond to the lower rates by reducing the quality of the services provided or by reducing the available supply of auto insurance written, thus rationing the insurance to the best drivers.

*Finally, in highly regulated states in which rates are inadequate, insurers will withdraw from the market entirely.* For example, because of inadequate rates, some insurers withdrew from the personal-lines market in South Carolina in 1990. In other states as well, several major insurers have reduced their auto insurance operations or have withdrawn from the market entirely.

SOURCE: Adapted from Robert J. Gibbons, George E. Rejda, and Michael W. Elliott, *Insurance Perspectives* (Malvern, Pa.: American Institute for Chartered Property Casualty Underwriters, 1992), pp. 121–23. Used by permission.

---

that the majority of the replacements were acceptable; that is, there were cost savings to policyowners. The authors concluded that their data provided no support for the commonly held viewpoint of state insurance commissioners that replacements are generally undesirable.[6] However, more recently, deceptive sales practices by agents in certain insurers have resulted in the replacement of life insurance policies that were financially harmful to the policyowners. Deceptive sales practices will be discussed later in the chapter.

**Rebating**  Most state insurance codes also forbid rebating. **Rebating** *is giving to an individual a premium reduction or some other financial advantage not*

*stated in the policy as an inducement to purchase the policy.* One obvious example is a partial refund of the agent's commission to the insured. The basic purpose of antirebate laws is to ensure fair and equitable treatment of all policyowners by preventing one insured from obtaining an unfair price advantage over another.

The desirability of antirebating laws is discussed later in greater detail.

**Unfair Trade Practices**  Insurance laws prohibit a wide variety of *unfair trade practices,* including misrepresentation, twisting, rebating, deceptive or false advertising, inequitable claim settlement, and unfair discrimination. The state insurance commissioner has the legal authority to stop insurers from engaging in unfair trade practices and deceptive advertising. Insurers can be fined, an injunction can be obtained, or, in serious cases, the insurer's license can be suspended or revoked.

**Complaint Division** State insurance departments typically have a complaint division or department for handling consumer complaints. The department or individual will investigate the complaint and try to obtain a response from the offending insurer or agency. Most consumer complaints involve claims. An insurer may refuse to pay a claim, or may dispute the amount payable. Although state insurance departments respond to individual complaints, the departments generally lack direct authority to order insurers to pay disputed claims where factual questions are an issue. *However, you should phone or write your state insurance department if you feel you are being treated unfairly by your insurer or agent.* This is especially true for auto insurance disputes where certain insurers have significantly higher complaint ratios than others (see Insight 27.2).

**Readable Policies** Greater protection of the consumer is also evidenced by the trend toward more *readable policies.* In order to make insurance contracts more understandable, the states have approved policies in which the language is less technical and is therefore simpler and easier to understand. The development of more readable policies will undoubtedly benefit most consumers.

**Shopper's Guides** A few states publish *shoppers' guides* for insurance consumers. The guides typically show the premiums charged by insurers for auto insurance and homeowners insurance, so that consumers can make meaningful cost comparisons. As a result, consumers may be able to purchase auto and homeowners insurance from low-cost insurers.

## Taxation of Insurers

Insurers pay numerous local, state, and federal taxes. Two important taxes are the federal income tax and state premium tax. Insurers pay federal income taxes based on complex formulas and rules established by federal legislation and the Internal Revenue Service. The states also levy a premium tax on gross premiums received from policyowners, such as 2 percent of the premium paid.

The primary purpose of the premium tax is to raise revenues for the states, not to provide funds for insurance regulation. However, many state insurance departments are underfunded and receive only a small fraction of the premium taxes collected. Critics of state regulation argue that if state regulation is to become more effective, more money must be spent on insurance regulation.

Most states also have retaliatory tax laws that affect premium taxes and other taxes. For example, assume that the premium tax is 2 percent in Nebraska and 3 percent in Iowa. If insurers domiciled in Nebraska are required to pay a 3 percent premium tax on business written in Iowa, then domestic insurers in Iowa doing business in Nebraska must also pay 3 percent even though Nebraska's rate is 2 percent. The purpose of a retaliatory tax law is to protect domestic insurers in the state from excessive taxation by other states where they do business.

## STATE VERSUS FEDERAL REGULATION

Critics of state regulation argue that the McCarran-Ferguson Act should be repealed and replaced by federal regulation. Certain advantages are claimed for federal regulation.

### Advantages of Federal Regulation

The following arguments are offered in support of federal regulation of insurance:

- *Uniformity of laws.* Federal regulation can provide greater uniformity of laws. Under state regulation, insurers doing business in more than one state must observe different state laws. Under federal regulation, the laws would be uniform.
- *Greater efficiency.* It is argued that federal regulation would be more efficient. Insurers doing business nationally would deal with only one federal agency rather than with numerous insurance departments. Also, the federal agency would be less likely to yield to industry pressures, especially those reflecting the views of local insurers. Federal regulation would also be less expensive to administer.

### INSIGHT 27.2

## Automobile Insurance Complaints in New York State

The New York State Insurance Department makes available an annual ranking of automobile insurers doing business in New York. The 1995 rankings shown here are based on the complaint ratios of 57 licensed automobile insurance companies or groups of companies.

The *complaint ratio* is the number of auto insurance complaints charged against an insurer and closed by the Consumer Services Bureau in 1995, divided by that insurer's 1994–95 average automobile premium volume in New York State. *Thus, the ratio represents the number of closed complaints per million dollars of premium writings for each insurer. The insurer with the lowest ratio is ranked first in the report; the insurer with the highest ratio is ranked last. The lower the ratio, the better the insurer's performance.*

All companies or groups of companies with at least $5 million in average annual automobile insurance premium writings for 1994–95 are included in the rankings. Companies or groups with less than $5 million in average premiums are not included unless they have ten or more complaints charged against them. The 25 best companies or groups with the lowest complaint ratios in 1995 are as follows:

| Company or group | 1995 complaint ratio[a] |
|---|---|
| State-Wide | 0.00 |
| Netherlands | 0.00 |
| Tri-State Consumer | 0.00 |
| CIGNA | 0.00 |
| Amica Mutual | 0.03 |
| Electric | 0.04 |
| Allianz | 0.05 |
| St. Paul | 0.06 |
| America | 0.06 |
| Chubb & Son | 0.06 |
| Executive | 0.07 |
| USAA | 0.07 |
| TIG | 0.07 |
| Government Employees | 0.08 |
| Nationwide | 0.08 |
| Liberty Mutual | 0.08 |
| Travelers | 0.09 |
| New York Central Mutual Fire | 0.10 |
| AMEX Assurance | 0.11 |
| National Grange Mutual | 0.11 |
| Integon | 0.12 |
| Lumbermans Mutual Casualty | 0.12 |
| CU Life | 0.13 |
| Motors | 0.13 |
| Preferred Mutual | 0.14 |

The ten worst companies or groups with the highest complaint ratios in 1995 are as follows:

| Company or group | 1995 complaint ratio[a] |
|---|---|
| Country-Wide | 1.29 |
| Continental[b] | 0.56 |
| Eagle | 0.56 |
| Winterthur Holdings | 0.54 |
| American International | 0.49 |
| American Financial | 0.49 |
| Interboro Mutual Indemnity | 0.48 |
| Eveready | 0.45 |
| Leucadia | 0.40 |
| U.S.F. & G. | 0.38 |

[a]The complaint ratio is the number of closed complaints per million dollars of automobile insurance premiums written directly in New York State.

[b]Continental was acquired by the CNA Financial Corp. in May 1995.

Source: New York State Insurance Department, *1995 Annual Ranking of Automobile Insurance Complaints.* Reprinted by permission.

• *More competent regulators.* Federal regulation would attract higher-quality personnel who would do a superior job of regulating the insurance industry. The higher salaries and prestige would attract more highly talented and skilled individuals.

## Advantages of State Regulation

Supporters of state regulation also offer convincing arguments for continued regulation of insurance by the states. The major advantages claimed for state regulation are as follows:

• *Greater responsiveness to local needs.* Local needs vary widely and state regulators can respond more quickly to local needs. In contrast, under federal regulation "red tape" and government bureaucracy would result in considerable delay in solving problems at the local level.

• *Uniformity of laws by NAIC.* Uniformity of laws can be achieved by the model laws and proposals of the NAIC. Thus, there is reasonable uniformity of state laws in important areas at the present time.

• *Greater opportunity for innovation.* State regulation provides greater opportunities for innovation in regulation. An individual state can experiment, and if the innovation fails, only that state is affected. In contrast, poor federal legislation would affect all states.

• *Unknown consequences of federal regulation.* State regulation is already in existence, and its strengths and weaknesses are well known. In contrast, the consequences of federal regulation on consumers and the insurance industry are unknown.

• *Decentralization of political power.* State regulation results in a decentralization of political power. Federal regulation would result in further encroachment of the federal government on the economy and a corresponding dilution of states' rights.

## Shortcomings of State Regulation

Congressional committees and the General Accounting Office (GAO) have assessed the effectiveness of state regulation of insurance and have found serious shortcomings, including the following:[7]

• *Inadequate regulation.* Critics argue that state regulation is inadequate, especially with respect to solvency regulation. Several property and liability insurers have failed because of inadequate regulation. Some property and liability insurers have been licensed to do business when they were under-capitalized, and state insurance departments have not carefully checked the background or monitored the activities of persons running the companies. Instead of demanding the highest character and financial references, many state insurance departments have been reluctant to deny or withdraw a license unless the person is guilty of criminal fraud.

• *Inadequate protection of consumers.* Critics argue that state insurance departments do not have systematic procedures for determining whether consumers are being treated properly with respect to claim payments, rate setting, and protection from unfair discrimination.

• *Improvements needed in handling complaints.* Although many states prepare complaint ratios (ratio of complaints to premiums) for each company, few states publicize the ratios or make them widely available to consumers.

• *Inadequate market conduct examinations.* Market conduct examinations refer to insurance department examinations of consumer matters such as claims handling, underwriting, advertising, and other trade practices. Serious deficiencies have been found in many market conduct examination reports. The most serious defect is the lack of explicit standards in evaluating the market conduct of insurers.

• *Insurance availability.* Many states have not conducted studies to determine if property and liability insurance availability is a serious problem in their states.

• *Regulators overly responsive to insurance industry.* State insurance departments are overly responsive to the insurance company at the expense of consumers. Insurance regulation is not characterized by an "arm's-length" relationship between regulators and the regulated. Many state insurance commissioners were previously employed in the insurance industry, and many return to the industry after leaving office.

Despite these shortcomings, however, the GAO points out some positive aspects of state regulation, which support the case for continued regulation of the insurance industry by the states. First, considerable uniformity in regulation is provided by the NAIC. Second, none of the insurance executives interviewed in the GAO study believes that compliance with different state laws imposes significant costs on insurers. Third, there is evidence that the threat of federal regulation has forced some state regulators to do a better job. Finally, there is considerable evidence that state insurance departments effectively respond to unique insurance needs at the local level, especially in the areas of medical malpractice and commercial liability insurance.

## CURRENT ISSUES IN INSURANCE REGULATION

Several timely issues are important in insurance regulation at the present time. They include the following:

- Banks in insurance
- Deceptive sales practices of insurers
- Insolvency of insurers
- Repeal of McCarran-Ferguson Act
- Unisex rating
- Rebating

### Banks in Insurance

A hotly debated issue is the extent to which commercial banks should be allowed to sell insurance. Many banks now sell annuities, life and health insurance, credit life insurance, and homeowners and auto insurance through subsidiary companies. In particular, the growth in market share of individual annuity premiums by commercial banks has been spectacular. Commercial banks accounted for about 37 percent of individual annuity premiums in the United States in 1994, up from about 18 percent in 1990.[8]

Because of deregulation, new computer technology, and the rapid growth of financial services, the distinction between commercial banks and other financial institutions is rapidly being blurred. As a result, banking representatives believe that remaining statutory and regulatory barriers that prevent banks from further entry into the insurance business should be abolished. The banking industry presents the following arguments to support its position:

1. *Consumers would have greater convenience.* Consumers should be given a choice of where they buy their insurance. The convenience of one-stop shopping for financial services should be made available through banks.

2. *Banks would be safer.* Banks would be safer if they were allowed to sell insurance and other financial services. It is argued that banks have been losing customers to competitors and that making loans is inherently risky. Banks would be financially stronger if they could offer new financial services that would generate additional income to supplement the earnings from loans.

3. *Companies in other industries own insurers.* Banks argue that companies in other industries have entered the insurance industry, including oil companies, department stores, baby-food companies, and railroads. Thus, commercial banks should be given the same right.

4. *Insurers can purchase banks.* Bankers argue that insurers can now acquire banks. Therefore, banks should have the right to acquire insurance companies.

The insurance industry, however, strongly opposes the further expansion of banks into the insurance business. The industry presents several arguments to support its position:

1. *Higher concentration of economic power.* The banking industry is now highly concentrated, since a relatively small proportion of large banks account for the bulk of the business. Critics argue that allowing banks to write or sell insurance will increase their economic power, and concentration in banking will be further increased. Big banks would also be big in insurance.

2. *Threat to survival of independent agents.* Independent agents argue that their financial survival is threatened if banks are allowed greater inroads into the insurance industry. Independent agents would lose their present customers to banks. The fear of being financially hurt is especially strong among independent agents who reside in small, rural areas. Because of unfair competition, agents fear the loss of their customers to local commercial banks.

3. *Coercion of debtors.* Insurers argue that debtors could be coerced into buying insurance from a

commercial bank as a tie-in sale. Although such tie-in sales are illegal, opponents argue that bank customers could be induced to buy credit life and health insurance, mortgage insurance, home-owners insurance, and auto insurance when they borrow from the bank. Since local banks control the market for bank loans, they would also control the local markets for insurance.

Who is winning the battle? So far, the banking industry appears to be winning. Favorable legislation and court decisions have firmly entrenched the presence of banks in the insurance business. The National Bank Act of 1916 and Bank Holding Act of 1956 allowed national banks to sell insurance in towns with population of 5000 or less. In 1983, South Dakota passed legislation that allowed state-chartered banks, including banks owned by out-of-state holding companies, to sell all lines of insurance nationally. In 1990, Delaware enacted legislation that allowed state-chartered banks to both sell and underwrite insurance. Responding to pressure from the insurance industry, Congress subsequently enacted legislation that would prohibit bank-holding companies from using state-chartered subsidiaries to underwrite insurance. However, sales were not touched.[9]

In 1996, in the *Barnett Bank* case, the Supreme Court ruled that the states cannot interfere with a federal law that allows nationally-chartered banks to sell insurance through small-town branches; this ruling cleared the way for banks to sell insurance policies nationally through branch banks in towns of 5000 or less. Finally, in late 1996, on a case-by-case basis, the Office of the Comptroller of the Currency (OCC) ruled that national banks could engage in insurance underwriting, securities underwriting, and other financial services by creating separate subsidiaries and by limiting investments to no more than 10 percent of capital. This latter ruling is a direct challenge to state regulation.

Based on the preceding discussion, banks in insurance are here to stay. The key regulatory issues that are unresolved at the time of this writing is how insurance and banking will be defined for regulatory purposes and which group of regulators will regulate the insurance activities of banks.

## Deceptive Sales Practices of Insurers

Regulating the market conduct of insurers remains an important issue. Since the last edition of this text, the life insurance industry has been rocked by a number of scandals involving deceptive sales practices. These practices included misrepresentation, churning of policies, lies, and fraud by agents of major life insurers.[10] In 1993, the Florida department of insurance charged 100 Metropolitan Life agents with fraudulent and deceptive sales practices. The agents sold life insurance contracts to nurses who believed they were buying retirement policies, which later resulted in a class action suit by the nurses against the company. In 1994, the Georgia department fined the Metropolitan $250,000 for deceiving nurses with retirement schemes. Later in 1994, the NAIC fined the Metropolitan an unprecedented $20 million in a global settlement of deceptive sales practices.

In 1994, Prudential was hit with a class action suit in Pennsylvania for churning policies. New York Life and John Hancock were hit with similar class action suits in Pennsylvania for churning policies. In 1995, Prudential faced class action law suits in other states. Also, in 1995, suits involving vanishing premiums that never vanished were filed against the Equitable and Equitable of Iowa.

In 1995, the New York and New Jersey insurance departments formed a multistate task force to investigate the sales practices of insurers; the task force begin its work by investigating the sales practices of Prudential. Also, in 1995, New York Life and Great-West Life agreed to settle vanishing premium class action suits with policyowners. In 1996, Phoenix Home Mutual and Connecticut General agreed to settle similar vanishing premium suits.

In 1996, the multistate task force continued its investigation of Prudential and announced that the company would be fined $35 million, and a remediation program would be available to 10.7 million policyowners. A number of states, however, did not agree to the settlement by the task force. Meanwhile, Prudential was separately negotiating a $410 million class action suit by policyowners involving misleading sales practices. Finally, in early 1997, all 50 states agreed to the task force's settlement agreement with Prudential.

As a result of these scandals and earlier misdeeds, the public's image of the life insurance industry is not good. According to the American Council of Life Insurance, in 1994, only 24 percent of the population agreed that life insurers had high ethical standards, down from 50 percent in 1968.[11] To deal with the image problem and negative impact on

## Exhibit 27.2
### Number of Multistate Insurance Company Insolvencies

| Year | Title | Fraternal | Life | Property & Casualty | Total |
|---|---|---|---|---|---|
| 1997 (as of 2/20/97) | 0 | 0 | 0 | 1 | 1 |
| 1996 | 0 | 0 | 3 | 5 | 8 |
| 1995 | 0 | 0 | 2 | 4 | 6 |
| 1994 | 0 | 0 | 8 | 11 | 19 |
| 1993 | 0 | 0 | 11 | 15 | 26 |
| 1992 | 0 | 0 | 12 | 29 | 41 |
| 1991 | 0 | 0 | 25 | 21 | 46 |
| 1990 | 0 | 1 | 20 | 23 | 44 |
| 1989 | 1 | 0 | 27 | 17 | 45 |
| **Total** | 1 | 1 | 108 | 126 | 236 |

NOTE: Above data include conservations, rehabilitations, and liquidations.
SOURCE: National Association of Insurance Commissioners (1997).

## Exhibit 27.3
### Number of Insolvencies by Insurers Operating in a Single State

| Year | Title | Life | Health, Medical, Dental & Indemnity | Property & Casualty | Fraternal | Total |
|---|---|---|---|---|---|---|
| 1997 (as of 1/22/97) | 0 | 0 | 0 | 2 | 0 | 2 |
| 1996 | 0 | 1 | 1 | 4 | 0 | 6 |
| 1995 | 1 | 1 | 0 | 5 | 0 | 7 |
| 1994 | 0 | 4 | 0 | 13 | 0 | 17 |
| 1993 | 0 | 5 | 0 | 10 | 0 | 15 |
| 1992 | 0 | 10 | 0 | 29 | 0 | 39 |
| 1991 | 1 | 15 | 0 | 15 | 0 | 31 |
| 1990 | 0 | 11 | 1 | 15 | 0 | 27 |
| 1989 | 0 | 20 | 2 | 20 | 2 | 44 |
| **Total** | 2 | 67 | 4 | 113 | 2 | 188 |

NOTE: Above data include conservations, rehabilitations, and liquidations.
SOURCE: National Association of Insurance Commissioners (1997).

sales, the American Council of Life Insurance proposed a system by which insurers would be certified by a third party for meeting certain ethical standards and a market code of conduct. In 1996, the Insurance Marketplace Standards Association was formed to do the certification.

## Insolvency of Insurers

Insolvency of insurers is another important issue in insurance regulation. Between 1989 and early 1997,

236 multistate insurers became insolvent (see Exhibit 27.2). During the same period, 188 single state insurers became insolvent (see Exhibit 27.3).

**Reasons for Insolvencies** The A. M. Best Company has published an insolvency study that identifies the major reasons insurers become insolvent or financially impaired.[12] Exhibit 27.4 identifies the primary causes of financial impairment for 290 life and health insurers that became financially

EXHIBIT 27.4

## Primary Causes of Financially Impaired Life and Health Insurers, 1976–1991

| Primary causes | Number of companies | % of total identified |
|---|---|---|
| **Inadequate Pricing/Surplus** | 47 | 23% |
| **Rapid Growth** | 41 | 20 |
| **Affiliate Problems** | 40 | 19 |
| **Overstated Assets** | 37 | 18 |
| **Alleged Fraud** | 16 | 8 |
| **Significant Change in Business** | 15 | 7 |
| **Reinsurance Failure** | 5 | 2 |
| **Miscellaneous** | 6 | 3 |
| Total Identified | 207 | 100% |
| Unidentified | 83 | |
| Total FICs | 290 | |

SOURCE: "Best's Insolvency Study Life/Health Insurers, 1976–1991, Executive Summary and Recommendations," *Best's Insurance Management Reports,* June 1992, p. 9, Exhibit 48. Copyright © 1992 A. M. Best Company. Used by permission.

EXHIBIT 27.5

## Primary Causes of Property-Liability Insurer Insolvencies, 1969–1990

| Primary causes | Number of companies | Percent of Total |
|---|---|---|
| **Deficient loss reserves (inadequate pricing)** | 86 | 28% |
| **Rapid growth** | 64 | 21 |
| **Alleged fraud** | 30 | 10 |
| **Overstated assets** | 30 | 10 |
| **Significant change in business** | 26 | 9 |
| **Reinsurance failure** | 21 | 7 |
| **Catastrophe losses** | 17 | 6 |
| **Miscellaneous** | 28 | 9 |
| **Total** | 302 | 100 |

SOURCE: J. David Cummins, Scott Harrington, and Greg Niehaus, *An Economic Overview of Risk-Based Capital Requirements for the Property-Liability Insurance Industry* (Schaumburg, Ill.: Alliance of American Insurers, 1992), p. 3. Table 1. Data are based on the insolvency study by the A. M. Best Company (1991). Reprinted by permission of Alliance of American Insurers.

impaired between 1976 and 1991. Inadequate pricing and surplus and rapid growth accounted for 43 percent of the insurers that became financially impaired. Other causes of failure include problems of affiliates, overstated assets, alleged fraud, a significant change in business, failure of reinsurers, and other miscellaneous reasons. Virtually all of the primary causes of financial impairment involved some form of company mismanagement.

Exhibit 27.5 summarizes the results of the study for 302 property and liability insurers included in the study. The two primary causes of insurer insolvency are deficient loss reserves (inadequate pricing) and rapid growth. These two reasons accounted for 49 percent of the insolvencies and failure of property and liability insurers included in the study. Other causes of insolvency include alleged fraud, overstated assets, a significant change in business, failure of reinsurers to pay claims, and catastrophe losses.

When an insurer becomes insolvent or financially impaired, state regulators must take appropriate action. With proper management, the insurer

may be rehabilitated. If rehabilitation is not feasible, the insurer may be involuntarily liquidated. Other regulatory actions include license revocation, cease-and-desist orders, and other actions that restrict an insurer's freedom to do business.

What happens to your policy or unpaid claim if your insurer becomes insolvent? Your policy may be sold to another insurer, and an unpaid claim may be paid by the state's guaranty fund. However, failure of a large insurer may result in a delay of several years before all claims are paid.

**Methods of Ensuring Solvency**    The principal methods of ensuring solvency are the following:

1. *Financial requirements.* Insurers must meet certain financial requirements that vary among the states, such as minimum capital and surplus requirements, restrictions on investments, and valuation of loss reserves.

2. *Risk-based capital standards.* As we noted earlier, life and health insurers must meet the risk-based capital standards based on a model law

developed by the NAIC. Insurers are graded by regulators based on how much capital they have to support the riskiness of their investments and operations. The increased capital requirements help to prevent insolvency.

3. *Annual financial statements.* Certain annual financial statements must be submitted to state insurance departments in a prescribed manner to provide information on premiums written, expenses, losses, investments, and other information. The financial statements are then reviewed by regulatory officials.

4. *Field examinations.* State laws require that insurers must be examined every three to five years. The NAIC coordinates the examination of insurers that do business in several states.

5. *Early warning system.* The NAIC administers an early warning system called the Insurance Regulatory Information System (IRIS). Financial ratios and other reports are developed based on information in the annual statement. Based on a review of this information, insurers may be designated for immediate attention or targeted for regulatory attention. The system, however, is not perfect. The financial ratios may not identify all troubled insurers. The system also has identified an increasing number of insurers, some of which do not require immediate regulatory attention.

6. *Accreditation program of NAIC.* To upgrade the quality of state regulation, the NAIC has enacted certain financial regulation standards. States meeting those standards are accredited by the NAIC. Most states have met the NAIC accreditation standards.

## Repeal of McCarran-Ferguson Act

Another regulatory issue is whether the McCarran-Ferguson Act should be repealed or substantially modified. As noted earlier, the McCarran Act gives the states primary responsibility for regulation of the insurance industry and also provides limited exemption from federal antitrust laws. In view of the trend toward deregulation and greater price competition, it is argued that insurers should not be exempt from federal antitrust laws that prohibit price fixing, collusion, and other activities harmful to competition.

Critics of state regulation present several arguments for repeal of the McCarran Act. They include the following:

1. *The insurance industry no longer needs broad antitrust exemption.* Critics argue that the "state action doctrine" has been fully developed and clarified by the Supreme Court. The state action doctrine defines certain activities required by state law that are exempt from federal antitrust activities. Since permissible actions of insurers have been clarified, exemption from the antitrust laws is no longer needed. In addition, it is argued that other industries are not exempt from antitrust laws, and this should also be true for insurers.

2. *Price collusion among insurers may create a problem of insurance affordability and availability.* Critics argue that collusive price fixing among insurers under the present system created the crisis in commercial liability insurance in the mid-1980s in which rates soared and availability of insurance was reduced.

3. *Federal regulation is needed because of the defects in state regulation.* Critics argue that federal minimum standards are needed to ensure nondiscrimination in insurance pricing, full availability of essential property and liability coverages, and elimination of unfair and excessive rate differentials among insureds.

The insurance industry, however, has strongly opposed any legislation that would repeal the McCarran Act. The industry believes that substantial harm to both insurers and the public will result from repeal of the act. The following arguments are presented in support of the industry's position:

1. *The insurance industry is already competitive.* There are more than 3300 property and liability insurers and more than 1700 life insurers that now compete for business.

2. *Small insurers would be harmed.* Smaller insurers would be unable to compete because they cannot develop accurate rates based on their limited loss and expense experience. Thus, smaller insurers may go out of business or be taken over by larger insurers. Hence a small number of large insurers will ultimately control

the business, a result exactly opposite of that intended by repeal of the McCarran Act.

3. *Insurers may be prevented from developing common coverage forms.* This could lead to costly gaps in coverage for insurance buyers and increased litigation between insurers and policyowners. Also, it would be difficult for insureds to know what is covered and excluded if nonstandard forms are used.

4. *Dual regulation may result from repeal of the McCarran Act.* However, the past record of federal regulation is poor. Federal regulators have done a poor job in regulating the savings and loan industry, which resulted in the insolvency of hundreds of thrifts with a cost to taxpayers of billions of dollars. Also, critics argue that federal regulation of railroads, airlines, and trucking has been destructive to competition. Federal regulation has also obstructed entry into an industry, entrenched the market power of large companies, and resulted in a cozy relationship between the regulators and the regulated.

5. *Sharing of information would be restricted.* Insurers would be restricted in the sharing of information through trade associations. Insurers would also experience greater expenses in developing new products and rates if information cannot be shared, which would increase the cost of insurance products to the public.

Numerous federal proposals have been introduced during the past 20 years to repeal or modify the McCarran Act. In general, these proposals would prohibit certain activities of insurers, including price fixing, tying the sale of one product to another, attempting to monopolize, and dividing up territories with competitors. In addition, insurers frequently act in concert to develop final rates. Depending on the proposed legislation, this type of activity would be restricted or prohibited.

## Unisex Rating

Unisex rating is another important issue. **Unisex rating** *means that the pooled loss experience of both sexes is used to determine the rates charged, and that the use of sex as a separate rating factor is not allowed.* Unisex rates are now used in group life and health insurance plans that are experience-rated since the aggregate

loss experience of both sexes is used to determine rates. Also, employer retirement plans are not a problem since retirement benefits are either based on unisex rates, or employers make up the difference in cost between male and female retirees. However, gender is an extremely important rating factor in individual life and health insurance and auto insurance. Activist groups would prohibit gender-based rates for these lines of insurance.

A small number of states have passed gender-neutral insurance laws that affect one or more lines of individual insurance, including Michigan, North Carolina, Hawaii, Massachusetts, and Montana. Montana's law applies to all lines of insurance.[13]

The insurance industry is strongly opposed to unisex rating on the basis of fairness and equity. *The industry argues that men and women should pay different rates because their claim experience is different.* Women pay 10 to 30 percent less for individual life insurance than men the same age, because, on average, women live about eight years longer than men. In addition, women are involved in relatively fewer fatal auto accidents than men and should pay less for auto insurance. However, women under age 55 generally pay more for individual health insurance because they tend to have more frequent and expensive claims. In addition, women pay more for individual disability income insurance because of higher disability rates; major insurers have discontinued the use of unisex rates for females because of higher disability rates. Finally, women are charged more for individual annuities because of a longer life expectancy.

In summary, under unisex rating, women would pay less for individual health and disability income insurance and substantially more for auto insurance. On balance, women as a group probably would benefit financially from unisex rating. However, one research study suggests that the overall lifetime financial impact is likely to be small. Using a discounted cash-flow methodology, Carney and Hardigree have attempted to measure the lifetime benefits and costs under unisex rating to women at six locations for auto, health, life, disability, and annuities. The authors concluded that the total lifetime benefits or costs for females would be small. For example, for the five benefits studied, women age 21 in Bozeman, Montana would receive lifetime benefits of $1679 under Montana's unisex rating law. Women age 40 would receive smaller lifetime benefits of only $255. However, for women age 50, unisex rates would increase their lifetime cost for the five benefits by $1264.[14]

## Rebating

Another controversial issue is whether state antirebating laws should be repealed. In recent years, numerous industries have been deregulated to stimulate competition, consumer protection laws have been enacted, and greater emphasis has been placed on price competition and free markets. Antirebating laws are viewed as being in opposition to these goals.

Rebating is now legal only in California and Florida. However, consumer groups in other states have challenged the legality of antirebating laws on the grounds that such laws discourage price competition and are harmful to consumers.

Most insurance companies and insurance agents believe that the antirebating laws should be kept in force. The industry maintains that rebating is harmful to both the insurance industry and consumers. Several arguments, summarized as follows, are presented in support of their position:

1. *Insurer insolvency may increase.* If rebating is allowed, consumers will be encouraged to replace their present policies. Insurers will then be forced to pay higher commissions and rebate allowances to agents to attract new business. Acquisition expenses will increase, and some financial weak insurers may become insolvent.

2. *Unfair price discrimination will increase.* Large policyowners would receive higher rebates than smaller policyowners. Thus, smaller policyowners would be subsidizing larger policyowners, which results in unfair price competition. It is also argued that personal price discrimination could increase. An agent may be more likely to give a discount if a friend or relative is applying for insurance.

3. *Service to policyowners will decline.* Since rebating will reduce an agent's commission, service to policyowners will decline.

4. *Concentration of sales in larger companies will increase.* In order to compete, agents will request discretionary dollars from their companies in order to offer higher rebates to clients. However,

only the larger insurers will be able to pay the additional funds for rebates. Smaller companies will not be able to compete. The result will be an increased concentration of sales for the larger companies.

5. *Misrepresentation and unethical sales practices may increase.* Some agents may be unethical and promise higher rebates that may not be possible. Deceptive advertising may also increase.

Consumer groups are not easily persuaded by the preceding arguments against rebating. Several arguments are presented in support of rebating, including the following:

1. *Consumers will benefit from lower prices.* Rebating will increase price competition that will ultimately lower insurance rates. This can only benefit consumers.

2. *Antirebating laws protect agents from competition.* It is argued that the real reason agents are opposed to rebating is to protect their incomes, which could be substantially reduced from rebating. It is argued further that antirebating laws should not shield agents from increased price competition that may result from rebating.

3. *Insurance purchasers are denied the right to negotiate price with the insurance agent.* Critics argue that consumers can negotiate purchase price with the sellers of other goods and services, and that insurance purchasers should not be exempt from such negotiation.

## Insurance Regulation in the Future

The regulation of the private insurance industry will continue to be an important public policy issue. Although it is speculative to forecast the future direction of insurance regulation, at least four comments are in order.

First, congressional interest in repealing the McCarran-Ferguson Act will continue. However, at the time of this writing, strong political pressures to repeal the McCarran-Ferguson Act have temporarily abated because of a Republican-controlled Congress. The issue is not likely to disappear soon.

Second, the recent scandals involving deceptive sales practices by life insurers will make regulators more aware of unethical market conduct of insurers. Insurers engaging in unethical sales practices can expect quicker retaliation by regulators than in the past.

Third, the quality of state regulation should continue to improve. The NAIC accreditation standards should upgrade the quality of state regulation.

Finally, the risk-based capital standards should reduce insurer insolvency in the future. Thus, policyowners should have greater protection because of these standards.

## SUMMARY

- The insurance industry is regulated for several reasons:

    To maintain insurer solvency

    To compensate for inadequate consumer knowledge

    To insure reasonable rates

    To make insurance available

- The insurance industry is regulated by the states. The McCarran-Ferguson Act states that continued regulation and taxation of the insurance industry by the states are in the public interest.

- Three principal methods are used to regulate the insurance industry:

    Legislation

    Courts

    State insurance departments

- The principal areas that are regulated include the following:

    Formation and licensing of insurers

    Financial regulation

    Rate regulation

    Policy forms

    Sales practices and consumer protection

- The states have rating laws that require rates to be adequate, reasonable (not excessive), and not unfairly discriminatory. The principal types of rating laws are as follows:

    Prior-approval laws

    File-and-use laws

    Open-competition laws

    Flex-rating laws

- Insurers must pay a state premium tax on gross premiums. The primary purpose is to raise revenues for the state, not to provide funds for insurance regulation.

- State versus federal regulation is an issue that has evoked considerable debate. The alleged advantages of federal regulation include the following:

    Uniformity of laws

    Greater efficiency

    More competent regulation

- The advantages of state regulation include the following:

    Greater responsiveness to local needs

    Uniformity of laws by the NAIC

    Greater opportunity for innovation

    Unknown consequences of federal regulation

    Decentralization of political power

- Critics argue that state regulation of insurance has serious shortcomings, including the following:

    Inadequate regulation

    Inadequate protection of consumers

    Defects in financial regulation

    Improvements needed in handling complaints

    Inadequate market conduct examinations

    Insurance availability studies conducted only in a minority of states

    Regulators overly responsive to the insurance industry

- Several current issues in insurance regulation include the following:

    Banks in insurance

    Deceptive sales practices of insurers

    Insolvency of insurers

    Repeal of McCarran-Ferguson Act

    Unisex rating

    Rebating

## KEY CONCEPTS AND TERMS

Admitted assets
Alien insurer
Assessment method
Domestic insurer
File-and-use law
Flex-rating law
Foreign insurer
Insurance guaranty funds
Kenney rule
McCarran-Ferguson Act
National Association of Insurance Commissioners (NAIC)

Open-competition law
*Paul v. Virginia*
Policyowners' surplus
Prior-approval law
Rebating
Reserves
Risk-based capital
Solidity
South-Eastern Underwriters Association Case
Twisting

## QUESTIONS FOR REVIEW

1. Explain the reasons insurance companies are regulated.

2. Describe briefly the historical development of insurance regulation by the states. Point out some important legal decisions in your answer.

3. What methods are used to regulate insurance companies?

4. Describe the areas of insurance company operations that are regulated by the states.

5. Explain the different types of rating laws.

6. Explain the principal arguments for federal regulation of the insurance industry. What are the major arguments in support of state regulation?

7. Explain the major arguments for and against repeal of the McCarran-Ferguson Act.

8. Identify the major techniques that regulators use to ensure insurance company solvency.

9. Explain the major arguments for and against expansion of commercial banks into the insurance business.

10. Explain the arguments for and against repeal of state antirebating laws.

## QUESTIONS FOR DISCUSSION

1. Certain legal cases are significant in insurance regulation. Explain the legal significance of each of the following United States Supreme Court decisions with respect to regulation of the insurance industry by the states:
   a. *Paul v. Virginia*
   b. South-Eastern Underwriters Association case
   c. McCarran-Ferguson Act

2. State rating laws vary. Some states have file-and-use laws, while others have prior-approval laws and open competition laws. Explain how a file-and-use law differs from the following:
   a. prior-approval law
   b. open-competition law

3. a. One important goal of insurance regulation is to maintain the solvency of insurers. Describe the specific financial areas of operations that are regulated by the states.
   b. Describe some specific areas of regulation or activities of state insurance departments that aim directly at protecting the consumer.
   c. Explain the major reasons for the insolvency of insurers.

---

### CASE APPLICATION

Assume that your state allows insurers to use gender as a rating variable in the calculation of insurance rates. If your state enacts a unisex rating law that applies to all personal lines of insurance, explain the likely direction of rates if individual insurance is purchased by each of the following:

a. Automobile insurance is purchased by a single female, age 23.

b. Automobile insurance is purchased by a single male, age 19.

c. Life insurance is purchased by a female, age 25.

d. Major medical insurance is purchased by a male, age 40.

e. Disability income insurance is purchased by a female, age 35.

---

4. The insurance industry contends that smaller insurers may become insolvent or may be merged with larger companies if the McCarran-Ferguson Act is repealed.
   a. Do you agree or disagree with the above statement? Explain your answer.
   b. Some observers maintain that the development of common coverage forms and standard forms will be accelerated if the McCarran-Ferguson Act is repealed. Do you agree or disagree with the statement? Explain your answer.

## SELECTED REFERENCES

"Best's Insolvency Study Life/Health Insurers, 1976–1991, Executive Summary and Recommendations," *Best's Insurance Management Reports* (July 1992).

Comptroller General of the United States, *Issues and Needed Improvements in State Regulation of the Insurance Business (Executive Summary)*. Washington, D.C.: General Accounting Office, 1979.

Cummins, J. David, Scott Harrington, and Greg Niehaus. *An Economic Overview of Risk-Based Capital Requirements for the Property-Liability Insurance Industry*. Schaumburg, Ill.: Alliance of American Insurers, 1992.

Harrington, Scott E. "Policyholder Runs, Life Insurance Company Failures, and Insurance Solvency Regulation." *Regulation: The Cato Review of Business and Government*, 15, no. 2 (Spring 1992): 27–37.

Hamilton, Karen L. *The Changing Nature of Insurance Regulation,* 2nd ed. (Malvern, Pa.: Insurance Institute of America, 1996).

Klein, Robert W, "Insurance Regulation in Transition," *The Journal of Risk and Insurance,* 62, no. 3 (September 1995): 363–404.

NAIC Insurance Availability and Affordability Task Force. *Improving Urban Insurance Markets, A Handbook on Available Options,* June 4, 1996.

United States General Accounting Office. *Insurer Failures: Differences in Property/Casualty Guaranty Fund Protection and Funding Limitation*s, GAO/GGD-92-55BR, March 1992.

———. *Insurer Failures: Life/Health Insurer Insolvencies and Limitations of State Guaranty Funds,* GAO/GGD-92–44, March 1992.

———. *Insurance Regulation: The Insurance Regulatory Information System Needs Improvement, GAO/GGD-91-20, November 1990.*

White, Michael D, "The Extent of U.S. Bank Insurance Powers and Activities," *Journal of the American Society of CLU & ChFC,* 50, no. 2 (March 1996): 56–61.

## NOTES

1. *Paul v. Virginia,* 8 Wall. 183 (1868).

2. *U.S v. South-Eastern Underwriters Association,* 322 U.S. 533 (1944).

3. See Roger Kenney, *Fundamentals of Fire and Casualty Insurance Strength,* 4th ed. (Dedham, Mass.: Kenney Insurance Studies, 1967).

4. S. S. Huebner, Kenneth Black, Jr., and Bernard L. Webb, *Property and Liability Insurance,* 4th ed. (Upper Saddle River, N.J.: Prentice Hall, 1996), pp. 653–54.

5. There are exceptions. Maximum credit life insurance rates are regulated in all states. New York has regulations concerning minimum group term insurance rates for groups not previously insured for life insurance.

6. William C. Scheel and Jack VanDerhei, "Replacement of Life Insurance: Its Regulation and Current Activity," *Journal of Risk and Insurance,* 45, no. 2 (June 1978).

7. See U.S. Congress, House, Subcommittee on Oversight and Investigations of the Committee on Energy and Commerce, *Failed Promises: Insurance Company Insolvencies.* (Washington, D.C.: U.S. Government Printing Office, 1990), pp. 72–75, and Comptroller General of the United States, *Issues and Needed Improvements in State Regulation of the Insurance Business (Executive Summary).* (Washington, D.C.: General Accounting Office, 1979), pp. i–viii.

8. Michael D. White, "The Extent of U.S. Bank Insurance Powers and Activities," *Journal of the American Society of CLU and ChFC,* 50, no. 2 (March 1996), p. 59.

9. Steven Brostoff, "The Bank-Insurance Issue's Long, Litigation-Filled History," *National Underwriter, The Last Word for 100 Years, Centennial Issue* (March 31, 1997), p. 96.

10. Discussion of this issue is based on Steven Piontek, "Company Failures, Sales Scandals Batter the Business," *National Underwriter, The Last Word for 100 Years, Centennial Issue* (March 31, 1997), p. 168.

11. "Editorial Comment, ACLI's Market Conduct Response," *National Underwriter,* Life & Health/Financial Services Edition, December 4, 1995, p. 42.

12. "Best's Insolvency Study Life/Health Insurers, 1976–1991, Executive Summary and Recommendations," *Best's Insurance Management Reports* (July 1992).

13. Robert J. Carney and Donald W. Hardigree, "The Economic Impact of Gender-Neutral Insurance Rating on Women," *Journal of Insurance Issues and Practices,* 13, no. 2 (June 1990): 2.

14. Ibid, pp. 1,18.

# *Appendix A*

# HOMEOWNERS 3 (SPECIAL FORM)

**HOMEOWNERS POLICY**

**Declarations applicable to all policy forms**

Policy Number

Policy Period: 12:01 a.m. Standard time     From:      To:
at the residence premises

Named Insured and mailing address

The residence premises covered by this policy is located at the above address unless otherwise stated:

Coverage is provided where a premium or limit of liability is shown for the coverage.

|  | Limit of Liability | Premium |
|---|---|---|
| SECTION I COVERAGES | | |
| A. Dwelling | | |
| B. Other structures | | |
| C. Personal property | | |
| D. Loss of use | | |
| SECTION II COVERAGES | | |
| E. Personal liability: each occurrence | | |
| F. Medical payments to others: each person | | |

Total premium for endorsements listed below

Policy Total

Forms and endorsements made part of this policy:

| Number | Edition Date | Title | Premium |
|---|---|---|---|

[Special State Provisions: South Carolina: Valuation Clause (Cov.A) $
Minnesota Insurable Value (Cov.A) $
New York: Coinsurance Clause Applies ___Yes ___No]

DEDUCTIBLE - Section I: $
In case of a loss under Section I, we cover only that part of the loss over the deductible stated.

Section II: Other insured locations:

[Mortgagee/Lienholder (Name and address)]

Countersignature of agent/date         Signature/title - company officer

Ed.4/84

## HOMEOWNERS 3
## SPECIAL FORM

### AGREEMENT

We will provide the insurance described in this policy in return for the premium and compliance with all applicable provisions of this policy.

### DEFINITIONS

In this policy, "you" and "your" refer to the "named insured" shown in the Declarations and the spouse if a resident of the same household. "We," "us" and "our" refer to the Company providing this insurance. In addition, certain words and phrases are defined as follows:

1. "Bodily injury" means bodily harm, sickness or disease, including required care, loss of services and death that results.

2. "Business" includes trade, profession or occupation.

3. "Insured" means you and residents of your household who are:

   a. Your relatives; or

   b. Other persons under the age of 21 and in the care of any person named above.

   Under Section II, "insured" also means:

   c. With respect to animals or watercraft to which this policy applies, any person or organization legally responsible for these animals or watercraft which are owned by you or any person included in 3.a. or 3.b. above. A person or organization using or having custody of these animals or watercraft in the course of any "business" or without consent of the owner is not an "insured";

   d. With respect to any vehicle to which this policy applies:

      (1) Persons while engaged in your employ or that of any person included in 3.a. or 3.b. above; or

      (2) Other persons using the vehicle on an "insured location" with your consent.

4. "Insured location" means:

   a. The "residence premises";

   b. The part of other premises, other structures and grounds used by you as a residence and:

      (1) Which is shown in the Declarations; or

      (2) Which is acquired by you during the policy period for your use as a residence;

   c. Any premises used by you in connection with a premises in 4.a. and 4.b. above;

   d. Any part of a premises:

      (1) Not owned by an "insured"; and

      (2) Where an "insured" is temporarily residing;

   e. Vacant land, other than farm land, owned by or rented to an "insured";

   f. Land owned by or rented to an "insured" on which a one or two family dwelling is being built as a residence for an "insured";

   g. Individual or family cemetery plots or burial vaults of an "insured"; or

   h. Any part of a premises occasionally rented to an "insured" for other than "business" use.

5. "Occurrence" means an accident, including continuous or repeated exposure to substantially the same general harmful conditions, which results, during the policy period, in:

   a. "Bodily injury"; or

   b. "Property damage."

6. "Property damage" means physical injury to, destruction of, or loss of use of tangible property.

7. "Residence employee" means:

   a. An employee of an "insured" whose duties are related to the maintenance or use of the "residence premises," including household or domestic services; or

   b. One who performs similar duties elsewhere not related to the "business" of an "insured."

8. "Residence premises" means:

   a. The one family dwelling, other structures, and grounds; or

   b. That part of any other building;

   where you reside and which is shown as the "residence premises" in the Declarations.

   "Residence premises" also means a two family dwelling where you reside in at least one of the family units and which is shown as the "residence premises" in the Declarations.

HO 00 03 04 91          Copyright, Insurance Services Office, Inc., 1990          **Page 1 of 18**

"Homeowners 3 Special Form" reprinted with permission. Copyright, Insurance Services Office, Inc., 1990.

HO 00 03 04 91

---

## SECTION I – PROPERTY COVERAGES

---

### COVERAGE A - Dwelling

We cover:

1. The dwelling on the "residence premises" shown in the Declarations, including structures attached to the dwelling; and

2. Materials and supplies located on or next to the "residence premises" used to construct, alter or repair the dwelling or other structures on the "residence premises."

This coverage does not apply to land, including land on which the dwelling is located.

### COVERAGE B - Other Structures

We cover other structures on the "residence premises" set apart from the dwelling by clear space. This includes structures connected to the dwelling by only a fence, utility line, or similar connection.

This coverage does not apply to land, including land on which the other structures are located.

We do not cover other structures:

1. Used in whole or in part for "business"; or

2. Rented or held for rental to any person not a tenant of the dwelling, unless used solely as a private garage.

The limit of liability for this coverage will not be more than 10% of the limit of liability that applies to Coverage A. Use of this coverage does not reduce the Coverage A limit of liability.

### COVERAGE C - Personal Property

We cover personal property owned or used by an "insured" while it is anywhere in the world. At your request, we will cover personal property owned by:

1. Others while the property is on the part of the "residence premises" occupied by an "insured";

2. A guest or a "residence employee," while the property is in any residence occupied by an "insured."

Our limit of liability for personal property usually located at an "insured's" residence, other than the "residence premises," is 10% of the limit of liability for Coverage C, or $1000, whichever is greater. Personal property in a newly acquired principal residence is not subject to this limitation for the 30 days from the time you begin to move the property there.

**Special Limits of Liability.** These limits do not increase the Coverage C limit of liability. The special limit for each numbered category below is the total limit for each loss for all property in that category.

1. $200 on money, bank notes, bullion, gold other than goldware, silver other than silverware, platinum, coins and medals.

2. $1000 on securities, accounts, deeds, evidences of debt, letters of credit, notes other than bank notes, manuscripts, personal records, passports, tickets and stamps. This dollar limit applies to these categories regardless of the medium (such as paper or computer software) on which the material exists.

   This limit includes the cost to research, replace or restore the information from the lost or damaged material.

3. $1000 on watercraft, including their trailers, furnishings, equipment and outboard engines or motors.

4. $1000 on trailers not used with watercraft.

5. $1000 for loss by theft of jewelry, watches, furs, precious and semi-precious stones.

6. $2000 for loss by theft of firearms.

7. $2500 for loss by theft of silverware, silver-plated ware, goldware, gold-plated ware and pewterware. This includes flatware, hollowware, tea sets, trays and trophies made of or including silver, gold or pewter.

8. $2500 on property, on the "residence premises," used at any time or in any manner for any "business" purpose.

9. $250 on property, away from the "residence premises," used at any time or in any manner for any "business" purpose. However, this limit does not apply to loss to adaptable electronic apparatus as described in Special Limits 10. and 11. below.

10. $1000 for loss to electronic apparatus, while in or upon a motor vehicle or other motorized land conveyance, if the electronic apparatus is equipped to be operated by power from the electrical system of the vehicle or conveyance while retaining its capability of being operated by other sources of power. Electronic apparatus includes:

    a. Accessories or antennas; or

    b. Tapes, wires, records, discs or other media;

    for use with any electronic apparatus.

Copyright, Insurance Services Office, Inc., 1990  HO 00 03 04 91

HO 00 03 04 91

11. $1000 for loss to electronic apparatus, while not in or upon a motor vehicle or other motorized land conveyance, if the electronic apparatus:

   a. Is equipped to be operated by power from the electrical system of the vehicle or conveyance while retaining its capability of being operated by other sources of power;

   b. Is away from the "residence premises"; and

   c. Is used at any time or in any manner for any "business" purpose.

   Electronic apparatus includes:

   a. Accessories and antennas; or

   b. Tapes, wires, records, discs or other media;

   for use with any electronic apparatus.

**Property Not Covered.** We do not cover:

1. Articles separately described and specifically insured in this or other insurance;

2. Animals, birds or fish;

3. Motor vehicles or all other motorized land conveyances. This includes:

   a. Their equipment and accessories; or

   b. Electronic apparatus that is designed to be operated solely by use of the power from the electrical system of motor vehicles or all other motorized land conveyances. Electronic apparatus includes:

      (1) Accessories or antennas; or

      (2) Tapes, wires, records, discs or other media;

      for use with any electronic apparatus.

      The exclusion of property described in **3.a.** and **3.b.** above applies only while the property is in or upon the vehicle or conveyance.

   We do cover vehicles or conveyances not subject to motor vehicle registration which are:

   a. Used to service an "insured's" residence; or

   b. Designed for assisting the handicapped;

4. Aircraft and parts. Aircraft means any contrivance used or designed for flight, except model or hobby aircraft not used or designed to carry people or cargo;

5. Property of roomers, boarders and other tenants, except property of roomers and boarders related to an "insured";

6. Property in an apartment regularly rented or held for rental to others by an "insured," except as provided in Additional Coverages **10.**;

7. Property rented or held for rental to others off the "residence premises";

8. "Business" data, including such data stored in:

   a. Books of account, drawings or other paper records; or

   b. Electronic data processing tapes, wires, records, discs or other software media;

   However, we do cover the cost of blank recording or storage media, and of pre-recorded computer programs available on the retail market; or

9. Credit cards or fund transfer cards except as provided in Additional Coverages **6.**

**COVERAGE D - Loss Of Use**

The limit of liability for Coverage D is the total limit for all the coverages that follow.

1. If a loss covered under this Section makes that part of the "residence premises" where you reside not fit to live in, we cover, at your choice, either of the following. However, if the "residence premises" is not your principal place of residence, we will not provide the option under paragraph **b.** below.

   a. **Additional Living Expense,** meaning any necessary increase in living expenses incurred by you so that your household can maintain its normal standard of living; or

   b. **Fair Rental Value,** meaning the fair rental value of that part of the "residence premises" where you reside less any expenses that do not continue while the premises is not fit to live in.

   Payment under **a.** or **b.** will be for the shortest time required to repair or replace the damage or, if you permanently relocate, the shortest time required for your household to settle elsewhere.

2. If a loss covered under this Section makes that part of the "residence premises" rented to others or held for rental by you not fit to live in, we cover the:

      **Fair Rental Value,** meaning the fair rental value of that part of the "residence premises" rented to others or held for rental by you less any expenses that do not continue while the premises is not fit to live in.

   Payment will be for the shortest time required to repair or replace that part of the premises rented or held for rental.

3. If a civil authority prohibits you from use of the "residence premises" as a result of direct damage to neighboring premises by a Peril Insured Against in this policy, we cover the Additional Living Expense and Fair Rental Value loss as provided under **1.** and **2.** above for no more than two weeks.

**HO 00 03 04 91**

The periods of time under **1.**, **2.** and **3.** above are not limited by expiration of this policy.

We do not cover loss or expense due to cancellation of a lease or agreement.

**ADDITIONAL COVERAGES**

**1. Debris Removal.** We will pay your reasonable expense for the removal of:

   **a.** Debris of covered property if a Peril Insured Against that applies to the damaged property causes the loss; or

   **b.** Ash, dust or particles from a volcanic eruption that has caused direct loss to a building or property contained in a building.

This expense is included in the limit of liability that applies to the damaged property. If the amount to be paid for the actual damage to the property plus the debris removal expense is more than the limit of liability for the damaged property, an additional 5% of that limit of liability is available for debris removal expense.

We will also pay your reasonable expense, up to $500, for the removal from the "residence premises" of:

   **a.** Your tree(s) felled by the peril of Windstorm or Hail;

   **b.** Your tree(s) felled by the peril of Weight of Ice, Snow or Sleet; or

   **c.** A neighbor's tree(s) felled by a Peril Insured Against under Coverage C;

provided the tree(s) damages a covered structure. The $500 limit is the most we will pay in any one loss regardless of the number of fallen trees.

**2. Reasonable Repairs.** In the event that covered property is damaged by an applicable Peril Insured Against, we will pay the reasonable cost incurred by you for necessary measures taken solely to protect against further damage. If the measures taken involve repair to other damaged property, we will pay for those measures only if that property is covered under this policy and the damage to that property is caused by an applicable Peril Insured Against.

This coverage:

   **a.** Does not increase the limit of liability that applies to the covered property;

   **b.** Does not relieve you of your duties, in case of a loss to covered property, as set forth in SECTION I - CONDITION **2.d.**

**3. Trees, Shrubs and Other Plants.** We cover trees, shrubs, plants or lawns, on the "residence premises," for loss caused by the following Perils Insured Against: Fire or lightning, Explosion, Riot or civil commotion, Aircraft, Vehicles not owned or operated by a resident of the "residence premises," Vandalism or malicious mischief or Theft.

We will pay up to 5% of the limit of liability that applies to the dwelling for all trees, shrubs, plants or lawns. No more than $500 of this limit will be available for any one tree, shrub or plant. We do not cover property grown for "business" purposes.

This coverage is additional insurance.

**4. Fire Department Service Charge.** We will pay up to $500 for your liability assumed by contract or agreement for fire department charges incurred when the fire department is called to save or protect covered property from a Peril Insured Against. We do not cover fire department service charges if the property is located within the limits of the city, municipality or protection district furnishing the fire department response.

This coverage is additional insurance. No deductible applies to this coverage.

**5. Property Removed.** We insure covered property against direct loss from any cause while being removed from a premises endangered by a Peril Insured Against and for no more than 30 days while removed. This coverage does not change the limit of liability that applies to the property being removed.

**6. Credit Card, Fund Transfer Card, Forgery and Counterfeit Money.**

We will pay up to $500 for:

   **a.** The legal obligation of an "insured" to pay because of the theft or unauthorized use of credit cards issued to or registered in an "insured's" name;

   **b.** Loss resulting from theft or unauthorized use of a fund transfer card used for deposit, withdrawal or transfer of funds, issued to or registered in an "insured's" name;

   **c.** Loss to an "insured" caused by forgery or alteration of any check or negotiable instrument; and

   **d.** Loss to an "insured" through acceptance in good faith of counterfeit United States or Canadian paper currency.

We do not cover use of a credit card or fund transfer card:

**a.** By a resident of your household;

**b.** By a person who has been entrusted with either type of card; or

**c.** If an "insured" has not complied with all terms and conditions under which the cards are issued.

All loss resulting from a series of acts committed by any one person or in which any one person is concerned or implicated is considered to be one loss.

We do not cover loss arising out of "business" use or dishonesty of an "insured."

This coverage is additional insurance. No deductible applies to this coverage.

Defense:

**a.** We may investigate and settle any claim or suit that we decide is appropriate. Our duty to defend a claim or suit ends when the amount we pay for the loss equals our limit of liability.

**b.** If a suit is brought against an "insured" for liability under the Credit Card or Fund Transfer Card coverage, we will provide a defense at our expense by counsel of our choice.

**c.** We have the option to defend at our expense an "insured" or an "insured's" bank against any suit for the enforcement of payment under the Forgery coverage.

**7.** **Loss Assessment.** We will pay up to $1000 for your share of loss assessment charged during the policy period against you by a corporation or association of property owners, when the assessment is made as a result of direct loss to the property, owned by all members collectively, caused by a Peril Insured Against under COVERAGE A - DWELLING, other than earthquake or land shock waves or tremors before, during or after a volcanic eruption.

This coverage applies only to loss assessments charged against you as owner or tenant of the "residence premises."

We do not cover loss assessments charged against you or a corporation or association of property owners by any governmental body.

The limit of $1000 is the most we will pay with respect to any one loss, regardless of the number of assessments.

Condition **1.** Policy Period, under SECTIONS I AND II CONDITIONS, does not apply to this coverage.

**8.** **Collapse.** We insure for direct physical loss to covered property involving collapse of a building or any part of a building caused only by one or more of the following:

**a.** Perils Insured Against in COVERAGE C - PERSONAL PROPERTY. These perils apply to covered buildings and personal property for loss insured by this additional coverage;

**b.** Hidden decay;

**c.** Hidden insect or vermin damage;

**d.** Weight of contents, equipment, animals or people;

**e.** Weight of rain which collects on a roof; or

**f.** Use of defective material or methods in construction, remodeling or renovation if the collapse occurs during the course of the construction, remodeling or renovation.

Loss to an awning, fence, patio, pavement, swimming pool, underground pipe, flue, drain, cesspool, septic tank, foundation, retaining wall, bulkhead, pier, wharf or dock is not included under items **b., c., d., e.,** and **f.** unless the loss is a direct result of the collapse of a building.

Collapse does not include settling, cracking, shrinking, bulging or expansion.

This coverage does not increase the limit of liability applying to the damaged covered property.

**9.** **Glass or Safety Glazing Material.**

We cover:

**a.** The breakage of glass or safety glazing material which is part of a covered building, storm door or storm window; and

**b.** Damage to covered property by glass or safety glazing material which is part of a building, storm door or storm window.

This coverage does not include loss on the "residence premises" if the dwelling has been vacant for more than 30 consecutive days immediately before the loss. A dwelling being constructed is not considered vacant.

Loss for damage to glass will be settled on the basis of replacement with safety glazing materials when required by ordinance or law.

This coverage does not increase the limit of liability that applies to the damaged property.

**HO 00 03 04 91**

10. **Landlord's Furnishings.** We will pay up to $2500 for your appliances, carpeting and other household furnishings, in an apartment on the "residence premises" regularly rented or held for rental to others by an "insured," for loss caused only by the following Perils Insured Against:

    a. **Fire or lightning.**

    b. **Windstorm or hail.**

    This peril does not include loss to the property contained in a building caused by rain, snow, sleet, sand or dust unless the direct force of wind or hail damages the building causing an opening in a roof or wall and the rain, snow, sleet, sand or dust enters through this opening.

    This peril includes loss to watercraft and their trailers, furnishings, equipment, and outboard engines or motors, only while inside a fully enclosed building.

    c. **Explosion.**

    d. **Riot or civil commotion.**

    e. **Aircraft,** including self-propelled missiles and spacecraft.

    f. **Vehicles.**

    g. **Smoke,** meaning sudden and accidental damage from smoke.

    This peril does not include loss caused by smoke from agricultural smudging or industrial operations.

    h. **Vandalism or malicious mischief.**

    i. **Falling objects.**

    This peril does not include loss to property contained in a building unless the roof or an outside wall of the building is first damaged by a falling object. Damage to the falling object itself is not included.

    j. **Weight of ice, snow or sleet** which causes damage to property contained in a building.

    k. **Accidental discharge or overflow of water or steam** from within a plumbing, heating, air conditioning or automatic fire protective sprinkler system or from within a household appliance.

    This peril does not include loss:

    (1) To the system or appliance from which the water or steam escaped;

    (2) Caused by or resulting from freezing except as provided in the peril of freezing below; or

    (3) On the "residence premises" caused by accidental discharge or overflow which occurs off the "residence premises."

    In this peril, a plumbing system does not include a sump, sump pump or related equipment.

    l. **Sudden and accidental tearing apart, cracking, burning or bulging** of a steam or hot water heating system, an air conditioning or automatic fire protective sprinkler system, or an appliance for heating water.

    We do not cover loss caused by or resulting from freezing under this peril.

    m. **Freezing** of a plumbing, heating, air conditioning or automatic fire protective sprinkler system or of a household appliance.

    This peril does not include loss on the "residence premises" while the dwelling is unoccupied, unless you have used reasonable care to:

    (1) Maintain heat in the building; or

    (2) Shut off the water supply and drain the system and appliances of water.

    n. **Sudden and accidental damage from artificially generated electrical current.**

    This peril does not include loss to a tube, transistor or similar electronic component.

    o. **Volcanic eruption** other than loss caused by earthquake, land shock waves or tremors.

    The $2500 limit is the most we will pay in any one loss regardless of the number of appliances, carpeting or other household furnishings involved in the loss.

---

## SECTION I – PERILS INSURED AGAINST

**COVERAGE A - DWELLING and COVERAGE B - OTHER STRUCTURES**

We insure against risk of direct loss to property described in Coverages A and B only if that loss is a physical loss to property. We do not insure, however, for loss:

1. Involving collapse, other than as provided in Additional Coverage 8.;

2. Caused by:

**a.** Freezing of a plumbing, heating, air conditioning or automatic fire protective sprinkler system or of a household appliance, or by discharge, leakage or overflow from within the system or appliance caused by freezing. This exclusion applies only while the dwelling is vacant, unoccupied or being constructed, unless you have used reasonable care to:

(1) Maintain heat in the building; or

(2) Shut off the water supply and drain the system and appliances of water;

**b.** Freezing, thawing, pressure or weight of water or ice, whether driven by wind or not, to a:

(1) Fence, pavement, patio or swimming pool;

(2) Foundation, retaining wall, or bulkhead; or

(3) Pier, wharf or dock;

**c.** Theft in or to a dwelling under construction, or of materials and supplies for use in the construction until the dwelling is finished and occupied;

**d.** Vandalism and malicious mischief if the dwelling has been vacant for more than 30 consecutive days immediately before the loss. A dwelling being constructed is not considered vacant;

**e.** Any of the following:

(1) Wear and tear, marring, deterioration;

(2) Inherent vice, latent defect, mechanical breakdown;

(3) Smog, rust or other corrosion, mold, wet or dry rot;

(4) Smoke from agricultural smudging or industrial operations;

(5) Discharge, dispersal, seepage, migration, release or escape of pollutants unless the discharge, dispersal, seepage, migration, release or escape is itself caused by a Peril Insured Against under Coverage C of this policy.

Pollutants means any solid, liquid, gaseous or thermal irritant or contaminant, including smoke, vapor, soot, fumes, acids, alkalis, chemicals and waste. Waste includes materials to be recycled, reconditioned or reclaimed;

(6) Settling, shrinking, bulging or expansion, including resultant cracking, of pavements, patios, foundations, walls, floors, roofs or ceilings;

(7) Birds, vermin, rodents, or insects; or

(8) Animals owned or kept by an "insured."

If any of these cause water damage not otherwise excluded, from a plumbing, heating, air conditioning or automatic fire protective sprinkler system or household appliance, we cover loss caused by the water including the cost of tearing out and replacing any part of a building necessary to repair the system or appliance. We do not cover loss to the system or appliance from which this water escaped.

**3.** Excluded under Section I - Exclusions.

Under items **1.** and **2.**, any ensuing loss to property described in Coverages A and B not excluded or excepted in this policy is covered.

## COVERAGE C - PERSONAL PROPERTY

We insure for direct physical loss to the property described in Coverage C caused by a peril listed below unless the loss is excluded in SECTION I - EXCLUSIONS.

**1. Fire or lightning.**

**2. Windstorm or hail.**

This peril does not include loss to the property contained in a building caused by rain, snow, sleet, sand or dust unless the direct force of wind or hail damages the building causing an opening in a roof or wall and the rain, snow, sleet, sand or dust enters through this opening.

This peril includes loss to watercraft and their trailers, furnishings, equipment, and outboard engines or motors, only while inside a fully enclosed building.

**3. Explosion.**

**4. Riot or civil commotion.**

**5. Aircraft,** including self-propelled missiles and spacecraft.

**6. Vehicles.**

**7. Smoke,** meaning sudden and accidental damage from smoke.

This peril does not include loss caused by smoke from agricultural smudging or industrial operations.

**8. Vandalism or malicious mischief.**

**9. Theft,** including attempted theft and loss of property from a known place when it is likely that the property has been stolen.

This peril does not include loss caused by theft:

**a.** Committed by an "insured";

**b.** In or to a dwelling under construction, or of materials and supplies for use in the construction until the dwelling is finished and occupied; or

**HO 00 03 04 91**

c. From that part of a "residence premises" rented by an "insured" to other than an "insured."

This peril does not include loss caused by theft that occurs off the "residence premises" of:

a. Property while at any other residence owned by, rented to, or occupied by an "insured," except while an "insured" is temporarily living there. Property of a student who is an "insured" is covered while at a residence away from home if the student has been there at any time during the 45 days immediately before the loss;

b. Watercraft, and their furnishings, equipment and outboard engines or motors; or

c. Trailers and campers.

**10. Falling objects.**

This peril does not include loss to property contained in a building unless the roof or an outside wall of the building is first damaged by a falling object. Damage to the falling object itself is not included.

**11. Weight of ice, snow or sleet** which causes damage to property contained in a building.

**12. Accidental discharge or overflow of water or steam** from within a plumbing, heating, air conditioning or automatic fire protective sprinkler system or from within a household appliance.

This peril does not include loss:

a. To the system or appliance from which the water or steam escaped;

b. Caused by or resulting from freezing except as provided in the peril of freezing below; or

c. On the "residence premises" caused by accidental discharge or overflow which occurs off the "residence premises."

In this peril, a plumbing system does not include a sump, sump pump or related equipment.

**13. Sudden and accidental tearing apart, cracking, burning or bulging** of a steam or hot water heating system, an air conditioning or automatic fire protective sprinkler system, or an appliance for heating water.

We do not cover loss caused by or resulting from freezing under this peril.

**14. Freezing** of a plumbing, heating, air conditioning or automatic fire protective sprinkler system or of a household appliance.

This peril does not include loss on the "residence premises" while the dwelling is unoccupied, unless you have used reasonable care to:

a. Maintain heat in the building; or

b. Shut off the water supply and drain the system and appliances of water.

**15. Sudden and accidental damage from artificially generated electrical current.**

This peril does not include loss to a tube, transistor or similar electronic component.

**16. Volcanic eruption** other than loss caused by earthquake, land shock waves or tremors.

---

## SECTION I – EXCLUSIONS

1. We do not insure for loss caused directly or indirectly by any of the following. Such loss is excluded regardless of any other cause or event contributing concurrently or in any sequence to the loss.

   a. **Ordinance or Law**, meaning enforcement of any ordinance or law regulating the construction, repair, or demolition of a building or other structure, unless specifically provided under this policy.

   b. **Earth Movement**, meaning earthquake including land shock waves or tremors before, during or after a volcanic eruption; landslide; mine subsidence; mudflow; earth sinking, rising or shifting; unless direct loss by:

      (1) Fire;

      (2) Explosion; or

      (3) Breakage of glass or safety glazing material which is part of a building, storm door or storm window;

      ensues and then we will pay only for the ensuing loss.

      This exclusion does not apply to loss by theft.

   c. **Water Damage**, meaning:

      (1) Flood, surface water, waves, tidal water, overflow of a body of water, or spray from any of these, whether or not driven by wind;

      (2) Water which backs up through sewers or drains or which overflows from a sump; or

HO 00 03 04 91

(3) Water below the surface of the ground, including water which exerts pressure on or seeps or leaks through a building, side-walk, driveway, foundation, swimming pool or other structure.

Direct loss by fire, explosion or theft resulting from water damage is covered.

d. **Power Failure,** meaning the failure of power or other utility service if the failure takes place off the "residence premises." But, if a Peril Insured Against ensues on the "residence premises," we will pay only for that ensuing loss.

e. **Neglect,** meaning neglect of the "insured" to use all reasonable means to save and preserve property at and after the time of a loss.

f. **War,** including the following and any conse-quence of any of the following:

(1) Undeclared war, civil war, insurrection, re-bellion or revolution;

(2) Warlike act by a military force or military personnel; or

(3) Destruction, seizure or use for a military purpose.

Discharge of a nuclear weapon will be deemed a warlike act even if accidental.

g. **Nuclear Hazard,** to the extent set forth in the Nuclear Hazard Clause of SECTION I - CON-DITIONS.

h. **Intentional Loss,** meaning any loss arising out of any act committed:

(1) By or at the direction of an "insured"; and

(2) With the intent to cause a loss.

2. We do not insure for loss to property described in Coverages A and B caused by any of the fol-lowing. However, any ensuing loss to property described in Coverages A and B not excluded or excepted in this policy is covered.

a. **Weather conditions.** However, this exclu-sion only applies if weather conditions con-tribute in any way with a cause or event excluded in paragraph **1.** above to produce the loss;

b. **Acts or decisions,** including the failure to act or decide, of any person, group, organiza-tion or governmental body;

c. **Faulty, inadequate or defective:**

(1) Planning, zoning, development, surveying, siting;

(2) Design, specifications, workmanship, re-pair, construction, renovation, remodeling, grading, compaction;

(3) Materials used in repair, construction, ren-ovation or remodeling; or

(4) Maintenance;

of part or all of any property whether on or off the "residence premises."

## SECTION I – CONDITIONS

1. **Insurable Interest and Limit of Liability.** Even if more than one person has an insurable interest in the property covered, we will not be liable in any one loss:

a. To the "insured" for more than the amount of the "insured's" interest at the time of loss; or

b. For more than the applicable limit of liability.

2. **Your Duties After Loss.** In case of a loss to covered property, you must see that the following are done:

a. Give prompt notice to us or our agent;

b. Notify the police in case of loss by theft;

c. Notify the credit card or fund transfer card company in case of loss under Credit Card or Fund Transfer Card coverage;

d. Protect the property from further damage. If repairs to the property are required, you must:

(1) Make reasonable and necessary repairs to protect the property; and

(2) Keep an accurate record of repair ex-penses;

e. Prepare an inventory of damaged personal property showing the quantity, description, actual cash value and amount of loss. Attach all bills, receipts and related documents that justify the figures in the inventory;

f. As often as we reasonably require:

(1) Show the damaged property;

(2) Provide us with records and documents we request and permit us to make copies; and

(3) Submit to examination under oath, while not in the presence of any other "insured," and sign the same;

HO 00 03 04 91

g. Send to us, within 60 days after our request, your signed, sworn proof of loss which sets forth, to the best of your knowledge and belief:

(1) The time and cause of loss;

(2) The interest of the "insured" and all others in the property involved and all liens on the property;

(3) Other insurance which may cover the loss;

(4) Changes in title or occupancy of the property during the term of the policy;

(5) Specifications of damaged buildings and detailed repair estimates;

(6) The inventory of damaged personal property described in **2.e.** above;

(7) Receipts for additional living expenses incurred and records that support the fair rental value loss; and

(8) Evidence or affidavit that supports a claim under the Credit Card, Fund Transfer Card, Forgery and Counterfeit Money coverage, stating the amount and cause of loss.

3. **Loss Settlement.** Covered property losses are settled as follows:

a. Property of the following types:

(1) Personal property;

(2) Awnings, carpeting, household appliances, outdoor antennas and outdoor equipment, whether or not attached to buildings; and

(3) Structures that are not buildings;

at actual cash value at the time of loss but not more than the amount required to repair or replace.

b. Buildings under Coverage A or B at replacement cost without deduction for depreciation, subject to the following:

(1) If, at the time of loss, the amount of insurance in this policy on the damaged building is 80% or more of the full replacement cost of the building immediately before the loss, we will pay the cost to repair or replace, after application of deductible and without deduction for depreciation, but not more than the least of the following amounts:

(a) The limit of liability under this policy that applies to the building;

(b) The replacement cost of that part of the building damaged for like construction and use on the same premises; or

(c) The necessary amount actually spent to repair or replace the damaged building.

(2) If, at the time of loss, the amount of insurance in this policy on the damaged building is less than 80% of the full replacement cost of the building immediately before the loss, we will pay the greater of the following amounts, but not more than the limit of liability under this policy that applies to the building:

(a) The actual cash value of that part of the building damaged; or

(b) That proportion of the cost to repair or replace, after application of deductible and without deduction for depreciation, that part of the building damaged, which the total amount of insurance in this policy on the damaged building bears to 80% of the replacement cost of the building.

(3) To determine the amount of insurance required to equal 80% of the full replacement cost of the building immediately before the loss, do not include the value of:

(a) Excavations, foundations, piers or any supports which are below the under-surface of the lowest basement floor;

(b) Those supports in (a) above which are below the surface of the ground inside the foundation walls, if there is no basement; and

(c) Underground flues, pipes, wiring and drains.

(4) We will pay no more than the actual cash value of the damage until actual repair or replacement is complete. Once actual repair or replacement is complete, we will settle the loss according to the provisions of **b.(1)** and **b.(2)** above.

However, if the cost to repair or replace the damage is both:

(a) Less than 5% of the amount of insurance in this policy on the building; and

(b) Less than $2500;

we will settle the loss according to the provisions of **b.(1)** and **b.(2)** above whether or not actual repair or replacement is complete.

Copyright, Insurance Services Office, Inc., 1990

HO 00 03 04 91

HO 00 03 04 91

**(5)** You may disregard the replacement cost loss settlement provisions and make claim under this policy for loss or damage to buildings on an actual cash value basis. You may then make claim within 180 days after loss for any additional liability according to the provisions of this Condition 3. Loss Settlement.

**4. Loss to a Pair or Set.** In case of loss to a pair or set we may elect to:

**a.** Repair or replace any part to restore the pair or set to its value before the loss; or

**b.** Pay the difference between actual cash value of the property before and after the loss.

**5. Glass Replacement.** Loss for damage to glass caused by a Peril Insured Against will be settled on the basis of replacement with safety glazing materials when required by ordinance or law.

**6. Appraisal.** If you and we fail to agree on the amount of loss, either may demand an appraisal of the loss. In this event, each party will choose a competent appraiser within 20 days after receiving a written request from the other. The two appraisers will choose an umpire. If they cannot agree upon an umpire within 15 days, you or we may request that the choice be made by a judge of a court of record in the state where the "residence premises" is located. The appraisers will separately set the amount of loss. If the appraisers submit a written report of an agreement to us, the amount agreed upon will be the amount of loss. If they fail to agree, they will submit their differences to the umpire. A decision agreed to by any two will set the amount of loss.

Each party will:

**a.** Pay its own appraiser; and

**b.** Bear the other expenses of the appraisal and umpire equally.

**7. Other Insurance.** If a loss covered by this policy is also covered by other insurance, we will pay only the proportion of the loss that the limit of liability that applies under this policy bears to the total amount of insurance covering the loss.

**8. Suit Against Us.** No action can be brought unless the policy provisions have been complied with and the action is started within one year after the date of loss.

**9. Our Option.** If we give you written notice within 30 days after we receive your signed, sworn proof of loss, we may repair or replace any part of the damaged property with like property.

**10.Loss Payment.** We will adjust all losses with you. We will pay you unless some other person is named in the policy or is legally entitled to receive payment. Loss will be payable 60 days after we receive your proof of loss and:

**a.** Reach an agreement with you;

**b.** There is an entry of a final judgment; or

**c.** There is a filing of an appraisal award with us.

**11.Abandonment of Property.** We need not accept any property abandoned by an "insured."

**12.Mortgage Clause.**

The word "mortgagee" includes trustee.

If a mortgagee is named in this policy, any loss payable under Coverage A or B will be paid to the mortgagee and you, as interests appear. If more than one mortgagee is named, the order of payment will be the same as the order of precedence of the mortgages.

If we deny your claim, that denial will not apply to a valid claim of the mortgagee, if the mortgagee:

**a.** Notifies us of any change in ownership, occupancy or substantial change in risk of which the mortgagee is aware;

**b.** Pays any premium due under this policy on demand if you have neglected to pay the premium; and

**c.** Submits a signed, sworn statement of loss within 60 days after receiving notice from us of your failure to do so. Policy conditions relating to Appraisal, Suit Against Us and Loss Payment apply to the mortgagee.

If we decide to cancel or not to renew this policy, the mortgagee will be notified at least 10 days before the date cancellation or nonrenewal takes effect.

If we pay the mortgagee for any loss and deny payment to you:

**a.** We are subrogated to all the rights of the mortgagee granted under the mortgage on the property; or

**b.** At our option, we may pay to the mortgagee the whole principal on the mortgage plus any accrued interest. In this event, we will receive a full assignment and transfer of the mortgage and all securities held as collateral to the mortgage debt.

Subrogation will not impair the right of the mortgagee to recover the full amount of the mortgagee's claim.

HO 00 03 04 91

13.**No Benefit to Bailee.** We will not recognize any assignment or grant any coverage that benefits a person or organization holding, storing or moving property for a fee regardless of any other provision of this policy.

14.**Nuclear Hazard Clause.**

a. "Nuclear Hazard" means any nuclear reaction, radiation, or radioactive contamination, all whether controlled or uncontrolled or however caused, or any consequence of any of these.

b. Loss caused by the nuclear hazard will not be considered loss caused by fire, explosion, or smoke, whether these perils are specifically named in or otherwise included within the Perils Insured Against in Section I.

c. This policy does not apply under Section I to loss caused directly or indirectly by nuclear hazard, except that direct loss by fire resulting from the nuclear hazard is covered.

15.**Recovered Property.** If you or we recover any property for which we have made payment under this policy, you or we will notify the other of the recovery. At your option, the property will be returned to or retained by you or it will become our property. If the recovered property is returned to or retained by you, the loss payment will be adjusted based on the amount you received for the recovered property.

16.**Volcanic Eruption Period.** One or more volcanic eruptions that occur within a 72-hour period will be considered as one volcanic eruption.

## SECTION II – LIABILITY COVERAGES

### COVERAGE E - Personal Liability

If a claim is made or a suit is brought against an "insured" for damages because of "bodily injury" or "property damage" caused by an "occurrence" to which this coverage applies, we will:

1. Pay up to our limit of liability for the damages for which the "insured" is legally liable. Damages include prejudgment interest awarded against the "insured"; and

2. Provide a defense at our expense by counsel of our choice, even if the suit is groundless, false or fraudulent. We may investigate and settle any claim or suit that we decide is appropriate. Our duty to settle or defend ends when the amount we pay for damages resulting from the "occurrence" equals our limit of liability.

### COVERAGE F - Medical Payments To Others

We will pay the necessary medical expenses that are incurred or medically ascertained within three years from the date of an accident causing "bodily injury." Medical expenses means reasonable charges for medical, surgical, x-ray, dental, ambulance, hospital, professional nursing, prosthetic devices and funeral services. This coverage does not apply to you or regular residents of your household except "residence employees." As to others, this coverage applies only:

1. To a person on the "insured location" with the permission of an "insured"; or

2. To a person off the "insured location," if the "bodily injury":

a. Arises out of a condition on the "insured location" or the ways immediately adjoining;

b. Is caused by the activities of an "insured";

c. Is caused by a "residence employee" in the course of the "residence employee's" employment by an "insured"; or

d. Is caused by an animal owned by or in the care of an "insured."

## SECTION II – EXCLUSIONS

1. **Coverage E - Personal Liability** and **Coverage F - Medical Payments to Others** do not apply to "bodily injury" or "property damage":

a. Which is expected or intended by the "insured";

b. Arising out of or in connection with a "business" engaged in by an "insured." This exclusion applies but is not limited to an act or omission, regardless of its nature or circumstance, involving a service or duty rendered, promised, owed, or implied to be provided because of the nature of the "business":

Page 12 of 18          Copyright, Insurance Services Office, Inc., 1990          HO 00 03 04 91

HO 00 03 04 91

c. Arising out of the rental or holding for rental of any part of any premises by an "insured." This exclusion does not apply to the rental or holding for rental of an "insured location":

   (1) On an occasional basis if used only as a residence;

   (2) In part for use only as a residence, unless a single family unit is intended for use by the occupying family to lodge more than two roomers or boarders; or

   (3) In part, as an office, school, studio or private garage;

d. Arising out of the rendering of or failure to render professional services;

e. Arising out of a premises:

   (1) Owned by an "insured";

   (2) Rented to an "insured"; or

   (3) Rented to others by an "insured";

   that is not an "insured location";

f. Arising out of:

   (1) The ownership, maintenance, use, loading or unloading of motor vehicles or all other motorized land conveyances, including trailers, owned or operated by or rented or loaned to an "insured";

   (2) The entrustment by an "insured" of a motor vehicle or any other motorized land conveyance to any person; or

   (3) Vicarious liability, whether or not statutorily imposed, for the actions of a child or minor using a conveyance excluded in paragraph (1) or (2) above.

   This exclusion does not apply to:

   (1) A trailer not towed by or carried on a motorized land conveyance.

   (2) A motorized land conveyance designed for recreational use off public roads, not subject to motor vehicle registration and:

      (a) Not owned by an "insured"; or

      (b) Owned by an "insured" and on an "insured location";

   (3) A motorized golf cart when used to play golf on a golf course;

   (4) A vehicle or conveyance not subject to motor vehicle registration which is:

      (a) Used to service an "insured's" residence;

      (b) Designed for assisting the handicapped; or

      (c) In dead storage on an "insured location";

g. Arising out of:

   (1) The ownership, maintenance, use, loading or unloading of an excluded watercraft described below;

   (2) The entrustment by an "insured" of an excluded watercraft described below to any person; or

   (3) Vicarious liability, whether or not statutorily imposed, for the actions of a child or minor using an excluded watercraft described below.

   Excluded watercraft are those that are principally designed to be propelled by engine power or electric motor, or are sailing vessels, whether owned by or rented to an "insured." This exclusion does not apply to watercraft:

   (1) That are not sailing vessels and are powered by:

      (a) Inboard or inboard-outdrive engine or motor power of 50 horsepower or less not owned by an "insured";

      (b) Inboard or inboard-outdrive engine or motor power of more than 50 horsepower not owned by or rented to an "insured";

      (c) One or more outboard engines or motors with 25 total horsepower or less;

      (d) One or more outboard engines or motors with more than 25 total horsepower if the outboard engine or motor is not owned by an "insured";

      (e) Outboard engines or motors of more than 25 total horsepower owned by an "insured" if:

         (i) You acquire them prior to the policy period; and

            (a) You declare them at policy inception; or

            (b) Your intention to insure is reported to us in writing within 45 days after you acquire the outboard engines or motors.

         (ii) You acquire them during the policy period.

         This coverage applies for the policy period.

   (2) That are sailing vessels, with or without auxiliary power:

      (a) Less than 26 feet in overall length;

      (b) 26 feet or more in overall length, not owned by or rented to an "insured."

HO 00 03 04 91

**(3)** That are stored;

**h.** Arising out of:

**(1)** The ownership, maintenance, use, loading or unloading of an aircraft;

**(2)** The entrustment by an "insured" of an aircraft to any person; or

**(3)** Vicarious liability, whether or not statutorily imposed, for the actions of a child or minor using an aircraft.

An aircraft means any contrivance used or designed for flight, except model or hobby aircraft not used or designed to carry people or cargo;

**i.** Caused directly or indirectly by war, including the following and any consequence of any of the following:

**(1)** Undeclared war, civil war, insurrection, rebellion or revolution;

**(2)** Warlike act by a military force or military personnel; or

**(3)** Destruction, seizure or use for a military purpose.

Discharge of a nuclear weapon will be deemed a warlike act even if accidental;

**j.** Which arises out of the transmission of a communicable disease by an "insured";

**k.** Arising out of sexual molestation, corporal punishment or physical or mental abuse; or

**l.** Arising out of the use, sale, manufacture, delivery, transfer or possession by any person of a Controlled Substance(s) as defined by the Federal Food and Drug Law at 21 U.S.C.A. Sections 811 and 812. Controlled Substances include but are not limited to cocaine, LSD, marijuana and all narcotic drugs. However, this exclusion does not apply to the legitimate use of prescription drugs by a person following the orders of a licensed physician.

Exclusions **e., f., g.,** and **h.** do not apply to "bodily injury" to a "residence employee" arising out of and in the course of the "residence employee's" employment by an "insured."

**2. Coverage E - Personal Liability,** does not apply to:

**a.** Liability:

**(1)** For any loss assessment charged against you as a member of an association, corporation or community of property owners;

**(2)** Under any contract or agreement. However, this exclusion does not apply to written contracts:

**(a)** That directly relate to the ownership, maintenance or use of an "insured location"; or

**(b)** Where the liability of others is assumed by the "insured" prior to an "occurrence";

unless excluded in **(1)** above or elsewhere in this policy;

**b.** "Property damage" to property owned by the "insured";

**c.** "Property damage" to property rented to, occupied or used by or in the care of the "insured." This exclusion does not apply to "property damage" caused by fire, smoke or explosion;

**d.** "Bodily injury" to any person eligible to receive any benefits:

**(1)** Voluntarily provided; or

**(2)** Required to be provided;

by the "insured" under any:

**(1)** Workers' compensation law;

**(2)** Non-occupational disability law; or

**(3)** Occupational disease law;

**e.** "Bodily injury" or "property damage" for which an "insured" under this policy:

**(1)** Is also an insured under a nuclear energy liability policy; or

**(2)** Would be an insured under that policy but for the exhaustion of its limit of liability.

A nuclear energy liability policy is one issued by:

**(1)** American Nuclear Insurers;

**(2)** Mutual Atomic Energy Liability Underwriters;

**(3)** Nuclear Insurance Association of Canada;

or any of their successors; or

**f.** "Bodily injury" to you or an "insured" within the meaning of part **a.** or **b.** of "insured" as defined.

**3. Coverage F - Medical Payments to Others,** does not apply to "bodily injury":

**a.** To a "residence employee" if the "bodily injury":

**(1)** Occurs off the "insured location"; and

**(2)** Does not arise out of or in the course of the "residence employee's" employment by an "insured";

   Copyright, Insurance Services Office, Inc., 1990   HO 00 03 04 91

HO 00 03 04 91

b. To any person eligible to receive benefits:

(1) Voluntarily provided; or

(2) Required to be provided;

under any:

(1) Workers' compensation law;

(2) Non-occupational disability law; or

(3) Occupational disease law;

c. From any:

(1) Nuclear reaction;

(2) Nuclear radiation; or

(3) Radioactive contamination;

all whether controlled or uncontrolled or however caused; or

(4) Any consequence of any of these; or

d. To any person, other than a "residence employee" of an "insured," regularly residing on any part of the "insured location."

## SECTION II – ADDITIONAL COVERAGES

We cover the following in addition to the limits of liability:

1. **Claim Expenses.** We pay:

   a. Expenses we incur and costs taxed against an "insured" in any suit we defend;

   b. Premiums on bonds required in a suit we defend, but not for bond amounts more than the limit of liability for Coverage E. We need not apply for or furnish any bond;

   c. Reasonable expenses incurred by an "insured" at our request, including actual loss of earnings (but not loss of other income) up to $50 per day, for assisting us in the investigation or defense of a claim or suit; and

   d. Interest on the entire judgment which accrues after entry of the judgment and before we pay or tender, or deposit in court that part of the judgment which does not exceed the limit of liability that applies.

2. **First Aid Expenses.** We will pay expenses for first aid to others incurred by an "insured" for "bodily injury" covered under this policy. We will not pay for first aid to you or any other "insured."

3. **Damage to Property of Others.** We will pay, at replacement cost, up to $500 per "occurrence" for "property damage" to property of others caused by an "insured."

   We will not pay for "property damage":

   a. To the extent of any amount recoverable under Section I of this policy;

   b. Caused intentionally by an "insured" who is 13 years of age or older;

   c. To property owned by an "insured";

   d. To property owned by or rented to a tenant of an "insured" or a resident in your household; or

   e. Arising out of:

   (1) A "business" engaged in by an "insured";

   (2) Any act or omission in connection with a premises owned, rented or controlled by an "insured," other than the "insured location"; or

   (3) The ownership, maintenance, or use of aircraft, watercraft or motor vehicles or all other motorized land conveyances.

   This exclusion does not apply to a motorized land conveyance designed for recreational use off public roads, not subject to motor vehicle registration and not owned by an "insured."

4. **Loss Assessment.** We will pay up to $1000 for your share of loss assessment charged during the policy period against you by a corporation or association of property owners, when the assessment is made as a result of:

   a. "Bodily injury" or "property damage" not excluded under Section II of this policy; or

   b. Liability for an act of a director, officer or trustee in the capacity as a director, officer or trustee, provided:

   (1) The director, officer or trustee is elected by the members of a corporation or association of property owners; and

   (2) The director, officer or trustee serves without deriving any income from the exercise of duties which are solely on behalf of a corporation or association of property owners.

   This coverage applies only to loss assessments charged against you as owner or tenant of the "residence premises."

    Copyright, Insurance Services Office, Inc., 1990

HO 00 03 04 91

We do not cover loss assessments charged against you or a corporation or association of property owners by any governmental body.

Regardless of the number of assessments, the limit of $1000 is the most we will pay for loss arising out of:

a. One accident, including continuous or repeated exposure to substantially the same general harmful condition; or

b. A covered act of a director, officer or trustee. An act involving more than one director, officer or trustee is considered to be a single act.

The following do not apply to this coverage:

1. Section II - Coverage E - Personal Liability Exclusion 2.a.(1);

2. Condition 1. Policy Period, under SECTIONS I AND II - CONDITIONS.

## SECTION II – CONDITIONS

1. **Limit of Liability.** Our total liability under Coverage E for all damages resulting from any one "occurrence" will not be more than the limit of liability for Coverage E as shown in the Declarations. This limit is the same regardless of the number of "insureds," claims made or persons injured. All "bodily injury" and "property damage" resulting from any one accident or from continuous or repeated exposure to substantially the same general harmful conditions shall be considered to be the result of one "occurrence."

   Our total liability under Coverage F for all medical expense payable for "bodily injury" to one person as the result of one accident will not be more than the limit of liability for Coverage F as shown in the Declarations.

2. **Severability of Insurance.** This insurance applies separately to each "insured." This condition will not increase our limit of liability for any one "occurrence."

3. **Duties After Loss.** In case of an accident or "occurrence," the "insured" will perform the following duties that apply. You will help us by seeing that these duties are performed:

   a. Give written notice to us or our agent as soon as is practical, which sets forth:

      (1) The identity of the policy and "insured";

      (2) Reasonably available information on the time, place and circumstances of the accident or "occurrence"; and

      (3) Names and addresses of any claimants and witnesses;

   b. Promptly forward to us every notice, demand, summons or other process relating to the accident or "occurrence";

   c. At our request, help us:

      (1) To make settlement;

      (2) To enforce any right of contribution or indemnity against any person or organization who may be liable to an "insured";

      (3) With the conduct of suits and attend hearings and trials; and

      (4) To secure and give evidence and obtain the attendance of witnesses;

   d. Under the coverage - Damage to Property of Others - submit to us within 60 days after the loss, a sworn statement of loss and show the damaged property, if in the "insured's" control;

   e. The "insured" will not, except at the "insured's" own cost, voluntarily make payment, assume obligation or incur expense other than for first aid to others at the time of the "bodily injury."

4. **Duties of an Injured Person - Coverage F - Medical Payments to Others.**

   The injured person or someone acting for the injured person will:

   a. Give us written proof of claim, under oath if required, as soon as is practical; and

   b. Authorize us to obtain copies of medical reports and records.

   The injured person will submit to a physical exam by a doctor of our choice when and as often as we reasonably require.

5. **Payment of Claim - Coverage F - Medical Payments to Others.** Payment under this coverage is not an admission of liability by an "insured" or us.

  Copyright, Insurance Services Office, Inc., 1990  HO 00 03 04 91

HO 00 03 04 91

**6. Suit Against Us.** No action can be brought against us unless there has been compliance with the policy provisions.

No one will have the right to join us as a party to any action against an "insured." Also, no action with respect to Coverage E can be brought against us until the obligation of the "insured" has been determined by final judgment or agreement signed by us.

**7. Bankruptcy of an Insured.** Bankruptcy or insolvency of an "insured" will not relieve us of our obligations under this policy.

**8. Other Insurance - Coverage E - Personal Liability.** This insurance is excess over other valid and collectible insurance except insurance written specifically to cover as excess over the limits of liability that apply in this policy.

## SECTIONS I AND II – CONDITIONS

**1. Policy Period.** This policy applies only to loss in Section I or "bodily injury" or "property damage" in Section II, which occurs during the policy period.

**2. Concealment or Fraud.** The entire policy will be void if, whether before or after a loss, an "insured" has:

a. Intentionally concealed or misrepresented any material fact or circumstance;

b. Engaged in fraudulent conduct; or

c. Made false statements;

relating to this insurance.

**3. Liberalization Clause.** If we make a change which broadens coverage under this edition of our policy without additional premium charge, that change will automatically apply to your insurance as of the date we implement the change in your state, provided that this implementation date falls within 60 days prior to or during the policy period stated in the Declarations.

This Liberalization Clause does not apply to changes implemented through introduction of a subsequent edition of our policy.

**4. Waiver or Change of Policy Provisions.**

A waiver or change of a provision of this policy must be in writing by us to be valid. Our request for an appraisal or examination will not waive any of our rights.

**5. Cancellation.**

a. You may cancel this policy at any time by returning it to us or by letting us know in writing of the date cancellation is to take effect.

b. We may cancel this policy only for the reasons stated below by letting you know in writing of the date cancellation takes effect. This cancellation notice may be delivered to you, or mailed to you at your mailing address shown in the Declarations.

Proof of mailing will be sufficient proof of notice.

(1) When you have not paid the premium, we may cancel at any time by letting you know at least 10 days before the date cancellation takes effect.

(2) When this policy has been in effect for less than 60 days and is not a renewal with us, we may cancel for any reason by letting you know at least 10 days before the date cancellation takes effect.

(3) When this policy has been in effect for 60 days or more, or at any time if it is a renewal with us, we may cancel:

(a) If there has been a material misrepresentation of fact which if known to us would have caused us not to issue the policy; or

(b) If the risk has changed substantially since the policy was issued.

This can be done by letting you know at least 30 days before the date cancellation takes effect.

(4) When this policy is written for a period of more than one year, we may cancel for any reason at anniversary by letting you know at least 30 days before the date cancellation takes effect.

c. When this policy is cancelled, the premium for the period from the date of cancellation to the expiration date will be refunded pro rata.

d. If the return premium is not refunded with the notice of cancellation or when this policy is returned to us, we will refund it within a reasonable time after the date cancellation takes effect.

**6. Nonrenewal.** We may elect not to renew this policy. We may do so by delivering to you, or mailing to you at your mailing address shown in the Declarations, written notice at least 30 days before the expiration date of this policy. Proof of mailing will be sufficient proof of notice.

**7. Assignment.** Assignment of this policy will not be valid unless we give our written consent.

HO 00 03 04 91

8. **Subrogation.** An "insured" may waive in writing before a loss all rights of recovery against any person. If not waived, we may require an assignment of rights of recovery for a loss to the extent that payment is made by us.

   If an assignment is sought, an "insured" must sign and deliver all related papers and cooperate with us.

   Subrogation does not apply under Section II to Medical Payments to Others or Damage to Property of Others.

9. **Death.** If any person named in the Declarations or the spouse, if a resident of the same household, dies:

a. We insure the legal representative of the deceased but only with respect to the premises and property of the deceased covered under the policy at the time of death;

b. "Insured" includes:

   (1) Any member of your household who is an "insured" at the time of your death, but only while a resident of the "residence premises"; and

   (2) With respect to your property, the person having proper temporary custody of the property until appointment and qualification of a legal representative.

# *Appendix B*

# PERSONAL AUTO POLICY

## Personal Auto Policy Declarations

POLICYHOLDER:      David M. and Joan G. Smith
(Named Insured)    216 Brookside Drive
                   Anytown, USA 40000

POLICY NUMBER:     296 S 468211

POLICY PERIOD:     FROM:   December 25, 1994
                   TO:     June 25, 1995

But only if the required premium for this period has been paid, and for six-month renewal periods if renewal premiums are paid as required. Each period begins and ends at 12:01 A.M. standard time at the address of the policyholder.

INSURED VEHICLES AND
SCHEDULE OF COVERAGES

| VEHICLE COVERAGES | LIMITS OF INSURANCE | PREMIUM |
|---|---|---|
| 1      1985 Toyota Tercel | ID #JT2AL21E8B3306553 | |
| Coverage A— Liability | $ 300,000 Each Occurrence | $ 101.50 |
| Coverage B—Medical Payments | $ 5,000 Each Person | $ 18.00 |
| Coverage C—Uninsured Motorists | $ 300,000 Each Occurrence | $ 30.90 |
| | TOTAL | $ 150.40 |
| 2      1993 Ford Taurus | ID #1FABP3OU7GG212619 | |
| Coverage A—Liability | $ 300,000 Each Occurrence | $ 101.50 |
| Coverage B—Medical Payments | $ 5,000 Each Person | $ 18.00 |
| Coverage C—Uninsured Motorists | $ 300,000 Each Occurrence | $ 30.90 |
| Coverage D—Other Than Collision | Actual Cash Value Less $ 100 | $ 20.80 |
| —Collision | Actual Cash Value Less $ 250 | $ 115.50 |
| | TOTAL | $ 286.70 |

POLICY FORM AND ENDORSEMENTS:      PP 00 01, PP 03 06

COUNTERSIGNATURE DATE:      December 1, 1994

AGENT:      A.M. Abel

**SAMPLE**

# PERSONAL AUTO POLICY

## AGREEMENT

In return for payment of the premium and subject to all the terms of this policy, we agree with you as follows:

## DEFINITIONS

**A.** Throughout this policy, "you" and "your" refer to:

   **1.** The "named insured" shown in the Declarations; and

   **2.** The spouse if a resident of the same household.

**B.** "We", "us" and "our" refer to the Company providing this insurance.

**C.** For purposes of this policy, a private passenger type auto shall be deemed to be owned by a person if leased:

   **1.** Under a written agreement to that person; and

   **2.** For a continuous period of at least 6 months.

Other words and phrases are defined. They are in quotation marks when used.

**D.** "Bodily injury" means bodily harm, sickness or disease, including death that results.

**E.** "Business" includes trade, profession or occupation.

**F.** "Family member" means a person related to you by blood, marriage or adoption who is a resident of your household. This includes a ward or foster child.

**G.** "Occupying" means in, upon, getting in, on, out or off.

**H.** "Property damage" means physical injury to, destruction of or loss of use of tangible property.

**I.** "Trailer" means a vehicle designed to be pulled by a:

   **1.** Private passenger auto; or

   **2.** Pickup or van.

   It also means a farm wagon or farm implement while towed by a vehicle listed in **1.** or **2.** above.

**J.** "Your covered auto" means:

   **1.** Any vehicle shown in the Declarations.

   **2.** Any of the following types of vehicles on the date you become the owner:

      **a.** A private passenger auto; or

      **b.** A pickup or van that:

         **(1)** Has a Gross Vehicle Weight of less than 10,000 lbs.; and

         **(2)** Is not used for the delivery or transportation of goods and materials unless such use is:

            **(a)** Incidental to your "business" of installing, maintaining or repairing furnishings or equipment; or

            **(b)** For farming or ranching.

      This provision (**J.2.**) applies only if:

      **a.** You acquire the vehicle during the policy period;

      **b.** You ask us to insure it within 30 days after you become the owner; and

      **c.** With respect to a pickup or van, no other insurance policy provides coverage for that vehicle.

      If the vehicle you acquire replaces one shown in the Declarations, it will have the same coverage as the vehicle it replaced. You must ask us to insure a replacement vehicle within 30 days only if you wish to add or continue Coverage for Damage to Your Auto.

      If the vehicle you acquire is in addition to any shown in the Declarations, it will have the broadest coverage we now provide for any vehicle shown in the Declarations.

   **3.** Any "trailer" you own.

   **4.** Any auto or "trailer" you do not own while used as a temporary substitute for any other vehicle described in this definition which is out of normal use because of its:

      **a.** Breakdown;          **d.** Loss; or
      **b.** Repair;             **e.** Destruction.
      **c.** Servicing;

      This provision (**J.4.**) does not apply to Coverage for Damage to Your Auto.

# SAMPLE

"Personal Auto Policy" reprinted with permission. Copyright, Insurance Services Office, Inc., 1994.

## PART A - LIABILITY COVERAGE

### INSURING AGREEMENT

**A.** We will pay damages for "bodily injury" or "property damage" for which any "insured" becomes legally responsible because of an auto accident. Damages include prejudgment interest awarded against the "insured". We will settle or defend, as we consider appropriate, any claim or suit asking for these damages. In addition to our limit of liability, we will pay all defense costs we incur. Our duty to settle or defend ends when our limit of liability for this coverage has been exhausted. We have no duty to defend any suit or settle any claim for "bodily injury" or "property damage" not covered under this policy.

**B.** "Insured" as used in this Part means:

1. You or any "family member" for the ownership, maintenance or use of any auto or "trailer"

2. Any person using "your covered auto".

3. For "your covered auto", any person or organization but only with respect to legal responsibility for acts or omissions of a person for whom coverage is afforded under this Part.

4. For any auto or "trailer", other than "your covered auto", any other person or organization but only with respect to legal responsibility for acts or omissions of you or any "family member" for whom coverage is afforded under this Part. This provision (**B.4.**) applies only if the person or organization does not own or hire the auto or "trailer".

### SUPPLEMENTARY PAYMENTS

In addition to our limit of liability, we will pay on behalf of an "insured":

1. Up to $250 for the cost of bail bonds required because of an accident, including related traffic law violations. The accident must result in "bodily injury" or "property damage" covered under this policy.

2. Premiums on appeal bonds and bonds to release attachments in any suit we defend.

3. Interest accruing after a judgment is entered in any suit we defend. Our duty to pay interest ends when we offer to pay that part of the judgment which does not exceed our limit of liability for this coverage.

4. Up to $50 a day for loss of earnings, but not other income, because of attendance at hearings or trials at our request.

5. Other reasonable expenses incurred at our request.

### EXCLUSIONS

**A.** We do not provide Liability Coverage for any "insured":

1. Who intentionally causes "bodily injury" or "property damage".

2. For "property damage" to property owned or being transported by that "insured".

3. For "property damage" to property:

   a. Rented to;

   b. Used by; or

   c. In the care of;

   that "insured".

   This exclusion (**A.3.**) does not apply to "property damage" to a residence or private garage.

4. For "bodily injury" to an employee of that "insured" during the course of employment. This exclusion (**A.4.**) does not apply to "bodily injury" to a domestic employee unless workers' compensation benefits are required or available for that domestic employee.

5. For that "insured's" liability arising out of the ownership or operation of a vehicle while it is being used as a public or livery conveyance. This exclusion (**A.5.**) does not apply to a share-the-expense car pool.

6. While employed or otherwise engaged in the "business" of:

   a. Selling;          d. Storing; or
   b. Repairing;        e. Parking;
   c. Servicing;

   vehicles designed for use mainly on public highways. This includes road testing and delivery. This exclusion (**A.6.**) does not apply to the ownership, maintenance or use of "your covered auto" by:

   a. You;

   b. Any "family member"; or

   c. Any partner, agent or employee of you or any "family member".

      Copyright, Insurance Services Office, Inc., 1994      PP 00 01 06 94

**SAMPLE**

7. Maintaining or using any vehicle while that "insured" is employed or otherwise engaged in any "business" (other than farming or ranching) not described in exclusion **A.6.**

   This exclusion (**A.7.**) does not apply to the maintenance or use of a:

   a. Private passenger auto;

   b. Pickup or van that:

      (1) You own; or

      (2) You do not own while used as a temporary substitute for "your covered auto" which is out of normal use because of its:

         (a) Breakdown;    (d) Loss; or
         (b) Repair;       (e) Destruction; or
         (c) Servicing;

   c. "Trailer" used with a vehicle described in a. or b. above.

8. Using a vehicle without a reasonable belief that that "insured" is entitled to do so.

9. For "bodily injury" or "property damage" for which that "insured":

   a. Is an insured under a nuclear energy liability policy; or

   b. Would be an insured under a nuclear energy liability policy but for its termination upon exhaustion of its limit of liability.

   A nuclear energy liability policy is a policy issued by any of the following or their successors:

   a. American Nuclear Insurers;

   b. Mutual Atomic Energy Liability Underwriters; or

   c. Nuclear Insurance Association of Canada.

B. We do not provide Liability Coverage for the ownership, maintenance or use of:

   1. Any vehicle which:

      a. Has fewer than four wheels; or

      b. Is designed mainly for use off public roads.

      This exclusion (**B.1.**) does not apply:

      a. While such vehicle is being used by an "insured" in a medical emergency; or

      b. To any "trailer".

   2. Any vehicle, other than "your covered auto", which is:

      a. Owned by you; or

      b. Furnished or available for your regular use.

3. Any vehicle, other than "your covered auto" which is:

   a. Owned by any "family member"; or

   b. Furnished or available for the regular use of any "family member".

   However, this exclusion (**B.3.**) does not apply to you while you are maintaining or "occupying" any vehicle which is:

   a. Owned by a "family member"; or

   b. Furnished or available for the regular use of a "family member".

4. Any vehicle, located inside a facility designed for racing, for the purpose of:

   a. Competing in; or

   b. Practicing or preparing for;

   any prearranged or organized racing or speed contest.

## LIMIT OF LIABILITY

A. The limit of liability shown in the Declarations for this coverage is our maximum limit of liability for all damages resulting from any one auto accident. This is the most we will pay regardless of the number of:

   1. "Insureds";

   2. Claims made;

   3. Vehicles or premiums shown in the Declarations; or

   4. Vehicles involved in the auto accident.

B. We will apply the limit of liability to provide any separate limits required by law for bodily injury and property damage liability. However, this provision (**B.**) will not change our total limit of liability.

C. No one will be entitled to receive duplicate payments for the same elements of loss under this coverage and:

   1. Part **B** or Part **C** of this policy; or

   2. Any Underinsured Motorists Coverage provided by this policy.

**SAMPLE**

## OUT OF STATE COVERAGE

If an auto accident to which this policy applies occurs in any state or province other than the one in which "your covered auto" is principally garaged, we will interpret your policy for that accident as follows:

A. If the state or province has:

1. A financial responsibility or similar law specifying limits of liability for "bodily injury" or "property damage" higher than the limit shown in the Declarations, your policy will provide the higher specified limit.

2. A compulsory insurance or similar law requiring a nonresident to maintain insurance whenever the nonresident uses a vehicle in that state or province, your policy will provide at least the required minimum amounts and types of coverage.

B. No one will be entitled to duplicate payments for the same elements of loss.

## FINANCIAL RESPONSIBILITY

When this policy is certified as future proof of financial responsibility, this policy shall comply with the law to the extent required.

## OTHER INSURANCE

If there is other applicable liability insurance we will pay only our share of the loss. Our share is the proportion that our limit of liability bears to the total of all applicable limits. However, any insurance we provide for a vehicle you do not own shall be excess over any other collectible insurance.

## PART B - MEDICAL PAYMENTS COVERAGE

### INSURING AGREEMENT

A. We will pay reasonable expenses incurred for necessary medical and funeral services because of "bodily injury":

1. Caused by accident; and

2. Sustained by an "insured".

We will pay only those expenses incurred for services rendered within 3 years from the date of the accident.

B. "Insured" as used in this Part means:

1. You or any "family member":

a. While "occupying"; or

b. As a pedestrian when struck by;

a motor vehicle designed for use mainly on public roads or a trailer of any type.

2. Any other person while "occupying" "your covered auto".

### EXCLUSIONS

We do not provide Medical Payments Coverage for any "insured" for "bodily injury":

1. Sustained while "occupying" any motorized vehicle having fewer than four wheels.

2. Sustained while "occupying" "your covered auto" when it is being used as a public or livery conveyance. This exclusion (2.) does not apply to a share-the-expense car pool.

3. Sustained while "occupying" any vehicle located for use as a residence or premises.

4. Occurring during the course of employment if workers' compensation benefits are required or available for the "bodily injury".

5. Sustained while "occupying", or when struck by, any vehicle (other than "your covered auto") which is:

a. Owned by you; or

b. Furnished or available for your regular use.

6. Sustained while "occupying", or when struck by, any vehicle (other than "your covered auto") which is:

a. Owned by any "family member"; or

b. Furnished or available for the regular use of any "family member".

However, this exclusion (6.) does not apply to you.

7. Sustained while "occupying" a vehicle without a reasonable belief that that "insured" is entitled to do so.

8. Sustained while "occupying" a vehicle when it is being used in the "business" of an "insured". This exclusion (8.) does not apply to "bodily injury" sustained while "occupying" a:

a. Private passenger auto;

b. Pickup or van that you own; or

c. "Trailer" used with a vehicle described in a. or b. above.

9. Caused by or as a consequence of:

a. Discharge of a nuclear weapon (even if accidental);

b. War (declared or undeclared);

c. Civil war;

d. Insurrection; or

e. Rebellion or revolution.

10. From or as a consequence of the following, whether controlled or uncontrolled or however caused:

a. Nuclear reaction;

b. Radiation; or

c. Radioactive contamination.

Copyright, Insurance Services Office, Inc., 1994   PP 00 01 06 94

**SAMPLE**

11. Sustained while "occupying" any vehicle located inside a facility designed for racing, for the purpose of:

   a. Competing in; or

   b. Practicing or preparing for;

   any prearranged or organized racing or speed contest.

### LIMIT OF LIABILITY

A. The limit of liability shown in the Declarations for this coverage is our maximum limit of liability for each person injured in any one accident. This is the most we will pay regardless of the number of:

1. "Insureds";

2. Claims made;

3. Vehicles or premiums shown in the Declarations; or

4. Vehicles involved in the accident.

B. No one will be entitled to receive duplicate payments for the same elements of loss under this coverage and:

1. Part A or Part C of this policy; or

2. Any Underinsured Motorists Coverage provided by this policy.

### OTHER INSURANCE

If there is other applicable auto medical payments insurance we will pay only our share of the loss. Our share is the proportion that our limit of liability bears to the total of all applicable limits. However, any insurance we provide with respect to a vehicle you do not own shall be excess over any other collectible auto insurance providing payments for medical or funeral expenses.

## PART C - UNINSURED MOTORISTS COVERAGE

### INSURING AGREEMENT

A. We will pay compensatory damages which an "insured" is legally entitled to recover from the owner or operator of an "uninsured motor vehicle" because of "bodily injury":

1. Sustained by an "insured"; and

2. Caused by an accident.

The owner's or operator's liability for these damages must arise out of the ownership, maintenance or use of the "uninsured motor vehicle".

Any judgment for damages arising out of a suit brought without our written consent is not binding on us.

B. "Insured" as used in this Part means:

1. You or any "family member".

2. Any other person "occupying" "your covered auto".

3. Any person for damages that person is entitled to recover because of "bodily injury" to which this coverage applies sustained by a person described in 1. or 2. above.

C. "Uninsured motor vehicle" means a land motor vehicle or trailer of any type:

1. To which no bodily injury liability bond or policy applies at the time of the accident.

2. To which a bodily injury liability bond or policy applies at the time of the accident. In this case its limit for bodily injury liability must be less than the minimum limit for bodily injury liability specified by the financial responsibility law of the state in which "your covered auto" is principally garaged.

3. Which is a hit-and-run vehicle whose operator or owner cannot be identified and which hits:

   a. You or any "family member";

   b. A vehicle which you or any "family member" are "occupying"; or

   c. "Your covered auto".

4. To which a bodily injury liability bond or policy applies at the time of the accident but the bonding or insuring company:

   a. Denies coverage; or

   b. Is or becomes insolvent.

However, "uninsured motor vehicle" does not include any vehicle or equipment:

1. Owned by or furnished or available for the regular use of you or any "family member".

2. Owned or operated by a self-insurer under any applicable motor vehicle law, except a self-insurer which is or becomes insolvent.

3. Owned by any governmental unit or agency.

4. Operated on rails or crawler treads.

5. Designed mainly for use off public roads while not on public roads.

6. While located for use as a residence or premises.

### EXCLUSIONS

A. We do not provide Uninsured Motorists Coverage for "bodily injury" sustained:

1. By an "insured" while "occupying", or when struck by, any motor vehicle owned by that "insured" which is not insured for this coverage under this policy. This includes a trailer of any type used with that vehicle.

**SAMPLE**

2. By any "family member" while "occupying", or when struck by, any motor vehicle you own which is insured for this coverage on a primary basis under any other policy.

B. We do not provide Uninsured Motorists Coverage for "bodily injury" sustained by any "insured":

1. If that "insured" or the legal representative settles the "bodily injury" claim without our consent.

2. While "occupying" "your covered auto" when it is being used as a public or livery conveyance. This exclusion (**B.2.**) does not apply to a share-the-expense car pool.

3. Using a vehicle without a reasonable belief that that "insured" is entitled to do so.

C. This coverage shall not apply directly or indirectly to benefit any insurer or self-insurer under any of the following or similar law:

1. Workers' compensation law; or

2. Disability benefits law.

D. We do not provide Uninsured Motorists Coverage for punitive or exemplary damages.

## LIMIT OF LIABILITY

A. The limit of liability shown in the Declarations for this coverage is our maximum limit of liability for all damages resulting from any one accident. This is the most we will pay regardless of the number of:

1. "Insureds";

2. Claims made;

3. Vehicles or premiums shown in the Declarations; or

4. Vehicles involved in the accident.

B. No one will be entitled to receive duplicate payments for the same elements of loss under this coverage and:

1. Part **A** or Part **B** of this policy; or

2. Any Underinsured Motorists Coverage provided by this policy.

C. We will not make a duplicate payment under this coverage for any element of loss for which payment has been made by or on behalf of persons or organizations who may be legally responsible.

D. We will not pay for any element of loss if a person is entitled to receive payment for the same element of loss under any of the following or similar law:

1. Workers' compensation law; or

2. Disability benefits law.

## OTHER INSURANCE

If there is other applicable insurance available under one or more policies or provisions of coverage:

1. Any recovery for damages under all such policies or provisions of coverage may equal but not exceed the highest applicable limit for any one vehicle under any insurance providing coverage on either a primary or excess basis.

2. Any insurance we provide with respect to a vehicle you do not own shall be excess over any collectible insurance providing coverage on a primary basis.

3. If the coverage under this policy is provided:

a. On a primary basis, we will pay only our share of the loss that must be paid under insurance providing coverage on a primary basis. Our share is the proportion that our limit of liability bears to the total of all applicable limits of liability for coverage provided on a primary basis.

b. On an excess basis, we will pay only our share of the loss that must be paid under insurance providing coverage on an excess basis. Our share is the proportion that our limit of liability bears to the total of all applicable limits of liability for coverage provided on an excess basis.

## ARBITRATION

A. If we and an "insured" do not agree:

1. Whether that "insured" is legally entitled to recover damages; or

2. As to the amount of damages which are recoverable by that "insured";

from the owner or operator of an "uninsured motor vehicle", then the matter may be arbitrated. However, disputes concerning coverage under this Part may not be arbitrated.

Both parties must agree to arbitration. If so agreed, each party will select an arbitrator. The two arbitrators will select a third. If they cannot agree within 30 days, either may request that selection be made by a judge of a court having jurisdiction.

B. Each party will:

1. Pay the expenses it incurs; and

2. Bear the expenses of the third arbitrator equally.

C. Unless both parties agree otherwise, arbitration will take place in the county in which the "insured" lives. Local rules of law as to procedure and evidence will apply. A decision agreed to by two of the arbitrators will be binding as to:

1. Whether the "insured" is legally entitled to recover damages; and

2. The amount of damages. This applies only if the amount does not exceed the minimum limit for bodily injury liability specified by the financial responsibility law of the state in which "your covered auto" is principally garaged. If the amount exceeds that limit, either party may demand the right to a trial. This demand must be made within 60 days of the arbitrators' decision. If this demand is not made, the amount of damages agreed to by the arbitrators will be binding.

**SAMPLE**

## PART D - COVERAGE FOR DAMAGE TO YOUR AUTO

### INSURING AGREEMENT

A. We will pay for direct and accidental loss to "your covered auto" or any "non-owned auto", including their equipment, minus any applicable deductible shown in the Declarations. If loss to more than one "your covered auto" or "non-owned auto" results from the same "collision", only the highest applicable deductible will apply. We will pay for loss to "your covered auto" caused by:

1. Other than "collision" only if the Declarations indicate that Other Than Collision Coverage is provided for that auto.

2. "Collision" only if the Declarations indicate that Collision Coverage is provided for that auto.

If there is a loss to a "non-owned auto", we will provide the broadest coverage applicable to any "your covered auto" shown in the Declarations.

B. "Collision" means the upset of "your covered auto" or a "non-owned auto" or their impact with another vehicle or object.

Loss caused by the following is considered other than "collision":

| | |
|---|---|
| 1. Missiles or falling objects; | 7. Malicious mischief or vandalism; |
| 2. Fire; | 8. Riot or civil commotion; |
| 3. Theft or larceny; | 9. Contact with bird or animal; or |
| 4. Explosion or earthquake; | 10. Breakage of glass |
| 5. Windstorm; | |
| 6. Hail, water or flood; | |

If breakage of glass is caused by a "collision", you may elect to have it considered a loss caused by "collision".

C. "Non-owned auto" means:

1. Any private passenger auto, pickup, van or "trailer" not owned by or furnished or available for the regular use of you or any "family member" while in the custody of or being operated by you or any "family member"; or

2. Any auto or "trailer" you do not own while used as a temporary substitute for "your covered auto" which is out of normal use because of its:

| | |
|---|---|
| a. Breakdown; | d. Loss; or |
| b. Repair; | e. Destruction. |
| c. Servicing; | |

### TRANSPORTATION EXPENSES

In addition, we will pay, without application of a deductible, up to $15 per day, to a maximum of $450, for:

1. Temporary transportation expenses incurred by you in the event of a loss to "your covered auto". We will pay for such expenses if the loss is caused by:

a. Other than "collision" only if the Declarations indicate that Other Than Collision Coverage is provided for that auto.

b. "Collision" only if the Declarations indicate that Collision Coverage is provided for that auto.

2. Loss of use expenses for which you become legally responsible in the event of loss to a "non-owned auto". We will pay for loss of use expenses if the loss is caused by:

a. Other than "collision" only if the Delcarations indicate that Other Than Collision Coverage is provided for any "your covered auto".

b. "Collision" only if the Declarations indicate that Collision Coverage is provided for any "your covered auto".

If the loss is caused by a total theft of "your covered auto" or a "non-owned auto", we will pay only expenses incurred during the period:

1. Beginning 48 hours after the theft; and

2. Ending when "your covered auto" or the "non-owned auto" is returned to use or we pay for its loss.

If the loss is caused by other than theft of a "your covered auto" or a "non-owned auto", we will pay only expenses beginning when the auto is withdrawn from use for more than 24 hours.

Our payment will be limited to that period of time reasonably required to repair or replace the "your covered auto" or the "non-owned auto".

### EXCLUSIONS

We will not pay for:

1. Loss to "your covered auto" or any "non-owned auto" which occurs while it is being used as a public or livery conveyance. This exclusion (1.) does not apply to a share-the-expense car pool.

2. Damage due and confined to:

a. Wear and tear;

b. Freezing;

c. Mechanical or electrical breakdown or failure; or

d. Road damage to tires.

This exclusion (2.) does not apply if the damage results from the total theft of "your covered auto" or any "non-owned auto".

3. Loss due to or as a consequence of:

a. Radioactive contamination;

b. Discharge of any nuclear weapon (even if accidental);

c. War (declared or undeclared);

d. Civil war;

PP 00 01 06 94          Copyright, Insurance Services Office, Inc., 1994          Page 7 of 11

**SAMPLE**

e. Insurrection; or

f. Rebellion or revolution.

4. Loss to:

a. Any electronic equipment designed for the reproduction of sound, including, but not limited to:

(1) Radios and stereos;

(2) Tape decks; or

(3) Compact disc players;

b. Any other electronic equipment that receives or transmits audio, visual or data signals, including, but not limited to:

(1) Citizens band radios;

(2) Telephones;

(3) Two-way mobile radios;

(4) Scanning monitor receivers;

(5) Television monitor receivers;

(6) Video cassette recorders;

(7) Audio cassette recorders; or

(8) Personal computers;

c. Tapes, records, discs, or other media used with equipment described in **a.** or **b.**; or

d. Any other accessories used with equipment described in **a.** or **b.**

This exclusion (**4.**) does not apply to:

a. Equipment designed solely for the reproduction of sound and accessories used with such equipment, provided:

(1) The equipment is permanently installed in "your covered auto" or any "non-owned auto"; or

(2) The equipment is:

(a) Removable from a housing unit which is permanently installed in the auto;

(b) Designed to be solely operated by use of the power from the auto's electrical system; and

(c) In or upon "your covered auto" or any "non-owned auto";

at the time of the loss.

b. Any other electronic equipment that is:

(1) Necessary for the normal operation of the auto or the monitoring of the auto's operating systems; or

(2) An integral part of the same unit housing any sound reproducing equipment described in **a.** and permanently installed in the opening of the dash or console of "your covered auto" or any "non-owned auto" normally used by the manufacturer for installation of a radio.

5. A total loss to "your covered auto" or any "non-owned auto" due to destruction or confiscation by governmental or civil authorities.

This exclusion (**5.**) does not apply to the interests of Loss Payees in "your covered auto".

6. Loss to a camper body or "trailer" you own which is not shown in the Declarations. This exclusion (**6.**) does not apply to a camper body or "trailer" you:

a. Acquire during the policy period; and

b. Ask us to insure within 30 days after you become the owner.

7. Loss to any "non-owned auto" when used by you or any "family member" without a reasonable belief that you or that "family member" are entitled to do so.

8. Loss to:

a. Awnings or cabanas; or

b. Equipment designed to create additional living facilities.

9. Loss to equipment designed or used for the detection or location of radar or laser.

10. Loss to any custom furnishings or equipment in or upon any pickup or van. Custom furnishings or equipment include but are not limited to:

a. Special carpeting and insulation, furniture or bars;

b. Facilities for cooking and sleeping;

c. Height-extending roofs; or

d. Custom murals, paintings or other decals or graphics.

11. Loss to any "non-owned auto" being maintained or used by any person while employed or otherwise engaged in the "business" of:

a. Selling;          d. Storing; or
b. Repairing;        e. Parking;
c. Servicing;

vehicles designed for use on public highways. This includes road testing and delivery.

12. Loss to any "non-owned auto" being maintained or used by any person while employed or otherwise engaged in any "business" not described in exclusion **11.** This exclusion (**12.**) does not apply to the maintenance or use by you or any "family member" of a "non-owned auto" which is a private passenger auto or "trailer".

13. Loss to "your covered auto" or any "non-owned auto", located inside a facility designed for racing, for the purpose of:

a. Competing in; or

b. Practicing or preparing for;

any prearranged or organized racing or speed contest.

Copyright, Insurance Services Office, Inc., 1994          **PP 00 01 06 94**

**SAMPLE**

14. Loss to, or loss of use of, a "non-owned auto" rented by:

    a. You; or

    b. Any "family member";

    if a rental vehicle company is precluded from recovering such loss or loss of use, from you or that "family member", pursuant to the provisions of any applicable rental agreement or state law.

## LIMIT OF LIABILITY

A. Our limit of liability for loss will be the lesser of the:

    1. Actual cash value of the stolen or damaged property;

    2. Amount necessary to repair or replace the property with other property of like kind and quality.

    However, the most we will pay for loss to any "non-owned auto" which is a trailer is $500.

B. An adjustment for depreciation and physical condition will be made in determining actual cash value in the event of a total loss.

C. If a repair or replacement results in better than like kind or quality, we will not pay for the amount of the betterment.

## PAYMENT OF LOSS

We may pay for loss in money or repair or replace the damaged or stolen property. We may, at our expense, return any stolen property to:

    1. You; or

    2. The address shown in this policy.

If we return stolen property we will pay for any damage resulting from the theft. We may keep all or part of the property at an agreed or appraised value.

If we pay for loss in money, our payment will include the applicable sales tax for the damaged or stolen property.

## NO BENEFIT TO BAILEE

This insurance shall not directly or indirectly benefit any carrier or other bailee for hire.

## OTHER SOURCES OF RECOVERY

If other sources of recovery also cover the loss, we will pay only our share of the loss. Our share is the proportion that our limit of liability bears to the total of all applicable limits. However, any insurance we provide with respect to a "non-owned auto" shall be excess over any other collectible source of recovery including, but not limited to:

    1. Any coverage provided by the owner of the "non-owned auto";

    2. Any other applicable physical damage insurance;

    3. Any other source of recovery applicable to the loss.

## APPRAISAL

A. If we and you do not agree on the amount of loss, either may demand an appraisal of the loss. In this event, each party will select a competent appraiser. The two appraisers will select an umpire. The appraisers will state separately the actual cash value and the amount of loss. If they fail to agree, they will submit their differences to the umpire. A decision agreed to by any two will be binding. Each party will:

    1. Pay its chosen appraiser; and

    2. Bear the expenses of the appraisal and umpire equally.

B. We do not waive any of our rights under this policy by agreeing to an appraisal.

## PART E - DUTIES AFTER AN ACCIDENT OR LOSS

We have no duty to provide coverage under this policy unless there has been full compliance with the following duties:

A. We must be notified promptly of how, when and where the accident or loss happened. Notice should also include the names and addresses of any injured persons and of any witnesses.

B. A person seeking any coverage must:

    1. Cooperate with us in the investigation, settlement or defense of any claim or suit.

    2. Promptly send us copies of any notices or legal papers received in connection with the accident or loss.

    3. Submit, as often as we reasonably require:

        a. To physical exams by physicians we select. We will pay for these exams.

        b. To examination under oath and subscribe the same.

    4. Authorize us to obtain:

        a. Medical reports; and

        b. Other pertinent records.

    5. Submit a proof of loss when required by us.

C. A person seeking Uninsured Motorists Coverage must also:

    1. Promptly notify the police if a hit-and-run driver is involved.

    2. Promptly send us copies of the legal papers if a suit is brought.

D. A person seeking Coverage for Damage to Your Auto must also:

    1. Take reasonable steps after loss to protect "your covered auto" or any "non-owned auto" and their equipment from further loss. We will pay reasonable expenses incurred to do this.

    2. Promptly notify the police if "your covered auto" or any "non-owned auto" is stolen.

    3. Permit us to inspect and appraise the damaged property before its repair or disposal.

SAMPLE

## PART F - GENERAL PROVISIONS

### BANKRUPTCY

Bankruptcy or insolvency of the "insured" shall not relieve us of any obligations under this policy.

### CHANGES

A. This policy contains all the agreements between you and us. Its terms may not be changed or waived except by endorsement issued by us.

B. If there is a change to the information used to develop the policy premium, we may adjust your premium. Changes during the policy term that may result in a premium increase or decrease include, but are not limited to, changes in:

1. The number, type or use classification of insured vehicles;

2. Operators using insured vehicles;

3. The place of principal garaging of insured vehicles;

4. Coverage, deductible or limits.

If a change resulting from A. or B. requires a premium adjustment, we will make the premium adjustment in accordance with our manual rules.

C. If we make a change which broadens coverage under this edition of your policy without additional premium charge, that change will automatically apply to your policy as of the date we implement the change in your state. This paragraph (C.) does not apply to changes implemented with a general program revision that includes both broadenings and restrictions in coverage, whether that general program revision is implemented through introduction of:

1. A subsequent edition of your policy; or

2. An Amendatory Endorsement.

### FRAUD

We do not provide coverage for any "insured" who has made fraudulent statements or engaged in fraudulent conduct in connection with any accident or loss for which coverage is sought under this policy.

### LEGAL ACTION AGAINST US

A. No legal action may be brought against us until there has been full compliance with all the terms of this policy. In addition, under Part A, no legal action may be brought against us until:

1. We agree in writing that the "insured" has an obligation to pay; or

2. The amount of that obligation has been finally determined by judgment after trial.

B. No person or organization has any right under this policy to bring us into any action to determine the liability of an "insured".

### OUR RIGHT TO RECOVER PAYMENT

A. If we make a payment under this policy and the person to or for whom payment was made has a right to recover damages from another we shall be subrogated to that right. That person shall do:

1. Whatever is necessary to enable us to exercise our rights; and

2. Nothing after loss to prejudice them.

However, our rights in this paragraph (A.) do not apply under Part D, against any person using "your covered auto" with a reasonable belief that that person is entitled to do so.

B. If we make a payment under this policy and the person to or for whom payment is made recovers damages from another, that person shall:

1. Hold in trust for us the proceeds of the recovery; and

2. Reimburse us to the extent of our payment.

### POLICY PERIOD AND TERRITORY

A. This policy applies only to accidents and losses which occur:

1. During the policy period as shown in the Declarations; and

2. Within the policy territory.

B. The policy territory is:

1. The United States of America, its territories or possessions;

2. Puerto Rico; or

3. Canada.

This policy also applies to loss to, or accidents involving, "your covered auto" while being transported between their ports.

### TERMINATION

A. **Cancellation.** This policy may be cancelled during the policy period as follows:

1. The named insured shown in the Declarations may cancel by:

   a. Returning this policy to us; or

   b. Giving us advance written notice of the date cancellation is to take effect.

2. We may cancel by mailing to the named insured shown in the Declarations at the address shown in this policy:

   a. At least 10 days notice:

   (1) If cancellation is for nonpayment of premium; or

   (2) If notice is mailed during the first 60 days this policy is in effect and this is not a renewal or continuation policy; or

   b. At least 20 days notice in all other cases.

   Copyright, Insurance Services Office, Inc., 1994   PP 00 01 06 94

**SAMPLE**

3. After this policy is in effect for 60 days, or if this is a renewal or continuation policy, we will cancel only:

   a. For nonpayment of premium; or

   b. If your driver's license or that of:

      (1) Any driver who lives with you; or

      (2) Any driver who customarily uses "your covered auto";

      has been suspended or revoked. This must have occurred:

      (1) During the policy period; or

      (2) Since the last anniversary of the original effective date if the policy period is other than 1 year; or

   c. If the policy was obtained through material misrepresentation.

B. **Nonrenewal.** If we decide not to renew or continue this policy, we will mail notice to the named insured shown in the Declarations at the address shown in this policy. Notice will be mailed at least 20 days before the end of the policy period. If the policy period is:

   1. Less than 6 months, we will have the right not to renew or continue this policy every 6 months, beginning 6 months after its original effective date.

   2. 1 year or longer, we will have the right not to renew or continue this policy at each anniversary of its original effective date.

C. **Automatic Termination.** If we offer to renew or continue and you or your representative do not accept, this policy will automatically terminate at the end of the current policy period. Failure to pay the required renewal or continuation premium when due shall mean that you have not accepted our offer.

   If you obtain other insurance on "your covered auto", any similar insurance provided by this policy will terminate as to that auto on the effective date of the other insurance.

D. **Other Termination Provisions.**

   1. We may deliver any notice instead of mailing it. Proof of mailing of any notice shall be sufficient proof of notice.

   2. If this policy is cancelled, you may be entitled to a premium refund. If so, we will send you the refund. The premium refund, if any, will be computed according to our manuals. However, making or offering to make the refund is not a condition of cancellation.

   3. The effective date of cancellation stated in the notice shall become the end of the policy period.

## TRANSFER OF YOUR INTEREST IN THIS POLICY

A. Your rights and duties under this policy may not be assigned without our written consent. However, if a named insured shown in the Declarations dies, coverage will be provided for:

   1. The surviving spouse if resident in the same household at the time of death. Coverage applies to the spouse as if a named insured shown in the Declarations; and

   2. The legal representative of the deceased person as if a named insured shown in the Declarations. This applies only with respect to the representative's legal responsibility to maintain or use "your covered auto".

B. Coverage will only be provided until the end of the policy period.

## TWO OR MORE AUTO POLICIES

If this policy and any other auto insurance policy issued to you by us apply to the same accident, the maximum limit of our liability under all the policies shall not exceed the highest applicable limit of liability under any one policy.

**SAMPLE**

# Appendix C

# WHOLE LIFE POLICY

29-3854-01(1-86) WHOLE LIFE
I/R 4400.00

This is a representative sample of Mutual Life's NN series Whole Life Policy. Policy benefits and wording may vary to comply with state regulations. The notations are to guide you through provisions of the policy. They do not modify the policy terms.

**Our promise to you.** ────────────────── Mutual Life Insurance Company agrees to pay the benefits provided in this policy, subject to its terms and conditions.

PRESIDENT AND C.E.O.                    SECRETARY

**WHOLE LIFE POLICY**

**Eligible For Annual Dividends.**

Insurance payable on death of Insured. Premiums payable for period shown on page 3.

**Return the policy** ──────────────────
**within ten days if you**
**don't like it, and your**
**money will be**
**refunded.**

**Right to Return Policy** — Please read this policy carefully. The policy may be returned by the Owner for any reason within ten days after it was received. The policy may be returned to your agent or to the Home Office of the Company at 720 East Wisconsin Avenue, Milwaukee, WI 53202. If returned, the policy will be considered void from the beginning. Any premium paid will then be refunded.

NN 1

**You, as a policyowner,**
**are also an owner of**
**this mutual company.** ──────────────────  **Mutual Life·**

"Whole Life Policy" reprinted with permission from Northwestern Mutual Life.

**This policy is a legal contract between the Owner and Mutual Life Insurance Company.**
**Read your policy carefully.**

**Table of Contents.** ————————————————— **GUIDE TO POLICY PROVISIONS**

NN 1, 4

**Page 4 shows our** ─────────────────────── BENEFITS AND PREMIUMS
**minimum guarantees.**

DATE OF ISSUE - JANUARY 1, 1986

| PLAN AND ADDITIONAL BENEFITS | AMOUNT | ANNUAL PREMIUM | PAYABLE FOR |
|---|---|---|---|
| WHOLE LIFE PAID-UP AT 90 | $ 100,000 | $ 1,533.00 | 55 YEARS |

A PREMIUM IS PAYABLE ON JANUARY 1, 1986 AND EVERY JANUARY 1 AFTER THAT.
THE FIRST PREMIUM IS $1,533.00.

THE OWNER MAY ELECT THE SPECIFIED RATE OR THE VARIABLE RATE LOAN INTEREST
OPTION.  SEE SECTIONS 6.4 THROUGH 6.6 OF THE POLICY.  THE VARIABLE RATE
LOAN INTEREST OPTION WAS ELECTED ON THE APPLICATION.

THIS POLICY IS ISSUED IN A SELECT PREMIUM CLASS.

DIRECT BENEFICIARY   JANE M DOE, WIFE OF THE INSURED

OWNER                JOHN J DOE, THE INSURED

| INSURED | JOHN J DOE | AGE AND SEX | 35    MALE |
|---|---|---|---|
| POLICY DATE | JANUARY 1, 1986 | POLICY NUMBER | 1 000 001 |
| PLAN | WHOLE LIFE PAID-UP AT 90 | AMOUNT | $ 100,000 |
| NN 1 | | PAGE 3 | |

**Type of policy you bought.** ──── WHOLE LIFE PAID-UP AT 90

**Your policy's "I.D."** ──────────

TABLE OF GUARANTEED VALUES

| END OF POLICY YEAR | JANUARY 1, | CASH VALUE | PAID-UP INSURANCE | $100,000 EXTENDED TERM INSURANCE TO |
|---|---|---|---|---|
| 1 | 1987 | $      0 | $      0 | JUN 15, 1991 |
| 2 | 1988 | 1,078 | 5,000 | APR 29, 1995 |
| 3 | 1989 | 2,291 | 9,800 | SEP 14, 1998 |
| 4 | 1990 | 4,588 | 14,400 | SEP 26, 2001 |
| 5 | 1991 | 4,588 | 18,700 | SEP 26, 2001 |
| 6 | 1992 | 5,852 | 22,900 | JUN 12, 2004 |
| 7 | 1993 | 7,135 | 26,800 | FEB 7, 2007 |
| 8 | 1994 | 8,528 | 30,500 | OCT 12, 2009 |
| 9 | 1995 | 9,942 | 34,100 | FEB 15, 2012 |
| 10 | 1996 | 11,411 | 37,400 | MAR 14, 2014 |
| 11 | 1997 | 12,933 | 40,600 | JAN 14, 2016 |
| 12 | 1998 | 14,515 | 43,700 | SEP 18, 2017 |
| 13 | 1999 | 16,156 | 46,600 | MAR 12, 2019 |
| 14 | 2000 | 17,860 | 49,300 | AUG 13, 2020 |
| 15 | 2001 | 19,629 | 51,900 | NOV 18, 2021 |
| 16 | 2002 | 21,466 | 54,400 | FEB 1, 2023 |
| 17 | 2003 | 23,370 | 56,800 | MAR 19, 2024 |
| 18 | 2004 | 25,341 | 59,000 | APR 7, 2025 |
| 19 | 2005 | 27,380 | 61,100 | APR 3, 2026 |
| 20 | 2006 | 29,486 | 63,100 | MAR 12, 2027 |
| AGE 60 | 2011 | 38,328 | 71,800 | OCT 30, 2030 |
| AGE 65 | 2016 | 47,545 | 78,800 | FEB 16, 2034 |
| AGE 70 | 2021 | 56,741 | 84,400 | FEB 18, 2037 |

VALUES ARE INCREASED BY PAID-UP ADDITIONS AND DIVIDEND ACCUMULATIONS
AND DECREASED BY POLICY DEBT. VALUES SHOWN AT END OF POLICY YEAR
DO NOT REFLECT ANY PREMIUM DUE ON THAT POLICY ANNIVERSARY.

| | | | |
|---|---|---|---|
| INSURED | JOHN J DOE | AGE AND SEX | 35    MALE |
| POLICY DATE | JANUARY 1, 1986 | POLICY NUMBER | 1 000 001 |
| PLAN | WHOLE LIFE PAID-UP AT 90 | AMOUNT | $    100,000 |

NN 1                                              PAGE 4

## SECTION 1. THE CONTRACT

**The contract is made up of the policy and the application.**

### 1.1 LIFE INSURANCE BENEFIT

The Northwestern Mutual Life Insurance Company will pay a benefit on the death of the Insured. Subject to the terms and conditions of the policy:

- payment of the death proceeds will be made after proof of the death of the Insured is received at the Home Office; and
- payment will be made to the beneficiary or other payee under Sections 8 and 9.

**The company's defense against misrepresentation ends two years after the policy is issued if the insured is still alive.**

The amount of the death proceeds when all premiums due have been paid will be:

- the plan Amount shown on page 3; plus
- the amount of any paid-up additions then in force (Section 4.2); plus
- the amount of any dividend accumulations (Section 4.2); plus
- the amount of any premium refund (Section 3.1) and any dividend at death (Section 4.4); less
- the amount of any policy debt (Section 6.3).

**The company's defense against suicide ends one year after the policy is issued if the insured is still alive.**

These amounts will be determined as of the date of death.

The amount of the death proceeds when the Insured dies during the grace period following the due date of any unpaid premium will be:

- the amount determined above assuming the overdue premium has been paid; less
- the amount of the unpaid premium.

The amount of the death proceeds when the Insured dies while the policy is in force as extended term or paid-up insurance will be determined under Sections 5.2 or 5.3.

### 1.2 ENTIRE CONTRACT; CHANGES

This policy with the attached application is the entire contract. Statements in the application are representations and not warranties. A change in the policy is valid only if it is approved by an officer of the Company. The Company may require that the policy be sent to it for endorsement to show a change. No agent has the authority to change the policy or to waive any of its terms.

### 1.3 INCONTESTABILITY

The Company will not contest this policy after it has been in force during the lifetime of the Insured for two years from the Date of Issue. In issuing the policy, the Company has relied on the application. While the policy is contestable, the Company, on the basis of a misstatement in the application, may rescind the policy or deny a claim.

### 1.4 SUICIDE

If the Insured dies by suicide within one year from the Date of Issue, the amount payable by the Company will be limited to the premiums paid, less the amount of any policy debt.

### 1.5 DATES

The contestable and suicide periods begin with the Date of Issue. Policy months, years and anniversaries are computed from the Policy Date. Both dates are shown on page 3.

### 1.6 MISSTATEMENT OF AGE OR SEX

If the age or sex of the Insured has been misstated, the amount payable will be the amount which the premiums paid would have purchased at the correct age and sex.

### 1.7 PAYMENTS BY THE COMPANY

All payments by the Company under this policy are payable at its Home Office.

## SECTION 2. OWNERSHIP

### 2.1 THE OWNER

The Owner is named on page 3. The Owner, his successor or his transferee may exercise policy rights without the consent of any beneficiary. After the death of the Insured, policy rights may be exercised only as provided in Sections 8 and 9.

**The policy can have a new owner.**

### 2.2 TRANSFER OF OWNERSHIP

The Owner may transfer the ownership of this policy. Written proof of transfer satisfactory to the Company must be received at its Home Office. The transfer will then take effect as of the date that it was signed. The Company may require that the policy be sent to it for endorsement to show the transfer.

NN 1,4

5

**The policy may be assigned as security for a loan.**

### 2.3 COLLATERAL ASSIGNMENT

The Owner may assign this policy as collateral security. The Company is not responsible for the validity or effect of a collateral assignment. The Company will not be responsible to an assignee for any payment or other action taken by the Company before receipt of the assignment in writing at its Home Office.

The interest of any beneficiary will be subject to any collateral assignment made either before or after the beneficiary is named.

A collateral assignee is not an Owner. A collateral assignment is not a transfer of ownership. Ownership can be transferred only by complying with Section 2.2.

## SECTION 3. PREMIUMS AND REINSTATEMENT

### 3.1 PREMIUM PAYMENT

**Payment.** All premiums after the first are payable at the Home Office or to an authorized agent. A receipt signed by an officer of the Company will be furnished on request. A premium must be paid on or before its due date. The date when each premium is due and the number of years for which premiums are payable are described on page 3.

**Frequency.** Premiums may be paid every 3, 6 or 12 months at the published rates of the Company. A change in premium frequency will take effect when the Company accepts a premium on a new frequency. Premiums may be paid on any other frequency approved by the Company.

**You have 31 days beyond the due date to pay your premium.**

**Grace Period.** A grace period of 31 days will be allowed to pay a premium that is not paid on its due date. The policy will be in full force during this period. If the Insured dies during the grace period, any overdue premium will be paid from the proceeds of the policy.

If the premium is not paid within the grace period, the policy will terminate as of the due date unless it continues as extended term or paid-up insurance under Section 5.2 or 5.3.

**How to reinstate your policy.**

**Premium Refund At Death.** The Company will refund a portion of a premium paid for the period beyond the date of the Insured's death. The refund will be part of the policy proceeds.

### 3.2 REINSTATEMENT

The policy may be reinstated within five years after the due date of the overdue premium. All unpaid premiums (and interest as required below) must be received by the Company while the Insured is alive. The policy may not be reinstated if the policy was surrendered for its cash surrender value. Any policy debt on the due date of the overdue premium, with interest from that date, must be repaid or reinstated.

In addition, for the policy to be reinstated more than 31 days after the end of the grace period:

- evidence of insurability must be given that is satisfactory to the Company; and
- all unpaid premiums must be paid with interest from the due date of each premium. Interest is at an annual effective rate of 6%.

## SECTION 4. DIVIDENDS

**You may receive dividends annually.**

### 4.1 ANNUAL DIVIDENDS

This policy will share in the divisible surplus of the Company. This surplus is determined each year. This policy's share will be credited as a dividend on the policy anniversary. The dividend will reflect the mortality, expense and investment experience of the Company and will be affected by any policy debt during the policy year.

### 4.2 USE OF DIVIDENDS

Annual dividends may be paid in cash or used for one of the following:

**This popular way to use dividends provides additional insurance.**

- **Paid-up Additions.** Dividends will purchase paid-up additional insurance. Paid-up additions share in the divisible surplus.
- **Dividend Accumulations.** Dividends will accumulate at interest. Interest is credited at an annual effective rate of 3 1/2%. The Company may set a higher rate.

**Another popular way to use dividends is to reduce premiums.**

- **Premium Payment.** Dividends will be used to reduce premiums. If the balance of a premium is

not paid, or if this policy is in force as paid-up insurance, the dividend will purchase paid-up additions.

Other uses of dividends may be made available by the Company.

If no direction is given for the use of dividends, they will purchase paid-up additions.

### 4.3 ADDITIONS AND ACCUMULATIONS

Paid-up additions and dividend accumulations increase the policy's cash value. They are payable as part of the policy proceeds. Additions may be surrendered and accumulations may be withdrawn unless they are used for a loan, for extended term insurance or for paid-up insurance.

### 4.4 DIVIDEND AT DEATH

A dividend for the period from the beginning of the policy year to the date of the Insured's death will be payable as part of the policy proceeds.

**The rights you have if you no longer want to pay premiums.**

# SECTION 5. CASH VALUES, EXTENDED TERM INSURANCE AND PAID-UP INSURANCE

## 5.1 CASH VALUE

The cash value for this policy, when all premiums due have been paid, will be the sum of:

- the cash value from the Table of Guaranteed Values;
- the cash value of any paid-up additions; and
- the amount of any dividend accumulations.

The cash value within three months after the due date of any unpaid premium will be the cash value on that due date reduced by any later surrender of paid-up additions and by any later withdrawal of dividend accumulations. After that, the cash value will be the cash value of the insurance then in force, including any paid-up additions and any dividend accumulations.

The cash value of any extended term insurance, paid-up insurance or paid-up additions will be the net single premium for that insurance at the attained age of the Insured.

**You can have term insurance for a period of time determined by the cash surrender value.**

## 5.2 EXTENDED TERM INSURANCE

If any premium is unpaid at the end of the grace period, this policy will be in force as extended term insurance. The amount of the death proceeds under this term insurance will be:

- the plan Amount shown on page 3; plus
- the amount of any paid-up additions in force (Section 4.2); plus
- the amount of any dividend accumulations (Section 4.2); less
- the amount of any policy debt (Section 6.3).

These amounts will be determined as of the due date of the unpaid premium. The term insurance will start as of the due date of the unpaid premium. The period of term insurance will be determined by using the cash surrender value as a net single premium at the attained age of the Insured. If the term insurance would extend to or beyond age 100, paid-up insurance will be provided instead. Extended term insurance does not share in divisible surplus.

If the extended term insurance is surrendered within 31 days after a policy anniversary, the cash value will not be less than the cash value on that anniversary.

**You can take a dividend paying policy, good for life, requiring no further premium payment, in an amount determined by the cash value.**

## 5.3 PAID-UP INSURANCE

Paid-up insurance may be selected in place of extended term insurance. A written request must be received at the Home Office no later than three months after the due date of an unpaid premium. The amount of insurance will be determined by using the cash value as a net single premium at the attained age of the Insured. Any policy debt will continue. Paid-up insurance will share in divisible surplus.

The amount of the death proceeds when this policy is in force as paid-up insurance will be:

- the amount of paid-up insurance determined above; plus

NN 1

- the amount of any in force paid-up additions purchased by dividends after the policy has become paid-up insurance (Section 4.2); plus
- the amount of any existing dividend accumulations (Section 4.2); plus
- the amount of any dividend at death (Section 4.4); less
- the amount of any policy debt (Section 6.3).

These amounts will be determined as of the date of death.

If paid-up insurance is surrendered within 31 days after a policy anniversary, the cash value will not be less than the cash value on that anniversary reduced by any later surrender of paid-up additions and by any later withdrawal of dividend accumulations.

## 5.4 CASH SURRENDER

The Owner may surrender this policy for its cash surrender value. The cash surrender value is the cash value less any policy debt. A written surrender of all claims, satisfactory to the Company, will be required. The date of surrender will be the date of receipt at the Home Office of the written surrender. The policy will terminate and the cash surrender value will be determined as of the date of surrender. The Company may require that the policy be sent to it.

## 5.5 TABLE OF GUARANTEED VALUES

Cash values, paid-up insurance and extended term insurance are shown on page 4 for the end of the policy years indicated. These values assume that all premiums due have been paid for the number of years stated. They do not reflect paid-up additions, dividend accumulations or policy debt. Values during a policy year will reflect any portion of the year's premium paid and the time elapsed in that year.

Values for policy years not shown are calculated on the same basis as those on page 4. A list of these values will be furnished on request. A detailed statement of the method of calculation of all values has been filed with the insurance supervisory official of the state in which this policy is delivered. The Company will furnish this statement at the request of the Owner. All values are at least as great as those required by that state.

## 5.6 BASIS OF VALUES

The cash value for each policy year not shown on page 4 equals the reserve for that year calculated on the Commissioners Reserve Valuation Method. Net single premiums are based on the Commissioners 1980 Standard Ordinary Mortality Table for the sex of the Insured; except that for extended term insurance, the Commissioners 1980 Extended Term Insurance Table for the sex of the Insured is used for the first 20 policy years. Interest is based on an annual effective rate of 5 1/2% for the first 20 policy years and 4% after that. Calculations assume the continuous payment of premiums and the immediate payment of claims.

7

**You can take out all of your cash value, less any policy debt.**

## SECTION 6. LOANS

**You can borrow money from the company, the maximum amount to be determined by the loan value.**

### 6.1 POLICY AND PREMIUM LOANS

The Owner may obtain a loan from the Company in an amount that is not more than the loan value.

**Policy Loan.** The loan may be obtained on written request. No loan will be made if the policy is in force as extended term insurance. The Company may defer making the loan for up to six months unless the loan is to be used to pay premiums due the Company.

**Premium Loan.** If the premium loan provision is in effect on this policy, a loan will be made to pay an overdue premium. If the loan value is not large enough to pay the overdue premium, a premium will be paid for any other frequency permitted by this policy for which the loan value is large enough. The Owner may elect or revoke the premium loan provision by written request received at the Home Office.

### 6.2 LOAN VALUE

**Two important facts about loans: Indebtedness is subtracted at death from the insurance proceeds. Despite the loan, the cash value continues to grow as guaranteed, and the policy continues to be eligible for dividends.**

The loan value is the smaller of a. or b., less any policy debt and any premium then due or billed; a. and b. are defined as:

a. the cash value one year after the date of the loan, assuming all premiums due within that year are paid, less interest to one year from the date of the loan.

b. the cash value on the due date of the first premium not yet billed that is due after the date of the loan, less interest from the date of the loan to that premium due date.

### 6.3 POLICY DEBT

Policy debt consists of all outstanding loans and accrued interest. It may be paid to the Company at any time. Policy debt affects dividends under Section 4.1. Any policy debt will be deducted from the policy proceeds.

If the policy debt equals or exceeds the cash value, this policy will terminate. Termination occurs 31 days after a notice has been mailed to the Owner and to any assignee on record at the Home Office.

**You can choose between a fixed or a variable loan rate and you may be able to change your option once a year.**

### 6.4 LOAN INTEREST

Interest accrues and is payable on a daily basis from the date of the loan on policy loans and from the premium due date on premium loans. Unpaid interest is added to the loan.

The Specified Rate loan interest option or the Variable Rate loan interest option is elected on the application.

**Change To Variable Rate Loan Interest Option.** The Owner may request a change to the Variable Rate loan interest option at any time, with the change to take effect on the January 1st following receipt of a written request at the Company's Home Office.

**Change To Specified Rate Loan Interest Option.** The Owner may request a change to the Specified Rate loan interest option if the interest rate set by the Company under Section 6.6 for the year beginning on the next January 1st is less than 8%. The written request to change must be received at the Home Office between November 15th and the last business day of the calendar year; the change will take effect on the January 1st following receipt of the request at the Home Office.

### 6.5 SPECIFIED RATE LOAN INTEREST OPTION

Interest is payable at an annual effective rate of 8%.

### 6.6 VARIABLE RATE LOAN INTEREST OPTION

Interest is payable at an annual effective rate that is set by the Company annually and applied to new or outstanding policy debt during the year beginning each January 1st. The highest loan interest rate that may be set by the Company is the greater of (i) 6 1/2% for the first 20 policy years and 5% after that or (ii) a rate based on the Moody's Corporate Bond Yield Averages-Monthly Average Corporates for the immediately preceding October. This Average is published by Moody's Investor's Service, Inc. If it is no longer published, the highest loan rate will be based on some other similar average established by the insurance supervisory official of the state in which this policy is delivered.

The loan interest rate set by the Company will not exceed the maximum rate permitted by the laws of the state in which this policy is delivered. The loan interest rate may be increased only if the increase in the annual effective rate is at least 1/2%. The loan interest rate will be decreased if the decrease in the annual effective rate is at least 1/2%.

The Company will give notice:
- of the initial loan interest rate in effect at the time a policy or premium loan is made.
- of an increase in loan interest rate on outstanding policy debt no later than 30 days before the January 1st on which the increase takes effect.

This policy will not terminate during a policy year as the sole result of an increase in the loan interest rate during that policy year.

**The fixed loan rate is 8%. The variable loan rate is based on Moody's Corporate Bond Yield Averages - Monthly Average Corporates.**

NN 1,4,9

8

## SECTION 7. CHANGE OF POLICY

**You can change the plan, keeping the original issue age.**

### 7.1 CHANGE OF PLAN

The Owner may change this policy to any permanent life insurance plan agreed to by the Owner and the Company by:

- paying the required costs; and

- meeting any other conditions set by the Company.

**You can change the policy to insure the life of another person, e.g., wife to husband, one business partner to another.**

### 7.2 CHANGE OF INSURED

**Change.** The Owner may change the insured under this policy by:

- paying the required costs; and

- meeting any other conditions set by the Company, including the following:

  a. on the date of change, the new insured's age may not be more than 75;

  b. the new insured must have been born on or before the Policy Date of this policy;

  c. the new insured must be insurable; and

  d. the Owner must have an insurable interest in the life of the new insured.

**Date Of Change.** The date of change will be the later of:

- the date of the request to change; or

- the date of the medical examination (or the non-medical application).

**Terms Of Policy After Change.** The policy will cover the new insured starting on the date of change. When coverage on the new insured starts, coverage on the prior insured will terminate.

The contestable and suicide periods for the new insured start on the date of change.

The amount of insurance on the new insured will be set so that there will be no change in the cash value of the policy at the time of change. If the policy has no cash value, the amount will be set so that premiums do not change.

Any policy debt or assignment will continue after the change.

NN 1,4,9

# SECTION 8. BENEFICIARIES

## 8.1 DEFINITION OF BENEFICIARIES

The term "beneficiaries" as used in this policy includes direct beneficiaries, contingent beneficiaries and further payees.

## 8.2 NAMING AND CHANGE OF BENEFICIARIES

**By Owner.** The Owner may name and change the beneficiaries of death proceeds:

**As an aid to estate and tax planning, a third-party policyowner can change beneficiaries after the death of the insured.**

- while the Insured is living.
- during the first 60 days after the date of death of the Insured, if the Insured just before his death was not the Owner. No one may change this naming of a direct beneficiary during this 60 days.

**By Direct Beneficiary.** A direct beneficiary may name and change the contingent beneficiaries and further payees of his share of the proceeds:

- if the direct beneficiary is the Owner;
- if, at any time after the death of the Insured, no contingent beneficiary or further payee of that share is living; or
- if, after the death of the Insured, the direct beneficiary elects a payment plan. The interest of any other beneficiary in the share of that direct beneficiary will end.

These direct beneficiary rights are subject to the Owner's rights during the 60 days after the date of death of the Insured.

**The marital deduction provision is valuable in cases in which the spouse is the direct beneficiary.**

**By Spouse (Marital Deduction Provision).**

- **Power To Appoint.** The spouse of the Insured will have the power alone and in all events to appoint all amounts payable to the spouse under the policy if:
  a. the Insured just before his death was the Owner; and
  b. the spouse is a direct beneficiary; and
  c. the spouse survives the Insured.
- **To Whom Spouse Can Appoint.** Under this power, the spouse can appoint:
  a. to the estate of the spouse; or
  b. to any other persons as contingent beneficiaries and further payees.
- **Effect Of Exercise.** As to the amounts appointed, the exercise of this power will:
  a. revoke any other designation of beneficiaries;
  b. revoke any election of payment plan as it applies to them; and
  c. cause any provision to the contrary in Section 8 or 9 of this policy to be of no effect.

NN 1,2,4,6,8,9                                         10

**Effective Date.** A naming or change of a beneficiary will be made on receipt at the Home Office of a written request that is acceptable to the Company. The request will then take effect as of the date that it was signed. The Company is not responsible for any payment or other action that is taken by it before the receipt of the request. The Company may require that the policy be sent to it to be endorsed to show the naming or change.

## 8.3 SUCCESSION IN INTEREST OF BENEFICIARIES

**Direct Beneficiaries.** The proceeds of this policy will be payable in equal shares to the direct beneficiaries who survive and receive payment. If a direct beneficiary dies before he receives all or part of his full share, the unpaid part of his share will be payable in equal shares to the other direct beneficiaries who survive and receive payment.

**Contingent Beneficiaries.** At the death of all of the direct beneficiaries, the proceeds, or the present value of any unpaid payments under a payment plan, will be payable in equal shares to the contingent beneficiaries who survive and receive payment. If a contingent beneficiary dies before he receives all or part of his full share, the unpaid part of his share will be payable in equal shares to the other contingent beneficiaries who survive and receive payment.

**Further Payees.** At the death of all of the direct and contingent beneficiaries, the proceeds, or the present value of any unpaid payments under a payment plan, will be paid in one sum:

- in equal shares to the further payees who survive and receive payment; or
- if no further payees survive and receive payment, to the estate of the last to die of all of the direct and contingent beneficiaries.

**Owner Or His Estate.** If no beneficiaries are alive when the Insured dies, the proceeds will be paid to the Owner or to his estate.

## 8.4 GENERAL

**Transfer Of Ownership.** A transfer of ownership of itself will not change the interest of a beneficiary.

**Claims Of Creditors.** So far as allowed by law, no amount payable under this policy will be subject to the claims of creditors of a beneficiary.

**Succession Under Payment Plans.** A direct or contingent beneficiary who succeeds to an interest in a payment plan will continue under the terms of the plan.

**Living successor beneficiaries can be provided for by contract.**

**This clause may safeguard policy proceeds.**

**A wide range of payment plans is available.**

## SECTION 9. PAYMENT OF POLICY BENEFITS

### 9.1 PAYMENT OF PROCEEDS

**Interest is paid on policy proceeds from the date of death.**

Death proceeds will be paid under the payment plan that takes effect on the date of death of the Insured. The Interest Income Plan (Option A) will be in effect if no payment plan has been elected. Interest will accumulate from the date of death until a payment plan is elected or the proceeds are withdrawn in cash.

Surrender proceeds will be the cash surrender value as of the date of surrender. These proceeds will be paid in cash or under a payment plan that is elected. The Company may defer paying the surrender proceeds for up to six months from the date of surrender. If payment is deferred for 30 days or more, interest will be paid on the surrender proceeds from the date of surrender to the date of payment. Interest will be at an annual effective rate of 5 1/2% during the first 20 policy years and 4% after that.

### 9.2 PAYMENT PLANS

**Interest Income Plan (Option A).** The proceeds will earn interest which may be received each month or accumulated. The first payment is due one month after the date on which the plan takes effect. Interest that has accumulated may be withdrawn at any time. Part or all of the proceeds may be withdrawn at any time.

**Beneficiaries, who have the right to withdraw from the chosen payment plan, can change payment plans.**

**Installment Income Plans.** Payments will be made each month on the terms of the plan that is elected. The first payment is due on the date that the plan takes effect.

- **Specified Period (Option B).** The proceeds with interest will be paid over a period of from one to 30 years. The present value of any unpaid installments may be withdrawn at any time.

- **Specified Amount (Option D).** Payments of not less than $10.00 per $1,000 of proceeds will be made until all of the proceeds with interest have been paid. The balance may be withdrawn at any time.

**Proceeds under these payment plans continue to earn interest.**

**Life Income Plans.** Payments will be made each month on the terms of the plan that is elected. The first payment is due on the date that the plan takes effect. Proof of the date of birth, acceptable to the Company, must be furnished for each person on whose life the payments are based.

- **Single Life Income (Option C).** Payments will be made for a chosen period and, after that, for the life of the person on whose life the payments are based. The choices for the period are:
  - a. zero years;
  - b. 10 years;
  - c. 20 years; or
  - d. a refund period which continues until the sum of the payments that have been made is equal to the proceeds that were placed under the plan.

NN 1,2,4,6,9

11

**Life income rates vary with investment conditions, but a minimum rate is guaranteed. Once a payment plan takes effect, that rate is assured thereafter.**

- **Joint And Survivor Life Income (Option E).** Payments are based on the lives of two persons. Level payments will be made for a period of 10 years and, after that, for as long as one or both of the persons are living.

- **Other Selections.** The Company may offer other selections under the Life Income Plans.

- **Withdrawal.** The present value of any unpaid payments that are to be made for the chosen period (Option C) or the 10 year period (Option E) may be withdrawn only after the death of all of the persons on whose lives the payments are based.

- **Limitations.** A direct or contingent beneficiary who is a natural person may be paid under a Life Income Plan only if the payments depend on his life. A corporation may be paid under a Life Income Plan only if the payments depend on the life of the Insured or, after the death of the Insured, on the life of his spouse or his dependent.

**Payment Frequency.** On request, payments will be made once every 3, 6 or 12 months instead of each month.

**Transfer Between Payment Plans.** A beneficiary who is receiving payment under a plan which includes the right to withdraw may transfer the amount withdrawable to any other plan that is available.

**Minimum Payment.** The Company may limit the election of a payment plan to one that results in payments of at least $50.

If payments under a payment plan are or become less than $50, the Company may change the frequency of payments. If the payments are being made once every 12 months and are less than $50, the Company may pay the present value or the balance of the payment plan.

### 9.3 PAYMENT PLAN RATES

**Interest Income And Installment Income Plans.** Proceeds will earn interest at rates declared each year by the Company. None of these rates will be less than an annual effective rate of 3 1/2%. Interest of more than 3 1/2% will increase the amount of the payments or, for the Specified Amount Plan (Option D), increase the number of payments. The present value of any unpaid installments will be based on the 3 1/2% rate of interest.

The Company may offer guaranteed rates of interest higher than 3 1/2% with conditions on withdrawal.

**Life Income Plans.** Payments will be based on rates declared by the Company. These rates will provide at least as much income as would the Company's rates, on the date that the payment plan takes effect, for a single premium immediate annuity contract, with no charge for issue expenses. Payments under these rates will not be less than the amounts that are described in Minimum Payment Rates.

**Minimum Payment Rates.** The minimum payment rates for the Installment Income Plans (Options B and D) and the Life Income Plans (Options C and E) are shown in the Minimum Payment Rate Tables.

The Life Income Plan payment rates in those tables depend on the sex and on the adjusted age of each person on whose life the payments are based. The adjusted age is:

- the age on the birthday that is nearest to the date on which the payment plan takes effect; plus

- the age adjustment shown below for the number of policy years that have elapsed from the Policy Date to the date that the payment plan takes effect. A part of a policy year is counted as a full year.

| POLICY YEARS ELAPSED | AGE ADJUSTMENT | POLICY YEARS ELAPSED | AGE ADJUSTMENT |
|---|---|---|---|
| 1 to 5 | + 8 | 31 to 35 | -2 |
| 6 to 10 | + 6 | 36 to 40 | -3 |
| 11 to 15 | + 4 | 41 to 45 | -4 |
| 16 to 20 | + 2 | 46 to 50 | -5 |
| 21 to 25 | 0 | 51 or more | -6 |
| 26 to 30 | -1 | | |

**9.4 EFFECTIVE DATE FOR PAYMENT PLAN**

A payment plan that is elected for death proceeds will take effect on the date of death of the Insured if:

- the plan is elected by the Owner; and

- the election is received at the Home Office while the Insured is living.

In all other cases, a payment plan that is elected will take effect:

- on the date the election is received at the Home Office; or

- on a later date, if requested.

**9.5 PAYMENT PLAN ELECTIONS**

**For Death Proceeds By Owner.** The Owner may elect payment plans for death proceeds:

- while the Insured is living.

- during the first 60 days after the date of death of the Insured, if the Insured just before his death was not the Owner. No one may change this election made during those 60 days.

**For Death Proceeds By Direct Or Contingent Beneficiary.** A direct or contingent beneficiary may elect payment plans for death proceeds payable to him if no payment plan that has been elected is in effect. This right is subject to the Owner's rights during the 60 days after the date of death of the Insured.

**For Surrender Proceeds.** The Owner may elect payment plans for surrender proceeds. The Owner will be the direct beneficiary.

**9.6 INCREASE OF MONTHLY INCOME**

A direct beneficiary who is to receive proceeds under a payment plan may increase the amount of the monthly payments. This is done by the payment of an annuity premium to the Company at the time the payment plan elected under Section 9.5 takes effect. The amount that will be applied under the payment plan will be the net premium. The net premium is the annuity premium less a charge of not more than 2% and less any premium tax. The net premium will be applied under the same payment plan and at the same rates as the proceeds. The Company may limit this net premium to an amount that is equal to the direct beneficiary's share of the proceeds payable under this policy.

**Beneficiaries can add funds to a payment plan when it takes effect.**

**Our minimum guarantees for installment income plans.**

## MINIMUM PAYMENT RATE TABLE
### Minimum Monthly Income Payments Per $1,000 Proceeds

INSTALLMENT INCOME PLANS (Options B and D)

| PERIOD (YEARS) | MONTHLY PAYMENT | PERIOD (YEARS) | MONTHLY PAYMENT | PERIOD (YEARS) | MONTHLY PAYMENT |
|---|---|---|---|---|---|
| 1 | $84.65 | 11 | $ 9.09 | 21 | $ 5.56 |
| 2 | 43.05 | 12 | 8.46 | 22 | 5.39 |
| 3 | 29.19 | 13 | 7.94 | 23 | 5.24 |
| 4 | 22.27 | 14 | 7.49 | 24 | 5.09 |
| 5 | 18.12 | 15 | 7.10 | 25 | 4.96 |
| 6 | 15.35 | 16 | 6.76 | 26 | 4.84 |
| 7 | 13.38 | 17 | 6.47 | 27 | 4.73 |
| 8 | 11.90 | 18 | 6.20 | 28 | 4.63 |
| 9 | 10.75 | 19 | 5.97 | 29 | 4.53 |
| 10 | 9.83 | 20 | 5.75 | 30 | 4.45 |

NN 1,2,4,6,9

**MINIMUM PAYMENT RATE TABLES**
Minimum Monthly Income Payments Per $1,000 Proceeds

**Our minimum guarantees for life income plans.** ━━━ LIFE INCOME PLAN (Option C)

| MALE ADJUSTED AGE* | SINGLE LIFE MONTHLY PAYMENTS | | | | FEMALE ADJUSTED AGE* | | | | |
|---|---|---|---|---|---|---|---|---|---|
| | CHOSEN PERIOD (YEARS) | | | | | CHOSEN PERIOD (YEARS) | | | |
| | ZERO | 10 | 20 | REFUND | | ZERO | 10 | 20 | REFUND |
| 55 | $ 4.99 | $ 4.91 | $ 4.66 | $ 4.73 | 55 | $ 4.54 | $ 4.51 | $ 4.38 | $ 4.40 |
| 56 | 5.09 | 5.00 | 4.72 | 4.81 | 56 | 4.62 | 4.58 | 4.44 | 4.47 |
| 57 | 5.20 | 5.10 | 4.78 | 4.90 | 57 | 4.71 | 4.66 | 4.51 | 4.54 |
| 58 | 5.32 | 5.20 | 4.85 | 4.99 | 58 | 4.80 | 4.75 | 4.57 | 4.62 |
| 59 | 5.44 | 5.31 | 4.91 | 5.08 | 59 | 4.90 | 4.84 | 4.64 | 4.70 |
| 60 | 5.57 | 5.42 | 4.97 | 5.18 | 60 | 5.00 | 4.93 | 4.70 | 4.78 |
| 61 | 5.71 | 5.54 | 5.04 | 5.29 | 61 | 5.11 | 5.03 | 4.77 | 4.87 |
| 62 | 5.86 | 5.67 | 5.10 | 5.40 | 62 | 5.23 | 5.14 | 4.84 | 4.96 |
| 63 | 6.02 | 5.80 | 5.16 | 5.51 | 63 | 5.36 | 5.25 | 4.91 | 5.06 |
| 64 | 6.20 | 5.94 | 5.22 | 5.63 | 64 | 5.49 | 5.37 | 4.98 | 5.17 |
| 65 | 6.38 | 6.08 | 5.28 | 5.76 | 65 | 5.64 | 5.50 | 5.05 | 5.28 |
| 66 | 6.54 | 6.23 | 5.33 | 5.90 | 66 | 5.79 | 5.63 | 5.12 | 5.39 |
| 67 | 6.70 | 6.38 | 5.38 | 6.04 | 67 | 5.94 | 5.77 | 5.19 | 5.52 |
| 68 | 6.87 | 6.54 | 5.43 | 6.19 | 68 | 6.09 | 5.91 | 5.25 | 5.65 |
| 69 | 7.05 | 6.71 | 5.48 | 6.35 | 69 | 6.25 | 6.07 | 5.32 | 5.79 |
| 70 | 7.21 | 6.87 | 5.52 | 6.52 | 70 | 6.42 | 6.23 | 5.37 | 5.94 |
| 71 | 7.40 | 7.05 | 5.55 | 6.69 | 71 | 6.59 | 6.40 | 5.43 | 6.09 |
| 72 | 7.58 | 7.21 | 5.59 | 6.88 | 72 | 6.78 | 6.58 | 5.48 | 6.26 |
| 73 | 7.77 | 7.40 | 5.62 | 7.07 | 73 | 6.96 | 6.76 | 5.52 | 6.44 |
| 74 | 7.95 | 7.57 | 5.64 | 7.28 | 74 | 7.16 | 6.95 | 5.57 | 6.63 |
| 75 | 8.14 | 7.75 | 5.66 | 7.49 | 75 | 7.35 | 7.14 | 5.60 | 6.83 |
| 76 | 8.32 | 7.92 | 5.68 | 7.72 | 76 | 7.56 | 7.34 | 5.63 | 7.04 |
| 77 | 8.49 | 8.09 | 5.70 | 7.96 | 77 | 7.77 | 7.54 | 5.66 | 7.26 |
| 78 | 8.84 | 8.26 | 5.71 | 8.21 | 78 | 7.97 | 7.74 | 5.68 | 7.51 |
| 79 | 9.18 | 8.42 | 5.72 | 8.47 | 79 | 8.18 | 7.94 | 5.70 | 7.76 |
| 80 | 9.51 | 8.57 | 5.73 | 8.74 | 80 | 8.37 | 8.13 | 5.71 | 8.03 |
| 81 | 9.84 | 8.71 | 5.74 | 9.04 | 81 | 8.57 | 8.32 | 5.72 | 8.32 |
| 82 | 10.18 | 8.85 | 5.74 | 9.34 | 82 | 8.93 | 8.50 | 5.73 | 8.61 |
| 83 | 10.49 | 8.97 | 5.75 | 9.65 | 83 | 9.28 | 8.67 | 5.74 | 8.93 |
| 84 | 10.82 | 9.09 | 5.75 | 9.98 | 84 | 9.62 | 8.83 | 5.74 | 9.27 |
| 85 and over | 11.13 | 9.20 | 5.75 | 10.34 | 85 and over | 9.96 | 8.97 | 5.75 | 9.62 |

**LIFE INCOME PLAN (OPTION E)**

| MALE ADJUSTED AGE* | JOINT AND SURVIVOR MONTHLY PAYMENTS | | | | | | |
|---|---|---|---|---|---|---|---|
| | FEMALE ADJUSTED AGE* | | | | | | |
| | 55 | 60 | 65 | 70 | 75 | 80 | 85 and over |
| 55 | $4.16 | $4.34 | $4.51 | $4.65 | $4.76 | $4.84 | $4.88 |
| 60 | 4.26 | 4.51 | 4.75 | 4.98 | 5.16 | 5.29 | 5.37 |
| 65 | 4.35 | 4.65 | 4.98 | 5.31 | 5.61 | 5.84 | 5.98 |
| 70 | 4.41 | 4.76 | 5.17 | 5.62 | 6.07 | 6.44 | 6.68 |
| 75 | 4.46 | 4.84 | 5.32 | 5.88 | 6.48 | 7.03 | 7.42 |
| 80 | 4.48 | 4.89 | 5.41 | 6.05 | 6.79 | 7.52 | 8.07 |
| 85 and over | 4.50 | 4.92 | 5.46 | 6.15 | 6.99 | 7.85 | 8.53 |

*See Section 9.3.

NN 1,2,4,6,8,9                    13

# WAIVER OF PREMIUM BENEFIT (LIFE & TERM)

### 1. THE BENEFIT

**Disability Before Age 60.** If total disability of the Insured starts on or before the policy anniversary nearest his 60th birthday, the Company will waive all premiums that come due on the policy as long as the total disability continues.

**Disability After Age 60.** If total disability of the Insured starts after the policy anniversary nearest his 60th birthday, the Company will waive those premiums that come due on the policy as long as the total disability continues, but only to the policy anniversary that is nearest his 65th birthday.

**Premium Waived On An Annual Basis.** Even if premiums have been paid more often than every 12 months, a premium waived on a policy anniversary will be an annual premium.

**Refund Of Premium.** The Company will refund that portion of a premium paid which applies to a period beyond the policy month in which the total disability began.

**Premium For Benefit.** The premium for this Benefit is shown on page 3.

### 2. TOTAL DISABILITY

**Definition Of Total Disability.** A total disability is one which prevents the Insured from engaging in an occupation. For the first 24 months of total disability, an occupation is the one that the Insured had at the time he became disabled. After 24 months, an occupation is one for which the Insured is qualified by education, training or experience. Due regard will be given to his vocation and earnings before he became disabled.

**Disabilities Covered By This Benefit.** Premiums are waived for total disability only if:

- the Insured becomes disabled while this Benefit is in force;

- the disability results from an accident or sickness; and

- the disability lasts for at least six months.

**Presumptive Total Disability.** Even if the Insured is able to work, he will be considered totally disabled if he incurs the total and irrecoverable loss of:

- sight of both eyes;
- use of both hands;
- use of both feet;
- use of one hand and one foot;
- speech; or
- hearing in both ears.

The loss must be the result of an accident that occurs, or from a sickness that first appears, while this Benefit is in force.

### 3. PROOF OF DISABILITY

Before any premium is waived, proof of total disability must be given to the Company within one year from the start of disability. However, the claim will not be affected if the proof is given as soon as reasonably possible.

### 4. PROOF THAT DISABILITY HAS CONTINUED

Proof that the total disability has continued may be required once a year. If the proof is not given when it is required, no more premiums will be waived. The Company will not require proof that the disability continues beyond the policy anniversary that is nearest the 65th birthday of the Insured.

### 5. PAYMENT OF PREMIUM

A premium that comes due while the Insured is disabled, but before the Company has approved the claim, is payable and should be paid. A premium that is paid and later waived will be refunded. A premium that is not paid will be waived if the total disability began before the end of the grace period.

### 6. TERMINATION OF BENEFIT

This Benefit will terminate on the policy anniversary that is nearest the 65th birthday of the Insured, unless he has been totally disabled since the policy anniversary that is nearest his 60th birthday. It will terminate earlier:

- when the policy terminates.
- when the policy becomes extended term or paid-up insurance.
- when the Owner's written request is received at the Home Office.

SPECIMEN
COPY
PROVISIONS MAY VARY SLIGHTLY
IN CERTAIN STATES

I/R 4400.00
29-3855-07 (12-85)

NN 1,2,4,5 WP

# ADDITIONAL PURCHASE BENEFIT

## 1. THE BENEFIT

The Company will issue additional permanent life insurance policies on the Insured, with no evidence of insurability, subject to the terms and conditions below.

The term "new policy" means each additional policy issued under this Benefit.

The premium for this Benefit is shown on page 3.

## 2. PURCHASE DATES

The Owner may purchase a new policy as of each Purchase Date. There is a Purchase Date on each policy anniversary that is nearest the 22nd, 25th, 28th, 31st, 34th, 37th, and 40th birthdays of the Insured.

The Company must receive an application and the first premium for each new policy:

- while the Insured is living; and
- not more than 60 days before, nor more than 30 days after, a Purchase Date.

The Owner of the new policy must have an insurable interest in the life of the Insured.

## 3. ADVANCE PURCHASE

A new policy may be purchased before a Purchase Date each time one of these events occurs:

- the marriage of the Insured.
- the birth of a child of the Insured.
- the completion, by the Insured, of the legal adoption of a child.

The event must occur while this policy is in force. To make an advance purchase of a new policy, there must be a future Purchase Date that has not been used. An advance purchase of a new policy cancels the next unused Purchase Date.

The Company must receive an application and the first premium for each new policy:

- while the Insured is living; and
- not more than 90 days after the marriage, birth or adoption.

The Company may require proof of the marriage, birth or adoption.

The Owner of the new policy must have an insurable interest in the life of the Insured.

## 4. AUTOMATIC TERM INSURANCE

The Company will provide term insurance on the life of the Insured during each 90 day period in which the Owner may purchase a new policy. The amount of the term insurance will be the largest amount of

insurance which could have been purchased as a new policy under this Benefit. The proceeds of the term insurance are payable on the death of the Insured only if:

- a new policy was not purchased within that period; or
- a new policy purchased within that period is surrendered to the Company for a refund of premiums.

The proceeds of the term insurance will be payable to the beneficiary and subject to the terms of this policy.

## 5. TERMS OF NEW POLICY

**Plan.** Each new policy will be on a level premium permanent life insurance plan being issued by the Company on the date of purchase of the new policy. An additional benefit that is made a part of the new policy will contain the provisions of that benefit as it is being issued by the Company on the date of issue of the new policy.

**Amount.** The minimum amount of each new policy on the Whole Life Paid Up at 90 plan will be $20,000. The amount of each new policy on any other plan must be at least the Company's minimum for policies being issued on that plan at that time. The maximum amount of each policy will be the Amount of the Additional Purchase Benefit shown on page 3. However, in the event of a multiple birth, the maximum amount which may be purchased as an advance purchase will be the Amount of this Benefit multiplied by the number of children of the birth.

**Waiver Of Premium Benefit.** If the Waiver of Premium Benefit is in force on this policy at the time that the Owner has the right to purchase a new policy:

- a new policy on a plan with a level death benefit on which premiums are payable to age 90 or later may be issued with the Waiver of Premium Benefit. If premiums are being waived for this policy at the time the new policy is purchased, premiums will also be waived for the new policy for as long as they are waived for this policy.
- a new policy on a plan with a nonlevel death benefit or a plan on which all premiums are payable before age 90 may be issued with the Waiver of Premium Benefit only if premiums are not then being waived for this policy. If the Waiver of Premium Benefit is a part of the new policy, it will apply only to a disability that starts after the new policy takes effect.

NN 1 Life APB

I/R 4400.00
29-3855-02 (12-85)

(Continued on reverse side)

SPECIMEN
COPY
PROVISIONS MAY VARY SLIGHTLY
IN CERTAIN STATES

**Accidental Death Benefit.** Each new policy may be issued with the Accidental Death Benefit, provided that:

- the Accidental Death Benefit is a part of this policy when the new policy is issued; and

- the Accidental Death Benefit amount is not more than the amount of the new policy. However, the total amount of Accidental Death Benefit in force with the Company on the life of the Insured may not be more than the Company's published limits.

**Provisions.** The Suicide and Incontestability provisions in each new policy will be in effect from the Date of Issue of this policy. Each new policy will contain any exclusion provision which is a part of this policy.

**Premiums.** The premium for each new policy, including any additional benefits, will be determined as of its date of issue based on:

- the Company's premium rates then in effect;

- the plan and amount of the new policy and any additional benefits; and

- the Insured's age on the policy date of the new policy.

If the Insured was age 18 or more on the Policy Date of this policy, the premium for the new policy will be based on the classification of risk of this policy. If the Insured was age 17 or less on the Policy Date of this policy, the premium for the new policy will be based on the classification of risk of this policy adjusted to reflect the Insured's cigarette smoking habits.

**Effective Date.** Each new policy will take effect on the later of:

- the date the Company receives the application; or

- the date the Company receives the first premium.

## 6. TERMINATION OF BENEFIT

This Benefit will terminate on the policy anniversary that is nearest the 40th birthday of the Insured. It will terminate earlier:

- when this policy terminates.

- when this policy becomes extended term or paid-up insurance.

- on the use of the final Purchase Date by an advance purchase.

- when the Owner's written request is received at the Home Office.

# ACCIDENTAL DEATH BENEFIT

## 1. THE BENEFIT

The Company will pay an Accidental Death Benefit upon receipt of proof that the Insured's death:

- resulted, directly and independently of all other causes, from accidental bodily injury; and
- occurred while this Benefit was in force.

## 2. PREMIUM AND AMOUNT OF BENEFIT

The premium for and the amount of this Benefit are shown on page 3. The Benefit will be payable as part of the policy proceeds.

## 3. RISKS NOT ASSUMED

This Benefit will not be payable if the Insured's death resulted from or was contributed to by:

- suicide.
- bodily or mental infirmity or disease.

- an act or incident of war, declared or undeclared.
- riding in any kind of aircraft:
    a. as a passenger in any aircraft operated by or for the armed forces.
    b. as a pilot, as a participant in training, or as a crew member. The term "crew member" includes anyone who has any duties at any time on the flight with respect to either the flight or the aircraft.

## 4. TERMINATION OF BENEFIT

This Benefit will terminate on the policy anniversary that is nearest the 70th birthday of the Insured. It will terminate earlier:

- when the policy terminates.
- when the policy becomes extended term or paid-up insurance.
- when the Owner's written request is received at the Home Office.

SPECIMEN COPY
PROVISIONS MAY VARY SLIGHTLY
IN CERTAIN STATES

NN 1 Life ADB

I/R 4400.00
29-3855-01 (12-85)

# Appendix D

# UNIVERSAL LIFE POLICY

---

**FLEXIBLE-PREMIUM (UNIVERSAL) LIFE INSURANCE POLICY**

### Flexible-Premium Life Insurance Policy

Life insurance payable if the insured dies before the Final Date of Policy. Accumulation Fund payable on the Final Date.

Adjustable death benefit.

Premiums payable while the insured is alive and before the Final Date of Policy. Premiums must be sufficient to keep the policy in force.

Not eligible for dividends.

**10-Day Right to Examine Policy**—Please read this policy. You may return this policy to us or to the sales representative through whom you bought it within 10 days from the date you receive it. If you return it within the 10-day period, the policy will be void from the beginning. We will refund any premium paid.

See Table of Contents and Company address on back cover.

POLICY SPECIFICATIONS

DATE OF POLICY..............................

INSURED'S AGE AND SEX....................

FINAL DATE OF POLICY......................POLICY ANNIVERSARY AT AGE 95

DEATH BENEFIT ...............................OPTION    (SEE PAGE 5)

OWNER ..........................................SEE APPLICATION

BENEFICIARY AND
CONTINGENT BENEFICIARY...................SEE APPLICATION

POLICY CLASSIFICATION......................

INSURED

SPECIFIED
FACE AMOUNT
OF INSURANCE .....      —AS OF DATE OF POLICY                    ..POLICY NUMBER

PLAN .................FLEXIBLE-PREMIUM LIFE

THIS POLICY PROVIDES LIFE INSURANCE COVERAGE UNTIL THE FINAL DATE IF SUFFICIENT PREMIUMS ARE PAID THE PLANNED PREMIUM SHOWN BELOW MAY NEED TO BE INCREASED TO KEEP THIS POLICY AND COVERAGE IN FORCE.

PLANNED PREMIUM OF          —PAYABLE

(TOTAL PREMIUM FOR LIFE INSURANCE BENEFIT. ANY SUPPLEMENTAL RATING AND ANY ADDITIONAL BENEFITS LISTED BELOW)

ADDITIONAL BENEFITS

FORM 7-82 MIAC                                    401. 402. 403. 404.

---

"Flexible-Premium (Universal) Life Insurance Policy" from *Policy Kit for Students of Insurance.* Reprinted with permission from Alliance of American Insurers.

**Table of Guaranteed Maximum Rates For Each $1,000 of Term Insurance**
**(See "Cost of Term Insurance" Provision on page 6.)**

| Age Male | Age Female | Monthly Rate* | Age Male | Age Female | Monthly Rate* | Age Male | Age Female | Monthly Rate* |
|---|---|---|---|---|---|---|---|---|
| 0 | — | .370 | 33 | 36 | .196 | 79 | 82 | 9.320 |
| 1 | — | .136 | 34 | 37 | .204 | 80 | 83 | 10.174 |
| 2 | — | .124 | 35 | 38 | .214 | 81 | 84 | 11.088 |
| 3 | — | .119 | 36 | 39 | .227 | 82 | 85 | 12.053 |
| 4 | — | .114 | 37 | 40 | .242 | 83 | 86 | 13.070 |
| 5 | — | .110 | 38 | 41 | .261 | 84 | 87 | 14.146 |
| 6 | — | .106 | 39 | 42 | .283 | 85 | 88 | 15.289 |
| 7 | — | .103 | 40 | 43 | .307 | 86 | 89 | 16.509 |
| 8 | — | .101 | 41 | 44 | .334 | 87 | 90 | 17.822 |
| 9 | — | .100 | 42 | 45 | .363 | 88 | 91 | 19.256 |
| 10 | — | .101 | 43 | 46 | .394 | 89 | 92 | 20.852 |
| 11 | — | .103 | 44 | 47 | .429 | 90 | 93 | 22.665 |
| — | 0 | .329 | 45 | 48 | .467 | 91 | 94 | 24.769 |
| — | 1 | .128 | 46 | 49 | .509 | 92 | — | 27.258 |
| — | 2 | .115 | 47 | 50 | .556 | 93 | — | 30.251 |
| — | 3 | .110 | 48 | 51 | .608 | 94 | — | 34.025 |
| — | 4 | .105 | 49 | 52 | .666 | | | |
| — | 5 | .101 | 50 | 53 | .729 | | | |
| — | 6 | .097 | 51 | 54 | .798 | | | |
| — | 7 | .094 | 52 | 55 | .873 | | | |
| — | 8 | .092 | 53 | 56 | .955 | | | |
| — | 9 | .092 | 54 | 57 | 1.044 | | | |
| — | 10 | .092 | 55 | 58 | 1.141 | | | |
| — | 11 | .094 | 56 | 59 | 1.249 | | | |
| — | 12 | .096 | 57 | 60 | 1.367 | | | |
| — | 13 | .099 | 58 | 61 | 1.496 | | | |
| — | 14 | .102 | 59 | 62 | 1.638 | | | |
| 12 | 15 | .107 | 60 | 63 | 1.794 | | | |
| 13 | 16 | .113 | 61 | 64 | 1.963 | | | |
| 14 | 17 | .118 | 62 | 65 | 2.148 | | | |
| 15 | 18 | .125 | 63 | 66 | 2.351 | | | |
| 16 | 19 | .131 | 64 | 67 | 2.573 | | | |
| 17 | 20 | .138 | 65 | 68 | 2.819 | | | |
| 18 | 21 | .143 | 66 | 69 | 3.091 | | | |
| 19 | 22 | .147 | 67 | 70 | 3.392 | | | |
| 20 | 23 | .151 | 68 | 71 | 3.722 | | | |
| 21 | 24 | .153 | 69 | 72 | 4.076 | | | |
| 22 | 25 | .156 | 70 | 73 | 4.452 | | | |
| 23 | 26 | .158 | 71 | 74 | 4.843 | | | |
| 24 | 27 | .160 | 72 | 75 | 5.248 | | | |
| 25 | 28 | .162 | 73 | 76 | 5.671 | | | |
| 26 | 29 | .164 | 74 | 77 | 6.124 | | | |
| 27 | 30 | .167 | 75 | 78 | 6.623 | | | |
| 28 | 31 | .171 | 76 | 79 | 7.183 | | | |
| 29 | 32 | .175 | 77 | 80 | 7.817 | | | |
| 30 | 33 | .180 | 78 | 81 | 8.532 | | | |
| 31 | 34 | .185 | | | | | | |
| 32 | 35 | .190 | | | | | | |

*If there is a supplemental rating for the life insurance benefit, as shown on page 3, the monthly deduction for such supplemental rating must be added to the monthly rate determined from this table.

401-82

## Understanding This Policy

"You" and "your" refer to the owner of this policy.

"We", "us" and "our" refer to Metropolitan Insurance and Annuity Company.

The "insured" named on page 3 is the person at whose death the insurance proceeds will be payable.

The "Specified Face Amount of Insurance" as of the date of policy is shown on page 3. A new page 3 will be issued to show any change in the Specified Face Amount of Insurance that has occurred at your request.

The "Date of Policy" is shown on page 3.

The "Final Date of Policy" is the policy anniversary on which the insured is age 95.

Policy years and months are measured from the date of policy. For example, if the date of policy is May 5, 1990, the first policy month ends June 4, 1990, and the first policy year ends May 4, 1991. Similarly, the first monthly anniversary is June 5, 1990, and the first policy anniversary is May 5, 1991.

The "accumulation fund" forms the basis for the benefits provided under your policy. Computation of the accumulation fund is described on page 6.

The "Designated Office" is our Executive Office at One Madison Avenue, New York, N. Y. 10010. We may, by written notice, name other offices within the United States to serve as Designated Offices.

To make this policy clear and easy to read, we have left out many cross-references and conditional statements. Therefore, the provisions of the policy must be read as a whole. For example, our payment of the insurance proceeds (see page 5) depends upon the payment of sufficient premiums (see page 7).

To exercise your rights, you should follow the procedures stated in this policy. If you want to request a payment, adjust the death benefit, change a beneficiary, change an address or request any other action by us, you should do so on the forms prepared for each purpose. You can get these forms from your sales representative or our Designated Office.

## Payment When Insured Dies

**Insurance Proceeds**—If the insured dies before the Final Date of Policy, an amount of money, called the insurance proceeds, will be payable to the beneficiary. The insurance proceeds are the sum of:

- The death benefit described below.

  PLUS

- Any insurance on the insured's life that may be provided by riders to this policy.

  MINUS

- Any policy loan and loan interest.

We will pay the insurance proceeds to the beneficiary after we receive proof of death and a proper written claim.

**Death Benefit**—The death benefit under the policy will be either (1) or (2) below, whichever is chosen and is in effect on the date of death:

1. Under Option A, the greater of:

   (a) the Specified Face Amount of Insurance;

   or

   (b) 110% of the accumulation fund on the date of death.

2. Under Option B:

   The Specified Face Amount of Insurance;

   PLUS

   The accumulation fund on the date of death.

**Death Benefit Adjustment**—At any time after the first policy year while this policy is in force, you may change the death benefit option or change (either increase or decrease) the Specified Face Amount of Insurance, subject to the following.

1. In the event of a change in the death benefit option, we will change the Specified Face Amount of Insurance as needed.

2. The Specified Face Amount of Insurance may not be reduced to less than $50,000 during the first 5 policy years or to less than $25,000 after the 5th policy year.

3. For any change which would increase the death benefit, you must provide evidence satisfactory to us of the insurability of the insured. Also, the increased death benefit will be subject to a charge of $3 for each $1,000 of insurance increase. We will deduct this charge from the accumulation fund as of the date the increase takes effect.

4. No change in the death benefit will take effect unless the accumulation fund, after the change, is sufficient to keep this policy in force for at least 2 months. Subject to this condition, a request for a change in the death benefit will take effect on the monthly anniversary which coincides with or next follows: (a) if evidence of insurability is required, the date we approve the request; or (b) if not, the date of the request.

5. We will issue a new page 3 for this policy showing the change. We may require that you send us this policy to make the change.

402-82

## Computation of Accumulation Fund

**Accumulation Fund**—The value of the accumulation fund is as follows:

- On the date of policy—91% of the first premium;

  MINUS

  The monthly deduction for the first month.

- On any monthly anniversary—The value on the last monthly anniversary;

  PLUS

  One month's interest on such value at the currently applicable rates;

  PLUS

  91% of the premiums received since the last monthly anniversary;

  MINUS

  The monthly deduction for the month beginning on the current monthly anniversary.

- On other than a monthly anniversary—The value on the last monthly anniversary;

  PLUS

  91% of the premiums received since the last monthly anniversary.

Note: The 9% deduction from premiums is an expense charge.

If you make a partial cash withdrawal (see page 7), the accumulation fund defined above will be reduced by the amount of such withdrawal.

**Monthly Deduction**—The deduction for any policy month is the sum of the following amounts, determined as of the beginning of that month:

- The monthly cost of the term insurance (See Cost of Term Insurance on page 6).
- The monthly cost of any benefits provided by riders.
- For each of the first 12 policy months only, a charge of $35 plus $.25 for each $1,000 of Specified Face Amount of Insurance.

**Interest Rate**—The guaranteed interest rate used to determine the accumulation fund is .32737% a month, compounded monthly. This is equivalent to a rate of 4% a year, compounded annually.

Interest will be credited to the accumulation fund each month as follows:

- At the guaranteed interest rate on the first $1,000 in the accumulation fund.
- In the manner and at the rate we set from time to time, on amounts in excess of $1,000 in the accumulation fund. The rate we set will never be less than the guaranteed interest rate.
- If there is a loan against this policy, interest on that portion of the accumulation fund in excess of $1,000 that equals the loan will be at a rate we set. The rate with respect to the amount of the loan will never be less than the guaranteed interest rate.

**Example**—Suppose the accumulation fund is $10,000 and there is a policy loan of $2,000. If we set the annual interest rates at 10% for amounts over $1,000 in the accumulation fund and at 6% for the amount of any loan, then interest would be credited: at the rate of 4% on the first $1,000; at the rate of 6% on the next $2,000 representing the amount of the loan; and at the rate of 10% on the remaining $7,000.

**Cost of Term Insurance**—Under either death benefit option, the amount of term insurance for any policy month is equal to:

- The death benefit divided by 1.0032737;

  MINUS

- The accumulation fund.

The accumulation fund used in this calculation is the accumulation fund at the beginning of the policy month before the deduction for the monthly cost of term insurance, but after the deductions for riders and any other charges.

The cost of the term insurance for any policy month is equal to the amount of term insurance multiplied by the monthly term insurance rate. Monthly term insurance rates will be set by us from time to time, based on the insured's age, sex, and underwriting class. But these rates will never be more than the maximum rates shown in the table on page 4.

402-82

## Payments During Insured's Lifetime

**Payment on Final Date of Policy**—If the insured is alive on the Final Date of Policy, we will pay you the accumulation fund minus any policy loan and loan interest. Coverage under this policy will then end.

**Cash Value**—Your policy has a cash value while the insured is alive.

The cash value at any time during the first policy year will equal:

- The accumulation fund;

    MINUS

- $35 times the number of full policy months left in that year;

    MINUS

- Any policy loan and loan interest.

After the first policy year, the cash value at any time will

    he accumulation fund;

    MINUS

- The interest in excess of the guaranteed rate credited to the fund during the last 12 policy months;

    MINUS

- Any policy loan and loan interest.

**Full and Partial Cash Withdrawal**—We will pay you all or part of the cash value after we receive your request at our Designated Office. The cash value will be determined as of the date we receive your request. If you request and are paid the full cash value, this policy and all our obligations under it will end. We may require surrender of this policy before we pay you the full cash value.

Each partial withdrawal of cash value must be at least $250. When a partial withdrawal is made, we will reduce the accumulation fund by the amount of the partial withdrawal. If Option A is in effect, we will also reduce the Specified Face Amount of Insurance by the amount of the partial withdrawal; and a new page 3 will then be issued. We may require that you send us this policy to make the change.

If you request a partial withdrawal which would reduce the cash value to less than $500, we will treat it as a request for a full cash withdrawal. Also, if Option A is in effect and the Specified Face Amount of Insurance would be reduced to less than $50,000 during the first 5 policy years, or to less than $25,000 thereafter, we will treat your request as a request for a full cash withdrawal.

**Policy Loan**—You may also get cash from us by taking a policy loan. If there is an existing loan you can increase it. The most you can borrow at any time is the cash value on the next monthly anniversary, less the monthly deduction for the following month.

Loan interest is charged daily at the rate of 8% a year, and is due at the end of each policy year. Interest not paid within 31 days after it is due will be added to the amount of the loan. It will be added as of the due date and will bear interest at the same rate as the rest of the loan.

A loan will affect the interest rate we credit to amounts over $1,000 in the accumulation fund (see "Interest Rate" on page 6).

**Loan Repayment**—You may repay all or part (but not less than $25) of a policy loan at any time while the insured is alive and this policy is in force. If any payment you make to us is intended as a loan repayment, rather than a premium payment, you must tell us this when you make the payment.

Failure to repay a policy loan or to pay loan interest will not terminate this policy unless the accumulation fund, minus the policy loan and loan interest, is insufficient to pay the monthly deduction due on a monthly anniversary. In that case, the Grace Period provision will apply (see page 8).

**Deferment**—We may delay paying a full or partial cash withdrawal for up to 6 months from the date we receive a request for payment. If we delay for 30 days or more, interest will be paid from the date we receive the request at a rate not less than 3% a year.

We also may delay making a policy loan, except for a loan to pay a premium, for up to 6 months from the date you request the loan.

## Premiums

**Premium Payments**—Premiums may be paid at our Designated Office or to our sales representative. A receipt signed by our President or Secretary and countersigned by the sales representative will be given for a premium paid to the sales representative.

The first premium is due on the date of policy and will be credited as of that date. No insurance will take effect before the first premium is paid. Other premiums may be paid at any time while the policy is in force and before the Final Date of Policy and in any amount and subject to the limits described below.

We will send premium notices, if you request in writing, according to the planned premium shown on page 3. You may skip planned premium payments or change their frequency and amount if the accumulation fund is large enough to keep your policy in force.

402-82

## Premiums (Continued)

**Limits**—The first premium may not be less than the planned premium shown on page 3. Each premium payment after the first must be at least $250 ($50 for a Check-O-Matic payment).

We may increase these minimum premium limits. No increase will take effect until 90 days after notice is sent

The total premiums paid in a policy year may not exceed the maximum we set for that year.

**Grace Period**—If the accumulation fund on any monthly anniversary, minus any policy loan and loan interest, is less than the monthly deduction for that month, there will be a grace period of 61 days after that anniversary to pay an amount that will cover the monthly deduction. We will send you a notice at the start of the grace period. We will also send a notice to any assignee on our records.

If we do not receive a sufficient amount by the end of the grace period, your policy will then end without value.

If the insured dies during the grace period, we will pay the insurance proceeds minus any overdue monthly deduction.

**Reinstatement**—If the grace period has ended and you have not paid the required premium and have not surrendered your policy for its cash value, you may reinstate this policy while the insured is alive if you:

1. Ask for reinstatement within 3 years after the end of the grace period;

2. Provide evidence of insurability satisfactory to us;

3. Pay a sufficient amount to keep the policy in force for at least 2 months after the date of reinstatement;

4. If the grace period began during the first policy year, pay: (a) an amount sufficient to cover the unpaid portion of the charges applicable during the first 12 policy months; plus (b) interest on such amount to the date of reinstatement at the rate of 6% a year.

The effective date of the reinstated policy will be the monthly anniversary following the date we approve the reinstatement application. If we approve it on a monthly anniversary, the effective date will be that anniversary.

## Ownership and Beneficiary

**Owner**—As owner, you may exercise all rights under your policy while the insured is alive. You may name a contingent owner who would become the owner if you should die before the insured.

**Change of Ownership**—You may name a new owner at any time. If a new owner is named, any earlier choice of a contingent owner, beneficiary, contingent beneficiary or optional income plan will be canceled, unless you specify otherwise.

**Beneficiary**—The beneficiary is the person or persons to whom the insurance proceeds are payable when the insured dies. You may name a contingent beneficiary to become the beneficiary if all the beneficiaries die while the insured is alive. If no beneficiary or contingent beneficiary is named, or if none is alive when the insured dies, the owner (or the owner's estate) will be the beneficiary. While the insured is alive, the owner may change any beneficiary or contingent beneficiary.

If more than one beneficiary is alive when the insured dies, we will pay them in equal shares, unless you have chosen otherwise.

**How to Change the Owner or the Beneficiary**—You may change the owner, contingent owner, beneficiary or contingent beneficiary of this policy by written notice or assignment of the policy. No change is binding on us until it is recorded at our Designated Office. Once recorded, the change binds us as of the date you signed it. The change will not apply to any payment made by us before we recorded your request. We may require that you send us this policy to make the change.

**Collateral Assignment**—Your policy may be assigned as collateral. All rights under the policy will be transferred to the extent of the assignee's interest. We are not bound by any assignment unless it is in writing and is recorded at our Designated Office. We are not responsible for the validity of any assignment.

402-82

# General Provisions

**The Contract**—This policy includes any riders and, with the application attached when the policy is issued, makes up the entire contract. All statements in the application will be representations and not warranties. No statement will be used to contest the policy unless it appears in the application.

**Limitation on Sales Representative's Authority**—No sales representative or other person except our President, a Vice-President, or the Secretary may (a) make or change any contract of insurance; or (b) make any binding promises about policy benefits; or (c) change or waive any of the terms of this policy. Any change is valid only if made in writing and signed by our President, a Vice-President, or the Secretary.

**Incontestability**—We will not contest the validity of your policy after it has been in force during the insured's lifetime for 2 years from the date of policy. We will not contest the validity of any increase in the death benefit after such increase has been in force during the insured's lifetime for 2 years from its effective date.

**Suicide**—The insurance proceeds will not be paid if the insured commits suicide, while sane or insane, within 2 years from the date of policy. Instead we will pay the beneficiary an amount equal to all premiums paid, without interest, less any policy loan and loan interest and less any partial cash withdrawals. If the insured commits suicide, while sane or insane, more than 2 years after the date of this policy but within 2 years from the effective date of any increase in the death benefit, our liability with respect to such increase will be limited to its cost.

**Age and Sex**—If the insured's age or sex on the date of the policy is not correct as shown on page 3, we will adjust the benefits under this policy. The adjusted benefits will be those that the premiums paid would have provided at the correct age and sex.

**Nonparticipation**—This policy is not eligible for dividends; it does not participate in any distribution of our surplus.

**Computation of Values**—The minimum accumulation fund and policy reserves are computed using interest at the rate of 4% a year. These values and the maximum term insurance rates shown on page 4 are based on the 1958 Commissioners Standard Ordinary Mortality Table, age last birthday for male lives. For female lives, they are based on that table set back 3 years at ages 15 and older and on the female extension of that table at ages under 15.

We have filed a detailed statement of the method of computation with the insurance supervisory official of the state in which this policy is delivered. The values under this policy are equal to or greater than those required by the law of that state.

**Annual Reports**—Each year we will send you a report showing the current death benefit, accumulation fund and cash value for this policy.

It will also show the amount and type of credits to and deductions from the accumulation fund during the past policy year.

The report will also include any other information required by state laws and regulations.

**Illustration of Future Benefits**—At any time, we will provide an illustration of the future benefits and values under your policy. You must ask in writing for this illustration and pay the service fee set by us.

## Optional Income Plans

The insurance proceeds when the insured dies, or the amount payable on the Final Date of Policy, instead of being paid in one sum may be applied under one or more of the following income plans. Also, at any time before the Final Date and while the insured is alive, you may ask us to:

(a) Apply the full cash value of this policy under a non-life income plan;

or

(b) Apply the accumulation fund of this policy, minus any policy loan and loan interest, under a life income plan.

### Non-Life Income Plans

**Option 1.** *Interest Income*
The amount applied will earn interest which will be paid monthly. Withdrawals of at least $500 each may be made at any time by written request.

**Option 2.** *Instalment Income for a Stated Period*
Monthly instalment payments will be made so that the amount applied, with interest, will be paid over the period chosen (from 1 to 30 years).

**Option 2A.** *Instalment Income of a Stated Amount*
Monthly instalment payments of a chosen amount will be made until the entire amount applied, with interest, is paid.

### Life Income Plans

**Option 3.** *Single Life Income—Guaranteed Payment Period*
Monthly payments will be made during the lifetime of the payee with a chosen guaranteed payment period of 10, 15 or 20 years.

**Option 3A.** *Single Life Income—Guaranteed Return*
Monthly payments will be made during the lifetime of the payee. If the payee dies before the total amount applied under this plan has been paid, the remainder will be paid in one sum as a death benefit.

**Option 4.** *Joint and Survivor Life Income*
Monthly payments will be made jointly to two persons while they are both alive and will continue during the remaining lifetime of the survivor. A total payment period of 10 years is guaranteed.

**Other Frequencies and Plans**—Instead of monthly payments, you may choose to have payments made quarterly, semiannually or annually. Other income plans may be arranged with us.

**Choice of Income Plans**—A choice of an income plan for insurance proceeds made by you in writing and recorded by us while the insured is alive will take effect when the insured dies. A choice of an income plan for the amount payable on the Final Date of Policy will take effect on such date. All other choices of income plans will take effect when recorded by us or later, if requested. When an income plan starts, we will issue a contract that will describe the terms of the plan. We may require that you send us this policy. We may also require proof of the payee's age

Income plans for insurance proceeds may be chosen

1. By you during the lifetime of the insured.

2. By the beneficiary, within one year after the date the insured died and before any payment has been made. if no election was in effect on the date of death.

Income plans for the amount payable on the Final Date of Policy may be chosen by you:

1. On or before the Final Date of Policy.

2. Within one year after the Final Date of Policy and before any payment has been made.

A choice of an income plan will not become effective unless each payment under the plan would be at least $50.

**Limitations**—If the payee is not a natural person. the choice of an income plan will be subject to our approval An assignment for a loan will modify a prior choice of income plan. The amount due the assignee will be payable in one sum and the balance will be applied under the income plan.

Income plan payments may not be assigned and, to the extent permitted by law, will not be subject to the claims of creditors.

**Income Plan Rates**—Amounts applied under non-life income plans will earn interest at a rate we set from time to time. That rate will never be less than 3% a year.

Life income plan payments will be based on a rate set by us and in effect on the date the amount to be applied becomes payable.

404-82

## Optional Income Plans (Continued)

**Minimum Payments under Optional Income Plans**—Monthly payments under Options 2, 3, 3A and 4 for each $1,000 applied will not be less than the amounts shown in the following Tables.

**Option 2.**   *Instalment Income for a Stated Period*
Monthly Payments for each $1,000 Applied

| Years Chosen | Minimum Amount of Each Monthly Payment | Years Chosen | Minimum Amount of Each Monthly Payment | Years Chosen | Minimum Amount of Each Monthly Payment |
|---|---|---|---|---|---|
| 1 | $84.47 | 11 | $8.86 | 21 | $5.32 |
| 2 | 42.86 | 12 | 8.24 | 22 | 5.15 |
| 3 | 28.99 | 13 | 7.71 | 23 | 4.99 |
| 4 | 22.06 | 14 | 7.26 | 24 | 4.84 |
| 5 | 17.91 | 15 | 6.87 | 25 | 4.71 |
| 6 | 15.14 | 16 | 6.53 | 26 | 4.59 |
| 7 | 13.16 | 17 | 6.23 | 27 | 4.47 |
| 8 | 11.68 | 18 | 5.96 | 28 | 4.37 |
| 9 | 10.53 | 19 | 5.73 | 29 | 4.27 |
| 10 | 9.61 | 20 | 5.51 | 30 | 4.18 |

To determine the minimum amount for quarterly payment, multiply the above monthly payment by 2.99; for semiannual by 5.96; and for annual by 11.84.

**Option 3.**   *Single Life Income*—Guaranteed Payment Period
Minimum Amount of each Monthly Payment for each $1,000 Applied

**Option 3A.**
*Single Life Income*—Guaranteed Return
Minimum Amount of each Monthly Payment for each $1,000 Applied

| Payee's Age | Guaranteed Payment Period | | | | | | | |
|---|---|---|---|---|---|---|---|---|
| | 10 years | | 15 years | | 20 years | | | |
| | Male | Female | Male | Female | Male | Female | Male | Female |
| 50 | $4.50 | $4.09 | $4.40 | $4.05 | $4.28 | $3.99 | $4.24 | $3.96 |
| 55 | 4.96 | 4.49 | 4.80 | 4.41 | 4.58 | 4.31 | 4.61 | 4.29 |
| 60 | 5.53 | 4.99 | 5.25 | 4.86 | 4.90 | 4.67 | 5.07 | 4.72 |
| 65 | 6.25 | 5.67 | 5.75 | 5.40 | 5.18 | 5.03 | 5.67 | 5.28 |
| 70 | 7.11 | 6.55 | 6.23 | 5.99 | 5.39 | 5.31 | 6.46 | 6.04 |
| 75 | 8.03 | 7.60 | 6.61 | 6.48 | 5.49 | 5.45 | 7.54 | 7.06 |
| 80 | 8.87 | 8.60 | 6.81 | 6.74 | 5.51 | 5.50 | 9.01 | 8.44 |
| 85 and over | 9.40 | 9.22 | 6.86 | 6.84 | 5.51 | 5.51 | 11.14 | 10.26 |

**Option 4.**   *Joint and Survivor Life Income*—Guaranteed Period of 10 years
Minimum Amount of each Monthly Payment for each $1,000 Applied

| Age of Both Payees | One Male and One Female | Two Males | Two Females |
|---|---|---|---|
| 50 | $3.77 | $3.92 | $3.67 |
| 55 | 4.09 | 4.27 | 3.97 |
| 60 | 4.52 | 4.73 | 4.37 |
| 65 | 5.10 | 5.35 | 4.91 |
| 70 | 5.90 | 6.18 | 5.68 |
| 75 | 6.95 | 7.21 | 6.72 |

On request, we will provide additional information about amounts of minimum payments.

404-82

# GLOSSARY

**Absolute liability** Liability for damages even though fault or negligence cannot be proven, for example, in such situations as occupational injury of employees under a workers compensation law.

**Accelerated death benefits rider** A rider that allows insureds who are terminally ill or who suffer from certain catastrophic diseases to collect part or all of their life insurance benefits before they die, primarily to pay for the care they require.

**Accident** A loss-causing event that is sudden, unforeseen, and unintentional. *See also* **Occurrence.**

**Accidental bodily injury** Bodily injury resulting from an act whose result was accidental or unexpected.

**Actual cash value** Value of property at the time of its damage or loss, determined by subtracting depreciation of the item from its replacement cost.

**Actual loss ratio** The ratio of incurred losses and loss-adjustment expenses to earned premiums.

**Add-on plan** Pays benefits to an accident victim without regard to fault, but the injured person still has the right to sue the negligent driver who caused the accident.

**Adjustable life insurance** Insurance contract that permits certain changes to be made in amount of life insurance, premiums, period of protection, and duration of the premium-paying period.

**Adjustment bureau** Organization for adjusting insurance claims that is supported by insurers using the bureau's services.

**Advance funding** Pension-funding method in which the employer systematically and periodically sets aside funds prior to the employee's retirement.

**Advance premium mutual** Mutual insurance company owned by the policyowners that does not issue assessable policies but charges premiums expected to be sufficient to pay all claims and expenses.

**Adverse selection** Tendency of persons with a higher-than-average chance of loss to seek insurance at standard (average) rates, which, if not controlled by underwriting, results in higher-than-expected loss levels.

**Agent** Someone who legally represents the insurer, has the authority to act on the insurer's behalf, and can bind the principal by expressed powers, by implied powers, and by apparent authority.

**Aggregate deductible** Deductible in some property and health insurance contracts in which all covered losses during a year are added together and the insurer pays only when the aggregate deductible amount is exceeded.

**Aleatory contract** One in which the values exchanged may not be equal but depend on an uncertain event.

**Alien insurer** Insurance company chartered by a foreign country and meeting certain licensing requirements.

**"All-risks" policy** Coverage by an insurance contract that promises to cover all losses except those losses specifically excluded in the policy. *See also* **Risk of direct loss to property.**

**Alternative dispute resolution (ADR) techniques** Techniques to resolve a legal dispute without litigation.

**Annuitant** Person who receives the periodic payment of an annuity.

**Annuity** Periodic payment to an individual that continues for a fixed period or for the duration of a designated life or lives.

**Appraisal clause** Used when the insured and insurer agree that the loss is covered, but the amount of the loss is in dispute.

**Assessment mutual** Mutual insurance company that has the right to assess policyowners for losses and expenses.

**Assumption-of-risk** Defense against a negligence claim that bars recovery for damages if a person understands and recognizes the danger inherent in a particular activity or occupation.

**Attractive nuisance** Condition that can attract and injure children. Occupants of land on which such a condition exists are liable for injuries to children.

**Automatic premium loan** Cash borrowed from a life insurance policy's cash value to pay an overdue premium after the grace period for paying the premium has expired.

**Automobile insurance plan** Formerly called assigned risk plan. Method for providing automobile insurance to persons considered to be high-risk drivers who cannot obtain protection in the voluntary markets. All automobile insurers in the state are assigned their share of such drivers based on the volume of automobile insurance business written in the state.

**Average indexed monthly earnings (AIME)** Under the OASDI program, the person's actual earnings are indexed to determine his or her primary insurance amount (PIA).

**Avoidance** *See* **Loss avoidance.**

**Bailee's customer policy** Policy that covers the loss or damage to property of customers regardless of a bailee's legal liability.

**Basic form** *See* **Dwelling Property 1.**

**Benefit period** A period of time, typically one to three years, during which major medical benefits are paid after the deductible is satisfied. When the benefit period ends, the insured must then satisfy a new deductible in order to establish a new benefit period.

**Binder** Authorization of coverage by an agent given before the company has formally approved a policy. Provides evidence that the insurance is in force.

**Blackout period** The period during which Social Security benefits are not paid to a surviving spouse—between the time the youngest child reaches age 16 and the surviving spouse's sixtieth birthday.

**Blue Cross plans** Typically nonprofit, community-oriented prepayment plans that provide health insurance coverage primarily for hospital services.

**Blue Shield plans** Typically nonprofit prepayment plans that provide health insurance coverage mainly for physicians' services.

**Boat owners package policy** A special package policy for boat owners that combines physical damage insurance, medical expense insurance, liability insurance, and other coverages in one contract.

**Branch office system** Type of life insurance marketing system under which branch offices are established in various areas. Salaried branch managers, who are employees of the company, are responsible for hiring and training new agents.

**Broad form** *See* **Dwelling Property 2; Homeowners 2 policy.**

**Broker** Someone who legally represents the insured, soliciting or accepting applications for insurance that are not in force until the company accepts the business.

**Burglary** Taking of property from within the premises by someone who unlawfully enters or leaves the premises, with marks of forcible entry or exit.

**Business income coverage form** Business income form drafted by the Insurance Services Office to cover the loss of business income regardless of whether the income is derived from retail or service operations, manufacturing, or rents.

**Businessowners policy** Package policy specifically designed to meet the basic property and liability insurance needs of smaller business firms in one contract.

**Cafeteria plan** Generic term for an employee benefit plan that allows employees to select among the various group life, medical expense, disability, dental, and other plans that best meet their specific needs. Also called flexible benefit plans.

**Calendar-year deductible** Amount payable by an insured during a calendar year before a group or individual health insurance policy begins to pay for medical expenses.

**Capital retention approach** A method used to estimate the amount of life insurance to own. Under this method, the insurance proceeds are retained and are not liquidated.

**Captive insurer** Insurance company established and owned by a parent firm in order to insure its loss exposures while reducing premium costs, providing easier access to a reinsurer, and perhaps easing tax burdens. *See also* **Association captive; Pure captive.**

**Cargo insurance** Type of ocean marine insurance that protects the shipper of the goods against financial loss if the goods are damaged or lost.

**Cash refund annuity** The balance is paid in one lump sum to the beneficiary after the death of the annuitant, if total payments not completed.

**Cash surrender value** Amount payable to the owner of a life insurance policy should he or she decide it is no longer wanted. Calculated separately from the legal reserve.

**Casualty insurance** Field of insurance that covers whatever is not covered by fire, marine, and life insurance. Includes automobile, liability, burglary and theft, workers compensation, glass, and health insurance.

**Catastrophic crop insurance** Guarantees 50 percent of the producer's average yield for each insured crop; the indemnity payment is 60 percent of the expected market price for that crop.

**Causes-of-loss form** Form added to commercial property insurance policy that indicates the causes of loss that are covered. There are four causes-of-loss forms: basic, broad, special, and earthquake.

**Ceding company** Insurer that writes the policy initially and later shifts part or all of the coverage to a reinsurer.

**Certified Financial Planner (CFP)** Professional who has attained a high degree of technical competency in financial planning and has passed a series of professional examinations by the College for Financial Planning.

**Certified Insurance Counselor (CIC)** Professional in property and liability insurance who has passed a series of examinations sponsored by the Society of Certified Insurance Counselors.

**Chance of loss** The probability that an event will occur.

**Change-of-plan provision** Allows policyowners to exchange their present policies for different contracts, provides flexibility.

**Chartered Financial Consultant (ChFC)** An individual who has attained a high degree of technical competency in the fields of financial planning, investments, and life and health insurance and has passed ten professional examinations administered by The American College.

**Chartered Life Underwriter (CLU)** An individual who has attained a high degree of technical competency in the fields of life and health insurance and who is expected to abide by a code of ethics. Must have minimum of three years of experience in life or health insurance sales and have passed ten professional examinations administered by The American College.

**Chartered Property Casualty Underwriter (CPCU)** Professional who has attained a high degree of technical competency in property and liability insurance and has passed ten professional examinations administered by the American Institute for Chartered Property Casualty Underwriters.

**Choice no-fault plans** Motorists can elect to be covered under the state's no-fault law with lower premiums or can retain the right to sue under the tort liability system with higher premiums.

**Claims adjustor** Person who settles claims: an agent, company adjustor, independent adjustor, adjustment bureau, or public adjustor.

**Claims-made policy** A liability insurance policy that only covers claims that are first reported during the policy period, provided the event occurred after the retroactive date (if any) stated in the policy.

**Class rating** Rate-making method in which similar insureds are placed in the same underwriting class and each is charged the same rate. Also called manual rating.

**CLU** *See* **Chartered Life Underwriter.**

**Coinsurance provision** Common provision in commercial property insurance contracts that requires the insured to maintain insurance on the property at a stated percentage of its actual cash value. Payment for a loss is determined by multiplying the amount of the loss by the fraction derived from the amount of insurance required. If the coinsurance requirement is not met at the time of loss, the insured will be penalized. Coinsurance is also used to refer to the percentage participation clause in health insurance. *See also* **Percentage participation clause.**

**Collateral source rule** Under this rule, the defendant cannot introduce any evidence that shows the injured party has received compensation from other collateral sources.

**Collision loss** Damages to an automobile caused by the upset of the automobile or its impact with another vehicle or object. Collision losses are paid by the insurer regardless of fault.

**Commercial general liability policy (CGL)** Commercial liability policy drafted by the Insurance Services Office containing two coverage forms—an occurrence form and a claims-made form.

**Commercial package policy (CPP)** A commercial policy that can be designed to meet the specific insurance needs of business firms. Property and liability coverage forms are combined to form a single policy.

**Commutative contract** One in which the values exchanged by both parties are theoretically even.

**Company adjustor** Claims adjustor who is a salaried employee representing only one company.

**Comparative negligence laws** Laws enacted by many jurisdictions permitting an injured person to recover damages even though he or she may have contributed to the accident. The financial burden is shared by both parties according to their respective degrees of fault.

**Completed operations** Liability arising out of faulty work performed away from the premises after the work or operations are completed; applicable to contractors, plumbers, electricians, repair shops, and similar firms.

**Comprehensive major medical insurance** Type of group plan combining basic plan benefits and major medical insurance in one policy.

**Compulsory insurance law** Law protecting accident victims against irresponsible motorists by requiring owners and op-erators of automobiles to carry certain amounts of liability insurance in order to license the vehicle and drive legally within the state.

**Concealment** Deliberate failure of an applicant for insurance to reveal a material fact to the insurer.

**Conditions** Provisions inserted in an insurance contract that qualify or place limitations on the insurer's promise to perform.

**Consequential loss** Financial loss occurring as the consequence of some other loss. Often called an indirect loss.

**Contingent beneficiary** Beneficiary of a life insurance policy who is entitled to receive the policy proceeds on the insured's death if the primary beneficiary dies before the insured; or the beneficiary who receives the remaining payments if the primary beneficiary dies before receiving the guaranteed number of payments.

**Contingent liability** Liability arising out of work done by independent contractors for a firm. A firm may be liable for the work done by an independent contractor if the activity is illegal, the situation does not permit delegation of authority, or the work is inherently dangerous.

**Contract bond** Type of surety bond guaranteeing that the principal will fulfill all contractual obligations.

**Contract of adhesion** The insured must accept the entire contract, with all of its terms and conditions.

**Contractual liability** Legal liability of another party that the business firm agrees to assume by a written or oral contract.

**Contribution by equal shares** Type of other-insurance provision often found in liability insurance contracts that requires each company to share equally in the loss until the share of each insurer equals the lowest limit of liability under any policy or until the full amount of loss is paid.

**Contributory negligence** Common law defense blocking an injured person from recovering damages if he or she has contributed in any way to the accident.

**Contributory plan** Group life, health, or pension plan in which the employees pay part of the premiums.

**Coordination-of-benefits provision** Provision of a group medical expense plan that prevents over-insurance and duplication of benefits when one person is covered under more than one group plan.

**Corridor deductible** Major medical plan deductible that excludes benefits provided by a basic plan if both a basic and a supplemental group major medical expense policy are in force.

**Cost-of-living rider** Benefit that can be added to a life insurance policy under which the policyowner can purchase one-year term insurance equal to the percentage change in the consumer price index with no evidence of insurability.

**Coverage for damage to your auto** That part of the personal auto policy insuring payment for damage or theft of the insured automobile. This optional coverage can be used to insure both collision and other-than-collision losses.

**CPCU** *See* **Chartered Property Casualty Underwriter.**

**Credit insurance** Protects a firm against abnormal credit losses because of customer insolvency or past due accounts when they are filed for collection within a specified time stated in the policy.

**Current assumption whole life insurance** Nonparticipating whole life policy in which the cash values are based on the insurer's current mortality, investment, and expense experience. An accumulation account is credited with a current interest rate that changes over time. Also called interest-sensitive whole life insurance.

**Currently insured** Status of a covered person under the Old-Age, Survivors, and Disability Insurance (OASDI) program who has at least six quarters of coverage out of the last thirteen quarters, ending with the quarter of death, disability, or entitlement to retirement benefits.

**Damage to property of others** Damage covered up to $500 per occurrence for an insured who damages another's property. Payment is made despite the lack of legal liability. Coverage is included in Section II of the homeowners policy.

**Declarations** Statements in an insurance contract that provide information about the property or life to be insured and used for underwriting and rating purposes and identification of the property or life to be insured.

**Deferred annuity** A retirement annuity that provides benefits at some future date.

**Defined-benefit plan** Type of pension plan in which the retirement benefit is known in advance but the contributions vary depending on the amount necessary to fund the desired benefit.

**Defined-contribution plan** Type of pension plan in which the contribution rate is fixed but the retirement benefit is variable.

**Dependency period** Period of time following the readjustment period during which the surviving spouse's children are under eighteen and therefore dependent on the parent.

**Deposit-administration plan** Type of pension plan in which all pension contributions are deposited in an unallocated fund. An annuity is purchased only when the employee retires.

**Diagnosis-related groups (DRGs)** Method for reimbursing hospitals under the Medicare program. Under this system, a flat, uniform amount is paid to each hospital for the same type of medical care or treatment.

**Difference in conditions insurance (DIC)** "All-risks" policy that covers other perils not insured by basic property insurance contracts, supplemental to and excluding the coverage provided by underlying contracts.

**Direct loss** Financial loss that results directly from an insured peril.

**Direct-response system** A marketing method where insurance is sold without the services of an agent. Potential customers are solicited by advertising in the mails, newspapers, magazines, television, radio, and other media.

**Direct writer** Insurance company in which the salesperson is an employee of the insurer, not an independent contractor, and which pays all selling expenses, including salary.

**Disability-insured** Status of an individual who is insured for disability benefits under the Old-Age, Survivors, and Disability Insurance (OASDI) program. The covered person must be disability-insured and have at least twenty quarters of coverage out of the last forty, ending with the quarter in which the disability occurs. Fewer quarters are required for persons under age thirty.

**Domestic insurer** Insurance company domiciled and licensed in the state in which it does business.

**Double indemnity rider** Benefit that can be added to a life insurance policy doubling the face amount of life insurance if death occurs as the result of an accident.

**Dram shop law** Law that imputes negligence to the owner of a business that sells liquor in the event that an intoxicated customer causes injury or property damage to another person; usually excluded from general liability policies.

**Driver education credit** Student discount or reduction in premium amount for which young drivers become eligible on completion of a driver education course.

**Dwelling Property 1** Property insurance policy that insures the dwelling at actual cash value, other structures, personal property, fair rental value, and certain other coverages; covers a limited number of perils.

**Dwelling Property 2** Property insurance policy that insures the dwelling and other structures at replacement cost. It adds additional coverages and has a greater list of covered perils than the Dwelling Property 1 policy.

**Dwelling Property 3** Property insurance policy that covers the dwelling and other structures against direct physical loss from any peril except for those perils otherwise excluded. However, personal property is covered on a named-perils basis.

**Dying intestate** Dying without a will.

**Earnings test (retirement test)** Test under the Old-Age, Survivors, and Disability Insurance (OASDI) program that reduces monthly benefits to those persons who have annual earned income in excess of the maximum allowed.

**Eligibility period** Brief period of time during which an employee can sign up for group insurance without furnishing evidence of insurability.

**Elimination period (waiting period)** Waiting period in health insurance during which benefits are not paid. Also a period of time that must be met before benefits are actually payable.

**Employee dishonesty coverage form** Commercial crime insurance form drafted by the Insurance Services Office that covers the loss of money, securities, and other covered property because of any dishonest act of a covered employee or employees.

**Employee Retirement Income Security Act (ERISA)** Legislation passed in 1974 applying to most private pension and welfare plans that requires certain standards to protect participating employees.

**Employers liability insurance** Covers employers against lawsuits by employees who are injured in the course of employment, but whose injuries (or disease) are not compensable under the state's workers compensation law.

**Endorsement** Written provision that adds to, deletes, or modifies the provisions in the original contract. *See also* **Rider.**

**Endowment insurance** Type of life insurance that pays the face amount of insurance to the beneficiary if the insured dies within a specified period or to the policyowner if the insured survives to the end of the period.

**Entire-contract clause** Provision in life insurance policies stating that the life insurance policy and attached application constitute the entire contract between the parties.

**Equity in the unearned premium reserve** Amount by which an unearned premium reserve is overstated because it is established on the basis of gross premium rather than net premium.

**ERISA** *See* **Employee Retirement Income Security Act.**

**Errors and omissions insurance** Liability insurance policy that provides protection against loss incurred by a client because of some negligent act, error, or omission by the insured.

**Essential insurance** Includes those coverages required by law or by contract, such as workers compensation insurance.

**Estate planning** Process designed to conserve estate assets before and after death, distribute property according to the individual's wishes, minimize federal estate and state inheritance taxes, provide estate liquidity to meet costs of estate settlement, and provide for the family's financial needs.

**Estoppel** Legal doctrine that prevents a person from denying the truth of a previous representation of fact, especially when such representation has been relied on by the one to whom the statement was made.

**Excess insurance** Under an excess insurance plan, the insurer does not participate in the loss until the actual loss exceeds a certain amount.

**Exclusions** Listing in an insurance contract of the perils, losses, and property excluded from coverage.

**Exclusive agency system** Type of insurance marketing system under which the agent represents only one company or group of companies under common ownership.

**Exclusive provider organization (EPO)** A plan that does not cover medical care received outside of a network of preferred providers.

**Exclusive remedy doctrine** Doctrine in workers compensation insurance that states that workers compensation benefits should be the exclusive or sole source of recovery for workers who have a job-related accident or disease; doctrine has been eroded by legal decisions.

**Expense loading** *See* **Loading.**

**Expense ratio** That proportion of the gross rate available for expenses and profit. Ratio of expenses incurred to premiums written.

**Experience rating** (1) Method of rating group life and health insurance plans that uses the loss experience of the group to determine the premiums to be charged. (2) As applied to property and liability insurance, the class or manual rate is adjusted upward or downward based on past loss experience. (3) As applied to state unemployment insurance programs, firms with favorable employment records pay lower tax rates.

**Exposure unit** Unit of measurement used in insurance pricing.

**Extended nonowned coverage** Endorsement that can be added to an automobile liability insurance policy that covers the insured while driving any nonowned automobile on a regular basis.

**Extra expense coverage form** A separate form that can be used to cover the extra expenses incurred by a firm to continue operations during a period of restoration.

**Factory mutual** Mutual insurance company insuring only properties that meet high underwriting standards; emphasizes loss prevention.

**Facultative reinsurance** Optional, case-by-case method of reinsurance used when the ceding company receives an application for insurance that exceeds its retention limit.

**Fair Access to Insurance Requirements (FAIR plan)** Federal property insurance plan that provides basic property insurance to property owners in areas where they are unable to obtain insurance in the normal markets. Each state with such a plan has a central placement facility.

**Fair rental value** Amount payable to an insured homeowner for loss of rental income due to damage that makes the premises uninhabitable.

**Family income policy** Special life insurance policy combining decreasing term and whole life insurance that pays a monthly income of $10 for each $1000 of life insurance if the insured dies within the specified period. The monthly income is paid to the end of the period, at which time the face amount of insurance is paid.

**Family purpose doctrine** Concept that imputes negligence committed by immediate family members while operating a family car to the owner of the car.

**Federal surety bond** Type of surety bond required by federal agencies that regulates the actions of business firms. It guarantees that the bonded party will comply with federal standards, pay all taxes or duties accrued, or pay any penalty if the bondholder fails to pay.

**Fidelity bond** Bond that protects an employer against dishonest or fraudulent acts of employees, such as embezzlement, fraud, or theft of money.

**File-and-use law** Law for regulating insurance rates under which companies are required only to file the rates with the state insurance department before putting them into effect.

**Financial responsibility law** Law that requires persons involved in automobile accidents under certain circumstances to furnish proof of financial responsibility up to a minimum dollar limit or face having driving privileges revoked or suspended.

**Fire legal liability** Liability of a firm or person for fire damage caused by negligence of and damage to property of others.

**Fixed-amount option** Life insurance settlement option in which the policy proceeds are paid out in fixed amounts.

**Fixed annuity** Annuity whose periodic payment is a guaranteed fixed amount.

**Fixed-period option** Life insurance settlement option in which the policy proceeds are paid out over a fixed period of time.

**Flexible-premium annuity** An annuity contract that permits the owner to vary the size and frequency of premium payments. The amount of retirement income depends on the accumulated sum in the annuity at retirement.

**Flexible-spending account** An arrangement by which the employee agrees to a salary reduction, which can be used to pay for plan benefits, unreimbursed medical and dental expenses, and other expenses permitted by the Internal Revenue Code.

**Flex-rating law** Type of rating law in which prior approval of the rates is required only if the rates exceed a certain percentage above and below the rates previously filed.

**Foreign insurer** Insurance company chartered by one state but licensed to do business in another.

**Fortuitous loss** Unforeseen and unexpected loss that occurs as a result of chance.

**Franchise deductible** Deductible found in some marine insurance contracts in which the insurer has no liability if the loss is under a certain amount, but once this amount is exceeded, the entire loss is paid in full.

**Fraternal insurer** Mutual insurance company that provides life and health insurance to members of a social organization.

**Fully insured** Insured status of a covered person under the Old-Age, Survivors, and Disability Insurance (OASDI) program. You must have one quarter of coverage for each year after 1950 (or after the year you attain age twenty-one, if later) up to the year of death, disability, or attainment of age sixty-two. A minimum of six quarters and a maximum of forty quarters are required.

**Fundamental risk** A risk that affects the entire economy or large numbers of persons or groups within the economy.

**Funding agency** A financial institution or individual that provides for the accumulation or administration of the pension contributions that will be used to pay pension benefits.

**Funding instrument** An insurance contract or trust agreement that states the terms under which the funding agency will accumulate, administer, and disburse the pension funds.

**General agency system** Type of life insurance marketing system in which the general agent is an independent businessperson who represents only one insurer, is in charge of a territory, and is responsible for hiring, training, and motivating new agents.

**General aggregate limit** The maximum amount the insurer will pay for the sum of the following—damages under Coverage A, B and medical expenses under Coverage C.

**General average** In ocean marine insurance, a loss incurred for the common good that is shared by all parties to the venture.

**Good student discount** Reduction of automobile premium for a young driver at least sixteen who ranks in the upper 20 percent of his or her class, has a B or 3.0 average, or is on the Dean's list or honor roll. It is based on the premise that good students are better drivers.

**Grace period** Period of time during which a policyowner may pay an overdue premium without causing the policy to lapse.

**Gross estate** The value of the property that you own when you die. Also includes value of jointly-owned property, life insurance, death proceeds, and certain other items.

**Gross premium** Amount paid by the insured, consisting of the gross rate multiplied by the number of exposure units.

**Gross rate** The sum of the pure premium and a loading element.

**Group deferred annuity** Type of allocated pension plan in which a single-premium deferred annuity is purchased each year and is equal to the retirement benefit for that year.

**Group life insurance** Life insurance provided on a number of persons in a single master contract. Physical examinations are not required, and certificates of insurance are issued to members of the group as evidence of insurance.

**Group term life insurance** Most common form of group life insurance. Yearly renewable term insurance on employees during their working careers.

**Group universal life products (GULP)** Universal life insurance plans sold to members of a group, such as individual employees of an employer. There are some differences between GULP plans and individual universal life plans; for instance, GULP expense charges are generally lower than those assessed against individual policies.

**Guaranteed investment contract** An investment contract with an insurer in which the insurer guarantees both principal and interest on a pension contribution.

**Guaranteed purchase option** Benefit that can be added to a life insurance policy permitting the insured to purchase additional amounts of life insurance at specified times in the future without requiring evidence of insurability.

**Guaranteed renewable** Continuance provision of a health insurance policy under which the company guarantees to renew the policy to a stated age, typically sixty-five, and whose renewal is at the insured's option. Premiums can be increased for broad classes of insureds.

**Guaranteed replacement cost** In the event of a total loss, the insurer agrees to replace the home exactly as it was before the loss even though the replacement cost exceeds the amount of insurance stated in the policy.

**Hazard** Condition that creates or increases the chance of loss.

**Health maintenance organization (HMO)** Organized system of health care that provides comprehensive health services to its members for a fixed prepaid fee.

**Hedging** Technique for transferring the risk of unfavorable price fluctuations to a speculator by purchasing and selling options and futures contracts on an organized exchange.

**HMO** *See* **Health maintenance organization.**

**Hold-harmless clause** Clause written into a contract by which one party agrees to release another party from all legal liability, such as a retailer who agrees to release the manufacturer from legal liability if the product injures someone.

**Home service life insurance** Industrial life insurance and monthly debit ordinary life insurance contracts that are serviced by agents who call on the policyowners at their homes to collect the premiums. The amount of life insurance per policy generally is larger than $1000.

**Homeowners 2 policy (broad form)** Homeowners insurance policy that provides coverage on a named-perils basis on the dwelling, other structures, and personal property. Personal liability insurance is also provided.

**Homeowners 3 policy (special form)** Homeowners insurance policy that covers the dwelling and other structures on a risk-of-direct-loss basis and personal property on a named-perils basis. Personal liability insurance is also provided.

**Homeowners 4 policy (contents broad form)** Homeowners insurance policy that applies to tenants renting a home or apartment. Covers the tenant's personal property and provides personal liability insurance.

**Homeowners 6 policy (unit-owners form)** Homeowners insurance policy that covers personal property of insured owners of condominium units and cooperative apartments on a broad form, named-perils basis. Personal liability insurance is also provided.

**Homeowners 8 policy (modified coverage form)** Homeowner policy that is designed for older homes. Dwelling and other structures are indemnified on the basis of repair cost using common construction materials and methods. Personal liability insurance is also provided.

**Hospital expense insurance** Individual health insurance that pays for medical expenses incurred while in a hospital—both a daily hospital benefit for room and board and benefits for miscellaneous expenses.

**HR-10 plan** *See* **Keogh plan for the self-employed.**

**Hull insurance** (1) Class of ocean marine insurance that covers physical damage to the ship or vessel insured. Typically written on an "all-risks" basis. (2) Physical damage insurance on aircraft—similar to collision insurance in an automobile policy.

**Human life value** For purposes of life insurance, the present value of the family's share of the deceased breadwinner's future earnings.

**Immediate annuity** An annuity where the first payment is due one payment interval from the date of purchase.

**Immediate-participation guarantee plan (IPG)** Type of pension plan in which all pension contributions are deposited in an unallocated fund and used directly to pay benefits to retirees.

**Imputed negligence** Case in which responsibility for damage can be transferred from the negligent party to another person, such as an employer.

**Incontestable clause** Contractual provision in a life insurance policy stating that the insurer cannot contest the policy after it has been in force two years during the insured's lifetime.

**Indemnification** Compensation to the victim of a loss, in whole or in part, by payment, repair, or replacement.

**Independent adjustor** Claims adjustor who offers his or her services to insurance companies and is compensated by a fee.

**Independent agency system** Type of property and liability insurance marketing system, sometimes called the American agency system, in which the agent is an independent businessperson representing several insurers. The agency owns the expirations or renewal rights to the business, and the agent is compensated by commissions that vary by line of insurance.

**Indeterminate-premium whole life insurance.** Nonparticipating whole life policy that permits the insurer to adjust premiums based on anticipated future experience. Initial premiums are guaranteed for a certain period. After the initial guaranteed period expires, the insurer can increase premiums up to some maximum limit.

**Indirect loss** *See* **Consequential loss.**

**Individual deductible** Amount that an insured and each person of his or her family covered by the policy must pay before the group or individual medical insurance policy begins to pay for medical expenses.

**Individual Retirement Account (IRA)** Individual retirement plan that can be established by a person with earned income. An IRA plan enjoys favorable income tax advantages.

**Industrial life insurance** Type of life insurance in which policies are sold in small amounts and the premiums are collected weekly or monthly by a debit agent at the policyowner's home.

**Inflation-guard endorsement** Endorsement added at the insured's request to a homeowners policy to increase periodically the face amount of insurance on the dwelling and other policy coverages by a specified percentage.

**Initial reserve** In life insurance, the reserve at the beginning of any policy year.

**Inland marine insurance** Transportation insurance that provides protection for goods shipped on land including imports, exports, domestic shipments, means of transportation, personal property floater risks, and commercial property floater risks.

**Installment refund annuity** Pays the annuitant a lifetime income, but if death occurs before receiving payments equal to the purchase price, the income payments continue to the beneficiary.

**Insurance** Pooling of fortuitous losses by transfer of risks to insurers who agree to indemnify insureds for such losses, to provide other pecuniary benefits on their occurrence, or to render services connected with the risk.

**Insurance exchange** Term used to describe a facility that existed in a few states to provide a market for reinsurance and for the insurance of large and unusual domestic and foreign risks that are difficult to insure in the normal markets.

**Insurance guaranty funds** State funds that provide for the payment of unpaid claims of insolvent insurers.

**Insurance Services Office (ISO)** Major rating organization in property and liability insurance that drafts policy forms for personal and commercial lines of insurance and provides rate data on loss costs for property and liability insurance lines.

**Insuring agreement** That part of an insurance contract that states the promises of the insurer.

**Interest-adjusted method** Method of determining cost to an insured of a life insurance policy that considers the time cost of money by applying an interest factor to each element of cost. *See also* **Net payment cost index; Surrender cost index.**

**Interest option** Life insurance settlement option in which the principal is retained by the insurer and interest is paid periodically.

**Invitee** Someone who is invited onto the premises for the benefit of the occupant.

**IPG plan** *See* **Immediate-participation guarantee plan.**

**IRA** *See* **Individual Retirement Account.**

**Irrevocable beneficiary** Beneficiary designation allowing no change to be made in the beneficiary of an insurance policy without the beneficiary's consent.

**ISO** *See* **Insurance Services Office.**

**Joint and several liability rule** Under which several people may be responsible for the injury, but a defendant who is only slightly responsible may be required to pay the full amount of damages.

**Joint-and-survivor annuity** Annuity based on the lives of two or more annuitants. The annuity income (either the full amount of the original income or only two-thirds or one-half of the original income when the first annuitant dies) is paid until the death of the last annuitant.

**Joint underwriting association (JUA)** Organization of automobile insurers operating in a state that makes automobile insurance available to high-risk drivers. All underwriting losses are proportionally shared by insurers on the basis of premiums written in the state.

**Judgment rating** Rate-making method for which each exposure is individually evaluated and the rate is determined largely by the underwriter's judgment.

**Judicial bond** Type of surety bond used for court proceedings and guaranteeing that the party bonded will fulfill certain obligations specified by law, for example, fiduciary responsibilities.

**Juvenile insurance** Life insurance purchased by parents for children under a specified age. Provides permanent life insurance that increases in face value five times at age twenty-one with no increase in premium.

**Keogh plan for the self-employed (HR-10 plan)** Retirement plan individually adopted by self-employed persons that allows a tax-deductible contribution to a deferred-contribution or defined-benefit plan.

**Lapsed policy** One that is not in force because premiums have not been paid.

**Last clear chance rule** Statutory modification of the contributory negligence law allowing the claimant endangered by his or her own negligence to recover damages from a defendant if the defendant has a last clear chance to avoid the accident but fails to do so.

**Law of large numbers** Concept that the greater the number of exposures, the more closely will actual results approach the probable results expected from an infinite number of exposures.

**Legal reserve** Liability item on a life insurer's balance sheet representing the redundant or excessive premiums paid under the level-premium method during the early years. Assets must be accumulated to offset the legal reserve liability. Purpose of the legal reserve is to provide lifetime protection.

**Liability coverage** That part of the personal auto policy that protects a covered person against a suit or claim for bodily injury or property damage arising out of negligent ownership or operation of an automobile. A single or split limit for bodily injury and property damage liability is applied on a per accident basis. Liability coverage is also included in a boat owners policy; it covers the insured for property damage and bodily injury liability from the negligent ownership and operation of the boat.

**Liability without fault** Principle on which workers compensation is based, holding the employer absolutely liable for occupational injuries or disease suffered by workers, regardless of who is at fault.

**License and permit bond** Type of surety bond guaranteeing that the person bonded will comply with all laws and regulations that govern his or her activities.

**Licensee** Someone who enters or remains on the premises with the occupant's expressed or implied permission.

**Life annuity with guaranteed payments** Pays a life income to the annuitant with a certain number of guaranteed payments.

**Life income option** Life insurance settlement option in which the policy proceeds are paid during the lifetime of the beneficiary. A certain number of guaranteed payments may also be payable.

**Life insurance planning** Systematic method of determining the insured's financial goals, which are translated into specific amounts of life insurance, then periodically reviewed for possible changes.

**Limited-payment policy** Type of whole life insurance providing protection throughout the insured's lifetime and for which relatively high premiums are paid only for a limited period.

**Liquor liability law** *See* **Dram shop law.**

**Loading** The amount that must be added to the pure premium for expenses, profit, and a margin for contingencies.

**Long-term-care insurance** A form of health insurance that pays a daily or monthly benefit for medical or custodial care received in a nursing facility or hospital.

**Loss control** Risk management activities that reduce both the frequency and severity of losses for a firm or organization.

**Loss frequency** The probable number of losses that may occur during some given time period.

**Loss ratio** *See* **Actual loss ratio.**

**Loss reserve** Amount set aside by property and liability insurers for claims reported and adjusted but not yet paid, claims reported and filed but not yet adjusted, and claims incurred but not yet reported to the insurer.

**Loss severity** The probable size of the losses that may occur.

**McCarran-Ferguson Act** Federal law passed in 1945 stating that continued regulation of the insurance industry by the states is in the public interest and that federal antitrust laws apply to insurance only to the extent that the industry is not regulated by state law.

**Major medical insurance** Health insurance designed to pay a large proportion of the covered expenses of a catastrophic illness or injury.

**Malpractice liability insurance** Covers acts of malpractice resulting in harm or injury to patients.

**Managed care** A generic name for medical expense plans that provide covered services to the members in a cost-effective manner.

**Manual rating** *See* **Class rating.**

**Manuscript policy** Policy designed for a firm's specific needs and requirements.

**Mass merchandising** Plan for insuring individual members of a group, such as employees of firms or members of labor unions, under a single program of insurance at reduced premiums. Property and liability insurance is sold to individual members using group insurance marketing methods.

**Master contract** Formed between the insurer and group policy-owner for the benefit of the individual members.

**Maximum possible loss** Worst loss that could possibly happen to a firm during its lifetime.

**Maximum probable loss** Worst loss that is likely to happen to a firm during its lifetime.

**Mean reserve** In life insurance, the average of the terminal and initial reserves.

**Medical Information Bureau (MIB)** Bureau whose purpose is to supply underwriting information in life insurance to member companies, which report any health impairments of an applicant for insurance.

**Medical payments coverage** That part of the personal auto policy that pays all reasonable medical and funeral expenses incurred by a covered person within three years from the date of an accident.

**Medical payments to others** Pays for medical expenses of others under the homeowners policy in the event that a person (not an insured) is accidentally injured on the premises, or by the activities of an insured, resident employee, or animal owned by or in the care of an insured.

**Merit rating** Rate-making method in which class rates are adjusted upward or downward based on individual loss experience.

**MIB** *See* **Medical Information Bureau.**

**Minimum coverage requirement** A test that must be met to prevent employers from establishing a qualified pension plan that covers only the highly compensated. *See also* **Ratio percentage test.**

**Misstatement of age or sex clause** Contractual provision in an insurance policy stating that if the insured's age or sex is misstated, the amount payable is the amount that the premium would have purchased at the correct age.

**Mobile-home insurance** A package policy that provides property insurance and personal liability insurance to the owners of mobile homes. A special endorsement is added to HO-2 or HO-3.

**Modified life policy** Whole life policy for which premiums are reduced for the first three to five years and are higher thereafter.

**Modified no-fault plan** An injured person has the right to sue a negligent driver only if the bodily injury claim exceeds the dollar or verbal threshold.

**Monetary threshold** An injured motorist would not be permitted to sue but would collect from his or her insurer, unless the claim exceeded the threshold amount.

**Morale hazard** Carelessness or indifference to a loss because of the existence of insurance.

**Moral hazard** Dishonesty or character defects in an individual that increase the chance of loss.

**Multicar discount** Reduction in automobile insurance premium for insured who owns two or more automobiles, on the assumption that two such autos owned by the same person will not be driven as frequently as only one.

**Multiple-line insurance** Type of insurance that combines several lines of insurance into one contract, for example, property insurance and casualty insurance.

**Multiple-peril crop insurance** Offers producers a choice of a 65 percent or a 75 percent yield guarantee, and producers can elect to be paid up to 100 percent of the expected market price.

**Mutual insurer** Insurance corporation owned by the policyowners, who elect the board of directors. The board appoints managing executives, and the company may pay a dividend or give a rate reduction in advance to insureds.

**NAIC** *See* **National Association of Insurance Commissioners.**

**NALP** *See* **Net annual level premium.**

**Named insured** The person or persons named in the declarations section of the policy, as opposed to someone who may have an interest in the policy but is not named as an insured.

**Named-perils policy** Coverage by an insurance contract that promises to pay only for those losses caused by perils specifically listed in the policy.

**National Association of Insurance Commissioners (NAIC)** Group founded in 1871 that meets periodically to discuss industry problems and draft model laws in various areas and recommends adoption of these proposals by state legislatures.

**Needs approach** Method for estimating amount of life insurance appropriate for a family by analyzing various family needs that must be met if the family head should die and converting them into specific amounts of life insurance. Financial assets are considered in determining the amount of life insurance needed.

**Negligence** Failure to exercise the standard of care required by law to protect others from harm.

**Net amount at risk** Concept associated with a level-premium life insurance policy. Calculated as the difference between the face amount of the policy and the legal reserve.

**Net annual level premium (NALP)** Annual level premium for a life insurance policy with no expense loading. Mathematically equivalent to the net single premium.

**Net payment cost index** Method of measuring the cost of an insurance policy to an insured if death occurs at the end of some specified time period. The time value of money is taken into consideration.

**Net retention** *See* **Retention limit.**

**Net single premium (NSP)** Present value of the future death benefit of a life insurance policy.

**No-fault insurance** A tort reform proposal in which the injured person would collect benefits from his or her insurer and would not have to sue a negligent third party who caused the accident and establish legal liability.

**Noncancellable** Continuance provision of a health insurance policy stipulating that the policy cannot be cancelled, that the renewal is guaranteed to a stated age, and that the premium rates cannot be increased.

**Noncontributory plan** Employer pays the entire cost of a group insurance or private pension plan. All eligible employees are covered.

**Nonforfeiture law** State law requiring insurance companies to provide at least a minimum nonforfeiture value to policyowners who surrender their cash value life insurance policies.

**Noninsurance transfers** Various methods other than insurance by which a pure risk and its potential financial consequences can be transferred to another party, for example, contracts, leases, and hold-harmless agreements.

**Nonoccupational disability** The accident or illness must occur off the job.

**Nonparticipating policy** Term used to describe a life insurance policy that does not pay dividends.

**Objective risk** Relative variation of actual loss from expected loss, which varies inversely with the square root of the number of cases under observation.

**Obligee** The party to a surety bond who is reimbursed for damages if the principal to the bond fails to perform.

**Occurrence** An accident, including continuous or repeated exposure to substantially the same general, harmful conditions, which results in bodily injury or property damage during the policy period. *See also* **Accident.**

**Occurrence policy** A liability insurance policy that covers claims arising out of occurrences that take place during the policy period, regardless of when the claim is made. *See also* **Claims-made policy.**

**Ocean marine insurance** Type of insurance that provides protection for all types of oceangoing vessels and their cargoes as well as legal liability of owners and shippers.

**Open-competition law** Law for regulating insurance rates under which insurers are not required to file rates at all with the state insurance department but may be required to furnish rate schedules and supporting data to state officials.

**Optionally renewable policy** The insurer has the right to terminate a policy on any anniversary date, or in some cases, on a premium date.

**Ordinary life insurance** Type of whole life insurance providing protection throughout the insured's lifetime and for which premiums are paid throughout the insured's lifetime.

**Other-insurance provisions** Provisions whose purpose is to prevent profiting from insurance and violation of the principle of indemnity.

**Other-than-collision loss** Part of the coverage available under Part D: Coverage for Damage to Your Auto in the personal auto policy. All physical damage losses to an insured vehicle are covered except collision losses and those losses specifically excluded.

**Ownership clause** Provision in life insurance policies under which the policyowner possesses all contractual rights in the policy while the insured is living. These rights can generally be exercised without the beneficiary's consent.

**P&I Insurance** *See* **Protection and indemnity insurance.**

**Package policy** Policy that combines two or more separate contracts of insurance in one policy, for example, homeowners insurance.

**Partial disability** Inability of the insured to perform one or more important duties of his or her occupation.

**Participating policy** Life insurance policy that pays dividends to the policyowners.

**Particular average** An ocean marine loss that falls entirely on a particular interest as contrasted with a general average loss that falls on all parties to the voyage.

**Particular risk** A risk that affects only individuals and not the entire community.

**Past-service credits** Pension benefits awarded to employees based on service with the employer prior to the inception of the plan.

***Paul* v. *Virginia*** Landmark legal decision of 1869 establishing the right of the states, and not the federal government, to regulate insurance. Ruled that insurance was not interstate commerce.

**Pension accrual benefit** A plan makes a pension contribution so that the disabled employee's pension benefit remains intact.

**Pension Benefit Guaranty Corporation (PBGC)** A federal corporation that guarantees the payment of vested or nonforfeitable benefits up to certain limits if a private pension plan is terminated.

**Percentage participation clause** Provision in a health insurance policy that requires the insured to pay a certain percentage of eligible medical expenses in excess of the deductible. Also called **coinsurance.**

**Peril** Cause or source of loss.

**Personal injury** Injury for which legal liability arises (such as for false arrest, detention or imprisonment, malicious prosecution, libel, slander, defamation of character, violation of the right of privacy, and unlawful entry or eviction) and which may be covered by an endorsement to the homeowners policy.

**Personal liability insurance** Liability insurance that protects the insured for an amount up to policy limits against a claim or suit for damages because of bodily injury or property damage caused by the insured's negligence. This coverage is provided by Section II of the homeowners policy.

**Personal-producing general agent** Term used to describe an above-average salesperson with a proven sales record who is hired primarily to sell life insurance under a contract that provides both direct and overriding commissions.

**Personal umbrella policy** Policy designed to provide protection against a catastrophic lawsuit or judgment, whose coverage ranges generally from $1 million to $10 million and extends to the entire family anywhere in the world. Insurance is excess over underlying coverages.

**Physical hazard** Physical condition that increases the chance of loss.

**PIA** *See* **Primary insurance amount.**

**Point-of-service plan (POS)** Establishes a network of preferred providers. If patients see a preferred provider, they pay little or nothing. Outside provider care is covered, but at a substantially higher deductible and copayment.

**Policy loan** Cash value of a life insurance policy that can be borrowed by the policyowner in lieu of surrendering the policy.

**Policyowners' surplus** Difference between an insurance company's assets and its liabilities.

**Pooling** Spreading of losses incurred by the few over the entire group, so that in the process, average loss is substituted for actual loss.

**Preexisting condition** Physical or mental condition of an insured that existed prior to issuance of a policy.

**Preexisting-conditions clause** Contractual provision in a health insurance policy stating that preexisting conditions are not covered or are covered only after the policy has been in force for a specified period.

**Preferred risks** Individuals whose mortality experience is expected to be lower than average.

**Premises burglary coverage form** Commercial crime insurance form by the Insurance Services Office that provides coverage for premises burglary and robbery of a guard.

**Primary and excess insurance** Type of other-insurance provision that requires the primary insurer to pay first in the case of a loss; when the policy limits under the primary policy are exhausted, the excess insurer pays.

**Primary beneficiary** Beneficiary of a life insurance policy who is first entitled to receive the policy proceeds on the insured's death.

**Primary insurance amount (PIA)** Monthly cash benefit paid to a retired worker at the normal retirement age, currently age 65, or to a disabled worker eligible for benefits under the Old-Age, Survivors, and Disability Insurance (OASDI) program.

**Principal** The bonded party in the purchase of a surety bond who agrees to perform certain acts or fulfill certain obligations.

**Principal of indemnity** States that the insured should not profit from a covered loss but should be restored to approximately the same financial position that existed prior to the loss.

**Prior-approval law** Law for regulating insurance rates under which the rates must be filed and approved by the state insurance department before they can be used.

**Pro rata liability clause** Clause in a property insurance policy that makes each company insuring the same interest in a property liable according to the proportion that its insurance bears to the total amount of insurance on the property.

**Probationary period** (1) Waiting period of one to six months required of an employee before he or she is allowed to participate in a group insurance plan. (2) Specified number of days after a health insurance policy is issued during which time sickness is not covered.

**Products-completed operations hazard** Liability losses that occur away from the premises and arise out of the insured's product or work after the insured has relinquished possession of the product, or the work has been completed.

**Products liability** The legal liability of manufacturers, wholesalers, and retailers to persons who are injured or who incur property damage from defective products.

**Prospective reserve** In life insurance, the difference between the present value of future benefits and the present value of future net premiums.

**Protection and indemnity insurance (P&I)** Coverage that can be added to an ocean marine insurance policy to provide broad, comprehensive liability insurance on an indemnity basis for property damage and bodily injury to third parties.

**Proximate cause** Factor causing damage to property for which there is an unbroken chain of events between the occurrence of an insured peril and damage or destruction of the property.

**Public adjustor** Claims adjustor who represents the insured rather than the insurance company and is paid a fee based on the amount of the claim settlement. A public adjustor may be employed in those cases where the insured and insurer cannot resolve a dispute over a claim, or if the insured needs technical assistance in a complex loss situation.

**Public official bond** Type of surety bond guaranteeing that public officials will faithfully perform their duties for the protection of the public.

**Pure no-fault plan** The injured person cannot sue at all, regardless of the seriousness of the claim, and no payments are made for pain and suffering.

**Pure premium** That portion of the insurance rate needed to pay losses and loss-adjustment expenses.

**Pure risk** Situation in which there are only the possibilities of loss or no loss.

**Rate** Price per unit of insurance.

**Rate making** Process by which insurance pricing or premium rates are determined for an insurance company.

**Ratio percentage test** A test that a qualified pension plan must meet to receive favorable income tax treatment. The pension plan must benefit a percentage of employees that is at least 70 percent of the highly compensated employees covered by the plan.

**Readjustment period** One- to two-year period immediately following the breadwinner's death during which time the family should receive approximately the same amount of income it received while the breadwinner was alive.

**Rebating** A practice—illegal in virtually all states—of giving a premium reduction or some other financial advantage to an individual as an inducement to purchase the policy.

**Reciprocal exchange** Unincorporated mutual insuring organization in which insurance is exchanged among members and which is managed by an attorney-in-fact.

**Reinstatement clause** Contractual provision in a life insurance policy that permits the owner to reinstate a lapsed policy within five years if certain requirements are fulfilled; for example, evidence of insurability is required and overdue premiums plus interest must be paid.

**Reinstatement provision** Provision of a health insurance policy that allows the insured to reinstate a lapsed policy by payment of premium either without an application or with an application.

**Reinsurance** The shifting of part or all of the insurance originally written by one insurer to another insurer.

**Reinsurance facility** Pool for placing high-risk automobile drivers that arranges for an insurer to accept all applicants for insurance. Underwriting losses are shared by all automobile insurers in the state.

**Relative-value schedule** Variation of the schedule approach in which units or points are assigned to each surgical operation on the basis of degree of difficulty, and a conversion factor is used to convert the relative value into a dollar amount paid to the surgeon.

**Replacement-cost insurance** Property insurance by which the insured is indemnified on the basis of replacement cost with no deduction for depreciation.

**Reporting form** Coverage for commercial property insurance that requires the insured to report monthly or quarterly the value of the insured inventory, with automatic adjustment of insurance amount to cover the accurately reported inventory.

**Representations** Statements made by an applicant for insurance regarding, for example, occupation, state of health, and family history.

**Residual disability** Residual disability means that a proportionate disability-income benefit is paid to an insured whose earned income is reduced because of an accident or illness.

**Residual market** The residual market refers to plans in which automobile insurers participate to make insurance available to high-risk drivers who are unable to obtain coverage in the standard markets. Examples include an automobile insurance plan, joint underwriting association, and reinsurance facility. Also called the shared market.

*Res ipsa loquitur* Literally, the thing speaks for itself. Under this doctrine, the very fact that the event occurred establishes a presumption of negligence on behalf of the defendant.

**Retained limit** Term found in an umbrella policy (also known as self-insured retention). If the loss is covered by the umbrella policy but not by any underlying contract, the insured must retain or pay a certain amount of the loss.

**Retention** Risk management technique in which the firm retains part or all of the losses resulting from a given loss exposure. Used when no other method is available, the worst possible loss is not serious, and losses are highly predictable.

**Retention limit** Amount of insurance retained by a ceding company for its own account in a reinsurance operation.

**Retirement test** *See* **Earnings test.**

**Retrocession** Process by which a reinsurer obtains reinsurance from another company.

**Retrospective rating** Type of merit-rating method in which the insured's loss experience during the current policy period determines the actual premium paid for that period.

**Retrospective reserve** In life insurance, the net premiums collected by the insurer for a particular block of policies, plus interest earnings at an assumed rate, less the amounts paid out as death claims.

**Revocable beneficiary** Beneficiary designation allowing the policyowner the right to change the beneficiary without consent of the beneficiary.

**Rider** Term used in insurance contracts to describe a document that amends or changes the original policy. *See also* **Endorsement.**

**Risk** Uncertainty concerning the occurrence of a loss.

**Risk-based capital** Under new NAIC standards, life and health insurers are graded based on how much capital they have to support the riskiness of their investments and operations.

**Risk management** Systematic process for the identification and evaluation of pure loss exposures faced by an organization or individual, and for the selection and implementation of the most appropriate techniques for treating such exposures.

**Robbery** Taking of property from a person by someone who has (1) caused or threatens to cause bodily harm to that person, or (2) committed an obviously unlawful act witnessed by that person.

**Safe driver plan** Plan in which the automobile premiums paid are based on the insured's driving record and on the records of those living with the insured.

**Savings bank life insurance** Life insurance sold over the counter in mutual savings banks to residents of Massachusetts, New York, and Connecticut.

**Scheduled personal property endorsement** Special coverage added at the insured's request to a homeowners policy to insure items specifically listed. Used to insure valuable property such as jewelry, furs, and paintings.

**Schedule rating** Type of merit-rating method in which each exposure is individually rated and given a basis rate that is then modified by debits or credits for undesirable or desirable physical features.

**Second-injury fund** State funds paying the excess amount of benefit awarded an employee for a second injury if the disability is greater than that caused by the second injury alone. Its purpose is to encourage employers to hire handicapped workers.

**Section 401(k) plan** A qualified profit-sharing or thrift plan that allows participants the option of putting money into the plan or receiving the funds as cash. The employee can voluntarily elect to have his or her salary reduced up to some maximum limit, which is then invested in the employer's Section 401(k) plan.

**Self-insurance** Retention program in which the employer self-funds or pays part or all of its losses.

**Self-insured retention** *See* **Retained limit.**

**SEP** *See* **Simplified Employee Pension.**

**Separate account** Variation of the deposit administration pension plan arrangement in which pension funds are segregated so that account assets are not commingled with insurance company's general assets and can be invested separately.

**Service benefits** Health insurance benefits that pay hospital charges or payment for care received by the insured directly to the hospital or providers of care. The plan provides service rather than cash benefits to the insured.

**Settlement options** Ways in which life insurance policy proceeds can be paid other than in a lump sum, including interest, fixed period, fixed amount, and life income options.

**SEUA case** *See* **South-Eastern Underwriters Association (SEUA) case.**

**Shared market** *See* **Residual market.**

**Short-rate table** Schedule used by insurers to refund premiums on policy cancelation. It refunds less than a pro rata amount to cover insurer's expenses in issuing and printing the policy and to offset adverse selection.

**Simplified Employee Pension (SEP)** An employer-sponsored individual retirement account that meets certain requirements. Paperwork is reduced for employers who wish to cover employees in a retirement plan. Under current law, the employer can make a maximum annual tax-deductible contribution equal to 15 percent of the employee's compensation or $30,000, whichever is lower.

**Single limit** The total amount of insurance applies to the entire accident without a separate limit for each person.

**Single-premium deferred annuity** A retirement annuity that is purchased with a single premium with benefits to start at some future date.

**Single-premium whole life insurance** A whole life policy that provides lifetime protection with a single premium payment.

**Social insurance** Government insurance programs with certain characteristics that distinguish them from other government insurance programs. Programs are generally compulsory; specific earmarked taxes fund the programs; benefits are heavily weighted in favor of low-income groups; and programs are designed to achieve certain social goals.

**South-Eastern Underwriters Association (SEUA) case** Legal landmark decision of 1944 overruling the *Paul* v. *Virginia* ruling and finding that insurance was interstate commerce when conducted across state lines and was subject to federal regulation.

**Speculative risk** Situation in which either profit or loss are clear possibilities.

**Split limits** The amounts of insurance for bodily injury liability and property damage liability are stated separately.

**Stop-loss limit** Modification of the coinsurance provision in major medical plans that places a dollar limit on the maximum amount that an individual must pay rather than requiring that the insured pay 20 percent of all expenses in excess of deductible.

**Straight deductible** Deductible in an insurance contract by which the insured must pay a certain number of dollars of loss before the insurer is required to make a payment.

**Subjective risk** Uncertainty based on one's mental condition or state of mind.

**Subrogation** Substitution of the insurer in place of the insured for the purpose of claiming indemnity from a negligent third person for a loss covered by insurance.

**Suicide clause** Contractual provision in a life insurance policy stating that if the insured commits suicide within two years after the policy is issued, the face amount of insurance will not be paid; only premiums paid will be refunded.

**Supplemental major medical insurance** Group health insurance plan that supplements the benefits provided by a basic medical expense plan. It provides more comprehensive benefits with higher limits and is designed for a catastrophic loss.

**Supplementary Medical Insurance** Part B of the Medicare program that covers physicians' fees and other related medical services. Most eligible Medicare recipients are automatically included unless they voluntarily refuse this coverage.

**Surety** Party who agrees to answer for the debt, default, or obligation of another in the purchase of a bond.

**Surety bond** Bond that provides monetary compensation if the bonded party fails to perform certain acts.

**Surgical expense insurance** Health insurance that provides for payment of physicians' fees for surgical operations performed in a hospital or elsewhere.

**Surplus line broker** Specialized insurance broker licensed to place business with a nonadmitted insurer (a company not licensed to do business in the state).

**Surrender cost index** Method of measuring the cost of an insurance policy to an insured if the policy is surrendered at the end of some specified time period. The time value of money is taken into consideration.

**Survivor income benefits** Monthly benefits paid to an eligible surviving spouse or children for a limited period following the disabled worker's death.

**Term insurance** Type of life insurance that provides temporary protection for a specified number of years. It is usually renewable and convertible.

**Terminal reserve** In life insurance, the reserve at the end of any given policy year.

**Theft** Any act of stealing; includes burglary, robbery. *See also* **Burglary; Robbery.**

**Time limit on certain defenses provision** Provision in a health insurance policy that prohibits the company from canceling the policy or denying a claim on the basis of a preexisting condition or misstatement in the application after the policy has been in force for two or three years, with the exception of fraudulent misstatement.

**Total disability** Condition of an insured that makes him or her completely unable to perform all duties of the insured's own occupation or unable to perform the duties of any occupation for which the insured is reasonably fitted by training, education, and experience.

**Traditional net cost method** Traditional method of determining cost to an insured of a life insurance policy, determined by subtracting the total dividends received and cash value at the end of a period from the total premiums paid during that period.

**Treaty reinsurance** Type of reinsurance in which the primary company must cede insurance to the reinsurer and the reinsurer must accept. The ceding company is automatically reinsured according to the terms of the reinsurance contract.

**Trespasser** A person who enters or remains on the owner's property without the owner's consent.

**Trust** Arrangement in which property is legally transferred to a trustee who manages it for the benefit of named beneficiaries for their security and to insure competent management of estate property.

**Trust-fund plan** Type of pension plan in which all pension contributions are deposited with a trustee who invests the funds according to a trust agreement between employer and trustee. Benefits are paid directly out of the trust fund.

**Twisting** Illegal practice of inducing a policyowner to drop an existing policy in one company and take out a new policy in another through misrepresentation or incomplete information.

**UCR** *See* **Usual, customary, and reasonable charges.**

**Ultimate net loss** The total amount that the insured is legally obligated to pay.

**Underinsured motorists coverage** Coverage that can be added to the personal auto policy. Coverage pays damages for a bodily injury to an insured caused by the ownership or operation of an underinsured vehicle by another driver. The negligent driver may have insurance that meets the state's financial responsibility or compulsory insurance law requirement, but the amount carried is insufficient to cover the loss sustained by the insured.

**Underwriting** The selection and classification of applicants for insurance through a clearly stated company policy consistent with company objectives.

**Unearned premium reserve**  Liability reserve of an insurance company that represents the unearned part of gross premiums on all outstanding policies at the time of valuation.

**Unified tax credit**  Tax credit that can be used to reduce the amount of the federal estate or gift tax.

**Unilateral contract**  Only one party makes a legally enforceable promise.

**Uninsured motorists coverage**  That part of the personal auto policy designed to insure against bodily injury caused by an uninsured motorist, a hit-and-run driver, or a driver whose company is insolvent.

**Unisex rating**  A rating system in which the pooled loss experience of both sexes is used to determine the rates charged.

**Unit-owners form**  *See* **Homeowners 6 policy**

**Universal life insurance**  A flexible-premium whole life policy that provides lifetime protection under a contract that separates the protection and saving components. The contract is an interest-sensitive product that unbundles the protection, saving, and expense components.

**Unsatisfied judgment fund**  Fund established by a state to compensate accident victims who have exhausted all other means of recovery. As of date of publication, only five states have such laws.

**Usual, customary, and reasonable charges (UCR)**  Amounts payable for health care referring, respectively, to the physician's normal charge for a specific procedure, the amount charged for the same procedure by physicians with similar training in the same geographical area, and the amount considered reasonable if the physician's usual charge does not exceed the customary charge.

**Utmost good faith**  That a higher degree of honesty is imposed on both parties to an insurance contract than is imposed on parties to other contracts.

**Valued policy**  Policy that pays the face amount of insurance, regardless of actual cash value, if a total loss occurs.

**Valued policy laws**  Laws requiring payment to an insured of the face amount of insurance if a total loss to real property oc-

curs from a peril specified in the law, even though the policy may state that only actual cash value will be paid.

**Vanishing-premium policy**  A whole life policy in which the premium vanishes or disappears after a number of years.

**Variable annuity**  Annuity whose periodic lifetime payments vary depending on the level of common stock prices (or other investments), based on the assumption that cost of living and common stock prices are correlated in the long run. Its purpose is to provide an inflation hedge.

**Variable life insurance**  Life insurance policy in which the death benefit and cash surrender values vary according to the investment experience of a separate account maintained by the insurer.

**Verbal threshold**  A suit for damages is allowed only in serious cases, such as those involving death, dismemberment etc.

**Vesting**  Characteristic of pension plans guaranteeing the employee's right to part or all of the benefits attributable to the employer's contributions if employment terminates prior to retirement.

**Vicarious liability**  Responsibility for damage done by the driver of an automobile that is imputed to the vehicle's owner.

**Waiver**  Voluntary relinquishment of a known legal right.

**Waiver-of-premium provision**  Benefit that can be added to a life insurance policy providing for waiver of all premiums coming due during a period of total disability of the insured.

**War clause**  Restriction in a life insurance policy that excludes payment if the insured dies as a direct result of war.

**Warranty**  Statement of fact or a promise made by the insured, which is part of the insurance contract and which must be true if the insurer is to be liable under the contract.

**Workers compensation insurance**  Insurance that covers payment of all workers compensation and other benefits that the employer must legally provide to covered employees who are occupationally disabled.

# Index

abandonment of property, 127
absolute assignment, 330
absolute liability, 93
abuse exclusion, 140
Acacia Mutual Life Insurance Co., 498
accelerated death benefits riders,
    342-343
Access Research Inc., 448
accident
    defining, 231
    victims of automobile, 195-201
accidental death benefit rider, 341-342,
    400
accidental discharge, 122-123
accidental loss, 21
accident-only policies, 403
accident points, 207
accounting department, 524
accounts receivable coverage form, 236
accumulation units, 317-318
action of civil authority, 226
actively at work, 413
active retention, 13
activities of daily living (ADLs), 394
acts or decisions exclusion, 124
actual cash value, 59, 130
actual deferral percentage (ADP), 445-447,
    449
actual loss sustained form, 231
actuary, 511
additional capital needed, 291-292
additional living expense, 118
add-on plan, 198
adequate liability insurance, 207-208
adjustment bureau, 517
advance funding, 441
advance premium mutual, 496
advance purchase privilege, 341
adverse selection, 24, 390-391
advertising injury, 248, 259
Advisory Council on Social Security,
    476-478
    *See also* Social Security
age
    auto premiums and, 203-204
    early retirement, 439, 468-469
    full or normal retirement, 467-468
Age Discrimination Act, 438
age of home, 144
agency relationship, 70, 98
agency rules, 70
agents
    authority of, 70
    as claims adjustor, 517

dealing with competent, 358-360
described, 501
field underwriting by, 512-513
increasing professionalism of,
    515-516
law and, 69-71
principal responsible for acts of, 70
special, 514
agent's authority, 70
agent's report, 513
aggregate benefits, 394
aggregate deductible, 82
agreed amount endorsement,
    84, 223
agreed value, 227
AIDS deaths, 284
AIDS patients, 343
air conditioning, 123
aircraft exclusion, 117, 139, 246
aircraft insurance, 121-122, 256-257
aleatory contract, 69
all-risks policy, 77-78
Allstate Insurance, 32, 210
alternations/new buildings, 226-227
alternative dispute resolution (ADR)
    techniques, 104
A.M. Best Company, 49, 357, 395
American agency system, 503
American Arbitration Association,
    105
American Association of Insurance Services
    (AAIS), 257
American Express, 357
American Family Assurance Co., 404
American Insurance Association, 185
American International Underwriter (AIU),
    275
American Lloyds, 500
American Re Corp., 209
AmerUs Life Holdings Inc., 498
animals, 99, 117
annual transit policy, 237
annuitant, 315
annuities, 315-319
annuity units, 318
anti-lock brakes, 210
apparent authority, 70
application, 513
appraisal clause, 126
appraisal provision, 186
arbitration, 105
architects, 102
Arthur Andersen & Co., 359
ASO contract, 416

assessment mutual, 496
assigned risk plan. *See* automobile insurance
    plan
assignment of policy, 128
Associated Aviation Underwriters (AAU),
    256, 257
association captive insurers, 45
assumption-of-risk doctrine, 96, 105,
    483-484
ATM card coverage, 119
attachment bond, 277
attained-age method, 298
attending physician's report, 513
attractive nuisance doctrine, 97
auctioneer's bond, 277
auto exclusion, 246-247
automatic fire protection sprinkler system,
    123
automatic premium loan provision, 331
automatic termination, 188
automobile accident victims, 195-201
automobile insurance
    damage to your auto (Part D), 179-186
    described, 26
    duties after accident/loss (Part E), 186,
        188
    general provisions (Part F), 188-189
    for high-risk drivers, 201-203
    liability coverage (Part A), 171-174
    medical payments coverage (Part B),
        174-176
    for motorcycles/other vehicles, 189
    no-fault, 198-201
    owned and nonowned vehicles, 173-174
    personal auto policy, 169-171
    society and, 194-211
    uninsured motorists coverage (Part C),
        176-179
automobile insurance plans, 201-202
automobiles
    high-risk drivers of, 201-203
    negligence and operation of, 98
    nonowned, 170-171, 180-182
    use of, 204
    *See also* motor vehicles
available insurance, 49
average benefits test, 437
average indexed monthly earnings (AIME),
    470
aviation exclusions, 329
aviation insurers, 256
avoidance, 12, 44
awnings, 184
Ayco Co., 314